LIFE-SPAN

DEVELOPMENT

Fifteenth Edition

JOHN W. SANTROCK
University of Texas at Dallas

Mc
Graw
Hill
Education

LIFE-SPAN DEVELOPMENT

www.mhhe.com

brief contents

contents

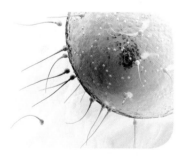

SECTION 3   INFANCY   101

SECTION 4 EARLY CHILDHOOD 196

SECTION 7 EARLY ADULTHOOD 399

SECTION 10 ENDINGS 592

about the **author**

John W. Santrock

John Santrock received his Ph.D. from the University of Minnesota. He taught at the University of Charleston and the University of Georgia before joining the Program in Psychology at the University of Texas at Dallas, where he currently teaches a number of undergraduate courses and was recently given the University's Effective Teaching Award. In 2010, he created the UT-Dallas Santrock undergraduate scholarship, an annual award that is given to outstanding undergraduate students majoring in developmental psychology to enable them to attend research conventions.

John Santrock, teaching in his undergraduate course in life-span development.

John has been a member of the editorial boards of *Child Development* and *Developmental Psychology*. His research on father custody is widely cited and used in expert witness testimony to promote flexibility and alternative considerations in custody disputes. John also has authored these exceptional McGraw-Hill texts: *Children* (13th edition), *Adolescence* (15th edition), *A Topical Approach to Life-Span Development* (7th edition), and *Educational Psychology* (5th edition).

For many years, John was involved in tennis as a player, teaching professional, and coach of professional tennis players. At the University of Miami (FL), the tennis team on which he played still holds the NCAA Division I record for most consecutive wins (137) in any sport. His wife, Mary Jo, has a master's degree in special education and has worked as a teacher and a Realtor. He has two daughters—Tracy, who also is a Realtor, and Jennifer, who is a medical sales specialist. He has one granddaughter, Jordan, age 21, currently a graduate student in Cox School of Business at Southern Methodist University, and two grandsons, Alex, age 9, and Luke, age 7. In the last two decades, John also has spent time painting expressionist art.

Dedication:

**With special appreciation to my mother,
Ruth Santrock, and my father, John Santrock.**

expert consultants

Life-span development has become an enormous, complex field, and no single author, or even several authors, can possibly keep up with all of the rapidly changing content in the many periods and different areas of life-span development. To solve this problem, author John Santrock has sought the input of leading experts about content in a number of areas of life-span development. These experts have provided detailed evaluations and recommendations in their area(s) of expertise.

The following individuals were among those who served as expert consultants for one or more of the previous editions of this text:

Urie Bronfenbrenner, *Cornell University*

K. Warner Schaie, *Pennsylvania State University*

Paul Baltes, *Max Planck Institute, Berlin*

Tiffany Field, *University of Miami*

James Birren, *University of Southern California*

Jean Berko Gleason, *Boston University*

Gilbert Gottlieb, *University of North Carolina—Chapel Hill*

Karen Adolph, *New York University*

Joseph Campos, *University of California—Berkeley*

Jean Mandler, *University of California—San Diego*

James Marcia, *Concordia University*

Andrew Meltzoff, *University of Washington*

Elizabeth Susman, *Pennsylvania State University*

David Almeida, *Pennsylvania State University*

John Schulenberg, *University of Michigan*

Margie Lachman, *Brandeis University*

Crystal Park, *University of Connecticut*

James Garbarino, *Cornell University*

Elena Grigorenko, *Yale University*

William Hoyer, *Syracuse University*

Ross Parke, *University of California—Riverside*

Ross Thompson, *University of California—Davis*

Phyllis Moen, *University of Minnesota*

Ravenna Helson, *University of California—Berkeley*

Toni Antonucci, *University of Michigan*

Arthur Kramer, *University of Illinois*

Karen Fingerman, *Purdue University*

Cigdem Kagitcibasi, *Koc University*

Robert Kastenbaum, *Arizona State University*

Following are the expert consultants for the fifteenth edition, who (like those of previous editions) literally represent a *Who's Who* in the field of life-span development.

K. Warner Schaie Dr. Schaie is widely recognized as one of the pioneers who created the field of life-span development and continues to be one of its leading experts. He is currently the Evan Pugh Professor Emeritus of Human Development and Psychology at Pennsylvania State University. Dr. Schaie also holds an appointment as Affiliate Professor of Psychiatry and Behavioral Sciences at the University of Washington. He received his Ph.D. in psychology from the University of Washington, an honorary Ph.D. from the Friedrich-Schiller University of Jena, Germany, and an honorary Sc.D. degree from West Virginia University. He received the Kleemeier Award for Distinguished Research Contributions and the Distinguished Career Contribution to Gerontology Award from the Gerontological Society of America, the MENSA lifetime career award, and the Distinguished Scientific Contributions award from the American Psychological Association. He is author or editor of 60 books, including the textbook *Adult Development and Aging* (5th ed., with S. L. Willis), the *Handbook of the Psychology of Aging* (7th ed., with Sherry Willis), and *Developmental Influences on Adult Intelligence* (2013, 2nd ed.). He has directed the Seattle Longitudinal Study of cognitive aging since 1956 and is the author of more than 300 journal articles and chapters on the psychology of aging. Dr. Schaie's current research interest focuses on the life course of adult intelligence, its antecedents and modifiability, the influence of cognitive behavior in midlife on the integrity of brain structures in old age, the early detection of risk for dementia, as well as methodological issues in the developmental sciences.

"In my view, this text continues to set the standard by which other texts on this topic must be measured. . . . It is my belief that the

15th edition will continue the tradition of providing the most comprehensive and user-friendly life-span developmental psychology textbook available for a large range of undergraduate students. It is soundly based on the current state of the scientific knowledge and continues to convey developing new concepts and content in a readily understandable manner." —**K. Warner Schaie**

Kirby Deater-Deckard Dr. Deater-Deckard is a leading expert on biological foundations of development, heredity-environment interaction, and parenting. He obtained his Ph.D. from the University of Virginia and currently is a professor of psychology and psychiatry and the director of developmental science graduate training at Virginia Tech. Dr. Deater-Deckard's research focuses on the development of individual differences in childhood and adolescence, with an emphasis on gene-environment processes. He has written papers, book chapters, and books in the areas of developmental psychology and psychopathology. His current research on parenting, schooling, and children's development is funded by the NIH and NSF. Dr. Deater-Deckard has been joint editor of the *Journal of Child Psychology and Psychiatry*, and currently is on the editorial boards of *Infant and Child Development, International Journal of Behavioral Development, Journal of Family Psychology*, and *Parenting: Science and Practice*.

"This book continues to be the standard against which other texts should be compared. The narrative provides a good balance between breadth of coverage and depth in certain topics that are foundational, as well as 'leading edge' new directions in the human development

research domain. Emphasis is properly placed on theories and classic/seminal concepts as well as recent ideas about how biology influences human development at the species level (i.e., evolutionary) and at the level of populations and individuals (e.g., gene-environment interaction). In addition, John Santrock provides adequate circumspection about the limitations of bio-social integration methods and theories in a clear and concise way. Students will come away from this chapter with a well-rounded understanding of why all that high school and college-level biology was useful for their understanding of human psychological development and functioning." **—Kirby Deater-Deckard**

Patricia Miller Dr. Patricia Miller is a leading expert in the cognitive development of children. She obtained her Ph.D. from the University of Minnesota and currently is Professor of Psychology at San Francisco State University, having previously been a professor at the University of Michigan, University of Georgia, and University of Florida. Her research focuses on children's executive function, memory, attention, and learning strategies. Current projects include the development of executive function in preschoolers, the effects of exercise on children's executive function and academic achievement, and the development of strategies in French and U.S. children. Dr. Miller is a recent president of the developmental psychology division of the American Psychological Association and is a Fellow of that organization as well as the Association for Psychological Science. She also has been an Associate Editor of *Child Development* and is on the Editorial Board at *Cognitive Development*. Her book, *Theories of Developmental Psychology*, is in its fifth edition, and she is co-author or co-editor of three other volumes. Dr. Miller's work has been published in journals such as *Child Development*, *Developmental Psychology*, and *Cognitive Development*.

"As in earlier editions of John Santrock's texts, the writing is clear and beautiful, and the topics are well chosen because of their interest to students and their importance. The research is up to date. The learning system and multiple summary/review sections keep the key ideas in front of the student throughout the chapter. (A strength is) connections to interesting and personally relevant real-life topics." **—Patricia Miller**

John Schulenberg Dr. Schulenberg is a leading expert on adolescent development and emerging adulthood. He currently is a professor of psychology in the Institute of Social Research and the Center for Human Growth and Development at the University of Michigan. His research expertise focuses on developmental transitions in adolescence and emerging adulthood that involve health and well-being, substance use and abuse, and conceptualization of developmental change. Dr. Schulenberg is one of the key members of the research team that conducts the ongoing Monitoring the Future study at the Institute of Social Research. He recently became President of the Society for Research on Adolescent Development. He is a Fellow of the American Psychological Association and President of the Society for Research on Adolescence. His work has been funded by NIDA, NIAAA, NICHD, NIMH, NSF, and the Robert Wood Johnson Foundation. Dr. Schulenberg serves on several editorial boards and has guest-edited special issues of *Addiction*, *Applied Developmental Science*, *Development and Psychopathology*, and *Journal of Longitudinal and Life Course Studies*. Finally, he has been a baseball and softball coach for community and travel youth teams for the past dozen years.

"I enjoyed reading these excellent chapters. I reviewed previous versions of these chapters for the previous edition of this book, and I see that these chapters continue to evolve in a positive and compelling way. I suspect that these chapters do well in capturing the attention of

college students, given the content and approach. In particular, the real-life examples, 'developmental connections,' various touchpoints throughout the chapters, and the review material at the end work well to encourage and maintain student interest and focus." **—John Schulenberg**

Patricia Reuter-Lorenz Dr. Reuter-Lorenz is one of the world's leading experts on cognitive neuroscience and aging. She received her Masters and Doctor of Philosophy degrees from the University of Toronto and did postdoctoral training in cognitive neuroscience at Cornell Medical Center (New York). Dr. Reuter-Lorenz is currently Professor of Psychology and Neuroscience at the University of Michigan—Ann Arbor where she directs the Cognitive and Affective Neuropsychology Laboratory. She is also the co-director of the International Max Planck Research School in Life Span Development, the Co-Editor-in-Chief of *Aging, Neuropsychology & Cognition*, and section editor for *Neuropsychologia*. Using imaging, behavioral, and case study approaches, she has published on a wide range of topics from neurocognitive aging to neuropsychological studies of attention, neglect and eye movement control, laterality, executive functions, and working memory. Dr. Reuter-Lorenz has received numerous awards for her research, mentorship and teaching, including the Outstanding Mentor Award from Division 20 of the American Psychological Association and the Justine Sergent Prize for International Research in Cognitive Neuroscience. Dr. Reuter-Lorenz is cofounder of the Cognitive Neuroscience Society and has played a leadership role in this organization for over twenty years.

"I found the chapter ("Cognitive Development in Late Adulthood") to be a pleasure to read and a valuable resource for students wanting to gain a broad perspective on life-span development. The organization was effective and the writing highly accessible." **—Patricia Reuter-Lorenz**

Scott Johnson Dr. Johnson is one of the world's leading experts on perceptual and cognitive development in infancy. He is currently a Professor of Psychology and Professor of Psychiatry and Biobehavioral Sciences at UCLA. Dr. Johnson obtained his Ph.D. from Arizona State University and then did postdoctoral work in the Center for Visual Science at the University of Rochester. His research interests center on mechanisms of perceptual, cognitive, motor, social, and cortical development, and relations among different developmental processes. Current research topics include object perception, face perception, intermodal perception, visual attention, early language development, and learning mechanisms in typical and at-risk populations. In studying infants, Dr. Johnson uses a combination of methods, including preferential looking, eye movements, electroencephalography, and connectionist modeling. He is currently Associate Editor of the journal *Cognition* and has served on the editorial boards of *Infancy*, *Infant Behavior & Development*, *Developmental Psychology*, the *British Journal of Developmental Psychology*, and *Frontiers in Neuroscience*.

"Dr. Santrock has expended great effort to update all of the chapters. . . . Overall, I thought Chapters 4 ("Physical Development in Infancy") and 5 ("Cognitive Development in Infancy") were great." **—Scott Johnson**

Amanda Rose Dr. Rose is a leading expert on children's socioemotional development. She currently is a Professor in the Department of Psychological Sciences at the University of Missouri—Columbia. She obtained her doctorate in developmental psychology from the University of Illinois. Dr. Rose's work focuses on friendships in childhood and adolescence, with particular attention to differences between girls and boys and to implications for emotional adjustment. She has published in a wide range of journals, including *Developmental Psychology, Child Development,* and *Psychological Bulletin,* and has held grants from the National Institute of Mental Health. Dr. Rose was awarded the Early Scientific Achievement Award from the Society for Research in Child Development and recently was awarded the University of Missouri's Chancellor's Award for Outstanding Research and Creative Activity. Dr. Rose also recently became a fellow in the American Psychological Association.

"Overall, based on the chapters I read, I thought the textbook had a number of strengths. The text is clear and engaging. Examples are used well and appropriately to illustrate points. In addition, real-world applications are incorporated throughout." —**Amanda Rose**

Ross Thompson Ross Thompson is one of the world's leading experts on children's socioemotional development. He currently is Professor of Psychology at the University of California–Davis, where he directs the Social and Emotional Development Lab. A developmental psychologist, Dr. Thompson studies early parent-child relationships, the development of emotion understanding and emotion regulation, early moral development, and the growth of self-understanding in young children. He also works on the applications of developmental research to public policy concerns, including school readiness and its development, early childhood investments, and early mental health. Dr. Thompson has published five books, several best-selling textbooks, and over 200 papers related to his work. He is a founding member of the National Scientific Council on the Developing Child, has twice been Associate Editor of *Child Development,* and has received the Boyd McCandless Young Scientist Award for Early Distinguished Achievement from the American Psychological Association. Dr. Thompson also recently was given the Ann Brown Award for Excellence in Developmental Research and the University of California–Davis Distinguished Scholarly Public Service Award.

". . . the chapters do a fine job of communicating the latest research clearly and engagingly, and by following a consistent outline, the reader is led through comparable topics at each chronological stage. As usual, John Santrock's writing is straightforward, easy to understand, and accessible." —**Ross Thompson**

Jerri Edwards Dr. Edwards is a leading expert in cognitive aging. She obtained her Ph.D. in life-span development from the University of Alabama at Birmingham and is currently a professor in the School of Aging Studies at the University of South Florida. Dr. Edwards' research seeks to discover how cognitive abilities can be maintained and even enhanced with advancing age. Ultimately, the goals of Dr. Edwards' research are to extend the mobility and independence of older adults, thereby improving their quality of life. Much of her work has focused on older adults' driving ability and cognitive training strategies to reduce the cognitive decline that results in driving difficulties. She is a member of the editorial board of *The Journals of Gerontology: Psychological Sciences.* Her work has been published in journals such as *Neurology, The Journal of the American Geriatrics Society, Psychology & Aging, Alzheimer's Disease and Associated Disorders,* and *Accident Analysis & Prevention.*

"I can't imagine the work and effort it takes to author a life-span development textbook. I admire Dr. Santrock's work, and he is well-known and respected among developmental psychology for his quality textbooks." —**Jerri Edwards**

Deborah Carr Dr. Carr is a leading expert on the social aspects of older adults' lives and on death, dying, and grieving. She obtained her Ph.D. from the University of Wisconsin and currently is a professor of sociology at Rutgers University. Dr. Carr is a life course sociologist who specializes in stress and health, widowhood, end-of-life issues, body weight, and later-life family relationships. She is the author of nearly 100 journal articles and book chapters, and is author or editor of five books including *Spousal Bereavement in Later Life, Encyclopedia of the Life Course and Human Development,* and *Worried Sick: Why Stress Hurts Us and What to Do About It* (2014). Dr. Carr is a fellow of the Gerontological Society of America.

"The new themes regarding 'connections' are integrative and thoughtful. I very much like the new features that emphasize cutting-edge research and careers . . . a truly impressive work; it's clear that John Santrock is not sitting on his laurels and really has made a Herculean effort in revising his book." —**Deborah Carr**

Santrock—connecting
research and *results!*

As a master teacher, John Santrock connects students to current research and real-world applications. His integrated, personalized learning program gives students the insight they need to study smarter and improve performance.

Better Data, Smarter Revision, Improved Results

Students helped inform the revision strategy of *Life-Span Development*.

STEP 1. Over the course of three years, data points showing concepts that caused students the most difficulty were anonymously collected from Connect Lifespan Development **LearnSmart** product.

STEP 2. The data from **LearnSmart** was provided to the author in the form of a *Heat Map*, which graphically illustrates "hot spots" in the text that impacts student learning (see image below).

STEP 3. The author used the *Heat Map* data to refine the content and reinforce student comprehension in the new edition. Additional quiz questions and assignable activities were created for use in Connect Lifespan Development to further support student success.

RESULT: Because the *Heat Map* gave the author empirically-based feedback at the paragraph and even sentence level, he was able to develop the new edition using precise student data that pinpointed concepts that gave students the most difficulty.

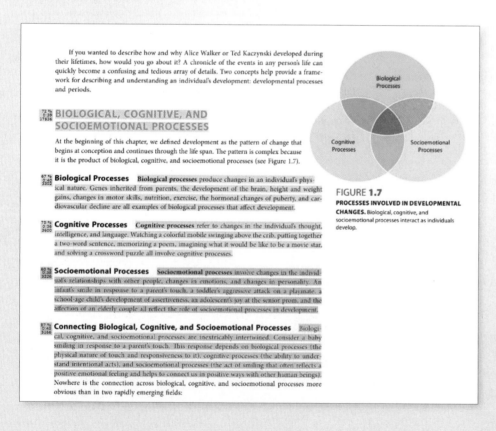

LearnSmart is an adaptive learning program designed to help students learn faster, study smarter, and retain more knowledge for greater success. Distinguishing what students know from what they don't, and focusing on concepts they are most likely to forget, LearnSmart continuously adapts to each student's needs by building an individual learning path. Millions of students have answered over a billion questions in LearnSmart since 2009, making it the most widely used and intelligent adaptive study tool that's proven to strengthen memory recall, keep students in class, and boost grades.

Fueled by LearnSmart, SmartBook is the first and only adaptive reading experience currently available.

- **Make It Effective.** SmartBook™ creates a personalized reading experience by highlighting the most impactful concepts a student needs to learn at that moment in time. This ensures that every minute spent with SmartBook™ is returned to the student as the most value-added minute possible.

- **Make It Informed.** The reading experience continuously adapts by highlighting content based on what the student knows and doesn't know. Real-time reports quickly identify the concepts that require more attention from individual students—or the entire class. SmartBook™ detects the content a student is most likely to forget and brings it back to improve long-term knowledge retention.

Personalized grading, on the go, made easier

Student performance reports show you about their progress. The first and only analytics tool of its kind, Connect Insight™ is a series of visual data displays—each framed by an intuitive question—to provide at-a-glance information regarding how your class is doing.

- **Make It Intuitive.** You receive an instant, at-a-glance view of student performance matched with student activity.

- **Make It Dynamic.** Connect Insight™ puts real-time analytics in your hands so you can take action early and keep struggling students from falling behind.

- **Make It Mobile.** Connect Insight™ travels from office to classroom, available on demand wherever and whenever it's needed.

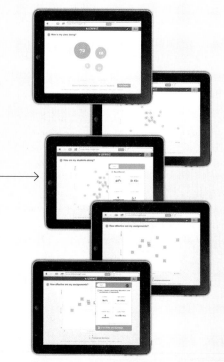

Real people, real world, real life

McGraw-Hill's Milestones is a powerful tool that allows students to experience life as it unfolds, from infancy through emerging adulthood. Students track the early stages of physical, social, and emotional development. By letting students observe one child over time or compare various children, Milestones provides a unique, experiential learning environment that can only be achieved by watching real human development as it happens.

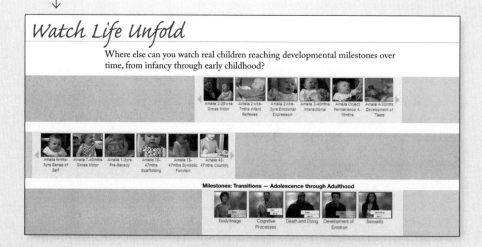

preface

Making Connections . . . From My Classroom to *Life-Span Development* to You

Having taught life-span development every semester for 30 years now, I'm always looking for ways to improve my course and *Life-Span Development*. Just as McGraw-Hill looks to those who teach the life-span development course for input, each year I ask the almost 200 students in my life-span development course to tell me what they like about the course and the text, and what they think could be improved. What have my students told me lately about my course and text? Students said that highlighting connections among the different aspects of life-span development would help them to better understand the concepts. As I thought about this, it became clear that a *connections* theme would provide a systematic, integrative approach to the course material. I used this theme to shape my current goals for my life-span development course, which, in turn, I've incorporated into *Life-Span Development:*

1. **Connecting with today's students** To help students learn about life-span development more effectively.
2. **Connecting research to what we know about development** To provide students with the best and most recent theory and research in the world today about each of the periods of the human life span.
3. **Connecting developmental processes** To guide students in making developmental connections across different points in the human life span.
4. **Connecting development to the real world** To help students understand ways to apply content about the human life span to the real world and improve people's lives; and to motivate them to think deeply about their own personal journey through life and better understand who they were, are, and will be.

Connecting with Today's Students

In *Life-Span Development,* I recognize that today's students are as different in some ways from the learners of the last generation as today's discipline of life-span development is different from the field 30 years ago. Students now learn in multiple modalities; rather than sitting down and reading traditional printed chapters in linear fashion from beginning to end, their work preferences tend to be more visual and more interactive, and their reading and study often occur in short bursts. For many students, a traditionally formatted printed textbook is no longer enough when they have instant, 24/7 access to news and information from around the globe. Two features that specifically support today's students are the adaptive ebook, Smartbook, (see pages xvi-xvii) and the learning goals system.

The Learning Goals System

My students often report that the life-span development course is challenging because of the amount of material covered. To help today's students focus on the key ideas, the Learning Goals System I developed for *Life-Span Development* provides extensive learning connections throughout the chapters. The learning

1 Physical Growth and Development in Infancy LG1 Discuss physical growth and development in infancy.

Patterns of Growth | Height and Weight | The Brain | Sleep | Nutrition

Physical Development in Infancy

1 Physical Growth and Development in Infancy **LG1** Discuss physical growth and development in infancy.

Patterns of Growth

Height and Weight

The Brain

- The cephalocaudal pattern is the sequence in which growth proceeds from top to bottom. The proximodistal pattern is the sequence in which growth starts at the center of the body and moves toward the extremities.
- The average North American newborn is 20 inches long and weighs 7 pounds. Infants grow about 1 inch per month in the first year and nearly triple their weight by their first birthday. The rate of growth slows in the second year.
- One of the most dramatic changes in the brain in the first two years of life is dendritic spreading, which increases the connections between neurons. Myelination, which speeds the conduction of nerve impulses, continues through infancy and even into adolescence. The cerebral cortex has two hemispheres (left and right). Lateralization refers to specialization of function in one hemisphere or the other. Early experiences play an important role in brain development. Neural connections are formed early in an infant's life. Before birth, genes mainly direct neurons to different locations. After birth, the inflowing stream of sights, sounds, smells, touches, language, and eye contact help shape the brain's neural connections, as does stimulation from caregivers and others. The

system connects the chapter opening outline, learning goals for the chapter, mini-chapter maps that open each main section of the chapter, *Review, Connect, and Reflect* questions at the end of each main section, and the chapter summary at the end of each chapter.

The learning system keeps the key ideas in front of the student from the beginning to the end of the chapter. The main headings of each chapter correspond to the learning goals that are presented in the chapter-opening spread. Mini-chapter maps that link up with the learning goals are presented at the beginning of each major section in the chapter.

Then, at the end of each main section of a chapter, the learning goal is repeated in *Review, Connect, and Reflect,* which prompts students to review the key topics in the section, connect to existing knowledge, and relate what they learned to their own personal journey through life. *Reach Your Learning Goals,* at the end of the chapter, guides students through the bulleted chapter review, connecting with the chapter outline/learning goals at the beginning of the chapter and the *Review, Connect, and Reflect* questions at the end of major chapter sections.

connecting through research

How Does the Quality and Quantity of Child Care Affect Children?

In 1991, the National Institute of Child Health and Human Development (NICHD) began a comprehensive, longitudinal study of child-care experiences. Data were collected on a diverse sample of almost 1,400 children and their families at 10 locations across the United States over a period of seven years. Researchers used multiple methods (trained observers, interviews, questionnaires, and testing) and measured many facets of children's development, including physical health, cognitive development, and socioemotional development. Following are some of the results of what is now referred to as the NICHD Study of Early Child Care and Youth Development or NICHD SECCYD (NICHD Early Child Care Research Network, 2001, 2002, 2003, 2004, 2005, 2006, 2010).

- **Patterns of use.** Many families placed their infants in child care very soon after the child's birth, and there was considerable instability in the child-care arrangements. By 4 months of age, nearly three-fourths of the infants had entered some form of nonmaternal child care. Almost half of the infants were cared for by a relative when they first entered care; only 12 percent were enrolled in child-care centers.

Socioeconomic factors were

What are some important findings from the national longitudinal study of child care conducted by the National Institute of Child Health and Human Development?

and flat affect, and language stimulation). Further, infants from low-income families experienced lower-quality child care than did infants from higher-income families. When quality of caregivers' care was high, children performed better on cognitive and language tasks, were more cooperative with their mothers during play, showed more positive and skilled interaction with peers, and had fewer behavior problems. Caregiver training and good child-staff ratios were linked with higher cognitive and social competence when children were 54 months of age. Using data collected as part of the NICHD early child care longitudinal study, a recent analysis indicated that higher-quality early childhood care, especially at 27 months of age, was linked to children's higher vocabulary scores in the fifth grade (Belsky & others, 2007).

Higher-quality child care was also related to higher-quality mother-child interaction among the families that used nonmaternal care. Further, poor-quality care was related to an increase of insecure attachment to the mother among infants who were 15 months of age, but only when the mother was low in sensitivity and responsiveness. However, child-care quality was not linked to attachment security at 36 months of age. A recent study revealed that

Connecting Research to What We Know about Development

Over the years, it has been important for me to include the most up-to-date research available. I continue that tradition in this edition by looking closely at specific areas of research, involving experts in related fields, and updating research throughout. *Connecting Through Research* describes a study or program to illustrate how research in life-span development is conducted and how it influences our understanding of the discipline. Topics range from *Do Children Conceived through In Vitro Fertilization Show Significant Differences in Developmental Outcomes in Adolescence?* (Chapter 2) to *How Much Does the Environment Affect Intelligence*? (Chapter 9) to *What Is the Relationship Between Fitness in Young Adults and Cardiovascular Health in Middle Age?* (Chapter 15).

The tradition of obtaining detailed, extensive input from a number of leading experts in different areas of life-span development also continues in this edition. Biographies and photographs of the leading experts in the field of life-span development appear on pages xiii to xiv, and the chapter-by-chapter highlights of new research content are listed on pages xxiii to xxvii. Finally, the research discussions have been updated in every period and topic. I expended every effort to make this edition of *Life-Span Development* as contemporary and up-to-date as possible. To that end, there are more than 1,900 citations from 2013, 2014, and 2015 in the text.

Connecting Developmental Processes

Development through the life span is a long journey, and too often we forget or fail to notice the many connections from one point in development to another. I have substantially increased these connections made in the text narrative and included features to help students connect topics across the periods of development.

developmental **connection**

Personality

Two key points in development when there is a strong push for independence are the second year of life and early adolescence. Chapter 12, p. 378

Developmental Connections, which appear multiple times in each chapter, point readers to where the topic is discussed in a previous or subsequent chapter. *Developmental Connections* highlight links across age periods of development *and* connections between biological, cognitive, and socioemotional processes. These key developmental processes are typically discussed in isolation from each other, and students often fail to see their connections. Included in the *Developmental Connections* is a brief description of the backward or forward connection. For example, consider the development of the brain. In recent editions, I have significantly expanded content on the changes in the brain through the life span, including new coverage of changes in the brain during prenatal development and an expanded discussion of the aging brain in older adults. The prenatal brain discussion appears in Chapter 3 and the aging brain is described in Chapter 17. An important brain topic that we discuss in Chapters 3 and 17 is neurogenesis, the production of new neurons. Connections between these topics in Chapters 3 and 17 are highlighted through *Developmental Connections.*

Topical Connections: Looking Back begin and conclude each chapter by placing the chapter's coverage in the larger context of development. The Looking Back section reminds the reader of what happened developmentally in previous periods of development.

Finally, a *Connect* question appears in the section self-reviews—*Review, Connect, and Reflect*—so students can practice making connections between topics. For example, in Chapter 9, students are asked to connect what they learned in Chapter 7 about the genetic links of autism to what they have just read about specific brain abnormalities associated with autism spectrum disorders.

> ## topical connections *looking back*
>
> In early childhood, according to Erikson, young children are in the stage of initiative versus guilt. Parents continue to play an important role in their development, and an authoritative parenting style is most likely to have positive outcomes for children. In early childhood, peer relations begin to take on a more significant role as children's social worlds widen. Play has a special place in young children's lives and is an important context for both cognitive and socioemotional development.

Connecting Development to the Real World

In addition to helping students make research and developmental connections, *Life-Span Development* shows the important connections between the concepts discussed and the real world. In recent years, students in my life-span development course have increasingly told me that they want more of this type of information. In this edition, real-life connections are explicitly made through the chapter opening vignette, *Connecting Development to Life,* the *Milestones* program that helps students watch life as it unfolds, and *Connecting with Careers.*

Each chapter also begins with a story designed to increase students' interest and motivation to read the chapter. For example, Chapter 18 begins with a description of the remarkable 93-year-old Helen Small, who published her first book at age 91 and completed her undergraduate degree 70 years after she started.

Connecting Development to Life describes the influence of development in a real-world context on topics including *From Waterbirth to Music Therapy* (Chapter 3), *Increasing Children's Self-Esteem* (Chapter 10), and *Health Care Providers and Older Adults* (Chapter 17).

The **Milestones** program, described on pg. xviii, shows students what developmental concepts look like by letting them watch actual humans develop. Starting from infancy, students track several individuals, seeing them achieve major developmental milestones, both physically and cognitively. Clips continue through adolescence and adulthood, capturing attitudes toward issues such as family, sexuality, and death and dying.

> ### connecting development to life
>
> **Coping and Adapting in the Aftermath of Divorce**
>
> Hetherington recommends the following strategies for divorced adults (Hetherington & Kelly, 2002):
>
> - Think of divorce as a chance to grow personally and to develop more positive relationships.
> - Make decisions carefully. The consequences of your decision making regarding work, lovers, and children may last a lifetime.
> - Focus more on the future than the past. Think about what is most important for you going forward in your life, set some challenging goals, and plan how to reach them.
> - Use your strengths and resources to cope with difficulties.
> - Don't expect to be successful and happy in everything you do. "The road to a more satisfying life is bumpy and will have many detours" (p. 109).
>
> - Remember that "you are never trapped by one pathway. Most of those who were categorized as defeated immediately after divorce gradually moved on to a better life, but moving onward usually requires some effort" (p. 109).
>
> Look back again at the six common pathways for exiting divorce that Hetherington proposes. Consider how someone on each of those pathways might particularly benefit from employing one or another of these strategies.

Connecting with Careers profiles careers ranging from an educational psychologist (Chapter 1) to a toy designer (Chapter 7) to a marriage and family therapist (Chapter 8) to the director of an organization that promotes positive adolescent development (Chapter 11)

Karen Fingerman, Professor, Department of Human Development and Family Sciences, and Researcher on Families and Aging

Dr. Karen Fingerman is a leading expert on aging, families, and socio-emotional development. She currently is a Professor in the Department of Human Development and Family Sciences within the School of Human Ecology at the University of Texas at Austin. Prior to coming to UT-Austin, she was the Berner Hanley Professor of Gerontology at Purdue University. Dr. Fingerman obtained her Ph.D. from the University of Michigan and did post-doctoral work at Stanford University. She has published numerous articles on the positive and negative aspects of relationships involving mothers and daughters, grandparents and grandchildren, friends, and acquaintances, and peripheral social ties. The National Institute of Aging, the Brookdale Foundation, and the MacArthur Transitions to Adulthood group have funded her research. Dr. Fingerman has received the Springer Award for Early Career Achievement in Research on Adult Development and Aging from the American Psychological Association, as well as the Margaret Baltes Award for Early Career Achievement in Behavioral and Social Gerontology from the Gerontological Association of America.

Dr. Karen Fingerman, leading expert on aging, families, and socioemotional development. Also you can use the following from what was in the previous Connecting with Careers on p. 528 of LSD 14th: *For more information on what professors and researchers do, see page 41 in the Careers in Life-Span Development appendix.*

to a geriatric nurse (Chapter 17), each of which requires knowledge about human development.

The careers highlighted extend from the Careers Appendix in Chapter 1 that provides a comprehensive overview of careers in life-span development to show students where knowledge of human development could lead them.

Part of applying development to the real world is understanding its impact on oneself. An important goal I have established for my life-span development course and this text is to motivate students to think deeply about their own journey of life. To further encourage students to make personal connections to content in the text, *Reflect: Your Own Personal Journey of Life* appears in the end-of-section review in each chapter. This feature involves a question that asks students to reflect on some aspect of the discussion in the section they have just read and connect it to their own life. For example, in Chapter 1, students are asked:

Do you think there is, was/will be a best age for you to be? If so, what is it? Why?

I always include this question in the first content lecture I give in life-span development and it generates thoughtful and interesting class discussion. Earlier in that section of Chapter 1 is a research discussion on whether there is a best age to be, which includes recent research on the topic and a self-assessment that lets students evaluate their own life satisfaction. In addition, students are asked a number of personal connections questions in the photograph captions.

Content Revisions

A significant reason why *Life-Span Development* has been successfully used by instructors for fifteen editions now is the painstaking effort and review that goes into making sure the text provides the latest research on all topic areas discussed in the classroom. This new edition is no exception, with more than 1,900 citations from 2013, 2014, and 2015.

New research highlights include very recent studies on outcomes of adoption; links of infant attachment (including attachment to both parents) to developmental outcomes; whether delay of gratification in early childhood can predict physical and mental health in adulthood; more precise discoveries about the adolescent's changing brain; cohabitation contexts that are or are not linked to divorce; the far-reaching benefits of exercise in the lives of older adults; and genetic, cellular, and lifestyle factors that characterize individuals with Alzheimer disease. **New techniques** are described, such as neurofeedback and mindfulness training to reduce ADHD symptoms; and **ongoing debates** are explored, such as whether supportive or tiger parenting is better for Chinese American children, and if adolescence is taking too long.

Below is a sample of the many chapter-by-chapter changes that were made in this new edition of *Life-Span Development*. A more extensive, detailed list of chapter-by-chapter changes can be obtained by contacting your McGraw-Hill sales representative.

Chapter 1: Introduction

- Expanded and updated coverage of ethnic minority children and children living in poverty
- Discussion of Ann Masten's recent research on resilience, including the lives of homeless children
- New description of Robert Siegler's microgenetic method for studying cognitive changes
- Expanded content on physiological assessment of development, including cortisol, EEG, heart rate, and eye movement

Chapter 2: Biological Beginnings

- Extensive editing and updating based on feedback from leading experts Kirby Deater-Deckard and David Moore
- Expanded coverage of recently developed genetic methods, including linkage analysis, next-generation sequencing, and the Thousand Genomes Project
- Updated and expanded content on gene-gene interaction to include alcoholism and Alzheimer disease
- Significantly updated information about adoption, including Harold Grotevant's recent research review on adoption outcomes, as well as "open adoption"
- New discussion of the challenges identical twins face in developing a unique identity
- Updated and expanded coverage of gene-environment interaction research, including some difficulties in replicating results

Chapter 3: Prenatal Development and Birth

- Updated research on substances and stress hormones that can cross the placenta
- New research on outcomes for offspring of women who drank various amounts of alcohol during pregnancy
- Inclusion of recent research on the negative effects on the fetus of maternal overweight and obesity during pregnancy
- Coverage of recent research on the effects of maternal stress and depression on the fetus and infant outcomes
- Extensive updating of research on prenatal care, including pregnant women's exercise and CenteringPregnancy outcomes

- Inclusion of recent research on doulas
- Discussion of an extensive number of new research studies on reducing negative outcomes for preterm and low birth weight infants
- Updated research on the positive effects of kangaroo care
- Much expanded and updated research on postpartum depression

Chapter 4: Physical Development in Infancy

- Inclusion of information on the development of the brain by leading expert Martha Ann Bell
- New Figure 4.3 that shows a new imaging device, magnetoencephalography (MEG), being used in Patricia Kuhl's laboratory while an infant listens to spoken words
- New section on links between infant sleep and cognitive development
- Editing and changes made to the material on infant perceptual development based on leading expert Scott Johnson's feedback
- Much expanded and updated coverage of the dramatic increase in the use of sophisticated eye-tracking equipment in the study of infant perception
- New coverage of Karen Adolph's recent research indicating why infants do or do not cross the visual cliff
- New discussion of Daphne Maurer's research on infants who have cataracts removed at different points in development and links to how deprivation and experience influence visual development

Chapter 5: Cognitive Development in Infancy

- Inclusion of recent research on how preverbal infants as young as 4 months of age may show an innate sense of morality
- Expanded criticism of the nativist approach to infant cognition
- Coverage of recent research on infant attention and links to executive function in the preschool years
- New discussion of how infants in the second half of the first year rely on the co-occurrence of phonemes and syllables to help them extract potential word forms
- Description of recent research on child-directed speech in low-SES Spanish-speaking families

Chapter 6: Socioemotional Development in Infancy

- Expanded and updated discussion of infants' biological recovery from stressors and the role that caregivers play in the recovery
- Inclusion of recent research on infants' possible display of jealousy-related behavior and changes in the infants' EEG patterns
- Description of recent research on infants' emotions, including how babies pick up on their mothers' stress and negative emotion, the role of maternal effortful control in infant emotion, and parents' elicitation of emotion talk and its link to toddlers' sharing and helping behaviors
- Updates on developmental outcomes of infant attachment, including a recent study showing that infants' insecure attachment to both their mother and father is linked to more externalizing problems later in childhood, along with a research review of stability and change in attachment from infancy to early adulthood
- New discussion of the inconsistency in gene-environment interaction studies related to infant attachment
- Inclusion of recent research on the role of fathers in infant development
- Updates on research on variations in child care and links to child outcomes

Chapter 7: Physical and Cognitive Development in Early Childhood

- New section on changes in perceptual development in early childhood
- Inclusion of a number of recent studies of sleep duration in early childhood and its link to various outcomes, as well as leading expert Mona El-Sheikh's recommendations for improving children's sleep environment
- Expanded and updated coverage of recent trends in overweight and obesity in early childhood and connections with later outcomes
- Coverage of a number of recent studies on the positive role of exercise and physical activity in young children's lives
- Inclusion of new information on young children's cognitive development based on leading expert Philip Zelazo's feedback
- Expanded discussion of Vygotsky's theory, including factors that influence the zone of proximal development and the positive role of scaffolding
- Expanded and updated coverage of sustained attention in young children
- New section on young children's autobiographical memories
- Expanded and updated coverage of delay of gratification, including recent research on connections of delay of gratification in early childhood to outcomes three decades later
- Inclusion of recent research on theory of mind, including the role of language and links to executive function
- Coverage of recent research on Head Start participation and Early Head Start outcomes

Chapter 8: Socioemotional Development in Early Childhood

- Discussion of recent research that found young children's ability to understand their own and others' emotions preceded advances in theory of mind
- Description of recent research on children's emotion regulation
- New *Connecting Through Research* box that details Dan McCoy and Cybele Raver's research on links between caregiver expressiveness, children's emotion expression, and children's internalizing and externalizing problems
- Coverage of recent research that found parents were more satisfied with their lives than were nonparents
- Updated discussion of punishment's effects on children, including commentary from a recent research review by Elizabeth Gershoff
- Expanded description of family-related factors that contribute to child maltreatment and recent research linking child maltreatment to depression in early adulthood
- Coverage of recent research on the positive aspects of gay and lesbian parenting, including higher rates of co-parenting compared with heterosexual parents
- Expanded and updated content on the stressors that immigrant families face, as well as a new discussion of transnational parents
- Description of a recent meta-analysis of research in 14 countries indicating positive effects of *Sesame Street* viewing in a number of areas of children's development

Chapter 9: Physical and Cognitive Development in Middle and Late Childhood

- Coverage of a number of recent research studies on the positive outcomes of exercise for elementary-school-aged children
- Inclusion of recent research on the negative outcomes of extensive screen time in the lives of children
- Updated research on ADHD, including executive function deficits, links of stimulant drug use to substance abuse later in development, and the role of neurofeedback, mindfulness training, and exercise in reducing ADHD symptoms
- New discussion of autobiographical memories, including how they change from early childhood to adolescence and cultural variations
- Description of recent research on children's working memory
- Inclusion of recent ideas on the use of mindfulness training, as well as other aspects of contemplative science such as yoga, to improve children's cognitive and socioemotional skills
- New coverage of the underrepresentation of ethnic minority children in programs for children who are gifted
- New discussion of the role that metacognitive strategies play in children's writing
- Updated and revised content on English language learners (ELL)

Chapter 10: Socioemotional Development in Middle and Late Childhood

- Expanded and updated coverage of the consequences of low self-esteem for children

- Discussion of recent research on the negative outcomes of giving inflated praise to children

- Recent research that revealed self-regulation was a protective factor in helping children in low-income circumstances to avoid developing emotional problems

- New content on gender in school and achievement contexts, including research on same-sex schools

- Updated information about gender differences in the brain

- New research linking low peer status in childhood with work and mental health problems in early adulthood

- Considerable research updates on bullying, including outcome for victims and also the increasing incidence of cyberbullying and its effects on children

- New coverage of two recent books on the strong disciplinarian orientation of Chinese parents

- New *Connecting Through Research* box that describes the research of Eva Pomerantz and her colleagues on the role of parenting in children's learning and achievement

- Inclusion of recent research that found supportive parenting, not tiger parenting, was the most common type of parenting used by Chinese American parents and tiger parenting was associated with negative academic and emotional outcomes

Chapter 11: Physical and Cognitive Development in Adolescence

- Inclusion of changes based on feedback from leading experts Elizabeth Susman and Bonnie Halpern-Felsher

- Revised definition of puberty to include neuroendocrine processes

- Description of recent research on negative sexual relationships of early-maturing girls

- New commentary on the developmental trajectory of the adolescent brain occurring in a bottom-up, top-down sequence

- Updated and revised content on changes in the limbic system and their role in the influence of reward during adolescence

- New discussion of increased focal activity within a brain region and increasing connectedness across more distant brain regions during adolescence

- New closing statement about research on the adolescent brain being correlational in nature

- Updated data on the sexual activity of U.S. adolescents, including risk factors, condom use, and pregnancy

- Coverage of a number of recent studies on the positive outcomes of exercise during adolescence and the negative outcomes for high levels of screen activity

- New discussion of the role peers play in adolescents' exercise

- Updated data on adolescent substance use and risk factors for substance abuse

- Inclusion of some changes in the description of cognitive development based on leading expert Valerie Reyna's feedback

- New content on whether social media serve as an amplification vehicle for adolescent egocentrism

- New *Connecting with Careers* box on an individual's work to improve young adolescents' science education

- Inclusion of recent research on the positive outcomes of volunteering in adolescence

Chapter 12: Socioemotional Development in Adolescence

- Substantially updated and expanded discussion of cultural and ethnic identity

- New research on the positive outcomes of parental monitoring

- Coverage of recent research on the positive outcomes of adolescent self-disclosure to parents

- Inclusion of recent research on parent-adolescent conflict, including such conflict in immigrant families and links to negative outcomes

- Considerably expanded and updated material on the role of immigration in adolescent development, including the complexity of immigration, parents' level of education, and stressful circumstances

- Updated data on the number of juvenile delinquency cases handled by U.S. courts

- New research on depression and suicide, including links to outcomes of adolescent depression later in development, family factors, victims of dating violence, peer victimization, and cyberbullying

- Updated research on outcomes of the Fast Track delinquency intervention study

Chapter 13: Physical and Cognitive Development in Early Adulthood

- New coverage of Joseph and Claudia Allen's book, *Escaping the Endless Adolescence*, which chronicles how adolescence today is taking too long

- New research on the negative outcomes of chronic sleep deprivation

- Updated content on overweight and obesity trends in college and early adulthood

- New research on binge drinking in emerging adulthood

- Inclusion of recent research on sexual risk factors, such as those involving hooking up and "friends with benefits" relationships in emerging adulthood, as well as gender differences in sexual encounters

- New commentary about how many individuals increasingly are working at a series of jobs and short-term jobs

- Updated data on the percentage of full-time and part-time college students who work while attending college

- Inclusion of recent research on factors that predict unemployment and links between unemployment and increased rates of cardiovascular disease

Chapter 14: Socioemotional Development in Early Adulthood

- Substantially updated discussion of research on connections between attachment earlier in development and adult attachment
- New content on whether online dating is a good idea and recent research on links between online dating and marital satisfaction
- Inclusion of recent research on various aspects of cohabitation, including contextual variations in whether prior cohabitation is likely to determine whether marriages survive or not
- New research on the high expectations newly married individuals have for the success of their marriage, including which individuals' forecasts are most often too optimistic
- Updated data on the percentage of marriages that are likely to end in divorce within 20 years, as well as other recent data on marriage and divorce rates
- Expanded discussion of the negative outcomes of divorce on physical and psychological well-being
- New research exploring how attitudes about divorce, marital quality, and divorce proneness differ for remarried individuals and couples in first marriages

Chapter 15: Physical and Cognitive Development in Middle Adulthood

- Coverage of a recent British study on when middle age begins and what characterizes it
- Discussion of recent research on many facets of obesity and cardiovascular disease in middle age, including new content on resistant hypertension
- New research on sleep-related problems in middle age
- New description of research by Sheldon Cohen and his colleagues showing that stress, emotion, and lack of social support interfere with immune system functioning
- Inclusion of recent research on chronic stress and its links to lower cognitive functioning and a decline in immune system functioning
- New research on factors such as aerobic training and yoga that are associated with a decrease in menopausal symptoms
- Description of recent research on various aspects of hormone replacement therapy (HRT) and its outcomes
- New coverage of the increased use of testosterone therapy with middle-aged men and its outcomes in areas such as sexual functioning and memory
- New discussion of leading Finnish expert Clas-Haken Nygard's research indicating that the ability to work effectively peaks in middle age and explaining why this is so
- Recent data on age variations in the percentage of U.S. adults who have a religious affiliation

Chapter 16: Socioemotional Development in Middle Adulthood

- New research on emotional reactivity to daily stressors and links to health outcomes
- Inclusion of recent research studies on daily stressors and their link to cortisol secretion
- Updated commentary on stability or changes in a positive direction (lower neuroticism, for example) being associated with better health and more competent functioning
- Coverage of recent research on individuals' perceptions of the extent to which their personality changed in the past and is likely to change in the future, as well as how accurate they were about such estimations
- Recent research on outcomes for women who get divorced in middle age
- Inclusion of recent research about middle-aged adults' views on providing support for emerging adult children and aging parents

Chapter 17: Physical Development in Late Adulthood

- Updated life expectancy data, including Latinos' higher life expectancy than non-Latino Whites and the narrowing life expectancy gap between men and women
- Coverage of a number of recent studies on centenarians, including genetic factors, compression of morbidity, as well as inclusion of the Georgia Centenarian Study and the Chinese Longitudinal Healthy Longevity Survey and comments by centenarians, including the person with the longest confirmed life span—Jeanne Louise Calment—about their views on life
- Expanded and updated discussion of sleep, including its link to falls and mild cognitive impairment
- Inclusion of recent research on hearing decline and cognitive functioning, language comprehension, and hearing aids
- New discussion and research on driving and its links to perceptual motor coupling, education, cognitive training, and processing speed
- Expanded and updated coverage of pain perception, persistent pain, most frequent pain complaints, and tolerance of pain
- Coverage of a number of recent studies on the benefits of exercise on aging, including the positive effects of long-term aerobic exercise and the stress-buffering aspects of exercise on mitochondrial functioning, cardiovascular and respiratory functioning, balance and strength, allocation of attention, and positive affect
- Recent research on obesity and links to mortality risk

Chapter 18: Cognitive Development in Late Adulthood

- Inclusion of recent research on allocation of attentional resources, selective attention and video game training to reduce distraction and increase alertness
- Coverage of a number of recent studies on memory, including episodic memory, working memory, and prospective memory
- New research on executive function, including links to falls and speed of processing training
- Inclusion of recent research on the influence of exercise on aging, including studies of tai chi training and executive function, cognitive flexibility, and mobility function

- Discussion of a recent research review on definitions of wisdom and links of wisdom to various outcomes in older adults
- Coverage of a recent research review indicating that exercise's positive link to cognition is associated with management of energy metabolism and synaptic plasticity
- Recent research by Denise Park and her colleagues on the positive effects of sustained engagement in cognitively demanding novel activities
- Discussion of recent research on the effects of video game training on older adults' cognitive skills
- Coverage of recent meta-examinations of four major longitudinal studies of cognitive aging
- Description of recent research on the positive effects of fish oil consumption on executive function
- Recent research on older adults working later in their lives and the role of working in a job with high cognitive demands
- New discussion of the role that bilingualism plays in delaying the onset of Alzheimer disease
- New discussion of the roles that tau and amyloid likely play in Alzheimer disease
- Inclusion of recent research on effects of attending religious services, links between religion/spirituality and longevity, and links between religious identification and health

Chapter 19: Socioemotional Development in Late Adulthood

- Recent research on the role of physical activity in life satisfaction and social interaction
- Inclusion of recent research on changes in peripheral social contacts and close relationships from 18 to 94 years of age

- New research on rates of positive emotion from 22 to 93 years of age, including the impact of the time of day when emotion is assessed
- Description of recent research on the role of self-control in older adults' engagement in physical activities
- Discussion of recent research on the Internet activity of older adults
- New section on attachment from early adulthood to late adulthood, including a recent research review of change across these age periods
- Inclusion of recent research on social activities, social isolation, and loneliness
- Description of recent studies on links between volunteering and mortality risk as well as the connection between psychological well-being and exercise

Chapter 20: Death, Dying, and Grieving

- Inclusion of recent research studies on advance care planning and the type of care people receive at the end of life
- Updated content on assisted suicide in various countries
- Recent research on links between older adults' bereavement and dysregulated cortisol patterns
- Updated discussion of prolonged grief disorder and the American Psychiatric Association's view on this disorder
- New description of what to say and what not to say to an individual who is grieving
- Coverage of recent research studies on widowhood and its links to longevity (including gender differences), depression and marital quality, bereavement, and expectations of being reunited with loved ones in the afterlife

Online Instructor Resources

The resources listed here accompany *Life-Span Development,* 15th edition. Please contact your McGraw-Hill representative for details concerning the availability of these and other valuable materials that can help you design and enhance your course.

Instructor's Manual   Broken down by chapter, these include chapter outlines, suggested lecture topics, classroom activities and demonstrations, suggested student research projects, essay questions, and critical thinking questions.

Test Bank and Computerized Test Bank   This comprehensive Test Bank includes more than 1,500 multiple-choice and approximately 75 essay questions. Organized by chapter, the questions are designed to test factual, applied, and conceptual understanding. All test questions are compatible with EZ Test, McGraw-Hill's Computerized Test Bank program.

PowerPoint Slides   These presentations cover the key points of each chapter and include charts and graphs from the text. They can be used as is, or you may modify them to meet your specific needs.

Acknowledgments

I very much appreciate the support and guidance provided to me by many people at McGraw-Hill. Krista Bettino, Executive Director, Products and Markets, has provided excellent guidance, vision, and direction for this book. Vicki Malinee provided considerable expertise in coordinating many aspects of the editorial process for this text. Janet Tilden again did an outstanding job as the book's copy editor. Sheila Frank did a terrific job in coordinating the book's production. Dawn Groundwater, Lead Product Developer, did excellent work on various aspects of the book's development, technology, and learning systems. Thanks also to Ann Helgerson and A.J. Laferrera for their extensive and outstanding work in marketing *Life-Span Development*. And Jennifer Blankenship provided me with excellent choices of new photographs for this edition of the book.

I also want to thank my parents, John and Ruth Santrock, my wife, Mary Jo, our children, Tracy and Jennifer, and our grandchildren, Jordan, Alex, and Luke, for their wonderful contributions to my life and for helping me to better understand the marvels and mysteries of life-span development.

EXPERT CONSULTANTS

As I develop a new edition of this text, I consult with leading experts in their respective areas of life-span development. Their invaluable feedback ensures that the latest research, knowledge, and perspectives are presented throughout the text. Their willingness to devote their time and expertise to this endeavor is greatly appreciated. The Expert Consultants who contributed to this edition, along with their biographies and commentary, can be found on pages xiii–xv.

REVIEWERS

I owe a special debt of gratitude to the reviewers who have provided detailed feedback on *Life-Span Development* over the years.

Patrick K. Ackles, *Michigan State University;* **Berkeley Adams,** *Jamestown Community College;* **Jackie Adamson,** *South Dakota School of Mines & Technology;* **Pamela Adelmann,** *Saint Paul Technical College;* **Joanne M. Alegre,** *Yavapai College;* **Gary L. Allen,** *University of South Carolina;* **Kristy Allen,** *Ozark Technical College;* **Lilia Allen,** *Charles County Community College;* **Ryan Allen,** *The Citadel;* **Susan E. Allen,** *Baylor University;* **Paul Anderer Castillo,** *SUNY Canton;* **Doreen Arcus,** *University of Massachusetts–Lowell;* **Frank R. Ashbur,** *Valdosta State College;* **Leslie Ault,** *Hostos Community College–CUNY;* **Renee L. Babcock,** *Central Michigan University;* **John Bauer,** *University of Dayton;* **Diana Baumrind,** *University of California–Berkeley;* **Daniel R. Bellack,** *Trident Technical College;* **Helen E. Benedict,** *Baylor University;* **Alice D. Beyrent,** *Hesser College;* **John Biondo,** *Community College of Allegheny County–Boyce Campus;* **James A. Blackburn,** *University of Wisconsin at Madison;* **William Blackston,** *Baltimore City Community College;* **Stephanie Blecharczyk,** *Keene State College;* **Belinda Blevins-Knabe,** *University of Arkansas–Little Rock;* **Marc H. Bornstein,** *National Institute of Child Health & Development;* **Karyn Mitchell Boutlin,** *Massasoit Community College;* **Donald Bowers,** *Community College of Philadelphia;* **Saundra Y. Boyd,** *Houston Community College;* **Michelle Boyer-Pennington,** *Middle Tennessee State University;* **Ann Brandt-Williams,** *Glendale Community College;* **Julia Braungart-Rieke,** *University of Notre Dame;* **Gregory Braswell,** *Illinois State University;* **Kathy Brown,** *California State University—Fullerton;* **Jack Busky,** *Harrisburg Area Community College;* **Marion Cahill,** *Our Lady of the Lake College;* **Joan B. Cannon,** *University of Lowell;* **Jeri Carter,** *Glendale Community College;* **Vincent Castranovo,** *Community College of Philadelphia;* **Ginny Chappeleau,** *Muskingum Area Technical College;* **Dominique Charlotteaux,** *Broward Community College;* **Rosalind Charlesworth,** *Weber State University;* **Yiwei Chen,** *Bowling Green State University;* **Bill Cheney,** *Crichton College;* **M. A. Christenberry,** *Augusta College;* **Saundra Ciccarelli,** *Florida Gulf University;* **Kevin Clark,** *Indiana*

University—Kokomo; **Andrea Clements**, *East Tennessee State University;* **Meredith Cohen**, *University of Pittsburgh;* **Diane Cook**, *Gainesville College;* **Pamela Costa**, *Tacoma Community College;* **Ava Craig**, *Sacramento City College;* **Kathleen Crowley-Long**, *College of Saint Rose;* **Cynthia Crown**, *Xavier University;* **Jennifer Dale**, *Community College of Aurora;* **Dana Davidson**, *University of Hawaii—Manoa;* **Diane Davis**, *Bowie State University;* **Karen Davis**, *Chippewa Valley Technical College;* **Tom L. Day**, *Weber State University;* **Mehgen Delaney**, *College of the Canyons;* **Doreen DeSantio**, *West Chester University;* **Jill De Villiers**, *Smith College;* **Darryl M. Dietrich**, *College of St. Scholastica;* **Alisa Diop**, *The Community College of Baltimore County;* **Bailey Drechsler**, *Cuesta College;* **Joseph Durlack**, *Loyola University;* **Mary B. Eberly**, *Oakland University;* **Margaret Sutton Edmonds**, *University of Massachusetts-Boston;* **Glen Elder**, *University of North Carolina—Chapel Hill;* **Martha M. Ellis**, *Collin County Community College;* **Lena Eriksen**, *Western Washington University;* **Richard Ewy**, *Pennsylvania State University;* **Dan Fawaz**, *Georgia Perimeter College;* **Shirley Feldman**, *Stanford University;* **Roberta Ferra**, *University of Kentucky;* **Tiffany Field**, *University of Miami;* **Linda E. Flickinger**, *St. Claire Community College;* **Alan Fogel**, *University of Utah;* **Lynne Andreozzi Fontaine**, *Community College of Rhode Island;* **Tom Frangicetto**, *Northampton Community College;* **Kathleen Corrigan Fuhs**, *J. Sargeant Reynolds Community College;* **J. Steven Fulks**, *Utah State University;* **Cathy Furlong**, *Tulsa Junior College;* **Duwayne Furman**, *Western Illinois University;* **John Gat**, *Humboldt State University;* **Marvin Gelman**, *Montgomery County College;* **G.R. Germo**, *University of California—Irvine;* **Rebecca J. Glare**, *Weber State College;* **David Goldstein**, *Temple University;* **Arthur Gonchar**, *University of LaVerne;* **Judy Goodell**, *National University;* **Mary Ann Goodwyn**, *Northeast Louisiana University;* **Caroline Gould**, *Eastern Michigan University;* **Julia Graber**, *Columbia University;* **Peter C. Gram**, *Pensacola Junior College;* **Dan Grangaard**, *Austin Community College;* **Tom Gray**, *Laredo Community College;* **Michele Gregoire**, *University of Florida—Gainesville;* **Michael Green**, *University of North Carolina;* **Rea Gubler**, *Southern Utah University;* **Gary Gute**, *University of Northern Iowa;* **Laura Hanish**, *Arizona State University;* **Ester Hanson**, *Prince George's Community College;* **Marian S. Harris**, *University of Illinois—Chicago;* **Yvette R. Harris**, *Miami University of Ohio;* **Amanda W. Harrist**, *Oklahoma State University;* **Robert Heavilin**, *Greater Hartford Community College;* **Donna Henderson**, *Wake Forest University;* **Debra Hollister**, *Valencia Community College;* **Heather Holmes-Lonergan**, *Metropolitan State College of Denver;* **Ramona O. Hopkins**, *Brigham Young University;* **Donna Horbury**, *Appalachian State University;* **Susan Horton**, *Mesa Community College;* **Sharon C. Hott**, *Allegany College of Maryland;* **John Hotz**, *Saint Cloud State University;* **Tasha Howe**, *Humboldt State University;* **Kimberley Howe-Norris**, *Cape Fear Community College;* **Stephen Hoyer**, *Pittsburgh State University;* **Charles H. Huber**, *New Mexico State University;* **Kathleen Day Hulbert**, *University of Massachusetts-Lowell;* **Derek Isaacowitz**, *Brandeis University;* **Kathryn French Iroz**, *Utah Valley State College;* **Terry Isbell**, *Northwestern State University of Louisiana;* **Erwin Janek**, *Henderson State University;* **Jamia Jasper Jacobsen**, *Indiana University-Purdue University Indianapolis;* **Christina Jose-Kampfner**, *Eastern Michigan University;* **Ursula Joyce**, *St. Thomas Aquinas College;* **Barbara Kane**, *Indiana State University;* **Ulas Kaplan**, *Harvard University;* **Kevin Keating**, *Broward Community College;* **James L. Keeney**, *Middle Georgia College;* **Elinor Kinarthy**, *Rio Hondo College;* **Karen Kirkendall**, *Sangamon State University;* **A. Klingner**, *Northwest Community College;* **Steven J. Kohn**, *Nazareth College;* **Amanda Kowal**, *University of Missouri;* **Jane Krump**, *North Dakota State College of Science;* **Nadene L'Amoreaux**, *Indiana University of Pennsylvania;* **Gisela Labouvie-Vief**, *Wayne State University;* **Joseph C. LaVoie**, *University of Nebraska—Omaha;* **Kathy Lein**, *Community College of Denver;* **Jean Hill Macht**, *Montgomery County Community College;* **Salvador Macias**, *University of South Carolina—Sumter;* **Karen Macrae**, *University of South Carolina;* **Christine Malecki**, *Northern Illinois University;* **Kathy Manuel**, *Bossier Parish Community College;* **James Marcia**, *Simon Fraser University;* **Myra Marcus**, *Florida Gulf Coast University;* **Carrie Margolin**, *The Evergreen State College;* **Allan Mayotte**, *Riverland Community College;* **Susan McClure**, *Westmoreland Community College;* **Dorothy H. McDonald**, *Sandhills Community College;* **Robert C. McGinnis**, *Ancilla College;* **Clara McKinney**, *Barstow College;* **Robert McLaren**, *California State University—Fullerton;* **Deborah H. McMurtrie**, *University of South Carolina—*

Aiken; **Sharon McNeeley,** *Northeastern Illinois University;* **Daysi Mejia,** *Florida Gulf Coast University;* **Kathleen Mentink,** *Chippewa Valley Technical College;* **James Messina,** *University of Phoenix;* **Heather E. Metcalfe,** *University of Windsor;* **Karla Miley,** *Black Hawk College;* **Jessica Miller,** *Mesa State College;* **Scott Miller,** *University of Florida;* **Teri M. Miller-Schwartz,** *Milwaukee Area Technical College;* **David B. Mitchell,** *Loyola University;* **Joann Montepare,** *Emerson College;* **Gary T. Montgomery,** *University of Texas—Pan American;* **Martin D. Murphy,** *University of Akron;* **Malinda Muzi,** *Community College of Philadelphia;* **Gordon K. Nelson,** *Pennsylvania State University;* **Michael Newton,** *Sam Houston State University;* **Charisse Nixon,** *Pennsylvania State University—Erie;* **Beatrice Norrie,** *Mount Royal College;* **Jean O'Neil,** *Boston College;* **Laura Overstreet,** *Tarrant County College–Northeast;* **Karla Parise,** *The Community College of Baltimore County—Essex;* **Jennifer Parker,** *University of South Carolina;* **Barba Patton,** *University of Houston–Victoria;* **Susan Perez,** *University of North Florida;* **Pete Peterson,** *Johnson County Community College;* **Richard Pierce,** *Pennsylvania State University–Altoona;* **David Pipes,** *Caldwell Community College;* **Leslee Pollina,** *Southeast Missouri State University;* **Robert Poresky,** *Kansas State University;* **Christopher Quarto,** *Middle Tennessee State University;* **Bob Rainey,** *Florida Community College;* **Nancy Rankin,** *University of New England;* **H. Ratner,** *Wayne State University;* **Cynthia Reed,** *Tarrant County College–Northeast;* **James Reid,** *Washington University;* **Amy Reesing,** *Arizona University;* **Russell Riley,** *Lord Fairfax Community College;* **Mark P. Rittman,** *Cuyahoga Community College;* **Cathie Robertson,** *Grossmont College;* **Clarence Romeno,** *Riverside Community College;* **Paul Roodin,** *SUNY–Oswego;* **Ron Rossac,** *University of North Florida;* **Peggy Russell,** *Indiana River State College;* **Julia Rux,** *Georgia Perimeter College;* **Carolyn Saarni,** *Sonoma State University;* **Karen Salekin,** *University of Alabama;* **Gayla Sanders,** *The Community College of Baltimore County–Essex;* **Toru Sato,** *Shippensburg University;* **Nancy Sauerman,** *Kirkwood Community College;* **Cynthia Scheibe,** *Ithaca College;* **Robert Schell,** *SUNY–Oswego;* **Rachel Schremp,** *Santa Fe Community College;* **Pamela Schuetze,** *Buffalo State College;* **Edythe Schwartz,** *California State University—Sacramento;* **Lisa Scott,** *University of Minnesota–Twin Cities;* **Owen Sharkey,** *University of Prince Edward Island;* **Elisabeth Shaw,** *Texarkana College;* **Susan Nakayama Siaw,** *California State Polytechnical University;* **Jessica Siebenbruner,** *Winona State College;* **Vicki Simmons,** *University of Victoria;* **Gregory Smith,** *University of Maryland;* **Jon Snodgrass,** *California State University–Los Angeles;* **Donald Stanley,** *North Dallas Community College;* **Jean A. Steitz,** *University of Memphis;* **Terre Sullivan,** *Chippewa Valley Technical College;* **Collier Summers,** *Florida Community College at Jacksonville;* **Barbara Thomas,** *National University;* **Stacy D. Thompson,** *Oklahoma State University;* **Debbie Tindell,** *Wilkes University;* **Stephen Truhon,** *Winston-Salem State University;* **James Turcott,** *Kalamazoo Valley Community College;* **Marian Underwood,** *University of Texas—Dallas;* **Dennis Valone,** *Pennsylvania State University—Erie;* **Gaby Vandergiessen,** *Fairmount State College;* **Elisa Velasquez,** *Sonoma State University;* **Stephen Werba,** *The Community College of Baltimore County—Catonsville;* **B. D. Whetstone,** *Birmingham Southern College;* **Susan Whitbourne,** *University of Massachusetts—Amherst;* **Nancy C. White,** *Reynolds Community College;* **Lyn W. Wickelgren,** *Metropolitan State College;* **Ann M. Williams,** *Luzerne County Community College;* **Myron D. Williams,** *Great Lakes Bible College;* **Linda B. Wilson,** *Quincy College;* **Mark Winkel,** *University of Texas—Pan American;* **Mary Ann Wisniewski,** *Carroll College.*

All the world's a stage,
And all the men and women merely players.
They have their exits and their entrances;
and one man in his time plays many parts.

—**WILLIAM SHAKESPEARE**
English Playwright, 17th Century

The Life-Span Perspective

This book is about human development—its universal features, its individual variations, its nature. Every life is distinct, a new biography in the world. Examining the shape of life-span development allows us to understand it better. *Life-Span Development* is about the rhythm and meaning of people's lives, about turning mystery into understanding, and about weaving a portrait of who each of us was, is, and will be. In Section 1, you will read the "Introduction" (Chapter 1).

INTRODUCTION

chapter **outline**

Ted Kaczynski sprinted through high school, not bothering with his junior year and making only passing efforts at social contact. Off to Harvard at age 16, Kaczynski was a loner during his college years.

One of his roommates at Harvard said that he avoided people by quickly shuffling by them and slamming the door behind him. After obtaining his Ph.D. in mathematics at the University of Michigan, Kaczynski became a professor at the University of California at Berkeley. His colleagues there remember him as hiding from social contact—no friends, no allies, no networking.

After several years at Berkeley, Kaczynski resigned and moved to a rural area of Montana where he lived as a hermit in a crude shack for 25 years. Town residents described him as a bearded eccentric. Kaczynski traced his own difficulties to growing up as a genius in a kid's body and sticking out like a sore thumb in his surroundings as a child. In 1996, he was arrested and charged as the notorious Unabomber, America's most-wanted killer. Over the course of 17 years, Kaczynski had sent 16 mail bombs that left 23 people wounded or maimed and 3 people dead. In 1998, he pleaded guilty to the offenses and was sentenced to life in prison.

A decade before Kaczynski mailed his first bomb, Alice Walker spent her days battling racism in Mississippi. She had recently won her first writing fellowship, but rather than use the money to follow her dream of moving to Senegal, Africa, she put herself into the heart and heat of the civil rights movement. Walker had grown up knowing the brutal effects of poverty and racism. Born in 1944, she was the eighth child of Georgia sharecroppers who earned $300 a year. When Walker was 8, her brother accidentally shot her in the left eye with a BB gun. By the time her parents got her to the hospital a week later (they had no car), she was blind in that eye, and it had developed a disfiguring layer of scar tissue. Despite the counts against her, Walker overcame pain and anger and went on to win a Pulitzer Prize for her book *The Color Purple*. She became not only a novelist but also an essayist, a poet, a short-story writer, and a social activist.

Ted Kaczynski, the convicted Unabomber, traced his difficulties to growing up as a genius in a kid's body and not fitting in when he was a child.

Ted Kaczynski, about age 15–16.

Alice Walker won the Pulitzer Prize for her book *The Color Purple*. Like the characters in her book, Walker overcame pain and anger to triumph and celebrate the human spirit.

Alice Walker, about age 8.

preview

What leads one individual, so full of promise, to commit brutal acts of violence and another to turn poverty and trauma into a rich literary harvest? If you have ever wondered why people turn out the way they do, you have asked yourself the central question we will explore in this book. This book is a window into the journey of human development—your own and that of every other member of the human species. In this first chapter, we will explore what it means to take a life-span perspective on development, examine the nature of development, and outline how science helps us to understand it.

1 The Life-Span Perspective

 LG1 Discuss the distinctive features of a life-span perspective on development.

The Importance of Studying Life-Span Development

Characteristics of the Life-Span Perspective

Some Contemporary Concerns

We reach backward to our parents and forward to our children, and through their children to a future we will never see, but about which we need to care.

—CARL JUNG
Swiss Psychiatrist, 20th Century

Each of us develops partly like all other individuals, partly like some other individuals, and partly like no other individual. Most of the time our attention is directed to an individual's uniqueness. But as humans, we have all traveled some common paths. Each of us—Leonardo da Vinci, Joan of Arc, George Washington, Martin Luther King, Jr., and you—walked at about 1 year, engaged in fantasy play as a young child, and became more independent as a youth. Each of us, if we live long enough, will experience hearing problems and the death of family members and friends. This is the general course of our **development,** the pattern of movement or change that begins at conception and continues through the human life span.

In this section, we will explore what is meant by the concept of development and why the study of life-span development is important. We will outline the main characteristics of the life-span perspective and discuss various sources of contextual influences. In addition, we will examine some contemporary concerns in life-span development.

THE IMPORTANCE OF STUDYING LIFE-SPAN DEVELOPMENT

How might people benefit from examining life-span development? Perhaps you are, or will be, a parent or teacher. If so, responsibility for children is, or will be, a part of your everyday life. The more you learn about them, the better you can deal with them. Perhaps you hope to gain some insight about your own history—as an infant, a child, an adolescent, or a young adult. Perhaps you want to know more about what your life will be like as you grow through the adult years—as a middle-aged adult, or as an adult in old age, for example. Or perhaps you just stumbled onto this course, thinking that it sounded intriguing and that the study of the human life span might raise some provocative issues. Whatever your reasons for taking this course, you will discover that the study of life-span development is intriguing and filled with information about who we are, how we came to be this way, and where our future will take us.

Most development involves growth, but it also includes decline (as in dying). In exploring development, we will examine the life span from the point of conception until the time when life (or at least life as we know it) ends. You will see yourself as an infant, as a child, and as an adolescent, and be stimulated to think about how those years influenced the kind of individual you are today. And you will see yourself as a young adult, as a middle-aged adult, and as an adult in old age, and be motivated to think about how

development The pattern of change that begins at conception and continues through the life span. Most development involves growth, although it also includes decline brought on by aging and dying.

life-span perspective The perspective that development is lifelong, multidimensional, multidirectional, plastic, multidisciplinary, and contextual; involves growth, maintenance, and regulation; and is constructed through biological, sociocultural, and individual factors working together.

your experiences today will influence your development through the remainder of your adult years.

CHARACTERISTICS OF THE LIFE-SPAN PERSPECTIVE

Although growth and development are dramatic during the first two decades of life, development is not something that happens only to children and adolescents. The traditional approach to the study of development emphasizes extensive change from birth to adolescence (especially during infancy), little or no change in adulthood, and decline in old age. But a great deal of change does occur in the five or six decades after adolescence. The life-span approach emphasizes developmental change throughout adulthood as well as childhood (Freund & others, 2013; Schaie & Willis, 2014).

Recent increases in human life expectancy contributed to the popularity of the life-span approach to development. The upper boundary of the human life span (based on the oldest age documented) is 122 years, as indicated in Figure 1.1; this maximum life span of humans has not changed since the beginning of recorded history. What has changed is life expectancy—the average number of years that a person born in a particular year can expect to live. In the twentieth century alone, life expectancy in the United States increased by 31 years, thanks to improvements in sanitation, nutrition, and medicine (see Figure 1.2). In the first half of the second decade of the twenty-first century, the life expectancy in the United States is 78 years of age (U.S. Census Bureau, 2013). Today, for most individuals in developed countries, childhood and adolescence represent only about one-fourth of their lives.

The belief that development occurs throughout life is central to the life-span perspective on human development, but this perspective has other characteristics as well. According to life-span development expert Paul Baltes (1939–2006), the **life-span perspective** views development as lifelong, multidimensional, multidirectional, plastic, multidisciplinary, and contextual, and as a process that involves growth, maintenance, and regulation of loss (Baltes, 1987, 2003; Baltes, Lindenberger, & Staudinger, 2006). In Baltes' view, it is important to understand that development is constructed through biological, sociocultural, and individual factors working together. Let's look at each of these components of the life-span perspective.

Development Is Lifelong In the life-span perspective, early adulthood is not the endpoint of development; rather, no age period dominates development. Researchers increasingly study the experiences and psychological orientations of adults at different points in their lives. Later in this chapter, we will describe the age periods of development and their characteristics.

Development Is Multidimensional No matter what your age might be, your body, mind, emotions, and relationships are changing and affecting each other. Consider the development of Ted Kaczynski, the Unabomber discussed at the beginning of this chapter. When he was 6 months old, he was hospitalized with a severe allergic reaction and his parents were rarely allowed to visit the baby. According to his mother, the previously happy baby was never the same after his hospitalization. The infant became withdrawn and unresponsive. As Ted grew up, he had periodic "shutdowns" accompanied by rage. In his mother's view, a biological event in infancy warped the development of her son's mind and emotions.

Development has biological, cognitive, and socioemotional dimensions. Even within a dimension, there are many components. For example, attention, memory, abstract thinking, speed of processing information, and social intelligence are just a few of the components of the cognitive dimension.

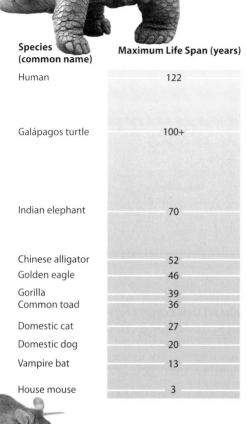

Species (common name)	Maximum Life Span (years)
Human	122
Galápagos turtle	100+
Indian elephant	70
Chinese alligator	52
Golden eagle	46
Gorilla	39
Common toad	36
Domestic cat	27
Domestic dog	20
Vampire bat	13
House mouse	3

FIGURE 1.1

MAXIMUM RECORDED LIFE SPAN FOR DIFFERENT SPECIES. Our only competitor for the maximum recorded life span is the Galápagos turtle.

Paul Baltes, a leading architect of the life-span perspective of development, conversing with one of the long-time research participants in the Berlin Aging Study that he directed. She joined the study in the early 1990s and participated six times in extensive physical, medical, psychological, and social assessments. In her professional life, she was a practicing medical doctor.

Time Period	Average Life Expectancy (years)
2013, USA	78
1954, USA	70
1915, USA	54
1900, USA	47
19th century, England	41
1620, Massachusetts Bay Colony	35
Middle Ages, England	33
Ancient Greece	20
Prehistoric times	18

FIGURE 1.2

HUMAN LIFE EXPECTANCY AT BIRTH FROM PREHISTORIC TO CONTEMPORARY TIMES. It took 5,000 years to extend human life expectancy from 18 to 41 years of age.

developmental **connection**

Exercise

What effect might exercise have on children's and older adults' ability to process information? Chapter 9, p. 269; Chapter 17, p. 530

What characterizes the life-span perspective on development?

Development Is Multidirectional Throughout life, some dimensions or components of a dimension expand and others shrink. For example, when one language (such as English) is acquired early in development, the capacity for acquiring second and third languages (such as Spanish and Chinese) decreases later in development, especially after early childhood (Levelt, 1989). During adolescence, as individuals establish romantic relationships, their time spent with friends may decrease. During late adulthood, older adults might become wiser because they have more experience than younger adults to draw upon to guide their decision making, but they perform more poorly on tasks that require speed in processing information (Manard & others, 2014; Salthouse, 2013).

Development Is Plastic Even at 10 years old, Ted Kaczynski was extraordinarily shy. Was he destined to remain forever uncomfortable with people? Developmentalists debate how much plasticity people have in various dimensions at different points in their development. Plasticity means the capacity for change. For example, can you still improve your intellectual skills when you are in your seventies or eighties? Or might these intellectual skills be fixed by the time you are in your thirties so that further improvement is impossible? Researchers have found that the cognitive skills of older adults can be improved through training and developing better strategies (Dixon & others, 2013; Rebok & others, 2014). However, possibly we possess less capacity for change as we grow older (Salthouse, 2013). The search for plasticity and its constraints is a key element on the contemporary agenda for developmental research (de Frias & Dixon, 2014; Yu & others, 2014).

Developmental Science Is Multidisciplinary Psychologists, sociologists, anthropologists, neuroscientists, and medical researchers all share an interest in unlocking the mysteries of development through the life span. How do your heredity and health limit your intelligence? Do intelligence and social relationships change with age in the same way around the world? How do families and schools influence intellectual development? These are examples of research questions that cut across disciplines.

Development Is Contextual All development occurs within a context, or setting. Contexts include families, schools, peer groups, churches, cities, neighborhoods, university laboratories, countries, and so on. Each of these settings is influenced by historical, economic, social, and cultural factors.

Contexts, like individuals, change (Clarke-Stewart & Parke, 2014; Gauvain, 2013). Thus, individuals are changing beings in a changing world. As a result of these changes, contexts exert three types of influences (Baltes, 2003): (1) normative age-graded influences, (2) normative history-graded influences, and (3) nonnormative or highly individualized life events. Each of these types can have a biological or environmental impact on development. **Normative age-graded influences** are similar for individuals in a particular age group. These influences include biological processes such as puberty and menopause. They also include sociocultural, environmental processes such as beginning formal education (usually at about age 6 in most cultures) and retirement from the workforce (which takes place during the fifties and sixties in most cultures).

Normative history-graded influences are common to people of a particular generation because of historical circumstances. For example, in their youth American baby boomers shared the experience of the Cuban missile crisis, the assassination of John F. Kennedy, and the Beatles invasion. Other examples of normative history-graded influences include economic, political, and social upheavals such as the Great Depression in the 1930s, World War II in the 1940s, the civil rights and women's rights movements of the 1960s and 1970s, the terrorist attacks of 9/11/2001, as well as the integration of computers and cell phones into everyday life during the 1990s (Schaie, 2013). Long-term changes in the genetic and cultural makeup of a population (due to immigration or changes in fertility rates) are also part of normative historical change.

Nonnormative life events are unusual occurrences that have a major impact on the lives of individual people. These events do not happen to everyone, and when they do occur they can influence people in different ways. Examples include the death of a parent when a child is young, pregnancy in early adolescence, a fire that destroys a home, winning the lottery, or getting an unexpected career opportunity.

Development Involves Growth, Maintenance, and Regulation of Loss

Baltes and his colleagues (2006) assert that the mastery of life often involves conflicts and competition among three goals of human development: growth, maintenance, and regulation of loss. As individuals age into middle and late adulthood, the maintenance and regulation of loss in their capacities takes center stage. Thus, a 75-year-old man might aim not to improve his memory or his golf swing but to maintain his independence and his ability to play golf at all. In Chapters 15 and 16, we will discuss these ideas about maintenance and regulation of loss in greater depth.

Development Is a Co-construction of Biology, Culture, and the Individual

Development is a co-construction of biological, cultural, and individual factors working together (Baltes, Reuter-Lorenz, & Rösler, 2011). For example, the brain shapes culture, but it is also shaped by culture and the experiences that individuals have or pursue. In terms of individual factors, we can go beyond what our genetic inheritance and environment give us. We can author a unique developmental path by actively choosing from the environment the things that optimize our lives (Rathunde & Csikszentmihalyi, 2006).

SOME CONTEMPORARY CONCERNS

Pick up a newspaper or magazine and you might see headlines like these: "Political Leanings May Be Written in the Genes," "Mother Accused of Tossing Children into Bay," "Gender Gap Widens," "FDA Warns About ADHD Drug," "Heart Attack Deaths Higher in African American Patients," "Test May Predict Alzheimer's Disease." Researchers using the life-span perspective are examining these and many other topics of contemporary concern. The roles that health and well-being, parenting, education, and sociocultural contexts play in life-span development, as well as how social policy is related to these issues, are a particular focus of this textbook.

Health and Well-Being   Health professionals today recognize the power of lifestyles and psychological states in health and well-being (Donatelle, 2015; Insel & Roth, 2014). In every chapter of this book, issues of health and well-being are integrated into our discussion.

Clinical psychologists are among the health professionals who help people improve their well-being. Read about one clinical psychologist who helps adolescents who have become juvenile delinquents or substance abusers in *Connecting with Careers*.

Parenting and Education   Can two gay men raise a healthy family? Are children harmed if both parents work outside the home? Are U.S. schools failing to teach children how to read and write and calculate adequately? We hear many questions like these involving pressures on the contemporary family and the problems of U.S. schools (Bredekamp, 2014; Cicchetti & Toth, 2015). In later chapters, we will analyze child care, the effects of divorce, parenting styles, child maltreatment, intergenerational relationships, early childhood education, links between childhood poverty and education, bilingual education, new educational efforts to improve lifelong learning, and many other issues related to parenting and education (Collins, Duncanson, & Burrows, 2014; Powell, 2015).

Sociocultural Contexts and Diversity   Health, parenting, and education—like development itself—are all shaped by their sociocultural context. To analyze this context, four concepts are especially useful: culture, ethnicity, socioeconomic status, and gender.

Nonnormative life events, such as Hurricane Sandy, are unusual circumstances that have a major impact on a person's life.

----------->
developmental **connection**
Middle Age
Adults typically face more losses in middle age than earlier in life. Chapter 15, p. 460

How might growth versus maintenance and regulation be reflected in the development of this grandfather and his grandchild?

normative age-graded influences Influences that are similar for individuals in a particular age group.

normative history-graded influences Influences that are common to people of a particular generation because of historical circumstances.

nonnormative life events Unusual occurrences that have a major impact on an individual's life.

Luis Vargas, Clinical Child Psychologist

Luis Vargas is Director of the Clinical Child Psychology Internship Program and a professor in the Department of Psychiatry at the University of New Mexico Health Sciences Center. He also is Director of Psychology at the University of New Mexico Children's Psychiatric Center.

Vargas obtained an undergraduate degree in psychology from St. Edward's University in Texas, a master's degree in psychology from Trinity University in Texas, and a Ph.D. in clinical psychology from the University of Nebraska-Lincoln.

Vargas' main interests are cultural issues and the assessment and treatment of children, adolescents, and families. He is motivated to find better ways to provide culturally responsive mental health services. One of his special interests is the treatment of Latino youth for delinquency and substance abuse.

Luis Vargas (*left*) conducting a child therapy session.

For more information about what clinical psychologists do, see page 42 in the Careers in Life-Span Development appendix immediately following this chapter.

Children learn to love when they are loved

culture The behavior patterns, beliefs, and all other products of a group that are passed on from generation to generation.

cross-cultural studies Comparison of one culture with one or more other cultures. These provide information about the degree to which development is similar, or universal, across cultures, and the degree to which it is culture-specific.

ethnicity A characteristic based on cultural heritage, nationality characteristics, race, religion, and language.

socioeconomic status (SES) Refers to the grouping of people with similar occupational, educational, and economic characteristics.

gender The characteristics of people as males or females.

social policy A national government's course of action designed to promote the welfare of its citizens.

Culture encompasses the behavior patterns, beliefs, and all other products of a particular group of people that are passed on from generation to generation. Culture results from the interaction of people over many years (Mistry, Contreras, & Dutta, 2013). A cultural group can be as large as the United States or as small as an isolated Appalachian town. Whatever its size, the group's culture influences the behavior of its members (Hooyman, Kiyak, & Kawamoto, 2015). **Cross-cultural studies** compare aspects of two or more cultures. The comparison provides information about the degree to which development is similar, or universal, across cultures, or is instead culture-specific (Gauvain, 2013).

Ethnicity (the word *ethnic* comes from the Greek word for "nation") is rooted in cultural heritage, nationality, race, religion, and language. African Americans, Latinos, Asian Americans, Native Americans, European Americans, and Arab Americans are a few examples of broad ethnic groups in the United States. Diversity exists within each ethnic group (Banks, 2014; Renzetti & Kennedy-Bergen, 2015). A special concern is the discrimination and prejudice experienced by ethnic minority children (Benner & Graham, 2013).

Socioeconomic status (SES) refers to a person's position within society based on occupational, educational, and economic characteristics. Socioeconomic status implies certain inequalities. Differences in the ability to control resources and to participate in society's rewards produce unequal opportunities (Huston, 2013).

Gender refers to the characteristics of people as males and females. Few aspects of our development are more central to our identity and social relationships than gender (Hyde, 2014; Leaper, 2013).

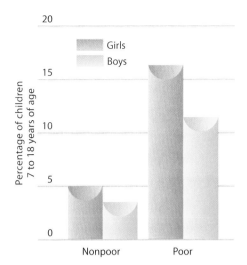

FIGURE **1.3**

PERCENTAGE OF CHILDREN 7 TO 18 YEARS OF AGE AROUND THE WORLD WHO HAVE NEVER BEEN TO SCHOOL OF ANY KIND.
When UNICEF (2004) surveyed the education that children around the world were receiving, it found that far more girls than boys received no formal schooling at all.

Two Korean-born children on the day they became United States citizens. Asian American and Latino children are the fastest-growing immigrant groups in the United States. *How diverse are the students in your life-span development class? How are their experiences in growing up likely to have been similar to or different from yours?*

Doly Akter, age 17, lives in a slum in Dhaka, Bangladesh, where sewers overflow, garbage rots in the streets, and children are undernourished. Nearly two-thirds of young women in Bangladesh get married before they are 18. Doly organized a club supported by UNICEF in which girls go door-to-door to monitor the hygiene habits of households in their neighborhood. The monitoring has led to improved hygiene and health in the families. Also, her group has managed to stop several child marriages by meeting with parents and convincing them that it is not in their daughters' best interests. When talking with parents in their neighborhoods, the girls in the club emphasize the importance of staying in school and how this will improve their daughters' future. Doly says that the girls in her UNICEF group are far more aware of their rights than their mothers ever were (UNICEF, 2007).

In the United States, the sociocultural context has become increasingly diverse in recent years (Koppelman, 2014). The U.S. population includes a greater variety of cultures and ethnic groups than ever before. This changing demographic tapestry promises not only the richness that diversity produces but also difficult challenges in extending the American dream to all individuals (Spring, 2014). We will discuss sociocultural contexts and diversity in each chapter.

A special cross-cultural concern is the educational and psychological conditions of women around the world (UNICEF, 2014). Inadequate educational opportunities, violence, and mental health issues are among the problems faced by many women.

One analysis found that a higher percentage of girls than boys around the world have never had any education (UNICEF, 2004) (see Figure 1.3). The countries with the fewest females being educated are in Africa, where girls and women in some areas are receiving no education at all. Canada, the United States, and Russia have the highest percentages of educated women. In developing countries, 67 percent of women over the age of 25 (compared with 50 percent of men) have never been to school. At the beginning of the twenty-first century, 80 million more boys than girls were in primary and secondary educational settings around the world (United Nations, 2002).

Social Policy **Social policy** is a government's course of action designed to promote the welfare of its citizens. Values, economics, and politics all shape a nation's social policy (Yeung & Mui-Teng, 2015). Out of concern that policy makers are doing too little to protect the well-being of children and older adults, life-span researchers are increasingly undertaking studies that they hope will lead to effective social policy (McLoyd, Mistry, & Hardaway, 2013; Ruzek & others, 2014).

Statistics such as infant mortality rates, mortality among children under 5, and the percentage of children who are malnourished or living in poverty provide benchmarks for evaluating how well children are doing in a particular society (Hernandez & Pressler, 2014). Marian Wright Edelman, a tireless advocate for children's rights, has pointed out that indicators like

Marian Wright Edelman, president of the Children's Defense Fund (shown here advocating for health care), has been a tireless advocate for children's rights and has been instrumental in calling attention to the needs of children. *What are some of these needs?*

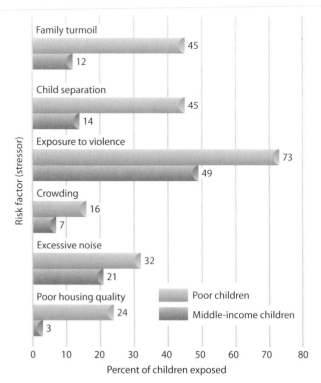

FIGURE **1.4**

EXPOSURE TO SIX STRESSORS AMONG POOR AND MIDDLE-INCOME CHILDREN. One study analyzed the exposure to six stressors among poor children and middle-income children (Evans & English, 2002). Poor children were much more likely to face each of these stressors.

Source	Characteristic
Individual	Good intellectual functioning Appealing, sociable, easygoing disposition Self-confidence, high self-esteem Talents Faith
Family	Close relationship to caring parent figure Authoritative parenting: warmth, structure, high expectations Socioeconomic advantages Connections to extended supportive family networks
Extrafamilial Context	Bonds to caring adults outside the family Connections to positive organizations Attending effective schools

FIGURE **1.5**

CHARACTERISTICS OF RESILIENT CHILDREN AND THEIR CONTEXTS

these place the United States at or near the lowest rank for industrialized nations in the treatment of children.

Children who grow up in poverty represent a special concern (Duncan, Magnuson, & Votruba-Drzal, 2015; McCartney & Yoshikawa, 2015). In 2012, 21.8 percent of U.S. children aged 18 years and younger were living in families with incomes below the poverty line, with African American and Latino families with children having especially high rates of poverty (more than 30 percent) (U.S. Census Bureau, 2013). This is an increase from 2001 (16 percent) but slightly down from a peak of 23 percent in 1993. As indicated in Figure 1.4, one study found that a higher percentage of U.S. children in poor families than in middle-income families were exposed to family turmoil, separation from a parent, violence, crowding, excessive noise, and poor housing (Evans & English, 2002). One study also revealed that the more years children spent living in poverty, the higher their physiological indices of stress (Evans & Kim, 2007).

The U.S. figure of 22 percent of children living in poverty is much higher than those of other industrialized nations. For example, Canada has a child poverty rate of 9 percent and Sweden has a rate of 2 percent.

Edelman says that parenting and nurturing the next generation of children is our society's most important function and that we need to take it more seriously than we have in the past. To read about efforts to improve the lives of children through social policies, see *Connecting Development to Life*.

Some children triumph over poverty or other adversities. They show *resilience* (Jackson & others, 2012; Masten, 2013, 2014). Think back to the chapter-opening story about Alice Walker. In spite of racism, poverty, her low socioeconomic status, and a disfiguring eye injury, she went on to become a successful author and champion for equality.

Are there certain characteristics that make children like Alice Walker resilient? Are there other characteristics that influence the development of children like Ted Kaczynski, who, despite his intelligence and education, became a killer? After analyzing research on this topic, Ann Masten and her colleagues (Masten, 2006, 2009, 2011, 2013, 2014; Masten, Burt, & Coatsworth, 2006; Masten, Liebkind, & Hernandez, 2012; Masten & Narayan, 2012; Motti-Stefanidi & Masten, 2014) concluded that a number of individual factors, such as good intellectual functioning, influence resiliency. In addition, as Figure 1.5 shows, the families and extrafamilial contexts of resilient individuals tend to share certain features. For example, resilient children are likely to have a close relationship to a caring parent figure and bonds to caring adults outside the family.

At the other end of the life span, the well-being of older adults also creates policy issues (Hooyman, Kiyak, & Kawamoto, 2015). Key concerns are escalating health care costs and the access of older adults to adequate health care (Lynch, Elmore, & Kotecki, 2015). One study found that the U.S. health care system fails older adults in many areas (Wenger & others, 2003). For example, older adults received the recommended care for general medical conditions such as heart disease only 52 percent of the time; they received appropriate care for undernutrition and Alzheimer disease only 31 percent of the time.

These concerns about the well-being of older adults are

Ann Masten (far right) with homeless children who are participating in her research on resilience. She and her colleagues have found that good parenting skills and good cognitive skills (especially attention and self-control) improve the likelihood that children in challenging circumstances will do better when they enter elementary school.

Improving Family Policy

In the United States, the actions of the national government, state governments, and city governments influence the well-being of children (Lerner & others, 2013; McCartney & Yoskikawa, 2015). When families seriously endanger a child's well-being, governments often step in to help. At the national and state levels, policy makers have debated for decades about whether helping poor parents ends up helping their children as well. Researchers are providing some answers by examining the effects of specific policies (Purtell & McLoyd, 2013; White & others, 2014).

For example, the Minnesota Family Investment Program (MFIP) was designed in the 1990s primarily to influence the behavior of adults—specifically, to move adults off the welfare rolls and into paid employment. A key element of the program was its guarantee that adults participating in the program would receive more income if they worked than if they did not. When the adults' income rose, how did that affect their children? A study of the effects of MFIP found that increased incomes of working poor parents were linked with benefits for their children (Gennetian & Miller, 2002). The children's achievement in school improved, and their behavior problems decreased. A current MFIP study is examining the influence of specific services on low-income families at risk for child maltreatment and other negative outcomes for children (Minnesota Family Investment Program, 2009).

A recent large-scale effort to help children escape from poverty is the *Ascend* two-generation education intervention being conducted by the Aspen Institute (2013). The focus of the intervention emphasizes education (increasing postsecondary education for mothers and improving the quality of their children's early childhood education), economic support (housing, transportation, financial education, health insurance, and food assistance), and social capital (peer support including friends and neighbors; participation in community and faith-based organizations; school and work contacts).

Developmental psychologists and other researchers have examined the effects of many other government policies. They are seeking ways to help families living in poverty improve their well-being, and they have offered many suggestions for improving government policies (Duncan & Magnuson, 2015; O'Brien & others, 2013).

Earlier, we learned that children who live in poverty experience higher levels of physiological stress. How might a child's stress level be affected by the implementation of MFIP?

heightened by two facts. First, the number of older adults in the United States is growing dramatically, as Figure 1.6 shows. Second, many of these older Americans are likely to need society's help (Viachantoni, 2012). Compared with earlier decades, U.S. adults today are less likely to be married, more likely to be childless, and more likely to be living alone. As the older population continues to expand during the twenty-first century, an increasing number

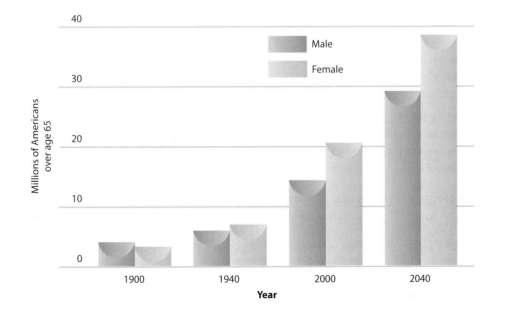

FIGURE **1.6**

THE AGING OF AMERICA. The number of Americans over age 65 has grown dramatically since 1900 and is projected to increase further from the present to the year 2040. A significant increase will also occur in the number of individuals in the 85-and-over group. Centenarians—persons 100 years of age or older—are the fastest-growing age group in the United States, and their numbers are expected to swell in the coming decades.

of older adults will be without either a spouse or children—traditionally the main sources of support for older adults. These individuals will need social relationships, networks, and other forms of support (Antonucci, Ajrouch, & Birditt, 2014).

Review *Connect* Reflect

LG1 Discuss the distinctive features of a life-span perspective on development.

Review
- What is meant by the concept of development? Why is the study of life-span development important?
- What are the main characteristics of the life-span perspective? What are three sources of contextual influences?
- What are some contemporary concerns in life-span development?

Connect
- Give your own example (not found in this chapter) of how biology, culture, and individual experience interact to affect development.

Reflect *Your Own Personal Journey of Life*
- Imagine what your development would have been like in a culture that offered fewer or distinctly different choices. How might your development have been different if your family had been significantly richer or poorer?

2 The Nature of Development

LG2 Identify the most important processes, periods, and issues in development.

| Biological, Cognitive, and Socioemotional Processes | Periods of Development | The Significance of Age | Developmental Issues |

In this section, we will explore what is meant by developmental processes and periods, as well as variations in the way age is conceptualized. We will examine key developmental issues and strategies we can use to evaluate them.

If you wanted to describe how and why Alice Walker or Ted Kaczynski developed during their lifetimes, how would you go about it? A chronicle of the events in any person's life can quickly become a confusing and tedious array of details. Two concepts help provide a framework for describing and understanding an individual's development: developmental processes and periods.

BIOLOGICAL, COGNITIVE, AND SOCIOEMOTIONAL PROCESSES

At the beginning of this chapter, we defined development as the pattern of change that begins at conception and continues through the life span. The pattern is complex because it is the product of biological, cognitive, and socioemotional processes (see Figure 1.7).

Biological Processes   **Biological processes** produce changes in an individual's physical nature. Genes inherited from parents, the development of the brain, height and weight gains, changes in motor skills, nutrition, exercise, the hormonal changes of puberty, and cardiovascular decline are all examples of biological processes that affect development.

Cognitive Processes   **Cognitive processes** refer to changes in the individual's thought, intelligence, and language. Watching a colorful mobile swinging above the crib, putting

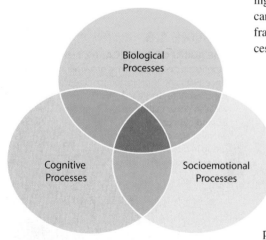

FIGURE 1.7

PROCESSES INVOLVED IN DEVELOPMENTAL CHANGES. Biological, cognitive, and socioemotional processes interact as individuals develop.

together a two-word sentence, memorizing a poem, imagining what it would be like to be a movie star, and solving a crossword puzzle all involve cognitive processes.

Socioemotional Processes   **Socioemotional processes** involve changes in the individual's relationships with other people, changes in emotions, and changes in personality. An infant's smile in response to a parent's touch, a toddler's aggressive attack on a playmate, a school-age child's development of assertiveness, an adolescent's joy at the senior prom, and the affection of an elderly couple all reflect the role of socioemotional processes in development.

Connecting Biological, Cognitive, and Socioemotional Processes
Biological, cognitive, and socioemotional processes are inextricably intertwined (Diamond, 2013). Consider a baby smiling in response to a parent's touch. This response depends on biological processes (the physical nature of touch and responsiveness to it), cognitive processes (the ability to understand intentional acts), and socioemotional processes (the act of smiling that often reflects a positive emotional feeling and helps to connect us in positive ways with other human beings). Nowhere is the connection across biological, cognitive, and socioemotional processes more obvious than in two rapidly emerging fields:

- *developmental cognitive neuroscience*, which explores links between development, cognitive processes, and the brain (Markant & Thomas, 2013)
- *developmental social neuroscience*, which examines connections between socioemotional processes, development, and the brain (Blakemore & Mills, 2014)

In many instances, biological, cognitive, and socioemotional processes are bidirectional. For example, biological processes can influence cognitive processes and vice versa. Thus, although usually we will study the different processes of development (biological, cognitive, and socioemotional) separately, keep in mind that we are talking about the development of an integrated individual with a mind and body that are interdependent. In many places throughout the book, we will call attention to these connections.

biological processes Changes in an individual's physical nature.

cognitive processes Changes in an individual's thought, intelligence, and language.

socioemotional processes Changes in an individual's relationships with other people, emotions, and personality.

developmental **connection**

Brain Development

Is there a link between changes in the adolescent's brain and their mood swings and increased risk taking? Chapter 11, p. 360

PERIODS OF DEVELOPMENT

The interplay of biological, cognitive, and socioemotional processes produces the periods of the human life span (see Figure 1.8). *A developmental period* refers to a time frame in a person's life that is characterized by certain features. For the purposes of organization and understanding, we commonly describe development in terms of these periods. The most widely used classification of developmental periods involves the eight-period sequence shown in Figure 1.8. Approximate age ranges are listed for the periods to provide a general idea of when a period begins and ends.

The prenatal period is the time from conception to birth. It involves tremendous growth—from a single cell to an organism complete with brain and behavioral capabilities—and takes place in approximately a 9-month period.

Infancy is the developmental period from birth to 18 or 24 months. Infancy is a time of extreme dependence upon adults. During this period, many psychological activities—language, symbolic thought, sensorimotor coordination, and social learning, for example—are just beginning.

The term *toddler* is often used to describe a child from about 1½ to 3 years of age. Toddlers are in a transitional period between infancy and the next period, *early childhood.*

Early childhood is the developmental period from 3 through 5 years of age. This period is sometimes called the "preschool years." During this time, young children learn to become more self-sufficient and to care for themselves, develop school readiness skills (following instructions, identifying letters), and spend many hours playing with peers. First grade typically marks the end of early childhood.

Periods of Development

| Prenatal period (conception to birth) | Infancy (birth to 18–24 months) | Early childhood (3–5 years) | Middle and late childhood (6–10/11 years) | Adolescence (10–12 to 18–21 years) | Early adulthood (20s and 30s) | Middle adulthood (40s and 50s) | Late adulthood (60s–70s to death) |

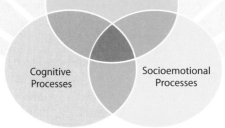

FIGURE 1.8

PROCESSES AND PERIODS OF DEVELOPMENT. The unfolding of life's periods of development is influenced by the interaction of biological, cognitive, and socioemotional processes.

Processes of Development

"This is the path to adulthood. You're here."

© Robert Weber/The New Yorker Collection/ www.cartoonbank.com

Middle and late childhood is the developmental period from about 6 to 10 or 11 years of age, approximately corresponding to the elementary school years. During this period, children master the fundamental skills of reading, writing, and arithmetic, and they are formally exposed to the larger world and its culture. Achievement becomes a more central theme of the child's world, and self-control increases.

Adolescence is the developmental period of transition from childhood to early adulthood, entered at approximately 10 to 12 years of age and ending at 18 to 21 years of age. Adolescence begins with rapid physical changes—dramatic gains in height and weight, changes in body contour, and the development of sexual characteristics such as enlargement of the breasts, growth of pubic and facial hair, and deepening of the voice. At this point in development, the pursuit of independence and an identity are preeminent. Thought is more logical, abstract, and idealistic. More time is spent outside the family.

Early adulthood is the developmental period that begins in the early twenties and lasts through the thirties. It is a time of establishing personal and economic independence, advancing in a career, and for many, selecting a mate, learning to live with that person in an intimate way, starting a family, and rearing children.

Middle adulthood is the developmental period from approximately 40 to about 60 years of age. It is a time of expanding personal and social involvement and responsibility; of assisting the next generation in becoming competent, mature individuals; and of reaching and maintaining satisfaction in a career.

Late adulthood is the developmental period that begins during the sixties or seventies and lasts until death. It is a time of life review, retirement, and adjustment to new social roles and diminishing strength and health.

Late adulthood has the longest span of any period of development, and as noted earlier, the number of people in this age group has been increasing dramatically. As a result, life-span developmentalists have been paying more attention to differences within late adulthood (Dixon & others, 2013). Paul Baltes and Jacqui Smith (2003) argue that a major change takes place in older adults' lives as they become the "oldest-old," on average at about 85 years of age. For example, the "young-old" (classified as 65 through 84 in this analysis) have substantial potential for physical and cognitive fitness, retain much of their cognitive capacity, and can develop strategies to cope with the gains and losses of aging. In contrast, the oldest-old (85 and older) show considerable loss in cognitive skills, experience an increase in chronic stress, and are more frail.

Thus, Baltes and Smith concluded that considerable plasticity and adaptability characterize adults from their sixties until their mid-eighties but that the oldest-old have reached the limits of their functional capacity, which makes interventions to improve their lives difficult. Nonetheless, as will be described in later chapters, considerable variation exists in how much the oldest-old retain their capabilities (Andersen & others, 2012; Rochan & others, 2014).

Four Ages   Life-span developmentalists who focus on adult development and aging increasingly describe life-span development in terms of four "ages" (Baltes, 2006; Willis & Schaie, 2006):

First age: Childhood and adolescence

Second age: Prime adulthood, ages 20 through 59

Third age: Approximately 60 to 79 years of age

Fourth age: Approximately 80 years and older

The major emphasis in this conceptualization is on the third and fourth ages, especially the increasing evidence that individuals in the third age are healthier and can lead more active, productive lives than their predecessors in earlier generations. However, when older adults reach their eighties (fourth age), especially 85 and over, health and well-being decline for many individuals.

Connections Across Periods of Development   A final important point needs to be made about the periods of the human life span. Just as there are many connections between biological, cognitive, and socioemotional processes, so are there many connections between the periods of the human life span. A key element in the study of life-span development is how development in one period is connected to development in another period. For example, when individuals reach adolescence, many developments and experiences have already taken place in their lives. If an adolescent girl becomes depressed, might her depression be linked to development early in her life, as well as recent and current development? Throughout the text we will call attention to such connections across periods of development through *Developmental Connection* inserts that guide you to earlier or later connections with the material you are currently reading.

THE SIGNIFICANCE OF AGE

In our description of developmental periods, we linked an approximate age range with each period. But we also have noted that there are variations in the capabilities of individuals of the same age, and we have seen how age-related changes can be exaggerated. How important is age in understanding the characteristics of an individual?

Age and Happiness   Is there a best age to be? An increasing number of studies indicate that in the United States adults are happier as they age. For example, a recent study of more than 300,000 U.S. adults revealed that psychological well-being increased after the age of 50 years (Stone & others, 2010). In this study, specific aspects of negative affect showed different age trends. When individuals were asked about affect experienced yesterday, stress and anger declined sharply from the early twenties, worry was elevated during

Which of these individuals is likely to be the happiest and to report the highest level of psychological well-being?

Below are five statements that you may agree or disagree with. Using the 1–7 scale below, indicate your agreement with each item by placing the appropriate number on the line preceding that item. Please be open and honest in your responding.

Scale		Response	Statement
7 Strongly agree		_____	In most ways my life is close to my ideal.
6 Agree			
5 Slightly agree		_____	The conditions of my life are excellent.
4 Neither agree nor disagree		_____	I am satisfied with my life.
3 Slightly disagree		_____	So far I have gotten the important things I want in life.
2 Disagree			
1 Strongly disagree		_____	If I could live my life over, I would change almost nothing.
		_____	Total score

Scoring

31–35 Extremely satisfied
26–30 Satisfied
21–25 Slightly satisfied
   20 Neutral
15–19 Slightly dissatisfied
10–14 Dissatisfied
  5–9 Extremely dissatisfied

FIGURE **1.9**

HOW SATISFIED AM I WITH MY LIFE?
Source: E. Diener, R. A. Emmons, R. J. Larson, & S. Griffin (1985). The Satisfaction with Life Scale. *Journal of Personality Assessment, 48,* 71–75.

How old would you be if you didn't know how old you were?

—SATCHEL PAIGE
American Baseball Pitcher, 20th Century

middle age and then declined, and sadness showed little change from 18 to 85 years of age.

Consider also a U.S. study of approximately 28,000 individuals from 18 to 88 that revealed happiness increased with age (Yang, 2008). About 33 percent were very happy at 88 years of age compared with only about 24 percent in their late teens and early twenties. Why might older people report being happier and more satisfied with their lives than younger people? Despite the increase in physical problems and losses older adults experience, they are more content with what they have in their lives, have better relationships with the people who matter to them, are less pressured to achieve, have more time for leisurely pursuits, and have many years of experience resulting in wisdom that may help them adapt better to their circumstances than younger adults do (Carstensen & others, 2011; Choi & Landeros, 2011). Also in the study, baby boomers (those born between 1946 and 1964) reported being less happy than individuals born earlier—possibly because they are not lowering their aspirations and idealistic hopes as they age, as did earlier generations. Because growing older is a certain outcome of living, it is good to know that we are likely to be happier as older adults than we were when we were younger.

Now that you have read about age variations in life satisfaction, think about how satisfied you are with your life. To help you answer this question, complete the items in Figure 1.9, which presents the most widely used measure in research on life satisfaction (Diener, 2014).

Conceptions of Age According to some life-span experts, chronological age is not very relevant to understanding a person's psychological development (Botwinick, 1978). *Chronological age* is the number of years that have elapsed since birth. But time is a crude index of experience, and it does not cause anything. Chronological age, moreover, is not the only way to measure age. Just as there are different domains of development, there are different ways of thinking about age.

Age has been conceptualized not just as chronological age but also as biological age, psychological age, and social age (Hoyer & Roodin, 2009). *Biological age* is a person's age in terms of biological health. Determining biological age involves knowing the functional capacities of a person's vital organs. One person's vital capacities may be better or worse than those of others of comparable age (Borrell & Samuel, 2014). The younger the person's biological age, the longer the person is expected to live, regardless of chronological age.

Psychological age is an individual's adaptive capacities compared with those of other individuals of the same chronological age. Thus, older adults who continue to learn, are flexible, are motivated, have positive personality traits, control their emotions, and think clearly are engaging in more adaptive behaviors than their chronological age-mates who do not continue to learn, are rigid, are unmotivated, do not control their emotions, and do not think clearly (Schaie, 2013). A longitudinal study of more than 1,200 individuals across seven decades revealed that the personality trait of conscientiousness (being organized, careful, and disciplined, for example) predicted lower mortality (frequency of death) risk from childhood through late adulthood (Martin, Friedman, & Schwartz, 2007).

Social age refers to connectedness with others and the social roles individuals adopt. Individuals who have better social relationships with others are happier and more likely to live longer than individuals who are lonely (Antonucci, Ajrouch, & Birditt, 2014).

Life-span expert Bernice Neugarten (1988) argues that in U.S. society chronological age is becoming irrelevant. The 28-year-old mayor, the 35-year-old grandmother, the 65-year-old father of a preschooler, the 55-year-old widow who starts a business, and the 70-year-old student

(*Left*) Dawn Russel, competing in the long jump in a Senior Olympics competition in Oregon; (*right*) a sedentary, overweight middle-aged man. *Even though Dawn Russel's chronological age is older, might her biological age be younger than the middle-aged man's?*

illustrate that old assumptions about the proper timing of life events no longer govern our lives. We still have some expectations for when certain life events—such as getting married, having children, and retiring—should occur. However, chronological age has become a less accurate predictor of these life events in our society. Moreover, issues such as how to deal with intimacy and how to cope with success and failure appear and reappear throughout the life span.

From a life-span perspective, an overall age profile of an individual involves not just chronological age but also biological age, psychological age, and social age. For example, a 70-year-old man (chronological age) might be in good physical health (biological age), be experiencing memory problems and not be coping well with the demands placed on him by his wife's recent hospitalization (psychological age), and have a number of friends with whom he regularly plays golf (social age).

developmental **connection**

Nature and Nurture

Can specific genes be linked to specific environmental experiences to influence development? Chapter 2, p. 51

DEVELOPMENTAL ISSUES

Was Ted Kaczynski born a killer, or did his life turn him into one? Kaczynski himself thought that his childhood was the root of his troubles. He grew up as a genius in a boy's body and never fit in with other children. Did his early experiences determine his later life? Is your own journey through life marked out ahead of time, or can your experiences change your path? Are the experiences you have early in your journey more important than later ones? Is your journey more like taking an elevator up a skyscraper with distinct stops along the way or more like a cruise down a river with smoother ebbs and flows? These questions point to three issues about the nature of development: the roles played by nature and nurture, stability and change, and continuity and discontinuity.

Nature and Nurture   The **nature-nurture issue** involves the extent to which development is influenced by nature and by nurture. Nature refers to an organism's biological inheritance, nurture to its environmental experiences.

According to those who emphasize the role of nature, just as a sunflower grows in an orderly way—unless flattened by an unfriendly environment—so too the human grows in an orderly way. An evolutionary and genetic foundation produces commonalities in growth and development (Durrant & Ellis, 2013). We walk before we talk, speak one word before two words, grow rapidly in infancy and less so in early childhood, experience a rush of sex hormones in puberty, reach the peak of our physical strength in late adolescence and early adulthood, and then physically decline. Proponents of the importance of nature acknowledge that extreme environments—those that are psychologically barren or hostile—can depress development. However, they believe that basic growth tendencies are genetically programmed into humans (Mader, 2014).

What are some key developmental issues?

nature-nurture issue Debate about whether development is primarily influenced by nature or nurture. Nature refers to an organism's biological inheritance, nurture to its environmental experiences.

developmental **connection**

Personality

How much does personality change as people go through the adult years? Chapter 16, p. 488

Continuity

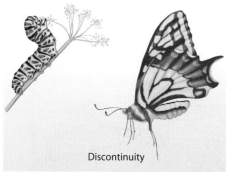

Discontinuity

FIGURE **1.10**

CONTINUITY AND DISCONTINUITY IN DEVELOPMENT. *Is our development like that of a seedling gradually growing into a giant oak? Or is it more like that of a caterpillar suddenly becoming a butterfly?*

stability-change issue Debate about whether we become older renditions of our early experience (stability) or whether we develop into someone different from who we were at an earlier point in development (change).

continuity-discontinuity issue Debate about the extent to which development involves gradual, cumulative change (continuity) or distinct stages (discontinuity).

By contrast, other psychologists emphasize the importance of nurture, or environmental experiences, in development (Clarke-Stewart & Parke, 2014). Experiences run the gamut from the individual's biological environment (nutrition, medical care, drugs, and physical accidents) to the social environment (family, peers, schools, community, media, and culture).

Stability and Change Is the shy child who hides behind the sofa when visitors arrive destined to become a wallflower at college dances, or might the child become a sociable, talkative individual? Is the fun-loving, carefree adolescent bound to have difficulty holding down a 9-to-5 job as an adult? These questions reflect the **stability-change issue,** which involves the degree to which early traits and characteristics persist through life or change.

Many developmentalists who emphasize stability in development argue that stability is the result of heredity and possibly early experiences in life. For example, many argue that if an individual is shy throughout life (as Ted Kaczynski was), this stability is due to heredity and possibly early experiences in which the infant or young child encountered considerable stress when interacting with people.

Developmentalists who emphasize change take the more optimistic view that later experiences can produce change. Recall that in the life-span perspective, plasticity, the potential for change, exists throughout the life span. Experts such as Paul Baltes (2003) argue that older adults often show less capacity for learning new things than younger adults do. However, many older adults continue to be good at practicing what they have learned earlier in life.

The roles of early and later experience are an aspect of the stability-change issue that has long been hotly debated (Easterbrooks & others, 2013). Some argue that warm, nurturant caregiving during infancy and toddlerhood predicts optimal development later in life (Cassidy & others, 2011). The later-experience advocates see children as malleable throughout development and believe later sensitive caregiving is just as important as earlier sensitive caregiving (Antonucci & others, 2013).

Continuity and Discontinuity When developmental change occurs, is it gradual or abrupt? Think about your own development for a moment. Did you gradually become the person you are today? Or did you experience sudden, distinct changes in your growth? For the most part, developmentalists who emphasize nurture describe development as a gradual, continuous process. Those who emphasize nature often describe development as a series of distinct stages.

The **continuity-discontinuity issue** focuses on the degree to which development involves either gradual, cumulative change (continuity) or distinct stages (discontinuity). In terms of continuity, as the oak grows from seedling to giant oak, it becomes more of an oak—its development is continuous (see Figure 1.10). Similarly, a child's first word, though seemingly an abrupt, discontinuous event, is actually the result of weeks and months of growth and practice. Puberty might seem abrupt, but it is a gradual process that occurs over several years.

In terms of discontinuity, as an insect grows from a caterpillar to a chrysalis to a butterfly, it passes through a sequence of stages in which change is qualitatively rather than quantitatively different. Similarly, at some point a child moves from not being able to think abstractly about the world to being able to do so. This is a qualitative, discontinuous change in development rather than a quantitative, continuous change.

Evaluating the Developmental Issues Most life-span developmentalists acknowledge that development is not all nature or all nurture, not all stability or all change, and not all continuity or all discontinuity. Nature and nurture, stability and change, continuity and discontinuity characterize development throughout the human life span.

Although most developmentalists do not take extreme positions on these three important issues, there is spirited debate regarding how strongly development is influenced by each of these factors (Moore, 2013; Raby & Roisman, 2014).

Review Connect Reflect

LG2 Identify the most important processes, periods, and issues in development.

Review

- What are three key developmental processes?
- What are eight main developmental periods?
- How is age related to development?
- What are three main developmental issues?

Connect

- In the previous section, we discussed biological, cognitive, and socioemotional processes. What concepts do these processes have in common with the issue of nature versus nurture, which was also discussed in this section?

Reflect *Your Own Personal Journey of Life*

- Do you think there was/is/will be a best age for you to be? If so, what is it? Why?

3 Theories of Development

LG3 Describe the main theories of human development.

Psychoanalytic Theories | Cognitive Theories | Behavioral and Social Cognitive Theories | Ethological Theory | Ecological Theory | An Eclectic Theoretical Orientation

How can we answer questions about the roles of nature and nurture, stability and change, and continuity and discontinuity in development? How can we determine, for example, whether deterioration of memory in older adults can be prevented or whether special care can repair the harm inflicted by child neglect? The scientific method is the best tool we have to answer such questions.

The **scientific method** is essentially a four-step process: (1) conceptualize a process or problem to be studied, (2) collect research information (data), (3) analyze the data, and (4) draw conclusions.

In step 1, when researchers are formulating a problem to study, they often draw on theories and develop hypotheses. A **theory** is an interrelated, coherent set of ideas that helps to explain phenomena and facilitate predictions. It may suggest **hypotheses,** which are specific assertions and predictions that can be tested. For example, a theory on mentoring might state that sustained support and guidance from an adult makes a difference in the lives of children from impoverished backgrounds because the mentor gives the children opportunities to observe and imitate the behavior and strategies of the mentor.

This section outlines key aspects of five theoretical orientations to development: psychoanalytic, cognitive, behavioral and social cognitive, ethological, and ecological. Each contributes an important piece to the life-span development puzzle. Although the theories disagree about certain aspects of development, many of their ideas are complementary rather than contradictory. Together they let us see the total landscape of life-span development in all its richness.

PSYCHOANALYTIC THEORIES

Psychoanalytic theories describe development as primarily unconscious (beyond awareness) and heavily colored by emotion. Psychoanalytic theorists emphasize that behavior is merely a surface characteristic and that a true understanding of development requires analyzing the symbolic meanings of behavior and the deep inner workings of the mind. Psychoanalytic theorists also stress that early experiences with parents extensively shape development. These characteristics are highlighted in the main psychoanalytic theory, that of Sigmund Freud (1856–1939).

> There is nothing quite so practical as a good theory.
>
> —**KURT LEWIN**
> *American Social Psychologist, 20th Century*

scientific method An approach that can be used to obtain accurate information. It includes the following steps: (1) conceptualize the problem, (2) collect data, (3) draw conclusions, and (4) revise research conclusions and theory.

theory An interrelated, coherent set of ideas that helps to explain phenomena and facilitate predictions.

hypotheses Specific assumptions and predictions that can be tested to determine their accuracy.

psychoanalytic theories Theories that describe development as primarily unconscious and heavily colored by emotion. Behavior is merely a surface characteristic, and the symbolic workings of the mind have to be analyzed to understand behavior. Early experiences with parents are emphasized.

Oral Stage	Anal Stage	Phallic Stage	Latency Stage	Genital Stage
Infant's pleasure centers on the mouth.	Child's pleasure focuses on the anus.	Child's pleasure focuses on the genitals.	Child represses sexual interest and develops social and intellectual skills.	A time of sexual reawakening; source of sexual pleasure becomes someone outside the family.
Birth to 1½ Years	**1½ to 3 Years**	**3 to 6 Years**	**6 Years to Puberty**	**Puberty Onward**

FIGURE **1.11**

FREUDIAN STAGES. Because Freud emphasized sexual motivation, his stages of development are known as psychosexual stages. In his view, if the need for pleasure at any stage is either undergratified or overgratified, an individual may become fixated, or locked in, at that stage of development.

Sigmund Freud, the pioneering architect of psychoanalytic theory. *How did Freud portray the organization of an individual's personality?*

Erik Erikson with his wife, Joan, an artist. Erikson generated one of the most important developmental theories of the twentieth century. *Which stage of Erikson's theory are you in? Does Erikson's description of this stage characterize you?*

Erikson's theory Includes eight stages of human development. Each stage consists of a unique developmental task that confronts individuals with a crisis that must be resolved.

Freud's Theory As Freud listened to, probed, and analyzed his patients, he became convinced that their problems were the result of experiences early in life. He thought that as children grow up, their focus of pleasure and sexual impulses shifts from the mouth to the anus and eventually to the genitals. As a result, we go through five stages of psychosexual development: oral, anal, phallic, latency, and genital (see Figure 1.11). Our adult personality, Freud (1917) claimed, is determined by the way we resolve conflicts between sources of pleasure at each stage and the demands of reality.

Freud's theory has been significantly revised by a number of psychoanalytic theorists. Many of today's psychoanalytic theorists maintain that Freud overemphasized sexual instincts; they place more emphasis on cultural experiences as determinants of an individual's development. Unconscious thought remains a central theme, but conscious thought plays a greater role than Freud envisioned. One of the most influential revisionists of Freud's ideas was Erik Erikson.

Erikson's Psychosocial Theory Erik Erikson (1902–1994) recognized Freud's contributions but believed that Freud misjudged some important dimensions of human development. For one thing, Erikson (1950, 1968) said we develop in psychosocial stages, rather than in psychosexual stages as Freud maintained. According to Freud, the primary motivation for human behavior is sexual in nature; according to Erikson, it is social and reflects a desire to affiliate with other people. According to Freud, our basic personality is shaped during the first five years of life; according to Erikson, developmental change occurs throughout the life span. Thus, in terms of the early-versus-later-experience issue described earlier in the chapter, Freud viewed early experience as being far more important than later experiences, whereas Erikson emphasized the importance of both early and later experiences.

In **Erikson's theory,** eight stages of development unfold as we go through life (see Figure 1.12). At each stage, a unique developmental task confronts individuals with a crisis that must be resolved. According to Erikson, this crisis is not a catastrophe but a turning point marked by both increased vulnerability and enhanced potential. The more successfully an individual resolves each crisis, the healthier development will be.

Trust versus mistrust is Erikson's first psychosocial stage, which is experienced in the first year of life. The development of trust during infancy sets the stage for a lifelong expectation that the world will be a good and pleasant place to live.

Autonomy versus shame and doubt is Erikson's second stage. This stage occurs in late infancy and toddlerhood (1 to 3 years). After gaining trust in their caregivers, infants begin to discover that their behavior is their own. They start to assert their sense of independence or autonomy. They realize their will. If infants and toddlers are restrained too much or punished too harshly, they are likely to develop a sense of shame and doubt.

Initiative versus guilt, Erikson's third stage of development, occurs during the preschool years. As preschool children encounter a widening social world, they face new challenges that require active, purposeful, responsible behavior. Feelings of guilt may arise, though, if the child is irresponsible and is made to feel too anxious.

Industry versus inferiority is Erikson's fourth developmental stage, occurring approximately during the elementary school years. Children now need to direct their energy toward mastering knowledge and intellectual skills. The negative outcome is that the child may develop a sense of inferiority—feeling incompetent and unproductive.

During the adolescent years, individuals need to find out who they are, what they are all about, and where they are going in life. This is Erikson's fifth developmental stage, *identity versus identity confusion*. If adolescents explore roles in a healthy manner and arrive at a positive path to follow in life, then they achieve a positive identity; if they do not, identity confusion reigns.

Intimacy versus isolation is Erikson's sixth developmental stage, which individuals experience during early adulthood. At this time, individuals face the developmental task of forming intimate relationships. If young adults form healthy friendships and an intimate relationship with another, intimacy will be achieved; if not, isolation will result.

Generativity versus stagnation, Erikson's seventh developmental stage, occurs during middle adulthood. By generativity Erikson means primarily a concern for helping the younger generation to develop and lead useful lives. The feeling of having done nothing to help the next generation is stagnation.

Integrity versus despair is Erikson's eighth and final stage of development, which individuals experience in late adulthood. During this stage, a person reflects on the past. If the person's life review reveals a life well spent, integrity will be achieved; if not, the retrospective glances likely will yield doubt or gloom—the despair Erikson described.

Evaluating Psychoanalytic Theories Contributions of psychoanalytic theories include an emphasis on a developmental framework, family relationships, and unconscious aspects of the mind. Criticisms include a lack of scientific support, too much emphasis on sexual underpinnings, and an image of people that is too negative.

COGNITIVE THEORIES

Whereas psychoanalytic theories stress the importance of the unconscious, cognitive theories emphasize conscious thoughts. Three important cognitive theories are Jean Piaget's cognitive developmental theory, Lev Vygotsky's sociocultural cognitive theory, and the information-processing theory.

Piaget's Cognitive Developmental Theory
Piaget's theory states that children go through four stages of cognitive development as they actively construct their understanding of the world. Two processes underlie this cognitive construction of the world: organization and adaptation. To make sense of our world, we organize our experiences. For example, we separate important ideas from less important ideas, and we connect one idea to another. In addition to organizing our observations and experiences, we adapt, adjusting to new environmental demands (Miller, 2011).

Piaget (1954) also held that we go through four stages in understanding the world (see Figure 1.13). Each stage is age-related and consists of a distinct way of thinking, a different way of understanding the

Jean Piaget, the famous Swiss developmental psychologist, changed the way we think about the development of children's minds. *What are some key ideas in Piaget's theory?*

Erikson's Stages	Developmental Period
Integrity versus despair	Late adulthood (60s onward)
Generativity versus stagnation	Middle adulthood (40s, 50s)
Intimacy versus isolation	Early adulthood (20s, 30s)
Identity versus identity confusion	Adolescence (10 to 20 years)
Industry versus inferiority	Middle and late childhood (elementary school years, 6 years to puberty)
Initiative versus guilt	Early childhood (preschool years, 3 to 5 years)
Autonomy versus shame and doubt	Infancy (1 to 3 years)
Trust versus mistrust	Infancy (first year)

FIGURE **1.12**

ERIKSON'S EIGHT LIFE-SPAN STAGES. Like Freud, Erikson proposed that individuals go through distinct, universal stages of development. Thus, in terms of the continuity-discontinuity issue discussed in this chapter, both favor the discontinuity side of the debate. Notice that the timing of Erikson's first four stages is similar to that of Freud's stages. *What are the implications of saying that people go through stages of development?*

Piaget's theory Theory stating that children actively construct their understanding of the world and go through four stages of cognitive development.

Sensorimotor Stage	**Preoperational Stage**	**Concrete Operational Stage**	**Formal Operational Stage**
The infant constructs an understanding of the world by coordinating sensory experiences with physical actions. An infant progresses from reflexive, instinctual action at birth to the beginning of symbolic thought toward the end of the stage.	The child begins to represent the world with words and images. These words and images reflect increased symbolic thinking and go beyond the connection of sensory information and physical action.	The child can now reason logically about concrete events and classify objects into different sets.	The adolescent reasons in more abstract, idealistic, and logical ways.
Birth to 2 Years of Age	**2 to 7 Years of Age**	**7 to 11 Years of Age**	**11 Years of Age Through Adulthood**

FIGURE **1.13**

PIAGET'S FOUR STAGES OF COGNITIVE DEVELOPMENT. According to Piaget, how a child thinks—not how much the child knows—determines the child's stage of cognitive development.

world. Thus, according to Piaget (1896–1980), the child's cognition is qualitatively different from one stage to another. What are Piaget's four stages of cognitive development?

- The *sensorimotor stage,* which lasts from birth to about 2 years of age, is the first Piagetian stage. In this stage, infants construct an understanding of the world by coordinating sensory experiences (such as seeing and hearing) with physical, motoric actions—hence the term *sensorimotor.*

- The *preoperational stage,* which lasts from approximately 2 to 7 years of age, is Piaget's second stage. In this stage, children begin to go beyond simply connecting sensory information with physical action and represent the world with words, images, and drawings. However, according to Piaget, preschool children still lack the ability to perform what he calls operations, which are internalized mental actions that allow children to do mentally what they previously could only do physically. For example, if you imagine putting two sticks together to see whether they would be as long as another stick, without actually moving the sticks, you are performing a concrete operation.

- The *concrete operational stage,* which lasts from approximately 7 to 11 years of age, is the third Piagetian stage. In this stage, children can perform operations that involve objects, and they can reason logically when the reasoning can be applied to specific or concrete examples. For instance, concrete operational thinkers cannot imagine the steps necessary to complete an algebraic equation, which is too abstract for thinking at this stage of development.

- The *formal operational stage,* which appears between the ages of 11 and 15 and continues through adulthood, is Piaget's fourth and final stage. In this stage, individuals move beyond concrete experiences and begin to think in abstract and more logical terms. As part of thinking more abstractly, adolescents develop images of ideal circumstances. They might think about what an ideal parent would be like and compare their parents to this ideal standard. They begin to entertain possibilities for the future and are fascinated with what they can be. In solving problems, they become more systematic, developing hypotheses about why something is happening the way it is and then testing these hypotheses. We will examine Piaget's cognitive developmental theory further in Chapters 5, 7, 9, and 11.

Vygotsky's Sociocultural Cognitive Theory   Like Piaget, the Russian developmentalist Lev Vygotsky (1896–1934) argued that children actively construct their knowledge. However, Vygotsky (1962) gave social interaction and culture far more important roles in cognitive development than Piaget did. **Vygotsky's theory** is a sociocultural cognitive theory that emphasizes how culture and social interaction guide cognitive development.

Vygotsky portrayed the child's development as inseparable from social and cultural activities (Gauvain, 2013). He maintained that cognitive development involves learning to use the inventions of society, such as language, mathematical systems, and memory strategies. Thus in one culture, children might learn to count with the help of a computer; in another, they might learn by using beads. According to Vygotsky, children's social interaction with more-skilled adults and peers is indispensable to their cognitive development. Through this interaction, they learn to use the tools that will help them adapt and be successful in their culture. (Mahn & John-Steiner, 2013). In Chapter 7, we examine ideas about learning and teaching that are based on Vygotsky's theory.

The Information-Processing Theory   **Information-processing theory** emphasizes that individuals manipulate information, monitor it, and strategize about it. Unlike Piaget's theory, but like Vygotsky's theory, information-processing theory does not describe development as stage-like. Instead, according to this theory, individuals develop a gradually increasing capacity for processing information, which allows them to acquire increasingly complex knowledge and skills (Siegler, 2013; Sternberg, 2014a, b).

Robert Siegler (2006, 2012, 2013), a leading expert on children's information processing, states that thinking is information processing. In other words, when individuals perceive, encode, represent, store, and retrieve information, they are thinking. Siegler emphasizes that an important aspect of development is learning good strategies for processing information. For example, becoming a better reader might involve learning to monitor the key themes of the material being read.

Siegler (2006) also argues that the best way to understand how children learn is to observe them while they are learning. He emphasizes the importance of using the *microgenetic method* to obtain detailed information about processing mechanisms as they are occurring from moment to moment. Siegler concludes that most research methods indirectly assess cognitive change, being more like snapshots than movies. The microgenetic method seeks to discover not just what children know but the cognitive processes involved in how they acquired the knowledge. A typical microgenetic study will be conducted across a number of trials assessed at various times over weeks or months (Miller, 2010). A number of microgenetic studies have focused on a specific aspect of academic learning, such as how children learn whole number arithmetic, fractions, and other areas of math (Siegler & others, 2013). Microgenetic studies also have been used to discover how children learn a particular issue in science or a key aspect of learning to read.

Evaluating Cognitive Theories   Contributions of cognitive theories include a positive view of development and an emphasis on the active construction of understanding. Criticisms include skepticism about the pureness of Piaget's stages and too little attention to individual variations.

BEHAVIORAL AND SOCIAL COGNITIVE THEORIES

Behaviorism essentially holds that we can study scientifically only what can be directly observed and measured. Out of the behavioral tradition grew the belief that development is observable behavior that can be learned through experience with the environment (Chance, 2014; Levy, 2013). In terms of the continuity-discontinuity issue discussed earlier in this

Lev Vygotsky was born the same year as Piaget, but he died much earlier, at the age of 37. There is considerable interest today in Vygotsky's sociocultural cognitive theory of child development. *What are some key characteristics of Vygotsky's theory?*

Vygotsky's theory A sociocultural cognitive theory that emphasizes how culture and social interaction guide cognitive development.

information-processing theory Emphasizes that individuals manipulate information, monitor it, and strategize about it. Central to this theory are the processes of memory and thinking.

B. F. Skinner was a tinkerer who liked to make new gadgets. The younger of his two daughters, Deborah, was raised in Skinner's enclosed Air-Crib, which he invented because he wanted to control her environment completely. The Air-Crib was sound-proofed and temperature controlled. Debbie, shown here as a child with her parents, is currently a successful artist, is married, and lives in London. *What do you think about Skinner's Air-Crib?*

Albert Bandura has been one of the leading architects of social cognitive theory. *How does Bandura's theory differ from Skinner's?*

developmental **connection**

Achievement

Bandura emphasizes that self-efficacy is a key person/cognitive factor in children's achievement. Chapter 10, p. 307

social cognitive theory The view of psychologists who emphasize behavior, environment, and cognition as the key factors in development.

chapter, the behavioral and social cognitive theories emphasize continuity in development and argue that development does not occur in stage-like fashion. Let's explore two versions of behaviorism: Skinner's operant conditioning and Bandura's social cognitive theory.

Skinner's Operant Conditioning   According to B. F. Skinner (1904–1990), through operant conditioning the consequences of a behavior produce changes in the probability of the behavior's occurrence. A behavior followed by a rewarding stimulus is more likely to recur, whereas a behavior followed by a punishing stimulus is less likely to recur. For example, when an adult smiles at a child after the child has done something, the child is more likely to engage in that behavior again than if the adult gives the child a disapproving look.

In Skinner's (1938) view, such rewards and punishments shape development. For Skinner the key aspect of development is behavior, not thoughts and feelings. He emphasized that development consists of the pattern of behavioral changes that are brought about by rewards and punishments. For example, Skinner would say that shy people learned to be shy as a result of experiences they had while growing up. It follows that modifications in an environment can help a shy person become more socially oriented.

Bandura's Social Cognitive Theory   Some psychologists agree with the behaviorists' notion that development is learned and is influenced strongly by environmental interactions. However, unlike Skinner, they also see cognition as important in understanding development (Mischel, 2004; Mischel & others, 2011). **Social cognitive theory** holds that behavior, environment, and cognition are the key factors in development.

American psychologist Albert Bandura (1925–) is the leading architect of social cognitive theory. Bandura (1986, 2004, 2010a, b, 2012) emphasizes that cognitive processes have important links with the environment and behavior. His early research program focused heavily on observational learning (also called imitation or modeling), which is learning that occurs through observing what others do. For example, a young boy might observe his father yelling in anger and treating other people with hostility; with his peers, the young boy later acts very aggressively, showing the same characteristics as his father's behavior. Social cognitive theorists stress that people acquire a wide range of behaviors, thoughts, and feelings through observing others' behavior and that these observations form an important part of life-span development.

What is cognitive about observational learning in Bandura's view? He proposes that people cognitively represent the behavior of others and then sometimes adopt this behavior themselves.

Bandura's (2004, 2010a, b, 2012) most recent model of learning and development includes three elements: behavior, the person/cognition, and the environment. An individual's confidence that he or she can control his or her success is an example of a person factor; strategies are an example of a cognitive factor. As shown in Figure 1.14, behavior, person/cognitive, and environmental factors operate interactively.

Evaluating Behavioral and Social Cognitive Theories   Contributions of the behavioral and social cognitive theories include an emphasis on scientific research and environmental determinants of behavior. Criticisms include too little emphasis on cognition in Skinner's view and inadequate attention paid to developmental changes.

ETHOLOGICAL THEORY

Ethology stresses that behavior is strongly influenced by biology, is tied to evolution, and is characterized by critical or sensitive periods. These are specific time frames during which, according to ethologists, the presence or absence of certain experiences has a long-lasting influence on individuals.

Konrad Lorenz, a pioneering student of animal behavior, is followed through the water by three imprinted greylag geese. Describe Lorenz's experiment with the geese. *Do you think his experiment would have had the same results with human babies? Explain.*

European zoologist Konrad Lorenz (1903–1989) helped bring ethology to prominence. In his best-known research, Lorenz (1965) studied the behavior of greylag geese, which will follow their mothers as soon as they hatch. Lorenz separated the eggs laid by one goose into two groups. One group he returned to the goose to be hatched by her. The other group was hatched in an incubator. The goslings in the first group performed as predicted. They followed their mother as soon as they hatched. However, those in the second group, which saw Lorenz when they first hatched, followed him everywhere, as though he were their mother. Lorenz marked the goslings and then placed both groups under a box. Mother goose and "mother" Lorenz stood aside as the box lifted. Each group of goslings went directly to its "mother." Lorenz called this process imprinting—the rapid, innate learning that involves attachment to the first moving object seen.

John Bowlby (1969, 1989) illustrated an important application of ethological theory to human development. Bowlby stressed that attachment to a caregiver over the first year of life has important consequences throughout the life span. In his view, if this attachment is positive and secure, the individual will likely develop positively in childhood and adulthood. If the attachment is negative and insecure, life-span development will likely not be optimal. In Chapter 6, we will explore the concept of infant attachment in much greater detail.

In Lorenz's view, imprinting needs to take place at a certain, very early time in the life of the animal, or else it will not take place. This point in time is called a critical period. A related concept is that of a sensitive period, and an example of this is the time during infancy when, according to Bowlby, attachment should occur in order to promote optimal development of social relationships.

Another theory that emphasizes biological foundations of development—evolutionary psychology—will be presented in Chapter 2, along with views on the role of heredity in development. In addition, we will examine a number of biological theories of aging in Chapter 17.

Contributions of ethological theory include a focus on the biological and evolutionary basis of development, and the use of careful observations in naturalistic settings. Criticisms include too much emphasis on biological foundations and a belief that the critical and sensitive period concepts might be too rigid.

ECOLOGICAL THEORY

While ethological theory stresses biological factors, ecological theory emphasizes environmental factors. One ecological theory that has important implications for understanding life-span development was created by Urie Bronfenbrenner (1917–2005). **Bronfenbrenner's ecological theory** (Bronfenbrenner, 1986, 2004; Bronfenbrenner & Morris, 1998, 2006) holds that development reflects the influence of several environmental systems. The theory identifies five environmental systems: microsystem, mesosystem, exosystem, macrosystem, and chronosystem (see Figure 1.15).

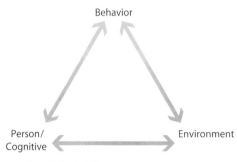

FIGURE 1.14

BANDURA'S SOCIAL COGNITIVE MODEL. The arrows illustrate how relations between behavior, person/cognitive, and environment are reciprocal rather than one-way. Person/cognitive refers to cognitive processes (for example, thinking and planning) and personal characteristics (for example, believing that you can control your experiences).

developmental **connection**

Attachment

Human babies go through a series of phases in developing an attachment to a caregiver. Chapter 6, p. 180

ethology Stresses that behavior is strongly influenced by biology, is tied to evolution, and is characterized by critical or sensitive periods.

Bronfenbrenner's ecological theory Bronfenbrenner's environmental systems theory that focuses on five environmental systems: microsystem, mesosystem, exosystem, macrosystem, and chronosystem.

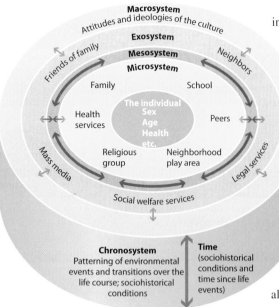

FIGURE **1.15**

BRONFENBRENNER'S ECOLOGICAL THEORY OF DEVELOPMENT.
Bronfenbrenner's ecological theory consists of five environmental systems: microsystem, mesosystem, exosystem, macrosystem, and chronosystem.

- - - - - - - - ->

developmental **connection**

Parenting

How are parent-child relationships and children's peer relations linked? Chapter 8, p. 258

Urie Bronfenbrenner developed ecological theory, a perspective that is receiving increased attention today. His theory emphasizes the importance of both micro and macro dimensions of the environment in which the child lives.

The *microsystem* is the setting in which the individual lives. These contexts include the person's family, peers, school, and neighborhood. It is in the microsystem that the most direct interactions with social agents take place—with parents, peers, and teachers, for example. The individual is not a passive recipient of experiences in these settings, but someone who helps to construct the settings.

The *mesosystem* involves relations between microsystems or connections between contexts. Examples are the relation of family experiences to school experiences, school experiences to religious experiences, and family experiences to peer experiences. For example, children whose parents have rejected them may have difficulty developing positive relations with teachers.

The *exosystem* consists of links between a social setting in which the individual does not have an active role and the individual's immediate context. For example, a husband's or child's experience at home may be influenced by a mother's experiences at work. The mother might receive a promotion that requires more travel, which might increase conflict with the husband and change patterns of interaction with the child.

The *macrosystem* involves the culture in which individuals live. Remember from earlier in the chapter that culture refers to the behavior patterns, beliefs, and all other products of a group of people that are passed on from generation to generation. Remember also that cross-cultural studies—the comparison of one culture with one or more other cultures—provide information about the generality of development.

The *chronosystem* consists of the patterning of environmental events and transitions over the life course, as well as sociohistorical circumstances. For example, divorce is one transition. Researchers have found that the negative effects of divorce on children often peak in the first year after the divorce (Hetherington, 1993, 2006). By two years after the divorce, family interaction has become more stable. As an example of sociohistorical circumstances, consider how career opportunities for women have increased since the 1960s.

Bronfenbrenner (2004; Bronfenbrenner & Morris, 2006) subsequently added biological influences to his theory, describing it as a bioecological theory. Nonetheless, it is still dominated by ecological, environmental contexts.

Contributions of the theory include a systematic examination of macro and micro dimensions of environmental systems, and attention to connections between environmental systems. A further contribution of Bronfenbrenner's theory is an emphasis on a range of social contexts beyond the family, such as neighborhood, religion, school, and workplace, as influential in children's development (Gauvain, 2013). Criticisms include inadequate attention to biological factors, as well as too little emphasis on cognitive factors.

AN ECLECTIC THEORETICAL ORIENTATION

No single theory described in this chapter can explain entirely the rich complexity of life-span development, but each has contributed to our understanding of development. Psychoanalytic theory best explains the unconscious mind. Erikson's theory best describes the changes that occur during adult development. Piaget's, Vygotsky's, and the information-processing views provide the most complete description of cognitive development. The behavioral and social cognitive and ecological theories have been the most adept at examining the environmental determinants of development. The ethological theories have highlighted biology's role and the importance of sensitive periods in development.

In short, although theories are helpful guides, relying on a single theory to explain development is probably a mistake. This book instead takes an **eclectic theoretical orientation,** which does not follow any one theoretical approach but rather selects from each theory whatever is considered its best features. In this way, you can view the study of development as it actually exists—with different theorists making different assumptions, stressing different empirical problems, and using different strategies to discover information. Figure 1.16 compares the main theoretical perspectives in terms of how they view important issues in life-span development.

THEORY	ISSUES	
	Continuity/discontinuity, early versus later experiences	**Biological and environmental factors**
Psychoanalytic	Discontinuity between stages—continuity between early experiences and later development; early experiences very important; later changes in development emphasized in Erikson's theory	Freud's biological determination interacting with early family experiences; Erikson's more balanced biological-cultural interaction perspective
Cognitive	Discontinuity between stages in Piaget's theory; continuity between early experiences and later development in Piaget's and Vygotsky's theories; no stages in Vygotsky's theory or information-processing theory	Piaget's emphasis on interaction and adaptation; environment provides the setting for cognitive structures to develop; information-processing view has not addressed this issue extensively but mainly emphasizes biological-environmental interaction
Behavioral and social cognitive	Continuity (no stages); experience at all points of development important	Environment viewed as the cause of behavior in both views
Ethological	Discontinuity but no stages; critical or sensitive periods emphasized; early experiences very important	Strong biological view
Ecological	Little attention to continuity/discontinuity; change emphasized more than stability	Strong environmental view

FIGURE **1.16**

A COMPARISON OF THEORIES AND ISSUES IN LIFE-SPAN DEVELOPMENT

eclectic theoretical orientation An orientation that does not follow any one theoretical approach but rather selects from each theory whatever is considered the best in it.

Review *Connect* Reflect

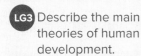 Describe the main theories of human development.

Review

- What are the four steps of the scientific method? How can theory and hypotheses be defined? What are two main psychoanalytic theories? What are some contributions and criticisms of the psychoanalytic theories?
- What are three main cognitive theories? What are some contributions and criticisms of the cognitive theories?
- What are two main behavioral and social cognitive theories? What are some contributions and criticisms of the behavioral and social cognitive theories?
- What is the nature of ethological theory? What are some contributions and criticisms of the theory?

- What characterizes ecological theory? What are some contributions and criticisms of the theory?
- What is an eclectic theoretical orientation?

Connect

- The beginning of this section started with a question about whether special care might be able to repair the harm inflicted by child neglect. How might this question be answered differently using the various theories outlined?

Reflect *Your Own Personal Journey of Life*

- Which of the life-span theories do you think best explains your own development? Why?

4 Research on Life-Span Development

LG4 Explain how research on life-span development is conducted.

| Methods for Collecting Data | Research Designs | Time Span of Research | Conducting Ethical Research | Minimizing Bias |

If they follow an eclectic orientation, how do scholars and researchers determine that one feature of a theory is somehow better than another? Through scientific research, the features of theories can be tested and refined (Smith & Davis, 2013).

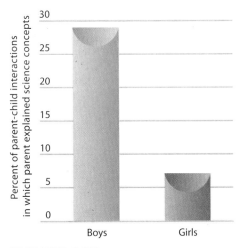

FIGURE **1.17**

**PARENTS' EXPLANATIONS OF SCIENCE
TO SONS AND DAUGHTERS AT A SCIENCE
MUSEUM.** In a naturalistic observation study at a children's science museum, parents were three times more likely to explain science to boys than to girls (Crowley & others, 2001). The gender difference occurred regardless of whether the father, the mother, or both parents were with the child, although the gender difference was greatest for fathers' science explanations to sons and daughters.

Generally, research on life-span development is designed to test hypotheses, which in some cases are derived from the theories just described. Through research, theories are modified to reflect new data, and occasionally new theories arise. How are data about life-span development collected? What types of research designs are used to study life-span development? And what are some ethical considerations in conducting research on life-span development?

METHODS FOR COLLECTING DATA

Whether we are interested in studying attachment in infants, the cognitive skills of children, or social relationships in older adults, we can choose from several ways of collecting data (Graziano & Raulin, 2013; Jackson, 2015). Here we outline the measures most often used, beginning with observation.

Observation   Scientific observation requires an important set of skills (Christensen, Johnson, & Turner, 2015; Reznick, 2013). For observations to be effective, they have to be systematic. We have to have some idea of what we are looking for. We have to know whom we are observing, when and where we will observe, how the observations will be made, and how they will be recorded.

Where should we make our observations? We have two choices: the laboratory and the everyday world.

When we observe scientifically, we often need to control certain factors that determine behavior but are not the focus of our inquiry (Stangor, 2015). For this reason, some research on life-span development is conducted in a **laboratory,** a controlled setting where many of the complex factors of the "real world" are absent. For example, suppose you want to observe how children react when they see other people act aggressively. If you observe children in their homes or schools, you have no control over how much aggression the children observe, what kind of aggression they see, which people they see acting aggressively, or how other people treat the children. In contrast, if you observe the children in a laboratory, you can control these and other factors and therefore have more confidence about how to interpret your observations.

Laboratory research does have some drawbacks, however, including the following:

1. It is almost impossible to conduct research without the participants knowing they are being studied.

2. The laboratory setting is unnatural and therefore can cause the participants to behave unnaturally.

3. People who are willing to come to a university laboratory may not accurately represent groups from diverse cultural backgrounds.

4. People who are unfamiliar with university settings and with the idea of "helping science" may be intimidated by the laboratory setting.

Naturalistic observation provides insights that sometimes cannot be attained in the laboratory (Leedy & Ormrod, 2013). **Naturalistic observation** means observing behavior in real-world settings, making no effort to manipulate or control the situation. Life-span researchers conduct naturalistic observations at sporting events, child-care centers, work settings, malls, and other places people live in and frequent.

Naturalistic observation was used in one study that focused on conversations in a children's science museum (Crowley & others, 2001). When visiting exhibits at the science museum, parents were far more likely to engage boys than girls in explanatory talk. This finding suggests a gender bias that encourages boys more than girls to be interested in science (see Figure 1.17).

What are some important strategies in conducting observational research with children?

Survey and Interview   Sometimes the best and quickest way to get information about people is to ask them for it. One technique is to interview them directly. A related method is the survey (sometimes referred to as a questionnaire), which is especially useful when information from many people is needed. A standard set of questions is used to obtain peoples' self-reported attitudes or beliefs about a particular topic. In a good survey, the questions are clear and unbiased, allowing respondents to answer unambiguously.

Surveys and interviews can be used to study topics ranging from religious beliefs to sexual habits to attitudes about gun control to beliefs about how to improve schools. Surveys and interviews may be conducted in person, over the telephone, and over the Internet.

One problem with surveys and interviews is the tendency of participants to answer questions in a way that they think is socially acceptable or desirable rather than to say what they truly think or feel (Madill, 2012). For example, on a survey or in an interview some individuals might say that they do not take drugs even though they do.

Standardized Test   A **standardized test** has uniform procedures for administration and scoring. Many standardized tests allow a person's performance to be compared with that of other individuals; thus they provide information about individual differences among people (Watson, 2012). One example is the Stanford-Binet intelligence test, which is described in Chapter 9. Your score on the Stanford-Binet test tells you how your performance compares with that of thousands of other people who have taken the test (Geisinger, 2012).

One criticism of standardized tests is that they assume a person's behavior is consistent and stable, yet personality and intelligence—two primary targets of standardized testing—can vary with the situation. For example, a person may perform poorly on a standardized intelligence test in an office setting but score much higher at home, where he or she is less anxious.

Case Study   A **case study** is an in-depth look at a single individual. Case studies are performed mainly by mental health professionals when, for either practical or ethical reasons, the unique aspects of an individual's life cannot be duplicated and tested in other individuals. A case study provides information about one person's experiences; it may focus on nearly any aspect of the subject's life that helps the researcher understand the person's mind, behavior, or other attributes (Yin, 2012). A researcher may gather information for a case study from interviews and medical records. In later chapters, we discuss vivid case studies, such as that of Michael Rehbein, who had much of the left side of his brain removed at 7 years of age to end severe epileptic seizures.

A case study can provide a dramatic, in-depth portrayal of an individual's life, but we must be cautious when generalizing from this information. The subject of a case study is unique, with a genetic makeup and personal history that no one else shares. In addition, case studies involve judgments of unknown reliability. Researchers who conduct case studies rarely check to see if other professionals agree with their observations or findings.

Mahatma Gandhi was the spiritual leader of India in the middle of the twentieth century. Erik Erikson conducted an extensive case study of Gandhi's life to determine what contributed to his identity development. *What are some limitations of the case study approach?*

Physiological Measures   Researchers are increasingly using physiological measures when they study development at different points in the life span (Bauer & Dunn, 2013; Chuang & others, 2014). Hormone levels are increasingly used in developmental research.

Cortisol is a hormone produced by the adrenal gland that is linked to the body's stress level and has been measured in studies of temperament, emotional reactivity, and peer relations (Gunnar & Herrera, 2013). Also, as puberty unfolds, the blood levels of certain hormones increase. To determine the nature of these hormonal changes, researchers analyze blood samples from adolescent volunteers (Susman & Dorn, 2013).

Another physiological measure that is increasingly being used is neuroimaging, especially *functional magnetic resonance imaging* (fMRI), in which electromagnetic waves are used to construct images of a person's brain tissue and biochemical activity (Fletcher & Rapp,

laboratory A controlled setting in which many of the complex factors of the "real world" are removed.

naturalistic observation Studies that involve observing behavior in real-world settings.

standardized test A test with uniform procedures for administration and scoring. Many standardized tests allow a person's performance to be compared with the performance of other individuals.

case study An in-depth look at a single individual.

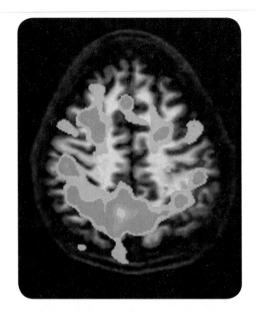

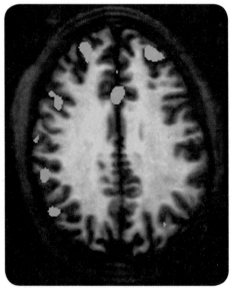

FIGURE **1.18**

BRAIN IMAGING OF 15-YEAR-OLD

ADOLESCENTS. These two brain images indicate how alcohol can influence the functioning of an adolescent's brain. Notice the pink and red coloring (which indicates effective brain functioning involving memory) in the brain of the 15-year-old non-drinker (*top*) while engaging in a memory task, and compare it with the lack of those colors in the brain of the 15-year-old heavy drinker (*bottom*) under the influence of alcohol.

descriptive research Studies designed to observe and record behavior.

correlational research Research that attempts to determine the strength of the relationship between two or more events or characteristics.

2013). Figure 1.18 compares the brain images of two adolescents—one a non-drinker and the other a heavy drinker—while they are engaged in a memory task.

Electroencephaly (EEG) is a physiological measure that has been used for many decades to monitor overall electrical activity in the brain (Reznick, 2013). Recent electroencephalograph research includes studies of infants' attention and memory (Rueda & Posner, 2013). In many chapters of this book, you will read about recent research on changes in the brain during prenatal development, infancy, childhood, adolescence, and aging.

Heart rate has been used as an indicator of infants' and children's development of perception, attention, and memory (Columbo, Brez, & Curtindale, 2013). Further, heart rate has served as an index of different aspects of emotional development, such as inhibition and anxiety (Reznick, 2013).

Researchers study eye movement to learn more about perceptual development and other developmental topics. Sophisticated eye-tracking equipment reveals detailed information about infants' perception, attention, and the development of autism (Bulf & Valenza, 2013; Xiao & others, 2014).

Researchers are increasingly using physiological measures when they study development at different points in the life span. For example, as puberty unfolds, the blood levels of certain hormones increase. To determine the nature of these hormonal changes, researchers analyze blood samples from adolescent volunteers (Susman & Dorn, 2013).

Yet another dramatic change in physiological methods is the advancement in methods to assess the actual units of hereditary information—genes—in studies of biological influences on development (Moore, 2013). For example, in Chapter 17 you will read about the role of the ApoE4 gene in Alzheimer disease (Kim, Vicenty, & Palmore, 2013; Ungar, Altmann, & Greicius, 2014).

RESEARCH DESIGNS

When you are conducting research on life-span development, in addition to selecting a method for collecting data, you also need to choose a research design. There are three main types of research designs: descriptive, correlational, and experimental.

Descriptive Research   All of the data-collection methods that we have discussed can be used in **descriptive research,** which aims to observe and record behavior. For example, a researcher might observe the extent to which people are altruistic or aggressive toward each other. By itself, descriptive research cannot prove what causes some phenomenon, but it can reveal important information about people's behavior (Leedy & Ormrod, 2013).

Correlational Research   In contrast with descriptive research, correlational research goes beyond describing phenomena to provide information that will help us to predict how people will behave. In **correlational research,** the goal is to describe the strength of the relationship between two or more events or characteristics. The more strongly the two events are correlated (or related or associated), the more accurately we can predict one event from the other (Levin, Fox, & Forde, 2015; Howell, 2014).

For example, to find out whether children of permissive parents have less self-control than other children, you would need to carefully record observations of parents' permissiveness and their children's self-control. You might observe that the higher a parent was in permissiveness, the lower the child was in self-control. You would then analyze these data statistically to yield a numerical measure called a **correlation coefficient,** which is a number based on a statistical analysis that describes the degree of association between two variables. The correlation coefficient ranges from -1.00 to $+1.00$. A negative number means an inverse relation. In this example, you might find an inverse correlation between permissive parenting and children's self-control with a coefficient of, say, $-.30$. By contrast, you might find a positive correlation of $+.30$ between parental monitoring of children and children's self-control.

The higher the correlation coefficient (whether positive or negative), the stronger the association between the two variables. A correlation of 0 means that there is no association between the variables. A correlation of $-.40$ is stronger than a correlation of $+.20$ because we disregard whether the correlation is positive or negative in determining the strength of the correlation.

Observed Correlation: As permissive parenting increases, children's self-control decreases.

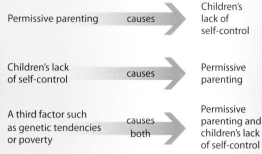

Possible explanations for this observed correlation

Permissive parenting → causes → Children's lack of self-control

Children's lack of self-control → causes → Permissive parenting

A third factor such as genetic tendencies or poverty → causes both → Permissive parenting and children's lack of self-control

An observed correlation between two events cannot be used to conclude that one event causes the second event. Other possibilities are that the second event causes the first event or that a third event causes the correlation between the first two events.

FIGURE 1.19

POSSIBLE EXPLANATIONS OF CORRELATIONAL DATA

A caution is in order, however. Correlation does not equal causation (Heiman, 2014, 2015). The correlational finding just mentioned does not mean that permissive parenting necessarily causes low self-control in children. It could have that meaning, but it also could indicate that a child's lack of self-control caused the parents to throw up their arms in despair and give up trying to control the child. It also could mean that other factors, such as heredity or poverty, caused the correlation between permissive parenting and low self-control in children. Figure 1.19 illustrates these possible interpretations of correlational data.

Experimental Research   To study causality, researchers turn to experimental research. An **experiment** is a carefully regulated procedure in which one or more factors believed to influence the behavior being studied are manipulated while all other factors are held constant. If the behavior under study changes when a factor is manipulated, we say that the manipulated factor has caused the behavior to change. In other words, the experiment has demonstrated cause and effect. The cause is the factor that was manipulated. The effect is the behavior that changed because of the manipulation. Nonexperimental research methods (descriptive and correlational research) cannot establish cause and effect because they do not involve manipulating factors in a controlled way.

Independent and Dependent Variables   Experiments include two types of changeable factors, or variables: independent and dependent. An independent variable is a manipulated, influential, experimental factor. It is a potential cause. The label "independent" is used because this variable can be manipulated independently of other factors to determine its effect. An experiment may include one independent variable or several of them.

A dependent variable is a factor that can change in an experiment, in response to changes in the independent variable. As researchers manipulate the independent variable, they measure the dependent variable for any resulting effect.

For example, suppose that you conducted a study to determine whether women could change the breathing and sleeping patterns of their newborn babies by meditating during pregnancy. You might require one group of pregnant women to engage in a certain amount and type of meditation each day while another group would not meditate; the meditation is thus the independent variable. When the infants are born, you would observe and measure their breathing and sleeping patterns. These patterns are the dependent variable, the factor that changes as the result of your manipulation.

Experimental and Control Groups   Experiments can involve one or more experimental groups and one or more control groups (Kirk, 2013). An experimental group is a group whose experience is manipulated. A control group is a comparison group that is as similar to the experimental group as possible and that is treated in every way like the experimental group except for the manipulated factor (independent variable). The control group serves as a baseline against which the effects of the manipulated condition can be compared.

Random assignment is an important principle for deciding whether each participant will be placed in the experimental group or in the control group. Random assignment means that researchers assign participants to experimental and control groups by chance. It reduces the likelihood that the experiment's results will be due to any preexisting differences between

- - - - - - - →

developmental **connection**

Cognitive Neuroscience and Aging

The cognitive neuroscience of aging involves the study of links between the brain's development in older adults and changes in their cognitive skills. Chapter 18, p. 551

- - - - - - - →

developmental **connection**

Gene × Environment (G × E) Interaction

Increasingly, researchers are exploring how the interaction of a specific gene and a specific aspect of the environment affects development. Chapter 2, p. 67

correlation coefficient A number based on statistical analysis that is used to describe the degree of association between two variables.

experiment A carefully regulated procedure in which one or more of the factors believed to influence the behavior being studied are manipulated while all other factors are held constant.

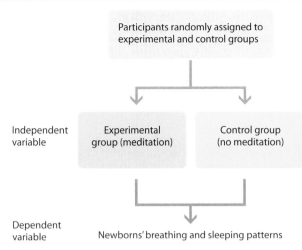

Participants randomly assigned to
experimental and control groups

Independent
variable

Experimental
group (meditation)

Control group
(no meditation)

Dependent
variable

Newborns' breathing and sleeping patterns

FIGURE **1.20**

PRINCIPLES OF EXPERIMENTAL RESEARCH.
Imagine that you decide to conduct an
experimental study of the effects of meditation by
pregnant women on their newborns' breathing
and sleeping patterns. You would randomly
assign pregnant women to experimental and
control groups. The experimental-group women
would engage in meditation over a specified
number of sessions and weeks. The control
group would not. Then, when the infants are
born, you would assess their breathing and
sleeping patterns. If the breathing and sleeping
patterns of newborns whose mothers were in the
experimental group are more positive than those
of the control group, you would conclude that
meditation caused the positive effects.

- - - - - - - - - ➤

developmental **connection**

Intelligence
Cohort effects help to explain differences
in the intelligence of people born at different points in time. Chapter 15, p. 471

cross-sectional approach A research strategy in
which individuals of different ages are compared
at one time.

longitudinal approach A research strategy in
which the same individuals are studied over a
period of time, usually several years or more.

cohort effects Effects due to a person's time of
birth, era, or generation rather than the person's
actual age.

groups (Kantowitz, Roediger, & Elmes, 2015). In the example involving the
effects of meditation by pregnant women on the breathing and sleeping patterns
of their newborns, you would randomly assign half of the pregnant women to
engage in meditation over a period of weeks (the experimental group) and the
other half to not meditate over the same number of weeks (the control group).
Figure 1.20 illustrates the nature of experimental research.

TIME SPAN OF RESEARCH

Researchers in life-span development have a special concern with studies that
focus on the relation of age to some other variable. We have several options:
Researchers can study different individuals of varying ages and compare them or
they can study the same individuals as they age over time.

Cross-Sectional Approach   The **cross-sectional approach** is a research
strategy that simultaneously compares individuals of different ages. A typical
cross-sectional study might include three groups of children: 5-year-olds, 8-year-
olds, and 11-year-olds. Another study might include groups of 15-year-olds, 25-year-olds, and
45-year-olds. The groups can be compared with respect to a variety of dependent variables:
IQ, memory, peer relations, attachment to parents, hormonal changes, and so on. All of this
can be accomplished in a short time. In some studies, data are collected in a single day. Even
in large-scale cross-sectional studies with hundreds of subjects, data collection does not usually take longer than several months to complete.

The main advantage of the cross-sectional study is that the researcher does not have to wait
for the individuals to grow up or become older. Despite its efficiency, though, the cross-sectional
approach has its drawbacks. It gives no information about how individuals change or about the
stability of their characteristics. It can obscure the increases and decreases of development—the
hills and valleys of growth and development. For example, a cross-sectional study of life satisfaction might reveal average increases and decreases, but it would not show how the life satisfaction
of individual adults waxed and waned over the years. It also would not tell us whether the same
adults who had positive or negative perceptions of life satisfaction in early adulthood maintained
their relative degree of life satisfaction as they became middle-aged or older adults.

Longitudinal Approach   The **longitudinal approach** is a research strategy in which
the same individuals are studied over a period of time, usually several years or more. For
example, in a longitudinal study of life satisfaction, the same adults might be assessed periodically over a 70-year time span—at the ages of 20, 35, 45, 65, and 90, for example.

Longitudinal studies provide a wealth of information about vital issues such as stability and
change in development and the influence of early experience on later development, but they do
have drawbacks (Windle, 2012). They are expensive and time consuming. The longer the study
lasts, the more participants drop out—they move, get sick, lose interest, and so forth. The participants who remain may be dissimilar to those who drop out, biasing the outcome of the study.
Those individuals who remain in a longitudinal study over a number of years may be more
responsible and conformity-oriented, for example, or they might lead more stable lives.

Cohort Effects   A *cohort* is a group of people who are born at a similar point in history
and share similar experiences as a result, such as living through the Vietnam War or growing
up in the same city around the same time. These shared experiences may produce a range of
differences among cohorts (Schaie, 2013). For example, people who were teenagers during
the Great Depression are likely to differ from people who were teenagers during the booming
1990s in their educational opportunities and economic status, in how they were raised, and
in their attitudes toward sex and religion. In life-span development research, **cohort effects**
are due to a person's time of birth, era, or generation but not to actual age.

Cohort effects are important because they can powerfully affect the dependent measures
in a study ostensibly concerned with age. Researchers have shown that it is especially important to be aware of cohort effects when assessing adult intelligence (Schaie, 2009, 2013).
Individuals born at different points in time—such as 1920, 1940, and 1960—have had varying

Cohort effects are due to a person's time of birth or generation but not actually to age. Think for a moment about growing up (a) during the Great Depression or (b) today. *How might your development differ depending on which of these time frames has dominated your life? your parents' lives? your grandparents' lives?*

opportunities for education. Individuals born in earlier years had less access to education, and this fact may have a significant effect on how this cohort performs on intelligence tests.

Cross-sectional studies can show how different cohorts respond, but they can confuse age changes and cohort effects. Longitudinal studies are effective in studying age changes but only within one cohort.

Various generations have been given labels by the popular culture. Figure 1.21 describes the labels given to various generations, their historical period, and the reasons for these labels. Consider the following description of the current generation of youth and think about how they differ from earlier youth generations:

> They are history's first "always connected" generation. Steeped in digital technology and social media, they treat their multi-tasking hand-held gadgets almost like a body part—for better or worse. More than 8 in 10 say they sleep with a cell phone glowing by the bed, poised to disgorge texts, phone calls, e-mails, songs, news, videos, games, and wake-up jingles. But sometimes convenience yields to temptation. Nearly two-thirds admit to texting while driving (Pew Research Center, 2010, p. 1).

So far we have discussed many aspects of research on life-span development, but where can you read about this research firsthand? Read *Connecting Through Research* to find out.

How are today's millennials experiencing youth differently from earlier generations?

FIGURE **1.21**

GENERATIONS, THEIR HISTORICAL PERIODS, AND CHARACTERISTICS

Generation	Historical Period	Reasons for Label
Millennials	Individuals born in 1980 and later	First generation to come of age and enter emerging adulthood (18 to 25 years of age) in the twenty-first century (the new millennium). Two main characteristics: (1) connection to technology, and (2) ethnic diversity.
Generation X	Individuals born between 1965 and 1980	Described as lacking an identity and savvy loners.
Baby Boomers	Individuals born between 1946 and 1964	Label used because this generation represents the spike in the number of babies born after World War II; the largest generation ever to enter late adulthood in the United States.
Silent Generation	Individuals born between 1928 and 1945	Children of the Great Depression and World War II; described as conformists and civic minded.

Where Is Life-Span Research Published?

Regardless of whether you pursue a career in life-span development, psychology, or some related scientific field, you can benefit by learning about the journal process. As a student, you might be required to look up original research in journals. As a parent, teacher, or nurse you might want to consult journals to obtain information that will help you understand and work more effectively with people. And, as an inquiring person, you might look up information in journals after you have heard or read something that piqued your curiosity.

A journal publishes scholarly and academic information, usually in a specific domain—like physics, math, sociology, or our current interest, life-span development. Scholars in these fields publish most of their research in journals, which are the source of core information in virtually every academic discipline.

An increasing number of journals publish information about life-span development. Among the leading journals in life-span development are *Developmental Psychology, Child Development, Pediatrics, Pediatric Nursing, The Journals of Gerontology, Infant Behavior and Development, Journal of Research on Adolescence, Journal of Adult Development, Journal of Gerontological Nursing, Psychology and Aging, Human Development,* and many others. Also, a number of journals that do not focus solely on development publish articles on various aspects of human development. These journals include *Journal of Educational Psychology, Sex Roles, Journal of Cross-Cultural Research, Journal of Marriage and the Family,* and *Journal of Consulting and Clinical Psychology.*

Every journal has a board of experts who evaluate articles submitted for publication. Each submitted paper is accepted or rejected on the basis of such factors as its contribution to the field, methodological excellence, and clarity of writing. Some of the most prestigious journals reject as many as 80 to 90 percent of the articles submitted.

Journal articles are usually written by professionals for other professionals in the specialized field of the journal's focus; therefore, they often contain technical language and terms specific to the discipline that are difficult for nonprofessionals to understand. Their structure often takes this format: abstract, introduction, method, results, discussion, and references.

The abstract is a brief summary that appears at the beginning of the article. The abstract lets readers quickly determine whether the article is relevant to their interests. The introduction introduces the

Research journals are the core of information in virtually every academic discipline. Those shown here are among the increasing number of research journals that publish information about life span development. *What are the main parts of a research article that presents findings from original research?*

problem or issue that is being studied. It includes a concise review of research relevant to the topic, theoretical ties, and one or more hypotheses to be tested. The method section consists of a clear description of the subjects evaluated in the study, the measures used, and the procedures that were followed. The method section should be sufficiently clear and detailed so that by reading it another researcher could repeat or replicate the study. The results section reports the analysis of the data collected. In most cases, the results section includes statistical analyses that are difficult for nonprofessionals to understand. The discussion section describes the author's conclusions, inferences, and interpretation of what was found. Statements are usually made about whether the hypotheses presented in the introduction were supported, limitations of the study, and suggestions for future research. The last part of the journal article, called references, includes bibliographic information for each source cited in the article. The references section is often a good resource for finding other articles relevant to a topic that interests you.

Where do you find journals such as those described above? Your college or university library likely has some of them, and some public libraries also carry journals. Online resources such as PsycINFO and PubMed, which can facilitate the search for journal articles, are available to students on many campuses.

The research published in the journals mentioned above shapes our lives. It not only informs the research of other life-span development researchers, but it also informs the practices of law and policy makers, physicians, educators, parents, and many others. In fact, much of what you will find that is new in this edition of this textbook comes directly from the research that can be found in the journals mentioned above.

Research journals are the core of information in virtually every academic discipline. Those shown here are among the increasing number of research journals that publish information about life-span development.

What are the main parts of a research article that presents findings from original research?

CONDUCTING ETHICAL RESEARCH

Ethics in research may affect you personally if you ever serve as a participant in a study. In that event, you need to know your rights as a participant and the responsibilities of researchers to assure that these rights are safeguarded.

If you ever become a researcher in life-span development yourself, you will need an even deeper understanding of ethics. Even if you only carry out experimental projects in psychology courses, you must consider the rights of the participants in those projects (Rosnow & Rosenthal, 2013). A student might think, "I volunteer in a home for the mentally retarded several hours per week. I can use the residents of the home in my study to see if a particular treatment helps improve their memory for everyday tasks." But without proper permissions, the most well-meaning, kind, and considerate studies still violate the rights of the participants.

Today, proposed research at colleges and universities must pass the scrutiny of a research ethics committee before the research can be initiated. In addition, the American Psychological Association (APA) has developed ethics guidelines for its members. The code of ethics instructs psychologists to protect their participants from mental and physical harm. The participants' best interests need to be kept foremost in the researcher's mind. APA's guidelines address four important issues:

1. *Informed consent.* All participants must know what their research participation will involve and what risks might develop. Even after informed consent is given, participants must retain the right to withdraw from the study at any time and for any reason.

2. *Confidentiality.* Researchers are responsible for keeping all of the data they gather on individuals completely confidential and, when possible, completely anonymous.

3. *Debriefing.* After the study has been completed, participants should be informed of its purpose and the methods that were used. In most cases, the experimenter also can inform participants in a general manner beforehand about the purpose of the research without leading participants to behave in a way they think that the experimenter is expecting.

4. *Deception.* In some circumstances, telling the participants beforehand what the research study is about substantially alters the participants' behavior and invalidates the researcher's data. In all cases of deception, however, the psychologist must ensure that the deception will not harm the participants and that the participants will be debriefed (told the complete nature of the study) as soon as possible after the study is completed.

MINIMIZING BIAS

Studies of life-span development are most useful when they are conducted without bias or prejudice toward any particular group of people. Of special concern is bias based on gender and bias based on culture or ethnicity.

Gender Bias   For most of its existence, our society has had a strong gender bias, a preconceived notion about the abilities of women and men that prevented individuals from pursuing their own interests and achieving their potential (Hyde, 2014). Gender bias also has had a less obvious effect within the field of life-span development. For example, it is not unusual for conclusions to be drawn about females' attitudes and behaviors from research conducted with males as the only participants.

Furthermore, when researchers find gender differences, their reports sometimes magnify those differences (Denmark & others, 1988). For example, a researcher might report that 74 percent of the men in a study had high achievement expectations versus only 67 percent of the women and go on to talk about the differences in some detail. In reality, this might be a rather small difference. It also might disappear if the study were repeated, or the study might have methodological problems that don't allow such strong interpretations.

Pam Reid is a leading researcher who studies the effects of gender and ethnic bias on development. You can read about Pam's interests in *Connecting with Careers*.

Pam Reid, Educational and Developmental Psychologist

When she was a child, Pam Reid liked to play with chemistry sets. Reid majored in chemistry during college and wanted to become a doctor. However, when some of her friends signed up for a psychology class as an elective, she decided to take the course. She was intrigued by learning about how people think, behave, and develop—so much so that she changed her major to psychology. Reid went on to obtain her Ph.D. in psychology (American Psychological Association, 2003, p. 16).

For a number of years, Reid was a professor of education and psychology at the University of Michigan, where she also was a research scientist at the Institute for Research on Women and Gender. Her main focus has been on how children and adolescents develop social skills, with a special interest in the development of African American girls (Reid & Zalk, 2001). She has been involved in numerous community activities, including the creation of a math and technology enrichment program for middle-school girls. In 2004, Reid became provost and executive vice-president at Roosevelt University in Chicago, and in 2008 became president of Saint Joseph College in Hartford, Connecticut.

Pam Reid (*center*), with students at Saint Joseph College in Hartford, Connecticut, where she is the president of the college.

For more information about what educational psychologists do, see page 42 in the Careers in Life-Span Development appendix.

Cultural and Ethnic Bias   Today there is a growing realization that research on life-span development needs to include more people from diverse ethnic groups (Leong & others, 2013). Historically, people from ethnic minority groups (African American, Latino, Asian American, and Native American) were excluded from most research in the United States and simply thought of as variations from the norm or average. If minority individuals were included in samples and their scores didn't fit the norm, they were viewed as confounds or "noise" in data and discounted. Given the fact that individuals from diverse ethnic groups were excluded from research on life-span development for so long, we might reasonably conclude that people's real lives are perhaps more varied than research data have indicated in the past.

Researchers also have tended to overgeneralize about ethnic groups (Parrillo, 2014; Schaefer, 2015). **Ethnic gloss** is using an ethnic label such as African American or Latino in a superficial way that portrays an ethnic group as being more homogeneous than it really is (Trimble, 1988). For example, a researcher might describe a research sample like this: "The participants were 60 Latinos." A more complete description of the Latino group might be something like this: "The 60 Latino participants were Mexican Americans from low-income neighborhoods in the southwestern area of Los Angeles. Thirty-six were from homes in which Spanish is the dominant language spoken, 24 from homes in which English is the main language spoken. Thirty were born in the United States, 30 in Mexico. Twenty-eight described themselves as Mexican American, 14 as Mexican, 9 as American, 6 as Chicano, and 3 as Latino." Ethnic gloss can cause researchers to obtain samples of ethnic groups that are not representative of the group's diversity, which can lead to overgeneralization and stereotyping.

Ross Parke and Raymond Buriel (2006) described how research on ethnic minority children and their families has not been given adequate attention, especially in light of their significant rates of growth. Until recently, ethnic minority families were combined in the category "minority," which masks important differences among ethnic groups as well as diversity within an ethnic group. When research has been conducted on ethnic groups, most often they are compared to non–Latino Whites to identify group differences. An assumption in two-group studies is that ethnic minority children have not advanced far enough to be the

ethnic gloss Using an ethnic label such as African American or Latino in a superficial way that portrays an ethnic group as being more homogeneous than it really is.

Look at these two photographs, one of all non-Latino White males, the other of a diverse group of females and males from different ethnic groups, including some non-Latino White males. Consider a topic in life-span development, such as parenting, love, or cultural values. *If you were conducting research on this topic, might the results of the study differ depending on whether the participants in your study were the individuals in the photograph on the left or on the right?*

same as non–Latino White children and that this developmental lag contributes to ethnic minority children's problems. Recently, some researchers have replaced two-group studies with more in-depth examination of variations within a single ethnic group. For example, a researcher might study how parents in an ethnic group adapt to the challenges they face as a minority in U.S. society and how these experiences contribute to the goals they have for their children.

The continued growth of minority families in the United States in approaching decades will mainly be due to the immigration of Latino and Asian families (Parrillo, 2014). Researchers need "to take into account their acculturation level and generational status of parents and children," and consider how these factors might influence family processes and child outcomes (Parke & Buriel, 2006, p. 487). More attention also needs to be given to biculturalism because the complexity of diversity means that some children of color identify with two or more ethnic groups (Schwartz & others, 2013). And language development research needs to focus more on second-language acquisition (usually English) and bilingualism and how they are linked to school achievement (Hall Haley & Austin, 2014; Herrera & Murry, 2015).

Review Connect Reflect

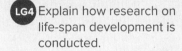

Explain how research on life-span development is conducted.

Review

- What methods do researchers use to collect data on life-span development?
- What research designs are used to study human development?
- How is research conducted on the time span of people's lives?
- What are researchers' ethical responsibilities to the people they study?
- How can gender, cultural, and ethnic bias affect the outcome of a research study?

Connect

- Earlier in the chapter, you read about normative age-graded influences, normative history-graded influences, and nonnormative life events. Describe how these influences relate to what you just read about cohort effects.

Reflect *Your Own Personal Journey of Life*

- You and your parents grew up at different points in time. Consider some ways that you are different from your parents. Do you think some of your differences might be due to cohort effects? Explain.

topical connections *looking forward*

In Chapter 2, you will continue to learn about theory and research as you explore the biological underpinnings of life-span development. The influence of human evolution on development will be covered, including a discussion of natural selection and adaptive behavior. You will examine how the human genome works, the collaborative nature of genes, and how DNA plays a role in the person each of us becomes. You also will explore the challenges and choices people encounter when deciding to reproduce, including infertility treatments and adoption. And you will read in greater depth about the many sides of the age-old nature-nurture debate, focusing on the way heredity and environment interact.

reach your **learning goals**

Introduction

1 The Life-Span Perspective

 Discuss the distinctive features of a life-span perspective on development.

- The Importance of Studying Life-Span Development

- Characteristics of the Life-Span Perspective

- Some Contemporary Concerns

- Development is the pattern of change that begins at conception and continues through the human life span. It includes both growth and decline. Studying life-span development helps prepare us to take responsibility for children, gives us insight about our own lives, and gives us knowledge about what our lives will be like as we age.

- The life-span perspective includes these basic conceptions: development is lifelong, multidimensional, multidirectional, and plastic; its study is multidisciplinary; it is contextual; it involves growth, maintenance, and regulation of loss; and it is a co-construction of biological, cultural, and individual factors. Three important sources of contextual influences are (1) normative age-graded influences, (2) normative history-graded influences, and (3) nonnormative life events.

- Health and well-being, parenting, education, sociocultural contexts and diversity, and social policy are all areas of contemporary concern that are closely tied to life-span development. Important dimensions of the sociocultural context include culture, ethnicity, socioeconomic status, and gender. There is increasing interest in social policy issues related to children and to older adults.

2 The Nature of Development

 Identify the most important processes, periods, and issues in development.

- Biological, Cognitive, and Socioemotional Processes

- Periods of Development

- Three key categories of developmental processes are biological, cognitive, and socioemotional. Throughout development, there are extensive connections between these types of processes.

- The life span is commonly divided into the following development periods: prenatal, infancy, early childhood, middle and late childhood, adolescence, early adulthood, middle adulthood, and late adulthood. Recently, life-span developmentalists have described the human life span in terms of four ages with a special focus on the third and fourth ages, as well as a distinction between the young-old and oldest-old. An important aspect of life-span development involves connections across periods of development.

The Significance of Age

- According to some experts on life-span development, too much emphasis is placed on chronological age. In studies covering adolescence through late adulthood, older people report the highest level of happiness. We often think of age only in terms of chronological age, but a full evaluation of age requires consideration of chronological, biological, psychological, and social age. Neugarten emphasizes that we are moving toward a society in which chronological age is only a weak predictor of development in adulthood.

Developmental Issues

- The nature-nurture issue focuses on the extent to which development is mainly influenced by nature (biological inheritance) or nurture (experience). The stability-change issue focuses on the degree to which we become older renditions of our early experience or develop into someone different from who we were earlier in development. A special aspect of the stability-change issue is the extent to which development is determined by early versus later experiences. Developmentalists describe development as continuous (gradual, or cumulative change) or as discontinuous (abrupt, or a sequence of stages). Most developmentalists recognize that extreme positions on the nature-nurture, stability-change, and continuity-discontinuity issues are unwise. Despite this consensus, there is still spirited debate on these issues.

3 Theories of Development

LG3 Describe the main theories of human development.

Psychoanalytic Theories

- The scientific method involves four main steps: (1) conceptualize a problem, (2) collect data, (3) analyze data, and (4) draw conclusions. Theory is often involved in conceptualizing a problem. A theory is a coherent set of interrelated ideas that helps to explain phenomena and to facilitate predictions. Hypotheses are specific assertions and predictions, often derived from theory, that can be tested. According to psychoanalytic theories, development primarily depends on the unconscious mind and is heavily couched in emotion. Freud argued that individuals go through five psychosexual stages. Erikson's theory emphasizes eight psychosocial stages of development: trust versus mistrust, autonomy versus shame and doubt, initiative versus guilt, industry versus inferiority, identity versus identity confusion, intimacy versus isolation, generativity versus stagnation, and integrity versus despair. Contributions of psychoanalytic theories include an emphasis on a developmental framework, family relationships, and unconscious aspects of the mind. Criticisms include a lack of scientific support, too much emphasis on sexual underpinnings, and an image of people that is too negative.

Cognitive Theories

- Three main cognitive theories are Piaget's, Vygotsky's, and information processing. Cognitive theories emphasize thinking, reasoning, language, and other cognitive processes. Piaget proposed a cognitive developmental theory in which children use their cognition to adapt to their world. In Piaget's theory, children go through four cognitive stages: sensorimotor, preoperational, concrete operational, and formal operational. Vygotsky's sociocultural cognitive theory emphasizes how culture and social interaction guide cognitive development. The information-processing approach emphasizes that individuals manipulate information, monitor it, and strategize about it. Contributions of cognitive theories include an emphasis on the active construction of understanding and a positive view of development. Criticisms include giving too little attention to individual variations and skepticism about the pureness of Piaget's stages.

Behavioral and Social Cognitive Theories

- Two main behavioral and social cognitive theories are Skinner's operant conditioning and Bandura's social cognitive theory. In Skinner's operant conditioning, the consequences of a behavior produce changes in the probability of the behavior's occurrence. In Bandura's social cognitive theory, observational learning is a key aspect of life-span development. Bandura emphasizes reciprocal interactions among person/cognition, behavior, and environment. Contributions of the behavioral and social cognitive theories include an emphasis on scientific research and a focus on environmental factors. Criticisms include inadequate attention to developmental changes and, in Skinner's theory, too little attention to cognition.

Ethological Theory

- Ethology stresses that behavior is strongly influenced by biology, is tied to evolution, and is characterized by critical or sensitive periods. Contributions of ethological theory include a focus on the biological and evolutionary basis of development. Criticisms include a belief that the concepts of critical and sensitive periods may be too rigid.

Ecological Theory

- Ecological theory emphasizes environmental contexts. Bronfenbrenner's environmental systems view of development proposes five environmental systems: microsystem, mesosystem, exosystem, macrosystem, and chronosystem. Contributions of the theory include a systematic examination of macro and micro dimensions of environmental systems and attention to connections between them. Criticisms include inadequate attention to biological factors, as well as a lack of emphasis on cognitive factors.

An Eclectic Theoretical Orientation

- An eclectic theoretical orientation does not follow any one theoretical approach but rather selects from each theory whatever is considered the best in it.

4 Research on Life-Span Development

 LG4 Explain how research on life-span development is conducted.

Methods for Collecting Data

- Methods for collecting data about life-span development include observation (in a laboratory or a naturalistic setting), survey (questionnaire) or interview, standardized test, case study, and physiological measures.

Research Designs

- Three main research designs are descriptive, correlational, and experimental. Descriptive research aims to observe and record behavior. In correlational research, the goal is to describe the strength of the relationship between two or more events or characteristics. Experimental research involves conducting an experiment, which can determine cause and effect. An independent variable is the manipulated, influential, experimental factor. A dependent variable is a factor that can change in an experiment, in response to changes in the independent variable. Experiments can involve one or more experimental groups and control groups. In random assignment, researchers assign participants to experimental and control groups by chance.

Time Span of Research

- When researchers decide about the time span of their research, they can conduct cross-sectional or longitudinal studies. Life-span researchers are especially concerned about cohort effects.

Conducting Ethical Research

- Researchers' ethical responsibilities include seeking participants' informed consent, ensuring their confidentiality, debriefing them about the purpose and potential personal consequences of participating, and avoiding unnecessary deception of participants.

Minimizing Bias

- Researchers need to guard against gender, cultural, and ethnic bias in research. Every effort should be made to make research equitable for both females and males. Individuals from varied ethnic backgrounds need to be included as participants in life-span research, and overgeneralization about diverse members within a group must be avoided.

key terms

key people

appendix

Careers in Life-Span Development

The field of life-span development offers an amazing breadth of careers that can provide extremely satisfying work. College and university professors teach courses in many areas of life-span development. Teachers impart knowledge, understanding, and skills to children and adolescents. Counselors, clinical psychologists, nurses, and physicians help people of different ages to cope more effectively with their lives and improve their well-being.

These and many other careers related to life-span development offer many rewards. By working in the field of life-span development, you can help people to improve their lives, understand yourself and others better, possibly advance the state of knowledge in the field, and have an enjoyable time while you are doing these things. Many careers in life-span development pay reasonably well. For example, psychologists earn well above the median salary in the United States.

If you are considering a career in life-span development, would you prefer to work with infants? children? adolescents? older adults? As you go through this term, try to spend some time with people of different ages. Observe their behavior. Talk with them about their lives. Think about whether you would like to work with people of this age in your life's work.

In addition, to find out about careers in life-span development you might talk with people who work in various jobs. For example, if you have some interest in becoming a school counselor, call a school, ask to speak with a counselor, and set up an appointment to discuss the counselor's career and work. If you have an interest in becoming a nurse, call the nursing department at a hospital and set up an appointment to speak with the nursing coordinator about a nursing career.

Another way of exploring careers in life-span development is to work in a related job while you are in college. Many colleges and universities offer internships or other work experiences for students who major in specific fields. Course credit or pay is given for some of these jobs. Take advantage of these opportunities. They can help you decide if this is the right career for you, and they can help you get into graduate school, if you decide you want to go.

An advanced degree is not absolutely necessary for some careers in life-span development, but usually you can considerably expand your opportunities (and income) by obtaining a graduate degree. If you think you might want to go to graduate school, talk with one or more professors about your interests, keep a high grade-point average, take appropriate courses, and realize that you likely will need to take the Graduate Record Examination at some point.

In the upcoming sections, we will profile a number of careers in four areas: education/research; clinical/counseling; medical/nursing/physical development; and families/relationships. These are not the only career options in life-span development, but the profiles should give you an idea of the range of opportunities available. For each career, we will describe the work and address the amount of education required and the nature of the training. We have provided page numbers after some entries telling you where within the text you can find *Connecting with Careers,* the career profiles of people who hold some of these positions. The Web site for this book gives more detailed information about these careers in life-span development.

Education/Research

Numerous careers in life-span development involve education or research. The opportunities range from college professor to preschool teacher to school psychologist.

College/University Professor

Professors teach courses in life-span development at many types of institutions, including research universities with master's or Ph.D. programs in life-span development, four-year colleges with no graduate programs, and community colleges. The courses in life-span development are offered in many different programs and schools, including psychology, education, nursing, child and family studies, social work, and medicine. In addition to teaching at the undergraduate or graduate level (or both), professors may conduct research, advise students or direct their research, and serve on college or university committees. Research is part of a professor's job description at most universities with master's and Ph.D. programs, but some college professors do not conduct research and focus instead on teaching.

Teaching life-span development at a college or university almost always requires a Ph.D. or master's degree. Obtaining a Ph.D. usually takes four to six years of graduate work; a master's degree requires approximately two years. The training involves taking graduate courses, learning to conduct research, and attending and presenting papers at professional meetings. Many graduate students work as teaching or research assistants for professors in an apprenticeship relationship that helps them to become competent teachers and researchers. **Read the profiles of professors on p. 479 and p. 504.**

Researcher

Some individuals in the field of life-span development work in research positions. They might work for a university, a government agency such as the National Institute of Mental Health, or private industry. They generate research ideas, plan studies, carry out the research, and usually attempt to publish the research in a scientific journal. A researcher often works in collaboration with other researchers. One researcher might spend much of his or her time in a laboratory; another researcher might work in the field, such as in schools, hospitals, and so on. Most researchers in life-span development have either a master's or a Ph.D.

Elementary or Secondary School Teacher

Elementary and secondary school teachers teach one or more subject areas, preparing the curriculum, giving tests, assigning grades, monitoring students' progress, conducting parent-teacher conferences, and attending workshops. Becoming an elementary or secondary school teacher requires a minimum of an undergraduate degree. The training involves taking a wide range of courses with a major or concentration in education as well as completing supervised practice teaching.

Exceptional Children (Special Education) Teacher

Teachers of exceptional children spend concentrated time with children who have a disability such as ADHD, intellectual disabilities, or cerebral palsy, or with children who are gifted. Usually some of their work occurs outside of the students' regular classroom and some of it inside the students' regular classroom. A teacher of exceptional children works closely with the student's regular classroom teacher and parents to create the best educational program for the student. Teachers of exceptional children often continue their education after obtaining their undergraduate degree and attain a master's degree.

Early Childhood Educator

Early childhood educators work on college faculties and usually teach in community colleges that award an associate degree in early childhood education. They have a minimum of a master's degree in their field. In graduate school, they take courses in early childhood education and receive supervisory training in child-care or early childhood programs.

Preschool/Kindergarten Teacher

Preschool teachers teach mainly 4-year-old children, and kindergarten teachers primarily teach 5-year-old children. They usually have an undergraduate degree in education, specializing in early childhood education. State certification to become a preschool or kindergarten teacher usually is required.

Family and Consumer Science Educator

Family and consumer science educators may specialize in early childhood education or instruct middle and high school students about such matters as nutrition, interpersonal relationships, human sexuality, parenting, and human development. Hundreds of colleges and universities throughout the United States offer two- and four-year degree programs in family and consumer science. These programs usually require an internship. Additional education courses may be needed to obtain a teaching certificate. Some family and consumer educators go on to graduate school for further training, which provides a background for possible jobs in college teaching or research. **Read a profile of a family and consumer science educator on p. 349.**

Educational Psychologist

Educational psychologists most often teach in a college or university and conduct research in various areas of educational psychology such as learning, motivation, classroom management, and assessment. They help train students for positions in educational psychology, school psychology, and teaching. Most educational psychologists have a doctorate in education, which takes four to six years of graduate work. **Read a profile of an educational psychologist on p. 36.**

School Psychologist

School psychologists focus on improving the psychological and intellectual well-being of elementary, middle/junior, and high school students. They give psychological tests, interview students and their parents, consult with teachers, and may provide counseling to students and their families. They may work in a centralized office in a school district or in one or more schools.

School psychologists usually have a master's or doctoral degree in school psychology. In graduate school, they take courses in counseling, assessment, learning, and other areas of education and psychology.

Gerontologist

Gerontologists usually work in research in some branch of the federal or state government. They specialize in the study of aging with a particular focus on government programs for older adults, social policy, and delivery of services to older adults. In their research, gerontologists define problems to be studied, collect data, interpret the results, and make recommendations for social policy. Most gerontologists have a master's or doctoral degree and have taken a concentration of coursework in adult development and aging.

Clinical/Counseling

There are a wide variety of clinical and counseling jobs that are linked with life-span development. These range from child clinical psychologist to adolescent drug counselor to geriatric psychiatrist.

Clinical Psychologist

Clinical psychologists seek to help people with psychological problems. They work in a variety of settings, including colleges and universities, clinics, medical schools, and private practice. Some clinical psychologists only conduct psychotherapy; others do psychological assessment and psychotherapy; some also do research. Clinical psychologists may specialize in a particular age group, such as children (child clinical psychologist) or older adults (often referred to as a geropsychologist).

Clinical psychologists have either a Ph.D. (which involves clinical and research training) or a Psy.D. degree (which only involves clinical training). This graduate training usually takes five to seven years and includes courses in clinical psychology and a one-year supervised internship in an accredited setting toward the end of the training. Many geropsychologists pursue a year or two of postdoctoral training. Most states require clinical psychologists to pass a test in order to become licensed in the state and to call themselves clinical psychologists. **Read a profile of a clinical psychologist on p. 96.**

Psychiatrist

Psychiatrists obtain a medical degree and then do a residency in psychiatry. Medical school takes approximately four years and the psychiatry residency another three to four years. Unlike most psychologists (who do not go to medical school), psychiatrists can administer drugs to clients. (Recently, several states gave clinical psychologists the right to prescribe drugs.)

Like clinical psychologists, psychiatrists might specialize in working with children (child psychiatry) or with older adults (geriatric psychiatry). Psychiatrists might work in medical schools in teaching and research roles, in a medical clinic or hospital, or in private practice. In addition to administering drugs to help improve the lives of people with psychological problems, psychiatrists also may conduct psychotherapy. **Read a profile of a child psychiatrist on p. 8.**

Counseling Psychologist

Counseling psychologists work in the same settings as clinical psychologists and may do psychotherapy, teach, or conduct research. Many counseling psychologists do not do therapy with individuals who have severe mental disorders, such as schizophrenia.

Counseling psychologists go through much the same training as clinical psychologists, although in a graduate program in counseling rather than clinical psychology. Counseling psychologists have either a master's degree or a doctoral degree. They also must go through a licensing procedure. One type of master's degree in counseling leads to the designation of licensed professional counselor.

School Counselor

School counselors help students cope with adjustment problems, identify their abilities and interests, develop academic plans, and explore career options. The focus of the job depends on the age of the children. High school counselors advise students about vocational and technical training and admissions requirements for college, as well as about taking entrance exams, applying for financial aid, and choosing a major. Elementary school counselors mainly counsel students about social and personal problems. They may observe children in the classroom and at play as part of their work. School counselors may work with students individually, in small groups, or even in a classroom. They often consult with parents, teachers, and school administrators when trying to help students. School counselors usually have a master's degree in counseling.

Career Counselor

Career counselors help individuals to identify their best career options and guide them in applying for jobs. They may work in private industry or at a college or university. They usually interview individuals and give them vocational and/or psychological tests to identify appropriate careers that fit their interests and abilities. Sometimes they help individuals to create résumés or conduct mock interviews to help them feel comfortable in a job interview. They might arrange and promote job fairs or other recruiting events to help individuals obtain jobs.

Rehabilitation Counselor

Rehabilitation counselors work with individuals to identify career options, develop adjustment and coping skills to maximize independence, and resolve problems created by a disability. A master's degree in rehabilitation counseling or guidance or counseling psychology is generally considered the minimum educational requirement.

Social Worker

Many social workers are involved in helping people with social or economic problems. They may investigate, evaluate, and attempt to rectify reported cases of abuse, neglect, endangerment, or domestic disputes. They may intervene in families and provide counseling and referral services to individuals and families. Some social workers specialize in a certain area. For example, a medical social worker might coordinate support services to people with a long-term disability; family-care social workers often work with families with children or an older adult who needs support services. Social workers often work for publicly funded agencies at the city, state, or national level, although increasingly they work in the private sector in areas such as drug rehabilitation and family counseling.

Social workers have a minimum of an undergraduate degree from a school of social work that includes coursework in sociology and psychology. Some social workers also have a master's or doctoral degree. For example, medical social workers have a master's degree in social work (M.S.W.) and complete graduate coursework and supervised clinical experiences in medical settings.

Drug Counselor

Drug counselors provide counseling to individuals with drug-abuse problems. Some drug counselors specialize in working with adolescents or older adults. They may work on an individual basis with a substance abuser or conduct group therapy. They may work in private practice, with a state or federal government agency, for a company, or in a hospital.

At a minimum, drug counselors complete an associate's or certificate program. Many have an undergraduate degree in substance-abuse counseling, and some have master's and doctoral degrees. Most states provide a certification procedure for obtaining a license to practice drug counseling.

Medical/Nursing/Physical Development

This third main area of careers in life-span development includes a wide range of choices in the medical and nursing areas, as well as jobs pertaining to improving some aspect of a person's physical development.

Obstetrician/Gynecologist

An obstetrician/gynecologist prescribes prenatal and postnatal care, performs deliveries in maternity cases, and treats diseases and injuries of the female reproductive system. Becoming an obstetrician/gynecologist requires a medical degree plus three to five years of residency in obstetrics/gynecology. Obstetricians may work in private practice, a medical clinic, a hospital, or a medical school.

Pediatrician

A pediatrician monitors infants' and children's health, works to prevent disease or injury, helps children attain optimal health, and treats children with health problems. Pediatricians have earned a medical degree and completed a three- to five-year residency in pediatrics.

Pediatricians may work in private practice or at a medical clinic, a hospital, or a medical school. Many pediatricians on the faculty of medical schools also teach and conduct research on children's health and diseases. **Read the profile of a pediatrician on p. 116.**

Geriatric Physician

Geriatric physicians diagnose medical problems of older adults, evaluate treatment options, and make recommendations for nursing care or other arrangements. They have a medical degree and specialized in geriatric medicine by doing a three- to five-year residency. Like other doctors, geriatric physicians may work in private practice or at a medical clinic, a hospital, or a medical school. Those in medical school settings may not only treat older adults but also teach future physicians and conduct research.

Neonatal Nurse

Neonatal nurses deliver care to newborn infants. They may work with infants born under normal circumstances or premature and critically ill neonates. A minimum of an undergraduate degree in nursing with a specialization in the newborn is required. This training involves coursework in nursing and the biological sciences, as well as supervised clinical experiences.

Nurse-Midwife

A nurse-midwife formulates and provides comprehensive care to expectant mothers as they prepare to give birth, guides them through the birth process, and cares for them after the birth. The nurse-midwife also may provide care to the newborn, counsel parents on the infant's development and parenting, and provide guidance about health practices. Becoming a nurse-midwife generally requires an undergraduate degree from a school of nursing. A nurse-midwife most often works in a hospital setting. **Read the profile of a perinatal nurse on p. 89.**

Pediatric Nurse

Pediatric nurses monitor infants' and children's health, work to prevent disease or injury, and help children attain optimal health. They may work in hospitals, schools of nursing, or with pediatricians in private practice or at a medical clinic.

Pediatric nurses have a degree in nursing that takes two to five years to complete. They take courses in biological sciences, nursing care, and pediatrics, usually in a school of nursing. They also undergo supervised clinical experiences in medical settings. Some pediatric nurses go on to earn a master's or doctoral degree in pediatric nursing.

Geriatric Nurse

Geriatric nurses seek to prevent or intervene in the chronic or acute health problems of older adults. They may work in hospitals, nursing homes, schools of nursing, or with geriatric medical specialists or psychiatrists in a medical clinic or in private practice. Like pediatric nurses, geriatric nurses take courses in a school of nursing and obtain a degree in nursing, which takes from two to five years. They complete courses in biological sciences, nursing care, and mental health as well as supervised clinical training in geriatric settings. They also may obtain a master's or doctoral degree in their specialty. **Read a profile of a geriatric nurse on p. 534.**

Physical Therapist

Physical therapists work with individuals who have a physical problem due to disease or injury to help them function as competently as possible. They may consult with other professionals and coordinate services for the individual. Many physical therapists work with people of all ages, although some specialize in working with a specific age group, such as children or older adults.

Physical therapists usually have an undergraduate degree in physical therapy and are licensed by a state. They take courses and experience supervised training in physical therapy.

Occupational Therapist

Occupational therapists initiate the evaluation of clients with various impairments and manage their treatment. They help people regain, develop, and build skills that are important for independent functioning, health, well-being, security, and happiness. An "Occupational Therapist Registered" (OTR) must have a master's and/or doctoral degree with education ranging from two to six years. Training includes occupational therapy courses in a specialized program. National certification is required and licensing/registration is required in some states.

Therapeutic/Recreation Therapist

Therapeutic/recreation therapists maintain or improve the quality of life for people with special needs through intervention, leisure education, and recreation. They work in hospitals, rehabilitation centers, local government agencies, at-risk youth programs, and other settings. Becoming a therapeutic/recreation therapist requires an undergraduate degree with coursework in leisure studies and a concentration in therapeutic recreation. National certification is usually required. Coursework in anatomy, special education, and psychology is beneficial.

Audiologist

Audiologists assess and identify the presence and severity of hearing loss, as well as problems in balance. They may work in a medical clinic, with a physician in private practice, in a hospital, or in a medical school.

An audiologist completes coursework and supervised training to earn a minimum of an undergraduate degree in hearing science. Some audiologists also go on to obtain a master's or doctoral degree.

Speech Therapist

Speech therapists identify, assess, and treat speech and language problems. They may work with physicians, psychologists, social workers, and other health care professionals in a team approach to help individuals with physical or psychological problems that involve speech and language. Some speech therapists specialize in working with individuals of a particular age or people with a particular type of speech disorder. Speech therapists have a minimum of an undergraduate degree in speech and hearing science or in a type of communication disorder. They may work in private practice, hospitals and medical schools, and government agencies.

Genetic Counselor

Genetic counselors identify and counsel families at risk for genetic disorders. They work as members of a health care team, providing information and support to families who have members who have genetic defects or disorders or are at risk for a variety of inherited conditions. They also serve as educators and resource people for other health care professionals and the public. Almost one-half of genetic counselors work in university medical centers; one-fourth work in private hospital settings.

Genetic counselors have specialized graduate degrees and experience in medical genetics and counseling. Most enter the field after majoring in undergraduate school in such disciplines as biology, genetics, psychology, nursing, public health, or social work. **Read a profile of a genetic counselor on p. 58.**

Families/Relationships

A number of careers and jobs related to life-span development focus on working with families and addressing relationship problems. These range from home health aide to marriage and family therapist.

Home Health Aide

A home health aide provides services to older adults in the older adults' homes, helping them with basic self-care tasks. No higher education is required for this position. There is brief training by an agency.

Child Welfare Worker

Child protective services in each state employ child welfare workers. They protect children's rights, evaluate any maltreatment, and may have children removed from their homes if necessary. A child social worker has a minimum of an undergraduate degree in social work.

Child Life Specialist

Child life specialists work with children and their families when the child needs to be hospitalized. They monitor the child's activities, seek to reduce the child's stress, and help the child to cope and to enjoy the hospital experience as much as possible. Child life specialists may provide parent education and develop individualized treatment plans based on an assessment of the child's development, temperament, medical plan, and available social supports. Child life specialists have an undergraduate degree. They have taken courses in child development and education and usually completed additional courses in a child life program. **Read a profile of a child life specialist on p. 272.**

Marriage and Family Therapist

Marriage and family therapists work on the principle that many individuals who have psychological problems benefit when psychotherapy is provided in the context of a marital or family relationship. Marriage and family therapists may provide marital therapy, couple therapy to individuals in a relationship who are not married, and family therapy to two or more members of a family.

Marriage and family therapists have a master's or a doctoral degree. They complete a training program in graduate school similar to a clinical psychologist's but with the focus on marital and family relationships. In most states, it is necessary to go through a licensing procedure to practice marital and family therapy. **Read the profile of a marriage and family therapist on p. 248.**

Further Careers

These are only a handful of careers that knowledge of developmental psychology can prepare you for. The *Connecting with Careers* profiles highlight additional careers, including an infant assessment specialist (p. 151), child care director (p. 190), toy designer (p. 218), health psychologist (p. 391), college/career counselor (p. 405), parent counselor (p. 451), pastoral counselor (p. 479), association director (p. 227), and home hospice nurse (p. 600). *What other careers can you think of that require a knowledge of human development?*

There are one hundred and ninety-three living species of monkeys and apes. One hundred and ninety-two of them are covered with hair. The exception is the naked ape, self-named Homo sapiens.

—**DESMOND MORRIS**
British Zoologist, 20th Century

Beginnings

The rhythm and meaning of life involve beginnings. Questions are raised about how, from so simple a beginning, endless forms develop, grow, and mature. What was this organism, what is this organism, and what will this organism be? In Section 2, you will read two chapters: "Biological Beginnings" (Chapter 2) and "Prenatal Development and Birth" (Chapter 3).

chapter 2

BIOLOGICAL BEGINNINGS

chapter **outline**

Jim Springer and Jim Lewis are identical twins. They were separated at 4 weeks of age and did not see each other again until they were 39 years old. Both worked as part-time deputy sheriffs, vacationed in Florida, drove Chevrolets, had dogs named Toy, and married and divorced women named Betty. One twin named his son James Allan, and the other named his son James Alan. Both liked math but not spelling, enjoyed carpentry and mechanical drawing, chewed their fingernails down to the nubs, had almost identical drinking and smoking habits, had hemorrhoids, put on 10 pounds at about the same point in development, first suffered headaches at the age of 18, and had similar sleep patterns.

Jim and Jim do have some differences. One wears his hair over his forehead, the other slicks it back and has sideburns. One expresses himself best orally; the other is more proficient in writing. But, for the most part, their profiles are remarkably similar.

Another pair of identical twins, Daphne and Barbara, are called the "giggle sisters" because after being reunited they were always making each other laugh. A thorough search of their adoptive families' histories revealed no gigglers. The giggle sisters ignored stress, avoided conflict and controversy whenever possible, and showed no interest in politics.

Jim and Jim and the giggle sisters were part of the Minnesota Study of Twins Reared Apart, directed by Thomas Bouchard and his colleagues. The study brings identical twins (identical genetically because they come from the same fertilized egg) and fraternal twins (who come from different fertilized eggs) from all over the world to Minneapolis to investigate their lives. There the twins complete personality and intelligence tests, and they provide detailed medical histories, including information about diet and smoking, exercise habits, chest X-rays, heart stress tests, and EEGs. The twins are asked more than 15,000 questions about their family and childhood, personal interests, vocational orientation, values, and aesthetic judgments (Bouchard & others, 1990).

topical connections *looking back*

The previous chapter introduced the field of life-span development, including discussion of three key categories of developmental processes: biological, cognitive, and socioemotional. In this chapter, we lay the foundation of the biological aspects of development. Biological processes, guided by genes, influence an individual's development in every period of the human life span. The forthcoming discussion of genetics and the previous discussion of theories (psychoanalytic, cognitive, behavioral and social cognitive, ethological, and ecological) in Chapter 1 provide a knowledge base from which to examine one of life-span development's major issues and debates—how strongly development is influenced by heredity (nature) and the environment (nurture).

When genetically identical twins who were separated as infants show such striking similarities in their tastes and habits and choices, can we conclude that their genes must have caused the development of those tastes and habits and choices? Other possible causes need to be considered. The twins shared not only the same genes but also some experiences. Some of the separated twins lived together for several months prior to their adoption; some of the twins had been reunited prior to testing (in some cases, many years earlier); adoption agencies often place twins in similar homes; and even strangers who spend several hours together and start comparing their lives are likely to come up with some coincidental similarities (Joseph, 2006). The Minnesota study of identical twins points to both the importance of the genetic basis of human development and the need for further research on genetic and environmental factors (Lykken, 2001). We will discuss twin studies in more detail in the section on behavior genetics later in this chapter.

preview

The examples of Jim and Jim and the giggle sisters stimulate us to think about our genetic heritage and the biological foundations of our existence. However, organisms are not like billiard balls, moved by simple external forces to predictable positions on life's table. Environmental experiences and biological foundations work together to make us who we are. Our coverage of life's biological beginnings focuses on evolution, genetic foundations, challenges and choices regarding reproduction, and the interaction of heredity and environment.

1 The Evolutionary Perspective

 LG1 Discuss the evolutionary perspective on life-span development.

Natural Selection and Adaptive Behavior

Evolutionary Psychology

In evolutionary time, humans are relative newcomers to Earth. As our earliest ancestors left the forest to feed on the savannahs and then to form hunting societies on the open plains, their minds and behaviors changed, and they eventually established humans as the dominant species on Earth. How did this evolution come about?

How does the attachment of this Vietnamese baby to its mother reflect the evolutionary process of adaptive behavior?

NATURAL SELECTION AND ADAPTIVE BEHAVIOR

Natural selection is the evolutionary process by which those individuals of a species that are best adapted are the ones that survive and reproduce. To understand what this means, let's return to the middle of the nineteenth century, when British naturalist Charles Darwin was traveling around the world, observing many different species of animals in their natural surroundings. Darwin, who published his observations and thoughts in *On the Origin of Species* (1859), noted that most organisms reproduce at rates that would cause enormous increases in the population of most species and yet populations remain nearly constant. He reasoned that an intense, constant struggle for food, water, and resources must occur among the many young born each generation, because many of the young do not survive. Those that do survive and reproduce pass on some of their characteristics to the next generation. Darwin argued that these survivors are better *adapted* to their world than are the nonsurvivors

(Hoefnagels, 2015). The best-adapted individuals survive to leave the most offspring. Over the course of many generations, organisms with the characteristics needed for survival make up an increasing percentage of the population. Over many, many generations, this could produce a gradual modification of the whole population. If environmental conditions change, however, other characteristics might become favored by natural selection, moving the species in a different direction (Mader, 2014).

All organisms must adapt to particular places, climates, food sources, and ways of life (Johnson, 2015). An eagle's claws are a physical adaptation that facilitates predation. *Adaptive behavior* is behavior that promotes an organism's survival in its natural habitat (Brooker & others, 2015). For example, attachment between a caregiver and a baby ensures the infant's closeness to a caregiver for feeding and protection from danger, thus increasing the infant's chances of survival.

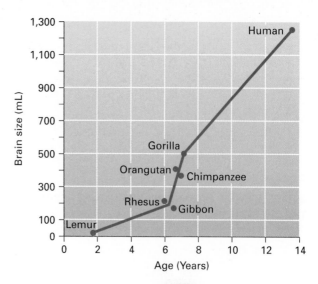

EVOLUTIONARY PSYCHOLOGY

Although Darwin introduced the theory of evolution by natural selection in 1859, his ideas only recently have become a popular framework for explaining behavior. Psychology's newest approach, **evolutionary psychology,** emphasizes the importance of adaptation, reproduction, and "survival of the fittest" in shaping behavior. "Fit" in this sense refers to the ability to bear offspring that survive long enough to bear offspring of their own. In this view, natural selection favors behaviors that increase reproductive success—the ability to pass your genes to the next generation (Durrant & Ellis, 2013).

David Buss (1995, 2004, 2008, 2012) has been especially influential in stimulating new interest in how evolution can explain human behavior. He reasons that just as evolution has contributed to our physical features such as body shape and height, it also pervasively influences our psychological makeup, such as how we make decisions, how aggressive we are, our fears, and our mating patterns. For example, assume that our ancestors were hunters and gatherers on the plains and that men did most of the hunting and women stayed close to home gathering seeds and plants for food. If you have to travel some distance from your home to find and slay a fleeing animal, you need certain physical traits along with the capacity for certain types of spatial thinking. Men with these traits would be more likely than men without them to survive, to bring home lots of food, and to be considered attractive mates—and thus to reproduce and pass on these characteristics to their children. In other words, if Buss' assumptions are correct, potentially these traits provide a reproductive advantage for males—over many generations, men with good spatial thinking skills might become more numerous in the population. Critics point out that these assumptions are not necessarily accurate and that this scenario might or might not have actually happened.

FIGURE **2.1**

THE BRAIN SIZES OF VARIOUS PRIMATES AND HUMANS IN RELATION TO THE LENGTH OF THE CHILDHOOD PERIOD. Compared with other primates, humans have both a larger brain and a longer childhood period. *What conclusions can you draw from the relationship indicated by this graph?*

Evolutionary Developmental Psychology Recently, interest has grown in using the concepts of evolutionary psychology to understand human development (Anderson & Finlay, 2014; Bjorklund, 2007, 2012). Here we discuss some ideas proposed by evolutionary developmental psychologists (Bjorklund & Pellegrini, 2002).

An extended childhood period might have evolved because humans require time to develop a large brain and learn the complexity of human societies. Humans take longer to become reproductively mature than any other mammal (see Figure 2.1). During this extended childhood period, they develop a large brain and have the experiences needed to become competent adults in a complex society.

Many of our evolved psychological mechanisms are domain-specific. That is, the mechanisms apply only to a specific aspect of a person's psychological makeup. According to evolutionary psychology, the mind is not a general-purpose device that can be applied equally to a vast array of problems. Instead, as our ancestors dealt with certain recurring problems such as hunting and finding shelter, specialized modules evolved to process information related to those problems. For example, such specialized modules might include a module

What endless questions vex the thought, of whence and whither, when and how.

—SIR RICHARD BURTON
British Explorer, 19th Century

evolutionary psychology Emphasizes the importance of adaptation, reproduction, and "survival of the fittest" in shaping behavior.

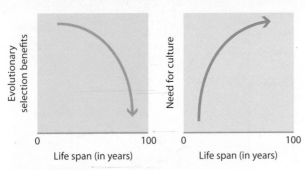

FIGURE **2.2**

BALTES' VIEW OF EVOLUTION AND CULTURE ACROSS THE LIFE SPAN. Benefits derived from evolutionary selection decrease as we age, whereas the need for culture increases with age.

developmental **connection**

Life-Span Perspective

Baltes described eight main characteristics of the life-span perspective. Chapter 1, p. 5

Children in all cultures are interested in the tools used by adults in their cultures. For example, this 11-month-old boy from the Efe culture in the Democratic Republic of the Congo in Africa is trying to cut a papaya with an apopau (a smaller version of a machete). *Might the infant's behavior be evolutionarily based or due to both biological and environmental conditions?*

for physical knowledge for tracking animals, a module for mathematical knowledge for trading, and a module for language.

Evolved mechanisms are not always adaptive in contemporary society. Some behaviors that were adaptive for our prehistoric ancestors may not serve us well today. For example, the food-scarce environment of our ancestors likely led to humans' propensity to gorge when food is available and to crave high-caloric foods, a trait that might lead to an epidemic of obesity when food is plentiful.

Connecting Evolution and Life-Span Development   In evolutionary theory, what matters is that individuals live long enough to reproduce and pass on their characteristics (Starr, Evers, & Starr, 2015). So why do humans live so long after reproduction? Perhaps evolution favored longevity because having older people around improves the survival rates of babies. Possibly having grandparents alive to care for the young while parents were out hunting and gathering food created an evolutionary advantage.

According to life-span developmentalist Paul Baltes (2003), the benefits conferred by evolutionary selection decrease with age. Natural selection has not weeded out many harmful conditions and nonadaptive characteristics that appear among older adults. Why? Natural selection operates primarily on characteristics that are tied to reproductive fitness, which extends through the earlier part of adulthood. Thus, says Baltes, selection primarily operates during the first half of life.

As an example, consider Alzheimer disease, an irreversible brain disorder characterized by gradual deterioration in thinking capacity. This disease typically does not appear until age 70 or later. If it were a disease that struck 20-year-olds, perhaps natural selection would have eliminated it eons ago.

Thus, unaided by evolutionary pressures against nonadaptive conditions, we suffer the aches, pains, and infirmities of aging. And as the benefits of evolutionary selection decrease with age, argues Baltes, the need for culture increases (see Figure 2.2). That is, as older adults weaken biologically, they need culture-based resources such as cognitive skills, literacy, medical technology, and social support. For example, older adults may need help and training from other people to maintain their cognitive skills (Rebok & others, 2014; Schaie & Willis, 2014).

Evaluating Evolutionary Psychology   Although the popular press gives a lot of attention to the ideas of evolutionary psychology, it remains just one theoretical approach among many. Like the theories described in Chapter 1, it has limitations, weaknesses, and critics (Hyde, 2014). Albert Bandura (1998), whose social cognitive theory was described in Chapter 1, acknowledges the important influence of evolution on human adaptation. However, he rejects what he calls "one-sided evolutionism," which sees social behavior as strictly the product of evolved biology. An alternative is a bidirectional view in which environmental and biological conditions influence each other. In this view, evolutionary pressures created changes in biological structures that allowed the use of tools, which enabled our ancestors to manipulate their environment, constructing new environmental conditions. In turn, environmental innovations produced new selection pressures that led to the evolution of specialized biological systems for consciousness, thought, and language.

In other words, evolution does not dictate behavior. People have used their biological capacities to produce diverse cultures—aggressive and peace-loving, egalitarian and autocratic. As American scientist Stephen Jay Gould (1981) concluded, in most domains of human functioning, biology allows a broad range of cultural possibilities.

The "big picture" idea of natural selection leading to the development of human traits and behaviors is difficult to refute or test because evolution occurs on a time scale that does not lend itself to empirical study. Thus, studying specific genes in humans and other species—and their links to traits and behaviors—may be the best approach for testing ideas coming out of evolutionary psychology.

Review

- How can natural selection and adaptive behavior be defined?
- What is evolutionary psychology? What are some basic ideas about human development proposed by evolutionary psychologists? How might evolutionary influences have different effects at different points in the life span? How can evolutionary psychology be evaluated?

Connect

- In the section on ethological theory in the previous chapter, you learned about critical time periods. How does the concept of critical period relate to what you learned about older adults and aging in this section?

Reflect *Your Own Personal Journey of Life*

- Which do you think is more persuasive in explaining your development: the views of evolutionary psychologists or their critics? Why?

2 Genetic Foundations of Development

LG2 Describe what genes are and how they influence human development.

| The Collaborative Gene | Genes and Chromosomes | Genetic Principles | Chromosomal and Gene-Linked Abnormalities |

Genetic influences on behavior evolved over time and across many species. The many traits and characteristics that are genetically influenced have a long evolutionary history that is retained in our DNA. Our DNA is not just inherited from our parents; it includes what we inherited as a species from other species that were our ancestors.

How are characteristics that suit a species for survival transmitted from one generation to the next? Darwin did not know the answer because genes and the principles of genetics had not yet been discovered. Each of us carries a "genetic code" that we inherited from our parents. Because a fertilized egg carries this human code, a fertilized human egg cannot grow into an egret, eagle, or elephant.

THE COLLABORATIVE GENE

Each of us began life as a single cell weighing about one twenty-millionth of an ounce! This tiny piece of matter housed our entire genetic code—information that helps us grow from that single cell to a person made of trillions of cells, each containing a replica of the original code. That code is carried by DNA, which includes our genes. What are genes and what do they do? For the answer, we need to look into our cells.

The nucleus of each human cell contains **chromosomes,** which are threadlike structures made up of deoxyribonucleic acid (DNA). **DNA** is a complex molecule that has a double helix shape, like a spiral staircase (shown in Figure 2.3) and contains genetic information. **Genes,** the units of hereditary information, are short segments of DNA. They help cells to reproduce themselves and to assemble proteins. Proteins, in turn, are the building blocks of cells as well as the regulators that direct the body's processes (Cowan, 2015; Willey, Sherwood, & Woolverton, 2014).

Each gene has its own location—its own designated place on a particular chromosome. Today, there is a great deal of enthusiasm about efforts to discover the specific locations of genes that are linked to certain functions and developmental outcomes (Mason & others, 2015; Raven & others, 2014). An important step in this direction is the Human Genome Project's efforts to map the human genome—the complete genetic content of our cells, which includes developmental information used for creating proteins that contribute to the making of a human organism (Brooker, 2015; Cummings, 2014).

---

developmental **connection**

Biological Processes

A current biological theory of aging emphasizes that changes in the tips of chromosomes play a key role in aging. Chapter 17, p. 516

---

chromosomes Threadlike structures that come in 23 pairs, with one member of each pair coming from each parent. Chromosomes contain the genetic substance DNA.

DNA A complex molecule that contains genetic information.

genes Units of hereditary information composed of DNA. Genes help cells to reproduce themselves and help manufacture the proteins that maintain life.

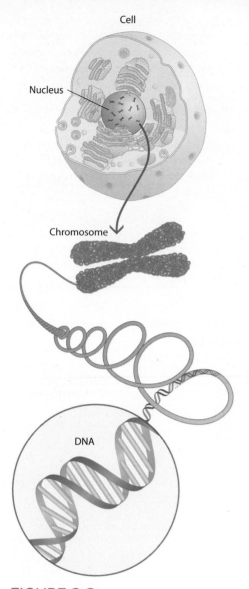

Cell

Nucleus

Chromosome

DNA

FIGURE **2.3**

CELLS, CHROMOSOMES, DNA, AND GENES.
(*Top*) The body contains trillions of cells. Each cell
contains a central structure, the nucleus. (*Middle*)
Chromosomes are threadlike structures located
in the nucleus of the cell. Chromosomes are
composed of DNA. (*Bottom*) DNA has the structure
of a spiral staircase. A gene is a segment of DNA.

Among the major approaches to gene identification and discovery that are being used today are the genome-wide association method, linkage analysis, next-generation sequencing, and the Thousand Genomes Project:

• Completion of the Human Genome Project has led to use of the *genome-wide association method* to identify genetic variations linked to a particular disease, such as obesity, cancer, cardiovascular disease, or Alzheimer disease (Brown & others, 2014; Guo & others, 2014). To conduct a genome-wide association study, researchers obtain DNA from individuals who have the disease and those who don't have it. Then, each participant's complete set of DNA, or genome, is purified from the blood or other cells and scanned on machines to determine markers of genetic variation. If the genetic variations occur more frequently in people who have the disease, the variations point to the region in the human genome with the disease. Genome-wide association studies have recently been conducted for childhood obesity (Zhao & others, 2014), cardiovascular disease (Malik & others, 2014), Alzheimer disease (Liu & others, 2014), and depression (He & others, 2014; Major Depressive Disorder Working Group of the Psychiatric GWAS Consortium, 2013).

• *Linkage analysis,* in which the goal is to discover the location of a gene (or genes) in relation to a marker gene (whose position is already known), is often used in the search for a disease-related gene(s) (Lyon & Wang, 2012). Genes transmitted to offspring tend to be in close proximity to each other so that the gene(s) involved in the disease are usually located near the marker gene. Gene linkage studies are now being conducted on a wide variety of disorders, including attention deficit hyperactivity disorder (Caylak, 2012), autism (Warrier, Baron-Cohen, & Chakrabarti, 2014), depression (Cohen-Woods, Craig, & McGuffin, 2012), and Alzheimer disease (Raj & others, 2014).

• *Next-generation sequencing* is a term used to describe the vast increase in genetic data generated at a much reduced cost and in a much shorter period of time. Next-generation sequencing has considerably increased knowledge about genetic influences on development in recent years (Kassahn, Scott, & Fletcher, 2014; Lango Allen & others, 2014).

• The human genome varies between individuals in small but very important ways. Understanding these variations will require examining the whole genomes of many individuals. A current project that began in 2008, the *Thousand Genomes Project*, is the most detailed study of human genetic variation to date. This project has the goal of determining the genomic sequences of at least 1,000 individuals from different ethnic groups around the world (Abyzov & others, 2013; Shibata & others, 2012). By compiling complete descriptions of the genetic variations of many people, studies of genetic variations in disease can be conducted in a more detailed manner.

One of the big surprises of the Human Genome Project was an early report indicating that humans have only about 30,000 genes (U.S. Department of Energy, 2001). More recently, the number of human genes has been revised further downward to approximately 20,700 (Ensembl Human, 2010; Flicek & others, 2013; Science Daily, 2008). Further recent analysis proposes that humans may actually have less than 20,000 protein-producing genes (Ezkurdia & others, 2014). Scientists had thought that humans had as many as 100,000 or more genes. They had also maintained that each gene programmed just one protein. In fact, humans have far more proteins than they have genes, so there cannot be a one-to-one correspondence between genes and proteins (Commoner, 2002). Each gene is not translated, in automaton-like fashion, into one and only one protein (Moore, 2013). A gene does not act independently, as developmental psychologist David Moore (2001) emphasized by titling his book *The Dependent Gene.*

Rather than being a group of independent genes, the human genome consists of many genes that collaborate both with each other and with nongenetic factors inside and outside the body (Moore, 2013). The collaboration operates at many points. For example, the cellular machinery mixes, matches, and links small pieces of DNA to reproduce the genes—and that machinery is influenced by what is going on around it.

Whether a gene is turned "on"—working to assemble proteins—is also a matter of collaboration. The activity of genes (genetic expression) is affected by their environment (Gottlieb, 2007; Moore, 2013). For example, hormones that circulate in the blood make their way into the cell where they can turn genes "on" and "off." And the flow of hormones can be affected by environmental conditions such as light, day length, nutrition, and behavior. Numerous studies have shown that external events outside of the original cell and the person, as well as events inside the cell, can excite or inhibit gene expression (Gottlieb, Wahlsten, & Lickliter, 2006). Recent research has documented that factors such as stress, radiation, and temperature can influence gene expression (Craft & others, 2014; Dedon & Begley, 2014). For example, one study revealed that an increase in the concentration of stress hormones such as cortisol produced a fivefold increase in DNA damage (Flint & others, 2007). Another study also found that exposure to radiation changed the rate of DNA synthesis in cells (Lee & others, 2011).

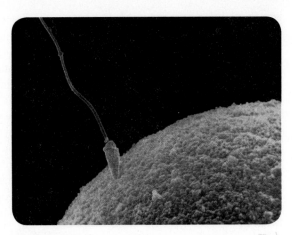

FIGURE **2.4**

A SINGLE SPERM PENETRATING AN EGG AT THE POINT OF FERTILIZATION

GENES AND CHROMOSOMES

Genes are not only collaborative, they are enduring. How do the genes manage to get passed from generation to generation and end up in all of the trillion cells in the body? Three processes explain the heart of the story: mitosis, meiosis, and fertilization.

Mitosis, Meiosis, and Fertilization   All of the cells in your body, except the sperm and egg, have 46 chromosomes arranged in 23 pairs. These cells reproduce through a process called **mitosis.** During mitosis, the cell's nucleus—including the chromosomes—duplicates itself and the cell divides. Two new cells are formed, each containing the same DNA as the original cell, arranged in the same 23 pairs of chromosomes.

However, a different type of cell division—**meiosis**—forms eggs and sperm (which also are called gametes). During meiosis, a cell of the testes (in men) or ovaries (in women) duplicates its chromosomes but then divides twice, thus forming four cells, each of which has only half of the genetic material of the parent cell. By the end of meiosis, each egg or sperm has 23 unpaired chromosomes.

During **fertilization,** an egg and a sperm fuse to create a single cell, called a **zygote** (see Figure 2.4). In the zygote, the 23 unpaired chromosomes from the egg and the 23 unpaired chromosomes from the sperm combine to form one set of 23 paired chromosomes—one chromosome of each pair having come from the mother's egg and the other from the father's sperm. In this manner, each parent contributes half of the offspring's genetic material.

Figure 2.5 shows 23 paired chromosomes of a male and a female. The members of each pair of chromosomes are both similar and different: Each chromosome in the pair contains varying forms of the same genes, at the same location on the chromosome. A gene that influences hair color, for example, is located on both members of one pair of chromosomes, in the same location on each. However, one of those chromosomes might carry a gene associated with blond hair; the other chromosome in the pair might carry a gene associated with brown hair.

Do you notice any obvious differences between the chromosomes of the male and the chromosomes of the female in Figure 2.5? The difference lies in the 23rd pair. Ordinarily, in females this pair consists of two chromosomes called X chromosomes; in males, the 23rd pair consists of an X and a Y chromosome. The presence of a Y chromosome is one factor that makes a person male rather than female.

Sources of Variability   Combining the genes of two parents in offspring increases genetic variability in the population, which is valuable for a species because it provides more characteristics for natural selection to operate on (Raven & others, 2014; Simon, 2015). In fact, the human genetic process creates several important sources of variability.

First, the chromosomes in the zygote are not exact copies of those in the mother's ovaries or the father's testes. During the formation of the sperm and egg in meiosis, the members of each pair of chromosomes are separated, but which chromosome in the pair goes to the

mitosis Cellular reproduction in which the cell's nucleus duplicates itself with two new cells being formed, each containing the same DNA as the parent cell, arranged in the same 23 pairs of chromosomes.

meiosis A specialized form of cell division that occurs to form eggs and sperm (also known as gametes).

fertilization A stage in reproduction when an egg and a sperm fuse to create a single cell, called a zygote.

zygote A single cell formed through fertilization.

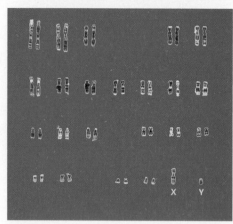

(a)

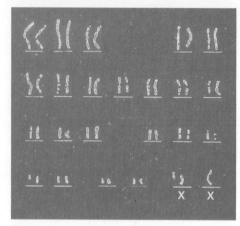

(b)

FIGURE **2.5**

THE GENETIC DIFFERENCE BETWEEN MALES AND FEMALES. Set (*a*) shows the chromosome structure of a male, and set (*b*) shows the chromosome structure of a female. The last pair of 23 pairs of chromosomes is in the bottom right box of each set. Notice that the Y chromosome of the male is smaller than the X chromosome of the female. To obtain this kind of chromosomal picture, a cell is removed from a person's body (an easy way to obtain a cell from a body is to swab the inside of the mouth with a Q-tip). The chromosomes are stained by chemical treatment, magnified extensively, and then photographed.

genotype A person's genetic heritage; the actual genetic material.

phenotype The way an individual's genotype is expressed in observed and measurable characteristics.

gamete is a matter of chance. In addition, before the pairs separate, pieces of the two chromosomes in each pair are exchanged, creating a new combination of genes on each chromosome (Mader & Windelspecht, 2015). Thus, when chromosomes from the mother's egg and the father's sperm are brought together in the zygote, the result is a truly unique combination of genes (Willey, Sherwood, & Woolverton, 2014).

If each zygote is unique, how do identical twins like those discussed in the opening of the chapter exist? *Identical twins* (also called monozygotic twins) develop from a single zygote that splits into two genetically identical replicas, each of which becomes a person. *Fraternal twins* (called dizygotic twins) develop when two eggs are fertilized by different sperm, creating two zygotes that are genetically no more similar than ordinary siblings.

Another source of variability comes from DNA. Chance events, a mistake by cellular machinery, or damage from an environmental agent such as radiation may produce a *mutated gene*, which is a permanently altered segment of DNA (Bauman, 2015).

There is increasing interest in studying *susceptibility genes*, those that make the individual more vulnerable to specific diseases or accelerated aging, and *longevity genes,* those that make the individual less vulnerable to certain diseases and more likely to live to an older age (Howard & Rogers, 2014; Stadler & others, 2014; Wei & others, 2014). Even when their genes are identical, however, people vary. The difference between genotypes and phenotypes helps us to understand this source of variability. All of a person's genetic material makes up his or her **genotype.** However, our observed and measurable characteristics reflect more than just genetic material. A **phenotype** consists of observable characteristics. Phenotypes include physical characteristics (such as height, weight, and hair color) and psychological characteristics (such as personality and intelligence).

How does the process from genotype to phenotype work? It's highly complex, but at a very basic level in a cell, DNA information is transcribed to RNA (ribonucleic acid), which in turn is translated into amino acids that will become proteins (Brooker, 2015; Cummings, 2014). Once proteins have been assembled, they become capable of producing phenotype traits and characteristics. Also, environments interact with genotypes to produce phenotypes.

Thus, for each genotype, a range of phenotypes can be expressed, providing another source of variability (Solomon & others, 2015). An individual can inherit the genetic potential to grow very large, for example, but environmental influences involving good nutrition, among other things, will be essential for achieving that potential.

GENETIC PRINCIPLES

What determines how a genotype is expressed to create a particular phenotype? Much is unknown about the answer to this question (Moore, 2013). However, a number of genetic principles have been discovered, among them those of dominant-recessive genes, sex-linked genes, genetic imprinting, and polygenically determined characteristics.

Dominant-Recessive Genes Principle In some cases, one gene of a pair always exerts its effects; it is *dominant,* overriding the potential influence of the other gene, called the recessive gene. This is the *dominant-recessive genes principle*. A recessive gene exerts its influence only if the two genes of a pair are both recessive. If you inherit a recessive gene for a trait from each of your parents, you will show the trait. If you inherit a recessive gene from only one parent, you may never know you carry the gene. Brown hair, farsightedness, and dimples rule over blond hair, nearsightedness, and freckles in the world of dominant-recessive genes.

Can two brown-haired parents have a blond-haired child? Yes, they can. Suppose that each parent has a dominant gene for brown hair and a recessive gene for blond hair. Since dominant genes override recessive genes, the parents have brown hair, but both are carriers of genes that can contribute to blondness and pass on their recessive genes for producing blond hair. With no dominant gene to override them, the recessive genes can make the child's hair blond.

Sex-Linked Genes Most mutated genes are recessive. When a mutated gene is carried on the X chromosome, the result is called *X-linked inheritance*. The implications for males may be very different from those for females (Guffanti & others, 2013; McClelland, Bowles, & Koopman, 2012). Remember that males have only one X chromosome. Thus, if there is an absent or altered disease-relevant gene on the X chromosome, males have no "backup" copy to counter the harmful gene and therefore may develop an X-linked disease. However, females have a second X chromosome, which is likely to be unchanged. As a result, they are not likely to have the X-linked disease. Thus, most individuals who have X-linked diseases are males. Females who have one abnormal copy of the gene on the X chromosome are known as "carriers," and they usually do not show any signs of the X-linked disease. Hemophilia and fragile X syndrome, which we will discuss later in the chapter, are examples of X-linked inheritance diseases (Bartel, Weinstein, & Schaffer, 2012).

Genetic Imprinting   Genetic imprinting occurs when the expression of a gene has different effects depending on whether the mother or the father passed on the gene (Schneider & others, 2014). A chemical process "silences" one member of the gene pair. For example, as a result of imprinting, only the maternally derived copy of the expressed gene might be active, while the paternally derived copy of the same expressed gene is silenced—or vice versa (Court & others, 2014). Only a small percentage of human genes appear to undergo imprinting, but it is a normal and important aspect of development. When imprinting goes awry, development is disturbed, as in the case of Beckwith-Wiedemann syndrome (a growth disorder) and Wilms tumor (a type of cancer) (Okun & others, 2014).

Polygenic Inheritance   Genetic transmission is usually more complex than the simple examples we have examined thus far (Moore, 2013). Few characteristics reflect the influence of only a single gene or pair of genes. Most are determined by the interaction of many different genes; they are said to be *polygenically determined* (Lu, Yu, & Deng, 2012). Even a simple characteristic such as height, for example, reflects the interaction of many genes as well as the influence of the environment. Most diseases, such as cancer and diabetes, develop as a consequence of complex gene interactions and environmental factors (Dastani & others, 2012).

The term *gene-gene interaction* is increasingly used to describe studies that focus on the interdependent process by which two or more genes influence characteristics, behavior, diseases, and development (Hu, Wang, & Wang, 2014; Sarlos & others, 2014). For example, recent studies have documented gene-gene interaction in children's immune system functioning (Reijmerink & others, 2011), asthma (Lee & others, 2014), alcoholism (Yokoyama & others, 2013), cancer (Mandal, Abebe, & Chaudhary, 2014), cardiovascular disease (Kumar & others, 2014), arthritis (Freytag & others, 2014), and Alzheimer disease (Koran & others, 2014).

CHROMOSOMAL AND GENE-LINKED ABNORMALITIES

Abnormalities characterize the genetic process in some individuals. Some of these abnormalities involve whole chromosomes that do not separate properly during meiosis. Other abnormalities are produced by harmful genes.

Chromosomal Abnormalities   Sometimes a gamete is formed in which the male's sperm and/or the female's ovum do not have their normal set of 23 chromosomes. The most notable examples involve Down syndrome and abnormalities of the sex chromosomes (see Figure 2.6).

Down Syndrome   **Down syndrome** is a form of intellectual disability caused by the presence of an extra copy of chromosome 21. It is not known why the extra chromosome is present, but the health of the male sperm or the female ovum may be involved. An individual with Down syndrome has a round face, a flattened skull, an extra fold of skin over the eyelids, a protruding tongue, short limbs, and retardation of motor and mental abilities (Peters & Petrill, 2011).

Down syndrome appears approximately once in every 700 live births. Women between the ages of 16 and 34 are less likely to give birth to a child with Down syndrome than are younger or older women. African American children are rarely born with Down syndrome.

Sex-Linked Chromosomal Abnormalities   Recall that a newborn normally has either an X and a Y chromosome, or two X chromosomes. Human embryos must possess at least one X chromosome to be viable. The most common sex-linked chromosomal abnormalities

These athletes, several of whom have Down syndrome, are participating in a Special Olympics competition. Notice the distinctive facial features of the individuals with Down syndrome, such as a round face and a flattened skull. *What causes Down syndrome?*

Down syndrome A form of intellectual disability that is caused by the presence of an extra copy of chromosome 21.

Name	Description	Treatment	Incidence
Down syndrome	An extra chromosome causes mild to severe intellectual disability and physical abnormalities.	Surgery, early intervention, infant stimulation, and special learning programs	1 in 1,900 births at age 20 1 in 300 births at age 35 1 in 30 births at age 45
Klinefelter syndrome (XXY)	An extra X chromosome causes physical abnormalities.	Hormone therapy can be effective	1 in 600 male births
Fragile X syndrome	An abnormality in the X chromosome can cause intellectual disability, learning disabilities, or short attention span.	Special education, speech and language therapy	More common in males than in females
Turner syndrome (XO)	A missing X chromosome in females can cause intellectual disability and sexual underdevelopment.	Hormone therapy in childhood and puberty	1 in 2,500 female births
XYY syndrome	An extra Y chromosome can cause above-average height.	No special treatment required	1 in 1,000 male births

FIGURE 2.6

SOME CHROMOSOMAL ABNORMALITIES. The treatments for these abnormalities do not necessarily erase the problem but may improve the individual's adaptive behavior and quality of life.

involve the presence of an extra chromosome (either an X or Y) or the absence of one X chromosome in females.

Klinefelter syndrome is a chromosomal disorder in which males have an extra X chromosome, making them XXY instead of XY. Males with this disorder have undeveloped testes, and they usually have enlarged breasts and become tall (Ross & others, 2012). Klinefelter syndrome occurs approximately once in every 600 live male births. Only 10 percent of individuals with Klinefelter syndrome are diagnosed before puberty, with the majority not identified until adulthood (Aksglaede & others, 2013).

Fragile X syndrome is a genetic disorder that results from an abnormality in the X chromosome, which becomes constricted and often breaks (Yudkin & others, 2014). An intellectual difficulty frequently is an outcome, which may take the form of an intellectual disability, autism, a learning disability, or a short attention span (Hall & others, 2014; Lipton & Sahin, 2013). One study revealed that boys with fragile X syndrome were characterized by cognitive deficits in inhibition, memory, and planning (Hooper & others, 2008). This disorder occurs more frequently in males than in females, possibly because the second X chromosome in females negates the effects of the abnormal X chromosome (McDuffie & others, 2014).

Turner syndrome is a chromosomal disorder in females in which either an X chromosome is missing, making the person XO instead of XX, or part of one X chromosome is deleted (Vlatkovic & others, 2014). Females with Turner syndrome are short in stature and have a webbed neck (Kaur & Phadke, 2012). They might be infertile and have difficulty in mathematics, but their verbal ability is often quite good (Lleo & others, 2012). Turner syndrome occurs in approximately 1 of every 2,500 live female births (Pinsker, 2012).

The **XYY syndrome** is a chromosomal disorder in which a male has an extra Y chromosome (Lepage & others, 2014). Early interest in this syndrome focused on the belief that the extra Y chromosome found in some males contributed to aggression and violence. However, researchers subsequently found that XYY males are no more likely to commit crimes than are normal XY males (Witkin & others, 1976).

Gene-Linked Abnormalities Abnormalities can be produced not only by an abnormal number of chromosomes but also by harmful genes. More than 7,000 such genetic disorders have been identified, although most of them are rare.

Phenylketonuria (PKU) is a genetic disorder in which the individual cannot properly metabolize phenylalanine, an amino acid. It results from a recessive gene and occurs about once in every 10,000 to 20,000 live births. Today, phenylketonuria is easily detected during infancy, and it is treated by a diet that prevents an excess accumulation of phenylalanine (Rohde & others, 2014). If phenylketonuria is left untreated, however, excess phenylalanine

Klinefelter syndrome A chromosomal disorder in which males have an extra X chromosome, making them XXY instead of XY.

fragile X syndrome A genetic disorder involving an abnormality in the X chromosome, which becomes constricted and often breaks.

Turner syndrome A chromosome disorder in females in which either an X chromosome is missing, making the person XO instead of XX, or the second X chromosome is partially deleted.

XYY syndrome A chromosomal disorder in which males have an extra Y chromosome.

phenylketonuria (PKU) A genetic disorder in which an individual cannot properly metabolize an amino acid called phenylalanine. PKU is now easily detected but, if left untreated, results in intellectual disability and hyperactivity.

builds up in the child, producing intellectual disability and hyperactivity. Phenylketonuria accounts for approximately 1 percent of institutionalized individuals with intellectual disabilities, and it occurs primarily in non-Latino Whites.

The story of phenylketonuria has important implications for the nature-nurture issue. Although phenylketonuria is often described as a genetic disorder (nature), how or whether a gene's influence in phenylketonuria is played out depends on environmental influences since the disorder can be treated (nurture) using an environmental manipulation (Di Ciommo, Forcella, & Cotugno, 2012). That is, the presence of a genetic defect does not inevitably lead to the development of the disorder if the individual develops in the right environment (one free of phenylalanine). This is one example of the important principle of heredity-environment interaction. Under one environmental condition (phenylalanine in the diet), intellectual disability results, but when other nutrients replace phenylalanine, intelligence develops in the normal range. The same genotype has different outcomes depending on the environment (in this case, the nutritional environment).

Sickle-cell anemia, which occurs most often in African Americans, is a genetic disorder that impairs the functioning of the body's red blood cells. Red blood cells carry oxygen to the body's other cells and are usually disk-shaped. In sickle-cell anemia, a recessive gene causes the red blood cell to become a hook-shaped "sickle" that cannot carry oxygen properly and dies quickly (Derebail & others, 2014). As a result, the body's cells do not receive adequate oxygen, causing anemia and early death (Mehari & others, 2012). About 1 in 400 African American babies is affected by sickle-cell anemia. One in 10 African Americans is a carrier, as is 1 in 20 Latin Americans. A National Institutes of Health (2008) panel concluded that the only FDA-approved drug (hydroxyurea) to treat sickle-cell anemia in adolescents and adults has been underutilized. Research is currently being conducted in a study named Baby HUG to determine whether the drug works with babies (Alvarez & others, 2012; Wang & others, 2013).

Other diseases that result from genetic abnormalities include cystic fibrosis, some forms of diabetes, hemophilia, Huntington disease, spina bifida, and Tay-Sachs disease. Figure 2.7 provides further information about these diseases. Someday scientists may be able to identify why these and other genetic abnormalities occur and discover how to cure them. The Human

sickle-cell anemia A genetic disorder that affects the red blood cells and occurs most often in people of African descent.

Name	Description	Treatment	Incidence
Cystic fibrosis	Glandular dysfunction that interferes with mucus production; breathing and digestion are hampered, resulting in a shortened life span.	Physical and oxygen therapy, synthetic enzymes, and antibiotics; most individuals live to middle age.	1 in 2,000 births
Diabetes	Body does not produce enough insulin, which causes abnormal metabolism of sugar.	Early onset can be fatal unless treated with insulin.	1 in 2,500 births
Hemophilia	Delayed blood clotting causes internal and external bleeding.	Blood transfusions/injections can reduce or prevent damage due to internal bleeding.	1 in 10,000 males
Huntington disease	Central nervous system deteriorates, producing problems in muscle coordination and mental deterioration.	Does not usually appear until age 35 or older; death likely 10 to 20 years after symptoms appear.	1 in 20,000 births
Phenylketonuria (PKU)	Metabolic disorder that, left untreated, causes intellectual disability.	Special diet can result in average intelligence and normal life span.	1 in 10,000 to 1 in 20,000 births
Sickle-cell anemia	Blood disorder that limits the body's oxygen supply; it can cause joint swelling, as well as heart and kidney failure.	Penicillin, medication for pain, antibiotics, blood transfusions, and hydroxyurea.	1 in 400 African American children (lower among other groups)
Spina bifida	Neural tube disorder that causes brain and spine abnormalities.	Corrective surgery at birth, orthopedic devices, and physical/medical therapy.	2 in 1,000 births
Tay-Sachs disease	Deceleration of mental and physical development caused by an accumulation of lipids in the nervous system.	Medication and special diet are used, but death is likely by 5 years of age.	1 in 30 American Jews is a carrier.

FIGURE **2.7**
SOME GENE-LINKED ABNORMALITIES

Holly Ishmael, Genetic Counselor

Holly Ishmael is a genetic counselor at Children's Mercy Hospital in Kansas City. She obtained an undergraduate degree in psychology and a master's degree in genetic counseling from Sarah Lawrence College.

Genetic counselors like Ishmael work as members of a health care team, providing information and support to families with birth defects or genetic disorders. They identify families at risk by analyzing inheritance patterns and then explore options with the family. Some genetic counselors, like Ishmael, specialize in prenatal and pediatric genetics while others focus on cancer genetics or psychiatric genetic disorders.

Ishmael says, "Genetic counseling is a perfect combination for people who want to do something science-oriented, but need human contact and don't want to spend all of their time in a lab or have their nose in a book" (Rizzo, 1999, p. 3).

Genetic counselors have specialized graduate degrees in medical genetics and counseling. They enter graduate school from undergraduate programs in a variety of disciplines, including biology, genetics, psychology, public health, and social work. There are approximately 30

Holly Ishmael (*left*) in a genetic counseling session.

graduate genetic counseling programs in the United States. If you are interested in this profession, you can obtain further information from the National Society of Genetic Counselors at www.nsgc.org.

For more information about what genetic counselors do, see page 44 in the Careers in Life-Span Development appendix.

Genome Project has already linked specific DNA variations with increased risk of a number of diseases and conditions, including Huntington disease (in which the central nervous system deteriorates), some forms of cancer, asthma, diabetes, hypertension, and Alzheimer disease (Cruchaga & others, 2014; Huang & others, 2014; Su & others, 2013).

Dealing with Genetic Abnormalities Every individual carries DNA variations that might predispose the person to serious physical disease or mental disorder. But not all individuals who carry an abnormal genetic variation develop the disorder. Other genes or developmental events sometimes compensate for genetic abnormalities (Pessia & others, 2012). For example, recall the earlier example of phenylketonuria: Even though individuals might carry the abnormal genetic variation associated with phenylketonuria, the abnormal phenotype does not develop when phenylalanine is replaced by other nutrients in their diet.

Thus, genes are not destiny, but genes that are missing, nonfunctional, or mutated can contribute to disorders (Fujita & others, 2014; Moore, 2013). Identifying such genetic flaws could enable doctors to predict an individual's risks, recommend healthy practices, and prescribe the safest and most effective drugs (Bennetts, 2014; Kassahn, Scott, & Fletcher, 2014). A decade or two from now, parents of a newborn baby may be able to leave the hospital with a full genome analysis of their offspring that identifies disease risks.

However, this knowledge might bring important costs as well as benefits. Who would have access to a person's genetic profile? An individual's ability to land and hold jobs or obtain insurance might be threatened if she or he is known to be at risk for some disease. For example, should an airline pilot or a neurosurgeon who is predisposed to develop a disorder that makes one's hands shake be required to leave that job early, before showing any symptoms of the disorder?

Genetic counselors, usually physicians or biologists who are well-versed in the field of medical genetics, understand the kinds of problems just described, the odds of encountering them, and helpful strategies for offsetting some of their effects (Mollee, 2014; Swanson, Ramos, & Snyder, 2014). To read about the career and work of a genetic counselor, see *Connecting with Careers*.

Review *Connect* Reflect

LG2 Describe what genes are and how they influence human development.

Review
- What are genes?
- How are genes passed on?
- What basic principles describe how genes interact?
- What are some chromosomal and gene-linked abnormalities?

Connect
- Would you want to be able to access a full genome analysis of your offspring? Why or why not?

Reflect *Your Own Personal Journey of Life*
- Can you identify in yourself or a friend the likelihood of the influence of dominant and/or recessive genes? Explain.

3 Reproductive Challenges and Choices

LG3 Identify some important reproductive challenges and choices.

Prenatal Diagnostic Tests   Infertility and Reproductive Technology   Adoption

The facts and principles we have discussed regarding meiosis, genetics, and genetic abnormalities are a small part of the recent explosion of knowledge about human biology. This knowledge not only helps us understand human development but also opens up many new choices to prospective parents—choices that can also raise ethical questions.

PRENATAL DIAGNOSTIC TESTS

One choice open to prospective mothers is the extent to which they will undergo prenatal testing. A number of tests can indicate whether a fetus is developing normally, including ultrasound sonography, fetal MRI, chorionic villus sampling, amniocentesis, maternal blood screening, and noninvasive prenatal diagnosis.

Ultrasound Sonography   An ultrasound test is often conducted seven weeks into a pregnancy and at various times later in pregnancy. *Ultrasound sonography* is a prenatal medical procedure in which high-frequency sound waves are directed into the pregnant woman's abdomen (Ekin & others, 2014). The echo from the sounds is transformed into a visual representation of the fetus's inner structures. This technique can detect many abnormalities in the fetus, including microencephaly, in which an abnormally small brain can produce intellectual disability (C. P. Chen & others, 2014); it can also determine the number of fetuses (that is, detect whether a woman is carrying twins or triplets) and give clues to the baby's sex (Masselli & others, 2011). There is virtually no risk to the woman or fetus in this test.

Brain-Imaging Techniques   The development of brain-imaging techniques has led to increasing use of *fetal MRI* to diagnose fetal malformations (Wu & others, 2014) (see Figure 2.8). MRI, which stands for magnetic resonance imaging, uses a powerful magnet and radio images to generate detailed images of the body's organs and structures. Currently, ultrasound is still the first choice in fetal screening, but fetal MRI can provide more detailed images than ultrasound. In many instances, ultrasound will indicate a possible

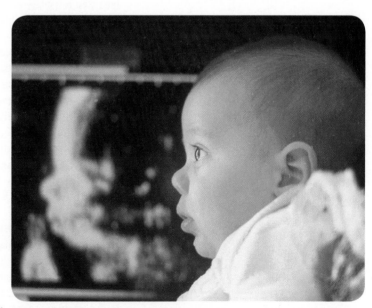

A 6-month-old infant poses with the ultrasound sonography record taken four months into the baby's prenatal development. *What is ultrasound sonography?*

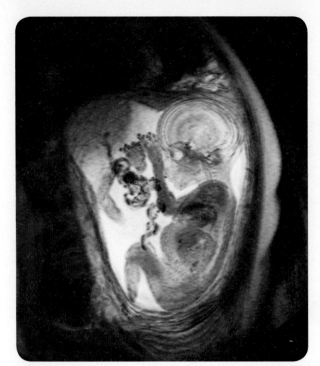

FIGURE **2.8**

A FETAL MRI, WHICH IS INCREASINGLY BEING USED IN PRENATAL DIAGNOSIS OF FETAL MALFORMATIONS

developmental **connection**

Biological Processes

Discover what the development of the fetus is like at the stages when chorionic villus sampling and amniocentesis can be used. Chapter 3, Figure 3.3, p. 77

abnormality and then fetal MRI will be used to obtain a clearer, more detailed image (Koelblinger & others, 2013). Among the fetal malformations that fetal MRI may be able to detect better than ultrasound sonography are certain abnormalities of the central nervous system, chest, gastrointestinal tract, genital/urinary organs, and placenta (Milesi & others, 2014).

Chorionic Villus Sampling At some point between the 10th and 12th weeks of pregnancy, chorionic villus sampling may be used to detect genetic defects and chromosomal abnormalities such as those discussed in the previous section. *Chorionic villus sampling (CVS) is a prenatal medical procedure in which a small sample of the placenta (the vascular organ that links the fetus to the mother's uterus) is removed* (Gimovsky & others, 2014). Diagnosis takes about 10 days. There is a small risk of limb deformity when CVS is used.

Amniocentesis Between the 15th and 18th weeks of pregnancy, amniocentesis may be performed. *Amniocentesis is a prenatal medical procedure in which a sample of amniotic fluid is withdrawn by syringe and tested for chromosomal or metabolic disorders* (Menon & others, 2014). The amniotic fluid is found within the amnion, a thin sac in which the embryo is suspended. Ultrasound sonography is often used during amniocentesis so that the syringe can be placed precisely. The later amniocentesis is performed, the better its diagnostic potential. The earlier it is performed, the more useful it is in deciding how to handle a pregnancy. It may take two weeks for enough cells to grow to allow amniocentesis test results to be obtained. Amniocentesis brings a small risk of miscarriage: About 1 woman in every 200 to 300 miscarries after amniocentesis.

Both amniocentesis and chorionic villus sampling provide valuable information about the presence of birth defects, but they also raise difficult issues for parents about whether an abortion should be obtained if birth defects are present (Zhang & others, 2010). Chorionic villus sampling allows a decision to be made earlier, near the end of the first 12 weeks of pregnancy, when abortion is safer and less traumatic.

Maternal Blood Screening During the 15th to 19th weeks of pregnancy, maternal blood screening may be performed. *Maternal blood screening* identifies pregnancies that have an elevated risk for birth defects such as spina bifida (a defect in the spinal cord) and Down syndrome (Bernard & others, 2013). The current blood test is called the *triple screen* because it measures three substances in the mother's blood. After an abnormal triple screen result, the next step is usually an ultrasound examination. If an ultrasound does not explain the abnormal triple screen results, amniocentesis is typically used.

Noninvasive Prenatal Diagnosis (NIPD) *Noninvasive prenatal diagnosis (NIPD)* is increasingly being explored as an alternative to procedures such as chorionic villus sampling and amniocentesis (Kantak & others, 2014; Li & others, 2014). At this point, NIPD has mainly focused on brain-imaging techniques, the isolation and examination of fetal cells circulating in the mother's blood, and analysis of cell-free fetal DNA in maternal plasma (Mersy & others, 2013; Papasavva & others, 2013).

Researchers already have used NIPD to successfully test for genes inherited from a father that cause cystic fibrosis and Huntington disease. They also are exploring the potential for using NIPD very early in fetal development to diagnose a baby's sex and detect Down syndrome (Lim, Park, & Ryu, 2013).

Fetal Sex Determination Chorionic villus sampling has often been used to determine the sex of the fetus at some point between 11 and 13 weeks of gestation. Recently, though, some noninvasive techniques have been able to detect the sex of the fetus at an earlier point (Moise & others, 2013). A meta-analysis of studies confirmed that a baby's sex can be detected as early as 7 weeks into pregnancy (Devaney & others, 2011). Being able to detect an offspring's sex as well as the presence of various diseases and defects at such an early stage raises ethical concerns about couples' motivation to terminate a pregnancy (Dickens, 2014).

INFERTILITY AND REPRODUCTIVE TECHNOLOGY

Recent advances in biological knowledge have also opened up many choices for infertile individuals (Asero & others, 2014). Approximately 10 to 15 percent of couples in the United States experience *infertility*, which is defined as the inability to conceive a child after 12 months of regular intercourse without contraception. The cause of infertility can rest with the woman or the man (Reindollar & Goldman, 2012). The woman may not be ovulating (releasing eggs to be fertilized), she may be producing abnormal ova, her fallopian tubes through which ova normally reach the womb may be blocked, or she may have a disease that prevents implantation of the embryo into the uterus. The man may produce too few sperm, the sperm may lack motility (the ability to move adequately), or he may have a blocked passageway (Guido & others, 2014; Takasaki & others, 2014).

In the United States, more than 2 million couples seek help for infertility every year. In some cases of infertility, surgery may correct the cause; in others, hormone-based drugs may improve the probability of having a child. Of the 2 million couples who seek help for infertility every year, about 40,000 try high-tech assisted reproduction. By far the most common technique used is *in vitro fertilization (IVF)*, in which eggs and sperm are combined in a laboratory dish. If any eggs are successfully fertilized, one or more of the resulting zygotes is transferred into the woman's uterus. A national study in the United States by the Centers for Disease Control and Prevention (2006) found the success rate of IVF depends on the mother's age (see Figure 2.9).

The creation of families by means of the new reproductive technologies raises important questions about the physical and psychological consequences for children (Parke, 2014). One result of fertility treatments is an increase in multiple births. Twenty-five to 30 percent of pregnancies achieved by fertility treatments—including in vitro fertilization—now result in multiple births. A *meta-analysis* (a statistical technique that combines the results of multiple studies to determine the strength of the effect) revealed that twins conceived by in vitro fertilization have a slightly increased risk of low birth weight (McDonald & others, 2010) and another meta-analysis found that in vitro fertilization singletons have a significant risk of low birth weight (McDonald & others, 2009). To read about a study that addresses longer-term consequences of in vitro fertilization, see *Connecting Through Research*.

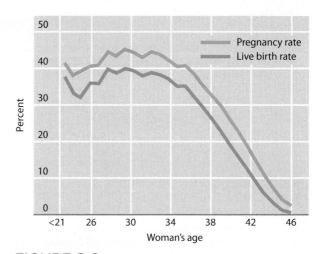

FIGURE **2.9**

SUCCESS RATES OF IN VITRO FERTILIZATION VARY ACCORDING TO THE WOMAN'S AGE

ADOPTION

Although surgery and fertility drugs can sometimes solve infertility problems, another choice is to adopt a child (Grotevant & McDermott, 2014). Adoption is a social and legal process that establishes a parent-child relationship between persons unrelated at birth.

The Increased Diversity of Adopted Children and Adoptive Parents A number of changes have characterized adoptive children and adoptive parents during the last three to four decades (Brodzinsky & Pinderhughes, 2002; Grotevant & McDermott, 2014). In the first half of the twentieth century, most U.S. adopted children were healthy, non–Latino White infants who were adopted at birth or soon after; however, in recent decades as abortion became legal and contraception increased, fewer of these infants became available for adoption. Increasingly, U.S. couples adopted a much wider diversity of children—from other countries, from other ethnic groups, children with physical and/or mental problems, and children who had been neglected or abused.

Changes also have characterized adoptive parents in the last three to four decades (Brodzinsky & Pinderhughes, 2002). In the first half of the twentieth century, most adoptive parents were from non–Latino White, middle or upper socioeconomic status backgrounds who were married and did not have any type of disability. However, in recent decades, increased diversity has characterized adoptive parents. Many adoption agencies today have no income requirements for adoptive parents and now allow adults from a wide range of backgrounds to adopt children, including single adults, gay and lesbian adults, and older adults. Further, many

connecting through research

Do Children Conceived Through In Vitro Fertilization Show Significant Differences in Developmental Outcomes in Adolescence?

A longitudinal study examined 34 in vitro fertilization families, 49 adoptive families, and 38 families with a naturally conceived child (Golombok, MacCallum, & Goodman, 2001). Each type of family included a similar proportion of boys and girls. Also, the ages of the young adolescents did not differ according to family type (mean age of 11 years, 11 months).

Children's socioemotional development was assessed by (1) interviewing the mother and obtaining detailed descriptions of any problems the child might have; (2) administering a strengths and difficulties questionnaire to the child's mother and teacher; and (3) administering the Social Adjustment Inventory for Children and Adolescents, which examines functioning in school, peer relationships, and self-esteem.

No significant differences between the children from in vitro fertilization, adoptive, and naturally conceiving families were found. The results from the Social Adjustment Inventory for Children and Adolescents are shown in Figure 2.10. Recent reviews by leading researchers conclude that children and adolescents conceived through new reproductive technologies—such as in vitro fertilization—are as

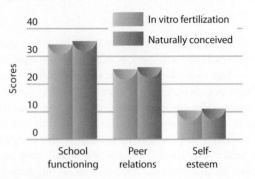

FIGURE 2.10

SOCIOEMOTIONAL FUNCTIONING OF CHILDREN CONCEIVED THROUGH IN VITRO FERTILIZATION OR NATURALLY CONCEIVED. This graph shows the results of a study that compared the socioemotional functioning of young adolescents who had either been conceived through in vitro fertilization (IVF) or naturally conceived (Golombok, MacCallum, & Goodman, 2001). For each type of family, the study included a similar proportion of boys and girls and children of similar age (mean age of 11 years, 11 months). Although the means for the naturally conceived group were slightly higher, this is likely due to chance: There were no significant differences between the groups.

well adjusted as their counterparts conceived by natural means (Golombok, 2011a, b; Golombok & Tasker, 2010).

adoptions involve other family members (aunts/uncles/grandparents); currently, 30 percent of U.S. adoptions are made by relatives (Ledesma, 2012). And slightly more than 50 percent of U.S. adoptions occur through the foster care system; recently, more than 100,000 children in the U.S. foster care system were waiting for someone to adopt them (Ledesma, 2012).

Three pathways to adoption are: (1) domestic adoption from the public welfare system, (2) domestic infant adoption through private agencies and intermediaries, and (3) international adoption (Grotevant & McDermott, 2014). In the next decade, the mix of U.S. adoptions is likely to include fewer domestic infant and international adoptions and more adoptions via the child welfare system (Grotevant & McDermott, 2014).

Outcomes for Adopted Children   How do adopted children fare after they are adopted? A recent research review concluded that adopted children are at higher risk for externalizing (aggression and conduct problems, for example), internalizing (anxiety and depression, for example), and attention problems (ADHD, for example) (Grotevant & McDermott, 2014). However, a majority of adopted children and adolescents (including those adopted at older ages, transracially, and across national borders) adjust effectively, and their parents report considerable satisfaction with their decision to adopt (Brodzinsky & Pinderhughes, 2002; Castle & others, 2010).

Adopted children fare much better than children raised in long-term foster care or in an institutional environment (Bernard & Dozier, 2008). A study of infants in China revealed that their cognitive development improved two to six months following their adoption from foster homes and institutions (van den Dries & others, 2010).

Children who are adopted very early in their lives are more likely to have positive outcomes than children adopted later in life (Bernard & Dozier, 2008; Julian, 2013). A Danish study indicated that being adopted was not a risk for juvenile delinquency if the individual was adopted at 12 months of age or earlier (Laubjerg & Petersson, 2011). However, those adopted after 12 months of age had a three to four times higher risk of becoming a juvenile delinquent than their nonadopted counterparts. Keep in mind that the changes in adoption

Parenting Adopted Children

Many of the keys to effectively parenting adopted children are no different from those for effectively parenting biological children: be supportive and caring, be involved and monitor the child's behavior and whereabouts, be a good communicator, and help the child learn to develop self-control. However, parents of adopted children face some unique circumstances (Fontenot, 2007; Grotevant & McDermott, 2014; Von Korff & Grotevant, 2011). These parents need to recognize the differences involved in adoptive family life, communicate about these differences, show respect for the birth family, and support the child's search for self and identity.

Following are some of the problems parents may face when their adopted children are at different points in development and some recommendations for how to handle these problems (Brodzinsky & Pinderhughes, 2002):

- **Infancy.** Researchers have found few differences in the attachment that adopted and nonadopted infants form with their parents. However, attachment can become problematic if parents have unresolved fertility issues or the child does not meet the parents' expectations. Counselors can help prospective adoptive parents develop realistic expectations.
- **Early childhood.** Because many children begin to ask where they came from when they are about 4 to 6 years old, this is a natural time to begin to talk in simple ways to children about their adoption status (Warshak, 2007). Some parents (although not as many as in the past) decide not to tell their children about the adoption. This secrecy may create psychological risks for the child if he or she later finds out about the adoption.

What are some strategies for parenting adopted children at different points in their development?

- **Middle and late childhood.** During the elementary school years, children begin to show more interest in their origins and may ask questions related to where they came from, what their birth parents looked like, and why their birth parents placed them for adoption. As they grow older, children may develop mixed feelings about being adopted and question their adoptive parents' explanations. It is important for adoptive parents to recognize that this ambivalence is normal. Also, problems may arise from the desire of adoptive parents to make life too perfect for the adoptive child and to present a perfect image of themselves to the child. The result too often is that adopted children feel that they cannot release any angry feelings or openly discuss problems.
- **Adolescence.** Adolescents are likely to develop more abstract and logical thinking, to focus their attention on their bodies, and to search for an identity. These characteristics provide the foundation for adopted adolescents to reflect on their adoption status in more complex ways, such as focusing on how they look so different from their adoptive parents. As they explore their identity, adopted adolescents may have difficulty incorporating their adopted status in positive ways into their identity. It is important for adoptive parents to understand the complexity of the adopted adolescent's identity exploration and be patient with the adolescent's lengthy identity search.

According to the information presented here and in the preceding text, how can mental health professionals help both adoptive parents and adopted children?

practice over the last several decades make it difficult to generalize about the average adopted child or average adoptive parent.

An ongoing issue in adopting children is whether there should be any contact with children's biological parents. Open adoption involves sharing identifying information and having contact with the biological parents; in contrast, closed adoption involves not having such sharing and contact. Most adoption agencies today offer adoptive parents the opportunity to have either an open or a closed adoption. A longitudinal study found that when their adopted children reached adulthood, adoptive parents described open adoption positively and saw it as serving the child's best interests (Siegel, 2013). Another longitudinal study found that birth mothers, adoptive parents, and adopted children who had contact were more satisfied with their arrangements than those who did not have contact (Grotevant & others, 2013). Also, in this study, contact was linked to more optimal adjustment for adolescents and emerging adults (Grotevant & others, 2013). Further, birth mothers who were more satisfied with their contact arrangements had less unresolved grief 12 to 20 years after placement.

To read more about adoption, see *Connecting Development to Life,* in which we discuss effective parenting strategies with adopted children.

Review
- What are some common prenatal diagnostic tests?
- What are some techniques that help infertile people to have children?
- How does adoption affect children's development?

Connect
- In Chapter 1, we learned different methods for collecting data. How would

you characterize the methods used in prenatal diagnostic testing?

Reflect *Your Own Personal Journey of Life*
- If you were an adult who could not have children, would you want to adopt a child? Why or why not?

4 Heredity-Environment Interaction: The Nature-Nurture Debate

LG4 Explain some of the ways that heredity and environment interact to produce individual differences in development.

| Behavior Genetics | Heredity-Environment Correlations | Shared and Nonshared Environmental Experiences | The Epigenetic View and Gene × Environment (G × E) Interaction | Conclusions about Heredity-Environment Interaction |

Is it possible to untangle the influence of heredity from that of environment and discover the role of each in producing individual differences in development? When heredity and environment interact, how does heredity influence the environment and vice versa?

BEHAVIOR GENETICS

Behavior genetics is the field that seeks to discover the influence of heredity and environment on individual differences in human traits and development (Krushkal & others, 2014; Maxson, 2013). Note that behavior genetics does not identify the extent to which genetics or the environment affects an individual's traits. Instead, what behavior geneticists try to do is to figure out what is responsible for the differences among people—that is, to what extent people vary because of differences in genes, environment, or a combination of these factors (Carlson, Mendle, & Harden, 2014; J. Chen & others, 2014). To study the influence of heredity on behavior, behavior geneticists often use either twins or adoption situations.

In the most common **twin study,** the behavioral similarity of identical twins (who are genetically identical) is compared with the behavioral similarity of fraternal twins. Recall that although fraternal twins share the same womb, they are no more genetically alike than non-twin siblings. Thus, by comparing groups of identical and fraternal twins, behavior geneticists capitalize on the basic knowledge that identical twins are more similar genetically than are fraternal twins (Lacourse & others, 2014; Matamura & others, 2014). For example, one study found that conduct problems were more prevalent in identical twins than fraternal twins; the researchers concluded that the study demonstrated an important role for heredity in conduct problems (Scourfield & others, 2004).

What are some of the thoughts and feelings people have about being a twin? In college freshman Colin Kunzweiler's (2007) view,

As a monozygotic individual, I am used to certain things. "Which one are you?" happens to be the most popular question I'm asked, which is almost always followed by "You're Colin. No, wait, you're Andy!" I have two names: one was given to me at birth, the other thrust on me in a random, haphazard way . . . My twin brother and I are as different from each other as caramel sauce is from gravy. We have different personalities, we enjoy different kind of music, and I am even taller than he is (by a quarter of an inch). We are

Twin studies compare identical twins with fraternal twins. Identical twins develop from a single fertilized egg that splits into two genetically identical organisms. Fraternal twins develop from separate eggs, making them genetically no more similar than nontwin siblings. *What is the nature of the twin study method?*

different; separate; individual. I have always been taught that I should maintain my own individuality; that I should be my own person. But if people keep constantly mistaking me for my twin, how can I be my own person with my own identity?

"Am I an 'I' or 'We'?" was the title of an article written by Lynn Perlman (2008) about the struggle twins have in developing a sense of being an individual. Of course, triplets have the same issue, possibly even more strongly so. One set of triplets entered a beauty contest as one person and won the contest!

Perlman, an identical twin herself, is a psychologist who works with twins (her identical twin also is a psychologist). She says that how twins move from a sense of "we" to "I" is a critical task for them as children and sometimes even as adults. For non-twins, separating oneself from a primary caregiver—mother and/or father—is an important developmental task in childhood, adolescence, and emerging adulthood. When a child has a twin, the separation process is likely more difficult because of the constant comparison with a twin. Because they are virtually identical in their physical appearance, identical twins are likely to have more problems in distinguishing themselves from their twin than are fraternal twins.

The twin separation process often accelerates in adolescence when one twin is likely to mature earlier than the other (Pearlman, 2013). However, for some twins it may not occur until emerging adulthood when they may go to different colleges and/or live apart separately for the first time. And for some twins, even as adults twin separation can be emotionally painful. One 28-year-old identical twin female got a new boyfriend but the new relationship caused a great deal of stress and conflict with her twin sister (Friedman, 2013).

In Lynn Perlman's (2008) view, helping twins develop their own identities needs to be done on a child-by-child basis, taking into account their preferences and what is in their best interests. She commented that most of the twins she has counseled consider having a twin a positive experience and while they also are usually strongly attached to each other they are intensely motivated to be considered a unique person.

However, several issues complicate interpretation of twin studies. For example, perhaps the environments of identical twins are more similar than the environments of fraternal twins. Adults might stress the similarities of identical twins more than those of fraternal twins, and identical twins might perceive themselves as a "set" and play together more than fraternal twins do. If so, the influence of the environment on the observed similarities between identical and fraternal twins might be very significant.

In an **adoption study,** investigators seek to discover whether the behavior and psychological characteristics of adopted children are more like those of their adoptive parents, who have provided a home environment, or more like those of their biological parents, who have contributed their DNA (Kendler & others, 2012). Another form of the adoption study compares adoptive and biological siblings.

HEREDITY-ENVIRONMENT CORRELATIONS

The difficulties that researchers encounter when they interpret the results of twin studies and adoption studies reflect the complexities of heredity-environment interaction. Some of these interactions are heredity-environment correlations, which means that individuals' genes may be systematically related to the types of environments to which they are exposed (Klahr & Burt, 2014). In a sense, individuals "inherit," seek out, or "construct" environments that may be related or linked to genetic "propensities." Behavior geneticist Sandra Scarr (1993) described three ways that heredity and environment can be correlated (see Figure 2.11):

- **Passive genotype-environment correlations** occur because biological parents, who are genetically related to the child, provide a rearing environment for the child. For example, the parents might have a genetic predisposition to be intelligent and read skillfully. Because they read well and enjoy reading, they provide their children with books to read. The likely outcome is that their children, because of both their own inherited predispositions and their book-filled environment, will become skilled readers.
- **Evocative genotype-environment correlations** occur because a child's genetically influenced characteristics elicit certain types of environments. For example, active, smiling children receive more social stimulation than passive, quiet children do.

behavior genetics The field that seeks to discover the influence of heredity and environment on individual differences in human traits and development.

twin study A study in which the behavioral similarity of identical twins is compared with the behavioral similarity of fraternal twins.

adoption study A study in which investigators seek to discover whether, in behavior and psychological characteristics, adopted children are more like their adoptive parents, who provided a home environment, or more like their biological parents, who contributed their heredity. Another form of the adoption study compares adoptive and biological siblings.

passive genotype-environment correlations Correlations that exist when the natural parents, who are genetically related to the child, provide a rearing environment for the child.

evocative genotype-environment correlations Correlations that exist when the child's genetically influenced characteristics elicit certain types of environments.

Heredity-Environment Correlation	Description	Examples
Passive	Children inherit genetic tendencies from their parents, and parents also provide an environment that matches their own genetic tendencies.	Musically inclined parents usually have musically inclined children and they are likely to provide an environment rich in music for their children.
Evocative	The child's genetic tendencies elicit stimulation from the environment that supports a particular trait. Thus genes evoke environmental support.	A happy, outgoing child elicits smiles and friendly responses from others.
Active (niche-picking)	Children actively seek out "niches" in their environment that reflect their own interests and talents and are thus in accord with their genotype.	Libraries, sports fields, and a store with musical instruments are examples of environmental niches children might seek out if they have intellectual interests in books, talent in sports, or musical talents, respectively.

FIGURE **2.11**

EXPLORING HEREDITY-ENVIRONMENT CORRELATIONS

Tennis stars Venus and Serena Williams. *What might be some shared and nonshared environmental experiences they had while they were growing up that contributed to their tennis stardom?*

Cooperative, attentive children evoke more pleasant and instructional responses from the adults around them than uncooperative, distractible children do.

- **Active (niche-picking) genotype-environment correlations** occur when children seek out environments that they find compatible and stimulating. *Niche-picking* refers to finding a setting that is suited to one's genetically influenced abilities. Children select from their surrounding environment certain aspects that they respond to, learn about, or ignore. Their active selections of environments are related to their particular genotype. For example, outgoing children tend to seek out social contexts in which to interact with people, whereas shy children don't. Children who are musically inclined are likely to select musical environments in which they can successfully perform their skills. How these "tendencies" come about will be discussed shortly under the topic of the epigenetic view.

Scarr observes that the relative importance of the three genotype-environment correlations changes as children develop from infancy through adolescence. In infancy, much of the environment that children experience is provided by adults. Thus, passive genotype-environment correlations are more common in the lives of infants and young children than they are in the lives of older children and adolescents who can extend their experiences beyond the family's influence and create or select their environments to a greater degree.

SHARED AND NONSHARED ENVIRONMENTAL EXPERIENCES

Behavior geneticists have argued that to understand the environment's role in differences between people, we should distinguish between shared and nonshared environments. That is, we should consider experiences that children share in common with other children living in the same home, and experiences that are not shared (Burt, 2014; White & others, 2014).

Shared environmental experiences are siblings' common experiences, such as their parents' personalities or intellectual orientation, the family's socioeconomic status, and the neighborhood in which they live. By contrast, **nonshared environmental experiences** consist of a child's unique experiences, both within the family and outside the family, that are not shared with a sibling. Even experiences occurring within the family can be part of the "nonshared environment." For example, parents often interact differently with each sibling, and siblings interact differently with parents. Siblings often have different peer groups, different friends, and different teachers at school, all of which contribute to their nonshared environments.

Behavior geneticist Robert Plomin (2004) has found that shared environment accounts for little of the variation in children's personality or interests. In other words, even though two children live under the same roof with the same parents, their personalities are often very different. Further, Plomin argues that heredity influences the nonshared environments of siblings through the heredity-environment correlations we described earlier. For example, a child who has inherited a tendency to be athletic is likely to spend more time in environments related to sports, and a child who has inherited a tendency to be musically inclined is more likely to spend time in environments related to music.

What are the implications of Plomin's interpretation of the role of shared and nonshared environments in development? In *The Nurture Assumption,* Judith Harris (1998, 2009) argued that what parents do does not make a difference in their children's and adolescents' behavior. Yell at them. Hug them. Read to them. Ignore them. Harris says it won't influence how they turn out. She argues based on data like Plomin's that genes and peers are far more important than parents in shaping children's and adolescents' development.

Genes and peers do matter, but Harris' descriptions of peer influences do not take into account the complexity of peer contexts and developmental trajectories (Hartup, 2009). In addition, Harris is wrong in saying that parents don't matter. For example, in the early childhood years parents play an important role in selecting children's peers and indirectly influencing children's development (Baumrind, 1999). A large volume of parenting literature with many research studies documents the importance of parents in children's development (Clarke-Stewart & Parke, 2014; McBride Murry & others, 2015). We will discuss parents' important roles throughout this book.

THE EPIGENETIC VIEW AND GENE × ENVIRONMENT (G × E) INTERACTION

Critics argue that the concept of heredity-environment correlation gives heredity too much of a one-sided influence in determining development because it does not consider the role of prior environmental influences in shaping the correlation itself (Gottlieb, 2007). Consistent with this view, earlier in the chapter we discussed how genes are collaborative, not determining an individual's traits in an independent manner but rather in an interactive manner with the environment.

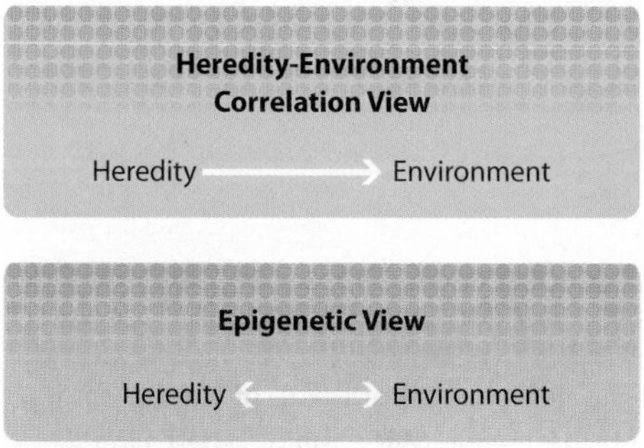

The Epigenetic View In line with the concept of a collaborative gene, Gilbert Gottlieb (2007) emphasizes the **epigenetic view,** which states that development reflects an ongoing, bidirectional interchange between heredity and the environment. Figure 2.12 compares the heredity-environment correlation and epigenetic views of development.

Let's look at an example that reflects the epigenetic view. A baby inherits genes from both parents at conception. During prenatal development, environmental experiences such as toxins, nutrition, and stress can influence some genes to stop functioning while others become more active or less active. During infancy, environmental experiences such as exposure to toxins, nutrition, stress, learning, and encouragement continue to modify genetic activity and influence the activity of the nervous system that directly underlies behavior. Heredity and environment operate together—or collaborate—to produce a person's intelligence, temperament, height, weight, ability to pitch a baseball, ability to read, and so on (Gottlieb, 2007).

Gene × Environment (G × E) Interaction An increasing number of studies are exploring how the interaction between heredity and environment influences development, including interactions that involve specific DNA sequences (Manuck & McCaffery, 2014). The epigenetic mechanisms involve the actual molecular modification of the DNA strand as a result of environmental inputs in ways that alter gene functioning (Davies & Cicchetti, 2014; Moore, 2013).

One study found that individuals who have a short version of a gene labeled 5-HTTLPR (a gene involving the neurotransmitter serotonin) have an elevated risk of developing depression only if they *also* lead stressful lives (Caspi & others, 2003). Thus, the specific gene did

developmental **connection**

Parenting

Is quantity or quality more important in parenting? Chapter 8, p. 244

FIGURE 2.12

COMPARISON OF THE HEREDITY-ENVIRONMENT CORRELATION AND EPIGENETIC VIEWS

active (niche-picking) genotype-environment correlations Correlations that exist when children seek out environments they find compatible and stimulating.

shared environmental experiences Siblings' common environmental experiences, such as their parents' personalities and intellectual orientation, the family's socioeconomic status, and the neighborhood in which they live.

nonshared environmental experiences The child's own unique experiences, both within the family and outside the family, that are not shared with another sibling. Thus, experiences occurring within the family can be part of the "nonshared environment."

epigenetic view Emphasizes that development is the result of an ongoing, bidirectional interchange between heredity and environment.

developmental **connection**

Attachment

One study revealed links between infant attachment, responsive parenting, and the 5-HTTLPR gene. Chapter 6, p. 183

not directly cause the development of depression; rather, the gene interacted with a stressful environment in a way that allowed the researchers to predict whether individuals would develop depression. A recent meta-analysis indicated that the short version of 5-HTTLPR was linked with higher cortisol stress reactivity (Miller & others, 2013). Recent studies also have found support for the interaction between the 5-HTTLPR gene and stress levels in predicting depression in adolescents and older adults (Petersen & others, 2012; Zannas & others, 2012).

Other research on interactions between genes and environmental experiences has focused on attachment, parenting, and supportive child rearing environments (Hostinar, Cicchetti, & Rogosch, 2014). In one study, adults who experienced parental loss as young children were more likely to have unresolved attachment issues as adults only when they had the short version of the 5-HTTLPR gene (Caspers & others, 2009). The long version of the serotonin transporter gene apparently provided some protection and ability to cope better with parental loss. Other recent research has found that variations in dopamine-related genes interact with supportive or unsupportive rearing environments to influence children's development (Bakermans-Kranenburg & van IJzendoorn, 2011). The type of research just described is referred to as studies of **gene × environment (G × E) interaction**—the interaction of a specific measured variation in DNA and a specific measured aspect of the environment (Manuck & McCaffery, 2014; Oppenheimer & others, 2013).

Although there is considerable enthusiasm about the concept of gene × environment interaction (G × E), a recent research review concluded that the area is plagued by difficulties in replicating results, inflated claims, and other weaknesses (Manuck & McCaffery, 2014). The science of G × E interaction is very young and over the next several decades it will likely produce more precise findings.

CONCLUSIONS ABOUT HEREDITY-ENVIRONMENT INTERACTION

developmental **connection**

Nature Versus Nurture

The relative importance of nature and nurture is one of the main debates in the study of life-span development. Chapter 1, p. 17

developmental **connection**

Life-Span Perspective

An important aspect of the life-span perspective is the co-construction of biology, environment, and the individual. Chapter 1, p. 7

If an attractive, popular, intelligent girl is elected president of her senior class in high school, is her success due to heredity or to environment? Of course, the answer is "both."

The relative contributions of heredity and environment are not additive. That is, we can't say that such-and-such a percentage of nature and such-and-such a percentage of experience make us who we are. Nor is it accurate to say that full genetic expression happens once, around conception or birth, after which we carry our genetic legacy into the world to see how far it takes us. Genes produce proteins throughout the life span, in many different environments. Or they don't produce these proteins, depending in part on how harsh or nourishing those environments are.

The emerging view is that complex behaviors are influenced by genes and environments in a way that gives people a propensity for a particular developmental trajectory (Asbury & Plomin, 2014). The actual development requires both genes and an environment. And that environment is complex, just like the mixture of genes we inherit (Cicchetti & Toth, 2015). Environmental influences range from the things we lump together under "nurture" (such as parenting, family dynamics, schooling, and neighborhood quality) to biological encounters (such as viruses, birth complications, and even biological events occurring at the cellular level).

In developmental psychologist David Moore's (2013) view, the biological systems that generate behaviors are extremely complex but too often these systems have been described in overly simplified ways that can be misleading. Thus, although genetic factors clearly contribute to behavior and psychological processes, they don't determine these phenotypes independently from the contexts in which they develop. From Moore's (2013) perspective, it is misleading to talk about "genes for" eye color, intelligence, personality, or other characteristics. Moore commented that in retrospect we should not have expected to be able to make the giant leap from DNA's molecules to a complete understanding of human behavior any more than we should anticipate being able to make the leap from understanding how sound waves move air molecules in a concert hall to a full-blown appreciation of a symphony's wondrous experience.

gene × environment (G × E) interaction The interaction of a specific measured variation in the DNA and a specific measured aspect of the environment.

Imagine for a moment a cluster of genes somehow associated with youth violence (this example is hypothetical because we don't know of any such combination). The adolescent who carries this genetic mixture might experience a world of loving parents, regular nutritious meals, lots of books, and a series of masterful teachers. Or the adolescent's world might include parental neglect, a neighborhood in which gunshots and crime are everyday occurrences, and inadequate schooling. In which of these environments is the adolescent likely to become a criminal?

If heredity and environment interact to determine the course of development, is that all there is to answering the question of what causes development? Are humans completely at the mercy of their genes and environment as they develop through the life span? Our genetic heritage and environmental experiences are pervasive influences on development (Brooker, 2015; Clarke-Stewart & Parke, 2014). But in thinking about what causes development, recall from Chapter 1 our discussion of development as the co-construction of biology, culture, *and* the individual. Not only are we the outcomes of our heredity and the environment we experience, but we also can author a unique developmental path by changing the environment. As one psychologist recently concluded:

> In reality, we are both the creatures and creators of our worlds. We are . . . the products of our genes and environments. Nevertheless, . . . the stream of causation that shapes the future runs through our present choices . . . Mind matters . . . Our hopes, goals, and expectations influence our future. (Myers, 2010, p. 168)

To what extent are this young girl's piano skills likely due to heredity, environment, or both?

Review Connect Reflect

LG4 Explain some of the ways that heredity and environment interact to produce individual differences in development.

Review
- What is behavior genetics?
- What are three types of heredity-environment correlations?
- What is meant by the concepts of shared and nonshared environmental experiences?
- What is the epigenetic view of development? What characterizes gene × environment (G × E) interaction?
- What conclusions can be reached about heredity-environment interaction?

Connect
- Of passive, evocative, and active genotype-environment correlations, which is the best explanation for the similarities discovered between the twins discussed in the chapter-opening story?

Reflect Your Own Personal Journey of Life
- Someone tells you that she has analyzed your genetic background and environmental experiences and concluded that environment definitely has had little influence on your intelligence. What would you say about this analysis?

topical connections *looking forward*

In the following chapters, we will continue to explore biological influences on development, especially in the chapters on physical development, but also in the chapters on cognitive and socioemotional development. For instance, biology's influence on infants' gross and fine motor skills (Chapter 4) may be obvious, but we will also discuss research questions such as "Is there a biological basis for sexual orientation?" (Chapter 13). In addition, we will examine reproduction when we look at adolescents (Chapter 11) and young adults (Chapter 14) who become parents. Finally, we will touch on the dual influence of nature and nurture in every period of life-span development.

reach your **learning goals**

Biological Beginnings

1 The Evolutionary Perspective

- Natural Selection and Adaptive Behavior
- Evolutionary Psychology

 LG1 Discuss the evolutionary perspective on life-span development.

- Natural selection is the process by which those individuals of a species that are best adapted survive and reproduce. Darwin proposed that natural selection fuels evolution. In evolutionary theory, adaptive behavior is behavior that promotes the organism's survival in a natural habitat.

- Evolutionary psychology holds that adaptation, reproduction, and "survival of the fittest" are important in shaping behavior. Ideas proposed by evolutionary developmental psychology include the view that an extended childhood period is needed to develop a large brain and learn the complexity of human social communities. According to Baltes, the benefits resulting from evolutionary selection decrease with age mainly because of a decline in reproductive fitness. At the same time, cultural needs increase. Like other theoretical approaches to development, evolutionary psychology has limitations. Bandura rejects "one-sided evolutionism" and argues for a bidirectional link between biology and environment. Biology allows for a broad range of cultural possibilities.

2 Genetic Foundations of Development

- The Collaborative Gene
- Genes and Chromosomes
- Genetic Principles
- Chromosomal and Gene-Linked Abnormalities

LG2 Describe what genes are and how they influence human development.

- Short segments of DNA constitute genes, the units of hereditary information that help cells to reproduce and manufacture proteins. Genes act collaboratively, not independently.

- Genes are passed on to new cells when chromosomes are duplicated during the processes of mitosis and meiosis, which are two ways in which new cells are formed. When an egg and a sperm unite in the fertilization process, the resulting zygote contains the genes from the chromosomes in the father's sperm and the mother's egg. Despite this transmission of genes from generation to generation, variability is created in several ways, including through the exchange of chromosomal segments during meiosis, through mutations, and through environmental influences.

- Genetic principles include those involving dominant-recessive genes, sex-linked genes, genetic imprinting, and polygenic inheritance.

- Chromosomal abnormalities produce Down syndrome, which is caused by the presence of an extra copy of chromosome 21. Other sex-linked conditions include Klinefelter syndrome, fragile X syndrome, Turner syndrome, and XYY syndrome. Gene-linked abnormalities involve harmful or absent genes. Gene-linked disorders include phenylketonuria (PKU) and sickle-cell anemia. Genetic counseling offers couples information about their risk of having a child with inherited abnormalities.

3 Reproductive Challenges and Choices

- Prenatal Diagnostic Tests
- Infertility and Reproductive Technology

 LG3 Identify some important reproductive challenges and choices.

- Ultrasound sonography, fetal MRI, chorionic villus sampling, amniocentesis, and maternal blood screening are used to determine whether a fetus is developing normally. Noninvasive prenatal diagnosis is increasingly being explored.

- Approximately 10 to 15 percent of U.S. couples have infertility problems, some of which can be corrected through surgery or fertility drugs. An additional option is in vitro fertilization.

| Adoption | • A majority of adopted children adapt effectively. When adoption occurs very early in development, the outcomes for the child are improved. Because of the dramatic changes that occurred in adoption in recent decades, it is difficult to generalize about the average adopted child or average adoptive family. |

4 Heredity-Environment Interaction: The Nature-Nurture Debate

 LG4 Explain some of the ways that heredity and environment interact to produce individual differences in development.

| Behavior Genetics | • Behavior genetics is the field concerned with the influence of heredity and environment on individual differences in human traits and development. Research methods used by behavior geneticists include twin studies and adoption studies. |

| Heredity-Environment Correlations | • In Scarr's heredity-environment correlations view, heredity directs the types of environments that children experience. She describes three genotype-environment correlations: passive, evocative, and active (niche-picking). Scarr argues that the relative importance of these three genotype-environment correlations changes as children develop. |

| Shared and Nonshared Environmental Experiences | • Shared environmental experiences refer to siblings' common experiences, such as their parents' personalities and intellectual orientation, the family's socioeconomic status, and the neighborhood in which they live. Nonshared environmental experiences involve the child's unique experiences, both within the family and outside the family, that are not shared with a sibling. Many behavior geneticists argue that differences in the development of siblings are due to nonshared environmental experiences (and heredity) rather than shared environmental experiences. |

| The Epigenetic View and Gene × Environment (G × E) Interaction | • The epigenetic view emphasizes that development is the result of an ongoing, bidirectional interchange between heredity and environment. Gene × environment interaction involves the interaction of a specific measured variation in the DNA and a specific measured aspect of the environment. An increasing number of G × E studies are being conducted. |

| Conclusions About Heredity-Environment Interaction | • Behaviors are influenced by genes and environments in a way that gives people a propensity for a particular developmental trajectory. The actual development requires both genes and an environment, and that environment is complex. The interaction of heredity and environment is extensive. Much remains to be discovered about the specific ways that heredity and environment interact to influence development. Although heredity and environment are pervasive influences on development, however, humans can author a unique developmental path by changing their environments. |

key terms

evolutionary psychology 49
chromosomes 51
DNA 51
genes 51
mitosis 53
meiosis 53
fertilization 53
zygote 53
genotype 54

phenotype 54
Down syndrome 55
Klinefelter syndrome 56
fragile X syndrome 56
Turner syndrome 56
XYY syndrome 56
phenylketonuria (PKU) 56
sickle-cell anemia 57
behavior genetics 65

twin study 65
adoption study 65
passive genotype-environment
    correlations 65
evocative genotype-environment
    correlations 65
active (niche-picking)
    genotype-environment
    correlations 67

shared environmental
    experiences 67
nonshared environmental
    experiences 67
epigenetic view 67
gene × environment (G × E)
    interaction 68

key people

Thomas Bouchard 47
Charles Darwin 48
David Buss 49

Paul Baltes 50
Albert Bandura 50
Stephen Jay Gould 50

David Moore 52
Sandra Scarr 65
Robert Plomin 67

Judith Harris 67
Gilbert Gottlieb 67

chapter 3

PRENATAL DEVELOPMENT AND BIRTH

chapter outline

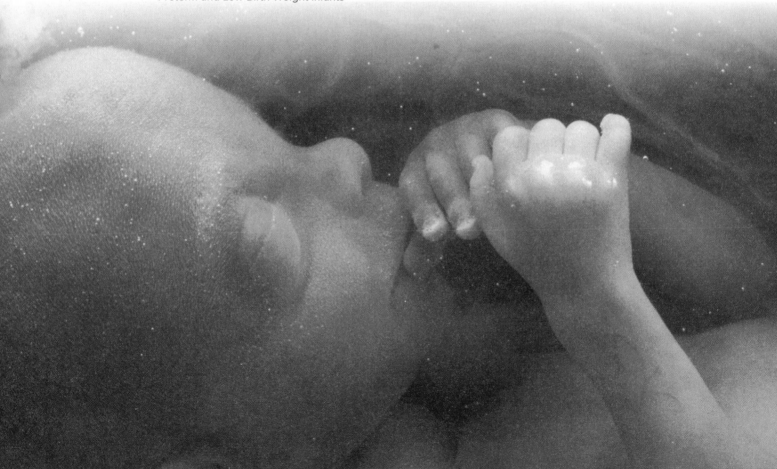

Diana and Roger married when he was 38 and she was 34. Both worked full-time and were excited when Diana became pregnant. Two months later, Diana began to have some unusual pains and bleeding. Just two months into her pregnancy she had lost the baby. Diana thought deeply about why she had been unable to carry the baby to full term. It was about the time she became pregnant that the federal government began to warn that eating certain types of fish with a high mercury content during pregnancy on a regular basis can cause a miscarriage. Now she eliminated those fish from her diet.

Six months later, Diana became pregnant again. She and Roger read about pregnancy and signed up for birth preparation classes. Each Friday night for eight weeks they practiced simulated contractions. They talked about what kind of parents they wanted to be and discussed what changes in their lives the baby would make. When they found out that their offspring was going to be a boy, they gave him a nickname: Mr. Littles.

This time, Diana's pregnancy went well, and Alex, also known as Mr. Littles, was born. During the birth, however, Diana's heart rate dropped precipitously, and she was given a stimulant to raise it. Apparently the stimulant also increased Alex's heart rate and breathing to a dangerous point, and he had to be placed in a neonatal intensive care unit (NICU).

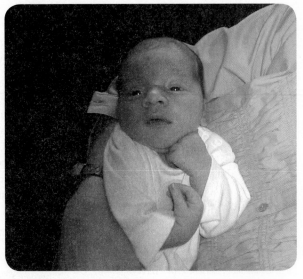

Alex, also known as "Mr. Littles."

Several times a day, Diana and Roger visited Alex in the NICU. A number of babies in the NICU with very low birth weights had been in intensive care for weeks, and some of the babies were not doing well. Fortunately, Alex was in better health. After he had spent several days in the NICU, his parents were permitted to take home a very healthy Alex.

topical connections *looking **back***

Genes form the biological basis of our development. They are passed on through mitosis, meiosis, and, ultimately, fertilization. The impact of our genes involves the genetic principles of dominant-recessive genes, sex-linked genes, genetic imprinting, and polygenically determined characteristics. Approximately 10 to 15 percent of U.S. couples have problems with fertility. Some of these problems can be solved through surgery, drugs, or in vitro fertilization. Whether a pregnancy occurs naturally or with assistance, the resulting infant's development is shaped both by his or her genes (nature) and environment (nurture).

preview

This chapter chronicles the truly remarkable developments from conception through birth. Imagine . . . at one time you were an organism floating in a sea of fluid in your mother's womb. Let's now explore what your development was like from the time you were conceived through the time you were born. We will explore normal development in the prenatal period, as well as the period's hazards (such as high levels of mercury that were mentioned in the preceding story). We also will study the birth process and tests used to assess the newborn; discuss parents' adjustment in the postpartum period; and evaluate parent-infant bonding.

1 Prenatal Development   **LG1** Describe prenatal development.

The Course of Prenatal Development

Teratology and Hazards to Prenatal Development

Prenatal Care

Normal Prenatal Development

The history of man for the nine months preceding his birth would, probably, be far more interesting, and contain events of greater moment, than all the three score and ten years that follow it.

—SAMUEL TAYLOR COLERIDGE
English Poet and Essayist, 19th Century

Imagine how Alex ("Mr. Littles") came to be. Out of thousands of eggs and millions of sperm, one egg and one sperm united to produce him. Had the union of sperm and egg come a day or even an hour earlier or later, he might have been very different—maybe even of the opposite sex. Conception occurs when a single sperm cell from the male unites with an ovum (egg) in the female's fallopian tube in a process called fertilization. Over the next few months, the genetic code discussed in Chapter 2 directs a series of changes in the fertilized egg, but many events and hazards will influence how that egg develops and becomes tiny Alex.

THE COURSE OF PRENATAL DEVELOPMENT

Typical prenatal development, which begins with fertilization and ends with birth, takes between 266 and 280 days (38 to 40 weeks). It can be divided into three periods: germinal, embryonic, and fetal.

The Germinal Period   The **germinal period** is the period of prenatal development that takes place in the first two weeks after conception. It includes the creation of the fertilized egg, called a zygote, cell division, and the attachment of the zygote to the uterine wall.

Rapid cell division by the zygote continues throughout the germinal period (recall from Chapter 2 that this cell division occurs through a process called mitosis). By approximately one week after conception, the differentiation of these cells—their specialization to perform various tasks—has already begun. At this stage, the group of cells, now called the **blastocyst,** consists of an inner mass of cells that will eventually develop into the embryo, and the **trophoblast,** an outer layer of cells that later provides nutrition and support for the embryo. Implantation, the attachment of the zygote to the uterine wall, takes place about 11 to 15 days after conception. Figure 3.1 illustrates some of the most significant developments during the germinal period.

The Embryonic Period   The **embryonic period** is the period of prenatal development that occurs from two to eight weeks after conception. During the embryonic period, the rate of cell differentiation intensifies, support systems for cells form, and organs appear.

This period begins as the blastocyst attaches to the uterine wall. The mass of cells is now called an *embryo,* and three layers of cells form. The embryo's *endoderm* is the inner layer of cells, which will develop into the digestive and respiratory systems. The *mesoderm* is the middle layer, which will become the circulatory system, bones, muscles, excretory system, and reproductive system. The *ectoderm* is the outermost layer, which will become the nervous system and brain, sensory receptors (ears, nose, and eyes, for example), and skin parts (hair and nails, for example). Every body part eventually develops from these three layers.

germinal period The period of prenatal development that takes place in the first two weeks after conception. It includes the creation of the zygote, continued cell division, and the attachment of the zygote to the uterine wall.

blastocyst The inner layer of cells that develops during the germinal period. These cells later develop into the embryo.

trophoblast The outer layer of cells that develops in the germinal period. These cells provide nutrition and support for the embryo.

embryonic period The period of prenatal development that occurs two to eight weeks after conception. During the embryonic period, the rate of cell differentiation intensifies, support systems for the cells form, and organs appear.

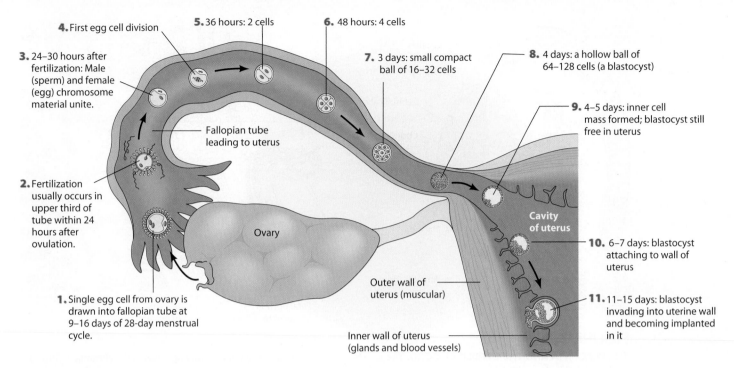

4. First egg cell division

5. 36 hours: 2 cells

6. 48 hours: 4 cells

3. 24–30 hours after fertilization: Male (sperm) and female (egg) chromosome material unite.

7. 3 days: small compact ball of 16–32 cells

8. 4 days: a hollow ball of 64–128 cells (a blastocyst)

Fallopian tube leading to uterus

9. 4–5 days: inner cell mass formed; blastocyst still free in uterus

2. Fertilization usually occurs in upper third of tube within 24 hours after ovulation.

Ovary

Cavity of uterus

10. 6–7 days: blastocyst attaching to wall of uterus

1. Single egg cell from ovary is drawn into fallopian tube at 9–16 days of 28-day menstrual cycle.

Outer wall of uterus (muscular)

11. 11–15 days: blastocyst invading into uterine wall and becoming implanted in it

Inner wall of uterus (glands and blood vessels)

FIGURE **3.1**

SIGNIFICANT DEVELOPMENTS IN THE GERMINAL PERIOD. Just one week after conception, cells of the blastocyst have already begun specializing. The germination period ends when the blastocyst attaches to the uterine wall. *Which of the steps shown in the drawing occur in the laboratory when IVF (described in Chapter 2) is used?*

The endoderm primarily produces internal body parts, the mesoderm primarily produces parts that surround the internal areas, and the ectoderm primarily produces surface parts.

As the embryo's three layers form, life-support systems for the embryo develop rapidly. These life-support systems include the amnion, the umbilical cord (both of which develop from the fertilized egg, not the mother's body), and the placenta. The **amnion** is like a bag or an envelope and contains a clear fluid in which the developing embryo floats. The amniotic fluid provides an environment that is temperature and humidity controlled, as well as shock-proof. The **umbilical cord** contains two arteries and one vein, and connects the baby to the placenta. The **placenta** consists of a disk-shaped group of tissues in which small blood vessels from the mother and the offspring intertwine but do not join.

Figure 3.2 illustrates the placenta, the umbilical cord, and the blood flow in the expectant mother and developing organism. Very small molecules—oxygen, water, salt, food from the mother's blood, as well as carbon dioxide and digestive wastes from the offspring's blood—pass back and forth between the mother and embryo or fetus (Woolett, 2011). Virtually any drug or chemical substance the pregnant woman ingests can cross the placenta to some degree, unless it is metabolized or altered during passage, or the molecules are too large to pass through the placental wall (Hutson & others, 2013; Iqbal & others, 2012). A recent study confirmed that ethanol crosses the human placenta and primarily reflects maternal alcohol use (Matlow & others, 2013). Another study revealed that cigarette smoke weakened and increased the oxidative stress of fetal membranes, from which the placenta develops (Menon & others, 2011). The stress hormone cortisol also can cross the placenta (Parrott & others, 2014). Large molecules that cannot pass through the placental wall include red blood cells and harmful substances, such as most bacteria, maternal wastes, and hormones. The complex mechanisms that govern the transfer of substances across the placental barrier are still not entirely understood (Antonucci & others, 2012).

By the time most women know they are pregnant, the major organs have begun to form. **Organogenesis** is the name given to the process of organ formation during the first two months of prenatal development. While they are being formed, the organs are especially vulnerable to environmental changes (Halt & Vainio, 2014; Wei & others, 2013). In the third week after conception, the neural tube that eventually becomes the spinal cord forms. At

amnion The life-support system that is a bag or envelope that contains a clear fluid in which the developing embryo floats.

umbilical cord A life-support system containing two arteries and one vein that connects the baby to the placenta.

placenta A life-support system that consists of a disk-shaped group of tissues in which small blood vessels from the mother and offspring intertwine.

organogenesis Organ formation that takes place during the first two months of prenatal development.

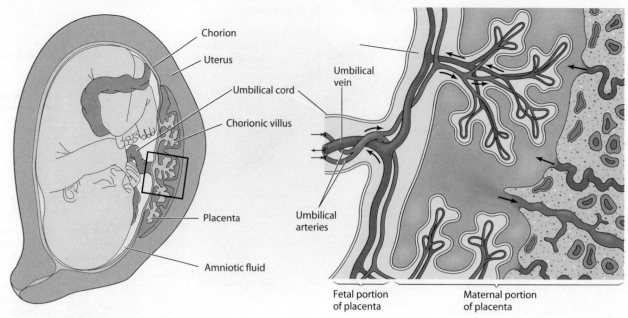

Chorion

Uterus

Umbilical cord

Chorionic villus

Umbilical vein

Placenta

Umbilical arteries

Amniotic fluid

Fetal portion of placenta

Maternal portion of placenta

FIGURE 3.2

THE PLACENTA AND THE UMBILICAL CORD. The area bound by the square is enlarged in the right half of the illustration. Arrows indicate the direction of blood flow. Maternal blood flows through the uterine arteries to the spaces housing the placenta, and it returns through the uterine veins to the maternal circulation. Fetal blood flows through the umbilical arteries into the capillaries of the placenta and returns through the umbilical vein to the fetal circulation. The exchange of materials takes place across the layer separating the maternal and fetal blood supplies, so the bloods never come into contact. *What is known about how the placental barrier works and its importance?*

about 21 days, eyes begin to appear, and at 24 days the cells for the heart begin to differentiate. During the fourth week, the urogenital system becomes apparent, and arm and leg buds emerge. Four chambers of the heart take shape, and blood vessels appear. From the fifth to the eighth week, arms and legs differentiate further; at this time, the face starts to form but still is not very recognizable. The intestinal tract develops and the facial structures fuse. At eight weeks, the developing organism weighs about 1/30 ounce and is just over 1 inch long.

The Fetal Period   The **fetal period,** lasting about seven months, is the prenatal period between two months after conception and birth in typical pregnancies. Growth and development continue their dramatic course during this time.

Three months after conception, the fetus is about 3 inches long and weighs about 3 ounces. It has become active, moving its arms and legs, opening and closing its mouth, and moving its head. The face, forehead, eyelids, nose, and chin are distinguishable, as are the upper arms, lower arms, hands, and lower limbs. In most cases, the genitals can be identified as male or female. By the end of the fourth month of pregnancy, the fetus has grown to 6 inches in length and weighs 4 to 7 ounces. At this time, a growth spurt occurs in the body's lower parts. For the first time, the mother can feel arm and leg movements.

By the end of the fifth month, the fetus is about 12 inches long and weighs close to a pound. Structures of the skin have formed—toenails and fingernails, for example. The fetus is more active, showing a preference for a particular position in the womb. By the end of the sixth month, the fetus is about 14 inches long and has gained another half pound to a pound. The eyes and eyelids are completely formed, and a fine layer of hair covers the head. A grasping reflex is present and irregular breathing movements occur.

As early as six months of pregnancy (about 24 to 25 weeks after conception), the fetus for the first time has a chance of surviving outside of the womb—that is, it is viable. Infants who are born early, or between 24 and 37 weeks of pregnancy, usually need help breathing because their lungs are not yet fully mature. By the end of the seventh month, the fetus is about 16 inches long and now weighs about 3 pounds.

During the last two months of prenatal development, fatty tissues develop, and the functioning of various organ systems—heart and kidneys, for example—steps up. During the eighth and

fetal period Lasting about seven months, the prenatal period between two months after conception and birth in typical pregnancies.

First trimester (first 3 months)

Conception to 4 weeks
- Is less than $^1/_{10}$ inch long
- Beginning development of spinal cord, nervous system, gastrointestinal system, heart, and lungs
- Amniotic sac envelops the preliminary tissues of entire body
- Is called a "zygote"

8 weeks
- Is just over 1 inch long
- Face is forming with rudimentary eyes, ears, mouth, and tooth buds
- Arms and legs are moving
- Brain is forming
- Fetal heartbeat is detectable with ultrasound
- Is called an "embryo"

12 weeks
- Is about 3 inches long and weighs about 1 ounce
- Can move arms, legs, fingers, and toes
- Fingerprints are present
- Can smile, frown, suck, and swallow
- Sex is distinguishable
- Can urinate
- Is called a "fetus"

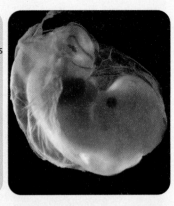

Second trimester (middle 3 months)

16 weeks
- Is about 6 inches long and weighs about 4 to 7 ounces
- Heartbeat is strong
- Skin is thin, transparent
- Downy hair (lanugo) covers body
- Fingernails and toenails are forming
- Has coordinated movements; is able to roll over in amniotic fluid

20 weeks
- Is about 12 inches long and weighs close to 1 pound
- Heartbeat is audible with ordinary stethoscope
- Sucks thumb
- Hiccups
- Hair, eyelashes, eyebrows are present

24 weeks
- Is about 14 inches long and weighs 1 to 1½ pounds
- Skin is wrinkled and covered with protective coating (vernix caseosa)
- Eyes are open
- Waste matter is collected in bowel
- Has strong grip

Third trimester (last 3 months)

28 weeks
- Is about 16 inches long and weighs about 3 pounds
- Is adding body fat
- Is very active
- Rudimentary breathing movements are present

32 weeks
- Is 16½ to 18 inches long and weighs 4 to 5 pounds
- Has periods of sleep and wakefulness
- Responds to sounds
- May assume the birth position
- Bones of head are soft and flexible
- Iron is being stored in liver

36 to 38 weeks
- Is 19 to 20 inches long and weighs 6 to 7½ pounds
- Skin is less wrinkled
- Vernix caseosa is thick
- Lanugo is mostly gone
- Is less active
- Is gaining immunities from mother

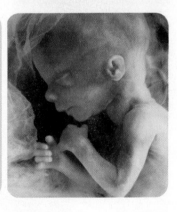

FIGURE **3.3**

THE THREE TRIMESTERS OF PRENATAL DEVELOPMENT. Both the germinal and embryonic periods occur during the first trimester. The end of the first trimester as well as the second and third trimesters are part of the fetal period.

ninth months, the fetus grows longer and gains substantial weight—about another 4 pounds. At birth, the average American baby weighs 7½ pounds and is about 20 inches long.

Figure 3.3 gives an overview of the main events during prenatal development. Notice that instead of describing development in terms of germinal, embryonic, and fetal periods, Figure 3.3 divides prenatal development into equal periods of three months, called trimesters. Remember that the three trimesters are not the same as the three prenatal periods we have discussed. The germinal and embryonic periods occur in the first trimester. The fetal period begins toward the end of the first trimester and continues through the second and third trimesters. Viability (the chances of surviving outside the womb) occurs at the very end of the second trimester.

The Brain One of the most remarkable aspects of the prenatal period is the development of the brain (Anderson & Thomason, 2013; Dubois & others, 2014). By the time babies are

developmental **connection**

Brain Development

At birth, infants' brains weigh approximately 25 percent of what they will weigh in adulthood. Chapter 4, p. 106

Yelyi Nordone, 12, of New York City, casts her line out into the pond during Camp Spifida at Camp Victory, near Millville, Pennsylvania, in July 2008. Camp Spifida is a week-long residential camp for children with spina bifida.

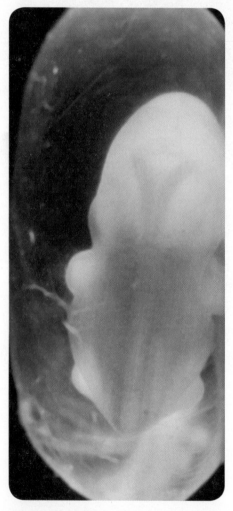

FIGURE **3.4**

EARLY FORMATION OF THE NERVOUS SYSTEM. The photograph shows the primitive, tubular appearance of the nervous system at six weeks in the human embryo.

born, they have approximately 100 billion **neurons,** or nerve cells, which handle information processing at the cellular level in the brain. During prenatal development, neurons spend time moving to the right locations and are starting to become connected. The basic architecture of the human brain is assembled during the first two trimesters of prenatal development. In typical development, the third trimester of prenatal development and the first two years of postnatal life are characterized by connectivity and functioning of neurons.

Four important phases of the brain's development during the prenatal period involve: (1) the neural tube, (2) neurogenesis, (3) neural migration, and (4) neural connectivity.

As the human embryo develops inside its mother's womb, the nervous system begins forming as a long, hollow tube located on the embryo's back. This pear-shaped neural tube, which forms at about 18 to 24 days after conception, develops out of the ectoderm. The tube closes at the top and bottom ends at about 24 days after conception. Figure 3.4 shows that the nervous system still has a tubular appearance six weeks after conception.

Two birth defects related to a failure of the neural tube to close are anencephaly and spina bifida. The highest regions of the brain fail to develop when fetuses have anencephaly or when the head end of the neural tube fails to close, and they die in the womb, during childbirth, or shortly after birth (Jin & others, 2013; Reynolds, 2014). Spina bifida results in varying degrees of paralysis of the lower limbs. Individuals with spina bifida usually need assistive devices such as crutches, braces, or wheelchairs. Both maternal diabetes and obesity place the fetus at risk for developing neural tube defects (McMahon & others, 2013). Also, one study found that maternal exposure to secondhand tobacco smoke was linked to neural tube defects (Suarez & others, 2011). Further, a recent study revealed that a high level of maternal stress during pregnancy was associated with neural tube defects in offspring (Li & others, 2013). A strategy that can help to prevent neural tube defects is for women to take adequate amounts of the B vitamin folic acid, a topic we will further discuss later in the chapter (Branum, Bailey, & Singer, 2013; Reynolds, 2014).

In a normal pregnancy, once the neural tube has closed, a massive proliferation of new immature neurons begins to takes place about the fifth prenatal week and continues throughout the remainder of the prenatal period. The generation of new neurons is called *neurogenesis* (Kronenberg & others, 2010). At the peak of neurogenesis, it is estimated that as many as 200,000 neurons are being generated every minute.

At approximately 6 to 24 weeks after conception, *neuronal migration* occurs (Nelson, 2013). This involves cells moving outward from their point of origin to their appropriate locations and creating the different levels, structures, and regions of the brain (Zeisel, 2011). Once a cell has migrated to its target destination, it must mature and develop a more complex structure.

At about the 23rd prenatal week, connections between neurons begin to occur, a process that continues postnatally (Kostovic, Judas, & Sedmak, 2011). We will have much more to say about the structure of neurons, their connectivity, and the development of the infant brain in Chapter 4.

TERATOLOGY AND HAZARDS TO PRENATAL DEVELOPMENT

For Alex, the baby discussed at the opening of this chapter, the course of prenatal development went smoothly. His mother's womb protected him as he developed. Despite this protection, the environment can affect the embryo or fetus in many well-documented ways.

General Principles A **teratogen** is any agent that can potentially cause a birth defect or negatively alter cognitive and behavioral outcomes. (The word comes from the Greek word *tera,* meaning "monster.") So many teratogens exist that practically every fetus is exposed to at least some teratogens. For this reason, it is difficult to determine which teratogen causes which problem. In addition, it may take a long time for the effects of a teratogen to show up. Only about half of all potential effects appear at birth.

The field of study that investigates the causes of birth defects is called teratology (Kancherla, Oakley, & Brent, 2014). Some exposures to teratogens do not cause physical birth

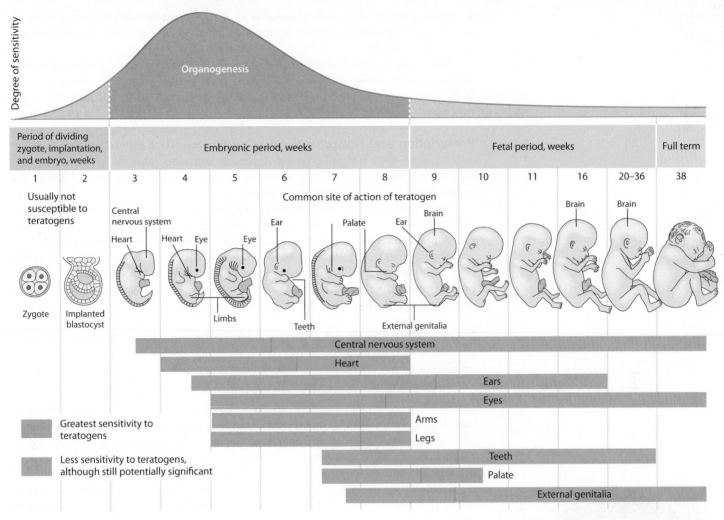

FIGURE **3.5**

TERATOGENS AND THE TIMING OF THEIR EFFECTS ON PRENATAL DEVELOPMENT.
The danger of structural defects caused by teratogens is greatest early in embryonic development. The period of organogenesis (red color) lasts for about six weeks. Later assaults by teratogens (blue-green color) mainly occur in the fetal period and instead of causing structural damage are more likely to stunt growth or cause problems of organ function.

defects but can alter the developing brain and influence cognitive and behavioral functioning, in which case the field of study is called behavioral teratology.

The dose, genetic susceptibility, and the time of exposure to a particular teratogen influence both the severity of the damage to an embryo or fetus and the type of defect:

- *Dose.* The dose effect is rather obvious—the greater the dose of an agent, such as a drug, the greater the effect.

- *Genetic susceptibility.* The type or severity of abnormalities caused by a teratogen is linked to the genotype of the pregnant woman and the genotype of the embryo or fetus (Charlet & others, 2012). For example, how a mother metabolizes a particular drug can influence the degree to which the drug effects are transmitted to the embryo or fetus. The extent to which an embryo or fetus is vulnerable to a teratogen may also depend on its genotype (de Planell-Saguer, Lovinsky-Desir, & Miller, 2014). Also, for unknown reasons, male fetuses are far more likely to be affected by teratogens than female fetuses.

- *Time of exposure.* Exposure to teratogens does more damage when it occurs at some points in development than at others (Holmes & Westgate, 2011). Damage during the germinal period may even prevent implantation. In general, the embryonic period is more vulnerable than the fetal period.

Figure 3.5 summarizes additional information about the effects of time of exposure to a teratogen. The probability of a structural defect is greatest early in the embryonic period, when organs are being formed (Holmes, 2011). Each body structure has its own critical period of formation. Recall from Chapter 1 that a critical period is a fixed time period very early in

neurons Nerve cells, which handle information processing at the cellular level in the brain.

teratogen From the Greek word *tera*, meaning "monster." Any agent that causes a birth defect. The field of study that investigates the causes of birth defects is called teratology.

development during which certain experiences or events can have a long-lasting effect on development. The critical period for the nervous system (week 3) is earlier than for arms and legs (weeks 4 and 5).

After organogenesis is complete, teratogens are less likely to cause anatomical defects. Instead, exposure during the fetal period is more likely to stunt growth or to create problems in the way organs function. To examine some key teratogens and their effects, let's begin with drugs.

Prescription and Nonprescription Drugs

Prescription and Nonprescription Drugs Many U.S. women are given prescriptions for drugs while they are pregnant—especially antibiotics, analgesics, and asthma medications. Prescription as well as nonprescription drugs, however, may have effects on the embryo or fetus that the women never imagine.

Prescription drugs that can function as teratogens include antibiotics, such as streptomycin and tetracycline; some antidepressants; certain hormones, such as progestin and synthetic estrogen; and Accutane (which often is prescribed for acne) (Koren & Nordeng, 2012).

Nonprescription drugs that can be harmful include diet pills and high dosages of aspirin (Wojtowicz & others, 2011). However, recent research indicated that low doses of aspirin pose no harm for the fetus but that high doses can contribute to maternal and fetal bleeding (Bennett, Bagot, & Arya, 2012).

Psychoactive Drugs *Psychoactive drugs* are drugs that act on the nervous system to alter states of consciousness, modify perceptions, and change moods. Examples include caffeine, alcohol, and nicotine, as well as illicit drugs such as cocaine, methamphetamine, marijuana, and heroin.

Caffeine People often consume caffeine when they drink coffee, tea, or cola, or when they eat chocolate. Somewhat mixed results have been found for the extent to which maternal caffeine intake influences an offspring's development (Jahanfar & Jaafar, 2013; Morgan, Koren, & Bozzo, 2013). However, a recent large-scale study of almost 60,000 women revealed that maternal caffeine intake was linked to lower birth weight and babies being born small for gestational age (Sengpiel & others, 2013). Also, the influence of increased consumption of energy drinks that typically have extremely high levels of caffeine on the development of offspring has not yet been studied. The U.S. Food and Drug Administration recommends that pregnant women either not consume caffeine or consume it only sparingly.

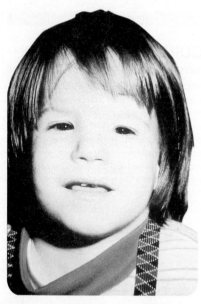

Fetal alcohol spectrum disorders (FASD) are characterized by a number of physical abnormalities and learning problems. Notice the wide-set eyes, flat cheekbones, and thin upper lip in this child with FASD.

fetal alcohol spectrum disorders (FASD) A cluster of abnormalities that appear in the offspring of mothers who drink alcohol heavily during pregnancy.

Alcohol Heavy drinking by pregnant women can be devastating to their offspring. **Fetal alcohol spectrum disorders (FASD)** are a cluster of abnormalities and problems that appear in the offspring of mothers who drink alcohol heavily during pregnancy. The abnormalities include facial deformities and defective limbs, face, and heart (Arnold & others, 2013). Most children with FASD have learning problems and many are below average in intelligence, with some having an intellectual disability (Grant & others, 2013; Harper & others, 2014). A recent study revealed that children with FASD have deficiencies in the brain pathways involved in working memory (Diwadkar & others, 2013). Although many mothers of FASD infants are heavy drinkers, many mothers who are heavy drinkers do not have children with FASD or have one child with FASD and other children who do not have it.

What are some guidelines for alcohol use during pregnancy? Even drinking just one or two servings of beer or wine or one serving of hard liquor a few days a week can have negative effects on the fetus, although it is generally agreed that this level of alcohol use will not cause fetal alcohol syndrome (Valenzuela & others, 2012). The U.S. Surgeon General recommends that no alcohol be consumed during pregnancy. However, in Great Britain, the National Institutes of Care and Health Excellence have concluded that it is safe to consume one to two drinks not more than twice a week during pregnancy (O'Keeffe, Greene, & Kearney, 2014). A recent study of more than 7,000 7-year-olds found that children born to mothers who were light drinkers during pregnancy (up to two drinks per week) did not show more developmental problems than children born to non-drinking mothers (Kelly & others, 2013). Nonetheless, some research suggests that it may not be wise to consume alcohol at the time of conception. One study revealed that intakes of alcohol by both men and women during the weeks of conception increased the risk of early pregnancy loss (Henriksen & others, 2004).

Nicotine Cigarette smoking by pregnant women can also adversely influence prenatal development, birth, and postnatal development (Wehby & others, 2011). Preterm births and low birth weights, fetal and neonatal deaths, respiratory problems, and sudden infant death syndrome (SIDS, also known as crib death) are all more common among the offspring of mothers who smoked during pregnancy (Burstyn & others, 2012; Grabenhenrich & others, 2014). Prenatal smoking has been implicated in as many as 25 percent of infants being born with a low birth weight (Brown & Graves, 2013).

Maternal smoking during pregnancy also has been identified as a risk factor for the development of attention deficit hyperactivity disorder in offspring (Abbott & Winzer-Serhan, 2012; Sagiv & others, 2012). Recent studies also indicate that environmental tobacco smoke is linked to an increased risk of low birth weight in offspring and to diminished ovarian functioning in female offspring (Kilic & others, 2012; Salama & others, 2013). And a recent study revealed that environmental tobacco smoke was associated with 114 deregulations of gene expression, especially those involving immune functioning, in the fetal cells of offspring (Votavova & others, 2012). Another recent study found that maternal exposure to environmental tobacco smoke during prenatal development increased the risk of stillbirth (Varner & others, 2014).

Cocaine Does cocaine use during pregnancy harm the developing embryo and fetus? A recent research review concluded that cocaine quickly crosses the placenta to reach the fetus (De Giovanni & Marchetti, 2012). The most consistent finding is that cocaine exposure during prenatal development is associated with reduced birth weight, length, and head circumference (Gouin & others, 2011). Also, in other studies, prenatal cocaine exposure has been linked to lower arousal, less effective self-regulation, higher excitability, and lower quality of reflexes at 1 month of age (Lester & others, 2002); to impaired motor development at 2 years of age and a slower rate of growth through 10 years of age (Richardson, Goldschmidt, & Willford, 2008); to deficits in behavioral self-regulation (Ackerman, Riggins, & Black, 2010); to elevated blood pressure at 9 years of age (Shankaran & others, 2010); to impaired language development and information processing (Beeghly & others, 2006), including attention deficits (especially impulsivity) (Accornero & others, 2006; Richardson & others, 2011); to learning disabilities at age 7 (Morrow & others, 2006); to increased likelihood of being in a special education program that involves support services (Levine & others, 2008); and to increased behavioral problems, especially externalizing problems such as high rates of aggression and delinquency (Minnes & others, 2010; Richardson & others, 2011).

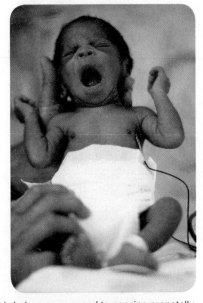

This baby was exposed to cocaine prenatally. *What are some of the possible effects on development of being exposed to cocaine prenatally?*

Some researchers argue that these findings should be interpreted cautiously (Accornero & others, 2006). Why? Because other factors in the lives of pregnant women who use cocaine (such as poverty, malnutrition, and other substance abuse) often cannot be ruled out as possible contributors to the problems found in their children (Hurt & others, 2005; Messiah & others, 2011). For example, cocaine users are more likely than nonusers to smoke cigarettes, use marijuana, drink alcohol, and take amphetamines.

Despite these cautions, the weight of research evidence indicates that children born to mothers who use cocaine are likely to have neurological, medical, and cognitive deficits (Cain, Bornick, & Whiteman, 2013; Field, 2007; Mayer & Zhang, 2009; Richardson & others, 2011). Cocaine use by pregnant women is never recommended.

Methamphetamine Methamphetamine, like cocaine, is a stimulant, speeding up an individual's nervous system. Babies born to mothers who use methamphetamine, or "meth," during pregnancy are at risk for a number of problems, including high infant mortality, low birth weight, and developmental and behavioral problems (Piper & others, 2011). One study revealed that prenatal meth exposure was associated with smaller head circumference, neonatal intensive care unit (NICU) admission, and referral to child protective services (Shah & others, 2012). Another study found that prenatal exposure to meth was linked to less brain activation in a number of areas, especially the frontal lobes, in 7- to 15-year-olds (Roussotte, 2011). And a recent study discovered that prenatal methamphetamine exposure was associated with risk for developing ADHD in 5-year-old children (Kiblawi & others, 2013).

Marijuana An increasing number of studies find that marijuana use by pregnant women also has negative outcomes for offspring. For example, researchers found that prenatal marijuana exposure was related to lower intelligence in children (Goldschmidt & others, 2008).

Another study indicated that prenatal exposure to marijuana was linked to marijuana use at 14 years of age (Day, Goldschmidt, & Thomas, 2006). And a recent study discovered that marijuana use by pregnant women was associated with stillbirth (Varner & others, 2014). In sum, marijuana use is not recommended for pregnant women.

Heroin   It is well documented that infants whose mothers are addicted to heroin show several behavioral difficulties at birth (Lindsay & Burnett, 2013). The difficulties include withdrawal symptoms, such as tremors, irritability, abnormal crying, disturbed sleep, and impaired motor control. Many still show behavioral problems at their first birthday, and attention deficits may appear later in development. The most common treatment for heroin addiction, methadone, is associated with very severe withdrawal symptoms in newborns (Blandthorn, Forster, & Love, 2011).

Incompatible Blood Types   Incompatibility between the mother's and father's blood types poses another risk to prenatal development (Matsuda & others, 2011). Blood types are created by differences in the surface structure of red blood cells. One type of difference in the surface of red blood cells creates the familiar blood groups—A, B, O, and AB. A second difference creates what is called Rh-positive and Rh-negative blood. If a surface marker, called the Rh-factor, is present in an individual's red blood cells, the person is said to be Rh-positive; if the Rh-marker is not present, the person is said to be Rh-negative. If a pregnant woman is Rh-negative and her partner is Rh-positive, the fetus may be Rh-positive. If the fetus' blood is Rh-positive and the mother's is Rh-negative, the mother's immune system may produce antibodies that will attack the fetus. This can result in any number of problems, including miscarriage or stillbirth, anemia, jaundice, heart defects, brain damage, or death soon after birth (Li & others, 2010).

Generally, the first Rh-positive baby of an Rh-negative mother is not at risk, but with each subsequent pregnancy the risk increases. A vaccine (RhoGAM) may be given to the mother within three days of the first child's birth to prevent her body from making antibodies that will attack any future Rh-positive fetuses in subsequent pregnancies. Also, babies affected by Rh incompatibility can be given blood transfusions before or right after birth (Goodnough & others, 2011).

Environmental Hazards   Many aspects of our modern industrial world can endanger the embryo or fetus. Some specific hazards to the embryo or fetus include radiation, toxic wastes, and other chemical pollutants (Lin & others, 2013).

X-ray radiation can affect the developing embryo or fetus, especially in the first several weeks after conception, when women do not yet know they are pregnant. Women and their physicians should weigh the risk of an X-ray when an actual or potential pregnancy is involved (Rajaraman & others, 2011). However, a routine diagnostic X-ray of a body area other than the abdomen, with the woman's abdomen protected by a lead apron, is generally considered safe (Brent, 2009, 2011).

Environmental pollutants and toxic wastes are also sources of danger to unborn children. Among the dangerous pollutants are carbon monoxide, mercury, and lead, as well as certain fertilizers and pesticides.

An explosion at the Chernobyl nuclear power plant in the Ukraine produced radioactive contamination that spread to surrounding areas. Thousands of infants were born with health problems and deformities as a result of the nuclear contamination, including this boy whose arm did not form. *Other than radioactive contamination, what are some other types of environmental hazards to prenatal development?*

Maternal Diseases   Maternal diseases and infections can produce defects in offspring by crossing the placental barrier, or they can cause damage during birth (Brunell, 2014). Rubella (German measles) is one disease that can cause prenatal defects. A recent study discovered that women who had measles during pregnancy had a higher risk of negative fetal and neonatal outcomes including spontaneous abortion and stillbirth (Ogbuanu & others, 2014). Women who plan to have children should have a blood test before they become pregnant to determine whether they are immune to the disease.

Syphilis (a sexually transmitted infection) is more damaging later in prenatal development—four months or more after conception. Damage to offspring includes stillbirth, eye lesions (which can cause blindness), skin lesions, and congenital syphilis (Qin & others, 2014).

Another infection that has received widespread attention is genital herpes. Newborns contract this virus when they are delivered through the birth canal of a mother with genital herpes (Sudfeld & others, 2013). About one-third of babies delivered through an infected birth canal die; another one-fourth become brain damaged. If an active case of genital herpes is detected in a pregnant woman close to her delivery date, a cesarean section can be performed (in which the infant is delivered through an incision in the mother's abdomen) to keep the virus from infecting the newborn (Pinninti & Kimberlin, 2013).

AIDS is a sexually transmitted infection that is caused by the human immunodeficiency virus (HIV), which destroys the body's immune system. A mother can infect her offspring with HIV/AIDS in three ways: (1) during gestation across the placenta, (2) during delivery through contact with maternal blood or fluids, and (3) postpartum (after birth) through breast feeding. The transmission of AIDS through breast feeding is especially a problem in many developing countries (UNICEF, 2013). Babies born to HIV-infected mothers can be (1) infected and symptomatic (show HIV symptoms), (2) infected but asymptomatic (not show HIV symptoms), or (3) not infected at all. An infant who is infected and asymptomatic may still develop HIV symptoms through 15 months of age.

The more widespread disease of diabetes, characterized by high levels of sugar in the blood, also affects offspring. A research review indicated that newborns with physical defects are more likely to have diabetic mothers (Eriksson, 2009). Women who have gestational diabetes also may deliver very large infants (weighing 10 pounds or more), and the infants are at risk for diabetes themselves (Alberico & others, 2014; Gluck & others, 2009). And a recent study found that 5- to 16-year-old Mexican American children were more likely to be obese if their mothers had gestational diabetes (women who have never had diabetes before but have high blood sugar levels during pregnancy) (Page & others, 2014).

Other Parental Factors   So far we have discussed a number of drugs, environmental hazards, maternal diseases, and incompatible blood types that can harm the embryo or fetus. Here we will explore other characteristics of the mother and father that can affect prenatal and child development, including nutrition, age, and emotional states and stress.

Maternal Diet and Nutrition   A developing embryo or fetus depends completely on its mother for nutrition, which comes from the mother's blood (Lowdermilk, Cashion, & Perry, 2014). The nutritional status of the embryo or fetus is determined by the mother's total caloric intake as well as her intake of proteins, vitamins, and minerals. Children born to malnourished mothers are more likely than other children to be malformed.

Maternal obesity adversely affects pregnancy outcomes through increased rates of hypertension, diabetes, respiratory complications, and infections in the mother (Mission, Marshall, & Caughey, 2013; Murray & McKinney, 2014). A recent study found that maternal overweight and obesity during pregnancy were associated with an increased risk of pre-term birth, especially extremely preterm delivery (Cnattingius & others, 2013). Further, research indicates that maternal obesity during pregnancy is linked to cardiovascular disease and type 2 diabetes in the adolescent and adult offspring of these mothers (Galliano & Bellver, 2013). Recent research studies have found that maternal obesity is linked to an increase in stillbirth (Gardosi & others, 2013) and increased like-lihood that the newborn will be placed in a neonatal intensive care unit (Minsart & others, 2013). Management of obesity that includes weight loss and increased exercise prior to pregnancy is likely to benefit the mother and the baby. Limiting gestational weight gain to 11 to 20 pounds among pregnant women is likely to improve outcomes for the mother and the child (Simmons, 2011).

One aspect of maternal nutrition that is important for normal prenatal development is folic acid, a B-complex vitamin (Branum & others, 2013; Kancherla, Oakley, & Brent, 2014). A study of more than 34,000 women showed that taking folic acid either alone or as part of a multivitamin for at least one year prior to conceiving was linked with a 70 percent lower risk of delivering between 20 and 28 weeks and a 50 percent lower risk of delivering between 28 and 32 weeks (Bukowski & others, 2008). One study revealed that toddlers of mothers

developmental **connection**

Conditions, Diseases, and Disorders

The greatest incidence of HIV/AIDS is in sub-Saharan Africa, where as many as 30 percent of mothers have HIV; many are unaware that they are infected with the virus. Chapter 4, p. 103

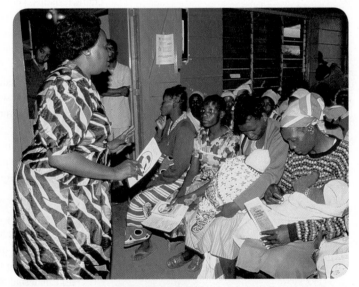

Because the fetus depends entirely on its mother for nutrition, it is important for pregnant women to have good nutritional habits. In Kenya, this government clinic provides pregnant women with information about how their diet can influence the health of their fetus and offspring. *What might the information about diet be like?*

developmental **connection**

Conditions, Diseases, and Disorders

What are some key factors that influence whether individuals will become obese? Chapter 13, p. 407

who did not use folic acid supplements in the first trimester of pregnancy had more behavior problems (Roza & others, 2010). Also, as indicated earlier in the chapter, a lack of folic acid is related to neural tube defects in offspring, such as spina bifida (a defect in the spinal cord) (Reynolds, 2014). The U.S. Department of Health and Human Services (2014) recommends that pregnant women consume a minimum of 400 micrograms of folic acid per day (about twice the amount the average woman gets in one day). Orange juice and spinach are examples of foods rich in folic acid.

Eating fish is often recommended as part of a healthy diet, but pollution has made many fish a risky choice for pregnant women. Some fish contain high levels of mercury, which is released into the air both naturally and by industrial pollution (Wells & others, 2011). When mercury falls into the water it can become toxic and accumulate in large fish, such as shark, swordfish, king mackerel, and some species of large tuna (American Pregnancy Association, 2014; Mayo Clinic, 2014). Mercury is easily transferred across the placenta, and the embryo's developing brain and nervous system are highly sensitive to the metal. Researchers have found that prenatal mercury exposure is linked to adverse outcomes, including miscarriage, preterm birth, and lower intelligence (Triche & Hossain, 2007; Xue & others, 2007).

Maternal Age When possible harmful effects on the fetus and infant are considered, two maternal ages are of special interest: (1) adolescence, and (2) 35 years and older (Rudang & others, 2012). The mortality rate of infants born to adolescent mothers is double that of infants born to mothers in their twenties. Adequate prenatal care decreases the probability that a child born to an adolescent girl will have physical problems. However, adolescents are the least likely of women in all age groups to obtain prenatal assistance from clinics and health services.

Maternal age is also linked to risk for adverse pregnancy outcomes. When the pregnant woman is older the risk that a child will have Down syndrome increases (Ghosh & others, 2010). As discussed in Chapter 2, an individual with *Down syndrome* has distinctive facial characteristics, short limbs, and retardation of motor and mental abilities. A baby with Down syndrome rarely is born to a mother 16 to 34 years of age. However, when the mother reaches 40 years of age, the probability is slightly over 1 in 100 that a baby born to her will have Down syndrome, and by age 50 it is almost 1 in 10. When mothers are 35 years and older, risks also increase for low birth weight, preterm delivery, and fetal death (Koo & others, 2012; Mbugua Gitau & others, 2009). A recent Norwegian study found that maternal age of 30 years or older was linked to the same level of increased risk for fetal deaths as 25- to 29-year-old pregnant women who were overweight/obese or were smokers (Waldenstrom & others, 2014).

We still have much to learn about the role of the mother's age in pregnancy and childbirth. As women remain active, exercise regularly, and are careful about their nutrition, their reproductive systems may remain healthier at older ages than was thought possible in the past.

Emotional States and Stress When a pregnant woman experiences intense fears, anxieties, and other emotions or negative mood states, physiological changes occur that may affect her fetus (Schuurmans & Kurrasch, 2013). A mother's stress may also influence the fetus indirectly by increasing the likelihood that the mother will engage in unhealthy behaviors, such as taking drugs and receiving poor prenatal care.

High maternal anxiety and stress during pregnancy can have long-term consequences for the offspring (Kleinhaus & others, 2013). A recent study found that high levels of depression, anxiety, and stress during pregnancy were linked to internalizing problems in adolescence (Betts & others, 2014). A research review indicated that pregnant women with high levels of stress are at increased risk for having a child with emotional or cognitive problems, attention deficit hyperactivity disorder (ADHD), and language delay (Taige & others, 2007). Also, a recent large-scale study found that a higher level of maternal stress in the period immediately prior to conception posed a risk for infant mortality (Class & others, 2013). Another study revealed that maternal stressful life events prior to conception increased the risk of having a very low birth weight infant (Witt & others, 2014).

Might maternal depression also have an adverse effect on birth outcomes? A recent research review concluded that maternal depression during pregnancy is linked to preterm birth (Mparmpakas & others, 2013). A recent study discovered that maternal depression during pregnancy was associated with low birth weight in full-term offspring (Chang & others, 2014). Another research review indicated that untreated prenatal maternal depression is associated with negative outcomes for offspring, including reduced empathy in childhood (Davalos, Yadon, & Tregellas, 2012). And a recent study revealed that maternal depression during pregnancy was related to increased risk for depression in 18-year-olds (Pearson & others, 2013).

Paternal Factors   So far, we have discussed how characteristics of the mother—such as drug use, disease, diet and nutrition, age, and emotional states—can influence prenatal development and the development of the child. Might there also be some paternal risk factors? Indeed, there are several. Men's exposure to lead, radiation, certain pesticides, and petrochemicals may cause abnormalities in sperm that lead to miscarriage or diseases, such as childhood cancer (Cordier, 2008). The father's smoking during the mother's pregnancy also can cause problems for the offspring. In one study, heavy paternal smoking was associated with the risk of early pregnancy loss (Venners & others, 2004). This negative outcome may be related to secondhand smoke. And in a recent study, paternal smoking around the time of the child's conception was linked to an increased risk of the child developing leukemia (Milne & others, 2012). Also, a recent research review concluded that there is an increased risk of spontaneous abortion, autism, and schizophrenic disorders when the father is 40 years of age or older (Reproductive Endocrinology and Infertility Committee & others, 2012). And a recent research study revealed that children born to fathers who were 40 years of age or older had increased risk of developing autism because of an increase in random gene mutations in the older fathers (Kong & others, 2012). However, the age of the offspring's mother was not linked to development of autism in the children.

In a study in China, the longer fathers smoked, the greater the risk that their children would develop cancer (Ji & others, 1997). *What are some other paternal factors that can influence the development of the fetus and the child?*

PRENATAL CARE

Although prenatal care varies enormously, it usually involves a defined schedule of visits for medical care, which typically includes screening for manageable conditions and treatable diseases that can affect the baby or the mother (Cypher & others, 2013; Novick & others, 2013). In addition to medical care, prenatal programs often include comprehensive educational, social, and nutritional services (Ickovics & others, 2011; Lowdermilk & others, 2014). A recent study revealed that group prenatal care provided pregnant women with a broad network of social support (McNeil & others, 2012).

Exercise increasingly is recommended as part of a comprehensive prenatal care program. Exercise during pregnancy helps prevent constipation, conditions the body, reduces the likelihood of excessive weight gain, and is associated with a more positive mental state, including a reduced level of depression (Bisson & others, 2013; Paul & Olson, 2013; Yan & others, 2014). Consider the positive outcomes of exercise during pregnancy found in these recent studies:

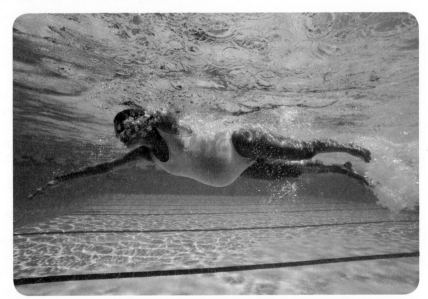

How might a woman's exercise during pregnancy benefit her and her offspring?

- Pregnant women who completed a three-month supervised aerobic exercise program showed improved health-related quality of life, including better physical functioning and reduced bodily pain, compared with their counterparts who did not participate in the program (Montoya Arizabaleta & others, 2010).

- Following 12 weeks of twice-weekly yoga or massage therapy, both therapy groups had a greater decrease in depression, anxiety, and back and leg pain than a control group (Field & others, 2012).

- A research review concluded that yoga during pregnancy was associated with a reduction in pregnancy discomforts, sleep disturbance, stress, and pain in mothers and a reduced incidence of low birth weight in offspring (Babbar & others, 2012).

- At 22 weeks gestation, prenatally depressed pregnant women were randomly assigned to participate in (1) a 20-minute group session of tai chi/yoga for 12 weeks, or (2) a wait list control group (Field & others, 2013). At the end of the treatment period, the exercise group had less depression, lower anxiety levels, less sleep disturbance, and fewer bodily complaints.

- Moderate exercise throughout pregnancy was not a risk for preterm delivery (Barakat & others, 2014; Tinloy & others, 2014).

Does prenatal care matter? Information about pregnancy, labor, delivery, and caring for the newborn can be especially valuable for first-time mothers (Yun & others, 2014). Prenatal care is also very important for women in poverty and immigrant women because it links them with other social services (Chandra-Mouli, Camacho, & Michaud, 2013).

A CenteringPregnancy program. This increasingly popular program alters routine prenatal care by bringing women out of exam rooms and into relationship-oriented groups.

An innovative program that is rapidly expanding in the United States is CenteringPregnancy (Benediktsson & others, 2013; Hale & others, 2014; Ickovics & others, 2011; McNeil & others, 2013). This program is relationship-centered and provides complete prenatal care in a group setting. CenteringPregnancy replaces traditional 15-minute physician visits with 90-minute peer group support settings and self-examination led by a physician or certified nurse-midwife. Groups of up to 10 women (and often their partners) meet regularly beginning at 12 to 16 weeks of pregnancy. The sessions emphasize empowering women to play an active role in experiencing a positive pregnancy. A recent study revealed that CenteringPregnancy group prenatal care was associated with a reduction in preterm birth (Novick & others, 2013). Another study revealed that Centering-Pregnancy groups made more prenatal visits, had higher breast feeding rates, and were more satisfied with their prenatal care than women in individual care (Klima & others, 2009). In another recent study, high-stress women were randomly assigned to a CenteringPregnancy Plus group, group prenatal care, or standard individual care from 18 weeks gestation to birth (Ickovics & others, 2011). The most stressed women in the CenteringPregnancy Plus group showed increased self-esteem and decreased stress and social conflict in their third trimester of pregnancy; their social conflict and depression also were lower at one year postpartum.

Some prenatal programs for parents focus on home visitation (Eckenrode & others, 2010; Tandon & others, 2011). A research review concluded that prenatal home visits were linked to improved use of prenatal care, although there was less evidence that they improve newborns' birth weight (Issel & others, 2011). However, a recent study found that use of home visiting services was associated with a reduced risk of low birth weight (Shah & Austin, 2014). Research evaluations indicate that the Nurse Family Partnership created by David Olds and his colleagues (2004, 2007, 2014) is successful. The Nurse Family Partnership involves home visits by trained nurses beginning in the second or third trimester of prenatal development. The extensive program consists of approximately 50 home visits from the prenatal period through two years of age. The home visits focus on the mother's health, access to health care, parenting, and improvement of the mother's life by providing her with guidance in education, work, and relationships. Research revealed that the Nurse Family Partnership has numerous positive outcomes including fewer pregnancies, better work circumstances, and stability in relationship partners for the mother, and improved academic success and social development for the child (Olds & others, 2004, 2007, 2014).

NORMAL PRENATAL DEVELOPMENT

Much of our discussion so far in this chapter has focused on what can go wrong with prenatal development. Prospective parents should take steps to avoid the vulnerabilities to fetal development that we have described. But it is important to keep in mind that most of the time, prenatal development does not go awry, and development occurs along the positive path that we described at the beginning of the chapter.

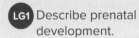
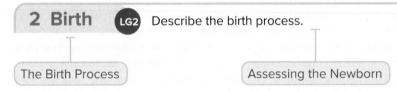

2 Birth   **LG2** Describe the birth process.

The Birth Process   Assessing the Newborn   Preterm and Low Birth Weight Infants

Nature writes the basic script for how birth occurs, but parents make important choices about conditions surrounding birth. We look first at the sequence of physical stages that occur when a child is born.

THE BIRTH PROCESS

The birth process occurs in stages, occurs in different contexts, and in most cases involves one or more attendants.

Stages of Birth   The birth process occurs in three stages. The first stage is the longest of the three. Uterine contractions are 15 to 20 minutes apart at the beginning and last up to a minute. These contractions cause the woman's cervix to stretch and open. As the first stage progresses, the contractions come closer together, appearing every two to five minutes. Their intensity increases. By the end of the first birth stage, contractions dilate the cervix to an opening of about 10 centimeters (4 inches), so that the baby can move from the uterus to the birth canal. For a woman having her first child, the first stage lasts an average of 6 to 12 hours; for subsequent children, this stage typically is much shorter.

The second birth stage begins when the baby's head starts to move through the cervix and the birth canal. It terminates when the baby completely emerges from the mother's body. With each contraction, the mother bears down hard to push the baby out of her body. By the time the baby's head is out of the mother's body, the contractions come almost every minute and last for about a minute. This stage typically lasts approximately 45 minutes to an hour.

Afterbirth is the third stage, at which time the placenta, umbilical cord, and other membranes are detached and expelled. This final stage is the shortest of the three birth stages, lasting only minutes.

Childbirth Setting and Attendants   In 2011 in the United States, 98.7 percent of births took place in hospitals (Martin & others, 2013). Of the 1.3 percent of births occurring outside of a hospital, approximately two-thirds took place in homes and almost 30 percent in

> There was a star danced, and under that I was born.

—**WILLIAM SHAKESPEARE**
English Playwright, 17th Century

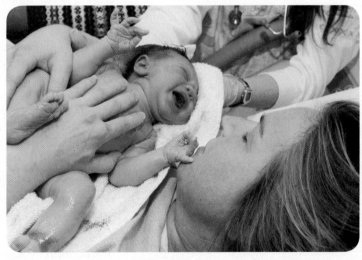

After the long journey of prenatal development, birth takes place. During birth the baby is on a threshold between two worlds. *What is the fetus/newborn transition like?*

afterbirth The third stage of birth, when the placenta, umbilical cord, and other membranes are detached and expelled.

In India, a midwife checks on the size, position, and heartbeat of a fetus. Midwives deliver babies in many countries around the world. *What are some cultural variations in prenatal care?*

free-standing birthing centers. The percentage of U.S. births at home is the highest since reporting of this context began in 1989. This increase in home births has occurred mainly among non-Latino White women, especially those who were older and married. For these non-Latino White women, two-thirds of their home births are attended by a midwife.

The people who help a mother during birth vary across cultures. In U.S. hospitals, it has become the norm for fathers or birth coaches to remain with the mother throughout labor and delivery. In the East African Nigoni culture, men are completely excluded from the childbirth process. When a woman is ready to give birth, female relatives move into the woman's hut and the husband leaves, taking his belongings (clothes, tools, weapons, and so on) with him. He is not permitted to return until after the baby is born. In some cultures, childbirth is an open, community affair. For example, in the Pukapukan culture in the Pacific Islands, women give birth in a shelter that is open for villagers to observe.

Midwives *Midwifery* is a profession that provides health care to women during pregnancy, birth, and the postpartum period (Avery, 2013; Walsh, 2013). Midwives also may give women information about reproductive health and annual gynecological examinations. They may refer women to general practitioners or obstetricians if a pregnant woman needs medical care beyond a midwife's expertise and skill.

Midwifery is practiced in most countries throughout the world (Dahlberg & Aune, 2013; Jesse & Kilpatrick, 2013). In Holland, more than 40 percent of babies are delivered by midwives rather than doctors. However, in 2010 only 8 percent of women who delivered a baby in the United States were attended by a midwife, a figure that is unchanged since 2000 (Martin & others, 2012). Nevertheless, the 8 percent figure for 2010 represents a substantial increase from less than 1 percent in 1975. A recent research review concluded that for low-risk women, midwife-led care was characterized by a reduction in procedures during labor and increased satisfaction with care (Sutcliffe & others, 2012). Also, in this study no adverse outcomes were found for midwife-led care compared with physician-led care.

Doulas In some countries, a doula attends a childbearing woman. *Doula* is a Greek word that means "a woman who helps." A **doula** is a caregiver who provides continuous physical, emotional, and educational support for the mother before, during, and after childbirth (Kang, 2014). Doulas remain with the parents throughout labor, assessing and responding to the mother's needs. Researchers have found positive effects when a doula is present at the birth of a child (Torres, 2013). A recent study found that doula-assisted mothers were four times less likely to have a low birth weight baby and two times less likely to have experienced a birth complication involving themselves or their baby (Gruber, Cupito, & Dobson, 2013). A recent study also revealed that for Medicaid recipients the odds of having a cesarean delivery were 41 percent lower for doula-supported births in the United States (Kozhimmanil & others, 2013). Thus, increasing doula-supported births could substantially lower the cost of a birth by reducing cesarean rates.

In the United States, most doulas work as independent providers hired by the expectant parents. Doulas typically function as part of a "birthing team," serving as an adjunct to the midwife or the hospital's obstetric staff.

Methods of Childbirth U.S. hospitals often allow the mother and her obstetrician a range of options regarding the method of delivery. Key choices involve the use of medication, whether to use any of a number of nonmedicated techniques to reduce pain, and when to have a cesarean delivery.

Medication Three basic kinds of drugs that are used for labor are analgesia, anesthesia, and oxytocin/pitocin.

Analgesia is used to relieve pain. Analgesics include tranquilizers, barbiturates, and narcotics (such as Demerol).

Anesthesia is used in late first-stage labor and during delivery to block sensation in an area of the body or to block consciousness. There is a trend toward not using general anesthesia, which blocks consciousness, in normal births because general anesthesia can be transmitted through the placenta to the fetus (Pennell & others, 2011). An *epidural block* is regional anesthesia that numbs the woman's body from the waist down. A recent research review concluded that epidural analgesia provides effective pain relief but at the cost of more

doula A caregiver who provides continuous physical, emotional, and educational support for the mother before, during, and after childbirth.

Linda Pugh, Perinatal Nurse

Perinatal nurses work with childbearing women to support health and growth during the childbearing experience. Linda Pugh, Ph.D., R.N.C., is a perinatal nurse on the faculty at The Johns Hopkins University School of Nursing. She is certified as an inpatient obstetric nurse and specializes in the care of women during labor and delivery. She teaches undergraduate and graduate students, educates professional nurses, and conducts research. In addition, Pugh consults with hospitals and organizations about women's health issues and topics we discuss in this chapter. Her research interests include nursing interventions with low-income breast feeding women, ways to prevent and ameliorate fatigue during childbearing, and the use of breathing exercises during labor.

likely having to use instruments during vaginal birth (Jones & others, 2012). Researchers are continuing to explore safer drug mixtures for use at lower doses to improve the effectiveness and safety of epidural anesthesia (Samhan & others, 2013).

Oxytocin is a hormone that promotes uterine contractions; a synthetic form called Pitocin™ is widely used to decrease the duration of first stage of labor. The relative benefits and risks of administering synthetic forms of oxytocin during childbirth continue to be debated (Bell, Erickson, & Carter, 2014; Buchanan & others, 2012).

Predicting how a drug will affect an individual woman and her fetus is difficult (Lowdermilk & others, 2014). A particular drug might have only a minimal effect on one fetus yet have a much stronger effect on another. The drug's dosage also is a factor (Weiner & Buhimschi, 2009). Stronger doses of tranquilizers and narcotics given to decrease the mother's pain potentially have a more negative effect on the fetus than mild doses. It is important for the mother to assess her level of pain and have a voice in deciding whether she receives medication.

Natural and Prepared Childbirth   For a brief time not long ago, the idea of avoiding all medication during childbirth gained favor in the United States. Instead, many women chose to reduce the pain of childbirth through techniques known as natural childbirth and prepared childbirth. Today, at least some medication is used in the typical childbirth, but elements of natural childbirth and prepared childbirth remain popular (Oates & Abraham, 2010).

Natural childbirth is the method that aims to reduce the mother's pain by decreasing her fear through education about childbirth and by teaching her and her partner to use breathing methods and relaxation techniques during delivery. One type of natural childbirth that is used today is the *Bradley Method,* which involves husbands as coaches, relaxation for easier birth, and prenatal nutrition and exercise.

French obstetrician Ferdinand Lamaze developed a method similar to natural childbirth that is known as **prepared childbirth,** or the Lamaze method. It includes a special breathing technique to control pushing in the final stages of labor, as well as more detailed education about anatomy and physiology. The Lamaze method has become very popular in the United States. The pregnant woman's partner usually serves as a coach who attends childbirth classes with her and helps her with her breathing and relaxation during delivery.

In sum, proponents of current natural and prepared childbirth methods conclude that when information and support are provided, women know how to give birth. To read about one nurse whose research focuses on fatigue during childbearing and breathing exercises during labor, see the *Connecting with Careers* profile. And to read about the increased variety of techniques now being used to reduce stress and control pain during labor, see *Connecting Development to Life.*

An instructor conducting a Lamaze class. *What characterizes the Lamaze method?*

natural childbirth This method attempts to reduce the mother's pain by decreasing her fear through education about childbirth and relaxation techniques during delivery.

prepared childbirth Developed by French obstetrician Ferdinand Lamaze, this childbirth strategy is similar to natural childbirth but includes a special breathing technique to control pushing in the final stages of labor and a more detailed anatomy and physiology course.

connecting development to life

From Waterbirth to Music Therapy

The effort to reduce stress and control pain during labor has recently led to an increase in the use of some older and some newer non-medicated techniques (Henderson & others, 2014; Jones & others, 2012; Kalder & others, 2011; Simkin & Bolding, 2004). These include waterbirth, massage, acupuncture, hypnosis, and music therapy.

Waterbirth

Waterbirth involves giving birth in a tub of warm water. Some women go through labor in the water and get out for delivery; others remain in the water for delivery. The rationale for waterbirth is that the baby has been in an amniotic sac for many months and that delivery in a similar environment is likely to be less stressful for the baby and the mother (Meyer, Weible, & Woeber, 2010). Mothers get into the warm water when contractions become closer together and more intense. Getting into the water too soon can cause labor to slow or stop. Reviews of research have indicated mixed results for waterbirths (Cluett & Burns, 2009; Dahlen & others, 2013; Field, 2007), but one study did find that waterbirth was linked with a shorter second stage of labor (Cortes, Basra, & Kelleher, 2011). Waterbirth has been practiced more often in European countries such as Switzerland and Sweden in recent decades than in the United States but is increasingly being included in U.S. birth plans.

Massage

Massage is increasingly used prior to and during delivery (Beckmann & Stock, 2013). Two recent research reviews concluded that massage therapy reduces pain during labor (Jones & others, 2012; Smith & others, 2012). One study revealed that massage therapy reduced pain in pregnant women and alleviated prenatal depression in both parents and improved their relationship (Field & others, 2008).

Acupuncture

Acupuncture, the insertion of very fine needles into specific locations in the body, is used as a standard procedure to reduce the pain of childbirth in China, although it only recently has begun to be used in the United States for this purpose. Recent research indicates that acupuncture can have positive effects on labor and delivery (Borup & others, 2009; Citkovitz, Schnyer, & Hoskins, 2011; Smith & others, 2012).

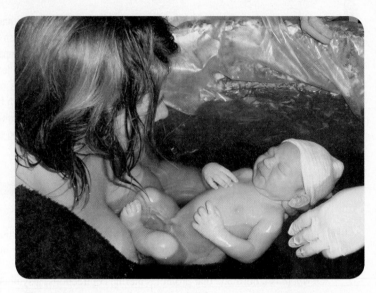

What characterizes the use of waterbirth in delivering a baby?

Hypnosis

Hypnosis, the induction of a psychological state of altered attention and awareness in which the individual is unusually responsive to suggestions, is also increasingly being used during childbirth (Werner & others, 2013). Some studies have indicated positive effects of hypnosis for reducing pain during childbirth (Abbasi & others, 2010), although a recent research review concluded that overall there is insufficient evidence to indicate that hypnosis reduces pain during labor (Smith & others, 2012).

Music Therapy

Music therapy during childbirth, which involves the use of music to reduce stress and manage pain, is becoming more common (Liu, Chang, & Chen, 2010). More research is needed to determine its effectiveness (Laopaiboon & others, 2009).

What are some reasons that natural childbirth methods such as these might be chosen instead of medication? What characterizes the use of waterbirth in delivering a baby?

---

breech position The baby's position in the uterus that causes the buttocks to be the first part to emerge from the vagina.

cesarean delivery Surgical procedure in which the baby is removed from the mother's uterus through an incision made in her abdomen.

Cesarean Delivery Normally, the baby's head comes through the vagina first. But if the baby is in a **breech position,** the baby's buttocks are the first part to emerge from the vagina. In 1 of every 25 deliveries, the baby's head is still in the uterus when the rest of the body is out. Breech births can cause respiratory problems. As a result, if the baby is in a breech position, a surgical procedure known as a cesarean section, or a cesarean delivery, is usually performed. In a **cesarean delivery,** the baby is removed from the mother's uterus through an incision made in her abdomen.

Score	0	1	2
Heart rate	Absent	Slow—less than 100 beats per minute	Fast—100–140 beats per minute
Respiratory effort	No breathing for more than one minute	Irregular and slow	Good breathing with normal crying
Muscle tone	Limp and flaccid	Weak, inactive, but some flexion of extremities	Strong, active motion
Body color	Blue and pale	Body pink, but extremities blue	Entire body pink
Reflex irritability	No response	Grimace	Coughing, sneezing and crying

FIGURE **3.6**

THE APGAR SCALE. A newborn's score on the Apgar Scale indicates whether the baby has urgent medical problems. *What are some trends in the Apgar scores of U.S. babies?*

The benefits and risks of cesarean deliveries continue to be debated (Furukawa, Sameshima, & Ikenoue, 2014; O'Neill & others, 2013). Some critics believe that too many babies are delivered by cesarean section in the United States and around the world (Gibbons & others, 2012). More cesarean deliveries are performed in the United States than in any other country in the world. In 2011, 32.8 percent of babies born in the United States were cesarean deliveries, unchanged from 2010 (Martin & others, 2013).

ASSESSING THE NEWBORN

Almost immediately after birth, after the baby and its parents have been introduced, a newborn is taken to be weighed, cleaned up, and tested for signs of developmental problems that might require urgent attention. The **Apgar Scale** is widely used to assess the health of newborns at one and five minutes after birth. The Apgar Scale evaluates an infant's heart rate, respiratory effort, muscle tone, body color, and reflex irritability. An obstetrician or a nurse does the evaluation and gives the newborn a score, or reading, of 0, 1, or 2 on each of these five health signs (see Figure 3.6). A total score of 7 to 10 indicates that the newborn's condition is good. A score of 5 indicates there may be developmental difficulties. A score of 3 or below signals an emergency and indicates that the baby might not survive.

The Apgar Scale is especially good at assessing the newborn's ability to cope with the stress of delivery and the demands of a new environment (Miyakoshi & others, 2013). It also identifies high-risk infants who need resuscitation. A recent study revealed that compared with children who have a high Apgar score (9 to 10), the risk of developing attention deficit hyperactivity disorder (ADHD) in childhood was 75 percent higher for newborns with a low Apgar score (1 to 4) and 63 percent higher for newborns with an Apgar score of 5 to 6 (Li, Olsen, & others, 2011). For a more thorough assessment of the newborn, the Brazelton Neonatal Behavioral Assessment Scale or the Neonatal Intensive Care Unit Network Neurobehavioral Scale may be used.

The **Brazelton Neonatal Behavioral Assessment Scale (NBAS)** is typically performed within 24 to 36 hours after birth. It is also used as a sensitive index of neurological competence up to one month after birth for typical infants and as a measure in many studies of infant development (Jones, 2012). The NBAS assesses the newborn's neurological development, reflexes, and reactions to people and objects. Sixteen reflexes, such as sneezing, blinking, and rooting, are assessed, along with reactions to animate (such as a face and voice) and inanimate stimuli (such as a rattle). (We will have more to say about reflexes in Chapter 4, when we discuss motor development in infancy.)

The NBAS is designed to assess normal, healthy, full-term infants. An "offspring" of the NBAS, the **Neonatal Intensive Care Unit Network Neurobehavioral Scale (NNNS)** provides another assessment of the newborn's behavior, neurological and stress responses, and regulatory capacities (Brazelton, 2004; Lester & others, 2011). T. Berry Brazelton, along with Barry Lester and Edward Tronick, developed the NNNS specifically to assess the "at-risk" infant. It is especially useful for evaluating preterm infants (although it may not be appropriate for those less than 30 weeks' gestational age) and substance-exposed infants (Montirosso & others, 2012).

Apgar Scale A widely used method of assessing the health of newborns at one and five minutes after birth. The Apgar Scale evaluates an infant's heart rate, respiratory effort, muscle tone, body color, and reflex irritability.

Brazelton Neonatal Behavioral Assessment Scale (NBAS) A measure that is used in the first month of life to assess the newborn's neurological development, reflexes, and reactions to people and objects.

Neonatal Intensive Care Unit Neurobehavioral Scale (NNNS) An "offspring" of the NBAS, the NNNS provides an assessment of the newborn's behavior, neurological and stress responses, and regulatory capacities.

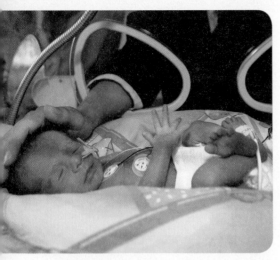

A "kilogram kid," weighing less than 2.3 pounds at birth. *What are some long-term outcomes for weighing so little at birth?*

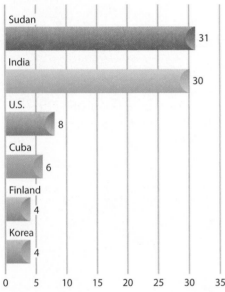

FIGURE **3.7**

PERCENTAGE OF INFANTS BORN WITH LOW BIRTH WEIGHT IN SELECTED COUNTRIES

low birth weight infants An infant that weighs less than 5½ pounds at birth.

preterm infants Those born before the completion of 37 weeks of gestation (the time between fertilization and birth).

small for date infants Also called small for gestational age infants, these infants' birth weights are below normal when the length of pregnancy is considered. Small for date infants may be preterm or full term.

kangaroo care Treatment for preterm infants that involves skin-to-skin contact.

PRETERM AND LOW BIRTH WEIGHT INFANTS

Different conditions that pose threats for newborns have been given different labels. We will examine these conditions and discuss interventions for improving outcomes of preterm infants.

Preterm and Small for Date Infants   Three related conditions pose threats to many newborns: low birth weight, being born preterm, and being small for date. **Low birth weight infants** weigh less than 5½ pounds at birth. *Very low birth weight* newborns weigh under 3½ pounds, and *extremely low birth weight* newborns weigh under 2 pounds. **Preterm infants** are those born three weeks or more before the pregnancy has reached its full term—in other words, before the completion of 37 weeks of gestation (the time between fertilization and birth). **Small for date infants** (also called *small for gestational age infants*) are those whose birth weight is below normal when the length of the pregnancy is considered. They weigh less than 90 percent of all babies of the same gestational age. Small for date infants may be preterm or full term. One study found that small for date infants had more than a fourfold increased risk of death (Regev & others, 2003).

In 2011, 11.7 percent of U.S. infants were born preterm—a 34 percent increase since the 1980s and a decrease of 1.1 percent since 2008 (Lynch, Dezen, & Brown, 2012). The increase in preterm birth since the 1980s is likely due to such factors as the increasing number of births to women 35 years and older, increasing rates of multiple births, increased management of maternal and fetal conditions (for example, inducing labor preterm if medical technology indicates it will increase the likelihood of survival), increased rates of substance abuse (tobacco, alcohol), and increased stress (Goldenberg & Culhane, 2007). Ethnic variations characterize preterm birth (Lhila & Long, 2011). For example, in 2011, the likelihood of being born preterm was 11.7 percent for all U.S. infants and 10.5 percent for non-Latino White infants, but the rate was 16.7 percent for African American infants and 11.6 for Latino infants (Martin & others, 2013).

Recently, considerable attention has been directed to the role that progestin might play in reducing preterm births (Hines, Lyseng-Williamson, & Deeks, 2013). Recent research reviews indicate that progestin is most effective in reducing preterm births when it is administered to women with a history of a previous spontaneous birth at less than 37 weeks (da Fonseca & others, 2009), to women who have a short cervical length of 15 millimeters or less (da Fonseca & others, 2009), and to women who are carrying a singleton rather than multiple offspring (Lucovnik & others, 2011). A recent study discovered that progestin treatment was associated with a decrease in preterm birth for women with a history of one or more spontaneous births (Markham & others, 2014).

Might exercise during pregnancy reduce the likelihood of preterm birth? One study found that compared with sedentary pregnant women, women who engaged in light leisure time physical activity had a 24 percent reduced likelihood of preterm delivery and those who participated in moderate to heavy leisure time physical activity had a 66 percent reduced risk of preterm delivery (Hegaard & others, 2008). As indicated earlier in the chapter, a recent study revealed that exercise during pregnancy did not increase the risk of late preterm birth or hospitalization during pregnancy (Tinloy & others, 2014).

The incidence of low birth weight varies considerably from country to country. In some countries, such as India and Sudan, where poverty is rampant and the health and nutrition of mothers are poor, the percentage of low birth weight babies reaches as high as 31 percent (see Figure 3.7). In the United States, there has been an increase in low birth weight infants in the last two decades, and the U.S. low birth weight rate of 8.1 percent in 2011 is considerably higher than that of many other developed countries (Martin & others, 2013). For example, only 4 percent of the infants born in Sweden, Finland, Norway, and Korea are low birth weight, and only 5 percent of those born in New Zealand, Australia, and France are low birth weight.

In both developed and developing countries, adolescents who give birth when their bodies have not fully matured are at risk for having low birth weight babies (Shuaib & others, 2011). In the United States, the increase in the number of low birth weight infants is due to factors such as the use of drugs, poor nutrition, multiple births, reproductive technologies, and improved technology and prenatal care that result in more high-risk babies surviving

(National Center for Health Statistics, 2012). Nonetheless, poverty still is a major factor in preterm births in the United States. Women living in poverty are more likely to be obese, have diabetes and hypertension, and to smoke cigarettes and use illicit drugs, and less likely to receive regular prenatal care (Timmermans & others, 2011).

Consequences of Preterm Birth and Low Birth Weight Although most preterm and low birth weight infants are healthy, as a group they have more health and developmental problems than normal birth weight infants (Bassil & others, 2014; Webb & others, 2014). For preterm birth, the terms *extremely preterm* and *very preterm* are increasingly used (Takayanagi & others, 2013). *Extremely preterm infants* are those born at less than 28 weeks gestation, and *very preterm infants* are those born at less than 33 weeks of gestational age. Figure 3.8 shows the results of a Norwegian study indicating that the earlier preterm infants are born, the more likely they are to drop out of school (Swamy, Ostbye, & Skjaerven, 2008).

The number and severity of these problems increase when infants are born very early and as their birth weight decreases (Castrodale & Rinehart, 2014). Survival rates for infants who are born very early and very small have risen, but with this improved survival rate have come increased rates of severe brain damage (McNicholas & others, 2014).

A recent study revealed that very preterm, low birth weight infants had abnormal axon development in their brains and impaired cognitive development at 9 years of age (Iwata & others, 2012). Children born low in birth weight are more likely than their normal birth weight counterparts to develop a learning disability, attention deficit hyperactivity disorder, autism spectrum disorders, or breathing problems such as asthma (Anderson & others, 2011; Maramara, He, & Ming, 2014). Approximately 50 percent of all low birth weight children are enrolled in special education programs.

Nurturing Low Birth Weight and Preterm Infants Two increasingly used interventions in the neonatal intensive care unit (NICU) are kangaroo care and massage therapy. **Kangaroo care** involves skin-to-skin contact in which the baby, wearing only a diaper, is held upright against the parent's bare chest, much as a baby kangaroo is carried by its mother (Ludington-Hoe & others, 2006). Kangaroo care is typically practiced for two to three hours per day, skin-to-skin over an extended time in early infancy (Ahmed & others, 2011).

Why use kangaroo care with preterm infants? Preterm infants often have difficulty coordinating their breathing and heart rate, and the close physical contact with the parent provided by kangaroo care can help to stabilize the preterm infant's heartbeat, temperature, and breathing (Cong, Ludington-Hoe, & Walsh, 2011; Mitchell & others, 2013). Preterm infants who experience kangaroo care gain more weight than their counterparts who are not given this care (Gathwala, Singh, & Singh, 2010). Also, a recent study discovered that preterm infants who experienced kangaroo care for 16 weeks had more complex electroencephalogram (EEG) patterns, which reflects neurological maturation, at 40 weeks of age postpartum than preterm infants who did not receive kangaroo care (Kaffashi & others, 2013). And a research review concluded that kangaroo care decreased the risk of mortality in low birth weight infants (Conde-Aguedelo, Belizan, & Diaz-Rossello, 2011). Further, a recent study demonstrated the positive long-term benefits of kangaroo care (Feldman, Rosenthal, & Eidelman, 2014). In this study, maternal-newborn kangaroo care with preterm infants was linked to better respiratory and cardiovascular functioning, sleep patterns, and cognitive functioning from 6 months to 10 years of age.

A recent U.S. survey found that mothers were much more likely to have a positive view of kangaroo care and to believe it should be provided daily than were neonatal intensive care nurses (Hendricks-Munoz & others, 2013). There is concern that kangaroo care is not used more in neonatal intensive care units (Davanzo & others, 2013; Stikes & Barbier, 2013). Increasingly, kangaroo care is recommended as standard practice for all newborns (Rodgers, 2013).

Many adults will attest to the therapeutic effects of receiving a massage. In fact, many will pay a premium to receive one at a spa on a regular basis. But can massage play a role in improving the developmental outcomes for preterm infants? To find out, see *Connecting Through Research.*

developmental **connection**

Environment

Poverty continues to negatively affect development throughout childhood. Chapter 8, p. 256; Chapter 10, p. 329

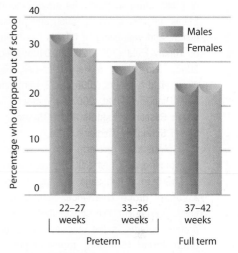

FIGURE **3.8**

PERCENTAGE OF PRETERM AND FULL-TERM BIRTH INFANTS WHO DROPPED OUT OF SCHOOL

A new mother practicing kangaroo care. *What is kangaroo care?*

developmental **connection**

Attachment

A classic study with surrogate cloth and wire monkeys demonstrated the important role that touch plays in infant attachment. Chapter 6, p. 180

How Does Massage Therapy Affect the Mood and Behavior of Babies?

Throughout history and in many cultures, caregivers have massaged infants. In Africa and Asia, infants are routinely massaged by parents or other family members for several months after birth. In the United States, interest in using touch and massage to improve the growth, health, and well-being of infants has been stimulated by the research of Tiffany Field (2001, 2007, 2010b; Diego, Field, & Hernandez-Reif, 2008; Field, Diego, & Hernandez-Reif, 2008, 2010; Field & others, 2006, 2012; Hernandez-Reif, Diego, & Field, 2007), director of the Touch Research Institute at the University of Miami School of Medicine.

In one study, preterm infants in a neonatal intensive care unit (NICU) were randomly assigned to a massage therapy group or a control group (Hernandez-Reif, Diego, & Field, 2007). For five consecutive days, the preterm infants in the massage group were given three 15-minute moderate-pressure massages. Behavioral observations of the following stress behaviors were made on the first and last days of the study: crying, grimacing, yawning, sneezing, jerky arm and leg movements, startles, and finger flaring. The various stress behaviors were summarized in a composite stress behavior index. As indicated in Figure 3.9, massage had a stress-reducing effect on the preterm infants, which is especially important because they encounter numerous stressors while they are hospitalized.

In another study, Field and her colleagues (Field, Hernandez-Reif, Diego, & others, 2004) tested a more cost-effective massage strategy. They taught mothers how to massage their full-term infants rather than having health care professionals do the massage. Beginning from day one of the newborn's life to the end of the first month, once a day before bedtime the mothers massaged the babies using either light or moderate pressure. Infants who were massaged with moderate pressure gained more weight, performed better on the orientation scale of the Brazelton, were less excitable and less depressed, and were less agitated during sleep.

Field has demonstrated the benefits of massage therapy for infants who face a variety of problems. For example, preterm infants exposed to cocaine in utero who received massage therapy gained weight and improved their scores on developmental tests (Wheeden & others, 1993). Another study investigated 1- to 3-month-old infants born to depressed adolescent mothers (Field & others, 1996). The infants of depressed mothers who received massage therapy had lower stress—as well as improved emotionality, sociability, and soothability—compared with the nonmassaged infants of depressed mothers.

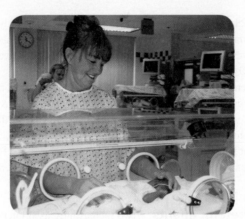

Shown here is Tiffany Field massaging a newborn infant. *What types of infants has massage therapy been shown to help?*

In a research review of massage therapy with preterm infants, Field and her colleagues (Field, Hernandez-Reif, & Freedman, 2004) concluded that the most consistent findings involve two positive results: (1) increased weight gain and (2) discharge from the hospital from three to six days earlier. A study revealed that the mechanisms responsible for increased weight gain as a result of massage therapy were stimulation of the vagus nerve (one of 12 cranial nerves leading to the brain) and in turn the release of insulin (a food absorption hormone) (Field, Diego, & Hernandez-Reif, 2010).

Infants are not the only ones who may benefit from massage therapy (Field, 2007). In other studies, Field and her colleagues have demonstrated the benefits of massage therapy with women in reducing labor pain (Field, Hernandez-Reif, Taylor, & others, 1997), with children who have asthma (Field, Henteleff, & others, 1998), with autistic children's attentiveness (Field, Lasko, & others, 1997), and with adolescents who have attention deficit hyperactivity disorder (Field, Quintino, & others, 1998).

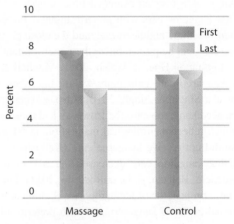

FIGURE **3.9**

PRETERM INFANTS SHOW REDUCED STRESS BEHAVIORS AND ACTIVITY AFTER FIVE DAYS OF MASSAGE THERAPY
Source: M. Hernandez-Reif, M. Diego, & T. Field (2007). Preterm infants show reduced stress behaviors and activity after 5 days of massage therapy. *Infant Behavior and Development, 30,* 557–561.

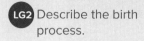

Review *Connect* Reflect

 Describe the birth process.

Review

- What are the three main stages of birth? What are some different birth strategies? What is the transition from fetus to newborn like for the infant?
- What are three measures of neonatal health and responsiveness?
- What are the outcomes for children if they are born preterm or with a low birth weight?

Connect

- What correlations have been found between birth weight and country of birth, and what might the causes be?

Reflect *Your Own Personal Journey of Life*

- If you are a female, which birth strategy do you prefer? Why? If you are a male, how involved would you want to be in helping your partner during the birth of your baby? Explain.

3 The Postpartum Period

LG3 Explain the changes that take place in the postpartum period.

Physical Adjustments | Emotional and Psychological Adjustments | Bonding

The weeks after childbirth present challenges for many new parents and their offspring. This is the **postpartum period,** the period after childbirth or delivery that lasts for about six weeks or until the mother's body has completed its adjustment and has returned to a nearly prepregnant state. It is a time when the woman adjusts, both physically and psychologically, to the process of childbearing.

The postpartum period involves a great deal of adjustment and adaptation (Haran & others, 2014). The adjustments needed are physical, emotional, and psychological.

PHYSICAL ADJUSTMENTS

A woman's body makes numerous physical adjustments in the first days and weeks after childbirth (Durham & Chapman, 2014). She may have a great deal of energy or feel exhausted and let down. Though these changes are normal, the fatigue can undermine the new mother's sense of well-being and confidence in her ability to cope with a new baby and a new family life.

A concern is the loss of sleep that the primary caregiver experiences in the postpartum period (Insana, Williams, & Montgomery-Downs, 2013; Ko & others, 2014). In the 2007 Sleep in America survey, a substantial percentage of women reported loss of sleep during pregnancy and in the postpartum period (National Sleep Foundation, 2007) (see Figure 3.10). The loss of sleep can contribute to stress, marital conflict, and impaired decision making (Meerlo, Sgoifo, & Suchecki, 2008). A recent study, though, found that it was poor-quality sleep (such as disrupted, fragmented sleep) rather than lesser amounts of sleep that were linked to postpartum depression (Park, Meltzer-Brody, & Stickgold, 2013).

After delivery, a mother's body undergoes sudden and dramatic changes in hormone production. When the placenta is delivered, estrogen and progesterone levels drop steeply and remain low until the ovaries start producing hormones again.

EMOTIONAL AND PSYCHOLOGICAL ADJUSTMENTS

Emotional fluctuations are common for mothers in the postpartum period. For some women, emotional fluctuations decrease within several weeks after the delivery, but other women experience more long-lasting emotional swings.

As shown in Figure 3.11, about 70 percent of new mothers in the United States have what are called the postpartum blues. About two to three days after birth, they begin to feel depressed, anxious, and upset. These feelings may come and go for several months after the

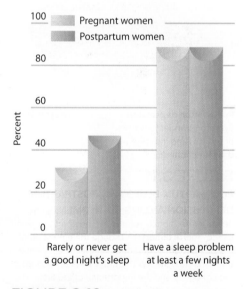

FIGURE 3.10

SLEEP DEPRIVATION IN PREGNANT AND POSTPARTUM WOMEN

postpartum period The period after childbirth when the mother adjusts, both physically and psychologically, to the process of childbirth. This period lasts for about six weeks or until her body has completed its adjustment and returned to a near prepregnant state.

Diane Sanford, Clinical Psychologist and Postpartum Expert

Diane Sanford has a doctorate in clinical psychology, and for many years she had a private practice that focused on marital and family relationships. But after she began collaborating with a psychiatrist whose clients included women with postpartum depression, Dr. Sanford, along with a women's health nurse, founded Women's Healthcare Partnership in St. Louis, Missouri, which specialized in women's adjustment during the postpartum period. Sanford (with Ann Dunnewold) authored *Life Will Never Be the Same: The Real Mom's Postpartum Survival Guide*. She also is a medical expert for BabyCenter.com.

Diane Sanford is a leading expert on postpartum depression.

For more information about what clinical psychologists do, see page 42 in the Careers in Life-Span Development appendix.

Postpartum blues
Symptoms appear 2 to 3 days after delivery and usually subside within 1 to 2 weeks.

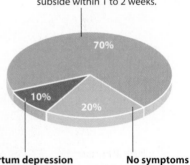

Postpartum depression
Symptoms linger for weeks or months and interfere with daily functioning.

No symptoms

FIGURE **3.11**

POSTPARTUM BLUES AND POSTPARTUM DEPRESSION AMONG U.S. WOMEN. Some health professionals refer to the postpartum period as the "fourth trimester." Though the time span of the postpartum period does not necessarily cover three months, the term "fourth trimester" suggests the continuity and the importance of the first several months after birth for the mother and baby.

postpartum depression Characteristic of women who have such strong feelings of sadness, anxiety, or despair that they have trouble coping with daily tasks in the postpartum period.

bonding The formation of a close connection, especially a physical bond, between parents and their newborn in the period shortly after birth.

birth, often peaking about three to five days after birth. Even without treatment, these feelings usually go away after one or two weeks.

However, some women develop **postpartum depression,** which involves a major depressive episode that typically occurs about four weeks after delivery. Women with postpartum depression have such strong feelings of sadness, anxiety, or despair that for at least a two-week period they have trouble coping with their daily tasks. Without treatment, postpartum depression may become worse and last for many months (Di Florio & others, 2014; O'Hara & McCabe, 2013). And many women with postpartum depression don't seek help. For example, one study found that 15 percent of the women surveyed had postpartum depression symptoms but less than half had sought help (McGarry & others, 2009). Estimates indicate that 10 to 14 percent of new mothers experience postpartum depression.

A recent research review concluded that the following are risk factors for developing postpartum depression: a history of depression, depression and anxiety during pregnancy, neuroticism, low self-esteem, postpartum blues, poor marital relationship, and a low level of social support (O'Hara & McCabe, 2013). Also, in this research review, a number of perinatal-related stressors such as perinatal complications, infant health and temperament, and type of delivery (cesarean section, for example) were found to be potential risk factors for postpartum depression. A subset of women are likely to develop postpartum depression in the context of hormonal changes associated with late pregnancy and childbirth (O'Hara & McCabe, 2013). Also, a recent study found that depression during pregnancy, a history of physical abuse, migrant status, and postpartum physical complications were major risk factors for postpartum depression (Gaillard & others, 2014).

Several antidepressant drugs are effective in treating postpartum depression and appear to be safe for breast feeding women (Logsdon, Wisner, & Hanusa, 2009). Psychotherapy, especially cognitive therapy, is effective in easing postpartum depression for many women (Bevan, Wittkowski, & Wells, 2013; O'Hara & McCabe, 2013). Also, engaging in regular exercise may help in treating postpartum depression (Ko & others, 2013).

Can a mother's postpartum depression affect the way she interacts with her infant? A recent research review concluded that the interaction difficulties of depressed mothers and their infants occur across cultures and socioeconomic status groups, and encompass less sensitivity of the mothers and less responsiveness on the part of their infants (Field, 2010a). Several caregiving activities also are compromised, including feeding (especially breast feeding), sleep routines, and safety practices. To read about one individual who specializes in women's adjustment during the postpartum period, see *Connecting with Careers*.

Fathers also undergo considerable adjustment in the postpartum period, even when they work away from home all day (Gawlick & others, 2014). When the mother develops postpartum depression, many fathers also experience feelings of depression (Roubinov & others, 2014; Serhan & others, 2013). Many fathers feel that the baby comes first and gets all of the mother's attention; some feel that they have been replaced by the baby.

The father's support and caring can play a role in whether the mother develops postpartum depression (Redshaw & Henderson, 2013). One study revealed that higher support by fathers was related to a lower incidence of postpartum depression in women (Smith & Howard, 2008).

BONDING

A special component of the parent-infant relationship is **bonding,** the formation of a connection, especially a physical bond between parents and the newborn in the period shortly after birth. Sometimes hospitals seem determined to deter bonding. Drugs given to the mother to make her delivery less painful can make the mother drowsy, interfering with her ability to respond to and stimulate the newborn. Mothers and newborns are often separated shortly after delivery, and preterm infants are isolated from their mothers even more than full-term infants.

Do these practices do any harm? Some physicians believe that during the period shortly after birth, the parents and newborn need to form an emotional attachment as a foundation for optimal development in years to come (Kennell, 2006; Kennell & McGrath, 1999). Is there evidence that close contact between mothers and babies in the first several days after birth is critical for optimal development later in life? Although some research supports this bonding hypothesis (Klaus & Kennell, 1976), a body of research challenges the significance of the first few days of life as a critical period (Bakeman & Brown, 1980; Rode & others, 1981). Indeed, the extreme form of the bonding hypothesis—that the newborn must have close contact with the mother in the first few days of life to develop optimally—simply is not true.

Nonetheless, the weakness of the bonding hypothesis should not be used as an excuse to keep motivated mothers from interacting with their newborns. Such contact brings pleasure to many mothers. In some mother-infant pairs—including preterm infants, adolescent mothers, and mothers from disadvantaged circumstances—early close contact may establish a climate for improved interaction after the mother and infant leave the hospital.

Many hospitals now offer a *rooming-in* arrangement, in which the baby remains in the mother's room most of the time during its hospital stay. However, if parents choose not to use this rooming-in arrangement, the weight of the research suggests that this decision will not harm the infant emotionally (Lamb, 1994).

The postpartum period is a time of considerable adjustment and adaptation for both the mother and the father. Fathers can provide an important support system for mothers, especially in helping mothers care for young infants. *What kinds of tasks might the father of a newborn do to support the mother?*

developmental **connection**

Attachment

Konrad Lorenz demonstrated the importance of early bonding in greylag geese, but the first few days of life are unlikely to be a critical period for bonding in human infants. Chapter 1, p. 25

Review Connect Reflect

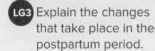 Explain the changes that take place in the postpartum period.

Review

- What does the postpartum period involve? What physical adjustments does the woman's body make during this period?
- What emotional and psychological adjustments characterize the postpartum period?
- Is bonding critical for optimal development?

Connect

- Compare and contrast what you learned about kangaroo care and breast feeding of preterm infants to what you learned about bonding and breast feeding when the mother is suffering from postpartum depression.

Reflect Your Own Personal Journey of Life

- If you are a female, what can you do to adjust effectively in the postpartum period? If you are a male, what can you do to help your partner during the postpartum period?

This chapter marks the beginning of our chronological look at the journey of life. In the next three chapters that comprise Section 3 of the book, we will follow the physical, cognitive, and socioemotional development of infants, including the theories, research, and milestones associated with the first 18 to 24 months of life. You will learn about the remarkable and complex physical development of infants' motor skills, such as learning to walk; trace the early development of infants' cognitive skills, such as the ability to form concepts; and explore infants' surprisingly sophisticated socioemotional capabilities, as reflected in the development of their motivation to share and to perceive others' actions as intentionally motivated.

reach your **learning goals**

Prenatal Development and Birth

1 Prenatal Development

LG1 Describe prenatal development.

The Course of Prenatal Development

- Prenatal development is divided into three periods: germinal (conception until 10 to 14 days later), which ends when the zygote (a fertilized egg) attaches to the uterine wall; embryonic (two to eight weeks after conception), during which the embryo differentiates into three layers, life-support systems develop, and organ systems form (organogenesis); and fetal (from two months after conception until about nine months, or when the infant is born), a time when organ systems have matured to the point at which life can be sustained outside the womb. The growth of the brain during prenatal development is nothing short of remarkable. By the time babies are born, they have approximately 100 billion neurons, or nerve cells. Neurogenesis is the term for the formation of new neurons. The nervous system begins with the formation of a neural tube at 18 to 24 days after conception. Proliferation and migration are two processes that characterize brain development in the prenatal period. The basic architecture of the brain is formed in the first two trimesters of prenatal development.

Teratology and Hazards to Prenatal Development

- Teratology is the field that investigates the causes of congenital (birth) defects. Any agent that causes birth defects is called a teratogen. The dose, genetic susceptibility, and time of exposure influence the severity of the damage to an unborn child and the type of defect that occurs. Prescription drugs that can be harmful include antibiotics. Nonprescription drugs that can be harmful include diet pills, aspirin, and caffeine. Legal psychoactive drugs that are potentially harmful to prenatal development include alcohol and nicotine. Fetal alcohol spectrum disorders are a cluster of abnormalities that appear in offspring of mothers who drink heavily during pregnancy. Even when pregnant women drink moderately (one to two drinks a few days a week), negative effects on their offspring have been found. Cigarette smoking by pregnant women has serious adverse effects on prenatal and child development, including low birth weight. Illegal psychoactive drugs that are potentially harmful to offspring include methamphetamine, marijuana, cocaine, and heroin. Incompatibility of the mother's and the father's blood types can also be harmful to the fetus. Environmental hazards include radiation, environmental pollutants, and toxic wastes. Syphilis, rubella (German measles), genital herpes, and AIDS are infectious diseases that can harm the fetus. Other parental factors include maternal diet and nutrition, age, emotional states and stress, and paternal factors. A developing fetus depends entirely on its mother for nutrition. Maternal age can negatively affect the offspring's development if the mother is an adolescent or over 35. High stress in the mother is linked with less than optimal prenatal and birth outcomes. Paternal factors that can adversely affect prenatal development include exposure to lead, radiation, certain pesticides, and petrochemicals, as well as smoking.

Prenatal Care

- Prenatal care varies extensively but usually involves health maintenance services with a defined schedule of visits.

Normal Prenatal Development

- It is important to remember that, although things can and do go wrong during pregnancy, most of the time pregnancy and prenatal development go well.

2 Birth

 Describe the birth process.

The Birth Process

- Childbirth occurs in three stages. The first stage, which lasts about 6 to 12 hours for a woman having her first child, is the longest stage. The cervix dilates to about 10 centimeters (4 inches) by the end of the first stage. The second stage begins when the baby's head starts to move through the cervix and ends with the baby's complete emergence. The third stage involves the delivery of the placenta after birth. Childbirth strategies involve the childbirth setting and attendants. In many countries, a doula attends a childbearing woman. Methods of delivery include medicated, natural or prepared, and cesarean.

Assessing the Newborn

- For many years, the Apgar Scale has been used to assess the newborn's health. The Brazelton Neonatal Behavioral Assessment Scale examines the newborn's neurological development, reflexes, and reactions to people. Recently, the Neonatal Intensive Care Unit Network Neurobehavioral Scale (NNNS) was created to assess at-risk infants.

Preterm and Low Birth Weight Infants

- Low birth weight infants weigh less than 5½ pounds, and they may be preterm (born before the completion of 37 weeks of gestation) or small for date (also called small for gestational age, which refers to infants whose birth weight is below normal when the length of pregnancy is considered). Small for date infants may be preterm or full term. Although most low birth weight and preterm infants are normal and healthy, as a group they have more health and developmental problems than normal birth weight infants. Kangaroo care and massage therapy have been shown to have benefits for preterm infants.

3 The Postpartum Period

Explain the changes that take place in the postpartum period.

Physical Adjustments

- The postpartum period is the name given to the period after childbirth or delivery. The period lasts for about six weeks or until the woman's body has completed its adjustment. Physical adjustments in the postpartum period include fatigue, involution (the process by which the uterus returns to its prepregnant size five or six weeks after birth), and hormonal changes.

Emotional and Psychological Adjustments

- Emotional fluctuations on the part of the mother are common in this period, and they can vary a great deal from one mother to the next. Postpartum depression characterizes women who have such strong feelings of sadness, anxiety, or despair that they have trouble coping with daily tasks in the postpartum period. Postpartum depression occurs in about 10 percent of new mothers. The father also goes through a postpartum adjustment.

Bonding

- Bonding is the formation of a close connection, especially a physical bond between parents and the newborn shortly after birth. Early bonding has not been found to be critical in the development of a competent infant.

key **terms**

germinal period 74
blastocyst 74
trophoblast 74
embryonic period 74
amnion 75
umbilical cord 75
placenta 75
organogenesis 75
fetal period 76

neurons 79
teratogen 79
fetal alcohol spectrum disorders
 (FASD) 80
afterbirth 87
doula 88
natural childbirth 89
prepared childbirth 89
breech position 90

cesarean delivery 90
Apgar Scale 91
Brazelton Neonatal
 Behavioral Assessment
 Scale (NBAS) 91
Neonatal Intensive Care Unit
 Network Neurobehavioral
 Scale (NNNS) 91
low birth weight infants 92

preterm infants 92
small for date infants 92
kangaroo care 92
postpartum period 95
postpartum depression 96
bonding 96

key **people**

David Olds 86

Ferdinand Lamaze 89

T. Berry Brazelton 91

Tiffany Field 94

section three

Babies are such a nice way to start people.

—Don Herold
American Writer, 20th Century

Infancy

As newborns, we were not empty-headed organisms. We had some basic reflexes, among them crying, kicking, and coughing. We slept a lot, and occasionally we smiled, although the meaning of our first smiles was not entirely clear. We ate and we grew. We crawled and then we walked, a journey of a thousand miles beginning with a single step. Sometimes we conformed; sometimes others conformed to us. Our development was a continuous creation of more complex forms. We needed the meeting eyes of love. We juggled the necessity of curbing our will with becoming what we could will freely. Section 3 contains three chapters: "Physical Development in Infancy" (Chapter 4), "Cognitive Development in Infancy" (Chapter 5), and "Socioemotional Development in Infancy" (Chapter 6).

chapter 4

PHYSICAL DEVELOPMENT IN INFANCY

chapter outline

Latonya is a newborn baby in Ghana. During her first days of life, she has been kept apart from her mother and bottle fed. Manufacturers of infant formula provide the hospital where she was born with free or subsidized milk powder. Her mother has been persuaded to bottle feed rather than breast feed her. When her mother bottle feeds Latonya, she overdilutes the milk formula with unclean water. Latonya's feeding bottles have not been sterilized. Latonya becomes very sick. She dies before her first birthday.

Ramona was born in a Nigerian hospital with a "baby-friendly" program. In this program, babies are not separated from their mothers when they are born, and the mothers are encouraged to breast feed them. The mothers are told of the perils that bottle feeding can bring because of unsafe water and unsterilized bottles. They also are informed about the advantages of breast milk, which include its nutritious and hygienic qualities, its ability to immunize babies against common illnesses, and the role of breast feeding in reducing the mother's risk of breast and ovarian cancer. Ramona's mother is breast feeding her. At 1 year of age, Ramona is very healthy.

For many years, maternity units in hospitals favored bottle feeding and did not give mothers adequate information about the benefits of breast feeding. In recent years, the World Health Organization and UNICEF have tried to reverse the trend toward bottle feeding of infants in many impoverished countries. They instituted "baby-friendly" programs in many countries (Grant, 1993). They also persuaded the International Association of Infant Formula Manufacturers to stop marketing their baby formulas to hospitals in countries where the governments support the baby-friendly initiatives (Grant, 1993). For the hospitals themselves, costs actually were reduced as infant formula, feeding bottles, and separate nurseries became unnecessary. For example, baby-friendly Jose Fabella Memorial Hospital in the Philippines reported saving 8 percent of its annual budget. Still, there are many places in the world where the baby-friendly initiatives have not been implemented.

The advantages of breast feeding in impoverished countries are substantial (Gopalappa & others, 2014; Tenthani & others, 2014; UNICEF, 2014). However, these advantages must be balanced against the risk of passing the human immunodeficiency virus (HIV) to babies through breast milk if the mothers have the

(*Top*) An HIV-infected mother breast feeding her baby in Nairobi, Kenya. (*Bottom*) A Rwandan mother bottle feeding her baby. *What are some concerns about breast versus bottle feeding in impoverished African countries?*

topical connections *looking back*

In the previous chapter, we followed the physical development that takes place from fertilization through the germinal, embryonic, and fetal periods of prenatal development. We learned that by the time the fetus has reached full gestational age (approximately 40 weeks), it has grown from a fertilized egg, barely visible to the human eye, to a fully formed human weighing approximately 7½ pounds and measuring 20 inches in length. Also remarkable is the fact that by the end of the prenatal period the brain has developed approximately 100 billion neurons.

virus (Fowler & others, 2014). In some areas of Africa, more than 30 percent of mothers have HIV, but the majority of these mothers don't know that they are infected (Mepham, Bland, and Newell, 2011). Later in the chapter, in the section on nutrition, we will look more closely at recent research on breast feeding in the United States, outlining the benefits for infants and mothers and discussing several life-threatening diseases that infants can contract as a result of malnutrition.

preview

It is very important for infants to get a healthy start. When they do, their first two years of life are likely to be a time of amazing development. In this chapter, we focus on the biological domain and the infant's physical development, exploring physical growth, motor development, and sensory and perceptual development.

1 Physical Growth and Development in Infancy

LG1 Discuss physical growth and development in infancy.

| Patterns of Growth | Height and Weight | The Brain | Sleep | Nutrition |

Infants' physical development in the first two years of life is extensive. Newborns' heads are quite large in comparison with the rest of their bodies. They have little strength in their necks and cannot hold their heads up, but they have some basic reflexes. In the span of 12 months, infants become capable of sitting anywhere, standing, stooping, climbing, and usually walking. During the second year, growth decelerates, but rapid increases in such activities as running and climbing take place. Let's now examine in greater detail the sequence of physical development in infancy.

PATTERNS OF GROWTH

An extraordinary proportion of the total body is occupied by the head during prenatal development and early infancy (see Figure 4.1). The **cephalocaudal pattern** is the sequence in which the earliest growth always occurs at the top—the head—with physical growth and differentiation of features gradually working their way down from top to bottom (for example, shoulders, middle trunk, and so on). This same pattern occurs in the head area, because the top parts of the head—the eyes and brain—grow faster than the lower parts, such as the jaw.

Motor development generally proceeds according to the cephalocaudal principle. For example, infants see objects before they can control their torso, and they can use their hands long before they can crawl or walk. However, development does not follow a rigid blueprint. One study found that infants reached for toys with their feet prior to reaching with their hands (Galloway & Thelen, 2004). On average, infants first touched the toy with their feet when they were 12 weeks old and with their hands when they were 16 weeks old.

Growth also follows the **proximodistal pattern,** the sequence in which growth starts at the center of the body and moves toward the extremities. For example, infants control the muscles of their trunk and arms before they control their hands and fingers, and they use their whole hands before they can control several fingers.

HEIGHT AND WEIGHT

The average North American newborn is 20 inches long and weighs 7 pounds. Ninety-five percent of full-term newborns are 18 to 22 inches long and weigh between 5 and 10 pounds.

In the first several days of life, most newborns lose 5 to 7 percent of their body weight before they adjust to feeding by sucking, swallowing, and digesting. Then they grow rapidly,

A baby is the most complicated object made by unskilled labor.

—ANONYMOUS

cephalocaudal pattern Developmental sequence in which the earliest growth always occurs at the top—the head—with physical growth in size, weight, and feature differentiation gradually working from top to bottom.

proximodistal pattern Developmental sequence in which growth starts at the center of the body and moves toward the extremities.

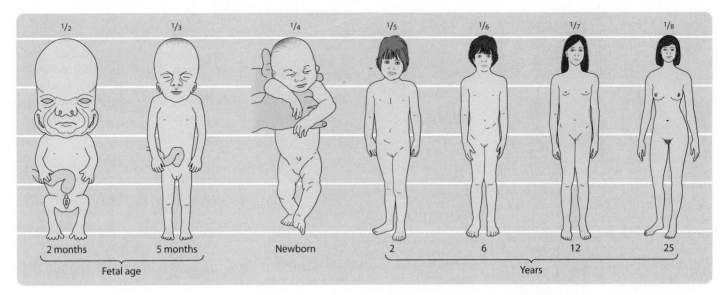

| 1/2 | 1/3 | 1/4 | 1/5 | 1/6 | 1/7 | 1/8 |

| 2 months | 5 months | Newborn | 2 | 6 | 12 | 25 |

Fetal age — Years

gaining an average of 5 to 6 ounces per week during the first month. They have doubled their birth weight by the age of 4 months and have nearly tripled it by their first birthday. Infants grow about 1 inch per month during the first year, approximately doubling their birth length by their first birthday.

Growth slows considerably in the second year of life (Burns & others, 2013; Marcdante & Kliegman, 2015). By 2 years of age, infants weigh approximately 26 to 32 pounds, having gained a quarter to half a pound per month during the second year to reach about one-fifth of their adult weight. At 2 years of age, infants average 32 to 35 inches in height, which is nearly half of their adult height.

THE BRAIN

We described the amazing growth of the brain from conception to birth in Chapter 3. By the time it is born, the infant that began as a single cell is estimated to have a brain that contains approximately 100 billion nerve cells, or neurons. Extensive brain development continues after birth, through infancy and later (Diamond, 2013; Gao & others, 2014; Zelazo, 2013). Because the brain is still developing so rapidly in infancy, the infant's head should be protected from falls or other injuries and the baby should never be shaken. *Shaken baby syndrome,* which includes brain swelling and hemorrhaging, affects hundreds of babies in the United States each year (Cohen & Ramsay, 2014; Squier, 2014). One analysis found that fathers were the most frequent perpetrators of shaken baby syndrome, followed by child care providers and boyfriends of the victim's mother (National Center on Shaken Baby Syndrome, 2012).

Researchers have been successful in using the electroencephalogram (EEG), a measure of the brain's electrical activity, to learn about the brain's development in infancy (Lusby & others, 2014) (See Figure 4.2). Recently Patricia Kuhl and her colleagues at the Institute for Learning and Brain Sciences at the University of Washington have been using magnetoencephalography, or MEG, brain-imaging machines to assess infants' brain activity. MEG maps brain activity by recording magnetic fields produced by electrical currents and is being used to assess such perceptual and cognitive activities as vision, hearing, and language in infants (see Figure 4.3).

Among the researchers who are making strides in finding out more about the brain's development in infancy are:

- Martha Ann Bell and her colleagues (Bell & Cuevas, 2012, 2014; Bell, Kraybill, & Diaz, 2014; Morasch, Raj, & Bell, 2013) who are studying brain-behavior links, emotion regulation, and the integration of cognition and emotion
- Charles Nelson and his colleagues (McLaughlin & others, 2014; Nelson, 2007, 2012, 2013a, b; Nelson, Fox, & Zeanah, 2014; Moulson & Nelson, 2008; Righi & others, 2014) who are exploring various aspects of memory development, face recognition and facial emotion, and

FIGURE 4.1

CHANGES IN PROPORTIONS OF THE HUMAN BODY DURING GROWTH. As individuals develop from infancy through adulthood, one of the most noticeable physical changes is that the head becomes smaller in relation to the rest of the body. The fractions listed refer to head size as a proportion of total body length at different ages.

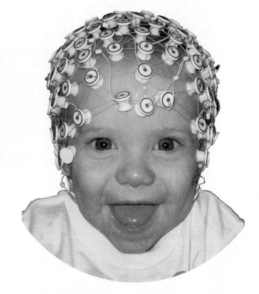

FIGURE 4.2

MEASURING THE ACTIVITY OF AN INFANT'S BRAIN WITH AN ELECTROENCEPHALOGRAM (EEG). By attaching up to 128 electrodes to a baby's scalp to measure the brain's activity, Charles Nelson and his colleagues (2006) have found that newborns produce distinctive brain waves that reveal they can distinguish their mother's voice from another woman's, even while they are asleep. *Why is it so difficult to measure infants' brain activity?*

FIGURE 4.3

MEASURING THE ACTIVITY OF AN INFANT'S BRAIN WITH MAGNETOENCEPHALOGRAPHY (MEG). This baby's brain activity is being assessed with a MEG brain-imaging device while the baby is listening to spoken words in a study at the Institute of Learning and Brain Sciences at the University of Washington. The infant sits under the machine and when he or she experiences a word, touch, sight, or emotion, the neurons working together in the infant's brain generate magnetic fields and MEG pinpoints the location of the fields in the brain.

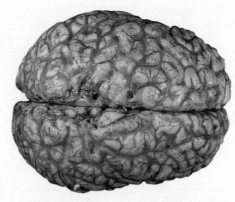

FIGURE 4.4

THE HUMAN BRAIN'S HEMISPHERES. The two hemispheres of the human brain are clearly seen in this photograph. It is a myth that the left hemisphere is the exclusive location of language and logical thinking and that the right hemisphere is the exclusive location of emotion and creative thinking.

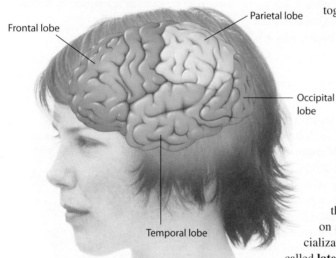

FIGURE 4.5

THE BRAIN'S FOUR LOBES. Shown here are the locations of the brain's four lobes: frontal, occipital, temporal, and parietal.

developmental **connection**

Brain Development

How does the brain change from conception to birth? Chapter 3, p. 77

lateralization Specialization of function in one hemisphere of the cerebral cortex or the other.

the role of experience in influencing the course of brain development

• John Richards and his colleagues (Richards, 2009, 2010, 2013; Richards, Reynolds, & Courage, 2010; Sanchez, Richards, & Almi, 2012) who are examining sustained attention, perception of TV programs, and eye movements

The Brain's Development At birth, the newborn's brain is about 25 percent of its adult weight. By the second birthday, the brain is about 75 percent of its adult weight. However, the brain's areas do not mature uniformly.

Mapping the Brain Scientists analyze and categorize areas of the brain in numerous ways (Blakemore & Mills, 2014; Dubois & others, 2014). The portion farthest from the spinal cord is known as the forebrain. This region includes the cerebral cortex and several structures beneath it. The cerebral cortex covers the forebrain like a wrinkled cap. The brain has two halves, or hemispheres (see Figure 4.4). Based on ridges and valleys in the cortex, scientists distinguish four main areas, called lobes, in each hemisphere. Although the lobes usually work together, each has a somewhat different primary function (see Figure 4.5):

• *Frontal lobes* are involved in voluntary movement, thinking, personality, and intentionality or purpose.

• *Occipital lobes* function in vision.

• *Temporal lobes* have an active role in hearing, language processing, and memory.

• *Parietal lobes* play important roles in registering spatial location, attention, and motor control.

To some extent, the type of information handled by neurons depends on whether they are in the left or right hemisphere of the cortex (Griffiths & others, 2013). Speech and grammar, for example, depend on activity in the left hemisphere in most people; humor and the use of metaphors depends on activity in the right hemisphere (Moore, Brendel, & Fiez, 2014). This specialization of function in one hemisphere of the cerebral cortex or the other is called **lateralization.** However, most neuroscientists agree that complex functions such as reading or performing music involve both hemispheres. Labeling people as "left-brained" because they are logical thinkers or "right-brained" because they are creative thinkers does not correspond to the way the brain's hemispheres work. Complex thinking in normal people is the outcome of communication between both hemispheres of the brain (Ibrahim & Eviatar, 2012).

At birth, the hemispheres of the cerebral cortex already have started to specialize: Newborns show greater electrical brain activity in the left hemisphere than the right hemisphere when they are listening to speech sounds (Telkemeyer & others, 2011). How are the areas of the brain different in the newborn and the infant from those in an adult, and why do the differences matter? Important differences have been documented at both the cellular and the structural levels.

Changes in Neurons Within the brain, the type of nerve cells called neurons send electrical and chemical signals, communicating with each other. As we indicated in Chapter 3, a *neuron* is a nerve cell that handles information processing (see Figure 4.6). Extending from the neuron's cell body are two types of fibers known as axons and dendrites. Generally, the axon carries signals away from the cell body and dendrites carry signals toward it. A *myelin sheath,* which is a layer of fat cells, encases many axons (see Figure 4.6). The myelin sheath insulates axons and helps electrical signals travel faster down the axon. Myelination also is involved in providing energy to neurons and in communication (White & Kramer-Albers, 2014). At the end of the axon are terminal buttons, which release chemicals called *neurotransmitters* into *synapses,* which are tiny gaps between neurons' fibers. Chemical interactions in synapses connect axons and dendrites, allowing information to pass from neuron to neuron (Emes & Grant, 2013; Zanella & others, 2014). Think of the synapse as a river that blocks a road. A grocery truck arrives at one bank of the river, crosses by ferry, and continues its journey to market. Similarly, a message in the brain is "ferried" across the synapse by a neurotransmitter, which pours out information contained in chemicals when it reaches the other side of the river.

Neurons change in two very significant ways during the first years of life. First, *myelination,* the process of encasing axons with fat cells, begins prenatally and continues after birth, even into adolescence (Blakemore & Mills, 2014; Markant & Thomas, 2013). Second, connectivity among neurons increases, creating new neural pathways. New dendrites grow, connections among dendrites increase, and synaptic connections between axons and dendrites proliferate. Whereas myelination speeds up neural transmissions, the expansion of dendritic connections facilitates the spreading of neural pathways in infant development.

Researchers have discovered an intriguing aspect of synaptic connections. Nearly twice as many of these connections are made as will ever be used (Huttenlocher & Dabholkar, 1997). The connections that are used become strengthened and survive, while the unused ones are replaced by other pathways or disappear. In the language of neuroscience, these connections will be "pruned" (Money & Stanwood, 2013). For example, the more babies engage in physical activity or use language, the more those pathways will be strengthened.

Changes in Regions of the Brain   Figure 4.7 vividly illustrates the dramatic growth and later pruning of synapses in the visual, auditory, and prefrontal cortex (Huttenlocher & Dabholkar, 1997). Notice that "blooming and pruning" vary considerably by brain region. For

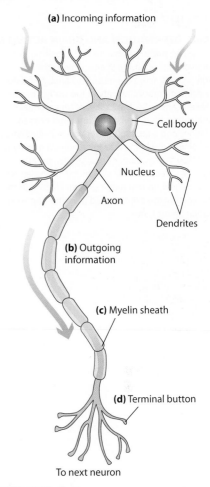

(a) Incoming information

Cell body

Nucleus

Axon

Dendrites

(b) Outgoing information

(c) Myelin sheath

(d) Terminal button

To next neuron

FIGURE **4.6**

THE NEURON. (*a*) The dendrites of the cell body receive information from other neurons, muscles, or glands through the axon. (*b*) Axons transmit information away from the cell body. (*c*) A myelin sheath covers most axons and speeds information transmission. (*d*) As the axon ends, it branches out into terminal buttons.

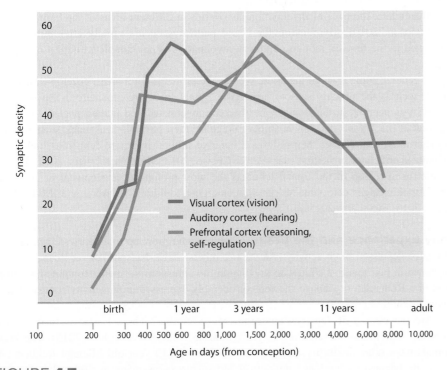

Visual cortex (vision)
Auditory cortex (hearing)
Prefrontal cortex (reasoning, self-regulation)

FIGURE **4.7**

SYNAPTIC DENSITY IN THE HUMAN BRAIN FROM INFANCY TO ADULTHOOD. The graph shows the dramatic increase followed by pruning in synaptic density for three regions of the brain: visual cortex, auditory cortex, and prefrontal cortex. Synaptic density is believed to be an important indication of the extent of connectivity between neurons.

FIGURE **4.8**

EARLY DEPRIVATION AND BRAIN ACTIVITY.
These two photographs are PET (positron emission tomography) scans, which use radioactive tracers to image and analyze blood flow and metabolic activity in the body's organs. These scans show the brains of (*a*) a normal child and (*b*) an institutionalized Romanian orphan who experienced substantial deprivation since birth. In PET scans, the highest to lowest brain activity is reflected in the colors of red, yellow, green, blue, and black, respectively. As can be seen, red and yellow show up to a much greater degree in the PET scan of the normal child than the deprived Romanian orphan.

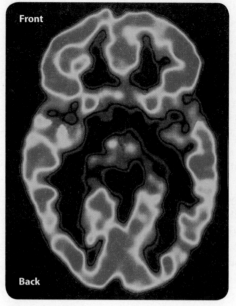

(a)

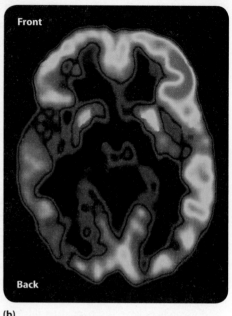

(b)

example, the peak of synaptic overproduction in the visual cortex occurs at about the fourth postnatal month, followed by a gradual retraction until the middle to end of the preschool years. In areas of the brain involved in hearing and language, a similar, though somewhat later, course is detected. However, in the prefrontal cortex, the area of the brain where higher-level thinking and self-regulation occur, the peak of overproduction takes place at about 1 year of age; it is not until middle to late adolescence that the adult density of synapses is achieved. Both heredity and environment are thought to influence the timing and course of synaptic overproduction and subsequent retraction.

Meanwhile, the pace of myelination also varies in different areas of the brain (Gogtay & Thompson, 2010). Myelination for visual pathways occurs rapidly after birth and is completed in the first six months. Auditory myelination is not completed until 4 or 5 years of age.

In general, some areas of the brain, such as the primary motor areas, develop earlier than others, such as the primary sensory areas. The frontal lobes are immature in the newborn. However, as neurons in the frontal lobes become myelinated and interconnected during the first year of life, infants develop an ability to regulate their physiological states, such as sleep, and gain more control over their reflexes. Cognitive skills that require deliberate thinking do not emerge until later in the first year (Bell & Cuevas, 2013; Morasch & others, 2013). Indeed, the prefrontal region of the frontal lobe has the most prolonged development of any brain region, with changes detectable at least into emerging adulthood (Blakemore & Mills, 2014; Casey, 2015; Steinberg, 2015a, b).

Early Experience and the Brain

Children who grow up in a deprived environment may have depressed brain activity (Narvaez & others, 2013; Nelson, Fox, & Zeanah, 2014). As shown in Figure 4.8, a child who grew up in the unresponsive and unstimulating environment of a Romanian orphanage showed considerably depressed brain activity compared with a normal child.

Are the effects of deprived environments reversible? There is reason to think that for some individuals the answer is "yes" (Sharma, Classen, & Cohen, 2013). The brain demonstrates both flexibility and resilience. Consider 14-year-old Michael Rehbein. At age 7, he began to experience uncontrollable seizures—as many as 400 a day. Doctors said the only solution was to remove the left hemisphere of his brain where the seizures were occurring. Recovery was slow, but his right hemisphere began to reorganize and take over functions that normally occur in the brain's left hemisphere, including speech (see Figure 4.9).

- - - - - - - - - - ->

developmental connection

Brain Development

Changes in the prefrontal cortex in adolescents and older adults have important implications for their cognitive development. Chapter 11, p. 359; Chapter 17, p. 518

(a)

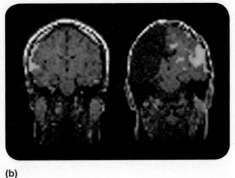
(b)

FIGURE **4.9**

PLASTICITY IN THE BRAIN'S HEMISPHERES. (*a*) Michael Rehbein at 14 years of age. (*b*) Michael's right hemisphere (*left*) has reorganized to take over the language functions normally carried out by corresponding areas in the left hemisphere of an intact brain (*right*). However, the right hemisphere is not as efficient as the left, and more areas of the brain are recruited to process speech.

Neuroscientists believe that what wires the brain—or rewires it, in the case of Michael Rehbein—is repeated experience. Each time a baby tries to touch an attractive object or gazes intently at a face, tiny bursts of electricity shoot through the brain, knitting together neurons into circuits. The results are some of the behavioral milestones we discuss in this chapter.

The Neuroconstructivist View   Not long ago, scientists thought that our genes determined how our brains were "wired" and that the cells in the brain responsible for processing information just maturationally unfolded with little or no input from environmental experiences. Whatever brain your heredity had dealt you, you were essentially stuck with. This view, however, turned out to be wrong. Instead, the brain has plasticity and its development depends on context (Markant & Thomas, 2013; Nelson, 2013a, b; Sale, Berardi, & Maffei, 2014; Zelazo, 2013).

The infant's brain depends on experiences to determine how connections are made (Nelson, Fox, & Zeanah, 2014; Nudo & McNeal, 2013). Before birth, it appears that genes mainly direct basic wiring patterns. Neurons grow and travel to distant places awaiting further instructions. After birth, the inflowing stream of sights, sounds, smells, touches, language, and eye contact help shape the brain's neural connections.

In the increasingly popular **neuroconstructivist view,** (a) biological processes (genes, for example) and environmental conditions (enriched or impoverished, for example) influence the brain's development; (b) the brain has plasticity and is context dependent; and (c) development of the brain and the child's cognitive development are closely linked. These factors constrain or advance the construction of cognitive skills (Westerman, Thomas, & Karmiloff-Smith, 2011). The neuroconstructivist view emphasizes the importance of considering interactions between experience and gene expression in the brain's development, much in the way the epigenetic view proposes (see Chapter 2, "Biological Beginnings") (Lopez, 2014).

SLEEP

When we were infants, sleep consumed more of our time than it does now (Lushington & others, 2014). The typical newborn sleeps approximately 18 hours a day, but newborns vary a lot in how much they sleep (Sadeh, 2008). The range is from about 10 hours to about 21 hours a day.

developmental **connection**

Nature and Nurture

In the epigenetic view, development is an ongoing, bidirectional interchange between heredity and the environment. Chapter 2, p. 68

Sleep that knits up the ravelled sleave of care . . . Balm of hurt minds, nature's second course. Chief nourisher in life's feast.

—**WILLIAM SHAKESPEARE**
English Playwright, 17th Century

neuroconstructivist view Perspective holding that biological processes and environmental conditions influence the brain's development; the brain has plasticity and is context dependent; and development of the brain and cognitive development are closely linked.

A recent research review concluded that infants 0 to 2 years of age slept an average of 12.8 hours out of the 24, within a range of 9.7 to 15.9 hours (Galland & others, 2012). And a recent study revealed that by 6 months of age the majority of infants slept through the night, awakening their parents only once or twice a week (Weinraub & others, 2012).

The most common infant sleep-related problem reported by parents is nighttime waking (Hospital for Sick Children & others, 2010). Surveys indicate that 20 to 30 percent of infants have difficulty going to sleep at night and staying asleep until morning (Sadeh, 2008). A recent study found that nighttime wakings at 1 year of age predicted lower sleep efficiency at 4 years of age (Tikotzky & Shaashua, 2012). Also, another study revealed that the mother's emotional availability at bedtime was linked to fewer infant sleep problems, supporting the premise that parents' emotional availability to infants in sleep contexts increases feelings of safety and security, and consequently better-regulated infant sleep (Teti & others, 2010). Another study found that a higher involvement of fathers in overall infant care was related to fewer infant sleep problems (Tikotzky, Sadeh, & Glickman-Gavrieli, 2010). However, infant nighttime waking problems have consistently been linked to excessive parental involvement in sleep-related interactions with their infant (Sadeh, 2008). Further research found that maternal depression during pregnancy, early introduction of solid foods, infant TV viewing, and child care attendance were related to shorter duration of infant sleep (Nevarez & others, 2010).

Cultural variations influence infant sleeping patterns. For example, in the Kipsigis culture in Kenya, infants sleep with their mothers at night and are permitted to nurse on demand (Super & Harkness, 1997). During the day, they are strapped to their mothers' backs, accompanying them on daily rounds of chores and social activities. As a result, the Kipsigis infants do not sleep through the night until much later than American infants do. During the first eight months of postnatal life, Kipsigis infants rarely sleep longer than three hours at a stretch, even at night. This sleep pattern contrasts with that of American infants, many of whom begin to sleep up to eight hours a night by 8 months of age.

REM Sleep   In REM sleep, the eyes flutter beneath closed lids; in non-REM sleep, this type of eye movement does not occur and sleep is more quiet (Sankupellay & others, 2011). Figure 4.10 shows developmental changes in the average number of total hours spent in REM and non-REM sleep. By the time they reach adulthood, individuals spend about one-fifth of their night in REM sleep, and REM sleep usually appears about one hour after non-REM sleep. However, about half of an infant's sleep is REM sleep, and infants often begin their sleep cycle with REM sleep rather than non-REM sleep. A much greater amount of time is taken up by REM sleep in infancy than at any other point in the life span. By the time infants reach 3 months of age, the percentage of time they spend in REM sleep falls to about 40 percent, and REM sleep no longer begins their sleep cycle.

Why do infants spend so much time in REM sleep? Researchers are not certain. The large amount of REM sleep may provide infants with added self-stimulation, since they spend less time awake than do older children. REM sleep also might promote the brain's development in infancy (Graven, 2006).

When adults are awakened during REM sleep, they frequently report that they have been dreaming, but when they are awakened during non-REM sleep, they are much less likely to report they have been dreaming (Cartwright & others, 2006). Since infants spend more time than adults in REM sleep, can we conclude that they dream a lot? We don't know whether infants dream or not, because they don't have any way of reporting dreams.

Shared Sleeping   Sleeping arrangements for newborns vary from culture to culture (Mindell & others, 2010a, b). For example, sharing a bed with a mother is a common practice in many cultures, such as Guatemala and China, whereas in others, such as the United States and Great Britain, newborns usually sleep in a crib, either in the same room as the parents or in a separate room. In some cultures, infants sleep with the mother until they are weaned, after which they sleep with siblings until middle and late childhood (Walker, 2006). Whatever

developmental **connection**

Sleep

What are some sleep problems that children encounter in early childhood? Chapter 7, p. 201

developmental **connection**

Sleep

Sleep patterns change in adolescence and are linked to changes in the brain. Chapter 11, p. 352

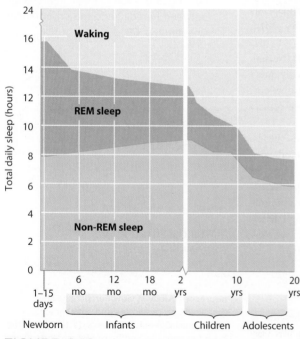

FIGURE 4.10

DEVELOPMENTAL CHANGES IN REM AND NON-REM SLEEP

the sleeping arrangements, it is recommended that the infant's bedding provide firm support and that cribs should have side rails.

In the United States, shared sleeping remains a controversial issue (Burnham, 2014). Some experts recommend it and others argue against it, although recently the recommendation trend has been to avoid infant-parent bed sharing, especially until the infant is at least 6 months of age (Byard, 2012a, b; Weber & others, 2012). The American Academy of Pediatrics Task Force on Infant Positioning and SIDS (AAPTFIPS) (2000) recommends against shared sleeping. Its members argue that in some instances bed sharing might lead to sudden infant death syndrome (SIDS), as could be the case if a sleeping mother rolls over on her baby. Recent studies have found that bed sharing is linked with a higher incidence of SIDS, especially when parents smoke (Senter & others, 2010).

SIDS   **Sudden infant death syndrome (SIDS)** is a condition that occurs when infants stop breathing, usually during the night, and die suddenly without any apparent reason. SIDS continues to be a leading cause of infant death in the United States, with nearly 3,000 infant deaths annually attributed to SIDS (Montagna & Chokroverty, 2011). Risk of SIDS is highest at 2 to 4 months of age (NICHD, 2013).

Since 1992, the American Academy of Pediatrics (AAP) has recommended that infants be placed to sleep on their backs (supine position) to reduce the risk of SIDS, and the frequency of prone sleeping (on the stomach) among U.S. infants has dropped dramatically (AAPTFIPS, 2000). Researchers have found that SIDS does indeed decrease when infants sleep on their backs rather than their stomachs or sides (Wong & others, 2013). Among the reasons given for prone sleeping being a risk factor for SIDS are that it impairs the infant's arousal from sleep and restricts the infant's ability to swallow effectively (Franco & others, 2010). One study revealed that 26 percent of U.S. mothers of 3-month-old infants did not use the recommended supine position for their infants' nighttime sleep (Hauck & others, 2008).

In addition to sleeping in a prone position, researchers have found that the following factors are linked to SIDS:

Is this a good sleep position for infants? Why or why not?

- SIDS occurs more often in infants with abnormal brain stem functioning involving the neurotransmitter serotonin (Rognum & others, 2014; Rubens & Sarnat, 2013).

- Heart arrhythmias are estimated to occur in as many as 15 percent of SIDS cases, and two recent studies found that gene mutations were linked to the occurrence of these arrhythmias (Brion & others, 2012; Van Norstrand & others, 2012).

- Six percent of infants with sleep apnea, a temporary cessation of breathing in which the airway is completely blocked, usually for 10 seconds or longer, die of SIDS (Ednick & others, 2010).

- Two reviews concluded that breast feeding is linked to a lower incidence of SIDS (Hauck & others, 2011; Zotter & Pichler, 2012).

- Low birth weight infants are 5 to 10 times more likely to die of SIDS than are their normal-weight counterparts (Horne & others, 2002).

- SIDS is more likely to occur in infants who do not use a pacifier when they go to sleep than in those who do use a pacifier (Moon & others, 2012).

- Infants whose siblings have died of SIDS are two to four times as likely to die of it (Lenoir, Mallet, & Calenda, 2000).

- African American and Eskimo infants are four to six times as likely as all others to die of SIDS (Kitsantas & Gaffney, 2010).

- SIDS is more common in lower socioeconomic groups (Hogan, 2014).

- SIDS is more common in infants who are passively exposed to cigarette smoke (Jarosinska & others, 2014).

- SIDS is more common when infants and parents share the same bed (Senter & others, 2010).

- SIDS is more common if infants sleep in soft bedding (McGarvey & others, 2006).

- SIDS is less common when infants sleep in a bedroom with a fan. One study revealed that sleeping in a bedroom with a fan lowers the risk of SIDS by 70 percent (Coleman-Phox, Odouli, & Li, 2008).

sudden infant death syndrome (SIDS) A condition that occurs when an infant stops breathing, usually during the night, and suddenly dies without an apparent cause.

Sleep and Cognitive Development   Might infant sleep be linked to children's cognitive development? A recent study revealed that 4-year-olds who had slept longer at night as infants engaged in a higher level of executive function (Bernier & others, 2013). The link between infant sleep and children's cognitive functioning likely occurs because of sleep's role in brain maturation and memory consolidation, which may improve daytime alertness and learning (Sadeh, 2007). Another recent study found that poor sleep consolidation in infancy was associated with language delays in early childhood (Dionne & others, 2011).

NUTRITION

From birth to 1 year of age, human infants nearly triple their weight and increase their length by 50 percent. What do they need to sustain this growth?

Nutritional Needs and Eating Behavior   Individual differences among infants in terms of their nutrient reserves, body composition, growth rates, and activity patterns make defining actual nutrient needs difficult (Thompson, Manore, & Vaughn, 2014). However, because parents need guidelines, nutritionists recommend that infants consume approximately 50 calories per day for each pound they weigh—more than twice an adult's requirement per pound.

A number of developmental changes involving eating characterize the infant's first year (Golley & others, 2012; Symon & Bammann, 2012). As infants' motor skills improve, they change from using suck-and-swallow movements with breast milk or formula to chew-and-swallow movements with semisolid and then more complex foods (van Dijk, Hunnius, & van Geert, 2012). As their fine motor control improves in the first year, they transition from being fed by others toward self-feeding. "By the end of the first year of life, children can sit independently, can chew and swallow a range of textures, are learning to feed themselves, and are making the transition to the family diet and meal patterns" (Black & Hurley, 2007, p. 1). At this point, infants need to have a diet that includes a variety of foods—especially fruits and vegetables.

Caregivers play very important roles in infants' early development of eating patterns (Brown, Pridham, & Brown, 2014; Daniels & others, 2014). Caregivers who are not sensitive to developmental changes in infants' nutritional needs, neglectful caregivers, and conditions of poverty can contribute to the development of eating problems in infants (Black & Lozoff, 2008). A recent study found that low maternal sensitivity when infants were 15 and 24 months of age was linked to a higher risk of obesity in adolescence (Anderson & others, 2012).

A national study of more than 3,000 randomly selected 4- to 24-month-olds documented that many U.S. parents aren't feeding their babies enough fruits and vegetables, but are feeding them too much junk food (Fox & others, 2004). Up to one-third of the babies ate no vegetables and fruit but frequently ate French fries, and almost half of the 7- to 8-month-old babies were fed desserts, sweets, or sweetened drinks. By 15 months, French fries were the most common vegetable the babies ate.

Such poor dietary patterns early in development can result in more infants being overweight (Blake, Munoz, & Volpe, 2014). In addition to consuming too many French fries, sweetened drinks, and desserts, are there other factors that might explain increased numbers of overweight U.S. infants? A mother's weight gain during pregnancy and a mother's own high weight before pregnancy may be factors (McKinney & Murray, 2013). One important factor likely is whether an infant is breast fed or bottle fed (Khalessi & Reich, 2014; Lawrence, 2012). Breast-fed infants have lower rates of weight gain than bottle-fed infants in childhood and adolescence, and it is estimated that breast feeding reduces the risk of obesity by approximately 20 percent (Li & others, 2007; Scott, Ng, & Cobiac, 2012). Also, one study found that the introduction of solid foods before 4 months of age was associated with an increased risk of obesity at 3 years of age (Huh & others, 2011).

Breast versus Bottle Feeding   For the first four to six months of life, human milk or an alternative formula is the baby's source of nutrients and energy. For years, debate has focused on whether breast feeding is better for the infant than bottle feeding. The growing consensus is that breast feeding is better for the baby's health (Gregory, Dubois, & Steele, 2014; Ho, 2013). Since the 1970s, breast feeding by U.S. mothers has soared (see Figure 4.11). In 2009 more than 77 percent of U.S. mothers breast fed their newborns, and 47 percent breast fed their 6-month-olds (Centers for Disease Control and Prevention, 2012). The American Academy of Pediatrics Section on Breastfeeding (2012) recently reconfirmed its recommendation of exclusive breast feeding in the first six months followed by continued breast feeding as complementary foods are introduced, and further breast feeding for one year or longer as mutually desired by the mother and infant.

What are some of the benefits of breast feeding? The following conclusions have been supported by research:

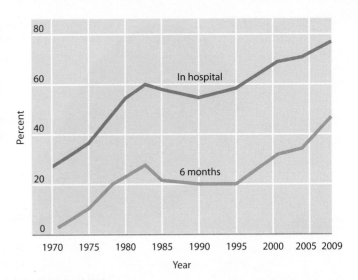

FIGURE **4.11**

TRENDS IN BREAST FEEDING IN THE UNITED STATES: 1970–2009

Outcomes for the Child

- *Gastrointestinal infections.* Breast-fed infants have fewer gastrointestinal infections (Garofalo, 2010).

- *Respiratory tract infections.* Breast-fed infants have fewer infections of the lower respiratory tract (Prameela, 2011).

- *Allergies.* A research review by the American Academy of Pediatrics indicated that there is no evidence that breast feeding reduces the risk of allergies in children (Greer & others, 2008).

- *Asthma.* The research review by the American Academy of Pediatrics concluded that exclusive breast feeding for three months protects against wheezing in babies, but whether it prevents asthma in older children is unclear (Greer & others, 2008).

- *Otitis media.* Breast-fed infants are less likely to develop this middle ear infection (Pelton & Leibovitz, 2009).

- *Overweight and obesity.* Consistent evidence indicates that breast-fed infants are less likely to become overweight or obese in childhood, adolescence, and adulthood (Khalessi & Reich, 2014; Minniti & others, 2014).

- *Diabetes.* Breast-fed infants are less likely to develop type 1 diabetes in childhood (Ping & Hagopian, 2006) and type 2 diabetes in adulthood (Minniti & others, 2014).

- *SIDS.* Breast-fed infants are less likely to experience SIDS (Byard, 2013).

In large-scale research reviews, no conclusive evidence for the benefits of breast feeding was found for children's cognitive development and cardiovascular health (Agency for Healthcare Research and Quality, 2007; Ip & others, 2009).

Outcomes for the Mother

- *Breast cancer.* Consistent evidence indicates a lower incidence of breast cancer in women who breast feed their infants (Akbari & others, 2011).

- *Ovarian cancer.* Evidence also reveals a reduction in ovarian cancer in women who breast feed their infants (Stuebe & Schwartz, 2010).

- *Type 2 diabetes.* Some evidence suggests a small reduction in type 2 diabetes in women who breast feed their infants (Stuebe & Schwartz, 2010).

In large-scale research reviews, no conclusive evidence could be found for the maternal benefits of breast feeding on return to prepregnancy weight, osteoporosis, and postpartum depression (Agency for Healthcare Research and Quality, 2007; Ip & others, 2009). However, one study revealed that women who breast fed their infants had a lower incidence of metabolic syndrome (a disorder characterized by obesity, hypertension, and insulin resistance) in midlife (Ram & others, 2008).

Many health professionals have argued that breast feeding facilitates the development of an attachment bond between the mother and infant (Britton, Britton, & Gronwaldt, 2006; Wittig & Spatz, 2008). However, a research review found that the positive role of breast feeding on the mother-infant relationship is not supported by research (Jansen, de Weerth, &

Human milk or an alternative formula is a baby's source of nutrients for the first four to six months. The growing consensus is that breast feeding is better for the baby's health, although controversy still surrounds the issue of breast feeding versus bottle feeding. *Why is breast feeding strongly recommended by pediatricians?*

developmental **connection**

Research Methods

How does a correlational study differ from an experimental study? Chapter 1, p. 30

marasmus A wasting away of body tissues in the infant's first year, caused by severe protein-calorie deficiency.

kwashiorkor A condition caused by severe protein deficiency in which the child's abdomen and feet become swollen with water; usually appears between 1 and 3 years of age.

Riksen-Walraven, 2008). The review concluded that recommending breast feeding should not be based on its role in improving the mother-infant relationship but rather on its positive effects on infant and maternal health.

Which women are least likely to breast feed? They include mothers who work full-time outside of the home, mothers under age 25, mothers without a high school education, African American mothers, and mothers in low-income circumstances (Merewood & others, 2007). In one study of low-income mothers in Georgia, interventions (such as counseling focused on the benefits of breast feeding and the free loan of a breast pump) increased the incidence of breast feeding (Ahluwalia & others, 2000). Increasingly, mothers who return to work in the infant's first year of life use a breast pump to extract breast milk that can be stored for later feeding of the infant when the mother is not present.

As mentioned earlier, the American Academy of Pediatrics Section on Breastfeeding (2012) strongly endorses exclusive breast feeding for the first 6 months and further recommends breast feeding for another year. Are there circumstances when mothers should not breast feed? Yes, a mother should not breast feed (1) when she is infected with HIV or some other infectious disease that can be transmitted through her milk, (2) if she has active tuberculosis, or (3) if she is taking any drug that may not be safe for the infant (D'Apolito, 2013; Fowler, 2014).

Some women cannot breast feed their infants because of physical difficulties; others feel guilty if they terminate breast feeding early. Mothers may also worry that they are depriving their infants of important emotional and psychological benefits if they bottle feed rather than breast feed. Some researchers have found, however, that there are no psychological differences between breast-fed and bottle-fed infants (Ferguson, Harwood, & Shannon, 1987; Young, 1990).

A further issue in interpreting the benefits of breast feeding was underscored in large-scale research reviews (Agency for Healthcare Research and Quality, 2007; Ip & others, 2009). While highlighting a number of breast feeding benefits for children and mothers, the report issued a caution about breast feeding research: None of the findings imply causality. Breast versus bottle feeding studies are correlational rather than experimental, and women who breast feed are wealthier, older, more educated, and likely more health-conscious than their bottle feeding counterparts, which could explain why breast-fed children are healthier.

Malnutrition in Infancy Many infants around the world are malnourished (UNICEF, 2014). Early weaning of infants from breast milk to inadequate sources of nutrients, such as unsuitable and unsanitary cow's milk formula, can cause protein deficiency and malnutrition in infants. However, as we saw in the chapter opening story, a concern in developing countries is the increasing number of women who are HIV-positive and the fear that they will transmit this virus to their offspring (Tenthani & others, 2014). Breast feeding is more optimal for mothers and infants in developing countries, except for mothers who have or are suspected of having HIV/AIDS.

A recent large-scale study that examined feeding practices in 28 developing countries found that the practices were far from optimal (Arabi & others, 2012). In this study, only 25 percent of infants 5 months of age and younger were breast fed. Also, feeding guidelines call for introducing complementary foods (solid and semisolid foods) beginning at 6 months. However, in this study, only 50 percent of the caregivers reported feeding their 6- to 8-month-olds complementary foods.

Two life-threatening conditions that can result from malnutrition are marasmus and kwashiorkor. **Marasmus** is caused by a severe protein-calorie deficiency and results in a wasting away of body tissues in the infant's first year. The infant becomes grossly underweight and his or her muscles atrophy. **Kwashiorkor,** caused by severe protein deficiency, usually

Improving the Nutrition of Infants and Young Children Living in Low-Income Families

Poor nutrition is a special concern in the lives of infants from low-income families. To address this problem in the United States, the WIC (Women, Infants, and Children) program provides federal grants to states for healthy supplemental foods, health care referrals, and nutrition education for women from low-income families beginning in pregnancy, and to infants and young children up to 5 years of age who are at nutritional risk (Campbell & others, 2014; Harrison & others, 2014; Langellier & others, 2014; Whaley & others, 2013). WIC serves approximately 7,500,000 participants in the United States.

Positive influences on infants' and young children's nutrition and health have been found for participants in WIC (Davis, Lazariu, & Sekhobo, 2010; Sekhobo & others, 2010). One study revealed that a WIC program that introduced peer counseling services for pregnant women increased breast feeding initiation by 27 percent (Olson & others, 2010a, b). Another study found that entry during the first trimester of pregnancy to the WIC program in Rhode Island reduced maternal cigarette smoking (Brodsky, Viner-Brown, & Handler, 2009). And a multiple-year literacy intervention with Spanish-speaking families in the WIC program in Los Angeles increased literacy resources and activities

Participants in the WIC program. *What are some changes the WIC program is trying to implement?*

at home, which in turn led to a higher level of school readiness in children (Whaley & others, 2011).

Why would the WIC program provide lactation counseling as part of its services?

---

appears between 1 and 3 years of age. Children with kwashiorkor sometimes appear to be well fed even though they are not because the disease can cause the child's abdomen and feet to swell with water. Kwashiorkor causes a child's vital organs to collect the nutrients that are present and deprive other parts of the body of them. The child's hair also becomes thin, brittle, and colorless, and the child's behavior often becomes listless.

Even if it is not fatal, severe and lengthy malnutrition is detrimental to physical, cognitive, and social development (Prado & others, 2014; UNICEF, 2014). One study found that Asian Indian children who had a history of chronic malnutrition performed more poorly on tests of attention and memory than their counterparts who were not malnourished (Kar, Rao, & Chandramouli, 2008). And a longitudinal study revealed that Barbadians who had experienced moderate to severe protein/energy malnutrition during infancy had persisting attention deficits when they were 40 years old (Galler & others, 2012). Researchers also have found that interventions can benefit individuals who have experienced malnutrition in infancy. For example, in one study standard nutritional care combined with a psychosocial intervention (group meetings with mothers and play sessions with infants, as well as six months of home visits) reduced the negative effects of malnutrition on severely malnourished Bangladesh 6- to 24-month-olds' cognitive development (Najar & others, 2008).

To read further about providing nutritional supplements to improve infants' and young children's nutrition, see *Connecting Development to Life*.

Adequate early nutrition is an important aspect of healthy development (Gorin & others, 2014). In addition to sound nutrition, children need a nurturing, supportive environment (Daniels & others, 2014). One individual who has stood out as an advocate of caring for children is T. Berry Brazelton, who is featured in *Connecting with Careers*.

T. Berry Brazelton, Pediatrician

T. Berry Brazelton is America's best-known pediatrician as a result of his numerous books, television appearances, and newspaper and magazine articles about parenting and children's health. He takes a family-centered approach to child development issues and communicates with parents in easy-to-understand ways.

Dr. Brazelton founded the Child Development Unit at Boston Children's Hospital and created the Brazelton Neonatal Behavioral Assessment Scale, a widely used measure of the newborn's health and well-being (which you read about in Chapter 3). He also has conducted a number of research studies on infants and children and has been president of the Society for Research in Child Development, a leading research organization.

T. Berry Brazelton, pediatrician, with a young child.

For more information about what pediatricians do, see page 43 in the Careers in Life-Span Development appendix.

Review *Connect* Reflect

LG1 Discuss physical growth and development in infancy

Review

- What are cephalocaudal and proximodistal patterns?
- What changes in height and weight take place in infancy?
- What are some key features of the brain and its development in infancy?
- What changes occur in sleep during infancy?
- What are infants' nutritional needs?

Connect

- What types of brain research technology can be used to study infants that cannot

be used to study them before they are born? Which can be used on adults but not infants? How might this affect our understanding of the human brain across the life span?

Reflect *Your Own Personal Journey of Life*

- What sleep and nutrition guidelines would you follow for enhancing the health and safety of your own infant?

---

2 Motor Development

LG2 Describe infants' motor development.

The Dynamic Systems View	Reflexes	Gross Motor Skills	Fine Motor Skills

As a newborn, Ramona, whom you read about in the chapter opening, could suck, fling her arms, and tightly grip a finger placed in her tiny hand. Within just two years, she would be toddling around on her own, opening doors and jars as she explored her little world. Are her accomplishments inevitable? How do infants develop their motor skills, and which skills do they develop when?

THE DYNAMIC SYSTEMS VIEW

Developmentalist Arnold Gesell (1934) thought his painstaking observations had revealed how people develop their motor skills. He had discovered that infants and children develop rolling, sitting, standing, and other motor skills in a fixed order and within specific time frames. These observations, said Gesell, show that motor development comes about through the unfolding of a genetic plan, or *maturation.*

Later studies, however, demonstrated that the sequence of developmental milestones is not as fixed as Gesell indicated and not due as much to heredity as Gesell argued (Adolph & Robinson, 2013; Berger, Chan, & Adolph, 2014). In the last two decades, the study of motor development experienced a renaissance as psychologists developed new insights about *how* motor skills develop (Gerson & Woodward, 2014; Kretch, Franchak, & Adolph, 2014). One increasingly influential perspective is dynamic systems theory, proposed by Esther Thelen (Thelen & Smith, 1998, 2006).

According to **dynamic systems theory,** infants assemble motor skills for perceiving and acting. Notice that perception and action are coupled, according to this theory (Keen, Lee, & Adolph, 2014; Thelen & Smith, 2006). To develop motor skills, infants must perceive something in their environment that motivates them to act and use their perceptions to fine-tune their movements. Motor skills represent solutions to the infant's goals (Gerson & Woodward, 2014; Keen, Lee, & Adolph, 2014).

How is a motor skill developed, according to this theory? When infants are motivated to do something, they might create a new motor behavior. The new behavior is the result of many converging factors: the development of the nervous system, the body's physical properties and its possibilities for movement, the goal the child is motivated to reach, and the environmental support for the skill. For example, babies learn to walk only when maturation of the nervous system allows them to control certain leg muscles, when their legs have grown enough to support their weight, and when they want to move.

Mastering a motor skill requires the infant's active efforts to coordinate several components of the skill. Infants explore and select possible solutions to the demands of a new task; they assemble adaptive patterns by modifying their current movement patterns. The first step occurs when the infant is motivated by a challenge—such as the desire to cross a room—and gets into the "ballpark" of the task demands by taking a couple of stumbling steps. Then, the infant "tunes" these movements to make them smoother and more effective. The tuning is achieved through repeated cycles of action and perception of the consequences of that action. According to the dynamic systems view, even universal milestones, such as crawling, reaching, and walking, are learned through this process of adaptation: Infants modulate their movement patterns to fit a new task by exploring and selecting possible configurations (Kretch, Franchak, & Adolph, 2014).

To see how dynamic systems theory explains motor behavior, imagine that you offer a new toy to a baby named Gabriel (Thelen & others, 1993). There is no exact program that can tell Gabriel ahead of time how to move his arm and hand and fingers to grasp the toy. Gabriel must adapt to his goal—grasping the toy—and the context. From his sitting position, he must make split-second adjustments to extend his arm, holding his body steady so that his arm and torso don't plow into the toy. Muscles in his arm and shoulder contract and stretch in a host of combinations, exerting a variety of forces. He improvises a way to reach out with one arm and wrap his fingers around the toy.

Thus, according to dynamic systems theory, motor development is not a passive process in which genes dictate the unfolding of a sequence of skills over time. Rather, the infant actively puts together a skill to achieve a goal within the constraints set by the infant's body and environment. Nature and nurture, the infant and the environment, are all working together as part of an ever-changing system.

As we examine the course of motor development, we will describe how dynamic systems theory applies to some specific skills. First, though, let's examine how the story of motor development begins with reflexes.

REFLEXES

The newborn is not completely helpless. Among other things, it has some basic reflexes. For example, when submerged in water, the newborn automatically holds its breath and contracts its throat to keep water out.

Reflexes are built-in reactions to stimuli; they govern the newborn's movements, which are automatic and beyond the newborn's control. Reflexes are genetically carried survival

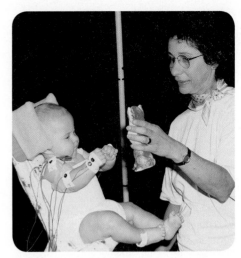

Esther Thelen is shown conducting an experiment to discover how infants learn to control their arm movements to reach and grasp for objects. A computer device is used to monitor the infant's arm movements and to track muscle patterns. Thelen's research is conducted from a dynamic systems perspective. *What is the nature of this perspective?*

How might dynamic systems theory explain the development of learning to walk?

dynamic systems theory The perspective on motor development that seeks to explain how motor behaviors are assembled for perceiving and acting.

reflexes Built-in reactions to stimuli that govern the newborn's movements, which are automatic and beyond the newborn's control.

rooting reflex A newborn's built-in reaction that occurs when the infant's cheek is stroked or the side of the mouth is touched. In response, the infant turns his or her head toward the side that was touched, in an apparent effort to find something to suck.

sucking reflex A newborn's built-in reaction to automatically suck an object placed in its mouth. The sucking reflex enables the infant to get nourishment before he or she has associated a nipple with food and also serves as a self-soothing or self-regulating mechanism.

Moro reflex A neonatal startle response that occurs in reaction to a sudden, intense noise or movement. When startled, the newborn arches its back, throws its head back, and flings out its arms and legs. Then the newborn rapidly pulls its arms and legs close to the center of the body.

grasping reflex A neonatal reflex that occurs when something touches the infant's palms. The infant responds by grasping tightly.

gross motor skills Motor skills that involve large-muscle activities, such as walking.

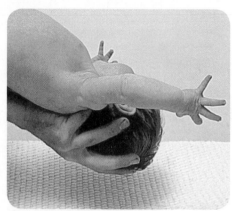

FIGURE **4.12**

NEWBORN REFLEXES. Young infants have several reflexes, including the Moro reflex (*top*) and grasping reflex (*bottom*).

mechanisms. They allow infants to respond adaptively to their environment before they have had the opportunity to learn. The rooting and sucking reflexes are important examples. Both have survival value for newborn mammals, who must find a mother's breast to obtain nourishment. The **rooting reflex** occurs when the infant's cheek is stroked or the side of the mouth is touched. In response, the infant turns its head toward the side that was touched in an apparent effort to find something to suck. The **sucking reflex** occurs when newborns automatically suck an object placed in their mouth. This reflex enables newborns to get nourishment before they have associated a nipple with food and also serves as a self-soothing or self-regulating mechanism.

Another example is the **Moro reflex,** which occurs in response to a sudden, intense noise or movement (see Figure 4.12). When startled, the newborn arches its back, throws back its head, and flings out its arms and legs. Then the newborn rapidly draws in its arms and legs. The Moro reflex is believed to be a way of grabbing for support while falling; it would have had survival value for our primate ancestors.

Some reflexes—coughing, sneezing, blinking, shivering, and yawning, for example—persist throughout life. They are as important for the adult as they are for the infant. Other reflexes, though, disappear several months following birth, as the infant's brain matures and voluntary control over many behaviors develops. The rooting and Moro reflexes, for example, tend to disappear when the infant is 3 to 4 months old.

The movements of some reflexes eventually become incorporated into more complex, voluntary actions. One important example is the **grasping reflex,** which occurs when something touches the infant's palms (see Figure 4.12). The infant responds by grasping tightly. By the end of the third month, the grasping reflex diminishes and the infant shows a more voluntary grasp. As its motor coordination becomes smoother, the infant will grasp objects, carefully manipulate them, and explore their qualities.

The old view of reflexes is that they were exclusively genetic, built-in mechanisms that governed the infant's movements. The new perspective on infant reflexes is that they are not automatic or completely beyond the infant's control. For example, infants can alternate the movement of their legs to make a mobile jiggle or change their sucking rate to listen to a recording (Adolph & Berger, 2013).

GROSS MOTOR SKILLS

Ask any parents about their baby, and sooner or later you are likely to hear about one or more motor milestones, such as "Cassandra just learned to crawl," "Jesse is finally sitting alone," or "Angela took her first step last week." Parents proudly announce such milestones as their children transform themselves from babies unable to lift their heads to toddlers who grab things off the grocery store shelf, chase a cat, and participate actively in the family's social life (Thelen, 2000). These milestones are examples of **gross motor skills,** which involve large-muscle activities such as moving one's arms and walking.

The Development of Posture How do gross motor skills develop? As a foundation, these skills require postural control (Adolph & Berger, 2013; Kretch & Adolph, 2013). For example, to track moving objects, you must be able to control the movement of your head in order to stabilize your gaze; before you can walk, you must be able to balance on one leg.

Posture is more than just holding still and straight. Posture is a dynamic process that is linked with sensory information in the skin, joints, and muscles, which tell us where we are in space; in vestibular organs in the inner ear that regulate balance and equilibrium; and in vision and hearing (Kretch, Franchak, & Adolph, 2014; Soska & Adolph, 2014; Thelen & Smith, 2006).

Newborn infants cannot voluntarily control their posture. Within a few weeks, though, they can hold their heads erect, and soon they can lift their heads while prone. By 2 months of age, babies can sit while supported on a lap or an infant seat, but they cannot sit independently until they are 6 or 7 months of age. Standing also develops gradually during the first year of life. By about 8 to 9 months of age, infants usually learn to pull themselves up and hold on to a chair, and they often can stand alone by about 10 to 12 months of age.

Newly crawling infant

Experienced walker

FIGURE 4.13

THE ROLE OF EXPERIENCE IN CRAWLING AND WALKING INFANTS' JUDGMENTS OF WHETHER TO GO DOWN A SLOPE. Karen Adolph (1997) found that locomotor experience rather than age was the primary predictor of adaptive responding on slopes of varying steepness. Newly crawling and walking infants could not judge the safety of the various slopes. With experience, they learned to avoid slopes where they would fall. When expert crawlers began to walk, they again made mistakes and fell, even though they had judged the same slope accurately when crawling. Adolph referred to this as the specificity of learning because it does not transfer across crawling and walking.

Learning to Walk Locomotion and postural control are closely linked, especially in walking upright (Adolph & Berger, 2013). To walk upright, the baby must be able both to balance on one leg as the other is swung forward and to shift the weight from one leg to the other.

Even young infants can make the alternating leg movements that are needed for walking. The neural pathways that control leg alternation are in place from a very early age, even at birth or before. Indeed, researchers have found that alternating leg movements occur during the fetal period and at birth (Adolph & Robinson, 2013).

If infants can produce forward stepping movements so early, why does it take them so long to learn to walk? The key skills in learning to walk appear to be stabilizing balance on one leg long enough to swing the other forward and shifting the weight without falling. These are difficult biomechanical problems to solve, and it takes infants about a year to do it.

In learning to locomote, infants learn what kinds of places and surfaces are safe for locomotion (Franchak & Adolph, 2014; Ishak, Franchak, & Adolph, 2014). Karen Adolph (1997) investigated how experienced and inexperienced crawling infants and walking infants go down steep slopes (see Figure 4.13). Newly crawling infants, who averaged about 8½ months in age, rather indiscriminately went down the steep slopes, often falling in the process (with their mothers next to the slope to catch them). After weeks of practice, the crawling babies became more adept at judging which slopes were too steep to crawl down and which ones they could navigate safely. New walkers also could not judge the safety of the slopes, but experienced walkers accurately matched their skills with the steepness of the slopes. They rarely fell downhill, either refusing to go down the steep slopes or going down backward in a cautious manner. Experienced walkers perceptually assessed the situation—looking, swaying, touching, and thinking before they moved down the slope. With experience, both the crawlers and the walkers learned to avoid the risky slopes where they would fall, integrating perceptual information with the development of a new motor behavior. In this research, we again see the importance of perceptual-motor coupling in the development of motor skills. Thus, practice is very important in the development of new motor skills (Berger, Chan, & Adolph, 2014).

Practice is especially important in learning to walk (Adolph & Robinson, 2013). "Thousands of daily walking steps, each step slightly different from the last because of variations in the terrain and the continually varying biomechanical constraints on the body, may help infants to identify the relevant" combination of strength and balance required to improve their walking skills (Adolph, Vereijken, & Shrout, 2003, p. 495). In a recent study, Adolph and her colleagues (2012) observed 12- to 19-month-olds during free play. Locomotor experience was extensive, with the infants averaging 2,368 steps and 17 falls per hour.

The First Year: Motor Development Milestones and Variations Figure 4.14 summarizes the range in which infants accomplish various gross motor skills during the first year, culminating in the ability to walk easily. The timing of these milestones, especially the

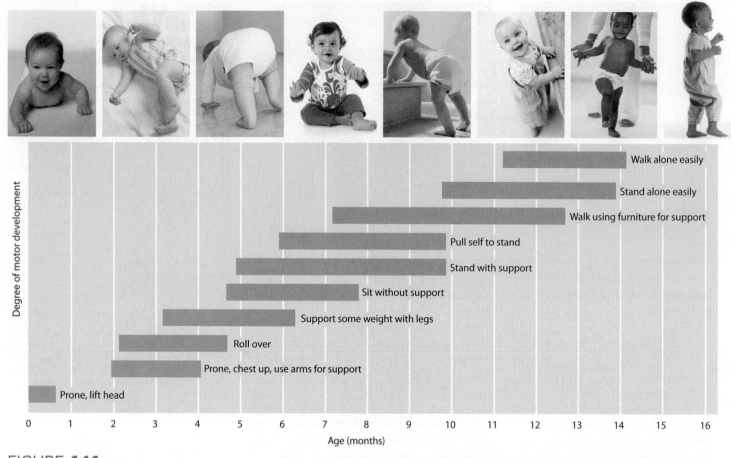

FIGURE **4.14**

MILESTONES IN GROSS MOTOR DEVELOPMENT. The horizontal red bars indicate the range in which most infants reach various milestones in gross motor development.

later ones, may vary by as much as two to four months, and experiences can modify the onset of these accomplishments (Adolph & Berger, 2013). For example, since 1992, when pediatricians began recommending that parents place their babies on their backs when they sleep, fewer babies crawled, and those who crawled did so later (Davis & others, 1998). Also, some infants do not follow the standard sequence of motor accomplishments. For example, many American infants never crawl on their belly or on their hands and knees. They may discover an idiosyncratic form of locomotion before walking, such as rolling, or they might never locomote until they get upright (Adolph & Robinson, 2013). In the African Mali tribe, most infants do not crawl (Bril, 1999). And in Jamaica, approximately one-fourth of babies skip crawling (Hopkins, 1991).

According to Karen Adolph and Sarah Berger (2005), "the old-fashioned view that growth and motor development reflect merely the age-related output of maturation is, at best, incomplete. Rather, infants acquire new skills with the help of their caregivers in a real-world environment of objects, surfaces, and planes."

Development in the Second Year   The motor accomplishments of the first year bring increasing independence, allowing infants to explore their environment more extensively and to initiate interaction with others more readily. In the second year of life, toddlers become more motorically skilled and mobile. Motor activity during the second year is vital to the child's competent development, and few restrictions, except for safety, should be placed on their adventures.

By 13 to 18 months, toddlers can pull a toy attached to a string and use their hands and legs to climb up a number of steps. By 18 to 24 months, toddlers can walk quickly or run stiffly for a short distance, balance on their feet in a squatting position while playing with

A baby is an angel whose wings decrease as his legs increase.

—FRENCH PROVERB

objects on the floor, walk backward without losing their balance, stand and kick a ball without falling, stand and throw a ball, and jump in place.

Can parents give their babies a head start on becoming physically fit and physically talented through structured exercise classes? Most infancy experts recommend against structured exercise classes for babies. But there are other ways to guide infants' motor development.

Mothers in developing countries tend to stimulate their infants' motor skills more than mothers in more developed countries (Hopkins, 1991). In many African, Indian, and Caribbean cultures, mothers massage and stretch their infants during daily baths (Adolph, Karasik, & Tamis-LeMonda, 2010). Mothers in the Gusii culture of Kenya also encourage vigorous movement in their babies.

Do these cultural variations make a difference in the infant's motor development? When caregivers provide babies with physical guidance by physically handling them in special ways (such as stroking, massaging, or stretching) or by giving them opportunities for exercise, the infants often reach motor milestones earlier than infants whose caregivers have not provided these activities (Adolph, Karasik, & Tamis-LeMonda, 2010). For example, Jamaican mothers expect their infants to sit and walk alone two to three months earlier than English mothers do (Hopkins & Westra, 1990). And in sub-Saharan Africa, traditional practices in many villages involve mothers and siblings engaging babies in exercises, such as frequent exercise for trunk and pelvic muscles (Super & Harkness, 1997).

Many forms of restricted movement—such as Chinese sandbags, orphanage restrictions, and failure of caregivers to encourage movement in Budapest—have been found to produce substantial delays in motor development (Adolph, Karasik, & Tamis-LeMonda, 2010). In some rural Chinese provinces, for example, babies are placed in a bag of fine sand, which acts as a diaper and is changed once a day. The baby is left alone, face up, and is visited only when being fed by the mother (Xie & Young, 1999). Some studies of swaddling show slight delays in motor development, but other studies show no delays. Cultures that do swaddle infants usually do so early in the infant's development when the infant is not mobile; when the infant becomes more mobile, swaddling decreases.

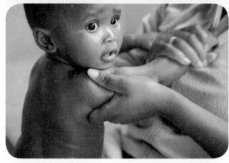

(*Top*) In the Algonquin culture in Quebec, Canada, babies are strapped to a cradle board for much of their infancy. (*Bottom*) In Jamaica, mothers massage and stretch their infants' arms and legs. *To what extent do cultural variations in the activity infants engage in influence the time at which they reach motor milestones?*

FINE MOTOR SKILLS

Whereas gross motor skills involve large muscle activity, **fine motor skills** involve finely tuned movements. Grasping a toy, using a spoon, buttoning a shirt, or anything that requires finger dexterity demonstrates fine motor skills. Infants have hardly any control over fine motor skills at birth, but newborns do have many components of what will become finely coordinated arm, hand, and finger movements (McCormack, Hoerl, & Butterfill, 2012).

The onset of reaching and grasping marks a significant achievement in infants' ability to interact with their surroundings (Libertus & others, 2013; Sacrey & others, 2014; Ziemer, Plumert, & Pick, 2012). During the first two years of life, infants refine how they reach and grasp (Needham, 2009). Initially, infants reach by moving their shoulders and elbows crudely, swinging toward an object. Later, when infants reach for an object they move their wrists, rotate their hands, and coordinate their thumb and forefinger. Infants do not have to see their own hands in order to reach for an object (Clifton & others, 1993). Cues from muscles, tendons, and joints, not sight of the limb, guide reaching by 4-month-old infants.

Infants refine their ability to grasp objects by developing two types of grasps. Initially, infants grip with the whole hand, which is called the *palmer grasp*. Later, toward the end of the first year, infants also grasp small objects with their thumb and forefinger, which is called the *pincer grip*. Their grasping system is very flexible. They vary their grip on an object depending on its size, shape, and texture, as well as the size of their own hands relative to the object's size. Infants grip small objects with their thumb and forefinger (and sometimes their middle finger too), whereas they grip large objects with all of the fingers of one hand or both hands.

Perceptual-motor coupling is necessary for the infant to coordinate grasping (Barrett, Traupman, & Needham, 2008). Which perceptual system the infant is most likely to use to coordinate grasping varies with age. Four-month-old infants rely greatly on touch to determine how they will grip an object; 8-month-olds are more likely to use vision as a guide (Newell & others, 1989). This developmental change is efficient because vision lets infants preshape their hands as they reach for an object.

A young girl using a pincer grip to pick up puzzle pieces.

fine motor skills Motor skills that involve more finely tuned movements, such as finger dexterity.

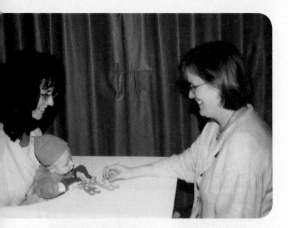

FIGURE **4.15**

INFANTS' USE OF "STICKY MITTENS" TO EXPLORE OBJECTS. Amy Needham and her colleagues (2002) found that "sticky mittens" enhanced young infants' object exploration skills.

Experience plays a role in reaching and grasping. In one study, 3-month-old infants participated in play sessions wearing "sticky mittens"—"mittens with palms that stuck to the edges of toys and allowed the infants to pick up the toys" (Needham, Barrett, & Peterman, 2002, p. 279) (see Figure 4.15). Infants who participated in sessions with the mittens grasped and manipulated objects earlier in their development than a control group of infants who did not receive the "mitten" experience. The infants who had worn the sticky mittens looked at the objects longer, swatted at them more during visual contact, and were more likely to mouth the objects. In a recent study, 5-month-old infants whose parents trained them to use the sticky mittens for 10 minutes a day over a two-week period showed advances in their reaching behavior at the end of the two weeks (Libertus & Needham, 2010).

Just as infants need to exercise their gross motor skills, they also need to exercise their fine motor skills (Needham, 2009). Especially when they can manage a pincer grip, infants delight in picking up small objects. Many develop the pincer grip and begin to crawl at about the same time, and infants at this time pick up virtually everything in sight, especially on the floor, and put the objects in their mouth. Thus, parents need to be vigilant in regularly monitoring what objects are within the infant's reach (Keen, 2005).

Rachel Keen (2011; Keen, Lee, & Adolph, 2014) emphasizes that tool use is an excellent context for studying problem solving in infants because tool use provides information about how infants plan to reach a goal. Researchers in this area have studied infants' intentional actions, which range from picking up a spoon in different orientations to retrieving rakes from inside tubes. A recent study explored motor origins of tool use by assessing developmental changes in banging movements in 6- to 15-month-olds (Kahrs, Jung, & Lockman, 2013). In this study, younger infants were inefficient and variable when banging an object but by one year of age infants showed consistent straight up-and-down hand movements that resulted in precise aiming and consistent levels of force.

Review Connect Reflect

 LG2 Describe infants' motor development.

Review

- What is the dynamic systems view?
- What are some reflexes that infants have?
- How do gross motor skills develop in infancy?
- How do fine motor skills develop in infancy?

Connect

- What are the differences between the grasping reflex present at birth and the

fine motor grasping skills an infant develops between 4 and 12 months of age?

Reflect *Your Own Personal Journey of Life*

- Think of a motor skill that you perform. How would dynamic systems theory explain your motor skill performance?

---

3 Sensory and Perceptual Development

LG3 Summarize the course of sensory and perceptual development in infancy.

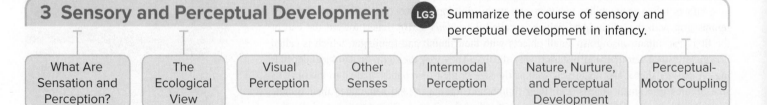

| What Are Sensation and Perception? | The Ecological View | Visual Perception | Other Senses | Intermodal Perception | Nature, Nurture, and Perceptual Development | Perceptual-Motor Coupling |

How do sensations and perceptions develop? Can a newborn see? If so, what can it perceive? What about the other senses—hearing, smell, taste, and touch? What are they like in the newborn, and how do they develop? Can an infant put together information from two modalities, such as sight and sound? These are among the intriguing questions that we will explore in this section.

WHAT ARE SENSATION AND PERCEPTION?

How does a newborn know that her mother's skin is soft rather than rough? How does a 5-year-old know what color his hair is? Infants and children "know" these things as a result of information that comes through the senses. Without vision, hearing, touch, taste, and smell, we would be isolated from the world; we would live in dark silence, a tasteless, colorless, feelingless void.

Sensation occurs when information interacts with sensory *receptors*—the eyes, ears, tongue, nostrils, and skin. The sensation of hearing occurs when waves of pulsating air are collected by the outer ear and transmitted through the bones of the inner ear to the auditory nerve. The sensation of vision occurs as rays of light contact the eyes, become focused on the retina, and are transmitted by the optic nerve to the visual centers of the brain.

Perception is the interpretation of what is sensed. The air waves that contact the ears might be interpreted as noise or as musical sounds, for example. The physical energy transmitted to the retina of the eye might be interpreted as a particular color, pattern, or shape, depending on how it is perceived.

THE ECOLOGICAL VIEW

For the past several decades, much of the research on perceptual development in infancy has been guided by the ecological view of Eleanor and James J. Gibson (E. J. Gibson, 1969, 1989, 2001; J. J. Gibson, 1966, 1979). They argue that we do not have to take bits and pieces of data from sensations and build up representations of the world in our minds. Instead, our perceptual system can select from the rich information that the environment itself provides.

According to the Gibsons' **ecological view,** we directly perceive information that exists in the world around us. This view is called *ecological* "because it connects perceptual capabilities to information available in the world of the perceiver" (Kellman & Arterberry, 2006, p. 112). Thus, perception brings us into contact with the environment so we can interact with and adapt to it. Perception is designed for action. Perception gives people such information as when to duck, when to turn their bodies as they move through a narrow passageway, and when to put their hands up to catch something.

In the Gibsons' view, objects have **affordances,** which are opportunities for interaction offered by objects that fit within our capabilities to perform activities. A pot may afford you something to cook with, and it may afford a toddler something to bang. Adults typically know when a chair is appropriate for sitting, when a surface is safe for walking, or when an object is within reach. We directly and accurately perceive these affordances by sensing information from the environment—the light or sound reflecting from the surfaces of the world—and from our own bodies through muscle receptors, joint receptors, and skin receptors, for example (Franchak & Adolph, 2014; Ishak, Franchak, & Adolph, 2014).

An important developmental question is: What affordances can infants or children detect and use? (Ishak, Franchak, & Adolph, 2014). In one study, for example, when babies who could walk were faced with a squishy waterbed, they stopped and explored it, then chose to crawl rather than walk across it (Gibson & others, 1987). They combined perception and action to adapt to the demands of the task.

Similarly, as we described earlier in the section on motor development, infants who were just learning to crawl or just learning to walk were less cautious when confronted with a steep slope than experienced crawlers or walkers were (Adolph, 1997). The more experienced crawlers and walkers perceived that a slope *affords* the possibility for not only faster locomotion but also for falling. Again, infants coupled perception and action to make a decision about what to do in their environment. Through perceptual development, children become more efficient at discovering and using affordances (Franchak & Adolph, 2014).

Studying infants' perceptions has not been an easy task. For instance, if newborns have limited communication abilities and are unable to verbalize what they are seeing, hearing, smelling, and so on, how can we study their perception? *Connecting Through Research* describes some of the ingenious ways researchers study infants' perceptions.

sensation The product of the interaction between information and the sensory receptors—the eyes, ears, tongue, nostrils, and skin.

perception The interpretation of what is sensed.

ecological view The view that perception functions to bring organisms in contact with the environment and to increase adaptation.

affordances Opportunities for interaction offered by objects that fit within our capabilities to perform functional activities.

How Can Newborns' Perception Be Studied?

The creature has poor motor coordination and can move itself only with great difficulty. Although it cries when uncomfortable, it uses few other vocalizations. In fact, it sleeps most of the time, about 16 to 17 hours a day. You are curious about this creature and want to know more about what it can do. You think to yourself, "I wonder if it can see. How could I find out?"

You obviously have a communication problem with the creature. You must devise a way that will allow the creature to "tell" you that it can see. While examining the creature one day, you make an interesting discovery. When you move an object horizontally in front of the creature, its eyes follow the object's movement.

The creature's eye movement suggests that it has at least some vision. In case you haven't already guessed, the creature you have been reading about is the human infant, and the role you played is that of a researcher interested in devising techniques to learn about the infant's visual perception. After years of work, scientists have developed research methods and tools sophisticated enough to examine the subtle abilities of infants and to interpret their complex actions (Bendersky & Sullivan, 2007).

Visual Preference Method

Robert Fantz (1963) was a pioneer in this effort. Fantz made an important discovery that advanced the ability of researchers to investigate infants' visual perception: Infants look at different things for different lengths of time. Fantz placed an infant in a "looking chamber," which had two visual displays on the ceiling above the infant's head. An experimenter viewed the infant's eyes by looking through a peephole. If the infant was fixating on one of the displays, the experimenter could see the display's reflection in the infant's eyes. This allowed the experimenter to determine how long the infant looked at each display. Fantz (1963) found that infants only two days old looked longer at patterned stimuli, such as

faces and concentric circles, than at red, white, or yellow discs. Infants 2 to 3 weeks old also preferred to look at patterns—a face, a piece of printed matter, or a bull's-eye—longer than at red, yellow, or white discs (see Figure 4.16). Fantz' research method—studying whether infants can distinguish one stimulus from another by measuring the length of time they attend to different stimuli—is referred to as the **visual preference method.**

Habituation and Dishabituation

Another way that researchers have studied infant perception is to present a stimulus (such as a sight or a sound) a number of times. If the infant decreases its response to the stimulus after several presentations, it indicates that the infant is no longer interested in looking at the stimulus. If the researcher now presents a new stimulus, the infant's response will recover—indicating the infant can discriminate between the old and new stimulus (Baker, Pettigrew, & Poulin-Dubois, 2014; Gerson & Woodward, 2014).

Habituation is the name given to decreased responsiveness to a stimulus after repeated presentations of the stimulus. **Dishabituation** is the recovery of a habituated response after a change in stimulation. Newborn infants can habituate to repeated sights, sounds, smells, or

visual preference method A method used to determine whether infants can distinguish one stimulus from another by measuring the length of time they attend to different stimuli.

habituation Decreased responsiveness to a stimulus after repeated presentations of the stimulus.

dishabituation Recovery of a habituated response after a change in stimulation.

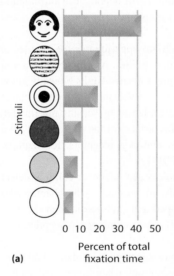

(a)

Stimuli

Percent of total fixation time

0 10 20 30 40 50

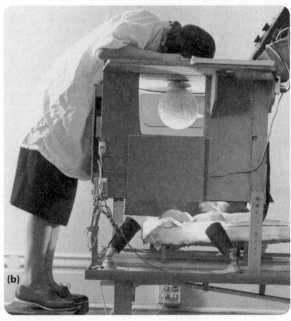

(b)

FIGURE **4.16**

FANTZ' EXPERIMENT ON INFANTS' VISUAL PERCEPTION. (*a*) Infants 2 to 3 weeks old preferred to look at some stimuli more than others. In Fantz' experiment, infants preferred to look at patterns rather than at color or brightness. For example, they looked longer at a face, a piece of printed matter, or a bull's-eye than at red, yellow, or white discs. (*b*) Fantz used a "looking chamber" to study infants' perception of stimuli.

(*continued*)

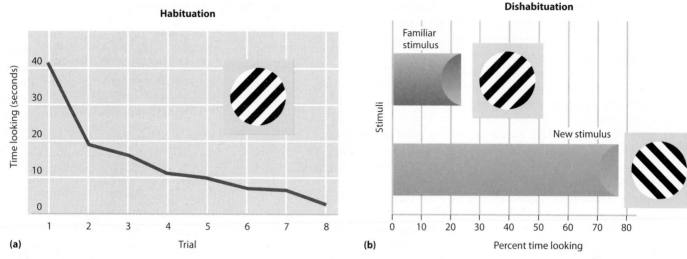

(a) Habituation — Time looking (seconds) vs Trial

(b) Dishabituation — Stimuli vs Percent time looking

FIGURE **4.17**

HABITUATION AND DISHABITUATION. In the first part of one study, (*a*) 7-hour-old newborns were shown a stimulus. As indicated, the newborns looked at it an average of 41 seconds when it was first presented to them (Slater, Morison, & Somers, 1988). Over seven more presentations of the stimulus, they looked at it less and less. In the second part of the study, (*b*) infants were presented with both the familiar stimulus to which they had just become habituated and a new stimulus (which was rotated 90 degrees). The newborns looked at the new stimulus three times as long as the familiar stimulus.

touches (Rovee-Collier, 2004). Among the measures researchers use in habituation studies are sucking behavior (sucking stops when the young infant attends to a novel object), heart and respiration rates, and the length of time the infant looks at an object. Figure 4.17 shows the results of one study of habituation and dishabituation with newborns (Slater, Morison, & Somers, 1988).

High-Amplitude Sucking

To assess an infant's attention to sound, researchers often use a method called high-amplitude sucking. In this method, infants are given a nonnutritive nipple to suck, and the nipple is connected to a sound-generating system. The researcher computes a baseline high-amplitude sucking rate in a one-minute silent period. Following the baseline, presentation of a sound is made contingent on the rate of high-amplitude sucking. Initially babies suck frequently so the sound occurs often. Gradually they lose interest in hearing the same sound, so they begin to suck less often. Then the researcher

FIGURE **4.18**

AN INFANT WEARING EYE-TRACKING HEADGEAR. Photo from Karen Adolph's laboratory at New York University.

changes the sound that is being presented. If the babies renew their vigorous sucking, the inference is that they have discriminated the sound change and are sucking more because they want to hear the interesting new sound (Menn & Stoel-Gammon, 2009).

The Orienting Response and Eye-Tracking

A technique that can be used to determine whether an infant can see or hear is the orienting response, which involves turning one's head toward a sight or sound. However, the most important recent advance in measuring infant perception is the development of sophisticated eye-tracking equipment (Eisner & others, 2013; Kretch, Franchak, & Adolph, 2014). Eye-tracking consists of measuring eye movements that follow (track) a moving object and can be used to evaluate an infant's early visual ability, or a startle response can determine an infant's reaction to a noise (Bendersky & Sullivan, 2007). Figure 4.18 shows an infant wearing an eye-tracking headgear in a

(conituned)

recent study on visually guided motor behavior and social interaction. Most studies of infant development use remote optics eye trackers that have a camera that is not attached to the infant's head.

One of the main reasons that infant perception researchers are so enthusiastic about the recent availability of sophisticated eye-tracking equipment is that looking time is among the most important measures of infant perceptual and cognitive development (Aslin, 2012). The new eye-tracking equipment allows for far greater precision in assessing various aspects of infant looking and gaze than is possible with human observation (Oakes, 2012). Among the areas of infant perception in which eye-tracking equipment is being used are memory, joint attention, and face processing (Oturai, Kolling, & Knopf, 2013; Pfeiffer, Vogeley, & Schilbach, 2013; Righi & others, 2014). Further, eye-tracking equipment is improving our understanding of atypically developing infants, such as those with autism (Guimard-Brunault & others, 2014).

A recent eye-tracking study shed light on the effectiveness of TV programs and DVDs that claim to educate infants (Kirkorian, Anderson, & Keen, 2012). In this study, 1-year-olds, 4-year-olds, and adults watched *Sesame Street* and the eye-tracking equipment recorded precisely what they looked at on the screen. The 1-year-olds were far less likely to consistently look at the same part of the screen as their older counterparts, suggesting that the 1-year-olds showed little understanding of the

Sesame Street video but instead were more likely to be attracted by what was salient than by what was relevant.

Equipment

Technology can facilitate the use of most methods for investigating the infant's perceptual abilities. Video-recording equipment allows researchers to investigate elusive behaviors. High-speed computers make it possible to perform complex data analysis in minutes. Other equipment records respiration, heart rate, body movement, visual fixation, and sucking behavior, which provide clues to what the infant is perceiving. For example, some researchers use equipment that detects whether a change in infants' respiration follows a change in the pitch of a sound. If so, it suggests that the infants heard the pitch change.

Scientists have had to be very creative when assessing the development of infants, discovering ways to "interview" them even though they cannot yet talk. Other segments of the population, such as adults who have suffered from a stroke, have difficulty communicating verbally. What kinds of methods or equipment do you think researchers might use to evaluate their perceptual abilities?

VISUAL PERCEPTION

What do newborns see? How does visual perception develop in infancy?

Visual Acuity and Human Faces Psychologist William James (1890/1950) called the newborn's perceptual world a "blooming, buzzing confusion." More than a century later, we can safely say that he was wrong (Atkinson & Braddick, 2013; Johnson & Hannon, 2015; Shirai & Imura, 2014). Even the newborn perceives a world with some order. That world, however, is far different from the one perceived by the toddler or the adult.

Just how well can infants see? At birth, the nerves and muscles and lens of the eye are still developing. As a result, newborns cannot see small things that are far away. The newborn's vision is estimated to be 20/240 on the well-known Snellen chart used for eye examinations, which means that a newborn can see at 20 feet what a normal adult can see at 240 feet (Aslin & Lathrop, 2008). In other words, an object 20 feet away is only as clear to the newborn as it would be if it were 240 feet away from an adult with normal vision (20/20). By 6 months of age, though, on *average* vision is 20/40 (Aslin & Lathrop, 2008).

Faces are possibly the most important visual stimuli in children's social environment, and it is important that they extract key information from others' faces (Lee & others, 2013). Infants show an interest in human faces soon after birth (Johnson & Hannon, 2015; Lee & others, 2013). Research shows that within hours after infants are born, they prefer to look at faces rather than other objects and to look at attractive faces more than at unattractive ones (Lee & others, 2013).

Figure 4.19 shows a computer estimation of what a picture of a face looks like to an infant at different ages from a distance of about 6 inches. Infants spend more time looking at their mother's face than a stranger's face as early as 12 hours after being born (Bushnell, 2003). By 3 months of age, infants match voices to faces, distinguish between male and female faces, and discriminate between faces of their own ethnic group and those of other ethnic groups (Gaither, Pauker, & Johnson, 2012; Kelly & others, 2005, 2007; Lee & others, 2013; Liu & others, 2011).

FIGURE **4.19**

VISUAL ACUITY DURING THE FIRST MONTHS OF LIFE. The four photographs represent a computer estimation of what a picture of a face looks like to a 1-month-old, 2-month-old, 3-month-old, and 1-year-old (which approximates the visual acuity of an adult).

As infants develop, they change the way they gather information from the visual world, including human faces (Otsuka & others, 2012; Simpson & others, 2014). One study recorded eye movements of 3-, 6-, and 9-month-old infants as they viewed clips from an animated film—*A Charlie Brown Christmas* (Frank, Vul, & Johnson, 2009). From 3 to 9 months of age, infants gradually began focusing their attention more on the faces in the animated film and less on salient background stimuli.

Experience plays an important role in face processing in infancy and later in development. One aspect of this experience involves the concept of *perceptual narrowing*, in which infants are more likely to recognize faces to which they have been exposed and are less likely to recognize faces to which they have not been exposed (Lee & others, 2013).

Also, as we discussed in the *Connecting Through Research* interlude, young infants can perceive certain patterns. With the help of his "looking chamber," Robert Fantz (1963) revealed that even 2- to 3-week-old infants prefer to look at patterned displays rather than nonpatterned displays. For example, they prefer to look at a normal human face rather than one with scrambled features, and prefer to look at a bull's-eye target or black-and-white stripes rather than a plain circle.

Color Vision The infant's color vision also improves (Brown & Lindsey, 2013). By 8 weeks, and possibly as early as 4 weeks, infants can discriminate some colors (Kelly, Borchert, & Teller, 1997). By 4 months of age, they have color preferences that mirror adults' in some cases, preferring saturated colors such as royal blue over pale blue, for example (Bornstein, 1975). In part, the changes in vision described here reflect maturation. Experience, however, is also necessary for color vision to develop normally (Sugita, 2004).

Perceptual Constancy Some perceptual accomplishments are especially intriguing because they indicate that the infant's perception goes beyond the information provided by the senses (Johnson, 2013; Slater & others, 2011). This is the case in perceptual constancy, in which sensory stimulation is changing but perception of the physical world remains constant. If infants did not develop perceptual constancy, each time they saw an object at a different distance or in a different orientation, they would perceive it as a different object. Thus, the development of perceptual constancy allows infants to perceive their world as stable. Two types of perceptual constancy are size constancy and shape constancy.

Size constancy is the recognition that an object remains the same even though the retinal image of the object changes as you move toward or away from the object. The farther away from us an object is, the smaller its image is on our eyes. Thus, the size of an object on the retina is not sufficient to tell us its actual size. For example, you perceive a bicycle standing right in front of you as smaller than the car parked across the street, even though the bicycle casts a larger image on your eyes than the car does. When you move away from the bicycle, you do not perceive it to be shrinking even though its image on your retinas shrinks; you perceive its size as constant.

But what about babies? Do they have size constancy? Researchers have found that babies as young as 3 months of age show size constancy (Bower, 1966; Day & McKenzie, 1973). However, at 3 months of age, this ability is not full-blown. It continues to develop until 10 or 11 years of age (Kellman & Banks, 1998).

size constancy The recognition that an object remains the same even though the retinal image of the object changes as you move toward or away from the object.

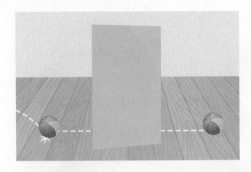

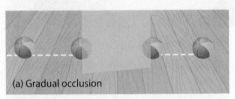

(a) Gradual occlusion

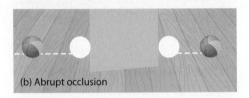

(b) Abrupt occlusion

(c) Implosion

FIGURE **4.20**

INFANTS' PREDICTIVE TRACKING OF A BRIEFLY OCCLUDED MOVING BALL. The top photograph shows the visual scene that infants experienced. At the beginning of each event, a multicolored ball bounced up and down with an accompanying bouncing sound, and then rolled across the floor until it disappeared behind the partition. The bottom drawing shows the three stimulus events that the 5- to 9-month-old infants experienced: (*a*) Gradual occlusion—the ball gradually disappears behind the right side of the occluding partition located in the center of the display. (*b*) Abrupt occlusion—the ball abruptly disappears when it reaches the location of the white circle and then abruptly reappears two seconds later at the location of the second white circle on the other side of the occluding partition. (*c*) Implosion—the rolling ball quickly decreases in size as it approaches the occluding partition and rapidly increases in size as it reappears on the other side of the occluding partition.

shape constancy The recognition that an object's shape remains the same even though its orientation to us changes.

Shape constancy is the recognition that an object remains the same shape even though its orientation to us changes. Look around the room you are in right now. You likely see objects of varying shapes, such as tables and chairs. If you get up and walk around the room, you will see these objects from different sides and angles. Even though your retinal image of the objects changes as you walk and look, you will still perceive the objects as having the same shape.

Do babies have shape constancy? As with size constancy, researchers have found that babies as young as 3 months of age have shape constancy (Bower, 1966; Day & McKenzie, 1973). Three-month-old infants, however, do not have shape constancy for irregularly shaped objects such as tilted planes (Cook & Birch, 1984).

Perception of Occluded Objects Look around where you are now. You likely see that some objects are partly occluded by other objects that are in front of them—possibly a desk behind a chair, some books behind a computer, or a car parked behind a tree. Do infants perceive an object as complete when it is occluded by an object in front of it?

In the first two months of postnatal development, infants don't perceive occluded objects as complete; instead, they perceive only what is visible (Johnson, 2013; Johnson & Hannon, 2015). Beginning at about 2 months of age, infants develop the ability to perceive that occluded objects are whole (Slater, Field, & Hernandez-Reif, 2007). How does perceptual completion develop? In Scott Johnson's research (2010, 2011, 2013), learning, experience, and self-directed exploration via eye movements play key roles in the development of perceptual completion in young infants.

Many objects that are occluded appear and disappear behind closer objects, as when you are walking down the street and see cars appear and disappear behind buildings as they move or you move. Infants develop the ability to track briefly occluded moving objects at about 3 to 5 months of age (Bertenthal, 2008). One study explored the ability of 5- to 9-month-old infants to track moving objects that disappeared gradually behind an occluded partition, disappeared abruptly, or imploded (shrank quickly in size) (Bertenthal, Longo, & Kenny, 2007) (see Figure 4.20). In this study, the infants were more likely to accurately predict the reappearance of the moving object when it disappeared gradually than when it vanished abruptly or imploded.

Depth Perception Might infants even perceive depth? To investigate this question, Eleanor Gibson and Richard Walk (1960) constructed a miniature cliff with a dropoff covered by glass in their laboratory. They placed infants on the edge of this visual cliff and had their mothers coax them to crawl onto the glass (see Figure 4.21). Most infants would not crawl out on the glass, choosing instead to remain on the shallow side, an indication that they could perceive depth.

In a recent research review, Karen Adolph and her colleagues (Adolph, Kretch, & LoBue, 2014) described how for many decades it was believed that crawling infants would not cross the clear glass indicating a dangerous dropoff because they have a fear of heights. However, they concluded that there is no research support for the view that infants have a fear of heights. Rather, recent research indicates that infants either crawl/walk across the glass precipice or don't do so because of their perception of the affordances it does or does not provide (Kretch & Adolph, 2013a, b). Research indicates that infants' exploration of the affordances increases on more challenging cliffs (deeper ones, for example) through such behaviors as patting the glass with their hands (Ueno & others, 2011).

Although researchers do not know precisely how early in life infants perceive depth, we do know that infants develop the ability to use binocular cues to depth by approximately 3 to 4 months of age.

OTHER SENSES

Other sensory systems besides vision also develop during infancy. We will explore development in hearing, touch and pain, smell, and taste.

Hearing During the last two months of pregnancy, as the fetus nestles in its mother's womb, it can hear sounds such as the mother's voice, music, and so on (Kisilevsky & others,

2009). Two psychologists wanted to find out if a fetus who heard Dr. Seuss' classic story *The Cat in the Hat* while still in the mother's womb would prefer hearing the story after birth (DeCasper & Spence, 1986). During the last months of pregnancy, 16 women read *The Cat in the Hat* to their fetuses. Then shortly after the babies were born, their mothers read either *The Cat in the Hat* or a story with a different rhyme and pace, *The King, the Mice and the Cheese* (which was not read to them during prenatal development). The infants sucked on a nipple in a different way when the mothers read the two stories, suggesting that the infants recognized the pattern and tone of *The Cat in the Hat* (see Figure 4.22). This study illustrates not only that a fetus can hear but also that it has a remarkable ability to learn and remember even before birth. A recent fMRI study confirmed capacity of the fetus to hear at 33 to 34 weeks into the prenatal period by assessing fetal brain response to auditory stimuli (Jardri & others, 2012).

The fetus can also recognize the mother's voice, as one study demonstrated (Kisilevsky & others, 2003). Sixty term fetuses (mean gestational age, 38.4 weeks) were exposed to a tape recording either of their mother or of a female stranger reading a passage. The sounds of the tape were delivered through a loudspeaker held just above the mother's abdomen. Fetal heart rate increased in response to the mother's voice but decreased in response to the stranger's voice.

What kind of changes in hearing take place during infancy? They involve perception of a sound's loudness, pitch, and localization:

- *Loudness.* Immediately after birth, infants cannot hear soft sounds quite as well as adults can; a stimulus must be louder to be heard by a newborn than by an adult (Trehub & others, 1991). For example, an adult can hear a whisper from about 4 to 5 feet away, but a newborn requires that sounds be closer to a normal conversational level to be heard at that distance. By three months of age, infants' perception of sounds improve, although some aspects of loudness perception do not reach adult levels until 5 to 10 years of age (Trainor & He, 2013).

- *Pitch.* Infants are also less sensitive to the pitch of a sound than adults are. *Pitch* is the perception of the frequency of a sound. A soprano voice sounds high-pitched, a bass voice low-pitched. Infants are less sensitive to low-pitched sounds and are more likely to hear high-pitched sounds (Aslin, Jusczyk, & Pisoni, 1998). A recent study revealed that by 7 months of age, infants can process simultaneous pitches when they hear voices but they are more likely to encode the higher-pitched voice (Marie & Trainor, 2013). By 2 years of age, infants have considerably improved their ability to distinguish sounds of different pitch.

- *Localization.* Even newborns can determine the general location from which a sound is coming, but by 6 months of age, they are more proficient at *localizing* sounds or detecting their origins. Their ability to localize sounds continues to improve during the second year (Burnham & Mattock, 2010).

Although infants can process variations in sound loudness, pitch, and localization, these aspects of hearing continue to improve during the childhood years (Trainor & He, 2013).

Touch and Pain
Do newborns respond to touch? Can they feel pain?

Newborns do respond to touch. A touch to the cheek produces a turning of the head; a touch to the lips produces sucking movements.

Newborns can also feel pain (Ganzewinkel & others, 2014; Rodkey & Pillai Riddell, 2013). If and when you have a son and consider whether he should be circumcised, the issue of an infant's pain perception probably will become important to you. Circumcision is usually performed on young boys about the third day after birth. Will your young son experience pain if he is circumcised when he is 3 days old? An investigation by Megan Gunnar and her colleagues (1987) found that newborn infant males cried intensely during circumcision. The circumcised

FIGURE **4.21**

EXAMINING INFANTS' DEPTH PERCEPTION ON THE VISUAL CLIFF. Eleanor Gibson and Richard Walk (1960) found that most infants would not crawl out on the glass, which, according to Gibson and Walk, indicated that they had depth perception. However, some critics point out that the visual cliff is a better indication of the infant's social referencing and fear of heights than of the infant's perception of depth.

(a)

(b)

FIGURE **4.22**

HEARING IN THE WOMB. (*a*) Pregnant mothers read *The Cat in the Hat* to their fetuses during the last few months of pregnancy. (*b*) When they were born, the babies preferred listening to a recording of their mothers reading *The Cat in the Hat*, as evidenced by their sucking on a nipple that produced this recording, rather than another story, *The King, the Mice and the Cheese.*

FIGURE **4.23**

NEWBORNS' PREFERENCE FOR THE SMELL OF THEIR MOTHER'S BREAST PAD. In the experiment by MacFarlane (1975), 6-day-old infants preferred to smell their mother's breast pad rather than a clean one that had never been used, but 2-day-old infants did not show this preference, indicating that odor preference requires several days of experience to develop.

infant also displays amazing resiliency. Within several minutes after the surgery, they can nurse and interact in a normal manner with their mothers. And, if allowed to, the newly circumcised newborn drifts into a deep sleep, which seems to serve as a coping mechanism.

For many years, doctors performed operations on newborns without anesthesia. This practice was accepted because of the dangers of anesthesia and because of the supposition that newborns do not feel pain. As researchers demonstrated that newborns can feel pain, the practice of operating on newborns without anesthesia is being challenged. Anesthesia now is used in some circumcisions (Morris & others, 2012).

Smell   Newborns can differentiate odors (Doty & Shah, 2008). The expressions on their faces seem to indicate that they like the way vanilla and strawberry smell but do not like the way rotten eggs and fish smell (Steiner, 1979). In one investigation, 6-day-old infants who were breast fed showed a clear preference for smelling their mother's breast pad rather than a clean breast pad (MacFarlane, 1975) (see Figure 4.23). However, when they were 2 days old, they did not show this preference, indicating that they require several days of experience to recognize this odor.

Taste   Sensitivity to taste is present even before birth (Doty & Shah, 2008). Human newborns learn tastes prenatally through the amniotic fluid and in breast milk after birth (Beauchamp & Mennella, 2009). In one study, even at only 2 hours of age, babies made different facial expressions when they tasted sweet, sour, and bitter solutions (Rosenstein & Oster, 1988). At about 4 months of age, infants begin to prefer salty tastes, which as newborns they had found to be aversive (Doty & Shah, 2008).

INTERMODAL PERCEPTION

Imagine yourself playing basketball or tennis. You are experiencing many visual inputs: the ball coming and going, other players moving around, and so on. However, you are experiencing many auditory inputs as well: the sound of the ball bouncing or being hit, the grunts and groans of other players, and so on. There is good correspondence between much of the visual and auditory information: When you see the ball bounce, you hear a bouncing sound; when a player stretches to hit a ball, you hear a groan. When you look at and listen to what is going on, you do not experience just the sounds or just the sights—you put all these things together. You experience a unitary episode. This is **intermodal perception,** which involves integrating information from two or more sensory modalities, such as vision and hearing (Bremner & others, 2012). Most perception is intermodal (Bahrick, 2010).

Early, exploratory forms of intermodal perception exist even in newborns (Bahrick & Hollich, 2008). For example, newborns turn their eyes and their head toward the sound of a voice or rattle when the sound is maintained for several seconds (Clifton & others, 1981), but the newborn can localize a sound and look at an object only in a crude way (Bechtold, Bushnell, & Salapatek, 1979). These early forms of intermodal perception become sharpened with experience in the first year of life (Kirkham & others, 2012). In one study, infants as young as 3 months old looked more at their mother when they also heard her voice and longer at their father when they also heard his voice (Spelke & Owsley, 1979). Thus, even young infants can coordinate visual-auditory information involving people.

Can young infants put vision and sound together as precisely as adults do? In the first six months, infants have difficulty connecting sensory input from different modes, but in the second half of the first year they show an increased ability to make this connection mentally.

NATURE, NURTURE, AND PERCEPTUAL DEVELOPMENT

Now that we have discussed many aspects of perceptual development, let's explore one of developmental psychology's key issues as it relates to perceptual development: the nature-nurture issue. There has been a longstanding interest in how strongly infants' perception is influenced by nature or nurture (Johnson, 2011, 2013; Johnson & Hannon, 2015; Slater & others, 2011). In the field of perceptual development, nature proponents are referred to as *nativists* and those who emphasize learning and experience are called *empiricists.*

intermodal perception The ability to relate and integrate information from two or more sensory modalities, such as vision and hearing.

In the nativist view, the ability to perceive the world in a competent, organized way is inborn or innate. At the beginning of our discussion of perceptual development, we examined the ecological view of the Gibsons because it has played such a pivotal role in guiding research in perceptual development. The Gibsons' ecological view leans toward a nativist explanation of perceptual development because it holds that perception is direct and evolved over time to allow the detection of size and shape constancy, a three-dimensional world, intermodal perception, and so on, early in infancy. However, the Gibsons' view is not entirely nativist because they emphasized that perceptual development involves distinctive features that are detected at different ages (Slater & others, 2011).

The Gibsons' ecological view is quite different from Piaget's constructivist view that reflects an empiricist approach to explaining perceptual development. According to Piaget, much of perceptual development in infancy must await the development of a sequence of cognitive stages for infants to construct more complex perceptual tasks. Thus, in Piaget's view the ability to perceive size and shape constancy, a three-dimensional world, intermodal perception, and so on, develops later in infancy than the Gibsons envision.

The longitudinal research of Daphne Maurer and her colleagues (Lewis & Maurer, 2005, 2009; Maurer & Lewis, 2013; Maurer & others, 1999) has focused on infants born with cataracts—a thickening of the lens of the eye that causes vision to become cloudy, opaque, and distorted and thus severely restricts infants' ability to experience their visual world. Studying infants whose cataracts were removed at different points in development, they discovered that those whose cataracts were removed and new lenses placed in their eyes in the first several months after birth showed a normal pattern of visual development. However, the longer the delay in removing the cataracts, the more their visual development was impaired. In their research, Maurer and her colleagues (2007) have found that experiencing patterned visual input early in infancy is important for holistic and detailed face processing after infancy. Maurer's research program illustrates how deprivation and experience influence visual development, including an early sensitive period in which visual input is necessary for normal visual development (Maurer & Lewis, 2013).

Much of early perception develops from innate (nature) foundations and the basic foundation of many perceptual abilities can be detected in newborns, whereas other abilities unfold maturationally (Bornstein, Arterberry, & Mash, 2011). However, as infants develop, environmental experiences (nurture) refine or calibrate many perceptual functions, and they may be the driving force behind some functions (Amso & Johnson, 2010). The accumulation of experience with and knowledge about their perceptual world contributes to infants' ability to process coherent perceptions of people and things (Johnson, 2013; Johnson & Hannon, 2015). Thus, a full portrait of perceptual development includes the influence of nature, nurture, and a developing sensitivity to information (Arterberry, 2008).

What roles do nature and nurture play in the infant's perceptual development?

PERCEPTUAL-MOTOR COUPLING

As we come to the end of this chapter, we return to the important theme of perceptual-motor coupling. The distinction between perceiving and doing has been a time-honored tradition in psychology. However, a number of experts on perceptual and motor development question whether this distinction makes sense (Adolph & Robinson, 2013; Thelen & Smith, 2006). The main thrust of research in Esther Thelen's dynamic systems approach is to explore how people assemble motor behaviors for perceiving and acting. The main theme of the ecological approach of Eleanor and James J. Gibson is to discover how perception guides action. Action can guide perception, and perception can guide action. Only by moving one's eyes, head, hands, and arms and by moving from one location to another can an individual fully experience his or her environment and learn how to adapt to it. Perception and action are coupled (Keen, Lee, & Adolph, 2014).

Babies, for example, continually coordinate their movements with perceptual information to learn how to maintain balance, reach for objects in space, and move across various surfaces and terrains (Ishak, Franchak, & Adolph, 2014; Thelen & Smith, 2006). They are motivated

> The infant is by no means as helpless as it looks and is quite capable of some very complex and important actions.
>
> **—HERB PICK**
> *Developmental Psychologist, University of Minnesota*

How are perception and action coupled in children's development?

to move by what they perceive. Consider the sight of an attractive toy across the room. In this situation, infants must perceive the current state of their bodies and learn how to use their limbs to reach the toy. Although their movements at first are awkward and uncoordinated, babies soon learn to select patterns that are appropriate for reaching their goals.

Equally important is the other part of the perception-action coupling. That is, action educates perception (Adolph & Robinson, 2013). For example, watching an object while exploring it manually helps infants to discriminate its texture, size, and hardness. Locomoting in the environment teaches babies about how objects and people look from different perspectives, or whether various surfaces will support their weight.

How do infants develop new perceptual-motor couplings? Recall from our discussion earlier in this chapter that in the traditional view of Gesell, infants' perceptual-motor development is prescribed by a genetic plan to follow a fixed and sequential progression of stages in development. The genetic determination view has been replaced by the dynamic systems view that infants learn new perceptual-motor couplings by assembling skills for perceiving and acting. New perceptual-motor coupling is not passively accomplished; rather, the infant actively develops a skill to achieve a goal within the constraints set by the infant's body and the environment (Gerson & Woodward, 2014).

Children perceive in order to move and move in order to perceive. Perceptual and motor development do not occur in isolation from each other but instead are coupled.

Review Connect Reflect

 LG3 Summarize the course of sensory and perceptual development in infancy

Review

- What are sensation and perception?
- What is the ecological view of perception?
- How does visual perception develop in infancy?
- How do hearing, touch and pain, smell, and taste develop in infancy?
- What is intermodal perception?
- What roles do nature and nurture play in perceptual development?
- How is perceptual-motor development coupled?

Connect

- Perceptual-motor coupling was discussed in the previous section as well as in this section. Describe how this concept could be linked to the concept of nature versus nurture.

Reflect *Your Own Personal Journey of Life*

- How much sensory stimulation would you provide your own baby? A little? A lot? Could you overstimulate your baby? Explain.

topical connections *looking forward*

In the next chapter, you will read about the remarkable cognitive changes that characterize infant development and how soon infants are able to competently process information about their world. Advances in infants' cognitive development—together with the development of the brain and perceptual-motor advances discussed in this chapter—allow infants to adapt more effectively to their environment. In Chapter 7, we will further explore physical development when we examine how children progress through the early childhood years (ages 3 to 5). Young children's physical development continues to change and to become more coordinated in early childhood, although gains in height and weight are not as dramatic in early childhood as in infancy.

Physical Development in Infancy

1 Physical Growth and Development in Infancy

LG1 Discuss physical growth and development in infancy.

Patterns of Growth

Height and Weight

The Brain

- The cephalocaudal pattern is the sequence in which growth proceeds from top to bottom. The proximodistal pattern is the sequence in which growth starts at the center of the body and moves toward the extremities.

- The average North American newborn is 20 inches long and weighs 7 pounds. Infants grow about 1 inch per month in the first year and nearly triple their weight by their first birthday. The rate of growth slows in the second year.

- One of the most dramatic changes in the brain in the first two years of life is dendritic spreading, which increases the connections between neurons. Myelination, which speeds the conduction of nerve impulses, continues through infancy and even into adolescence. The cerebral cortex has two hemispheres (left and right). Lateralization refers to specialization of function in one hemisphere or the other. Early experiences play an important role in brain development. Neural connections are formed early in an infant's life. Before birth, genes mainly direct neurons to different locations. After birth, the inflowing stream of sights, sounds, smells, touches, language, and eye contact help shape the brain's neural connections, as does stimulation from caregivers and others. The neuroconstructivist view is an increasingly popular perspective on the brain's development.

Sleep

- Newborns usually sleep about 18 hours a day. By 6 months of age, many American infants approach adult-like sleeping patterns. REM sleep—during which dreaming occurs—is present more in early infancy than in childhood and adulthood. Sleeping arrangements for infants vary across cultures. In America, infants are more likely to sleep alone than in many other cultures. Some experts believe shared sleeping can lead to sudden infant death syndrome (SIDS), a condition that occurs when a sleeping infant suddenly stops breathing and dies without an apparent cause.

Nutrition

- Infants need to consume about 50 calories per day for each pound they weigh. The growing consensus is that in most instances breast feeding is superior to bottle feeding for both the infant and the mother, although the correlational nature of studies must be considered. Severe infant malnutrition is still prevalent in many parts of the world. A special concern in impoverished countries is early weaning from breast milk and the misuse and hygiene problems associated with bottle feeding in these countries. The Women, Infants, and Children (WIC) program has produced positive benefits in low-income families.

2 Motor Development

LG2 Describe infants' motor development.

The Dynamic Systems View

- Thelen's dynamic systems theory seeks to explain how motor behaviors are assembled for perceiving and acting. Perception and action are coupled. According to this theory, motor skills are the result of many converging factors, such as the development of the nervous system, the body's physical properties and its movement possibilities, the goal the child is motivated to reach, and environmental support for the skill. In the dynamic systems view, motor development is far more complex than the result of a genetic blueprint.

Reflexes

- Reflexes—automatic movements—govern the newborn's behavior. They include the sucking, rooting, and Moro reflexes. The rooting and Moro reflexes disappear after three to four months. Permanent reflexes include coughing and blinking. For infants, sucking is an especially important reflex because it provides a means of obtaining nutrition.

Gross Motor Skills

- Gross motor skills involve large-muscle activities. Key skills developed during infancy include control of posture and walking. Although infants usually learn to walk by their first birthday, the neural pathways that allow walking begin to form earlier. The age at which infants reach milestones in the development of gross motor skills may vary by as much as two to four months, especially for milestones in late infancy.

Fine Motor Skills

- Fine motor skills involve finely tuned movements. The onset of reaching and grasping marks a significant accomplishment, and this becomes more refined during the first two years of life.

3 Sensory and Perceptual Development

 LG3 Summarize the course of sensory and perceptual development in infancy.

What Are Sensation and Perception?

The Ecological View

Visual Perception

Other Senses

Intermodal Perception

Nature, Nurture, and Perceptual Development

Perceptual-Motor Coupling

- Sensation occurs when information interacts with sensory receptors. Perception is the interpretation of sensation.

- Created by the Gibsons, the ecological view states that we directly perceive information that exists in the world around us. Perception brings people in contact with the environment to interact with and adapt to it. Affordances provide opportunities for interaction offered by objects that fit within our capabilities to perform activities.

- Researchers have developed a number of methods to assess the infant's perception, including the visual preference method (which Fantz used to determine young infants' preference for looking at patterned over nonpatterned displays), habituation and dishabituation, and tracking. The infant's visual acuity increases dramatically in the first year of life. Infants' color vision improves as they develop. Young infants systematically scan human faces. As early as 3 months of age, infants show size and shape constancy. At approximately 2 months of age, infants develop the ability to perceive that occluded objects are complete. In Gibson and Walk's classic study, infants as young as 6 months of age indicated they could perceive depth.

- The fetus can hear during the last two months of pregnancy. Immediately after birth, newborns can hear, but their sensory threshold is higher than that of adults. Developmental changes in the perception of loudness, pitch, and localization of sound occur during infancy. Newborns can respond to touch and feel pain. Newborns can differentiate odors, and sensitivity to taste may be present before birth.

- Early, exploratory forms of intermodal perception—the ability to relate and integrate information from two or more sensory modalities—are present in newborns and become sharpened over the first year of life.

- In perception, nature advocates are referred to as nativists and nurture proponents are called empiricists. The Gibsons' ecological view that has guided much of perceptual development research leans toward a nativist approach but still allows for developmental changes in distinctive features. Piaget's constructivist view leans toward an empiricist approach, emphasizing that many perceptual accomplishments must await the development of cognitive stages in infancy. A strong empiricist approach is unwarranted. A full account of perceptual development includes the roles of nature, nurture, and the developing sensitivity to information.

- Perception and action are often not isolated but rather are coupled. Individuals perceive in order to move and move in order to perceive.

key **terms**

key **people**

chapter 5

COGNITIVE DEVELOPMENT IN INFANCY

chapter outline

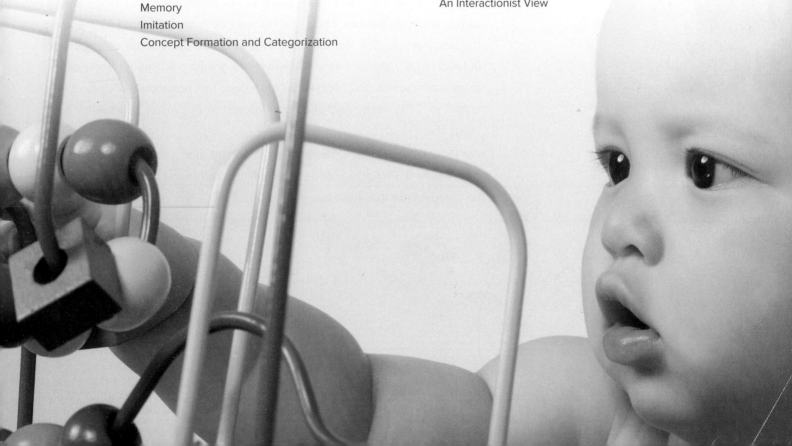

Jean Piaget, the famous Swiss psychologist, was a meticulous observer of his three children—Laurent, Lucienne, and Jacqueline. His books on cognitive development are filled with these observations. Here are a few of Piaget's observations of his children in infancy (Piaget, 1952):

- At 21 days of age, "Laurent found his thumb after three attempts: prolonged sucking begins each time. But, once he has been placed on his back, he does not know how to coordinate the movement of the arms with that of the mouth and his hands draw back even when his lips are seeking them" (p. 27).

- During the third month, thumb sucking becomes less important to Laurent because of new visual and auditory interests. But, when he cries, his thumb goes to the rescue.

- Toward the end of Lucienne's fourth month, while she is lying in her crib, Piaget hangs a doll above her feet. Lucienne thrusts her feet at the doll and makes it move. "Afterward, she looks at her motionless foot for a second, then recommences. There is no visual control of her foot, for the movements are the same when Lucienne only looks at the doll or when I place the doll over her head. On the other hand, the tactile control of the foot is apparent: after the first shakes, Lucienne makes slow foot movements as though to grasp and explore" (p. 159).

- At 11 months, "Jacqueline is seated and shakes a little bell. She then pauses abruptly in order to delicately place the bell in front of her right foot; then she kicks hard. Unable to recapture it, she grasps a ball which she then places at the same spot in order to give it another kick" (p. 225).

- At 1 year, 2 months, "Jacqueline holds in her hands an object which is new to her: a round, flat box which she turns all over, shakes, [and] rubs against the bassinet. . . . She lets it go and tries to pick it up. But she only succeeds in touching it with her index finger, without grasping it. She nevertheless makes an attempt and presses on the edge. The box then tilts up and falls again" (p. 273). Jacqueline shows an interest in this result and studies the fallen box.

For Piaget, these observations reflect important changes in the infant's cognitive development. Piaget maintained that infants go through a series of substages as they progress in less than two short years.

preview

Piaget's descriptions of infants are just the starting point for our exploration of cognitive development. Excitement and enthusiasm about the study of infant cognition have been fueled by an interest in what newborns and infants know, by continued fascination about innate and learned factors in the infant's cognitive development, and by controversies about whether infants construct their knowledge (Piaget's view) or know their world more directly. In this chapter, you will not only study Piaget's theory of infant development but also explore how infants learn, remember, and conceptualize; learn about some of their individual differences; and trace their language development.

1 Piaget's Theory of Infant Development

 LG1 Summarize and evaluate Piaget's theory of infant development.

Cognitive Processes   The Sensorimotor Stage   Evaluating Piaget's Sensorimotor Stage

Poet Nora Perry asks, "Who knows the thoughts of a child?" As much as anyone, Piaget knew. Through careful observations of his own three children—Laurent, Lucienne, and Jacqueline—and observations of and interviews with other children, Piaget changed perceptions of the way children think about the world.

Piaget's theory is a general, unifying story of how biology and experience sculpt cognitive development. Piaget thought that, just as our physical bodies have structures that enable us to adapt to the world, we build mental structures that help us adjust to new environmental demands. Piaget stressed that children actively construct their own cognitive worlds; information is not just poured into their minds from the environment. He sought to discover how children at different points in their development think about the world and how systematic changes in their thinking occur.

We are born capable of learning.

—**JEAN-JACQUES ROUSSEAU**
Swiss-Born French Philosopher, 18th Century

COGNITIVE PROCESSES

What processes do children use as they construct their knowledge of the world? Piaget developed several concepts to answer this question; especially important are schemes, assimilation, accommodation, organization, equilibrium, and equilibration.

Schemes   As the infant or child seeks to construct an understanding of the world, said Piaget (1954), the developing brain creates **schemes.** These are actions or mental representations

schemes In Piaget's theory, actions or mental representations that organize knowledge.

In Piaget's view, what is a scheme? What schemes might this young infant be displaying?

that organize knowledge. In Piaget's theory, behavioral schemes (physical activities) characterize infancy, and mental schemes (cognitive activities) develop in childhood (Lamb, Bornstein, & Teti, 2002). A baby's schemes are structured by simple actions that can be performed on objects, such as sucking, looking, and grasping. Older children have schemes that include strategies and plans for solving problems. For example, in the descriptions at the opening of this chapter, Laurent displayed a scheme for sucking; Jacqueline displayed a problem-solving scheme when she was able to open the door without losing her blades of grass. By the time we have reached adulthood, we have constructed an enormous number of diverse schemes, ranging from driving a car to balancing a budget to understanding the concept of fairness.

Assimilation and Accommodation   To explain how children use and adapt their schemes, Piaget offered two concepts: assimilation and accommodation. **Assimilation** occurs when children use their existing schemes to deal with new information or experiences. **Accommodation** occurs when children adjust their schemes to take new information and experiences into account.

Think about a toddler who has learned the word *car* to identify the family vehicle. The toddler might call all moving vehicles on roads "cars," including motorcycles and trucks; the child has assimilated these objects to his or her existing scheme. But the child soon learns that motorcycles and trucks are not cars and fine-tunes the category to exclude motorcycles and trucks, accommodating the scheme.

Assimilation and accommodation operate even in very young infants. Newborns reflexively suck everything that touches their lips; they assimilate all sorts of objects into their sucking scheme. By sucking different objects, they learn about their taste, texture, shape, and so on. After several months of experience, though, they construct their understanding of the world differently. Some objects, such as fingers and the mother's breast, can be sucked, and others, such as fuzzy blankets, should not be sucked. In other words, they accommodate their sucking scheme.

Organization   To make sense out of their world, said Piaget, children cognitively organize their experiences. **Organization** in Piaget's theory is the grouping of isolated behaviors and thoughts into a higher-order system. Continual refinement of this organization is an inherent part of development. A boy who has only a vague idea about how to use a hammer may also have a vague idea about how to use other tools. After learning how to use each one, he relates these uses, organizing his knowledge.

Equilibration and Stages of Development   Assimilation and accommodation always take the child to a higher ground, according to Piaget. In trying to understand the world, the child inevitably experiences cognitive conflict, or *disequilibrium*. That is, the child is constantly faced with counterexamples to his or her existing schemes and with inconsistencies. For example, if a child believes that pouring water from a short and wide container into a tall and narrow container changes the amount of water, then the child might be puzzled by where the "extra" water came from and whether there is actually more water to drink. The puzzle creates disequilibrium; for Piaget, an internal search for equilibrium creates motivation for change. The child assimilates and accommodates, adjusting old schemes, developing new schemes, and organizing and reorganizing the old and new schemes. Eventually, the new organization has become fundamentally different from the old organization; it is a new way of thinking.

In short, according to Piaget, children constantly assimilate and accommodate as they seek equilibrium. There is considerable movement between states of cognitive equilibrium and disequilibrium as assimilation and accommodation work in concert to produce cognitive change. **Equilibration** is the name Piaget gave to this mechanism by which children shift from one stage of thought to the next.

The result of these processes, according to Piaget, is that individuals go through four stages of development. A different way of understanding the world makes one stage more

assimilation Piagetian concept of using existing schemes to deal with new information or experiences.

accommodation Piagetian concept of adjusting schemes to fit new information and experiences.

organization Piaget's concept of grouping isolated behaviors and thoughts into a higher-order, more smoothly functioning cognitive system.

equilibration A mechanism that Piaget proposed to explain how children shift from one stage of thought to the next.

Substage	Age	Description	Example
1 Simple reflexes	Birth to 1 month	Coordination of sensation and action through reflexive behaviors.	Rooting, sucking, and grasping reflexes; newborns suck reflexively when their lips are touched.
2 First habits and primary circular reactions	1 to 4 months	Coordination of sensation and two types of schemes: habits (reflex) and primary circular reactions (reproduction of an event that initially occurred by chance). Main focus is still on the infant's body.	Repeating a body sensation first experienced by chance (sucking thumb, for example); then infants might accommodate actions by sucking their thumb differently from how they suck on a nipple.
3 Secondary circular reactions	4 to 8 months	Infants become more object-oriented, moving beyond self-preoccupation; repeat actions that bring interesting or pleasurable results.	An infant coos to make a person stay near; as the person starts to leave, the infant coos again.
4 Coordination of secondary circular reactions	8 to 12 months	Coordination of vision and touch—hand-eye coordination; coordination of schemes and intentionality.	Infant manipulates a stick in order to bring an attractive toy within reach.
5 Tertiary circular reactions, novelty, and curiosity	12 to 18 months	Infants become intrigued by the many properties of objects and by the many things they can make happen to objects; they experiment with new behavior.	A block can be made to fall, spin, hit another object, and slide across the ground.
6 Internalization of schemes	18 to 24 months	Infants develop the ability to use primitive symbols and form enduring mental representations.	An infant who has never thrown a temper tantrum before sees a playmate throw a tantrum; the infant retains a memory of the event, then throws one himself the next day.

FIGURE 5.1

PIAGET'S SIX SUBSTAGES OF SENSORIMOTOR DEVELOPMENT

advanced than another. Cognition is *qualitatively* different in one stage compared with another. In other words, the way children reason at one stage is different from the way they reason at another stage. Here our focus is on Piaget's stage of infant cognitive development. In later chapters, when we study cognitive development in early childhood, middle and late childhood, and adolescence (Chapters 7, 9, and 11) we will explore the last three Piagetian stages.

THE SENSORIMOTOR STAGE

The **sensorimotor stage** lasts from birth to about 2 years of age. In this stage, infants construct an understanding of the world by coordinating sensory experiences (such as seeing and hearing) with physical, motoric actions—hence the term "sensorimotor." At the beginning of this stage, newborns have little more than reflexes with which to work. At the end of the sensorimotor stage, 2-year-olds can produce complex sensorimotor patterns and use primitive symbols. We first will summarize Piaget's descriptions of how infants develop. Later we will consider criticisms of his view.

Substages   Piaget divided the sensorimotor stage into six substages: (1) simple reflexes; (2) first habits and primary circular reactions; (3) secondary circular reactions; (4) coordination of secondary circular reactions; (5) tertiary circular reactions, novelty, and curiosity; and (6) internalization of schemes (see Figure 5.1).

Simple reflexes, the first sensorimotor substage, corresponds to the first month after birth. In this substage, sensation and action are coordinated primarily through reflexive behaviors, such as rooting and sucking. Soon the infant produces behaviors that resemble reflexes in the absence of the usual stimulus for the reflex. For example, a newborn will suck a nipple or bottle only when it is placed directly in the baby's mouth or touched to the lips. But soon the infant might suck when a bottle or nipple is only nearby. Even in the first month of life, the infant is initiating action and actively structuring experiences.

First habits and primary circular reactions is the second sensorimotor substage, which develops between 1 and 4 months of age. In this substage, the infant coordinates sensation

developmental **connection**

Cognitive Theory

Recall the main characteristics of Piaget's four stages of cognitive development. Chapter 1, p. 21

sensorimotor stage The first of Piaget's stages, which lasts from birth to about 2 years of age; infants construct an understanding of the world by coordinating sensory experiences with motoric actions.

simple reflexes Piaget's first sensorimotor substage, which corresponds to the first month after birth. In this substage, sensation and action are coordinated primarily through reflexive behaviors.

first habits and primary circular reactions Piaget's second sensorimotor substage, which develops between 1 and 4 months of age. In this substage, the infant coordinates sensation and two types of schemes: habits and primary circular reactions.

SECTION 3   Infancy   **13**

primary circular reaction A scheme based on the attempt to reproduce an event that initially occurred by chance.

secondary circular reactions Piaget's third sensorimotor substage, which develops between 4 and 8 months of age. In this substage, the infant becomes more object-oriented, moving beyond preoccupation with the self.

coordination of secondary circular reactions Piaget's fourth sensorimotor substage, which develops between 8 and 12 months of age. Actions become more outwardly directed, and infants coordinate schemes and act with intentionality.

tertiary circular reactions, novelty, and curiosity Piaget's fifth sensorimotor substage, which develops between 12 and 18 months of age. In this substage, infants become intrigued by the many properties of objects and by the many things that they can make happen to objects.

internalization of schemes Piaget's sixth and final sensorimotor substage, which develops between 18 and 24 months of age. In this substage, the infant develops the ability to use primitive symbols.

developmental **connection**

Cognitive Theory

What are some changes in symbolic thought in young children? Chapter 7, p. 206

This 17-month-old is in Piaget's stage of tertiary circular reactions. *What might the infant do to suggest that he is in this stage?*

and two types of schemes: habits and primary circular reactions. A *habit* is a scheme based on a reflex that has become completely separated from its eliciting stimulus. For example, infants in substage 1 suck when bottles are put to their lips or when they see a bottle. Infants in substage 2 might suck even when no bottle is present. A *circular reaction* is a repetitive action.

A **primary circular reaction** is a scheme based on the attempt to reproduce an event that initially occurred by chance. For example, suppose an infant accidentally sucks his fingers when they are placed near his mouth. Later, he searches for his fingers to suck them again, but the fingers do not cooperate because the infant cannot coordinate visual and manual actions.

Habits and circular reactions are stereotyped—that is, the infant repeats them the same way each time. During this substage, the infant's own body remains the infant's center of attention. There is no outward pull by environmental events.

Secondary circular reactions is the third sensorimotor substage, which develops between 4 and 8 months of age. In this substage, the infant becomes more object-oriented, moving beyond preoccupation with the self. The infant's schemes are not intentional or goal-directed, but they are repeated because of their consequences. By chance, an infant might shake a rattle. The infant repeats this action for the sake of its fascination. This is a *secondary circular reaction:* an action repeated because of its consequences. The infant also imitates some simple actions, such as the baby talk or burbling of adults, and some physical gestures. However, the baby imitates only actions that he or she is already able to produce.

Coordination of secondary circular reactions is Piaget's fourth sensorimotor substage, which develops between 8 and 12 months of age. To progress into this substage the infant must coordinate vision and touch, eye and hand. Actions become more outwardly directed. Significant changes during this substage involve the coordination of schemes and intentionality. Infants readily combine and recombine previously learned schemes in a coordinated way. They might look at an object and grasp it simultaneously, or they might visually inspect a toy, such as a rattle, and finger it simultaneously, exploring it tactilely. Actions are even more outwardly directed than before. Related to this coordination is the second achievement—the presence of intentionality. For example, infants might manipulate a stick in order to bring a desired toy within reach, or they might knock over one block to reach and play with another one. Similarly, when 11-month-old Jacqueline, as described in the chapter opening, placed the ball in front of her and kicked it, she was demonstrating intentionality.

Tertiary circular reactions, novelty, and curiosity is Piaget's fifth sensorimotor substage, which develops between 12 and 18 months of age. In this substage, infants become intrigued by the many properties of objects and by the many things that they can make happen to objects. A block can be made to fall, spin, hit another object, and slide across the ground. *Tertiary circular reactions* are schemes in which the infant purposely explores new possibilities with objects, continually doing new things to them and exploring the results. Piaget says that this stage marks the starting point for human curiosity and interest in novelty.

Internalization of schemes is Piaget's sixth and final sensorimotor substage, which develops between 18 and 24 months of age. In this substage, the infant develops the ability to use primitive symbols. For Piaget, a *symbol* is an internalized sensory image or word that represents an event. Primitive symbols permit the infant to think about concrete events without directly acting them out or perceiving them. Moreover, symbols allow the infant to manipulate and transform the represented events in simple ways. In a favorite Piagetian example, Piaget's young daughter saw a matchbox being opened and closed. Later, she mimicked the event by opening and closing her mouth. This was an obvious expression of her image of the event.

Object Permanence   Imagine how chaotic and unpredictable your life would be if you could not distinguish between yourself and your world. This is what the life of a newborn must be like, according to Piaget. There is no differentiation between the self and world; objects have no separate, permanent existence.

By the end of the sensorimotor period, objects are both separate from the self and permanent. **Object permanence** is the understanding that objects continue to exist even

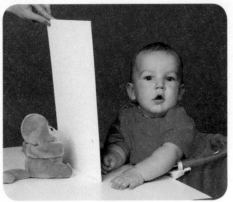

FIGURE **5.2**

OBJECT PERMANENCE. Piaget argued that object permanence is one of infancy's landmark cognitive accomplishments. For this 5-month-old boy, "out-of-sight" is literally out of mind. The infant looks at the toy monkey (*left*), but, when his view of the toy is blocked (*right*), he does not search for it. Several months later, he will search for the hidden toy monkey, an action reflecting the presence of object permanence.

when they cannot be seen, heard, or touched. Acquiring the sense of object permanence is one of the infant's most important accomplishments, according to Piaget.

How could anyone know whether an infant had a sense of object permanence or not? The principal way that object permanence is studied is by watching an infant's reaction when an interesting object disappears (see Figure 5.2). If infants search for the object, it is assumed that they believe it continues to exist.

Object permanence is just one of the basic concepts that babies develop about the physical world. To Piaget, children, even infants, are much like little scientists, examining the world to see how it works. But how can adult scientists determine what these "baby scientists" are finding out about the world and at what age they're finding it out? Read *Connecting Through Research* to find out.

EVALUATING PIAGET'S SENSORIMOTOR STAGE

Piaget opened up a new way of looking at infants with his view that their main task is to coordinate their sensory impressions with their motor activity. However, the infant's cognitive world is not as neatly packaged as Piaget portrayed it, and some of Piaget's explanations for the cause of change are debated. In the past several decades, sophisticated experimental techniques have been devised to study infants, and a large number of research studies have focused on infant development. Much of the new research suggests that Piaget's view of sensorimotor development needs to be modified (Baillargeon, 2014; Brooks & Meltzoff, 2014; Diamond, 2013; Johnson & Hannon, 2015).

The A-not-B Error One modification concerns Piaget's claim that certain processes are crucial in transitions from one stage to the next. The data do not always support his explanations. For example, in Piaget's theory, an important feature in the progression into substage 4, *coordination of secondary circular reactions,* is an infant's inclination to search for a hidden object in a familiar location rather than to look for the object in a new location. If a toy is hidden twice, initially at location A and subsequently at location B, 8- to 12-month-old infants search correctly at location A initially. But when the toy is subsequently hidden at location B, they make the mistake of continuing to search for it at location A. **A-not-B error** is the term used to describe this common mistake. Older infants are less likely to make the A-not-B error because their concept of object permanence is more complete.

Researchers have found, however, that the A-not-B error does not show up consistently (Sophian, 1985). The evidence indicates that A-not-B errors are sensitive to the delay between hiding the object at B and the infant's attempt to find it (Diamond, 1985). Thus, the A-not-B error might be due to a failure in memory. Another explanation is that infants tend to repeat a previous motor behavior (Clearfield & others, 2006).

Perceptual Development and Expectations A number of theorists, such as Eleanor Gibson (2001) and Elizabeth Spelke (1991, 2011, 2013), argue that infants' perceptual

object permanence The Piagetian term for understanding that objects and events continue to exist even when they cannot directly be seen, heard, or touched.

A-not-B error Error that occurs when infants make the mistake of selecting the familiar hiding place (A) rather than the new hiding place (B) of an object as they progress into substage 4 in Piaget's sensorimotor stage.

connecting through research

How Do Researchers Study Infants' Understanding of Object Permanence and Causality?

Two accomplishments of infants that Piaget examined were the development of object permanence and the child's understanding of causality. Let's examine two research studies that address these topics.

In both studies, Renée Baillargeon and her colleagues used a research method that involves violation of expectations. In this method, infants see an event happen as it normally would. Then, the event is changed, often in a way that creates a physically impossible event. That an infant looks longer at the changed event indicates he or she is surprised by it. In other words, the reaction is interpreted to indicate that the infant had certain expectations about the world that were violated.

In one study that focused on object permanence, researchers showed infants a toy car that moved down an inclined track, disappeared behind a screen, and then reemerged at the other end, still on the track (Baillargeon & DeVos, 1991) (a). After this sequence was repeated several times, something different occurred: A toy mouse was placed behind the track but was hidden by the screen while the car rolled by (b). This was the "possible" event. Then, the researchers created an "impossible event": The toy mouse was placed on the track but was secretly removed after the screen was lowered so that the car seemed to go through the mouse (c). In this study, infants as young as 3 months of age took a longer look at the impossible event than at the possible event, indicating that they were surprised by it. Their surprise suggested that they remembered not only that the toy mouse still existed (object permanence) but also recalled its location.

Another study focused on the infant's understanding of causality (Kotovsky & Baillargeon, 1994). In this research, a cylinder rolls down a ramp and hits a toy bug at the bottom of the ramp. By 5 and 6 months of age, after infants have seen how far the bug will be pushed by a medium-sized cylinder, their reactions indicate that they understand that the bug will roll farther if it is hit by a large cylinder than if it is hit by a small cylinder. Thus, by the middle of the first year of life these infants understood that the size of a moving object determines how far it will move a stationary object that it collides with.

In Baillargeon's (2008, 2014; Baillargeon & Carey, 2012; Baillargeon & others, 2011, 2012; Luo & Baillargeon, 2010) view, infants have a pre-adapted, innate bias called the principle of persistence that explains their assumption that objects don't change their properties—including how solid they are, their location, their color, and their form—unless some external factor (a person moves the object, for example) obviously intervenes. Shortly, we will revisit the extent to which nature and nurture are at work in the changes that take place in the infant's cognitive development.

The research findings discussed in this interlude and other research indicate that infants develop object permanence and causal reasoning much earlier than Piaget proposed (Baillargeon & others, 2011; Luo & Baillargeon, 2010). Indeed, as you will see in the next section, a major theme of infant cognitive development today is that infants are more cognitively competent than Piaget envisioned.

developmental connection

Perceptual Development

Eleanor Gibson was a pioneer in crafting the ecological perception view of development. Chapter 4, p. 128

abilities are highly developed at a very early stage. Spelke concludes that young infants interpret the world as having predictable occurrences. For example, in Chapter 4 we discussed research that demonstrated the presence of intermodal perception—the ability to coordinate information from two or more sensory modalities, such as vision and hearing—by 3½ months of age, much earlier than Piaget would have predicted (Spelke & Owsley, 1979).

Research also suggests that infants develop the ability to understand how the world works at a very early age (Baillargeon, 2014; Huang & Spelke, 2014; Rakison & Lawson, 2013). For example, by the time they are 3 months of age, infants develop expectations about future events. Marshall Haith and his colleagues (Canfield & Haith, 1991; Haith, Hazen, & Goodman, 1988) presented pictures to infants in either a regular alternating sequence (such as left, right, left, right) or an unpredictable sequence (such as right, right, left, right). When the sequence was predictable, the 3-month-old infants began to anticipate the location of the picture, looking at the side on which it was expected to appear. However, younger infants did not develop expectations about where a picture would be presented.

What kinds of expectations do infants form? Experiments by Spelke (1991, 2000; Spelke & Hespos, 2001) have addressed this question. She placed babies before a puppet stage and showed them a series of actions that are unexpected if you know how the physical world works—for example, one ball seemed to roll through a solid barrier, another seemed to leap between two platforms, and a third appeared to hang in midair (Spelke, 1979). Spelke measured and compared the babies' looking times for unexpected and expected actions. She concluded that by 4 months of age, even though infants do not yet have the ability to talk about objects, move around objects, manipulate objects, or even see objects with high resolution, they expect objects to be solid and continuous. However, at 4 months of age, infants do not expect an object to obey gravitational constraints (Spelke & others, 1992). Similarly, research by Renée Baillargeon and her colleagues (Baillargeon, 1995, 2004) documents that infants as young as 3 to 4 months expect objects to be substantial (in the sense that other objects cannot move through them) and permanent (in the sense that objects continue to exist when they are hidden).

In sum, researchers conclude that infants see objects as bounded, unitary, solid, and separate from their background, possibly at birth or shortly thereafter, but definitely by 3 to 4 months of age—much earlier than Piaget envisioned. Young infants still have much to learn about objects, but the world appears both stable and orderly to them.

However, some critics, such as Andrew Meltzoff (2008; Meltzoff & Moore, 1998), argue that Spelke's and Baillargeon's research relies on how long infants look at unexpected events and thus assess infants' *perceptual expectations* about where and when objects will reappear rather than tapping their *knowledge* about where the objects are when they are out of sight. Meltzoff points out that whether infants act on their perception is an important aspect of assessing object permanence; he states that it does not appear that young infants can act on the information. Thus, Meltzoff (2008) concludes that whether longer looking time is a valid measure of object permanence and how early infants develop object permanence remains controversial.

By 6 to 8 months, infants have learned to perceive gravity and support—that an object hanging on the end of a table should fall, that ball bearings will travel farther when rolled down a longer rather than a shorter ramp, and that cup handles will not fall when attached to a cup (Slater, Field, & Hernandez-Reif, 2007). As infants develop, their experiences and actions on objects help them to understand physical laws (Johnson, 2013; Johnson & Hammon, 2015).

The Nature-Nurture Issue   In considering the big issue of whether nature or nurture plays the more important role in infant development, Elizabeth Spelke (Spelke, 2003, 2011, 2013) comes down clearly on the side of nature, a position often referred to as *nativist*. Spelke endorses a **core knowledge approach,** which states that infants are born with domain-specific innate knowledge systems. Among these domain-specific knowledge systems are those involving space, number sense, object permanence, and language (which we will discuss later in this chapter). Strongly influenced by evolution, the core knowledge domains are theorized to be prewired to allow infants to make sense of their world (Coubart & others, 2014). After all, Spelke concludes, how could infants possibly grasp the complex world in which they live if they didn't come into the world equipped with core sets of knowledge? In this approach, the innate core knowledge domains form a foundation around which more mature cognitive functioning and learning develop (Baillargeon, 2014). The core knowledge approach argues that Piaget greatly underestimated the cognitive abilities of infants, especially young infants (Huang & Spelke, 2014).

An intriguing domain of core knowledge that has been investigated in young infants is whether they have a sense of number. Spelke and her colleagues conclude that they do (Coubart & others, 2014; Hyde & Spelke, 2012). Using the violation of expectations method discussed in this chapter's *Connecting Through Research,* Karen Wynn (1992) conducted an early experiment on infants' sense of number. Five-month-old infants were shown one or two Mickey Mouse dolls on a puppet stage. Then the experimenter hid the doll(s) behind a screen and visibly removed or added one. Next, when the screen was lifted, the infants looked longer when they saw the incorrect number of dolls. Spelke and her colleagues (Coubart & others, 2014; de Hevia & Spelke, 2010; Hyde & Spelke, 2012; Lipton & Spelke, 2004; Spelke & Kinzler, 2007; Xu, Spelke, & Goddard, 2005) have found that infants can distinguish between different numbers of objects, actions, and sounds. Efforts to find further support for infants' sense of number are extending to assessments of brain activity (Hyde & Spelke, 2012). For example, one study of 3-month-olds observing changes either in the identity of objects or in the number of objects revealed that changes in the type of objects activated a region of the brain's temporal lobe while changes in the number of objects activated an additional region of the parietal lobe (Izard, Dehaene-Lambertz, & Dehaene, 2008). In older children and adults, number sense activates the same region of the parietal lobe activated in the 3-month-old infants in this study.

Of course, not everyone agrees with Spelke's conclusions about young infants' math skills (Cohen, 2002). One criticism is that infants in the number experiments are merely responding to changes in the display that violated their expectations.

developmental **connection**

Nature Versus Nurture

The nature-nurture debate is one of developmental psychology's main issues. Chapter 1, p. 17

core knowledge approach States that infants are born with domain-specific innate knowledge systems.

What are some conclusions that can be reached about infant learning and cognition?

Recently, researchers also have explored whether preverbal infants might have a built-in, innate sense of morality. In this research, infants as young as 4 months of age are more likely to make visually guided reaches toward a puppet who has acted as a helper (such as helping someone get up a hill, assisting in opening a box, or giving a ball back) rather than toward a puppet who has acted as a hinderer to others' efforts to achieve such goals (Hamlin, 2013, 2014).

In criticizing the core knowledge approach, British developmental psychologist Mark Johnson (2008) says that the infants Spelke and other core knowledge advocates study already have accumulated hundreds, and in some cases even thousands, of hours of experience in grasping what the world is about, which gives considerable room for the environment's role in the development of infant cognition (Highfield, 2008). According to Johnson (2008), infants likely come into the world with "soft biases to perceive and attend to different aspects of the environment, and to learn about the world in particular ways." A major criticism is that nativists completely neglect the infant's social immersion in the world and instead focus only on what happens inside the infant's head apart from the environment (Nelson, 2013).

Although debate about the cause and course of infant cognitive development continues, most developmentalists today agree that Piaget underestimated the early cognitive accomplishments of infants and that both nature and nurture are involved in infants' cognitive development.

Conclusions   In sum, many researchers conclude that Piaget wasn't specific enough about how infants learn about their world and that infants, especially young infants, are more competent than Piaget thought (Baillargeon, 2014; Diamond, 2013; Johnson & Hannon, 2015). As they have examined the specific ways that infants learn, the field of infant cognition has become very specialized. There are many researchers working on different questions, with no general theory emerging that can connect all of the different findings (Nelson, 1999). These theories often are local theories, focused on specific research questions, rather than grand theories like Piaget's (Kuhn, 1998). Among the unifying themes in the study of infant cognition are seeking to understand more precisely how developmental changes in cognition take place, the big issue of nature and nurture, and the brain's role in cognitive development (Baillargeon, 2014; Brooks & Meltzoff, 2014). Recall from Chapter 1 that exploring connections between brain, cognition, and development involves the recently emerging field of *developmental cognitive neuroscience* (Bell & Cuevas, 2014; Bell, Kraybill, & Diaz, 2014; Righi & others, 2014; Vanderwert & Nelson, 2014; Zelazo, 2013).

Review Connect Reflect

 Summarize and evaluate Piaget's theory of infant development.

Review
- What cognitive processes are important in Piaget's theory?
- What are some characteristics of Piaget's stage of sensorimotor development?
- What are some contributions and criticisms of Piaget's sensorimotor stage?

Connect
- You just read that by the age of 6 to 8 months infants have learned to perceive gravity and support. What physical developments occurring around this same time period (discussed in Chapter 4) might contribute to infants' exploration and understanding of these concepts?

Reflect *Your Own Personal Journey of Life*
- What are some implications of Piaget's theory for parenting your own baby?

Conditioning · Attention · Memory · Imitation · Concept Formation and Categorization

When Piaget hung a doll above 4-month-old Lucienne's feet, as described in the chapter opening, did she remember the doll? If Piaget had rewarded her for moving the doll with her foot, would that have affected Lucienne's behavior? If he had shown her how to shake the doll's hand, could she have imitated him? If he had shown her a different doll, could she have formed the concept of a "doll"?

Questions like these might be examined by researchers taking the behavioral and social cognitive or information-processing approaches introduced in Chapter 1. In contrast with Piaget's theory, these approaches do not describe infant development in terms of stages. Instead, they document gradual changes in the infant's ability to understand and process information about the world (Brooks & Meltzoff, 2014; Diamond, 2013). In this section, we explore what researchers using these approaches can tell us about how infants learn, remember, and conceptualize.

CONDITIONING

In Chapter 1, we described Skinner's operant conditioning (in which the consequences of a behavior produce changes in the probability of the behavior's occurrence). For example, if an infant's behavior is followed by a rewarding stimulus, the behavior is likely to recur.

Operant conditioning has been especially helpful to researchers in their efforts to determine what infants perceive (Rovee-Collier & Barr, 2010). For example, infants will suck faster on a nipple when the sucking behavior is followed by a visual display, music, or a human voice (Rovee-Collier, 1987, 2007).

Carolyn Rovee-Collier (1987) has also demonstrated how infants can retain information from the experience of being conditioned. In a characteristic experiment, she places a 2½-month-old baby in a crib under an elaborate mobile (see Figure 5.3). She then ties one end of a ribbon to the baby's ankle and the other end to the mobile. Subsequently, she observes that the baby kicks and makes the mobile move. The movement of the mobile is the reinforcing stimulus (which increases the baby's kicking behavior) in this experiment. Weeks later, the baby is returned to the crib, but its foot is not tied to the mobile. The baby kicks, which suggests it has retained the information that if it kicks a leg, the mobile will move.

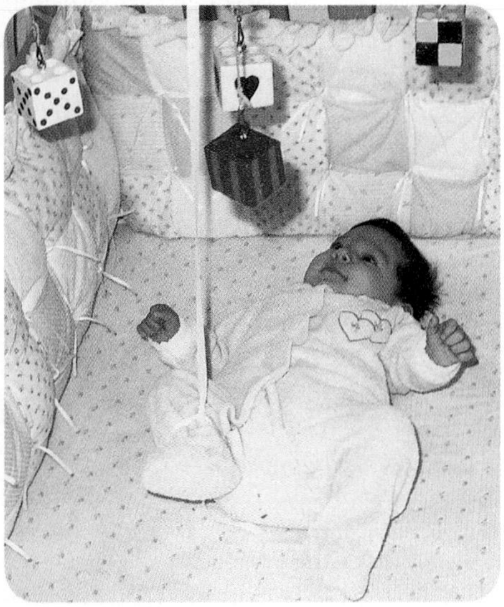

ATTENTION

Attention, the focusing of mental resources on select information, improves cognitive processing on many tasks (Columbo, Brez, & Curtindale, 2013; Rueda & Posner, 2013). At any one time, though, people can pay attention to only a limited amount of information. Even newborns can detect a contour and fix their attention on it. Older infants scan patterns more thoroughly. By 4 months, infants can selectively attend to an object. Also, a recent study examined 7- and 8-month-old infants' visual attention to sequences of events that varied in complexity (Kidd, Piantadosi, & Aslin, 2012). The infants tended to look away from events that were overly simple or complex, preferring instead to attend to events of intermediate complexity. Also, in recent research, 5-month-olds whose attention involved more efficient speed of processing information (called "short lookers") engaged in a higher level of executive function (higher-level cognitive functioning, such as being cognitively flexible and having better inhibitory control) in the preschool years than their counterparts who were less efficient in attending to information (referred to as "long lookers") (Cuevas & Bell, 2014).

In adults, when individuals orient their attention to an object or event, the parietal lobes in the cerebral cortex are involved (Goldberg & others, 2012). It is likely that the parietal lobes are active when infants orient their attention, although research has not yet documented this. (Figure 4.5 in the previous chapter illustrates the location of the parietal lobes in the brain.)

developmental **connection**

Theories

The behavioral and social cognitive approaches emphasize continuity rather than discontinuity in development. Chapter 1, p. 23

FIGURE **5.3**

THE TECHNIQUE USED IN ROVEE-COLLIER'S INVESTIGATION OF INFANT MEMORY. In Rovee-Collier's experiment, operant conditioning was used to demonstrate that infants as young as 2½ months of age can retain information from the experience of being conditioned. *What did infants recall in Rovee-Collier's experiment?*

attention The focusing of mental resources on select information.

developmental **connection**

Attention

In early childhood, children make significant advances in sustained attention. Chapter 7, p. 214

Attention in the first year of life is dominated by an *orienting/investigative process* (Rothbart, 2011). This process involves directing attention to potentially important locations in the environment (that is, *where*) and recognizing objects and their features (such as color and form) (that is, *what*) (Richards, 2010). From 3 to 9 months of age, infants can deploy their attention more flexibly and quickly. Another important type of attention is *sustained attention,* also referred to as *focused attention* (Richards, 2010). New stimuli typically elicit an orienting response followed by sustained attention. It is sustained attention that allows infants to learn about and remember characteristics of a stimulus as it becomes familiar. Researchers have found that infants as young as 3 months of age engage in 5 to 10 seconds of sustained attention. From this age through the second year, the length of sustained attention increases (Courage & Richards, 2008).

Habituation and Dishabituation Closely linked with attention are the processes of habituation and dishabituation that we discussed in Chapter 4 (Kavsek, 2004, 2013). If you say the same word or show the same toy to a baby several times in a row, the baby usually pays less attention to it each time. This is *habituation*—decreased responsiveness to a stimulus after repeated presentations of the stimulus. *Dishabituation* is the increase in responsiveness after a change in stimulation. Chapter 4 described some of the measures that researchers use to study whether habituation is occurring, such as sucking behavior (sucking stops when an infant attends to a novel object), heart rates, and the length of time the infant looks at an object.

Infants' attention is strongly governed by novelty and habituation (Richards, 2010). When an object becomes familiar, attention becomes shorter, and infants become more vulnerable to distraction (Oakes, Kannass, & Shaddy, 2002).

Researchers study habituation to determine the extent to which infants can see, hear, smell, taste, and experience touch (Slater, Field, & Hernandez-Reif, 2007). Studies of habituation can also indicate whether infants recognize something they have previously experienced. Habituation provides a measure of an infant's maturity and well-being. Infants who have brain damage do not habituate well.

Knowing about habituation and dishabituation can help parents interact effectively with infants. Infants respond to changes in stimulation. Wise parents sense when an infant shows an interest and realize that they may have to repeat something many times for the infant to process information. But if the stimulation is repeated often, the infant stops responding to the parent. In parent-infant interaction, it is important for parents to do novel things and to repeat them often until the infant stops responding. The parent stops or changes behaviors when the infant redirects his or her attention (Rosenblith, 1992).

This young infant's attention is riveted on the blue frog. The young infant's attention to the toy will be strongly regulated by the processes of habituation and dishabituation. *What characterizes these processes?*

Joint Attention Another aspect of attention that is an important aspect of infant development is **joint attention,** in which two or more individuals focus on the same object or event. Joint attention requires (1) an ability to track another's behavior, such as following the gaze of someone; (2) one person's directing another's attention, and (3) reciprocal interaction (Butterworth, 2004). Early in infancy, joint attention involves a caregiver pointing, turning the infant's head, snapping fingers, or using words to direct the infant's attention. Emerging forms of joint attention occur at about 7 to 8 months, but it is not until toward the end of the first year that joint attention skills are frequently observed (Heimann & others, 2006). In a study conducted by Andrew Meltzoff and Rechele Brooks (2006), at 10 to 11 months of age infants first began engaging in "gaze following," looking where another person has just looked (see Figure 5.4). And by their first birthday, infants have begun to direct adults' attention to objects that capture their interest (Heimann & others, 2006).

Joint attention plays important roles in many aspects of infant development and considerably increases infants' ability to learn from other people (Brooks & Meltzoff, 2014; Mateus & others, 2013). Nowhere is this more apparent than in observations of interchanges between caregivers and infants as infants are learning language (Tomasello, 2011, 2014). When caregivers and infants frequently engage in joint attention, infants say their first word earlier and develop a larger vocabulary (Beuker & others, 2013; Carpenter, Nagell, & Tomasello, 1998; Flom & Pick, 2003).

joint attention Process that occurs when individuals focus on the same object and are able to track another's behavior, one individual directs another's attention, and reciprocal interaction takes place.

memory A central feature of cognitive development, pertaining to all situations in which an individual retains information over time.

implicit memory Memory without conscious recollection; involves skills and routine procedures that are automatically performed.

explicit memory Memory of facts and experiences that individuals consciously know and can state.

(a)   (b)

FIGURE **5.4**

GAZE FOLLOWING IN INFANCY. Researcher Rechele Brooks shifts her eyes from the infant to a toy in the foreground (*a*). The infant then follows her eye movement to the toy (*b*). Brooks and colleague Andrew Meltzoff (2005) found that infants begin to engage in this kind of behavior, called "gaze following," at 10 to 11 months of age. Why might gaze following be an important accomplishment for an infant?

Later in this chapter in our discussion of language, we further discuss joint attention as an early predictor of language development in older infants and toddlers (Tomasello & Hamann, 2012).

The following studies also document the role of joint attention in children's memory and self-regulation:

- The extent to which 9-month-old infants engaged in joint attention was linked to their long-term memory (a one-week delay), possibly because joint attention enhances the relevance of attended items (Kopp & Lindenberger, 2011).
- Responding to joint attention at 12 months of age was linked to self-regulation skills at 3 years of age that involved delaying gratification for an attractive object (Van Hecke & others, 2012).

MEMORY

Memory involves the retention of information over time. Attention plays an important role in memory as part of a process called encoding, which is the process by which information is transferred to memory. What can infants remember, and when?

Some researchers such as Rovee-Collier (2008) have concluded that infants as young as 2 to 6 months of age can remember some experiences through 1½ to 2 years of age. However, critics such as Jean Mandler (2004), a leading expert on infant cognition, argue that the infants in Rovee-Collier's experiments were displaying only implicit memory. **Implicit memory** refers to memory without conscious recollection—memories of skills and routine procedures that are performed automatically. In contrast, **explicit memory** refers to conscious remembering of facts and experiences.

When people think about memory, they are usually referring to explicit memory. Most researchers find that babies do not show explicit memory until the second half of the first year (Bauer, 2013; Bauer & Fivush, 2014; Bauer & others, 2000). Then, explicit memory improves substantially during the second year of life (Bauer, 2013; Lukowski & Bauer, 2014). In one longitudinal study, infants were assessed several times during their second year (Bauer & others, 2000). Older infants showed more accurate memory and required fewer prompts to demonstrate their memory than younger infants. Figure 5.5 summarizes how long researchers have found infants of different ages can remember information (Bauer, 2009). As indicated in Figure 5.5, researchers have documented that 6-month-olds can remember information for 24 hours but by 20 months of age infants can remember information they encountered 12 months earlier.

What changes in the brain are linked to infants' memory development? From about 6 to 12 months of age, the maturation of the hippocampus and the surrounding cerebral cortex, especially the frontal lobes, makes explicit memory possible (Nelson, 2013; Nelson, Thomas, & de Haan, 2006) (see Figure 5.6). Explicit memory continues to improve in the second year as these brain structures further mature and connections between them increase. Less is known about the areas of the brain involved in implicit memory in infancy.

Let's examine another aspect of memory. Do you remember your third birthday party? Probably not. Most adults can remember little if anything from their first three years of life.

Age Group	Length of Delay
6-month-olds	24 hours
9-month-olds	1 month
10–11-month-olds	3 months
13–14-month-olds	4–6 months
20-month-olds	12 months

FIGURE **5.5**

AGE-RELATED CHANGES IN THE LENGTH OF TIME OVER WHICH MEMORY OCCURS

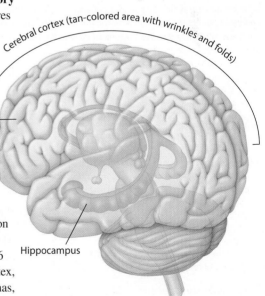

Cerebral cortex (tan-colored area with wrinkles and folds)

Frontal lobe

Hippocampus

FIGURE **5.6**

KEY BRAIN STRUCTURES INVOLVED IN EXPLICIT MEMORY DEVELOPMENT IN INFANCY

This is called *infantile* or *childhood amnesia.* The few reported adult memories of life at age 2 or 3 are at best very sketchy (Fivush, 2011; Newcombe, 2008; Riggins, 2012). Elementary school children also do not remember much of their early childhood years (Lie & Newcombe, 1999).

What is the cause of infantile amnesia? One reason older children and adults have difficulty recalling events from their infancy and early childhood is that during these early years the prefrontal lobes of the brain are immature; this area of the brain is believed to play an important role in storing memories of events (Boyer & Diamond, 1992).

In sum, most of young infants' conscious memories appear to be rather fragile and short-lived, although their implicit memory of perceptual-motor actions can be substantial (Bauer, 2013; Mandler, 2004). By the end of the second year, long-term memory is more substantial and reliable (Bauer, 2013; Lukowski & Bauer, 2014).

IMITATION

Can infants imitate someone else's emotional expressions? If an adult smiles, for example, will the baby respond with a smile? If an adult protrudes her lower lip, wrinkles her forehead, and frowns, will the baby show a sad face?

Infant development researcher Andrew Meltzoff (2004, 2005, 2011; Meltzoff & Moore, 1999; Meltzoff & Williamson, 2010, 2013; Meltzoff, Williamson, & Marshall, 2013) has conducted numerous studies of infants' imitative abilities. He sees infants' imitative abilities as biologically based, because infants can imitate a facial expression within the first few days after birth. He also emphasizes that the infant's imitative abilities do not resemble a hardwired response but rather involve flexibility and adaptability. In Meltzoff's observations of infants throughout their first 72 hours of life, the infants gradually displayed more complete imitation of an adult's facial expression, such as protruding the tongue or opening the mouth wide (see Figure 5.7).

Meltzoff (2007) concludes that infants don't blindly imitate everything they see and often make creative errors. He also argues that beginning at birth there is an interplay between learning by observing and learning by doing (Piaget emphasized learning by doing).

Not all experts on infant development accept Meltzoff's conclusions that newborns are capable of imitation. Some say that these babies were engaging in little more than automatic responses to a stimulus.

Meltzoff (2005, 2011) also has studied **deferred imitation,** which occurs after a time delay of hours or days. Piaget held that deferred imitation doesn't occur until about 18 months of age. Meltzoff's research suggested that it occurs much earlier. In one study, Meltzoff (1988) demonstrated that 9-month-old infants could imitate actions—such as pushing a recessed button in a box, which produced a beeping sound—that they had seen performed 24 hours earlier. Also, in one study, engagement in deferred imitation at 9 months of age was a strong predictor of more extensive production of communicative gestures at 14 months of age (Heimann & others, 2006). Two of the most common infant gestures are (1) extending the arm to show the caregiver something the infant is holding, and (2) pointing with the arm and index finger extended at some interesting object or event.

CONCEPT FORMATION AND CATEGORIZATION

Along with attention, memory, and imitation, concepts are key aspects of infants' cognitive development (Gelman, 2013; Quinn, 2014; Rakison & Lawson, 2013). **Concepts** are cognitive groupings of similar objects, events, people, or ideas. Without concepts, you would see each object and event as unique; you would not be able to make any generalizations.

Do infants have concepts? Yes, they do, although we do not know precisely how early concept formation begins (Quinn & others, 2013).

Using habituation experiments like those described earlier in the chapter, some researchers have found that infants as young as 3 to 4 months of age can group together objects with similar appearances, such as animals (Quinn, 2014; Rakison & Lawson, 2013). This research

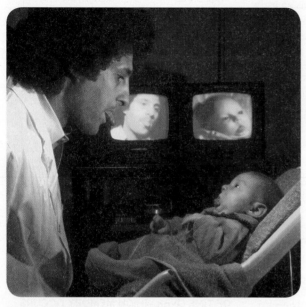

FIGURE 5.7

INFANT IMITATION. Infant development researcher Andrew Meltzoff protrudes his tongue in an attempt to get the infant to imitate his behavior. *How do Meltzoff's findings about imitation compare with Piaget's descriptions of infants' abilities?*

deferred imitation Imitation that occurs after a delay of hours or days.

concepts Cognitive groupings of similar objects, events, people, or ideas.

capitalizes on the knowledge that infants are more likely to look at a novel object than a familiar object. Jean Mandler (2004, 2009) argues that these early categorizations are best described as *perceptual categorization*. That is, the categorizations are based on similar perceptual features of objects, such as size, color, and movement, as well as parts of objects, such as legs for animals. Mandler (2004) concludes that it is not until about 7 to 9 months of age that infants form *conceptual* categories rather than just making perceptual discriminations between different categories. In one study of 9- to 11-month-olds, infants classified birds as animals and airplanes as vehicles even though the objects were perceptually similar—airplanes and birds with their wings spread (Mandler & McDonough, 1993).

In addition to infants categorizing items on the basis of external, perceptual features such as shape, color, and parts, they also may categorize items on the basis of prototypes, or averages, that they extract from the structural regularities of items (Rakison & Lawson, 2013).

Further advances in categorization occur in the second year of life (Booth, 2006; Rakison & Lawson, 2013). Many infants' "first concepts are broad and global in nature, such as 'animal' or 'indoor thing.' Gradually, over the first two years these broad concepts become more differentiated into concepts such as 'land animal,' then 'dog,' or to 'furniture,' then 'chair'" (Mandler, 2009, p. 1). Also in the second year, infants often categorize objects on the basis of their shape (Landau, Smith, & Jones, 1998).

Learning to put things into the correct categories—what makes something one kind of thing rather than another kind of thing, such as what makes a bird a bird, or a fish a fish—is an important aspect of learning (Rakison & Lawson, 2013). As infant development researcher Alison Gopnik (2010, p. 159) pointed out, "If you can sort the world into the right categories—put things in the right boxes—then you've got a big advance on understanding the world."

Do some very young children develop an intense, passionate interest in a particular category of objects or activities? A recent study confirmed that they do (DeLoache, Simcock, & Macari, 2007). A striking finding was the large gender difference in categories, with an intense interest in particular categories stronger for boys than girls. Categorization of boys' intense interests focused on vehicles, trains, machines, dinosaurs, and balls; girls' intense interests were more likely to involve dress-ups and books/reading (see Figure 5.8). When your author's grandson Alex was 18 to 24 months old, he already had developed an intense, passionate interest in the category of vehicles. For example, at this age, he categorized vehicles into such subcategories as cars, trucks, earth-moving equipment, and buses. In addition to common classifications of cars into police cars, jeeps, taxis, and such, and trucks into fire trucks, dump trucks, and the like, his categorical knowledge of earth-moving equipment included bulldozers and excavators, and he categorized buses into school buses, London buses, and funky Malta buses (retro buses on the island of Malta). Later, at 3 years of age, Alex developed an intense, passionate interest in categorizing dinosaurs.

In sum, the infant's advances in processing information—through attention, memory, imitation, and concept formation—is much richer, more gradual and less stage-like, and occurs earlier than was envisioned by earlier theorists, such as Piaget (Johnson & Hannon, 2015; Lukowski & Bauer, 2014; Quinn, 2014). As leading infant researcher Jean Mandler (2004) concluded, "The human infant shows a remarkable degree of learning power and complexity in what is being learned and in the way it is represented" (p. 304).

> Infants are creating concepts and organizing their world into conceptual domains that will form the backbone of their thought throughout life.
>
> —JEAN MANDLER
> *Contemporary Psychologist, University of California–San Diego*

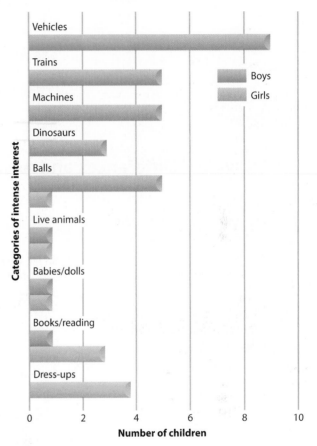

FIGURE **5.8**

CATEGORIZATION OF BOYS' AND GIRLS' INTENSE INTERESTS

The author's grandson Alex at 2 years of age showing his intense, passionate interest in the category of vehicles while playing with a London taxi and a funky Malta bus.

> I wish I could travel down by the road that crosses the baby's mind where reason makes kites of her laws and flies them. . . .
>
> —RABINDRANATH TAGORE
> *Bengali Poet and Essayist, 20th Century*

Review *Connect* **Reflect**

LG2 Describe how infants learn, remember, and conceptualize.

Review

- How do infants learn through conditioning?
- What is attention? What characterizes attention in infants?
- To what extent can infants remember?
- How is imitation involved in infant learning?
- When do infants develop concepts, and how does concept formation change during infancy?

Connect

- In this section, we learned that explicit memory improves in the second year as

the hippocampus and frontal lobes mature and as connections between them increase. What did you learn in the text associated with Figure 4.6 in the previous chapter that might also contribute to improvements in a mental process such as memory during this same time frame?

Reflect *Your Own Personal Journey of Life*

- If a friend told you that she remembers being abused by her parents when she was 2 years old, would you believe her? Explain your answer.

3 Individual Differences and Assessment

LG3 Discuss infant assessment measures and the prediction of intelligence.

Measures of Infant Development   Predicting Intelligence

So far, we have discussed how the cognitive development of infants generally progresses. We have emphasized what is typical of the largest number of infants or the average infant, but the results obtained for most infants do not apply to all infants. It is advantageous to know whether an infant is developing at a slow, normal, or advanced pace during the course of infancy. If an infant advances at an especially slow rate, then some form of enrichment may be necessary. If an infant develops at an advanced pace, parents may be advised to provide toys that stimulate cognitive growth in slightly older infants. How is an infant's cognitive development assessed?

MEASURES OF INFANT DEVELOPMENT

Individual differences in infant cognitive development have been studied primarily through the use of developmental scales or infant intelligence tests. For example, in Chapter 3 we discussed the Brazelton Neonatal Behavioral Assessment Scale (NBAS) and the Neonatal Intensive Care Unit Network Neurobehavioral Scale (NNNS), which are used to evaluate newborns. To read about the work of one infant assessment specialist, see *Connecting with Careers.*

The most important early contributor to the testing of infants was Arnold Gesell (1934). He developed a measure that helped sort out babies with normal functioning from ones with abnormal functioning. This was especially useful to adoption agencies, which had large numbers of babies awaiting placement. Gesell's examination was used widely for many years and still is frequently employed by pediatricians to distinguish normal and abnormal functioning in infants. The current version of the Gesell test has four categories of behavior: motor, language, adaptive, and personal-social. The **developmental quotient (DQ)** combines subscores in these categories to provide an overall score.

The widely used **Bayley Scales of Infant Development** were developed by Nancy Bayley (1969) to assess infant behavior and predict later development. The current version, Bayley-III, has five scales: cognitive, language, motor, socioemotional, and adaptive (Bayley, 2006). The first three scales are administered directly to the infant, while the latter two are questionnaires given to the caregiver. The Bayley-III also is more appropriate for use in clinical settings than were the two previous editions (Lennon & others, 2008).

developmental connection

Intelligence

Tests that assess older children's intelligence use more verbal items than do developmental assessments of infants. Chapter 9, p. 286

developmental quotient (DQ) An overall score that combines subscores in motor, language, adaptive, and personal-social domains in the Gesell assessment of infants.

Bayley Scales of Infant Development Scales developed by Nancy Bayley that are widely used to assess infant development. The current version has three components: a mental scale, a motor scale, and an infant behavior profile.

Toosje Thyssen Van Beveren, Infant Assessment Specialist

Toosje Thyssen Van Beveren is a developmental psychologist at the University of Texas Medical Center in Dallas. She has a master's degree in child clinical psychology and a Ph.D. in human development. Van Beveren has been involved for a number of years in a 12-week program called New Connections, which is a comprehensive intervention for infants who were affected by substance abuse prenatally and for their caregivers.

In the New Connections program, Van Beveren assesses infants' developmental status and progress. She might refer the infants to a speech, physical, or occupational therapist and monitor the infants' services and progress. Van Beveren trains the program staff and encourages them to use the exercises she recommends. She also discusses the child's problems with the primary caregivers, suggests activities, and assists them in enrolling infants in appropriate programs.

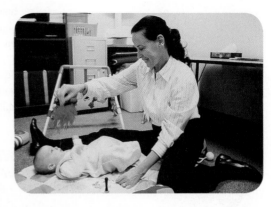

Toosje Thyssen Van Beveren conducting an infant assessment.

During her graduate work at the University of Texas at Dallas, Van Beveren was author John Santrock's teaching assistant in his undergraduate course on life-span development for four years. As a teaching assistant, she attended classes, graded exams, counseled students, and occasionally gave lectures. Van Beveren returns periodically to give a lecture on prenatal development and infancy. She also teaches courses in infant development and in child development in the psychology department at UT–Dallas. In Van Beveren's words, "My days are busy and full. The work is often challenging. There are some disappointments but mostly the work is enormously gratifying."

How should a 6-month-old perform on the Bayley mental scale? The 6-month-old infant should be able to vocalize pleasure and displeasure, persistently search for objects that are just out of immediate reach, and approach a mirror that is placed in front of the infant by the examiner. By 12 months of age, the infant should be able to inhibit behavior when commanded to do so, imitate words the examiner says (such as "Mama"), and respond to simple requests (such as "Take a drink").

The explosion of interest in infant development has produced many new measures, especially tasks that evaluate the ways infants process information (Fogel, 2010). The Fagan Test of Infant Intelligence is increasingly being used (Fagan, 1992). This test focuses on the infant's ability to process information in such ways as encoding the attributes of objects, detecting similarities and differences between objects, forming mental representations, and retrieving these representations. For example, to estimate intelligence, it uses the amount of time babies look at a new object compared with the amount of time they spend looking at a familiar object.

Items in the Bayley-III Scales of Infant Development.

PREDICTING INTELLIGENCE

The infant-testing movement grew out of the tradition of IQ testing. However, IQ tests of older children pay more attention to verbal ability. Tests for infants contain far more items related to perceptual-motor development and include measures of social interaction.

One longitudinal study examined the intelligence of 200 children ranging in age from 12 months (using the Bayley scales) to 4 years (using the Stanford Binet test) (Blaga & others, 2009). The results indicated considerable stability from late infancy through the preschool years. However, overall scores on such tests as the Gesell and the Bayley scales do not correlate highly with IQ scores obtained later in childhood. This result is not surprising because the components tested in infancy are not the same as the components assessed by IQ tests.

Unlike the Gesell and Bayley scales, the Fagan test is correlated with measures of intelligence in older children. In fact, evidence is accumulating that measures of habituation and dishabituation are linked to intelligence in childhood, adolescence, and even adulthood (Fagan,

Holland, and Wheeler, 2007; Kavsek, 2004). One study revealed that habituation assessed at 3 and 6 months of age was linked to verbal skills and intelligence assessed at 32 months of age (Domasch, Lohaus, & Thomas, 2009). And a longitudinal study revealed that four information-processing domains (attention, processing speed, memory, and representational competence) assessed in infancy and early childhood were linked to general intelligence scores on the Wechsler Intelligence Scale for Children–III at 11 years of age (Rose & others, 2012).

It is important, however, not to go too far and think that connections between cognitive development in early infancy and later cognitive development are so strong that no discontinuity takes place. Some important changes in cognitive development occur after infancy, changes that we will describe in later chapters.

Review Connect Reflect

 LG3 Discuss infant assessment measures and the prediction of intelligence.

Review
- What are some measures of infant development?
- Do tests of infants predict intelligence later in life?

Connect
- In this section, you learned that measures of habituation and dishabituation are linked to intelligence. In Section 2 of this chapter, what advice was given to parents regarding habituation and dishabituation?

Reflect *Your Own Personal Journey of Life*
- Imagine that you had your 1-year-old assessed with a developmental scale and the baby did very well on it. How confident should you be that your baby is going to be a genius when he or she grows up?

4 Language Development

 LG4 Describe the nature of language and how it develops in infancy.

| Defining Language | Language's Rule Systems | How Language Develops | Biological and Environmental Influences | An Interactionist View |

Language allows us to communicate with others. *What are some important characteristics of language?*

In 1799, a nude boy was observed running through the woods in France. The boy was captured when he was 11 years old. He was called the Wild Boy of Aveyron and was believed to have lived in the woods alone for six years (Lane, 1976). When found, he made no effort to communicate. He never learned to communicate effectively. Sadly, a modern-day wild child named Genie was discovered in Los Angeles in 1970. Despite intensive intervention, Genie has never acquired more than a primitive form of language. Both cases—the Wild Boy of Aveyron and Genie—raise questions about the biological and environmental determinants of language, topics that we also will examine later in the chapter. First, though, we need to define language.

DEFINING LANGUAGE

Language is a form of communication—whether spoken, written, or signed—that is based on a system of symbols. Language consists of the words used by a community and the rules for varying and combining them.

Think how important language is in our everyday lives. We need language to speak with others, listen to others, read, and write. Our language enables us to describe past events in detail and to plan for the future. Language lets us pass down information from one generation to the next and create a rich cultural heritage.

All human languages have some common characteristics (Berko Gleason, 2009; Waxman & others, 2014; Werker & Gervain, 2013). These include infinite generativity and organizational rules. **Infinite generativity** is the ability to produce an endless number of meaningful sentences using a finite set of words and rules. Rules describe the way language works. Let's explore what these rules involve.

LANGUAGE'S RULE SYSTEMS

When nineteenth-century American writer Ralph Waldo Emerson said, "The world was built in order, and the atoms march in tune," he must have had language in mind. Language is highly ordered and organized (Song, 2013). The organization involves five systems of rules: phonology, morphology, syntax, semantics, and pragmatics.

Phonology   Every language is made up of basic sounds. **Phonology** is the sound system of the language, including the sounds that are used and how they may be combined (Vihman, 2014). For example, English has the initial consonant cluster *spr* as in *spring,* but no words begin with the cluster *rsp.*

Phonology provides a basis for constructing a large and expandable set of words out of two or three dozen phonemes. A *phoneme* is the basic unit of sound in a language; it is the smallest unit of sound that affects meaning. For example, in English the sound represented by the letter *p,* as in the words *pot* and *spot,* is a phoneme. The /p/ sound is slightly different in the two words, but this variation is not distinguished in English, and therefore the /p/ sound is a single phoneme. In some languages, such as Hindi, the variations of the /p/ sound represent separate phonemes.

Morphology   **Morphology** refers to the units of meaning involved in word formation. A *morpheme* is a minimal unit of meaning; it is a word or a part of a word that cannot be broken into smaller meaningful parts (Booij, 2013). Every word in the English language is made up of one or more morphemes. Some words consist of a single morpheme (for example, *help*), whereas others are made up of more than one morpheme (for example, *helper* has two morphemes, *help* and *er,* with the morpheme *-er* meaning "one who"—in this case, "one who helps"). Thus, not all morphemes are words by themselves; for example, *pre-, -tion,* and *-ing* are morphemes.

Just as the rules that govern phonology describe the sound sequences that can occur in a language, the rules of morphology describe the way meaningful units (morphemes) can be combined in words (Brown, 2013). Morphemes have many jobs in grammar, such as marking tense (for example, "she walks" versus "she walked") and number ("she walks" versus "they walk").

Syntax   **Syntax** involves the way words are combined to form acceptable phrases and sentences (de Villiers & de Villiers, 2013). If someone says to you, "Bob slugged Tom" or "Bob was slugged by Tom," you know who did the slugging and who was slugged in each case because you have a syntactic understanding of these sentence structures. You also understand that the sentence, "You didn't stay, did you?" is a grammatical sentence, but that "You didn't stay, didn't you?" is unacceptable and ambiguous.

If you learn another language, English syntax will not get you very far. For example, in English an adjective usually precedes a noun (as in *blue sky*), whereas in Spanish the adjective usually follows the noun *(cielo azul).* Despite the differences in their syntactic structures, however, syntactic systems in all of the world's languages have some common ground (Whaley, 2013). For example, no language we know of permits sentences like the following one:

> *The mouse the cat the farmer chased killed ate the cheese.*

It appears that language users cannot process subjects and objects arranged in too complex a fashion in a sentence.

Semantics   **Semantics** refers to the meaning of words and sentences. Every word has a set of semantic features, which are required attributes related to meaning (Parish-Morris, Golinkoff, & Hirsh-Pasek, 2013). *Girl* and *woman,* for example, share many semantic features, but they differ semantically in regard to age.

Words have semantic restrictions on how they can be used in sentences (de Villiers & de Villiers, 2013). The sentence *The bicycle talked the boy into buying a candy bar* is syntactically correct but semantically incorrect. The sentence violates our semantic knowledge that bicycles don't talk.

Pragmatics   A final set of language rules involves **pragmatics,** the appropriate use of language in different contexts. Pragmatics covers a lot of territory (Elbourne, 2012). When you take turns speaking in a discussion or use a question to convey a command ("Why is it so

language A form of communication, whether spoken, written, or signed, that is based on a system of symbols. Language consists of the words used by a community and the rules for varying and combining them.

infinite generativity The ability to produce an endless number of meaningful sentences using a finite set of words and rules.

phonology The sound system of the language, including the sounds that are used and how they may be combined.

morphology Units of meaning involved in word formation.

syntax The ways words are combined to form acceptable phrases and sentences.

semantics The meaning of words and sentences.

pragmatics The appropriate use of language in different contexts.

Rule System	Description	Examples
Phonology	The sound system of a language. A phoneme is the smallest sound unit in a language.	The word *chat* has three phonemes or sounds: /ch/ /ā/ /t/. An example of phonological rule in the English language is while the phoneme /r/ can follow the phonemes /t/ or /d/ in an English consonant cluster (such as *track* or *drab*), the phoneme /l/ cannot follow these letters.
Morphology	The system of meaningful units involved in word formation.	The smallest sound units that have a meaning are called morphemes, or meaning units. The word *girl* is one morpheme, or meaning unit; it cannot be broken down any further and still have meaning. When the suffix *s* is added, the word becomes *girls* and has two morphemes because the *s* changed the meaning of the word, indicating that there is more than one girl.
Syntax	The system that involves the way words are combined to form acceptable phrases and sentences.	Word order is very important in determining meaning in the English language. For example, the sentence "Sebastian pushed the bike" has a different meaning than "The bike pushed Sebastian."
Semantics	The system that involves the meaning of words and sentences.	Knowing the meaning of individual words—that is, vocabulary. For example, semantics includes knowing the meaning of such words as *orange*, *transportation*, and *intelligent*.
Pragmatics	The system of using appropriate conversation and knowledge of how to effectively use language in context.	An example is using polite language in appropriate situations, such as being mannerly when talking with one's teacher. Taking turns in a conversation involves pragmatics.

FIGURE **5.9**

THE RULE SYSTEMS OF LANGUAGE

noisy in here? What is this, Grand Central Station?"), you are demonstrating knowledge of pragmatics. You also apply the pragmatics of English when you use polite language in appropriate situations (for example, when talking to your teacher) or tell stories that are interesting, jokes that are funny, and lies that convince. In each of these cases, you are demonstrating that you understand the rules of your culture for adjusting language to suit the context.

At this point, we have discussed five important rule systems involved in language. An overview of these rule systems is presented in Figure 5.9.

HOW LANGUAGE DEVELOPS

According to an ancient historian, in the thirteenth century the emperor of Germany, Frederick II, had a cruel idea. He wanted to know what language children would speak if no one talked to them. He selected several newborns and threatened their caregivers with death if they ever talked to the infants. Frederick never found out what language the children spoke because they all died. Today, we are still curious about infants' development of language, although our experiments and observations are, to say the least, far more humane than the evil Frederick's.

Whatever language they learn, infants all over the world follow a similar path in language development. What are some key milestones in this development?

Recognizing Language Sounds   Long before they begin to learn words, infants can make fine distinctions among the sounds of the language. In Patricia Kuhl's (1993, 2000, 2007, 2009, 2011) research, phonemes from languages all over the world are piped through a speaker for infants to hear (see Figure 5.10). A box with a toy bear in it is placed where the infant can see it. A string of identical syllables is played; then the syllables are changed (for example, *ba ba ba ba*, and then *pa pa pa pa*). If the infant turns its head when the

FIGURE **5.10**

FROM UNIVERSAL LINGUIST TO LANGUAGE-SPECIFIC LISTENER. In Patricia Kuhl's research laboratory babies listen to tape-recorded voices that repeat syllables. When the sounds of the syllables change, the babies quickly learn to look at the bear. Using this technique, Kuhl has demonstrated that babies are universal linguists until about 6 months of age, but in their next six months they become language-specific listeners. *Does Kuhl's research give support to the view that either "nature" or "nurture" is the source of language acquisition?*

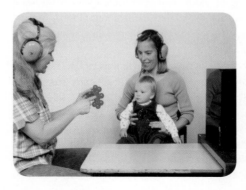

syllables change, the box lights up and the bear dances and drums, rewarding the infant for noticing the change.

Kuhl's (2007, 2009, 2011) research has demonstrated that from birth up to about 6 months of age, infants are "citizens of the world": They recognize when sounds change most of the time, no matter what language the syllables come from. But over the next six months, infants get even better at perceiving the changes in sounds from their "own" language (the one their parents speak) and gradually lose the ability to recognize differences that are not important in their own language (Kuhl & Damasio, 2012).

Also, in the second half of the first year, infants begin to segment the continuous stream of speech they encounter into words (Werker & Gervain, 2013). Initially, they likely rely on statistical information such as the co-occurrence patterns of phonemes and syllables, which allows them to extract potential word forms. For example, discovering that the sequence *br* occurs more often at the beginning of words while *nt* is more common at the end of words helps infants detect word boundaries. And as infants extract an increasing number of potential word forms from the speech stream they hear, they begin to associate these with concrete, perceptually available objects in their world (Zamuner, Fais, & Werker, 2014).

Babbling and Other Vocalizations Long before infants speak recognizable words, they produce a number of vocalizations. The functions of these early vocalizations are to practice making sounds, to communicate, and to attract attention (Parish-Morris, Golinkoff & Hirsh-Pasek, 2013). Babies' sounds go through the following sequence during the first year:

- *Crying.* Babies cry even at birth. Crying can signal distress, but, as we will discuss in Chapter 6, different types of cries signal different things.
- *Cooing.* Babies first coo at about 2 to 4 months (Menn & Stoel-Gammon, 2009). These are gurgling sounds that are made in the back of the throat and usually express pleasure during interaction with the caregiver.
- *Babbling.* In the middle of the first year, babies babble—that is, they produce strings of consonant-vowel combinations, such as "ba, ba, ba, ba."

Long before infants speak recognizable words, they communicate by producing a number of vocalizations and gestures. *At approximately what ages do infants begin to produce different types of vocalizations and gestures?*

Gestures Infants start using gestures, such as showing and pointing, at about 7 to 15 months of age with a mean age of approximately 11 to 12 months (Colonnesi & others, 2010). They may wave bye-bye, nod to mean "yes," show an empty cup to ask for more milk, and point to a dog to draw attention to it. Some early gestures are symbolic, as when an infant smacks her lips to indicate food/drink. Pointing is regarded by language experts as an important index of the social aspects of language, and it follows this developmental sequence: from pointing without checking on adult gaze to pointing while looking back and forth between an object and the adult (Goldin-Meadow, 2014a, b; Goldin-Meadow & Alibali, 2013). Lack of pointing is a significant indicator of problems in the infant's communication system. For example, failure to engage in pointing characterizes many autistic children. The ability to use the pointing gesture effectively improves in the second year of life as advances in other aspects of language communication occur (Colonnesi & others, 2010).

One study found that parents in high socioeconomic status (SES) families were more likely to use gestures when communicating with their 14-month-old infants (Rowe & Goldin-Meadow, 2009). Further, the infants' use of gestures at 14 months of age in high-SES families was linked to a larger vocabulary at 54 months of age.

First Words Infants understand their first words earlier than they speak them (Parish-Morris, Golinkoff, & Hirsh-Pasek, 2013). As early as 5 months of age, infants recognize their name when someone says it. On the average, infants understand about 50 words at about 13 months, but they can't say this many words until about 18 months (Menyuk, Liebergott, & Schultz, 1995). Thus, in infancy *receptive vocabulary* (words the child understands) considerably exceeds *spoken* (or *expressive*) *vocabulary* (words the child uses).

A child's first words include those that name important people (*dada*), familiar animals (*kitty*), vehicles (*car*), toys (*ball*), food (*milk*), body parts (*eye*), clothes (*hat*), household items

What characterizes the infant's early word learning?

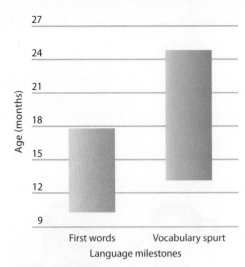

FIGURE **5.11**

VARIATION IN LANGUAGE MILESTONES.
What are some possible explanations for variations in the timing of language milestones?

Around the world, most young children learn to speak in two-word utterances at about 18 to 24 months of age. *What are some examples of these two-word utterances?*

telegraphic speech The use of short and precise words without grammatical markers such as articles, auxiliary verbs, and other connectives.

(*clock*), and greeting terms (*bye*). These were the first words of babies 50 years ago, and they are the first words of babies today. Children often express various intentions with their single words, so that "cookie" might mean, "That's a cookie" or "I want a cookie." Nouns are easier to learn because the majority of words in this class are more perceptually accessible than words not in this class (Parish-Morris, Golinkoff, & Hirsh-Pasek, 2013). Think how the noun "car" is so much more concrete and imaginable than the verb "goes," making the word "car" much easier to acquire than the word "goes."

The infant's spoken vocabulary rapidly increases after the first word is spoken (Werker & Gervain, 2013). The average 18-month-old can speak about 50 words, but most 2-year-olds can speak about 200 words. This rapid increase in vocabulary that begins at approximately 18 months is called the *vocabulary spurt* (Bloom, Lifter, & Broughton, 1985).

Like the timing of a child's first word, the timing of the vocabulary spurt varies (Lieven, 2008). Figure 5.11 shows the range for these two language milestones in 14 children. On average, these children said their first word at 13 months and had a vocabulary spurt at 19 months. However, the ages for the first spoken word of individual children varied from 10 to 17 months and for their vocabulary spurt from 13 to 25 months.

Cross-linguistic differences occur in word learning (Waxman & others, 2014). Children learning Mandarin Chinese, Korean, and Japanese acquire more verbs earlier in their development than do children learning English. This cross-linguistic difference reflects the greater use of verbs in the language input to children in these Asian languages.

Children sometimes overextend or underextend the meanings of the words they use (Woodward & Markman, 1998). *Overextension* is the tendency to apply a word to objects that are inappropriate for the word's meaning. For example, children at first may say "dada" not only for "father" but also for other men, strangers, or boys. With time, overextensions decrease and eventually disappear. *Underextension* is the tendency to apply a word too narrowly; it occurs when children fail to use a word to name a relevant event or object. For example, a child might use the word *boy* to describe a 5-year-old neighbor but not apply the word to a male infant or to a 9-year-old male.

Two-Word Utterances By the time children are 18 to 24 months of age, they usually speak in two-word utterances. To convey meaning with just two words, the child relies heavily on gesture, tone, and context. The wealth of meaning children can communicate with a two-word utterance includes the following (Slobin, 1972):

- Identification: "See doggie."
- Location: "Book there."
- Repetition: "More milk."
- Negation: "Not wolf."
- Possession: "My candy."
- Attribution: "Big car."
- Agent-action: "Mama walk."
- Action-direct object: "Hit you."
- Action-indirect object: "Give Papa."
- Action-instrument: "Cut knife."
- Question: "Where ball?"

These are examples from children whose first language is English, German, Russian, Finnish, Turkish, or Samoan.

Notice that the two-word utterances omit many parts of speech and are remarkably succinct. In fact, in every language, a child's first combinations of words have this economical quality; they are telegraphic. **Telegraphic speech** is the use of short and precise words without grammatical markers such as articles, auxiliary verbs, and other connectives. Telegraphic speech is not limited to two words. "Mommy give ice cream" and "Mommy give Tommy ice cream" also are examples of telegraphic speech.

We have discussed a number of language milestones in infancy; Figure 5.12 summarizes the approximate ages at which infants typically reach these milestones.

BIOLOGICAL AND ENVIRONMENTAL INFLUENCES

What makes the milestones of infant language developed described in Figure 5.12 possible? Everyone who uses language in some way "knows" its rules and has the ability to create an infinite number of words and sentences. Where does this knowledge come from? Is it the product of biology? Is language learned and influenced by experiences?

Biological Influences   The ability to speak and understand language requires a certain vocal apparatus as well as a nervous system with certain capabilities. The nervous system and vocal apparatus of humanity's predecessors changed over hundreds of thousands or millions of years. With advances in the nervous system and vocal structures, *Homo sapiens* went beyond the grunting and shrieking of other animals to develop speech. Although estimates vary, many experts believe that humans acquired language about 100,000 years ago, which in evolutionary time represents a very recent acquisition. It gave humans an enormous edge over other animals and increased the chances of human survival (Arbib, 2012).

Some language scholars view the remarkable similarities in how children acquire language all over the world as strong evidence that language has a biological basis. There is evidence that particular regions of the brain are predisposed to be used for language (Tando & others, 2014). Two regions involved in language were first discovered in studies of brain-damaged individuals: **Broca's area**, an area in the left frontal lobe of the brain involved in producing words, and **Wernicke's area**, a region of the brain's left hemisphere involved in language comprehension (see Figure 5.13). Damage to either of these areas produces types of **aphasia**, which is a loss or impairment of language processing. Individuals with damage to Broca's area have difficulty producing words correctly; individuals

Typical Age	Language Milestones
Birth	Crying
2 to 4 months	Cooing begins
5 months	Understands first word
6 months	Babbling begins
7 to 11 months	Change from universal linguist to language-specific listener
8 to 12 months	Uses gestures, such as showing and pointing Comprehension of words appears
13 months	First word spoken
18 months	Vocabulary spurt starts
18 to 24 months	Uses two-word utterances Rapid expansion of understanding of words

FIGURE **5.12**
SOME LANGUAGE MILESTONES IN INFANCY. Despite great variations in the language input received by infants, around the world they follow a similar path in learning to speak.

developmental **connection**
Language
Much of language is processed in the brain's left hemisphere. Chapter 4, p. 106

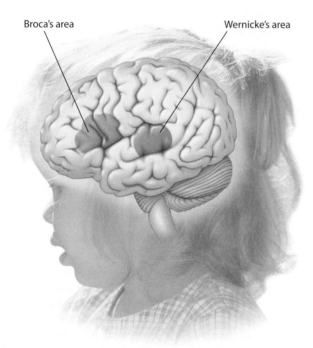

FIGURE **5.13**
BROCA'S AREA AND WERNICKE'S AREA. Broca's area is located in the frontal lobe of the brain's left hemisphere, and it is involved in the control of speech. Wernicke's area is a portion of the left hemisphere's temporal lobe that is involved in understanding language. *How does the role of these areas of the brain relate to lateralization, which was discussed in Chapter 4?*

Broca's area An area in the brain's left frontal lobe that is involved in speech production.

Wernicke's area An area in the brain's left hemisphere that is involved in language comprehension.

aphasia A loss or impairment of language ability caused by brain damage.

FIGURE 5.14

SOCIAL INTERACTION AND BABBLING. One study focused on two groups of mothers and their 8-month-old infants (Goldstein, King, & West, 2003). One group of mothers was instructed to smile and touch their infants immediately after the babies cooed and babbled; the other group was also told to smile and touch their infants but in a random manner, unconnected to sounds the infants made. The infants whose mothers immediately responded in positive ways to their babbling subsequently made more complex, speechlike sounds, such as "da" and "gu." The research setting for this study, which underscores how important caregivers are in the early development of language, is shown above.

language acquisition device (LAD) Chomsky's term that describes a biological endowment enabling the child to detect the features and rules of language, including phonology, syntax, and semantics.

with damage to Wernicke's area have poor comprehension and often produce fluent but incomprehensible speech.

Linguist Noam Chomsky (1957) proposed that humans are biologically prewired to learn language at a certain time and in a certain way. He said that children are born into the world with a **language acquisition device (LAD),** a biological endowment that enables the child to detect certain features and rules of language, including phonology, syntax, and semantics. Children are equipped by nature with the ability to detect the sounds of language, for example, and to follow rules such as how to form plurals and ask questions.

Chomsky's LAD is a theoretical construct, not a physical part of the brain. Is there evidence for the existence of a LAD? Supporters of the LAD concept cite the uniformity of language milestones across languages and cultures, evidence that children create language even in the absence of well-formed input, and biological substrates of language. But, as we will see, critics argue that even if infants have something like a LAD, it cannot explain the whole story of language acquisition.

Environmental Influences   Decades ago, behaviorists opposed Chomsky's hypothesis and argued that language represents nothing more than chains of responses acquired through reinforcement (Skinner, 1957). A baby happens to babble "Ma-ma"; Mama rewards the baby with hugs and smiles; the baby says "Mama" more and more. Bit by bit, said the behaviorists, the baby's language is built up. According to behaviorists, the use of language is a complex, learned skill, much like playing the piano or dancing.

The behaviorist view of language learning has several problems. First, it does not explain how people create novel sentences—sentences that people have never heard or spoken before. Second, children learn the syntax of their native language even if they are not reinforced for doing so. Social psychologist Roger Brown (1973) spent long hours observing parents and their young children. He found that parents did not directly or explicitly reward or correct the syntax of most children's utterances. That is, parents did not say "good," "correct," "right," "wrong," and so on. Also, parents did not offer direct corrections such as "You should say *two shoes,* not *two shoe.*" However, as we will see shortly, many parents do expand on their young children's grammatically incorrect utterances and recast many of those that have grammatical errors (Clark, 2009).

The behaviorist view is no longer considered a viable explanation of how children acquire language. But a great deal of research describes ways in which children's environmental experiences influence their language skills (Hirsh-Pasek & Golinkoff, 2014). Many language experts argue that a child's experiences, the particular language to be learned, and the context in which learning takes place can strongly influence language acquisition (Giorgis & Glazer, 2013).

Language is not learned in a social vacuum. Most children are bathed in language from a very early age, unlike the Wild Boy of Aveyron, who never learned to communicate effectively, having lived in social isolation for years. The support and involvement of caregivers and teachers greatly facilitate a child's language learning (Giorgis & Glazer, 2013; Hirsh-Pasek & Golinkoff, 2014). For example, one study found that when mothers immediately smiled and touched their 8-month-old infants after they babbled, the infants subsequently made more complex speech-like sounds than when mothers responded to their infants in a random manner (Goldstein, King, & West, 2003) (see Figure 5.14).

Michael Tomasello (2003, 2006, 2011, 2014) stresses that young children are intensely interested in their social world and that early in their development they can understand the intentions of other people. His *interaction view* of language emphasizes that children learn language in specific contexts. For example, when a toddler and a father are jointly focused on a book, the father might say, "See the birdie." In this case, even a toddler understands that the father intends to name something and knows to look in the direction of the pointing. Through this kind of joint attention, early in their development children are able to use their social skills to acquire language (Carpenter, 2011; Tomasello, 2014). One study revealed that joint attention at 12 and 18 months predicted language skills at 24 months of age (Mundy & others, 2007).

Researchers have also found that the child's vocabulary development is linked to the family's socioeconomic status and the type of talk that parents direct to their children. Betty

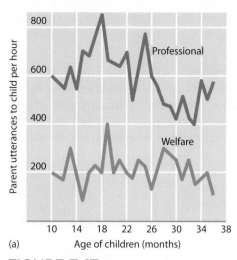

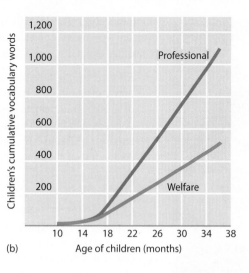

FIGURE **5.15**

LANGUAGE INPUT IN PROFESSIONAL AND WELFARE FAMILIES AND YOUNG CHILDREN'S VOCABULARY DEVELOPMENT. (*a*) In this study (Hart & Rísley, 1995), parents from professional families talked with their young children more than parents from welfare families. (*b*) All of the children learned to talk, but children from professional families developed vocabularies that were twice as large as those from welfare families. Thus, by the time children go to preschool, they already have experienced considerable differences in language input in their families and developed different levels of vocabulary that are linked to their socioeconomic context. *Does this study indicate that poverty caused deficiencies in vocabulary development?*

Hart and Todd Risley (1995) observed the language environments of children whose parents were professionals and children whose parents were on welfare (public assistance). Compared with the professional parents, the parents on welfare talked much less to their young children, talked less about past events, and provided less elaboration. As indicated in Figure 5.15, the children of the professional parents had a much larger vocabulary at 36 months of age than the children of the welfare parents.

Other research has linked how much mothers speak to their infants with the size of the infants' vocabularies. For example, in one study by Janellen Huttenlocher and her colleagues (1991), infants whose mothers spoke more often to them had markedly higher vocabularies. By the second birthday, vocabulary differences were substantial. A recent study of low-SES Spanish-speaking families found that infants who experienced more child-directed speech were better at processing familiar words in real time and had larger vocabularies at 2 years of age (Weisleder & Fernald, 2014).

However, a study of 1- to 3-year-old children living in low-income families found that the sheer amount of maternal talk was not the best predictor of a child's vocabulary growth (Pan & others, 2005). Rather, it was maternal language and literacy skills and mothers' diversity of vocabulary use that best predicted children's vocabulary development. For example, when mothers used a more diverse vocabulary when talking with their children, their children's vocabulary benefited, but their children's vocabulary was not related to the total amount of their talkativeness with their children. Also, mothers who frequently used pointing gestures had children with a greater vocabulary. Pointing usually occurs in concert with speech, and it may enhance the meaning of mothers' verbal input to their children. These research studies and others (Perkins, Finegood, & Swain, 2013; NICHD Early Child Care Research Network, 2005) demonstrate the important effect that early speech input and poverty can have on the development of a child's language skills.

One intriguing component of the young child's linguistic environment is **child-directed speech,** language spoken in a higher pitch than normal with simple words and sentences (Houston & others, 2014). It is hard to use child-directed speech when not in the presence of a baby, but parents shift into it when they start talking to a baby. Much of this is automatic and something most parents are not aware they are doing. Even 4-year-olds speak in simpler ways to 2-year-olds than to their 4-year-old friends. Child-directed speech has the important function of capturing the infant's attention and maintaining

child-directed speech Language spoken in a higher pitch than normal, with simple words and sentences.

What characterizes shared reading in the lives of infants, toddlers, and young children?

communication (Ratner, 2013). Adults often use strategies other than child-directed speech to enhance the child's acquisition of language, including recasting, expanding, and labeling:

- *Recasting* is rephrasing something the child has said, perhaps turning it into a question or restating the child's immature utterance in the form of a fully grammatical sentence. For example, if the child says, "The dog was barking," the adult can respond by asking, "When was the dog barking?" Effective recasting lets the child indicate an interest and then elaborates on that interest.

- *Expanding* is restating, in a linguistically sophisticated form, what a child has said. For example, a child says, "Doggie eat," and the parent replies, "Yes, the doggie is eating."

- *Labeling* is identifying the names of objects. Young children are forever being asked to identify the names of objects. Roger Brown (1958) called this "the original word game" and claimed that much of a child's early vocabulary is motivated by this adult pressure to identify the words associated with objects.

Parents use these strategies naturally and in meaningful conversations. Parents do not need to use a particular method to teach their children to talk, even for children who are slow in learning language. Children usually benefit when parents follow the child's lead, talking about things the child is interested in at the moment, and when parents provide information that children can process. If children are not ready to take in some information, they are likely to tell you (perhaps by turning away). Thus, giving the child more information is not always better.

Remember, the encouragement of language development, not drill and practice, is the key. Language development is not a simple matter of imitation and reinforcement.

Infants, toddlers, and young children benefit when adults read books to and with them (shared reading) (Hirsh-Pasek & Golinkoff, 2014). Storybook reading especially benefits children when parents extend the meaning of the text by discussing it with children and encouraging them to ask and answer questions (Harris, Golinkoff, & Hirsh-Pasek, 2011). In one study, a majority of U.S. mothers in low-income families reported that they were reading to their infants and toddlers with some regularity (Raikes & others, 2006). In this study, non-Latino White, more highly educated mothers who were parenting a first-born child were more likely to read books to their infants and toddlers than were African American and Latino mothers who were parenting later-born children. Reading daily to children at 14 to 24 months of age was positively related to the children's language and cognitive development at 36 months of age. To read further about ways that parents can facilitate children's language development, see *Connecting Development to Life*.

AN INTERACTIONIST VIEW

If language acquisition depended only on biology, then the Wild Boy of Aveyron and Genie (discussed earlier in the chapter) should have talked without difficulty. A child's experiences influence language acquisition. But we have seen that language does have strong biological foundations. No matter how much you converse with a dog, it won't learn to talk. In contrast, children are biologically prepared to learn language. Children all over the world acquire language milestones at about the same time and in about the same order. However, there are cultural variations in the type of support given to children's language development. For example, caregivers in the Kaluli culture prompt young children to use a loud voice and particular morphemes that direct the speech act performed (calling out) and to refer to names, kinship relations, and places where there has been a shared past experience that indicates a closeness to the person being addressed (Ochs & Schieffelin, 2008; Schieffelin, 2005).

Environmental influences are also very important in developing competence in language (Hirsh-Pasek & Golinkoff, 2014). Children whose parents provide them with a rich verbal

How Parents Can Facilitate Infants' and Toddlers' Language Development

Linguist Naomi Baron (1992) in *Growing Up with Language,* and more recently Ellen Galinsky (2010) in *Mind in the Making,* provided ideas to help parents facilitate their infants' and toddlers' language development. Their ideas are summarized below:

- *Be an active conversational partner.* Talk to your baby from the time it is born. Initiate conversation with the baby. If the baby is in an all-day child-care program, ensure that the baby receives adequate language stimulation from adults.
- *Talk in a slowed-down pace and don't worry about how you sound to other adults when you talk to your baby.* Talking in a slowed-down pace will help your baby detect words in the sea of sounds they experience. Babies enjoy and attend to the high-pitched sound of child-directed speech.
- *Use parent-look and parent-gesture, and name what you are looking at.* When you want your child to pay attention to something, look at it and point to it. Then name it—for example, you might say, "Look, Alex, there's an airplane."
- *When you talk with infants and toddlers, be simple, concrete, and repetitive.* Don't try to talk to them in abstract, high-level ways and think you have to say something new or different all of the time. Using familiar words often will help them remember the words.
- *Play games.* Use word games like peek-a-boo and pat-a-cake to help infants learn words.
- *Remember to listen.* Since toddlers' speech is often slow and laborious, parents are often tempted to supply words and thoughts for them. Be patient and let toddlers express themselves, no matter how painstaking the process is or how great a hurry you are in.
- *Expand and elaborate language abilities and horizons with infants and toddlers.* Ask questions that encourage answers other than "yes" or "no." Actively repeat, expand, and recast the utterances. Your toddler might say, "Dada." You could follow with, "Where's Dada?" and then you might continue, "Let's go find him."
- *Adjust to your child's idiosyncrasies instead of working against them.* Many toddlers have difficulty pronouncing words and making themselves understood. Whenever possible, make toddlers feel that they are being understood.

It is a good idea for parents to begin talking to their babies at the start. The best language teaching occurs when the talking begins before the infant becomes capable of intelligible speech. *What are some other guidelines for parents to follow in helping their infants and toddlers develop their language skills?*

- *Resist making normative comparisons.* Be aware of the ages at which your child reaches specific milestones (such as the first word, first 50 words), but do not measure this development rigidly against that of other children. Such comparisons can bring about unnecessary anxiety.

The first suggestion above to parents of infants is to "be an active conversational partner." What did you learn earlier in the chapter about the amount of conversation mothers have with their infants? Does the amount of conversation or the mother's literacy skills and vocabulary diversity have more of a positive effect on infants' vocabulary?

environment show many positive benefits (Beaty & Pratt, 2015; Tamis-LeMonda & Song, 2013). Parents who pay attention to what their children are trying to say, expand their children's utterances, read to them, and label things in the environment, are providing valuable benefits for them (Parish-Morris, Golinkoff, & Hirsh-Pasek, 2013; Senechal & Lefevre, 2014).

An interactionist view emphasizes that both biology and experience contribute to language development (Hoff, 2014). How much of language acquisition is biologically determined and how much depends on interaction with others is a subject of debate among linguists and psychologists. However, all agree that both biological capacity and relevant experience are necessary (Tomasello, 2014; Werker & Gervain, 2013).

LG4 Describe the nature of language and how it develops in infancy.

Review
- What is language?
- What are language's rule systems?
- How does language develop in infancy?
- What are some biological and environmental influences on language?
- To what extent do biological and environmental influences interact to produce language development?

Connect
- In Chapter 1, you learned that the more years children spend living in poverty, the more their physiological indices of stress are elevated. In this chapter, you learned about the effects of SES on children's language acquisition and vocabulary building. How might these effects influence children's school performance?

Reflect *Your Own Personal Journey of Life*
- Would it be a good idea for you as a parent to hold large flash cards of words in front of your baby for several hours each day to help the baby learn language and improve the baby's intelligence? Why or why not? What do you think Piaget would say about this activity?

topical connections *looking forward*

Advances in infants' cognitive development are linked to their socioemotional development. In Chapter 6 you will learn about the infant's developing social orientation and understanding, which involve perceiving people as engaging in intentional and goal-directed behavior, joint attention, and cooperation. In Chapter 7 you will read about two major theorists—Piaget and Vygotsky—and compare their views of how young children's thinking advances. You will see how young children become more capable of sustaining their attention; learn about the astonishing rate at which preschool children's vocabulary expands; and explore variations in early childhood education.

reach your **learning goals**

Cognitive Development in Infancy

1 Piaget's Theory of Infant Development

LG1 Summarize and evaluate Piaget's theory of infant development.

Cognitive Processes

- In Piaget's theory, children actively construct their own cognitive worlds, building mental structures to adapt to their world. Schemes are actions or mental representations that organize knowledge. Behavioral schemes (physical activities) characterize infancy, whereas mental schemes (cognitive activities) develop in childhood. Assimilation occurs when children use their existing schemes to deal with new information; accommodation refers to children's adjustment of their schemes in the face of new information. Through organization, children group isolated behaviors into a higher-order, more smoothly functioning cognitive system. Equilibration is a mechanism Piaget proposed to explain how children shift from one cognitive stage to the next. As children experience cognitive conflict in trying to understand the world, they use assimilation and accommodation to attain equilibrium. The result is a new stage of thought. According to Piaget, there are four qualitatively different stages of thought. The first of these, the sensorimotor stage, is described in this chapter. The other three stages are discussed in subsequent chapters.

The Sensorimotor Stage	• In sensorimotor thought, the first of Piaget's four stages, the infant organizes and coordinates sensations with physical movements. The stage lasts from birth to about 2 years of age. Sensorimotor thought has six substages: simple reflexes; first habits and primary circular reactions; secondary circular reactions; coordination of secondary circular reactions; tertiary circular reactions, novelty, and curiosity; and internalization of schemes. One key accomplishment of this stage is object permanence, the ability to understand that objects continue to exist even when the infant is no longer observing them. Another aspect involves infants' understanding of cause and effect.
Evaluating Piaget's Sensorimotor Stage	• Piaget opened up a whole new way of looking at infant development in terms of coordinating sensory input with motoric actions. In the past decades, revisions of Piaget's view have been proposed based on research. For example, researchers have found that a stable and differentiated perceptual world is established earlier than Piaget envisioned, and infants begin to develop concepts earlier as well. The nature-nurture issue in regard to infant cognitive development continues to be debated. Spelke endorses a core knowledge approach, which states that infants are born with domain-specific innate knowledge systems. Critics argue that Spelke has not given adequate attention to early experiences that infants have.

2 Learning, Remembering, and Conceptualizing

 LG2 Describe how infants learn, remember, and conceptualize.

Conditioning

• Operant conditioning techniques have been especially useful to researchers in demonstrating infants' perception and retention of information about perceptual-motor actions.

Attention

• Attention is the focusing of mental resources on select information, and in infancy attention is closely linked with habituation. In the first year, much of attention is of the orienting/ investigative type, but sustained attention also becomes important. Habituation is the repeated presentation of the same stimulus, causing reduced attention to the stimulus. If a different stimulus is presented and the infant pays increased attention to it, dishabituation is occurring. Joint attention plays an important role in infant development, especially in the infant's acquisition of language.

Memory

• Memory is the retention of information over time. Infants as young as 2 to 6 months of age can retain information about perceptual-motor actions. However, many experts argue that what we commonly think of as memory (consciously remembering the past) does not occur until the second half of the first year of life. By the end of the second year, long-term memory is more substantial and reliable. The hippocampus and frontal lobes of the brain are involved in development of explicit memory in infancy. The phenomenon of not being able to remember events that occurred before the age of 3—known as infantile or childhood amnesia—may be due to the immaturity of the prefrontal lobes of the brain at that age.

Imitation

• Meltzoff has shown that newborns can match their behaviors (such as protruding their tongue) to those of a model. His research also shows that deferred imitation occurs as early as 9 months of age.

Concept Formation and Categorization

• Mandler argues that it is not until about 7 to 9 months of age that infants form conceptual categories, although we do not know precisely when concept formation begins. Infants' first concepts are broad. Over the first two years of life, these broad concepts gradually become more differentiated.

3 Individual Differences and Assessment

 LG3 Discuss infant assessment measures and the prediction of intelligence.

Measures of Infant Development

• Gesell's scale is still widely used by pediatricians to distinguish normal and abnormal infants; it provides a developmental quotient (DQ). The Bayley Scales of Infant Development, developed by Nancy Bayley, continue to be widely used to assess infant development. The current version, the Bayley-III, consists of five scales: cognitive, language, motor, socioemotional, and adaptive. Increasingly used, the Fagan Test of Infant Intelligence assesses how effectively the infant processes information.

Predicting Intelligence

- Developmental scales for infants grew out of the tradition of IQ testing of older children. These scales are less verbally oriented than IQ tests. Global scores on the Gesell and Bayley scales are not good predictors of IQ scores in later childhood. However, measures of information processing such as speed of habituation and degree of dishabituation do correlate with intelligence later in childhood. There is both continuity and discontinuity between infant cognitive development and cognitive development later in childhood.

4 Language Development

LG4 Describe the nature of language and how it develops in infancy.

Defining Language

- Language is a form of communication, whether spontaneous, written, or signed, that is based on a system of symbols. Language consists of the words used by a community and the rules for varying and combining them. Language is characterized by infinite generativity.

Language's Rule Systems

- Phonology is the sound system of the language, including the sounds that are used and how they may be combined. Morphology refers to the units of meaning involved in word formation. Syntax is the way words are combined to form acceptable phrases and sentences. Semantics involves the meaning of words and sentences. Pragmatics is the appropriate use of language in different contexts.

How Language Develops

- Among the milestones in infant language development are crying (birth), cooing (1 to 2 months), babbling (6 months), making the transition from universal linguist to language-specific listener (6 to 12 months), using gestures (8 to 12 months), comprehending words (8 to 12 months), speaking one's first word (13 months), undergoing a vocabulary spurt (19 months), rapidly expanding one's understanding of words (18 to 24 months), and producing two-word utterances (18 to 24 months).

Biological and Environmental Influences

- In evolution, language clearly gave humans an enormous advantage over other animals and increased their chances of survival. Broca's area and Wernicke's area are important locations for language processing in the brain's left hemisphere. Chomsky argues that children are born with the ability to detect basic features and rules of language. In other words, they are biologically equipped to learn language with a prewired language acquisition device (LAD). The behaviorist view—that children acquire language as a result of reinforcement—has not been supported. Adults help children acquire language by engaging in child-directed speech, recasting, expanding, and labeling. Environmental influences are demonstrated by differences in the language development of children as a consequence of being exposed to different language environments in the home. Parents should talk extensively with an infant, especially about what the baby is attending to.

An Interactionist View

- Today, most language researchers believe that children everywhere arrive in the world with special social and linguistic capacities that make language acquisition not just likely but inevitable for virtually all children. How much of the language is biologically determined, and how much depends on interaction with others, is a subject of debate among linguists and psychologists. However, all agree that both biological capacity and relevant experience are necessary.

key **terms**

schemes 137
assimilation 138
accommodation 138
organization 138
equilibration 138
sensorimotor stage 139
simple reflexes 139
first habits and primary circular
    reactions 139
primary circular reaction 140
secondary circular reactions 140

coordination of secondary circular
    reactions 140
tertiary circular reactions, novelty,
    and curiosity 140
internalization of schemes 140
object permanence 141
A-not-B error 141
core knowledge approach 143
attention 145
joint attention 146
memory 146

implicit memory 146
explicit memory 146
deferred imitation 148
concepts 148
developmental quotient (DQ) 150
Bayley Scales of Infant
    Development 150
language 153
infinite generativity 153
phonology 153
morphology 153

syntax 153
semantics 153
pragmatics 153
telegraphic speech 156
Broca's area 157
Wernicke's area 157
aphasia 157
language acquisition device
    (LAD) 158
child-directed speech 159

key people

chapter 6

SOCIOEMOTIONAL DEVELOPMENT IN INFANCY

chapter **outline**

1 Emotional and Personality Development

Learning Goal 1 Discuss the development of emotions and personality in infancy.

Emotional Development
Temperament
Personality Development

2 Social Orientation/ Understanding and Attachment

Learning Goal 2 Describe social orientation/ understanding and the development of attachment in infancy.

Social Orientation/Understanding
Attachment and Its Development
Individual Differences in Attachment
Caregiving Styles and Attachment
Developmental Social Neuroscience and Attachment

3 Social Contexts

Learning Goal 3 Explain how social contexts influence the infant's development.

The Family
Child Care

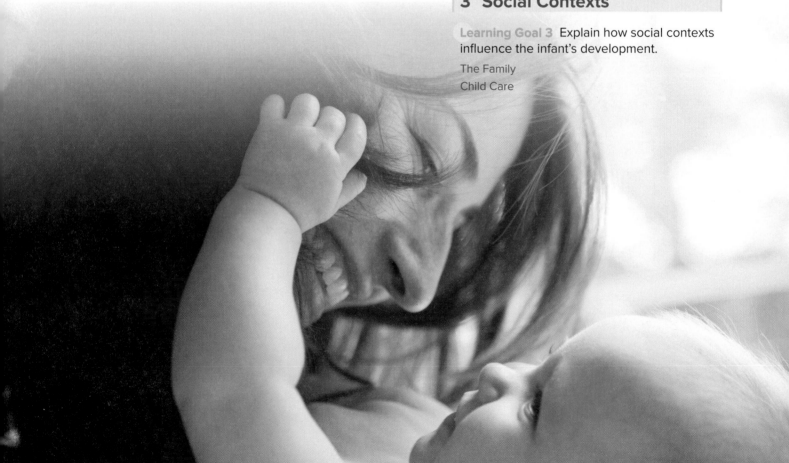

An increasing number of fathers are staying home to care for their children (Lamb, 2013; Shwalb, Shwalb, & Lamb, 2013). Consider 17-month-old Darius. On weekdays, Darius' father, a writer, cares for him during the day while his mother works full-time as a landscape architect. Darius' father is doing a great job of caring for him. He keeps Darius nearby while he is writing and spends lots of time talking to him and playing with him. From their interactions, it is clear that they genuinely enjoy each other.

Last month, Darius began spending one day a week at a child-care center. His parents carefully selected the center after observing a number of centers and interviewing teachers and center directors. His parents placed him in the center one day a week because they wanted to help Darius get some experience with peers and to give his father some time out from his caregiving.

Darius' father looks to the future and imagines the Little League games Darius will play in and the many other activities he can enjoy with Darius. Remembering how little time his own father spent with him, he is dedicated to making sure that Darius has an involved, nurturing experience with his father.

When Darius' mother comes home in the evenings, she spends considerable time with him. Darius has a secure attachment with both his mother and his father.

Many fathers are spending more time with their infants today than in the past.

topical **connections** *looking **back***

Until now, we have only discussed the social situations and emotions of parents before and after the arrival of their infants, focusing on such topics as parents' feelings of joy, anticipation, anxiety, and stress during pregnancy; how a mother's optimism may lead to better outcomes for her fetus; and parents' emotional and psychological adjustments during the postpartum period. In this chapter, we will explore the infant's socio-emotional development.

preview

In Chapters 4 and 5, you read about how the infant perceives, learns, and remembers. Infants also are socioemotional beings, capable of displaying emotions and initiating social interaction with people close to them. The main topics that we will explore in this chapter are emotional and personality development, social understanding and attachment, and the social contexts of the family and child care.

1 Emotional and Personality Development

LG1 Discuss the development of emotions and personality in infancy.

| Emotional Development | Temperament | Personality Development |

Blossoms are scattered by
the wind
And the wind cares nothing, but
The blossoms of the heart
No wind can touch.

—YOSHIDA KENKO
Buddhist Monk, 14th Century

How do biological and environmental factors influence the infant's emotional development?

emotion Feeling, or affect, that occurs when a person is in a state or interaction that is important to him or her. Emotion is characterized by behavior that reflects (expresses) the pleasantness or unpleasantness of the state a person is in or the transactions being experienced.

Anyone who has been around infants for even a brief time detects that they are emotional beings. Not only do infants express emotions, but they also vary in their temperaments. Some are shy and others are outgoing. Some are active and others much less so. In this section, we will explore these and other aspects of emotional and personality development in infants.

EMOTIONAL DEVELOPMENT

Imagine your life without emotion. Emotion is the color and music of life, as well as the tie that binds people together. How do psychologists define and classify emotions, and why are they important to development? How do emotions develop during the first two years of life?

What Are Emotions?   For our purposes, we will define **emotion** as feeling, or affect, that occurs when a person is in a state or an interaction that is important to him or her, especially to his or her well-being. Especially in infancy, emotions play important roles in (1) communication with others, and (2) behavioral organization. Through emotions, infants communicate important aspects of their lives such as joy, sadness, interest, and fear (Witherington & others, 2010). In terms of behavioral organization, emotions influence infants' social responses and adaptive behavior as they interact with others in their world (Easterbrooks & others, 2013; Thompson, 2015).

Psychologists classify the broad range of emotions in many ways, but almost all classifications designate an emotion as either positive or negative (Izard, 2009; Shuman & Scherer, 2014). Positive emotions include enthusiasm, joy, and love. Negative emotions include anxiety, anger, guilt, and sadness.

Biological and Environmental Influences   Emotions are influenced both by biological foundations and by a person's experience (Calkins, 2012; Thompson, 2013c, d; Easterbrooks & others, 2013). Biology's importance to emotion is apparent in the changes in a baby's emotional capacities (Kagan, 2010, 2013). Certain regions of the brain that develop early in life (such as the brain stem, hippocampus, and amygdala) play a role in distress, excitement, and rage, and even infants display these emotions (Fox, Reeb-Sutherland, & Degnan, 2013; Kagan, 2013). But, as we discuss later in the chapter, infants only gradually develop the ability to regulate their emotions, and this ability seems tied to the gradual maturation of the frontal regions of the cerebral cortex (discussed in Chapter 4) that can exert control over other areas of the brain (Cuevas & others, 2012; Morasch & Bell, 2012).

Biological evolution has endowed human beings to be *emotional,* but embeddedness in relationships and culture with others provides diversity in emotional experiences (Thompson, 2014b). Emotional development and coping with stress are influenced by whether caregivers have maltreated or neglected children and whether children's caregivers are depressed or not (Hostinar & Gunnar, 2013). When infants become stressed, infants show better biological recovery from the stressors when their caregivers engage in sensitive caregiving with them (Gunnar & Herrera, 2013; Waters, West, & Mendes, 2014).

Social relationships provide the setting for the development of a rich variety of emotions (Easterbrooks & others, 2013; Thompson, 2014a, b; 2015). When toddlers hear their parents quarreling, they often react with distress and inhibit their play. Well-functioning families make each other laugh and may develop a light mood to defuse conflicts.

Cultural differences occur in emotional experiences (Tamis-LeMonda & Song, 2013; Thompson & Virmani, 2010). For example, researchers have found that East Asian infants display less frequent and less intense positive and negative emotions than non-Latino White infants (Cole & Tan, 2007). Further, Japanese parents try to prevent their children from experiencing negative emotions, whereas non-Latino White mothers are more likely to respond after their children become distressed and then help them cope (Cole & Tan, 2007).

Early Emotions   A leading expert on infant emotional development, Michael Lewis (2007, 2008, 2010) distinguishes between primary emotions and self-conscious emotions. **Primary emotions** are present in humans and other animals; these emotions appear in the first 6 months of the human infant's development. Primary emotions include surprise, interest, joy, anger, sadness, fear, and disgust (see Figure 6.1 for infants' facial expressions of some of these early emotions). In Lewis' classification, **self-conscious emotions** require self-awareness that involves consciousness and a sense of "me." Self-conscious emotions include jealousy, empathy, embarrassment, pride, shame, and guilt, most of these occurring for the first time at some point in the second half of the first year through the second year. Some experts on emotion call self-conscious emotions such as embarrassment, shame, guilt, and pride *other-conscious emotions* because they involve the emotional reactions of others when they are generated (Saarni & others, 2006). For example, approval from parents is linked to toddlers beginning to show pride when they successfully complete a task.

Researchers such as Joseph Campos (2005) and Michael Lewis (2007) debate how early in the infant and toddler years the emotions that we have described first appear and in what sequence. As an indication of the controversy regarding when certain emotions first are displayed by infants, consider jealousy. Some researchers argue that jealousy does not emerge until approximately 15 to 18 months of age (Lewis, 2007), whereas others assert that it is displayed much earlier (Draghi-Lorenz, 2007; Hart & Behrens, 2013).

Consider the results of two research studies. In the first one, 9-month-old infants engaged in more approach-style, jealousy-related behaviors when their mothers gave attention to a social rival (a lifelike doll) than to a non-social rival (a book) (Mize & others, 2014). Further, in this study, the infants showed EEG activity during the social-rival condition that is associated with jealousy. In a second study, 6-month-old infants observed their mothers in situations similar to the first study: either giving attention to a lifelike baby doll (hugging or gently rocking it, for example) or to a book (Hart & Carrington, 2002). When mothers directed their attention to the doll, the infants were more likely to display negative emotions, such as anger and sadness, which may have indicated their jealousy (see Figure 6.2). On the other hand, their expressions of anger and sadness may have reflected frustration in not being able to have the novel doll to play with.

Debate about the onset of an emotion such as jealousy illustrates the complexity and difficulty in indexing early emotions. That said, some experts on infant socioemotional development, such as Jerome Kagan (2010), conclude that the structural immaturity of the infant brain make it unlikely that emotions which require thought—such as guilt, pride, despair, shame, empathy, and jealousy—can be experienced during the first year.

Joy   Sadness

Fear   Surprise

FIGURE 6.1

EXPRESSION OF DIFFERENT EMOTIONS IN INFANTS

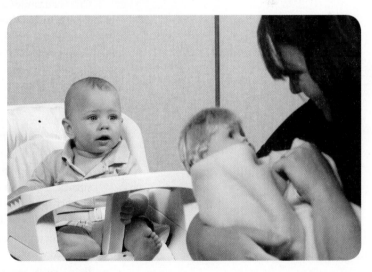

FIGURE 6.2

IS THIS THE EARLY EXPRESSION OF JEALOUSY? In the study by Hart and Carrington (2002), the researchers concluded that the 6-month-old infants who observed their mothers giving attention to a baby doll displayed negative emotions—such as anger and sadness—which may indicate the early appearance of jealousy. However, experts on emotional development, such as Michael Lewis (2007) and Jerome Kagan (2010), argue that it is unlikely emotions such as jealousy appear in the first year. *Why do they conclude that it is unlikely jealousy occurs in the first year?*

primary emotions Emotions that are present in humans and other animals and emerge early in life; examples are joy, anger, sadness, fear, and disgust.

self-conscious emotions Emotions that require self-awareness, especially consciousness and a sense of "me"; examples include jealousy, empathy, and embarrassment.

What are some different types of cries?

basic cry A rhythmic pattern usually consisting of a cry, a briefer silence, a shorter inspiratory whistle that is higher pitched than the main cry, and then a brief rest before the next cry.

anger cry A variation of the basic cry, with more excess air forced through the vocal cords.

pain cry A sudden appearance of a long, initial loud cry without preliminary moaning, followed by breath holding.

reflexive smile A smile that does not occur in response to external stimuli. It happens during the first month after birth, usually during sleep.

social smile A smile in response to an external stimulus, which early in development is typically a face.

Emotional Expression and Social Relationships Emotional expressions are involved in infants' first relationships. The ability of infants to communicate emotions permits coordinated interactions with their caregivers and the beginning of an emotional bond between them (Easterbrooks & others, 2013; Thompson, 2014a, b, 2015). Not only do parents change their emotional expressions in response to infants' emotional expressions, but infants also modify their emotional expressions in response to their parents' emotional expressions (Slatcher & Trentacosta, 2012). In other words, these interactions are mutually regulated. Because of this coordination, the interactions are described as reciprocal, or synchronous, when all is going well. Sensitive, responsive parents help their infants grow emotionally, whether the infants respond in distressed or happy ways (Wilson, Havighurst, & Harley, 2012). A recent study revealed that parents' elicitation of talk about emotion with toddlers was associated with the toddlers' sharing and helping (Brownell & others, 2013).

A recent study documented how babies pick up on their mothers' stress (Waters, West, & Mendes, 2014). In this study, mothers were separated from their babies and asked to give a 5-minute speech on which half of the mothers received a positive evaluation, the other half a negative evaluation. Mothers who received negative feedback reported an increase in negative emotion and cardiac stress, while those who were given positive feedback reported an increase in positive emotion. The babies quickly detected and responded to their mothers' stress, as reflected in an increased heart rate when reunited with them. And the greater the mother's stress response, the more her baby's heart rate increased.

Cries and smiles are two emotional expressions that infants display when interacting with parents. These are babies' first forms of emotional communication.

Crying Crying is the most important mechanism newborns have for communicating with their world. The first cry verifies that the baby's lungs have filled with air. Cries also may provide information about the health of the newborn's central nervous system. Newborns even tend to respond with cries and negative facial expressions when they hear other newborns cry (Dondi, Simion, & Caltran, 1999). However, a recent study revealed that newborns of depressed mothers showed less vocal distress when another infant cried, reflecting emotional and physiological dysregulation (Jones, 2012).

Babies have at least three types of cries:

- **Basic cry.** A rhythmic pattern that usually consists of a cry, followed by a briefer silence, then a shorter whistle that is somewhat higher in pitch than the main cry, then another brief rest before the next cry. Some infancy experts believe that hunger is one of the conditions that incites the basic cry.
- **Anger cry.** A variation of the basic cry in which more excess air is forced through the vocal cords.
- **Pain cry.** A sudden long, initial loud cry followed by breath holding; no preliminary moaning is present. The pain cry is stimulated by a high-intensity stimulus.

Most adults can determine whether an infant's cries signify anger or pain (Zeskind, Klein, & Marshall, 1992). Parents can distinguish the cries of their own baby better than those of another baby.

Smiling Smiling is a key social signal and a very important aspect of positive social interaction in developing a new social skill (Sauter & others, 2014). The power of the infant's smiles was appropriately captured by British theorist John Bowlby (1969): "Can we doubt that the more and better an infant smiles the better he is loved and cared for? It is fortunate for their survival that babies are so designed by nature that they beguile and enslave mothers." Two types of smiling can be distinguished in infants:

- **Reflexive smile.** A smile that does not occur in response to external stimuli and appears during the first month after birth, usually during sleep.
- **Social smile.** A smile that occurs in response to an external stimulus, typically a face in the case of the young infant. Social smiling occurs as early as 2 months of age.

The infant's social smile can have a powerful impact on caregivers (Sauter & others, 2014). Following weeks of seemingly endless demands, fatigue, and little reinforcement, an infant starts smiling at them and all of the caregivers' efforts are rewarded. A recent study found that higher maternal effortful control and positive emotionality predicted more initial infant smiling and laughter, while a higher level of parenting stress predicted a lower trajectory of infant smiling and laughter (Bridgett & others, 2013).

Fear One of a baby's earliest emotions is fear, which typically first appears at about 6 months of age and peaks at about 18 months. However, abused and neglected infants can show fear as early as 3 months (Witherington & others, 2010). Researchers have found that infant fear is linked to guilt, empathy, and low aggression at 6 to 7 years of age (Rothbart, 2007).

The most frequent expression of an infant's fear involves **stranger anxiety,** in which an infant shows a fear and wariness of strangers. Stranger anxiety usually emerges gradually. It first appears at about 6 months of age in the form of wary reactions. By age 9 months, the fear of strangers is often more intense, reaching a peak toward the end of the first year of life and then decreasing thereafter (Scher & Harel, 2008).

Not all infants show distress when they encounter a stranger. Besides individual variations, whether an infant shows stranger anxiety also depends on the social context and the characteristics of the stranger.

Infants show less stranger anxiety when they are in familiar settings. For example, in one study 10-month-olds showed little stranger anxiety when they met a stranger in their own home but much greater fear when they encountered a stranger in a research laboratory (Sroufe, Waters, & Matas, 1974). Thus, it appears that when infants feel secure, they are less likely to show stranger anxiety.

Who the stranger is and how the stranger behaves also influence stranger anxiety in infants. Infants are less fearful of child strangers than adult strangers. They also are less fearful of friendly, outgoing, smiling strangers than of passive, unsmiling strangers (Bretherton, Stolberg, & Kreye, 1981).

In addition to stranger anxiety, infants experience fear of being separated from their caregivers. The result is **separation protest**—crying when the caregiver leaves. Separation protest is initially displayed by infants at approximately 7 to 8 months and peaks at about 15 months among U.S. infants (Kagan, 2008). In fact, one study found that separation protest peaked at about 13 to 15 months in four different cultures (Kagan, Kearsley, & Zelazo, 1978). As indicated in Figure 6.3, the percentage of infants who engaged in separation protest varied across cultures, but the infants reached a peak of protest at about the same age—just before the middle of the second year of life.

Emotional Regulation and Coping During the first year of life, the infant gradually develops an ability to inhibit, or minimize, the intensity and duration of emotional reactions (Calkins & Dollar, 2014; Ekas, Lickenbrock, & Braungart-Rieker, 2014). From early in infancy, babies put their thumbs in their mouths to soothe themselves. But at first, infants mainly depend on caregivers to help them soothe their emotions, as when a caregiver rocks an infant to sleep, sings lullabyes to the infant, gently strokes the infant, and so on.

The caregivers' actions influence the infant's neurobiological regulation of emotions (Calkins & Dollar, 2014; Thompson, 2015). By soothing the infant, caregivers help infants to modulate their emotion and reduce the level of stress hormones. Many developmentalists stress that it is a good strategy for a caregiver to soothe an infant before the infant gets into an intense, agitated, uncontrolled state (McElwain & Booth-LaForce, 2006).

Later in infancy, when they become aroused, infants sometimes redirect their attention or distract themselves in order to reduce their arousal. By 2 years of age, toddlers can use language to define their feeling states and the context that is upsetting them. A toddler might say, "Doggy scary." This type of communication may help caregivers to assist the child in regulating emotion.

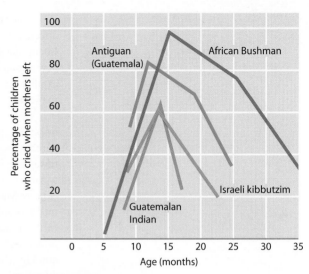

FIGURE **6.3**

SEPARATION PROTEST IN FOUR CULTURES. Note that separation protest peaked at about the same age in all four cultures in this study (13 to 15 months) (Kagan, Kearsley, & Zelazo, 1978). However, a higher percentage (100 percent) of infants in an African Bushman culture engaged in separation protest compared with only about 60 percent of infants in Guatemalan Indian and Israeli kibbutzim cultures. *What might explain the fact that separation protest peaks at about the same time in different cultures?* Reprinted by permission of the publisher from *Infancy: Its Place in Human Development* by Jerome Kagan, Richard B. Kearsley, and Philip R. Zelazo, p. 107, Cambridge, Mass.: Harvard University Press. Copyright © 1978 by the President and Fellows of Harvard College.

stranger anxiety An infant's fear and wariness of strangers; it tends to appear during the second half of the first year of life.

separation protest An infant's distressed crying when the caregiver leaves.

Contexts can influence emotional regulation (Thompson, 2014b). Infants are often affected by fatigue, hunger, time of day, which people are around them, and where they are. Infants must learn to adapt to different contexts that require emotional regulation. Further, new demands appear as the infant becomes older and parents modify their expectations. For example, a parent may take it in stride if a 6-month-old infant screams in a restaurant but may react very differently if a 6-year-old starts screaming.

To soothe or not to soothe—should a crying baby be given attention and soothed, or does this spoil the infant? Many years ago, the behaviorist John Watson (1928) argued that parents spend too much time responding to infant crying. As a consequence, he said, parents reward crying and increase its incidence. Also, behaviorist Jacob Gewirtz (1977) found that a caregiver's quick, soothing response to crying increased crying. In contrast, infancy experts Mary Ainsworth (1979) and John Bowlby (1989) stress that you can't respond too much to infant crying in the first year of life. They believe that a quick, comforting response to the infant's cries is an important ingredient in developing a strong bond between the infant and caregiver. In one of Ainsworth's studies, infants whose mothers responded quickly when they cried at 3 months of age cried less later in the first year of life (Bell & Ainsworth, 1972).

Controversy still surrounds the question of whether or how parents should respond to an infant's cries. However, developmentalists increasingly argue that an infant cannot be spoiled in the first year of life, which suggests that parents should soothe a crying infant. This response should help infants develop a sense of trust and secure attachment to the caregiver. One study revealed that mothers' negative emotional reactions (anger and anxiety) to crying increased the risk of subsequent attachment insecurity (Leerkes, Parade, & Gudmundson, 2011). Another study found that problems in infant soothability at 6 months of age were linked to insecure attachment at 12 months of age (Mills-Koonce, Propper, & Barnett, 2012). And in a recent study, researchers discovered that emotionally reactive infants who also showed a high level of emotion regulation were more likely to have primary caregivers who engaged in positive parenting behavior during a parent-child interaction task (Ursache & others, 2013).

TEMPERAMENT

Do you get upset a lot? Does it take much to get you angry, or to make you laugh? Even at birth, babies seem to have different emotional styles. One infant is cheerful and happy much of the time; another baby seems to cry constantly. These tendencies reflect **temperament,** which involves individual differences in behavioral styles, emotions, and characteristic ways of responding. With regard to its link to emotion, temperament refers to individual differences in how quickly the emotion is shown, how strong it is, how long it lasts, and how quickly it fades away.

Describing and Classifying Temperament How would you describe your temperament or the temperament of a friend? Researchers have described and classified the temperament of individuals in different ways (Goodvin, Winer, & Thompson, 2014). Here we will examine three of those ways.

Chess and Thomas' Classification Psychiatrists Alexander Chess and Stella Thomas (Chess & Thomas, 1977; Thomas & Chess, 1991) identified three basic types, or clusters, of temperament:

- An **easy child** is generally in a positive mood, quickly establishes regular routines in infancy, and adapts easily to new experiences.
- A **difficult child** reacts negatively and cries frequently, engages in irregular daily routines, and is slow to accept change.
- A **slow-to-warm-up child** has a low activity level, is somewhat negative, and displays a low intensity of mood.

temperament Involves individual differences in behavioral styles, emotions, and characteristic ways of responding.

easy child A child who is generally in a positive mood, quickly establishes regular routines in infancy, and adapts easily to new experiences.

difficult child A child who tends to react negatively and cry frequently, engages in irregular daily routines, and is slow to accept change.

slow-to-warm-up child A child who has a low activity level, is somewhat negative, and displays a low intensity of mood.

In their longitudinal investigation, Chess and Thomas found that 40 percent of the children they studied could be classified as easy, 10 percent as difficult, and 15 percent as slow to warm up. Notice that 35 percent did not fit any of the three patterns. Researchers have found that these three basic clusters of temperament are moderately stable across the childhood years.

Kagan's Behavioral Inhibition   Another way of classifying temperament focuses on the differences between a shy, subdued, timid child and a sociable, extraverted, bold child. Jerome Kagan (2002, 2008, 2010, 2013) regards shyness with strangers (peers or adults) as one feature of a broad temperament category called inhibition to the unfamiliar. Inhibited children react to many aspects of unfamiliarity with initial avoidance, distress, or subdued affect, beginning about 7 to 9 months of age.

Kagan has found that inhibition shows considerable stability from infancy through early childhood. One study classified toddlers into extremely inhibited, extremely uninhibited, and intermediate groups (Pfeifer & others, 2002). Follow-up assessments occurred at 4 and 7 years of age. Continuity was demonstrated for both inhibition and lack of inhibition, although a substantial number of the inhibited children moved into the intermediate groups at 7 years of age. One study revealed that behavioral inhibition at 3 years of age was linked to shyness four years later (Volbrecht & Goldsmith, 2010). Another study found that 24-month-olds who were fearful in situations relatively low in threat were likely to experience higher than average anxiety levels in kindergarten (Buss, 2011). And in another study, shyness/inhibition in infancy/childhood was linked to social anxiety at 21 years of age (Bohlin & Hagekull, 2009).

What are some characteristics of an inhibited temperament?

Rothbart and Bates' Classification   New classifications of temperament continue to be forged. Mary Rothbart and John Bates (2006) argue that prior classifications of temperament have not included a key temperament style: effortful control (self-regulation). They conclude that the following three broad dimensions best represent what researchers have found to characterize the structure of temperament: extraversion/surgency, negative affectivity, and effortful control (self-regulation):

- *Extraversion/surgency* includes "positive anticipation, impulsivity, activity level, and sensation seeking" (Rothbart, 2004, p. 495). Kagan's uninhibited children fit into this category.

- *Negative affectivity* includes "fear, frustration, sadness, and discomfort" (Rothbart, 2004, p. 495). These children are easily distressed; they may fret and cry often. Kagan's inhibited children fit this category.

- *Effortful control (self-regulation)* includes "attentional focusing and shifting, inhibitory control, perceptual sensitivity, and low-intensity pleasure" (Rothbart, 2004, p. 495). Infants who are high on effortful control show an ability to keep their arousal from getting too high and have strategies for soothing themselves. By contrast, children low on effortful control are often unable to control their arousal; they become easily agitated and intensely emotional. A recent study found that young children higher in effortful control were more likely to wait longer to express anger and were more likely to use a self-regulatory strategy, distraction (Tan, Armstrong, & Cole, 2013).

In Rothbart's (2004, p. 497) view, "early theoretical models of temperament stressed the way we are moved by our positive and negative emotions or level of arousal, with our actions driven by these tendencies." The more recent focus on effortful control, however, emphasizes that individuals can engage in a more cognitive, flexible approach to stressful circumstances. It is Rothbart and Bates' addition of effortful control (self-regulation) that is their most important contribution to our understanding of temperament.

An important point about temperament classifications such as those of Chess and Thomas or Rothbart and Bates is that children should not be pigeonholed as having only one temperament dimension, such as "difficult" or "negative affectivity." A good strategy when attempting to classify a child's temperament is to think of temperament as consisting of multiple dimensions (Bates, 2012a, b). For example, a child might be extraverted, show little emotional negativity, and have good self-regulation. Another child might be introverted, show little emotional negativity, and have a low level of self-regulation.

The development of temperament capabilities such as effortful control allows individual differences to emerge. For example, although maturation of the brain's prefrontal lobes must occur for any child's attention to improve and the child to achieve effortful control, some children develop effortful control while others do not. And it is these individual differences in children that are at the heart of what temperament is (Bates, 2012a, b).

Biological Foundations and Experience   How does a child acquire a certain temperament? Kagan (2002, 2010, 2013) argues that children inherit a physiology that biases them to have a particular type of temperament. However, through experience they may learn to modify their temperament to some degree. For example, children may inherit a physiology that biases them to be fearful and inhibited, but they can learn to reduce their fear and inhibition to some degree.

Biological Influences   Physiological characteristics have been linked with different temperaments (Bates, 2012a, b; Kagan, 2013; Mize & Jones, 2012). In particular, an inhibited temperament is associated with a unique physiological pattern that includes high and stable heart rate, high level of the hormone cortisol, and high activity in the right frontal lobe of the brain (Kagan, 2008, 2010). This pattern may be tied to the excitability of the amygdala, a structure of the brain that plays an important role in fear and inhibition.

What is heredity's role in the biological foundations of temperament? Twin and adoption studies suggest that heredity has a moderate influence on differences in temperament within a group of people (Plomin & others, 2009). The contemporary view is that temperament is a biologically based but evolving aspect of behavior; it evolves as the child's experiences are incorporated into a network of self-perceptions and behavioral preferences that characterize the child's personality (Goodvin, Winer, & Thompson, 2014).

Too often the biological foundations of temperament are interpreted to mean that temperament cannot develop or change. However, important self-regulatory dimensions

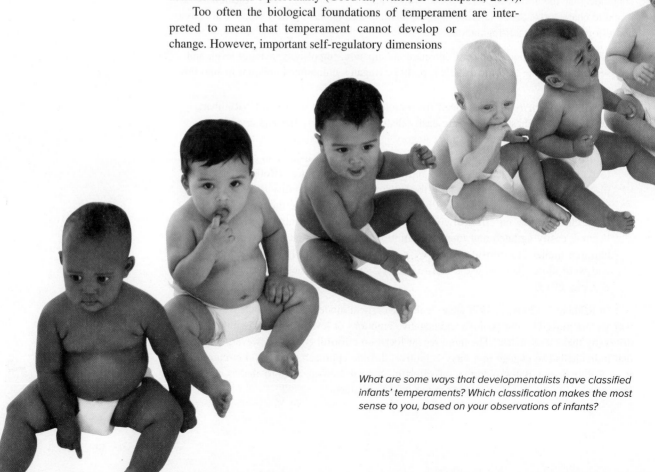

What are some ways that developmentalists have classified infants' temperaments? Which classification makes the most sense to you, based on your observations of infants?

of temperament such as adaptability, soothability, and persistence look very different in a 1-year-old and a 5-year-old (Easterbrooks & others, 2013). These temperament dimensions develop and change with the growth of the neurobiological foundations of self-regulation.

Gender, Culture, and Temperament Gender may be an important factor shaping the environmental context that influences temperament (Gaias & others, 2012). Parents might react differently to an infant's temperament depending on whether the baby is a boy or a girl. For example, in one study, mothers were more responsive to the crying of irritable girls than to the crying of irritable boys (Crockenberg, 1986).

Similarly, the caregiver's reaction to an infant's temperament may depend in part on culture (Chen & others, 2011; Gartstein & others, 2014). For example, behavioral inhibition is more highly valued in China than in North America, and researchers have found that Chinese children are more inhibited than Canadian infants are (Chen & others, 1998). The cultural differences in temperament were linked to parent attitudes and behaviors. Canadian mothers of inhibited 2-year-olds were less accepting of their infants' inhibited temperament, whereas Chinese mothers were more accepting. Also, a recent study revealed that U.S infants showed more temperamental fearfulness while Finnish infants engaged in more positive affect, such as effortful control (Gaias & others, 2012).

In short, many aspects of a child's environment can encourage or discourage the persistence of temperament characteristics (Bates, 2012a, b; Gartstein & others, 2014; Shiner & DeYoung, 2013). For example, a recent study found that fathers' internalizing problems

goodness of fit Refers to the match between a child's temperament and the environmental demands with which the child must cope.

developmental **connection**

Community and Culture

Cross-cultural studies seek to determine culture-universal and culture-specific aspects of development. Chapter 1, p. 8

(anxiety and depression, for example) were linked to a higher level of negative affectivity in 6-month-olds (Potapova, Gartstein, & Bridgett, 2014). One useful way of thinking about these relationships applies the concept of goodness of fit, which we examine next.

Goodness of Fit and Parenting **Goodness of fit** refers to the match between a child's temperament and the environmental demands the child must cope with. Suppose Jason is an active toddler who is made to sit still for long periods of time, and Jack is a slow-to-warm-up toddler who is abruptly pushed into new situations on a regular basis. Both Jason and Jack face a lack of fit between their temperament and environmental demands. Lack of fit can produce adjustment problems (Rothbart, 2011).

Some temperament characteristics pose more parenting challenges than others, at least in modern Western societies (Goodvin, Winer, & Thompson, 2014; Rothbart, 2011). When children are prone to distress, as exhibited by frequent

An infant's temperament can vary across cultures. *What do parents need to know about a child's temperament?*

Parenting and the Child's Temperament

What are the implications of temperamental variations for parenting? Although answers to this question necessarily are speculative, these conclusions regarding the best parenting strategies to use in relation to children's temperament were reached by temperament experts Ann Sanson and Mary Rothbart (1995):

- *Attention to and respect for individuality.* Good parenting involves sensitivity to the child's individual characteristics. A goal might be accomplished in one way with one child and in another way with another child, depending on the child's temperament.
- *Structuring the child's environment.* Crowded, noisy environments can pose greater problems for some children (such as a "difficult child") than others (such as an "easy child"). We might also expect that a fearful, withdrawing child would benefit from slower entry into new contexts.
- *The "difficult child" and packaged parenting programs.* Programs for parents often focus on dealing with children who have "difficult" temperaments. In some cases, "difficult child" refers to Thomas and Chess' description of a child who reacts negatively, cries frequently, engages in irregular daily routines, and is slow to accept change. In others, the concept might be used to describe a child who is irritable, displays anger frequently, does not follow directions well, or shows some other negative characteristic. Acknowledging that some children are harder than others to parent is often helpful, and advice on how to handle particular difficult characteristics can be useful. However, whether a particular characteristic is difficult depends on its fit with the environment. Labeling a child "difficult" can create a self-fulfilling prophecy. If a child is identified as "difficult," people may treat the child in a way that actually elicits "difficult" behavior.

Too often, we pigeonhole children into categories without considering the context (Bates, 2012a, b; Rothbart, 2011). Instead of doing

What are some good strategies for parents to adopt when responding to their infant's temperament?

this, caregivers need to take children's temperament into account. Research does not yet allow for many highly specific recommendations, but, in general, caregivers should (1) be sensitive to the individual characteristics of the child, (2) be flexible in responding to these characteristics, and (3) avoid applying negative labels to the child.

How does the advice to "structure the child's environment" relate to what you learned about the concept of "goodness of fit"?

crying and irritability, their parents may eventually respond by ignoring the child's distress or trying to force the child to "behave." In one research study, though, extra support and training for mothers of distress-prone infants improved the quality of mother-infant interaction (van den Boom, 1989). The training led the mothers to alter their demands on the child, improving the fit between the child and the environment. Researchers also have found that decreases in infants' negative emotionality are linked to higher levels of parental sensitivity, involvement, and responsiveness (Bates, 2012a, b; Penela & others, 2012). To read further about some positive strategies for parenting that take into account the child's temperament, see the *Connecting Development to Life* interlude.

PERSONALITY DEVELOPMENT

Emotions and temperament form key aspects of *personality,* the enduring personal characteristics of individuals. Let's now examine characteristics that often are thought of as central to personality development during infancy: trust and the development of self and independence.

Trust   According to Erik Erikson (1968), the first year of life is characterized by the trust-versus-mistrust stage of development. Following a life of regularity, warmth, and protection in the mother's womb, the infant faces a world that is less secure. Erikson proposed that infants learn trust when they are cared for in a consistent, warm manner. If the infant is not well fed and kept warm on a consistent basis, a sense of mistrust is likely to develop.

The issue of trust versus mistrust is not resolved once and for all in the first year of life. It arises again at each successive stage of development, which can have positive or negative outcomes. For example, children who leave infancy with a sense of trust can still have their sense of mistrust activated at a later stage, perhaps if their parents are separated or divorced under conflictual circumstances.

The Developing Sense of Self   When does the individual begin to sense a separate existence from others? Studying the development of a sense of self in infancy is difficult mainly because infants cannot verbally express their thoughts and impressions. They also cannot understand complex instructions from researchers.

One ingenious strategy to test infants' visual self-recognition is the use of a mirror technique, in which an infant's mother first puts a dot of rouge on the infant's nose. Then an observer watches to see how often the infant touches its nose. Next, the infant is placed in front of a mirror, and observers detect whether nose touching increases. Why does this matter? The idea is that increased nose touching indicates that the infant recognizes the self in the mirror and is trying to touch or rub off the rouge because the rouge violates the infant's view of the self. Increased touching indicates that the infant realizes that it is the self in the mirror but that something is not right since the real self does not have a dot of rouge on it.

Figure 6.4 displays the results of two investigations that used the mirror technique. The researchers found that before they were 1 year old, infants did not recognize themselves in the mirror (Amsterdam, 1968; Lewis & Brooks-Gunn, 1979). Signs of self-recognition began to appear among some infants when they were 15 to 18 months old. By the time they were 2 years old, most children recognized themselves in the mirror. In sum, infants begin to develop a self-understanding called self-recognition at approximately 18 months of age (Hart & Karmel, 1996; Lewis, 2005).

However, mirrors are not familiar to infants in all cultures (Rogoff, 2003). Thus, physical self-recognition may be a more important marker of self-recognition in Western than non–Western cultures (Thompson & Virmani, 2010). Supporting this cultural variation view, one study revealed that 18- to 20-month-old toddlers from urban middle-SES German families were more likely to recognize their mirror images than were toddlers from rural Cameroon farming families (Keller & others, 2005).

Late in the second year and early in the third year, toddlers show other emerging forms of self-awareness that reflect a sense of "me" (Goodvin, Winer, & Thompson, 2014). For

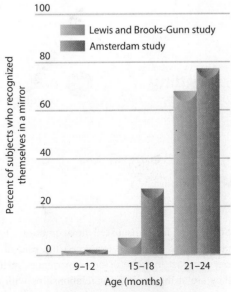

Age (months)

FIGURE 6.4

THE DEVELOPMENT OF SELF-RECOGNITION IN INFANCY. The graph shows the findings of two studies in which infants less than 1 year of age did not recognize themselves in a mirror. A slight increase in the percentage of infant self-recognition occurred around 15 to 18 months of age. By 2 years of age, a majority of children recognized themselves. *Why do researchers study whether infants recognize themselves in a mirror?*

developmental **connection**

Personality

Erikson proposed that individuals go through eight stages in the course of human development. Chapter 1, p. 20

developmental **connection**

Personality

Two key points in development when there is a strong push for independence are the second year of life and early adolescence. Chapter 12, p. 378

example, they refer to themselves by making statements such as "me big"; they label their internal experiences such as emotions; they monitor themselves, as when a toddler says, "do it myself"; and they declare that things are theirs (Bates, 1990; Fasig, 2000).

Independence   Erik Erikson (1968) stressed that independence is an important issue in the second year of life. Erikson describes the second stage of development as the stage of autonomy versus shame and doubt. Autonomy builds as the infant's mental and motor abilities develop. At this point in development, not only can infants walk, but they can also climb, open and close, drop, push and pull, and hold and let go. Infants feel pride in these new accomplishments and want to do everything themselves, whether the activity is flushing a toilet, pulling the wrapping off a package, or deciding what to eat. It is important for parents to recognize the motivation of toddlers to do what they are capable of doing at their own pace. Then they can learn to control their muscles and their impulses themselves. But when caregivers are impatient and do for toddlers what they are capable of doing themselves, shame and doubt develop. Every parent has rushed a child from time to time. It is only when parents consistently overprotect toddlers or criticize accidents (wetting, soiling, spilling, or breaking, for example) that children develop an excessive sense of shame and doubt about their ability to control themselves and their world. As we discuss in later chapters, Erikson emphasized that the stage of autonomy versus shame and doubt has important implications for the individual's future development.

Review *Connect* Reflect

 LG1 Discuss the development of emotions and personality in infancy.

Review

- What are emotions? What is the nature of an infant's emotions and how do they change?
- What is temperament, and how does it develop in infancy?
- What are some important aspects of personality in infancy, and how do they develop?

Connect

- In this section, you read that twin and adoption studies have been used to sort out the influences of heredity and environment on temperament. In Chapter 2, you learned how twin and adoption studies are conducted. Discuss the characteristics of twin and adoption studies.

Reflect *Your Own Personal Journey of Life*

- How would you describe your temperament? Does it fit one of Chess and Thomas' three styles—easy, slow to warm up, or difficult? If you have siblings, is your temperament similar to or different from theirs?

2 Social Orientation/Understanding and Attachment

LG2 Describe social orientation/understanding and the development of attachment in infancy.

Social Orientation/ Understanding	Attachment and Its Development	Individual Differences in Attachment	Caregiving Styles and Attachment	Developmental Social Neuroscience and Attachment

So far, we have discussed how emotions and emotional competence change as children develop. We have also examined the role of emotional style; in effect, we have seen how emotions set the tone of our experiences in life. But emotions also write the lyrics because they are at the core of our relationships with others.

SOCIAL ORIENTATION/UNDERSTANDING

In Ross Thompson's (2006, 2011, 2013, 2014a, 2015) view, infants are socioemotional beings who show a strong interest in their social world and are motivated to orient to it and understand it. In previous chapters, we described many of the biological and cognitive foundations that contribute to the infant's development of social orientation and understanding. In this chapter, we will call attention to relevant biological and cognitive factors as we explore social orientation; locomotion; intention and goal-directed behavior; social referencing; and social sophistication and insight. Discussing biological, cognitive, and social processes together reminds us of an important aspect of development that was pointed out in Chapter 1: These processes are intricately intertwined (Diamond, 2013).

developmental **connection**
Life-Span Perspective
Biological, cognitive, and socioemotional processes are often linked as individuals go through the life span. Chapter 1, p. 12

A mother and her baby engaging in face-to-face play. *At what age does face-to-face play usually begin, and when does it typically start decreasing in frequency?*

Social Orientation   From early in their development, infants are captivated by the social world. As we discussed in our coverage of infant perception in Chapter 4, young infants stare intently at faces and are attuned to the sounds of human voices, especially the voices of their caregivers (Lowe & others, 2012; Sugden, Mohamed-Ali, & Moulson, 2014). Later, they become adept at interpreting the meaning of facial expressions.

Face-to-face play often begins to characterize caregiver-infant interactions when the infant is about 2 to 3 months of age. The focused social interaction of face-to-face play may include vocalizations, touch, and gestures (Lee & others, 2013). Such play illustrates many mothers' motivation to create a positive emotional state in their infants (Thompson, 2013c, d).

In part because of such positive social interchanges between caregivers and infants, by 2 to 3 months of age infants respond in different ways to people and objects, showing more positive emotion to people than to inanimate objects such as puppets (Legerstee, 1997). At this age, most infants expect people to react positively when the infants initiate a behavior, such as a smile or a vocalization. This finding has been discovered using a method called the *still-face paradigm,* in which the caregiver alternates between engaging in face-to-face interaction with the infant and remaining still and unresponsive (Bigelow & Power, 2012). As early as 2 to 3 months of age, infants show more withdrawal, negative emotions, and self-directed behavior when their caregivers are still and unresponsive (Adamson & Frick, 2003). The frequency of face-to-face play decreases after 7 months of age as infants become more mobile (Thompson, 2006). A meta-analysis revealed that infants' higher positive affect and lower negative affect as displayed during the still-face paradigm were linked to secure attachment at one year of age (Mesman, van IJzendoorn, & Bakermans-Kranenburg, 2009).

Infants also learn about their social world through contexts other than face-to-face play with a caregiver (Thompson, 2014a, b, 2015). Even though infants as young as 6 months of age show an interest in each other, their interaction with peers increases considerably in the last half of the second year. Between 18 and 24 months of age, children markedly increase their imitative and reciprocal play, such as imitating nonverbal actions like jumping and running (Eckerman & Whitehead, 1999). One study involved presenting 1- and 2-year-olds with a simple cooperative task that consisted of pulling a lever to get an attractive toy (Brownell, Ramani, & Zerwas, 2006) (see Figure 6.5). Any coordinated actions of the 1-year-olds appeared to be coincidental rather than cooperative, whereas the 2-year-olds' behavior was characterized by active cooperation to reach a goal.

Locomotion   Recall from earlier in the chapter the growing importance of independence for infants, especially during the second year of life. As infants develop the ability to crawl, walk, and run, they are able to explore and expand their social world. These newly developed, self-produced locomotion skills allow the infant to independently initiate social interchanges on a more frequent basis (Laible & Thompson, 2007). Remember from Chapter 4 that the development of these gross motor skills results from factors such as the development of the nervous system, the goal the infant is motivated to reach, and environmental support for the skill (Adolph & Kretch, 2014; Adolph & Robinson, 2015).

The infant's and toddler's push for independence also is likely paced by the development of locomotion skills. Of further importance is locomotion's

FIGURE **6.5**

THE COOPERATION TASK. The cooperation task consisted of two handles on a box, atop which was an animated musical toy, surreptitiously activated by remote control when both handles were pulled. The handles were placed far enough apart that one child could not pull both handles. The experimenter demonstrated the task, saying, "Watch! If you pull the handles, the doggie will sing" (Brownell, Ramani, & Zerwas, 2006).

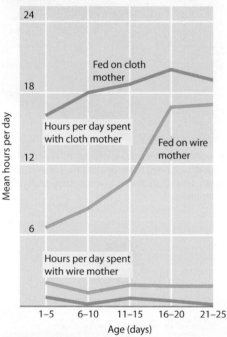

FIGURE **6.6**

CONTACT TIME WITH WIRE AND CLOTH SURROGATE MOTHERS. Regardless of whether the infant monkeys were fed by a wire or a cloth mother, they overwhelmingly preferred to spend contact time with the cloth mother. *How do these results compare with what Freud's theory and Erikson's theory would predict about human infants?*

social referencing "Reading" emotional cues in others to help determine how to act in a particular situation.

attachment A close emotional bond between two people.

motivational implications. Once infants have the ability to move in goal-directed pursuits, the rewards from these pursuits lead to further efforts to explore and develop skills.

Intention and Goal-Directed Behavior Perceiving people as engaging in intentional and goal-directed behavior is an important social cognitive accomplishment that initially occurs toward the end of the first year (Thompson, 2010). Joint attention and gaze-following help the infant to understand that other people have intentions (Deak & others, 2014; Tomasello, 2014). Recall from Chapter 5 that *joint attention* occurs when the caregiver and infant focus on the same object or event. We indicated that emerging aspects of joint attention occur at about 7 to 8 months, but at about 10 to 11 months of age joint attention intensifies and infants begin to follow the caregiver's gaze. By their first birthday, infants have begun to direct the caregiver's attention to objects that capture their interest (Heimann & others, 2006).

Social Referencing Another important social cognitive accomplishment in infancy is developing the ability to "read" the emotions of other people (Cornew & others, 2012). **Social referencing** is the term used to describe "reading" emotional cues in others to help determine how to act in a particular situation. The development of social referencing helps infants to interpret ambiguous situations more accurately, as when they encounter a stranger and need to know whether to fear the person (Pelaez, Virues-Ortega, & Gewirtz, 2012). By the end of the first year, a mother's facial expression—either smiling or fearful—influences whether an infant will explore an unfamiliar environment.

Infants become better at social referencing in the second year of life. At this age, they tend to "check" with their mother before they act; they look at her to see if she is happy, angry, or fearful. For example, in one study 14- to 22-month-old infants were more likely to look at their mother's face to get information about how to act in a situation than were 6- to 9-month-old infants (Walden, 1991).

Infants' Social Sophistication and Insight In sum, researchers are discovering that infants are more socially sophisticated and insightful at younger ages than was previously envisioned (Thompson, 2013, 2014a, b, 2015). This sophistication and insight is reflected in infants' perceptions of others' actions as intentionally motivated and goal-directed and their motivation to share and participate in that intentionality by their first birthday. The more advanced social cognitive skills of infants likely influence their understanding and awareness of attachment to a caregiver.

ATTACHMENT AND ITS DEVELOPMENT

Attachment is a close emotional bond between two people. There is no shortage of theories about infant attachment. Three theorists discussed in Chapter 1—Freud, Erikson, and Bowlby—proposed influential views.

Freud emphasized that infants become attached to the person or object that provides oral satisfaction. For most infants, this is the mother, since she is most likely to feed the infant. Is feeding as important as Freud thought? A classic study by Harry Harlow (1958) reveals that the answer is no (see Figure 6.6).

Harlow removed infant monkeys from their mothers at birth; for six months they were reared by surrogate (substitute) "mothers." One surrogate mother was made of wire, the other of cloth. Half of the infant monkeys were fed by the wire mother, half by the cloth mother. Periodically, the amount of time the infant monkeys spent with either the wire or the cloth mother was computed. Regardless of which mother fed them, the infant monkeys spent far more time with the cloth mother. Even if the wire mother, but not the cloth mother, provided nourishment, the infant monkeys spent more time with the cloth mother. And when Harlow frightened the monkeys, those "raised" by the cloth mother ran to the mother and clung to it; those raised by the wire mother did not. Whether the mother provided comfort seemed to determine whether the monkeys associated the mother with security. This study clearly demonstrated that feeding is not the crucial element in the attachment process and that contact comfort is important.

Physical comfort also plays a role in Erik Erikson's (1968) view of the infant's development. Recall Erikson's proposal that the first year of life represents the stage of trust versus mistrust. Physical comfort and sensitive care, according to Erikson (1968), are key to establishing a basic sense of trust in infants. The infant's sense of trust, in turn, is the foundation for attachment and sets the stage for a lifelong expectation that the world will be a good and pleasant place to be.

The ethological perspective of British psychiatrist John Bowlby (1969, 1989) also stresses the importance of attachment in the first year of life and the responsiveness of the caregiver. Bowlby maintains that both infants and their primary caregivers are biologically predisposed to form attachments. He argues that the newborn is biologically equipped to elicit attachment behavior. The baby cries, clings, coos, and smiles. Later, the infant crawls, walks, and follows the mother. The immediate result is to keep the primary caregiver nearby; the long-term effect is to increase the infant's chances of survival.

Attachment does not emerge suddenly but rather develops in a series of phases, moving from a baby's general preference for human beings to a partnership with primary caregivers. Following are four such phases based on Bowlby's conceptualization of attachment (Schaffer, 1996):

- *Phase 1: From birth to 2 months.* Infants instinctively direct their attachment to human figures. Strangers, siblings, and parents are equally likely to elicit smiling or crying from the infant.
- *Phase 2: From 2 to 7 months.* Attachment becomes focused on one figure, usually the primary caregiver, as the baby gradually learns to distinguish familiar from unfamiliar people.
- *Phase 3: From 7 to 24 months.* Specific attachments develop. With increased locomotor skills, babies actively seek contact with regular caregivers, such as the mother or father.
- *Phase 4: From 24 months on.* Children become aware of others' feelings, goals, and plans and begin to take these into account in forming their own actions.

Bowlby argued that infants develop an *internal working model* of attachment, a simple mental model of the caregiver, their relationship, and the self as deserving of nurturant care. The infant's internal working model of attachment with the caregiver influences the infant's and later the child's subsequent responses to other people (Roisman & Groh, 2011). The internal model of attachment also has played a pivotal role in the discovery of links between attachment and subsequent emotional understanding, conscience development, and self-concept (Thompson, 2015).

INDIVIDUAL DIFFERENCES IN ATTACHMENT

Although attachment to a caregiver intensifies midway through the first year, isn't it likely that the quality of babies' attachment experiences varies? Mary Ainsworth (1979) thought so. Ainsworth created the **Strange Situation,** an observational measure of infant attachment that takes about 20 minutes in which the infant experiences a series of introductions, separations, and reunions with the caregiver and an adult stranger in a prescribed order. In using the Strange Situation, researchers hope that their observations will provide information about the infant's motivation to be near the caregiver and the degree to which the caregiver's presence provides the infant with security and confidence (Brownell & others, 2015).

Based on how babies respond in the Strange Situation, they are described as being securely attached or insecurely attached (in one of three ways) to the caregiver:

- **Securely attached babies** use the caregiver as a secure base from which to explore the environment. When they are in the presence of their caregiver, securely attached infants explore the room and examine toys that have been placed in it. When the caregiver departs, securely attached infants might protest mildly, and when the caregiver returns these infants reestablish positive interaction with her, perhaps by smiling or climbing onto her lap. Subsequently, they often resume playing with the toys in the room.

Strange Situation An observational measure of infant attachment that requires the infant to move through a series of introductions, separations, and reunions with the caregiver and an adult stranger in a prescribed order.

securely attached babies Babies who use the caregiver as a secure base from which to explore the environment.

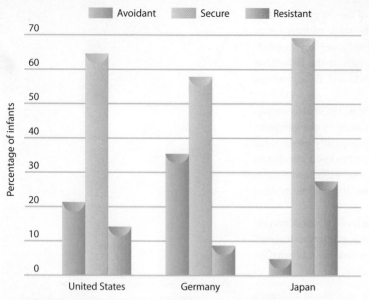

FIGURE **6.7**

CROSS-CULTURAL COMPARISON OF ATTACHMENT. In one study, infant attachment in three countries—the United States, Germany, and Japan—was measured in the Ainsworth Strange Situation (van IJzendoorn & Kroonenberg, 1988). The dominant attachment pattern in all three countries was secure attachment. However, German infants were more avoidant and Japanese infants were less avoidant and more resistant than U.S. infants. *What are some explanations for differences in how German, Japanese, and American infants respond to the Strange Situation?*

What is the nature of secure and insecure attachment?

insecure avoidant babies Babies who show insecurity by avoiding the caregiver.

insecure resistant babies Babies who often cling to the caregiver, then resist the caregiver by fighting against the closeness, perhaps by kicking or pushing away.

insecure disorganized babies Babies who show insecurity by being disorganized and disoriented.

- **Insecure avoidant babies** show insecurity by avoiding the caregiver. In the Strange Situation, these babies engage in little interaction with the caregiver, are not distressed when she leaves the room, usually do not reestablish contact when she returns, and may even turn their back on her. If contact is established, the infant usually leans away or looks away.
- **Insecure resistant babies** often cling to the caregiver and then resist her by fighting against the closeness, perhaps by kicking or pushing away. In the Strange Situation, these babies often cling anxiously to the caregiver and don't explore the playroom. When the caregiver leaves, they often cry loudly and then push away if she tries to comfort them on her return.
- **Insecure disorganized babies** appear disoriented. In the Strange Situation, these babies might seem dazed, confused, and fearful. To be classified as disorganized, babies must show strong patterns of avoidance and resistance or display certain specified behaviors, such as extreme fearfulness around the caregiver.

Evaluating the Strange Situation Does the Strange Situation capture important differences among infants? As a measure of attachment, it may be culturally biased. For example, German and Japanese babies often show patterns of attachment different from those of American infants. As illustrated in Figure 6.7, German infants are more likely to show an avoidant attachment pattern and Japanese infants are less likely to display this pattern than U.S. infants (van IJzendoorn & Kroonenberg, 1988). The avoidant pattern in German babies likely occurs because their caregivers encourage them to be independent (Grossmann & others, 1985). Also as shown in Figure 6.7, Japanese babies are more likely than American babies to be categorized as resistant. This may have more to do with the Strange Situation as a measure of attachment than with attachment insecurity itself. Japanese mothers rarely let anyone unfamiliar with their babies care for them. Thus, the Strange Situation might create considerably more stress for Japanese infants than for American infants, who are more accustomed to separation from their mothers (Miyake, Chen, & Campos, 1985). Even though there are cultural variations in attachment classification, the most frequent classification in every culture studied so far is secure attachment (Jin & others, 2012; Thompson, 2006; van IJzendoorn & Kroonenberg, 1988).

Interpreting Differences in Attachment Do individual differences in attachment matter? Ainsworth argues that secure attachment in the first year of life provides an important foundation for psychological development later in life. The securely attached infant moves freely away from the mother but keeps track of where she is through periodic glances. The securely attached infant responds positively to being picked up by others, and when put back down, freely moves away to play. An insecurely attached infant, by contrast, avoids the mother or is ambivalent toward her, fears strangers, and is upset by minor, everyday separations.

If early attachment to a caregiver is important, it should be linked to a child's social behavior later in development. For some children, early attachments seem to foreshadow later functioning (Bretherton, 2012; Kok & others, 2013; Moutsiana & others, 2014). In the extensive longitudinal study conducted by Alan Sroufe and his colleagues (2005), early secure attachment (assessed by the Strange Situation at 12 and 18 months) was linked with positive emotional health, high self-esteem, self-confidence, and socially competent interaction with peers, teachers, camp counselors, and romantic partners through adolescence. Another study discovered that attachment security at 2 years of age was linked to lower rates of peer conflict at 3 years of age (Raikes & others, 2013).

Few studies have assessed infants' attachment security to the mother and the father separately. However, a recent study revealed that infants who were insecurely attached to their mother and father ("double-insecure") at 15 months of age had more externalizing problems (out-of-control behavior, for example) during their elementary school years than their counterparts who were securely attached to at least one parent (Kochanska & Kim, 2013).

An important issue regarding attachment is whether infancy is a critical or sensitive period for development. The studies just described show continuity, with secure attachment in infancy predicting subsequent positive development in childhood and adolescence. For some children, though, there is little continuity. Not all research reveals the power of infant attachment to predict subsequent development (Groh & others, 2014; Roisman & Groh, 2011; Thompson, 2014a, 2015). In one longitudinal study, attachment classification in infancy did not predict attachment classification at 18 years of age (Lewis, Feiring, & Rosenthal, 2000). In this study, the best predictor of an insecure attachment classification at 18 was the occurrence of parental divorce in the intervening years.

Consistently positive caregiving over a number of years is likely an important factor in connecting early attachment with the child's functioning later in development. Indeed, researchers have found that early secure attachment and subsequent experiences, especially maternal care and life stresses, are linked with children's later behavior and adjustment (Thompson, 2013a). For example, a longitudinal study revealed that changes in attachment security/insecurity from infancy to adulthood were linked to stresses and supports in socio-emotional contexts (Van Ryzin, Carlson, & Sroufe, 2011). These results suggest that attachment continuity may be a reflection of stable social contexts as much as early working models. The study just described (Van Ryzin, Carlson, & Sroufe, 2011) reflects an increasingly accepted view of the development of attachment and its influence on development. That is, it is important to recognize that attachment security in infancy does not always by itself produce long-term positive outcomes, but rather is linked to later outcomes through connections with the way children and adolescents subsequently experience various social contexts as they develop.

The Van Ryzin, Carlson, and Sroufe (2011) study reflects a **developmental cascade model,** which involves connections across domains over time that influence developmental pathways and outcomes (Cicchetti, 2013; Groh & others, 2014; Masten, 2013). Developmental cascades can include connections between a wide range of biological, cognitive, and socioemotional processes (attachment, for example), and also can involve social contexts such as families, peers, schools, and culture. Further, links can produce positive or negative outcomes at different points in development, such as infancy, early childhood, middle and late childhood, adolescence, and adulthood.

A recent meta-analysis supported the views just described (Pinquart, Feubner, & Ahnert, 2013). In this analysis of 127 research reports, the following conclusions were reached: (1) moderate stability of attachment security occurred from early infancy to adulthood, (2) no significant stability of attachment occurred over time intervals of more than 15 years, (3) attachment stability was greater when the time span was less than 2 years than when it was more than 5 years, and (4) securely attached children at risk were less likely to maintain attachment security, while insecurely attached children at risk were likely to continue to be insecurely attached.

In addition to challenging the assumption that infancy is a critical or sensitive period for creating a secure attachment with a caregiver, some developmentalists argue that the secure attachment concept does not adequately consider certain biological factors in development, such as genes and temperament. For example, Jerome Kagan (1987, 2002) points out that infants are highly resilient and adaptive; he argues that they are evolutionarily equipped to stay on a positive developmental course even in the face of wide variations in parenting. Kagan and others stress that genetic characteristics and temperament play more important roles in a child's social competence than the attachment theorists, such as Bowlby and Ainsworth, are willing to acknowledge (Bakermans-Kranenburg & van IJzendoorn, 2011). For example, if some infants inherit a low tolerance for stress, this characteristic, rather than an insecure attachment bond, may be responsible for an inability to get along with peers. One study found links between disorganized attachment in infancy, a specific gene, and levels of maternal responsiveness (Spangler & others, 2009). In this study, infants with the short version of the serotonin transporter gene, 5-HTTLPR, developed a disorganized attachment style only when mothers were slow in responding to them. Also, in a longitudinal study, infant attachment security only predicted adult attachment security when individuals were in their twenties if they had a particular variant of the oxytocin receptor gene (OXTR G/G) (Raby &

To what extent might this adolescent girl's development be linked to how securely or insecurely attached she was during infancy?

developmental **connection**

Attachment

How might secure and insecure attachment be reflected in the relationships of young adults? Chapter 14, p. 433

developmental cascade model Involves connections across domains over time that influence developmental pathways and outcomes.

developmental connection

Nature Versus Nurture

What is involved in gene × environment (G × E) interaction? Chapter 2, p. 67

In the Hausa culture, siblings and grandmothers provide a significant amount of care for infants. *How might these variations in care affect attachment?*

others, 2013). In this study, the 5-HTTLPR gene and a dopamine gene (DRD4) did not consistently influence the link between infant attachment and adult attachment. Shortly, we will discuss the role of the hormone oxytocin in attachment. It is important to note that some researchers have not found support for gene-environment interactions related to infant attachment (Fraley & others, 2013a; Luijk & others, 2011; Roisman & Fraley, 2012).

A third criticism of attachment theory (in addition to the critical/sensitive period issue and inadequate attention to biological-based factors) is that it ignores the diversity of socializing agents and contexts that exists in an infant's world. A culture's value system can influence the nature of attachment. In some cultures, infants show attachments to many people. Among the Hausa (who live in Nigeria), both grandmothers and siblings provide a significant amount of care for infants (Harkness & Super, 1995). Infants in agricultural societies tend to form attachments to older siblings, who are assigned a major responsibility for younger siblings' care. Researchers recognize the influence of competent, nurturant caregivers on an infant's development (Cicchetti & Toth, 2015). At issue, though, is whether or not secure attachment, especially to a single caregiver, is critical (Lamb, 2013; Fraley, Roisman, & Haltigan, 2013; Thompson, 2014a).

Despite such criticisms, there is ample evidence that secure attachment is important in development (Thompson, 2014a, 2015; Powell & others, 2014; Sroufe, Coffino, & Carlson, 2010). Is secure attachment the sole predictor of positive developmental outcomes for infants? No, and neither is any other single factor. Nonetheless, secure attachment in infancy is important because it reflects a positive parent-infant relationship and provides a foundation that supports healthy socioemotional development in the years that follow.

CAREGIVING STYLES AND ATTACHMENT

Is the style of caregiving linked with the quality of the infant's attachment? Securely attached babies have caregivers who are sensitive to their signals and are consistently available to respond to their infants' needs (Powell & others, 2014). These caregivers often let their babies have an active part in determining the onset and pacing of interaction in the first year of life. One study revealed that maternal sensitive responding was linked to infant attachment security (Finger & others, 2009). Another study found that maternal sensitivity—but not infants' temperament—when infants were 6 months old was linked to subsequent attachment security (Leerkes, 2011).

How do the caregivers of insecurely attached babies interact with them? Caregivers of avoidant babies tend to be unavailable or rejecting (Posada & Kaloustian, 2010). They often don't respond to their babies' signals and have little physical contact with them. When they do interact with their babies, they may behave in an angry and irritable way. Caregivers of resistant babies tend to be inconsistent; sometimes they respond to their babies' needs and sometimes they don't. In general, they tend not to be very affectionate with their babies and show little synchrony when interacting with them. Caregivers of disorganized babies often neglect or physically abuse them (Bernard & others, 2012). In some cases, these caregivers are depressed.

DEVELOPMENTAL SOCIAL NEUROSCIENCE AND ATTACHMENT

In Chapter 1, we described the emerging field of developmental social neuroscience that examines connections between socioemotional processes, development, and the brain (Singer, 2012). Attachment has been a major focus of theory and research on developmental social neuroscience. The connections between attachment and the brain involve the neuroanatomy of the brain, neurotransmitters, and hormones.

Theory and research on the role of the brain's regions in mother-infant attachment is just emerging (De Haan & Gunnar, 2009). One theoretical view proposed that the prefrontal cortex likely has an important role in maternal attachment behavior, as do the subcortical (areas of the brain lower than the cortex) regions of the amygdala (which is strongly involved in emotion) and the hypothalamus (Gonzalez, Atkinson, & Fleming, 2009).

Research on the role of hormones and neurotransmitters in attachment has emphasized the importance of two neuropeptide hormones—oxytocin and vasopressin—in forming the maternal-infant bond (Strathearn & others, 2012). Oxytocin, a mammalian hormone that also acts as a neurotransmitter in the brain, is released during breast feeding and by contact and warmth (Carter, 2014). Oxytocin is especially thought to be a likely candidate in the formation of infant-mother attachment (Feldman, 2012). A recent research review indicated strong links between levels or patterns of maternal oxytocin and aspects of mother-infant attachment (Galbally & others, 2011). The influence of these neuropeptides on the neurotransmitter dopamine in the nucleus accumbens (a collection of neurons in the forebrain that are involved in pleasure) likely is important in motivating approach to the attachment object (de Haan & Gunnar, 2009). Figure 6.8 shows the regions of the brain we have described that have been proposed as important in infant-mother attachment.

Although oxytocin release is stimulated by birth and lactation in mothers, might it also be released in fathers? Oxytocin is secreted in males, and one research study found that at both 6 weeks and 6 months after birth, when fathers engaged in more stimulation contact with babies, encouraged their exploration, and directed their attention to objects, the fathers' oxytocin levels increased (Gordon & others, 2010). In this study, mothers' behaviors that increased their oxytocin levels involved more affectionate parenting, such as gazing at their babies, expressing positive affect toward them, and touching them. Another study found that fathers with lower testosterone levels engaged in more optimal parenting with their infants (Weisman, Zagoory-Sharon, & Feldman, 2014). Also in this study, when fathers were administered oxytocin, their parenting behavior improved as evidenced in increased positive affect, social gaze, touch, and vocal synchrony when interacting with their infants.

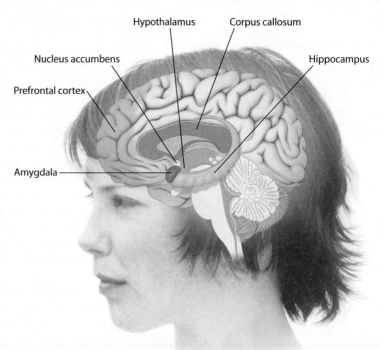

FIGURE **6.8**

REGIONS OF THE BRAIN PROPOSED AS LIKELY TO BE IMPORTANT IN INFANT-MOTHER ATTACHMENT

Review *Connect* Reflect

 Describe social orientation/understanding and the development of attachment in infancy.

Review

- How do infants orient to the social world?
- What is attachment, and how is it conceptualized?
- What are some individual variations in attachment? What are some criticisms of attachment theory?
- How are caregiving styles related to attachment?

Connect

- Do the different theories of attachment complement or contradict each other? Describe how the concept of nature versus nurture is involved.

Reflect *Your Own Personal Journey of Life*

- What can you do as a parent to improve the likelihood that your baby will form a secure attachment with you?

3 Social Contexts

LG3 Explain how social contexts influence the infant's development.

The Family   Child Care

Now that we have explored the infant's emotional and personality development and attachment to caregivers, let's examine the social contexts in which these occur. We will begin by studying a number of aspects of the family and then turn to a social context in which infants increasingly spend time—child care.

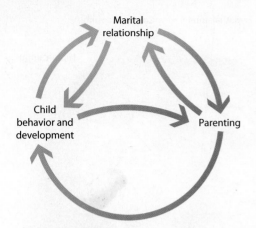

FIGURE **6.9**

INTERACTION BETWEEN CHILDREN AND THEIR PARENTS: DIRECT AND INDIRECT EFFECTS

What characterizes the transition to parenting?

- - - - - - - - - →

developmental **connection**

Cognitive Theory

A version of scaffolding is an important aspect of Lev Vygotsky's sociocultural cognitive theory of development. Chapter 7, p. 210

reciprocal socialization Socialization that is bidirectional; children socialize parents, just as parents socialize children.

scaffolding Practice in which parents time interactions so that infants experience turn taking with the parents.

THE FAMILY

The family can be thought of as a constellation of subsystems—a complex whole made up of interrelated, interacting parts—defined in terms of generation, gender, and role. Each family member participates in several subsystems (Clarke-Stewart & Parke, 2014; Parfitt, Pike, & Ayers, 2014). The father and child represent one subsystem, the mother and father another, the mother-father-child yet another, and so on.

These subsystems have reciprocal influences on each other (Cummings, Bergman, & Kuznicki, 2014; Emery, 2014). For example, Jay Belsky (1981) emphasizes that marital relations, parenting, and infant behavior and development can have both direct and indirect effects on each other (see Figure 6.9). An example of a direct effect is the influence of the parents' behavior on the child. An indirect effect is how the relationship between the spouses mediates the way a parent acts toward the child (Cummings, Koss, & Cheung, 2015; McCoy & others, 2014). For example, marital conflict might reduce the efficiency of parenting, in which case marital conflict would indirectly affect the child's behavior. The simple fact that two people are becoming parents may have profound effects on their relationship.

The Transition to Parenthood   When people become parents through pregnancy, adoption, or stepparenting, they face disequilibrium and must adapt. Parents want to develop a strong attachment with their infant, but they also want to maintain strong attachments to their spouse and friends, and possibly continue their careers. Parents ask themselves how the presence of this new individual will change their lives. A baby places new restrictions on partners; no longer will they be able to rush out to a movie on a moment's notice, and money may not be readily available for vacations and other luxuries. Dual-career parents ask, "Will it harm our baby if we place her in child care? Will we be able to find responsible babysitters?"

In a longitudinal investigation that tracked couples from late pregnancy until 3½ years after their baby was born, couples enjoyed more positive marital relations before the baby was born than after (Cowan & Cowan, 2000; Cowan & others, 2005). Still, almost one-third reported an increase in marital satisfaction. Some couples said that the baby had both brought them closer together and moved them farther apart; being parents enhanced their sense of themselves and also gave them a new, more stable identity as a couple. Babies opened men up to a concern with intimate relationships, and the demands of juggling work and family roles stimulated women to manage family tasks more efficiently and to pay attention to their own personal growth.

Other studies have explored the transition to parenthood (Brown, Feinberg, & Kan, 2012; Menendez & others, 2011). One study found similar negative change in relationship satisfaction for married and cohabiting women during the transition to parenthood (Mortensen & others, 2012). Another study revealed that mothers experienced unmet expectations in the transition to parenting, with fathers doing less than they had anticipated (Biehle & Mickelson, 2012).

The Bringing Home Baby project is a workshop that helps new parents to strengthen their relationship, understand and become acquainted with their baby, resolve conflict, and develop parenting skills (Gottman, 2014). Evaluations of the project revealed that parents who participated improved their ability to work together as parents; fathers became more involved with their baby and sensitive to the baby's behavior; mothers had a lower incidence of postpartum depression symptoms; and babies showed better overall development than infants whose parents were part of a control group (Gottman, Shapiro, & Parthemer, 2004; Shapiro & Gottman, 2005).

Reciprocal Socialization   The mutual influence that parents and children exert on each other goes beyond specific interactions in games such as peek-a-boo; it extends to the whole process of socialization (Deater-Deckard, 2013). Socialization between parents and children is not a one-way process (Ram & others, 2014). Parents do socialize children, but socialization in families is reciprocal. **Reciprocal socialization** is socialization that is bidirectional; children socialize parents just as parents socialize children. These reciprocal interchanges and mutual influence processes are sometimes referred to as *transactional* (Sameroff, 2009, 2012).

When reciprocal socialization has been studied in infancy, mutual gaze or eye contact plays an important role in early social interaction (Stern, 2010). In one investigation, the mother and infant engaged in a variety of behaviors while they looked at each other (Stern & others, 1977). By contrast, when they looked away from each other, the rate of such behaviors dropped considerably. In sum, the behaviors of mothers and infants involve substantial interconnection, mutual regulation, and synchronization (Laurent, Ablow, & Measelle, 2012; Tronick, 2010). One study revealed that *parent-infant synchrony*—the temporal coordination of social behavior—played an important role in children's development (Feldman, 2007). In this study, parent-infant synchrony at 3 and 9 months of age was positively linked to children's self-regulation from 2 to 6 years of age.

An important form of reciprocal socialization is **scaffolding,** in which parents time interactions in such a way that the infant experiences turn taking with the parents. Scaffolding involves parental behavior that supports children's efforts, allowing them to be more skillful than they would be if they had to rely only on their own abilities (Erickson & others, 2013). In using scaffolding, caregivers provide a positive, reciprocal framework in which they and their children interact. For example, in the game peek-a-boo, the mother initially covers the baby. Then she removes the cover and registers "surprise" at the infant's reappearance. As infants become more skilled at peek-a-boo, pat-a-cake, and so on, caregivers initiate other games that exemplify scaffolding and turn-taking sequences. Turn taking and games like peek-a-boo reflect the development of joint attention by the caregiver and infant, which we discussed in Chapter 5 (Melzi, Schick, & Kennedy, 2011).

Increasingly, genetic and epigenetic factors are being studied to discover not only parental influences on children but also children's influence on parents (Asbury & Plomin, 2014; Beach & Whisman, 2013; Brody & others, 2013; Deater-Deckard, 2013; Harold & others, 2013). Recall from Chapter 2 that the *epigenetic view* emphasizes that development is the result of an ongoing, bidirectional interchange between heredity and the environment (Gottlieb, 2007; Lickliter, 2013; Moore, 2013). For example, harsh, hostile parenting is associated with negative outcomes for children, such as being defiant and oppositional (Deater-Deckard, 2013). This likely reflects bidirectional influences rather than a unidirectional parenting effect. That is, the parents' harsh, hostile parenting and the children's defiant, oppositional behavior may influence each other. In this bidirectional influence, the parents' and children's behavior may have genetic linkages as well as experiential connections.

Managing and Guiding Infants' Behavior

In addition to sensitive parenting that involves warmth and caring that can help babies become securely attached to their parents, other important aspects of parenting infants involve managing and guiding their behavior in an attempt to reduce or eliminate undesirable behaviors (Holden, Vittrup, & Rosen, 2011). This management process includes (1) being proactive and childproofing the environment so infants won't encounter potentially dangerous objects or situations, and (2) engaging in corrective methods when infants engage in undesirable behaviors such as excessive fussing and crying, throwing objects, and so on.

One study assessed results of disciplinary and corrective methods that parents had used by the time infants were 12 and 24 months old (Vittrup, Holden, & Buck, 2006). As indicated in Figure 6.10, the main method parents used by the time infants were 12 months old was diverting the infants' attention, followed by reasoning, ignoring, and negotiating. Also note in Figure 6.10 that more than one-third of parents had yelled at their infant, about one-fifth had slapped the infant's hands or threatened the infant, and approximately one-sixth had spanked the infant before his or her first birthday.

As infants move into the second year of life and become more mobile and capable of exploring a wider range of environments, parental management of the toddler's behavior often triggers even more corrective feedback and discipline (Holden, Vittrup, & Rosen, 2011). As indicated in Figure 6.10, in the study just described, yelling increased from 36 percent at 1 year of age to 81 percent at 2 years of age, slapping the infant's hands increased from 21 percent at 1 year to 31 percent at age 2, and spanking increased from 14 percent at 1 year to 45 percent at age 2 (Vittrup, Holden, & Buck, 2006).

Children socialize parents, just as parents socialize children.

Caregivers often play games such as peek-a-boo and pat-a-cake. *How is scaffolding involved in these games?*

Method	12 Months	24 Months
Spank with hand	14	45
Slap infant's hand	21	31
Yell in anger	36	81
Threaten	19	63
Withdraw privileges	18	52
Time-out	12	60
Reason	85	100
Divert attention	100	100
Negotiate	50	90
Ignore	64	90

FIGURE 6.10

PARENTS' METHODS FOR MANAGING AND CORRECTING INFANTS' UNDESIRABLE BEHAVIOR. Shown here are the percentage of parents who had used various corrective methods by the time the infants were 12 and 24 months old.
Source: After data presented by Vittrup, Holden & Buck, 2006, Table 1.

developmental connection

Parenting

Psychologists give a number of reasons why harsh physical punishment can be harmful to children's development. Chapter 8, p. 246

An Aka pygmy father with his infant son. In the Aka culture, fathers were observed to be holding or near their infants 47 percent of the time (Hewlett, 1991).

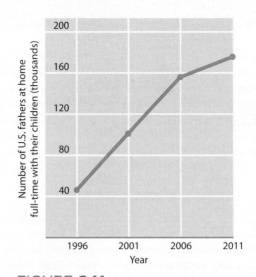

FIGURE 6.11

THE INCREASE IN THE NUMBER OF U.S. FATHERS STAYING AT HOME FULL-TIME WITH THEIR CHILDREN

A special concern is that such corrective discipline tactics not become abusive. Too often what starts out as mild to moderately intense discipline on the part of parents can move into highly intense anger. In Chapter 8, you will read more extensively about the use of punishment with children and child abuse.

Maternal and Paternal Caregiving

An increasing number of U.S. fathers stay home full-time with their children (Lamb & Lewis, 2013). As indicated in Figure 6.11, there was a 300-plus percent increase in stay-at-home fathers in the United States from 1996 to 2011 (U.S. Census Bureau, 2012). A large portion of the full-time fathers have career-focused wives who provide most of the family income. One study revealed that the stay-at-home fathers were as satisfied with their marriage as traditional parents, although they indicated that they missed their daily life in the workplace (Rochlen & others, 2008). In this study, the stay-at-home fathers reported that they tended to be ostracized when they took their children to playgrounds and often were excluded from parent groups.

Can fathers take care of infants as competently as mothers can? Observations of fathers and their infants suggest that fathers have the ability to act as sensitively and responsively as mothers with their infants (Lamb & Lewis, 2013; Shwalb, Shwalb, & Lamb, 2013). Consider the Aka pygmy culture in Africa where fathers spend as much time interacting with their infants as do their mothers (Hewlett, 1991, 2000; Hewlett & MacFarlan, 2010). Also, one study also found that marital intimacy and partner support during prenatal development were linked to father-infant attachment following childbirth (Yu & others, 2012). And another study revealed that fathers with a college-level education engaged in more stimulating physical activities with their infants and that fathers in a conflicting couple relationship participated in less caregiving and physical play with their infants (Cabrera, Hofferth, & Chae, 2011). Further, a recent study found that infants who showed a higher level of externalizing, disruptive problems at one year of age had fathers who displayed a low level of engagement with them as early as the third month of life (Ramchandani & others, 2013).

Remember, however, that although fathers can be active, nurturing, involved caregivers with their infants, as Aka pygmy fathers are, in many cultures men have not chosen to follow this pattern (Parkinson, 2010). Also, if fathers have mental health problems, they may not interact as effectively with their infants. A recent study revealed that depressed fathers focused more on their own needs than their infants' needs, directing more negative and critical speech toward infants (Sethna, Murray, & Ramchandani, 2012).

Do fathers and mothers interact with their infants in different ways? Maternal interactions usually center on child-care activities such as feeding, changing diapers, or bathing. Paternal interactions are more likely to include play (Lamb & Lewis 2013). Fathers engage in more rough-and-tumble play than mothers do. They bounce infants, throw them up in the air, tickle them, and so on (Lamb, 2000). Mothers do play with infants, but their play is less physical and arousing than that of fathers.

In one study, fathers were interviewed about their caregiving responsibilities when their children were 6, 15, 24, and 36 months of age (NICHD Early Child Care Research Network, 2000). Some of the fathers were videotaped while playing with their children at 6 and 36 months. Fathers were more involved in caregiving—bathing, feeding, dressing the child, taking the child to child care, and so on—when they worked fewer hours and mothers worked more hours, when mothers and fathers were younger, when mothers reported greater marital intimacy, and when the children were boys.

CHILD CARE

Many U.S. children today experience multiple caregivers. Most do not have a parent staying home to care for them; instead, the children have some type of care provided by others—"child care." Many parents worry that child care will reduce their infants' emotional attachment to them, harm the infants' cognitive development, fail to teach them how to control anger, and allow them to become unduly influenced by their peers. How extensively is child care used by families? Are the worries of these parents justified?

Parental Leave   Today far more young children are in child care than at any other time in history. About 2 million children in the United States currently receive formal, licensed child care, and uncounted millions of children are cared for by unlicensed babysitters. In part, these numbers reflect the fact that U.S. adults do not receive paid leave from their jobs to care for their young children.

Child-care policies around the world vary (Coley & others, 2013; Lamb, 2013). Europe led the way in creating new standards of parental leave: The European Union (EU) mandated a paid 14-week maternity leave in 1992. In most European countries today, working parents on leave receive from 70 to 100 percent of their prior wage, and paid leave averages about 16 weeks (Tolani & Brooks-Gunn, 2008). The United States currently grants up to 12 weeks of unpaid leave to workers caring for a newborn.

Most countries provide parental benefits only to women who have been employed for a minimum time prior to childbirth. In Denmark, however, even unemployed mothers are eligible for extended parental leave related to childbirth. In Germany, child-rearing leave is available to almost all parents. The Nordic countries (Denmark, Norway, and Sweden) have extensive gender-equity family leave policies for childbirth that emphasize the contributions of both women and men (O'Brien & Moss, 2010; Tolani & Brooks-Gunn, 2008). For example, in Sweden, parents can take an 18-month job-protected parental leave with benefits that can be shared by parents and applied to full-time or part-time work.

Variations in Child Care   Because the United States does not have a policy of paid leave for child care, child care in the United States has become a major national concern (Lamb, 2013). Many factors influence the effects of child care, including the age of the child, the type of child care, and the quality of the program.

In the United States, approximately 15 percent of children 5 years of age and younger attend more than one child-care arrangement. One study of 2- and 3-year-old children revealed that an increase in the number of child-care arrangements the children experienced was linked to an increase in behavioral problems and a decrease in prosocial behavior (Morrissey, 2009).

The type of child care varies extensively (Berlin, 2012; Hillemeier & others, 2012; Lamb, 2013). Child care is provided in large centers with elaborate facilities and in private homes. Some child-care centers are commercial operations; others are nonprofit centers run by churches, civic groups, and employers. Some child-care providers are professionals; others are mothers who want to earn extra money. Figure 6.12 presents the primary care arrangements for children under 5 years of age with employed mothers (Clarke-Stewart & Miner, 2008).

How do most fathers and mothers interact differently with infants?

How are child-care policies in many European countries, such as Sweden, different from those in the United States?

Wanda Mitchell, Child-Care Director

Wanda Mitchell is the Center Director at the Hattie Daniels Day Care Center in Wilson, North Carolina. Her responsibilities include directing the operation of the center, which involves creating and maintaining an environment in which young children can learn effectively, and ensuring that the center meets state licensing requirements. Wanda obtained her undergraduate degree from North Carolina A & T University, majoring in Child Development. Prior to her current position, she was an education coordinator for Head Start and an instructor at Wilson Technical Community College. Describing her work, Wanda says, "I really enjoy working in my field. This is my passion. After graduating from college, my goal was to advance in my field."

For more information about what early childhood educators do, see page 41 in the Careers in Life-Span Development appendix.

Wanda Mitchell, child-care director, working with some of the children at her center.

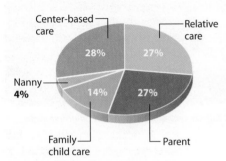

FIGURE **6.12**

PRIMARY CARE ARRANGEMENTS IN THE UNITED STATES FOR CHILDREN UNDER 5 YEARS OF AGE WITH EMPLOYED MOTHERS

Child-care quality makes a difference (Berlin, 2012; Lamb, 2012). What constitutes a high-quality child-care program for infants? In high-quality child care (Clarke-Stewart & Miner, 2008, p. 273):

> Caregivers encourage the children to be actively engaged in a variety of activities, have frequent, positive interactions that include smiling, touching, holding, and speaking at the child's eye level, respond properly to the child's questions or requests, and encourage children to talk about their experiences, feelings, and ideas.

Children are more likely to experience poor-quality child care if they come from families with few resources (psychological, social, and economic) (Carta & others, 2012). Many researchers have examined the role of poverty in the quality of child care (Hillemeier & others, 2012). One study found that extensive child care was harmful to low-income children only when the care was of low quality (Votruba-Drzal, Coley, & Chase-Lansdale, 2004). Even if the child was in child care more than 45 hours a week, high-quality care was linked with fewer internalizing problems (anxiety, for example) and externalizing problems (aggressive and destructive behaviors, for example). Another study revealed that children from low-income families benefited in terms of school readiness and language development when their parents selected higher-quality child care (McCartney & others, 2007).

High-quality child care also involves providing children with a safe environment, access to age-appropriate toys and participation in age-appropriate activities, and a low caregiver-to-child ratio that allows caregivers to spend considerable time with children on an individual basis. Quality of child care matters in children's development and according to UNICEF, the United States meets or exceeds only 3 of 10 child care quality benchmarks. An analysis of U.S. child care studies found that a greater quantity of child care was a strong predictor of socioemotional problems (Jacob, 2009). However, a recent study in Norway (a country that meets or exceeds 8 of 10 UNICEF benchmarks) revealed that a high quantity of child care there was not linked to children's externalizing problems (Zachrisson & others, 2013).

To read about one individual who provides quality child care to individuals from impoverished backgrounds, see *Connecting with Careers*. Do children in low-income families usually get quality child care? To answer that question and to learn more about the effects of child care, read *Connecting Through Research*.

How Does the Quality and Quantity of Child Care Affect Children?

In 1991, the National Institute of Child Health and Human Development (NICHD) began a comprehensive, longitudinal study of child-care experiences. Data were collected on a diverse sample of almost 1,400 children and their families at 10 locations across the United States over a period of seven years. Researchers used multiple methods (trained observers, interviews, questionnaires, and testing) and measured many facets of children's development, including physical health, cognitive development, and socioemotional development. Following are some of the results of what is now referred to as the NICHD Study of Early Child Care and Youth Development or NICHD SECCYD (NICHD Early Child Care Research Network, 2001, 2002, 2003, 2004, 2005, 2006, 2010).

- *Patterns of use.* Many families placed their infants in child care very soon after the child's birth, and there was considerable instability in the child-care arrangements. By 4 months of age, nearly three-fourths of the infants had entered some form of nonmaternal child care. Almost half of the infants were cared for by a relative when they first entered care; only 12 percent were enrolled in child-care centers.

  What are some important findings from the national longitudinal study of child care conducted by the National Institute of Child Health and Human Development?

  Socioeconomic factors were linked to the amount and type of care. For example, mothers with higher incomes and families that were more dependent on the mother's income placed their infants in child care at an earlier age. Mothers who believed that maternal employment has positive effects on children were more likely than other mothers to place their infant in nonmaternal care for more hours. Low-income families were more likely than more affluent families to use child care, but infants from low-income families who were in child care averaged as many hours as other income groups. In the preschool years, mothers who were single, those with more education, and families with higher incomes used more hours of center care than other families. Minority families and mothers with less education used more hours of care by relatives.

- *Quality of care.* Evaluations of quality of care were based on characteristics such as group size, child-adult ratio, physical environment, caregiver characteristics (such as formal education, specialized training, and child-care experience), and caregiver behavior (such as sensitivity to children). An alarming conclusion is that a majority of the child care in the first three years of life was of unacceptably low quality. Positive caregiving by nonparents in child-care settings was infrequent—only 12 percent of the children studied experienced positive nonparental child care (such as positive talk, lack of detachment and flat affect, and language stimulation). Further, infants from low-income families experienced lower-quality child care than did infants from higher-income families. When quality of caregivers' care was high, children performed better on cognitive and language tasks, were more cooperative with their mothers during play, showed more positive and skilled interaction with peers, and had fewer behavior problems. Caregiver training and good child-staff ratios were linked with higher cognitive and social competence when children were 54 months of age. Using data collected as part of the NICHD early child care longitudinal study, a recent analysis indicated that higher-quality early childhood care, especially at 27 months of age, was linked to children's higher vocabulary scores in the fifth grade (Belsky & others, 2007).

  Higher-quality child care was also related to higher-quality mother-child interaction among the families that used nonmaternal care. Further, poor-quality care was related to an increase of insecure attachment to the mother among infants who were 15 months of age, but only when the mother was low in sensitivity and responsiveness. However, child-care quality was not linked to attachment security at 36 months of age. A recent study revealed that higher-quality child care from birth to 4½ years of age was linked to higher cognitive-academic achievement at 15 years of age (Vandell & others, 2010). In this study, early higher-quality care also was related to youth reports of less externalizing behavior (lower rates of delinquency, for example). In a recent study, high quality infant-toddler child care was linked to better memory skills at the end of the preschool years (Li & others, 2013).

- *Amount of child care.* In general, when children spent 30 hours or more per week in child care, their development was less than optimal (Ramey, 2005). In a recent study, more time spent in early non-relative child care was related to higher levels of risk taking and impulsivity at 15 years of age (Vandell & others, 2010).

- *Family and parenting influences.* The influence of families and parenting was not weakened by extensive child care. Parents played a significant role in helping children to regulate their emotions. Especially important parenting influences were being sensitive to children's needs, being involved with children, and cognitively stimulating them. Indeed, parental sensitivity has been the most consistent predictor of a secure attachment, with child-care experiences being relevant in many cases only when mothers engage in insensitive parenting (Friedman, Melhuish, & Hill, 2010).

(continued)

(continued)

An important point about the extensive NICHD research is that findings show that family factors are considerably stronger and more consistent predictors of a wide variety of child outcomes than are child-care experiences (such as quality, quantity, type). The worst outcomes for children occur when both home and child care settings are of poor quality. For example, a recent study involving the NICHD SECCYD data revealed that worse socioemotional outcomes (more problem behavior, lower levels of prosocial behavior) for children occurred when they experienced both home and child care environments that conferred risk (Watamura & others, 2011).

This study reinforces the conclusion reached by other researchers cited earlier in this section of the chapter—it is not the quantity as much as the quality of child care a child receives that is important. What is also significant to note is the emphasis on the positive effect families and parents can have on children's child-care experiences.

> We have all the knowledge necessary to provide absolutely first-rate child care in the United States. What is missing is the commitment and the will.
>
> **—Edward Zigler**
> *Contemporary Developmental Psychologist, Yale University*

What are some strategies parents can follow in regard to child care? Child-care expert Kathleen McCartney (2003, p. 4) offered this advice:

- *Recognize that the quality of your parenting is a key factor in your child's development.*
- *Monitor your child's development.* "Parents should observe for themselves whether their children seem to be having behavior problems." They need to talk with their child-care providers and pediatricians about their child's behavior.
- *Take some time to find the best child care.* Observe different child-care facilities and be certain that you like what you see. "Quality child care costs money, and not all parents can afford the child care they want. However, state subsidies, and other programs like Head Start, are available for families in need."

Review *Connect* Reflect

 Explain how social contexts influence the infant's development.

Review

- What are some important family processes in infant development?
- How does child care influence infant development?

Connect

- In Chapter 4, you learned about a fine motor skills experiment involving 3-month-olds and grasping. What concept in this section of the chapter is related to the use of "sticky gloves" in the experiment described in Chapter 4?

Reflect *Your Own Personal Journey of Life*

- Imagine that a friend of yours is getting ready to put her baby in child care. What advice would you give her? Do you think she should stay home with the baby? Why or why not? What type of child care would you recommend?

topical connections *looking forward*

In Chapter 8 we will discuss socioemotional development in early childhood. Babies no more, young children make considerable progress in the development of their self, their emotions, and their social interactions. In early childhood, they show increased self-understanding and understanding of others, as well as an increased capacity to regulate their emotions. Many of the advances in young children's socioemotional development become possible because of the remarkable changes in their brain and cognitive development, which you will read about in Chapter 7. In early childhood, relationships and interactions with parents and peers expand their knowledge of and connections with the social world. Additionally, play becomes something they not only enjoy doing on a daily basis but also a wonderful context for advancing both their socioemotional and cognitive development.

reach your learning goals

Socioemotional Development in Infancy

1 Emotional and Personality Development

LG1 Discuss the development of emotions and personality in infancy.

Emotional Development

- Emotion is feeling, or affect, that occurs when a person is in a state or an interaction that is important to him or her. The broad range of emotions includes enthusiasm, joy, and love (positive emotions) and anxiety, anger, and sadness (negative emotions). Psychologists stress that emotions, especially facial expressions of emotions, have a biological foundation. Biological evolution endowed humans to be emotional, but embeddedness in culture and relationships provides diversity in emotional experiences. Emotions are the first language with which parents and infants communicate, and emotions play key roles in parent-child relationships. Infants display a number of emotions early in their development, although researchers debate the onset and sequence of these emotions. Lewis distinguishes between primary emotions and self-conscious emotions. Crying is the most important mechanism newborns have for communicating with the people in their world. Babies have at least three types of cries—basic, anger, and pain cries. Controversy swirls about whether babies should be soothed when they cry, although increasingly experts recommend immediately responding in a caring way during the first year. Social smiling occurs as early as 2 months of age. Two fears that infants develop are stranger anxiety and separation from a caregiver (which is reflected in separation protest). As infants develop, it is important for them to engage in emotion regulation.

Temperament

- Temperament involves individual differences in behavioral styles, emotions, and characteristic ways of responding. Chess and Thomas classified infants as (1) easy, (2) difficult, or (3) slow to warm up. Kagan proposed that inhibition to the unfamiliar is an important temperament category. Rothbart and Bates' view of temperament emphasizes this classification: (1) extraversion/surgency, (2) negative affectivity, and (3) effortful control (self-regulation). Physiological characteristics are associated with different temperaments. Children inherit a physiology that biases them to have a particular type of temperament, but through experience they learn to modify their temperament style to some degree. Goodness of fit refers to the match between a child's temperament and the environmental demands the child must cope with. Goodness of fit can be an important aspect of a child's adjustment. Although research evidence is sketchy at this point, some general recommendations are that caregivers should (1) be sensitive to the individual characteristics of the child, (2) be flexible in responding to these characteristics, and (3) avoid negatively labeling the child.

Personality Development

- Erikson argued that an infant's first year is characterized by the stage of trust versus mistrust. The infant begins to develop a self-understanding called self-recognition at about 18 months of age. Independence becomes a central theme in the second year of life. Erikson stressed that the second year of life is characterized by the stage of autonomy versus shame and doubt.

2 Social Orientation/Understanding and Attachment

LG2 Describe social orientation/understanding and the development of attachment in infancy.

Social Orientation/ Understanding

- Infants show a strong interest in their social world and are motivated to understand it. Infants orient to the social world early in their development. Face-to-face play with a caregiver begins to occur at about 2 to 3 months of age. Newly developed self-produced locomotion skills significantly expand the infant's ability to initiate social interchanges and explore their social world more independently. Perceiving people as engaging in intentional and goal-directed behavior is an important social cognitive accomplishment that occurs toward the end of the first year. Social referencing increases in the second year of life.

Attachment and Its Development

- Attachment is a close emotional bond between two people. In infancy, contact comfort and trust are important in the development of attachment. Bowlby's ethological theory stresses that the caregiver and the infant are biologically predisposed to form an attachment. Attachment develops in four phases during infancy.

Individual Differences in Attachment

- Securely attached babies use the caregiver, usually the mother, as a secure base from which to explore the environment. Three types of insecure attachment are avoidant, resistant, and disorganized. Ainsworth created the Strange Situation, an observational measure of attachment. Ainsworth points out that secure attachment in the first year of life provides an important foundation for psychological development later in life. The strength of the link found between early attachment and later development has varied somewhat across studies. Three criticisms of the concept of secure attachment in infancy are (1) there is insufficient support for the assertion that infancy serves as a critical/sensitive period for later development; (2) biologically based factors such as genes and temperament have not been given adequate consideration; and (3) diversity of social agents and contexts have received insufficient attention. A current trend in attachment research reflects the developmental cascade model by considering not only attachment but also stability and change in stresses and social contexts as children and adolescents develop. Despite these criticisms, there is ample evidence that attachment is an important aspect of human development. Cultural variations in attachment have been found, but in all cultures studied to date secure attachment is the most common classification.

Caregiving Styles and Attachment

- Caregivers of secure babies are sensitive to the babies' signals and are consistently available to meet their needs. Caregivers of avoidant babies tend to be unavailable or rejecting. Caregivers of resistant babies tend to be inconsistently available to their babies and usually are not very affectionate. Caregivers of disorganized babies often neglect or physically abuse their babies.

Developmental Social Neuroscience and Attachment

- Increased interest has been directed toward the role of the brain in the development of attachment. The hormone oxytocin is a key candidate for influencing the development of maternal-infant attachment.

3 Social Contexts

 LG3 Explain how social contexts influence the infant's development.

The Family

- The transition to parenthood requires considerable adaptation and adjustment on the part of parents. Children socialize parents, just as parents socialize children. Parent-infant synchrony and scaffolding are important aspects of reciprocal socialization. Belsky's model describes direct and indirect effects of marital relations, parenting, and infant behavior. Parents use a wide range of methods to manage and guide infants' behavior. The mother's primary role when interacting with the infant usually is caregiving; the father's is playful interaction.

Child Care

- More U.S. children are in child care now than at any earlier point in history. The quality of child care is uneven, and child care remains a controversial topic. Quality child care can be achieved and seems to have few adverse effects on children. In the NICHD child-care study, infants from low-income families were more likely to receive the lowest quality of care. Also, higher-quality child care was linked with fewer problems in children.

key terms

emotion 168
primary emotions 169
self-conscious emotions 169
basic cry 170
anger cry 170
pain cry 170
reflexive smile 170

social smile 170
stranger anxiety 171
separation protest 171
temperament 172
easy child 172
difficult child 172
slow-to-warm-up child 172

goodness of fit 175
social referencing 180
attachment 180
Strange Situation 181
securely attached babies 181
insecure avoidant babies 182
insecure resistant babies 182

insecure disorganized babies 182
developmental cascade model 183
reciprocal socialization 186
scaffolding 186

key people

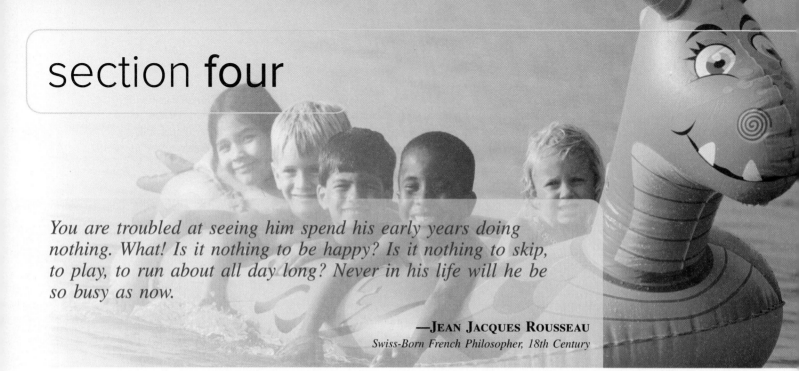

section four

You are troubled at seeing him spend his early years doing nothing. What! Is it nothing to be happy? Is it nothing to skip, to play, to run about all day long? Never in his life will he be so busy as now.

—JEAN JACQUES ROUSSEAU
Swiss-Born French Philosopher, 18th Century

Early Childhood

In early childhood, our greatest untold poem was being only 4 years old. We skipped and ran and played all the sun long, never in our lives so busy, busy being something we had not quite grasped yet. Who knew our thoughts, which we worked up into small mythologies all our own? Our thoughts and images and drawings took wings. The blossoms of our heart, no wind could touch. Our small world widened as we discovered new refuges and new people. When we said, "I," we meant something totally unique, not to be confused with any other. Section 4 consists of two chapters: "Physical and Cognitive Development in Early Childhood" (Chapter 7) and "Socioemotional Development in Early Childhood" (Chapter 8).

chapter 7

PHYSICAL AND COGNITIVE DEVELOPMENT IN EARLY CHILDHOOD

chapter outline

1 Physical Changes

Learning Goal 1 Identify physical changes in early childhood.

Body Growth and Change
Motor and Perceptual Development
Sleep
Nutrition and Exercise
Illness and Death

2 Cognitive Changes

Learning Goal 2 Describe three views of the cognitive changes that occur in early childhood.

Piaget's Preoperational Stage
Vygotsky's Theory
Information Processing

3 Language Development

Learning Goal 3 Summarize how language develops in early childhood.

Understanding Phonology and Morphology
Changes in Syntax and Semantics
Advances in Pragmatics
Young Children's Literacy

4 Early Childhood Education

Learning Goal 4 Evaluate different approaches to early childhood education.

Variations in Early Childhood Education
Education for Young Children Who Are Disadvantaged
Controversies in Early Childhood Education

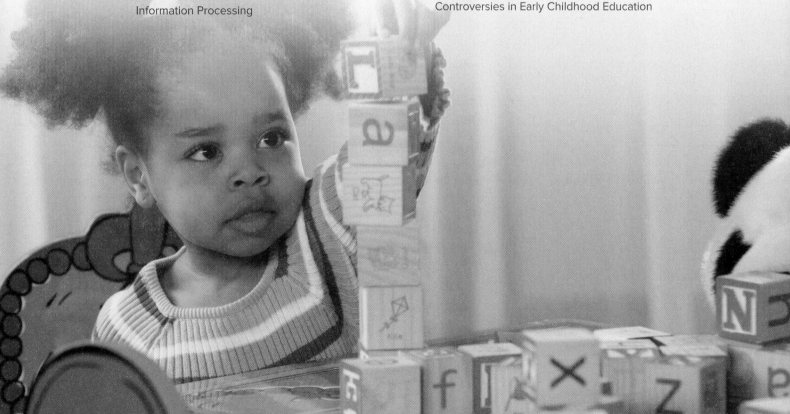

The Reggio Emilia approach is an educational program for young children that was developed in the northern Italian city of Reggio Emilia. Children of single parents and children with disabilities have priority in admission; other children are admitted according to a scale of needs. Parents pay on a sliding scale based on income.

The children are encouraged to learn by investigating and exploring topics that interest them. A wide range of stimulating media and materials is available for children to use as they learn music, movement, drawing, painting, sculpting, collages, puppets and disguises, and photography, for example (Freeman, 2011).

In this program, children often explore topics in a group, which fosters a sense of community, respect for diversity, and a collaborative approach to problem solving. Two co-teachers are present to serve as guides for children. The Reggio Emilia teachers consider a project as an adventure, which can start from an adult's suggestion, from a child's idea, or from an event, such as a snowfall or something else unexpected. The teachers allow children enough time to think about a topic and craft a project.

At the core of the Reggio Emilia approach is the image of children who are competent and have rights, especially the right to receive outstanding care and education. Parent participation is considered essential, and cooperation is a major theme in the schools. Many early childhood education experts believe the Reggio Emilia approach provides a supportive, stimulating context in which children are motivated to explore their world in a competent and confident manner (Martin & Evaldsson, 2012).

A Reggio Emilia classroom in which young children explore topics that interest them.

topical connections _looking **back**_

Physical growth in infancy is dramatic. Even though physical growth in early childhood slows, it is not difficult to distinguish young children from infants when you look at them. Most young children lose their "baby fat," and their legs and trunks become longer. In addition to what you can see with the naked eye, much development also continues below the surface in the brain. In infancy, myelination of axons in the brain paved the way for development of such functions as full visual capacity. Continued myelination in early childhood provides children with much better hand-eye coordination. In terms of cognitive development, you learned that infants make amazing progress in their attentional, memory, concept formation, and language skills. In this chapter, you will discover that these information-processing skills continue to show remarkable advances in early childhood.

preview

Parents and educators who clearly understand how young children develop can play an active role in creating programs that foster their natural interest in learning, rather than stifling it. In this chapter, we will explore the physical, cognitive, and language changes that typically occur as the toddler develops into the preschooler, and then examine different approaches to early childhood education.

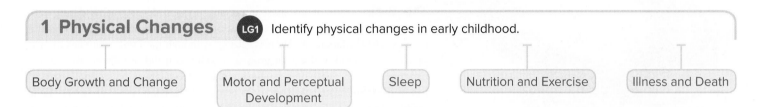

1 Physical Changes **LG1** Identify physical changes in early childhood.

| Body Growth and Change | Motor and Perceptual Development | Sleep | Nutrition and Exercise | Illness and Death |

Remember from Chapter 4 that an infant's growth in the first year is rapid and follows cephalocaudal and proximodistal patterns. Improvement in fine motor skills—such as being able to turn the pages of a book one at a time—also contributes to the infant's sense of mastery in the second year. The growth rate continues to slow down in early childhood. If it did not, we would be a species of giants.

BODY GROWTH AND CHANGE

Growth in height and weight is the obvious physical change that characterizes early childhood. Unseen changes in the brain and nervous system are no less significant, however, in preparing children for advances in cognition and language.

Height and Weight   The average child grows 2½ inches in height and gains between 5 and 7 pounds a year during early childhood. As the preschool child grows older, the percentage of increase in height and weight decreases with each additional year (Wilson & Hockenberry, 2012). Girls are only slightly smaller and lighter than boys during these years, a difference that continues until puberty. During the preschool years, both boys and girls slim down as the trunks of their bodies lengthen. Although their heads are still somewhat large for their bodies, by the end of the preschool years most children have lost their top-heavy look. Body fat also shows a slow, steady decline during the preschool years. The chubby baby often looks much leaner by the end of early childhood. Girls have more fatty tissue than boys; boys have more muscle tissue.

Growth patterns vary individually (Burns & others, 2013). Think back to your preschool years. This was probably the first time you noticed that some children were taller than you, some shorter; some were fatter, some thinner; some were stronger, some weaker. Much of the variation was due to heredity, but environmental experiences were also involved. A review of the height and weight of children around the world concluded that the two most important contributors to height differences are ethnic origin and nutrition (Meredith, 1978). Urban, middle-socioeconomic-status, and firstborn children were taller than rural, lower-socioeconomic-status, and later-born children. In the United States, African American children are taller than non-Latino White children.

Why are some children unusually short? The primary contributing influences are congenital factors (genetic or prenatal problems), growth hormone deficiency, a physical problem that develops in childhood, maternal smoking during pregnancy, or an emotional difficulty (Ball, Bindler, & Cowan, 2014; Wit, Kiess, & Mullis, 2011).

Growth hormone deficiency is the absence or deficiency of growth hormone produced by the pituitary gland to stimulate the body to grow. Growth hormone deficiency may occur during infancy or later in childhood (Chae & others, 2013; Ross & others, 2014). As many as 10,000 to 15,000 U.S. children may have growth hormone deficiency (Stanford University

The bodies of 5-year-olds and 2-year-olds are different. Notice that the 5-year-old not only is taller and weighs more, but also has a longer trunk and legs than the 2-year-old. *Can you think of some other physical differences between 2- and 5-year-olds?*

growth hormone deficiency Absence or deficiency of growth hormone produced by the pituitary gland to stimulate the body to grow.

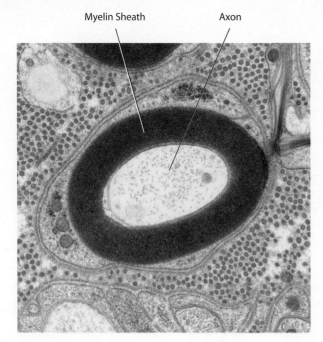

FIGURE 7.1

A MYELINATED NERVE FIBER. The myelin sheath, shown in brown, encases the axon (white). This image was produced by an electron microscope that magnified the nerve fiber 12,000 times. *What role does myelination play in the brain's development and children's cognition?*

- - - - - - - - - - →

developmental **connection**

Brain Development

In middle and late childhood, cortical thickening occurs in the frontal lobes, which may be linked to improvements in language abilities such as reading. Chapter 9, p. 268

myelination The process by which the nerve cells are covered and insulated with a layer of fat cells, which increases the speed at which information travels through the nervous system.

Medical Center, 2012). Without treatment, most children with growth hormone deficiency will not reach a height of five feet. Twice as many boys as girls are treated with growth hormone, likely because there is a greater stigma attached to boys being short. A research review concluded that growth hormone therapy with children of short stature was partially effective in reducing their height deficit in adulthood (Deodati & Cianfarani, 2011). And one study also revealed that growth hormone treatment of children who were very short in stature was linked to an increase in height as well as improvements in self-esteem and mood (Chaplin & others, 2012).

The Brain   One of the most important physical developments during early childhood is the continuing development of the brain and nervous system (Bell & Cuevas, 2014; Markant & Thomas, 2013). Although the brain continues to grow in early childhood, it does not grow as rapidly as it did in infancy. By the time children reach 3 years of age, the brain is three-quarters of its adult size. By age 6, the brain has reached about 95 percent of its adult size (Lenroot & Giedd, 2006). Thus, the brain of a 5-year-old is nearly the size it will be when the child reaches adulthood, but as we will see in later chapters, the development that occurs inside the brain continues through the remaining years of childhood and adolescence (Raznahan & others, 2014).

Some of the brain's interior changes involve increases in dendritic connections as well as **myelination,** in which nerve cells are covered and insulated with a layer of fat cells (see Figure 7.1). Myelination has the effect of increasing the speed and efficiency of information traveling through the nervous system. Myelination is important in the development of a number of abilities during childhood (Diamond, 2013; Yates, 2014). For example, myelination in the areas of the brain related to hand-eye coordination is not complete until about 4 years of age.

Researchers also have discovered that children's brains undergo dramatic anatomical changes between the ages of 3 and 15 (Gogtay & Thompson, 2010; Steinberg, 2011, 2015a, b). By repeatedly obtaining brain scans of the same children for up to four years, they have found that children's brains experience rapid, distinct spurts of growth. The amount of brain material in some areas can nearly double within as little as a year, followed by a drastic loss of tissue as unneeded cells are purged and the brain continues to reorganize itself. The scientists have revealed that the overall size of the brain does not show dramatic growth in the 3- to 15-year age range. However, what does dramatically change are local patterns within the brain. Researchers have found that in children from 3 to 6 years of age the most rapid growth takes place in the frontal lobe areas involved in planning and organizing new actions, and in maintaining attention to tasks (Carlson, Zelazo, & Faja, 2013; Gogtay & Thompson, 2010).

MOTOR AND PERCEPTUAL DEVELOPMENT

Most preschool children are as active as they will ever be in the life span. Let's explore what this activity involves in young children's lives, as well as advances in their perceptual skills.

Gross Motor Skills   The preschool child no longer has to make an effort simply to stay upright and to move around. As children move their legs with more confidence and carry themselves more purposefully, moving around in the environment becomes more automatic (Burns & others, 2013). However, there are large individual differences in young children's gross motor skills (Ball, Bindler, & Cowan, 2014).

At 3 years of age, children enjoy simple movements, such as hopping, jumping, and running back and forth, just for the sheer delight of performing these activities. They take considerable pride in showing how they can run across a room and jump all of 6 inches. The run-and-jump will win no Olympic gold medals, but for the 3-year-old the activity is a source of considerable pride in accomplishment.

At 4 years of age, children are still enjoying the same kind of activities, but they have become more adventurous. They scramble over low jungle gyms as they display their athletic prowess.

At 5 years of age, children are even more adventuresome than when they were at 4. It is not unusual for self-assured 5-year-olds to perform hair-raising stunts on practically any climbing object. Five-year-olds run hard and enjoy races with each other and their parents.

Fine Motor Skills   At 3 years of age, although children have had the ability to pick up the tiniest objects between their thumb and forefinger for some time, they are still somewhat clumsy at it. Three-year-olds can build surprisingly high block towers, placing each block with intense concentration but often not in a completely straight line. When 3-year-olds play with a simple jigsaw puzzle, they are rather rough in placing the pieces. Even when they recognize the hole a piece fits into, they are not very precise in positioning the piece. They often try to force the piece into the hole or pat it vigorously.

By 4 years of age, children's fine motor coordination has improved substantially and become much more precise. Sometimes 4-year-old children have trouble building high towers with blocks because, in their desire to place each of the blocks perfectly, they may upset those already stacked. By age 5, children's fine motor coordination has improved further. Hand, arm, and body all move together under better command of the eye.

Perceptual Development   Changes in children's perceptual development continue in childhood (Atkinson & Braddick, 2013; Lee & others, 2013). Children become increasingly efficient at detecting the boundaries between colors (such as red and orange) at 3 to 4 years of age (Gibson, 1969). When children are about 4 or 5 years old, their eye muscles usually are developed enough that they can move their eyes efficiently across a series of letters. Many preschool children are farsighted, unable to see close up as well as they can see far away. By the time they enter the first grade, though, most children can focus their eyes and sustain their attention effectively on close-up objects.

What are the signs of vision problems in children? They include rubbing the eyes, blinking or squinting excessively, appearing irritable when playing games that require good distance vision, shutting or covering one eye, and tilting the head or thrusting it forward when looking at something. A child who shows any of these behaviors should be examined by an ophthalmologist.

After infancy, children's visual expectations about the physical world continue to develop. In one study, 2- to 4½-year-old children were given a task in which the goal was to find a ball that had been dropped through an opaque tube (Hood, 1995). As shown in Figure 7.2, if the ball is dropped into the tube at the top left, it will land in the box at the bottom right. However, in this task, most of the 2-year-olds, and even some of the 4-year-olds, persisted in searching in the box directly beneath the dropping point. For them, gravity ruled and they had failed to perceive the end location of the curved tube.

In one study 3-year-olds were presented with the same task shown in Figure 7.2 (Joh, Jaswal, & Keen, 2011). In the group that was told to imagine the various paths the ball might take, the young children were more accurate in predicting where the ball would land. In another recent study, 3-year-olds improved their performance on the ball-dropping task shown in Figure 7.2 when they were instructed to follow the tube with their eyes to the bottom (Bascandziev & Harris, 2011). Thus, in these two studies, 3-year-olds were able to overcome the gravity bias and their impulsive tendencies when they were given verbal instructions from a knowledgeable adult (Keen, 2011).

How do children learn to deal with situations like that in Figure 7.2, and how do they come to understand other laws of the physical world? These questions are addressed by studies of cognitive development, which we discuss later in this chapter.

SLEEP

Getting a good night's sleep is important for children's development (El-Sheikh & others, 2013; Lushington & others, 2014). Experts recommend that young children get 11 to 13 hours of sleep each night (National Sleep Foundation, 2014). Most young children sleep through the night and have one daytime nap. Not only do children need a certain amount of sleep, but also uninterrupted sleep (Owens & Mindell, 2011). However, it sometimes is difficult to

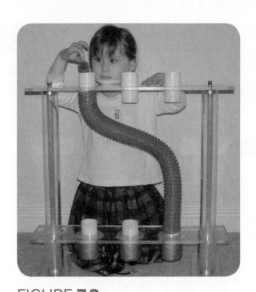

FIGURE 7.2

VISUAL EXPECTATIONS ABOUT THE PHYSICAL WORLD. When young children see the ball dropped into the tube, many of them will search for it immediately below the dropping point.

developmental **connection**

Sleep

What sleep disorder in infancy leads to the most infant deaths and at what age is the infant most at risk for this disorder? Chapter 4, p. 111

What characterizes young children's sleep problems?

get young children to go to sleep as they drag out their bedtime routine. Studies often report that young children don't get adequate sleep (Caldwell & Redeker, 2014; Palermo, 2014).

Children can experience a number of sleep problems, including narcolepsy (extreme daytime sleepiness), insomnia (difficulty getting to sleep or staying asleep), and nightmares (Ivanenko & Larson, 2014; Roane & Taylor, 2014). One estimate indicates that more than 40 percent of children experience a sleep problem at some point in their development (Boyle & Cropley, 2004). The following research studies indicate links between children's sleep problems and negative developmental outcomes:

- Sleep problems in early childhood were a subsequent indicator of attention problems that in some cases persisted into early adolescence (O'Callaghan & others, 2010).
- Preschool children who had a longer sleep duration were more likely to have better peer acceptance, social skills, and receptive vocabulary (Vaughn & others, 2014).
- Short sleep duration in children was linked with being overweight (Hart, Cairns, & Jelalian, 2011).
- Inadequate sleep duration at 4 years of age predicted inadequate sleep duration at 6 years of age (Koulouglioti & others, 2014).

To improve children's sleep, Mona El-Sheikh (2013) recommends making sure that the bedroom is cool, dark, and comfortable; maintaining consistent bed times and wake times; and building positive family relationships. Also, helping the child slow down before bedtime often contributes to less resistance in going to bed. Reading the child a story, playing quietly with the child in the bath, and letting the child sit on the caregiver's lap while listening to music are quieting activities.

NUTRITION AND EXERCISE

Eating habits are important aspects of development during early childhood (Schiff, 2015; Sorte, Daeschel, & Amador, 2014). What children eat affects their skeletal growth, body shape, and susceptibility to disease. Exercise and physical activity also are very important aspects of young children's lives (Graham, Holt/Hale, & Parker, 2013).

Overweight Young Children   Being overweight has become a serious health problem in early childhood (Cunningham, Kramer, & Narayan, 2014; Stein, 2014). A national study revealed that 45 percent of children's meals exceed recommendations for saturated and trans fats, which can raise cholesterol levels and increase the risk of heart disease (Center for Science in the Public Interest, 2008). The same study found that one-third of children's daily caloric intake comes from restaurants—twice the percentage consumed away from home in the 1980s. Further, 93 percent of almost 1,500 possible choices at 13 major fast-food chains exceeded 430 calories—one-third of what the National Institute of Medicine recommends that 4- to 8-year-old children consume in a day. Nearly all of the children's meal options at KFC, Taco Bell, Sonic, Jack in the Box, and Chick-fil-A were too high in calories. One study of U.S. 2- and 3-year-olds found that French fries and other fried potatoes were the vegetable they were most likely to consume (Fox & others, 2010).

Young children's eating behavior is strongly influenced by their caregivers' behavior (Black & Hurley, 2007; Burns & others, 2013). Young children's eating behavior improves when caregivers eat with children on a predictable schedule, model choosing nutritious food, make mealtimes pleasant occasions, and engage in certain feeding styles. Distractions from television, family arguments, and competing activities should be minimized so that children can focus on eating. A sensitive/responsive caregiver feeding style, in which the caregiver is nurturant, provides clear information about what is expected, and appropriately responds to children's cues, is recommended (Black & Lozoff, 2008). Forceful and restrictive caregiver behaviors are not recommended (Holland & others, 2014; Riesch & others, 2013).

What are some trends in the eating habits and weight of young children?

The Centers for Disease Control and Prevention (2014) has established categories for obesity, overweight, and at risk for being overweight. These categories are determined by body mass index (BMI), which is computed using a formula that takes into account height and weight. Only children and adolescents at or above the 97th percentile are classified as obese; those at the 95th or 96th percentile as overweight; and those from the 85th to the 94th percentile as at risk of being overweight.

The percentages of young children who are overweight or at risk of being overweight in the United States have increased dramatically in recent decades, but in the last several years there are indications that fewer preschool children are obese (Wardlaw, Smith, & Collene, 2015). In 2009–2010, 12.1 percent of U.S. 2- to 5-year-olds were classified as obese, compared with 5 percent in 1976–1980 and 10.4 percent in 2007–2008 (Ogden & others, 2012). However, in 2011–2012, a substantial drop (43 percent) in the obesity rate of 2- to 5-year-old children occurred in comparison with their counterparts in 2003–2004 (Ogden & others, 2014). In 2011–2012, 8 percent of 2- to 5-year-olds were obese compared with 14 percent in 2004. It is not clear precisely why this drop occurred, but among the possibilities are families buying lower-calorie foods and the Special Supplementation Program for Women, Infants, and Children (which subsidizes food for women in low-income families) emphasizing reduced consumption of fruit juice, cheese, and eggs and increased consumption of whole fruits and vegetables.

The risk that overweight children will continue to be overweight when they are older was documented in a recent U.S. study of nearly 8,000 children (Cunningham & others, 2014). In this study, overweight 5-year-olds were four times more likely to be obese at 14 years of age than their 5-year-old counterparts who began kindergarten at a normal weight. Also, in the recent study described earlier in which obesity rates were decreasing among preschool children, preschool children who were obese were five times more likely to be overweight or obese as adults (Ogden & others, 2014).

One comparison of 34 countries revealed that the United States had the second highest rate of child obesity (Janssen & others, 2005). Childhood obesity contributes to a number of health problems in young children (Anspaugh & Ezell, 2013). For example, physicians are now seeing type 2 (adult-onset) diabetes (a condition directly linked with obesity and a low level of fitness) and hypertension in children as young as 5 years of age (Chaturvedi & others, 2014; Riley & Bluhm, 2012).

Prevention of obesity in children includes helping children and parents see food as a way to satisfy hunger and meet nutritional needs, not as proof of love or as a reward for good behavior. Snack foods should be low in fat, in simple sugars, and in salt, as well as high in fiber. Routine physical activity should be a daily occurrence (Espana-Romero & others, 2013; Wuest & Fisette, 2015). A recent research review concluded that a higher level of screen time (watching TV, using a computer) at 4 to 6 years of age was linked to a lower activity level and being overweight from preschool through adolescence (te Velde & others, 2012). A recent intervention study with children attending Head Start programs found that getting parents involved in such activities as nutrition counseling, becoming more aware of their child's weight status, and developing healthy life styles was effective in lowering children's rate of obesity, increasing children's physical activity, reducing children's TV viewing, and improving children's eating habits (Davison & others, 2013). Other researchers also are finding that interventions with parents can reduce children's likelihood of being overweight or obese (Holland & others, 2014; Rauner, Mess, & Woll, 2013). A recent research review concluded that family-based interventions were often effective in helping obese children lose weight (Kothandan, 2014). We will have much more to consider about children's eating behavior and weight status in Chapter 9.

Malnutrition in Young Children from Low-Income Families

Malnutrition is a problem for many U.S. children, with approximately 11 million preschool children experiencing malnutrition that places their health at risk. Poverty is an especially strong risk factor for malnutrition in young children (Black & others, 2013). One of the most common nutritional problems in early childhood is iron deficiency anemia, which results in chronic fatigue. This problem results from the failure to eat adequate amounts of quality meats and dark green vegetables. Young children from low-income families are the most likely to develop iron deficiency anemia (Shamah & Villalpando, 2006).

How much physical activity should preschool children engage in per day?

---- ➤

developmental **connection**

Health

As boys and girls reach and progress through adolescence, they exercise less. Chapter 11, p. 351

Exercise Routine physical activity should be a daily occurrence for young children (Lumpkin, 2014; Wuest & Fisette, 2015). Guidelines recommend that preschool children engage in two hours of physical activity per day, consisting of one hour of structured activity and one hour of unstructured free play (National Association for Sport and Physical Education, 2002). The child's life should center around activities, not meals (Graber & Woods, 2013). Following are some recent research studies that examine young children's exercise and activities:

- In preschoolers, more time spent in vigorous physical activity was strongly linked to lower probability of being overweight or obese (Collings & others, 2013).

  - A recent research review of 17 studies concluded that exercise was an effective strategy for reducing body fat in overweight and obese children (Kelley & Kelley, 2014).

  - Observations of 3- to 5-year-old children during outdoor play at preschools revealed that the preschool children were mainly sedentary even when participating in outdoor play (Brown & others, 2009). In this study, throughout the day the preschoolers were sedentary 89 percent of the time, engaged in light activity 8 percent of the time, and participated in moderate to vigorous physical activity only 3 percent of the time.

  - Preschool children's physical activity was enhanced by family members engaging in sports together and by parents' perception that it was safe for their children to play outside (Beets & Foley, 2008).

  - Incorporation of a "move and learn" physical activity curriculum increased the activity level of 3- to 5-year-old children in a half-day preschool program (Trost, Fees, & Dzewaltowski, 2008).

ILLNESS AND DEATH

What are the greatest risks to the health of young children in the United States? How pervasive is death among young children around the world?

The United States Young children's active and exploratory nature, coupled with their unawareness of danger in many instances, often puts them in situations in which they are at risk for injuries. In the United States, motor vehicle accidents are the leading cause of death in young children, followed by cancer and cardiovascular disease (National Vital Statistics Report, 2004) (see Figure 7.3). In addition to motor vehicle accidents, other causes of

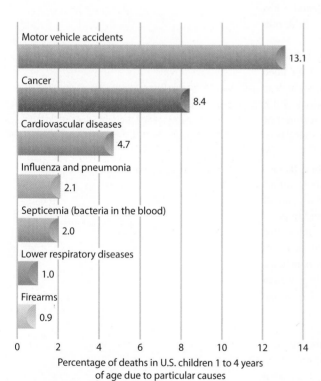

FIGURE 7.3

MAIN CAUSES OF DEATH IN CHILDREN 1 THROUGH 4 YEARS OF AGE. These figures show the percentage of deaths in U.S. children 1 to 4 years of age due to particular causes in 2002 (National Vital Statistics Reports, 2004).

accidental death in children include drowning, falls, burns, and poisoning (Theurer & Bhavsar, 2013; Zielinski, Rochette, & Smith, 2012).

Children's Safety Children's safety is influenced not only by their own skills and safety behaviors but also by characteristics of their family and home, school and peers, and the community's actions (Sorte, Daeschel, & Amador, 2014). Figure 7.4 describes steps that can be taken in each of these contexts to enhance children's safety and prevent injury (Sleet & Mercy, 2003). Children in poverty have higher rates of accidents, death, and asthma than children from higher-income families (Doob, 2013; Green, Muir, & Maher, 2011).

Environmental Tobacco Smoke Estimates indicate that approximately 22 percent of children and adolescents in the United States are exposed to tobacco smoke in the home. An increasing number of studies reach the conclusion that children are at risk for health problems when they live in homes in which a parent smokes (Carlsson & others, 2013; Jarosinska & others, 2014). Children exposed to tobacco smoke in the home are more likely to develop wheezing symptoms and asthma than children in nonsmoking families (Gonzales-Barcala & others, 2013; Hur, Liang, & Lin, 2014). One study found that parental smoking was a risk factor for higher blood pressure in children (Simonetti & others, 2011). And a recent study revealed that maternal cigarette smoking and alcohol consumption when children were 5 years of age were linked to onset of smoking in early adolescence (Hayatbakhsh & others, 2013). Further, a recent study revealed that children living in low-income families are more likely to be exposed to environmental tobacco smoke than their counterparts in middle-income families (Kit & others, 2013).

The State of Illness and Health of the World's Children

Devastating effects on the health of young children occur in countries where poverty rates are high (UNICEF, 2014). The poor are the majority in nearly one of every five nations in the world. They often experience hunger, malnutrition, illness, inadequate access to health care, unsafe water, and a lack of protection from harm (Gaiha & others, 2012).

In the last decade, there has been a dramatic increase in the number of young children who have died because HIV/AIDS was transmitted to them by their parents (UNICEF, 2014). Deaths of young children due to HIV/AIDS especially occur in countries with high rates of poverty and low levels of education (Toure & others, 2012).

Many of the deaths of young children around the world could be prevented by reductions in poverty and improvements in nutrition, sanitation, education, and health services (UNICEF, 2014).

Individual

Development of social skills and ability to regulate emotions

Impulse control (such as not darting out into a street to retrieve a ball)

Frequent use of personal protection (such as bike helmets and safety seats)

Family/Home

High awareness and knowledge of child management and parenting skills

Frequent parent protective behaviors (such as use of child safety seats)

Presence of home safety equipment (such as smoke alarms and cabinet locks)

School/Peers

Promotion of home/school partnerships

Absence of playground hazards

Injury prevention and safety promotion policies and programs

Community

Availability of positive activities for children and their parents

Active surveillance of environmental hazards

Effective prevention policies in place (such as pool fencing)

FIGURE 7.4

CHARACTERISTICS THAT ENHANCE YOUNG CHILDREN'S SAFETY. In each context of a child's life, steps can be taken to create conditions that enhance the child's safety and reduce the likelihood of injury. *How are the contexts listed in the figure related to Bronfenbrenner's theory (described in Chapter 1)?*

Many children in impoverished countries die before reaching the age of 5 from dehydration and malnutrition brought about by diarrhea. *What are some of the other main causes of death in young children around the world?*

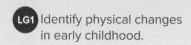

Review *Connect* Reflect

LG1 Identify physical changes in early childhood.

Review

- How does the body grow and change during early childhood?
- What changes take place in motor and perceptual development during early childhood?
- What are some problems associated with sleep in young children?
- What roles do nutrition and exercise play in early childhood?
- What are some major causes of illness and death among young children in the United States and around the world?

Connect

- In this section you learned that experts recommend that children get 11 to 13 hours of sleep a night during early childhood. How does that compare with what you learned about the sleep patterns of infants in Chapter 4?

Reflect *Your Own Personal Journey of Life*

- What were your eating habits like as a young child? In what ways are they similar or different from your current eating habits? Did your early eating habits predict whether or not you have weight problems today?

---

2 Cognitive Changes

LG2 Describe three views of the cognitive changes that occur in early childhood.

| Piaget's Preoperational Stage | Vygotsky's Theory | Information Processing |

The cognitive world of the preschool child is creative, free, and fanciful. Preschool children's imaginations work overtime, and their mental grasp of the world improves. Our coverage of cognitive development in early childhood focuses on three theories: Piaget's, Vygotsky's, and information processing.

PIAGET'S PREOPERATIONAL STAGE

developmental **connection**

Cognitive Theory

Object permanence is an important accomplishment in the sensorimotor stage. Chapter 5, p. 140

preoperational stage Piaget's second stage, lasting from about 2 to 7 years of age, during which children begin to represent the world with words, images, and drawings, and symbolic thought goes beyond simple connections of sensory information and physical action; stable concepts are formed, mental reasoning emerges, egocentrism is present, and magical beliefs are constructed.

operations In Piaget's theory, these are reversible mental actions that allow children to do mentally what they formerly did physically.

symbolic function substage Piaget's first substage of preoperational thought, in which the child gains the ability to mentally represent an object that is not present (between about 2 and 4 years of age).

Remember from Chapter 5 that, during Piaget's first stage of development, the sensorimotor stage, the infant progresses in the ability to organize and coordinate sensations and perceptions with physical movements and actions. The **preoperational stage,** which lasts from approximately 2 to 7 years of age, is the second Piagetian stage. In this stage, children begin to represent the world with words, images, and drawings. They form stable concepts and begin to reason. At the same time, the young child's cognitive world is dominated by egocentrism and magical beliefs.

Because Piaget called this stage "preoperational," it might sound like an unimportant waiting period. Not so. Instead, the label *preoperational* emphasizes that the child does not yet perform **operations,** which are reversible mental actions that allow children to do mentally what before they could do only physically. Adding and subtracting numbers mentally are examples of operations. *Preoperational thought* is the beginning of the ability to reconstruct in thought what has been established in behavior. This developmental stage can be divided into two substages: the symbolic function substage and the intuitive thought substage.

The Symbolic Function Substage The **symbolic function substage** is the first substage of preoperational thought, occurring roughly between the ages of 2 and 4. During this substage, the young child gains the ability to mentally represent an object that is not present. This ability vastly expands the child's mental world (Mandler & DeLoache, 2012). Young children use scribble designs to represent people, houses, cars, clouds, and so on; they begin to use language and engage in pretend play. However, although young children make distinct progress during this substage, their thought still has important limitations, two of which are egocentrism and animism.

Model of Mountains

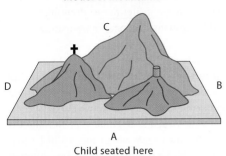

Photo 1
(View from A)

Photo 2
(View from B)

Photo 3
(View from C)

Photo 4
(View from D)

FIGURE 7.5

THE THREE MOUNTAINS TASK. View 1 shows the child's perspective from where he or she is sitting. View 2 is an example of one of the photographs the child would be shown, along with other photographs taken from different perspectives. It shows what the mountains look like to a person sitting at spot B. When asked what a view of the mountains looks like from position B, the preoperational child selects a photograph taken from location A, the child's view at the time. A child who thinks in a preoperational way cannot take the perspective of a person sitting at another spot.

Egocentrism is the inability to distinguish between one's own perspective and someone else's perspective. Piaget and Barbel Inhelder (1969) initially studied young children's egocentrism by devising the three mountains task (see Figure 7.5). The child walks around the model of the mountains and becomes familiar with what the mountains look like from different perspectives, and she can see that there are different objects on the mountains. The child is then seated on one side of the table on which the mountains are placed. The experimenter moves a doll to different locations around the table, at each location asking the child to select from a series of photos the one photo that most accurately reflects the view that the doll is seeing. Children in the preoperational stage often pick their own view rather than the doll's view. Preschool children frequently show the ability to take another's perspective on some tasks but not others.

Animism, another limitation of preoperational thought, is the belief that inanimate objects have lifelike qualities and are capable of action. A young child might show animism by saying, "That tree pushed the leaf off, and it fell down," or "The sidewalk made me mad; it made me fall down." A young child who uses animism fails to distinguish the appropriate occasions for using human and nonhuman perspectives (Opfer & Gelman, 2011).

Possibly because young children are not very concerned about reality, their drawings are fanciful and inventive. Suns are blue, skies are yellow, and cars float on clouds in their symbolic, imaginative world. One 3½-year-old looked at a scribble he had just drawn and described it as a pelican kissing a seal (see Figure 7.6a). The symbolism is simple but strong,

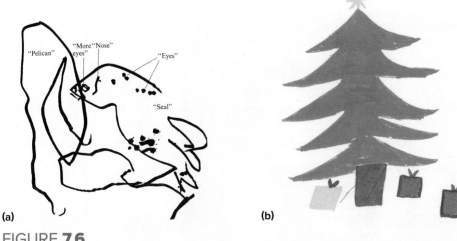

(a)

(b)

FIGURE 7.6

THE SYMBOLIC DRAWINGS OF YOUNG CHILDREN. (*a*) A 3½-year-old's symbolic drawing. Halfway into his drawing, the 3½-year-old artist said it was a "pelican kissing a seal." (*b*) This 11-year-old's drawing is neater and more realistic but also less inventive.

egocentrism The inability to distinguish between one's own perspective and someone else's (salient feature of the first substage of preoperational thought).

animism The belief that inanimate objects have lifelike qualities and are capable of action.

intuitive thought substage Piaget's second substage of preoperational thought, in which children begin to use primitive reasoning and want to know the answers to all sorts of questions (between 4 and 7 years of age).

centration Focusing attention on one characteristic to the exclusion of all others.

conservation In Piaget's theory, awareness that altering an object's or a substance's appearance does not change its basic properties.

"I still don't have all the answers, but I'm beginning to ask the right questions."
© Lee Lorenz/The New Yorker Collection/ www.cartoon.bank.

like abstractions found in some modern art. Twentieth-century Spanish artist Pablo Picasso commented, "I used to draw like Raphael but it has taken me a lifetime to draw like young children." During the elementary school years, a child's drawings become more realistic, neat, and precise (see Figure 7.6b) (Winner, 1986).

The Intuitive Thought Substage   The **intuitive thought substage** is the second substage of preoperational thought, occurring between approximately 4 and 7 years of age. In this substage, children begin to use primitive reasoning and want to know the answers to all sorts of questions. Consider 4-year-old Tommy, who is at the beginning of the intuitive thought substage. Although he is starting to develop his own ideas about the world he lives in, his ideas are still simple, and he is not very good at thinking things out. He has difficulty understanding events that he knows are taking place but that he cannot see. His fantasized thoughts bear little resemblance to reality. He cannot yet answer the question "What if?" in any reliable way. For example, he has only a vague idea of what would happen if a car were to hit him. He also has difficulty negotiating traffic because he cannot do the mental calculations necessary to estimate whether an approaching car will hit him when he crosses the road.

By the age of 5, children have just about exhausted the adults around them with "why" questions. The child's questions signal the emergence of interest in reasoning and in figuring out why things are the way they are. Following are some samples of the questions children ask during the questioning period of 4 to 6 years of age (Elkind, 1976): "What makes you grow up?" "Who was the mother when everybody was a baby?" "Why do leaves fall?" "Why does the sun shine?" Piaget called this substage intuitive because young children seem so sure about their knowledge and understanding yet are unaware of how they know what they know. That is, they know something but know it without the use of rational thinking.

Centration and the Limits of Preoperational Thought   One limitation of preoperational thought is **centration,** a centering of attention on one characteristic to the exclusion of all others. Centration is most clearly evidenced in young children's lack of **conservation,** the awareness that altering an object's or a substance's appearance does not change its basic properties. For example, to adults, it is obvious that a certain amount of liquid stays the same, regardless of a container's shape. But this is not at all obvious to young children. Instead, they are struck by the height of the liquid in the container; they focus on that characteristic to the exclusion of others.

The situation that Piaget devised to study conservation is his most famous task. In the conservation task, children are presented with two identical beakers, each filled to the same level with liquid (see Figure 7.7). They are asked if these beakers have the same amount of liquid, and they usually say yes. Then the liquid from one beaker is poured into a third beaker,

FIGURE **7.7**

PIAGET'S CONSERVATION TASK. The beaker test is a well-known Piagetian test to determine whether a child can think operationally—that is, can mentally reverse actions and show conservation of the substance. (*a*) Two identical beakers are presented to the child. Then the experimenter pours the liquid from B into C, which is taller and thinner than A or B. (*b*) The child is asked if these beakers (A and C) have the same amount of liquid. The preoperational child says "no." When asked to point to the beaker that has more liquid, the preoperational child points to the tall, thin beaker.

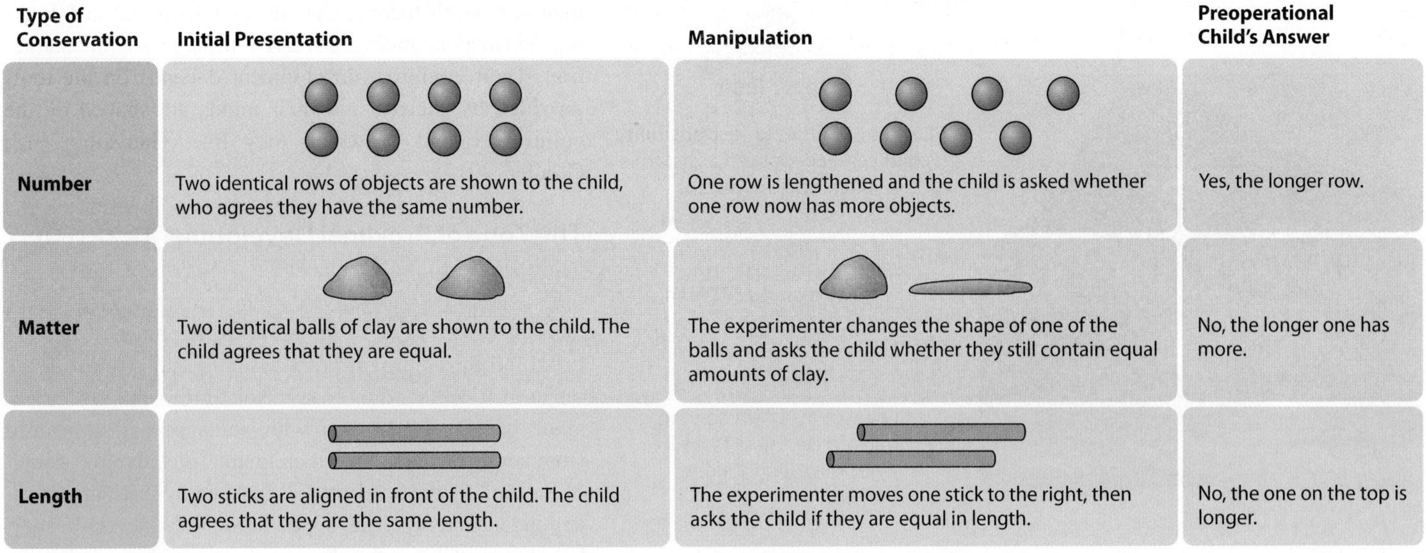

Type of Conservation	Initial Presentation	Manipulation	Preoperational Child's Answer
Number	Two identical rows of objects are shown to the child, who agrees they have the same number.	One row is lengthened and the child is asked whether one row now has more objects.	Yes, the longer row.
Matter	Two identical balls of clay are shown to the child. The child agrees that they are equal.	The experimenter changes the shape of one of the balls and asks the child whether they still contain equal amounts of clay.	No, the longer one has more.
Length	Two sticks are aligned in front of the child. The child agrees that they are the same length.	The experimenter moves one stick to the right, then asks the child if they are equal in length.	No, the one on the top is longer.

FIGURE 7.8

SOME DIMENSIONS OF CONSERVATION: NUMBER, MATTER, AND LENGTH. *What characteristics of preoperational thought do children demonstrate when they fail these conservation tasks?*

which is taller and thinner than the first two. The children are then asked if the amount of liquid in the tall, thin beaker is equal to that which remains in one of the original beakers. Children who are less than 7 or 8 years old usually say no and justify their answers in terms of the differing height or width of the beakers. Older children usually answer yes and justify their answers appropriately ("If you poured the water back, the amount would still be the same").

In Piaget's theory, failing the conservation-of-liquid task is a sign that children are at the preoperational stage of cognitive development. The failure demonstrates not only centration but also an inability to mentally reverse actions. For example, in the conservation of matter example shown in Figure 7.8, preoperational children say that the longer shape has more clay because they assume that "longer is more." Preoperational children cannot mentally reverse the clay-rolling process to see that the amount of clay is the same in both the shorter ball shape and the longer stick shape.

In addition to failing to conserve volume, preoperational children also fail to conserve number, matter, length, and area. However, children often vary in their performance on different conservation tasks. Thus, a child might be able to conserve volume but not number. A recent fMRI brain-imaging study of conservation of number revealed that advances in a network in the parietal and frontal lobes were linked to 9- and 10-year-olds' conservation success in comparison with non-conserving 5- and 6-year-olds (Houde & others, 2011).

Some developmentalists disagree with Piaget's estimate of when children's conservation skills emerge. For example, Rochel Gelman (1969) showed that when the child's attention to relevant aspects of the conservation task is improved, the child is more likely to conserve. Gelman has also demonstrated that attentional training on one dimension, such as number, improves the preschool child's performance on another dimension, such as mass. Thus, Gelman argues that conservation appears earlier than Piaget thought and that attention is especially important in explaining conservation.

VYGOTSKY'S THEORY

Piaget's theory is a major developmental theory. Another developmental theory that focuses on children's cognition is Vygotsky's theory. Like Piaget, Vygotsky (1962) emphasized that children actively construct their knowledge and understanding. In Piaget's theory, children develop ways of thinking and understanding by their actions and interactions with the physical world. In Vygotsky's theory, children are more often described as social creatures

FIGURE **7.9**

VYGOTSKY'S ZONE OF PROXIMAL DEVELOPMENT. Vygotsky's zone of proximal development has a lower limit and an upper limit. Tasks in the ZPD are too difficult for the child to perform alone. They require assistance from an adult or a more-skilled child. As children experience the verbal instruction or demonstration, they organize the information in their existing mental structures so that they can eventually perform the skill or task alone.

developmental **connection**

Parenting

Scaffolding also is an effective strategy for parents to adopt in interacting with their infants. Chapter 6, p. 187

Upper limit

Level of additional responsibility child can accept with assistance of an able instructor

Zone of proximal development (ZPD)

Lower limit

Level of problem solving reached on these tasks by child working alone

than in Piaget's theory. They develop their ways of thinking and understanding primarily through social interaction. Their cognitive development depends on the tools provided by society, and their minds are shaped by the cultural context in which they live (Gauvain, 2013; Gredler, 2012).

The Zone of Proximal Development   Vygotsky's belief in the role of social influences, especially instruction, in children's cognitive development is reflected in his concept of the zone of proximal development. **Zone of proximal development (ZPD)** is Vygotsky's term for the range of tasks that are too difficult for the child to master alone but can be learned with guidance and assistance from adults or more-skilled children. Thus, the lower limit of the ZPD is the level of skill reached by the child working independently. The upper limit is the level of additional responsibility the child can accept with the assistance of an able instructor (see Figure 7.9). The ZPD captures the child's cognitive skills that are in the process of maturing and can be accomplished only with the assistance of a more-skilled person (Mahn & John-Steiner, 2013; Petrick-Steward, 2012). Vygotsky (1962) called these the "buds" or "flowers" of development, to distinguish them from the "fruits" of development, which the child already can accomplish independently.

What are some factors that can influence the effectiveness of the ZPD in children's learning and development? Researchers have found that the following factors can enhance the ZPD's effectiveness (Gauvain, 2013): better emotion regulation, secure attachment, absence of maternal depression, and child compliance.

Scaffolding   Closely linked to the idea of the ZPD is the concept of scaffolding. *Scaffolding* means changing the level of support. Over the course of a teaching session, a more-skilled person (a teacher or advanced peer) adjusts the amount of guidance to fit the child's current performance (Daniels, 2011). When the student is learning a new task, the skilled person may use direct instruction. As the student's competence increases, less guidance is given. As the student's competence increases, the person gives less guidance. A recent study found that scaffolding techniques that heighten engagement, direct exploration, and facilitate "sense-making," such as guided play, improved 4- to 5-year-old children's acquisition of geometric knowledge (Fisher & others, 2013).

Language and Thought   The use of dialogue as a tool for scaffolding is only one example of the important role of language in a child's development. According to Vygotsky, children use speech not only to communicate socially but also to help them solve tasks. Vygotsky (1962) further believed that young children use language to plan, guide, and monitor their behavior. This use of language for self-regulation is called *private speech*. For Piaget, private speech is egocentric and immature, but for Vygotsky it is an important tool of thought during the early childhood years (John-Steiner, 2007).

Vygotsky said that language and thought initially develop independently of each other and then merge. He emphasized that all mental functions have external, or social, origins. Children must use language to communicate with others before they can focus inward on their own thoughts. Children also must communicate externally and use language for a long period of time before they can make the transition from external to internal speech. This transition period occurs between 3 and 7 years of age and involves talking to oneself. After a while, the self-talk becomes second nature to children, and

zone of proximal development (ZPD) Vygotsky's term for tasks that are too difficult for children to master alone but can be mastered with the assistance of adults or more-skilled children.

they can act without verbalizing. When they gain this skill, children have internalized their egocentric speech in the form of *inner speech,* which becomes their thoughts.

Vygotsky reasoned that children who use a lot of private speech are more socially competent than those who don't. He argued that private speech represents an early transition in becoming more socially communicative. In Vygotsky's view, when young children talk to themselves they are using language to govern their behavior and guide themselves. For example, a child working on a puzzle might say to herself, "Which pieces should I put together first? I'll try those green ones first. Now I need some blue ones. No, that blue one doesn't fit there. I'll try it over here."

Piaget maintained that self-talk is egocentric and reflects immaturity. However, researchers have found support for Vygotsky's view that private speech plays a positive role in children's development (Winsler, Carlton, & Barry, 2000). Researchers have found that children use private speech more often when tasks are difficult, after they have made errors, and when they are not sure how to proceed (Berk, 1994). They also have revealed that children who use private speech are more attentive and improve their performance more than children who do not use private speech (Berk & Spuhl, 1995).

Lev Vygotsky (1896–1934), shown here with his daughter, reasoned that children's cognitive development is advanced through social interaction with more-skilled individuals embedded in a sociocultural backdrop. *How is Vygotsky's theory different from Piaget's?*

Teaching Strategies Vygotsky's theory has been embraced by many teachers and has been successfully applied to education (Costley, 2012; Gauvain, 2013). Here are some ways Vygotsky's theory can be incorporated in classrooms:

1. *Assess the child's ZPD.* Like Piaget, Vygotsky did not recommend formal, standardized tests as the best way to assess children's learning. Rather, Vygotsky argued that assessment should focus on determining the child's zone of proximal development. The skilled helper presents the child with tasks of varying difficulty to determine the best level at which to begin instruction.

2. *Use the child's ZPD in teaching.* Teaching should begin toward the zone's upper limit, so that the child can reach the goal with help and move to a higher level of skill and knowledge. Offer just enough assistance. You might ask, "What can I do to help you?" Or simply observe the child's intentions and attempts and provide support when it is needed. When the child hesitates, offer encouragement. And encourage the child to practice the skill. You may watch and appreciate the child's practice or offer support when the child forgets what to do.

3. *Use more-skilled peers as teachers.* Remember that it is not just adults who are important in helping children learn. Children also benefit from the support and guidance of more-skilled children.

4. *Place instruction in a meaningful context.* Educators today are moving away from abstract presentations of material; instead, they provide students with opportunities to experience learning in real-world settings. For example, rather than just memorizing math formulas, students work on math problems with real-world implications.

5. *Transform the classroom with Vygotskian ideas.* What does a Vygotskian classroom look like? The Kamehameha Elementary Education Program (KEEP) in Hawaii is based on Vygotsky's theory (Tharp, 1994). The ZPD is the key element of instruction in this program. Children might read a story and then interpret its meaning. Many of the learning activities take place in small groups. All children spend at least 20 minutes each morning in a setting called "Center One." In this context, scaffolding is used to improve children's literary skills. The instructor asks questions, responds to students' queries, and builds on the ideas that students generate.

Connecting Development to Life further explores the implications of Vygotsky's theory for children's education.

Tools of the Mind

Tools of the Mind is an early childhood education curriculum that emphasizes children's development of self-regulation and the cognitive foundations of literacy. The curriculum was created by Elena Bodrova and Deborah Leong (2007) and has been implemented in more than 200 classrooms. Most of the children in the Tools of the Mind programs are at risk because of their living circumstances, which in many instances involve poverty and other difficult conditions such as being homeless and having parents with drug problems.

Tools of the Mind is grounded in Vygotsky's (1962) theory with special attention given to cultural tools, development of self-regulation, use of the zone of proximal development, scaffolding, private speech, shared activity, and play as important activity. In a Tools of the Mind classroom, dramatic play has a central role. Teachers guide children in creating themes that are based on the children's interests, such as treasure hunt, store, hospital, and restaurant. Teachers also incorporate field trips, visitor presentations, videos, and books in the development of children's play. They help children develop a play plan, which increases the maturity of their play. Play plans describe what the children expect to do in the play period, including the imaginary context, roles, and props to be used. The play plans increase the quality of their play and self-regulation.

Scaffolding writing is another important theme in the Tools of the Mind classroom. Teachers guide children in planning their own message by drawing a line to stand for each word the child says. Children then repeat the message, pointing to each line as they say the word. Then, the child writes on the lines, trying to represent each word with some letters or symbols. Figure 7.10 shows how the scaffolding writing process improved a 5-year-old child's writing over the course of two months.

Research assessments of children's writing in Tools of the Mind classrooms revealed that they have more advanced writing skills than children in other early childhood programs (Bodrova & Leong, 2007) (see Figure 7.10). For example, they write more complex messages, use more words, spell more accurately, show better letter recognition, and have a better understanding of the concept of a sentence.

One study assessed the effects of the Tools of the Mind curriculum on at-risk preschool children (Diamond & others, 2007). The results indicated that the Tools of the Mind curriculum improved the self-regulatory and cognitive control skills (such as resisting distractions and temptations) of the at-risk children. Other research on the Tools of the Mind curriculum also has found that it improves young children's cognitive skills (Barnett & others, 2006; Bodrova, Leong, & Akhutina, 2011; Saifer, 2007).

How does the Reggio Emilia approach to education that you read about in the story that opened this chapter compare with the Tools of the Mind approach described here?

(a) Five-year-old Aaron's independent journal writing prior to using the scaffolded writing technique.

(b) Aaron's journal two months after using the scaffolded writing technique.

FIGURE **7.10**

WRITING PROGRESS OF A 5-YEAR-OLD BOY OVER TWO MONTHS USING THE SCAFFOLDING WRITING PROCESS IN TOOLS OF THE MIND. (a) Five-year-old Aaron's independent journal writing prior to using the scaffolded writing technique. (b) Aaron's journal two months after beginning to use the scaffolded writing technique.

	Vygotsky		Piaget
Sociocultural Context	Strong emphasis		Little emphasis
Constructivism	Social constructivist		Cognitive constructivist
Stages	No general stages of development proposed		Strong emphasis on stages (sensorimotor, preoperational, concrete operational, and formal operational)
Key Processes	Zone of proximal development, language, dialogue, tools of the culture		Schema, assimilation, accommodation, operations, conservation, classification
Role of Language	A major role; language plays a powerful role in shaping thought		Language has a minimal role; cognition primarily directs language
View on Education	Education plays a central role, helping children learn the tools of the culture		Education merely refines the child's cognitive skills that have already emerged
Teaching Implications	Teacher is a facilitator and guide, not a director; establish many opportunities for children to learn with the teacher and more-skilled peers		Also views teacher as a facilitator and guide, not a director; provide support for children to explore their world and discover knowledge

FIGURE 7.11
COMPARISON OF VYGOTSKY'S AND PIAGET'S THEORIES

Evaluating Vygotsky's Theory   Even though their theories were proposed at about the same time, most of the world learned about Vygotsky's theory later than they learned about Piaget's theory. Thus, Vygotsky's theory has not yet been evaluated as thoroughly. However, Vygotsky's view of the importance of sociocultural influences on children's development fits with the current belief that it is important to evaluate the contextual factors in learning (Gauvain, 2013; Gredler, 2012).

We already have compared several aspects of Vygotsky's and Piaget's theories, such as Vygotsky's emphasis on the importance of inner speech in development and Piaget's view that such speech is immature. Although both theories are constructivist, Vygotsky's theory takes a **social constructivist approach,** which emphasizes the social contexts of learning and the construction of knowledge through social interaction (O'Donnell, 2011).

In moving from Piaget to Vygotsky, the conceptual shift is one from the individual to collaboration, social interaction, and sociocultural activity (Gauvain, 2013). The endpoint of cognitive development for Piaget is formal operational thought. For Vygotsky, the endpoint can differ depending on which skills are considered to be the most important in a particular culture. In Piaget's theory, children construct knowledge by transforming, organizing, and reorganizing previous knowledge. From Vygotsky's perspective, children construct knowledge through social interaction (Costley, 2012; Gauvain, 2013). The implication of Piaget's theory for teaching is that children need support to explore their world and discover knowledge. The main implication of Vygotsky's theory for teaching is that students need many opportunities to learn with the teacher and more-skilled peers. In both Piaget's and Vygotsky's theories, teachers serve as facilitators and guides, rather than as directors and molders of learning. Figure 7.11 compares Vygotsky's and Piaget's theories.

Criticisms of Vygotsky's theory also have surfaced. Some critics point out that Vygotsky was not specific enough about age-related changes. Another criticism is that Vygotsky did not adequately describe how changes in socioemotional capabilities contribute to cognitive development (Gauvain, 2008). Yet another criticism is that he overemphasized the role of language in thinking. Also, his emphasis on collaboration and guidance has potential pitfalls. Might facilitators be too helpful in some cases, as when a parent becomes too overbearing and controlling? Further, some children might become lazy and expect help when they might have done something on their own.

social constructivist approach An approach that emphasizes the social contexts of learning and asserts that knowledge is mutually built and constructed. Vygotsky's theory reflects this approach.

INFORMATION PROCESSING

Piaget's and Vygotsky's theories provided important ideas about how young children think and how their thinking changes. More recently, the information-processing approach has generated research that illuminates how children process information during the preschool years (Bjorklund, 2013; Feldman, 2013). What are the limitations and advances in young children's ability to pay attention to the environment, to remember, to develop strategies and solve problems, and to understand their own mental processes and those of others?

What are some advances in children's attention in early childhood?

Attention   Recall from Chapter 6, "Cognitive Development in Infancy," that *attention* was defined as the focusing of mental resources on select information. The child's ability to pay attention improves significantly during the preschool years (Bell & Cuevas, 2013; Rueda & Posner, 2013). Toddlers wander around, shift attention from one activity to another, and seem to spend little time focusing on any one object or event. By comparison, the preschool child might be observed watching television for a half hour or longer. A recent research study revealed that watching television and playing video games were both linked to attention problems in children (Swing & others, 2010).

Young children especially make advances in two aspects of attention—executive attention and sustained attention (Bell & Cuevas, 2013; Rothbart, 2011). **Executive attention** involves action planning, allocating attention to goals, error detection and compensation, monitoring progress on tasks, and dealing with novel or difficult circumstances. **Sustained attention** is focused and extended engagement with an object, task, event, or other aspect of the environment. Sustained attention also is called *vigilance*. Research indicates that although older children and adolescents show increases in vigilance, it is during the preschool years that individuals show the greatest increase in vigilance (Rueda & Posner, 2013).

Mary Rothbart and Maria Gartstein (2008, p. 332) explained why advances in executive and sustained attention are so important in early childhood:

> The development of the . . . executive attention system supports the rapid increases in effortful control in the toddler and preschool years. Increases in attention are due, in part, to advances in comprehension and language development. As children are better able to understand their environment, this increased appreciation of their surroundings helps them to sustain attention for longer periods of time.

In at least two ways, however, the preschool child's control of attention is still deficient:

- *Salient versus relevant dimensions.* Preschool children are likely to pay attention to stimuli that stand out, or are *salient,* even when those stimuli are not relevant to solving a problem or performing a task. For example, if a flashy, attractive clown presents the directions for solving a problem, preschool children are likely to pay more attention to the clown than to the directions. After the age of 6 or 7, children attend more efficiently to the dimensions of the task that are relevant, such as the directions for solving a problem. This change reflects a shift to cognitive control of attention, so that children behave less impulsively and reflect more.

- *Planfulness.* When experimenters ask children to judge whether two complex pictures are the same, preschool children tend to use a haphazard comparison strategy, not examining all of the details before making a judgment. By comparison, elementary-school-age children are more likely to systematically compare the details across the pictures, one detail at a time (Vurpillot, 1968) (see Figure 7.12).

In Central European countries such as Hungary, kindergarten children participate in exercises designed to improve their attention (Mills & Mills, 2000; Posner & Rothbart, 2007). For example, in one eye-contact exercise, the teacher sits in the center of a circle of children and each child is required to catch the teacher's eye before being permitted to leave the group. In other exercises created to improve attention, teachers have children participate in stop-go activities during which they have to listen for a specific signal, such as a drumbeat or an exact number of rhythmic beats, before stopping the activity.

Computer exercises recently have been developed to improve children's attention (Jaeggi, Berman, & Jonides, 2009; Rueda & Posner, 2013; Stevens & Bavelier, 2012; Tang & Posner,

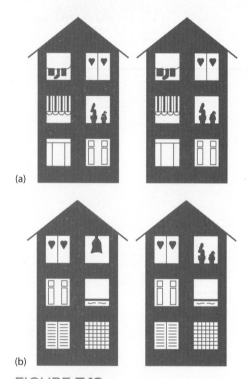

(a)

(b)

FIGURE 7.12

THE PLANFULNESS OF ATTENTION. In one study, children were given pairs of houses to examine, like the ones shown here (Vurpillot, 1968). For three pairs of houses, what was in the windows was identical (*a*). For the other three pairs, the windows had different items in them (*b*). By filming the reflection in the children's eyes, it could be determined what they were looking at, how long they looked, and the sequence of their eye movements. Children under 6 examined only a fragmentary portion of each display and made their judgments on the basis of insufficient information. By contrast, older children scanned the windows in more detailed ways and were more accurate in their judgments of which windows were identical.

2009). For example, one study revealed that five days of computer exercises that involved learning how to use a joystick, working memory, and conflict resolution skills improved the attention of 4- to 6-year-old children (Rueda & others, 2005). Although not commercially available, further information about computer exercises for improving children's attention is available at www.teach-the-brain.org/learn/attention/index.

The ability of preschool children to control and sustain their attention is related to school readiness (Posner & Rothbart, 2007). For example, a study of more than 1,000 children revealed that their ability to sustain their attention at 54 months of age was linked to their school readiness (which included achievement and language skills) (NICHD Early Child Care Research Network, 2005). And in another study children whose parents and teachers rated them higher on a scale of having attention problems at 54 months of age had a lower level of social skills in peer relations in the first and third grades than their counterparts who were rated lower on the attention problems scale at 54 months of age (NICHD Early Child Care Research Network, 2009). And in yet another study, the ability to focus attention better at age 5 was linked to a higher level of school achievement at age 9 (Razza, Martin, & Brooks-Gunn, 2012).

Memory   *Memory*—the retention of information over time—is a central process in children's cognitive development. In Chapter 5, we saw that most of a young infant's memories are fragile and, for the most part, short-lived—except for the memory of perceptual-motor actions, which can be substantial (Bauer, 2013; Bauer & Fivush, 2014). Thus, we saw that to understand the infant's capacity to remember we need to distinguish *implicit memory* from *explicit memory*. Explicit memory itself, however, comes in many forms. One distinction occurs between relatively permanent or long-term memory and short-term memory.

Short-Term Memory   In **short-term memory,** individuals retain information for up to 30 seconds if there is no rehearsal of the information. Using rehearsal (repeating information after it has been presented), we can keep information in short-term memory for a much longer period. One method of assessing short-term memory is the memory-span task. You hear a short list of stimuli—usually digits—presented at a rapid pace (one per second, for example). Then you are asked to repeat the digits.

Research with the memory-span task suggests that short-term memory increases during early childhood. For example, in one investigation memory span increased from about 2 digits in 2- to 3-year-old children to about 5 digits in 7-year-old children, yet between 7 and 13 years of age memory span increased only by 2 more digits (Dempster, 1981) (see Figure 7.13). Keep in mind, though, that memory span varies from one individual to another.

Why does memory span change with age? Rehearsal of information is important; older children rehearse the digits more than younger children do. Speed—especially the speed with which memory items can be identified—and efficiency of processing information are important, too (Schneider, 2011).

The speed-of-processing explanation highlights a key point in the information-processing perspective: The speed with which a child processes information is an important aspect of the child's cognitive abilities, and there is abundant evidence that the speed with which many cognitive tasks are completed improves dramatically across the childhood years (Kail, 2007).

How Accurate Are Young Children's Long-Term Memories?   While toddlers' short-term memory span increases during the early childhood years, their memory also becomes more accurate. Young children can remember a great deal of information if they are given appropriate cues and prompts (Bruck & Ceci, 2012, 2014). Increasingly, young children are even being allowed to testify in court, especially if they are the sole witnesses to abuse, a crime, and so forth (Cederborg & others, 2014; Lamb & others, 2015). Several factors can influence the accuracy of a young child's memory (Bruck & Ceci, 1999):

- *There are age differences in children's susceptibility to suggestion.* Preschoolers are the most suggestible age group in comparison with older children and adults (Lehman & others, 2010). For example, preschool children are more susceptible to believing misleading or incorrect information given after an event (Ghetti & Alexander, 2004). Despite these differences among various age groups, there is still concern about the reaction of older children when they are subjected to suggestive interviews (Ahern & Lamb, 2014; Bruck & Ceci, 2012).

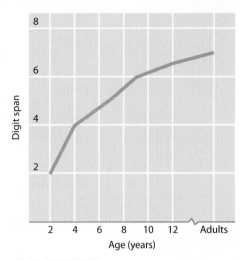

FIGURE **7.13**

DEVELOPMENTAL CHANGES IN MEMORY SPAN. In one study, from 2 years of age to 7 years of age children's memory span increased about 2 digits to 5 digits (Dempster, 1981). Between 7 and 13 years of age, memory span had increased on average only another 2 digits, to 7 digits. *What factors might contribute to the increase in memory span during childhood?*

executive attention Involves action planning, allocating attention to goals, error detection and compensation, monitoring progress on tasks, and dealing with novel or difficult circumstances.

sustained attention Focused and extended engagement with an object, task, event, or other aspect of the environment.

short-term memory The memory component in which individuals retain information for up to 30 seconds, assuming there is no rehearsal of the information.

- *There are individual differences in susceptibility.* Some preschoolers are highly resistant to interviewers' suggestions, whereas others immediately succumb to the slightest suggestion (Ceci & Klemfuss, 2010; Sim & Lamb, 2014). One study revealed that preschool children's ability to produce a high-quality narrative was linked to their resistance to suggestion (Kulkofsky & Klemfuss, 2008).
- *Interviewing techniques can produce substantial distortions in children's reports about highly salient events.* Children are suggestible not just about peripheral details but also about the central aspects of an event (Bruck & Ceci, 2012; Cederborg & others, 2014). In some cases, children's false reports can be tinged with sexual connotations. In laboratory studies, young children have made false claims about "silly events" that involved body contact (such as "Did the nurse lick your knee?" or "Did she blow in your ear?"). A significant number of preschool children have falsely reported that someone touched their private parts, kissed them, and hugged them, when these events clearly did not happen in the research. Nonetheless, young children are capable of recalling much that is relevant about an event (Fivush, 1993). Young children are more likely to accurately recall information about an event if the interviewer has a neutral tone, there is limited use of misleading questions, and there no motivation for the child to make a false report (Bruck & Ceci, 2012; Principe, Greenhoot, & Ceci, 2014).

In sum, whether a young child's eyewitness testimony is accurate or not may depend on a number of factors such as the type, number, and intensity of the suggestive techniques the child has experienced (Lamb & others, 2015). It appears that the reliability of young children's reports has as much to do with the skills and motivation of the interviewer as with any natural limitations on young children's memory (Bruck & Ceci, 2012, 2014).

Autobiographical Memory   Another aspect of long-term memory that has been extensively studied in research on children's development is autobiographical memory (Pathman & St. Jacques, 2014). *Autobiographical memory* involves memory of significant events and experiences in one's life. You are engaging in autobiographical memory when you answer questions such as: Who was your first-grade teacher and what was s/he like? What is the most traumatic event that happened to you as a child?

During the preschool years, young children's memories increasingly take on more autobiographical characteristics (Bauer, 2013; Bauer & Fivush, 2014; Miller, 2014). In some areas, such as remembering a story, a movie, a song, or an interesting event or experience, young children have been shown to have reasonably good memories. From 3 to 5 years of age, they (1) increasingly remember events as occurring at a specific time and location, such as "on my birthday at Chuck E. Cheese's last year" and (2) include more elements that are rich in detail in their narratives (Bauer, 2013). In one study, children went from including 4 descriptive items per event at 3½ years of age to 12 such items at 6 years of age (Fivush & Haden, 1997).

Executive Function   Recently, increasing attention has been given to the development of children's **executive function,** an umbrella-like concept that consists of a number of higher-level cognitive processes linked to the development of the brain's prefrontal cortex. Executive function involves managing one's thoughts to engage in goal-directed behavior and self-control. Earlier in this chapter, we described the recent interest in *executive attention*, which comes under the umbrella of executive function.

In early childhood, executive function especially involves developmental advances in cognitive inhibition (such as inhibiting a strong tendency that is incorrect), cognitive flexibility (such as shifting attention to another item or topic), goal-setting (such as sharing a toy or mastering a skill like catching a ball), and delay of gratification (waiting longer to get a more attractive reward, for example) (Carlson, Zelazo, & Faja, 2013; Zelazo & Muller, 2011). During early childhood, the relatively stimulus-driven toddler is transformed into a child capable of flexible, goal-directed problem solving that characterizes executive function (Zelazo & Muller, 2011). Researchers have found that advances in executive function during the preschool years are linked with school readiness (Bierman & others, 2008).

Walter Mischel and his colleagues (Berman & others, 2013; Mischel, Cantor, & Feldman, 1996; Mischel & Moore, 1980; Mischel & others, 2011; Schlam & others, 2013) have conducted a number of studies of delay of gratification with young children. One way they assess

executive function An umbrella-like concept that consists of a number of higher-level cognitive processes linked to the development of the brain's prefrontal cortex. Executive function involves managing one's thoughts to engage in goal-directed behavior and self-control.

delay of gratification is to place a young child alone in a room with an alluring marshmallow that is in their reach. The children are told that they either can ring a bell at any time and eat the marshmallow or they can wait until the experimenter returns and they then will get two marshmallows. Among the young children who were able to wait for the experimenter to return, what did they do to help them wait? They engaged in a number of strategies to distract their attention from the marshmallows, including singing songs, picking their noses, or doing other things to keep from looking at the marshmallows. Mischel and his colleagues labeled these strategies "cool thoughts" (that is, doing non-marshmallow-related thoughts and activities), whereas they said that young children who looked at the marshmallow were engaging in "hot thoughts." The young children who engaged in cool thoughts were more likely to eat the marshmallow later or wait until the experimenter returned to the room. In one study using the delay of gratification task just described, longer delay of gratification at 4 years of age was linked to a lower body mass index (BMI) three decades later (Schlam & others, 2013).

Stephanie Carlson and her colleagues (2010, 2011; Carlson, Claxton, & Moses, 2014; Carlson & White, 2013; Carlson, White, & Davis-Unger, 2014) have conducted a number of research studies on young children's executive function. In one study, young children listened as an adult read aloud either *Planet Opposite*—a fantasy book in which everything is turned upside down—or *Fun Town*—a reality-oriented fiction book (Carlson & White, 2011). After hearing the adult read one of the books, the young children completed the Less Is More Task, in which they were shown two trays of candy—one with five pieces, the other with two—and told that the tray they picked would be given to the stuffed animal seated at the table (see Figure 7.14). This task was difficult for the 3-year-olds, who tended to pick the tray that they themselves wanted (and so ended up losing the tray to the stuffed animal). Sixty percent of the 3-year-olds who heard the *Planet Opposite* story selected the smaller number of candies (hence keeping the five pieces of candy) compared with only 20 percent of their counterparts who heard the more straightforward story. The results indicated that learning about a topsy-turvy imaginary world likely helped the young children become more flexible in their thinking.

What are some predictors of young children's executive function? Parenting practices are linked to children's development of executive function (Carlson, Zelazo, & Faja, 2013; Cuevas & others, 2014). For example, several studies have linked greater use of verbal scaffolding by parents (providing age-appropriate support during cognitive tasks) to children's more advanced executive function (Bernier, Carlson, & Whipple, 2010; Bibok, Carpendale, & Muller, 2009; Hammond & others, 2012; Hughes & Ensor, 2009). Another study found that preschool children who were securely attached to their mothers had a higher level of executive function than their insecurely attached counterparts (Bernier & others, 2011).

Other predictors of better executive function in children include higher socioeconomic status (Obradovic, 2010); some aspects of language, including vocabulary size, verbal labeling, and bilingualism (Bell, Wolfe, & Adkins, 2007; Bialystok, 2010; Muller & others, 2008); imagination (generating novel ideas, for example) (Carlson & White, 2013); cultural background (Asian children, especially urban Chinese and Korean children, show better executive function than U.S. children) (Lan & others, 2011; Sabbagh & others, 2006); and fewer sleep problems (Friedman & others, 2009).

Some developmental psychologists use their training in areas such as cognitive development to pursue careers in applied areas. To read about the work of Helen Hadani, an individual who has followed this path, see the *Connecting with Careers* profile.

The Child's Theory of Mind Even young children are curious about the nature of the human mind (Astington & Hughes, 2013; Buttelmann & others, 2014; Ronfard & Harris, 2014; Wellman, 2011). They have a **theory of mind,** which refers to awareness of one's own mental processes and the mental processes of others. Studies of theory of mind view the child as "a thinker who is trying to explain, predict, and understand people's thoughts, feelings, and utterances" (Harris, 2006, p. 847).

Developmental Changes Children's theory of mind changes as they develop through childhood (Gelman, 2013; Lillard & Kavanaugh, 2014; Wellman, 2011). Although whether

FIGURE **7.14**

STUDYING EXECUTIVE FUNCTION IN YOUNG CHILDREN. Researcher Stephanie Carlson administers the Less Is More task to a 4-year-old boy. *What were the results of Carlson's research?*

theory of mind Awareness of one's own mental processes and the mental processes of others.

Helen Hadani, Ph.D., Developmental Psychologist, Toy Designer, and Associate Director of Research for the Center for Childhood Creativity

Helen Hadani obtained a Ph.D. from Stanford University in developmental psychology. As a graduate student at Stanford, she worked part-time for Hasbro Toys and Apple testing children's software and computer products for young children. Her first job after graduate school was with Zowie Intertainment, which was subsequently bought by LEGO. In her work as a toy designer there, Helen conducted experiments and focus groups at different stages of a toy's development, and she also studied the age-effectiveness of each toy. In Helen's words, "Even in a toy's most primitive stage of development . . . you see children's creativity in responding to challenges, their satisfaction when a problem is solved or simply their delight in having fun" (Schlegel, 2000, p. 50).

More recently, she began working with the Bay Area Discovery Museum's Center for Childhood Creativity (CCC) in Sausalito California, an education-focused think tank that pioneers new research, thought-leadership, and teacher training programs that advance creative thinking in all children. Helen is currently the Associate Director of Research for the CCC.

Helen Hadani, who has worked as both a toy designer and in a museum position that involves thinking of ways to increase children's creative thinking.

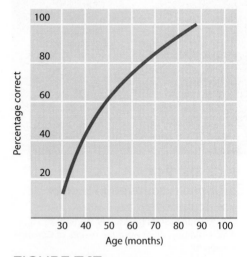

FIGURE 7.15

DEVELOPMENTAL CHANGES IN FALSE-BELIEF PERFORMANCE. False-belief performance—the child's understanding that a person may have a false belief that contradicts reality—dramatically increases from 2½ years of age through the middle of the elementary school years. In a summary of the results of many studies, 2½-year-olds gave incorrect responses about 80 percent of the time (Wellman, Cross, & Watson, 2001). At 3 years, 8 months, they were correct about 50 percent of the time, and after that, they gave increasingly correct responses.

infants have a theory of mind continues to be questioned by some (Rakoczy, 2012), the consensus is that some changes occur quite early in development, as we will see next.

From 18 months to 3 years of age, children begin to understand three mental states:

- *Perceptions.* By 2 years of age, a child recognizes that another person will see what's in front of her own eyes instead of what's in front of the child's eyes (Lempers, Flavell, & Flavell, 1977), and by 3 years of age, the child realizes that looking leads to knowing what's inside a container (Pratt & Bryant, 1990).
- *Emotions.* The child can distinguish between positive (for example, happy) and negative (sad, for example) emotions. A child might say, "Tommy feels bad."
- *Desires.* All humans have some sort of desires. But when do children begin to recognize that someone else's desires may differ from their own? Toddlers recognize that if people want something, they will try to get it. For instance, a child might say, "I want my mommy."

Two- to three-year-olds understand the way that desires are related to actions and to simple emotions. For example, they understand that people will search for what they want and that if they obtain it, they are likely to feel happy, but if they don't, they will keep searching for it and are likely to feel sad or angry (Wellman & Woolley, 1990). Children also refer to desires earlier and more frequently than they refer to cognitive states such as thinking and knowing (Bartsch & Wellman, 1995).

One of the landmark developments in understanding others' desires is recognizing that someone else may have different desires from one's own (Doherty, 2008). Eighteen-month-olds understand that their own food preferences may not match the preferences of others—they will give an adult the food to which she says "Yummy!" even if the food is something that the infants detest (Repacholi & Gopnik, 1997). As they get older, they can verbalize that they themselves do not like something but an adult might (Flavell & others, 1992).

Between the ages of 3 and 5, children come to understand that the mind can represent objects and events accurately or inaccurately (Low & Simpson, 2012). The realization that people can have *false beliefs*—beliefs that are not true—develops in a majority of children by the time they are 5 years old (Wellman, Cross, & Watson, 2001) (see Figure 7.15). This point is often described as a pivotal one in understanding the mind—recognizing that beliefs are not just mapped directly into the mind from the surrounding world, but that different people can also have different, and sometimes incorrect, beliefs (Gelman, 2009). In a classic false-belief task, young children were shown a Band-Aids box and asked what was inside (Jenkins & Astington, 1996). To the children's surprise, the box actually contained pencils. When asked what a child who had never seen the box would think was inside, 3-year-olds typically responded, "Pencils." However, the 4- and 5-year-olds, grinning in anticipation of the false beliefs of other children who had not seen what was inside the box, were more likely to say "Band-Aids."

In a similar task, children are told a story about Sally and Anne: Sally places a toy in a basket and then leaves the room (see Figure 7.16). In her absence, Anne takes the toy from the basket and places it in a box. Children are asked where Sally will look for the toy when she returns. The major finding is that 3-year-olds tend to fail false-belief tasks, saying that Sally will look in the box (even though Sally could not have known that the toy has moved to this new location). Four-year-olds and older children tend to perform the task correctly, saying that Sally will have a "false belief"—she will think the object is in the basket, even though that belief is now false. The conclusion from these studies is that children younger than 4 years old do not understand that it is possible to have a false belief.

However, there are many reasons to question the focus on this one supposedly pivotal moment in the development of a theory of mind. For example, the false-belief task is a complicated one that involves a number of factors such as the characters in the story and all of their individual actions (Bloom & German, 2000).

It is only beyond the preschool years—at approximately 5 to 7 years of age—that children have a deepening appreciation of the mind itself rather than just an understanding of mental states. For example, they begin to recognize that people's behaviors do not necessarily reflect their thoughts and feelings (Flavell, Green, & Flavell, 1993). Not until middle and late childhood do children see the mind as an active constructor of knowledge or processing center (Flavell, Green, & Flavell, 1998) and move from understanding that beliefs can be false to realizing that the same event can be open to multiple interpretations (Carpendale & Chandler, 1996). For example, in one study, children saw an ambiguous line drawing (for example, a drawing that could be seen as either a duck or a rabbit); one puppet told the child she believed the drawing was a duck while another puppet told the child he believed the drawing was a rabbit (see Figure 7.17). Before the age of 7, children said that there was one right answer and that it was not okay for the two puppets to have different opinions.

Although most research on children's theory of mind focuses on children around or before their preschool years, at 7 years of age and beyond there are important developments in the ability to understand the beliefs and thoughts of others (Apperly, 2012; Miller, 2012). Although it is important to understand that people may have different interpretations, it is also necessary to recognize that some interpretations and beliefs may be evaluated on the basis of the merits of arguments and evidence (Kuhn, Cheney, & Weinstock, 2000). In early adolescence, children begin to understand that people can have ambivalent feelings (Flavell & Miller, 1998). They start to recognize that the same person can feel both happy and sad about the same event. They also engage in more recursive thinking: thinking about what other people are thinking about.

Individual Differences   As in other developmental research, there are individual differences in the ages when children reach certain milestones in their theory of mind (Wellman, 2011). For example, *executive function,* which describes several functions discussed earlier in this chapter, such as planning and inhibition, that are important for flexible, future-oriented behavior, also is connected to theory of mind development (Astington & Hughes, 2013; Benson & others, 2014; Fizke & others, 2014). In one executive function task, children are asked to say the word *night* when they see a picture of a sun, and the word *day* when they see a picture of a moon and stars. To do this correctly, children have to engage in inhibitory

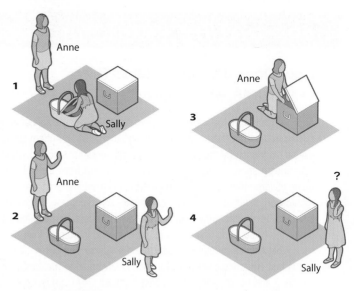

FIGURE **7.16**

THE SALLY AND ANNE FALSE-BELIEF TASK. In the false-belief task, the skit above in which Sally has a basket and Anne has a box is shown to children. Sally places a toy in her basket and then leaves. While Sally is gone and can't watch, Anne removes the toy from Sally's basket and places it in her box. Sally then comes back and the children are asked where they think Sally will look for her toy. Children are said to "pass" the false-belief task if they understand that Sally looks in her basket first before realizing the toy isn't there.

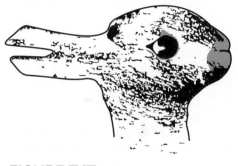

FIGURE **7.17**
AMBIGUOUS LINE DRAWING

How Does Theory of Mind Differ in Children with Autism?

Approximately 1 in 150 children is estimated to have some sort of autism spectrum disorder (National Autism Association, 2011). Autism can usually be diagnosed by the age of 3 years, and sometimes earlier. Children with autism show a number of behaviors different from typically developing children their age, including deficits in social interaction and communication skills as well as higher rates of repetitive behaviors or interests. They often show indifference toward others, in many instances preferring to be alone and showing more interest in objects than people.

What causes the autism spectrum disorders? The current consensus is that autism is a brain dysfunction involving abnormalities in brain structure and neurotransmitters (Bosl & others, 2011; Shukla & others, 2011). Genetic factors likely play a role in the development of the autism spectrum disorders (Ronald & Hoekstra, 2011).

Children and adults with autism have difficulty in social interactions (Luiselli, 2014). These deficits are generally greater than deficits in children of the same mental age with intellectual disabilities (O'Reilly & others, 2014). Researchers have found that children with autism have difficulty in developing a theory of mind, especially in understanding others' beliefs and emotions (Boucher, 2012a). Although children with autism tend to do poorly when reasoning about false-belief tasks and task sequencing (Peterson, Wellman, & Slaughter, 2012), they can perform much better on reasoning tasks that require an understanding of physical causality.

However, it is important to consider individual variations in children with autism and particular aspects of theory of mind (Matthews & others, 2012). Children with autism are not a homogeneous group, and some have less severe social and communication problems than others. Thus, it is not surprising that children who have less severe forms of autism do better than those who have more severe forms of the disorder on some theory of mind tasks. For example, higher-functioning children with autism show reasonable progress in understanding others' desires (Harris, 2006).

A young boy with autism. *What are some characteristics of autistic children? What are some deficits in autistic children's theory of mind?*

A further important consideration in thinking about autism and theory of mind is that children with autism might have difficulty in understanding others' beliefs and emotions not solely due to theory of mind deficits but to other aspects of cognition such as problems in focusing attention, eye gaze, face recognition, memory, language impairment, or some general intellectual impairment (Boucher, 2012b; Elsabbagh & others, 2012).

Some recent theories of autism suggest that weaknesses in executive function are linked to autism and may relate to the difficulty that those with autism have in performing theory of mind tasks (Just & others, 2012). Other theories have pointed out that typically developing individuals process information by extracting the big picture, whereas those with autism process information in a very detailed, almost obsessive way (Wang & others, 2012). It may be that in autism, a number of different but related deficits lead to social cognitive deficits.

control by suppressing the most realistic responses (saying the word *day* when seeing a picture of a sun, for example).

Children who perform better at such executive function tasks show a better understanding of theory of mind (Astington & Hughes, 2013; Sabbagh & others, 2006). In a recent study, 3½-year-old children who showed poor performance on false-belief tasks were given training to improve their executive function (Benson & others, 2014). Improvements in children's executive function as a result of the training were linked to improvements in theory of mind. The researchers concluded that executive function skills promote advances in theory of mind by facilitating children's ability to reflect on and learn from relevant experience.

Language development also likely plays a prominent role in the increasing reflective nature of theory of mind as children go through the early childhood and middle and late childhood years (Astington & Hughes, 2013; Meins & others, 2013). Researchers have found that differences in children's language skills predict performance on theory of mind tasks (Hughes & Ensor, 2007).

Another individual difference in understanding the mind involves autism. To learn how theory of mind differs in children with autism, see *Connecting Through Research.*

Review Connect Reflect

 Describe three views of the cognitive changes that occur in early childhood.

Review

- What characterizes Piaget's stage of preoperational thought?
- What does Vygotsky's theory suggest about how preschool children construct knowledge?
- What are some important ways in which information processing changes during early childhood? What characterizes children's theory of mind?

Connect

- In this section, you learned that children who frequently engage in pretend play perform better on theory of mind tasks. During which substage of Piaget's preoperational stage do children begin to engage in pretend play? What mental ability does it signify?

Reflect *Your Own Personal Journey of Life*

- If you were the parent of a 4-year-old child, would you try to train the child to develop conservation skills? Explain.

3 Language Development

 Summarize how language develops in early childhood.

| Understanding Phonology and Morphology | Changes in Syntax and Semantics | Advances in Pragmatics | Young Children's Literacy |

Toddlers move rather quickly from producing two-word utterances to creating three-, four-, and five-word combinations. Between 2 and 3 years of age, they begin the transition from saying simple sentences that express a single proposition to saying complex sentences.

As young children learn the special features of their own language, there are extensive regularities in how they acquire that particular language (Berko Gleason, 2009; Hoff, 2014; Wagner & Hoff, 2013). For example, all children learn the prepositions *on* and *in* before other prepositions. Children learning other languages, such as Russian or Chinese, also acquire the particular features of those languages in a consistent order.

UNDERSTANDING PHONOLOGY AND MORPHOLOGY

During the preschool years, most children gradually become more sensitive to the sounds of spoken words and become increasingly capable of producing all the sounds of their language (Vihman, 2014; Zhou & others, 2012). By the time children are 3 years of age, they can produce all the vowel sounds and most of the consonant sounds (Menn & Stoel-Gammon, 2009).

As children move beyond two-word utterances, they demonstrate a knowledge of morphology rules (Park & others, 2012). Children begin using the plural and possessive forms of nouns (such as *dogs* and *dog's*). They put appropriate endings on verbs (such as *-s* when the subject is third-person singular and *-ed* for the past tense). They use prepositions (such as *in* and *on*), articles (such as *a* and *the*), and various forms of the verb *to be* (such as "I *was* going to the store"). Some of the best evidence for changes in children's use of morphological rules occurs in their overgeneralization of the rules, as when a preschool child says "foots" instead of "feet," or "goed" instead of "went."

In a classic experiment that was designed to study children's knowledge of morphological rules, such as how to make a plural, Jean Berko (1958) presented preschool children and first-grade children with cards such as the one shown in Figure 7.18. Children were asked to look at the card while the experimenter read aloud the words on the card. Then the children were asked to supply the missing word. This might sound easy, but Berko was interested in the children's ability to apply the appropriate morphological rule—in this case to say "wugs" with the *z* sound that indicates the plural.

Although the children's answers were not perfect, they were much better than chance. What makes Berko's study impressive is that most of the words were made up for the

The greatest poem ever known
Is one all poets have outgrown;
The poetry, innate, untold,
Of being only four years old.

—CHRISTOPHER MORLEY
American Novelist, 20th Century

This is a wug.

Now there is another one.
There are two of them.
There are two _____.

FIGURE **7.18**

STIMULI IN BERKO'S STUDY OF YOUNG CHILDREN'S UNDERSTANDING OF MORPHOLOGICAL RULES. In Jean Berko's (1958) study, young children were presented cards, such as this one with a "wug" on it. Then the children were asked to supply the missing word; in supplying the missing word, they had to say it correctly, too. "Wugs" is the correct response here.

developmental **connection**

Language

The average 2-year-old can speak about 200 words. Chapter 5, p. 155

fast mapping A process that helps to explain how young children learn the connection between a word and its referent so quickly.

experiment. Thus, the children could not base their responses on remembering past instances of hearing the words. That they could make the plurals or past tenses of words they had never heard before was proof that they knew the morphological rules.

CHANGES IN SYNTAX AND SEMANTICS

Preschool children also learn and apply rules of syntax (de Villiers & de Villiers, 2013). They show a growing mastery of complex rules for how words should be ordered. Consider *wh*-questions, such as "Where is Daddy going?" or "What is that boy doing?" To ask these questions properly, the child must know two important differences between *wh*- questions and affirmative statements (for instance, "Daddy is going to work" and "That boy is waiting for the school bus"). First, a *wh*- word must be added at the beginning of the sentence. Second, the auxiliary verb must be inverted—that is, exchanged with the subject of the sentence. Young children learn quite early where to put the *wh*- word, but they take much longer to learn the auxiliary-inversion rule. Thus, preschool children might ask, "Where Daddy is going?" and "What that boy is doing?"

Gains in semantics also characterize early childhood. Vocabulary development is dramatic (Parrish-Morris, Golinkoff, & Hirsh-Pasek, 2013). Some experts have concluded that between 18 months and 6 years of age, young children learn approximately one new word every waking hour (Gelman & Kalish, 2006). By the time they enter first grade, it is estimated that children know about 14,000 words (Clark, 1993).

Why can children learn so many new words so quickly? One possibility is **fast mapping,** which involves children's ability to make an initial connection between a word and its referent after only limited exposure to the word (Kan, 2014; Trueswell & others, 2013; Woodward, Markman, & Fitzsimmons, 1994). Researchers have found that exposure to words on multiple occasions over several days results in more successful word learning than the same number of exposures in a single day (Childers & Tomasello, 2002). Recent research using eye-tracking found that even 15-month-old infants fast map words (Puccini & Liszkowski, 2012).

What are some important aspects of how word learning optimally occurs? Kathy Hirsh-Pasek, Robert Golinkoff, and Justin Harris (Harris, Golinkoff, & Hirsh-Pasek, 2011; Hirsh-Pasek & Golinkoff, 2014) emphasize six key principles in young children's vocabulary development:

1. *Children learn the words they hear most often.* They learn the words that they encounter when interacting with parents, teachers, siblings, and peers, as well as words that they hear when books are read aloud to them. They especially benefit from encountering words that they do not know.

2. *Children learn words for things and events that interest them.* Parents and teachers can direct young children to experience words in contexts that interest the children; playful peer interactions are especially helpful in this regard.

3. *Children learn words better in responsive and interactive contexts than in passive contexts.* Children who experience turn-taking opportunities, joint focusing experiences, and positive, sensitive socializing contexts with adults encounter the scaffolding necessary for optimal word learning. They learn words less effectively when they are passive learners.

4. *Children learn words best in contexts that are meaningful.* Young children learn new words more effectively when new words are encountered in integrated contexts rather than as isolated facts.

5. *Children learn words best when they access clear information about word meaning.* Children whose parents and teachers are sensitive to words the children might not understand and provide support and elaboration with hints about word meaning learn words better than those whose parents and teachers quickly state a new word and don't monitor whether children understand its meaning.

6. *Children learn words best when grammar and vocabulary are considered.* Children who experience a large number of words and diversity in verbal stimulation develop a richer vocabulary and better understanding of grammar. In many cases, vocabulary and grammar development are connected.

ADVANCES IN PRAGMATICS

Changes in pragmatics, the appropriate use of language in different contexts, also characterize young children's language development (Waxman, 2013). A 6-year-old is simply a much better conversationalist than a 2-year-old is. What are some of the improvements in pragmatics during the preschool years?

Young children begin to engage in extended discourse (Akhtar & Herold, 2008, p. 581). For example, they learn culturally specific rules of conversation and politeness and become sensitive to the need to adapt their speech in different settings. Their developing linguistic skills and increasing ability to take the perspective of others contribute to their generation of more competent narratives.

As children get older, they become increasingly able to talk about things that are not here (Grandma's house, for example) and not now (what happened to them yesterday or might happen tomorrow, for example). A preschool child can tell you what she wants for lunch tomorrow, something that would not have been possible at the two-word stage of language development.

Around 4 to 5 years of age, children learn to change their speech style to suit the situation. For example, even 4-year-old children speak to a 2-year-old differently from the way they speak to a same-aged peer; they use shorter sentences with the 2-year-old. They also speak differently to an adult and to a same-aged peer, using more polite and formal language with the adult (Shatz & Gelman, 1973).

YOUNG CHILDREN'S LITERACY

The concern about the ability of U.S. children to read and write has led to a careful examination of preschool and kindergarten children's experiences, with the hope that a positive orientation toward reading and writing can be developed early in life (Beaty & Pratt, 2015). Parents and teachers need to provide young children with a supportive environment for developing literacy skills (Tamis-LeMonda & Song, 2013; Tompkins, 2015). Children should be active participants and be immersed in a wide range of interesting listening, talking, writing, and reading experiences (Senechal & LeFevre, 2014). One study revealed that children whose mothers had more education acquired more advanced emergent literacy levels than children whose mothers had less education (Korat, 2009). Another study found that literacy experiences (such as how often the child was read to), the quality of the mother's engagement with her child (such as attempts to cognitively stimulate the child), and provision of learning materials (such as

What are some positive strategies for improving young children's literacy?

age-appropriate books) were important home literacy experiences in low-income families that were linked to the children's language development in positive ways (Rodriguez & others, 2009). Instruction should be built on what children already know about oral language, reading, and writing. Further, early precursors of literacy and academic success include language skills, phonological and syntactic knowledge, letter identification, and conceptual knowledge about print and its conventions and functions (Christie & others, 2014; Jalongo, 2014).

The following three longitudinal studies indicate the relationship between early language skills and children's school readiness:

- Phonological awareness, letter name and sound knowledge, and naming speed in kindergarten were linked to reading success in the first and second grade (Schattschneider & others, 2004).
- Children's early home environment influenced their early language skills, which in turn predicted their readiness for school (Forget-Dubois & others, 2009).
- The number of letters children knew in kindergarten was highly correlated (.52) with their reading achievement in high school (Stevenson & Newman, 1986).

So far, our discussion of early literacy has focused on U.S. children. These findings may not apply to children in other countries. For example, the extent to which phonological awareness is linked to learning to read effectively varies across languages to some degree (McBride-Chang, 2004). Rates of dyslexia (severe reading disability) differ across countries and are linked with the spelling and phonetic rules that characterize the language (McCardle & others, 2011). English is one of the more difficult languages to learn because of its irregular spellings and pronunciations. In countries where English is spoken, the rate of dyslexia is higher than in countries where the alphabet script is more phonetically pronounced.

Books can be valuable in enhancing children's communication skills (Beaty & Pratt, 2015). What are some strategies for using books effectively with preschool children? Ellen Galinsky (2010) suggests the following strategies:

- *Use books to initiate conversation with young children.* Ask them to put themselves in the book characters' places and imagine what they might be thinking or feeling.
- *Use what and why questions.* Ask young children what they think is going to happen next in a story and then to see if it occurs.
- *Encourage children to ask questions about stories.*
- *Choose some books that play with language.* Creative books on the alphabet, including those with rhymes, often interest young children.

The advances in language that take place in early childhood lay the foundation for later development in the elementary school years, as we will discuss in Chapter 9.

Review Connect Reflect

 LG3 Summarize how language develops in early childhood.

Review
- How do phonology and morphology change during early childhood?
- What characterizes young children's understanding of syntax and semantics in early childhood?
- What advances in pragmatics occur in early childhood?
- What are some effective ways to guide young children's literacy?

Connect
- In this section, you learned that children can sometimes overgeneralize the rules for morphology. How is this different from or similar to the concept of overextension as it relates to infants' speech (covered in Chapter 5)?

Reflect *Your Own Personal Journey of Life*
- As a parent, what could you to do to improve the likelihood that your child would enter first grade with excellent literacy skills?

---

4 Early Childhood Education

LG4 Evaluate different approaches to early childhood education.

| Variations in Early Childhood Education | Education for Young Children Who Are Disadvantaged | Controversies in Early Childhood Education |

child-centered kindergarten Education that involves the whole child by considering both the child's physical, cognitive, and socioemotional development and the child's needs, interests, and learning styles.

To the teachers in a Reggio Emilia program (described in the chapter opening), preschool children are active learners who are engaged in exploring the world with their peers, constructing their knowledge of the world in collaboration with their community, and aided but not directed by their teachers. In many ways, the Reggio Emilia approach applies ideas consistent with the views of Piaget and Vygotsky that were discussed earlier in this chapter. Our exploration of early childhood education focuses on variations in programs, education for young children who are disadvantaged, and some controversies in early childhood education.

VARIATIONS IN EARLY CHILDHOOD EDUCATION

Attending preschool is rapidly becoming the norm for U.S. children. There are many variations in the way young children are educated (Feeney, Moravcik, & Nolte, 2013; Henninger, 2013). The foundation of early childhood education has been the child-centered kindergarten.

The Child-Centered Kindergarten   Nurturing is a key aspect of the **child-centered kindergarten,** which emphasizes the education of the whole child and concern for his or her physical, cognitive, and socioemotional development (Morrison, 2014, 2015). Instruction is organized around the child's needs, interests, and learning styles. Emphasis is on the process of learning, rather than what is learned (Kostelnik & others, 2015; Weissman & Hendrick, 2014). The child-centered kindergarten honors three principles: (1) each child follows a unique developmental pattern; (2) young children learn best through firsthand experiences with people and materials; and (3) play is extremely important in the child's total development. *Experimenting, exploring, discovering, trying out, restructuring, speaking,* and *listening* are frequent activities in excellent kindergarten programs. Such programs are closely attuned to the developmental status of 4- and 5-year-old children.

The Montessori Approach   Montessori schools are patterned after the educational philosophy of Maria Montessori (1870–1952), an Italian physician-turned-educator who at the beginning of the twentieth century crafted a revolutionary approach to young children's education. The **Montessori approach** is a philosophy of education in which children are given considerable freedom and spontaneity in choosing activities. They are allowed to move from one activity to another as they desire. The teacher acts as a facilitator rather than a director. The teacher shows the child how to perform intellectual activities, demonstrates interesting ways to explore curriculum materials, and offers help when the child requests it (Isaacs, 2012; Murray, 2011). "By encouraging children to make decisions from an early age, Montessori programs seek to develop self-regulated problem solvers who can make choices and manage their time effectively" (Hyson, Copple, & Jones, 2006, p. 14). The number of Montessori schools in the United States has expanded dramatically in recent years, from 1 school in 1959 to 355 schools in 1970 and more than 4,000 today.

Some developmentalists favor the Montessori approach, but others believe that it neglects children's socioemotional development. For example, although Montessori fosters independence and the development of cognitive skills, it deemphasizes verbal interaction between the teacher and child and between peers. Montessori's critics also argue that it restricts imaginative play and that its heavy reliance on self-corrective materials may not adequately allow for creativity and for a variety of learning styles.

Developmentally Appropriate and Inappropriate Education   Many educators and psychologists conclude that preschool and young elementary school children learn best through active, hands-on teaching methods such as games and dramatic play. They know that children develop at varying rates and that schools need to allow for these individual differences. They also argue that schools should focus on supporting children's socioemotional development as well as their cognitive development. Educators refer to this type of schooling as **developmentally appropriate practice (DAP),** which is based on knowledge of the typical development of children within an age span (age-appropriateness), as well as the uniqueness of the child (individual-appropriateness). DAP emphasizes the importance of creating settings that encourage active learning and reflect children's interests and capabilities (Bredekamp, 2011, 2014; Follari, 2015). Desired outcomes for DAP include thinking critically, working cooperatively, solving problems, developing self-regulatory skills, and enjoying learning. The emphasis in DAP is on the process of learning rather than its content (Bredekamp, 2011, 2014). The most recent developmentally appropriate guidelines provided by the National Association for the Education of Young Children (NAEYC, 2009) are summarized in Figure 7.19.

Do developmentally appropriate educational practices improve young children's development? Some researchers have found that young children in developmentally appropriate

Montessori approach An educational philosophy in which children are given considerable freedom and spontaneity in choosing activities and are allowed to move from one activity to another as they desire.

developmentally appropriate practice Education that focuses on the typical developmental patterns of children (age-appropriateness) and the uniqueness of each child (individual-appropriateness).

Larry Page and Sergey Brin, founders of the highly successful Internet search engine Google, said that their early years at Montessori schools were a major factor in their success (International Montessori Council, 2006). During an interview with Barbara Walters, they said they learned how to be self-directed and self-starters at Montessori (ABC News, 2005). They commented that Montessori experiences encouraged them to think for themselves and allowed them the freedom to develop their own interests.

What are some differences in developmentally appropriate and inappropriate practice?

Core Considerations in Developmentally Appropriate Practice

1 Knowledge to Consider in Making Decisions

In all aspects of working with children, early childhood practitioners need to consider these three areas of knowledge: 1) What is known about child development and learning; 2) What is known about each child as an individual; and 3) What is known about the social and cultural contexts in which children live.

2 Challenging and Achievable Goals

Keeping in mind desired goals and what is known about the children as a group and individually, the teacher plans experiences to promote children's learning and development.

Principles of Child Development and Learning That Inform Practice

1 All the domains of development and learning—physical, cognitive, and social—are important, and they are closely interrelated.

2 Many aspects of children's learning and development follow well-documented sequences, with later abilities, skills, and knowledge building on those already acquired.

3 Development and learning proceed at varying rates from child to child, as well as at uneven rates across different areas of a child's individual functioning.

4 Development and learning result from a dynamic and continuous interaction of biological maturation and experience.

5 Early experiences have profound effects—, both cumulative and delayed—, on a child's development and learning; and optimal periods exist for certain types of development and learning to occur.

6 Development proceeds toward greater complexity, self-regulation, and symbolic or representational capacities.

7 Children develop best when they have secure, consistent relationships with responsive adults and opportunities for positive relationships with peers.

8 Development and learning occur in and are influenced by multiple social and cultural contexts.

9 Always mentally active in seeking to understand the world around them, children learn in a variety of ways; a wide range of teaching strategies and interactions are effective in supporting all these kinds of learning.

10 Play is an important vehicle for developing self-regulation as well as for promoting language, cognition, and social competence.

11 Development and learning advance when children are challenged to achieve at a level just beyond their current mastery, and also when they have many opportunities to practice newly acquired skills.

12 Children's experiences shape their motivation and approaches to learning, such as persistence, initiative, and flexibility; in turn, these dispositions and behaviors affect their learning and development.

Guidelines for Developmentally Appropriate Practice

1 Creating a Caring Community of Learners

Each member of the community is valued by the others; relationships are an important context through which children develop and learn; practitioners ensure that members of the community feel psychologically safe.

2 Teaching to Enhance Development and Learning

Teachers are responsible for fostering the caring community through their teaching.

3 Planning Curriculum to Achieve Important Goals

Teachers use the curriculum and their knowledge of children's interests in planning relevant, engaging learning experiences.

4 Assessing Children's Development and Learning

Assessment focuses on children's progress toward goals that are developmentally and educationally significant.

5 Establishing Reciprocal Relationships with Families

In reciprocal relationships between practitioners and families, there is mutual respect, cooperation, shared responsibility, and negotiation of shared goals.

FIGURE **7.19**

RECOMMENDATIONS BY NAEYC FOR DEVELOPMENTALLY APPROPRIATE PRACTICE IN EARLY CHILDHOOD PROGRAMS SERVING CHILDREN FROM BIRTH THROUGH AGE 8.
Source: NAEYC (2009). *Developmentally appropriate practice in early childhood programs serving children from birth through age 8.* Washington, DC: NAEYC.

classrooms are likely to have less stress, be more motivated, be more skilled socially, have better work habits, be more creative, have better language skills, and demonstrate better math skills than children in developmentally inappropriate classrooms (Hart & others, 2003). However, not all studies show significant positive benefits for developmentally appropriate education (Hyson, Copple, & Jones, 2006). Among the reasons it is difficult to generalize about research on developmentally appropriate education is that individual programs often vary, and developmentally appropriate education is an evolving concept. Recent changes in the concept have given more attention to sociocultural factors, to the teacher's active involvement and implementation of systematic intentions, and to the degree to which academic skills should be emphasized and how they should be taught.

EDUCATION FOR YOUNG CHILDREN WHO ARE DISADVANTAGED

For many years, U.S. children from low-income families did not receive any education before they entered the first grade. Often, they began first grade already several steps behind their classmates in their readiness to learn. In the summer of 1965, the federal government began an effort to break the cycle of poverty and poor education for young children in the United States through

Project Head Start. It is a compensatory program designed to provide children from low-income families the opportunity to acquire the skills and experiences important for success in school (Hustedt, Friedman, & Barnett, 2012; Zigler & Styfco, 2010). After almost half a century, Head Start continues to be the largest federally funded program for U.S. children, with almost 1 million U.S. children enrolled annually (Hagen & Lamb-Parker, 2008). In 2007, 3 percent of Head Start children were 5 years old, 51 percent were 4 years old, 36 percent were 3 years old, and 10 percent were under 3 years of age (Administration for Children & Families, 2008).

Early Head Start was established in 1995 to serve children from birth to 3 years of age. In 2007, half of all new funds appropriated for Head Start programs were used for the expansion of Early Head Start. Researchers have found positive effects for Early Head Start (Hoffman & Ewen, 2007). A recent study revealed that Early Head Start had a protective effect on risks young children might experience related to parenting stress, language development, and self-control (Ayoub, Vallotton, & Mastergeorge, 2011).

Head Start programs are not all created equal. One estimate is that 40 percent of the 1,400 Head Start programs are of questionable quality (Zigler & Styfco, 1994). More attention needs to be given to developing consistently high-quality Head Start programs (Hillemeier & others, 2013). One individual who is strongly motivated to make Head Start a valuable learning experience for young children from disadvantaged backgrounds is Yolanda Garcia. To read about her work, see *Connecting with Careers*.

Evaluations support the positive influence of quality early childhood programs on both the cognitive and social worlds of disadvantaged young children (Bierman & others, 2014; Phillips & Lowenstein, 2011). A national evaluation of Head Start revealed that the program had a positive influence on the language and cognitive development of 3- and 4-year-olds (Puma & others, 2010). However, by the end of the first grade, there were few lasting outcomes. One exception was a larger vocabulary for those who went to Head Start as 4-year-olds and better oral comprehension for those who went to Head Start as 3-year-olds. Another study found that when young children initially began Head Start, they were well below their more academically advantaged peers in literacy and math (Hindman & others, 2010). However, by the end of the first grade, the Head Start children were on par with national averages in literacy and math. A recent national study found mixed results for Head Start participation (Lee & others, 2013). In this study, Head Start children had higher early reading and math scores than children in other nonparental care or parental care but also higher levels of conduct problems than children in parental care. Also in this study, Head Start children had lower reading scores than children in prekindergarten and showed no differences compared with children in other center-based care. Head Start benefits occurred more often with children who had low initial cognitive

Project Head Start A government-funded program that is designed to provide children from low-income families with the opportunity to acquire the skills and experiences important for school success.

ability, whose parents had low levels of education, and who attended Head Start more than 20 hours per week.

Positive outcomes for Early Head Start have been found. In an experimental study of low-income families, data were collected when the children were 1, 2, and 3 years of age in Early Head Start, and also at 5 years of age (2 years after leaving Early Head Start) (Love & others, 2013). In this study, positive outcomes for the Early Head Start children (compared with a control group who did not receive the Early Head Start experience) occurred at 2, 3, and 5 years of age. At 2 and 3 years of age, Early Head Start children showed a higher level of cognition, language, attention, and health, and fewer behavior problems; at age 5, the Early Head Start children had better attention and approaches to learning as well as fewer behavior problems, but they did not differ from control group children in early school achievement. Also, a recent study revealed that Early Head Start had a protective effect on risks young children might experience in regard to parenting stress, language development, and self-control (Ayoub, Vallotton, & Mastergeorge, 2011).

One high-quality early childhood education program (although not a Head Start program) is the Perry Preschool program in Ypsilanti, Michigan, a two-year preschool program that includes weekly home visits from program personnel. In analyses of the long-term effects of the program, adults who had been in the Perry Preschool program were compared with a control group of adults from the same background who had not received the enriched early childhood education (Schweinhart & others, 2005; Weikert, 1993). Those who had been in the Perry Preschool program had fewer teen pregnancies and higher rates of high school graduation, and at age 40 more were in the workforce, owned their own homes, had a savings account, and had fewer arrests than adults in the control group.

CONTROVERSIES IN EARLY CHILDHOOD EDUCATION

Two current controversies in early childhood education involve (1) what the curriculum for early childhood education should be (Bredekamp, 2014; Morrison, 2015), and (2) whether preschool education should be universal in the United States (Zigler, Gilliam, & Barnett, 2011).

What is the curriculum controversy in early childhood education?

Curriculum Controversy   A current controversy in early childhood education involves what the curriculum for early childhood education should be (Follari, 2015). On one side are those who advocate a child-centered, constructivist approach much like that emphasized by the National Association for the Education of Young Children (NAEYC), along the lines of developmentally appropriate practice. On the other side are those who advocate an academic, direct-instruction approach.

In reality, many high-quality early childhood education programs include both academic and constructivist approaches. Many education experts like Lilian Katz (1999), though, worry about academic approaches that place too much pressure on young children to achieve and don't provide any opportunities to actively construct knowledge. Competent early childhood programs also should focus on cognitive development *and* socioemotional development, not exclusively on cognitive development (NAEYC, 2009).

Universal Preschool Education   Another early childhood education controversy focuses on whether preschool education should be instituted for all U.S. 4-year-old children. Edward Zigler and his colleagues (2011) recently have argued that the United States should have universal preschool education. They emphasize that quality preschools prepare children for school readiness and academic success. Zigler and his colleagues (2006) cite research that shows quality preschool programs decrease the likelihood that once children go to elementary and secondary school they will be retained in a grade or drop out of school. They also point to analyses indicating that universal preschool would bring cost savings on the order of billions of dollars because of a diminished need for remedial and justice services (Karoly & Bigelow, 2005).

Critics of universal preschool education argue that the gains attributed to preschool and kindergarten education are often overstated. They especially stress that research has not proven that nondisadvantaged children benefit from attending a preschool. Thus, the critics say it is more important to improve preschool education for young children who are disadvantaged than to fund preschool education for all 4-year-old children. Some critics, especially homeschooling advocates, emphasize that young children should be educated by their parents, not by schools. Thus, controversy continues to surround questions about whether universal preschool education should be implemented.

Review Connect Reflect

LG4 Evaluate different approaches to early childhood education.

Review
- What are some variations in early childhood education?
- What are the main efforts to educate young children who are disadvantaged?
- What are two controversies about early childhood education?

Connect
- In Chapter 1 you learned about cross-sectional and longitudinal research designs. Which type of research design is the Perry Preschool program?

Reflect *Your Own Personal Journey of Life*
- What type of early childhood education program would you want your child to attend? Why?

topical connections *looking forward*

In the next chapter, you will read about the many advances that take place during the socioemotional development of young children. The cognitive advances we discussed in this chapter, combined with the socioemotional experiences young children have in interacting with others, pave the way for social cognitive advances in understanding the self and others. Then, in Chapter 9 you will read about the continuing changes in children's physical and cognitive development in middle and late childhood. In terms of physical development, their motor skills become smoother and more coordinated. The development of their brain—especially the prefrontal cortex—provides the foundation for a number of cognitive advances, including the development of learning strategies and reading skills.

reach your **learning goals**

Physical and Cognitive Development in Early Childhood

1 Physical Changes

 LG1 Identify physical changes in early childhood.

Body Growth and Change

- The average child grows 2½ inches in height and gains between 5 and 7 pounds a year during early childhood. Growth patterns vary individually, though. Some of the brain's interior changes in early childhood are due to myelination. From 3 to 6 years of age, the most rapid growth in the brain occurs in the frontal lobes.

Motor and Perceptual Development

- Gross motor skills increase dramatically during early childhood. Children become increasingly adventuresome as their gross motor skills improve. Fine motor skills also improve substantially during early childhood. Young children also make advances in perceptual development.

Sleep

- Experts recommend that young children get 11 to 13 hours of sleep each night. Most young children sleep through the night and have one daytime nap. Helping the young child slow down before bedtime often leads to less resistance in going to bed. Sleep problems in young children are linked to other problems, such as being overweight and being depressed. Disruptions in sleep in early childhood are related to less optimal adjustment in preschool.

Nutrition and Exercise

- Too many young children in the United States are being raised on diets that are too high in fat. The child's life should be centered on activities, not meals. Other nutritional concerns include malnutrition in early childhood and the inadequate diets of many children living in poverty. Young children are not getting nearly as much exercise as they need.

Illness and Death

- In recent decades, vaccines have virtually eradicated many diseases that once resulted in the deaths of many young children. The disorders still most likely to be fatal for young children in the United States are cancer and cardiovascular disease, but accidents are the leading cause of death in young children. A special concern is the poor health status of many young children in low-income families. There has been a dramatic increase in HIV/AIDS in young children in developing countries in the last decade.

2 Cognitive Changes

LG2 Describe three views of the cognitive changes that occur in early childhood.

Piaget's Preoperational Stage

- According to Piaget, in the preoperational stage children cannot yet perform operations, which are reversible mental actions, but they begin to represent the world with symbols, to form stable concepts, and to reason. During the symbolic function substage, which occurs between about 2 and 4 years of age, children begin to mentally represent an object that is not present, but their thought is limited by egocentrism and animism. During the intuitive thought substage, which stretches from about 4 to 7 years of age, children begin to reason and to bombard adults with questions. Thought at this substage is called intuitive because children seem so sure about their knowledge yet are unaware of how they know what they know. Centration and a lack of conservation also characterize the preoperational stage.

Vygotsky's Theory

- Vygotsky's theory represents a social constructivist approach to development. According to Vygotsky, children construct knowledge through social interaction, and they use language not only to communicate with others but also to plan, guide, and monitor their own behavior and to help them solve problems. His theory suggests that adults should assess and use the child's zone of proximal development (ZPD), which is the range of tasks that are too difficult for children to master alone but that can be learned with the guidance and assistance of adults or more-skilled children. The theory also suggests that adults and peers should teach through scaffolding, which involves changing the level of support over the course of a teaching session, with the more-skilled person adjusting guidance to fit the student's current performance level.

Information Processing

- The child's ability to attend to stimuli dramatically improves during early childhood. Advances in executive attention and sustained attention are especially important in early childhood, but young children still attend to the salient rather than the relevant features of a task. Significant improvement in short-term memory occurs during early childhood. With good prompts, young children's long-term memories can be accurate, although young children can be led into developing false memories. Advances in executive function, an umbrella-like concept that consists of a number of higher-level cognitive processes linked to the development of the prefrontal cortex, occur in early childhood. Executive function involves managing one's thoughts to engage in goal-directed behavior and self-control. Young children express curiosity about the human mind, and this has been studied under the topic of theory of mind. A number of developmental changes characterize children's theory of mind, including those involved in false beliefs. Individual variations also are involved in theory of mind. For example, autistic children have difficulty developing such a theory.

3 Language Development

 LG3 Summarize how language develops in early childhood.

Understanding Phonology and Morphology

Changes in Syntax and Semantics

Advances in Pragmatics

Young Children's Literacy

- Young children increase their grasp of language's rule systems. In terms of phonology, most young children become more sensitive to the sounds of spoken language. Berko's classic experiment demonstrated that young children understand morphological rules.

- Preschool children learn and apply rules of syntax and of how words should be ordered. In terms of semantics, vocabulary development increases dramatically during early childhood.

- Young children's conversational skills improve, they increase their sensitivity to the needs of others in conversation, and they learn to change their speech style to suit the situation.

- Parents and teachers need to provide young children with a supportive environment in which to develop literacy skills. Children should be active participants and be immersed in a wide range of interesting experiences that involve listening, talking, writing, and reading.

4 Early Childhood Education

 LG4 Evaluate different approaches to early childhood education.

Variations in Early Childhood Education

Education for Young Children Who Are Disadvantaged

Controversies in Early Childhood Education

- The child-centered kindergarten emphasizes educating the whole child, with particular attention to individual variation, the process of learning, and the importance of play in development. The Montessori approach allows children to choose from a range of activities while teachers serve as facilitators. Developmentally appropriate practice focuses on the typical patterns of children (age-appropriateness) and the uniqueness of each child (individual-appropriateness). Such practice contrasts with developmentally inappropriate practice, which ignores the concrete, hands-on approach to learning.

- The U.S. government has tried to break the poverty cycle with programs such as Head Start. The Early Head Start program began in 1995. Model programs have been shown to have positive effects on children who live in poverty.

- Controversy characterizes early childhood education curricula. On the one side are the child-centered, constructivist advocates; on the other are those who advocate an instructivist, academic approach. Another controversy focuses on whether preschool education makes a difference, especially for children who are not disadvantaged.

key terms

growth hormone deficiency 199
myelination 200
preoperational stage 206
operations 206
symbolic function substage 206
egocentrism 207

animism 207
intuitive thought substage 208
centration 208
conservation 208
zone of proximal development (ZPD) 210

social constructivist approach 213
executive attention 215
sustained attention 215
short-term memory 215
executive function 216
theory of mind 217

fast mapping 222
child-centered kindergarten 224
Montessori approach 225
developmentally appropriate practice 225
Project Head Start 227

key people

Mona El-Sheikh 202
Jean Piaget 206
Barbel Inhelder 207
Rochel Gelman 209

Lev Vygotsky 209
Mary Rothbart 214
Maria Gartstein 214
Walter Mischel 216

Stephanie Carlson 217
Jean Berko 221
Kathy Hirsh-Pasek 222
Robert Golinkoff 222

Justin Harris 222
Ellen Galinsky 224
Maria Montessori 225

chapter 8

SOCIOEMOTIONAL DEVELOPMENT IN EARLY CHILDHOOD

chapter outline

1 Emotional and Personality Development

Learning Goal 1 Discuss emotional and personality development in early childhood.

The Self
Emotional Development
Moral Development
Gender

2 Families

Learning Goal 2 Explain how families can influence young children's development.

Parenting
Child Maltreatment
Sibling Relationships and Birth Order
The Changing Family in a Changing Society

3 Peer Relations, Play, and Media/Screen Time

Learning Goal 3 Describe the roles of peers, play, and media/screen time in young children's development.

Peer Relations
Play
Media/Screen Time

Like many children, Sara Newland loves animals.

During a trip to the zoo when she was four years old, Sarah learned about an animal that was a member of an endangered species and became motivated to help. With her mother's guidance, she baked lots of cakes and cookies, then sold them on the sidewalk outside her home. She was excited about making $35 from the cake and cookie sales, which soon after she mailed to the World Wildlife Fund. Several weeks later, the fund wrote back to Sarah, requesting more money. Sarah was devastated because she thought she had taken care of the animal problem. Her mother consoled her and told her that the endangered animal problem and many others are so big that it takes continued help from many people to solve them. Her mother's guidance when Sarah was a young child must have worked because by the end of elementary school, Sarah had begun helping out at a child care center and working with her mother to provide meals to the homeless.

As with Sarah's mother, sensitive parents can make a difference in encouraging young children's sense of morality. Just as parents support and guide their children to become good readers, musicians, or athletes, they also play key roles in young children's socioemotional development. (Source: Kantowitz, 1991).

topical connections *looking back*

During infancy, children's socioemotional development makes considerable progress as their caregivers (especially their parents) socialize them and they develop more sophisticated ways of initiating social interactions with others. Development of a secure attachment is a key aspect of infant development, and the development of autonomy in the second year of life also signals an important accomplishment. As children move through infancy, it is important for caregivers to guide them in regulating their emotions. Temperament also is a central characteristic of the infant's profile, and some temperament styles are more adaptive than others. The use of child care has become increasingly common in recent years, and the quality of this care varies considerably. Parents continue to play key roles in children's development in the early childhood period, but peers begin to play more important roles as well.

preview

In early childhood, children's emotional lives and personalities develop in significant ways, and their small worlds widen. In addition to the continuing influence of family relationships, peers take on a more significant role in children's development, and play as well as media and screen time fill the days of many young children's lives.

1 Emotional and Personality Development

LG1 Discuss emotional and personality development in early childhood.

The Self — Emotional Development — Moral Development — Gender

Many changes characterize young children's socioemotional development in early childhood. Their developing minds and social experiences produce remarkable advances in the development of their self, emotional maturity, moral understanding, and gender awareness.

THE SELF

We learned in Chapter 6 that during the second year of life children make considerable progress in self-recognition. In the early childhood years, young children develop in many ways that enable them to enhance their self-understanding.

Initiative Versus Guilt   In Chapter 1, you read about Erik Erikson's (1968) eight developmental stages that are encountered during certain time periods in the human life span. As you learned in Chapter 6, Erikson's first two stages—trust versus mistrust and autonomy versus shame and doubt—describe what he considers to be the main developmental tasks of infancy. Erikson's psychosocial stage associated with early childhood is initiative versus guilt. By now, children have become convinced that they are persons in their own right; during early childhood, they begin to discover what kind of person they will become. They identify intensely with their parents, who most of the time appear to them to be powerful and beautiful, although often unreasonable, disagreeable, and sometimes even dangerous. During early childhood, children use their perceptual, motor, cognitive, and language skills to make things happen. They have a surplus of energy that permits them to forget failures quickly and to approach new areas that seem desirable—even if dangerous—with undiminished zest and some increased sense of direction. On their own initiative, then, children at this stage exuberantly move out into a wider social world.

The great governor of initiative is conscience. Young children's initiative and enthusiasm may bring them not only rewards but also guilt, which lowers self-esteem.

Self-Understanding and Understanding Others   Recent research studies have revealed that young children are more psychologically aware—of themselves and others—than used to be thought (Easterbrooks & others, 2013). This psychological awareness reflects expanding psychological sophistication.

Self-Understanding   In Erikson's portrait of early childhood, the young child clearly has begun to develop **self-understanding,** which is the representation of self, the substance and content of self-conceptions (Harter, 2012). Though not the whole of personal identity, self-understanding provides its rational underpinnings. Mainly through interviews, researchers have probed children's conceptions of many aspects of self-understanding.

As we saw in Chapter 6, "Socioemotional Development in Infancy," early self-understanding involves self-recognition. In early childhood, young children think that the self can be described by material characteristics, such as size, shape, and color. They distinguish themselves from others through physical and material attributes. Says 4-year-old Sandra, "I'm different from Jennifer because I have brown hair and she has blond hair." Says 4-year-old

self-understanding The child's cognitive representation of self, the substance and content of the child's self-conceptions.

Ralph, "I am different from Hank because I am taller, and I am different from my sister because I have a bicycle." Physical activities are also a central component of the self in early childhood (Keller, Ford, & Meacham, 1978). For example, preschool children often describe themselves in terms of activities such as play. In sum, during early childhood, children often provide self-descriptions that involve body attributes, material possessions, and physical activities.

Although young children mainly describe themselves in terms of concrete, observable features and action tendencies, at about 4 to 5 years of age as they hear others use words describing psychological traits and emotions, they begin to include these in their own self-descriptions (Marsh, Ellis, & Craven, 2002). Thus, in a self-description, a 4-year-old might say, "I'm not scared. I'm always happy." Young children's self-descriptions are typically unrealistically positive, as reflected in the comment of this 4-year-old who says he is always happy, which he is not (Harter, 2012). They express this optimism because they don't yet distinguish between their desired competence and their actual competence, tend to confuse ability and effort (thinking that differences in ability can be changed as easily as can differences in effort), don't engage in spontaneous social comparison of their abilities with those of others, and tend to compare their present abilities with what they could do at an earlier age (which usually makes their abilities look quite good). This overestimation of their attributes helps to protect young children from negative self-evaluations.

However, as in virtually all areas of human development, there are individual variations in young children's self-conceptions, and there is increasing evidence that some children are vulnerable to negative self-attributions (Thompson, 2011). For example, one study revealed that insecurely attached preschool children whose mothers reported a high level of parenting stress and depressive symptoms had a lower self-concept than other young children in more positive family circumstances (Goodvin & others, 2008). This research indicates that young children's generally optimistic self-ascriptions do not buffer them from adverse, stressful family conditions (Thompson, 2011).

In recent research studies, young children's ability to understand their own and others' emotions preceded advances in their theory of mind (Nelson & others, 2013a; O'Brien & others, 2011). These studies indicated that a better basic understanding of emotions in early childhood enabled them to develop a more advanced understanding of others' perspectives.

What characterizes young children's self-understanding?

Understanding Others Children also make advances in their understanding of others and learn from others in early childhood (Harter, 2012; Mills, 2013; Thompson, 2014a, 2015). As we saw in Chapter 7, "Physical and Cognitive Development in Early Childhood," young children's theory of mind includes understanding that other people have emotions and desires. And, at about 4 to 5 years, children not only start describing themselves in terms of psychological traits, but they also begin to perceive others in terms of psychological traits. Thus, a 4-year-old might say, "My teacher is nice."

As they mature, young children need to develop an understanding that people don't always give accurate reports of their beliefs (Landrum, Mills, & Johnston, 2013; Mills, 2013; Mills, Elashi, & Archacki, 2011; Mills & Landrum, 2012). Researchers have found that even 4-year-olds understand that people may make statements that aren't true to obtain what they want or to avoid trouble (Lee & others, 2002). For example, one study revealed that 4- and 5-year-olds were increasingly skeptical of another child's claim to be sick when the children were informed that the child was motivated to avoid having to go to camp (Gee & Heyman, 2007). Also, a recent study compared preschool children's trust in an expert's comments under different conditions (Landrum, Mills, & Johnston, 2013). In this study, in one condition, 5-year-olds trusted the expert's claim more than 3-year-olds did. However, in other conditions, preschoolers tended to trust a nice non-expert more than a mean expert, indicating that young children often are likely to believe someone who is nice to them rather than someone who is an expert.

Young children are more psychologically aware of themselves and others than used to be thought. Some children are better than others at understanding people's feelings and desires—and, to some degree, these individual differences are influenced by conversations caregivers have with young children about feelings and desires.

Another important aspect of understanding others involves understanding joint commitments. As children approach their third birthday, their collaborative interactions with others increasingly involve obligations to the partner (Tomasello & Hamann, 2012). A recent study revealed that 3-year-olds, but not 2-year-olds, recognized when an adult is committed and when they themselves are committed to joint activity that involves obligation to a partner (Grafenhain & others, 2009).

Both the extensive theory of mind research and the recent research on young children's social understanding underscore that young children are not as egocentric as Piaget envisioned (Sokol, Snjezana, & Muller, 2010; Thompson, 2012). Piaget's concept of egocentrism has become so ingrained in people's thinking about young children that too often the current research on social awareness in infancy and early childhood has been overlooked. Research increasingly shows that young children are more socially sensitive and perceptive than was previously envisioned, suggesting that parents and teachers can help them to better understand and interact in the social world by how they interact with them (Thompson 2014a). If young children are seeking to better understand various mental and emotional states (intentions, goals, feelings, desires) that underlie people's actions, then talking with them about these internal states can improve young children's understanding of them (Thompson, 2011, 2014a, 2015).

However, debate continues to surround the question of whether young children are socially sensitive or basically egocentric. Ross Thompson (2012, 2014a, 2015) comes down on the side of viewing young children as socially sensitive, while Susan Harter (2012, 2013) argues that there is still evidence to support the conclusion that young children are essentially egocentric.

EMOTIONAL DEVELOPMENT

The young child's growing awareness of self is linked to the ability to feel an expanding range of emotions. Young children, like adults, experience many emotions during the course of a day. Their emotional development in early childhood allows them to try to make sense of other people's emotional reactions and to begin to control their own emotions (Cummings, Braungart-Rieker, & Du Rocher-Schudlich, 2013; Thompson, 2014a, 2015).

Expressing Emotions Recall from Chapter 6 that even young infants experience emotions such as joy and fear, but to experience *self-conscious emotions* children must be able to refer to themselves and be aware of themselves as distinct from others (Lewis, 2010). Pride, shame, embarrassment, and guilt are examples of self-conscious emotions. Self-conscious emotions do not appear to develop until self-awareness appears at approximately 15 to 18 months of age.

During the early childhood years, emotions such as pride and guilt become more common. They are especially influenced by parents' responses to children's behavior. For example, a young child may experience shame when a parent says, "You should feel bad about biting your sister." A recent study revealed that young children's emotional expression was linked to their parents' own expressive behavior (Nelson & others, 2012). In this study, mothers who expressed a high incidence of positive emotions and a low incidence of negative emotions at home had children who were observed to use more positive emotion words during mother-child interactions than mothers who expressed few positive emotions at home.

A young child expressing the emotion of shame, which occurs when a child evaluates his or her actions as not living up to standards. A child experiencing shame wishes to hide or disappear. *Why is shame called a self-conscious emotion?*

Understanding Emotions One of the most important advances in emotional development in early childhood is an increased understanding of emotion (Denham & others, 2012; Easterbrooks & others, 2013; Goodvin, Winer, & Thompson, 2014). During early childhood, young children increasingly understand that certain situations are likely to evoke particular emotions, facial expressions indicate specific emotions, emotions affect behavior, and emotions can be used to influence others' emotions (Cole & others, 2009). Researchers have found that young children's understanding of emotions is linked to their prosocial behavior (Ensor, Spencer, & Hughes, 2011).

Between 2 and 4 years of age, children considerably increase the number of terms they use to describe emotions. During this time, they are also learning about the causes and consequences of feelings (Denham & others, 2011).

When they are 4 to 5 years of age, children show an increased ability to reflect on emotions. They also begin to understand that the same event can elicit different feelings in

Caregivers' Emotional Expressiveness, Children's Emotion Regulation, and Behavior Problems in Head Start Children

A recent study by Dana McCoy and Cybele Raver (2011) explored links between caregivers' reports of their positive and negative emotional expressiveness, observations of young children's emotion regulation, and teachers' reports of the children's internalizing and externalizing behavior problems. The participants were 97 mostly African American and Latino children whose mean age was 4 years and 3 months, along with their primary caregivers (90 mothers, 5 fathers, and 2 grandmothers).

To assess caregiver expressiveness, caregivers were asked to provide ratings from 1 (never/rarely) to 9 (very frequently) on 7 items that reflect caregiver expressiveness, such as "telling family members how happy you are" and "expressing anger at someone's carelessness." Children's emotion regulation was assessed with (a) the emotion regulation part of the PSRA (preschool self-regulation assessment) in which observers rated young children's behavior on 4 delay tasks, 3 executive function tasks, and 3 compliance tasks; (b) an assessment report on children's emotion and emotion regulation; and (c) observations of the children's real-time emotion regulation related to positive emotion (expressions of happiness, for example) and negative emotion (expressions of anger or irritability,

How might young children's emotion regulation be linked to caregivers' expressiveness?

for example). Children's internalizing and externalizing behaviors were rated by their teachers on the extent to which the children had shown such behavioral problems in the last 3 months.

The researchers found that a higher level of caregiver negativity and a lower level of children's emotion regulation independently were linked to more internalizing behavior problems in the young Head Start children. Also, caregivers' reports of their positive emotional expressiveness were associated with a lower level of young children's externalizing behavior problems. The findings demonstrate the importance of family emotional climate and young children's emotion regulation in the development of young children.

The study you just read about was correlational in nature. If you were interested in conducting an experimental study of the effects of caregivers' emotional expressiveness and children's emotion regulation on children's problem behaviors, how would you conduct the study differently?

---

different people. Moreover, they show a growing awareness that they need to manage their emotions to meet social standards.

Regulating Emotions   As we saw in Chapter 6, "Socioemotional Development in Infancy," emotion regulation is an important aspect of development. Emotion regulation especially plays a key role in children's ability to manage the demands and conflicts they face in interacting with others (Lewis, 2013; Thompson, 2011, 2013c, d). Many researchers consider the growth of emotion regulation in children as fundamental to becoming socially competent (Cole & Hall, 2012; Perry & others, 2012; Thompson, 2014a, 2015). Emotion regulation can be conceptualized as an important component of self-regulation or of executive function. Recall from Chapter 7 that executive function is increasingly thought to be a key concept in describing the young child's higher-level cognitive functioning (Carlson, White, & Davis-Unger, 2014; Carlson, Zelazo, & Faja, 2013).

Cybele Raver and her colleagues (Blair & Raver, 2012, 2015; Raver & others, 2011, 2012, 2013; Zhai, Raver, & Jones, 2012) have conducted a number of studies that explore the role of emotion regulation in young children's development. They use various interventions, such as increasing caregiver emotional expressiveness, to improve young children's emotion regulation and reduce behavior problems in children growing up in poverty conditions. To read in greater detail about one of Cybele Raver's recent studies, see *Connecting through Research.*

Emotion-Coaching and Emotion-Dismissing Parents   Parents can play an important role in helping young children regulate their emotions (Dunsmore, Booker, & Ollendick, 2013). Depending on how they talk with their children about emotion, parents can be described as taking an *emotion-coaching* or an *emotion-dismissing* approach (Gottman, 2013). The

developmental **connection**

Executive Function

In early childhood, executive function especially involves developmental advances in cognitive inhibition, cognitive flexibility, goal-setting, and delay of gratification. Chapter 7, p. 216

An emotion-coaching parent. *What are some differences between emotion-coaching and emotion-dismissing parents?*

distinction between these approaches is most evident in the way the parent deals with the child's negative emotions (anger, frustration, sadness, and so on). *Emotion-coaching parents* monitor their children's emotions, view their children's negative emotions as opportunities for teaching, assist them in labeling emotions, and coach them in how to deal effectively with emotions. In contrast, *emotion-dismissing parents* view their role as to deny, ignore, or change negative emotions. Emotion-coaching parents interact with their children in a less rejecting manner, use more scaffolding and praise, and are more nurturant than are emotion-dismissing parents. Moreover, the children of emotion-coaching parents are better at soothing themselves when they get upset, more effective in regulating their negative affect, focus their attention better, and have fewer behavior problems than the children of emotion-dismissing parents (Gottman, 2014). Recent researcher studies found that fathers' emotion coaching was related to children's social competence (Baker, Fenning, & Crnic, 2011) and that mothers' emotion coaching was linked to less oppositional behavior (Dunsmore, Booker, & Ollendick, 2013).

Parents' knowledge of their children's emotional world can help them to guide their children's emotional development and to teach their children how to cope effectively with problems. One study found that mothers' knowledge about what distresses and comforts their children predicted the children's coping, empathy, and prosocial behavior (Vinik, Almas, & Grusec, 2011).

A challenge parents face is that young children typically don't want to talk about difficult emotional topics, such as being distressed or engaging in negative behaviors. Among the strategies young children use to avoid these conversations is to not talk at all, change the topic, push away, or run away. In one study, Ross Thompson and his colleagues (2009) found that young children were more likely to openly discuss difficult emotional circumstances when they were securely attached to their mother and when their mother conversed with them in a way that validated and accepted the child's views.

Emotion Regulation and Peer Relations   Emotions play a strong role in determining the success of a child's peer relationships (Denham & others, 2011). Specifically, the ability to modulate one's emotions is an important skill that benefits children in their relationships with peers. Moody and emotionally negative children are more likely to experience rejection by their peers, whereas emotionally positive children are more popular. One study revealed that 4-year-olds recognized and generated strategies for controlling their anger more than did 3-year-olds (Cole & others, 2009). Also, a recent study found that children who regulated their frustration and distress at an earlier age during preschool (3 years) had a more rapid decline in externalizing problem behavior when interacting with peers across the early childhood period (3 to 5 years of age) (Perry & others, 2013). Emotion regulation at ages 4 and 5 did not reduce the problem behavior to the same extent that it did at 3 years of age, suggesting that earlier emotion regulation puts children on a more adaptive trajectory in interacting with peers.

MORAL DEVELOPMENT

Moral development involves thoughts, feelings, and behaviors regarding rules and conventions about what people should do in their interactions with other people. Major developmental theories have focused on different aspects of moral development (Vozzola, 2014).

Moral Feelings   Feelings of anxiety and guilt are central to the account of moral development provided by Freud's psychoanalytic theory (introduced in Chapter 1). According to Freud, children attempt to reduce anxiety, avoid punishment, and maintain parental affection by identifying with parents and internalizing their standards of right and wrong, thus forming the superego—the moral element of personality.

Freud's ideas are not backed by research, but guilt certainly can motivate moral behavior. Other emotions, however, also contribute to the child's moral development, including positive feelings. One important example is empathy, which involves responding to another person's feelings with an emotion that echoes the other's feelings (Denham & others, 2011).

Infants have the capacity for some purely empathic responses, but empathy often requires the ability to discern another's inner psychological states, which is also known as perspective

developmental connection

Theories

Freud theorized that individuals go through five psychosexual stages. Chapter 1, p. 20

moral development Development that involves thoughts, feelings, and behaviors regarding rules and conventions about what people should do in their interactions with other people.

taking. Learning how to identify a wide range of emotional states in others and to anticipate what kinds of action will improve another person's emotional state helps to advance children's moral development (Thompson, 2011, 2015).

Today, many child developmentalists believe that both positive feelings—such as empathy, sympathy, admiration, and self-esteem—and negative feelings—such as anger, outrage, shame, and guilt—contribute to children's moral development (Eisenberg, Spinrad, & Morris, 2013). When these emotions are strongly experienced, they influence children to act in accord with standards of right and wrong. *Sympathy*—an other-oriented emotional response in which an observer experiences emotions that are similar or identical to what the other person is feeling—often motivates prosocial behavior (Eisenberg, Spinrad, & Morris, 2013).

Moral Reasoning   Interest in how children think about moral issues was stimulated by Piaget (1932), who extensively observed and interviewed children between the ages of 4 and 12. Piaget watched children play marbles to learn how they applied and thought about the game's rules. He also asked children about ethical issues—theft, lies, punishment, and justice, for example. Piaget concluded that children go through two distinct stages in how they think about morality.

- From about 4 to 7 years of age, children display **heteronomous morality,** the first stage of moral development in Piaget's theory. Children think of justice and rules as unchangeable properties of the world, removed from the control of people.
- From 7 to 10 years of age, children are in a transition showing some features of the first stage of moral reasoning and some stages of the second stage, autonomous morality.
- At about 10 years of age and older, children show **autonomous morality.** They become aware that rules and laws are created by people, and in judging an action they consider the actor's intentions as well as the consequences.

Because young children are heteronomous moralists, they judge the rightness or goodness of behavior by considering its consequences, not the intentions of the actor. For example, to the heteronomous moralist, breaking 12 cups accidentally is worse than breaking one cup intentionally. As children develop into moral autonomists, intentions become more important than consequences.

The heteronomous thinker also believes that rules are unchangeable and are handed down by all-powerful authorities. When Piaget suggested to young children that they use new rules in a game of marbles, they resisted. By contrast, older children—moral autonomists—accept change and recognize that rules are merely convenient conventions, subject to change.

The heteronomous thinker also believes in **immanent justice,** the concept that if a rule is broken, punishment will be meted out immediately. The young child believes that a violation is connected automatically to its punishment. Immanent justice also implies that if something unfortunate happens to someone, the person must have transgressed earlier. Older children, who are moral autonomists, recognize that punishment occurs only if someone witnesses the wrongdoing and that even then, punishment is not inevitable.

How do these changes in moral reasoning occur? Piaget concluded that the changes come about through the mutual give-and-take of peer relations. In the peer group, where others have power and status similar to the child's, plans are negotiated and coordinated, and disagreements are reasoned about and eventually settled. Parent-child relations, in which parents have the power and children do not, are less likely to advance moral reasoning, because rules are often handed down in an authoritarian way.

Earlier in this chapter you read about Ross Thompson's view that young children are not as egocentric as Piaget envisioned. Thompson (2012) recently further elaborated on this view, arguing that recent research indicates that young children often show a nonegocentric awareness of others' goals, feelings, and desires and how such internal states are influenced by the actions of others. Theory of mind research indicates that young children possess cognitive resources that allow them to be aware of others' intentions and to recognize when someone violates a moral prohibition. One study of 3-year-olds found that they were less likely to offer assistance to an adult they had previously observed being harmful to another person (Vaish, Carpenter, & Tomasello, 2010). However, because of limitations in their self-control skills, social understanding, and cognitive flexibility, young children's moral advancements often are

heteronomous morality The first stage of moral development in Piaget's theory, occurring from approximately 4 to 7 years of age. Justice and rules are conceived of as unchangeable properties of the world, removed from the control of people.

autonomous morality In Piaget's theory, older children (about 10 years of age and older) become aware that rules and laws are created by people and that in judging an action one should consider the actor's intentions as well as the consequences.

immanent justice The concept that if a rule is broken, punishment will be meted out immediately.

How will this child's moral thinking about stealing a cookie differ according to whether he is in Piaget's heteronomous or autonomous stage?

developmental **connection**

Development

Kohlberg's theory, like Piaget's, emphasizes that peers play more important roles in children's moral development than parents do. Chapter 10, p. 310

developmental connection

Theories

What are the main themes of Bandura's social cognitive theory? Chapter 1, p. 24

◀ - - - - - - - - - - - - - -

What are some aspects of relationships between parents and children that contribute to children's moral development?

conscience An internal regulation of standards of right and wrong that involves integrating moral thought, feeling, and behavior.

inconsistent and vary across situations. They still have a long way to go before they have the capacity to develop a consistent moral character and to make ethical judgments.

Moral Behavior   The behavioral and social cognitive approaches initially described in Chapter 1 focus on moral behavior rather than moral reasoning. Advocates of these perspectives hold that the processes of reinforcement, punishment, and imitation explain the development of moral behavior. When children are rewarded for behavior that is consistent with laws and social conventions, they are likely to repeat that behavior. When models who behave morally are provided, children are likely to adopt their actions. And, when children are punished for immoral behavior, those behaviors are likely to be reduced or eliminated. However, because punishment may have adverse side effects, as discussed later in this chapter, it should be used judiciously and cautiously.

In the moral behavior view, the situation also influences behavior. More than a half century ago, a comprehensive study of thousands of children in many situations—at home, at school, and at church, for example—found that the totally honest child was virtually nonexistent; so was the child who cheated in all situations (Hartshorne & May, 1928–1930). Behavioral and social cognitive researchers emphasize that what children do in one situation is often only weakly related to what they do in other situations. A child might cheat in class but not in a game; a child might steal a piece of candy when alone but not steal it when others are present.

And when children observe people behaving morally, they are likely to copy their actions. In a recent study, 2-year-olds watched a video of an adult engaging in prosocial behavior in response to another person's distress (Williamson, Donohue, & Tully, 2013). Children who saw the prosocial video were more likely than children who did not see it to imitate the prosocial behavior in response to their own parents' distress.

Social cognitive theorists also stress that the ability to resist temptation is closely tied to the development of self-control. To achieve this self-control, children must learn to delay gratification. According to social cognitive theorists, cognitive factors are important in the child's development of self-control (Bandura, 2009, 2010a, b, 2012).

Conscience   **Conscience** refers to an internal regulation of standards of right and wrong that involves an integration of all three components of moral development we have described so far—moral thought, feeling, and behavior (Kochanska & others, 2010). Reflecting the presence of a conscience in young children, researchers have found that young children are aware of right and wrong, have the capacity to show empathy toward others, experience guilt, indicate discomfort following a transgression, and are sensitive to violating rules (Kochanska & Aksan, 2007; Kochanska & others, 2009).

A major interest regarding young children's conscience focuses on children's relationships with their caregivers (Kochanska & Kim, 2012, 2013). Especially important in this regard is the emergence of young children's willingness to embrace the values of their parents, an orientation that flows from a positive, close relationship (Kochanska & Aksan, 2007). For example, children who are securely attached are more likely to internalize their parents' values and rules (Kochanska & Kim, 2012, 2013; Thompson, 2014a, 2015).

Parenting and Young Children's Moral Development   In Ross Thompson's (2006, 2009, 2012) view, young children are moral apprentices, striving to understand what is moral. Among the most important aspects of the relationship between parents and children that contribute to children's moral development are relational quality, parental discipline, proactive strategies, and conversational dialogue.

Parent-child relationships introduce children to the mutual obligations of close relationships (Kim & others, 2014; Kochanska & Kim, 2012, 2013). Parents' obligations include engaging in positive caregiving and guiding children to become competent human beings. Children's obligations include responding appropriately to parents' initiatives and maintaining a positive relationship with parents.

An important parenting strategy involves proactively averting potential misbehavior by children before it takes place (Thompson, 2009). With younger children, being proactive means using diversion, such as distracting their attention or moving them to alternative activities. With older children, being proactive may involve talking with them about values that the parents deem important.

Conversations related to moral development can benefit children, regardless of whether they occur as part of a discipline encounter or outside the encounter in the everyday stream of parent-child interaction (Thompson, Meyer, & McGinley, 2006; Thompson & Newton, 2013). The conversations can be planned or spontaneous and can focus on topics such as past events (for example, a child's prior misbehavior or positive moral conduct), shared future events (for example, going somewhere that may involve a temptation and will require positive moral behavior), and immediate events (for example, talking with the child about a sibling's tantrums).

GENDER

Recall from Chapter 1 that *gender* refers to the characteristics of people as males and females. **Gender identity** involves a sense of one's own gender, including knowledge, understanding, and acceptance of being male or female (Egan & Perry, 2001; Perry, 2012). One aspect of gender identity involves knowing whether you are a girl or boy, an awareness that most children develop by about 2½ years of age (Blakemore, Berenbaum, & Liben, 2009). **Gender roles** are sets of expectations that prescribe how females or males should think, act, and feel. During the preschool years, most children increasingly act in ways that match their culture's gender roles. **Gender typing** refers to acquisition of a traditional masculine or feminine role. For example, fighting is more characteristic of a traditional masculine role and crying is more characteristic of a traditional feminine role. One study revealed that sex-typed behavior (boys playing with cars and girls with jewelry, for example) increased during the preschool years and that children who engaged in the most sex-typed behavior during the preschool years still did so at 8 years of age (Golombok & others, 2008).

How is gender influenced by biology? by children's social experiences? by cognitive factors?

Biological Influences Biology clearly plays a role in gender development (Arnold, 2012; Hines, 2013). Among the possible biological influences are chromosomes, hormones, and evolution.

Chromosomes and Hormones Biologists have learned a great deal about how sex differences develop. Recall that humans normally have 46 chromosomes arranged in pairs (see Chapter 2). The 23rd pair consists of a combination of X and Y chromosomes, usually two X chromosomes in a female and an X and a Y in a male. In the first few weeks of gestation, however, female and male embryos look alike.

Males start to differ from females when genes on the Y chromosome in the male embryo trigger the development of testes rather than ovaries; the testes secrete copious amounts of the class of hormones known as androgens. Low levels of androgens in the female embryo allow the normal development of female sex organs.

Thus, hormones play a key role in the development of sex differences (Hines, 2013). The two main classes of sex hormones, estrogens and androgens, are secreted by the *gonads* (ovaries in females, testes in males). *Estrogens,* such as estradiol, influence the development of female physical sex characteristics. *Androgens,* such as testosterone, promote the development of male physical sex characteristics. Sex hormones also can influence children's socioemotional development.

The Evolutionary Psychology View How might physical differences between the sexes give rise to psychological differences between males and females? Evolutionary psychology (introduced in Chapter 2) offers one answer. According to evolutionary psychology, adaptation during human evolution produced psychological differences between males and females (Brooker & others, 2015; Buss, 2012). Because of their differing roles in reproduction, males and females faced differing pressures when the human species was evolving. In particular, because having multiple sexual liaisons improves the likelihood that males will pass on their genes, natural selection favored males who adopted short-term mating strategies. These are strategies that allow a male to win the competition with other males for sexual access to females. Therefore, say evolutionary psychologists, males evolved dispositions that favor violence, competition, and risk taking.

gender identity The sense of being male or female, which most children acquire by the time they are 3 years old.

gender role A set of expectations that prescribes how females or males should think, act, and feel.

gender typing Acquisition of a traditional masculine or feminine role.

First imagine that this is a photograph of a baby girl. *What expectations would you have of her?* Then imagine that this is a photograph of a baby boy. *What expectations would you have of him?*

"How is it gendered?"
© Edward Koren/The New Yorker Collection/
www.cartoonbank.com

social role theory A theory that gender differences result from the contrasting roles of men and women.

psychoanalytic theory of gender A theory deriving from Freud's view that the preschool child develops a sexual attraction to the opposite-sex parent, by approximately 5 or 6 years of age renounces this attraction because of anxious feelings, and subsequently identifies with the same-sex parent, unconsciously adopting the same-sex parent's characteristics.

In contrast, according to evolutionary psychologists, females' contributions to the gene pool were improved when they secured resources that ensured that their offspring would survive. As a consequence, natural selection favored females who devoted effort to parenting and chose successful, ambitious mates who could provide their offspring with resources and protection.

Critics of evolutionary psychology argue that its hypotheses are backed by speculations about prehistory, not evidence, and that in any event people are not locked into behavior that was adaptive in the evolutionary past. Critics also claim that the evolutionary view pays little attention to cultural and individual variations in gender differences (Hyde & Else-Quest, 2013).

Social Influences   Many social scientists do not locate the cause of psychological gender differences in biological dispositions. Rather, they argue that these differences reflect social experiences. Explanations for how gender differences come about through experience include both social and cognitive theories.

Social Theories of Gender   Three main social theories of gender have been proposed—social role theory, psychoanalytic theory, and social cognitive theory. Alice Eagly (2001, 2010, 2012) proposed **social role theory,** which states that gender differences result from the contrasting roles of women and men. In most cultures around the world, women have less power and status than men, and they control fewer resources (UNICEF, 2011). Compared with men, women perform more domestic work, spend fewer hours in paid employment, receive lower pay, and are more thinly represented in the highest levels of organizations. In Eagly's view, as women adapted to roles with less power and less status in society, they showed more cooperative, less dominant profiles than men. Thus, the social hierarchy and division of labor are important causes of gender differences in power, assertiveness, and nurturing.

The **psychoanalytic theory of gender** stems from Freud's view that the preschool child develops a sexual attraction to the opposite-sex parent. This is the process known as the Oedipus (for boys) or Electra (for girls) complex. At 5 or 6 years of age, the child renounces this attraction because of anxious feelings. Subsequently, the child identifies with the same-sex parent, unconsciously adopting the same-sex parent's characteristics. However, developmentalists have observed that gender development does not proceed as Freud proposed. Children become gender-typed much earlier than 5 or 6 years of age, and they become masculine or feminine even when the same-sex parent is not present in the family.

The social cognitive approach discussed in Chapter 1 provides an alternative explanation of how children develop gender-typed behavior. According to the **social cognitive theory of gender,** children's gender development occurs through observing and imitating what other people say and do, and through being rewarded and punished for gender-appropriate and gender-inappropriate behavior (Bussey & Bandura, 1999). From birth onward, males and females are treated differently from one another. When infants and toddlers show gender-appropriate behavior, adults tend to reward them. Parents often use rewards and punishments to teach their daughters to be feminine ("Karen, you are being a good girl when you play gently with your doll") and their sons to be masculine ("Keith, a boy as big as you is not supposed to cry"). Parents, however, are only one of many sources through which children learn gender roles (Leaper, 2013; Leaper & Bigler, 2011). Culture, schools, peers, the media, and other family members also provide gender role models. For example, children also learn about gender by observing the behavior of other adults in the neighborhood and on television (Bugental & Grusec, 2006). As children get older, peers become increasingly important. Let's take a closer look at the influence of parents and peers.

Parental Influences   Parents, by action and by example, influence their children's gender development (Liben, Bigler, & Hilliard, 2014; Leaper, 2013). Both mothers and fathers are psychologically important to their children's gender development (Hyde & Else-Quest, 2013; Leaper, 2013; Tenenbaum & May, 2014). Cultures around the world, however, tend to give mothers and fathers different roles (Chen & others, 2011). A research review yielded the following conclusions (Bronstein, 2006):

- *Mothers' socialization strategies.* In many cultures, mothers socialize their daughters to be more obedient and responsible than their sons. They also place more restrictions on daughters' autonomy.

What role does gender play in children's peer relations?

- *Fathers' socialization strategies.* Fathers show more attention to sons than to daughters, engage in more activities with sons, and put forth more effort to promote sons' intellectual development.

Thus, according to Bronstein (2006, pp. 269–270), "Despite an increased awareness in the United States and other Western cultures of the detrimental effects of gender stereotyping, many parents continue to foster behaviors and perceptions that are consonant with traditional gender role norms."

Peer Influences   Parents provide the earliest discrimination of gender roles, but before long peers join the process of responding to and modeling masculine and feminine behavior (Goble & others, 2012). In fact, peers become so important to gender development that the playground has been called "gender school" (Luria & Herzog, 1985).

Peers extensively reward and punish gender behavior (Leaper, 2013; Leaper & Bigler, 2011). For example, when children play in ways that the culture says are sex-appropriate, their peers tend to reward them. But peers often reject children who act in a manner that is considered more characteristic of the other gender (Handrinos & others, 2012). A little girl who brings a doll to the park may find herself surrounded by new friends; a little boy might be jeered at. However, there is greater pressure for boys to conform to a traditional male role than for girls to conform to a traditional female role (Fagot, Rogers, & Leinbach, 2000). For example, a preschool girl who wants to wear boys' clothing receives considerably more approval than a boy who wants to wear a dress. The very term "tomboy" implies broad social acceptance of girls' adopting traditional male behaviors.

Gender molds important aspects of peer relations (Field & others, 2012; Zozuls & others, 2012). It influences the composition of children's groups, the size of groups, and interactions within a group (Maccoby, 1998, 2002):

- *Gender composition of children's groups.* Around the age of 3, children already show a preference to spend time with same-sex playmates. From 4 to 12 years of age, this preference for playing in same-sex groups increases, and during the elementary school years children spend a large majority of their free time with children of their own sex (see Figure 8.1). A recent study found that when preschool children select a playmate both the sex of the playmate and the playmate's level of gender-typed activity are important but sex of the playmate is more important (Martin & others, 2013).

- *Group size.* From about 5 years of age onward, boys are more likely to associate together in larger clusters than girls are. Boys are also more likely to participate in organized group games than girls are. In one study, same-sex groups of six children were permitted to use play materials in any way they wished (Benenson, Apostolaris, & Parnass, 1997). Girls were more likely than boys to play in dyads or triads, while boys were more likely to interact in larger groups and seek to attain a group goal.

- *Interaction in same-sex groups.* Boys are more likely than girls to engage in rough-and-tumble play, competition, conflict, ego displays, risk taking, and seeking dominance. By contrast, girls are more likely to engage in "collaborative discourse," in which they talk and act in a more reciprocal manner.

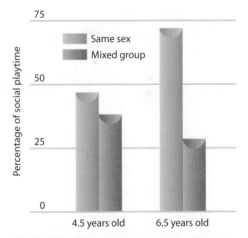

FIGURE **8.1**

DEVELOPMENTAL CHANGES IN PERCENTAGE OF TIME SPENT IN SAME-SEX AND MIXED-GROUP SETTINGS. Observations of children show that they are more likely to play in same-sex than mixed-sex groups. This tendency increases between 4 and 6 years of age.

social cognitive theory of gender A theory emphasizing that children's gender development occurs through the observation and imitation of gender behavior and through the rewards and punishments children experience for gender-appropriate and gender-inappropriate behavior.

gender schema theory The theory that gender typing emerges as children develop gender schemas of their culture's gender-appropriate and gender-inappropriate behavior.

Cognitive Influences   One influential cognitive theory is **gender schema theory,** which states that gender typing emerges as children gradually develop gender schemas of what is gender-appropriate and gender-inappropriate in their culture (Blakemore, Berenbaum, & Liben, 2009; Miller & others, 2013). A *schema* is a cognitive structure, a network of associations that guides an individual's perceptions. A *gender schema* organizes the world in terms of female and male. Children are internally motivated to perceive the world and to act in accordance with their developing schemas. Bit by bit, children pick up what is gender-appropriate and gender-inappropriate in their culture, and develop gender schemas that shape how they perceive the world and what they remember (Conry-Murray, Kim, & Turiel, 2012). Children are motivated to act in ways that conform to these gender schemas. Thus, gender schemas fuel gender typing.

Review Connect Reflect

 LG1 Discuss emotional and personality development in early childhood.

Review
- What changes in the self occur during early childhood?
- What changes take place in emotional development in early childhood?
- What are some key aspects of moral development in young children?
- How does gender develop in young children?

Connect
- In the previous section, you read about the influence of parents on children's gender development. How does this compare with what you learned about parental influences on children's temperament in Chapter 6?

Reflect *Your Own Personal Journey of Life*
- Imagine that you are the parent of a 4-year-old child. What strategies would you use to increase your child's understanding of others?

2 Families   **LG2** Explain how families can influence young children's development.

| Parenting | Child Maltreatment | Sibling Relationships and Birth Order | The Changing Family in a Changing Society |

Parenting is a very important profession, but no test of fitness for it is ever imposed in the interest of children.

—**George Bernard Shaw**
Irish Playwright, 20th Century

Attachment to a caregiver is a key social relationship during infancy, but we saw in Chapter 6 that some experts maintain that secure attachment and other aspects of the infant years have been overdramatized as determinants of life-span development. Social and emotional development is also shaped by other relationships and by temperament, contexts, and social experiences during the early childhood years and later. In this section, we will discuss social relationships in early childhood beyond attachment. We will explore different types of parenting, sibling relationships, and variations in family structures.

PARENTING

Some recent media accounts portray many parents as unhappy, feeling little joy in caring for their children. However, recent research found that parents were more satisfied with their lives than were nonparents, felt relatively better on a daily basis than did nonparents, and had more positive feelings related to caring for their children than toward doing other daily activities (Nelson & others, 2013b). Also, a recent research review concluded that parents are unhappy when they experience more negative emotions, financial problems, sleep problems, and troubled marriages (Nelson, Kushley, & Lyubomirsky, 2014). In this review, it was concluded that parents are happy when they experienced meaning in life, satisfaction of basic needs, more positive emotions, and positive social roles.

Good parenting takes time and effort (Grusec & others, 2013). You can't do it in a minute here and a minute there. You can't do it with CDs or DVDs. Of course, it's not just the quantity of time parents spend with children that is important for children's development—the quality of the parenting is clearly important (Clarke-Stewart & Parke, 2014). For example, a recent study found that maternal scaffolding, sensitivity, and support for autonomy were linked to better executive function in preschool children (Blair, Raver, & Berry, 2014). To understand variations in parenting, let's consider the styles parents use when they interact with their children, how they discipline their children, and coparenting.

Baumrind's Parenting Styles   Diana Baumrind (1971, 2012) argues that parents should be neither punitive nor aloof. Rather, they should develop rules for their children and be affectionate with them. She has described four types of parenting styles:

- **Authoritarian parenting** is a restrictive, punitive style in which parents exhort the child to follow their directions and respect their work and effort. The authoritarian parent places firm limits and controls on the child and allows little verbal exchange. For example, an authoritarian parent might say, "You do it my way or else." Authoritarian parents also might spank the child frequently, enforce rules rigidly but not explain them, and show rage toward the child. Children of authoritarian parents are often unhappy, fearful, and anxious about comparing themselves with others, fail to initiate activity, and have weak communication skills.

- **Authoritative parenting** encourages children to be independent but still places limits and controls on their actions. Extensive verbal give-and-take is allowed, and parents are warm and nurturing toward the child. An authoritative parent might put his arm around the child in a comforting way and say, "You know you should not have done that. Let's talk about how you can handle the situation better next time." Authoritative parents show pleasure and support in response to children's constructive behavior. They also expect mature, independent, and age-appropriate behavior from their children. Children whose parents are authoritative are often cheerful, self-controlled and self-reliant, and achievement-oriented; they tend to maintain friendly relations with peers, cooperate with adults, and cope well with stress.

  As was just indicated, authoritative parents do exercise some direction and control over their children. The children of authoritative parents who engage in behavioral or psychological control without being coercive or punitive often show positive developmental outcomes (Baumrind, Larzelere, & Owens, 2010).

- **Neglectful parenting** is a style in which the parent is uninvolved in the child's life. Children whose parents are neglectful develop the sense that other aspects of the parents' lives are more important than they are. These children tend to be socially incompetent. Many have poor self-control and don't handle independence well. They frequently have low self-esteem, are immature, and may be alienated from the family. In adolescence, they may show patterns of truancy and delinquency.

- **Indulgent parenting** is a style in which parents are highly involved with their children but place few demands or controls on them. Such parents let their children do what they want. As a result, the children never learn to control their own behavior and always expect to get their way. Some parents deliberately rear their children in this way because they believe the combination of warm involvement and few restraints will produce a creative, confident child. However, children whose parents are indulgent rarely learn respect for others and have difficulty controlling their behavior. They might be domineering, egocentric, noncompliant, and have difficulties in peer relations.

These four classifications of parenting involve combinations of acceptance and responsiveness on the one hand and demand and control on the other (Maccoby & Martin, 1983). How these dimensions combine to produce authoritarian, authoritative, neglectful, and indulgent parenting is shown in Figure 8.2.

Keep in mind that research on parenting styles and children's development is *correlational*, not causal, in nature. Thus, if a study reveals that authoritarian parenting is linked to higher

authoritarian parenting A restrictive, punitive style in which parents exhort the child to follow their directions and to respect their work and effort. The authoritarian parent places firm limits and controls on the child and allows little verbal exchange. Authoritarian parenting is associated with children's social incompetence.

authoritative parenting A parenting style in which parents encourage their children to be independent but still place limits and controls on their actions. Extensive verbal give-and-take is allowed, and parents are warm and nurturing toward the child. Authoritative parenting is associated with children's social competence.

neglectful parenting A style of parenting in which the parent is uninvolved in the child's life; it is associated with children's social incompetence, especially a lack of self-control.

indulgent parenting A style of parenting in which parents are highly involved with their children but place few demands or controls on them. Indulgent parenting is associated with children's social incompetence, especially a lack of self-control.

	Accepting, responsive	Rejecting, unresponsive
Demanding, controlling	Authoritative	Authoritarian
Undemanding, uncontrolling	Indulgent	Neglectful

FIGURE 8.2

CLASSIFICATION OF PARENTING STYLES. The four types of parenting styles (authoritative, authoritarian, indulgent, and neglectful) involve the dimensions of acceptance and responsiveness, on the one hand, and demand and control on the other. For example, authoritative parenting involves being both accepting/responsive and demanding/controlling.

According to Ruth Chao, which type of parenting style do many Asian American parents use?

levels of children's aggression, the possibility that aggressive children elicited authoritarian parenting is just as likely as the possibility that authoritarian parenting produced aggressive children (Bush & Peterson, 2013). Also recall from Chapter 1 that, in correlational studies, a third factor may influence the correlation between two factors. Thus, in the example involving the correlation between authoritarian parenting and children's aggression, possibly authoritarian parents (first factor) and aggressive children (second factor) share genes (third factor) that predispose them to behave in ways that produced the correlation.

Parenting Styles in Context Do the benefits of authoritative parenting transcend the boundaries of ethnicity, socioeconomic status (SES), and household composition? Although occasional exceptions have been found, evidence linking authoritative parenting with competence on the part of the child occurs in research across a wide range of ethnic groups, social strata, cultures, and family structures (Steinberg & Silk, 2002).

Nonetheless, researchers have found that in some ethnic groups, aspects of the authoritarian style may be associated with more positive child outcomes than Baumrind predicts (Parke & Clarke-Stewart, 2011). Elements of the authoritarian style may take on different meanings and have different effects depending on the context. For example, Asian American parents often continue aspects of traditional Asian child-rearing practices that have sometimes been described as authoritarian. The parents exert considerable control over their children's lives. However, Ruth Chao (2001, 2005, 2007; Chao & Otsuki-Clutter, 2011; Chao & Tseng, 2002) argues that the style of parenting used by many Asian American parents is distinct from the domineering control of the authoritarian style. Instead, Chao argues, this type of parental control reflects concern and involvement in their children's lives and is best conceptualized as a type of training. The high academic achievement of Asian American children may be a consequence of their "training" parents (Stevenson & Zusho, 2002). In recent research involving Chinese American adolescents and their parents, parental control was endorsed, as were the Confucian parental goals of perseverance, working hard in school, obedience, and being sensitive to parents' wishes (Russell, Crockett, & Chao, 2010).

An emphasis on requiring respect and obedience is also associated with the authoritarian style, but in Latino child rearing this focus may be positive rather than punitive. Rather than suppressing the child's development, it may encourage the development of a self and an identity that are embedded in the family and require respect and obedience (Dixon, Graber, & Brooks-Gunn, 2008). In these circumstances, emphasizing respect and obedience may be part of maintaining a harmonious family and important in shaping the child's identity (Umana-Taylor & Updegraff, 2013; Umana-Taylor & others, 2014).

Punishment For centuries, corporal (physical) punishment, such as spanking, has been considered a necessary and even desirable method of disciplining children. Use of corporal punishment is legal in every state in America. A national survey of U.S. parents with 3- and 4-year-old children found that 26 percent of parents reported spanking their children frequently, and 67 percent of the parents reported yelling at their children frequently (Regalado & others, 2004). A recent study of more than 11,000 U.S. parents indicated that 80 percent of the parents reported spanking their children by the time they reached kindergarten (Gershoff & others, 2012). A cross-cultural comparison found that individuals in the United States were among those with the most favorable attitudes toward corporal punishment and were the most likely to remember it being used by their parents (Curran & others, 2001) (see Figure 8.3).

An increasing number of studies have examined the outcomes of physically punishing children, although those that have been conducted are correlational (Gershoff, 2013; Lansford & Deater-Deckard, 2012; Lansford & others, 2012). Clearly, it would be highly unethical to randomly assign parents to either spank or not spank their children in an experimental study. Recall that cause and effect cannot be determined in a correlational study. In one correlational study, spanking by parents was linked with children's antisocial behavior, including cheating, telling lies, being mean to others, bullying, getting into fights, and being disobedient (Strauss, Sugarman, & Giles-Sims, 1997).

What are some reasons for avoiding spanking or similar harsh punishments? The reasons include the following:

- When adults punish a child by yelling, screaming, or spanking, they are presenting children with out-of-control models for handling stressful situations. Children may imitate this aggressive, out-of-control behavior.

- Punishment can instill fear, rage, or avoidance. For example, spanking the child may cause the child to avoid being around the parent and to fear the parent.

- Punishment tells children what not to do rather than what to do. Children should be given feedback, such as "Why don't you try this?"

- Punishment can be abusive. Parents might unintentionally become so angry when they are punishing the child that they become abusive (Knox, 2010).

Most child psychologists recommend handling misbehavior by reasoning with the child, especially explaining the consequences of the child's actions for others. Time out, in which the child is removed from a setting that offers positive reinforcement, can also be effective. For example, when the child has misbehaved, a parent might take away TV viewing for a specified time.

Debate about the effects of punishment on children's development continues (Deater-Deckard, 2013; Ferguson, 2013; Gershoff, 2013; Grusec & others, 2013; Knox, 2010). A research review concluded that corporal punishment by parents is associated with higher levels of immediate compliance and aggression by the children (Gershoff, 2002). The review also found that corporal punishment is linked to lower levels of moral internalization and mental health (Gershoff, 2002). A study in six countries revealed that mothers' use of physical punishment was linked to high rates of aggression in their children (Gershoff & others, 2010). Another study also discovered that a history of harsh physical discipline was related to adolescent depression and externalized problems, such as juvenile delinquency (Bender & others, 2007). And several recent longitudinal studies also have found that physical punishment of young children is associated with higher levels of aggression later in childhood and adolescence (Berlin & others, 2009; Gershoff & others, 2012; Lansford & others, 2011; Taylor & others, 2010). However, a research review of 26 studies concluded that only severe or predominant use of spanking, not mild spanking, compared unfavorably with alternative discipline practices with children (Larzelere & Kuhn, 2005). Also, a recent meta-analysis focused on longitudinal studies revealed that the negative outcomes of punishment on children's internalizing and externalizing problems were small (Ferguson, 2013).

Some experts (including Diana Baumrind) argue that much of the evidence for the negative effects of physical punishment is based on studies in which parents acted in an abusive manner (Baumrind, Larzelere, & Cowan, 2002). She concludes from her research that when parents use punishment in a calm, reasoned manner (which she says characterized most of the authoritative parents in her studies), children's development benefits. Thus, she emphasizes that physical punishment does not need to present children with an out-of-control adult who is yelling and screaming, as well as spanking.

In a recent research review, Elizabeth Gershoff (2013) concluded that the defenders of spanking have not produced any evidence that spanking produces positive outcomes for children, and she noted that negative outcomes of spanking have been replicated in many studies. Also, one thing that is clear regarding research on punishment of children is that if physical punishment is used it needs to be mild, infrequent, age-appropriate, and used in the context of a positive parent-child relationship (Grusec, 2011). It is also clear that when physical punishment involves abuse, it can be very harmful to children's development (Cicchetti, 2013).

In addition to considering whether physical punishment is mild or out-of-control, another factor in evaluating punishment's effects on children's development involves cultural contexts. Recent research has indicated that in countries such as Kenya where physical punishment is considered normal and necessary for handling children's transgressions, the effects of physical

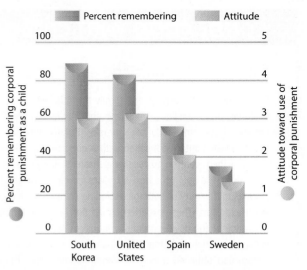

FIGURE **8.3**

CORPORAL PUNISHMENT IN DIFFERENT COUNTRIES. A five-point scale was used to assess attitudes toward corporal punishment, with scores closer to 1 indicating an attitude against its use and scores closer to 5 suggesting an attitude favoring its use. *Why are studies of corporal punishment correlational studies, and how does that affect their usefulness?*

Darla Botkin, Marriage and Family Therapist

Darla Botkin is a marriage and family therapist who teaches, conducts research, and engages in marriage and family therapy. She is on the faculty of the University of Kentucky. Botkin obtained a bachelor's degree in elementary education with a concentration in special education and then went on to receive a master's degree in early childhood education. She spent the next six years working with children and their families in a variety of settings, including child care, elementary school, and Head Start. These experiences led Botkin to recognize the interdependence of the developmental settings that children and their parents experience (such as home, school, and work). She returned to graduate school and obtained a Ph.D. in family studies from the University of Tennessee. She then became a faculty member in the Family Studies program at the University of Kentucky. Completing further coursework and clinical training in marriage and family therapy, she became certified as a marriage and family therapist.

Botkin's current interests include working with young children in family therapy, addressing gender and ethnic issues in family therapy, and exploring the role of spirituality in family wellness.

Darla Botkin (*left*) conducting a family therapy session.

For more information about what marriage and family therapists do, see page 44 in the Careers in Life-Span Development appendix.

What characterizes coparenting?

> Child maltreatment involves grossly inadequate and destructive aspects of parenting.
>
> —**Dante Cicchetti**
> *Contemporary Developmental Psychologist, University of Minnesota*

coparenting Support parents provide for each other in jointly raising their children.

punishment are less harmful than in countries such as Thailand where physical punishment is perceived as more harmful to children's development (Lansford & others, 2005, 2012).

Coparenting   The support that parents provide one another in jointly raising a child is called **coparenting.** Poor coordination between parents, undermining of the other parent, lack of cooperation and warmth, and disconnection by one parent are conditions that place children at risk for problems (McHale & Sullivan, 2008; Solmeyer & others, 2011). For example, one study revealed that coparenting influenced young children's effortful control above and beyond maternal and paternal parenting by themselves (Karreman & others, 2008). And a recent study found that greater father involvement in young children's play was linked to an increase in supportive coparenting (Jia & Schoppe-Sullivan, 2011).

Parents who do not spend enough time with their children or who have problems in child rearing can benefit from counseling and therapy. To read about the work of marriage and family counselor Darla Botkin, see *Connecting with Careers.*

CHILD MALTREATMENT

Unfortunately, punishment sometimes leads to the abuse of infants and children (Cicchetti & Toth, 2015; McCoy & Keen, 2014). In 2009, approximately 702,000 U.S. children were found to be victims of child abuse at least once during that year (U.S. Department of Health and Human Services, 2010). Eighty-one percent of these children were abused by a parent or parents. Laws in many states now require physicians and teachers to report suspected cases of child abuse, yet many cases go unreported, especially those involving battered infants.

Whereas the public and many professionals use the term *child abuse* to refer to both abuse and neglect, developmentalists increasingly use the term *child maltreatment* (Cicchetti, 2011, 2013; Cicchetti & others, 2012). This term does not have quite the emotional impact of the term *abuse* and acknowledges that maltreatment includes diverse conditions.

Types of Child Maltreatment   The four main types of child maltreatment are physical abuse, child neglect, sexual abuse, and emotional abuse (National Clearinghouse on Child Abuse and Neglect, 2004):

- *Physical abuse* is characterized by the infliction of physical injury as a result of punching, beating, kicking, biting, burning, shaking, or otherwise harming a child. The parent or other person may not have intended to hurt the child; the injury may have resulted from excessive physical punishment (Flaherty & others, 2014; Redford & others, 2013).

- *Child neglect* is characterized by failure to provide for the child's basic needs (Ross & Juarez, 2014). Neglect can be physical (abandonment, for example), educational (allowing chronic truancy, for example), or emotional (marked inattention to the child's needs, for example) (Horner, 2014). Child neglect is by far the most common form of child maltreatment. In every country where relevant data have been collected, neglect occurs up to three times as often as abuse (Dubowitz, 2013).

- *Sexual abuse* includes fondling a child's genitals, intercourse, incest, rape, sodomy, exhibitionism, and commercial exploitation through prostitution or the production of pornographic materials (Fergusson, McLeod, & Horwood, 2013; Zollner, Fuchs, & Fegert, 2014; Williams & others, 2014).

- *Emotional abuse (psychological/verbal abuse/mental injury)* includes acts or omissions by parents or other caregivers that have caused, or could cause, serious behavioral, cognitive, or emotional problems (Potthast, Neuner, & Catani, 2014).

Although any of these forms of child maltreatment may be found separately, they often occur in combination. Emotional abuse is almost always present when other forms are identified.

The Contexts of Abuse   No single factor causes child maltreatment (Cicchetti, 2011, 2013; Cicchetti & others, 2014; Cicchetti & Toth, 2015). A combination of factors, including the culture, family, and developmental characteristics of the child, likely contribute to child maltreatment.

The extensive violence that takes place in American culture, including TV violence, is reflected in the occurrence of violence in the family (Durrant, 2008). The family itself is obviously a key part of the context of abuse (Cicchetti & Toth, 2015; Trickett & Negriff, 2011). Among the family and family-associated characteristics that may contribute to child maltreatment are parenting stress, substance abuse, social isolation, single parenting, and socioeconomic difficulties (especially poverty) (Cicchetti, 2013). The interactions of all family members need to be considered, regardless of who performs the violent acts against the child. For example, even though the father may be the one who physically abuses the child, the behavior of the mother, the child, and siblings also should be evaluated.

Were parents who abuse children abused by their own parents? About one-third of parents who were abused themselves when they were young go on to abuse their own children (Cicchetti & Toth, 2006). Thus, some, but not a majority, of parents are involved in an intergenerational transmission of abuse.

Developmental Consequences of Abuse   Among the consequences of child maltreatment in childhood and adolescence are poor emotion regulation, attachment problems, problems in peer relations, difficulty in adapting to school, and other psychological problems such as depression and delinquency (Cicchetti, 2011, 2013; Cicchetti & Banny, 2014). As shown in Figure 8.4, maltreated young children in foster care were more likely to show abnormal stress hormone levels than middle-SES young children living with their birth family (Gunnar, Fisher, & The Early Experience, Stress, and Prevention Network, 2006). In this study, the abnormal stress hormone levels were mainly present in the foster children who were neglected, best described as "institutional neglect" (Fisher, 2005). Abuse also may have this effect on young children (Gunnar & others, 2006). Adolescents who experienced abuse or neglect as children are more likely than adolescents who were not maltreated as children

Eight-year-old Donnique Hein lovingly holds her younger sister, 6-month-old Maria Paschel, after a meal at Laura's Home, a crisis shelter in Westpark (Ohio) run by the City Mission, in March 2010.

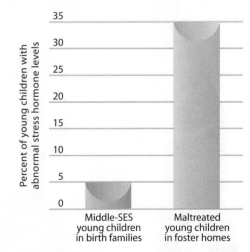

FIGURE 8.4

ABNORMAL STRESS HORMONE LEVELS IN YOUNG CHILDREN IN DIFFERENT TYPES OF REARING CONDITIONS

to engage in violent romantic relationships, delinquency, sexual risk taking, and substance abuse (Shin, Hong, & Hazen, 2010; Trickett, Negriff, & Peckins, 2011). And a recent study revealed that a significant increase in suicide attempts before age 18 occurred with repeated child maltreatment (Jonson-Reid, Kohl, & Drake, 2012).

Later, during the adult years, individuals who were maltreated as children are more likely to experience physical ailments, mental illness, and sexual problems (Lacelle & others, 2012). A 30-year longitudinal study found that middle-aged adults who had experienced maltreatment in childhood were at increased risk for diabetes, lung disease, malnutrition, and vision problems (Widom & others, 2012). Another study revealed that child maltreatment was linked to depression in adulthood and to unfavorable outcomes for treatment of depression (Nanni, Uher, & Danese, 2012). Also, a recent study revealed that young adults who experienced child maltreatment, especially physical abuse, at any age were more likely to be depressed and engage in suicidal ideation as adults (Dunn & others, 2013). Further, adults who were maltreated as children often have difficulty establishing and maintaining healthy intimate relationships (Dozier, Stovall-McClough, & Albus, 2009). As adults, maltreated children are also at higher risk for violent behavior toward other adults—especially dating partners and marital partners—as well as substance abuse, anxiety, and depression (Miller-Perrin, Perrin, & Kocur, 2009). One study also revealed that adults who had experienced child maltreatment were at increased risk for financial and employment-related difficulties (Zielinski, 2009).

An important research agenda is to discover how to prevent child maltreatment or to intervene in children's lives when they have been maltreated (Cicchetti, 2013; Cicchetti & Toth, 2015; McCoy & Keen, 2014; Toth & others, 2014). In one study of maltreating mothers and their 1-year-olds, two treatments were effective in reducing child maltreatment: (1) home visitation that emphasized improved parenting, coping with stress, and increasing support for the mother; and (2) parent-infant psychotherapy that focused on improving maternal-infant attachment (Cicchetti, Toth, & Rogosch, 2005).

SIBLING RELATIONSHIPS AND BIRTH ORDER

How do developmentalists characterize sibling relationships? How extensively does birth order influence behavior?

Sibling Relationships Approximately 80 percent of American children have one or more siblings—that is, sisters and brothers (Dunn, 2007). If you grew up with siblings, you probably have a rich memory of aggressive, hostile interchanges. Siblings in the presence of each other when they are 2 to 4 years of age, on average, have a conflict once every 10 minutes and then the conflicts go down somewhat from 5 to 7 years of age (Kramer, 2006). What do parents do when they encounter siblings having a verbal or physical confrontation? One study revealed that they do one of three things: (1) intervene and try to help them resolve the conflict, (2) admonish or threaten them, or (3) do nothing at all (Kramer & Perozynski, 1999). Of interest is that in families with two siblings 2 to 5 years of age, the most frequent parental reaction is to do nothing at all.

Laurie Kramer (2006), who has conducted a number of research studies on siblings, says that not intervening and letting sibling conflict escalate are not good strategies. She developed a program titled "More Fun with Sisters and Brothers" that teaches 4- to 8-year-old siblings social skills for developing positive interactions (Kramer & Radey, 1997). Among the social skills taught in the program are how to appropriately initiate play, how to accept and refuse invitations to play, how to take another person's perspective, how to deal with angry feelings, and how to manage conflict.

However, conflict is only one of the many dimensions of sibling relations (Buist, Dekovic, & Prinzie, 2013; Feinberg & others, 2013; McHale, Updegraff, & Whiteman, 2013). Sibling relations include helping, sharing, teaching, fighting, and playing, and siblings can act as emotional supports, rivals, and communication partners.

Do parents usually favor one sibling over others—and if so, does it make a difference in an adolescent's development? One study of 384 sibling pairs revealed that 65 percent of their mothers and 70 percent of their fathers showed favoritism toward one sibling (Shebloski, Conger, & Widaman, 2005). When favoritism of one sibling occurred, it

developmental **connection**

Family

Siblings who are psychologically close to each other in adulthood tended to be that way in childhood. Chapter 16, p. 499

What characterizes children's sibling relationships?

was linked to lower self-esteem and sadness in the less-favored sibling. Indeed, equality and fairness are major concerns of siblings' relationships with each other and how they are treated by their parents (Campione-Barr, 2011; Campione-Barr, Greer, & Kruse, 2013; Campione-Barr & Smetana, 2010).

Judy Dunn (2007), a leading expert on sibling relationships, recently described three important characteristics of sibling relationships:

- *Emotional quality of the relationship.* Intense positive and negative emotions are often expressed by siblings toward each other. Many children and adolescents have mixed feelings toward their siblings.
- *Familiarity and intimacy of the relationship.* Siblings typically know each other very well, and this intimacy suggests that they can either provide support or tease and undermine each other, depending on the situation.
- *Variation in sibling relationships.* Some siblings describe their relationships more positively than others. Thus, there is considerable variation in sibling relationships. We just discussed that many siblings have mixed feelings about each other, but some children and adolescents mainly describe their siblings in warm, affectionate ways, whereas others primarily talk about how irritating and mean a sibling is. Research indicates that a high level of sibling conflict is linked to negative developmental outcomes (Fosco & others, 2012).

Birth Order Whether a child has older or younger siblings has been linked to development of certain personality characteristics. For example, a recent review concluded that "firstborns are the most intelligent, achieving, and conscientious, while later-borns are the most rebellious, liberal, and agreeable" (Paulhus, 2008, p. 210). Compared with later-born children, firstborn children have also been described as more adult-oriented, helpful, conforming, and self-controlled. However, when such birth-order differences are reported, they often are small.

What accounts for differences related to birth order? Proposed explanations usually point to variations in interactions with parents and siblings associated with being in a particular position in the family. In one study, mothers became more negative, coercive, and restraining and played less with the firstborn following the birth of a second child (Dunn & Kendrick, 1982).

What is the only child like? The popular conception is that the only child is a "spoiled brat" with such undesirable characteristics as dependency, lack of self-control, and self-centered behavior. But researchers present a more positive portrayal of the only child. Only children often are achievement-oriented and display a desirable personality, especially in comparison with later-borns and children from large families (Falbo & Poston, 1993; Jiao, Ji, & Jing, 1996).

So far, our discussion suggests that birth order might be a strong predictor of behavior. However, an increasing number of family researchers stress that when all of the factors that influence behavior are considered, birth order by itself shows limited accuracy in predicting behavior. Think about some of the other important factors beyond birth order in children's lives that influence their behavior. They include heredity, models of competency or incompetency that parents present to children on a daily basis, peer influences, school influences, socioeconomic factors, sociohistorical factors, and cultural variations. When someone says firstborns are always like this but last-borns are always like that, the person is making overly simplistic statements that do not adequately take into account the complexity of influences on a child's development.

THE CHANGING FAMILY IN A CHANGING SOCIETY

Beyond variations in the number of siblings, the families that children experience differ in many important ways (Parke, 2013). The number of children growing up in single-parent families is staggering. As shown in Figure 8.5, the United States has one of the highest percentages of single-parent families in the world. Among two-parent families, there are those in which both parents work outside the home, one or both parents had a previous marriage that ended in divorce, or the parents are gay or lesbian. Differences in culture and socioeconomic status (SES) also influence families. How do these variations in families affect children?

FIGURE **8.5**

SINGLE-PARENT FAMILIES IN DIFFERENT COUNTRIES

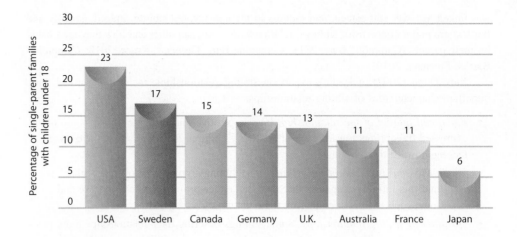

How does work affect parenting?

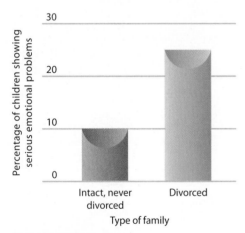

FIGURE **8.6**

DIVORCE AND CHILDREN'S EMOTIONAL PROBLEMS. In Hetherington's research, 25 percent of children from divorced families showed serious emotional problems compared with only 10 percent of children from intact, never-divorced families. However, keep in mind that a substantial majority (75 percent) of the children from divorced families did not show serious emotional problems.

Working Parents More than one of every two U.S. mothers with a child under the age of 5 is in the labor force; more than two of every three with a child from 6 to 17 years of age is employed. Maternal employment is a part of modern life, but its effects continue to be debated.

Most research on parental work has focused on the role of maternal employment on young children's development (Brooks-Gunn, Han, & Waldfogel, 2010; O'Brien & others, 2014). However, the effects of working parents involve the father as well as the mother when such matters as work schedules and work-family stress are considered (Clarke-Stewart & Parke, 2014; O'Brien & Moss, 2010). Recent research indicates that the nature of parents' work has more influence on children's development than the fact that one parent works outside the home (Clarke-Stewart & Parke, 2014; Han, 2009; O'Brien & others, 2014). Work can produce positive and negative effects on parenting (Crouter & McHale, 2005). Ann Crouter (2006) described how parents bring their experiences at work into their homes. She concluded that parents who face poor working conditions such as long hours, overtime work, stressful work, and lack of autonomy on the job are likely to be more irritable at home and to engage in less effective parenting than their counterparts with better working conditions. A consistent finding is that children (especially girls) of working mothers engage in less gender stereotyping and have more egalitarian views of gender than children whose mothers are not employed outside the home (Goldberg & Lucas-Thompson, 2008).

Children in Divorced Families Divorce rates changed rather dramatically in the United States and many countries around the world in the late twentieth century (Amato & Dorius, 2010; Braver & Lamb, 2013). The U.S. divorce rate increased dramatically in the 1960s and 1970s but has declined since the 1980s. However, the divorce rate in the United States remains much higher than it is in most other countries.

It is estimated that 40 percent of children born to married parents in the United States will experience their parents' divorce (Hetherington & Stanley-Hagan, 2002). Let's examine some important questions about children in divorced families.

Are children better adjusted in intact, never-divorced families than in divorced families? Most researchers agree that children from divorced families show poorer adjustment than their counterparts in nondivorced families (Amato & Dorius, 2010; Hetherington, 2006; Lansford, 2012, 2013; Robbers & others, 2012; Wallerstein, 2008) (see Figure 8.6). Those who have experienced multiple divorces are at greater risk. Children in divorced families are more likely than children in nondivorced families to have academic problems, to show externalized problems (such as acting out and delinquency) and internalized problems (such as anxiety and depression), to be less socially responsible, to have less competent intimate relationships, to drop out of school, to become sexually active at an early age, to take drugs, to associate with antisocial peers, to have low self-esteem, and to be less securely attached as young adults (Conger & Chao, 1996). Nonetheless, keep in mind that a majority of children in divorced families do not have significant adjustment problems (Ahrons, 2007). One study found that 20 years after their parents had divorced when they were children, approximately 80 percent of adults concluded that their parents' decision to divorce was a wise one (Ahrons, 2004).

Should parents stay together for the sake of the children? Whether parents should stay in an unhappy marriage for the sake of their children is one of the most commonly asked questions about divorce (Hetherington, 2006). If the stresses and disruptions in family relationships associated with an unhappy, conflictual marriage that erode the well-being of children are reduced by the move to a divorced, single-parent family, divorce can be advantageous. However, if the diminished resources and increased risks associated with divorce also are accompanied by inept parenting and sustained or increased conflict, not only within the divorced couple but also among the parents, children, and siblings, the best choice for the children would be for an unhappy marriage to be retained (Hetherington & Stanley-Hagan, 2002). It is difficult to determine how these "ifs" will play out when parents either remain together in an acrimonious marriage or become divorced.

Note that marital conflict may have negative consequences for children in the context of marriage or divorce (El-Sheikh & others, 2013). And many of the problems that children from divorced homes experience begin during the predivorce period, a time when parents are often in active conflict with each other. Thus, when children from divorced homes show problems, the problems may not be due only to the divorce but also to the marital conflict that led to it.

E. Mark Cummings and his colleagues (Cummings & Davies, 2010; Cummings, El-Sheikh, & Kouros, 2009; Cummings & Schatz, 2012; Koss & others, 2011, 2013, 2014; McCoy & others, 2014) have proposed *emotion security theory*, which has its roots in attachment theory and states that children appraise marital conflict in terms of their sense of security and safety in the family. They make a distinction between marital conflict that is negative for children (such as hostile emotional displays and destructive conflict tactics) and marital conflict that can be positive for children (such as marital disagreement that involves calmly discussing each person's perspective and then working together to reach a solution).

How much do family processes matter in divorced families? Family processes matter a great deal (Lansford, 2012; Parke, 2013; Warshak, 2014). For example, when divorced parents' relationship with each other is harmonious and when they use authoritative parenting, the adjustment of children improves (Hetherington, 2006). When the divorced parents can agree on childrearing strategies and can maintain a cordial relationship with each other, frequent visits by the noncustodial parent usually benefit the child (Fabricius & others, 2010). Following a divorce, father involvement with children drops off more than mother involvement, especially for fathers of girls. Also, a recent study in divorced families revealed that an intervention focused on improving the mother-child relationship was linked to improvements in relationship quality that increased children's coping skills over the short term (6 months) and long term (6 years) (Velez & others, 2011).

What factors influence an individual child's vulnerability to suffering negative consequences from living in a divorced family? Among the factors involved in the child's risk and vulnerability is the child's adjustment prior to the divorce, as well as the child's personality and temperament, gender, and custody situation (Hetherington, 2006). Children whose parents later divorce often show poor adjustment before the breakup (Amato & Booth, 1996). Children who are socially mature and responsible, who show few behavioral problems, and who have an easy temperament are better able to cope with their parents' divorce. Children with a difficult temperament often have problems coping with their parents' divorce (Hetherington, 2000).

Earlier studies reported gender differences in response to divorce, with divorce being more negative for boys than girls in mother-custody families. However, more recent studies have shown that gender differences are less pronounced and consistent than was previously believed. Some of the inconsistency may be due to the increase in father custody, joint custody, and increased involvement of noncustodial fathers, especially in their sons' lives (Ziol-Guest, 2009).

Research on whether different types of custodial arrangements are better for children in divorced families has yielded inconsistent results (Parke, 2013). An analysis of studies found that children in joint-custody families were better adjusted than children in sole-custody families (Bauserman, 2002). However, joint custody works best for children when the parents can get along with each other (Clarke-Stewart & Parke, 2014).

What role does socioeconomic status play in the lives of children in divorced families? Custodial mothers experience the loss of about one-fourth to one-half of their predivorce income, in comparison with a loss of only one-tenth by custodial fathers. This income loss for

What concerns are involved in whether parents should stay together for the sake of the children or become divorced?

developmental **connection**

Family

Early marriage, low educational level, low income, not having a religious affiliation, having parents who are divorced, and having a baby before marriage are factors linked to an increased probability of divorce. Chapter 14, p. 446

As marriage has become a more optional, less permanent institution in contemporary America, children and adolescents are encountering stresses and adaptive challenges associated with their parents' marital transitions.

—E. MAVIS HETHERINGTON
Contemporary Psychologist, University of Virginia

Communicating with Children About Divorce

Ellen Galinsky and Judy David (1988) developed a number of guidelines for communicating with children about divorce.

- **Explain the separation.** As soon as daily activities in the home make it obvious that one parent is leaving, tell the children. If possible, both parents should be present when children are told about the separation to come. The reasons for the separation are very difficult for young children to understand. No matter what parents tell children, children can find reasons to argue against the separation. It is extremely important for parents to tell the children who will take care of them and to describe the specific arrangements for seeing the other parent.
- **Explain that the separation is not the child's fault.** Young children often believe their parents' separation or divorce is their own fault. Therefore, it is important to tell children that they are not the cause of the separation. Parents need to repeat this statement a number of times.
- **Explain that it may take time to feel better.** Tell young children that it's normal to not feel good about what is happening and that many other children feel this way when their parents become separated. It is also okay for divorced parents to share some of their emotions with children, by saying something like "I'm having a hard time since the separation just like you, but I know it's going to get better after a while." Such statements are best kept brief and should not criticize the other parent.

- **Keep the door open for further discussion.** Tell your children to come to you anytime they want to talk about the separation. It is healthy for children to express their pent-up emotions in discussions with their parents and to learn that the parents are willing to listen to their feelings and fears.
- **Provide as much continuity as possible.** The less children's worlds are disrupted by the separation, the easier their transition to a single-parent family will be. Thus, parents should maintain the rules already in place as much as possible. Children need parents who care enough not only to give them warmth and nurturance but also to set reasonable limits.
- **Provide support for your children and yourself.** After a divorce or separation, parents are as important to children as before the divorce or separation. Divorced parents need to provide children with as much support as possible. Parents function best when other people are available to give them support as adults and as parents. Divorced parents can find people who provide practical help and with whom they can talk about their problems.

How does the third bullet point above ("Explain that it may take time to feel better.") relate to what you learned earlier in this chapter about emotion coaching?

What are the research findings regarding the development and psychological well-being of children raised by gay and lesbian couples?

divorced mothers is accompanied by increased workloads, high rates of job instability, and residential moves to less desirable neighborhoods with inferior schools (Braver & Lamb, 2013).

In sum, many factors are involved in determining how divorce influences a child's development (Hetherington, 2006; Lansford, 2012; Parke, 2013). To read about some strategies for helping children cope with the divorce of their parents, see *Connecting Development to Life.*

Gay and Lesbian Parents Increasingly, gay and lesbian couples are creating families that include children (Parke, 2013; Patterson, 2013a, b, 2014; Patterson & D'Augelli, 2013; Patterson & Farr, 2014). Approximately 20 percent of lesbians and 10 percent of gays are parents. There may be more than 1 million gay and lesbian parents in the United States today.

Like heterosexual couples, gay and lesbian parents vary greatly. They may be single or they may have same-gender partners. Many lesbian mothers and gay fathers are noncustodial parents because they lost custody of their children to heterosexual spouses after a divorce. In addition, gays and lesbians are increasingly choosing parenthood through donor insemination or adoption. Researchers have found that the children conceived through new reproductive technologies—such as in vitro fertilization—are as well adjusted as their counterparts conceived by natural means (Golombok, 2011a, b; Golombok & Tasker, 2010).

Parenthood among lesbians and gays is controversial. Opponents claim that being raised by gay or lesbian parents harms the child's development. But researchers have found few differences between children growing up with lesbian mothers or gay fathers on the one hand, and children growing up with heterosexual parents on the other (Golombok & Tasker, 2010; Patterson, 2013a, b; Patterson & Farr, 2014). For example, children growing up in gay or lesbian families are just as popular with their peers, and no differences are found in the adjustment and mental health of children living in these families when they are compared with children in heterosexual families (Hyde & DeLamater, 2014). Further, a recent study revealed more positive parenting in adoptive gay father families and fewer child externalizing problems in these families than in heterosexual families (Golombok & others, 2014). Contrary to the once-popular expectation that being raised by a gay or lesbian parent would result in the child growing up to be gay or lesbian, in reality the overwhelming majority of children from gay or lesbian families have a heterosexual orientation (Golombok & Tasker, 2010; Tasker & Golombok, 1997).

Also, a recent study compared the incidence of coparenting in adoptive heterosexual, lesbian, and gay couples with preschool-aged children (Farr & Patterson, 2013). Both self-reports and observations found that lesbian and gay couples shared child care more than heterosexual couples, with lesbian couples being the most supportive and gay couples the least supportive.

Cultural, Ethnic, and Socioeconomic Variations   Parenting can be influenced by culture, ethnicity, and socioeconomic status (Berry & others, 2013; Parke, 2013; Schaefer, 2013). Recall from Bronfenbrenner's ecological theory (see Chapter 1) that a number of social contexts influence the child's development. In Bronfenbrenner's theory, culture, ethnicity, and socioeconomic status are classified as part of the macrosystem because they represent broader, societal contexts.

Cross-Cultural Studies   Different cultures often give different answers to basic questions such as what the father's role in the family should be, what support systems are available to families, and how children should be disciplined (Bekman & Aksu-Koc, 2012). There are important cross-cultural variations in parenting and the value placed on children (Trommsdorff, 2012). In some cultures, such as rural areas of many countries, authoritarian parenting is widespread.

Cultural change, brought about by factors such as increasingly frequent international travel, access to the Internet and electronic communications, and economic globalization, is coming to families in many countries around the world. There are trends toward greater family mobility, migration to urban areas, separation as some family members work in cities or countries far from their homes, smaller families, fewer extended-family households, and increased maternal employment (Brown & Larson, 2002). These trends can change the resources that are available to children. For example, when several generations no longer live near each other, children may lose support and guidance from grandparents, aunts, and uncles. On the positive side, smaller families may produce more openness and communication between parents and children.

Ethnicity   Families within different ethnic groups in the United States differ in their typical size, structure, composition, reliance on kinship networks, and levels of income and education (Parke, 2013). Large and extended families are more common among minority groups than among the non-Latino White majority. For example, 19 percent of Latino families have three or more children, compared with 14 percent of African American and 10 percent of White families. African American and Latino children interact more with grandparents, aunts, uncles, cousins, and more distant relatives than do White children.

Single-parent families are more common among African Americans and Latinos than among White Americans (Doob, 2013). In comparison with two-parent households, single parents often have more limited resources of time, money, and energy (Evans, Li, & Sepanski Whipple, 2013). Ethnic minority parents also are less educated and more likely to live in low-income circumstances than their non-Latino White counterparts. Still, many impoverished ethnic minority families manage to find ways to raise competent children (Hurst, 2013).

A major change in families in the last several decades has been the dramatic increase in the immigration of Latino and Asian families into the United States (Kiang & others, 2013; Marks, Godoy, & Garcia Coll, 2014; Nieto & Yoshikawa, 2014; Umana-Taylor & Updegraff, 2013). Immigrant families often experience stressors uncommon to or less prominent among longtime residents, such as

What are some characteristics of families within different ethnic groups?

What are some of the stressors immigrant families experience when they come to the United States?

language barriers, dislocations and separations from support networks, the dual struggle to preserve identity and to acculturate, and changes in SES status (Marks, Godoy, & Garcia Coll, 2014; Parke, 2013; Phinney & others, 2013a, b).

Further, an increasing number of children are growing up in transnational families, who move back and forth between the United States and Mexico or China (Dreby, 2010; Mazzucato & Schans, 2011). In some cases these children are left behind in their home country, and in other cases (especially in China), they are sent back to China to be raised by grandparents during their early childhood years. Such children might benefit from economic remittances but suffer emotionally from prolonged separation from their parents.

Of course, individual families vary, and how ethnic minority families deal with stress depends on many factors (Berry & others, 2013; Parke, 2013; Nieto & Yoshikawa, 2014). Whether the parents are native-born or immigrants, how long the family has been in this country, and their socioeconomic status and national origin all make a difference (Parke, 2013). The characteristics of the family's social context also influence its adaptation. What are the attitudes toward the family's ethnic group within its neighborhood or city? Can the family's children attend good schools? Are there community groups that welcome people from the family's ethnic group? Do members of the family's ethnic group form community groups of their own?

Ethnic minority/immigrant children and their parents are expected to move beyond their own cultural background and identify with aspects of the dominant culture. They undergo varying degrees of acculturation, which refers to cultural changes that occur when one culture comes in contact with another. Asian American parents, for example, may feel pressed to modify the traditional training style of parental control discussed earlier as they encounter the more permissive parenting typical of the dominant culture.

Recent research indicates that many members of families that have recently immigrated to the United States adopt a bicultural orientation, selecting characteristics of the U.S. culture that help them to survive and advance, while still retaining aspects of their culture of origin (Moro, 2014). In adopting characteristics of the U.S. culture, Latino families are increasingly embracing its emphasis on education (Cooper, 2011). Although their school dropout rates have remained higher than those of other ethnic groups, toward the end of the first decade of the twenty-first century they declined considerably (National Center for Education Statistics, 2013). However, while many ethnic/immigrant families adopt a bicultural orientation, parenting in many ethnic minority families also focuses on issues associated with promoting children's ethnic pride, knowledge of their ethnic group, and awareness of discrimination (Ho, 2014; Simpkins & others, 2013; Umana-Taylor & others, 2014).

Socioeconomic Status   Low-income families have less access to resources than higher-income families do (Coley & others, 2014; Evans & Kim, 2013; Weisner & Duncan, 2014). The differential in access to resources encompasses nutrition, health care, protection from danger, and enriching educational and socialization opportunities such as tutoring and lessons in various activities (Huston, 2012). These differences are compounded in low-income families characterized by long-term poverty (Maholmes & King, 2012; McLoyd, Mistry, & Hardaway, 2014). A recent study found that persistent economic hardship and very early poverty were linked to lower cognitive functioning in children at 5 years of age (Schoon & others, 2012). An in another recent study, poverty-related adversity in family and school contexts in early childhood were linked to less effective executive function in second and third grades (Raver & others, 2013).

In the United States and most Western cultures, differences have been found in child rearing among families with different socioeconomic statuses (SES) (Hoff, Laursen, & Tardif, 2002, p. 246):

- "Lower-SES parents (1) are more concerned that their children conform to society's expectations, (2) create a home atmosphere in which it is clear that parents have authority over children," (3) use physical punishment more in disciplining their children, and (4) are more directive and less conversational with their children.

- "Higher-SES parents (1) are more concerned with developing children's initiative" and delay of gratification, "(2) create a home atmosphere in which children are more nearly equal participants and in which rules are discussed as opposed to being laid down" in an authoritarian manner, (3) are less likely to use physical punishment, and (4) "are less directive and more conversational" with their children.

Review

- What are the four main parenting styles, and what aspects of parenting are linked with young children's development?
- What are the types and consequences of child maltreatment?
- How are sibling relationships and birth order related to young children's development?
- How is young children's development affected by having two wage-earning parents, having divorced parents, having gay or lesbian parents, and being part of a particular cultural, ethnic, and socioeconomic group?

Connect

- In Chapter 4, you learned that fathers were most often the perpetrators in shaken baby syndrome. Given what you learned in this chapter, which family interactions would a researcher or marriage and family therapist be likely to explore in such a case of child maltreatment?

Reflect *Your Own Personal Journey of Life*

- Which style or styles of parenting did your mother and father use in rearing you? What effects do you think their parenting styles have had on your development?

3 Peer Relations, Play, and Media/Screen Time

LG3 Describe the roles of peers, play, and media/screen time in young children's development.

| Peer Relations | Play | Media/Screen Time |

The family is a very important social context for children's development. However, children's development also is strongly influenced by what goes on in other social contexts, such as in peer groups and when children are playing or spending time with the media, computers, and other electronic devices.

PEER RELATIONS

As children grow older, they spend an increasing amount of time with their *peers*—children of about the same age or maturity level.

Peer Group Functions   What are the functions of a child's peer group? One of its most important functions is to provide a source of information and comparison about the world outside the family. Children receive feedback about their abilities from their peer group. Children evaluate what they do in terms of whether it is better than, as good as, or worse than what other children do. It is hard to make these judgments at home because siblings are usually older or younger.

Good peer relations promote normal socioemotional development (Coley & others, 2013). Special concerns in peer relations focus on children who are withdrawn or aggressive (Rubin & others, 2013). Withdrawn children who are rejected by peers or are victimized and feel lonely are at risk for depression. Children who are aggressive with their peers are at risk for developing a number of problems, including delinquency and dropping out of school (Bukowski, Buhrmester, & Underwood, 2011).

Developmental Changes   Recall from our discussion of gender that, by about the age of 3, children already prefer to spend time with same-sex rather than opposite-sex play-mates, and this preference increases in early childhood. During these same years the frequency of peer interaction, both positive and negative, picks up considerably (Cillessen & Bellmore, 2011). Many preschool children spend considerable time in peer interaction conversing with playmates about such matters as "negotiating roles and rules in play, arguing, and agreeing"

What are some characteristics of peer relations in early childhood?

developmental **connection**

Peers

Children's peer relations have been classified in terms of five peer statuses. Chapter 10, p. 323

(Rubin, Bukowski, & Parker, 2006). And during early childhood children's interactions with peers become more coordinated and involve longer turns and sequences (Coplan & Arbeau, 2009).

Friends   In early childhood, children distinguish between friends and nonfriends (Howes, 2009). For most young children, a friend is someone to play with. Young preschool children are more likely than older children to have friends who are of a different gender and ethnicity (Howes, 2009).

The Connected Worlds of Parent-Child and Peer Relations   Parents may influence their children's peer relations in many ways, both directly and indirectly (Tilton-Weaver & others, 2013). Parents affect such relations through their interactions with their children, how they manage their children's lives, and the opportunities they provide to their children (Brown & Bakken, 2011). For example, a recent study found that when mothers coached their preschool daughters about the negative aspects of peer conflicts involving relational aggression (harming someone by manipulating a relationship), the daughters engaged in lower rates of relational aggression (Werner & others, 2014).

Basic lifestyle decisions by parents—their choices of neighborhoods, churches, schools, and their own friends—largely determine the pool from which their children select possible friends. These choices in turn affect which children their children meet, their purpose in interacting, and eventually which children become their friends.

Researchers also have found that children's peer relations are linked to attachment security and parents' marital quality (Booth-LaForce & Kerns, 2009). Early attachments to caregivers provide a connection to children's peer relations not only by creating a secure base from which children can explore social relationships beyond the family but also by conveying a working model of relationships (Hartup, 2009).

Do these results indicate that children's peer relations always are wedded to parent-child relationships? Although parent-child relationships influence children's subsequent peer relations, children also learn other modes of relating through their relationships with peers. For example, rough-and-tumble play occurs mainly with other children, not in parent-child interaction. In times of stress, children often turn to parents rather than peers for support. In parent-child relationships, children learn how to relate to authority figures. With their peers, children are likely to interact on a much more equal basis and to learn a mode of relating based on mutual influence. We will have much more to say about peer relations in Chapter 10, "Socioemotional Development in Middle and Late Childhood."

PLAY

An extensive amount of peer interaction during childhood involves play, but social play is only one type of play. Play is a pleasurable activity in which children engage for its own sake, and its functions and forms vary (Hirsh-Pasek & Golinkoff, 2014).

Play's Functions   Play makes important contributions to young children's cognitive and socioemotional development (Coplan & Arbeau, 2009; Smith & Pellegrini, 2013). Theorists have focused on different aspects of play and highlighted a long list of functions.

According to Freud and Erikson, play helps children master anxieties and conflicts. Because tensions are relieved in play, children can cope with life's problems. Play permits children to work off excess physical energy and to release pent-up tensions. Therapists use *play therapy* both to allow children to work off frustrations and to analyze children's conflicts and ways of coping with them. Children may feel less threatened and be more likely to express their true feelings in the context of play (Yanof, 2013).

Play also is an important context for cognitive development (Power, 2011). Both Piaget and Vygotsky concluded that play is a child's work. Piaget (1962) maintained that play advances children's cognitive development. At the same time, he said, children's cognitive development *constrains* the way they play. Play permits children to practice their competencies and acquired skills in a relaxed, pleasurable way. Piaget thought that cognitive structures need to be exercised, and play provides the perfect setting for this exercise.

Let us play, for it is yet day
And we cannot go to sleep;
Besides, in the sky the little
birds fly
And the hills are all covered
with sheep.

—**WILLIAM BLAKE**
English Poet, 19th Century

developmental **connection**

Sociocultural Cognitive Theory
Vygotsky emphasized that children develop their ways of thinking and understanding mainly through social interaction. Chapter 7, p. 209

sensorimotor play Behavior engaged in by infants that lets them derive pleasure from exercising their existing sensorimotor schemas.

practice play Play that involves repetition of behavior when new skills are being learned or when physical or mental mastery and coordination of skills are required for games or sports.

Vygotsky (1962) also considered play to be an excellent setting for cognitive development. He was especially interested in the symbolic and make-believe aspects of play, as when a child substitutes a stick for a horse and rides the stick as if it were a horse. For young children, the imaginary situation is real. Parents should encourage such imaginary play, because it advances the child's cognitive development, especially creative thought.

Daniel Berlyne (1960) described play as exciting and pleasurable in itself because it satisfies our exploratory drive. This drive involves curiosity and a desire for information about something new or unusual. Play encourages exploratory behavior by offering children the possibilities of novelty, complexity, uncertainty, surprise, and incongruity.

More recently, play has been described as an important context for the development of language and communication skills (Harris, Golinkoff, & Hirsh-Pasek, 2011; Hirsh-Pasek & Golinkoff, 2013). Language and communication skills may be enhanced through discussions and negotiations regarding roles and rules in play as young children practice various words and phrases. These types of social interactions during play can benefit young children's literacy skills (Gunning, 2013). And, as we saw in Chapter 7, play is a central focus of the child-centered kindergarten and is thought to be an essential aspect of early childhood education (Feeney, Moravcik, & Nolte, 2013; Henninger, 2013).

Types of Play   The contemporary perspective on play emphasizes both the cognitive and the social aspects of play (Hirsh-Pasek & Golinkoff, 2013; Vong, 2012). Among the most widely studied types of children's play today are sensorimotor and practice play, pretense/symbolic play, social play, constructive play, and games (Bergen, 1988).

Sensorimotor and Practice Play   **Sensorimotor play** is behavior by infants that lets them derive pleasure from exercising their sensorimotor schemes. The development of sensorimotor play follows Piaget's description of sensorimotor thought, which we discussed in Chapter 5. Infants initially engage in exploratory and playful visual and motor transactions in the second quarter of the first year of life. At about 9 months of age, infants begin to select novel objects for exploration and play, especially responsive objects such as toys that make noise or bounce.

Practice play involves the repetition of behavior when new skills are being learned or when physical or mental mastery and coordination of skills are required for games or sports. Sensorimotor play, which often involves practice play, is primarily confined to infancy, whereas practice play can be engaged in throughout life. During the preschool years, children often engage in practice play.

Pretense/Symbolic Play   **Pretense/symbolic play** occurs when the child transforms the physical environment into a symbol. Between 9 and 30 months of age, children increase their use of objects in symbolic play. They learn to transform objects—substituting them for other objects and acting toward them as if they were those other objects. For example, a preschool child treats a table as if it were a car and says, "I'm fixing the car," as he grabs a leg of the table.

Many experts on play consider the preschool years the "golden age" of symbolic/pretense play that is dramatic or sociodramatic in nature. This type of make-believe play often appears at about 18 months of age and reaches a peak at 4 to 5 years of age, then gradually declines.

Some child psychologists conclude that pretend play is an important aspect of young children's development and often reflects advances in their cognitive development, especially as an indication of symbolic understanding. For example, Catherine Garvey (2000) and Angeline Lillard (2006) emphasize that hidden in young children's pretend play narratives are remarkable capacities for role-taking, balancing of social roles, metacognition (thinking about thinking), testing of the reality-pretense distinction, and numerous nonegocentric capacities that reveal the remarkable cognitive skills of young children. In one recent analysis, a major accomplishment in early childhood is the development of children's ability to share their pretend play with peers (Coplan & Arbeau, 2009). And researchers have found that pretend play contributes to young children's self-regulation, mainly because of the self-monitoring and social sensitivity that is required in creating and enacting a sociodramatic narrative in cooperation with other children (Diamond & others, 2007).

A preschool "superhero" at play.

And that park grew up with me; that small world widened as I learned its secrets and boundaries, as I discovered new refuges in its woods and jungles: hidden homes and lairs for the multitudes of imagination, for cowboys and Indians. . . . I used to dawdle on half holidays along the bent and Devon-facing seashore, hoping for gold watches or the skull of a sheep or a message in a bottle to be washed up with the tide.

—DYLAN THOMAS
Welsh Poet, 20th Century

pretense/symbolic play Play in which the child transforms the physical environment into a symbol.

What characterizes social play?

Social Play   **Social play** involves interaction with peers. Social play increases dramatically during the preschool years. For many children, social play is the main context for young children's social interactions with peers (Power, 2011).

Constructive Play   **Constructive play** combines sensorimotor/practice play with symbolic representation. It occurs when children engage in the self-regulated creation of a product or a solution. Constructive play increases in the preschool years as symbolic play increases and sensorimotor play decreases. It also becomes a frequent form of play in the elementary school years, both in and out of the classroom.

Games   **Games** are activities that children engage in for pleasure and that have rules. Often they involve competition. Preschool children may begin to participate in social games that involve simple rules of reciprocity and turn taking. However, games take on a much stronger role in the lives of elementary school children. In one study, the highest incidence of game playing occurred between 10 and 12 years of age (Eiferman, 1971). After age 12, games decline in popularity (Bergen, 1988).

Kathy Hirsh-Pasek interacting with a young child in a play context. *What are some of the benefits of play for children according to Hirsh-Pasek and her colleagues?*

social play Play that involves social interactions with peers.

constructive play Play that combines sensorimotor and repetitive activity with symbolic representation of ideas. Constructive play occurs when children engage in self-regulated creation or construction of a product or a solution.

games Activities engaged in for pleasure that include rules and often involve competition with one or more individuals.

Trends in Play   Kathy Hirsh-Pasek, Roberta Golinkoff, and Dorothy Singer (Hirsh-Pasek & others, 2009; Singer, Golinkoff, & Hirsh-Pasek, 2006) are concerned about the small amount of time for free play that young children have, reporting that it has declined considerably in recent decades. They especially are worried about young children's playtime being restricted at home and school so they can spend more time on academic subjects. They also point out that many schools have eliminated recess. And it is not just the declining time for free play that bothers them. They underscore that learning in playful contexts captivates children's minds in ways that enhance their cognitive and socioemotional development—Singer, Golinkoff, and Hirsh-Pasek's (2006) first book on play was titled: *Play = Learning*. Among the cognitive benefits of play they described are skills in the following areas: creativity; abstract thinking; imagination; attention, concentration, and persistence; problem-solving; social cognition, empathy, and perspective taking; language; and mastery of new concepts. Among the socioemotional experiences and development they believe play promotes are enjoyment, relaxation, and self-expression; cooperation, sharing, and turn-taking; anxiety reduction; and self-confidence. With so many positive cognitive and socioemotional outcomes of play, clearly it is important that we find more time for play in young children's lives.

MEDIA/SCREEN TIME

Few developments in society in the second half of the twentieth century had a greater impact on children than television (Maloy & others, 2014). Television continues to have a strong influence on children's development, but children's use of other media and information/communication devices has led very recently to the use of the term *screen time,* which includes how much time individuals spend with television, DVDs, computers, video games, and mobile media such as iPhones (Sterin, 2014). Television is still the elephant in young children's media lives, with 2- to 4-year-old children watching TV approximately 2 to 4 hours per day (Roberts & Foehr, 2008). However, a recent study revealed that 12 percent of 2- to 4-year-old U.S. children use computers every day and 22 percent of 5- to 8-year-olds use computers daily (Common Sense Media, 2011). A recent recommendation stated that for children 2 to 4 years of age, screen time should be limited to no more than 1 hour per day (Tremblay & others, 2012). Many children spend more time with various screen media than they do interacting with their parents and peers.

What are some concerns about the increase in children's media and screen time?

Some types of TV shows are linked to positive outcomes for children. For example, a recent meta-analysis of studies in 14 countries found that watching the TV show *Sesame Street* produced positive outcomes in three areas: cognitive skills, learning about the world, and social reasoning and attitudes toward outgroups (Mares & Pan, 2013).

However, too much screen time can have a negative influence on children by making them passive learners, distracting them from doing homework, teaching them stereotypes, providing them with violent models of aggression, and presenting them with unrealistic views of the world. Among other concerns about young children having so much screen time are decreasing time spent in play, less time interacting with peers, decreased physical activity, an increased tendency to become overweight or obese, poor sleep habits, and higher rates of aggression. A research review concluded that a higher level of screen time at 4 to 6 years of age was linked to increased obesity and reduced physical activity from preschool through adolescence (te Velde & others, 2012). Another study found that sleep problems were more common in 3- to 5-year-old children who (1) watched TV after 7 p.m. and (2) watched TV shows with violence (Garrison, Liekweg, & Christakis, 2011). Next, let's take a closer look at the effects of television on children's aggression.

Effects of Television on Children's Aggression   The extent to which children are exposed to violence and aggression on television raises special concerns (Matos, Ferreira, & Haase, 2012). For example, Saturday morning cartoon shows average more than 25 violent acts per hour. In one experiment, preschool children were randomly assigned to one of two groups: One group watched television shows taken directly from violent Saturday morning cartoons on 11 days; the second group watched television cartoon shows with all of the violence removed (Steur, Applefield, & Smith, 1971). The children were then observed during play at their preschool. The preschool children who had seen the TV cartoon shows with violence kicked, choked, and pushed their playmates more than did the preschool children who watched nonviolent TV cartoon shows. Because the children were randomly assigned to the two conditions (TV cartoons with violence versus nonviolent TV cartoons), we can conclude that exposure to TV violence caused the increased aggression in the children in this investigation.

Other research has found links between watching television violence as a child and acting aggressively years later. For example, in one study, exposure to media violence at 6 to 10 years of age was linked with aggressive behavior in young adulthood (Huesmann & others, 2003).

In addition to television violence, there is increased concern about children who play violent video games, especially those that are highly realistic (Escobar-Chaves & Anderson, 2008). Research reviews have concluded that playing violent video games is linked to aggression in both males and females (Gentile, 2011; Holtz & Appel, 2011).

Effects of Television on Children's Prosocial Behavior   Television can have a positive influence on children's development by presenting motivating educational programs, providing information about the world beyond their immediate environment, and displaying models of prosocial behavior (Maloy & others, 2014). Researchers have found that when children watch positive social interchanges on the TV show *Sesame Street,* they subsequently are likely to imitate these positive social behaviors (Bryant, 2007; Truglio & Kotler, 2014).

Review *Connect* Reflect

LG3 Describe the roles of peers, play, and media/screen time in young children's development.

Review
- How do peers affect young children's development?
- What are some theories and types of play?
- How does television influence young children's development?

Connect
- Earlier in this chapter, you learned about Laurie Kramer's program for teaching

siblings social skills to develop positive interactions. Do you think her recommendations would be relevant or irrelevant to peer relationships? Why?

Reflect *Your Own Personal Journey of Life*
- What guidelines would you adopt for your own children's television viewing?

topical **connections** *looking forward*

The middle and late childhood years bring further changes in children's socioemotional development. Development of self-understanding and understanding of others becomes more sophisticated, emotional understanding improves, and moral reasoning advances. Children now spend less time with parents, but parents continue to play very important roles in children's lives, especially in guiding their academic achievement and managing their opportunities. Peer status and friendship become more important in children's peer relations, and school takes on a stronger academic focus.

reach your **learning goals**

Socioemotional Development in Early Childhood

1 Emotional and Personality Development

LG1 Discuss emotional and personality development in early childhood.

The Self

- In Erikson's theory, early childhood is a period when development involves resolving the conflict of initiative versus guilt. The toddler's rudimentary self-understanding develops into the preschooler's representation of the self in terms of body parts, material possessions, and physical activities. At about 4 to 5 years of age, children also begin to use trait-like self-descriptions. Young children display more sophisticated self-understanding and understanding of others than was previously thought.

Emotional Development

- Advances in young children's emotional development involve expressing emotions, understanding emotions, and regulating emotions. Young children's range of emotions expands during early childhood as they increasingly experience self-conscious emotions such as pride, shame, and guilt. Between 2 and 4 years old, children use an increasing number of terms to describe emotion and learn more about the causes and consequences of feelings. At 4 to 5 years of age, children show an increased ability to reflect on emotions and understand that a single event can elicit different emotions in different people. They also show a growing awareness of the need to manage emotions to meet social standards. Emotion-coaching parents have children who engage in more effective self-regulation of their emotions than do emotion-dismissing parents. Emotion regulation plays an important role in successful peer relations.

Moral Development	• Moral development involves thoughts, feelings, and behaviors regarding rules and conventions about what people should do in their interactions with others. Freud's psychoanalytic theory emphasizes the importance of feelings in the development of the superego, the moral branch of personality. Positive emotions, such as empathy, also contribute to the child's moral development. Piaget analyzed moral reasoning and concluded that children from about 4 to 7 years of age display heteronomous morality, judging behavior by its consequences; then, at about 10 years of age and older, they develop autonomous morality. According to behavioral and social cognitive theorists, moral behavior develops as a result of reinforcement, punishment, and imitation, and there is considerable situational variability in moral behavior. Conscience refers to an internal regulation of standards of right and wrong that involves an integration of moral thought, feeling, and behavior. Young children's conscience emerges out of relationships with parents. Parents influence young children's moral development through the quality of parent-child relationships, by being proactive in helping children avert misbehavior, and by engaging children in conversational dialogue about moral issues.
Gender	• Gender refers to the social and psychological dimensions of being male or female. Gender identity is acquired by 2½ years of age for most children. A gender role is a set of expectations that prescribes how females or males should think, act, and feel. Gender typing refers to the acquisition of a traditional masculine or feminine role. Biological influences on gender development include chromosomes and hormones. However, biology does not completely dictate destiny in gender development; children's socialization experiences matter a great deal. Social role theory, psychoanalytic theory, and social cognitive theory emphasize various aspects of social experiences in the development of gender characteristics. Parents influence children's gender development, and peers are especially adept at rewarding gender-appropriate behavior. Gender schema theory emphasizes the role of cognition in gender development.

2 Families

LG2 Explain how families can influence young children's development.

Parenting	• Authoritarian, authoritative, neglectful, and indulgent are four main parenting styles. Authoritative parenting is the most widely used style around the world and is the style most often associated with children's social competence. However, ethnic variations in parenting styles suggest that in Asian American families, some aspects of control may benefit children. Physical punishment is widely used by U.S. parents, but some experts conclude that there are a number of reasons it should not be used with children. However, there currently is controversy about the effects of physical punishment on children, with few studies making a distinction between abusive and mild physical punishment. Coparenting has positive effects on children's development.
Child Maltreatment	• Child maltreatment may take the form of physical abuse, child neglect, sexual abuse, and emotional abuse. Child maltreatment places the child at risk for academic, emotional, and social problems. Adults who suffered child maltreatment are also vulnerable to a range of problems.
Sibling Relationships and Birth Order	• Siblings interact with each other in positive and negative ways. Birth order is related in certain ways to personality characteristics—for example, firstborns are more adult-oriented and self-controlled than later-born children. Only children often are achievement-oriented. By itself, however, birth order is not a good predictor of behavior.
The Changing Family in a Changing Society	• In general, having both parents employed full-time outside the home has not been shown to have negative effects on children. However, the nature of parents' work can affect their parenting quality. Divorce can have negative effects on children's adjustment, but so can an acrimonious relationship between parents who stay together for their children's sake. If divorced parents develop a harmonious relationship and practice authoritative parenting, children's adjustment improves. Researchers have found few differences between children growing up in gay or lesbian families and children growing up in heterosexual families. Cultures vary on a number of issues regarding families. African American and Latino children are more likely than White American children to live in single-parent families and larger families and to have extended family connections. Low-income families have less access to resources than higher-income families do. Lower-SES parents create a home atmosphere with more parental authority and greater use of physical punishment, while higher-SES parents are more concerned about developing children's initiative and ability to delay gratification.

3 Peer Relations, Play, and Media/Screen Time

 LG3 Describe the roles of peers, play, and media/screen time in young children's development.

Peer Relations

- Peers are powerful socialization agents. Peers provide a source of information and comparison about the world outside the family. In early childhood, children distinguish between friends and nonfriends, with a friend often described as someone to play with. Parent-child and peer relationships are often connected. Parents influence their children's peer relations by how they manage children's lives and the opportunities they provide for interacting with peers. Rough-and-tumble play is more likely to occur in peer relations, whereas in times of stress children often turn to parents rather than peers for support.

Play

- Play's functions include affiliation with peers, tension release, advances in cognitive development, exploration, and provision of a safe haven. The contemporary perspective on play emphasizes both the cognitive and the social aspects of play. Among the most widely studied types of children's play are sensorimotor play, practice play, pretense/symbolic play, social play, constructive play, and games. There is concern about the decreasing number of hours children spend in free play and in recess at school. Because play is a powerful positive context for the development of children's cognitive and socioemotional skills, it is important that we find more time for play in children's lives.

Media/Screen Time

- Young children watch 2 to 4 hours of TV per day on average, but experts recommend that they watch 1 hour or less. Young children increasingly are spending time with other media and information/communication devices such as computers, DVDs, video games, and iPhones, which has given rise to the term *screen time*. Screen time can have both negative influences (such as turning children into passive learners, presenting them with aggressive models, and decreasing time spent with peers and in play and physical activity) and positive influences (such as providing models of prosocial behavior) on children's development. Both watching TV violence and playing violent video games have been linked to children's aggressive behavior. Watching prosocial behavior on TV can teach children positive social skills.

key terms

self-understanding 234
moral development 238
heteronomous morality 239
autonomous morality 239
immanent justice 239
conscience 240
gender identity 241

gender role 241
gender typing 241
social role theory 242
psychoanalytic theory of gender 242
social cognitive theory of gender 243

gender schema theory 244
authoritarian parenting 245
authoritative parenting 245
neglectful parenting 245
indulgent parenting 245
coparenting 248
sensorimotor play 258

practice play 258
pretense/symbolic play 259
social play 260
constructive play 260
games 260

key people

Erik Erikson 234
Ross Thompson 236
Cybele Raver 237
Jean Piaget 236
Sigmund Freud 238

Diana Baumrind 245
Ruth Chao 246
Elizabeth Gershoff 247
Laurie Kramer 250
Judy Dunn 251

Ann Crouter 252
E. Mark Cummings 253
Lev Vygotsky 258
Daniel Berlyne 259
Dorothy Singer 260

Kathy Hirsh-Pasek 260
Roberta Golinkoff 260

Each forward step we take we leave some phantom of ourselves behind.

—JOHN LANCASTER SPALDING
American Educator, 19th Century

Middle and Late Childhood

In middle and late childhood, children are on a different plane, belonging to a generation and feeling all their own. It is the wisdom of the human life span that at no time are children more ready to learn than during the period of expansive imagination at the end of early childhood. Children develop a sense of wanting to make things—and not just to make them, but to make them well and even perfectly. They seek to know and to understand. They are remarkable for their intelligence and for their curiosity. Their parents continue to be important influences in their lives, but their growth also is shaped by peers and friends. They don't think much about the future or about the past, but they enjoy the present moment. Section 5 consists of two chapters: "Physical and Cognitive Development in Middle and Late Childhood" (Chapter 9) and "Socioemotional Development in Middle and Late Childhood" (Chapter 10).

chapter 9

PHYSICAL AND COGNITIVE DEVELOPMENT IN MIDDLE AND LATE CHILDHOOD

chapter outline

1 Physical Changes and Health

Learning Goal 1 Describe physical changes and health in middle and late childhood.

Body Growth and Change
The Brain
Motor Development
Exercise
Health, Illness, and Disease

2 Children with Disabilities

Learning Goal 2 Identify children with different types of disabilities and discuss issues in educating them.

The Scope of Disabilities
Educational Issues

3 Cognitive Changes

Learning Goal 3 Explain cognitive changes in middle and late childhood.

Piaget's Cognitive Developmental Theory
Information Processing
Intelligence
Extremes of Intelligence

4 Language Development

Learning Goal 4 Discuss language development in middle and late childhood.

Vocabulary, Grammar, and Metalinguistic Awareness
Reading
Writing
Bilingualism and Second-Language Learning

The following comments were made by Angie, an elementary-school-aged girl:

When I was 8 years old, I weighed 125 pounds. My clothes were the size that large teenage girls wear. I hated my body, and my classmates teased me all the time. I was so overweight and out of shape that when I took a P.E. class my face would get red and I had trouble breathing. I was jealous of the kids who played sports and weren't overweight like I was.

I'm 9 years old now and I've lost 30 pounds. I'm much happier and proud of myself. How did I lose the weight? My mom said she had finally decided enough was enough. She took me to a pediatrician who specializes in helping children lose weight and keep it off. The pediatrician counseled my mom about my eating and exercise habits, then had us join a group that he had created for overweight children and their parents. My mom and I go to the group once a week and we've now been participating in the program for 6 months. I no longer eat fast food meals and my mom is cooking more healthy meals. Now that I've lost weight, exercise is not as hard for me and I don't get teased by the kids at school. My mom's pretty happy too because she's lost 15 pounds herself since we've been in the counseling program.

Not all overweight children are as successful as Angie at reducing their weight. Indeed, being overweight or obese in childhood has become a major national concern in the United States. Later in this chapter, we will further explore being overweight and obese in childhood, including obesity's causes and outcomes.

topical connections *looking* **back**

Children grow more slowly in early childhood than in infancy, but they still grow an average of 2.5 inches and gain 4 to 7 pounds a year. In early childhood, the most rapid growth in the brain occurs in the prefrontal cortex. The gross and fine motor skills of children also become smoother and more coordinated. In terms of cognitive development, early childhood is a period in which young children increasingly engage in symbolic thought. Young children's information-processing skills also improve considerably—executive and sustained attention advance, short-term memory gets better, executive function increases, and their understanding of the human mind makes considerable progress. Young children also increase their knowledge of language's rule systems, and their literacy benefits from being active participants in a wide range of language experiences. Most young children attend an early childhood education program, and there are many variations in these programs.

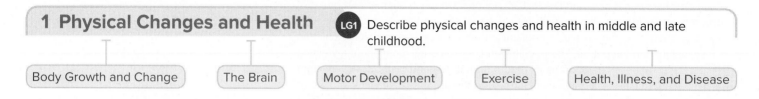

preview

During the middle and late childhood years, children grow taller, heavier, and stronger. They become more adept at using their physical skills, and they develop new cognitive skills. This chapter is about physical and cognitive development in middle and late childhood. To begin, we will explore aspects of physical development.

1 Physical Changes and Health

LG1 Describe physical changes and health in middle and late childhood.

Body Growth and Change   The Brain   Motor Development   Exercise   Health, Illness, and Disease

Continued change characterizes children's bodies during middle and late childhood, and their motor skills improve. As children move through the elementary school years, they gain greater control over their bodies and can sit and keep their attention focused for longer periods of time. Regular exercise is one key to making these years a time of healthy growth and development.

BODY GROWTH AND CHANGE

The period of middle and late childhood involves slow, consistent growth (Burns & others, 2013). This is a period of calm before the rapid growth spurt of adolescence. During the elementary school years, children grow an average of 2 to 3 inches a year until, at the age of 11, the average girl is 4 feet, 10 inches tall, and the average boy is 4 feet, 9 inches tall. During the middle and late childhood years, children gain about 5 to 7 pounds a year. The weight increase is due mainly to increases in the size of the skeletal and muscular systems, as well as the size of some body organs.

What characterizes children's physical growth in middle and late childhood?

Proportional changes are among the most pronounced physical changes in middle and late childhood. Head circumference and waist circumference decrease in relation to body height (Kliegman & others, 2012). A less noticeable physical change is that bones continue to ossify during middle and late childhood but yield to pressure and pull more than mature bones.

THE BRAIN

The development of brain-imaging techniques, such as magnetic resonance imaging (MRI), has led to increased research on changes in the brain during middle and late childhood and links between these brain changes and cognitive development (Diamond, 2013). Total brain volume stabilizes by the end of late childhood, but significant changes in various structures and regions of the brain continue to occur. In particular, the brain pathways and circuitry involving the prefrontal cortex, the highest level in the brain, continue to increase during middle and late childhood (see Figure 9.1). These advances in the prefrontal cortex are linked to children's improved attention, reasoning, and cognitive control (Markant & Thomas, 2013).

Leading developmental neuroscientist Mark Johnson and his colleagues (2009) proposed that the prefrontal cortex likely orchestrates the functions of many other brain regions during development. As part of this neural leadership role, the prefrontal cortex may provide an advantage to neural networks and connections that include the prefrontal cortex. In their view, the prefrontal cortex coordinates the best neural connections for solving a problem at hand.

Changes also occur in the thickness of the cerebral cortex (cortical thickness) in middle and late childhood (Thomason & Thompson, 2011). One study used brain scans to assess cortical thickness in 5- to 11-year-old children (Sowell & others, 2004). Cortical thickening across a two-year time period was observed in the temporal and frontal lobe areas that function in language, which may reflect improvements in language abilities such as reading. Figure 4.4 in Chapter 4 shows the locations of the temporal and frontal lobes in the brain.

As children develop, some brain areas become more active while others become less so (Diamond, 2013; Nelson, 2013; Raznahan & others, 2014). One shift in activation that occurs as children develop is from diffuse, larger areas to more focal, smaller areas (Turkeltaub & others, 2003). This shift is characterized by synaptic pruning, a process in which areas of the brain not being used lose synaptic connections and those being used show increased connections. In one study, researchers found less diffusion and more focal activation in the prefrontal cortex from 7 to 30 years of age (Durston & others, 2006).

MOTOR DEVELOPMENT

During middle and late childhood, children's motor skills become much smoother and more coordinated than they were in early childhood. For example, only one child in a thousand can hit a tennis ball over the net at the age of 3, yet by the age of 10 or 11 most children can learn to play the sport. Running, climbing, skipping rope, swimming, bicycle riding, and skating are just a few of the many physical skills elementary school children can master. In gross motor skills involving large muscle activity, boys usually outperform girls.

Increased myelination of the central nervous system is reflected in the improvement of fine motor skills during middle and late childhood. Children can more adroitly use their hands as tools. Six-year-olds can hammer, paste, tie shoes, and fasten clothes. By 7 years of age, children's hands have become steadier. At this age, children prefer a pencil to a crayon for printing, and reversal of letters is less common. Printing becomes smaller. At 8 to 10 years of age, the hands can be used independently with more ease and precision. Fine motor coordination develops to the point at which children can write rather than print words. Cursive letter size becomes smaller and more even. At 10 to 12 years of age, children begin to show manipulative skills similar to the abilities of adults. They can master the complex, intricate, and rapid movements needed to produce fine-quality crafts or to play a difficult piece on a musical instrument. Girls usually outperform boys in their use of fine motor skills.

EXERCISE

American children and adolescents are not getting enough exercise (Beets & others, 2014; Graber & Woods, 2013; Lumpkin, 2014). Increasing children's exercise levels has positive outcomes (Graham, Holt/Hale, & Parker, 2013; Wuest & Fisette, 2015).

An increasing number of studies document the importance of exercise in children's physical development (McCormack & others, 2014; Shin & others, 2014). A recent experimental study revealed positive effects for aerobic training on the insulin resistance and body fat levels of overweight/obese elementary school children (Davis & others, 2012). One study revealed that a high-intensity resistance training program decreased children's body fat and increased their muscle strength (Benson, Torode, & Fiatarone Singh, 2008). Also, a study of 9-year-olds revealed that a higher level of physical activity was linked to a lower level of metabolic disease risk based on measures such as cholesterol, waist circumference, and insulin (Parrett & others, 2011). A recent research review found that diet-only and diet-plus exercise interventions produced weight loss and metabolic profile improvement (Ho & others, 2013). However, adding exercise to dietary intervention resulted in more improvement in levels of high-density lipoprotein cholesterol, fasting glucose, and fasting insulin. Further, another recent research review concluded that exercise programs with

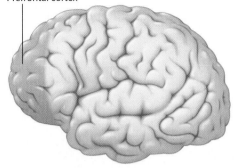

Prefrontal cortex

FIGURE 9.1

THE PREFRONTAL CORTEX. The brain pathways and circuitry involving the prefrontal cortex (shaded in purple) show significant advances in development during middle and late childhood. *What cognitive processes are linked to these changes in the prefrontal cortex?*

developmental **connection**

Brain Development

Synaptic pruning is an important aspect of the brain's development, and the pruning varies by brain region across children's development. Chapter 4, p. 107

What are some good strategies for increasing children's exercise?

developmental **connection**

Exercise

Experts recommend that preschool children engage in two hours of physical activity per day. Chapter 8, p. 258

a frequency of three weekly sessions lasting longer than 60 minutes were effective in lowering both systolic and diastolic blood pressure (Garcia-Hermoso, Saavedra, & Escalante, 2013).

A research review concluded that aerobic exercise also increasingly is linked to children's cognitive skills (Best, 2010). Researchers have found that aerobic exercise benefits children's attention, memory, effortful and goal-directed thinking and behavior, and creativity (Budde & others, 2008; Davis & Cooper, 2011; Davis & others, 2011; Hinkle, Tuckman, & Sampson, 1993; Krafft & others, 2014; Monti, Hillman, & Cohen, 2012; Pesce & others, 2009). In a recent fMRI study of physically unfit 8- to 11-year-old overweight children, a daily instructor-led aerobic exercise program that lasted 8 months was effective in improving the efficiency or flexible modulation of neural circuits that support better cognitive functioning (Krafft & others, 2014). Further, a recent study found that moderately intensive aerobic exercise improved children's cognitive inhibitory control (Drollette & others, 2014).

Parents and schools play important roles in determining children's exercise levels (Gilbertson & Graves, 2014; Meyer & others, 2014). Growing up with parents who exercise regularly provides positive models of exercise for children (Crawford & others, 2010). One study revealed that mothers were more likely than fathers to limit sedentary behavior in boys and girls (Edwardson & Gorely, 2010). In this study, fathers did have an influence on their sons' physical activity, but primarily through explicit modeling of physical activity, such as showing their sons how to shoot a basketball. A research review found that school-based physical activity was successful in improving children's fitness and lowering their fat levels (Kriemler & others, 2011).

Screen time also is linked with low activity and obesity in children (Saunders, 2014; Taverno Ross & others, 2013). Recall from Chapter 8 that a research review concluded that a higher level of screen time at 4 to 6 years of age was linked to increased obesity and lower physical activity from preschool through adolescence (te Velde & others, 2012). And recent research found that a higher level of screen time increased the risk of obesity for low- and high-activity children (Lane, Harrison, & Murphy, 2014).

Here are some ways to get children to exercise more:

- Offer more physical activity programs run by volunteers at school facilities.
- Improve physical fitness activities in schools.
- Have children plan community and school activities that interest them.
- Encourage families to focus more on physical activity, and encourage parents to exercise more.

HEALTH, ILLNESS, AND DISEASE

For the most part, middle and late childhood is a time of excellent health. Disease and death are less prevalent at this time than during other periods in childhood and in adolescence. However, many children in middle and late childhood face health problems that harm their development.

Accidents and Injuries   Injuries are the leading cause of death during middle and late childhood, and the most common cause of severe injury and death in this period is motor vehicle accidents, either as a pedestrian or as a passenger (Committee on Injury, Violence, and Poison Prevention, 2011). For this reason, safety advocates recommend the use of safety-belt restraints and child booster seats in vehicles because they can greatly reduce the severity of motor vehicle injuries (Theurer & Bhavsar, 2013). For example, a recent study found that child booster seats reduced the risk for serious injury by 45 percent for 4- to 8-year-old children (Sauber-Schatz & others, 2014). Other serious injuries involve bicycles, skateboards, roller skates, and other sports equipment.

Overweight Children   Being overweight is an increasingly prevalent health problem in children (Blake, Munoz, & Volpe, 2014; Schiff, 2015). Recall from Chapter 7, "Physical and Cognitive Development in Early Childhood," that being overweight is defined in terms of body mass index (BMI), which is computed by a formula that takes into account height and weight—children at or above the 97th percentile are included in the obesity category, at or above the 95th percentile in the overweight category, and children at or above the 85th percentile are described as at risk for being overweight (Centers for Disease Control and Prevention, 2014). Over the last three decades, the percentage of U.S. children who are at risk for being overweight has increased dramatically (Orsi, Hale, & Lynch, 2011). In Chapter 7, we indicated that there recently has been a decrease in the percentage of 2- to 5-year-old children who are obese, going from 12.1 percent in 2009–2010 to 8 percent in 2011–2012 (Ogden & others, 2014). In 2011–2012, 17.5 percent of U.S. 6- to 11-year-old U.S. children were classified as obese, which is essentially unchanged from 2009–2010 (Ogden & others, 2014).

It is not just in the United States that children are becoming more overweight (Gordon-Larsen, Wang, & Popkin, 2014; Ma & others, 2014). For example, a study found that general and abdominal obesity in Chinese children increased significantly from 1993 to 2009 (Liang & others, 2012). Further, a recent study revealed that overweight and obese Chinese children had a greater risk of having high blood pressure than children who were not overweight (Dong & others, 2013).

What are some concerns about increased numbers of overweight and obese children?

Causes of Children Being Overweight   Heredity and environmental contexts are related to being overweight in childhood (Gortmaker & Taveras, 2014; Thompson, Manore, & Vaughn, 2014; Wardlaw & Smith, 2015). Genetic analysis indicates that heredity is an important factor in children becoming overweight (Llewellyn & others, 2014). Overweight parents tend to have overweight children (Pufal & others, 2012). For example, one study found that the greatest risk factor for being overweight at 9 years of age was having an overweight parent (Agras & others, 2004). Parents and their children often have similar body types, height, body fat composition, and metabolism (Pereira-Lancha & others, 2012).

Environmental factors that influence whether children become overweight include the greater availability of food (especially food high in fat content), energy-saving devices, declining physical activity, parents' eating habits and monitoring of children's eating habits, the context in which a child eats, and heavy screen time (Hendrie & others, 2013; Turner & others, 2014). A recent behavior modification study of overweight and obese children made watching TV contingent on their engagement in exercise (Goldfield, 2012). The intervention markedly increased their exercise and reduced their TV viewing time.

Consequences of Being Overweight   The increase in overweight children in recent decades is cause for great concern because being overweight raises the risk for many medical and psychological problems (Buttitta & others, 2014; Thompson, Manore, & Vaughn, 2014). Diabetes, hypertension (high blood pressure), and elevated blood cholesterol levels are common in children who are overweight (Prendergast & Gidding, 2014). A research review concluded that obesity was linked with low self-esteem in children (Gomes & others, 2011). And in one study, overweight children were more likely than normal-weight children to report being teased by their peers and family members (McCormack & others, 2011).

Intervention Programs   A combination of diet, exercise, and behavior modification is often recommended to help children lose weight (Rauner, Mess, & Woll, 2013). Intervention programs that emphasize getting parents to engage in healthier lifestyles themselves, as well as to feed their children healthier food and get them to exercise more, can produce weight reduction in overweight and obese children (Lumpkin, 2014; Stovitz & others, 2014). For example, one study found that a combination of a child-centered activity program and a parent-centered dietary modification program were successful in helping overweight children lose pounds over a two-year period (Collins & others, 2011).

Cardiovascular Disease   Cardiovascular disease is uncommon in children. Nonetheless, environmental experiences and behavior in the childhood years can sow the seeds for cardiovascular disease in adulthood (Zhang, Zhang, & Xie, 2014). Many elementary-school-aged children already possess one or more of the risk factors for cardiovascular disease, such as hypertension and obesity (Abdulle, Al-Junaibi, & Nagelkerke, 2014; Bell & others, 2013;

developmental **connection**

Conditions, Diseases, and Disorders
Metabolic syndrome has increased in middle-aged adults in recent years and is linked to early death. Chapter 15, p. 464

connecting with careers

Sharon McLeod, Child Life Specialist

Sharon McLeod is a child life specialist who is senior clinical director in the Division of Child Life and Division of Integrative Care at the Children's Hospital Medical Center in Cincinnati.

Under McLeod's direction, the goals of her department are to promote children's optimal growth and development, reduce the stress of health care experiences, and provide support to child patients and their families. These goals are accomplished by facilitating therapeutic play and developmentally appropriate activities, educating and psychologically preparing children for medical procedures, and serving as a resource for parents and other professionals regarding children's development and health care issues.

McLeod says that human growth and development provides the foundation for her profession as a child life specialist. She also says her best times as a student were when she conducted fieldwork, had an internship, and experienced hands-on applications of the theories and concepts that she learned in her courses.

Sharon McLeod, child life specialist, working with a child at Children's Hospital Medical Center in Cincinnati.

For more information about what child life specialists do, see page 44 in the Careers in Life-Span Development appendix.

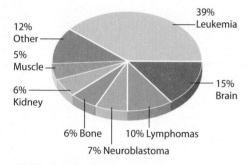

FIGURE **9.2**

TYPES OF CANCER IN CHILDREN. Cancers in children have a different profile from adult cancers, which attack mainly the lungs, colon, breast, prostate, and pancreas.

learning disability Difficulty in understanding or using spoken or written language or in doing mathematics. To be classified as a learning disability, the learning problem is not primarily the result of visual, hearing, or motor disabilities; intellectual disability; emotional disorders; or due to environmental, cultural, or economic disadvantage.

Zhao & others, 2014). A national study found that an increasing percentage of U.S. children and adolescents had elevated blood pressure from 1988 to 2006 (Ostchega & others, 2009). In this study, children who were obese were more likely to have elevated blood pressure. Another study revealed that high blood pressure goes undiagnosed in 75 percent of children with the disease (Hansen, Gunn, & Kaelber, 2007). Yet another study revealed that more than 2 hours of TV viewing per day was associated with higher blood pressure in children (Stamatakis & others, 2013). And other research found that children with a high body mass index and waist circumference are at risk for *metabolic syndrome*—a constellation of factors, including obesity, high blood pressure, and type 2 diabetes—placing them at risk for developing cardiovascular disease in adulthood (Sun & others, 2008).

Cancer Cancer is the second leading cause of death in U.S. children 5 to 14 years of age. One in every 330 children in the United States develops cancer before the age of 19. The incidence of cancer in children has increased slightly in recent years (National Cancer Institute, 2014).

Childhood cancers mainly attack the white blood cells (leukemia), brain, bone, lymph system, muscles, kidneys, and nervous system. All types of cancer are characterized by an uncontrolled proliferation of abnormal cells (Bleeker & others, 2014; Fabbri & others, 2012). As indicated in Figure 9.2, the most common cancer in children is leukemia, a cancer in which bone marrow manufactures an abundance of abnormal white blood cells that crowd out normal cells, making the child highly susceptible to bruising and infection (Alkayed, Al Hmood, & Madanat, 2013).

Because of advancements in cancer treatment, children with cancer are surviving longer than in the past (National Cancer Institute, 2014). Approximately 80 percent of children with acute lymphoblastic leukemia are cured with current chemotherapy treatment (Wayne, 2011).

Child life specialists are among the health professionals who work to make the lives of children with diseases less stressful. To read about the work of child life specialist Sharon McLeod, see *Connecting with Careers.*

Review *Connect* Reflect

LG1 Describe physical changes and health in middle and late childhood.

Review

- What are some changes in body growth and proportions in middle and late childhood?
- What characterizes the development of the brain in middle and late childhood?
- How do children's motor skills develop in middle and late childhood?
- What role does exercise play in children's lives?
- What are some characteristics of health, illness, and disease in middle and late childhood?

Connect

- In this section, you learned that increased myelination of the central nervous system is reflected in the improvement of fine motor skills during middle and late childhood. What developmental advances were connected with increased myelination in infancy and early childhood?

Reflect *Your Own Personal Journey of Life*

- One way that children get exercise is to play a sport. If you played a sport as a child, was it a positive or negative experience? Do you think that playing a sport as a child likely made a difference in whether you continue to exercise on a regular basis today? Explain. If you did not play a sport, do you wish you had? Explain.

2 Children with Disabilities

LG2 Identify children with different types of disabilities and discuss issues in educating them.

The Scope of Disabilities

Educational Issues

What are some of the disabilities that children have? What characterizes the education of children with disabilities?

THE SCOPE OF DISABILITIES

Of all children in the United States, 13 percent from 3 to 21 years of age in the United States received special education or related services in 2011–2012, an increase of 3 percent since 1980–1981 (Condition of Education, 2014). Figure 9.3 shows the four largest groups of students with a disability who were served by federal programs during the 2011–2012 school year (Condition of Education, 2014). As indicated in Figure 9.3, students with a learning disability were by far the largest group of students with a disability to be given special education, followed by children with speech or language impairments, intellectual disability, autism, and emotional disturbance. Note that the U.S. Department of Education includes both students with a learning disability and students with ADHD in the category of learning disability.

Learning Disabilities   The U.S. government created a definition of learning disabilities in 1997 and then reauthorized the definition with a few minor changes in 2004. Following is a summary of the government's definition of what determined whether a child should be classified as having a learning disability. A child with a **learning disability** has difficulty in learning that involves understanding or using spoken or written language, and the difficulty can appear in listening, thinking, reading, writing, and spelling. A learning disability also may involve difficulty in doing mathematics (Jitendra & Montague, 2013). To be classified as a learning disability, the learning problem is not primarily the result of visual, hearing, or motor disabilities; intellectual disability; emotional disorders; or environmental, cultural, or economic disadvantage (Swanson, 2014).

About three times as many boys as girls are classified as having a learning disability. Among the explanations for this gender difference are a greater biological vulnerability among boys and *referral bias*. That is, boys are more likely to be referred by teachers for treatment because of troublesome behavior.

Disability	Percentage of All Children in Public Schools
Learning disabilities	4.7
Speech or hearing impairments	2.8
Intellectual disability	0.9
Autism	0.9
Emotional disturbance	0.8

FIGURE 9.3

U.S. CHILDREN WITH A DISABILITY WHO RECEIVE SPECIAL EDUCATION SERVICES. Figures are for the 2011–2012 school year and represent the five categories with the highest number and percentage of children. Both learning disability and attention deficit hyperactivity disorder are combined in the learning disabilities category (Condition of Education, 2014).

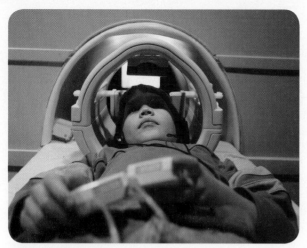

FIGURE **9.4**

BRAIN SCANS AND LEARNING DISABILITIES. An increasing number of studies are using MRI brain scans to examine the brain pathways involved in learning disabilities. Shown here is 9-year-old Patrick Price, who has dyslexia. Patrick is going through an MRI scanner disguised by drapes to look like a child-friendly castle. Inside the scanner, children must lie virtually motionless as words and symbols flash on a screen, and they are asked to identify them by clicking different buttons.

Approximately 80 percent of children with a learning disability have a reading problem (Shaywitz, Gruen, & Shaywitz, 2007). Three types of learning disabilities are dyslexia, dysgraphia, and dyscalculia:

- **Dyslexia** is a category reserved for individuals who have a severe impairment in their ability to read and spell (Allor & Al Otaiba, 2013; Ramus, 2014).
- **Dysgraphia** is a learning disability that involves difficulty in handwriting (Fischer-Baum & Rapp, 2014; Mason, Harris, & Graham, 2013). Children with dysgraphia may write very slowly, their writing products may be virtually illegible, and they may make numerous spelling errors because of their inability to match up sounds and letters (Hayes & Berninger, 2013).
- **Dyscalculia,** also known as developmental arithmetic disorder, is a learning disability that involves difficulty in math computation (Bryant & others, 2013; Cowan & Powell, 2014).

The precise causes of learning disabilities have not yet been determined (Friend, 2014; Vaughn & Bos, 2015). Researchers also use brain-imaging techniques, such as magnetic resonance imaging, to reveal any regions of the brain that might be involved in learning disabilities (Shaywitz, Lyon, & Shaywitz, 2006) (see Figure 9.4). This research indicates that it is unlikely learning disabilities reside in a single, specific brain location. More likely, learning disabilities are due to difficulty integrating information from multiple brain regions or subtle impairments in brain structures and functions.

Interventions with children who have a learning disability often focus on improving reading ability (Carlisle, Kenney, & Vereb, 2013; Templeton & Gehsmann, 2014). Intensive instruction over a period of time by a competent teacher can help many children (Berninger & Dunn, 2012).

Attention Deficit Hyperactivity Disorder (ADHD)

Attention deficit hyperactivity disorder (ADHD) is a disability in which children consistently show one or more of the following characteristics over a period of time: (1) inattention, (2) hyperactivity, and (3) impulsivity. Children who are inattentive have such difficulty focusing on any one thing that they may get bored with a task after only a few minutes—or even seconds. Children who are hyperactive show high levels of physical activity, seeming to be almost constantly in motion. Children who are impulsive have difficulty curbing their reactions; they do not do a good job of thinking before they act. Depending on the characteristics that children with ADHD display, they can be diagnosed as having (1) ADHD with predominantly inattention, (2) ADHD with predominantly hyperactivity/impulsivity, or (3) ADHD with both inattention and hyperactivity/impulsivity.

The number of children diagnosed and treated for ADHD has increased substantially in recent decades. The disorder occurs as much as four to nine times more frequently in boys than in girls. There is controversy, however, about the increased diagnosis of ADHD (Friend, 2014). Some experts attribute the increase mainly to heightened awareness of the disorder; others are concerned that many children are being incorrectly diagnosed (Watson & others, 2014).

A recent study examined the possible misdiagnosis of ADHD (Bruchmiller, Margraf, & Schneider, 2012). In this study, child psychologists, psychiatrists, and social workers were given vignettes of children with ADHD. Some vignettes matched the diagnostic criteria for the disorder, while others did not. The child in each vignette was sometimes identified as male and sometimes as female. The researchers assessed whether the mental health professionals gave a diagnosis of ADHD to the child described in the vignette. The professionals overdiagnosed ADHD almost 20 percent of the time, and regardless of the symptoms described, boys were twice as likely as girls to be diagnosed as having ADHD.

Adjustment and optimal development are difficult for children who have ADHD, so it is important that the diagnosis be accurate (Bolea-Alamanac & others, 2014; Feldman & Reiff, 2014). Children diagnosed with ADHD have an increased risk of school dropout, adolescent pregnancy, substance use problems, and antisocial behavior (Chang, Lichtenstein, & Larsson, 2012; Von Polier, Vioet, & Herpertz-Dahlmann, 2012).

Definitive causes of ADHD have not been found. However, a number of possible causes have been proposed (American Academy of Pediatrics & Reiff, 2011). Some children likely inherit a tendency to develop ADHD from their

Many children with ADHD show impulsive behavior, such as this boy reaching to pull a girl's hair. *How would you handle this situation if you were a teacher and this happened in your classroom?*

parents (Lee & Song, 2014). Other children likely develop ADHD because of damage to their brain during prenatal or postnatal development (Lindblad & Hjern, 2010). Among early possible contributors to ADHD are cigarette and alcohol exposure, as well as a high level of maternal stress during prenatal development and low birth weight (Glover, 2014; Yochum & others, 2014). For example, one study revealed that cigarette smoking during pregnancy was linked to ADHD in 6- to 7-year-old children (Sciberras, Ukoumunne, & Efron, 2011).

As with learning disabilities, the development of brain-imaging techniques is leading to a better understanding of ADHD (Dunn & Kronenberger, 2013; Lawrence & others, 2013; Posner, Park, & Wang, 2014). One study revealed that peak thickness of the cerebral cortex occurred three years later (10.5 years) in children with ADHD than in children without ADHD (peak at 7.5 years) (Shaw & others, 2007). The delay was more prominent in the prefrontal regions of the brain that especially are important in attention and planning (see Figure 9.5). Another study also found delayed development of the brain's frontal lobes in children with ADHD, likely due to delayed or decreased myelination (Nagel & others, 2011). Researchers also are exploring the roles that various neurotransmitters, such as serotonin and dopamine, might play in ADHD (Dalley & Roiser, 2012; Gold & others, 2014; Kollins & Adcock, 2014).

The delays in brain development just described are in areas linked to executive function. An increasing interest in the study of children with ADHD is their difficulty with tasks involving executive function, such as behavioral inhibition when necessary, use of working memory, and effective planning (Dunn & Kronenberger, 2013; Langberg, Dvorsky, & Evans, 2013; Saarinen & others, 2014). Researchers also have found deficits in theory of mind in children with ADHD (Buhler & others, 2011; Shuai, Chan, & Wang, 2011). And research indicates that children with ADHD are at risk for engaging in antisocial behavior (Miller, Loya, & Hinshaw, 2013).

Stimulant medication such as Ritalin or Adderall (which has fewer side effects than Ritalin) is effective in improving the attention of many children with ADHD, but it usually does not improve their attention to the same level as children who do not have ADHD (Wong & Stevens, 2012). A meta-analysis concluded that behavior management treatments are useful in reducing the effects of ADHD (Fabiano & others, 2009). Researchers have often found that a combination of medication (such as Ritalin) and behavior management improves the behavior of some but not all children with ADHD better than medication alone or behavior management alone (Parens & Johnston, 2009).

The sheer number of ADHD diagnoses has prompted speculation that psychiatrists, parents, and teachers are in fact labeling normal childhood behavior as psychopathology (Mash & Wolfe, 2013; Molina & Pelham, 2014). One reason for concern about overdiagnosing ADHD is that the form of treatment in well over 80 percent of cases is psychoactive drugs, including stimulants such as Ritalin and Adderall (Garfield & others, 2012). Further, there is increasing concern that children who are given stimulant drugs such as Ritalin or Adderall are at risk for developing substance abuse problems, although evidence regarding this concern so far has been mixed (Groenman & others, 2013; Molina & others, 2013; Nogueira & others, 2014; Zulauf & others, 2014).

Recently, researchers have been exploring the possibility that neurofeedback might improve the attention of children with ADHD (Gevensleben & others, 2014; Maurizio & others, 2013; Steiner & others, 2014). Neurofeedback trains individuals to become more aware of their physiological responses so they can attain better control over their brain's prefrontal cortex, where executive control primarily occurs. Individuals with ADHD have higher levels of electroencephalogram (EEG) abnormalities, such as lower beta waves that involve attention and memory and lower sensorimotor rhythms that involve control of movements. Neurofeedback produces audiovisual profiles of these brain waves so that individuals can learn how to achieve normal EEG functioning. In a recent study, 7- to 14-year-olds with ADHD were randomly assigned to either receive a neurofeedback treatment that consisted of 40 sessions or to take Ritalin (Meisel & others, 2013). Both groups showed a lower level of ADHD symptoms 6 months after the treatment, but only the neurofeedback group performed better academically.

Recently, mindfulness training also has been given to children and adolescents with ADHD (Cassone, 2014; Converse & others, 2014). In a recent study, 11- to 15-year-old adolescents with ADHD were given 8 weeks of mindfulness training (van de Weijer-Bergsma & others, 2012). Immediately after and 8 weeks following the training, the adolescents' attention improved and they engaged in fewer behavioral problems, although by 16 weeks post-training the effects had waned.

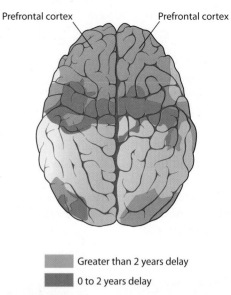

Prefrontal cortex   Prefrontal cortex

■ Greater than 2 years delay
■ 0 to 2 years delay

FIGURE 9.5

REGIONS OF THE BRAIN IN WHICH CHILDREN WITH ADHD HAD A DELAYED PEAK IN THE THICKNESS OF THE CEREBRAL CORTEX. *Note:* The greatest delays occurred in the prefrontal cortex.

dyslexia A category of learning disabilities involving a severe impairment in the ability to read and spell.

dysgraphia A learning disability that involves difficulty in handwriting.

dyscalculia Also known as developmental arithmetic disorder; a learning disability that involves difficulty in math computation.

attention deficit hyperactivity disorder (ADHD) A disability in which children consistently show one or more of the following characteristics: (1) inattention, (2) hyperactivity, and (3) impulsivity.

developmental **connection**

Cognitive Processes

Mindfulness training is being used to improve students' executive function. Chapter 12, p. 395

developmental **connection**

Conditions, Diseases, and Disorders

Autistic children have difficulty in developing a theory of mind, especially in understanding others' beliefs and emotions. Chapter 7, p. 220

What characterizes children with autism?

emotional and behavioral disorders Serious, persistent problems that involve relationships, aggression, depression, fears associated with personal or school matters, as well as other inappropriate socioemotional characteristics.

autism spectrum disorders (ASD) Also called pervasive developmental disorders, they range from the severe disorder labeled autistic disorder to the milder disorder called Asperger syndrome. Children with these disorders are characterized by problems in social interaction, verbal and nonverbal communication, and repetitive behaviors.

autistic disorder A severe autism spectrum disorder that has its onset in the first three years of life and includes deficiencies in social relationships, abnormalities in communication, and restricted, repetitive, and stereotyped patterns of behavior.

Exercise also is being investigated as a possible treatment for children with ADHD (Berwid & Halperin, 2012). A recent study found that a single 20-minute bout of moderately intense aerobic exercise improved the neurocognitive function and inhibitory control of children with ADHD (Pontifex & others, 2013). Among the reasons given as to why exercise might reduce ADHD symptoms in children are (1) better allocation of attention resources, (2) positive influence on prefrontal cortex functioning, and (3) exercise-induced dopamine release (Chang & others, 2012).

Emotional and Behavioral Disorders   Most children have minor emotional difficulties at some point during their school years. A small percentage have problems so serious and persistent that they are classified as having an emotional or behavioral disorder (Jolivette & others, 2013). These problems may include internalized disorders, such as depression, or externalized disorders, such as aggression (Kamphaus & Mays, 2014; Lane & others, 2013; Volpe & Chafouleas, 2014).

Emotional and behavioral disorders consist of serious, persistent problems that involve relationships, aggression, depression, and fears associated with personal or school matters, as well as other inappropriate socioemotional characteristics (Gueldner & Merrell, 2014; Jensen, Harward, & Bowen, 2014). Approximately 8 percent of children who have a disability and require an individualized education plan fall into this classification. Boys are three times as likely as girls to have these disorders.

Autism Spectrum Disorders   Autism spectrum disorders (ASD), also called pervasive developmental disorders, range from the severe disorder labeled autistic disorder to the milder disorder called Asperger syndrome. Autism spectrum disorders are characterized by problems in social interaction, problems in verbal and nonverbal communication, and repetitive behaviors (Hall, 2013; Wheeler, Mayton, & Carter, 2015; Wilcynski & others, 2014). Children with these disorders may also show atypical responses to sensory experiences (National Institute of Mental Health, 2014). Intellectual disability is present in some children with autism; others show average or above-average intelligence (Memari & others, 2012; Volkmar & others, 2014). Autism spectrum disorders can often be detected in children as young as 1 to 3 years of age.

Recent estimates of autism spectrum disorders indicate that they are dramatically increasing in occurrence (or are increasingly being detected). Once thought to affect only 1 in 2,500 children decades ago, they were estimated to be present in about 1 in 150 children in 2002 (Centers for Disease Control and Prevention, 2007). However, the most recent estimate is that 1 in 88 children had an autism spectrum disorder in 2008 (Centers for Disease Control & Prevention, 2012). In the most recent survey, autism spectrum disorders were identified five times more often in boys than in girls.

Autistic disorder is a severe developmental autism spectrum disorder that has its onset during the first three years of life and includes deficiencies in social relationships, abnormalities in communication, and restricted, repetitive, and stereotyped patterns of behavior.

Asperger syndrome is a relatively mild autism spectrum disorder in which the child has relatively good verbal language skills, milder nonverbal language problems, and a restricted range of interests and relationships (Soares & Patel, 2012). Children with Asperger syndrome often engage in obsessive, repetitive routines and preoccupations with a particular subject. For example, a child may be obsessed with baseball scores or specific videos on YouTube.

In 2013, the American Psychiatric Association published the new edition (DSM-V) of its psychiatric classification of disorders. In the new classification, autistic disorder, Asperger's syndrome, and several other autistic variations were consolidated in the overarching category of autism spectrum disorder (Autism Research Institute, 2013). Distinctions are made in terms of the severity of problems based on amount of support needed due to challenges involving social communication, restricted interests, and repetitive behaviors. Critics argue that the umbrella category proposed for autism spectrum disorder masks the heterogeneity that characterizes the subgroups of autism (Lai & others, 2013).

What causes autism spectrum disorders? The current consensus is that autism is a brain dysfunction characterized by abnormalities in brain structure and neurotransmitters (Catarino

& others, 2013; Doll & Broadie, 2014). Recent interest has focused on a lack of connectivity between brain regions as a key factor in autism (Just & others, 2012; Verly & others, 2014).

Genetic factors also are likely to play a role in the development of autism spectrum disorders (Nijmeijer & others, 2014; Rutter & Thapar, 2014). One study revealed that mutations—missing or duplicated pieces of DNA on chromosome 16—can raise a child's risk of developing autism 100-fold (Weiss & others, 2008). There is no evidence that family socialization causes autism.

Boys are estimated to be five times more likely to have autism spectrum disorders than girls are (Centers for Disease Control and Prevention, 2012). Expanding on autism's male linkage, Simon Baron-Cohen (2008, 2011) argues that autism reflects an extreme male brain, especially indicative of males' less effective ability to show empathy and read facial expressions and gestures than girls. In an attempt to improve these skills in 4- to 8-year-old autistic boys, Baron-Cohen and his colleagues (2007) produced a number of animations on a DVD that place faces with different emotions on toy trains and tractor characters in a boy's bedroom. (See www.thetransporters.com for a look at a number of facial expression animations.) After the autistic children had watched the animations 15 minutes every weekday for one month, their ability to interpret expressions on real faces in a different context equaled that of children without autism.

Children with autism benefit from a well-structured classroom, individualized teaching, and small-group instruction (Simmons, Lanter, & Lyons, 2014). Behavior modification techniques are sometimes effective in helping autistic children learn (Iovannone, 2013; Koehler-Platten & others, 2013; Odom & others, 2014).

EDUCATIONAL ISSUES

Until the 1970s most U.S. public schools either refused enrollment to children with disabilities or inadequately served them. This changed in 1975 when Public Law 94-142, the Education for All Handicapped Children Act, required that all students with disabilities be given a free, appropriate public education. In 1990, Public Law 94-142 was recast as the Individuals with Disabilities Education Act (IDEA). IDEA was amended in 1997 and then reauthorized in 2004 and renamed the Individuals with Disabilities Education Improvement Act.

IDEA spells out broad mandates for services to children with disabilities of all kinds (Kirk, Gallagher, & Coleman, 2015; Turnbull & others, 2013). These services include evaluation and eligibility determination, appropriate education and an individualized education plan (IEP), and education in the least restrictive environment (LRE) (Hallahan, Kauffman, & Pullen, 2015).

An **individualized education plan (IEP)** is a written statement that spells out a program that is specifically tailored for the student with a disability. The **least restrictive environment (LRE)** is a setting that is as similar as possible to the one in which children who do not have a disability are educated. This provision of the IDEA has given a legal basis to efforts to educate children with a disability in the regular classroom. The term **inclusion** describes educating a child with special educational needs full-time in the regular classroom (Friend & Bursuck, 2015; Vaughn, Bos, & Shumm, 2014). In a 2011–2012 assessment, 61 percent of U.S. students with a disability spent more than 80 percent of their school day in a general classroom, the highest percentage since 1990–1991, the first year for which data were collected (Condition of Education, 2014). Only 33 percent of students with a disability spent most of their school day in the general classroom in 1990–1991.

The outcomes of many legal changes regarding children with disabilities have been extremely positive (Smith & Tyler, 2014). Compared with several decades ago, far more children today are receiving competent, specialized services. For many children, inclusion in the regular classroom, with modifications or supplemental services, is appropriate (Friend & Bursuck, 2015). However, some leading experts on special education argue that in some cases the effort to educate children with disabilities in the regular classroom has become too extreme. For example, James Kauffman and his colleagues (Kauffman, McGee, & Brigham, 2004) state that inclusion too often has meant making accommodations in the regular classroom that do not always benefit children with disabilities. They advocate a more individualized approach that does not always involve full inclusion but allows options such as special education outside the regular classroom. Kauffman and

IDEA mandates free, appropriate education for all children. *What services does IDEA mandate for children with disabilities?*

Asperger syndrome A relatively mild autism spectrum disorder in which the child has relatively good verbal language skills, milder nonverbal language problems, and a restricted range of interests and relationships.

individualized education plan (IEP) A written statement that spells out a program specifically tailored to a child with a disability.

least restrictive environment (LRE) A setting that is as similar as possible to the one in which children who do not have a disability are educated.

inclusion Educating a child with special education needs full-time in the regular classroom.

his colleagues (2004, p. 620) acknowledge that children with disabilities "*do* need the services of specially trained professionals" and "*do* sometimes need altered curricula or adaptations to make their learning possible." However, they believe "we sell students with disabilities short when we pretend that they are not different from typical students. We make the same error when we pretend that they must *not* be expected to put forth extra effort if they are to learn to do some things—or learn to do something in a different way." Like general education, special education should challenge students with disabilities "to become all they can be."

Review *Connect* Reflect

 LG2 Identify children with different types of disabilities and discuss issues in educating them.

Review

- Who are children with disabilities? What characterizes children with learning disabilities?
- How would you describe children with attention deficit hyperactivity disorder?
- What are autism spectrum disorders, what causes them, and how are they characterized?
- What are some issues in educating children with disabilities?

Connect

- In Chapters 5 and 7, you learned about the development of attention in infancy and early childhood. How might ADHD be linked to earlier attention difficulties in infancy and early childhood?

Reflect *Your Own Personal Journey of Life*

- Think about your own schooling and how children with learning disabilities or ADHD either were or were not diagnosed. Were you aware of such individuals in your classes? Were they helped by specialists? You may know one or more individuals with a learning disability or ADHD. Ask them about their educational experiences and whether they think schools could have done a better job of helping them.

3 Cognitive Changes

 LG3 Explain cognitive changes in middle and late childhood.

| Piaget's Cognitive Developmental Theory | Information Processing | Intelligence | Extremes of Intelligence |

Do children enter a new stage of cognitive development in middle and late childhood? How do children process information during this age period? What is the nature of children's intelligence? Let's explore some answers to these questions.

PIAGET'S COGNITIVE DEVELOPMENTAL THEORY

According to Piaget (1952), the preschool child's thought is preoperational. Preschool children can form stable concepts, and they have begun to reason, but their thinking is flawed by egocentrism and magical belief systems. As we discussed in Chapter 7, however, Piaget may have underestimated the cognitive skills of preschool children. Some researchers argue that under the right conditions, young children may display abilities that are characteristic of Piaget's next stage of cognitive development, the stage of concrete operational thought (Gelman, 1969). Here we will cover the characteristics of concrete operational thought and evaluate Piaget's portrait of this stage.

The Concrete Operational Stage Piaget proposed that the *concrete operational stage* lasts from approximately 7 to 11 years of age. In this stage, children can perform concrete operations, and they can reason logically as long as reasoning can be applied to specific or concrete examples. Remember that *operations* are mental actions that are reversible, and *concrete operations* are operations that are applied to real, concrete objects.

The conservation tasks described in Chapter 7 indicate whether children are capable of concrete operations. For example, recall that in one task involving conservation of matter, the child is presented with two identical balls of clay. The experimenter rolls one ball into a long,

developmental connection

Centration

Centration, a centering of attention on one characteristic to the exclusion of all others, is present in young children's lack of conservation. Chapter 7, p. 208

seriation The concrete operation that involves ordering stimuli along a quantitative dimension (such as length).

transitivity The ability to logically combine relations to understand certain conclusions.

thin shape; the other remains in its original ball shape. The child is then asked if there is more clay in the ball or in the long, thin piece of clay. By the time children reach the age of 7 or 8, most answer that the amount of clay is the same. To answer this problem correctly, children have to imagine the clay rolling back into a ball. This type of imagination involves a reversible mental action applied to a real, concrete object. Concrete operations allow the child to consider several characteristics rather than focusing on a single property of an object. In the clay example, the preoperational child is likely to focus on height *or* width. The concrete operational child coordinates information about both dimensions.

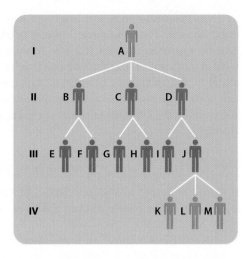

FIGURE **9.6**

CLASSIFICATION: AN IMPORTANT ABILITY IN CONCRETE OPERATIONAL THOUGHT. A family tree of four generations (I to IV): The preoperational child has trouble classifying the members of the four generations, while the concrete operational child can classify the members vertically, horizontally, and obliquely (up and down and across). For example, the concrete operational child understands that a family member can be a son, a brother, and a father, all at the same time.

What other abilities are characteristic of children who have reached the concrete operational stage? One important skill is the ability to classify or divide things into different sets or subsets and to consider their interrelationships. Consider the family tree of four generations that is shown in Figure 9.6 (Furth & Wachs, 1975). This family tree suggests that the grandfather (A) has three children (B, C, and D), each of whom has two children (E through J), and that one of these children (J) has three children (K, L, and M). A child who comprehends the classification system can move up and down a level, across a level, and up and down and across within the system. The concrete operational child understands that person J can at the same time be father, brother, and grandson, for example.

Children who have reached the concrete operational stage are also capable of **seriation,** which is the ability to order stimuli along a quantitative dimension (such as length). To see if students can serialize, a teacher might haphazardly place eight sticks of different lengths on a table. The teacher then asks the students to order the sticks by length. Many young children end up with two or three small groups of "big" sticks or "little" sticks, rather than a correct ordering of all eight sticks. Another mistaken strategy they use is to evenly line up the tops of the sticks but ignore the bottoms. The concrete operational thinker simultaneously understands that each stick must be longer than the one that precedes it and shorter than the one that follows it.

Another aspect of reasoning about the relations between classes is **transitivity,** which is the ability to logically combine relations to understand certain conclusions. In this case, consider three sticks (A, B, and C) of differing lengths. A is the longest, B is intermediate in length, and C is the shortest. Does the child understand that if A is longer than B and B is longer than C, then A is longer than C? In Piaget's theory, concrete operational thinkers do, while preoperational thinkers do not.

Evaluating Piaget's Concrete Operational Stage
Has Piaget's portrait of the concrete operational child withstood the test of research? According to Piaget, various aspects of a stage should emerge at the same time. In fact, however, some concrete operational abilities do not appear in synchrony. For example, children do not learn to conserve at the same time they learn to cross-classify.

Furthermore, education and culture exert stronger influences on children's development than Piaget reasoned (Morrison, 2015). Some preoperational children can be trained to reason at a concrete operational stage. And the age at which children acquire conservation skills is related to how much practice their culture provides in these skills.

Thus, although Piaget was a giant in the field of developmental psychology, his conclusions about the concrete operational stage have been challenged. In Chapter 11, after examining the final stage in his theory of cognitive development, we will further evaluate Piaget's contributions and examine various criticisms of his theory.

We owe to Piaget the present field of cognitive development with its image of the developing child, who through its own active and creative commerce with its environment, builds an orderly succession of cognitive structures en route to intellectual maturity.

—JOHN FLAVELL
Contemporary Developmental Psychologist, Stanford University

An outstanding teacher and instruction in the logic of science and mathematics are important cultural experiences that promote the development of operational thought. *Might Piaget have underestimated the roles of culture and schooling in children's cognitive development?*

neo-Piagetians Developmentalists who argue that Piaget got some things right but that his theory needs considerable revision. They have elaborated on Piaget's theory, giving more emphasis to information processing, strategies, and precise cognitive steps.

long-term memory A relatively permanent type of memory that holds huge amounts of information for a long period of time.

working memory A mental "workbench" where individuals manipulate and assemble information when making decisions, solving problems, and comprehending written and spoken language.

Neo-Piagetians argue that Piaget got some things right but that his theory needs considerable revision. They give more emphasis to how children use attention, memory, and strategies to process information (Case & Mueller, 2001). They especially believe that a more accurate portrayal of children's thinking requires attention to children's strategies, the speed at which children process information, the particular task involved, and the division of problem solving into smaller, more precise steps (Morra & others, 2008). These are issues addressed by the information-processing approach, and we discuss some of them later in this chapter.

INFORMATION PROCESSING

If instead of describing children's stages of thinking we were to examine how they process information during middle and late childhood, what would we find? During these years, most children dramatically improve their ability to sustain and control attention (Siegler, 2012). As we discussed in Chapter 7, they pay more attention to task-relevant stimuli than to salient stimuli. Other changes in information processing during middle and late childhood involve memory, thinking, metacognition, and executive function (Bauer & Zelazo, 2013; Cowan, 2014; Friedman, 2014).

Memory   In Chapter 7, we concluded that short-term memory increases considerably during early childhood but after the age of 7 does not show as much increase. **Long-term memory,** a relatively permanent and unlimited type of memory, increases with age during middle and late childhood. In part, improvements in memory reflect children's increased knowledge and their increased use of strategies. Keep in mind that it is important not to view memory in terms of how children add something to it but rather to underscore how children actively construct their memory (Bjorklund, 2013; Cohen, 2012; Willoughby & others, 2012).

Working Memory   Short-term memory is like a passive storehouse with shelves to store information until it is moved to long-term memory. Alan Baddeley (1990, 2001, 2007, 2010, 2012) defines **working memory** as a kind of mental "workbench" where individuals manipulate and assemble information when they make decisions, solve problems, and comprehend written and spoken language (see Figure 9.7). Working memory is described as more active and powerful in modifying information than short-term memory. Working memory involves bringing information to mind and mentally working with or updating it, as when you link one idea to another and relate what you are reading now to something you read earlier.

Note in Figure 9.8 that a key component of working memory is the *central executive*, which supervises and controls the flow of information. The central executive is especially at work in selective attention and inhibition, planning and decision making, and trouble shooting. Recall from Chapter 7 our description of *executive function* as an umbrella-like concept that encompasses a number of higher-level cognitive processes. One of those cognitive processes is working memory, especially its central executive dimension.

Working memory is linked to many aspects of children's development (Cowan, 2014; Myatchin & Lagae, 2013; Reznick, 2014). The following studies illustrate the importance of working memory to children's cognitive and language development:

- A recent research review concluded that children with learning difficulties in reading and math have working memory deficits (Peng & Fuchs, 2014).
- Working memory capacity at 9 to 10 years of age predicted foreign language comprehension two years later at 11 to 12 years of age (Andersson, 2010).

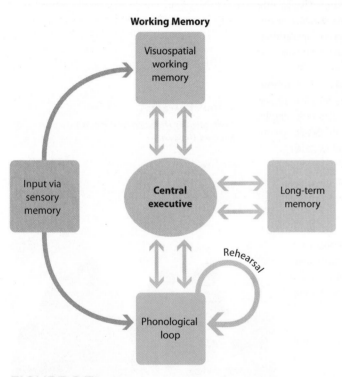

Working Memory

FIGURE **9.7**

WORKING MEMORY. In Baddeley's working memory model, working memory is like a mental workbench where a great deal of information processing is carried out. Working memory consists of three main components with the phonological loop and visuospatial working memory helping the central executive do its work. Input from sensory memory goes to the phonological loop, where information about speech is stored and rehearsal takes place, and visuospatial working memory, where visual and spatial information, including imagery, are stored. Working memory is a limited-capacity system, and information is stored there for only a brief time. Working memory interacts with long-term memory, using information from long-term memory in its work and transmitting information to long-term memory for longer storage.

- Working memory capacity predicted how many items on a to-be-remembered list that fourth-grade children forgot (Aslan, Zellner, & Bauml, 2010).
- A computerized working memory intervention with 9- to 11-year-old children improved their reading performance (Loosli & others, 2012).

Knowledge and Expertise   Much of the research on the role of knowledge in memory has compared experts and novices. Experts have acquired extensive knowledge about a particular content area; this knowledge influences what they notice and how they organize, represent, and interpret information (Siegler, 2013). These aspects in turn affect their ability to remember, reason, and solve problems. When individuals have expertise about a particular subject, their memory also tends to be good regarding material related to that subject (Staszewski, 2013).

For example, one study found that 10- and 11-year-olds who were experienced chess players ("experts") were able to remember more information about the location of chess pieces on a chess board than college students who were not chess players ("novices") (Chi, 1978) (see Figure 9.8). In contrast, when the college students were presented with other stimuli, they were able to remember them better than the children were. Thus, the children's expertise in chess gave them superior memories, but only in chess.

There are developmental changes in expertise (Blair & Somerville, 2009; Ericsson, 2014). Older children usually have more expertise about a subject than younger children do, which can contribute to their better memory for the subject.

Autobiographical Memory   Recall that we discussed *autobiographical memory,* which involves memory of significant events and experiences in one's life, in Chapter 7. You are engaging in autobiographical memory when you answer questions such as: Who was your first-grade teacher and what was s/he like? What is the most traumatic event that happened to you as a child?

As children go through middle and late childhood, and through adolescence, their autobiographical narratives broaden and become more elaborated (Bauer, 2013; Bauer & Fivush, 2014; DeMarie & Lopez, 2014; Pathman & St. Jacques, 2014). Researchers have found that children develop more detailed, coherent, and evaluative autobiographical memories when their mothers reminisce with them in elaborated and evaluative ways (Fivush, 2010).

Culture influences children's autobiographical memories. American children, especially American girls, produce autobiographical narratives that are longer, more detailed, more specific, and more personal than narratives by children from China and Korea (Bauer, 2013). In their conversations about past events, American mothers and their children are more elaborative and more focused on themes related to being independent while Korean mothers and their children less often engage in detailed conversations about the past. Possibly the more elaborated content of American children's narratives contributes to the earlier first memories researchers have found in American adults (Han, Leichtman, & Wang, 1998).

Strategies   If we know anything at all about long-term memory, it is that long-term memory depends on the learning activities individuals engage in when they are learning and remembering information (Friedman, 2014). A key learning activity involves **strategies,** which consist of deliberate mental activities to improve the processing of information. For example, organizing is a strategy that older children, adolescents, and adults use to remember more effectively. Strategies do not occur automatically; they require effort and work.

Following are some effective strategies for adults to use when attempting to improve children's memory skills:

- *Advise children to elaborate on what is to be remembered.* **Elaboration** is an important strategy that involves engaging in more extensive processing of information. When individuals engage in elaboration, their memory benefits (Schneider, 2011). Thinking of examples and relating information to one's own self and experiences are good ways to elaborate information. Forming personal associations with information makes the information more meaningful and helps children to remember it. For example, if the word *win* is on a list of words a child is asked to remember, the child might think of the last time he won a bicycle race with a friend.

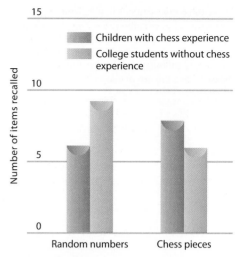

FIGURE 9.8

THE ROLE OF EXPERTISE IN MEMORY. Notice that when 10- to 11-year-old children and college students were asked to remember a string of random numbers that had been presented to them, the college students fared better. However, the 10- to 11-year-olds who had experience playing chess ("experts") had better memory for the location of chess pieces on a chess board than college students with no chess experience ("novices") (Chi, 1978).

strategies Deliberate mental activities that improve the processing of information.

elaboration An important strategy for remembering that involves engaging in more extensive processing of information.

fuzzy trace theory States that memory is best understood by considering two types of memory representations: (1) verbatim memory trace, and (2) gist. In this theory, older children's better memory is attributed to the fuzzy traces created by extracting the gist of information.

- *Encourage children to engage in mental imagery.* Mental imagery can help even young schoolchildren to remember pictures. However, for remembering verbal information, mental imagery works better for older children than for younger children (Schneider, 2011).

- *Motivate children to remember material by understanding it rather than by memorizing it.* Children will remember information better over the long term if they understand the information rather than just rehearse and memorize it. Rehearsal works well for encoding information into short-term memory, but when children need to retrieve the information from long-term memory, it is much less efficient. For most information, encourage children to understand it, give it meaning, elaborate it, and personalize it. Give children concepts and ideas to remember and then ask them how they can relate the concepts and ideas to their own personal experiences and meanings. Give them practice on elaborating a concept so they will process the information more deeply.

- *Repeat with variation on the instructional information and link early and often.* These are memory development research expert Patricia Bauer's (2009) recommendations to improve children's consolidation and reconsolidation of the information they are learning. Variations on a lesson theme increase the number of associations in memory storage, and linking expands the network of associations in memory storage; both strategies expand the routes for retrieving information from storage.

- *Embed memory-relevant language when instructing children.* Teachers vary considerably in how much they use memory-relevant language that encourages students to remember information. In research that involved extensive observations of a number of first-grade teachers in the classroom, Peter Ornstein and his colleagues (Ornstein, Coffman, & Grammer, 2007, 2009; Ornstein & others, 2010) found that during the time segments observed, the teachers rarely used strategy suggestions or metacognitive (thinking about thinking) questions. In this research, when lower-achieving students were placed in classrooms in which teachers were categorized as "high-mnemonic teachers" who frequently embedded memory-relevant information in their teaching, the students' achievement increased (Ornstein, Coffman, & Grammer, 2007).

Fuzzy Trace Theory   Might something other than knowledge and strategies be responsible for the improvement in memory during the elementary school years? Charles Brainerd and Valerie Reyna (1993, 2014; Reyna, 2004) argue that fuzzy traces account for much of this improvement. Their **fuzzy trace theory** states that memory is best understood by considering two types of memory representations: (1) verbatim memory trace, and (2) gist. The *verbatim memory trace* consists of the precise details of the information, whereas *gist* refers to the central idea of the information. When gist is used, fuzzy traces are built up. Although individuals of all ages extract gist, young children tend to store and retrieve verbatim traces. At some point during the early elementary school years, children begin to use gist more and, according to the theory, this contributes to the improved memory and reasoning of older children because fuzzy traces are more enduring and less likely to be forgotten than verbatim traces.

Thinking   Four important aspects of thinking are executive function, critical thinking, thinking creatively, and thinking scientifically.

Executive Function   In Chapter 7, you read about executive function and its characteristics in early childhood (Carlson, Claxton, & Moses, 2014; Carlson, White, & Davis-Unger, 2014; Carlson, Zelazo, & Faja, 2013). Some of the cognitive topics we already have discussed in this chapter—working memory, critical thinking, creative thinking, and metacognition—can be considered under the umbrella of executive function and linked to the development of the brain's prefrontal cortex. Also, earlier in the chapter in the coverage of brain development in middle and late childhood, you read about the increase in cognitive control, which involves flexible and effective control in a number of areas such as focusing attention, reducing interfering thoughts, inhibiting motor actions, and exercising flexibility in deciding between competing choices.

developmental **connection**

Cognitive Processes

In early childhood, executive function especially involves advances in cognitive inhibition, cognitive flexibility, and goal-setting. Chapter 7, p. 216

Adele Diamond and Kathleen Lee (2011) highlighted the following dimensions of executive function that they conclude are the most important for 4- to 11-year-old children's cognitive development and school success:

- *Self-control/inhibition.* Children need to develop self-control that will allow them to concentrate and persist on learning tasks, to inhibit their tendencies to repeat incorrect responses, and to resist the impulse to do something now that they later would regret.
- *Working memory.* Children need an effective working memory to mentally work with the masses of information they will encounter as they go through school and beyond.
- *Flexibility.* Children need to be flexible in their thinking to consider different strategies and perspectives.

What are some key dimensions of executive function that are linked to children's cognitive development and school success?

Researchers have found that executive function is a better predictor of school readiness than general IQ (Blair & Razza, 2007). A number of diverse activities have been found to increase children's executive function, such as computerized training that uses games to improve working memory (CogMed, 2013), aerobic exercise (Chang & others, 2012), mindfulness (the Tools of the Mind program discussed in Chapter 7, for example) (Bodrova, Leong, & Akhutina, 2011), and some types of school curricula (the Montessori curriculum, for example) (Diamond, 2013; Diamond & Lee, 2011).

As discussed in Chapter 1, Ann Masten and her colleagues (Herbers & others, 2011, 2014; Masten, 2013, 2014a, b; Masten & others, 2008) have found that executive function and parenting skills are linked to homeless children's success in school. Masten believes that executive function and good parenting skills are related. In her words, "When we see kids with good executive function, we often see adults around them that are good self-regulators. . . Parents model, they support, and they scaffold these skills" (Masten, 2012, p. 11).

Critical Thinking   Currently, there is considerable interest among psychologists and educators in critical thinking (Barnett & Francis, 2012). **Critical thinking** involves thinking reflectively and productively and evaluating evidence. In this book, the second and third parts of the *Review, Connect, Reflect* sections of each chapter challenge you to think critically about a topic or an issue related to the discussion.

According to Ellen Langer (2005), **mindfulness**—being alert, mentally present, and cognitively flexible while going through life's everyday activities and tasks—is an important aspect of thinking critically. Mindful children and adults maintain an active awareness of the circumstances in their life and are motivated to find the best solutions to tasks. Mindful individuals create new ideas, are open to new information, and explore multiple strategies and perspectives. By contrast, mindless individuals are entrapped in old ideas, engage in automatic behavior, and often use a single strategy or adopt a single perspective.

Jacqueline and Martin Brooks (2001) lament that few schools really teach students to think critically and develop a deep understanding of concepts. Deep understanding occurs when students are stimulated to rethink previously held ideas. In Brooks and Brooks' view, schools spend too much time getting students to give a single correct answer in an imitative way, rather than encouraging them to expand their thinking by coming up with new ideas and rethinking earlier conclusions. They observe that too often teachers ask students to recite, define, describe, state, and list, rather than to analyze, infer, connect, synthesize, criticize, create, evaluate, think, and rethink. Many successful students complete their assignments, do well on tests and get good grades, yet they don't ever learn to think critically and deeply. They think superficially, staying on the surface of problems rather than stretching their minds and becoming deeply engaged in meaningful thinking.

Recently, Robert Roeser and Philip Zelazo (2012) have emphasized that mindfulness is an important mental process that children can engage in to improve a number of cognitive and socioemotional skills, such as executive function, focused attention, emotion regulation, and empathy (Roeser & Zelazo, 2012). It has been proposed that mindfulness training could be implemented in schools through practices such as using age-appropriate activities that increase children's reflection on moment-to-moment experiences and result in improved self-regulation (Zelazo & Lyons, 2012).

"For God's sake, think! Why is he being so nice to you?"
© Sam Gross/The New Yorker Collection/
www.cartoonbank.com

critical thinking Thinking reflectively and productively, as well as evaluating evidence.

mindfulness Being alert, mentally present, and cognitively flexible while going through life's everyday activities and tasks.

What do you mean, "What is it?" It's the spontaneous, unfettered expression of a young mind not yet bound by the restraints of narrative or pictorial representation.
Science Cartoons Plus.com

developmental **connection**

Creativity

How can you cultivate your curiosity and interest to live a more creative life? Chapter 13, p. 420

creative thinking The ability to think in novel and unusual ways and to come up with unique solutions to problems.

convergent thinking Thinking that produces one correct answer and is characteristic of the kind of thinking tested by standardized intelligence tests.

divergent thinking Thinking that produces many answers to the same question and is characteristic of creativity.

metacognition Cognition about cognition, or knowing about knowing.

In addition to mindfulness, activities such as yoga, meditation, and tai chi have been recently suggested as candidates for improving children's cognitive and socioemotional development. Together these activities are being grouped under the topic of *contemplative science*, a cross-disciplinary term that involves the study of how various types of mental and physical training might enhance children's development (Roeser & Zelazo, 2012).

Creative Thinking   Cognitively competent children not only think critically, but also creatively (Kaufman & Sternberg, 2013). **Creative thinking** is the ability to think in novel and unusual ways and to come up with unique solutions to problems. Thus, intelligence and creativity are not the same thing. This difference was recognized by J. P. Guilford (1967), who distinguished between **convergent thinking,** which produces one correct answer and characterizes the kind of thinking that is required on conventional tests of intelligence, and **divergent thinking,** which produces many different answers to the same question and characterizes creativity. For example, a typical item on a conventional intelligence test is "How many quarters will you get in return for 60 dimes?" In contrast, the following question has many possible answers: "What image comes to mind when you hear the phrase 'sitting alone in a dark room' or 'some unique uses for a paper clip'?"

A special concern is that children's creative thinking appears to be declining. A study of approximately 300,000 U.S. children and adults found that creativity scores rose until 1990, but since then have been steadily declining (Kim, 2010). Among the likely causes of the creativity decline are the number of hours U.S. children spend watching TV and playing video games instead of engaging in creative activities, as well as the lack of emphasis on creative thinking skills in schools (Gregorson, Kaufman, & Snyder, 2013; Kaufman & Sternberg, 2013). Some countries, though, are placing increasing emphasis on creative thinking in schools. For example, historically, creative thinking has been discouraged in Chinese schools. However, Chinese educators are now encouraging teachers to spend more classroom time on creative activities (Plucker, 2010).

It is important to recognize that children will show more creativity in some domains than others (Kaufman & Sternberg, 2013). A child who shows creative thinking skills in mathematics may not exhibit these skills in art, for example. An important goal is to help children become more creative. The *Connecting Development to Life* interlude offers some recommended ways to accomplish this goal.

Scientific Thinking   Like scientists, children ask fundamental questions about reality and seek answers to problems that may seem utterly trivial or unanswerable to many adults (such as "Why is the sky blue?"). Do children generate hypotheses, perform experiments, and reach conclusions about their data in ways resembling those of scientists?

Scientific reasoning often is aimed at identifying causal relations. Like scientists, children place a great deal of emphasis on causal mechanisms. Their understanding of how events are caused weighs more heavily in their causal inferences than even such strong influences as whether the cause happened immediately before the effect.

There also are important differences between the reasoning of children and the reasoning of scientists (Kuhn, 2011, 2013). For example, children have difficulty designing experiments that can distinguish among alternative causes. Instead, they tend to bias the experiments in favor of whatever hypothesis they began with. Sometimes they see the results as supporting their original hypothesis even when the results directly contradict it.

Too often, the skills scientists use, such as careful observation, graphing, self-regulatory thinking, and knowing when and how to apply one's knowledge to solve problems, are not routinely taught in schools. Children have many concepts that are incompatible with science and reality. Good teachers perceive and understand a child's underlying scientific concepts, then use the concepts as a scaffold for learning (DeRosa & Abruscato, 2015). Effective science teaching helps children distinguish between fruitful errors and misconceptions and detect plainly wrong ideas that need to be replaced by more accurate conceptions (Contant, Bass, & Carin, 2015).

Metacognition   **Metacognition** is cognition about cognition, or knowing about knowing (Flavell, 2004). Metacognition can take many forms, including thinking about and knowing

Strategies for Increasing Children's Creative Thinking

Below are some strategies for increasing children's creative thinking.

Encourage Brainstorming

Brainstorming is a technique in which people are encouraged to come up with creative ideas in a group, play off each other's ideas, and say practically whatever comes to mind that seems relevant to a particular issue. Facilitators usually tell participants to hold off from criticizing others' ideas at least until the end of the brainstorming session.

Provide Environments That Stimulate Creativity

Some environments nourish creativity, while others inhibit it. Parents and teachers who encourage creativity often rely on children's natural curiosity. They provide exercises and activities that stimulate children to find insightful solutions to problems, rather than ask a lot of questions that require rote answers (Baer & Kaufman, 2013). Teachers also encourage creativity by taking students on field trips to locations where creativity is valued. Science, discovery, and children's museums offer rich opportunities to stimulate creativity.

Don't Overcontrol Children

Teresa Amabile (1993) says that telling children exactly how to do things leaves them feeling that originality is a mistake and exploration is a waste of time. Instead of dictating which activities they should engage in, teachers and parents who let children follow their interests and who support their inclinations are less likely to stifle their natural curiosity (Hennessey, 2011).

Encourage Internal Motivation

Parents and teachers should avoid excessive use of prizes, such as gold stars, money, or toys, which can stifle creativity by undermining the intrinsic pleasure students derive from creative activities (Hennessey, 2011). Creative children's motivation is the satisfaction generated by the work itself.

Build Children's Confidence

To expand children's creativity, teachers and parents should encourage children to believe in their own ability to create something innovative and worthwhile. Building children's confidence in their creative skills aligns with Bandura's (2010a, 2012) concept of self-efficacy, the belief that one can master a situation and produce positive outcomes.

What are some good strategies for guiding children in thinking more creatively?

Guide Children to Be Persistent and Delay Gratification

Parents and teachers need to be patient and understand that most highly successful creative products take years to develop. Most creative individuals work on ideas and projects for months and years without being rewarded for their efforts.

Encourage Children to Take Intellectual Risks

Parents and teachers should encourage children to take intellectual risks. Creative individuals take intellectual risks and seek to discover or invent something never before discovered or invented. Creative people are not afraid of failing or getting something wrong (Baer & Kaufman, 2013).

Introduce Children to Creative People

Teachers can invite creative people to their classrooms and ask them to describe what helps them become creative or to demonstrate their creative skills. A writer, poet, musician, scientist, and many others can bring their props and productions to the classroom, turning it into a forum for stimulating students' creativity.

You learned that it is important to recognize that children will show more creativity in some domains than others. Choose one of the strategies mentioned above and describe how you would implement it differently to encourage creativity in writing, science, math, and art in children in middle and late childhood.

when and where to use particular strategies for learning or solving problems. Conceptualization of metacognition consists of several dimensions of executive function, such as planning (deciding how much time to spend focusing on a task, for example) and self-regulation (modifying strategies as work on a task progresses, for example) (Dimmitt & McCormick, 2012; McCormick, Dimmitt, & Sullivan, 2013).

brainstorming A technique in which individuals are encouraged to come up with creative ideas in a group, play off each other's ideas, and say almost anything that comes to mind.

developmental connection

Cognitive Theory

Theory of mind—awareness of one's own mental processes and the mental processes of others—involves metacognition. Chapter 7, p. 217

Cognitive developmentalist John Flavell is a pioneer in providing insights about children's thinking. Among his many contributions are establishing the field of metacognition and conducting numerous studies in this area, including metamemory and theory of mind studies.

The thirst to know and understand. . . . These are the good in life's rich hand.

—Sir William Watson

English Poet, 20th Century

intelligence Problem-solving skills and the ability to learn from and adapt to the experiences of everyday life.

individual differences The stable, consistent ways in which people differ from each other.

Many studies classified as "metacognitive" have focused on *metamemory,* or knowledge about memory. This includes general knowledge about memory, such as knowing that recognition tests are easier than recall tests. It also encompasses knowledge about one's own memory, such as a student's ability to monitor whether she has studied enough for a test that is coming up next week or a child's confidence in eyewitness judgments (Buratti, Allwood, & Johansson, 2014).

Young children do have some general knowledge about memory (Lukowski & Bauer, 2014). By 5 or 6 years of age, children usually know that familiar items are easier to learn than unfamiliar ones, that short lists are easier to memorize than long ones, that recognition is easier than recall, and that forgetting is more likely to occur over time (Lyon & Flavell, 1993). However, in other ways young children's metamemory is limited. They don't understand that related items are easier to remember than unrelated ones and that remembering the gist of a story is easier than remembering information verbatim (Kreutzer, Leonard, & Flavell, 1975). By the fifth grade, students understand that gist recall is easier than verbatim recall.

Young children also have only limited knowledge about their own memory. They have an inflated opinion of their memory abilities. For example, in one study a majority of young children predicted that they would be able to recall all 10 items on a list of 10 items. When tested for this, none of the young children managed this feat (Flavell, Friedrichs, & Hoyt, 1970). As they move through the elementary school years, children give more realistic evaluations of their memory skills (Schneider, 2011).

In addition to metamemory, metacognition includes knowledge about strategies (McCormick, Dimmitt, & Sullivan, 2013; Sperling & others, 2012). Strategies have been the focus of a number of microgenetic investigations (Kuhn, 2013). Recall from Chapter 1 that the *microgenetic method* involves obtaining detailed information about processing mechanisms as they are occurring moment to moment (Siegler, 2013). Using the microgenetic approach, researchers have shown that developing effective strategies doesn't occur abruptly but occurs gradually. This research has found considerable variability in children's use of strategies, even revealing that they may use an incorrect strategy in solving a math problem for which they had used a correct strategy several trials earlier (Siegler & others, 2013).

In the view of Michael Pressley (2003), the key to education is helping students learn a rich repertoire of strategies that produce solutions to problems. Good thinkers routinely use strategies and effective planning to solve problems. Good thinkers also know when and where to use strategies. Understanding when and where to use strategies often results from monitoring the learning situation (Serra & Metcalfe, 2010).

Pressley and his colleagues (Pressley & others, 2003, 2004, 2007) spent considerable time in recent years observing strategy instruction by teachers and strategy use by students in elementary and secondary school classrooms. They conclude that strategy instruction is far less complete and intense than what students need to receive in order to learn how to use strategies effectively. They argue that education ought to be restructured so that students are provided with more opportunities to become competent strategic learners.

INTELLIGENCE

How can intelligence be defined? **Intelligence** is the ability to solve problems and to adapt and learn from experiences. Interest in intelligence has often focused on individual differences and assessment. **Individual differences** are the stable, consistent ways in which people differ from each other. We can talk about individual differences in personality or any other domain, but it is in the domain of intelligence that the most attention has been directed at individual differences (Kehle & Bray, 2014). For example, an intelligence test purports to inform us about whether a student can reason better than others who have taken the test. Let's go back in history and see what the first intelligence test was like.

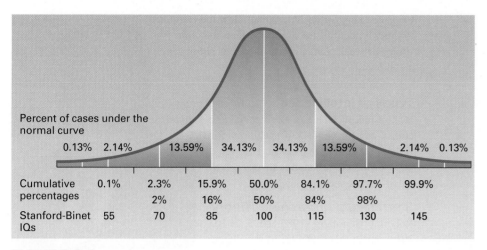

Percent of cases under the normal curve								
0.13%	2.14%	13.59%	34.13%	34.13%	13.59%	2.14%	0.13%
Cumulative percentages	0.1%	2.3%	15.9%	50.0%	84.1%	97.7%	99.9%	
		2%	16%	50%	84%	98%		
Stanford-Binet IQs	55	70	85	100	115	130	145	

FIGURE 9.9

THE NORMAL CURVE AND STANFORD-BINET IQ SCORES. The distribution of IQ scores approximates a normal curve. Most of the population falls in the middle range of scores. Notice that extremely high and extremely low scores are very rare. Slightly more than two-thirds of the scores fall between 85 and 115. Only about 1 in 50 individuals has an IQ higher than 130, and only about 1 in 50 individuals has an IQ lower than 70.

The Binet Tests   In 1904, the French Ministry of Education asked psychologist Alfred Binet to devise a method of identifying children who were unable to learn in school. School officials wanted to reduce crowding by placing students who did not benefit from regular classroom teaching in special schools. Binet and his student Theophile Simon developed an intelligence test to meet this request. The test is called the 1905 Scale. It consisted of 30 questions on topics ranging from the ability to touch one's ear to the ability to draw designs from memory and define abstract concepts.

Binet developed the concept of **mental age (MA),** an individual's level of mental development relative to others. Not much later, in 1912, William Stern created the concept of **intelligence quotient (IQ),** a person's mental age divided by chronological age (CA), multiplied by 100; that is, $IQ = MA/CA \times 100$. If mental age is the same as chronological age, then the person's IQ is 100. If mental age is above chronological age, then IQ is more than 100. If mental age is below chronological age, then IQ is less than 100.

The Binet test has been revised many times to incorporate advances in the understanding of intelligence and intelligence tests. These revisions are called the *Stanford-Binet tests* (Stanford University is where the revisions have been done). In 2004, the test—now called the Stanford-Binet 5—was revised to analyze an individual's response in five content areas: fluid reasoning, knowledge, quantitative reasoning, visual-spatial reasoning, and working memory. A general composite score also is still obtained.

By administering the test to large numbers of people of different ages (from preschool through late adulthood) from different backgrounds, researchers have found that scores on the Stanford-Binet approximate a normal distribution (see Figure 9.9). A **normal distribution** is symmetrical, with a majority of the scores falling in the middle of the possible range of scores and few scores appearing toward the extremes of the range.

The Wechsler Scales   Another set of tests widely used to assess students' intelligence is called the Wechsler scales, developed by psychologist David Wechsler. They include the Wechsler Preschool and Primary Scale of Intelligence—Third Edition (WPPSI-III) to test children from 2.5 years to 7.25 years of age; the Wechsler Intelligence Scale for Children—Fourth Edition (WISC-IV) for children and adolescents 6 to 16 years of age; and the Wechsler Adult Intelligence Scale—Third Edition (WAIS-III).

The Wechsler scales not only provide an overall IQ score but also yield several composite indexes (for example, the Verbal Comprehension Index, the Working Memory Index, and

Alfred Binet constructed the first intelligence test after being asked to create a measure to determine which children could benefit from instruction in France's schools and which could not.

developmental **connection**

Intelligence

Does intelligence decrease when individuals become middle-aged? Chapter 15, p. 470

mental age (MA) Binet's measure of an individual's level of mental development, compared with that of others.

intelligence quotient (IQ) A person's mental age divided by chronological age, multiplied by 100.

normal distribution A symmetrical distribution with most scores falling in the middle of the possible range of scores and a few scores appearing toward the extremes of the range.

Similarities

A child must think logically and abstractly to answer a number of questions about how things might be similar.

Example: "In what way are a lion and a tiger alike?"

Comprehension

This subscale is designed to measure an individual's judgment and common sense.

Example: "What is the advantage of keeping money in a bank?"

Nonverbal Subscales

Block Design

A child must assemble a set of multicolored blocks to match designs that the examiner shows. Visual-motor coordination, perceptual organization, and the ability to visualize spatially are assessed.

Example: "Use the four blocks on the left to make the pattern on the right."

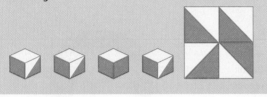

FIGURE 9.10

SAMPLE SUBSCALES OF THE WECHSLER INTELLIGENCE SCALE FOR CHILDREN—FOURTH EDITION (WISC-IV). The Wechsler includes 11 subscales—6 verbal and 5 nonverbal. Three of the subscales are shown here. Simulated items are similar to those found in the Wechsler Intelligence Scale for Children—Fourth Edition. Copyright © 2004 by NCS Pearson, Inc. Reproduced by permission. All rights reserved. "Wechsler Intelligence Scale for Children" and "WISC" are trademarks of Harcourt Assessment, Inc. registered in the United States of America and/or other jurisdictions.

"You're wise, but you lack tree smarts."
© Donald Reilly/The New Yorker Collection/ www.cartoonbank.com

triarchic theory of intelligence Sternberg's theory that intelligence consists of analytical intelligence, creative intelligence, and practical intelligence.

the Processing Speed Index) that allow the examiner to quickly identify the areas in which the child is strong or weak. Three of the Wechsler subscales are shown in Figure 9.10.

Types of Intelligence Is it more appropriate to think of a child's intelligence as a general ability or as a number of specific abilities? Robert Sternberg and Howard Gardner have proposed influential theories oriented to this second viewpoint.

Sternberg's Triarchic Theory Robert J. Sternberg (1986, 2004, 2010, 2011, 2012, 2013, 2014a, b) developed the **triarchic theory of intelligence,** which states that intelligence comes in three forms: (1) *analytical intelligence,*

Robert J. Sternberg, who developed the triarchic theory of intelligence.

which refers to the ability to analyze, judge, evaluate, compare, and contrast; (2) *creative intelligence,* which consists of the ability to create, design, invent, originate, and imagine; and (3) *practical intelligence,* which involves the ability to use, apply, implement, and put ideas into practice.

Sternberg (2013, 2014a, b) says that children with different triarchic patterns "look different" in school. Students with high analytic ability tend to be favored in conventional schooling. They often do well under direct instruction, in which the teacher lectures and gives students objective tests. They often are considered to be "smart" students who get good grades, show up in high-level tracks, do well on traditional tests of intelligence and the SAT, and later get admitted to competitive colleges.

In contrast, children who are high in creative intelligence often are not on the top rung of their class. Many teachers have specific expectations about how assignments should be done, and creatively intelligent students may not conform to those expectations. Instead of giving conformist answers, they give unique answers, for which they might get reprimanded or marked down. No teacher wants to discourage creativity, but Sternberg stresses that too often a teacher's desire to increase students' knowledge suppresses creative thinking.

Like children high in creative intelligence, children who are practically intelligent often do not relate well to the demands of school. However, many of these children do well outside of the classroom's walls. They may have excellent social skills and good common sense. As adults, some become successful managers, entrepreneurs, or politicians in spite of having undistinguished school records.

Gardner's Eight Frames of Mind Howard Gardner (1983, 1993, 2002) suggests there are eight types of intelligence, or "frames of mind." These are described here, with examples of the types of vocations in which they are regarded as strengths (Campbell, Campbell, & Dickinson, 2004):

Verbal: The ability to think in words and use language to express meaning. Occupations: authors, journalists, speakers.

Mathematical: The ability to carry out mathematical operations. Occupations: scientists, engineers, accountants.

Spatial: The ability to think three-dimensionally. Occupations: architects, artists, sailors.

Bodily-kinesthetic: The ability to manipulate objects and be physically adept. Occupations: surgeons, craftspeople, dancers, athletes.

Musical: A sensitivity to pitch, melody, rhythm, and tone. Occupations: composers and musicians.

Interpersonal: The ability to understand and interact effectively with others. Occupations: successful teachers, mental health professionals.

Intrapersonal: The ability to understand oneself. Occupations: theologians, psychologists.

Naturalist: The ability to observe patterns in nature and understand natural and human-made systems. Occupations: farmers, botanists, ecologists, landscapers.

According to Gardner, everyone has all of these intelligences to varying degrees. As a result, we prefer to learn and process information in different ways. People learn best when they can do so in a way that uses their stronger intelligences.

Evaluating the Multiple-Intelligence Approaches Sternberg's and Gardner's approaches have much to offer. They have stimulated teachers to think more broadly about what makes up children's competencies. And they have motivated educators to develop programs that instruct students in multiple domains. These approaches have also contributed to interest in assessing intelligence and classroom learning in innovative ways, such as by evaluating student portfolios (Moran & Gardner, 2006, 2007).

However, doubts about multiple-intelligence approaches persist. A number of psychologists think that the multiple-intelligence views have taken the concept of specific intelligences too far (Reeve & Charles, 2008). Some argue that a research base to support the three intelligences of Sternberg or the eight intelligences of Gardner has not yet emerged. One expert on intelligence, Nathan Brody (2007), observes that people who excel at one type of intellectual task are likely to excel in others. Thus, individuals who do well at memorizing lists of digits are also likely to be good at solving verbal problems and spatial layout problems. Other critics suggest that if musical skill reflects a distinct type of intelligence, why not label the skills of outstanding chess players, prizefighters, painters, and poets as types of intelligence?

The argument between those who support the concept of general intelligence and those who advocate the multiple-intelligence view is ongoing (Gardner, 2014; Irwing & others, 2012; Traskowski & others, 2013). Sternberg (2013, 2014a, b) acknowledges the existence of a general intelligence for the kinds of analytical tasks that traditional IQ tests assess but thinks that the range of tasks those tests measure is far too narrow.

Culture and Intelligence
Differences in conceptions of intelligence occur not only among psychologists but also among cultures. What is viewed as intelligent in one culture may not be thought of as intelligent in another. For example, people in Western cultures tend to view intelligence in terms of reasoning and thinking skills, whereas people in Eastern cultures see intelligence as a way for members of a community to engage successfully in social roles (Nisbett, 2003).

Interpreting Differences in IQ Scores
The IQ scores that result from tests such as the Stanford-Binet and Wechsler scales provide information about children's mental abilities. However, interpreting what performance on an intelligence test means is a subject of debate among researchers.

The Influence of Genetics How strong is the effect of genetics on intelligence? This question is difficult to answer because (as we discussed in Chapter 2) making clear-cut distinctions between the influences of heredity and environment is virtually impossible. Also, most research on heredity and environment does not include environments that differ radically. Thus, it is not surprising that many genetic studies show environment to be a fairly weak influence on intelligence.

Have scientists been able to pinpoint specific genes that are linked to intelligence? A recent research review concluded that there may be more than 1,000 genes that affect intelligence, each possibly having a small influence on an individual's intelligence (Davies & others, 2011). However, researchers have not been able to identify the specific genes that contribute to intelligence (Deary, 2012; Zhao, Kong, & Qu, 2014).

One strategy for examining the role of heredity in intelligence is to compare the IQs of identical and fraternal twins, which we initially discussed in Chapter 2. Recall that identical twins have exactly the same genetic makeup but fraternal twins do not. If intelligence is

Howard Gardner, here working with a young child, developed the view that intelligence consists of eight kinds of skills: verbal, mathematical, spatial, bodily-kinesthetic, musical, intrapersonal, interpersonal, and naturalist.

developmental **connection**

Intelligence

Polygenic inheritance is the term used to describe the effects of multiple genes on a particular characteristic. Chapter 2, p. 55

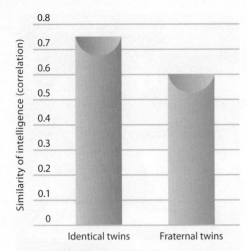

FIGURE **9.11**

CORRELATION BETWEEN INTELLIGENCE TEST SCORES AND TWIN STATUS. The graph represents a summary of research findings that have compared the intelligence test scores of identical and fraternal twins. An approximate .15 difference has been found, with a higher correlation for identical twins (.75) and a lower correlation for fraternal twins (.60).

developmental **connection**

Nature Versus Nurture

The epigenetic view emphasizes that development is an ongoing, bidirectional interchange between heredity and environment. Chapter 2, p. 67

genetically determined, say some investigators, the IQs of identical twins should be more similar than the IQs of fraternal twins. A research review of many studies found that the difference between the average correlation of IQs of identical and fraternal twins was .15, a relatively small difference (Grigorenko, 2000) (see Figure 9.11).

Today, most researchers agree that genetics and environment interact to influence intelligence. For most people, this means that modifications in environment can change their IQ scores considerably. Although genetic endowment may always influence a person's intellectual ability, the environmental influences and opportunities we provide to children and adults do make a difference (Sternberg, 2013, 2014a, b).

Environmental Influence In Chapter 5 we described one study that demonstrated the influence of parents on cognitive abilities. Researchers went into homes and observed how extensively parents from welfare and middle-income professional families talked and communicated with their young children (Hart & Risley, 1995). They found that the middle-income professional parents were much more likely to communicate with their young children than the welfare parents were. How much the parents communicated with their children in the first three years of their lives was correlated with the children's Stanford-Binet IQ scores at age 3. The more parents communicated with their children, the higher the children's IQs were.

The environment's role in intelligence is reflected in the 12- to 18-point increase in IQ that occurs when children are adopted from lower-SES to middle-SES families (Nisbett & others, 2012). Environmental influences on intelligence also involve schooling (Gustafsson, 2007). The biggest effects have been found when large groups of children have been deprived of formal education for an extended period, resulting in lower intelligence (Ceci & Gilstrap, 2000). Another possible effect of education can be seen in rapidly increasing IQ test scores around the world (Flynn, 1999, 2007, 2011, 2013). IQ scores have been increasing so quickly that a high percentage of people regarded as having average intelligence at the turn of the century would be considered below average in intelligence today (see Figure 9.12). If a representative sample of people today took the Stanford-Binet test version used in 1932, about 25 percent would be defined as having very superior intelligence, a label usually accorded to fewer than 3 percent of the population. Because the increase has taken place in a relatively short time, it can't be due to heredity, but rather may be due to increasing levels of education attained by a much greater percentage of the world's population, or to other environmental factors such as the explosion of information to which people are exposed. The worldwide increase in intelligence test scores that has occurred over a short time frame has been called the *Flynn effect* after the researcher who discovered it, James Flynn.

Researchers are increasingly concerned about finding ways to improve the early environment of children who are at risk for impoverished intelligence and poor developmental outcomes (Love & others, 2013; Maholmes, 2014). For various reasons, many low-income parents have difficulty providing an intellectually stimulating environment for their children. Programs that educate parents to be more sensitive caregivers and better teachers, as well as support services such as quality child care and early childhood education programs, can make a difference in a child's intellectual development (Bredekamp, 2014; Follari, 2015; Morrison, 2015). Thus, the efforts to counteract a deprived early environment's effect on intelligence emphasize prevention rather than remediation.

FIGURE **9.12**

INCREASING IQ SCORES FROM 1932 TO 1997. As measured by the Stanford-Binet intelligence test, American children seem to be getting smarter. Scores of a group tested in 1932 fell along a bell-shaped curve with half below 100 and half above. Studies show that if children took that same test today, half would score above 120 on the 1932 scale. Very few of them would score in the "intellectually deficient" end on the left side, and about one-fourth would rank in the "very superior" range on the right side.

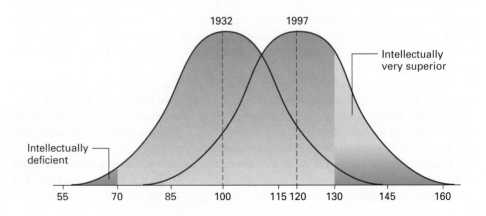

How Much Does Environment Affect Intelligence?

Each morning a young mother waited with her child for the bus that would take the child to school. The child was only 2 months old, and "school" was an experimental program at the University of North Carolina at Chapel Hill. There the child experienced a number of interventions designed to improve her intellectual development—everything from bright objects dangled in front of her eyes while she was a baby to language instruction and counting activities when she was a toddler (Wickelgren, 1999). The child's mother had an IQ of 40 and could not read signs or determine how much change she should receive from a cashier. Her grandmother had a similarly low IQ.

Today, at age 20, the child's IQ measures 80 points higher than her mother's did when the child was 2 months old. Not everyone agrees that IQ can be affected this extensively, but environment can make a substantial difference in a child's intelligence. As behavior geneticist Robert Plomin (1999) says, even something that is highly heritable (like intelligence) may be malleable through interventions.

The child we just described was part of the Abecedarian Intervention program at the University of North Carolina at Chapel Hill conducted by Craig Ramey and his associates (Ramey & Campbell, 1984; Ramey & Ramey, 1998; Ramey, Ramey, & Lanzi, 2001). They randomly assigned 111 young children from low-income, poorly educated families to either an intervention group, which received full-time, year-round child care along with medical and social work services, or to a control group, which received medical and social benefits but no child care. The child-care program included game-like learning activities aimed at improving language, motor, social, and cognitive skills.

The success of the program in improving IQ was evident by the time the children were 3 years old. At that age, the experimental group showed normal IQs averaging 101, a 17-point advantage over the control group. Recent follow-up results suggest that the effects are long-lasting. More than a decade later at age 15, children from the intervention group still maintained an IQ advantage of 5 points over the control-group children (97.7 to 92.6) (Campbell & others, 2001; Ramey, Ramey, & Lanzi, 2001). They also did better on standardized tests of reading and math, and were less likely to be held back a year in school. Also, the greatest IQ gains were made by the children whose mothers had especially low IQs—below 70. At age 15, these children showed a 10-point IQ advantage over a group of children whose mothers' IQs were below 70 but who had not experienced the child-care intervention. In a recent analysis of the long-term influence of Abecedarian intervention, at age 30 the children who experienced the early intervention had attained more years of education but the intervention did not lead to any benefits involving social adjustment and criminal activity (Campbell & others, 2012).

This research reinforces the research mentioned earlier that found prevention rather than remediation is important in counteracting a deprived early environment's effect on intelligence. It also supports the conclusion that modifications in environment can change IQ scores considerably. Therefore, it is important to consider the types of environments we provide for children—both those in the general population and those with disabilities (Waber, 2010).

A review of the research on early interventions concluded that (1) high-quality interventions based in child-care centers are associated with increases in children's intelligence and school achievement; (2) the interventions are most successful with poor children and children whose parents have little education; (3) the positive benefits continue through adolescence but are not as strong as they are in early childhood or at the beginning of elementary school; and (4) the programs that continue into middle and late childhood have the best long-term results (Brooks-Gunn, 2003). To read further about environmental influences on intelligence, see *Connecting Through Research*.

In sum, there is a consensus among psychologists that both heredity and environment influence intelligence (Grigorenko & Takanishi, 2012). This consensus reflects the nature-nurture issue that was highlighted in Chapter 1. Recall that the nature-nurture issue focuses on the extent to which development is influenced by nature (heredity) and nurture (environment). Although psychologists agree that intelligence is the product of both nature and nurture, there is still disagreement about how strongly each influences intelligence.

Group Differences   On average, African American schoolchildren in the United States score 10 to 15 points lower on standardized intelligence tests than non–Latino White American schoolchildren do (Brody, 2000). Children from Latino families also score lower than non–Latino White children. These are average scores, however; there is significant overlap in the distribution of scores. About 15 to 25 percent of African American schoolchildren score higher than half of White schoolchildren do, and many White schoolchildren score lower than most African American schoolchildren. As African Americans have gained social, economic,

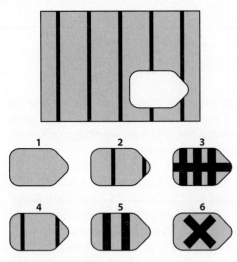

FIGURE 9.13

SAMPLE ITEM FROM THE RAVEN'S PROGRESSIVE MATRICES TEST. Individuals are presented with a matrix arrangement of symbols, such as the one at the top of this figure, and must then complete the matrix by selecting the appropriate missing symbol from a group of symbols, such as the ones at the bottom. These symbols and the matrix are similar to those found in the Raven's Progressive Matrices. Copyright © 1998 by NCS Pearson, Inc. Reproduced with permission. All rights reserved.

developmental connection

Conditions, Diseases, and Disorders

Down syndrome is caused by the presence of an extra copy of chromosome 21. Chapter 2, p. 55

culture-fair tests Tests of intelligence that are designed to be free of cultural bias.

intellectual disability A condition of limited mental ability in which the individual (1) has a low IQ, usually below 70 on a traditional intelligence test, (2) has difficulty adapting to the demands of everyday life, and (3) first exhibits these characteristics by age 18.

organic intellectual disability A genetic disorder or condition involving brain damage that is linked to a low level of intellectual functioning.

cultural-familial intellectual disability Condition in which there is no evidence of organic brain damage but the individual's IQ generally is between 50 and 70.

gifted Having above-average intelligence (an IQ of 130 or higher) and/or superior talent for something.

and educational opportunities, the gap between African Americans and Whites on standardized intelligence tests has narrowed (Nisbett & others, 2012). This gap especially narrows in college, where African American and White students often experience more similar environments than in the elementary and high school years (Myerson & others, 1998).

Creating Culture-Fair Tests **Culture-fair tests** are tests of intelligence that are intended to be free of cultural bias. Two types of culture-fair tests have been devised. The first includes items that are familiar to children from all socioeconomic and ethnic backgrounds, or items that at least are familiar to the children taking the test. For example, a child might be asked how a bird and a dog are different, on the assumption that all children have been exposed to birds and dogs. The second type of culture-fair test has no verbal questions. Figure 9.13 shows a sample question from the Raven's Progressive Matrices Test. Even though tests such as the Raven's Progressive Matrices are designed to be culture-fair, people with more education still score higher on them than do those with less education.

Why is it so hard to create culture-fair tests? Most tests tend to reflect what the dominant culture thinks is important. If tests have time limits, that will bias the test against groups not concerned with time. If languages differ, the same words might have different meanings for different language groups. Even pictures can produce bias because some cultures have less experience with drawings and photographs. Because of such difficulties in creating culture-fair tests, Robert Sternberg concludes that there are no culture-fair tests, only *culture-reduced tests*.

Using Intelligence Tests   Here are some cautions about IQ that can help you avoid the pitfalls of using information about a child's intelligence in negative ways:

- *Avoid stereotyping and expectations.* A special concern is that the scores on an IQ test easily can lead to stereotypes and expectations about students. Sweeping generalizations are too often made on the basis of an IQ score. An IQ test should always be considered a measure of current performance. It is not a measure of fixed potential. Maturational changes and enriched environmental experiences can advance a student's intelligence.

- *Know that IQ is not a sole indicator of competence.* Another concern about IQ tests occurs when they are used as the main or sole assessment of competence. A high IQ is not the ultimate human value. As we have seen in this chapter, it is important to consider not only students' intellectual competence in such areas as verbal skills but also their creative and practical skills.

- *Use caution in interpreting an overall IQ score.* In evaluating a child's intelligence, it is wiser to think of intelligence as consisting of a number of domains. Keep in mind the different types of intelligence described by Sternberg and Gardner. Remember that by considering the different domains of intelligence you can find that every child has at least one area of strength.

EXTREMES OF INTELLIGENCE

Intelligence tests have been used to discover indications of intellectual disability or intellectual giftedness, the extremes of intelligence. At times, intelligence tests have been misused for this purpose. Keeping in mind the theme that an intelligence test should not be used as the sole indicator of intellectual disability or giftedness, we will explore the nature of these intellectual extremes.

Intellectual Disability   The most distinctive feature of intellectual disability (formerly called mental retardation) is inadequate intellectual functioning. Long before formal tests were developed to assess intelligence, individuals with an intellectual disability were identified by a lack of age-appropriate skills in learning and caring for themselves. Once intelligence tests were developed, they were used to identify the degree of intellectual disability. But of two individuals with an intellectual disability who have the same low IQ, one might be married, employed, and involved in the community and the other might require constant supervision in an institution. Such differences in social competence led psychologists to include deficits in adaptive behavior in their definition of intellectual disability.

Intellectual disability is a condition of limited mental ability in which the individual (1) has a low IQ, usually below 70 on a traditional intelligence test; (2) has difficulty adapting to the demands of everyday life; and (3) first exhibits these characteristics by age 18 (Hodapp & others, 2011). The age limit is included in the definition of intellectual disability because, for example, we don't usually think of a college student who suffers massive brain damage in a car accident, resulting in an IQ of 60, as having an "intellectual disability." The low IQ and low adaptiveness should be evident in childhood, not after normal functioning is interrupted by damage of some form. About 5 million Americans fit this definition of intellectual disability.

Some cases of intellectual disability have an organic cause. **Organic intellectual disability** describes a genetic disorder or a lower level of intellectual functioning caused by brain damage. Down syndrome is one form of organic intellectual disability, and it occurs when an extra chromosome is present. Other causes of organic intellectual disability include fragile X syndrome, an abnormality in the X chromosome that was discussed in Chapter 2, "Biological Beginnings"; prenatal malformation; metabolic disorders; and diseases that affect the brain. Most people who suffer from organic intellectual disability have IQs between 0 and 50.

When no evidence of organic brain damage can be found, cases are labeled **cultural-familial intellectual disability**. Individuals with this type of disability have IQs between 55 and 70. Psychologists suspect that this type of disability often results from growing up in a below-average intellectual environment. Children with this type of disability can be identified in schools, where they often fail, need tangible rewards (candy rather than praise), and are highly sensitive to what others expect of them. However, as adults, they are usually not noticeable, perhaps because adult settings don't tax their cognitive skills as sorely. It may also be that they increase their intelligence as they move toward adulthood.

Giftedness There have always been people whose abilities and accomplishments outshine those of others—the whiz kid in class, the star athlete, the natural musician. People who are **gifted** have above-average intelligence (an IQ of 130 or higher) and/or superior talent for something. When it comes to programs for the gifted, most school systems select children who have intellectual superiority and academic aptitude, whereas children who are talented in the visual and performing arts (art, drama, dance), who demonstrate skill in athletics, or who have other special aptitudes tend to be overlooked (Olszewski-Kubilius & Thomson, 2013).

Estimates vary but indicate that approximately 3 to 5 percent of U.S. students are gifted (National Association for Gifted Children, 2009). This percentage is likely conservative because it focuses more on children who are gifted intellectually and academically, often failing to include those who are gifted in creative thinking or the visual and performing arts (Ford, 2012).

Characteristics What are the characteristics of children who are gifted? Despite speculation that giftedness is linked with having a mental disorder, no relation between giftedness and mental disorder has been found. Similarly, the idea that gifted children are maladjusted is a myth, as Lewis Terman (1925) found when he conducted an extensive study of 1,500 children whose Stanford-Binet IQs averaged 150. The children in Terman's study were socially well adjusted, and many went on to become successful doctors, lawyers, professors, and scientists. Studies support the conclusion that gifted people tend to be more mature than others, have fewer emotional problems than others, and grow up in a positive family climate (Davidson, 2000).

Ellen Winner (1996) described three criteria that characterize gifted children, whether in art, music, or academic domains:

1. *Precocity.* Gifted children are precocious. They begin to master an area earlier than their peers. Learning in their domain is more effortless for them than for ordinary children. In most instances, these gifted children are precocious because they have an inborn high ability in a particular domain or domains.

2. *Marching to their own drummer.* Gifted children learn in a qualitatively different way from ordinary children. One way that they march to a different drummer is that they need minimal help, or scaffolding, from adults to learn. In many instances, they resist

A child with Down syndrome. *What causes a child to develop Down syndrome? In which major classification of intellectual disability does the condition fall?*

At 2 years of age, art prodigy Alexandra Nechita colored in coloring books for hours and also took up pen and ink. She had no interest in dolls or friends. By age 5 she was using watercolors. Once she started school, she would start painting as soon as she got home. At the age of 8, in 1994, she saw the first public exhibit of her work. In succeeding years, working quickly and impulsively on canvases as large as 5 feet by 9 feet, she has completed hundreds of paintings, some of which sell for close to $100,000 apiece. As a teenager, she continues to paint—relentlessly and passionately. It is, she says, what she loves to do. *What are some characteristics of children who are gifted?*

any kind of explicit instruction. They often make discoveries on their own and solve problems in unique ways.

3. *A passion to master.* Gifted children are driven to understand the domain in which they have high ability. They display an intense, obsessive interest and an ability to focus. They motivate themselves, says Winner, and do not need to be "pushed" by their parents.

Nature-Nurture   Is giftedness a product of heredity or environment? Likely both (Duggan & Friedman, 2014; Johnson & Bouchard, 2014). Individuals who are gifted recall that they had signs of high ability in a particular area at a very young age, prior to or at the beginning of formal training. This suggests the importance of innate ability in giftedness. However, researchers have also found that individuals with world-class status in the arts, mathematics, science, and sports all report strong family support and years of training and practice (Bloom, 1985). Deliberate practice is an important characteristic of individuals who become experts in a particular domain. For example, in one study the best musicians engaged in twice as much deliberate practice over their lives as did the least successful ones (Ericsson, Krampe, & Tesch-Romer, 1993).

Domain-Specific Giftedness and Development   Individuals who are highly gifted are typically not gifted in many domains, and research on giftedness is increasingly focused on domain-specific developmental trajectories (Kell & Lubinski, 2014; Sternberg & Bridges, 2014; Thagard, 2014; Winner, 2009, 2014). During the childhood years, the domain(s) in which individuals are gifted usually emerges. Thus, at some point in the childhood years the child who is to become a gifted artist or the child who is to become a gifted mathematician begins to show expertise in that domain. Regarding domain-specific giftedness, software genius Bill Gates (1998), the founder of Microsoft and one of the world's richest persons, commented that sometimes you have to be careful when you are good at something and resist the urge to think that you will be good at everything. Gates says that because he has been so successful at software development, people expect him to be brilliant about other domains in which he is far from being a genius.

A young Bill Gates, founder of Microsoft and now one of the world's richest people. Like many highly gifted students, Gates was not especially fond of school. He hacked a computer security system when he was 13, and as a high school student he was allowed to take some college math classes. He dropped out of Harvard University and began developing a plan for what was to become Microsoft Corporation. *What are some ways that schools can enrich the education of such highly talented students as Gates to make it a more challenging, interesting, and meaningful experience?*

Identifying an individual's domain-specific talent and providing individually appropriate and optional educational opportunities need to be accomplished at the very latest by adolescence (Keating, 2009). During adolescence, individuals who are talented become less reliant on parental support and increasingly pursue their own interests.

Education of Children Who Are Gifted   An increasing number of experts argue that the education of children who are gifted in the United States requires a significant overhaul (Ambrose, Sternberg, & Sriraman, 2012; Reis & Renzulli, 2014). Ellen Winner (1996, 2006) argues that too often children who are gifted are socially isolated and underchallenged in the classroom. It is not unusual for them to be ostracized and labeled "nerds" or "geeks." Many eminent adults report that school was a negative experience for them, that they were bored and sometimes knew more than their teachers (Bloom, 1985). Winner argues that American education will benefit when standards are raised for all children. When some children are still underchallenged, she recommends that they be allowed to attend advanced classes in their domain of exceptional ability. Some especially precocious middle school students may benefit from taking college classes in their area of expertise. For example, Bill Gates took college math classes at 13; Yo-Yo Ma, a famous cellist, graduated from high school at 15 and attended Juilliard School of Music in New York City.

A final concern is that African American, Latino, and Native American children are underrepresented in gifted programs (Ford, 2012). Much of the underrepresentation involves the lower test scores for these children compared with non-Latino White and Asian American children, which may be due to reasons such as test bias and fewer opportunities to develop language skills such as vocabulary and comprehension (Ford, 2012).

Review Connect Reflect

LG3 Explain cognitive changes in middle and late childhood.

Review

- What characterizes Piaget's stage of concrete operational thought? What are some contributions and criticisms of Piaget?
- How do children process information in the middle and late childhood years?
- What is intelligence, and how is it assessed? What characterizes links between neuroscience and intelligence? What determines individual and group differences in IQ scores?
- What are the key characteristics of intellectual disability and giftedness?

Connect

- In discussing memory, thinking, and intelligence, the topic of recommended educational strategies often came. Compare these recommendations to those you learned about in the "Early Childhood Education" section of Chapter 7.

Reflect *Your Own Personal Journey of Life*

- A CD-ROM, *Children's IQ and Achievement Test,* now lets parents test their child's IQ and identify how well the child is performing in relation to his or her grade in school. Would you want to personally test your own child's IQ? What might be some problems with parents giving their children an IQ test?

4 Language Development

LG4 Discuss language development in middle and late childhood.

| Vocabulary, Grammar, and Metalinguistic Awareness | Reading | Writing | Bilingualism and Second-Language Learning |

Children gain new skills as they enter school that make it possible for them to learn to read and write. These skills include increased use of language to talk about things that are not physically present, learning what a word is, and learning how to recognize and talk about sounds. Children also learn the *alphabetic principle*—that the letters of the alphabet represent sounds of the language.

VOCABULARY, GRAMMAR, AND METALINGUISTIC AWARENESS

During middle and late childhood, changes occur in the way children's mental vocabulary is organized. When asked to say the first word that comes to mind when they hear a word, preschool children typically provide a word that often follows the word in a sentence. For example, when asked to respond to *dog,* the young child may say "barks," or to the word *eat* respond with "lunch." At about 7 years of age, children begin to respond with a word that is the same part of speech as the stimulus word. For example, a child may now respond to the word *dog* with "cat" or "horse." To *eat,* they now might say "drink." This is evidence that children now have begun to categorize their vocabulary by parts of speech.

The process of categorizing becomes easier as children increase their vocabulary (Clark, 2012). Children's vocabulary increases from an average of about 14,000 words at age 6 to an average of about 40,000 words by age 11.

Children make similar advances in grammar (Behrens, 2012). During the elementary school years, children's improvement in logical reasoning and analytical skills helps them understand such constructions as the appropriate use of comparatives *(shorter, deeper)* and subjectives ("If you were president . . ."). During the elementary school years, children become increasingly able to understand and use complex grammar, such as the following

How do vocabulary, grammar, and metalinguistic awareness change in middle and late childhood?

sentence: *The boy who kissed his mother wore a hat.* They also learn to use language in a more connected way, producing connected discourse. They become able to relate sentences to one another to produce descriptions, definitions, and narratives that make sense. Children must be able to do these things orally before they can be expected to deal with them in written assignments.

These advances in vocabulary and grammar during the elementary school years are accompanied by the development of **metalinguistic awareness,** which is knowledge about language, such as understanding what a preposition is or being able to discuss the sounds of a language (Tong, Deacon, & Cain, 2014). Metalinguistic awareness allows children "to think about their language, understand what words are, and even define them" (Berko Gleason, 2009, p. 4). It improves considerably during the elementary school years (Pan & Uccelli, 2009). Defining words becomes a regular part of classroom discourse, and children increase their knowledge of syntax as they study and talk about the components of sentences such as subjects and verbs (Crain, 2012).

Children also make progress in understanding how to use language in culturally appropriate ways—a process called pragmatics (Bryant, 2012). By the time they enter adolescence, most children know the rules for using language in everyday contexts—that is, what is appropriate and inappropriate to say.

This teacher is helping a student sound out words. Researchers have found that phonics instruction is a key aspect of teaching students to read, especially beginning readers and students with weak reading skills.

metalinguistic awareness Refers to knowledge about language, such as understanding what a preposition is or being able to discuss the sounds of a language.

whole-language approach An approach to reading instruction based on the idea that instruction should parallel children's natural language learning. Reading materials should be whole and meaningful.

phonics approach The idea that reading instruction should teach the basic rules for translating written symbols into sounds.

READING

Before learning to read, children learn to use language to talk about things that are not present; they learn what a word is; and they learn how to recognize sounds and talk about them. Children who begin elementary school with a robust vocabulary have an advantage when it comes to learning to read.

How should children be taught to read? Currently, debate focuses on the whole-language approach versus the phonics approach (Lloyd & others, 2015; Reutzel & Cooter, 2015).

The **whole-language approach** stresses that reading instruction should parallel children's natural language learning. In some whole-language classes, beginning readers are taught to recognize whole words or even entire sentences, and to use the context of what they are reading to guess at the meaning of words. Reading materials that support the whole-language approach are whole and meaningful—that is, children are given material in its complete form, such as stories and poems, so that they learn to understand language's communicative function. Reading is connected with listening and writing skills. Although there are variations in whole-language programs, most share the premise that reading should be integrated with other skills and subjects, such as science and social studies, and that it should focus on real-world material. Thus, a class might read newspapers, magazines, or books, and then write about and discuss them.

In contrast, the **phonics approach** emphasizes that reading instruction should teach basic rules for translating written symbols into sounds. Early phonics-centered reading instruction should involve simplified materials. Only after children have learned correspondence rules that relate spoken phonemes to the alphabet letters that are used to represent them should they be given complex reading materials, such as books and poems (Fox, 2014).

Which approach is better? Research suggests that children can benefit from both approaches, but instruction in phonics needs to be emphasized (Tompkins, 2013). An increasing number of experts in the field of reading now conclude that direct instruction in phonics is a key aspect of learning to read (Cunningham, 2013; Fox, 2014).

Beyond the phonics/whole language issue in learning to read, becoming a good reader includes learning to read fluently (Allington, 2015). Many beginning or poor readers do not recognize words automatically. Their processing capacity is consumed by the demands of word recognition, so they have less capacity to devote to comprehension of groupings of words as phrases or sentences. As their processing of words and passages becomes more automatic, it is said that their reading becomes more *fluent*. Metacognitive strategies, such as learning to monitor one's reading progress, getting the gist of what is being read, and summarizing also are important in becoming a good reader (Nash-Ditzel, 2010).

WRITING

As they begin to write, children often invent spellings. Parents and teachers should encourage children's early writing but not be overly concerned about the formation of letters or spelling. Corrections of spelling and printing should be selective and made in positive ways that do not discourage the child's writing and spontaneity.

Like becoming a good reader, becoming a good writer takes many years and lots of practice (Tompkins, 2015). Children should be given many writing opportunities. As their language and cognitive skills improve with good instruction, so will their writing skills. For example, developing a more sophisticated understanding of syntax and grammar serves as an underpinning for better writing. So do such cognitive skills as organization and logical reasoning. Through the course of the school years, students develop increasingly sophisticated methods of organizing their ideas.

The metacognitive strategies needed to be a competent writer are linked with those required to be a competent reader because the writing process involves competent reading and rereading during composition and revision (McCormick, Dimmitt, & Sullivan, 2013). Further, researchers have found that strategy instruction involving planning, drafting, revising, and editing improves older elementary school children's metacognitive awareness and writing competence (Harris & others, 2009).

Major concerns about students' writing competence are increasingly being voiced (Soter, 2013). One study revealed that 70 to 75 percent of U.S. students in grades 4 through 12 are low-achieving writers (Persky, Dane, & Jin, 2003). College instructors report that 50 percent of high school graduates are not prepared for college-level writing (Achieve, Inc., 2005).

BILINGUALISM AND SECOND-LANGUAGE LEARNING

Are there sensitive periods in learning a second language? That is, if individuals want to learn a second language, how important is the age at which they begin to learn it? What is the best way to teach children who come from homes in which English is not the primary language?

Second-Language Learning   For many years, it was claimed that if individuals did not learn a second language prior to puberty they would never reach native-language learners' proficiency in the second language (Johnson & Newport, 1991). However, recent research indicates a more complex conclusion: Sensitive periods likely vary across different language systems (Thomas & Johnson, 2008). Thus, for late language learners, such as adolescents and adults, new vocabulary is easier to learn than new sounds or new grammar (Neville, 2006). For example, children's ability to pronounce words with a native-like accent in a second language typically decreases with age, with an especially sharp drop occurring after the age of about 10 to 12. Also, adults tend to learn a second language faster than children, but their final level of second-language attainment is not as high as children's. And the way children and adults learn a second language differs somewhat. Compared with adults, children are less sensitive to feedback, less likely to use explicit strategies, and more likely to learn a second language from large amounts of input (Thomas & Johnson, 2008).

Students in the United States are far behind their counterparts in many developed countries in learning a second language. For example, in Russia, schools have 10 grades, called forms, which roughly correspond to the 12 grades in American schools. Russian children begin school at age 7 and begin learning English in the third form. Because of this emphasis on teaching English, most Russian citizens under the age of 40 today are able to speak at least some English. The United States is the only technologically advanced Western nation that does not have a national foreign language requirement at the high school level, even for students in rigorous academic programs.

U.S. students who do not learn a second language may be missing more than the chance to acquire a skill. Bilingualism—the ability to speak two languages—has a positive effect on children's cognitive development (Tompkins, 2013). Children who are fluent in two languages perform better than their single-language counterparts on tests of control of attention, concept formation, analytical reasoning, cognitive flexibility, and cognitive complexity (Bialystok, 2001, 2007, 2011; Bialystok & Craik, 2010). They also are more conscious of the structure of spoken and written language and better at noticing errors of grammar and meaning, skills that benefit their reading ability (Bialystok, 1997; Kuo & Anderson, 2012). However, recent research indicates that bilingual children have a smaller vocabulary in each language than monolingual children do (Bialystok, 2011).

In the United States, many immigrant children go from being monolingual in their home language to bilingual in that language and in English, only to end up as monolingual speakers of English. This is called *subtractive bilingualism,* and it can have negative effects on children, who often become ashamed of their home language.

Bilingual Education A current controversy related to bilingualism involves the millions of U.S. children who come from homes in which English is not the primary language (Echevarria, Richards-Tutor, & Vogt, 2015; Lessow-Hurley, 2013). What is the best way to teach these English language learners (ELLs)?

ELLs have been taught in one of two main ways: (1) instruction in English only, or (2) a *dual-language* (used to be called *bilingual*) approach that involves instruction in their home language and English (Haley & Austin, 2014; Horowitz, 2013). In a dual-language approach, instruction is given in both the ELL child's home language and English for varying amounts of time at certain grade levels. One of the arguments for the dual-language approach is the research discussed earlier demonstrating that bilingual children have more advanced information processing skills than monolingual children (Genesee & Lindholm-Leary, 2012).

If a dual-language instructional strategy is used, too often it has been thought that immigrant children need only one or two years of this type of instruction. However, in general it takes immigrant children approximately three to five years to develop speaking proficiency and seven years to develop reading proficiency in English (Hakuta, Butler, & Witt, 2000). Also, immigrant children vary in their ability to learn English (Horowitz, 2013). Children who come from lower socioeconomic backgrounds have more difficulty than those from higher socioeconomic backgrounds (Hakuta, 2001; Hoff & Place, 2013). Thus, especially for immigrant children from lower socioeconomic backgrounds, more years of dual-language instruction may be needed than they currently are receiving.

What have researchers found regarding outcomes of ELL programs? Drawing conclusions about the effectiveness of ELL programs is difficult because of variations across programs in the number of years they are in effect, type of instruction, quality of schooling other than ELL instruction, teachers, children, and other factors. Further, no effective experiments have been conducted that compare bilingual education with English-only education in the United States (Snow & Kang, 2006). Some experts have concluded that the quality of instruction is more important in determining outcomes than the language in which it is delivered (Lesaux & Siegel, 2003).

Nonetheless, other experts, such as Kenji Hakuta (2001, 2005), support the combined home language and English approach because (1) children have difficulty learning a subject when it is taught in a language they do not understand; and (2) when both languages are integrated in the classroom, children learn the second language more readily and participate more actively. In support of Hakuta's view, most large-scale studies have found that the academic achievement of ELLs is higher in dual-language programs than English-only programs (Genesee & Lindholm-Leary, 2012). To read about the work of one dual-language teacher, see *Connecting with Careers.*

A first- and second-grade dual-language English-Cantonese teacher instructing students in Chinese in Oakland, California. *What have researchers found about the effectiveness of dual-language instruction?*

Salvador Tamayo, Teacher of English Language Learners

Salvador Tamayo is an ELL fifth-grade teacher at Turner Elementary School in West Chicago. He recently was given a National Educator Award by the Milken Family Foundation for his work in educating ELLs. Tamayo is especially adept at integrating technology into his ELL classes. He and his students have created several award-winning Web sites about the West Chicago City Museum, the local Latino community, and the history of West Chicago. His students also developed an "I Want to Be an American Citizen" Web site to assist family and community members in preparing for the U.S. Citizenship Test. Tamayo also teaches an ELL class at Wheaton College.

Salvador Tamayo working with dual-language students.

For more information about what elementary school teachers do, see page 41 in the Careers in Life-Span Development appendix.

Review Connect Reflect

LG4 Discuss language development in middle and late childhood.

Review
- What are some changes in vocabulary and grammar in the middle and late childhood years?
- What controversy characterizes how to teach children to read?
- What characterizes children's writing skills and their development?
- What is dual-language instruction? What issues are involved in this approach?

Connect
- Earlier in the chapter you learned about metacognition. Compare that with metalinguistic awareness.

Reflect *Your Own Personal Journey of Life*
- Did you learn a second language as a child? If you did, do you think it was beneficial to you? If so, how? If you did not learn a second language as a child, do you wish you had? Why or why not?

topical connections *looking forward*

The slow physical growth of middle and late childhood gives way to the dramatic changes of puberty in early adolescence. Significant changes also occur in the adolescent's brain in which earlier maturation of the amygdala (emotion processing) and later maturation of the prefrontal cortex (decision making, self-regulation) are likely linked to increases in risk-taking and sensation seeking. Sexual development is a normal aspect of adolescence, but having sexual intercourse early in adolescence is associated with a number of problems. Adolescence is a critical juncture in health because many poor health habits begin in adolescence. Despite recent declines, the United States has one of the highest rates of illicit drug use of any developed nation. Adolescent thought is more abstract, idealistic, and logical than children's. The transition from elementary school to middle school or junior high is difficult for many individuals because it coincides with so many physical, cognitive, and socioemotional changes in development.

Physical and Cognitive Development in Middle and Late Childhood

1 Physical Changes and Health

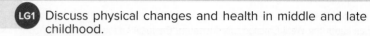 **LG1** Discuss physical changes and health in middle and late childhood.

Body Growth and Change

- The period of middle and late childhood involves slow, consistent growth. During this period, children grow an average of 2 to 3 inches a year. Muscle mass and strength gradually increase. Among the most pronounced changes in body growth and proportion are decreases in head circumference and waist circumference in relation to body height.

The Brain

- Changes in the brain in middle and late childhood include advances in functioning in the prefrontal cortex, which are reflected in improved attention, reasoning, and cognitive control. During middle and late childhood, less diffusion and more focal activation occurs in the prefrontal cortex, a change that is associated with an increase in cognitive control.

Motor Development

- During the middle and late childhood years, motor development becomes much smoother and more coordinated. Children gain greater control over their bodies and can sit and pay attention for longer periods of time. However, their lives should include abundant physical activity. Increased myelination of the central nervous system is reflected in improved motor skills. Improved fine motor skills appear in the form of handwriting development. Boys are usually better at gross motor skills, girls at fine motor skills.

Exercise

- Most American children do not get nearly enough exercise. Parents play an especially important role in guiding children to increase their exercise. Heavy television viewing and computer use are linked to lower activity levels in children.

Health, Illness, and Disease

- For the most part, middle and late childhood is a time of excellent health. The most common cause of severe injury and death in childhood is motor vehicle accidents. Being overweight or obese is an increasingly prevalent child health problem, raising the risk for many medical and psychological problems. Cardiovascular disease is uncommon in children, but the precursors to adult cardiovascular disease are often already apparent during childhood. Cancer is the second leading cause of death in children (after accidents). Leukemia is the most common childhood cancer.

2 Children with Disabilities

 LG2 Identify children with different types of disabilities and discuss issues in educating them.

The Scope of Disabilities

- Approximately 14 percent of U.S. children from 3 to 21 years of age receive special education or related services. A child with a learning disability has difficulty in learning that involves understanding or using spoken or written language, and the difficulty can appear in listening, thinking, reading, writing, and spelling. A learning disability also may involve difficulty in doing mathematics. To be classified as a learning disability, the learning problem is not primarily the result of visual, hearing, or motor disabilities; intellectual disabilities; emotional disorders; or due to environmental, cultural, or economic disadvantage. Dyslexia is a category of learning disabilities that involves a severe impairment in the ability to read and spell. Dysgraphia is a learning disability that involves having difficulty in handwriting. Dyscalculia is a learning disability that involves difficulties in math computation. Attention deficit hyperactivity disorder (ADHD) is a disability in which individuals consistently show problems in one or more of these areas: (1) inattention, (2) hyperactivity, and (3) impulsivity. ADHD has been increasingly diagnosed. Emotional and behavioral disorders consist of serious, persistent problems that involve relationships, aggression, depression, fears associated with personal or school matters, as well as other inappropriate socioemotional characteristics. Autism spectrum disorders (ASD), also called pervasive developmental disorders, range from autistic disorder, a severe developmental disorder, to Asperger syndrome, a relatively mild autism spectrum disorder. The current consensus is that autism is a brain dysfunction involving abnormalities in brain structure and neurotransmitters. Children with autism spectrum disorders are characterized by problems in social interaction, verbal and nonverbal communication, and repetitive behaviors.

Educational Issues

- In 1975, Public Law 94-142, the Education for All Handicapped Children Act, required that all children with disabilities be given a free, appropriate public education. This law was renamed the Individuals with Disabilities Education Act (IDEA) in 1990 and updated in 2004. IDEA includes requirements that children with disabilities receive an individualized education plan (IEP), which is a written plan that spells out a program tailored to the child and requires that they be educated in the least restrictive environment (LRE), which is a setting that is as similar as possible to the one in which children without disabilities are educated. The term *inclusion* means educating children with disabilities full-time in the regular classroom.

3 Cognitive Changes

LG3 Explain cognitive changes in middle and late childhood.

Piaget's Cognitive Developmental Theory

- Piaget said that the stage of concrete operational thought characterizes children from about 7 to 11 years of age. During this stage, children are capable of concrete operations, conservation, classification, seriation, and transitivity. Critics argue that some abilities emerge earlier than Piaget thought, that elements of a stage do not appear at the same time, and that education and culture have more influence on development than Piaget predicted. Neo-Piagetians place more emphasis on how children process information, their use of strategies, speed of information processing, and division of cognitive problems into more precise steps.

Information Processing

- Long-term memory increases in middle and late childhood. Working memory is an important memory process. Knowledge and expertise influence memory. Changes in autobiographical memory occur in middle and late childhood. Strategies can be used by children to improve their memory, and it is important for adults who instruct children to encourage children's strategy use. Fuzzy trace theory has been proposed to explain developmental changes in memory. Among the key dimensions of executive function that are important in cognitive development and school success are self-control/inhibition, working memory, and flexibility. Critical thinking involves thinking reflectively and productively, as well as evaluating available evidence. Mindfulness is an important aspect of critical thinking. A special concern is the lack of emphasis on critical thinking in many schools. Creative thinking is the ability to think in novel and unusual ways and to come up with unique solutions to problems. Guilford distinguished between convergent and divergent thinking. A number of strategies can be used to encourage children's creative thinking, including brainstorming. Children think like scientists in some ways, but in others they don't. Metacognition is knowing about knowing. Many metacognitive studies have focused on metamemory. Pressley views the key to education as helping students learn a rich repertoire of strategies for problem solving.

Intelligence

- Intelligence consists of problem-solving skills and the ability to adapt to and learn from life's everyday experiences. Interest in intelligence often focuses on individual differences and assessment. Widely used intelligence tests today include the Stanford-Binet tests and Wechsler scales. Results on these tests may be reported in terms of an overall IQ or in terms of performance on specific areas of the tests. Sternberg proposed that intelligence comes in three main forms: analytical, creative, and practical. Gardner proposes that there are eight types of intelligence: verbal, mathematical, spatial, bodily-kinesthetic, interpersonal, intrapersonal, musical, and naturalist. The multiple-intelligence approaches have expanded our conception of intelligence, but critics argue that the research base for these approaches is not well established. IQ scores are influenced by both genetics and characteristics of the environment. Parents, home environments, schools, and intervention programs can influence these scores. Intelligence test scores have risen considerably around the world in recent decades. This phenomenon is called the Flynn effect, and it supports the role of environment in intelligence. Group differences in IQ scores may reflect many influences, including cultural bias. Tests may be biased against certain groups that are not familiar with a standard form of English, with the content tested, or with the testing situation. Tests are likely to reflect the values and experience of the dominant culture.

Extremes of Intelligence

- Intellectual disability involves a low level of intellectual functioning as well as difficulty adapting to the demands of everyday life, and these characteristics occur prior to age 18. One classification of intellectual disability distinguishes between organic and cultural-familial types. Individuals who are gifted have above-average intelligence (an IQ of 130 or higher) and/or superior talent for something. Three characteristics of gifted children are precocity, marching to their own drummer, and a passion to master their domain. Giftedness is likely a consequence of both heredity and environment. Developmental changes characterize giftedness, and increasingly the domain-specific aspect of giftedness is emphasized. Concerns exist about the education of children who are gifted.

4 Language Development

 LG4 Discuss language development in middle and late childhood.

Vocabulary, Grammar, and Metalinguistic Awareness

- Children gradually become more analytical and logical in their approach to words and grammar. In terms of grammar, children now better understand comparatives and subjectives. They become increasingly able to use complex grammar and produce narratives that make sense. Improvements in metalinguistic awareness—knowledge about language—are evident during the elementary school years as children increasingly define words, expand their knowledge of syntax, and understand better how to use language in culturally appropriate ways.

Reading

- A current debate in reading focuses on the phonics approach versus the whole-language approach. The phonics approach advocates phonetics instruction and giving children simplified materials. The whole-language approach stresses that reading instruction should parallel children's natural language learning and that children should be given whole-language materials such as books and poems. Three key processes in learning to read a printed word are being aware of sound units in words, decoding words, and accessing word meaning.

Writing

- Advances in children's language and cognitive development provide the underpinnings for improved writing. Major concerns are increasingly being voiced about children's writing competence. Teachers play a key role in improving children's writing skills.

Bilingualism and Second-Language Learning

- Recent research indicates the complexity of determining whether there are sensitive periods in learning a second language. The dual-language approach (formerly called "bilingual") aims to teach academic subjects to immigrant children in their native languages while gradually adding English instruction. Researchers have found that the dual-language approach does not interfere with performance in either language.

key **terms**

learning disability 272
dyslexia 275
dysgraphia 275
dyscalculia 275
attention deficit hyperactivity disorder (ADHD) 275
emotional and behavioral disorders 276
autism spectrum disorders (ASD) 276
autistic disorder 276
Asperger syndrome 277

individualized education plan (IEP) 277
least restrictive environment (LRE) 277
inclusion 277
seriation 278
transitivity 278
neo-Piagetians 280
long-term memory 280
working memory 280
strategies 281
elaboration 281

fuzzy trace theory 282
critical thinking 283
mindfulness 283
creative thinking 284
convergent thinking 284
divergent thinking 284
metacognition 284
brainstorming 285
intelligence 286
individual differences 286
mental age (MA) 287
intelligence quotient (IQ) 287

normal distribution 287
triarchic theory of intelligence 288
culture-fair tests 292
intellectual disability 292
organic intellectual disability 292
cultural-familial intellectual disability 292
gifted 292
metalinguistic awareness 296
whole-language approach 296
phonics approach 296

key **people**

Mark Johnson 268
Simon Baron-Cohen 277
James Kauffman 277
Jean Piaget 278
Alan Baddeley 280
Patricia Bauer 282
Charles Brainerd 282

Valerie Reyna 282
Adele Diamond 283
Ellen Langer 283
Jacqueline Brooks 283
Martin Brooks 283
Robert Roeser 283
Philip Zelazo 283

J. P. Guilford 284
Teresa Amabile 285
Michael Pressley 286
Alfred Binet 287
Theophile Simon 287
David Wechsler 287
Robert J. Sternberg 288

Howard Gardner 288
Nathan Brody 289
James Flynn 290
Craig Ramey 291
Lewis Terman 293
Ellen Winner 293

chapter 10

SOCIOEMOTIONAL DEVELOPMENT IN MIDDLE AND LATE CHILDHOOD

chapter outline

1 Emotional and Personality Development

Learning Goal 1 Discuss emotional and personality development in middle and late childhood.

The Self
Emotional Development
Moral Development
Gender

2 Families

Learning Goal 2 Describe developmental changes in parent-child relationships, parents as managers, attachment in families, and stepfamilies.

Developmental Changes in Parent-Child Relationships
Parents as Managers
Attachment in Families
Stepfamilies

3 Peers

Learning Goal 3 Identify changes in peer relationships in middle and late childhood.

Developmental Changes
Peer Status
Social Cognition
Bullying
Friends

4 Schools

Learning Goal 4 Characterize aspects of schooling in children's development in middle and late childhood.

Contemporary Approaches to Student Learning
Socioeconomic Status, Ethnicity, and Culture

In *The Shame of the Nation,* Jonathan Kozol (2005) described his visits to 60 U.S. schools in urban low-income areas in 11 states. He saw many schools in which minorities totaled 80 to 90 percent of the student population. Kozol observed numerous inequities—unkempt classrooms, hallways, and restrooms; inadequate textbooks and supplies; and lack of resources. He also saw teachers mainly instructing students to memorize material by rote, especially as preparation for mandated tests, rather than stimulating them to engage in higher-level thinking. Kozol also frequently observed teachers using threatening disciplinary tactics to control the classroom.

However, some teachers Kozol observed were effective in educating children in these undesirable conditions. At P.S. 30 in the South Bronx, Mr. Bedrock teaches fifth grade. One student in his class, Serafina, recently lost her mother to AIDS. When author Jonathan Kozol visited the class, he was told that two other children had taken the role of "allies in the child's struggle for emotional survival" (Kozol, 2005, p. 291). Textbooks are in short supply for the class, and the social studies text is so out of date it claims that Ronald Reagan is the country's president. But Mr. Bedrock told Kozol that it's a "wonderful" class this year. About their teacher, 56-year-old Mr. Bedrock, one student said, "'He's getting old, . . . but we love him anyway'" (p. 292). Kozol observed the students in Mr. Bedrock's class to be orderly, interested, and engaged.

What are some of the challenges faced by children growing up in the South Bronx?

topical connections *looking back*

In early childhood, according to Erikson, young children are in the stage of initiative versus guilt. Parents continue to play an important role in their development, and an authoritative parenting style is most likely to have positive outcomes for children. In early childhood, peer relations begin to take on a more significant role as children's social worlds widen. Play has a special place in young children's lives and is an important context for both cognitive and socioemotional development.

preview

The years of middle and late childhood bring many changes to children's social and emotional lives. Transformations in their relationships with parents and peers occur, and schooling takes on a more academic flavor. The development of their self-conceptions, moral reasoning, and moral behavior is also significant.

1 Emotional and Personality Development   **LG1** Discuss emotional and personality development in middle and late childhood.

The Self   Emotional Development   Moral Development   Gender

In this section, we will explore how the self continues to develop during middle and late childhood and the emotional changes that take place during these years. We will also discuss children's moral development and many aspects of the role that gender plays in their development in middle and late childhood.

THE SELF

What is the nature of the child's self-understanding, understanding of others, and self-esteem during the elementary school years? What roles do self-efficacy and self-regulation play in children's achievement?

The Development of Self-Understanding   In middle and late childhood, especially from 8 to 11 years of age, children increasingly describe themselves in terms of psychological characteristics and traits, in contrast with the more concrete self-descriptions of younger children. For example, older children are more likely to describe themselves using adjectives such as "*popular, nice, helpful, mean, smart,* and *dumb*" (Harter, 2006, p. 526).

In addition, during the elementary school years, children become more likely to recognize social aspects of the self (Harter, 2012, 2013). They include references to social groups in their self-descriptions, such as referring to themselves as Girl Scouts, as Catholics, or as someone who has two close friends (Livesly & Bromley, 1973).

Children's self-understanding in the elementary school years also includes increasing reference to social comparison (Harter, 2012, 2013). At this point in development, children are more likely to distinguish themselves from others in comparative rather than in absolute terms. That is, elementary-school-age children are no longer as likely to think about what they do or do not do, but are more likely to think about what they can do in comparison with others.

Consider a series of studies in which Diane Ruble (1983) investigated children's use of social comparison in their self-evaluations. Children were given a difficult task and then offered feedback on their performance, as well as information about the performances of other children their age. The children were then asked for self-evaluations. Children younger than 7 made virtually no reference to the information about other children's performances. However, many children older than 7 included socially comparative information in their self-descriptions.

In sum, in middle and late childhood, self-description increasingly involves psychological and social characteristics, including social comparison.

Understanding Others   In Chapter 8, we described the advances and limitations of young children's social understanding. In middle and late childhood, **perspective taking,** the social cognitive process involved in assuming the perspective of others and understanding their thoughts and feelings, improves. Executive function, discussed in Chapter 7, "Physical and Cognitive Development in Early Childhood," is at work in perspective taking (Galinsky, 2010). Among the executive functions called on when children engage in perspective taking are cognitive inhibition (controlling one's own thoughts to consider the perspective of others) and cognitive flexibility (seeing situations in different ways).

> Children are busy becoming something they have not quite grasped yet, something which keeps changing.
>
> —**ALASTAIR REID**
> *American Poet, 20th Century*

developmental **connection**

Identity

In adolescence, individuals become more introspective and reflective in their self-understanding as they search for an identity. Chapter 12, p. 372

perspective taking The social cognitive process involved in assuming the perspective of others and understanding their thoughts and feelings.

What are some changes in children's understanding of others in middle and late childhood?

In Robert Selman's (1980) view, at about 6 to 8 years of age, children begin to understand that others may have a different perspective because some people have more access to information. Then, he says, in the next several years, children begin to realize that each individual is aware of the other's perspective and that putting oneself in the other's place is a way of judging the other person's intentions, purposes, and actions.

Perspective taking is thought to be especially important in determining whether children develop prosocial or antisocial attitudes and behavior. In terms of prosocial behavior, taking another's perspective improves children's likelihood of understanding and sympathizing with others when they are distressed or in need. A recent study revealed that in children characterized as being emotionally reactive, good perspective-taking skills were linked to being able to regain a neutral emotional state after being emotionally aroused (Bengtsson & Arvidsson, 2011). In this study, children who made gains in perspective-taking skills reduced their emotional reactivity over a two-year period.

In middle and late childhood, children also become more skeptical of others' claims (Heyman, Fu, & Lee, 2013; Mills, Elashi, & Archacki, 2011). In Chapter 8, we indicated that even 4-year-old children show some skepticism of others' claims. In middle and late childhood, children become increasingly skeptical of some sources of information about psychological traits. For example, in one study, 10- to 11-year-olds were more likely to reject other children's self-reports that they were *smart* and *honest* than were 6- to 7-year-olds (Heyman & Legare, 2005). The more psychologically sophisticated 10- to 11-year-olds also showed a better understanding that others' self-reports may focus on socially desirable tendencies than the 6- to 7-year-olds did.

Self-Esteem and Self-Concept   High self-esteem and a positive self-concept are important characteristics of children's well-being (Marsh, Martin, & Xu, 2012). Investigators sometimes use the terms *self-esteem* and *self-concept* interchangeably or do not precisely define them, but there is a meaningful difference between them. **Self-esteem** refers to global evaluations of the self; it is also called *self-worth* or *self-image*. For example, a child may perceive that she is not merely a person but a *good* person. **Self-concept** refers to domain-specific evaluations of the self. Children can make self-evaluations in many domains of their lives—academic, athletic, appearance, and so on. In sum, *self-esteem* refers to global self-evaluations, *self-concept* to domain-specific evaluations.

The foundations of self-esteem and self-concept emerge from the quality of parent-child interaction in infancy and early childhood. Thus, if children have low self-esteem in middle and late childhood, they may have experienced neglect or abuse in relationships with their parents earlier in development. Children with high self-esteem are more likely to be securely attached to parents and have parents who engage in sensitive caregiving (Thompson, 2011, 2013a, b, c, d).

Self-esteem reflects perceptions that do not always match reality (Baumeister & others, 2003; Jordan & Zeigler-Hill, 2013). A child's self-esteem might reflect a belief about whether he or she is intelligent and attractive, for example, but that belief is not necessarily accurate. Thus, high self-esteem may refer to accurate, justified perceptions of one's worth as a person and one's successes and accomplishments, but it can also refer to an arrogant, grandiose, unwarranted sense of superiority over others (Gerstenberg & others, 2014). In the same manner, low self-esteem may reflect either an accurate perception of one's shortcomings or a distorted, even pathological insecurity and inferiority.

What are the consequences of low self-esteem? Low self-esteem has been implicated in overweight and obesity, anxiety, depression, suicide, and delinquency (Blanco & others, 2014; O'Brien, Bartoletti, & Leitzel, 2013; Ziegler-Hill, 2013). A recent study revealed that youths with low self-esteem had lower life satisfaction at 30 years of age (Birkeland & others, 2012). Another recent study found that low and decreasing self-esteem in adolescence was linked to adult depression two decades later (Steiger & others, 2014).

Although variations in self-esteem have been linked with many aspects of children's development, much of the research is *correlational* rather than *experimental*. Recall from Chapter 1 that correlation does not equal causation. Thus, if a correlational study finds an

self-esteem The global evaluative dimension of the self. Self-esteem is also referred to as self-worth or self-image.

self-concept Domain-specific evaluations of the self.

Increasing Children's Self-Esteem

Ways to improve children's self-esteem include identifying the causes of low self-esteem, providing emotional support and social approval, helping children achieve, and helping children cope (Bednar, Wells, & Peterson, 1995; Harter, 2006, 2012).

- *Identify the causes of low self-esteem.* Intervention should target the causes of low self-esteem. Children have the highest self-esteem when they perform competently in domains that are important to them. Therefore, children should be encouraged to identify and value areas of competence. These areas might include academic skills, athletic skills, physical attractiveness, and social acceptance.

- *Provide emotional support and social approval.* Some children with low self-esteem come from conflicted families or conditions in which they experienced abuse or neglect—situations in which support was not available. In some cases, alternative sources of support can be arranged either informally through the encouragement of a teacher, a coach, or another significant adult, or more formally, through programs such as Big Brothers and Big Sisters.

- *Help children achieve.* Achievement also can improve children's self-esteem. For example, the straightforward teaching of real skills to children often results in increased achievement and, thus, in enhanced self-esteem. Children develop higher self-esteem because they know the important tasks that will achieve their goals, and they have performed them or similar behaviors in the past.

- *Help children cope.* Self-esteem often increases when children face a problem and try to cope with it, rather than avoid it. If coping rather than avoidance prevails, children face problems realistically, honestly, and nondefensively. This produces favorable self-evaluative thoughts, which lead to the self-generated approval that raises self-esteem.

How can parents help children develop higher self-esteem?

As discussed in the "Emotional Development" section of Chapter 8, which parenting approach might help accomplish the last goal mentioned here? How? How can parents help children develop higher self-esteem?

association between children's low self-esteem and low academic achievement, low academic achievement could cause the low self-esteem as much as low self-esteem causes low academic achievement.

In fact, there are only moderate correlations between school performance and self-esteem, and these correlations do not suggest that high self-esteem produces better school performance (Baumeister & others, 2003). Efforts to increase students' self-esteem have not always led to improved school performance (Davies & Brember, 1999).

Children with high self-esteem have greater initiative, but this can produce positive or negative outcomes (Baumeister & others, 2003). Children with high self-esteem are prone to both prosocial and antisocial actions (Krueger, Vohs, & Baumeister, 2008).

In addition, a current concern is that too many of today's children grow up receiving praise for mediocre or even poor performance and as a consequence have inflated self-esteem (Graham, 2005; Stipek, 2005). They may have difficulty handling competition and criticism. This theme is vividly captured by the title of a book, *Dumbing Down Our Kids: Why American Children Feel Good About Themselves But Can't Read, Write, or Add* (Sykes, 1995). In a series of studies, researchers found that inflated praise, although well intended, may cause children with low self-esteem to avoid important learning experiences, such as tackling challenging tasks (Brummelman & others, 2014).

What are some good strategies for effectively increasing children's self-esteem? See the *Connecting Development to Life* interlude for some answers to this question.

Self-Efficacy   The belief that one can master a situation and produce favorable outcomes is called **self-efficacy.** Albert Bandura (2001, 2008, 2010a, 2012), whose social cognitive

self-efficacy The belief that one can master a situation and produce favorable outcomes.

theory we described in Chapter 1, states that self-efficacy is a critical factor in whether or not students achieve. Self-efficacy is the belief that "I can"; helplessness is the belief that "I cannot." Students with high self-efficacy endorse such statements as "I know that I will be able to learn the material in this class" and "I expect to be able to do well at this activity."

Dale Schunk (2012) has applied the concept of self-efficacy to many aspects of students' achievement. In his view, self-efficacy influences a student's choice of activities. Students with low self-efficacy for learning may avoid many learning tasks, especially those that are challenging. By contrast, their counterparts with high self-efficacy eagerly work at learning tasks (Schunk, 2012). Students with high self-efficacy are more likely to expend effort and persist longer at a learning task than students with low self-efficacy.

Self-Regulation   One of the most important aspects of the self in middle and late childhood is an increased capacity for self-regulation (Carlson, Zelazo, & Faja, 2013; Flouri, Midouhas, & Joshi, 2014). This increased capacity is characterized by deliberate efforts to manage one's behavior, emotions, and thoughts, leading to increased social competence and achievement (Schunk & Zimmerman, 2013; Thompson, 2014c, 2015). One study found that self-control increased from 4 years to 10 years of age and that high self-control was linked to lower levels of deviant behavior (Vazsonyi & Huang, 2010). In this study, parenting characterized by warmth and positive affect predicted the developmental increase in self-control. Also, a recent study of almost 17,000 3- to 7-year-old children revealed that self-regulation was a protective factor for children growing up in low socioeconomic (SES) conditions (Flouri, Midouhas, & Joshi, 2014). In this study, 7-year-old children with low self-regulation living in low-SES conditions had more emotional problems than their 3-year-old counterparts with higher self-regulation. Thus, low self-regulation was linked to a widening gap in low-SES children's emotional problems over time. Another study revealed that children from low-income families who had a higher level of self-regulation earned better grades in school than their counterparts who had a lower level of self-regulation (Buckner, Mezzacappa, & Beardslee, 2009).

The increased capacity for self-regulation is linked to developmental advances in the brain's prefrontal cortex, as discussed in Chapter 9, "Physical and Cognitive Development in Middle and Late Childhood" (Markant & Thomas, 2013). Recall our discussion there of the increased focal activation in the prefrontal cortex that is linked to improved cognitive control, which includes self-regulation (Diamond, 2013).

Industry Versus Inferiority   In Chapter 1, we described Erik Erikson's (1968) eight stages of human development. His fourth stage, industry versus inferiority, appears during middle and late childhood. The term *industry* expresses a dominant theme of this period: Children become interested in how things are made and how they work. When children are encouraged in their efforts to make, build, and work—whether building a model airplane, constructing a tree house, fixing a bicycle, solving an addition problem, or cooking—their sense of industry increases. However, parents who see their children's efforts at making things as "mischief" or "making a mess" encourage children's development of a sense of inferiority.

Children's social worlds beyond their families also contribute to a sense of industry. School becomes especially important in this regard. Consider children who are slightly below average in intelligence. They are too bright to be in special classes but not bright enough to be in gifted classes. They fail frequently in their academic efforts, developing a sense of inferiority. By contrast, consider children whose sense of industry is derogated at home. A series of sensitive and committed teachers may revitalize their sense of industry (Elkind, 1970).

What characterizes Erikson's stage of industry versus inferiority?

developmental **connection**

Erikson's Theory

Initiative versus guilt is Erikson's early childhood stage and identity versus identity confusion is his adolescence stage. Chapter 1, p. 21

EMOTIONAL DEVELOPMENT

In Chapter 8, we saw that preschoolers become more adept at talking about their own and others' emotions. They also show a growing awareness of the need to control and manage their emotions to meet social standards. In middle and late childhood, children further develop their understanding and self-regulation of emotion (McRae & others, 2012; Thompson, 2013c, d).

Developmental Changes

Developmental changes in emotions during the middle and late childhood years include the following (Denham, Bassett, & Wyatt, 2007; Denham & others, 2011; Kuebli, 1994; Thompson, 2014c, 2015):

- *Improved emotional understanding.* For example, children in elementary school develop an increased ability to understand such complex emotions as pride and shame. These emotions become less tied to the reactions of other people; they become more self-generated and integrated with a sense of personal responsibility.

- *Increased understanding that more than one emotion can be experienced in a particular situation.* A third-grader, for example, may realize that achieving something might involve both anxiety and joy.

- *Increased tendency to be aware of the events leading to emotional reactions.* A fourth-grader may become aware that her sadness today is influenced by her friend moving to another town last week.

- *Ability to suppress or conceal negative emotional reactions.* A fifth-grader has learned to tone down his anger better than he used to when one of his classmates irritates him.

- *The use of self-initiated strategies for redirecting feelings.* In the elementary school years, children become more reflective about their emotional lives and increasingly use strategies to control their emotions. They become more effective at cognitively managing their emotions, such as soothing themselves after an upset.

- *A capacity for genuine empathy.* For example, a fourth-grader feels sympathy for a distressed person and experiences vicariously the sadness the distressed person is feeling.

What are some changes in emotion during the middle and late childhood years?

Coping with Stress

An important aspect of children's emotional lives is learning how to cope with stress (Masten, 2013, 2014a, b; Morris, Thompson, & Morris, 2013). As children get older, they are able to more accurately appraise a stressful situation and determine how much control they have over it. Older children generate more coping alternatives to stressful conditions and use more cognitive coping strategies (Saarni & others, 2006). They are better than younger children at intentionally shifting their thoughts to something that is less stressful and at reframing, or changing their perception of a stressful situation. For example, younger children may be very disappointed that their teacher did not say hello to them when they arrived at school. Older children may reframe this type of situation and think, "She may have been busy with other things and just forgot to say hello."

By 10 years of age, most children are able to use these cognitive strategies to cope with stress (Saarni, 1999). However, in families that have not been supportive and are characterized by turmoil or trauma, children may be so overwhelmed by stress that they do not use such strategies.

Disasters can especially harm children's development and produce adjustment problems (Scheerings, Cobham, & McDermott, 2014). Among the outcomes for children who experience disasters are acute stress reactions, depression, panic disorder, and post-traumatic stress disorder (Pfefferbaum, Newman, & Nelson, 2014). The likelihood that a child will face these problems following a disaster depends on factors such as the nature and severity of the disaster and the type of support available to the child.

In research on disasters/trauma, the term *dose-response effects* is often used. A widely supported finding in this research area is that the more severe the disaster/trauma (dose), the worse the adaptation and adjustment (response) following the disaster/trauma (Masten, 2013; Masten & Narayan, 2012).

The terrorist attacks on the World Trade Center in New York City and the Pentagon in Washington, D.C., on September 11, 2001, and hurricanes Katrina and Rita in September 2005 raised special concerns about how to help children cope with such stressful events.

--->

developmental connection

Biological Processes

In older adults, stress hormones stay elevated in the bloodstream longer, which can accelerate aging and harm immune system functioning. Chapter 17, p. 516

What are some effective strategies to help children cope with traumatic events such as the mass shooting in December, 2012 at Sandy Hook Elementary School in Connecticut?

Researchers have offered the following recommendations for parents, teachers, and other adults caring for children after a disaster (Gurwitch & others, 2001, pp. 4–11):

- Reassure children (numerous times, if necessary) of their safety and security.
- Allow children to retell events and be patient in listening to them.
- Encourage children to talk about any disturbing or confusing feelings, reassuring them that such feelings are normal after a stressful event.
- Protect children from re-exposure to frightening situations and reminders of the trauma—for example, by limiting discussion of the event in front of the children.
- Help children make sense of what happened, keeping in mind that children may misunderstand what took place. For example, young children "may blame themselves, believe things happened that did not happen, believe that terrorists are in the school, etc. Gently help children develop a realistic understanding of the event" (p. 10).

Traumatic events may cause individuals to think about the moral aspects of life. Hopelessness and despair may short-circuit moral development when a child is confronted by the violence of war zones and impoverished inner cities (Nader, 2001). Let's further explore children's moral development.

MORAL DEVELOPMENT

Remember from Chapter 8 our description of Piaget's view of moral development. Piaget proposed that younger children are characterized by heteronomous morality—but that by 10 years of age they have moved into a higher stage called autonomous morality. According to Piaget, older children consider the intentions of the individual, believe that rules are subject to change, and are aware that punishment does not always follow wrongdoing.

A second major perspective on moral development was proposed by Lawrence Kohlberg (1958, 1986). Piaget's cognitive stages of development serve as the underpinnings for Kohlberg's theory, but Kohlberg suggested that there are six stages of moral development. These stages, he argued, are universal. Development from one stage to another, said Kohlberg, is fostered by opportunities to take the perspective of others and to experience conflict between one's current stage of moral thinking and the reasoning of someone at a higher stage.

Kohlberg arrived at his view after 20 years of using a unique interview with children. In the interview, children are presented with a series of stories in which characters face moral dilemmas. The following is the most popular Kohlberg dilemma:

> In Europe a woman was near death from a special kind of cancer. There was one drug that the doctors thought might save her. It was a form of radium that a druggist in the same town had recently discovered. The drug was expensive to make, but the druggist was charging ten times what the drug cost him to make. He paid $200 for the radium and charged $2,000 for a small dose of the drug. The sick woman's husband, Heinz, went to everyone he knew to borrow the money, but he could only get together $1,000 which is half of what it cost. He told the druggist that his wife was dying and asked him to sell it cheaper or let him pay later. But the druggist said, "No, I discovered the drug, and I am going to make money from it." So Heinz got desperate and broke into the man's store to steal the drug for his wife. (Kohlberg, 1969, p. 379)

This story is one of 11 that Kohlberg devised to investigate the nature of moral thought. After reading the story, the interviewee answers a series of questions about the moral dilemma. Should Heinz have stolen the drug? Was stealing it right or wrong? Why? Is it a husband's duty to steal the drug for his wife if he can get it no other way? Would a good husband steal? Did the druggist have the right to charge that much when there was no law setting a limit on the price? Why or why not?

The Kohlberg Stages   Based on the answers interviewees gave for this and other moral dilemmas, Kohlberg described three levels of moral thinking, each of which is characterized by two stages (see Figure 10.1). A key concept in understanding progression through the levels and stages is that the person's morality gradually becomes more internal or mature. That is, their reasons for moral decisions or values begin to go beyond the external or superficial reasons they gave when they were younger. Let's further examine Kohlberg's stages.

Lawrence Kohlberg, the architect of a provocative cognitive developmental theory of moral development. *What is the nature of his theory?*

preconventional reasoning The lowest level in Kohlberg's theory of moral development. The individual's moral reasoning is controlled primarily by external rewards and punishment.

heteronomous morality Kohlberg's first stage of preconventional reasoning in which moral thinking is tied to punishment.

LEVEL 1	LEVEL 2	LEVEL 3
Preconventional Level **No Internalization**	**Conventional Level** **Intermediate Internalization**	**Postconventional Level** **Full Internalization**
Stage 1 Heteronomous Morality *Children obey because adults tell them to obey. People base their moral decisions on fear of punishment.* **Stage 2** Individualism, Instrumental Purpose, and Exchange *Individuals pursue their own interests but let others do the same. What is right involves equal exchange.*	**Stage 3** Mutual Interpersonal Expectations, Relationships, and Interpersonal Conformity *Individuals value trust, caring, and loyalty to others as a basis for moral judgments.* **Stage 4** Social System Morality *Moral judgments are based on understanding and the social order, law, justice, and duty.*	**Stage 5** Social Contract or Utility and Individual Rights *Individuals reason that values, rights, and principles undergird or transcend the law.* **Stage 6** Universal Ethical Principles *The person has developed moral judgments that are based on universal human rights. When faced with a dilemma between law and conscience, a personal, individualized conscience is followed.*

FIGURE 10.1

KOHLBERG'S THREE LEVELS AND SIX STAGES OF MORAL DEVELOPMENT.
Kohlberg argued that people everywhere develop their moral reasoning by passing through these age-based stages. *Where does Kohlberg's theory stand on the nature-nurture and continuity-discontinuity issues discussed in Chapter 1?*

Kohlberg's Level 1: Preconventional Reasoning

Preconventional reasoning is the lowest level of moral reasoning in Kohlberg's theory and consists of two stages: heteronomous morality (stage 1) and individualism, instrumental purpose, and exchange (stage 2).

- *Stage 1.* **Heteronomous morality** is the first Kohlberg stage of moral development. At this stage, moral thinking is often tied to punishment. For example, children and adolescents obey adults because adults tell them to obey.

- *Stage 2.* **Individualism, instrumental purpose, and exchange** is the second stage of Kohlberg's theory. At this stage, individuals pursue their own interests but also let others do the same. Thus, what is right involves an equal exchange. People are nice to others so that others will be nice to them in return.

Kohlberg's Level 2: Conventional Reasoning

Conventional reasoning is the second, or intermediate, level in Kohlberg's theory of moral development. Individuals abide by certain standards (internal), but they are the standards of others, such as parents or the laws of society. The conventional reasoning level consists of two stages: mutual interpersonal expectations, relationships, and interpersonal conformity (stage 3) and social systems morality (stage 4).

- *Stage 3.* **Mutual interpersonal expectations, relationships, and interpersonal conformity** is Kohlberg's third stage of moral development. At this stage, individuals value trust, caring, and loyalty to others as a basis of moral judgments. Children and adolescents often adopt their parents' moral standards at this stage, seeking to be thought of by their parents as a "good girl" or a "good boy."

- *Stage 4.* **Social systems morality** is the fourth stage in Kohlberg's theory of moral development. At this stage, moral judgments are based on understanding the social order, law, justice, and duty. For example, adolescents may reason that in order for a community to work effectively, it needs to be protected by laws that are adhered to by its members.

Kohlberg's Level 3: Postconventional Reasoning

Postconventional reasoning is the third and highest level in Kohlberg's theory. At this level, morality is more internal. The postconventional level of morality consists of two stages: social contract or utility and individual rights (stage 5) and universal ethical principles (stage 6).

- *Stage 5.* **Social contract or utility and individual rights** is the fifth Kohlberg stage. At this stage, individuals reason that values, rights, and principles undergird or transcend the law. A person evaluates the validity of actual laws and examines social systems in terms of the degree to which they preserve and protect fundamental human rights and values.

individualism, instrumental purpose, and exchange Kohlberg's second stage of preconventional reasoning, in which individuals pursue their own interests but also let others do the same.

conventional reasoning The second, or intermediate, level in Kohlberg's theory of moral development. At this level, individuals abide by certain standards, but these are standards set by others such as parents or society.

mutual interpersonal expectations, relationships, and interpersonal conformity Kohlberg's third stage of moral development. At this stage, individuals value trust, caring, and loyalty to others as a basis of moral judgments.

social systems morality The fourth stage in Kohlberg's theory of moral development, in which moral judgments are based on understanding the social order, law, justice, and duty.

postconventional reasoning The highest level in Kohlberg's theory of moral development. At this level, the individual recognizes alternative moral courses, explores the options, and then decides on a personal moral code.

social contract or utility and individual rights The fifth Kohlberg stage. At this stage, individuals reason that values, rights, and principles undergird or transcend the law.

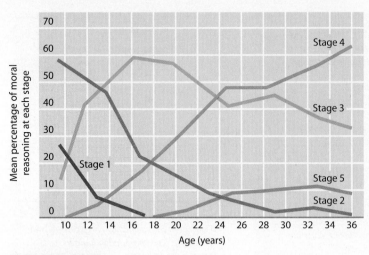

FIGURE **10.2**

AGE AND THE PERCENTAGE OF INDIVIDUALS AT EACH KOHLBERG STAGE. In one longitudinal study of males from 10 to 36 years of age, at age 10 most moral reasoning was at stage 2 (Colby & others, 1983). At 16 to 18 years of age, stage 3 became the most frequent type of moral reasoning, and it was not until the mid-twenties that stage 4 became the most frequent. Stage 5 did not appear until 20 to 22 years of age, and it never characterized more than 10 percent of the individuals. In this study, the moral stages appeared somewhat later than Kohlberg envisioned and stage 6 was absent. *Do you think it matters that all of the participants in this study were males? Why or why not?*

developmental **connection**

Peers

Piaget argued that the mutual give-and-take of peer relations is more important than parenting in enhancing children's moral reasoning. Chapter 8, p. 239

universal ethical principles The sixth and highest stage in Kohlberg's theory of moral development, in which individuals develop a moral standard based on universal human rights.

justice perspective A moral perspective that focuses on the rights of the individual and in which individuals independently make moral decisions.

care perspective The moral perspective of Carol Gilligan, which views people in terms of their connectedness with others and emphasizes interpersonal communication, relationships with others, and concern for others.

domain theory of moral development Theory that identifies different domains of social knowledge and reasoning, including moral, social conventional, and personal domains. These domains arise from children's and adolescents' attempts to understand and deal with different forms of social experience.

• *Stage 6.* **Universal ethical principles** is the sixth and highest stage in Kohlberg's theory of moral development. At this stage, the person has developed a moral standard based on universal human rights. When faced with a conflict between law and conscience, the person will follow conscience, even though the decision might involve personal risk.

Kohlberg maintained that these levels and stages occur in a sequence and are age-related: Before age 9, most children use level 1, preconventional reasoning based on external rewards and punishments, when they consider moral choices. By early adolescence, their moral reasoning is increasingly based on the application of standards set by others. Most adolescents reason at stage 3, with some signs of stages 2 and 4. By early adulthood, a small number of individuals reason in postconventional ways.

What evidence supports this description of development? A 20-year longitudinal investigation found that use of stages 1 and 2 decreased with age (Colby & others, 1983) (see Figure 10.2). Stage 4, which did not appear at all in the moral reasoning of 10-year-olds, was reflected in the moral thinking of 62 percent of the 36-year-olds. Stage 5 did not appear until age 20 to 22 and never characterized more than 10 percent of the individuals.

Thus, the moral stages appeared somewhat later than Kohlberg initially envisioned, and reasoning at the higher stages, especially stage 6, was rare. Although stage 6 has been removed from the Kohlberg moral judgment scoring manual, it still is considered to be theoretically important in the Kohlberg scheme of moral development.

Influences on the Kohlberg Stages   What factors influence movement through Kohlberg's stages? Although moral reasoning at each stage presupposes a certain level of cognitive development, Kohlberg argued that advances in children's cognitive development did not ensure development of moral reasoning. Instead, moral reasoning also reflects children's experiences in dealing with moral questions and moral conflict.

Several investigators have tried to advance individuals' levels of moral development by having a model present arguments that reflect moral thinking one stage above each individual's established level. This approach applies the concepts of equilibrium and conflict that Piaget used to explain cognitive development. By presenting arguments slightly beyond the children's level of moral reasoning, the researchers created a disequilibrium that motivated the children to restructure their moral thought. The upshot of studies using this approach is that virtually any plus-stage discussion, for any length of time, seems to promote more advanced moral reasoning (Walker, 1982).

Kohlberg emphasized that peer interaction and perspective taking are critical aspects of the social stimulation that challenges children to change their moral reasoning. Whereas adults characteristically impose rules and regulations on children, the give-and-take among peers gives children an opportunity to take the perspective of another person and to generate rules democratically.

Kohlberg's Critics   Kohlberg's theory has provoked debate, research, and criticism (Gibbs, 2014; Killen & Smetana, 2014; Lapsley & Yeager, 2013; Narváez, 2014). Key criticisms involve the link between moral thought and moral behavior, the roles of culture and the family in moral development, and the significance of concern for others.

Moral Thought and Moral Behavior   Kohlberg's theory has been criticized for placing too much emphasis on moral thought and not enough emphasis on moral behavior (Walker, 2004). Moral reasons can sometimes be a shelter for immoral behavior. Corrupt CEOs and politicians endorse the loftiest of moral virtues in public before their own behavior is exposed. Whatever the latest public scandal, you will probably find that the culprits displayed virtuous thoughts but engaged in immoral behavior. No one wants a nation of cheaters and thieves who can reason at the postconventional level. The cheaters and thieves may know what is right yet still do what is wrong. Heinous actions can be cloaked in a mantle of moral virtue.

Culture and Moral Reasoning   Kohlberg emphasized that his stages of moral reasoning are universal, but some critics claim his theory is culturally biased (Gibbs, 2014; Miller & Bland, 2014). Both Kohlberg and his critics may be partially correct. In one study, individuals in diverse cultures developed through the first four stages in sequence as Kohlberg predicted. Stages 5 and 6, however, have not been found in all cultures (Gibbs & others, 2007; Snarey, 1987). In sum, although Kohlberg's approach does capture much of the moral reasoning voiced in various cultures around the world, his approach misses or misconstrues some important moral concepts in particular cultures (Gibbs, 2014; Miller & Bland, 2014).

Families and Moral Development   Kohlberg argued that family processes are essentially unimportant in children's moral development. As noted earlier, he argued that parent-child relationships usually provide children with little opportunity for give-and-take or perspective taking. Rather, Kohlberg said that such opportunities are more likely to be provided by children's peer relationships. However, most experts on children's moral development conclude that parents' moral values and actions influence children's development of moral reasoning (Grusec & others, 2014; Thompson, 2014a). Nonetheless, most developmentalists agree with Kohlberg and Piaget that peers play an important role in the development of moral reasoning.

Gender and the Care Perspective   The most publicized criticism of Kohlberg's theory has come from Carol Gilligan (1982, 1992, 1996), who argues that Kohlberg's theory reflects a gender bias. According to Gilligan, Kohlberg's theory is based on a male norm that puts abstract principles above relationships and concern for others and sees the individual as standing alone and independently making moral decisions. It puts justice at the heart of morality. In contrast with Kohlberg's **justice perspective,** Gilligan argues for a **care perspective,** which is a moral perspective that views people in terms of their connectedness with others and emphasizes interpersonal communication, relationships with others, and concern for others. According to Gilligan, Kohlberg greatly underplayed the care perspective, perhaps because he was a male, because most of his research was with males rather than females, and because he used male responses as a model for his theory.

However, questions have been raised about Gilligan's gender conclusions (Walker & Frimer, 2009). For example, a meta-analysis (a statistical analysis that combines the results of many different studies) casts doubt on Gilligan's claim of substantial gender differences in moral judgment (Jaffee & Hyde, 2000). And a research review concluded that girls' moral orientations are "somewhat more likely to focus on care for others than on abstract principles of justice, but they can use both moral orientations when needed (as can boys . . .)" (Blakemore, Berenbaum, & Liben, 2009, p. 132).

Domain Theory: Moral, Social Conventional, Personal Reasoning   The **domain theory of moral development** states that there are different domains of social knowledge and reasoning, including moral, social conventional, and personal domains. In domain theory, children's and adolescents' moral, social conventional, and personal knowledge and reasoning emerge from their attempts to understand and deal with different forms of social experience (Smetana, 2011a, b, 2013; Turiel, 2014).

Some theorists and researchers argue that Kohlberg did not adequately distinguish between moral reasoning and social conventional reasoning (Killen & Smetana, 2014; Smetana, 2013; Turiel, 2014). **Social conventional reasoning** focuses on conventional rules that have been established by social consensus in order to control behavior and maintain the social system. The rules themselves are arbitrary, such as raising your hand in class before speaking, using one staircase at school to go up and the other to go down, not cutting in front of someone standing in line to buy movie tickets, and stopping at a stop sign when driving. There are sanctions if we violate these conventions, although they can be changed by consensus.

In contrast, moral reasoning focuses on ethical issues and rules of morality. Unlike conventional rules, moral rules are not arbitrary. They are obligatory, widely accepted, and

This 14-year-old boy in Nepal is thought to be the sixth-holiest Buddhist in the world. In one study of 20 adolescent male Buddhist monks in Nepal, the issue of justice, a basic theme in Kohlberg's theory, was not a central focus in the monks' moral views (Huebner & Garrod, 1993). Also, the monks' concerns about prevention of suffering and the importance of compassion are not captured in Kohlberg's theory.

Carol Gilligan. *What is Gilligan's view of moral development?*

social conventional reasoning Thoughts about social consensus and convention, in contrast with moral reasoning, which stresses ethical issues.

somewhat impersonal (Helwig & Turiel, 2011). Rules pertaining to lying, cheating, stealing, and physically harming another person are moral rules because violation of these rules affronts ethical standards that exist apart from social consensus and convention. Moral judgments involve concepts of justice, whereas social conventional judgments are concepts of social organization. Violating moral rules is usually more serious than violating conventional rules.

The social conventional approach is a serious challenge to Kohlberg's approach because Kohlberg argued that social conventions are a stop-over on the road to higher moral sophistication. For social conventional reasoning advocates, social conventional reasoning is not lower than postconventional reasoning but rather something that needs to be disentangled from the moral thread (Smetana, 2013; Smetana, Jambon, & Ball, 2014).

Recently, a distinction also has been made between moral and conventional issues, which are viewed as legitimately subject to adult social regulation, and personal issues, which are more likely subject to the child's or adolescent's independent decision making and personal discretion (Smetana, 2011a, b, 2013). Personal issues include control over one's body, privacy, and choice of friends and activities. Thus, some actions belong to a *personal* domain and are not governed by moral reasoning or social norms.

How does children's sharing change from the preschool to the elementary school years?

Prosocial Behavior Whereas Kohlberg's and Gilligan's theories have focused primarily on the development of moral reasoning, the study of prosocial moral behavior has placed more emphasis on the behavioral aspects of moral development (Eisenberg, Spinrad, & Morris, 2013; Padilla-Walker & Carlo, 2014). Children engage in immoral, antisocial acts such as lying and cheating and also display prosocial moral behavior such as showing empathy or acting altruistically (Eisenberg & Spinrad, 2014; Padilla-Walker & Carlo, 2014). Even during the preschool years, children may care for others or comfort others in distress (Laible & Karahuta, 2014), but prosocial behavior occurs more often in adolescence than in childhood (Eisenberg & others, 2009).

William Damon (1988) described how sharing develops. During their first years, when children share, it is usually not for reasons of empathy but for the fun of the social play ritual or out of imitation. Then, at about 4 years of age, a combination of empathic awareness and adult encouragement produces a sense of obligation on the part of the child to share with others. Most 4-year-olds are not selfless saints, however. Children believe they have an obligation to share but do not necessarily think they should be as generous to others as they are to themselves.

Children's sharing comes to reflect a more complex sense of what is just and right during middle and late childhood. By the start of the elementary school years, children begin to express objective ideas about fairness. It is common to hear 6-year-old children use the word *fair* as synonymous with *equal* or *same*. By the mid- to late elementary school years, children believe that equity can sometimes mean that people with special merit or special needs deserve special treatment.

Moral Personality Beyond the development of moral reasoning and specific moral feelings and prosocial behaviors, do children also develop a pattern of moral characteristics that is distinctively their own? In other words, do children develop a *moral personality,* and if so, what are its components? Researchers have focused attention on three possible components: (1) moral identity, (2) moral character, and (3) moral exemplars:

- *Moral identity*. Individuals have a moral identity when moral notions and moral commitments are central to their lives (Matsuba, Murazyn, & Hart, 2014; Walker, 2014a, b). They construct the self with reference to moral categories. Violating their moral commitment would place the integrity of their self at risk (Hardy & others, 2014). A mature moral individual cares about morality and being a moral person.

- *Moral character*. A person with moral character has the willpower, desire, and integrity to stand up to pressure, overcome distractions and disappointments, and behave morally. A person of good moral character displays moral virtues such as "honesty, truthfulness, and trustworthiness, as well as those of care, compassion, thoughtfulness, and considerateness. Other salient traits revolve around virtues of dependability, loyalty, and conscientiousness" (Walker, 2002, p. 74).

- *Moral exemplars*. Moral exemplars are people who have lived exemplary moral lives. Their moral personality, identity, character, and set of virtues reflect moral excellence and commitment (Walker, 2014a, b).

In sum, moral development is a multifaceted, complex concept. Included in this complexity are an individual's thoughts, feelings, behaviors, and personality.

GENDER

Gilligan's claim that Kohlberg's theory of moral development reflects gender bias reminds us of the pervasive influence of gender on development. Long before elementary school, boys and girls show preferences for different toys and activities. As we discussed in Chapter 8, preschool children display a gender identity and gender-typed behavior that reflects biological, cognitive, and social influences. Here we will examine gender stereotypes, gender similarities and differences, and gender-role classification.

Gender Stereotypes   According to the old ditty, boys are made of "frogs and snails" and girls are made of "sugar and spice and all that is nice." In the past, a well-adjusted boy was supposed to be independent, aggressive, and powerful. A well-adjusted girl was supposed to be dependent, nurturing, and uninterested in power. These notions reflect **gender stereotypes,** which are broad categories that reflect general impressions and beliefs about females and males.

Recent research has found that gender stereotypes are, to a great extent, still present in today's world, both in the lives of children and adults (Hyde, 2014; Leaper, 2013; Liben, Bigler, & Hilliard, 2014). Gender stereotyping continues to change during middle and late childhood and adolescence (Blakemore, Berenbaum, & Liben, 2009). By the time children enter elementary school, they have considerable knowledge about which activities are linked with being male or female. Until about 7 to 8 years of age, gender stereotyping is extensive because young children don't recognize individual variations in masculinity and femininity. By 5 years of age, both boys and girls stereotype boys as powerful and in more negative terms, such as mean, and girls in more positive terms, such as nice (Martin & Ruble, 2010). Across the elementary school years, children become more flexible in their gender attitudes (Trautner & others, 2005).

A study of 3- to 10-year-old U.S. children revealed that girls and older children used a higher percentage of gender stereotypes (Miller & others, 2009). In this study, appearance stereotypes were more prevalent on the part of girls while activity (sports, for example) and trait (aggressive, for example) stereotyping was more commonly engaged in by boys. Another recent study of 6- to 10-year-olds found that both boys and girls indicated math is for boys (Cvencek, Meltzoff, & Greenwald, 2011). Researchers also have found that boys' gender stereotypes are more rigid than girls' (Blakemore, Berenbaum, & Liben, 2009).

Gender Similarities and Differences   What is the reality behind gender stereotypes? Let's examine some of the similarities and differences between the sexes, keeping in mind that (1) the differences are averages—not all females versus all males; (2) even when differences are reported, there is considerable overlap between the sexes; and (3) the differences may be due primarily to biological factors, sociocultural factors, or both. First, we will examine physical similarities and differences, and then we will turn to cognitive and socio-emotional similarities and differences.

Physical Development   Women have about twice the body fat of men, most of it concentrated around their breasts and hips. In males, fat is more likely to go to the abdomen. On the average, males grow to be 10 percent taller than females. Other physical differences are less obvious. From conception on, females have a longer life expectancy than males, and females are less likely than males to develop physical or mental disorders. Males have twice the risk of coronary disease as females.

Does gender matter when it comes to brain structure and function? Human brains are much alike, whether the brain belongs to a male or a female (Halpern & others, 2007).

What are little boys made of?
Frogs and snails
And puppy-dogs' tails.
What are little girls made of?
Sugar and spice
And all that is nice.

—J. O. HALLIWELL
English Author, 19th Century

gender stereotypes Broad categories that reflect our impressions and beliefs about females and males.

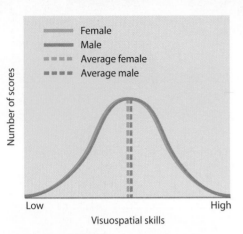

FIGURE **10.3**

VISUOSPATIAL SKILLS OF MALES AND

FEMALES. Notice that although an average male's visuospatial skills are higher than an average female's, the scores for the two sexes almost entirely overlap. Not all males have better visuospatial skills than all females—the overlap indicates that although the average male score is higher, many females outperform most males on such tasks.

"So according to the stereotype, you can put two and two together, but I can read the handwriting on the wall." © Joel Pett. Author rights reserved.

What are some recent changes in single-sex education in the United States? What does research say about whether single-sex education is beneficial?

However, researchers have found some differences in the brains of males and females (Hofer & others, 2007). Female brains are approximately 10 percent smaller than male brains (Giedd, 2012; Giedd & others, 2012). However, female brains have more folds; the larger folds (called convolutions) allow more surface brain tissue within the skulls of females than males (Luders & others, 2004). An area of the parietal lobe that functions in visuospatial skills is larger in males than females (Frederikse & others, 2000). And the areas of the brain involved in emotional expression show more metabolic activity in females than males (Gur & others, 1995).

Although some differences in brain structure and function have been found, many of these differences are small or research is inconsistent regarding the differences. Also, when sex differences in the brain have been revealed, in many cases they have not been directly linked to psychological differences (Blakemore, Berenbaum, & Liben, 2009). Although research on sex differences in the brain is still in its infancy, it is likely that there are far more similarities than differences in the brains of females and males. A further point is worth noting: Anatomical sex differences in the brain may be due to the biological origins of these differences, behavioral experiences (which underscores the brain's continuing plasticity), or a combination of these factors.

Cognitive Development No gender differences in general intelligence have been revealed, but some gender differences have been found in some cognitive areas (Halpern, 2012). Research has shown that in general girls and women have slightly better verbal skills than boys and men, although in some verbal skill areas the differences are substantial (Blakemore, Berenbaum, & Liben, 2009).

Are there gender differences in math skills? A recent very large-scale study of more than 7 million U.S. students in grades 2 through 11 revealed no differences in math test scores for boys and girls (Hyde & others, 2008). And a recent meta-analysis found no gender differences in math for adolescents (Lindberg & others, 2010). A recent research review concluded that girls have more negative math attitudes and that parents' and teachers' expectancies for children's math competence are often gender-biased in favor of boys (Gunderson & others, 2012).

One area of math that has been examined for possible gender differences is visuospatial skills, which include being able to rotate objects mentally and to determine what they would look like when rotated (Halpern, 2012). These types of skills are important in courses such as plane and solid geometry and geography. A research review revealed that boys have better visuospatial skills than girls (Halpern & others, 2007). For example, despite equal participation in the National Geography Bee, in most years all 10 finalists are boys (Liben, 1995). A recent research review found that having a stronger masculine gender role was linked to better spatial ability in males and females (Reilly & Neumann, 2013). However, some experts argue that the gender difference in visuospatial skills is small (Hyde, 2014; Hyde & Else-Quest, 2013) (see Figure 10.3).

Are there gender differences in reading and writing skills? There is strong evidence that females outperform males in reading and writing. In national studies, girls have had higher reading achievement than have boys (National Assessment of Educational Progress, 2012). An international study in 65 countries found that girls had higher reading achievement than did boys in every country (Reilly, 2012). In this study, the gender difference in reading was stronger in countries with less gender equity and lower economic prosperity. In the United States, girls also have consistently outperformed boys in writing skills in the National Assessment of Educational Progress in fourth-, eighth-, and twelfth-grade assessments.

Are there gender differences in school contexts and achievement? With regard to school achievement, girls earn better grades and complete high school at a higher rate, and they are less likely to drop out of school than boys are (Halpern, 2012). Males are more likely than females to be assigned to special/remedial education classes. Girls are more likely than boys to be engaged with academic material, be attentive in class, put forth more academic effort, and participate more in class (DeZolt & Hull, 2001).

Might single-sex education be better for children than coed education? The argument for single-sex education is that it eliminates distraction from the other sex and reduces sexual harassment. Single-sex public education has increased dramatically in recent years. In 2002, only 12 public schools in the United States provided single-sex education; in the 2011–2012 school year, 116 public schools were single-sex and an additional 390 provided such experiences (NASSPE, 2012).

The increase in single-sex education has especially been fueled by its inclusion in the No Child Left Behind legislation as a means of improving the educational experiences and academic achievement of low-income students of color. It appears that many of the public schools offering single-sex education have a high percentage of such youth (Klein, 2012). However, two recent research reviews concluded that there have been no documented benefits of single-sex education for low-income students of color (Goodkind, 2014; Halpern & others, 2011). One review, titled "The Pseudoscience of Single-Sex Schooling," by Diane Halpern and her colleagues (2011) concluded that single-sex education is highly misguided, misconstrued, and unsupported by any valid scientific evidence. They emphasize that among the many arguments against single-sex education, the strongest is its reduction in the opportunities for boys and girls to work together in a supervised, purposeful environment.

There has been a special call for single-sex public education for one group of adolescents—African American boys—because of their historically poor academic achievement and high dropout rate from school (Mitchell & Stewart, 2013). In 2010, Urban Prep Academy for Young Men became the first all-male, all African American public charter school. One hundred percent of its first graduates enrolled in college, despite the school's location in a section of Chicago where poverty, gangs, and crime predominate. Because so few public schools focus solely on educating African American boys, it is too early to tell whether this type of single-sex education can be effective across a wide range of participants.

Socioemotional Development   Three areas of socioemotional development in which gender similarities and differences have been studied extensively are aggression, emotion, and prosocial behavior.

One of the most consistent gender differences found is that boys are more physically aggressive than girls are (Coyne, Nelson, & Underwood, 2011; Hyde, 2014). The difference occurs in all cultures and appears very early in children's development (White, 2001). The physical aggression difference is especially pronounced when children are provoked. Both biological and environmental factors have been proposed to account for gender differences in aggression. Biological factors include heredity and hormones. Environmental factors include cultural expectations, adult and peer models, and social agents that reward aggression in boys and punish aggression in girls.

What gender differences characterize aggression?

Although boys are consistently more physically aggressive than girls, might girls show levels of verbal aggression, such as yelling, that equal or exceed the levels shown by boys? When verbal aggression is considered, gender differences often disappear, although sometimes verbal aggression is more pronounced in girls (Eagly & Steffen, 1986).

Recently, increased attention has been directed to *relational aggression*, which involves harming someone by manipulating a relationship. Relational aggression includes such behaviors as spreading malicious rumors about someone in order to make others dislike that person (Kawabata & others, 2012; Underwood, 2004, 2011). Relational aggression increases in middle and late childhood (Dishion & Piehler, 2009). Mixed findings have characterized research on whether girls show more relational aggression than boys, but one consistent finding is that relational aggression comprises a greater percentage of girls' overall aggression than is the case for boys (Putallaz & others, 2007). And a recent research review revealed that girls engage in more relational aggression than boys in adolescence but not in childhood (Smith, Rose, & Schwartz-Mette, 2010).

What gender differences characterize children's prosocial behavior?

FIGURE **10.4**

THE BEM SEX-ROLE INVENTORY. These items are from the Bem Sex-Role Inventory (BSRI). When taking the BSRI, an individual is asked to indicate on a 7-point scale how well each of the 60 characteristics describes herself or himself. The scale ranges from 1 (never or almost never true) to 7 (always or almost always true). The items are scored on independent dimensions of masculinity and femininity. Individuals who score high on the masculine items and low on the feminine items are categorized as masculine; those who score high on the feminine items and low on the masculine items are categorized as feminine; and those who score high on both the masculine and feminine items are categorized as androgynous.

Examples of masculine items

Defends own beliefs

Forceful

Willing to take risks

Dominant

Aggressive

Examples of feminine items

Does not use harsh language

Affectionate

Loves children

Understanding

Gentle

Gender differences occur in some aspects of emotion (Leaper, 2013). Females express emotion more than do males, are better than males at decoding emotion, smile more, cry more, and are happier (Gross, Fredrickson, & Levenson, 1994; LaFrance, Hecht, & Paluck, 2003). Males report experiencing and expressing more anger than do females (Kring, 2000). A recent meta-analysis found that overall gender differences in children's emotional expression were small, with girls showing more positive emotions (sympathy, for example) and more internalized emotions (sadness and anxiety, for example) (Chaplin & Aldao, 2013). In this analysis, the gender difference in positive emotions became more pronounced with age as girls more strongly expressed positive emotions than boys in middle and late childhood and in adolescence.

An important skill is to be able to regulate and control one's emotions and behavior (Thompson, Winer, & Goodvin, 2014). Boys usually show less self-regulation than girls do (Eisenberg, Spinrad, & Eggum, 2010). This low self-control can translate into behavior problems.

Are there gender differences in prosocial behavior? Females view themselves as more prosocial and empathic (Eisenberg & Spinrad, 2014; Eisenberg & Morris, 2004). Across childhood and adolescence, females engage in more prosocial behavior (Hastings, Utendale, & Sullivan, 2007). The biggest gender difference occurs for kind and considerate behavior, with a smaller difference in sharing.

developmental connection

Gender

The nature and extent of gender differences in communication in relationships is controversial. Chapter 14, p. 439

Gender-Role Classification Not long ago, it was accepted that boys should grow up to be masculine and girls to be feminine. In the 1970s, however, as both females and males became dissatisfied with the burdens imposed by their stereotypical roles, alternatives to femininity and masculinity were proposed. Instead of describing masculinity and femininity based on a continuum in which more of one means less of the other, it was proposed that individuals could have both masculine and feminine traits.

This thinking led to the development of the concept of **androgyny,** the presence of positive masculine and feminine characteristics in the same person (Bem, 1977; Spence & Helmreich, 1978). The androgynous boy might be assertive (masculine) and nurturant (feminine). The androgynous girl might be powerful (masculine) and sensitive to others' feelings (feminine). Measures have been developed to assess androgyny (see Figure 10.4).

Gender experts such as Sandra Bem argue that androgynous individuals are more flexible, competent, and mentally healthy than their masculine or feminine counterparts. To some degree, though, which gender-role classification is best depends on the context involved. For example, in close relationships, feminine and androgynous orientations might be more desirable. One study found that girls and individuals high in femininity showed a stronger interest in caring than did boys and individuals high in masculinity (Karniol, Grosz, & Schorr, 2003). However, masculine and androgynous orientations might be more desirable in traditional academic and work settings because of the achievement demands in these contexts.

developmental connection

Community and Culture

Bronfenbrenner's ecological theory emphasizes the importance of contexts; in his theory the macrosystem includes cross-cultural comparisons. Chapter 1, p. 25

Despite talk about the "sensitive male," William Pollack (1999) argues that little has been done to change traditional ways of raising boys. He says that the "boy code" tells boys that they should show little if any emotion and should act tough. Boys learn the boy code in many contexts—sandboxes, playgrounds, schoolrooms, camps, hangouts. The result, according to Pollack, is a "national crisis of boyhood." Pollack and others suggest that boys would benefit from being socialized to express their anxieties and concerns and to better regulate their aggression.

androgyny The presence of positive masculine and feminine characteristics in the same individual.

Gender in Context Both the concept of androgyny and gender stereotypes describe people in terms of personality traits such as "aggressive" or "caring." However, the traits people display may vary with the situation (Leaper, 2013). Thus, the nature and extent of gender differences may depend on the context (Gershoff, Mistry, & Crosby, 2014; Liben, Bigler, & Hilliard, 2014).

Consider helping behavior. The stereotype is that females are better than males at helping. But it depends on the situation. Females are more likely than males to volunteer their time to help children with personal problems and to engage in care-giving behavior. However, in situations in which males feel a sense of competence and in circumstances that involve danger, males are more likely than females to help (Eagly & Crowley, 1986). For example, a male is more likely than a female to stop and help a person stranded by the roadside with a flat tire. Indeed, one study documented that males are more likely to help when the context is masculine in nature (MacGeorge, 2003).

The importance of considering gender in context is nowhere more apparent than when examining what is culturally prescribed behavior for females and males in different countries around the world (Hyde & Else-Quest, 2013). Although there has been greater acceptance of androgyny and similarities in male and female behavior in the United States in recent years, in many countries gender roles have remained gender-specific. For example, in many Middle Eastern countries, the division of labor between males and females is dramatic. Males are socialized and schooled to work in the public sphere, females in the private world of home and child rearing. Also, in Iran the dominant view is that the man's duty is to provide for his family and the woman's is to care for her family and household. China also has been a male-dominant culture. Although women have made some strides in China, especially in urban areas, the male role is still dominant. Most males in China do not accept androgynous behavior or gender equity.

In China, females and males are usually socialized to behave, feel, and think differently. The old patriarchal traditions of male supremacy have not been completely uprooted. Chinese women still make considerably less money than Chinese men do, and in rural China (such as here in the Lixian Village of Sichuan) male supremacy still governs many women's lives.

Review Connect Reflect

 LG1 Discuss emotional and personality development in middle and late childhood.

Review
- What changes take place in the self during the middle and late childhood years?
- How does emotional expression change during middle and late childhood?
- What characterizes moral development in middle and late childhood? What are gender stereotypes, and what are some important gender differences?

Connect
- In Chapter 5, you learned about the concept of joint attention. How is joint attention similar to or different from the concept of perspective taking you learned about here?

Reflect *Your Own Personal Journey of Life*
- A young man who had been sentenced to serve 10 years for selling a small amount of marijuana escaped from a prison six months after he was sent there. He is now in his fifties and has been a model citizen. Should he be sent back to prison? Why or why not? At which Kohlberg stage should your response be placed? Do you think the stage at which you placed your response accurately captures the level of your moral thinking? Explain.

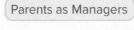
Developmental Changes in Parent-Child Relationships	Parents as Managers	Attachment in Families	Stepfamilies

What are some changes in the focus of parent-child relationships in middle and late childhood?

Our discussion of parenting and families in this section focuses on how parent-child interactions typically change in middle and late childhood, the importance of parents being effective managers of children's lives, the role of attachment in family relationships, and how children are affected by living with stepparents.

DEVELOPMENTAL CHANGES IN PARENT-CHILD RELATIONSHIPS

As children move into the middle and late childhood years, parents spend considerably less time with them (Grusec & others, 2013). In one study, parents spent less than half as much time with their children aged 5 to 12 in caregiving, instruction, reading, talking, and playing as they did when the children were younger (Hill & Stafford, 1980). Although parents spend less time with their children in middle and late childhood than in early childhood, parents continue to be extremely important in their children's lives. In a recent analysis of the contributions of parents in middle and late childhood, the following conclusion was reached: "Parents serve as gatekeepers and provide scaffolding as children assume more responsibility for themselves and . . . regulate their own lives" (Huston & Ripke, 2006, p. 422).

Parents especially play an important role in supporting and stimulating children's academic achievement in middle and late childhood (Eccles, 2014; Pomerantz & Kempner, 2013). The value parents place on education can determine whether children do well in school. Parents not only influence children's in-school achievement, but they also make decisions about children's out-of-school activities. Whether children participate in sports, music, and other activities is heavily influenced by the extent to which parents sign up children for such activities and encourage their participation (Simpkins & others, 2006).

Elementary school children tend to receive less physical discipline than they did as preschoolers. Instead of spanking or coercive holding, their parents are more likely to use deprivation of privileges, appeals to the child's self-esteem, comments designed to increase the child's sense of guilt, and statements that the child is responsible for his or her actions.

During middle and late childhood, some control is transferred from parent to child. The process is gradual, and it produces coregulation rather than control by either the child or the parent alone. Parents continue to exercise general supervision and control, while children are allowed to engage in moment-to-moment self-regulation. The major shift to autonomy does not occur until about the age of 12 or later. A key developmental task as children move toward autonomy is learning to relate to adults outside the family on a regular basis—adults such as teachers who interact with children much differently from their parents.

PARENTS AS MANAGERS

Parents can play important roles as managers of children's opportunities, as monitors of their behavior, and as social initiators and arrangers (Grusec & others, 2013; Parke & Clarke-Stewart, 2011). Mothers are more likely than fathers to engage in a managerial role in parenting.

Researchers have found that family management practices are positively related to students' grades and self-responsibility, and negatively to school-related problems (Eccles, 2007; Taylor & Lopez, 2005). Among the most important family management practices in this regard are maintaining a structured and organized family environment, such as establishing routines for homework, chores, bedtime, and so on, and effectively monitoring the child's behavior. A research review of the role of family functioning in determining African American students' academic achievement found that when African American parents monitored their son's academic achievement by ensuring that homework was completed, by restricting time spent on nonproductive distractions (such as video games and TV), and by participating in a consistent, positive dialogue with teachers and school officials, their son's academic achievement benefited (Mandara, 2006).

ATTACHMENT IN FAMILIES

In Chapter 6, you read about the importance of secure attachment in infancy and the role of sensitive parenting in attachment (Bretherton, 2012; Thompson, 2014b, 2015). The attachment process continues to be an important aspect of children's development during the childhood years. In middle and late childhood, attachment becomes more sophisticated and as children's social worlds expand to include peers, teachers, and others, they typically spend less time with parents.

Kathryn Kerns and her colleagues (Brumariu & Kerns, 2014; Brumariu, Kerns, & Seibert, 2012; Kerns & Seibert, 2012; Kerns, Siener, & Brumariu, 2011; Siener & Kerns, 2012; West, Mathews, & Kerns, 2013) have studied links between attachment to parents and various child outcomes in the middle and late childhood years. They have found that during this period of development, secure attachment is associated with a lower level of internalized symptoms, anxiety, and depression in children (Brumariu & Kerns, 2010). For example, a recent study revealed that children who were less securely attached to their mothers reported having more anxiety (Brumariu, Kerns, & Seibert, 2012). Also in this study, secure attachment was linked to a higher level of children's emotion regulation and less difficulty in identifying emotions.

STEPFAMILIES

Not only has divorce become commonplace in the United States, so has remarriage. It takes time for parents to marry, have children, get divorced, and then remarry. Consequently, stepfamilies include far more elementary and secondary school children than infants or preschool children.

The number of remarriages involving children has grown steadily in recent years. Also, divorces occur at a 10 percent higher rate in remarriages than in first marriages (Cherlin & Furstenberg, 1994). About half of all children whose parents divorce will have a stepparent within four years of the separation.

Remarried parents face some unique tasks (de Jong Gierveld & Merz, 2013). The couple must define and strengthen their marriage and at the same time renegotiate the biological parent-child relationships and establish stepparent-stepchild and stepsibling relationships (Coleman, Ganong, & Fine, 2004). The complex histories and multiple relationships make adjustment difficult in a stepfamily (Dodson & Davies, 2014; Higginbotham & others, 2012). Only one-third of stepfamily couples stay remarried.

In some cases, the stepfamily may have been preceded by the death of a spouse. However, by far the largest number of stepfamilies are preceded by divorce rather than death (Pasley & Moorefield, 2004). Three common types of stepfamily structure are (1) stepfather, (2) stepmother, and (3) blended or complex. In stepfather families, the mother typically had custody of the children and remarried, introducing a stepfather into her children's lives. In stepmother families, the father usually had custody and remarried, introducing a stepmother into his children's lives. In a blended or complex stepfamily, both parents bring children from previous marriages to live in the newly formed stepfamily.

In E. Mavis Hetherington's (2006) longitudinal analyses, children and adolescents who had been in a simple stepfamily (stepfather or stepmother) for a number of years were adjusting better than in the early years of the remarried family and were functioning well in comparison with children and adolescents in conflictual nondivorced families and children and adolescents in complex (blended) stepfamilies. More than 75 percent of the adolescents in long-established simple stepfamilies described their relationships with their stepparents as "close" or "very close." Hetherington (2006) concluded that in long-established simple stepfamilies adolescents seem to eventually benefit from the presence of a stepparent and the resources provided by the stepparent.

- - - - - - - - - ->
developmental **connection**

Family

Approximately 50 percent of remarried women bear children within their newly formed union. Chapter 14, p. 447

How does living in a stepfamily influence a child's development?

Children often have better relationships with their custodial parents (mothers in stepfather families, fathers in stepmother families) than with stepparents (Santrock, Sitterle, & Warshak, 1988). Also, children in simple stepfamilies (stepmother, stepfather) often show better adjustment than their counterparts in complex (blended) families (Hetherington & Kelly, 2002). As in divorced families, children in stepfamilies show more adjustment problems than children in nondivorced families (Hetherington & Kelly, 2002). The adjustment problems are similar to those found among children of divorced parents—academic problems and lower self-esteem, for example (Anderson & others, 1999). However, it is important to recognize that a majority of children in stepfamilies do not have such problems. In one analysis, 25 percent of children from stepfamilies showed adjustment problems compared with 10 percent in intact, never-divorced families (Hetherington & Kelly, 2002).

Adolescence is an especially difficult time for the formation of a stepfamily (Gosselin, 2010). This difficulty may occur because becoming part of a stepfamily exacerbates normal adolescent concerns about identity, sexuality, and autonomy.

Review Connect Reflect

 LG2 Describe developmental changes in parent-child relationships, parents as managers, attachment in families, and stepfamilies.

Review

- What changes characterize parent-child relationships in middle and late childhood?
- How can parents be effective managers of their children's lives?
- How is attachment linked to children's development in middle and late childhood?
- How does being in a stepfamily influence children's development?

Connect

- In this section you learned how being part of a stepfamily affects the development of children. What did you learn in Chapter 8 about children in divorced families, parenting style, and children's adjustment?

Reflect *Your Own Personal Journey of Life*

- What was your relationship with your parents like when you were in elementary school? How do you think it influenced your development?

3 Peers   **LG3** Identify changes in peer relationships in middle and late childhood.

Developmental Changes   Peer Status   Social Cognition   Bullying   Friends

Having positive relationships with peers is especially important in middle and late childhood (Lansford & others, 2014; Rubin & others, 2013). Engaging in positive interactions with peers, resolving conflicts with peers in nonaggressive ways, and maintaining quality friendships in middle and late childhood not only produce positive outcomes at this time in children's lives, but also are linked to more positive relationship outcomes in adolescence and adulthood (Huston & Ripke, 2006). For example, in one longitudinal study, being popular with peers and engaging in low levels of aggression at 8 years of age were related to higher levels of occupational status at 48 years of age (Huesmann & others, 2006). Another study found that peer competence (a composite measure that included social contact with peers, popularity with peers, friendship, and social skills) in middle and late childhood was linked to having better relationships with coworkers in early adulthood (Collins & van Dulmen, 2006). And a recent study indicated that low peer status in childhood (low acceptance/likeability) was linked to increased probability of being unemployed and having mental health problems in adulthood (Almquist & Brannstrom, 2014).

DEVELOPMENTAL CHANGES

As children enter the elementary school years, reciprocity becomes especially important in peer interchanges. Researchers estimate that the percentage of time spent in social interaction with peers increases from approximately 10 percent at 2 years of age to more than 30 percent in middle and late childhood (Rubin, Bukowski, & Parker, 2006). In an early classic study, a typical day in elementary school included approximately 300 episodes with peers (Barker & Wright, 1951). As children move through middle and late childhood, the size of their peer group increases, and peer interaction is less closely supervised by adults. Until about 12 years of age, children's preference for same-sex peer groups increases.

PEER STATUS

Which children are likely to be popular with their peers and which ones tend to be disliked? Developmentalists address this and similar questions by examining *sociometric status,* a term that describes the extent to which children are liked or disliked by their peer group (Cillessen & van den Berg, 2012). Sociometric status is typically assessed by asking children to rate how much they like or dislike each of their classmates. Or it may be assessed by asking children to name the children they like the most and those they like the least.

What are some statuses that children have with their peers?

Developmentalists have distinguished five peer statuses (Wentzel & Asher, 1995):

- **Popular children** are frequently nominated as a best friend and are rarely disliked by their peers.
- **Average children** receive an average number of both positive and negative nominations from their peers.
- **Neglected children** are infrequently nominated as a best friend but are not disliked by their peers.
- **Rejected children** are infrequently nominated as someone's best friend and are actively disliked by their peers.
- **Controversial children** are frequently nominated both as someone's best friend and as being disliked.

Popular children have a number of social skills that contribute to their being well liked. They give out reinforcements, listen carefully, maintain open lines of communication with peers, are happy, control their negative emotions, act like themselves, show enthusiasm and concern for others, and are self-confident without being conceited (Hartup, 1983; Rubin, Bukowski, & Parker, 1998). Rejected children often have serious adjustment problems (Rubin & others, 2013).

John Coie (2004, pp. 252–253) provided three reasons why aggressive, peer-rejected boys have problems in social relationships:

- "First, the rejected, aggressive boys are more impulsive and have problems sustaining attention. As a result, they are more likely to be disruptive of ongoing activities in the classroom and in focused group play.
- Second, rejected, aggressive boys are more emotionally reactive. They are aroused to anger more easily and probably have more difficulty calming down once aroused. Because of this they are more prone to become angry at peers and attack them verbally and physically. . . .
- Third, rejected children have fewer social skills in making friends and maintaining positive relationships with peers."

Not all rejected children are aggressive (Rubin & others, 2013). Although aggression and its related characteristics of impulsiveness and disruptiveness underlie rejection about half the time, approximately 10 to 20 percent of rejected children are shy.

How can rejected children be trained to interact more effectively with their peers? Rejected children may be taught to more accurately assess whether the intentions of their peers are negative (Bierman & Powers, 2009). They may be asked to engage in role playing or to discuss hypothetical situations involving negative encounters with peers, such as when a peer cuts into

popular children Children who are frequently nominated as a best friend and are rarely disliked by their peers.

average children Children who receive an average number of both positive and negative nominations from peers.

neglected children Children who are infrequently nominated as a best friend but are not disliked by their peers.

rejected children Children who are infrequently nominated as a best friend and are actively disliked by their peers.

controversial children Children who are frequently nominated both as a best friend and as being disliked by their peers.

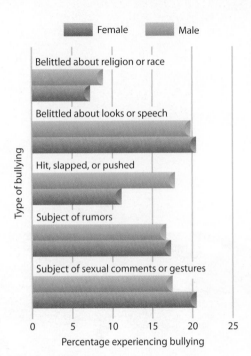

Female   Male

Belittled about religion or race

Belittled about looks or speech

Hit, slapped, or pushed

Subject of rumors

Subject of sexual comments or gestures

Type of bullying

0   5   10   15   20   25
Percentage experiencing bullying

FIGURE 10.5

BULLYING BEHAVIORS AMONG U.S. YOUTH. This graph shows the type of bullying most often experienced by U.S. youth. The percentages reflect the extent to which bullied students said that they had experienced a particular type of bullying. In terms of gender, note that when they were bullied, boys were more likely to be hit, slapped, or pushed than girls were.

Who is likely to be bullied? What are some outcomes of bullying?

a line ahead of them. In some programs, children are shown videotapes of appropriate peer interaction and asked to draw lessons from what they have seen (Ladd, Buhs, & Troop, 2004).

SOCIAL COGNITION

A boy accidentally trips and knocks another boy's soft drink out of his hand. That boy misinterprets the encounter as hostile, which leads him to retaliate aggressively against the boy who tripped. Through repeated encounters of this kind, the aggressive boy's classmates come to perceive him as habitually acting in inappropriate ways.

This encounter demonstrates the importance of *social cognition*—thoughts about social matters, such as the aggressive boy's interpretation of an encounter as hostile and his classmates' perception of his behavior as inappropriate (Crone & Dahl, 2012; Vetter & others, 2014). Children's social cognition about their peers becomes increasingly important for understanding peer relationships in middle and late childhood. Of special interest are the ways in which children process information about peer relations and their social knowledge (Dodge, 2011a, b).

Kenneth Dodge (1983, 2011a, b) argues that children go through six steps in processing information about their social world: they selectively attend to social cues, attribute intent, generate goals, access behavioral scripts from memory, make decisions, and enact behavior. Dodge has found that aggressive boys are more likely to perceive another child's actions as hostile when the child's intention is ambiguous. And when aggressive boys search for cues to determine a peer's intention, they respond more rapidly, less efficiently, and less reflectively than do nonaggressive children. These are among the social cognitive factors believed to be involved in children's conflicts.

Social knowledge also is involved in children's ability to get along with peers. They need to know what goals to pursue in poorly defined or ambiguous situations, how to initiate and maintain a social bond, and what scripts to follow to get other children to be their friends. For example, as part of the script for getting friends, it helps to know that saying nice things, regardless of what the peer does or says, will make the peer like the child more.

BULLYING

Significant numbers of students are victimized by bullies (Olweus, 2013; Thornberg & Jungert, 2014; Tsitsika & others, 2014). In a national survey of more than 15,000 sixth-through tenth-grade students, nearly one of every three students said that they had experienced occasional or frequent involvement as a victim or perpetrator in bullying (Nansel & others, 2001). In this study, bullying was defined as verbal or physical behavior intended to disturb someone less powerful. As shown in Figure 10.5, being belittled about looks or speech was the most frequent type of bullying. Boys are more likely to be bullies than girls, but gender differences regarding victims of bullies are less clear (Peets, Hodges, & Salmivalli, 2011).

Who is likely to be bullied? In the study just described, boys and younger middle school students were most likely to be affected (Nansel & others, 2001). Children who said they were bullied reported more loneliness and difficulty in making friends, while those who did the bullying were more likely to have low grades and to smoke cigarettes and drink alcohol.

Researchers have found that anxious, socially withdrawn, and aggressive children are often the victims of bullying (Hanish & Guerra, 2004; Rubin & others, 2013). Anxious and socially withdrawn children may be victimized because they are nonthreatening and unlikely to retaliate if bullied, whereas aggressive children may be the targets of bullying because their behavior is irritating to bullies (Rubin & others, 2013). Overweight and obese children are often bullied (Puhl & King, 2013).

Social contexts such as poverty, family, school, and peer groups also influence bullying (Hilliard & others, 2014; Schwartz & others, 2010; Troop-Gordon & Ladd, 2014). A recent meta-analysis indicated that positive parenting behavior (including having good communication, a warm relationship, being involved, and engaging in supervision of their children) and negative parenting behavior (including child maltreatment—physical abuse and neglect), was related to a greater likelihood of becoming either a bully/victim or a victim at school (Lereya, Samara, & Wolke, 2013).

The social context of the peer group also plays an important role in bullying (Salmivalli, Peets, & Hodges, 2011). Recent research indicates that 70 to 80 percent of victims and their bullies are in the same school classroom (Salmivalli & Peets, 2009). Classmates are often aware of bullying incidents and in many cases witness bullying. In many cases, bullies torment victims to gain higher status in the peer group and bullies need others to witness their power displays. Many bullies are not rejected by the peer group. A recent longitudinal study explored the costs and benefits of bullying in the context of the peer group (Reijntjes & others, 2013). In this study children were initially assessed at 10 years of age and then followed into early adolescence. The results indicated that although young bullies may be on a developmental trajectory that over the long run is problematic, in the shorter term personal benefits of bullying often outweigh disadvantages. Frequent bullying was linked to high social status as indexed by perceived popularity in the peer group, and bullies also were characterized by self-perceived personal competence. Also, a recent study revealed that having supportive friends was linked to a lower level of bullying and victimization (Kendrick, Jutengren, & Stattin, 2012).

What are the outcomes of bullying? A recent study revealed that peer victimization in the fifth grade was associated with worse physical and mental health in the tenth grade (Bogart & others, 2014). Researchers have found that children who are bullied are more likely to experience depression, engage in suicidal ideation, and attempt suicide than their counterparts who have not been the victims of bullying (Undheim & Sund, 2013; Yen & others, 2014). A recent study indicated that peer victimization during the elementary school years was a leading indicator of internalizing problems (depression, for example) in adolescence (Schwartz & others, 2014). Also, a recent longitudinal study of more than 6,000 children found that children who were the victims of peer bullying from 4 to 10 years of age were more likely to engage in suicide ideation at 11½ years of age (Winsper & others, 2012). Consider these cases in which bullying was linked to suicide: an 8-year-old jumped out of a two-story building in Houston; a 13-year-old hanged himself in Houston; and teenagers harassed a girl so mercilessly that she killed herself in Massachusetts. A recent study also revealed that 11-year-olds who were victims of peer bullying were more likely to have a heightened risk of developing borderline personality disorder symptoms (a pervasive pattern of unstable interpersonal relationships, low self-image, and emotional difficulties) (Wolke & others, 2012).

An increasing concern is peer bullying and harassment on the Internet (called *cyberbullying*) (Bonanno & Hymel, 2013; Donnerstein, 2012; Wright & Li, 2013; Yang & others, 2013). A recent study involving third- to sixth-graders revealed that engaging in cyber aggression was related to loneliness, lower self-esteem, fewer mutual friendships, and lower peer popularity (Schoffstall & Cohen, 2011). Another recent study revealed that cyberbullying contributed to depression and suicidal ideation above and beyond the contribution of involvement in traditional types of bullying (physical and verbal bullying in school and in neighborhood contexts, for example) (Bonanno & Hymel, 2013). And a recent meta-analysis concluded that being the victim of cyberbullying was most likely to be associated with stress and suicidal ideation (Kowalski & others, 2014). Information about preventing cyberbullying can be found at www.stopcyberbullying.org/.

Increasing interest is being directed to finding ways to prevent and treat bullying and victimization (Low & others, 2013; Olweus, 2013; Saarento, Boulton, & Salmivalli, 2014). School-based interventions vary greatly, ranging from involving the whole school in an anti-bullying campaign to providing individualized social skills training (Alsaker & Valanover, 2012). One of the most promising bullying intervention programs has been created by Dan Olweus (2003, 2013). This program focuses on 6- to 15-year-olds with the goal of decreasing opportunities and rewards for bullying. School staff are instructed in ways to improve peer relations and make schools safer. When properly implemented, the program reduces bullying by 30 to 70 percent (Ericson, 2001; Olweus, 2003). Information on how to implement the program can be obtained from the Center for the Prevention of Violence at the University of Colorado (www.colorado.edu/espv/blueprints).

FRIENDS

Friendship is an important aspect of children's development (Neal, Neal, & Cappella, 2014; Rose & others, 2012). Like adult friendships, children's friendships are typically characterized by similarity (Brechwald & Prinstein, 2011). Throughout childhood, friends are more similar than dissimilar

developmental **connection**

Peers

Beginning in early adolescence, teenagers typically prefer to have a smaller number of friendships that are more intense and intimate. Chapter 12, p. 381

What are some characteristics of children's friendships?

intimacy in friendships Self-disclosure and the sharing of private thoughts.

in terms of age, sex, race, and many other factors. Friends often have similar attitudes toward school, similar educational aspirations, and closely aligned achievement orientations.

Why are children's friendships important? Willard Hartup (1983, 1996, 2009) has studied peer relations and friendship for more than three decades. He recently concluded that friends can provide cognitive and emotional resources from childhood through old age. For example, friends can foster self-esteem and a sense of well-being.

More specifically, children's friendships can serve six functions (Gottman & Parker, 1987):

- *Companionship.* Friendship provides children with a familiar partner and playmate, someone who is willing to spend time with them and join in collaborative activities.
- *Stimulation.* Friendship provides children with interesting information, excitement, and amusement.
- *Physical support.* Friendship provides time, resources, and assistance.
- *Ego support.* Friendship provides the expectation of support, encouragement, and feedback, which helps children maintain an impression of themselves as competent, attractive, and worthwhile individuals.
- *Social comparison.* Friendship provides information about where the child stands vis-à-vis others and whether the child is doing okay.
- *Affection and intimacy.* Friendship provides children with a warm, close, trusting relationship with another individual. **Intimacy in friendships** is characterized by self-disclosure and the sharing of private thoughts. Research reveals that intimate friendships may not appear until early adolescence (Berndt & Perry, 1990).

Although having friends can be a developmental advantage, not all friendships are alike (Vitaro, Boivin, & Bukowski, 2009; Wentzel, 2013). People differ in the company they keep—that is, who their friends are. Developmental advantages occur when children have friends who are socially skilled and supportive. However, it is not developmentally advantageous to have coercive and conflict-ridden friendships (Laursen & Pursell, 2009). A recent study found that students who engaged in classroom aggressive-disruptive behavior were more likely to have aggressive friends (Powers & Bierman, 2013).

Friendship also plays an important role in children's emotional well-being and academic success. Students with friends who are academically oriented are more likely to achieve success in school themselves (Wentzel, 2013). In one study, sixth-grade students who did not have a friend engaged in less prosocial behavior (cooperation, sharing, helping others), had lower grades, and were more emotionally distressed (depression, lower levels of well-being) than their counterparts who had one or more friends (Wentzel, Barry, & Caldwell, 2004). In this study, two years later, in the eighth grade, the students who did not have a friend in the sixth grade continued to be more emotionally distressed.

Review *Connect* Reflect

 Identify changes in peer relationships in middle and late childhood.

Review

- What developmental changes characterize peer relations in middle and late childhood?
- How does children's peer status influence their development?
- How is social cognition involved in children's peer relations?
- What is the nature of bullying?
- What are children's friendships like?

Connect

- Earlier in the chapter, you read that most developmentalists agree that peers play an important role in the development of

moral reasoning. Of the five peer status groups you learned about in this section of the chapter, in which group do you think children would have the least opportunity to fully develop their moral reasoning capacities and why?

Reflect *Your Own Personal Journey of Life*

- Which of the five peer statuses characterized you as a child? Did your peer status change in adolescence? How do you think your peer status as a child has influenced your development?

Contemporary Approaches to Student Learning   Socioeconomic Status, Ethnicity, and Culture

For most children, entering the first grade signals new obligations. They develop new relationships and adopt new standards by which to judge themselves. School provides children with a rich source of new ideas to shape their sense of self. They will spend many years in schools as members of small societies in which there are tasks to be accomplished, people to socialize with and be socialized by, and rules that define and limit behavior, feelings, and attitudes. By the time students graduate from high school, they have spent 12,000 hours in the classroom.

CONTEMPORARY APPROACHES TO STUDENT LEARNING

Controversy swirls about the best way to teach children and how to hold schools and teachers accountable for whether children are learning (Lynch, 2015; Powell, 2015).

Constructivist and Direct Instruction Approaches The **constructivist approach** to instruction is a learner-centered approach that emphasizes the importance of individuals actively constructing their knowledge and understanding with guidance from the teacher. In the constructivist view, teachers should not attempt to simply pour information into children's minds. Rather, children should be encouraged to explore their world, discover knowledge, reflect, and think critically with careful monitoring and meaningful guidance from the teacher (Robinson-Zanartu, Doerr, & Portman, 2015). Constructivists believe that for too long in American education children have been required to sit still, be passive learners, and rotely memorize irrelevant as well as relevant information.

Today, constructivism may include an emphasis on collaboration—children working with each other in their efforts to know and understand (Borich, 2014). A teacher with a constructivist instructional philosophy would not have children memorize information rotely but would give them opportunities to meaningfully construct the knowledge and understand the material while guiding their learning (Webb, Metha, & Jordan, 2013).

By contrast, the **direct instruction approach** is a structured, teacher-centered approach that is characterized by teacher direction and control, high teacher expectations for students' progress, maximum time spent by students on academic tasks, and efforts by the teacher to keep negative affect to a minimum. An important goal in the direct instruction approach is maximizing student learning time (Kilbane & Milman, 2014).

Advocates of the constructivist approach argue that the direct instruction approach turns children into passive learners and does not adequately challenge them to think in critical and creative ways (Robinson-Zanartu, Doerr, & Portman, 2015). Direct instruction enthusiasts say that the constructivist approaches do not give enough attention to the content of a discipline, such as history or science. They also believe that the constructivist approaches are too relativistic and vague.

Some experts in educational psychology believe that many effective teachers use both a constructivist *and* a direct instruction approach rather than relying exclusively on one or the other (Bransford & others, 2006; Parkay, 2013). Further, some circumstances may call more for a constructivist approach, others for a direct instruction approach. For example, experts increasingly recommend an explicit, intellectually engaging direct instruction approach when teaching students who have a reading or a writing disability (Berninger & O'Malley, 2011).

Is this classroom more likely constructivist or direct instruction? Explain.

constructivist approach A learner-centered approach that emphasizes the importance of individuals actively constructing their knowledge and understanding with guidance from the teacher.

direct instruction approach A structured, teacher-centered approach that is characterized by teacher direction and control, mastery of academic skills, high expectations for students' progress, maximum time spent on learning tasks, and efforts to keep negative affect to a minimum.

What are some issues involved in the No Child Left Behind legislation?

Accountability Since the 1990s, the U.S. public and governments at every level have demanded increased accountability from schools. One result was the spread of state-mandated testing to measure just what students had or had not learned (Brookhart & Nitko, 2015; McMillan, 2014). Many states identified objectives for students in their state and created tests to measure whether students were meeting those objectives. This approach became national policy in 2002 when the No Child Left Behind (NCLB) legislation was signed into law.

Advocates argue that statewide standardized testing will have a number of positive effects. These include improved student performance; more time spent teaching the subjects that are tested; high expectations for all students; identification of poorly performing schools, teachers, and administrators; and improved confidence in schools as test scores rise.

Critics argue that the NCLB legislation is doing more harm than good (Noddings, 2007; Sadker & Zittleman, 2012). One criticism stresses that using a single test as the sole indicator of students' progress and competence presents a very narrow view of students' skills (Lewis, 2007). This criticism is similar to the one leveled at IQ tests, which we described in Chapter 9. To assess student progress and achievement, many psychologists and educators emphasize that a number of measures should be used, including tests, quizzes, projects, portfolios, classroom observations, and so on. Also, the tests used as part of NCLB don't measure creativity, motivation, persistence, flexible thinking, and social skills (Stiggins, 2008). Critics point out that teachers end up spending far too much class time "teaching to the test" by drilling students and having them memorize isolated facts at the expense of teaching that focuses on the development of thinking skills, which students need for success in life (Pressley, 2007). Also, recall from Chapter 9 that some individuals are concerned that in the era of No Child Left Behind policy there is a neglect of gifted students in the effort to raise the achievement level of students who are not doing well (Clark, 2008).

Consider also the following: Each state is allowed to establish different criteria for what constitutes passing or failing grades on tests designated for NCLB inclusion. An analysis of NCLB data indicated that almost every fourth-grade student in Mississippi knows how to read but only half of Massachusetts' students do (Birman & others, 2007). Because state standards vary greatly, state-by-state comparisons of success on NCLB tests are likely to be unreliable. In the analysis of state-by-state comparisons, many states have taken the safe route and kept the standard for passing low. Thus, while one of NCLB's goals is to raise standards for achievement in U.S. schools, apparently allowing states to set their own standards has lowered achievement standards.

Despite such criticisms, the U.S. Department of Education is committed to implementing No Child Left Behind, and schools are making accommodations to meet the requirements of this law. Indeed, most educators endorse the value of establishing high expectations and high standards of excellence for students and teachers. At issue, however, is whether the tests and procedures mandated by NCLB are the best route for achieving these high standards (McMillan, 2014).

SOCIOECONOMIC STATUS, ETHNICITY, AND CULTURE

Children from low-income, ethnic minority backgrounds have more difficulties in school than do their middle-socioeconomic-status, White counterparts. Why? Critics argue that schools have not done a good job of educating low-income, ethnic minority students to overcome the barriers to their achievement (Spring, 2014). Let's further explore the roles of socioeconomic status, ethnicity, and culture in schools.

The Education of Students from Low-Income Backgrounds Many children living in poverty face problems that present barriers to their learning (Crosnoe & Leventhal, 2014). They might have parents who don't set high educational standards for them, who are incapable of reading to them, or who don't have enough money to pay for educational materials and experiences, such as books and trips to zoos and museums. They may be malnourished or live in areas where crime and violence are a way of life. One study revealed that the longer children experienced poverty, the more detrimental the poverty was to their cognitive development (Najman & others, 2009).

In *The Shame of a Nation,* Jonathan Kozol (2005) criticized the inadequate quality and lack of resources in many U.S. schools, especially those in the poverty areas of inner cities that have high concentrations of ethnic minority children. Kozol praises teachers like Angela Lively (*above*), who keeps a box of shoes in her Indianapolis classroom for students in need.

Compared with schools in higher-income areas, schools in low-income areas are more likely to have more students with low achievement test scores, low graduation rates, and smaller percentages of students going to college; they are more likely to have young teachers with less experience; and they are more likely to encourage rote learning (Nelson, Palonsky, & McCarthy, 2013; Weisner & Duncan, 2014). Many of the schools' buildings and classrooms are old and crumbling. These are the types of undesirable conditions Jonathan Kozol (2005) observed in many inner-city schools, including the South Bronx in New York City, as described at the beginning of the chapter. In sum, far too many schools in low-income neighborhoods provide students with environments that are not conducive to effective learning (McLoyd, Mistry, & Hardaway, 2014).

Much of the focus on the lives of children living in poverty has emphasized improving their future prospects in educational and economic development. A recent analysis concluded that their social and emotional functioning has often been ignored and should be given more attention (Crosnoe & Leventhal, 2014). Further, efforts to intervene in the lives of children living in poverty need to jointly focus on schools and neighborhoods (Gershoff & Benner, 2014).

Ethnicity in Schools More than one-third of all African American and almost one-third of all Latino students attend schools in the 47 largest city school districts in the United States, compared with only 5 percent of all White and 22 percent of all Asian American students. Many of these inner-city schools continue to be racially segregated, are grossly underfunded, and do not provide adequate opportunities for children to learn effectively. Thus, the effects of SES and the effects of ethnicity are often intertwined (Banks, 2014; Koppelman, 2014).

The school experiences of students from different ethnic groups vary considerably (Crosnoe & Leventhal, 2014). African American and Latino students are much less likely than non-Latino White or Asian American students to be enrolled in academic, college preparatory programs and are much more likely to be enrolled in remedial and special education programs. Asian American students are far more likely than other ethnic minority groups to take advanced math and science courses in high school. African American students are twice as likely as Latinos, Native Americans, or non-Latino Whites to be suspended from school.

However, it is very important to note that diversity characterizes every ethnic group (Cushner, McClelland, & Safford, 2015; Spring, 2014). For example, the higher percentage of Asian American students in advanced classes is mainly true for students with Chinese, Taiwanese, Japanese, Korean, and East Indian cultural backgrounds, but students with Hmong and Vietnamese cultural backgrounds have had less academic success.

Following are some strategies for improving relationships among ethnically diverse students:

- *Turn the class into a jigsaw classroom.* When Eliot Aronson was a professor at the University of Texas at Austin, the school system contacted him for ideas on how to reduce the increasing racial tension in classrooms. Aronson (1986) developed the concept of a "jigsaw classroom" in which students from different cultural backgrounds are placed in a cooperative group in which they have to construct different parts of a project to reach a common goal. Aronson used the term *jigsaw* because he saw the technique as much like a group of students cooperating to put different pieces together to complete a jigsaw puzzle. How might this work? Team sports, drama productions, and musical performances are examples of contexts in which students participate cooperatively to reach a common goal; however, the jigsaw technique also lends itself to group science projects, history reports, and other learning experiences with a variety of subject matter.

- *Encourage students to have positive personal contact with diverse other students.* Mere contact does not do the job of improving relationships with diverse others. For example, busing ethnic minority students to predominantly White schools, or vice versa, has not reduced prejudice or improved interethnic relations. What matters is what happens after children get to school. Especially beneficial in improving interethnic relations is sharing one's worries, successes, failures, coping strategies, interests, and other personal information with people of other ethnicities. When this happens, people tend to look at others as individuals rather than as members of a homogeneous group.

- *Reduce bias.* Teachers can reduce bias by displaying images of children from diverse ethnic and cultural groups, selecting play materials and classroom activities that encourage cultural understanding, helping students resist stereotyping, and working with parents to reduce children's exposure to bias and prejudice at home.

- *View the school and community as a team.* James Comer (1988, 2004, 2006, 2010) advocates a community-based, team approach as the best way to educate children. Three important aspects of the Comer Project for Change are (1) a governance and management team that develops a comprehensive school plan, assessment strategy, and staff development plan; (2) a mental health or school support team; and (3) a parents' program. Comer believes that the entire school community should have a cooperative rather than an adversarial attitude. The Comer program is currently operating in more than 600 schools in 26 states. Read further about James Comer's work in the *Connecting with Careers* profile.

- *Be a competent cultural mediator.* Teachers can play a powerful role as cultural mediators by being sensitive to biased content in materials and classroom interactions, learning more about different ethnic groups, being aware of children's ethnic attitudes, viewing students of color positively, and thinking of positive ways to get parents of color more involved as partners with teachers in educating children.

Cross-Cultural Comparisons In the past three decades, the poor performance of American children in math and science has been well publicized. In a large-scale comparison of math and science achievement by fourth-grade students in 2007, the average fourth-grade math score in the United States was higher than in 23 of the 35 countries and lower than in 8 countries (all in Asia and Europe) (National Center for Education Statistics, 2009). Fourth-graders from Hong Kong had the highest average math score. The average fourth-grade U.S. math score did improve slightly (11 points) from the same assessment in 1995, but some Asian countries improved their scores considerably more—the Hong Kong score was 50 points higher and the Slovenia score 40 points higher in 2007 than in 1995, for example.

In 2007, the average fourth-grade U.S. science score was higher than those in 25 countries and lower than those in 4 countries (all in Asia). However, the average U.S. fourth-grade science score decreased 3 points from 1995 to 2007 while the average science scores in some countries increased dramatically—63 points in Singapore, 56 points in Latvia, and 55 points in Iran, for example.

Harold Stevenson's (1995, 2000; Stevenson, Hofer, & Randel, 1999; Stevenson & others, 1990) research explores possible reasons for the poor performance of American

James Comer, Child Psychiatrist

James Comer grew up in a low-income neighborhood in East Chicago, Indiana, and credits his parents with leaving him with no doubt about the importance of education. He earned a BA degree from Indiana University and went on to obtain a medical degree from Howard University College of Medicine, a Master of Public Health degree from the University of Michigan School of Public Health, and psychiatry training at the Yale University School of Medicine's Child Study Center. He currently is the Maurice Falk professor of Child Psychiatry at the Yale University Child Study Center and an associate dean at the Yale University Medical School. During his years at Yale, Comer has concentrated his career on promoting a focus on child development as a way of improving schools. His efforts in support of healthy development of young people have received international recognition.

Comer is, perhaps, best known for founding the School Development Program in 1968, which promotes the collaboration of parents, educators, and communities to improve social, emotional, and academic outcomes for children.

James Comer is shown with some of the inner-city children who attend a school that became a better learning environment because of Comer's intervention.

For more information about what child psychiatrists do, see page 42 in the Careers in Life-Span Development appendix.

For more information about what child psychiatrists do, see page 42 in the Careers in Life-Span Development appendix.

students compared with students in selected Asian countries. Stevenson and his colleagues have completed five cross-cultural comparisons of students in the United States, China, Taiwan, and Japan. In these studies, Asian students consistently outperform American students. And, the longer the students are in school, the wider the gap becomes between Asian and American students—the lowest difference is in the first grade, the highest in the eleventh grade (the highest grade studied).

To learn more about the reasons for these large cross-cultural differences, Stevenson and his colleagues spent thousands of hours observing in classrooms, as well as interviewing and surveying teachers, students, and parents. They found that the Asian teachers spent more of their time teaching math than did the American teachers. For example, more than one-fourth of total classroom time in the first grade was spent on math instruction in Japan, compared with only one-tenth of the time in the U.S. first-grade classrooms. Also, the Asian students were in school an average of 240 days a year, compared with 178 days in the United States.

How do U.S. students fare against Asian students in math and science achievement? What were some findings in Stevenson's research that might explain the results of those international comparisons?

In addition to the substantially greater time spent on math instruction in the Asian schools than the American schools, differences were found between the Asian and American parents. The American parents had much lower expectations for their children's education and achievement than did the Asian parents. Also, the American parents were more likely to believe that their children's math achievement was due to innate ability, while the Asian parents were more likely to say that their children's math achievement was the consequence of effort and training (see Figure 10.6). The Asian students were more likely to do math homework than were the American students, and the Asian parents were far more likely to help their children with their math homework than were the American parents (Chen & Stevenson, 1989).

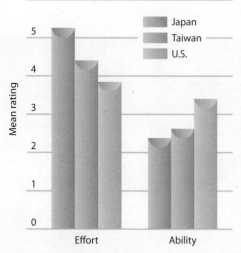

FIGURE **10.6**

MOTHERS' BELIEFS ABOUT THE FACTORS RESPONSIBLE FOR CHILDREN'S MATH ACHIEVEMENT IN THREE COUNTRIES. In one study, mothers in Japan and Taiwan were more likely to believe that their children's math achievement was due to effort rather than innate ability, while U.S. mothers were more likely to believe their children's math achievement was due to innate ability (Stevenson, Lee, & Stigler, 1986). If parents believe that their children's math achievement is due to innate ability and their children are not doing well in math, the implication is that they are less likely to think their children will benefit from putting forth more effort.

Related to the differences between Asian and U.S. parents in explaining the roles of effort and ability, Carol Dweck (2006, 2013, 2014) described the importance of children's **mindset,** which she defines as the cognitive view individuals develop for themselves. She concludes that individuals have one of two mindsets: (1) a *fixed mindset,* in which they believe that their qualities are carved in stone and cannot change; or (2) a *growth mindset,* in which they believe their qualities can change and improve through their effort.

Dweck (2006, 2013, 2014) argued that individuals' mindsets influence whether they will be optimistic or pessimistic, what their goals will be and how hard they will strive to reach those goals, and what they will achieve. Dweck says that mindsets begin to be shaped in childhood as children interact with parents, teachers, and coaches, who themselves have either a fixed mindset or a growth mindset.

Related to her emphasis on encouraging students to develop a growth mindset, Dweck and her colleagues (Blackwell & Dweck, 2008; Blackwell & others, 2007; Dweck, 2013; Dweck & Master, 2009) have recently incorporated information about the brain's plasticity into their effort to improve students' motivation to achieve and succeed. In one study, they assigned two groups of students to eight sessions of either (1) study skills instruction or (2) study skills instruction plus information about the importance of developing a growth mindset (called incremental theory in the research) (Blackwell & others, 2007). One of the exercises in the growth mindset group was titled "You Can Grow Your Brain" and emphasized that the brain is like a muscle that can change and grow as it is exercised and develops new connections. Students were informed that the more you challenge your brain to learn, the more your brain cells grow. Both groups had a pattern of declining math scores prior to the intervention. Following the intervention, the group who only received the study skills instruction continued to decline, but the group that received the combination of study skills instruction plus the growth mindset emphasis reversed the downward trend and improved their math achievement.

In other work, Dweck has been creating a computer-based workshop, "Brainology," to teach students that their intelligence can change (Blackwell & Dweck, 2008; Dweck, 2013). Students experience six modules about how the brain works and how they can make their brain improve (see Figure 10.7). After the program was tested in 20 New York City schools, students strongly endorsed the value of the computer-based brain modules. Said one student, "I will try harder because I know that the more you try the more your brain knows" (Dweck & Master, 2009, p. 137).

In the *Connecting Through Research* interlude, you can read further about efforts to discover why parenting practices are likely to be an important aspect of the lower achievement of U.S. children compared to East Asian children, as well as have possible implications for other aspects of children's development.

FIGURE **10.7**

DWECK'S BRAINOLOGY PROGRAM. A screen shot from Carol Dweck's Brainology program, which is designed to cultivate children's growth mindset.

mindset The cognitive view, either fixed or growth, that individuals develop for themselves.

connecting through research

Parenting and Children's Achievement: My Child Is My Report Card, Tiger Moms, and Tiger Babies Strike Back

There is rising concern that U.S. children are not reaching their full academic potential, which ultimately will reduce the success of the United States in competing with other countries (Pomerantz, 2013). Eva Pomerantz is interested in identifying how parents can maximize their children's motivation and achievement in school while also maintaining positive emotional adjustment. To this end, Pomerantz and her colleagues are conducting research with children and their parents not only in the United States but also in China, where children often attain higher levels of achievement than their U.S. counterparts (Pomerantz, Cheung, & Qin, 2012; Pomerantz & Kempner, 2013; Pomerantz, Kim, & Cheung, 2012).

As indicated earlier in Harold Stevenson's research, East Asian parents spend considerably more time helping their children with homework than do U.S. parents (Chen & Stevenson, 1989). Pomerantz's research indicates that East Asian parental involvement in children's learning is present as early as the preschool years and continues during the elementary school years (Cheung & Pomerantz, 2012; Ng, Pomerantz, & Deng, 2014; Ng, Pomerantz, & Lam, 2013; Siegler & Mu, 2008). In East Asia, children's learning is considered to be a far greater responsibility of parents than in the United States (Ng, Pomerantz, & Lam, 2013; Pomerantz, Kim, & Cheung, 2012). However, a recent study revealed that when U.S. parents are more involved in their children's learning, the children's achievement benefits (Cheung & Pomerantz, 2012). In this study, more than 800 U.S. and Chinese children (average age = 12.73 years) reported on their parents' involvement in their learning and their motivation in school every six months from the

Qing Zhou, who has recently conducted research on authoritarian parenting of immigrant children, with her children. *What are the results of her research?*

fall of seventh grade to the end of eighth grade. The researchers also collected data on children's self-regulated learning strategies and grades. Over time, the more involved parents were in children's learning, the more strongly motivated children were to do well academically for parent-oriented reasons, which improved children's self-regulated learning and grades.

In addition to studying parental involvement in children's learning, Pomerantz and her colleagues also are conducting research on the role of parental control in children's achievement. In a recent study in which the title of the research study included the phrase "My Child Is My Report Card," Chinese mothers exerted more control (especially psychological control) over their children than did U.S. mothers (Ng, Pomerantz, & Deng, 2014). Also in this study, Chinese mothers' self-worth was more contingent on their children's achievement than was the case for U.S. mothers.

Pomerantz's research reflects the term "training parents," a variation of authoritarian parenting, that was described in Chapter 8, in which the parenting strategy of many Asian parents is to train their children to achieve high levels of academic success. In 2011, Amy Chua's book, *Battle Hymn of the Tiger Mom,* sparked considerable interest in the role of parenting in children's achievement. Chua uses the term *Tiger Mom* to mean a mother who engages in strict disciplinarian practices. In another recent book, *Tiger Babies Strike Back*, Kim Wong Keltner (2013) argues that the Tiger Mom parenting style can be so demanding and confining that being an Asian American child is like being in an "emotional jail." She says that the Tiger Mom authoritarian style does provide some advantages for children, such as learning to go for what you want and not to take no for an answer, but that too often the results are not worth the emotional costs.

Recent research on Chinese-American immigrant families with first- and second-grade children has found that the children with authoritarian (highly controlling parents) are more aggressive, are more depressed, have a higher anxiety level, and show poorer social skills than children whose parents had non-authoritarian styles (Zhou & others, 2012). Qing Zhou (2013), lead author on the study just described and the director of the University of California's Culture and Family Laboratory, is conducting workshops to teach Chinese mothers positive parenting strategies such as listening skills, praising their children for good behavior, and spending more time with their children in fun activities.

Further, a longitudinal study involving students from adolescence to emerging adulthood found that four parenting styles were primarily used in Chinese American families: supportive, tiger, easygoing, and harsh (Kim & others, 2013). In this study, the supportive style was the most common and was linked to the best outcomes, followed by easygoing, tiger, and harsh styles. Compared with a supportive style, the tiger style was associated with a lower grade point average, more depressive symptoms, and greater alienation.

In sum, there are concerns that an intensely authoritarian, highly controlling style may produce more negative outcomes for not only U.S. children and adolescents, but also for Asian American children and adolescents (Kim & others, 2013).

What do you think: What are the best parenting strategies overall for rearing children to reach high levels of achievement and be emotionally healthy?

Review *Connect* Reflect

 Characterize aspects of schooling in children's development in middle and late childhood.

Review

- What are two major contemporary issues in educating children?
- How do socioeconomic status, ethnicity, and culture influence schooling?

Connect

- One of Carol Dweck's exercises in the growth-mindset group was titled "You Can Grow Your Brain." Can you actually grow your brain? What physical changes, if any, are still occurring in the brain in middle and late childhood?

Reflect *Your Own Personal Journey of Life*

- How would you rate the quality of your teachers in elementary school? Were their expectations for your achievement too low or too high?

---

topical connections *looking forward*

In adolescence, children begin spending more time thinking about their identity—who they are, what they are all about, and where they are going in life. Time spent with peers increases in adolescence, and friendships become more intense and intimate. Dating and romantic relationships also become more central to the lives of most adolescents. Parents continue to have an important influence on adolescent development. Having good relationships with parents provides support for adolescents as they seek more autonomy and explore a widening social world. Problems that adolescents can develop include juvenile delinquency and depression.

---

reach your **learning goals**

Socioemotional Development in Middle and Late Childhood

1 Emotional and Personality Development

 Discuss emotional and personality development in middle and late childhood.

> The Self

- In middle and late childhood, self-understanding increasingly involves social and psychological characteristics, including social comparison. Children increase their perspective taking in middle and late childhood, and their social understanding shows increasing psychological sophistication as well. Self-concept refers to domain-specific evaluations of the self. Self-esteem refers to global evaluations of the self and is also referred to as self-worth or self-image. Self-esteem is only moderately related to school performance but is more strongly linked to initiative. Four ways to increase self-esteem are to (1) identify the causes of low self-esteem, (2) provide emotional support and social approval, (3) help children achieve, and (4) help children cope. Self-efficacy is the belief that one can master a situation and produce positive outcomes. Bandura believes that self-efficacy is a critical factor in whether students will achieve. Schunk argues that self-efficacy influences a student's choice of tasks, with low-efficacy students avoiding many learning tasks. The development of self-regulation is an important aspect of children's development. Erikson's fourth stage of development, industry versus inferiority, characterizes the middle and late childhood years.

Emotional Development

- Developmental changes in emotion include increased understanding of complex emotions such as pride and shame, detecting that more than one emotion can be experienced in a particular situation, taking into account the circumstances that led up to an emotional reaction, improvements in the ability to suppress and conceal negative emotions, and the use of self-initiated strategies to redirect feelings. As children get older, they use a greater variety of coping strategies and more cognitive strategies.

Moral Development

- Kohlberg argued that moral development occurs on three levels—preconventional, conventional, and postconventional—and six stages (two at each level). Kohlberg maintained that these stages were age-related. Influences on movement through the stages include cognitive development, imitation and cognitive conflict, peer relations, and perspective taking. Criticisms of Kohlberg's theory have been made, especially by Gilligan, who advocates a stronger care perspective. Other criticisms focus on the inadequacy of moral reasoning to predict moral behavior, culture, and family influences. The domain theory of moral development states that there are different domains of social knowledge and reasoning, including moral, social conventional, and personal. Prosocial behavior involves positive moral behaviors such as sharing. Most sharing in the first three years is not done for empathy, but at about 4 years of age empathy contributes to sharing. By the start of the elementary school years, children express objective ideas about fairness. By the mid- to late elementary school years, children believe equity can mean that others with special needs/merit deserve special treatment. Recently, there has been a surge of interest in moral personality.

Gender

- Gender stereotypes are prevalent around the world. A number of physical differences exist between males and females. Some experts argue that cognitive differences between males and females have been exaggerated. In terms of socioemotional differences, males are more physically aggressive than females, whereas females regulate their emotions better and engage in more prosocial behavior than males do. Gender-role classification focuses on the degree to which individuals are masculine, feminine, or androgynous. Androgyny means having positive feminine and masculine characteristics. It is important to think about gender in terms of context.

2 Families

LG2 Describe developmental changes in parent-child relationships, parents as managers, attachment in families, and stepfamilies.

Developmental Changes in Parent-Child Relationships

- Parents spend less time with children during middle and late childhood than in early childhood. Parents especially play an important role in supporting and stimulating children's academic achievement. Discipline changes, and control becomes more coregulatory.

Parents as Managers

- Parents have important roles as managers of children's opportunities, as monitors of their behavior, and as social initiators and arrangers. Mothers are more likely to function in these parental management roles than fathers are.

Attachment in Families

- Secure attachment to parents is linked to a lower level of internalized symptoms, anxiety, and depression in children during middle and late childhood. Also in middle and late childhood, attachment becomes more complex as children's social worlds expand.

Stepfamilies

- As in divorced families, children living in stepparent families face more adjustment problems than their counterparts in nondivorced families. However, a majority of children in stepfamilies do not have adjustment problems. Children in complex (blended) stepfamilies have more problems than children in simple stepfamilies or nondivorced families.

3 Peers

LG3 Identify changes in peer relationships in middle and late childhood.

Developmental Changes

- Among the developmental changes in peer relations in middle and late childhood are increased preference for same-sex groups, increased time spent in peer relations, and less supervision of the peer group by adults.

Peer Status

- Popular children are frequently named as a best friend and are rarely disliked by their peers. Average children receive an average number of both positive and negative nominations from their peers. Neglected children are infrequently named as a best friend but are not disliked by their peers. Rejected children are infrequently named as a best friend and are actively disliked by their peers. Controversial children are frequently named both as a best friend and as being disliked by peers. Rejected children are especially at risk for a number of problems.

- Social information-processing skills and social knowledge are two important dimensions of social cognition in peer relations.

- Significant numbers of children are bullied, and this can result in short-term and long-term negative effects for both the victims and bullies.

- Like adult friends, children who are friends tend to be similar to each other. Children's friendships serve six functions: companionship, stimulation, physical support, ego support, social comparison, and intimacy/affection.

Social Cognition

Bullying

Friends

4 Schools

LG4 Characterize aspects of schooling in children's development in middle and late childhood.

Contemporary Approaches to Student Learning

Socioeconomic Status, Ethnicity, and Culture

- Two contemporary issues involve whether it is best to educate students by using a constructivist approach (a learner-centered approach) or a direct instruction approach (a teacher-centered approach) and how to hold teachers accountable for whether children are learning. In the United States, standardized testing of elementary school students has been mandated by many state governments and by the No Child Left Behind federal legislation. Numerous criticisms of NCLB have been made.

- Children in poverty face many barriers to learning at school as well as at home. The effects of SES and ethnicity on schools are intertwined, and many U.S. schools are segregated. Low expectations for ethnic minority children represent one of the barriers to their learning. American children are more achievement-oriented than children in many countries but are less achievement-oriented than many children in Asian countries such as China, Taiwan, and Japan. Mindset is the cognitive view, either fixed or growth, that individuals develop for themselves. Dweck argues that a key aspect of supporting children's development is to guide them in developing a growth mindset. Pomerantz emphasizes that parental involvement is a key aspect of children's achievement.

key terms

perspective taking 305
self-esteem 306
self-concept 306
self-efficacy 307
preconventional reasoning 310
heteronomous morality 310
individualism, instrumental
   purpose, and exchange 311
conventional reasoning 311

mutual interpersonal
   expectations, relationships,
   and interpersonal
   conformity 311
social systems morality 311
postconventional
   reasoning 311
social contract or utility and
   individual rights 311

universal ethical principles 312
justice perspective 312
care perspective 312
domain theory of moral
   development 312
social conventional
   reasoning 313
gender stereotypes 315
androgyny 318

popular children 323
average children 323
neglected children 323
rejected children 323
controversial children 323
intimacy in friendships 326
constructivist approach 327
direct instruction approach 327
mindset 332

key people

Diane Ruble 305
Albert Bandura 307
Dale Schunk 308
Jonathan Kozol 304
Erik Erikson 308
Lawrence Kohlberg 310

Carol Gilligan 313
William Damon 314
Sandra Bem 318
William Pollack 318
Kathryn Kerns 321
E. Mavis Hetherington 321

John Coie 323
Kenneth Dodge 324
Dan Olweus 325
Willard Hartup 326
Eliot Aronson 329
James Comer 330

Harold Stevenson 330
Carol Dweck 332
Eva Pomerantz 333

In no order of things is adolescence the simple time of life.

—JEAN ERSKINE STEWART
American Writer, 20th Century

Adolescence

Adolescents try on one face after another, seeking to find a face of their own. Their generation of young people is the fragile cable by which the best and the worst of their parents' generation is transmitted to the present. In the end, there are only two lasting bequests parents can leave youth— one is roots, the other wings. Section 6 contains two chapters: "Physical and Cognitive Development in Adolescence" (Chapter 11) and "Socioemotional Development in Adolescence" (Chapter 12).

chapter 11

PHYSICAL AND COGNITIVE DEVELOPMENT IN ADOLESCENCE

chapter outline

1 The Nature of Adolescence

Learning Goal 1 Discuss the nature of adolescence.

2 Physical Changes

Learning Goal 2 Describe the changes involved in puberty, as well as changes in the brain and sexuality during adolescence.

Puberty
The Brain
Adolescent Sexuality

3 Issues in Adolescent Health

Learning Goal 3 Identify adolescent problems related to health, substance use and abuse, and eating disorders.

Adolescent Health
Substance Use and Abuse
Eating Disorders

4 Adolescent Cognition

Learning Goal 4 Explain cognitive changes in adolescence.

Piaget's Theory
Adolescent Egocentrism
Information Processing

5 Schools

Learning Goal 5 Summarize some key aspects of how schools influence adolescent development.

The Transition to Middle or Junior High School
Effective Schools for Young Adolescents
High School
Extracurricular Activities
Service Learning

Fifteen-year-old Latisha developed a drinking problem, and she was kicked off the cheerleading squad for missing too many practice sessions—but that didn't make her stop drinking. She and her friends began skipping school regularly so they could drink.

Fourteen-year-old Arnie is a juvenile delinquent. Last week he stole a TV set, struck his mother and bloodied her face, broke some streetlights in the neighborhood, and threatened a boy with a wrench and hammer.

Twelve-year-old Katie, more than just about anything else, wanted a playground in her town. She knew that the other kids also wanted one, so she put together a group that generated funding ideas for the playground. They presented their ideas to the town council. Her group attracted more youth, and they raised money by selling candy and sandwiches door-to-door. The playground became a reality, a place where, as Katie says, "People have picnics and make friends." Katie's advice: "You won't get anywhere if you don't try."

Adolescents like Latisha and Arnie are the ones we hear about the most. But there are many adolescents like Katie who contribute in positive ways to their communities and competently make the transition through adolescence. Indeed, for most young people, adolescence is not a time of rebellion, crisis, pathology, and deviance. A far more accurate vision of adolescence is that it is a time of evaluation, decision making, commitment, and carving out a place in the world. Most of the problems of today's youth are not with the youth themselves, but with needs that go unmet. To reach their full potential, adolescents need a range of legitimate opportunities as well as long-term support from adults who care deeply about them (Fisher & others, 2013; Lerner & others, 2013).

Katie Bell (*front*) and some of her volunteers.

topical connections *looking back*

In middle and late childhood, physical growth continues but at a slower pace than in infancy and early childhood. Gross motor skills become much smoother and more coordinated, and fine motor skills also improve. Significant advances in the development of the prefrontal cortex occur. Cognitive and language skills also improve considerably. In terms of cognitive development, most children become concrete operational thinkers, long-term memory increases, and metacognitive skills improve, especially if children learn a rich repertoire of strategies. In terms of language development, children's understanding of grammar and syntax increases, and learning to read becomes an important achievement.

preview

Adolescence is a transitional period in the human life span, linking childhood and adulthood. We begin the chapter by examining some general characteristics of adolescence and then explore the major physical changes and health issues of adolescence. Next, we consider the significant cognitive changes that characterize adolescence and conclude the chapter by describing various aspects of schools for adolescents.

1 The Nature of Adolescence   LG1 Discuss the nature of adolescence.

As in development during childhood, genetic/biological and environmental/social factors influence adolescent development. During their childhood years, adolescents experienced thousands of hours of interactions with parents, peers, and teachers, but now they face dramatic biological changes, new experiences, and new developmental tasks. Relationships with parents take a different form, moments with peers become more intimate, and dating occurs for the first time, as do sexual exploration and possibly intercourse. The adolescent's thoughts become more abstract and idealistic. Biological changes trigger a heightened interest in body image. Adolescence has both continuity and discontinuity with childhood.

There is a long history of worrying about how adolescents will "turn out." In 1904, G. Stanley Hall proposed the "storm-and-stress" view that adolescence is a turbulent time charged with conflict and mood swings. However, when Daniel Offer and his colleagues (1988) studied the self-images of adolescents in the United States, Australia, Bangladesh, Hungary, Israel, Italy, Japan, Taiwan, Turkey, and West Germany, at least 73 percent of the adolescents displayed a healthy self-image. Although there were differences among them, the adolescents were happy most of the time, they enjoyed life, they perceived themselves as able to exercise self-control, they valued work and school, they felt confident about their sexual selves, they expressed positive feelings toward their families, and they felt they had the capability to cope with life's stresses—not exactly a storm-and-stress portrayal of adolescence.

Public attitudes about adolescence emerge from a combination of personal experience and media portrayals, neither of which produces an objective picture of how normal adolescents develop (Feldman & Elliott, 1990). Some of the readiness to assume the worst about adolescents likely involves the short memories of adults. Many adults measure their current perceptions of adolescents by their memories of their own adolescence. Adults may portray

Growing up has never been easy. However, adolescence is not best viewed as a time of rebellion, crisis, pathology, and deviance. A far more accurate vision of adolescence describes it as a time of evaluation, of decision making, of commitment, and of carving out a place in the world. Most of the problems of today's youth are not with the youth themselves. What adolescents need is access to a range of legitimate opportunities and to long-term support from adults who care deeply about them. *What might be some examples of such support and caring?*

today's adolescents as more troubled, less respectful, more self-centered, more assertive, and more adventurous than they were.

However, in matters of taste and manners, the young people of every generation have seemed unnervingly radical and different from adults—different in how they look, in how they behave, in the music they enjoy, in their hairstyles, and in the clothing they choose. It would be an enormous error, though, to confuse adolescents' enthusiasm for trying on new identities and enjoying moderate amounts of outrageous behavior with hostility toward parental and societal standards. Acting out and boundary testing are time-honored ways in which adolescents move toward accepting, rather than rejecting, parental values.

Most adolescents negotiate the lengthy path to adult maturity successfully, but too large a group does not. Ethnic, cultural, gender, socioeconomic, age, and lifestyle differences influence the actual life trajectory of each adolescent (Huston, 2014; McLoyd, Mistry, & Hardaway, 2014). Different portrayals of adolescence emerge, depending on the particular group of adolescents being described. Today's adolescents are exposed to a complex menu of lifestyle options through the media, and many face the temptations of drug use and sexual activity at increasingly young ages. Too many adolescents are not provided with adequate opportunities and support to become competent adults (Crosnoe & Leventhal, 2014; Lerner & others, 2013).

Recall from Chapter 1 that *social policy* is the course of action designed by the national government to influence the welfare of its citizens. Currently, many researchers in adolescent development are designing studies that they hope will lead to wise and effective social policy decision making (Eccles & Roeser, 2013; Granger, Tseng, & Wilcox, 2014).

Research indicates that youth benefit enormously when they have caring adults in their lives in addition to parents or guardians (Nieto & Yoshikawa, 2014). Caring adults—such as coaches, neighbors, teachers, mentors, and after-school leaders—can serve as role models, confidants, advocates, and resources. Relationships with caring adults are powerful when youth know they are respected, that they matter to the adult, and that the adult wants to be a resource in their lives. However, in a recent survey, only 20 percent of U.S. 15-year-olds reported having meaningful relationships with adults outside their family who are helping them to succeed in life (Search Institute, 2010).

Review Connect Reflect

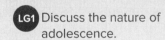 Discuss the nature of adolescence.

Review
- What characterizes adolescent development? What especially needs to be done to improve the lives of adolescents?

Connect
- In this section you read about how important it is for adolescents to have caring adults in their lives. In previous chapters, what did you learn about the role parents play in their children's lives leading up to adolescence that might influence adolescents' development?

Reflect *Your Own Personal Journey of Life*
- Was your adolescence better described as a stormy and stressful time or as one of trying out new identities as you sought to find an identity of your own? Explain.

2 Physical Changes

LG2 Describe the changes involved in puberty, as well as changes in the brain and sexuality during adolescence.

Puberty   The Brain   Adolescent Sexuality

One father remarked that the problem with his teenage son was not that he grew, but that he did not know when to stop growing. As we will see, there is considerable variation in the timing of the adolescent growth spurt. In addition to pubertal changes, other physical changes we will explore involve sexuality and the brain.

PUBERTY

Puberty is not the same as adolescence. For most of us, puberty ends long before adolescence does, although puberty is the most important marker of the beginning of adolescence.

Puberty is a brain-neuroendocrine process occurring primarily in early adolescence that provides stimulation for the rapid physical changes that take place during this period of development (Susman & Dorn, 2013). Puberty is not a single, sudden event. We know whether a young boy or girl is going through puberty, but pinpointing puberty's beginning and end is difficult. Among the most noticeable changes are signs of sexual maturation and increases in height and weight.

Sexual Maturation, Height, and Weight

Think back to the onset of your puberty. Of the striking changes that were taking place in your body, what was the first to occur? Researchers have found that male pubertal characteristics typically develop in this order: increase in penis and testicle size, appearance of straight pubic hair, minor voice change, first ejaculation (which usually occurs through masturbation or a wet dream), appearance of kinky pubic hair, onset of maximum growth in height and weight, growth of hair in armpits, more detectable voice changes, and, finally, growth of facial hair.

What is the order of appearance of physical changes in females? First, either the breasts enlarge or pubic hair appears. Later, hair appears in the armpits. As these changes occur, the female grows in height and her hips become wider than her shoulders. **Menarche**—a girl's first menstruation—comes rather late in the pubertal cycle. Initially, her menstrual cycles may be highly irregular. For the first several years, she may not ovulate every menstrual cycle; some girls do not ovulate at all until a year or two after menstruation begins. No voice changes comparable to those in pubertal males occur in pubertal females. By the end of puberty, the female's breasts have become more fully rounded.

Marked weight gains coincide with the onset of puberty. During early adolescence, girls tend to outweigh boys, but by about age 14 boys begin to surpass girls. Similarly, at the beginning of the adolescent period, girls tend to be as tall as or taller than boys of their age, but by the end of the middle school years most boys have caught up or, in many cases, surpassed girls in height.

As indicated in Figure 11.1, the growth spurt occurs approximately two years earlier for girls than for boys. The mean age at the beginning of the growth spurt in girls is 9; for boys, it is 11. The peak rate of pubertal change occurs at 11½ years for girls and 13½ years for boys. During their growth spurt, girls increase in height about 3½ inches per year, boys about 4 inches. Boys and girls who are shorter or taller than their peers before adolescence are likely to remain so during adolescence; however, as much as 30 percent of an individual's height in late adolescence is unexplained by his or her height in the elementary school years.

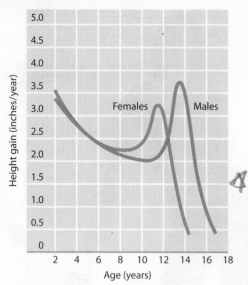

FIGURE 11.1

PUBERTAL GROWTH SPURT. On average, the peak of the growth spurt during puberty occurs two years earlier for girls (11½) than for boys (13½). *How are hormones related to the growth spurt and to the difference between the average height of adolescent boys and that of girls?*

puberty A period of rapid physical maturation, occurring primarily in early adolescence, that involves hormonal and bodily changes.

menarche A girl's first menstruation.

ZITS By Jerry Scott and Jim Borgman

ZITS © ZITS Partnership. King Features Syndicate.

Hormonal Changes

Behind the first whisker in boys and the widening of hips in girls is a flood of **hormones,** powerful chemical substances secreted by the endocrine glands and carried through the body by the bloodstream.

The concentrations of certain hormones increase dramatically during adolescence (Koolschijn, Peper & Crone, 2014; Nguyen & others, 2013). *Testosterone* is a hormone associated in boys with genital development, increased height, and deepening of the voice. *Estradiol* is a type of estrogen that in girls is associated with breast, uterine, and skeletal development. In one study, testosterone levels increased eighteen-fold in boys but only twofold in girls during puberty; estradiol increased eightfold in girls but only twofold in boys (Nottelmann & others, 1987). Thus, both testosterone and estradiol are present in the hormonal makeup of both boys and girls, but testosterone dominates in male pubertal development, estradiol in female pubertal development.

The same influx of hormones that grows hair on a male's chest and increases the fatty tissue in a female's breasts may also contribute to psychological development in adolescence (Holder & Blaustein, 2014; Susman & Dorn, 2013). In one study of boys and girls ranging in age from 9 to 14, a higher concentration of testosterone was present in boys who rated themselves as more socially competent (Nottelmann & others, 1987). However, hormonal effects by themselves do not account for adolescent development (Susman & Dorn, 2013). For example, in one study, social factors were much better predictors of young adolescent girls' depression and anger than hormonal factors (Brooks-Gunn & Warren, 1989). Behavior and moods also can affect hormones (DeRose & Brooks-Gunn, 2008). Stress, eating patterns, exercise, sexual activity, tension, and depression can activate or suppress various aspects of the hormonal system (Marceau, Dorn, & Susman, 2012). In sum, the hormone-behavior link is complex (Susman & Dorn, 2013).

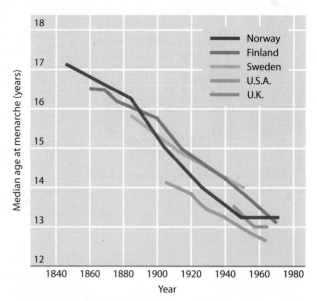

FIGURE 11.2

AGE AT MENARCHE IN NORTHERN EUROPEAN COUNTRIES AND THE UNITED STATES IN THE NINETEENTH AND TWENTIETH CENTURIES. Notice the steep decline in the age at which girls experienced menarche in four northern European countries and the United States from 1845 to 1969. Recently the age at which girls experience menarche has been leveling off.

Timing and Variations in Puberty

In the United States—where children mature up to a year earlier than children in European countries—the average age of menarche has declined significantly since the mid-nineteenth century (see Figure 11.2). Fortunately, however, we are unlikely to see pubescent toddlers, since what has happened in the past century is likely the result of improved nutrition and health.

Why do the changes of puberty occur when they do, and how can variations in their timing be explained? The basic genetic program for puberty is wired into the species (Dvornyk & Waqar-ul-Haq, 2012). A recent cross-cultural study in 29 countries found that childhood obesity was linked to early puberty in girls (Currie & others, 2012).

Experiences that are linked to earlier pubertal onset include an urban environment, low socioeconomic status, adoption, father absence, family conflict, maternal harshness, child maltreatment, and early substance use (Ellis & others, 2011). In many cases, puberty comes months earlier in these situations, and this earlier onset of puberty is likely explained by high rates of conflict and stress in these social contexts.

For most boys, the pubertal sequence may begin as early as age 10 or as late as 13½, and it may end as early as age 13 or as late as 17. Thus, the normal range is wide enough that, given two boys of the same chronological age, one might complete the pubertal sequence before the other one has begun it. For girls, menarche is considered within the normal range if it appears between the ages of 9 and 15. An increasing number of U.S. girls are beginning puberty at 8 and 9 years of age, with African American girls developing earlier than non-Latino White girls (Herman-Giddens, 2007; Sorensen & others, 2012).

What are some of the differences in the ways girls and boys experience pubertal growth?

Body Image

One psychological aspect of physical change in puberty is universal: Adolescents are preoccupied with their bodies and develop images of what their bodies are like (Leone & others, 2014). Preoccupation with body image is strong throughout adolescence but is especially acute during early adolescence, a time when adolescents are more dissatisfied with their bodies than in late adolescence.

hormones Powerful chemical substances secreted by the endocrine glands and carried through the body by the bloodstream.

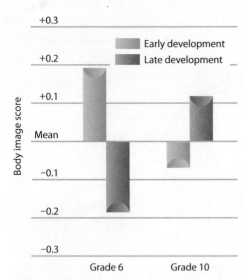

FIGURE 11.3

EARLY- AND LATE-MATURING ADOLESCENT GIRLS' PERCEPTIONS OF BODY IMAGE IN EARLY AND LATE ADOLESCENCE. The sixth-grade girls in this study had positive body image scores if they were early maturers but negative body image scores if they were late maturers (Simmons & Blyth, 1987). Positive body image scores indicated satisfaction with their figures. By the tenth grade, however, it was the late maturers who had positive body image scores.

corpus callosum The location where fibers connect the brain's left and right hemispheres.

Gender differences characterize adolescents' perceptions of their bodies (de Guzman & Nishina, 2014). In general, girls are less happy with their bodies and have more negative body images than boys throughout puberty (Bearman & others, 2006). Girls' more negative body images may be due to media portrayals of the attractiveness of being thin and the increase in body fat in girls during puberty (Benowitz-Fredericks & others, 2012). A recent study found that both boys' and girls' body images became more positive as they moved from the beginning to the end of adolescence (Holsen, Carlson Jones, & Skogbrott Birkeland, 2012).

Early and Late Maturation   You may have entered puberty earlier or later than average, or perhaps you were right on schedule. Adolescents who mature earlier or later than their peers perceive themselves differently (Susman & Dorn, 2013). In the Berkeley Longitudinal Study some years ago, early-maturing boys perceived themselves more positively and had more successful peer relations than did their late-maturing counterparts (Jones, 1965). When the late-maturing boys were in their thirties, however, they had developed a stronger sense of identity than the early-maturing boys had (Peskin, 1967). This identity development may have occurred because the late-maturing boys had more time to explore life's options, or because the early-maturing boys continued to focus on their advantageous physical status instead of on career development and achievement. More recent research confirms, though, that at least during adolescence it is advantageous to be an early-maturing rather than a late-maturing boy (Graber, Brooks-Gunn, & Warren, 2006).

Early and late maturation have been linked with body image. In one study, in the sixth grade, early-maturing girls showed greater satisfaction with their figures than do late-maturing girls, but by the tenth grade late-maturing girls were more satisfied (Simmons & Blyth, 1987) (see Figure 11.3). A possible reason for this is that in late adolescence early-maturing girls are shorter and stockier, whereas late-maturing girls are taller and thinner. Thus, late-maturing girls in late adolescence have bodies that more closely approximate the current American ideal of feminine beauty—tall and thin. Also, a recent study found that in the early high school years, late-maturing boys had a more negative body image than early-maturing boys (de Guzman & Nishina, 2014).

An increasing number of researchers have found that early maturation increases girls' vulnerability to a number of problems (Graber, 2013; Hamilton & others, 2014). Early-maturing girls are more likely to smoke, drink, be depressed, have an eating disorder, engage in delinquency, struggle for earlier independence from their parents, and have older friends; and their bodies are likely to elicit responses from males that lead to earlier dating and earlier sexual experiences (Baker & others, 2012; Verhoef & others, 2014). Further, early-maturing girls have sexual intercourse earlier and have more unstable sexual relationships (Moore, Harden, & Mendle, 2014). And early-maturing girls are less likely to graduate from high school and tend to cohabit and marry earlier (Cavanagh, 2009). Apparently as a result of their social and cognitive immaturity, combined with early physical development, early-maturing girls are easily lured into problem behaviors, not recognizing the possible long-term negative effects on their development.

THE BRAIN

Along with the rest of the body, the brain changes during adolescence, but the study of adolescent brain development is still in its infancy. As advances in technology take place, significant strides will also likely be made in charting developmental changes in the adolescent brain (Blakemore & Mills, 2014; Reyna & Zayas, 2014). What do we know now?

The dogma of the unchanging brain has been discarded and researchers are mainly focused on context-induced plasticity of the brain over time (Zelazo, 2013). The development of the brain mainly changes in a bottom-up, top-down sequence with sensory, appetitive (eating, drinking), sexual, sensation-seeking, and risk-taking brain linkages maturing first and higher-level brain linkages such as self-control, planning, and reasoning maturing later (Zelazo, 2013).

Using fMRI brain scans, scientists have recently discovered that adolescents' brains undergo significant structural changes (Blakemore & Mills, 2014; Raznahan & others, 2014). The **corpus callosum,** where fibers connect the brain's left and right hemispheres, thickens in adolescence, and this improves adolescents' ability to process information (Chavarria & others, 2014; Gilliam & others, 2011). We described advances in the development of the prefrontal cortex—the highest level of the frontal lobes involved in reasoning, decision making, and self-control—in

Chapter 9. However, the prefrontal cortex doesn't finish maturing until the emerging adult years, approximately 18 to 25 years of age, or later (Luna, Padmanabhan, & Geier, 2014; Steinberg, 2015a, b).

At a lower, subcortical level, the **limbic system,** which is the seat of emotions and where rewards are experienced, matures much earlier than the prefrontal cortex and is almost completely developed in early adolescence (Blakemore & Mills, 2014; Steinberg, 2015a, b). The limbic system structure that is especially involved in emotion is the **amygdala.** Figure 11.4 shows the locations of the corpus callosum, prefrontal cortex, and the limbic system.

In Chapter 9, "Physical Development in Middle and Late Childhood," we described the increased focal activation that is linked to synaptic pruning in a specific region, such as the prefrontal cortex. In middle and late childhood, while there is increased focal activation within a specific brain region such as the prefrontal cortex, there are limited connections across distant brain regions. By the time individuals reach emerging adulthood, there are more connections across brain areas (Markant & Thomas, 2013). The increased connectedness (referred to as brain networks) is especially prevalent across more distant brain regions. Thus, as children develop, greater efficiency and focal activation occurs in close-by areas of the brain, and simultaneously there is an increase in brain networks connecting more distant brain regions (Markant & Thomas, 2013).

Many of the changes in the adolescent brain that have been described here involve the rapidly emerging fields of *developmental cognitive neuroscience* and *developmental social neuroscience,* in which connections between development, the brain, and cognitive or socioemotional processes are studied (Blakemore & Mills, 2014; Yap & others, 2013). For example, consider leading researcher Charles Nelson's (2003) view that, although adolescents are capable of very strong emotions, their prefrontal cortex hasn't adequately developed to the point at which they can control these passions. It is as if their brain doesn't have the brakes to slow down their emotions. Or consider this interpretation of the development of emotion and cognition in adolescents: "early activation of strong 'turbo-charged' feelings with a relatively unskilled set of 'driving skills' or cognitive abilities to modulate strong emotions and motivations" (Dahl, 2004, p. 18).

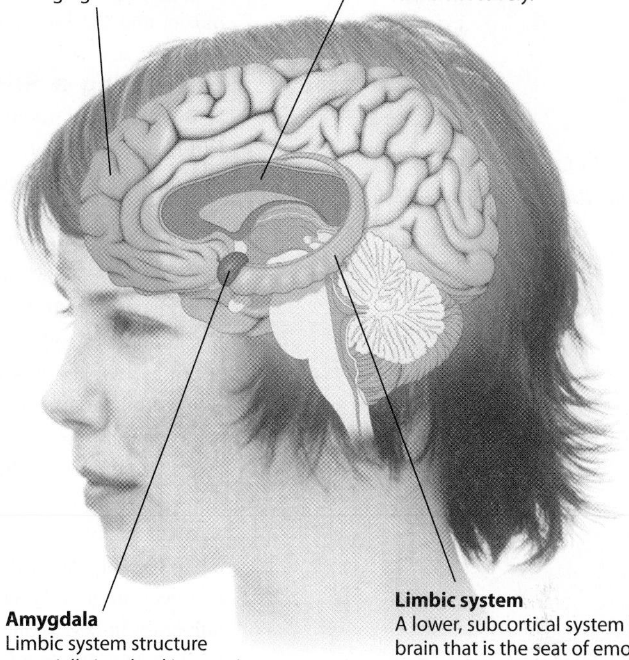

Of course, a major question is which comes first, biological changes in the brain or experiences that stimulate these changes (Lerner, Boyd, & Du, 2008; Steinberg, 2015a, b). Consider a study in which the prefrontal cortex thickened and more brain connections formed when adolescents resisted peer pressure (Paus & others, 2007). Scientists have yet to determine whether the brain changes come first or whether they result from experiences with peers, parents, and others. Once again, we encounter the nature-nurture issue that is so prominent in an examination of development through the life span. Nonetheless, there is adequate evidence that environmental experiences make important contributions to the brain's development (Monahan & others, 2014; Zelazo, 2013).

In closing this section on the development of the brain in adolescence, a further caution is in order. Much of the research on neuroscience and the development of the brain in adolescence is correlational in nature, and thus causal statements need to be scrutinized. This caution, of course, applies to any period in the human life span.

ADOLESCENT SEXUALITY

Not only is adolescence characterized by substantial changes in physical growth and the development of the brain, but adolescence also is a bridge between the asexual child and the sexual adult. Adolescence is a time of sexual exploration and experimentation, of sexual fantasies and realities, of incorporating sexuality into one's identity. Adolescents have an almost insatiable curiosity about sexuality. They are concerned about whether they are sexually attractive, how

Prefrontal cortex
This "judgment" region reins in intense emotions but doesn't finish developing until at least emerging adulthood.

Corpus callosum
These nerve fibers connect the brain's two hemispheres; they thicken in adolescence to process information more effectively.

Amygdala
Limbic system structure especially involved in emotion.

Limbic system
A lower, subcortical system in the brain that is the seat of emotions and experience of rewards. This system is almost completely developed in early adolescence.

FIGURE **11.4**

THE CHANGING ADOLESCENT BRAIN: PREFRONTAL CORTEX, LIMBIC SYSTEM, AND CORPUS CALLOSUM

developmental **connection**

Brain Development

Although the prefrontal cortex shows considerable development in childhood, it is still not fully mature even in adolescence. Chapter 9, p. 268

limbic system The part of the brain where emotions and rewards are processed.

amygdala The region of the brain that is the seat of emotions.

to do sex, and what the future holds for their sexual lives. Although most adolescents experience times of vulnerability and confusion, the majority will eventually develop a mature sexual identity. In the United States, information about sexuality is widely available to adolescents. They learn a great deal about sex from television, videos, magazines, the lyrics of popular music, and the Internet (Herdt & Polen-Petit, 2014; King & Regan, 2014).

Developing a Sexual Identity   Mastering emerging sexual feelings and forming a sense of sexual identity are multifaceted and lengthy processes (Diamond, 2013; Savin-Williams, 2015; Savin-Williams & Cohen, 2015). They involve learning to manage sexual feelings (such as sexual arousal and attraction), developing new forms of intimacy, and learning how to regulate sexual behavior to avoid undesirable consequences.

An adolescent's sexual identity involves activities, interests, styles of behavior, and an indication of sexual orientation (whether an individual has same-sex or other-sex attractions, or both) (Buzwell & Rosenthal, 1996). For example, some adolescents have a high anxiety level about sex, others a low level. Some adolescents are strongly aroused sexually, others less so. Some adolescents are very active sexually, others not at all (Hyde & DeLamater, 2014). Some adolescents are sexually inactive in response to their strong religious upbringing; others go to church regularly and yet their religious training does not inhibit their sexual activity.

It is commonly thought that most gays and lesbians quietly struggle with same-sex attractions in childhood, do not engage in heterosexual dating, and gradually recognize that they are a gay or lesbian in mid- to late adolescence. Many youth do follow this developmental pathway, but others do not (Diamond & Savin-Williams, 2015). For example, many youth have no recollection of early same-sex attractions and experience a more abrupt sense of their same-sex attraction in late adolescence. The majority of adolescents with same-sex attractions also experience some degree of other-sex attractions (Hock, 2012). Even though some adolescents who are attracted to individuals of their same sex fall in love with these individuals, others claim that their same-sex attractions are purely physical (Diamond & Savin-Willlams, 2015).

The Timing of Adolescent Sexual Behaviors   What is the current profile of sexual activity of adolescents? In a U.S. national survey conducted in 2011, 63 percent of twelfth-graders reported having experienced sexual intercourse, compared with 33 percent of ninth-graders (Eaton & others, 2012). By age 20, 77 percent of U.S. youth report having engaged in sexual intercourse (Dworkin & Santelli, 2007). Nationally, 47.5 percent of twelfth-graders, 39 percent of eleventh-graders, 30 percent of tenth-graders, and 21 percent of ninth-graders recently reported that they were currently sexually active (Eaton & others, 2012). A recent analysis of more than 12,000 adolescents in the Longitudinal Study of Adolescent Health found a predominant overall pattern of vaginal sex first, average age of sexual initiation of 16 years, and spacing of more than 1 year between initiation of first and second sexual behaviors (Haydon & others, 2012). In this study, about a third of the adolescents initiated sex slightly later but initiated oral-genital and vaginal sex within the same year. Further, compared with non-Latino adolescents, African American adolescents were more likely to engage in vaginal sex first. Also, adolescents from low-SES backgrounds were characterized by earlier sexual initiation.

What trends in adolescent sexual activity have occurred in the last two decades? From 1991 to 2011, fewer adolescents reported any of the following: ever having had sexual intercourse, currently being sexually active, having had sexual intercourse before the age of 13, and having had sexual intercourse with four or more persons during their lifetime (Eaton & others, 2012) (see Figure 11.5).

Until very recently, at all grade levels adolescent males have been more likely than adolescent females to report having had sexual intercourse and being sexually active (MMWR, 2006). However, the 2009 national survey was the first time that a higher percentage of twelfth-grade females than twelfth-grade males reported having experienced sexual intercourse (Eaton & others, 2010). This reversal continued in 2011 (Eaton & others, 2012). Also, a higher percentage of ninth-grade males (38 percent) than ninth-grade females (28 percent) reported having experienced sexual intercourse. Adolescent males also are more likely than their female counterparts to describe sexual intercourse as an enjoyable experience.

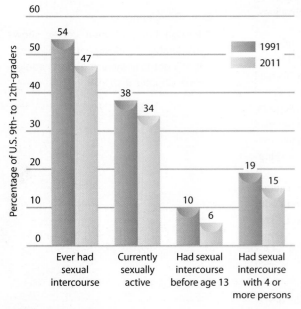

FIGURE **11.5**

SEXUAL ACTIVITY OF U.S. ADOLESCENTS FROM 1991 TO 2011.

Source: After Eaton & others (2012). U.S. government data.

Sexual initiation varies by ethnic group in the United States (Eaton & others, 2012). African Americans are likely to engage in sexual behavior earlier than other ethnic groups, whereas Asian Americans are likely to engage in them later (Feldman, Turner, & Araujo, 1999). In a more recent national U.S. survey (2011) of ninth- to twelfth-graders, 60 percent of African Americans, 49 percent of Latinos, and 44 percent of non-Latino Whites said they had experienced sexual intercourse (Eaton & others, 2012). In this study, 14 percent of African Americans (compared with 7 percent of Latinos and 3 percent of non-Latino Whites) said they had their first sexual experience before 13 years of age.

Recent research indicates that oral sex is now a common occurrence among U.S. adolescents (Fava & Bay-Cheng, 2012; Song & Halpern-Felsher, 2010). In a national survey, 55 percent of U.S. 15- to 19-year-old boys and 54 percent of girls said they had engaged in oral sex (National Center for Health Statistics, 2002). A recent study also found that among female adolescents who reported having vaginal sex first, 31 percent reported having a teen pregnancy, whereas among those who initiated oral-genital sex first, only 8 percent reported having a teen pregnancy (Reese & others, 2013). Thus, how adolescents initiate their sex lives may have positive or negative consequences for their sexual health.

Risk Factors in Adolescent Sexual Behavior   Many adolescents are not emotionally prepared to handle sexual experiences, especially in early adolescence (Coley & others, 2013). Early sexual activity is linked with risky behaviors such as drug use, delinquency, and school-related problems (Chan & others, 2014). A recent study confirmed that early engagement in sexual intercourse (prior to 14 years of age) is associated with high-risk sexual factors (forced sex, using drugs/alcohol at last sex, not using a condom at last sex, having multiple partners in last month, and becoming pregnant or causing a pregnancy), as well as experiencing dating violence (Kaplan & others, 2013). Other risk factors for sexual problems in adolescence include contextual factors such as socioeconomic status (SES) and poverty, family/parenting and peer factors (Van Ryzin & others, 2011). A recent study revealed that neighborhood poverty concentrations predicted 15- to 17-year-old girls' and boys' sexual initiation (Cubbin & others, 2010). The percentage of sexually active adolescents is especially high in low-income areas of major cities (Morrison-Beedy & others, 2013).

developmental **connection**
Sexuality
What characterizes the sexual activity of emerging adults (18 to 25 years of age)? Chapter 13, p. 412

What are some risks associated with early initiation of sexual intercourse?

A number of family factors are linked to sexuality outcomes for adolescents (de Looze & others, 2014; Widman & others, 2014). A research review indicated that the following aspects of connectedness predicted sexual and reproductive health outcomes for youth: family connectedness, parent-adolescent communication about sexuality, parental monitoring, and partner connectedness (Markham & others, 2010). A recent study found that difficulties and disagreements between Latino adolescents and their parents were linked to the adolescents' early sex initiation (Cordova & others, 2014). Also, having older sexually active siblings or pregnant/parenting teenage sisters placed adolescent girls at increased risk for pregnancy (Miller, Benson, & Galbraith, 2001). Further, recent research indicated that associating with more deviant peers in early adolescence was related to having more sexual partners at age 16 (Lansford & others, 2010). And a research review found that school connectedness was linked to positive sexuality outcomes (Markham & others, 2010). A recent study also found that a high level of impulsiveness was linked to early adolescent sexual risk-taking (Khurana & others, 2012).

Psychologists are exploring ways to encourage adolescents to make less risky sexual decisions. Here an adolescent participates in an interactive video session developed by Julie Downs and her colleagues at the Department of Social and Decision Making Sciences at Carnegie Mellon University. The videos help adolescents evaluate their responses and decisions in high-risk sexual contexts.

Contraceptive Use   Are adolescents increasingly using condoms? A recent national study revealed a substantial increase in the use of contraceptives (60 percent in 2011 compared with 46 percent in 1991) by U.S. high school students the last time they had sexual intercourse

sexually transmitted infections (STIs) Infections that are contracted primarily through sexual contact, including oral-genital and anal-genital contact.

- - - - - - - - - →

developmental **connection**

Conditions, Diseases, and Disorders

What are some good strategies for protecting against HIV and other sexually transmitted infections? Chapter 13, p. 415

(Eaton & others, 2012). However, in this study, condom use by U.S. adolescents did not significantly change from 2003 through 2009.

Many sexually active adolescents still do not use contraceptives, or they use them inconsistently (Finer & Philbin, 2013). In 2011, 34 percent of sexually active adolescents did not use a condom the last time they had sexual intercourse (Eaton & others, 2012). Younger adolescents are less likely than older adolescents to take contraceptive precautions. Also, a recent study found that a greater age difference between sexual partners in adolescence is associated with less consistent condom use (Volpe & others, 2013).

Sexually Transmitted Infections   Some forms of contraception, such as birth control pills or implants, do not protect against sexually transmitted infections, or STIs. **Sexually transmitted infections (STIs)** are contracted primarily through sexual contact, including oral-genital and anal-genital contact. Every year more than 3 million American adolescents (about one-fourth of those who are sexually experienced) acquire an STI (Centers for Disease Control and Prevention, 2014). In a single act of unprotected sex with an infected partner, a teenage girl has a 1 percent risk of getting HIV, a 30 percent risk of acquiring genital herpes, and a 50 percent chance of contracting gonorrhea (Glei, 1999). Yet another very widespread STI is chlamydia. In Chapter 13, we will consider these and other sexually transmitted infections.

Adolescent Pregnancy   In cross-cultural comparisons, the United States continues to have one of the highest adolescent pregnancy and childbearing rates in the industrialized world, despite a considerable decline in the 1990s. The U.S. adolescent pregnancy rate is eight times as high as that in the Netherlands. Although U.S. adolescents are no more sexually active than their counterparts in the Netherlands, their adolescent pregnancy rate is dramatically higher. In the United States, 82 percent of pregnancies to mothers 15 to 19 years of age are unintended (Koh, 2014).

Despite the negative comparisons of the United States with many other developed countries, there have been some encouraging trends in U.S. adolescent pregnancy rates. In 2012, the U.S. birth rate for 15- to 19-year-olds was 29.4 births per 1,000 females, the lowest rate ever recorded, which represents a 52 percent decrease from 61.8 births for the same age range in 1991 (Hamilton, Martin, & Ventura, 2013) (see Figure 11.6). Reasons for the decline include school/community health classes, increased contraceptive use, and fear of sexually transmitted infections such as AIDS.

What are some consequences of adolescent pregnancy?

Ethnic variations characterize birth rates for U.S. adolescents (Centers for Disease Control and Prevention, 2012). Latina adolescents are more likely than African American and non-Latina White adolescents to have a child (Ventura & Hamilton, 2011). Latina and African American adolescent girls who have a child are also more likely to have a second child than are non-Latina White adolescent girls (Rosengard, 2009). And daughters of teenage mothers are at increased risk for teenage childbearing, thus perpetuating an intergenerational cycle (Meade, Kershaw, & Ickovics, 2008).

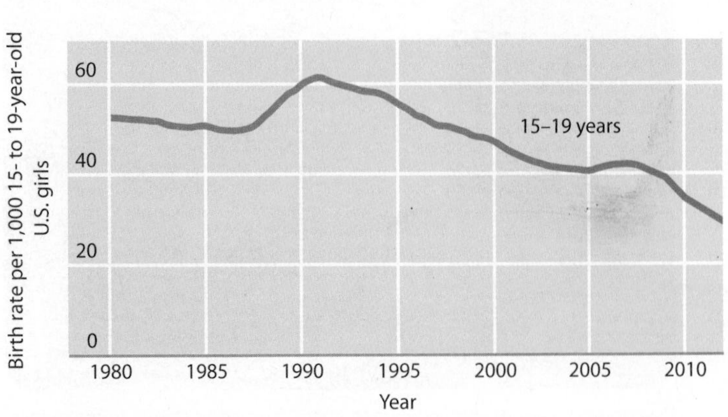

Adolescent pregnancy creates health risks for both the baby and the mother (Bartlett & others, 2014; Kappeler & Farb, 2014). Infants born to adolescent mothers are more likely to have low birth weights—a prominent factor in infant mortality—as well as neurological problems and childhood illness (Khashan, Baker, & Kenny, 2010). Adolescent mothers also are more likely to be depressed and to drop out of school than their peers (Siegel & Brandon, 2014). Although many adolescent mothers resume their education later in life, they generally never catch up economically with women who postpone childbearing until their twenties. One longitudinal study found that the children of women who had their first birth during their teens had lower achievement test scores and

FIGURE 11.6

BIRTH RATES FOR U.S. 15- TO 19-YEAR-OLD GIRLS FROM 1980 TO 2012.
Source: Hamilton, Martin, & Ventura (2013).

Lynn Blankinship, Family and Consumer Science Educator

Lynn Blankinship is a family and consumer science educator with an undergraduate degree in this field from the University of Arizona. She has taught for more than 20 years, the last 14 at Tucson High Magnet School.

Blankinship was honored as the Tucson Federation of Teachers Educator of the Year for 1999–2000 and the Arizona Teacher of the Year in 1999. Blankinship especially enjoys teaching life skills to adolescents. One of her favorite activities is having students care for an automated baby that imitates the needs of real babies. She says that this program has a profound impact on students because the baby must be cared for around the clock for the duration of the assignment. Blankinship also coordinates real-world work experiences and training for students in several child-care facilities in the Tucson area.

Lynn Blankinship (*center*) teaching life skills to students.

For more information about what family and consumer science educators do, see page 42 in the Careers in Life-Span Development appendix.

more behavioral problems than did children whose mothers had their first birth as adults (Hofferth & Reid, 2002).

Researchers have found that adolescent mothers interact less effectively with their infants than do adult mothers. A recent study revealed that adolescent mothers spent more time negatively interacting and less time in play and positive interaction with their infants than did adult mothers (Riva Crugnola & others, 2014). A recent intervention, "My Baby and Me," that involved frequent (55), intensive home visitation coaching sessions with adolescent mothers across three years resulted in improved maternal behavior and child outcomes (Guttentag & others, 2014).

Although the consequences of America's high adolescent pregnancy rate are cause for great concern, it often is not pregnancy alone that leads to negative consequences for an adolescent mother and her offspring. Adolescent mothers are more likely to come from low-SES backgrounds (Molina & others, 2010). Many adolescent mothers also were not good students before they became pregnant (Malamitsi-Puchner & Boutsikou, 2006). However, not every adolescent female who bears a child lives a life of poverty and low achievement. Thus, although adolescent pregnancy is a high-risk circumstance, and adolescents who do not become pregnant generally fare better than those who do, some adolescent mothers do well in school and have positive outcomes (Schaffer & others, 2012).

Serious, extensive efforts are needed to help pregnant adolescents and young mothers enhance their educational and occupational opportunities (Asheer & others, 2014). Adolescent mothers also need help obtaining competent child care and planning for the future.

Adolescents can benefit from age-appropriate family-life education. Family and consumer science educators teach life skills, such as effective decision making, to adolescents. To read about the work of one family and consumer science educator, see *Connecting with Careers*. And to learn more about ways to reduce adolescent pregnancy, see *Connecting Development to Life*.

Reducing Adolescent Pregnancy

One strategy for reducing adolescent pregnancy, called the Teen Outreach Program (TOP), focuses on engaging adolescents in volunteer community service and stimulates discussions that help adolescents appreciate the lessons they learn through volunteerism.

Girls, Inc., has four programs that are intended to increase adolescent girls' motivation to avoid pregnancy until they are mature enough to make responsible decisions about motherhood (Roth & others, 1998). Growing Together, a series of five two-hour workshops for mothers and adolescents, and Will Power/Won't Power, a series of six two-hour sessions that focus on assertiveness training, are for 12- to 14-year-old girls. For older adolescent girls, Taking Care of Business provides nine sessions that emphasize career planning as well as information about sexuality, reproduction, and contraception. Health Bridge coordinates health and education services—girls can participate in this program as one of their club activities. Girls who participated in these programs were less likely to get pregnant than girls who did not participate (Girls, Inc., 1991).

In 2010, the U.S. government launched the Teen Pregnancy Prevention (TPP) Program under the direction of the newly created Office of Adolescent Health (Koh, 2014). Currently, a number of studies are being funded by the program in an effort to find ways to reduce the rate of adolescent pregnancy.

The sources and the accuracy of adolescents' sexual information are linked to adolescent pregnancy. Adolescents can get information about sex from many sources, including parents, siblings, schools, peers, magazines, television, and the Internet. A special concern is the accuracy of sexual information to which adolescents have access on the Internet.

Currently, a major controversy in sex education is whether schools should have an abstinence-only program or a program that emphasizes contraceptive knowledge (Erkut & others, 2013; Kraft & others, 2012).

A number of leading experts on adolescent sexuality now conclude that sex education programs that emphasize contraceptive knowledge do not increase the incidence of sexual intercourse and are more likely to reduce the risk of adolescent pregnancy and sexually transmitted infections than abstinence-only programs (Carroll, 2013; Eisenberg & others, 2008, 2013; Hyde & DeLamater, 2014). Some sex education programs are starting to include abstinence-plus sexuality by promoting abstinence while also providing instructions on contraceptive use (Nixon & others, 2011; Realini & others, 2010).

Based on the information you read earlier about risk factors in adolescent sexual behavior, which segments of the adolescent population would benefit most from the types of sex education programs described here?

Review Connect Reflect

 Describe the changes involved in puberty, as well as changes in the brain and sexuality during adolescence.

Review

- What are some key aspects of puberty?
- What changes typically occur in the brain during adolescence?
- What are some important aspects of sexuality in adolescence?

Connect

- How might adolescent brain development be linked to adolescents' decisions to engage in sexual activity or to abstain from it?

Reflect *Your Own Personal Journey of Life*

- Did you experience puberty earlier or later than your peers? How did this timing affect your development?

---

3 Issues in Adolescent Health

 Identify adolescent problems related to health, substance use and abuse, and eating disorders.

Adolescent Health   Substance Use and Abuse   Eating Disorders

Many health experts argue that whether adolescents are healthy depends primarily on their own behavior. To improve adolescent health, adults should aim to (1) increase adolescents' *health-enhancing* behaviors, such as eating nutritious foods, exercising, wearing seat belts, and getting adequate sleep; and (2) reduce adolescents' *health-compromising* behaviors, such as drug abuse, violence, unprotected sexual intercourse, and dangerous driving.

ADOLESCENT HEALTH

Adolescence is a critical juncture in the adoption of behaviors that are relevant to health (Kadivar & others, 2014; Quinlan-Davidson & others, 2014). Many of the behaviors that are linked to poor health habits and early death in adults begin during adolescence. Conversely, the early formation of healthy behavior patterns, such as regular exercise and a preference for foods low in fat and cholesterol, not only has immediate health benefits but helps in adulthood to delay or prevent disability and mortality from heart disease, stroke, diabetes, and cancer (Blake, Munoz, & Volpe, 2014).

Nutrition and Exercise   Concerns are growing about adolescents' nutrition and exercise habits (Chen & others, 2014; Dowdy & others, 2013). National data indicated that the percentage of overweight U.S. 12- to 19-year-olds increased from 11 percent in the early 1990s to nearly 21 percent in 2011–2012 (Ogden & others, 2014). In another recent study, 12.4 percent of U.S. kindergarten children were obese, but by 14 years of age, 20.8 percent were obese (Cunningham, Kramer, & Narayan, 2014).

A special concern in American culture is the amount of fat we consume. Many of today's adolescents virtually live on fast-food meals, which are high in fat. A comparison of adolescents in 28 countries found that U.S. and British adolescents were more likely to eat fried food and less likely to eat fruits and vegetables than adolescents in most other countries that were studied (World Health Organization, 2000). One study found that eating regular family meals during early adolescence was linked to healthy eating habits five years later (Burgess-Champoux & others, 2009).

Being obese in adolescence predicts obesity in emerging adulthood. For example, a longitudinal study of more than 8,000 adolescents found that obese adolescents were more likely to develop severe obesity in emerging adulthood than were overweight or normal-weight adolescents (The & others, 2010). In another longitudinal study, the percentage of overweight individuals increased from 20 percent at 14 years of age to 33 percent at 24 years of age (Patton & others, 2011).

Researchers have found that individuals become less active as they reach and progress through adolescence (Alberga & others, 2012). A national study of U.S. adolescents revealed that physical activity increased until 13 years of age in boys and girls but then declined through 18 years of age (Kahn & others, 2008).

A national study revealed that only 28.7 percent of U.S. adolescents met the federal government's exercise recommendations (a minimum of 60 minutes of moderate to vigorous exercise per day) (Eaton & others, 2012). This national study also found that adolescent boys were much more likely to engage in 60 minutes or more of vigorous exercise per day than were girls (38.3 percent versus 18.5 percent) (Eaton & others, 2012). Ethnic differences in exercise participation rates of U.S. adolescents also occur, and these rates vary by gender. In the national study just mentioned, non-Latino White boys exercised the most, African American and Latino girls the least (Eaton & others, 2012).

Exercise is linked to a number of positive physical outcomes in adolescence. For example, regular exercise has a positive effect on adolescents' weight status (Davison & others, 2013; Hoare & others, 2014). Other positive outcomes of exercise in adolescence are reduced triglyceride levels, lower blood pressure, and a lower incidence of type II diabetes (Anyaegu & Dharnidharka, 2014). Low levels of exercise are related to depressive symptoms in adolescents (Gosmann & others, 2014). In another study, young adolescents who exercised regularly had higher academic achievement (Hashim, Freddy, & Rosmatunisah, 2012). Yet another study found that adolescents who were high in physical fitness had better connectivity between brain regions than adolescents who were low in physical fitness (Herting & others, 2014). A recent study also revealed that playing on a sports team was an important factor in adolescents' weight. In this study, among a wide range of activities (other physical activity, physical education, screen time, and diet quality, for example), team sports participation was the strongest predictor of lower risk for being overweight or obese (Drake & others, 2012).

Adolescents' exercise is increasingly being found to be associated with parenting and peer relationships. For example, a recent study revealed that female adolescents' physical activity was linked to their male and female friends' physical activity, while male adolescents'

What are some characteristics of adolescents' exercise patterns?

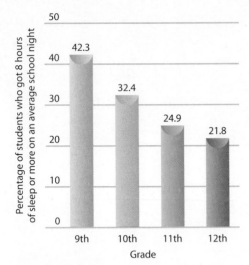

FIGURE **11.7**

DEVELOPMENTAL CHANGES IN U.S. ADOLESCENTS' SLEEP PATTERNS ON AN AVERAGE SCHOOL NIGHT

physical activity was associated with their female friends' physical activity (Sirard & others, 2013). In a recent research review, peer/friend support of exercise, presence of peers and friends, peer norms, friendship quality and acceptance, peer crowds, and peer victimization were linked to adolescents' physical activity (Fitzgerald, Fitzgerald, & Aherne, 2012).

A recent research review concluded that screen-based activity is linked to a number of adolescent health problems (Costigan & others, 2013). In this review, a higher level of screen-based sedentary behavior was associated with being overweight, having sleep problems, being depressed, and having lower levels of physical activity/fitness and psychological well-being (higher stress levels, for example).

Sleep Patterns   Like nutrition and exercise, sleep is an important influence on well-being. Might changing sleep patterns in adolescence contribute to adolescents' health-compromising behaviors? Recently there has been a surge of interest in adolescent sleep patterns (Doane & Thurston, 2014; Telzer & others, 2013). A longitudinal study in which adolescents completed a 24-hour diary every 14 days in ninth, tenth, and twelfth grades found that regardless of how much students studied each day, when the students sacrificed sleep time to study more than usual they had difficulty understanding what was taught in class and were more likely to struggle with class assignments the next day (Gillen-O'Neel, Huynh, & Fuligni, 2013).

In a national survey of youth, only 31 percent of U.S. adolescents got eight or more hours of sleep on an average school night (Eaton & others, 2010). In this study, the percentage of adolescents getting this much sleep on an average school night decreased as they got older (see Figure 11.7).

The National Sleep Foundation (2006) conducted a U.S. survey of 1,602 caregivers and their 11- to 17-year-olds. Forty-five percent of the adolescents got less than eight hours of sleep on school nights. Older adolescents (ninth- to twelfth-graders) got markedly less sleep on school nights than younger adolescents (sixth- to eighth-graders)—62 percent of the older adolescents got inadequate sleep compared with 21 percent of the younger adolescents. Adolescents who got inadequate sleep (eight hours or less) on school nights were more likely to feel more tired or sleepy, to be more cranky and irritable, to fall asleep in school, to be in a depressed mood, and to drink caffeinated beverages than their counterparts who got optimal sleep (nine or more hours). Also, a longitudinal study of more than 6,000 adolescents found that sleep problems were linked to subsequent suicidal thoughts and attempts in adolescence and early adulthood (Wong & Brower, 2012). Further, a recent study found that adolescents who got less than 7.7 hours of sleep per night on average had more emotional and peer-related problems, high anxiety, and a higher level of suicidal ideation than their peers who got 7.7 hours of sleep or more (Sarchiapone & others, 2014).

Mary Carskadon and her colleagues (2004, 2005, 2011a, b; Crowley & Carskadon, 2010; Tarokh & Carskadon, 2010) have conducted a number of research studies on adolescent sleep patterns. They found that when given the opportunity, adolescents will sleep an average of 9 hours and 25 minutes a night. Most get considerably less than nine hours of sleep, however, especially during the week. This shortfall creates a sleep deficit, which adolescents often attempt to make up on the weekend. The researchers also found that older adolescents tend to be sleepier during the day than younger adolescents. They theorized that this sleepiness was not due to academic work or social pressures. Rather, their research suggests that adolescents' biological clocks undergo a shift as they get older, delaying their period of sleepiness by about one hour. A delay in the nightly release of the sleep-inducing hormone melatonin, which is produced in the brain's pineal gland, seems to underlie this shift. Melatonin is secreted at about 9:30 p.m. in younger adolescents and approximately an hour later in older adolescents.

Carskadon concludes that early school starting times may cause grogginess, inattention in class, and poor performance on tests. Based on her research, school officials in Edina, Minnesota, decided to start classes at 8:30 a.m. rather than the usual 7:25 a.m. Since then there have been fewer referrals for discipline problems, and the number of students who report being ill or depressed has decreased. The school system reports that test scores have improved for high school students, but not for middle school students. This finding supports Carskadon's

In Mary Carskadon's sleep laboratory at Brown University, an adolescent girl's brain activity is being monitored. Carskadon (2005) says that in the morning, sleep-deprived adolescents' "brains are telling them it's night time . . . and the rest of the world is saying it's time to go to school" (p. 19).

suspicion that early start times are likely to be more stressful for older than for younger adolescents.

Do sleep patterns change in emerging adulthood? Research indicates that they do (Galambos, Howard, & Maggs, 2011). One study revealed that more than 60 percent of college students were categorized as poor-quality sleepers (Lund & others, 2010). In this study, the weekday bedtimes and rise times of first-year college students were approximately 1 hour and 15 minutes later than those of seniors in high school (Lund & others, 2010). However, the first-year college students had later bedtimes and rise times than third- and fourth-year college students, indicating that at about 20 to 22 years of age, a reverse in the timing of bedtimes and rise times occurs.

Leading Causes of Death in Adolescence   The three leading causes of death in adolescence are unintentional injuries, homicide, and suicide (National Center for Health Statistics, 2014). Almost half of all deaths from 15 to 24 years of age are due to unintentional injuries, the majority of them involving motor vehicle accidents. Risky driving habits, such as speeding, tailgating, and driving under the influence of alcohol or other drugs, may be more important contributors to these accidents than lack of driving experience (Marcotte & others, 2012). In about 50 percent of motor vehicle fatalities involving adolescents, the driver has a blood alcohol level of 0.10 percent—twice the level at which a driver is designated as "under the influence" in some states. A high rate of intoxication is also found in adolescents who die as pedestrians or while using vehicles other than automobiles.

Homicide is the second leading cause of death in adolescence, especially among African American males (National Center for Health Statistics, 2014). Also notable is the adolescent suicide rate, which has tripled since the 1950s. Suicide accounts for 6 percent of the deaths in the 10-to-14 age group and 12 percent of deaths in the 15-to-19 age group. We will discuss suicide further in Chapter 12.

SUBSTANCE USE AND ABUSE

Each year since 1975, Lloyd Johnston and his colleagues at the Institute of Social Research at the University of Michigan have monitored the drug use of America's high school seniors in a wide range of public and private high schools. Since 1991, they also have surveyed drug use by eighth- and tenth-graders. In 2012, the study surveyed more than 45,000 secondary school students in more than 400 public and private schools (Johnston & others, 2013).

According to this study, the proportions of eighth-, tenth-, and twelfth-grade U.S. students who used any illicit drug declined during the late 1990s and the first decade of the twenty-first century (Johnston & others, 2014) (see Figure 11.8). The use of drugs among

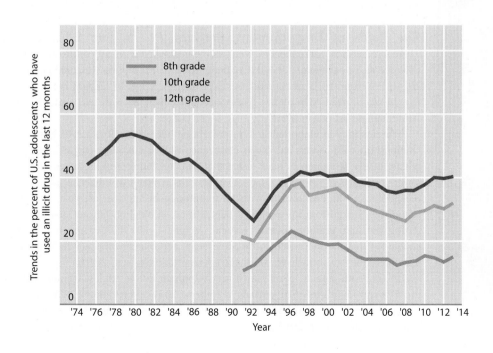

FIGURE **11.8**

TRENDS IN DRUG USE BY U.S. EIGHTH-, TENTH-, AND TWELFTH-GRADE STUDENTS. This graph shows the percentage of U.S. eighth-, tenth-, and twelfth-grade students who reported having taken an illicit drug in the last 12 months from 1991 to 2013 (for eighth- and tenth-graders) and from 1975 to 2013 (for twelfth-graders) (Johnston & others, 2014).

What are some trends in alcohol use by U.S. adolescents?

developmental **connection**

Substance Abuse

Does substance abuse increase or decrease in emerging adulthood? Chapter 13, p. 409

What are some of the ways that parents influence whether their adolescents take drugs?

U.S. secondary school students declined in the 1980s but began to increase in the early 1990s (Johnston & others, 2014). In the late 1990s and the early part of the twenty-first century, the proportion of secondary school students reporting the use of any illicit drug declined. The overall decline in the use of illicit drugs by adolescents during this time frame was approximately one-third for eighth-graders, one-fourth for tenth-graders, and one-eighth for twelfth-graders. The most notable declines in drug use by U.S. adolescents in the first decade of the twenty-first century occurred for LSD, cocaine, cigarettes, sedatives, tranquilizers, and Ecstasy.

As shown in Figure 11.8, in which marijuana is included, an increase in illicit drug use by U.S. adolescents occurred from 2008 to 2013. However, when marijuana use is subtracted from the illicit drug index, no increase in U.S. adolescent drug use occurred in this time frame (Johnston & others, 2014). However, the United States still has one of the highest rates of adolescent drug use of any industrialized nation.

How extensive is alcohol use by U.S. adolescents? Sizable declines in adolescent alcohol use have occurred in recent years (Johnston & others, 2014). The percentage of U.S. eighth-graders who reported having had any alcohol to drink in the past 30 days fell from a 1996 high of 26 percent to 10 percent in 2013. The 30-day prevalence fell among tenth-graders from 39 percent in 2001 to 26 percent in 2013 and among high school seniors from 72 percent in 1980 to 39 percent in 2013. Binge drinking (defined in the University of Michigan surveys as having five or more drinks in a row in the last two weeks) by high school seniors declined from 41 percent in 1980 to 26 percent in 2013. Binge drinking by eighth- and tenth-graders also has dropped in recent years. A consistent gender difference occurs in binge drinking, with males engaging in this behavior more than females do (Johnston & others, 2014).

A special concern is adolescents who drive while they are under the influence of alcohol or other substances (Catalano & others, 2012). In the University of Michigan Monitoring the Future Study, 30 percent of high school seniors said they had been in a vehicle with a drugged or drinking driver in the past two weeks (Johnston & others, 2008).

Cigarette smoking among U.S. adolescents peaked in 1996 and has gradually declined since then (Johnston & others, 2014). Following peak use in 1996, smoking rates for U.S. eighth-graders have fallen by 50 percent. In 2013, the percentage of twelfth-graders who reported having smoked cigarettes in the last 30 days was 16 percent, a 3 percent decrease from 2011, while the rate for tenth-graders was 9 percent and the rate for eighth-graders was 4.5 percent. Since the mid-1990s an increasing percentage of adolescents have reported that they perceive cigarette smoking as dangerous, that they disapprove of it, that they are less accepting of being around smokers, and that they prefer to date nonsmokers (Johnston & others, 2014).

The Roles of Development, Parents, Peers, and Education

There are serious consequences when adolescents begin to use drugs early in adolescence or even in childhood (Conduct Problems Prevention Research Group, 2014). For example, a recent study revealed that the onset of alcohol use before age 11 was linked to a higher risk of alcohol dependence in early adulthood (Guttmannova & others, 2012).

Parents play an important role in preventing adolescent drug abuse. Positive relationships with parents and others can reduce adolescents' drug use (Broning & others, 2014). Researchers have found that parental monitoring is linked with a lower incidence of drug use (Hurt & others, 2013; Wang & others, 2014). In a recent study, a higher level of parental monitoring during the last year of high school was linked to a lower risk of dependence on alcohol, but not marijuana, during the first year of college (Kaynak & others, 2013). A research review concluded that the more frequently adolescents ate dinner with their family, the less likely they were to have substance abuse problems (Sen, 2010).

Along with parents, peers play a very important role in adolescent substance use (Valente & others, 2013; Wang & others, 2014). For example, one study found that peer network drinking increased adolescents' alcohol use (Cruz, Emery, & Turkheimer, 2012).

connecting through research

What Can Families Do to Reduce Drinking and Smoking by Young Adolescents?

Experimental studies have been conducted to determine whether family programs can reduce drinking and smoking by young adolescents. In one experimental study, 1,326 families with 12- to 14-year-old adolescents living in various parts of the United States were interviewed (Bauman & others, 2002). After the baseline interviews, participants were randomly assigned either to go through the Family Matters program (experimental group) or not to experience the program (control group) (Bauman & others, 2002).

The families assigned to the Family Matters program received four mailings of booklets. Each mailing was followed by a telephone call from a health educator to "encourage participation by all family members, answer any questions, and record information" (Bauman & others, 2002, pp. 36–37). The first booklet focused on the negative consequences of adolescent substance abuse to the family. The second emphasized "supervision, support, communication skills, attachment, time spent together, educational achievement, conflict reduction, and how well adolescence is understood." The third booklet asked parents to list things that they do that might inadvertently encourage their child's use of tobacco or alcohol, identify rules that might influence the child's use, and consider ways to monitor use. Then adult family members and the child met "to agree upon rules and sanctions related to adolescent use." Booklet four dealt with "what the child can do to resist peer and media pressures for use."

Two follow-up interviews with the parents and adolescents were conducted three months and one year after the experimental group had completed the program. Adolescents in the Family Matters program reported lower alcohol and cigarette use at three months and at one year after the program had been completed. Figure 11.9 shows the results for alcohol.

The topics covered in the second booklet underscore the importance of parental influence earlier in development. For instance, staying

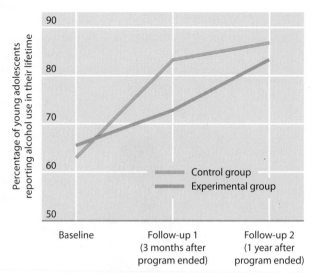

FIGURE **11.9**

YOUNG ADOLESCENTS' REPORTS OF ALCOHOL USE IN THE FAMILY MATTERS PROGRAM. Note that at baseline (before the program started) the young adolescents in the Family Matters program (experimental group) and their counterparts who did not go through the program (control group) reported approximately the same lifetime use of alcohol (slightly higher use by the experimental group). However, three months after the program ended, the experimental group reported lower alcohol use, and this reduction was still present one year after the program had ended, although at a reduced level.

actively involved and establishing an authoritative, as opposed to a neglectful, parenting style early in children's lives will better ensure that children have a clear understanding of the parents' level of support and expectations when the children reach adolescence.

Educational success is also a strong buffer for the emergence of drug problems in adolescence (Balsa, Giuliano, & French, 2011). An analysis by Jerald Bachman and his colleagues (2008) revealed that early educational achievement considerably reduced the likelihood that adolescents would develop drug problems. But what can families do to educate themselves and their children and reduce adolescent drinking and smoking behavior? To find out, see *Connecting Through Research*.

EATING DISORDERS

Let's now examine two eating problems—anorexia nervosa and bulimia nervosa—that are far more common in adolescent girls than boys.

Anorexia Nervosa   Although most U.S. girls have been on a diet at some point, slightly less than 1 percent ever develop anorexia nervosa. **Anorexia nervosa** is an eating disorder that involves the relentless pursuit of thinness through starvation. It is a serious

anorexia nervosa An eating disorder that involves the relentless pursuit of thinness through starvation.

disorder that can lead to death. Four main characteristics apply to people suffering from anorexia nervosa: (1) weight below 85 percent of what is considered normal for their age and height; (2) an intense fear of gaining weight that does not decrease with weight loss; (3) a distorted image of their body shape (Stewart & others, 2012), and (4) *amenorrhea* (lack of menstruation) in girls who have reached puberty.

Obsessive thinking about weight and compulsive exercise also are linked to anorexia nervosa (Simpson & others, 2013). Even when they are extremely thin, they see themselves as too fat. They never think they are thin enough, especially in the abdomen, buttocks, and thighs. They usually weigh themselves frequently, often take their body measurements, and gaze critically at themselves in mirrors.

Anorexia nervosa typically begins in the early to middle adolescent years, often following an episode of dieting and some type of life stress (Fitzpatrick, 2012). It is about 10 times more likely to occur in females than males. When anorexia nervosa does occur in males, the symptoms and other characteristics (such as a distorted body image and family conflict) are usually similar to those reported by females who have the disorder (Ariceli & others, 2005).

Most anorexics are non-Latina White adolescent or young adult females from well-educated middle- and upper-income families and are competitive and high-achieving (Darcy, 2012). They set high standards, become stressed about not being able to reach the standards, and are intensely concerned about how others perceive them. Unable to meet these high expectations, they turn to something they can control: their weight. Offspring of mothers with anorexia nervosa are at risk for becoming anorexic themselves (Machado & others, 2014). Problems in family functioning are increasingly being found to be linked to the appearance of anorexia nervosa in adolescent girls (Machado & others, 2014; Stiles-Shields & others, 2012), and a research review concluded that family therapy is often the most effective treatment for adolescent girls with anorexia nervosa (Bulik & others, 2007).

Biology and culture are involved in anorexia nervosa. Genes play an important role in anorexia nervosa (Boraska & others, 2014; Lock, 2012a). Also, the physical effects of dieting may change neural networks and thus sustain the disordered pattern (Lock, 2012b; Fuglset & others, 2014). The fashion image in U.S. culture likely contributes to the incidence of anorexia nervosa (Benowitz-Fredericks & others, 2012). The media portray thin as beautiful in their choice of fashion models, whom many adolescent girls strive to emulate.

Anorexia nervosa has become an increasing problem for adolescent girls and young adult women. *What are some possible causes of anorexia nervosa?*

Bulimia Nervosa

Whereas anorexics control their weight by restricting food intake, most bulimics cannot. **Bulimia nervosa** is an eating disorder in which the individual consistently follows a binge-and-purge pattern. The bulimic goes on an eating binge and then purges by self-inducing vomiting or using a laxative. Although many people binge and purge occasionally and some experiment with it, a person is considered to have a serious bulimic disorder only if the episodes occur at least twice a week for three months (Cuzzolaro, 2014; Uher & Rutter, 2012).

As with anorexics, most bulimics are preoccupied with food, have a strong fear of becoming overweight, are depressed or anxious, and have a distorted body image. A recent study found that bulimics have difficulty controlling their emotions (Lavender & others, 2014). Like adolescents who are anorexic, bulimics are highly perfectionistic (Lampard & others, 2012). Unlike anorexics, individuals who binge and purge typically fall within a normal weight range, which makes bulimia more difficult to detect.

Approximately 1 to 2 percent of U.S. women are estimated to develop bulimia nervosa, and about 90 percent of bulimics are women. Bulimia nervosa typically begins in late adolescence or early adulthood. Many women who develop bulimia nervosa were somewhat overweight before the onset of the disorder, and the binge eating often began during an episode of dieting. As with anorexia nervosa, about 70 percent of individuals who develop bulimia nervosa eventually recover from the disorder (Agras & others, 2004). Drug therapy and psychotherapy have been effective in treating anorexia nervosa and bulimia nervosa (Hagman & Frank, 2012). Cognitive behavior therapy has especially been helpful in treating bulimia nervosa (Hay, 2013).

bulimia nervosa An eating disorder in which the individual consistently follows a binge-and-purge pattern.

4 Adolescent Cognition

 LG4 Explain cognitive changes in adolescence.

Piaget's Theory   Adolescent Egocentrism   Information Processing

Adolescents' developing power of thought opens up new cognitive and social horizons. Let's examine some explanations of how their power of thought develops, beginning with Piaget's theory (1952).

PIAGET'S THEORY

As we discussed in Chapter 9, Jean Piaget proposed that around 7 years of age children enter the *concrete operational stage* of cognitive development. They can reason logically about concrete events and objects, and they make gains in their ability to classify objects and to reason about the relationships between classes of objects. Around age 11, according to Piaget, the fourth and final stage of cognitive development—the formal operational stage—begins.

The Formal Operational Stage   What are the characteristics of the formal operational stage? Formal operational thought is more abstract than concrete operational thought. Adolescents are no longer limited to actual, concrete experiences as anchors for thought. They can conjure up make-believe situations, abstract propositions, and events that are purely hypothetical, and can try to reason logically about them.

The abstract quality of thinking during the formal operational stage is evident in the adolescent's verbal problem-solving ability. Whereas the concrete operational thinker needs to see the concrete elements A, B, and C to be able to make the logical inference that if A = B and B = C, then A = C, the formal operational thinker can solve this problem merely through verbal presentation.

Another indication of the abstract quality of adolescents' thought is their increased tendency to think about thought itself. One adolescent commented, "I began thinking about why I was thinking what I was. Then I began thinking about why I was thinking about what I was thinking about what I was." If this sounds abstract, it is, and it characterizes the adolescent's enhanced focus on thought and its abstract qualities.

Accompanying the abstract nature of formal operational thought is thought full of idealism and possibilities, especially during the beginning of the formal operational stage, when assimilation dominates. Adolescents engage in extended speculation about ideal characteristics—qualities they desire in themselves and in others. Such thoughts often lead adolescents to compare themselves with others in regard to such ideal standards. And their thoughts are often fantasy flights into future possibilities.

"Ben is in his first year of high school, and he's questioning all the right things."

© Edward Koren/The New Yorker Collection/ www.cartoonbank.com.

Might adolescents' ability to reason hypothetically and to evaluate what is ideal versus what is real lead them to engage in demonstrations such as this protest related to improving education? What other causes might be attractive to adolescents' newfound cognitive abilities of hypothetical-deductive reasoning and idealistic thinking?

At the same time that adolescents think more abstractly and idealistically, they also think more logically. Children are likely to solve problems through trial and error; adolescents begin to think more as a scientist thinks, devising plans to solve problems and systematically testing solutions. This type of problem solving requires **hypothetical-deductive reasoning,** which involves creating a hypothesis and deducing its implications, steps that provide ways to test the hypothesis. Thus, formal operational thinkers develop hypotheses about ways to solve problems and then systematically deduce the best path to follow to solve the problem.

Evaluating Piaget's Theory   Researchers have challenged some of Piaget's ideas about the formal operational stage (Reyna & Zayas, 2014). Among their findings is that there is much more individual variation than Piaget envisioned: Only about one in three young adolescents is a formal operational thinker, and many American adults (and adults in other cultures) never become formal operational thinkers.

Furthermore, education in the logic of science and mathematics promotes the development of formal operational thinking. This point recalls a criticism of Piaget's theory that we discussed in Chapter 9: Culture and education exert stronger influences on cognitive development than Piaget maintained (Gauvain, 2013).

Piaget's theory of cognitive development has been challenged on other points as well (Diamond, 2013). As we noted in Chapter 9, Piaget conceived of stages as unitary structures of thought, with various aspects of a stage emerging at the same time. However, most contemporary developmentalists agree that cognitive development is not as stage-like as Piaget thought (Siegler & others, 2013). Some cognitive abilities can emerge earlier than Piaget thought, others later than he believed (Brynes, 2012). As we just noted, many adolescents still think in concrete operational ways or are just beginning to master formal operations, and even many adults are not formal operational thinkers.

Despite these challenges to Piaget's ideas, we owe him a tremendous debt (Miller, 2011). Piaget was the founder of the present field of cognitive development, and he developed a long list of masterful concepts of enduring power and fascination: assimilation, accommodation, object permanence, egocentrism, conservation, and others. Psychologists also owe him the current vision of children as active, constructive thinkers. And they are indebted to him for creating a theory that has generated a huge volume of research on children's cognitive development.

Piaget also was a genius when it came to observing children. His careful observations demonstrated inventive ways to discover how children act on and adapt to their world. He showed us how children need to make their experiences fit their schemes yet simultaneously adapt their schemes to accommodate their experiences. And Piaget revealed how cognitive change is likely to occur if the context is structured to allow gradual movement to the next higher level.

ADOLESCENT EGOCENTRISM

Adolescent egocentrism is the heightened self-consciousness of adolescents. David Elkind (1976) points out that adolescent egocentrism has two key components—the imaginary audience and personal fable. The **imaginary audience** is reflected in adolescents' belief that others are as interested in them as they themselves are, as well as attention-getting behavior—attempts to be noticed, visible, and "on stage." For example, an eighth-grade boy might walk into a classroom and think that all eyes are riveted on his spotty complexion. Adolescents sense that they are "on stage" in early adolescence, believing they are the main actors and all others are the audience.

- - - - - - - - - - ▶

developmental **connection**

Cognitive Theory

Is there a fifth, postformal stage of cognitive development that characterizes young adults? Chapter 13, p. 420

developmental **connection**

Cognitive Theory

Piaget described a form of egocentrism that characterizes young children. Chapter 7, p. 206

◀ - - - - - - - - - - -

hypothetical-deductive reasoning Piaget's formal operational concept that adolescents have the cognitive ability to develop hypotheses, or best guesses, about ways to solve problems.

adolescent egocentrism The heightened self-consciousness of adolescents.

imaginary audience Adolescents' belief that others are as interested in them as they themselves are, as well as attention-getting behavior motivated by a desire to be noticed, visible, and "on stage."

According to Elkind, the **personal fable** is the part of adolescent egocentrism involving a sense of uniqueness and invincibility (or invulnerability). For example, 13-year-old Adrienne says this about herself: "No one understands me, particularly my parents. They have no idea of what I am feeling." Adolescents' sense of personal uniqueness makes them believe that no one can understand how they really feel. As part of their effort to retain a sense of personal uniqueness, adolescents might craft a story about the self that is filled with fantasy, immersing themselves in a world that is far removed from reality. Personal fables frequently show up in adolescent diaries.

Adolescents often have been portrayed as having a sense of invincibility or invulnerability. For example, during a conversation with a girl who is the same age, 14-year-old Margaret says, "Are you kidding? I won't get pregnant." This sense of invincibility may lead adolescents to believe that they themselves are invulnerable to dangers and catastrophes (such as deadly car wrecks) that happen to other people. As a result, some adolescents engage in risky behaviors such as drag racing, drug use, suicide attempts, and having sexual intercourse without using contraceptives or barriers against STIs (Alberts, Elkind, & Ginsberg, 2007).

Might social media be an amplification tool for adolescent egocentrism? Earlier generations of adolescents did not have social media to connect with large numbers of people; instead, they connected with fewer people, either in person or via telephone. Might today's teens be drawn to social media and its virtually unlimited friend base to express their imaginary audience and sense of uniqueness? One analysis concluded that amassing a large number of friends (audience) may help to validate adolescents' perception that their life is on stage and everyone is watching them (Psychster Inc, 2010).

What about having a sense of invulnerability—is that aspect of adolescent egocentrism as accurate as Elkind argues? An increasing number of research studies suggest that rather than perceiving themselves to be invulnerable, adolescents tend to portray themselves as vulnerable to experiencing a premature death (Reyna & Rivers, 2008). For example, in a recent study, 12- to 18-year-olds were asked about their chances of dying in the next year and prior to age 20 (Fischhoff & others, 2010). The adolescents greatly overestimated their chance of dying prematurely.

Many adolescent girls spend long hours in front of the mirror, depleting cans of hairspray, tubes of lipstick, and jars of cosmetics. *How might this behavior be related to changes in adolescent cognitive and physical development?*

Might frequent use of social media, such as Facebook, increase adolescents' egocentrism?

INFORMATION PROCESSING

Deanna Kuhn (2009) identified some important characteristics of adolescents' information processing and thinking. In her view, in the later years of childhood and continuing in adolescence, individuals approach cognitive levels that may or may not be achieved, in contrast to the largely universal cognitive levels that young children attain. By adolescence, considerable variation in cognitive functioning is present across individuals. This variability supports the argument that adolescents are producers of their own development to a greater extent than are children.

Kuhn (2009) further argues that the most important cognitive change in adolescence is improvement in *executive function,* which we discussed in Chapters 7 and 9. Recall from Chapters 7 and 9 the description of *executive function* as an umbrella-like concept that consists of a number of higher-level cognitive processes linked to the development of the prefrontal cortex. Executive function involves managing one's thoughts to engage in goal-directed behavior and to exercise self-control. Our further coverage of executive function in adolescence focuses on cognitive control, decision making, and critical thinking.

Cognitive Control   In Chapter 9, you read about the increase in cognitive control that occurs in middle and late childhood. Recall that **cognitive control** involves effective control in a number of areas, including controlling attention, reducing interfering thoughts, and being cognitively flexible (Carlson, Zelazo, & Faja, 2013). Cognitive control continues to increase in adolescence and emerging adulthood (Casey, Jones, & Somerville, 2011).

developmental **connection**

The Brain

The prefrontal cortex is the location in the brain where much of executive function occurs. Chapter 7, p. 216

personal fable The part of adolescent egocentrism that involves an adolescent's sense of uniqueness and invincibility (or invulnerability).

cognitive control Effective control of thinking in a number of areas, including controlling attention, reducing interfering thoughts, and being cognitively flexible.

Think about all the times adolescents need to engage in cognitive control, such as the following situations (Galinsky, 2010):

- making a real effort to stick with a task, avoiding interfering thoughts or environmental events, and instead doing what is most effective;
- stopping and thinking before acting to avoid blurting out something that a minute or two later they wished they hadn't said;
- continuing to work on something that is important but boring when there is something a lot more fun to do, inhibiting their behavior and doing the boring but important task, saying to themselves, "I have to show the self-discipline to finish this."

Control Attention and Reduce Interfering Thoughts   Controlling attention is a key aspect of learning and thinking in adolescence and emerging adulthood (Bjorklund, 2012). Distractions that can interfere with attention in adolescence and emerging adulthood come from the external environment (other students talking while the student is trying to listen to a lecture, or the student turning on a laptop or tablet PC during a lecture and looking at a new friend request on Facebook, for example) or intrusive distractions from competing thoughts in the individual's mind. Self-oriented thoughts, such as worrying, self-doubt, and intense emotionally laden thoughts may especially interfere with focusing attention on thinking tasks (Gillig & Sanders, 2011; Walsh, 2011).

Be Cognitively Flexible   *Cognitive flexibility* involves being aware that options and alternatives are available and adapting to the situation. Before adolescents and emerging adults adapt their behavior in a situation, they must be aware that they need to change their way of thinking and be motivated to do. Having confidence in their ability to adapt their thinking to a particular situation, an aspect of *self-efficacy*, also is important in being cognitively flexible (Bandura, 2012). To evaluate how cognitively flexible you are, see Figure 11.10 (Galinsky, 2010).

Decision Making   Adolescence is a time of increased decision making—which friends to choose; which person to date; whether to have sex, buy a car, go to college, and so on (Reyna & Zayas, 2014; Steinberg, 2015a, b). How competent are adolescents at making decisions? Older adolescents are described as more competent than younger adolescents, who in turn are more competent than children (Keating, 1990). Compared with children, young adolescents are more likely to generate different options, examine a situation from a variety of perspectives, anticipate the consequences of decisions, and consider the credibility of sources.

Most people make better decisions when they are calm than when they are emotionally aroused. That may especially be true for adolescents, who have a tendency to be emotionally

Circle the number that best reflects how you think for each of the four items:

	Exactly Like You	Very Much Like You	Somewhat Like You	Not Too Much Like You	Not At All Like You
1. When I try something that doesn't work, it's hard for me to give it up and try another solution.	1	2	3	4	5
2. I adapt to change pretty easily.	5	4	3	4	5
3. When I can't convince someone of my point of view, I can usually understand why not.	5	4	3	4	5
4. I am not very quick to take on new ideas.	1	2	3	4	5

Add your numbers for each of the four items: Total Score: _____
If your overall score is between 20 and 15, then you rate high on cognitive flexibility. If you scored between 9 and 14, you are in the middle category, and if you scored 8 or below, you likely could improve your cognitive flexibility considerably.

FIGURE **11.10**
HOW COGNITIVELY FLEXIBLE ARE YOU?

intense. The same adolescent who makes a wise decision when calm may make an unwise decision when emotionally aroused (Albert & Steinberg, 2011a, b). In the heat of the moment, emotions may overwhelm decision-making ability.

The social context plays a key role in adolescent decision making (Smith, Chein, & Steinberg, 2014). For example, adolescents' willingness to make risky decisions is more likely to occur in contexts where substances and other temptations are readily available (Reyna & Rivers, 2008). Recent research reveals that the presence of peers in risk-taking situations increases the likelihood that adolescents will make risky decisions (Albert & Steinberg, 2011a, b; Steinberg, 2015a, b).

One proposal to explain effective adolescent decision making is the **dual-process model,** which states that decision making is influenced by two cognitive systems—one analytical and one experiential—which compete with each other (Klaczynski, 2001; Reyna & Farley, 2006; Reyna & others, 2011; Reyna & Zayas, 2014; Wilhelms & Reyna, 2013). The dual-process model emphasizes that it is the experiential system—monitoring and managing actual experiences—that benefits adolescents' decision making, not the analytical system. In this view, adolescents don't benefit from engaging in reflective, detailed, higher-level cognitive analysis about a decision, especially in high-risk, real-world contexts. In such contexts, adolescents just need to know that there are some circumstances that are so dangerous that they need to be avoided at all costs (Mills, Reyna, & Estrada, 2008).

In the experiential system, in risky situations it is important for an adolescent to quickly get the *gist,* or meaning, of what is happening and glean that the situation is a dangerous context, which can cue personal values that will protect the adolescent from making a risky decision (Reyna & Zayas, 2014; Wilhelms & Reyna, 2013). Further, adolescents who have a higher level of trait inhibition (self-control that helps them to manage their impulses effectively) and find themselves in risky contexts are less likely to engage in risk-taking behavior than their adolescent counterparts who have a lower level of trait inhibition (Chick & Reyna, 2012). However, some experts on adolescent cognition argue that in many cases adolescents benefit from both analytical and experiential systems (Kuhn, 2009).

Adolescents need more opportunities to practice and discuss realistic decision making. Many real-world decisions on matters such as sex, drugs, and daredevil driving occur in an atmosphere of stress that includes time constraints and emotional involvement. One strategy for improving adolescent decision making is to provide more opportunities for them to engage in role playing and peer group problem solving.

Critical Thinking Adolescence is an important transitional period in the development of critical thinking (Keating, 1990). In one study of fifth-, eighth-, and eleventh-graders, critical thinking increased with age but still occurred in only 43 percent of even the eleventh-graders, and many adolescents showed self-serving biases in their reasoning.

dual-process model A view of thinking in which decision making is influenced by two systems—one analytical and one experiential—that compete with each other.

If fundamental skills (such as literacy and math skills) are not developed during childhood, critical-thinking skills are unlikely to mature in adolescence. For the subset of adolescents who lack such fundamental skills, potential gains in adolescent thinking are unlikely. For other adolescents, however, cognitive changes that allow improved critical thinking in adolescence include the following: (1) increased speed, automaticity, and capacity of information processing, which free cognitive resources for other purposes; (2) more breadth of content knowledge in a variety of domains; (3) increased ability to construct new combinations of knowledge; and (4) a greater range and more spontaneous use of strategies or procedures for applying or obtaining knowledge, such as planning, considering alternatives, and cognitive monitoring.

Review Connect Reflect

LG4 Explain cognitive changes in adolescence.

Review

- What is Piaget's theory of adolescent cognitive development?
- What is adolescent egocentrism?
- What are some important aspects of information processing in adolescence?

Connect

- Egocentrism was also mentioned in Chapter 7 in the context of early childhood cognitive development. How is adolescent egocentrism similar to or different from egocentrism in early childhood?

Reflect *Your Own Personal Journey of Life*

- Evaluate the level of your thinking as you made the transition to adolescence and through adolescence. Does Piaget's stage of formal operational thinking accurately describe the changes that occurred in your thinking? Explain.

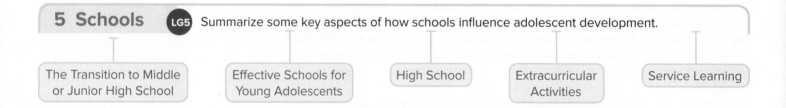

5 Schools

LG5 Summarize some key aspects of how schools influence adolescent development.

The Transition to Middle or Junior High School | Effective Schools for Young Adolescents | High School | Extracurricular Activities | Service Learning

What is the transition from elementary to middle or junior high school like? What are the characteristics of effective schools for adolescents? How can adolescents benefit from service learning?

THE TRANSITION TO MIDDLE OR JUNIOR HIGH SCHOOL

The first year of middle school or junior high school can be difficult for many students (Anderman, 2012; Duchesne, Ratelle, & Feng, 2014). For example, in one study of the transition from sixth grade in an elementary school to seventh grade in a junior high school, adolescents' perceptions of the quality of their school life plunged in the seventh grade (Hirsch & Rapkin, 1987). Compared with their earlier feelings as sixth-graders, the seventh-graders were less satisfied with school, were less committed to school, and liked their teachers less. The drop in school satisfaction occurred regardless of how academically successful the students were. The transition to middle or junior high school is less stressful when students have positive relationships with friends and go through the transition in team-oriented schools where 20 to 30 students take the same classes together (Hawkins & Berndt, 1985).

Katherine McMillan Culp, Research Scientist at an Educational Center

Katherine McMillan Culp wanted mainly to live in New York City when she graduated from college and became a receptionist at a center that focused on children and technology. More than 20 years later she is leading research projects at the center (Center for Children and Technology). Not long after her receptionist job, she combined work at the center with graduate school at Columbia University. Culp became especially interested in how content and instruction can best be created to link with the developmental level of children and adolescents.

Today she holds the position of principal research scientist at Education Development Center, directing a number of projects. One of her main current interests is middle-school students' science learning. In this area, she consults with game designers, teachers, and policy makers to improve their understanding of how adolescents think and learn.

Her advice to anyone wanting to do this type of work outside of academia is to get the best education and training possible, then become connected with schools, work with teachers, and obtain experience related to practical problems involved with schools and learning (Culp, 2012).

The transition to middle or junior high school takes place at a time when many changes—in the individual, in the family, and in school—are occurring simultaneously (Eccles & Roeser, 2013). These changes include puberty and related concerns about body image; the emergence of at least some aspects of formal operational thought, including accompanying changes in social cognition; increased responsibility and decreased dependency on parents; change to a larger, more impersonal school structure; change from one teacher to many teachers and from a small, homogeneous set of peers to a larger, more heterogeneous set of peers; and an increased focus on achievement and performance. Moreover, when students make the transition to middle or junior high school, they experience the **top-dog phenomenon,** moving from being the oldest, biggest, and most powerful students in the elementary school to being the youngest, smallest, and least powerful students in the middle or junior high school.

The transition to middle or junior high school also can have positive aspects. Students are more likely to feel grown up, have more subjects from which to select, have more opportunities to spend time with peers and locate compatible friends, and enjoy increased independence from direct parental monitoring. They also may be more challenged intellectually by academic work.

The transition from elementary to middle or junior high school occurs at the same time as a number of other developmental changes. *What are some of these other developmental changes?*

EFFECTIVE SCHOOLS FOR YOUNG ADOLESCENTS

Critics argue that middle and junior high schools should offer activities that reflect a wide range of individual differences in biological and psychological development among young adolescents. In 1989 the Carnegie Corporation issued an extremely negative evaluation of our nation's middle schools. It concluded that most young adolescents attended massive, impersonal schools; were taught from irrelevant curricula; trusted few adults in school; and lacked access to health care and counseling. It recommended that the nation develop smaller "communities" or "houses" to lessen the impersonal nature of large middle schools, have lower student-to-counselor ratios (10 to 1 instead of several hundred to 1), involve parents and community leaders in schools, develop new curricula, have teachers team teach in more flexibly designed curriculum blocks that integrate several disciplines, boost students' health and fitness with more in-school programs, and help students who need public health care to get it. Twenty years later, experts are still finding that middle schools throughout the nation need a major redesign if they are to be effective in educating adolescents (Anderman, 2012; Eccles & Roeser, 2013).

To read about one individual whose main career focus is improving middle school students' learning and education, see *Connecting with Careers*.

top-dog phenomenon The circumstance of moving from the top position in elementary school to the lowest position in middle or junior high school.

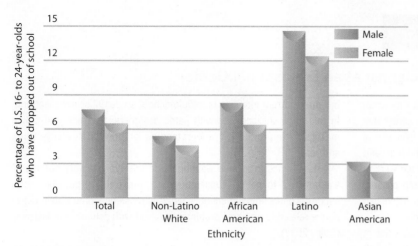

FIGURE **11.11**

SCHOOL DROPOUT RATES OF U.S. 16- TO 24-YEAR-OLDS BY GENDER AND ETHNICITY.

Source: National Center for Education Statistics (2012). Note: Data were collected in 2011.

HIGH SCHOOL

Just as there are concerns about U.S. middle school education, so are there concerns about U.S. high school education (Lauff, Ingels, & Christopher, 2014). Critics stress that in many high schools expectations for success and standards for learning are too low. Critics also argue that too often high schools foster passivity and that schools should create a variety of pathways for students to achieve an identity. Many students graduate from high school with inadequate reading, writing, and mathematical skills—including many who go on to college and must enroll in remediation classes there. Other students drop out of high school and do not have skills that will allow them to obtain decent jobs, much less to be informed citizens.

Robert Crosnoe's (2011) recent book, *Fitting In, Standing Out,* highlighted another major problem with U.S. high schools: how the negative social aspects of adolescents' lives undermine their academic achievement. In his view, adolescents become immersed in complex peer group cultures that demand conformity. High school is supposed to be about getting an education, but for many youth it is about navigating the social worlds of peer relations that may or may not value education and academic achievement. Adolescents who fail to fit in, especially those who are obese or gay, become stigmatized. Crosnoe recommends increased school counseling services, expanded extracurricular activities, and improved parental monitoring to reduce such problems.

Dropout Rates In the last half of the twentieth century and the first several years of the twenty-first century, U.S. high school dropout rates declined (National Center for Education Statistics, 2012). In the 1940s, more than half of U.S. 16- to 24-year-olds had dropped out of school; by 2011, this figure had decreased to 7.1 percent. The dropout rate of Latino adolescents remains high, although it has been decreasing in the twenty-first century (from 28 percent in 2000 to 13.6 percent in 2011). Asian American adolescents have the lowest dropout rate (2.8 percent) followed by non-Latino White adolescents (5 percent), African American adolescents (7.3 percent), and Latino adolescents (13.6 percent).

Gender differences characterize U.S. dropout rates, with males more likely to drop out than females (7.7 versus 6.5 percent) (National Center for Education Statistics, 2012). The gender gap in dropout rates is especially large for Latinos and African Americans. Figure 11.11 shows the dropout rates of 16- to 24-year-olds by gender and ethnicity.

National data on Native American adolescents are inadequate because statistics have been collected sporadically and/or from small samples. However, there are some indications that Native American adolescents may have the highest school dropout rate. Also, the average U.S. high school dropout rates described in Figure 11.11 mask some very high dropout rates in low-income areas of inner cities. For example, in cities such as Detroit, Cleveland, and Chicago, dropout rates are higher than 50 percent. Also, the percentages cited in Figure 11.11 are for 16- to 24-year-olds. When dropout rates are calculated in terms of students who do not graduate from high school within four years, the percentage of students is also much higher than in Figure 11.11. Thus, in considering high school dropout rates, it is important to examine age, the number of years it takes to complete high school, and various contexts including ethnicity, gender, and school location.

Students are shown using the technology training center at Wellpinit Elementary/High School located on the Spokane Indian Reservation in the state of Washington. An important educational goal is to increase the high school graduation rate of Native American adolescents.

Students drop out of school for many reasons (Fall & Roberts, 2012; Schoeneberger, 2012). In one study, almost 50 percent of the dropouts cited school-related reasons for leaving school, such as not liking school or being expelled or suspended (Rumberger, 1983). Twenty percent of the dropouts (but 40 percent of the Latino students) cited economic reasons for leaving school. One-third of the female students dropped out for personal reasons such as pregnancy or marriage.

According to a research review, the most effective programs to discourage dropping out of high school provide early intervention for reading problems, tutoring, counseling, and mentoring (Lehr & others, 2003). Clearly, then, early detection of children's school-related difficulties and getting children engaged with school in positive ways are important strategies for reducing the dropout rate (Fall & Roberts, 2012).

One program that has been very effective in reducing school dropout rates is "I Have a Dream" (IHAD), an innovative, comprehensive, long-term dropout prevention program administered by the National "I Have a Dream" Foundation in New York ("I Have a Dream" Foundation, 2013). Local IHAD projects around the country "adopt" entire grades (usually the third or fourth) from public elementary schools, or corresponding age cohorts from public housing developments. These children—"Dreamers"—are then provided with a program of academic, social, cultural, and recreational activities throughout their elementary, middle school, and high school years. Evaluations of IHAD programs have found improvements in grades, test scores, and school attendance, as well as a reduction in behavioral problems among Dreamers (Davis, Hyatt, & Arrasmith, 1998).

These adolescents are participating in the "I Have a Dream" Program, a comprehensive, long-term dropout prevention program that has been very successful. *What are some other strategies for reducing high school dropout rates?*

EXTRACURRICULAR ACTIVITIES

Adolescents in U.S. schools usually can choose from a wide array of extracurricular activities in addition to their academic courses. These adult-sanctioned activities typically occur during the after-school hours and can be sponsored either by the school or by the community. They include such diverse activities as sports, academic clubs, band, drama, and math clubs. Researchers have found that participation in extracurricular activities is linked to higher grades, greater school engagement, less likelihood of dropping out of school, improved probability of going to college, higher self-esteem, and lower rates of depression, delinquency, and substance abuse (Eccles & Roeser, 2013; Fredricks & Eccles, 2010). A recent study revealed that immigrant adolescents who participated in extracurricular activities improved their academic achievement and increased their school engagement (Camacho & Fuligni, 2014). Adolescents gain more benefit from a breadth of extracurricular activities than from focusing on a single extracurricular activity.

Of course, the quality of the extracurricular activities matters (Eccles & Roeser, 2013). High-quality extracurricular activities that are likely to promote positive adolescent development provide competent, supportive adult mentors; opportunities for increasing school connectedness; challenging and meaningful activities; and opportunities for improving skills.

SERVICE LEARNING

Service learning is a form of education that promotes social responsibility and service to the community. In service learning, adolescents engage in activities such as tutoring, helping older adults, working in a hospital, assisting at a child-care center, or cleaning up a vacant lot to make a play area. An important goal of service learning is that adolescents become less self-centered and more strongly motivated to help others (Davidson & others, 2010). Service learning is often more effective when two conditions are met (Nucci, 2006): (1) giving students some degree of choice in the service activities in which they participate, and (2) providing students opportunities to reflect about their participation.

Researchers have found that service learning benefits adolescents in a number of ways (Gonsalves, 2011; Kielsmeier, 2011). Improvements in adolescent development related to service learning include higher grades in school, increased goal setting, higher self-esteem, a greater sense of being able to make a difference for others, and a recent study revealed that adolescents' volunteer activities provided opportunities to explore and reason about moral issues (van Goethem & others, 2012).

What are some of the positive effects of service learning?

service learning A form of education that promotes social responsibility and service to the community.

Review *Connect* Reflect

Summarize some key aspects of how schools influence adolescent development.

Review
- What is the transition to middle or junior high school like?
- What are some characteristics of effective schools for young adolescents?
- What are some important things to know about high school dropouts and improving high schools?
- How does participation in extracurricular activities influence adolescent development?
- What is service learning, and how does it affect adolescent development?

Connect
- Compare the optimal school learning environments for adolescents described in this chapter with those described for younger children in previous chapters. Aside from age-appropriate curricula, what else is similar or different?

Reflect *Your Own Personal Journey of Life*
- What was your middle or junior high school like? How did it measure up to the Carnegie Corporation's recommendations?

---

topical **connections** *looking forward*

From 18 to 25 years of age, individuals make a transition from adolescence to adulthood. This transitional period, called emerging adulthood, is characterized by identity exploration, instability, and awareness of possibilities. Individuals often reach the peak of their physical skills between 19 and 26 years of age, followed by declining physical development during the early thirties. Cognitive development becomes more pragmatic and realistic, as well as more reflective and relativistic. Work becomes a more central aspect of individuals' lives.

---

reach your **learning goals**

Physical and Cognitive Development in Adolescence

1 The Nature of Adolescence

 Discuss the nature of adolescence.

- Many stereotypes of adolescents are too negative. Most adolescents today successfully negotiate the path from childhood to adulthood. However, too many of today's adolescents are not provided with adequate opportunities and support to become competent adults. It is important to view adolescents as a heterogeneous group because different portraits of adolescents emerge, depending on the particular set of adolescents being described. Social policy regarding adolescents too often has focused on health-compromising behaviors and not enough on strength-based approaches. Adolescents need more caring adults in their lives.

2 Physical Changes

 Describe the changes involved in puberty, as well as changes in the brain and sexuality during adolescence.

Puberty

- Puberty is a period of rapid physical maturation involving hormonal and bodily changes that occur primarily during early adolescence. Puberty's determinants include nutrition, health, and heredity. The initial onset of the pubertal growth spurt occurs on the average at 9 years for girls and 11 for boys, reaching a peak change for girls at 11½ and for boys at 13½.

Individual variation in pubertal changes is substantial. Adolescents show considerable interest in their body image, with girls having more negative body images than boys do. For boys, early maturation brings benefits, at least during early adolescence. Early-maturing girls are vulnerable to a number of risks.

The Brain

- Changes in the brain during adolescence involve the thickening of the corpus callosum and a gap in maturation between the limbic system and the prefrontal cortex, which functions in reasoning and self-regulation.

Adolescent Sexuality

- Adolescence is a time of sexual exploration and sexual experimentation. Having sexual intercourse in early adolescence is associated with negative developmental outcomes. Contraceptive use by adolescents is increasing. About one in four sexually experienced adolescents acquires a sexually transmitted infection (STI). America's adolescent pregnancy rate is higher than in other industrialized nations but has been decreasing in recent years.

3 Issues in Adolescent Health

LG3 Identify adolescent problems related to health, substance use and abuse, and eating disorders.

Adolescent Health

- Adolescence is a critical juncture in health because many of the factors related to poor health habits and early death in the adult years begin during adolescence. Poor nutrition, lack of exercise, and inadequate sleep are concerns. The three leading causes of death in adolescence are unintentional injuries, homicide, and suicide.

Substance Use and Abuse

- Despite recent declines, the United States has one of the highest rates of adolescent illicit drug use of any industrialized nation. Alcohol abuse is a major adolescent problem, although its rate has been dropping in recent years, as has the rate of cigarette smoking. Parents, peers, social support, and educational success play important roles in determining whether adolescents take drugs.

Eating Disorders

- Eating disorders have increased in adolescence, along with the percentage of adolescents who are overweight. Two eating disorders that may emerge in adolescence are anorexia nervosa and bulimia nervosa. Anorexia nervosa typically starts in the early to middle adolescent years following a dieting episode, and involves the relentless pursuit of thinness through starvation. Bulimia nervosa involves a binge-and-purge pattern, but—unlike anorexics—bulimics typically fall within a normal weight range.

4 Adolescent Cognition

LG4 Explain cognitive changes in adolescence.

Piaget's Theory

- During the formal operational stage, Piaget's fourth stage of cognitive development, thinking becomes more abstract, idealistic, and logical than during the concrete operational stage. However, many adolescents are not formal operational thinkers but are consolidating their concrete operational thought.

Adolescent Egocentrism

- Elkind describes adolescent egocentrism as the heightened self-consciousness of adolescents that consists of two parts: the imaginary audience and the personal fable. Recent research questions whether adolescents perceive themselves to be invulnerable.

Information Processing

- Adolescence is characterized by a number of advances in executive functioning. Cognitive control involves effective control and flexible thinking in a number of areas, including controlling attention, reducing interfering thoughts, remaining cognitively flexible, making decisions, and thinking critically.

5 Schools

LG5 Summarize some key aspects of how schools influence adolescent development.

The Transition to Middle or Junior High School

- The transition to middle or junior high school coincides with many social, familial, and individual changes in the adolescent's life, and this transition is often stressful. One source of stress is the move from the top-dog position to the lowest position in school.

Effective Schools for Young Adolescents

- Some critics argue that a major redesign of U.S. middle schools is needed. Critics say that U.S. high schools foster passivity and do not develop students' academic skills adequately. Characteristics of effective schools include lower student-to-counselor ratios, involvement of

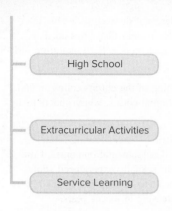

High School

Extracurricular Activities

Service Learning

parents and community leaders in schools, team teaching, and efforts to boost students' health and fitness.

- A number of strategies have been proposed for improving U.S. high schools, including raising expectations and providing better support. The overall high school dropout rate declined considerably in the last half of the twentieth century, but the dropout rates among Latino and Native American youth remain very high.

- Participation in extracurricular activities is associated with positive academic and psychological outcomes. Adolescents benefit from participating in a variety of extracurricular activities; the quality of the activities also matters.

- Service learning, a form of education that promotes social responsibility and service to the community, has been linked with positive benefits for adolescents such as higher grades, increased goal setting, and improved self-esteem.

key **terms**

puberty 342
menarche 342
hormones 343
corpus callosum 344
limbic system 345

amygdala 345
sexually transmitted infections
   (STIs) 348
anorexia nervosa 355
bulimia nervosa 356

hypothetical-deductive
   reasoning 358
adolescent egocentrism 358
imaginary audience 358
personal fable 359

cognitive control 359
dual-process model 361
top-dog phenomenon 363
service learning 365

key **people**

Lloyd Johnston 353

Jean Piaget 357

David Elkind 358

Deanna Kuhn 359

chapter 12

SOCIOEMOTIONAL DEVELOPMENT IN ADOLESCENCE

chapter **outline**

1 The Self, Identity, and Religious/Spiritual Development

Learning Goal 1 Discuss self, identity, and religious/spiritual development in adolescence.

Self-Esteem
Identity
Religious/Spiritual Development

2 Families

Learning Goal 2 Describe changes that take place in adolescents' relationships with their parents.

Parental Monitoring and Information Management
Autonomy and Attachment
Parent-Adolescent Conflict

3 Peers

Learning Goal 3 Characterize the changes that occur in peer relationships during adolescence.

Friendships
Peer Groups
Dating and Romantic Relationships

4 Culture and Adolescent Development

Learning Goal 4 Explain how culture influences adolescent development.

Cross-Cultural Comparisons
Ethnicity
The Media

5 Adolescent Problems

Learning Goal 5 Identify adolescent problems in socioemotional development and strategies for helping adolescents with problems.

Juvenile Delinquency
Depression and Suicide
The Interrelation of Problems and Successful Prevention/Intervention Programs

Jewel Cash seated next to her mother participating in a crime watch meeting at a community center.

The mayor of the city says she is "everywhere." She recently persuaded the city's school committee to consider ending the practice of locking tardy students out of their classrooms. She also swayed a neighborhood group to support her proposal for a winter jobs program. According to one city councilman, "People are just impressed with the power of her arguments and the sophistication of the argument" (Silva, 2005, pp. B1, B4). She is Jewel E. Cash, and she is only 16 years old.

A junior at Boston Latin Academy, Jewel was raised in one of Boston's housing projects by her mother, a single parent. Today she belongs to the Boston Student Advisory Council, mentors children, volunteers at a women's shelter, manages and dances in two troupes, and participates in a neighborhood watch group—among other activities. Jewel is far from typical, but her activities illustrate that cognitive and socioemotional development allows adolescents to be capable, effective individuals.

topical connections *looking back*

In middle and late childhood, development of self-understanding and understanding others becomes more sophisticated, emotional understanding improves, and moral reasoning advances. In Erikson's view, children now are in the industry versus inferiority stage, with their industry expressed as an interest in building things and figuring out how things work. Children now spend more time with peers, but parents continue to play important roles in their development, especially in guiding their academic achievement and managing their opportunities. Peer status and friendship become more important in children's peer relations, and school takes on a stronger academic focus.

preview

Significant changes characterize socioemotional development in adolescence. These changes include increased efforts to understand themselves and to find their identity. Changes also occur in the social contexts of adolescents' lives, with transformations occurring in relationships with families and peers in cultural contexts. Adolescents also may develop socioemotional problems such as delinquency and depression.

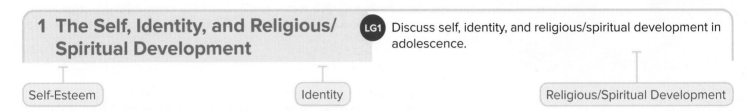

1 The Self, Identity, and Religious/ Spiritual Development

LG1 Discuss self, identity, and religious/spiritual development in adolescence.

Self-Esteem   Identity   Religious/Spiritual Development

Jewel Cash told an interviewer from the *Boston Globe,* "I see a problem and I say, 'How can I make a difference?' . . . I can't take on the world, even though I can try. . . . I'm moving forward but I want to make sure I'm bringing people with me" (Silva, 2005, pp. B1, B4). Jewel's confidence and positive identity sound at least as impressive as her activities. This section examines how adolescents develop characteristics like these. How much did you understand yourself during adolescence, and how did you acquire the stamp of your identity? Is your identity still developing?

SELF-ESTEEM

Recall from Chapter 10 that self-esteem is the overall way we evaluate ourselves. Controversy characterizes the extent to which self-esteem changes during adolescence and whether there are gender differences in adolescents' self-esteem (Harter, 2006, 2012, 2013). In one study, both boys and girls had particularly high self-esteem in childhood, but their self-esteem dropped considerably during adolescence (Robins & others, 2002). The self-esteem of girls declined more than the self-esteem of boys during adolescence in this study.

Does self-esteem in adolescence foreshadow adjustment and competence in adulthood? A New Zealand longitudinal study assessed the self-esteem of adolescents at 11, 13, and 15 years of age and then assessed the adjustment and competence of the same individuals when they were 26 years old (Trzesniewski & others, 2006). The results revealed that adults with poorer mental and physical health, worse economic prospects, and higher levels of criminal behavior were more likely to have had low self-esteem in adolescence than their better adjusted, more competent adult counterparts.

Some critics argue that developmental changes and gender differences in self-esteem during adolescence have been exaggerated (Harter, 2006, 2012, 2013). Despite the differing results and interpretations, the self-esteem of girls is likely to decline at least somewhat during early adolescence.

Why would the self-esteem of girls decline during early adolescence? One explanation points to girls' negative body images during pubertal change. Another explanation involves the greater interest young adolescent girls take in social relationships and society's failure to reward that interest (Impett & others, 2008).

Self-esteem reflects perceptions that do not always match reality (Jordan & Ziegler-Hill, 2013; Krueger, Vohs, & Baumeister, 2008). An adolescent's self-esteem might indicate a perception about whether he or she is intelligent and attractive, for example, but that perception may not be accurate. Thus, high self-esteem may refer to accurate, justified perceptions of one's worth as a person and one's successes and accomplishments, but it can also indicate an arrogant, grandiose, unwarranted sense of superiority over others. In the same manner, low self-esteem may suggest either an accurate perception of one's shortcomings or a distorted, even pathological insecurity and inferiority.

What characterizes narcissistic adolescents? Are today's adolescents more narcissistic than their counterparts in earlier generations?

"Who are you?" said the Caterpillar. Alice replied, rather shyly, "I—I hardly know, Sir, just at present—at least I know who I was when I got up this morning, but I must have changed several times since then."

—LEWIS CARROLL
English Writer, 19th Century

What are some important dimensions of identity?

narcissism A self-centered and self-concerned approach toward others.

Narcissism refers to a self-centered and self-concerned approach toward others. Typically, narcissists are unaware of their actual self and how others perceive them. This lack of awareness contributes to their adjustment problems. Narcissists are excessively self-centered and self-congratulatory, viewing their own needs and desires as paramount.

Are today's adolescents and emerging adults more self-centered and narcissistic than their counterparts in earlier generations? Research by Jean Twenge and her colleagues (2008a, b) indicated that compared with Baby Boomers who were surveyed in 1975, twelfth-graders surveyed in 2006 were more self-satisfied overall and far more confident that they would be very good employees, mates, and parents. However, other recent large-scale analyses have revealed no increase in high school and college students' narcissism from the 1980s through the first decade of the twenty-first century (Roberts, Edmonds, & Grijalva, 2010; Trzesniewski & Donnellan, 2010; Trzesniewski, Donnellan, & Robins, 2008a, b, 2013).

IDENTITY

Who am I? What am I all about? What am I going to do with my life? What is different about me? How can I make it on my own? These questions reflect the search for an identity. By far the most comprehensive and provocative theory of identity development is Erik Erikson's. In this section, we examine his views on identity. We also discuss contemporary research on how identity develops and how social contexts influence that development.

What Is Identity? Identity is a self-portrait composed of many pieces, including these:

- The career and work path the person wants to follow (vocational/career identity)
- Whether the person is conservative, liberal, or middle-of-the-road (political identity)
- The person's spiritual beliefs (religious identity)
- Whether the person is single, married, divorced, and so on (relationship identity)
- The extent to which the person is motivated to achieve and is intellectually oriented (achievement, intellectual identity)
- Whether the person is heterosexual, homosexual, or bisexual (sexual identity)
- Which part of the world or country a person is from and how intensely the person identifies with his or her cultural heritage (cultural/ethnic identity)
- The kind of things a person likes to do, which can include sports, music, hobbies, and so on (interests)
- The individual's personality characteristics, such as being introverted or extroverted, anxious or calm, friendly or hostile, and so on (personality)
- The individual's body image (physical identity)

Synthesizing the identity components can be a long and drawn-out process, with many negations and affirmations of various roles and faces (Kroger, 2012). Identity development takes place in bits and pieces. Decisions are not made once and for all, but have to be made again and again. Identity development does not happen neatly, and it does not happen cataclysmically (Azmitia, Syed, & Radmacher, 2014; Rivas-Drake & others, 2014a, b; Schwartz & others, 2013, 2014a, b, c).

Erikson's View It was Erik Erikson (1950, 1968) who first understood how central questions about identity are to understanding adolescent development.

Recall from Chapter 1 that Erikson's fifth developmental stage, which individuals experience during adolescence, is *identity versus identity confusion.* During this time, said Erikson, adolescents are faced with deciding who they are, what they are all about, and where they are going in life.

The search for an identity during adolescence is aided by a *psychosocial moratorium,* which is Erikson's term for the gap between childhood security and adult autonomy. During this period, society leaves adolescents relatively free of responsibilities and able to try out different identities. Adolescents experiment with different roles and personalities. They may want to pursue one career one month (lawyer, for example) and another career the next month (doctor, actor, teacher, social worker, or astronaut, for example). They may dress neatly one day, sloppily the next. This experimentation is a deliberate effort on the part of adolescents to find out where they fit in the world. Most adolescents eventually discard undesirable roles.

Youth who successfully cope with conflicting identities emerge with a new sense of self that is both refreshing and acceptable. Adolescents who do not successfully resolve this identity crisis suffer what Erikson calls identity confusion. The confusion takes one of two courses: Individuals withdraw, isolating themselves from peers and family, or they immerse themselves in the world of peers and lose their identity in the crowd.

Developmental Changes   Although questions about identity may be especially important during adolescence, identity formation neither begins nor ends during these years. What is important about identity development in adolescence, especially late adolescence, is that for the first time, physical development, cognitive development, and socioemotional development advance to the point at which the individual can sort through and synthesize childhood identities and identifications to construct a viable path toward adult maturity.

How do individual adolescents go about the process of forming an identity? Eriksonian researcher James Marcia (1980, 1994) reasons that Erikson's theory of identity development contains four statuses of identity, or ways of resolving the identity crisis: identity diffusion, identity foreclosure, identity moratorium, and identity achievement. What determines an individual's identity status? Marcia classifies individuals based on the existence or extent of their crisis or commitment (see Figure 12.1). **Crisis** is defined as a period of identity development during which the individual is exploring alternatives. Most researchers use the term *exploration* rather than *crisis*. **Commitment** is personal investment in identity.

The four statuses of identity are described below:

- **Identity diffusion** is the status of individuals who have not yet experienced a crisis or made any commitments. Not only are they undecided about occupational and ideological choices, they are also likely to show little interest in such matters.

- **Identity foreclosure** is the status of individuals who have made a commitment but not experienced a crisis. This occurs most often when parents hand down commitments to their adolescents, usually in an authoritarian way, before adolescents have had a chance to explore different approaches, ideologies, and vocations on their own.

- **Identity moratorium** is the status of individuals who are in the midst of a crisis but whose commitments are either absent or are only vaguely defined.

- **Identity achievement** is the status of individuals who have undergone a crisis and made a commitment.

Earlier in this chapter we described a number of dimensions of identity. To explore your identity status on a number of dimensions, see Figure 12.1.

developmental **connection**

Cognitive Theory

Erikson's stage for middle and late childhood is industry versus inferiority and for early adulthood is intimacy versus isolation. Chapter 10, p. 308; Chapter 14, p. 438

Once formed, an identity furnishes individuals with a historical sense of who they have been, a meaningful sense of who they are now, and a sense of who they might become in the future.

—**James Marcia**
Contemporary Psychologist, Simon Fraser University

crisis Marcia's term for a period of identity development during which the adolescent is exploring alternatives.

commitment Marcia's term for the part of identity development in which adolescents show a personal investment in identity.

identity diffusion Marcia's term for the status of individuals who have not yet experienced a crisis (explored meaningful alternatives) or made any commitments.

identity foreclosure Marcia's term for the status of individuals who have made a commitment but have not experienced a crisis.

identity moratorium Marcia's term for the status of individuals who are in the midst of a crisis, but their commitments are either absent or vaguely defined.

identity achievement Marcia's term for the status of individuals who have undergone a crisis and have made a commitment.

Position on Occupation and Ideology	Identity Status			
	Identity Diffusion	Identity Foreclosure	Identity Moratorium	Identity Achievement
Crisis	Absent	Absent	Present	Present
Commitment	Absent	Present	Absent	Present

FIGURE **12.1**

MARCIA'S FOUR STATUSES OF IDENTITY. According to Marcia, an individual's status in developing an identity can be categorized as identity diffusion, identity foreclosure, identity moratorium, or identity achievement. The status depends on the presence or absence of (1) a crisis or exploration of alternatives and (2) a commitment to an identity. *What is the identity status of most young adolescents?*

How does identity change in emerging adulthood?

Emerging Adulthood and Beyond   One study found that as individuals matured from early adolescence to emerging adulthood, they increasingly pursued in-depth exploration of their identity (Klimstra & others, 2010). And a recent meta-analysis of 124 studies by Jane Kroger and her colleagues (2010) revealed that during adolescence and emerging adulthood, identity moratorium status rose steadily to age 19 and then declined; identity achievement rose across late adolescence and emerging adulthood; and foreclosure and diffusion statuses declined across the high school years but fluctuated in the late teens and emerging adulthood. The studies also found that a large portion of individuals were not identity achieved by the time they reached their twenties.

Indeed, a consensus is developing that the key changes in identity are more likely to take place in emerging adulthood (18 to 25 years of age) or later than during adolescence (Schwartz & others, 2013, 2014a, c; Walker & Syed, 2013). College upperclassmen are more likely to be identity achieved than college freshmen or high school students. Many young adolescents, on the other hand, are identity diffused.

Why might college produce some key changes in identity? Increased complexity in the reasoning skills of college students, combined with a wide range of new experiences that highlight contrasts between home and college and between themselves and others, stimulate them to reach a higher level of integrating various dimensions of their identity (Phinney, 2008). College contexts serve as a virtual "laboratory" for identity development through such experiences as diverse coursework and exposure to peers from diverse backgrounds. Also, one of emerging adulthood's key themes is not having many social commitments, which gives individuals considerable independence in developing a life path (Arnett & Fishel, 2013).

Resolution of the identity issue during adolescence and emerging adulthood does not mean that identity will be stable throughout the remainder of life. Many individuals who develop positive identities follow what are called "MAMA" cycles; that is, their identity status changes from moratorium to achievement to moratorium to achievement (Marcia, 1994). These cycles may be repeated throughout life (Francis, Fraser, & Marcia, 1989).

Marcia (2002) points out that the first identity is just that—it is not, and should not be expected to be, the final product.

Cultural and Ethnic Identity   Most research on identity development has historically been based on data obtained from adolescents and emerging adults in the United States and Canada, especially those who are non-Latino Whites (Schwartz, Cano, & Zamboanga, 2014; Schwartz & others, 2012, 2014b). Many of these individuals have grown up in cultural contexts that value individual autonomy. However, in many countries around the world, adolescents and emerging adults have grown up influenced by a collectivist emphasis on fitting in with the group and connecting with others (Juang, Syed, & Cookston, 2012; Schwartz & others, 2014b, c). The collectivist emphasis is especially prevalent in East Asian countries such as China. Researchers have found that self-oriented identity exploration may not be the main process through which identity achievement is attained in East Asian countries (Schwartz & others, 2012). Rather, East Asian adolescents and emerging adults may develop their identity through identification with and imitation of others in their cultural group (Bosma & Kunnen, 2001).

Identity development may take longer in some countries than in others (Schwartz & others, 2012, 2014c). For example, research indicates that Italian youth may postpone significant identity exploration beyond adolescence and emerging adulthood, not settling on an identity until their mid- to late twenties (Crocetti, Rabaglietti, & Sica, 2012). This delayed identity development is strongly influenced by many Italian youth living at home with their parents until 30 years of age and older.

Seth Schwartz and his colleagues (2012) recently pointed out that while everyone identifies with a particular "culture," many individuals in cultural majority groups take their cultural identity for granted. Thus, many adolescents and emerging adults in the cultural majority of non-Latino Whites in the United States likely don't spend much time

One adolescent girl, 16-year-old Michelle Chin, made these comments about ethnic identity development: "My parents do not understand that teenagers need to find out who they are, which means a lot of experimenting, a lot of mood swings, a lot of emotions and awkwardness. Like any teenager, I am facing an identity crisis. I am still trying to figure out whether I am a Chinese American or an American with Asian eyes."

thinking of themselves as "White American." However, for many adolescents and emerging adults who have grown up within an ethnic minority group in the United States or emigrated from another country, cultural dimensions likely are an important aspect of their identity.

Throughout the world, ethnic minority groups have struggled to maintain their ethnic identities while blending in with the dominant culture (Erikson, 1968). **Ethnic identity** is an enduring aspect of the self that includes a sense of membership in an ethnic group, along with the attitudes and feelings related to that membership (Phinney & others, 2013a, b; Syed & Juang, 2014; Umana-Taylor & others, 2014). Most adolescents from ethnic minority groups develop a *bicultural identity*. That is, they identify in some ways with their ethnic group and in other ways with the majority culture (Basilio & others, 2014; Berry & others, 2013; Knight & others, 2014).

For ethnic minority individuals, adolescence and emerging adulthood are often special junctures in their development (Rivas-Drake & others, 2014a; Schwartz & others, 2014c; Syed, 2013; Syed & Juang, 2014). Although children are aware of some ethnic and cultural differences, individuals consciously confront their ethnicity for the first time in adolescence or emerging adulthood. Unlike children, adolescents and emerging adults have the ability to interpret ethnic and cultural information, to reflect on the past, and to speculate about the future. With their advancing cognitive skills of abstract thinking and self-reflection, adolescents (especially older adolescents) increasingly consider the meaning of their ethnicity and also have more ethnic-related experiences (O'Hara & others, 2012).

The indicators of identity change often differ for each succeeding generation (Phinney & Ong, 2007). First-generation immigrants are likely to be secure in their identities and unlikely to change much; they may or may not develop a new identity. The degree to which they begin to feel "American" appears to be related to whether or not they learn English, develop social networks beyond their ethnic group, and become culturally competent in their new country. Second-generation immigrants are more likely to think of themselves as "American," possibly because citizenship is granted at birth. Their ethnic identity is likely to be linked to retention of their ethnic language and social networks. In the third and later generations, the issues become more complex. Historical, contextual, and political factors that are unrelated to acculturation may affect the extent to which members of this generation retain their ethnic identities. For non-European ethnic groups, racism and discrimination influence whether ethnic identity is retained.

Researchers are also increasingly finding that a positive ethnic identity is related to positive outcomes for ethnic minority adolescents (Rivas-Drake & others, 2014b; Williams & others, 2014). Consider the following studies:

- Asian American adolescents' ethnic identity was associated with high self-esteem, positive relationships, academic motivation, and lower levels of depression over time (Kiang, Witkow, & Champagne, 2013).

- Having a positive ethnic identity helped to buffer some of the negative effects of discrimination experienced by Mexican American adolescents (Umana-Taylor & others, 2012).

- Navajo adolescents' positive ethnic heritage was linked to higher self-esteem, school connectedness, and social functioning (Jones & Galliher, 2007).

RELIGIOUS/SPIRITUAL DEVELOPMENT

In Chapter 11, we described the many positive benefits of service learning. A number of studies have found that adolescents who are involved in religious institutions are more likely to engage in service learning than their counterparts who don't participate in religious institutions (Lerner & others, 2013; Saroglou, 2013). Let's explore adolescents' religious and spiritual experiences.

Religious issues are important to many adolescents, but during the twenty-first century religious interest among adolescents has declined. In a 2010 national study of American college freshmen, 73 percent said they had attended religious services frequently or occasionally during their senior year in high school, down from a high of 85 percent in 1997 (Pryor, DeAngelo, & Blake, 2011).

A developmental study revealed that religiousness declined from 14 to 20 years of age in the United States (Koenig, McGue, & Iacono, 2008) (see Figure 12.2). In this study, religiousness was assessed with items such as frequency of prayer, frequency of discussing

ethnic identity An enduring, basic aspect of the self that includes a sense of membership in an ethnic group and the attitudes and feelings related to that membership.

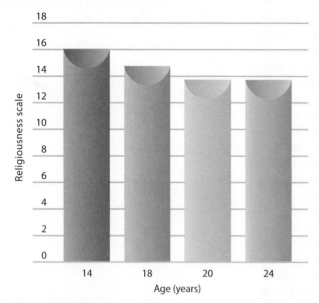

FIGURE 12.2

DEVELOPMENTAL CHANGES IN RELIGIOUSNESS FROM 14 TO 24 YEARS OF AGE. *Note:* The religiousness scale ranged from 0 to 32, with higher scores indicating stronger religiousness.

religious teachings, frequency of deciding moral actions for religious reasons, and the overall importance of religion in everyday life. As indicated in Figure 12.2, more change in religiousness occurred from 14 to 18 years of age than from 20 to 24 years of age. Also in this study, attending religious services declined from 14 to 18 years of age and then began to increase at 20 years of age.

Researchers have found that adolescent girls are more religious than are adolescent boys (King & Roeser, 2009). One study of 13- to 17-year-olds revealed that girls are more likely to attend religious services frequently, to perceive that religion shapes their daily lives, to participate in religious youth groups, to pray alone, and to feel closer to God (Smith & Denton, 2005).

Analysis of the World Values Survey of 18- to 24-year-olds revealed that emerging adults in less developed countries were more likely to be religious than their counterparts in more developed countries (Lippman & Keith, 2006). For example, emerging adults' reports that religion was very important in their lives ranged from a low of 0 in Japan to 93 percent in Nigeria, and belief in God ranged from a low of 40 percent in Sweden to a high of 100 percent in Pakistan.

Religion and Identity Development   As we saw earlier in this chapter, identity development becomes a central focus during adolescence and emerging adulthood (Rivas-Drake & others, 2014a, b; Schwartz & others, 2014a, b, c). As part of their search for identity, adolescents and emerging adults begin to grapple in more sophisticated, logical ways with such questions as "Why am I on this planet?" "Is there really a God or higher spiritual being, or have I just been believing what my parents and the church imprinted in my mind?" "What really are my religious views?"

Cognitive Development and Religion in Adolescence   Many of the cognitive changes thought to influence religious development involve Piaget's cognitive developmental theory. More so than in childhood, adolescents think abstractly, idealistically, and logically. The increase in abstract thinking lets adolescents consider various ideas about religious and spiritual concepts. For example, an adolescent might ask how a loving God can possibly exist

Many children and adolescents show an interest in religion, and many religious institutions created by adults (such as this Muslim school in Malaysia) are designed to introduce them to religious benefits and ensure that they will carry on a religious tradition.

given the extensive suffering of many people in the world (Good & Willoughby, 2008). Adolescents' increased idealistic thinking provides a foundation for thinking about whether religion provides the best route to a better world. And adolescents' increased logical reasoning gives them the ability to develop hypotheses and systematically sort through different answers to spiritual questions (Good & Willoughby, 2008).

The Positive Role of Religion in Adolescents' Lives   Researchers have found that various aspects of religion are linked with positive outcomes for adolescents (Shek, 2012). Religion plays a role in adolescents' health and has an influence on whether they engage in problem behaviors (King, Ramos, & Clardy, 2013). A recent meta-analysis found that spirituality/religiosity was positively related to well-being, self-esteem, and three of the Big Five factors of personality (conscientiousness, agreeableness, openness) (Yonker, Schnabelrauch, & DeHaan, 2012). In this meta-analysis, spirituality/religion was negatively associated with higher levels of risk-taking and depression. And a study of ninth- to twelfth-graders revealed that more frequent religious attendance in one grade predicted lower levels of substance abuse in the next grade (Good & Willoughby, 2010).

Many religious adolescents also adopt their religion's message about caring and concern for people (Lerner & others, 2013; Saroglou, 2013; Shek, 2012). For example, in one survey religious youth were almost three times as likely to engage in community service as nonreligious youth (Youniss, McLellan, & Yates, 1999).

developmental **connection**

Religion

Religion plays an important role in the lives of many individuals in adulthood and is linked to their health and coping. Chapter 15, p. 478; Chapter 18, p. 563

Review Connect Reflect

 Discuss self, identity, and religious/spiritual development in adolescence.

Review

- What are some changes in self-esteem that take place during adolescence?
- How does identity develop in adolescence?
- What characterizes religious and spiritual development in adolescence?

Connect

- Compare what is said about inflated self-esteem in middle and late childhood in Chapter 10 to what is said in this section about potential narcissism in adolescence. What are your conclusions?

Reflect *Your Own Personal Journey of Life*

- What role did religion/spiritual development play in your life during adolescence? Has your religious/spiritual thinking changed since you were an adolescent? If so, how?

2 Families   LG2   Describe changes that take place in adolescents' relationships with their parents.

Parental Monitoring and Information Management	Autonomy and Attachment	Parent-Adolescent Conflict

Adolescence typically alters the relationship between parents and their children. Among the most important aspects of family relationships in adolescence are those that involve parental monitoring and information management, autonomy and attachment, and parent-adolescent conflict.

PARENTAL MONITORING AND INFORMATION MANAGEMENT

In Chapter 10, we discussed the importance of parents as managers of children's development. A key aspect of the managerial role of parenting is effective monitoring, which is especially important as children move into the adolescent years (Kaynak & others, 2013;

What role does parental monitoring and information management play in adolescent development?

Metzger & others, 2013). Monitoring includes supervising adolescents' choice of social settings, activities, and friends, as well as their academic efforts. A recent study found that high level of parental monitoring within the context of parental warmth was linked to positive academic outcomes for ethnic minority youth (Lowe & Dotterer, 2013). A recent meta-analysis also concluded that low parental monitoring was associated with adolescent depression (Yap & others, 2014). And in another recent study, low parental monitoring was a key factor in predicting a developmental trajectory of delinquency and substance use in adolescence (Wang & others, 2014). Later in this chapter, we will describe lack of adequate parental monitoring as the parental factor most likely to be linked to juvenile delinquency.

A current interest involving parental monitoring focuses on adolescents' management of their parents' access to information, especially strategies used in disclosing or concealing information about their activities (Marshall, Tilton-Weaver, & Bosdet, 2005; Tilton-Weaver & Marshall, 2008). A recent study of U.S. and Chinese young adolescents found that adolescents' disclosure to parents was linked with a higher level of academic competence (better learning strategies, autonomous motivation, and better grades) over time (Cheung, Pomerantz, & Dong, 2012). When parents engage in positive parenting practices, adolescents are more likely to disclose information (Rote & others, 2012). For example, disclosure increases when parents ask adolescents questions and when adolescents' relationship with parents is characterized by a high level of trust, acceptance, and quality (Keijsers & Laird, 2010; McElvaney, Greene, & Hogan, 2014). Researchers have found that adolescents' disclosure to parents about their whereabouts, activities, and friends is linked to positive adolescent adjustment (Smetana, 2011a, b).

AUTONOMY AND ATTACHMENT

With most adolescents, parents are likely to find themselves engaged in a delicate balancing act, weighing competing needs for autonomy and control, for independence and connection.

The typical adolescent's push for autonomy and responsibility puzzles and angers many parents. Most parents anticipate that their teenager will have some difficulty adjusting to the changes that adolescence brings, but few parents imagine and predict just how strong an adolescent's desires will be to spend time with peers or how intensely adolescents will want to show that it is they—not their parents—who are responsible for their successes and failures.

Adolescents' ability to attain autonomy and gain control over their behavior is acquired through appropriate adult reactions to their desire for control (McElhaney & Allen, 2012). At the onset of adolescence, the average individual does not have the knowledge to make appropriate or mature decisions in all areas of life. As the adolescent pushes for autonomy, the wise adult relinquishes control in those areas where the adolescent can make reasonable decisions, but continues to guide the adolescent to make reasonable decisions in areas where the adolescent's knowledge is more limited. Gradually, adolescents acquire the ability to make mature decisions on their own.

Gender differences characterize autonomy-granting in adolescence. Boys are given more independence than girls. In one study, this was especially true in U.S. families with a traditional gender-role orientation (Bumpus, Crouter, & McHale, 2001).

Expectations about the appropriate timing of adolescent autonomy often vary across cultures, parents, and adolescents (McElhaney & Allen, 2012; Romo, Mireles-Rios, & Lopez-Tello, 2014). For example, expectations for early autonomy on the part of adolescents are more prevalent among non-Latino Whites, single parents, and adolescents themselves than they are among Asian Americans or Latinos, married parents, and parents themselves (Feldman & Rosenthal, 1999). Nonetheless, although Latino cultures may place a stronger emphasis on parental authority and restrict adolescent autonomy, a recent study revealed that regardless of where they were born, Mexican-origin adolescent girls

developmental **connection**

Parenting

In authoritative parenting, parents encourage children and adolescents to be independent but still place limits and controls on their actions. Extensive verbal give-and-take is allowed, and parents are warm and nurturant. Chapter 8, p. 245

When I was a boy of 14, my father was so ignorant I could hardly stand to have the man around. But when I got to be 21, I was astonished at how much the old man had learnt in 7 years.

—MARK TWAIN
American Writer and Humorist, 19th Century

living in the United States expected autonomy at an earlier age than their mothers preferred (Bamaca-Colbert & others, 2012).

The Role of Attachment   Recall from Chapter 6 that one of the most widely discussed aspects of socioemotional development in infancy is secure attachment to caregivers (Easterbrooks & others, 2013; Milan & Acker, 2014). In the past decade, researchers have explored whether secure attachment also might be an important concept in adolescents' relationships with their parents (Sheftall & others, 2013). Researchers have found that securely attached adolescents are less likely than those who are insecurely attached to have emotional difficulties and to engage in problem behaviors such as juvenile delinquency and drug abuse (Dykes & Cassidy, 2011; Hoeve & others, 2012). In a longitudinal study, Joseph Allen and colleagues (2009) found that secure attachment at 14 years of age was linked to a number of positive outcomes at 21 years of age, including relationship competence, financial/career competence, and fewer problematic behaviors. In a recent analysis, it was concluded that the most consistent outcomes of secure attachment in adolescence involve positive peer relations and development of the adolescent's capacity to regulate emotions (Allen & Miga, 2010).

Balancing Freedom and Control   We have seen that parents play very important roles in adolescent development (Morris, Cui, & Steinberg, 2013). Although adolescents are moving toward independence, they still need to stay connected with their family (Schwarz, Stutz, & Ledermann, 2012). For example, the National Longitudinal Study on Adolescent Health of more than 12,000 adolescents found that those who did not eat dinner with a parent five or more days a week had dramatically higher rates of smoking, drinking, using marijuana, getting into fights, and initiating sexual activity (Council of Economic Advisors, 2000).

According to one adolescent girl, Stacey Christensen, age 16: "I am lucky enough to have open communication with my parents. Whenever I am in need or just need to talk, my parents are there for me. My advice to parents is to let your teens grow at their own pace, be open with them so that you can be there for them. We need guidance; our parents need to help but not be too overwhelming."

PARENT-ADOLESCENT CONFLICT

Although parent-adolescent conflict increases in early adolescence, it does not reach the tumultuous proportions G. Stanley Hall envisioned at the beginning of the twentieth century (Bornstein, Jager, & Steinberg, 2013). Rather, much of the conflict involves the everyday events of family life, such as keeping a bedroom clean, dressing neatly, getting home by a certain time, and not talking endlessly on the phone. The conflicts rarely involve major dilemmas such as drugs or delinquency.

Conflict with parents often escalates during early adolescence, remains somewhat stable during the high school years, and then lessens as the adolescent reaches 17 to 20 years of age. Parent-adolescent relationships become more positive if adolescents go away to college than if they attend college while living at home (Sullivan & Sullivan, 1980).

The everyday conflicts that characterize parent-adolescent relationships may actually serve a positive developmental function. These minor disputes and negotiations facilitate the adolescent's transition from being dependent on parents to becoming an autonomous individual. Recognizing that conflict and negotiation can serve a positive developmental function can tone down parental hostility.

The old model of parent-adolescent relationships suggested that as adolescents mature they detach themselves from parents and move into a world of autonomy apart from parents. The old model also suggested that parent-adolescent conflict is intense and stressful throughout adolescence. The new model emphasizes that parents serve as important attachment figures and support systems while adolescents explore a wider, more complex social world. The new model also emphasizes that in most families parent-adolescent conflict is moderate rather than severe and that the everyday negotiations and minor disputes not only are normal but also can serve the positive developmental function of helping the adolescent make the transition from childhood dependency to adult independence (see Figure 12.3).

Still, a high degree of conflict characterizes some parent-adolescent relationships (Rengasamy & others, 2013; Schwarz, Stutz, & Ledermann, 2012).

Conflict with parents increases in early adolescence. *What is the nature of this conflict in a majority of American families?*

developmental **connection**

Attachment

In secure attachment during infancy, babies use the caregiver as a secure base from which to explore the environment. Chapter 6, p. 181

Old Model		New Model
Autonomy, detachment from parents; parent and peer worlds are isolated Intense, stressful conflict throughout adolescence; parent-adolescent relationships are filled with storm and stress on virtually a daily basis		Attachment and autonomy; parents are important support systems and attachment figures; adolescent-parent and adolescent-peer worlds have some important connections Moderate parent-adolescent conflict is common and can serve a positive developmental function; conflict greater in early adolescence

FIGURE 12.3

OLD AND NEW MODELS OF PARENT-ADOLESCENT RELATIONSHIPS

And this prolonged, intense conflict is associated with various adolescent problems: movement out of the home, juvenile delinquency, school dropout, pregnancy and early marriage, membership in religious cults, and drug abuse (Brook & others, 1990). A recent study revealed that a higher level of parent-adolescent conflict was related to peer-reported aggression and delinquency (Ehrlich, Dykas, & Cassidy, 2012).

Cross-cultural studies reveal that parent-adolescent conflict is lower in some countries than in the United States. Two countries where parent-adolescent conflict is lower than in the United States are Japan and India.

When families emigrate to another country, adolescents typically acculturate more quickly to the norms and values of their new country than do their parents (Fuligni, 2012). This likely occurs because of immigrant adolescents' exposure in school to the language and culture of the host country. The norms and values immigrant adolescents experience are especially likely to diverge from those of their parents in areas such as autonomy and romantic relationships. Such divergences are likely to increase parent-adolescent conflict in immigrant families. Andrew Fuligni (2012) argues that these conflicts aren't always expressed openly but are often present in underlying, internal feelings. For example, immigrant adolescents may feel that their parents want them to give up their personal interests for the sake of the family, and the adolescents don't think this is fair. Such acculturation-based conflict focuses on issues related to core cultural values and is likely to occur in immigrant families, such as Latino and Asian American families, who come to the United States to live (Juang & Umana-Taylor, 2012).

Review Connect Reflect

 Describe changes that take place in adolescents' relationships with their parents.

Review

- What roles do parental managing and monitoring play in adolescent development?
- How do needs for autonomy and attachment develop in adolescence?
- What characterizes parent-adolescent conflict?

Connect

- Adolescence is identified as the second time in an individual's life when the quest for independence is especially strong. When is the other time, and what characterizes that stage of development?

Reflect *Your Own Personal Journey of Life*

- How much autonomy did your parents give you in adolescence? Too much? Too little? How intense was your conflict with your parents during adolescence? What were the conflicts mainly about? Would you interact with your own adolescents differently from the way your parents did with you? If so, how?

Friendships · Peer Groups · Dating and Romantic Relationships

Peers play powerful roles in the lives of adolescents (Bornstein, Jager, & Steinberg, 2013; Rancourt & others, 2014; Trucco & others, 2014; Wentzel, 2013). Peer relations undergo important changes in adolescence, including changes in friendships and in peer groups, as well as the beginning of romantic relationships.

FRIENDSHIPS

For most children, being popular with their peers is a strong motivator. Beginning in early adolescence, however, teenagers typically prefer to have a smaller number of friendships that are more intense and intimate than those of young children.

Harry Stack Sullivan (1953) was the most influential theorist to discuss the importance of adolescent friendships. During adolescence, said Sullivan, friends become increasingly important in meeting social needs. In particular, Sullivan argued, the need for intimacy intensifies during early adolescence, motivating teenagers to seek out close friends. If adolescents fail to develop such close friendships, they experience loneliness and a reduced sense of self-worth.

Many of Sullivan's ideas have withstood the test of time. For example, adolescents report disclosing intimate and personal information to their friends more often than do younger children (Buhrmester, 1998) (see Figure 12.4). Adolescents also say they depend more on friends than on parents to satisfy their needs for companionship, reassurance of worth, and intimacy. The ups and downs of experiences with friends shape adolescents' well-being (Cook, Buehler, & Blair, 2013). Adolescent girls are more likely to disclose information about problems to a friend than are adolescent boys (Rose & others, 2012).

Although having friends can be a developmental advantage, not all friendships are alike and the quality of friendship matters (Mason & others, 2014; Sirard & others, 2013). People differ in the company they keep—that is, who their friends are. It is a developmental disadvantage to have coercive, conflict-ridden, and poor-quality friendships (Poulin & others, 2011). Developmental advantages occur when adolescents have friends who are socially skilled, supportive, and oriented toward academic achievement (Rodkin & Ryan, 2012). Positive friendship relationships in adolescence are associated with a host of positive outcomes, including lower rates of delinquency, substance abuse, risky sexual behavior, and bullying victimization, and a higher level of academic achievement (Jones & Magee, 2014; Wentzel, 2013; Yu & others, 2013).

Although most adolescents develop friendships with individuals who are close to their own age, some adolescents become best friends with younger or older individuals. Do older friends encourage adolescents to engage in delinquent behavior or early sexual behavior? Adolescents who interact with older youth do engage in more problem behaviors, such as delinquency and early sexual behavior (Poulin & Pedersen, 2007).

To read about strategies for helping adolescents develop friendships, see *Connecting Development to Life*.

PEER GROUPS

How extensive is peer pressure in adolescence? What roles do cliques and crowds play in adolescents' lives? As we see next, researchers have found that the standards of peer groups and the influence of crowds and cliques become increasingly important during adolescence.

Peer Pressure   Young adolescents conform more to peer standards than children do (Badaly, 2013; Teunissen & others, 2014). Around the eighth and ninth grades, conformity

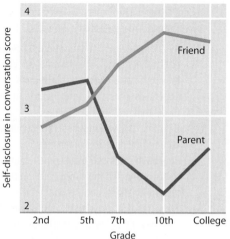

FIGURE **12.4**

DEVELOPMENTAL CHANGES IN SELF-DISCLOSING CONVERSATIONS. Self-disclosing conversations with friends increased dramatically in adolescence while declining in an equally dramatic fashion with parents. However, self-disclosing conversations with parents began to pick up somewhat during the college years. The measure of self-disclosure involved a 5-point rating scale completed by the children and youth, with a higher score representing greater self-disclosure. The data shown represent the means for each age group.

How do characteristics of an adolescent's friends influence whether the friends have a positive or negative influence on the adolescent?

Effective and Ineffective Strategies for Making Friends

Here are some strategies for making friends that adults can recommend to adolescents (Wentzel, 1997):

- Initiate interaction. Learn about a friend: Ask for his or her name, age, favorite activities. Use these prosocial overtures: introduce yourself, start a conversation, and invite him or her to do things.
- Be nice. Show kindness, be considerate, and compliment the other person.
- Engage in prosocial behavior. Be honest and trustworthy: Tell the truth, keep promises. Be generous, share, and be cooperative.
- Show respect for yourself and others. Have good manners, be polite and courteous, and listen to what others have to say. Have a positive attitude and personality.
- Provide social support. Show you care.

What are some effective and ineffective strategies for making friends?

And here are some inappropriate strategies for making friends that adults can recommend that adolescents avoid using (Wentzel, 1997):

- Be psychologically aggressive. Show disrespect and have bad manners. Use others, be uncooperative, don't share, ignore others, gossip, and spread rumors.
- Present yourself negatively. Be self-centered, snobby, conceited, and jealous; show off; care only about yourself. Be mean, have a bad attitude, be angry, throw temper tantrums, and start trouble.
- Behave antisocially. Be physically aggressive, yell at others, pick on them, make fun of them, be dishonest, tell secrets, and break promises.

Based on what you read earlier in this chapter, what might you recommend to an adolescent about whom to approach as a potential friend?

---

to peers—especially to their antisocial standards—peaks (Brown & Larson, 2009; Brown & others, 2008). At this point, adolescents are most likely to go along with a peer to steal hubcaps off a car, draw graffiti on a wall, or steal cosmetics from a store counter. One study found that U.S. adolescents are more likely than Japanese adolescents to put pressure on their peers to resist parental influence (Rothbaum & others, 2000).

Which adolescents are most likely to conform to peers? Mitchell Prinstein and his colleagues (Cohen & Prinstein, 2006; Prinstein, 2007; Prinstein & Dodge, 2008) have conducted research that found adolescents who feel uncertain about their social identity, which may be evident in low self-esteem and high social anxiety, are most likely to conform to peers. This uncertainty often increases during times of transition, such as changing circumstances in school and family life. Also, adolescents are more likely to conform to peers whom they perceive to have higher status than they do.

Cliques and Crowds   Cliques and crowds assume more important roles during adolescence than during childhood (Brown, 2011). **Cliques** are small groups that range from 2 to about 12 individuals and average about 5 or 6 individuals. The clique members are usually of the same sex and about the same age.

Cliques can form because adolescents engage in similar activities, such as belonging to a club or playing on a sports team. Some cliques also form because of friendship. Several adolescents may form a clique because they have spent time with each other, share mutual interests, and enjoy each other's company.

Crowds are larger than cliques and less personal. Adolescents are usually members of a crowd based on reputation, and they may or may not spend much time together. Many crowds are defined by the activities adolescents engage in (such as "jocks" who are good at sports or "druggies" who take drugs) (Brown, 2011).

What characterizes peer pressure in adolescence?

clique A small group of about 5 or 6 individuals that may form among adolescents who engage in similar activities.

DATING AND ROMANTIC RELATIONSHIPS

Adolescents spend considerable time either dating or thinking about dating (Ogolsky, Lloyd, & Cate, 2013; Young, Furman, & Laursen, 2014). Dating can be a form of recreation, a source of status, or a setting for learning about close relationships, as well as a way of finding a mate.

Developmental Changes in Dating and Romantic Relationships Three stages characterize the development of romantic relationships in adolescence (Connolly & McIsaac, 2009):

1. *Entry into romantic attractions and affiliations at about 11 to 13 years of age.* This initial stage is triggered by puberty. From 11 to 13, adolescents become intensely interested in romance and it dominates many conversations with same-sex friends. Developing a crush on someone is common and the crush often is shared with a same-sex friend. Young adolescents may or may not interact with the individual who is the object of their infatuation. When dating occurs, it usually occurs in a group setting.

2. *Exploring romantic relationships at approximately 14 to 16 years of age.* At this point in adolescence, two types of romantic involvement occur: (a) Casual dating emerges between individuals who are mutually attracted. These dating experiences are often short-lived, lasting a few months at best, and usually endure for only a few weeks. (b) Dating in groups is common and reflects embeddedness in the peer context. Friends often act as third-party facilitators of a potential dating relationship by communicating their friend's romantic interest and determining whether this attraction is reciprocated.

3. *Consolidating dyadic romantic bonds at about 17 to 19 years of age.* At the end of the high school years, more serious romantic relationships develop. This is characterized by strong emotional bonds more closely resembling those in adult romantic relationships. These bonds often are more stable and enduring than earlier bonds, typically lasting one year or more.

What are some developmental changes in romantic relationships in adolescence?

Two variations on these stages in the development of romantic relationships in adolescence involve early and late bloomers (Connolly & McIsaac, 2009). *Early bloomers* include 15 to 20 percent of 11- to 13-year-olds who say that they currently are in a romantic relationship and 35 percent who indicate that they have had some prior experience in romantic relationships. A recent study found that early bloomers externalized problem behaviors through adolescence more than their on-time and later-bloomer counterparts (Connolly & others, 2013). *Late bloomers* comprise approximately 10 percent of 17- to 19-year-olds who say that they have had no experience with romantic relationships and another 15 percent who report that they have not engaged in any romantic relationships that lasted more than four months.

Dating in Gay and Lesbian Youth Recently, researchers have begun to study romantic relationships among gay and lesbian youth (Diamond & Savin-Williams, 2015; Savin-Williams, 2015). Many sexual minority youth date other-sex peers, which can help them to clarify their sexual orientation or disguise it from others (Cohen & Savin-Williams, 2013). Most gay and lesbian youth have had some same-sex sexual experience, often with peers who are "experimenting." Some gay and lesbian youth continue to have a same-sex orientation while others have a primarily heterosexual orientation (Savin-Williams & Cohen, 2015; Vrangalova & Savin-Williams, 2013). In one study, gay and lesbian youth rated the breakup of a current romance as their second most stressful problem, second only to disclosure of their sexual orientation to their parents (D'Augelli, 1991).

Sociocultural Contexts and Dating The sociocultural context exerts a powerful influence on adolescents' dating patterns (Cheng & others, 2012). This influence may be seen in differences in dating patterns among ethnic groups within the United States. For example,

crowd A larger group structure than a clique that is usually based on reputation; members may or may not spend much time together.

one study found that Asian American adolescents were less likely to have been involved in a romantic relationship in the past 18 months than African American or Latino adolescents were (Carver, Joyner, & Udry, 2003).

Values, religious beliefs, and traditions often dictate the age at which dating begins, how much freedom in dating is allowed, whether dates must be chaperoned by adults or parents, and the roles of males and females in dating. For example, Latino and Asian American cultures have more conservative standards regarding adolescent dating than does the Anglo-American culture. Dating may become a source of conflict within a family if the parents grew up in cultures where dating begins at a late age, little freedom in dating is allowed, dates are chaperoned, and dating by adolescent girls is especially restricted. When immigrant adolescents choose to adopt the ways of the dominant U.S. culture (such as unchaperoned dating), they often clash with parents and extended-family members who have more traditional values.

Dating and Adjustment   Researchers have linked dating and romantic relationships with various measures of how well adjusted adolescents are (Collins, Welsh, & Furman, 2009; Soller, 2014). For example, a study of tenth-graders revealed that the more romantic experiences they had experienced, the more likely they were to report high levels of social acceptance, friendship competence, and romantic competence; however, having more romantic experience also was linked with a higher level of substance use, delinquency, and sexual behavior (Furman, Low, & Ho, 2009). In another study conducted among adolescent girls but not adolescent males, having an older romantic partner was linked with an increase in depressive symptoms, largely influenced by an increase in substance use (Haydon & Halpern, 2010).

Dating and romantic relationships at an early age can be especially problematic (Connolly & McIsaac, 2009). A recent study found that romantic activity was linked to depression in early adolescent girls (Starr & others, 2012). Researchers also have found that early dating and "going with" someone are linked with adolescent pregnancy and problems at home and school (Florsheim, Moore, & Edgington, 2003).

Review *Connect* Reflect

 LG3 Characterize the changes that occur in peer relationships during adolescence.

Review

- What changes take place in friendship during adolescence?
- What are adolescents' peer groups like?
- What is the nature of adolescent dating and romantic relationships?

Connect

- Relational aggression was discussed here and in Chapter 10. In one of the studies described in Chapter 10, what connection was made between parents and the relational aggression of their children?

Reflect *Your Own Personal Journey of Life*

- What were your peer relationships like during adolescence? What peer groups were you involved in? How did they influence your development? What were your dating and romantic relationships like in adolescence? If you could change anything about the way you experienced peer relations in adolescence, what would it be?

4 Culture and Adolescent Development

 LG4 Explain how culture influences adolescent development.

| Cross-Cultural Comparisons | Ethnicity | The Media |

In this section, we will discuss cross-cultural variations in a number of aspects of adolescent development. We also will examine how ethnicity affects U.S. adolescents and influences their development. And we will explore an important aspect of the cultural worlds of adolescents—the media.

CROSS-CULTURAL COMPARISONS

What traditions continue to influence the lives of adolescents around the globe? What circumstances are changing adolescents' lives? Depending on the culture, adolescence may involve many different experiences (Arnett, 2012).

Muslim school in Middle East with boys only.

Health   Adolescent health and well-being have improved in some respects but not in others. Overall, fewer adolescents around the world die from infectious diseases and malnutrition now than in the past (UNICEF, 2014). However, a number of adolescent health-compromising behaviors (especially illicit drug use and unprotected sex) are increasing in frequency. Extensive increases in the rates of HIV in adolescents have occurred in many sub-Saharan countries (UNICEF, 2014).

Gender   Around the world, the experiences of male and female adolescents continue to be quite different (Brown & Larson, 2002; Larson, Wilson, & Rickman, 2009). Except in a few regions, such as Japan, the Philippines, and Western countries, males have far greater access to educational opportunities than females do (UNICEF, 2014). In many countries, adolescent females have less freedom than males to pursue a variety of careers and engage in various leisure activities. Gender differences in sexual expression are widespread, especially in India, Southeast Asia, Latin America, and Arab countries where far more restrictions are placed on the sexual activity of adolescent females than on males. These gender differences do appear to be narrowing over time, however. In some countries, educational and career opportunities for women are expanding, and control over adolescent girls' romantic and sexual relationships is weakening.

Family   In some countries, adolescents grow up in closely knit families with extensive kin networks that retain a traditional way of life. For example, in Arab countries "adolescents are taught strict codes of conduct and loyalty" (Brown & Larson, 2002, p. 6). However, in Western countries such as the United States, parenting is less authoritarian than in the past, and much larger numbers of adolescents are growing up in divorced families and stepfamilies.

In many countries around the world, current trends "include greater family mobility, migration to urban areas, family members working in distant cities or countries, smaller families, fewer extended-family households, and increases in mothers' employment" (Brown & Larson, 2002, p. 7). Unfortunately, many of these changes may reduce the ability of families to spend time with their adolescents.

Peers   Some cultures give peers a stronger role in adolescence than other cultures do (Brown & others, 2008). In most Western nations, peers figure prominently in adolescents' lives, in some cases taking on roles that in other cultures are assumed by parents. Among street youth in South America, the peer network serves as a surrogate family that supports survival in dangerous and stressful settings. In other regions of the world, such as in Arab countries, peer relations are restricted, especially for girls (Booth, 2002).

Time Allocation to Different Activities   Reed Larson and his colleagues (Larson, 2001; Larson & Angus, 2011; Larson & Dawes, 2014; Larson, Shernoff, & Bempechat, 2014; Larson & Verma, 1999) have examined how adolescents spend their time in work, play, and developmental activities such as school. U.S. adolescents spend about 60 percent as much time on schoolwork as East Asian adolescents do, which is mainly due to U.S. adolescents doing less homework (Larson & Verma, 1999).

U.S. adolescents have greater quantities of discretionary time than adolescents in other industrialized countries do (Larson & Wilson, 2004; Larson, Wilson, & Rickman, 2009). About 40 to 50 percent of U.S. adolescents' waking hours (not counting summer vacations) is spent in discretionary activities, compared with 25 to 35 percent in East Asia and 35 to 45 percent in Europe. Whether this additional discretionary time is a liability or an asset for U.S. adolescents, of course, depends on how they use it.

According to Larson (2001), U.S. adolescents may have too much unstructured time because when they are given a choice they typically engage in unchallenging activities such as hanging out and watching TV. Although relaxation and social interaction are important aspects of adolescence, it seems unlikely that spending large numbers of hours per week in unchallenging activities would foster development. Structured voluntary activities may provide more promise for adolescent development than unstructured time, especially if adults give responsibility to adolescents, challenge them, and provide competent guidance in these activities (Larson & Dawes, 2014).

In sum, adolescents' lives are characterized by a combination of change and tradition. Researchers have found both similarities and differences in the experiences of adolescents in different countries (Chen & Liu, 2014; Schwartz & others, 2014a, c).

Rites of Passage   Another variation in the experiences of adolescents in different cultures is whether the adolescents go through a rite of passage. Some societies have elaborate ceremonies that signal the adolescent's move to maturity and achievement of adult status (Kottak & Kozaitis, 2012). A **rite of passage** is a ceremony or ritual that marks an individual's transition from one status to another. Most rites of passage focus on the transition to adult status. In some traditional cultures, rites of passage are the avenue through which adolescents gain access to sacred adult practices, to knowledge, and to sexuality. These rites often involve dramatic practices intended to facilitate the adolescent's separation from the immediate family, especially the mother. The transformation is usually characterized by some form of ritual death and rebirth, or by means of contact with the spiritual world. Bonds are forged between the adolescent and the adult instructors through shared rituals, hazards, and secrets to allow the adolescent to enter the adult world. This kind of ritual provides a forceful and discontinuous entry into the adult world at a time when the adolescent is perceived to be ready for the change.

These Congolese Kota boys painted their faces as part of a rite of passage to adulthood. *What rites of passage do American adolescents have?*

An especially rich tradition of rites of passage for adolescents has prevailed in African cultures, especially sub-Saharan Africa. Under the influence of Western industrialized culture, many of these rites are disappearing today, although they are still prevalent in locations where formal education is not readily available.

Do we have such rites of passage for American adolescents? We certainly do not have universal formal ceremonies that mark the passage from adolescence to adulthood. Certain religious and social groups do, however, have initiation ceremonies that indicate that an advance in maturity has been reached: the Jewish bar and bat mitzvah, the Catholic confirmation, and social debuts, for example. School graduation ceremonies come the closest to being culture-wide rites of passage in the United States. The high school graduation ceremony has become nearly universal for middle-class adolescents and increasing numbers of adolescents from low-income backgrounds.

ETHNICITY

Earlier in this chapter, we explored the identity development of ethnic minority adolescents. Here we will further examine immigration and the relationship between ethnicity and socioeconomic status.

rite of passage A ceremony or ritual that marks an individual's transition from one status to another. Most rites of passage focus on the transition to adult status.

Immigration   Relatively high rates of immigration are contributing to the growing proportion of ethnic minority adolescents and emerging adults in the United States (Camacho & Fuligni, 2014; Potochnick, 2014). Immigrant families are those in which at least one of the parents is born outside of the country of residence. Variations in immigrant families involve whether one or both parents are foreign born, whether the child was born in the host country, and the ages at which immigration took place for both the parents and the children. As recently concluded by Robert Crosnoe and Andrew Fuligni (2012, p. 1473):

> Some children from immigrant families are doing quite well, some less so, depending on the characteristics of migration itself (including the nation of origin) and their families' circumstances in their new country (including their position in socioeconomic and race-ethnic stratification systems)."

What are some of the circumstances immigrants face that challenge their adjustment? Immigrants often experience stressors uncommon to or less prominent among longtime residents, such as language barriers, dislocations and separations from support networks, the dual struggle to preserve identity and to acculturate, and changes in SES status (Rivas-Drake & others, 2014a; Schwartz, Cano, & Zamboanga, 2014; Schwartz & others, 2014c). Many individuals in immigrant families are dealing with the problem of being undocumented. Living in an undocumented family can affect children's and adolescents' developmental outcomes through parents being unwilling to sign up for services for which they are eligible, through conditions linked to low-wage work and lack of benefits, through stress, and through a lack of cognitive stimulation in the home (Yoshikawa, 2012). Consequently, when working with adolescents and their immigrant families, counselors need to adapt intervention programs to optimize cultural sensitivity (Sue & others, 2013, 2014).

What are some cultural adaptations Mexican American girls likely will have to make as immigrants to the United States?

Ethnicity and Socioeconomic Status Much of the research on ethnic minority adolescents has failed to tease apart the influences of ethnicity and socioeconomic status. Ethnicity and socioeconomic status can interact in ways that exaggerate the influence of ethnicity because ethnic minority individuals are overrepresented in the lower socioeconomic levels of American society (Cushner, McClelland, & Safford, 2015; Banks, 2014). Consequently, researchers too often have given ethnic explanations for aspects of adolescent development that were largely due instead to socioeconomic status.

Not all ethnic minority families are poor. However, poverty contributes to the stressful life experiences of many ethnic minority adolescents (Evans & Kim, 2013). Thus, many ethnic minority adolescents experience a double disadvantage: (1) prejudice, discrimination, and bias because of their ethnic minority status; and (2) the stressful effects of poverty (Crosnoe & Leventhal, 2014; Koppelman, 2014). Although some ethnic minority youth have middle-income backgrounds, economic advantage does not entirely enable them to escape the prejudice, discrimination, and bias associated with being a member of an ethnic minority group (McLoyd, Mistry, & Hardaway, 2014).

developmental **connection**

Environment

Poverty is linked to family turmoil, separation from a parent, violence, crowding, excessive noise, and poor housing. Chapter 1, p. 9

THE MEDIA

The culture adolescents experience not only involves values, socioeconomic status, and ethnicity, but also media influences. First, we will explore adolescents' use of various media and then we will discuss the role of digital media in adolescents' lives.

Media Use If the amount of time spent in an activity is any indication of its importance, there is no doubt that media play important roles in adolescents' lives (Calvert & Wartella, 2014). To better understand various aspects of U.S. adolescents' media use, the Kaiser Family Foundation funded three national surveys in 1999, 2004, and 2009. The 2009 survey included more than 2,000 8- to 18-year-olds and documented that adolescent media

How much time do adolescents spend using different types of media?

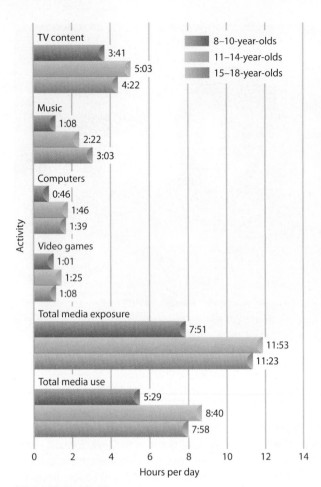

TV content
3:41
5:03
4:22

Music
1:08
2:22
3:03

Computers
0:46
1:46
1:39

Video games
1:01
1:25
1:08

Total media exposure
7:51
11:53
11:23

Total media use
5:29
8:40
7:58

■ 8–10-year-olds
■ 11–14-year-olds
■ 15–18-year-olds

Activity

0   2   4   6   8   10   12   14
Hours per day

FIGURE 12.5

DEVELOPMENTAL CHANGES IN THE AMOUNT OF TIME U.S. 8- TO 18-YEAR-OLDS SPEND WITH DIFFERENT TYPES OF MEDIA

What characterizes the online social environment of adolescents and emerging adults?

use has increased dramatically in the last decade (Rideout, Foehr, & Roberts, 2010). In this survey, in 2009, 8- to 11-year-olds used media 5 hours and 29 minutes a day, 11- to 14-year-olds used media an average of 8 hours and 40 minutes a day, and 15- to 18-year-olds an average of 7 hours and 58 minutes a day (see Figure 12.5). Thus, media use jumps more than 3 hours in early adolescence! The largest increases in media use in early adolescence are for TV and video games. TV use by youth increasingly has involved watching TV on the Internet, an iPod/MP3 player, and on a cell phone. As indicated in Figure 12.5, listening to music and using computers also increase considerably among 11- to 14-year-old adolescents. And based on the 2009 survey, adding up the daily media use figures to obtain weekly media use leads to the staggering levels of more than 60 hours a week of media use by 11- to 14-year-olds and almost 56 hours a week by 15- to 18-year-olds!

A major trend in the use of technology is the dramatic increase in media multitasking (Calvert & Wartella, 2014; Sanbonmatsu & others, 2013). In the 2009 survey, when the amount of time spent multitasking was included in computing media use, 11- to 14-year-olds spent nearly 12 hours a day (compared with almost 9 hours a day when multitasking was not included) exposed to media (Rideout, Foehr, & Roberts, 2010)! In this survey, 39 percent of seventh- to twelfth-graders said "most of the time" they use two or more media concurrently, such as surfing the Web while listening to music. In some cases, media multitasking—such as text messaging, listening to an iPod, and updating a YouTube site—is engaged in while doing homework. It is hard to imagine that this allows a student to do homework efficiently, although there is little research on media multitasking. A study that compared heavy and light media multitaskers revealed that heavy media multitaskers were more susceptible to interference from irrelevant information (Ophir, Nass, & Wagner, 2009). A recent study of 8- to 12-year-old girls also found that a higher level of media multitasking was linked to negative social well-being while a higher level of face-to-face communication was associated with positive social-wellbeing indicators such as greater social success, feeling more normal, and having fewer friends whom parents thought were a bad influence (Pea & others, 2012).

Technology and Digitally Mediated Communication Culture involves change, and nowhere is that change greater than in the technological revolution individuals are experiencing with increased use of computers and the Internet (Lever-Duffy & McDonald, 2015; Smaldino & others, 2015). Society still relies on some basic nontechnological competencies—for example, good communication skills, positive attitudes, and the ability to solve problems and to think deeply and creatively. But how people pursue these competencies is changing in ways and at speeds that few people had to cope with in previous eras. For youth to be adequately prepared for tomorrow's jobs, technology needs to become an integral part of their lives (Jackson & others, 2012).

The digitally mediated social environment of adolescents and emerging adults includes e-mail, instant messaging, social networking sites such as Facebook, chat rooms, video sharing and photo sharing, multiplayer online computer games, and virtual worlds. Most of these digitally mediated social interactions began on computers but more recently have also shifted to cell phones, especially smartphones.

Text messaging has become the main way that adolescents connect with their friends, surpassing face-to-face contact, e-mail, instant messaging, and voice calling (Lenhart & others, 2010). In the national survey and a further update (Lenhart, 2012), daily text messaging increased from 38 percent who texted friends daily in 2008 to 54 percent in 2009 to 60 percent in 2012. However, voice mailing is the primary way that most adolescents prefer to connect with parents.

Review Connect Reflect

Review
- What are some comparisons of adolescents in different cultures? How do adolescents around the world spend their time? What is the purpose of rites of passage?
- How does ethnicity influence adolescent development?
- What characterizes media use by adolescents?

Connect
- How might what you learned about school dropout rates and extracurricular activities in Chapter 11 be linked to the view of Reed Larson and his colleagues regarding adolescents' lack of adequate self-initiative?

Reflect *Your Own Personal Journey of Life*
- What is your ethnicity? Have you ever been stereotyped because of your ethnicity? How different is your identity from the mainstream culture?

5 Adolescent Problems

LG5 Identify adolescent problems in socioemotional development and strategies for helping adolescents with problems.

| Juvenile Delinquency | Depression and Suicide | The Interrelation of Problems and Successful Prevention/Intervention Programs |

In Chapter 11, we described several adolescent problems: substance abuse, sexually transmitted infections, and eating disorders. In this chapter, we will examine the problems of juvenile delinquency, depression, and suicide. We will also explore interrelationships among adolescent problems and describe how such problems can be prevented or remediated.

JUVENILE DELINQUENCY

The label **juvenile delinquent** is applied to an adolescent who breaks the law or engages in behavior that is considered illegal. Like other categories of disorders, juvenile delinquency is a broad concept, encompassing legal infractions that range from littering to murder.

Delinquency Rates The number of juvenile court delinquency caseloads in the United States increased dramatically from 1960 to 1996 but has decreased slightly since 1996 (see Figure 12.6) (Puzzanchera & Robson, 2014). Note that this figure reflects only adolescents

juvenile delinquent An adolescent who breaks the law or engages in behavior that is considered illegal.

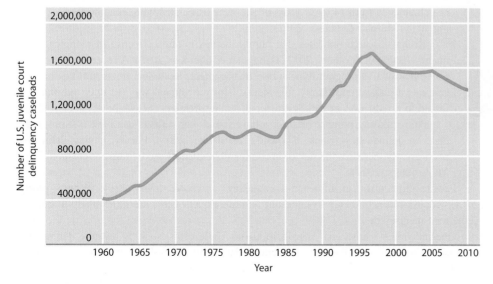

FIGURE **12.6**

NUMBER OF U.S. JUVENILE COURT DELINQUENCY CASELOADS FROM 1960 TO 2010.
Source: Puzzanchera & Robson (2014).

who have been arrested and assigned to juvenile court delinquency caseloads and does not include those who were arrested but not assigned to the delinquency caseloads, nor does the figure include youth who committed offenses but were not apprehended. In 2010, U.S. juvenile courts had nearly 1.4 million delinquency cases that involved juveniles charged with violating criminal laws. As indicated in Figure 12.6, there has been a decrease in juvenile court cases in the last two decades.

Males are more likely to engage in delinquency than are females. However, U.S. government statistics revealed that the percentage of delinquency caseloads involving females increased from 19 percent in 1985 to 28 percent in 2005 (Puzzanchera & Robson, 2014).

Delinquency rates among minority groups and lower-socioeconomic-status youth are higher than the proportion of these groups within the general population. However, such groups have less influence over the judicial decision-making process in the United States and therefore may be judged delinquent more readily than their White, middle-socioeconomic-status counterparts.

A distinction is made between early-onset—before age 11—and late-onset—after 11—antisocial behavior. Early-onset antisocial behavior is associated with more negative developmental outcomes than late-onset antisocial behavior (Schulenberg & Zarrett, 2006; Wiecko, 2014). Not only is it more likely to persist into emerging adulthood but it is also associated with more mental health and relationship problems (Loeber & Burke, 2011; Pechorro & others, 2014).

Causes of Delinquency   Although delinquency is less exclusively a phenomenon of lower socioeconomic status than it was in the past, some characteristics of lower-SES culture might promote delinquency (Thompson & Bynum, 2013). The norms of many lower-SES peer groups and gangs are antisocial, or counterproductive, to the goals and norms of society at large. Getting into and staying out of trouble are prominent features of life for some adolescents in low-income neighborhoods. Being "tough" and "masculine" are high-status traits for lower-SES boys, and these traits are often measured by the adolescent's success in performing and getting away with delinquent acts. And adolescents in communities with high crime rates observe many models who engage in criminal activities. These communities may be characterized by poverty, unemployment, and feelings of alienation toward the middle class. Quality schooling, educational funding, and organized neighborhood activities often are lacking in these communities (Crosnoe & Leventhal, 2014). One study found that youth whose families had experienced repeated poverty were more than twice as likely to be delinquent at 14 and 21 years of age (Najman & others, 2010).

What are some factors that are linked to whether adolescents engage in delinquent acts?

Certain characteristics of families are also associated with delinquency (Connell, Dishion, & Klostermann, 2012). Parental monitoring of adolescents is especially important in determining whether an adolescent becomes a delinquent (Fosco & others, 2012). Family discord and inconsistent and inappropriate discipline are also associated with delinquency (Bor, McGee, & Fagan, 2004). And one study found that low rates of delinquency from 14 to 23 years of age were associated with an authoritative parenting style (Murphy & others, 2012).

Recent research indicates that family therapy is often effective in reducing delinquency (Baldwin & others, 2012; Henggeler & Sheidow, 2012). A recent meta-analysis found that of five program types (case management, individual treatment, youth court, restorative justice, and family treatment), family treatment was the only one that was linked to a reduction in recidivism for juvenile offenders (Schwalbe & others, 2012).

An increasing number of studies have found that siblings can have a strong influence on delinquency (Bank, Burraston, & Snyder, 2004). Finally, having delinquent peers greatly increases the risk of becoming delinquent (Fosco, Frank, & Dishion, 2012; Yu & others, 2013).

Peer relations also can influence delinquency (Trucco & others, 2014; Wang & others, 2014). Adolescents who begin to hang out with delinquent peers are more likely to become delinquent themselves.

One individual whose goal is to help at-risk adolescents, such as juvenile delinquents, cope more effectively with their lives is Rodney Hammond. Read about his work in *Connecting with Careers.*

Rodney Hammond, Health Psychologist

Rodney Hammond described how his college experiences led to his career choice:

> When I started as an undergraduate at the University of Illinois, Champaign-Urbana, I hadn't decided on my major. But to help finance my education, I took a part-time job in a child development research program sponsored by the psychology department. There, I observed inner-city children in settings designed to enhance their learning. I saw firsthand the contribution psychology can make, and I knew I wanted to be a psychologist (American Psychological Association, 2003, p. 26).

Rodney Hammond went on to obtain a doctorate in school and community psychology with a focus on children's development. For a number of years, he trained clinical psychologists at Wright State University in Ohio and directed a program to reduce violence in ethnic minority youth. There, he and his associates taught at-risk youth how to use social skills to effectively manage conflict and to recognize situations that could lead to violence. Today, Hammond is Director of Violence Prevention at the Centers for Disease Control and Prevention in Atlanta. Hammond says that if you are interested in people and problem solving, psychology is a wonderful way to put these topics together.

Rodney Hammond, counseling an adolescent girl about the risks of adolescence and how to cope with them effectively.

DEPRESSION AND SUICIDE

What is the nature of depression in adolescence? What causes an adolescent to commit suicide?

Depression   How extensive is depression in adolescence? Rates of ever experiencing major depressive disorder range from 15 to 20 percent for adolescents (Graber & Sontag, 2009). By about age 15, adolescent females have a rate of depression that is twice that of adolescent males. Among the reasons for this gender difference are that females tend to ruminate on their depressed mood and amplify it; females' self-images, especially their body images, are more negative than those of males; females face more discrimination than males do; and puberty occurs earlier for girls than for boys (Nolen-Hoeksema, 2011). As a result, girls experience a piling up of changes and life experiences in the middle school years that can increase depression.

Do gender differences in adolescent depression hold for other cultures? In many cultures females experience depression more often than males do, but one study of more than 17,000 Chinese 11- to 22-year-olds revealed that the male adolescents and emerging adults experienced more depression than their female counterparts did (Sun & others, 2010). Explanation of the higher rates of depression among males in China focused on stressful life events and a less positive coping style.

Is adolescent depression linked to problems in emerging and early adulthood? A recent study initially assessed U.S. adolescents when they were 16 to 17 years of age and then again every two years until they were 26 to 27 years of age (Naicker & others, 2013). In this study, significant effects that persisted after 10 years were depression recurrence, stronger depressive symptoms, migraine headaches, poor self-rated health, and low levels of social support. In another longitudinal study of young people from 14 to 24 years of age, mild to moderate levels of early adolescent depressive behaviors were linked to lower maternal relationship quality, less positive romantic relationships, and greater loneliness in emerging adulthood (Allen & others, 2014).

developmental connection

The Epigenetic Approach

The epigenetic approach states that development is an ongoing, bidirectional interaction between heredity and the environment. Chapter 2, p. 67

Genes are linked to adolescent depression (Hansell & others, 2012). A recent study found that certain dopamine-related genes were associated with depressive symptoms in adolescents (Adkins & others, 2012). And another recent study revealed that the link between adolescent girls' perceived stress and depression occurred only when the girls had the short version of the serotonin-related gene—5HTTLPR (Beaver & others, 2012).

Certain family factors place adolescents at risk for developing depression (Morris & others, 2014; Yap & others, 2014). These include having a depressed parent, emotionally unavailable parents, parents who have high marital conflict, and parents with financial problems. One study also revealed that mother-daughter co-rumination (extensively discussing, rehashing, and speculating about problems) was linked to an increase in anxiety and depression in adolescent girls (Waller & Rose, 2010).

Poor peer relationships also are associated with adolescent depression (Vanhalst & others, 2012). Not having a close relationship with a best friend, having less contact with friends, and being rejected by peers increase depressive tendencies in adolescents (Platt & others, 2013). One study found that relational aggression was linked to depression for girls (Spieker & others, 2012). And as indicated earlier in this chapter, problems in adolescent romantic relationships can also trigger depression (Starr & others, 2012).

Friendship often provides social support. However, whether friendship is linked with a lower level of depression among girls and boys depends on the type of friendship. For example, in one study young adolescents with nondepressed friends were less likely to be depressed than young adolescents without friends, whereas young adolescents with depressed friends were more likely to be depressed (Brendgen & others, 2010). And a study of third- through ninth-graders revealed that girls' co-rumination predicted not only an increase in the positive quality of the friendship, but also an increase in further co-rumination and in depressive and anxiety symptoms (Rose, Carlson, & Waller, 2007).

Being stressed about weight-related concerns is increasingly thought to contribute to the greater incidence of depression in adolescent girls than in adolescent boys (Marmorstein, Iacono, & Legrand, 2014). One study revealed that adolescent girls' higher level of depressive symptoms was linked to a heightened tendency to perceive oneself as overweight and to diet (Vaughan & Halpern, 2010).

What type of treatment is most likely to reduce depression in adolescence? A recent research review concluded that drug therapy using serotonin reuptake inhibitors, cognitive behavior therapy, and interpersonal therapy are effective in treating adolescent depression (Maalouf & Brent, 2012). However, in this review, the most effective treatment was a combination of drug therapy and cognitive behavior therapy.

Suicide   Suicide behavior is rare in childhood but escalates in adolescence and then increases further in emerging adulthood (Park & others, 2006). Suicide is the third-leading cause of death in 10- to 19-year-olds today in the United States (National Center for Health Statistics, 2014). Approximately 4,400 adolescents commit suicide each year (Eaton & others, 2010).

Although a suicide threat should always be taken seriously, far more adolescents contemplate or attempt it unsuccessfully than actually commit it. As indicated in Figure 12.7, in

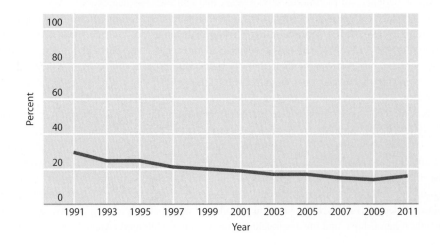

What are some characteristics of adolescents who become depressed?

FIGURE **12.7**

PERCENTAGE OF U.S. NINTH- TO TWELFTH-GRADE STUDENTS WHO SERIOUSLY CONSIDERED ATTEMPTING SUICIDE IN THE PREVIOUS 12 MONTHS FROM 1991 TO 2011

the last two decades there has been a considerable decline in the percentage of adolescents who think about committing suicide, although from 2009 to 2011 this percentage increased from 14 to 16 percent (Youth Risk Behavior Survey, 2011). In this national study, in 2011, 8 percent attempted suicide and 2 percent engaged in suicide attempts that required medical attention.

Females are more likely to attempt suicide than males, but males are more likely to succeed in committing suicide. Males use more lethal means, such as guns, in their suicide attempts, whereas adolescent females are more likely to cut their wrists or take an overdose of sleeping pills—methods less likely to result in death.

Distal, or earlier, experiences often are involved in suicide attempts as well. The adolescent may have a long-standing history of family instability and unhappiness (Wan & Leung, 2010). Just as a lack of affection and emotional support, high control, and parental pressure for achievement during childhood are related to adolescent depression, such combinations of family experiences also are likely to show up as distal factors in adolescents' suicide attempts. Adolescents who have experienced abuse also are at risk for suicidal ideation and attempts (Rhodes & others, 2012). A recent study revealed that adolescents who engaged in suicidal ideation perceived their family functioning to be significantly worse than did their caregivers (Lipschitz & others, 2012). Another recent study found that family discord and negative relationships with parents were associated with increased suicide attempts by depressed adolescents (Consoli & others, 2013).

Recent and current stressful circumstances, such as getting poor grades in school or experiencing the breakup of a romantic relationship, may trigger suicide attempts (Antai-Otong, 2003; Thompson & others, 2012). Also, a recent study found that adolescent females who were the victims of dating violence were at a higher risk for planning and/or attempting suicide than were their counterparts who had not been victimized (Belshaw & others, 2012).

Adolescent suicide attempts also vary across ethnic groups in the United States (Wong & others, 2012). As indicated in Figure 12.8, more than 20 percent of American Indian/ Alaska Native (AI/AN) female adolescents reported that they had attempted suicide in the previous year, and suicide accounts for almost 20 percent of AI/AN deaths in 15- to 19-year-olds (Goldston & others, 2008). As indicated in Figure 12.8, African American and non-Latino White males reported the lowest incidence of suicide attempts. A major risk factor in the high rate of suicide attempts by AI/AN adolescents is their elevated rate of alcohol abuse.

Just as genetic factors are associated with depression, they also are associated with suicide (Kapornai & Vetro, 2008). The closer a person's genetic relationship to someone who has committed suicide, the more likely that person is to also commit suicide.

What is the psychological profile of the suicidal adolescent? Suicidal adolescents often have depressive symptoms (Fried & others, 2013; Zetterqvist, Lundh, & Svedin, 2013). Although not all depressed adolescents are suicidal, depression is the most frequently cited factor associated with adolescent suicide (Thapar & others, 2012). Further, one study indicated that adolescents' use of alcohol while they were sad or depressed was linked with risk for making a suicide attempt (Schilling & others, 2009). A recent study also found that the strong link between self-reported adolescent suicide attempts and drug use was any lifetime use of tranquilizers or sedatives (Kokkevi & others, 2012). Further, a recent study found that peer victimization was linked to suicidal ideation and suicide attempts, with cyberbullying more strongly associated with suicidal ideation than traditional bullying (van Geel, Vedder, & Tanilon, 2014). And the National Longitudinal Study of Adolescent Health identified the following indicators of suicide risk: depressive symptoms, a sense of hopelessness, engaging in suicidal ideation, having a family background of suicidal behavior, and having friends with a history of suicidal behavior (Thompson, Kuruwita, & Foster, 2009). Also, a recent study revealed that playing sports predicted lower suicidal ideation in boys, and venting by talking with others was associated with lower suicidal ideation in girls (Kim & others, 2014).

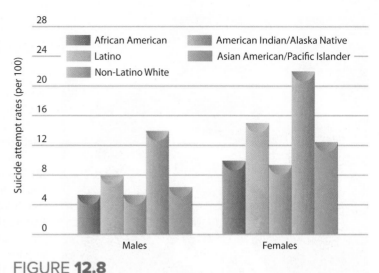

FIGURE **12.8**

SUICIDE ATTEMPTS BY U.S. ADOLESCENTS FROM DIFFERENT ETHNIC GROUPS. *Note:* Data shown are for one-year rates of self-reported suicide attempts.

developmental **connection**

Conditions, Diseases, and Disorders

What characterizes depression and suicide in older adults? Chapter 18, p. 558

THE INTERRELATION OF PROBLEMS AND SUCCESSFUL PREVENTION/INTERVENTION PROGRAMS

How are problems interrelated in adolescence?

We have described some of the major adolescent problems in this chapter and in Chapter 11: substance abuse; juvenile delinquency; school-related problems such as dropping out of school; adolescent pregnancy and sexually transmitted infections; eating disorders; depression; and suicide.

The four problems that affect the most adolescents are (1) drug abuse, (2) juvenile delinquency, (3) sexual problems, and (4) school-related problems (Dryfoos, 1990; Dryfoos & Barkin, 2006). The adolescents most at risk have more than one of these problems. Researchers are increasingly finding that problem behaviors in adolescence are interrelated (Milburn & others, 2012; Passini, 2012). For example, heavy substance abuse is related to early sexual activity, lower grades, dropping out of school, and delinquency (Grigsby & others, 2014). Early initiation of sexual activity is associated with the use of cigarettes and alcohol, the use of marijuana and other illicit drugs, lower grades, dropping out of school, and delinquency (Chan & others, 2014). Delinquency is related to early sexual activity, early pregnancy, substance abuse, and dropping out of school (Pedersen & Mastekaasa, 2011). As many as 10 percent of adolescents in the United States have been estimated to engage in all four of these problem behaviors (for example, adolescents who have dropped out of school are behind in their grade level, are users of heavy drugs, regularly use cigarettes and marijuana, and are sexually active but do not use contraception). In 1990, it was estimated that another 15 percent of high-risk youth engage in two or three of the four main problem behaviors (Dryfoos, 1990). Sixteen years later, this figure increased to 20 percent of all U.S. adolescents (Dryfoos & Barkin, 2006).

A review of the programs that have been successful in preventing or reducing adolescent problems found these common components (Dryfoos, 1990; Dryfoos & Barkin, 2006):

1. *Intensive individualized attention.* In successful programs, high-risk adolescents are attached to a responsible adult who gives the adolescent attention and deals with the adolescent's specific needs. This theme occurs in a number of programs. In a successful substance-abuse program, a student assistance counselor is available full-time for individual counseling and referral for treatment.

2. *Community-wide multiagency collaborative approaches.* The basic philosophy of community-wide programs is that a number of different programs and services have to be in place. In one successful substance-abuse program, a community-wide health promotion campaign has been implemented that uses local media and community education, in concert with a substance-abuse curriculum in the schools.

3. *Early identification and intervention.* Reaching younger children and their families before children develop problems or at the onset of their problems is a successful strategy. One preschool program serves as an excellent model for the prevention of delinquency, pregnancy, substance abuse, and dropping out of school. Operated by the High/Scope Foundation in Ypsilanti, Michigan, the Perry Preschool (discussed in Chapter 7) has had a long-term positive impact on its students. This enrichment program, directed by David Weikart, serves disadvantaged African American children. They attend a high-quality two-year preschool program and receive weekly home visits from program personnel. Based on official police records, by age 19, individuals who had attended the Perry Preschool program were less likely to have been

What are some strategies for preventing and intervening in adolescent problems?

Which Children Are Most Likely to Benefit From Early Intervention?

Fast Track is an intervention that attempts to lower the risk of juvenile delinquency and other problems (Conduct Problems Prevention Research Group, 2010, 2011, 2013; Dodge, Godwin, & Conduct Problems Prevention Research Group, 2013; Dodge & McCourt, 2010; Jones & others, 2010; Miller & others, 2010). Schools in four areas (Durham, North Carolina; Nashville, Tennessee; Seattle, Washington; and rural central Pennsylvania) were identified as high-risk based on neighborhood crime and poverty data. Researchers screened more than 9,000 kindergarten children in the four schools and randomly assigned 891 of the highest-risk and moderate-risk children to intervention or control groups. The average age of the children when the intervention began was 6.5 years.

The 10-year intervention consisted of parent behavior management training, child social cognitive skills training, reading tutoring, home visitations, mentoring, and a revised classroom curriculum that was designed to increase socioemotional competence and decrease aggression. Outcomes were assessed in the third, sixth, and ninth grades for conduct disorder (multiple instances of behaviors such as truancy, running away, fire setting, cruelty to animals, breaking and entering, and excessive fighting across a 6-month period), oppositional defiant disorder (an ongoing pattern of disobedient, hostile, and defiant behavior toward authority figures), attention deficit hyperactivity disorder (as described in Chapter 9, having one or more of these characteristics

over a period of time: inattention, hyperactivity, and impulsivity), any externalizing disorder (presence of any of the three disorders previously described), and self-reported antisocial behavior (a list of 34 behaviors, such as skipping school, stealing, and attacking someone with an intent to hurt them).

The extensive intervention was successful only for children and adolescents who were identified as having the highest risk in kindergarten, lowering their incidence of conduct disorder, attention deficit hyperactivity disorder, any externalized disorder, and antisocial behavior (Dodge & McCourt, 2010). Positive outcomes for the intervention occurred as early as the third grade and continued through the ninth grade. For example, in the ninth grade the intervention reduced the likelihood that the highest-risk kindergarten children would develop conduct disorder by 75 percent, attention deficit hyperactivity disorder by 53 percent, and any externalized disorder by 43 percent. Recently, data have been reported through age 19 (Miller & others, 2010). Findings indicate that the comprehensive Fast Track intervention was successful in reducing youth arrest rates (Conduct Problems Prevention Research Group, 2011). Also, a recent study found that the intervention's impact on adolescents' antisocial behavior was linked to three social cognitive processes: reducing hostile-attribution biases, improving responses to social problems, and devaluing aggression (Dodge, Godwin, & Conduct Problems Prevention Research Group, 2013).

arrested and reported fewer adult offenses than a control group did. The Perry Preschool students also were less likely to drop out of school, and teachers rated their social behavior as more competent than that of a control group who had not received the enriched preschool experience (High/Scope Resource, 2005). To read further about which children are most likely to benefit from an early intervention, see *Connecting Through Research*.

Review *Connect* Reflect

 Identify adolescent problems in socioemotional development and strategies for helping adolescents with problems.

Review
- What is juvenile delinquency? What causes it?
- What is the nature of depression and suicide in adolescence?
- How are adolescent problems interrelated? What are some components of successful prevention/intervention programs for adolescents?

Connect
- In Chapter 10, what did you learn about the connection between bullying in middle and late childhood and problems in adolescence?

Reflect *Your Own Personal Journey of Life*
- When you were an adolescent, did you have any of the problems discussed in this chapter or Chapter 11—such as substance abuse, eating disorders, juvenile delinquency, depression, and attempted suicide? If you had one or more of the problems, why do you think you developed the problem? If you did not have one of the problems, why do you think you didn't develop one or more of them?

┌─ topical **connections** *looking forward* ─┐

The transitional time frame between adolescence and adulthood that is labeled emerging adulthood occurs between approximately 18 and 25 years of age. Many emerging adults explore their identity and experience instability in different contexts with greater intensity than they did as adolescents. As adults, they benefit from a secure attachment style in close relationships. Love and possibly marriage become central aspects of many young adults' socioemotional development. Many young adults not only are marrying later or not at all but also are having children later than in past decades. Many young adults also cohabit with a romantic partner.

reach your **learning goals**

Socioemotional Development in Adolescence

1 The Self, Identity, and Religious/ Spiritual Development

 LG1 Discuss self, identity, and religious/spiritual development in adolescence.

Self-Esteem

- Some researchers have found that self-esteem declines in early adolescence for both boys and girls, but the drop for girls is greater. Other researchers caution that these declines are often exaggerated and actually are small. Self-esteem reflects perceptions that do not always match reality. Thus, high self-esteem may be justified or it might reflect an arrogant, grandiose self-image that is not warranted. Controversy surrounds the question of whether today's adolescents and emerging adults are more narcissistic than their counterparts in earlier generations.

Identity

- Identity development is complex and takes place in bits and pieces. Erikson argues that identity versus identity confusion is the fifth stage of the human life span, which individuals experience during adolescence. A psychosocial moratorium during adolescence allows the personality and role experimentation that are important aspects of identity development. James Marcia proposed four identity statuses—identity diffusion, foreclosure, moratorium, and achievement—that are based on crisis (exploration) and commitment. Increasingly, experts argue that the main changes in identity occur in emerging adulthood rather than adolescence. Individuals often follow moratorium-achievement-moratorium-achievement (MAMA) cycles in their lives. Throughout the world, ethnic minority groups have struggled to maintain their identities while blending into the majority culture.

Religious/Spiritual Development

- Many adolescents show an interest in religious and spiritual development. As part of their search for identity, many adolescents and emerging adults begin to grapple with more complex aspects of religion. Various aspects of religion are linked with positive outcomes in adolescent development.

2 Families

 LG2 Describe changes that take place in adolescents' relationships with their parents.

Parental Monitoring and Information Management

- A key aspect of parenting in adolescence is effectively monitoring the adolescent's development. Monitoring includes supervising adolescents' choice of social settings, activities, friends, and academic efforts. Adolescents' management of information involves the extent to which adolescents disclose information to parents about their whereabouts. This disclosure, which is more likely when parents engage in positive parenting practices, is linked to positive adolescent adjustment.

| Autonomy and Attachment | • | Many parents have a difficult time handling the adolescent's push for autonomy, even though the push is one of the hallmarks of adolescence. Adolescents do not simply move into a world isolated from parents; attachment to parents increases the probability that an adolescent will be socially competent. |

• Parent-adolescent conflict increases in adolescence. The conflict is usually moderate rather than severe, and the increased conflict may serve the positive developmental function of promoting autonomy and identity. A subset of adolescents experiences high parent-adolescent conflict, which is linked with negative outcomes.

3 Peers

LG3 Characterize the changes that occur in peer relationships during adolescence.

Friendships

• Harry Stack Sullivan was the most influential theorist to discuss the importance of adolescent friendships. He argued that there is a dramatic increase in the psychological importance and intimacy of close friends in early adolescence. Friends become increasingly important in meeting social needs.

Peer Groups

• The pressure to conform to peers is strong during adolescence, especially during the eighth and ninth grades. Cliques and crowds assume more importance in the lives of adolescents than in the lives of children.

Dating and Romantic Relationships

• Dating can have many functions. Three stages characterize the development of romantic relationships in adolescence: (1) entry into romantic attractions and affiliations at about 11 to 13 years of age; (2) exploring romantic relationships at approximately 14 to 16 years of age; and (3) consolidating dyadic romantic bonds at about 17 to 19 years of age. Many gay and lesbian youth date other-sex peers, which can help them to clarify their sexual orientation or disguise it from others. Culture can exert a powerful influence on adolescent dating. Dating shows mixed connections with adjustment during adolescence. Early dating is linked with developmental problems.

4 Culture and Adolescent Development

LG4 Explain how culture influences adolescent development.

Cross-Cultural Comparisons

• There are both similarities and differences in adolescents across different countries. In some countries, traditions are being continued in the socialization of adolescents, whereas in others, substantial changes in the experiences of adolescents are taking place. Adolescents often fill their time with different activities, depending on the culture in which they live. A rite of passage is a ceremony or ritual that marks an individual's transition from one status to another, especially into adulthood. In primitive cultures, rites of passage are often well defined. In contemporary America, rites of passage to adulthood are ill-defined.

Ethnicity

• Many of the families that have immigrated to the United States in recent decades come from collectivist cultures in which there is a strong sense of family obligation. Much of the research on ethnic minority adolescents has not teased apart the influences of ethnicity and socioeconomic status. Because of this failure, too often researchers have given ethnic explanations for characteristics that were largely due to socioeconomic factors. Although not all ethnic minority families are poor, poverty contributes to the stress experienced by many ethnic minority adolescents.

The Media

• In terms of media exposure, the average U.S. 8- to 18-year-old spends 6½ hours a day using electronic media. If media multitasking is taken into account, adolescents use electronic media 8 hours a day. Adolescents are rapidly increasing the time they spend online. Older adolescents reduce their TV viewing and video game playing and increase their music listening and computer use. Large numbers of adolescents and college students engage in social networking.

5 Adolescent Problems

LG5 Identify adolescent problems in socioemotional development and strategies for helping adolescents with problems.

Juvenile Delinquency

Depression and Suicide

The Interrelation of Problems and Successful Prevention/Intervention Programs

- A juvenile delinquent is an adolescent who breaks the law or engages in conduct that is considered illegal. Low socioeconomic status, negative family experiences (especially a low level of parental monitoring and having a sibling who is a delinquent), and negative peer influences have been linked to juvenile delinquency.

- Adolescents and emerging adults have higher rates of depression than children do. Female adolescents and emerging adults are more likely to have mood and depressive disorders than their male counterparts. Suicide is the third-leading cause of death in U.S. adolescents.

- Researchers are increasingly finding that problem behaviors in adolescence are interrelated, and at-risk adolescents have one or more of these problems: (1) drug abuse, (2) juvenile delinquency, (3) sexual problems, and (4) school-related problems. Dryfoos found a number of common components in successful programs designed to prevent or reduce adolescent problems: These programs provide individual attention to high-risk adolescents, they develop community-wide intervention strategies, and they include early identification and intervention.

key terms

narcissism 372	identity diffusion 373	identity achievement 373	crowd 383
crisis 373	identity foreclosure 373	ethnic identity 375	rite of passage 386
commitment 373	identity moratorium 373	clique 382	juvenile delinquent 389

key people

Erik Erikson 372	Jane Kroger 374	Andrew Fuligni 380	Harry Stack Sullivan 381
James Marcia 373	Seth Schwartz 374		

section seven

How many roads must a man walk down before you call him a man?

—**Bob Dylan**
American Folk Singer, 20th Century

Early Adulthood

Early adulthood is a time for work and a time for love, sometimes leaving little time for anything else. For some of us, finding our place in adult society and committing to a more stable life take longer than we imagine. We still ask ourselves who we are and wonder if it isn't enough just to be. Our dreams continue and our thoughts are bold, but at some point we become more pragmatic. Sex and love are powerful passions in our lives—at time angels of light, at others fiends of torment. And we possibly will never fully know the love of our parents until we become parents ourselves. Section 7 contains two chapters: "Physical and Cognitive Development in Early Adulthood" (Chapter 13) and "Socioemotional Development in Early Adulthood" (Chapter 14).

chapter 13

PHYSICAL AND COGNITIVE DEVELOPMENT IN EARLY ADULTHOOD

chapter **outline**

1 The Transition from Adolescence to Adulthood

Learning Goal 1 Describe the transition from adolescence to adulthood.

Becoming an Adult
The Transition from High School to College

2 Physical Development

Learning Goal 2 Identify the changes in physical development in young adults.

Physical Performance and Development
Health
Eating and Weight
Regular Exercise
Substance Abuse

3 Sexuality

Learning Goal 3 Discuss sexuality in young adults.

Sexual Activity in Emerging Adulthood
Sexual Orientation and Behavior
Sexually Transmitted Infections
Forcible Sexual Behavior and Sexual Harassment

4 Cognitive Development

Learning Goal 4 Characterize cognitive changes in early adulthood.

Cognitive Stages
Creativity

5 Careers and Work

Learning Goal 5 Explain the key dimensions of career and work in early adulthood.

Developmental Changes
Finding a Path to Purpose
Monitoring the Occupational Outlook
The Impact of Work
Diversity in the Workplace

He was a senior in college when both of his parents died of cancer within five weeks of each other. What would he do? He and his 8-year-old brother left Chicago to live in California where their older sister was entering law school. Dave would take care of his younger brother, but he needed a job. That first summer, he took a class in furniture painting; then he worked for a geological surveying company, re-creating maps on a computer. Soon, though, he did something very different: with friends from high school, Dave Eggers started *Might,* a satirical magazine for twenty-somethings. It was an edgy, highly acclaimed publication, but not a moneymaker. After a few years, Eggers had to shut down the magazine, and he abandoned California for New York.

This does not sound like a promising start for a career. But within a decade after his parents' death, Eggers had not only raised his young brother but had also founded a quarterly journal and Web site, *McSweeney's,* and had written a best-seller, *A Heartbreaking Work of Staggering Genius,* which received the National Book Critics Circle Award and was nominated for a Pulitzer Prize. It is a slightly fictionalized account of Eggers' life as he helped care for his dying mother, raised his brother, and searched for his own place in the world. Despite the pain of his loss and the responsibility for his brother, Eggers quickly built a record of achievement as a young adult.

Dave Eggers, talented and insightful author.

topical connections *looking back*

Early adolescence is a time of dramatic physical change as puberty unfolds. Pubertal change also brings considerable interest in one's body image. And pubertal change ushers in an intense interest in sexuality. Although most adolescents develop a positive sexual identity, many encounter sexual risk factors that can lead to negative developmental outcomes. Adolescence also is a critical time in the development of behaviors related to health, such as good nutrition and regular exercise, which are health enhancing, and drug abuse, which is health compromising. Significant changes occur in the adolescent's brain—the early development of the amygdala and the delayed development of the prefrontal cortex—that may contribute to risk taking and sensation seeking. Adolescent thinking becomes more abstract, idealistic, and logical—which Piaget described as the key aspects of formal operational thought. The brain's development and social contexts influence adolescents' decision making.

preview

In this chapter we will explore many aspects of physical and cognitive development in early adulthood. These include some of the areas that were so important in Dave Eggers' life, such as using his creative talents and pursuing a career. We also will examine changes in physical development, sexuality, and cognitive development. We will begin where we left off in Section 6, "Adolescence," and address the transition from adolescence to adulthood, a time during which Dave Eggers displayed resilience in the face of intense stress.

---

1 The Transition from Adolescence to Adulthood

 LG1 Describe the transition from adolescence to adulthood.

> Becoming an Adult

> The Transition from High School to College

When does an adolescent become an adult? In Chapter 11, we saw that it is not easy to tell when a girl or a boy enters adolescence. The task of determining when an individual becomes an adult is even more difficult.

BECOMING AN ADULT

For most individuals, becoming an adult involves a lengthy transition period. Recently, the transition from adolescence to adulthood has been referred to as **emerging adulthood,** which occurs from approximately 18 to 25 years of age (Arnett, 2006, 2007, 2010, 2012; Arnett & Fishel, 2013). Experimentation and exploration characterize the emerging adult. At this point in their development, many individuals are still exploring which career path they want to follow, what they want their identity to be, and which lifestyle they want to adopt (for example, single, cohabiting, or married).

Key Features   Jeffrey Arnett (2006) concluded that five key features characterize emerging adulthood:

- *Identity exploration, especially in love and work.* Emerging adulthood is a time during which key changes in identity take place for many individuals (Schwartz & others, 2013, 2015a, b).
- *Instability.* Residential changes peak during early adulthood, a time during which instability also is common in love, work, and education.
- *Self-focused.* According to Arnett (2006, p. 10), emerging adults "are self-focused in the sense that they have little in the way of social obligations, little in the way of duties and commitments to others, which leaves them with a great deal of autonomy in running their own lives."
- *Feeling in-between.* Many emerging adults don't consider themselves adolescents or full-fledged adults.
- *The age of possibilities, a time when individuals have an opportunity to transform their lives.* Arnett (2006) describes two ways in which emerging adulthood is the age of possibilities: (1) many emerging adults are optimistic about their future; and (2) for emerging adults who have experienced difficult times while growing up, emerging adulthood presents an opportunity to chart their life course in a more positive direction.

Research indicates that these five aspects characterize not only individuals in the United States as they make the transition from adolescence to early adulthood, but also their counterparts in European countries and Australia (Arnett, 2012; Buhl & Lanz, 2007; Sirsch &

emerging adulthood The transition from adolescence to adulthood (occurring from approximately 18 to 25 years of age), which is characterized by experimentation and exploration.

others, 2009). Although emerging adulthood does not characterize development in all cultures, it does appear to occur in cultures that postpone assuming adult roles and responsibilities (Kins & Beyers, 2010). The concept of emerging adulthood has been criticized as applying mainly to privileged adolescents and not being a self-determined choice for many young people, especially those in limiting socioeconomic conditions (Cote & Bynner, 2008). A recent study revealed that U.S. at-risk youth entered emerging adulthood slightly earlier than the general population of youth (Lisha & others, 2014).

An important aspect of emerging adulthood is the resilience that some individuals have shown in moving their life in a positive direction following a troubled adolescence (Masten, 2013, 2014; Masten & Tellegen, 2012). A recent review and analysis of research on resilience in the transition to adulthood concluded that the increased freedom that is available to emerging adults in Western society places a premium on the capacity to plan ahead, delay gratification, and make positive choices (Burt & Paysnick, 2012). Also emphasized in resilient adaptation during emerging adulthood was the importance of forming positive close relationships—to some degree with parents, but more often with supportive romantic partners, close friends, and mentors.

Joseph and Claudia Allen (2009), authors of *Escaping the Endless Adolescence: How We Can Help Our Teenagers Grow Up Before They Grow Old,* opened their book with a chapter titled, "Is Twenty-five the New Fifteen?" They argue that in recent decades adolescents have experienced a world that places more challenges on maturing into a competent adult. In their words (p. 17),

> Generations ago, fourteen-year-olds used to drive, seventeen-year-olds led armies, and even average teens contributed labor and income that helped keep their families afloat. While facing other problems, those teens displayed adultlike maturity far more quickly than today's, who are remarkably well kept, but cut off from most of the responsibility, challenge, and growth-producing feedback of the adult world. Parents of twenty-somethings used to lament, "They grow up so fast." But that seems to be replaced with, "Well, . . . Mary's living at home a bit while she sorts things out."

What are some strategies parents can adopt to help adolescents gain adult maturity sooner?

The Allens conclude that what is happening to the current generation of adolescents is that after adolescence, they are experiencing "more adolescence" instead of adequately being launched into the adult years. Even many adolescents who have gotten good grades and then as emerging adults continued to achieve academic success in college later find themselves in their mid-twenties not having a clue about how to find a meaningful job, manage their finances, or live independently.

The Allens offer the following suggestions for helping adolescents become more mature on their way to adulthood:

- *Provide them with opportunities to be contributors.* Help them move away from being consumers by creating more effective work experiences (quality work apprenticeships, for example), or service learning opportunities that allow adolescents to make meaningful contributions.

- *Give candid, quality feedback to adolescents.* Don't just shower praise and material things on them, but let them see how the real world works. Don't protect them from criticism, constructive or negative. Protecting them in this way only leaves them ill-equipped to deal with the ups and downs of the real world of adulthood.

- *Create positive adult connections with adolescents.* Many adolescents deny that they need parental support or attachment to parents, but to help them develop maturity on the way to adulthood, they do. Exploring a wider social world than in childhood, adolescents need to be connected to parents and other adults in positive ways to be able to handle autonomy maturely.

- *Challenge adolescents to become more competent.* Adults need to do fewer things for adolescents that they can accomplish for themselves. Providing adolescents with opportunities to engage in tasks that are just beyond their current level of ability stretches their minds and helps them to make progress along the road to maturity.

developmental connection

Community

Service learning is linked to many positive outcomes for adolescents. Chapter 11, p. 365

developmental connection

Families

Secure attachment to parents increases the likelihood that adolescents will be socially competent. Chapter 11, p. 340

The transition from high school to college often involves positive as well as negative features. In college, students are likely to feel grown up, be able to spend more time with peers, have more opportunities to explore different lifestyles and values, and enjoy greater freedom from parental monitoring. However, college involves a larger, more impersonal school structure and an increased focus on achievement and its assessment. *What was your transition to college like?*

Markers of Becoming an Adult In the United States, the most widely recognized marker of entry into adulthood is holding a more or less permanent, full-time job, which usually happens when an individual finishes school—high school for some, college for others, graduate or professional school for still others. However, other criteria are far from clear. Economic independence is one marker of adult status, but achieving it is often a long process. College graduates are increasingly returning to live with their parents as they attempt to establish themselves economically. However, one study revealed that continued co-residence with parents during emerging adulthood slowed down the process of becoming a self-sufficient and independent adult (Kins & Beyers, 2010).

Other studies suggest that taking responsibility for oneself may be an important marker of adult status for many individuals. In one study, both parents and college students agreed that taking responsibility for one's actions and developing emotional control are important aspects of becoming an adult (Nelson & others, 2007).

What we have identified as markers of adult status mainly characterize individuals in industrialized societies, especially Americans. Are the criteria for adulthood the same in developing countries as they are in the United States? In developing countries, marriage is more often a significant marker for entry into adulthood, and this usually occurs much earlier than the adulthood markers in the United States (Arnett, 2004). In one study, the majority of 18- to 26-year-olds in India felt that they had achieved adulthood (Seiter & Nelson, 2011).

THE TRANSITION FROM HIGH SCHOOL TO COLLEGE

For many individuals in developed countries, graduating from high school and going to college is an important aspect of the transition to adulthood (Bowman, 2010). Just as the transition from elementary school to middle or junior high school involves change and possible stress, so does the transition from high school to college. The two transitions have many parallels. Going from being a senior in high school to being a freshman in college replays the top-dog phenomenon of transferring from the oldest and most powerful group of students to the youngest and least powerful group of students that occurred as adolescence began. For many students, the transition from high school to college involves movement to a larger, more impersonal school structure; interaction with peers from more diverse geographical and sometimes more diverse ethnic backgrounds; and increased focus on achievement and its assessment. And like the transition from elementary to middle or junior high school, the transition from high school to college can involve positive features. Students are more likely to feel grown up, have more subjects from which to select, have more time to spend with peers, have more opportunities to explore different lifestyles and values, enjoy greater independence from parental monitoring, and be challenged intellectually by academic work (Halonen & Santrock, 2013).

Today's college students experience more stress and depression than students in previous generations, according to a national study of more than 165,000 freshmen at more than 230 colleges and universities (Eagan & others, 2013). And a national survey conducted by the American College Health Association (2008) of more than 90,000 students on 177 campuses revealed that feeling things are hopeless, feeling overwhelmed with all they have to do, feeling mentally exhausted, feeling sad, and feeling depressed are not uncommon among college students. Figure 13.1 indicates the percentage of students who had these feelings and how many times a year they experienced them.

Most college campuses have a counseling center that provides access to mental health professionals who can help students learn effective ways to cope with stress. Counselors can provide good information about coping with stress and dealing with academic challenges. To read about the work of college counselor Grace Leaf, see *Connecting with Careers*.

Mental Health Difficulty	1–4 Times	5–8 Times	9 or More Times
Felt things were hopeless	39	11	12
Felt overwhelmed with all I had to do	31	25.5	37
Felt mentally exhausted	32	24.5	36
Felt so depressed it was difficult to function	27	7	9
Seriously contemplated suicide	7	1	1
Attempted suicide	1	0.1	0.1

FIGURE 13.1

COLLEGE STUDENTS' MENTAL HEALTH DIFFICULTIES IN THE PAST YEAR. *Note:* Figure shows the percentage of college students who responded to the question: "Within the last school year, how many times have you . . . ?"

connecting with careers

Grace Leaf, College/Career Counselor

Grace Leaf is a counselor at Spokane Community College in Washington. She has a master's degree in educational leadership and is working toward a doctoral degree in educational leadership at Gonzaga University in Washington. Her job involves providing orientation sessions for international students, advising individuals and groups, and facilitating individual and group career planning. Leaf tries to connect students with their own goals and values and to help them design an educational program that fits their needs and visions. Following a long career as a counselor, she is now vice-president for Instruction at Lower Columbia College in Washington.

Grace Leaf, counseling college students at Spokane Community College about careers.

For more information about what career counselors do, see page 45 in the Careers in Life-Span Development appendix.

Review Connect Reflect

LG1 Describe the transition from adolescence to adulthood.

Review
- What is the nature of emerging adulthood? What are two main criteria for becoming an adult?
- What are some positive and negative aspects of the transition from high school to college?

Connect
- In Chapter 12, you learned about a number of effective strategies for parenting adolescents. Which of those strategies might provide a foundation for individuals to experience a more successful adulthood?

Reflect *Your Own Personal Journey of Life*
- What do you think is the most important criterion for becoming an adult? Does it make sense to describe becoming an adult in terms of "emerging adulthood" over a period of years, or is there a specific age at which someone becomes an adult? Explain.

2 Physical Development

LG2 Identify the changes in physical development in young adults.

| Physical Performance and Development | Health | Eating and Weight | Regular Exercise | Substance Abuse |

As more information becomes available about healthy lifestyles and how they contribute to a longer life span, emerging and young adults are increasingly interested in learning about physical performance, health, nutrition, exercise, and addiction.

PHYSICAL PERFORMANCE AND DEVELOPMENT

Most of us reach our peak levels of physical performance before the age of 30, often between the ages of 19 and 26. This peak of physical performance occurs not only for the average young adult, but for outstanding athletes as well. Different types of athletes, however, reach their peak performances at different ages. Most swimmers and gymnasts peak in their late teens. Golfers and marathon runners tend to peak in their late twenties. In other areas of

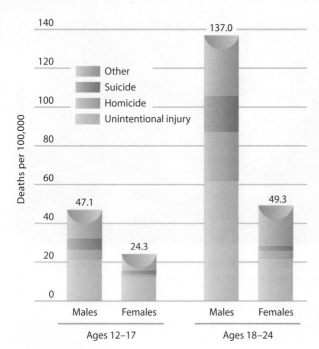

140 — 137.0

120 —

Other
Suicide
Homicide
Unintentional injury

100 —

80 —

60 —

47.1   49.3

40 —

24.3

20 —

0 —

Deaths per 100,000

Males   Females   Males   Females

Ages 12–17   Ages 18–24

FIGURE **13.2**

MORTALITY RATES OF U.S. ADOLESCENTS AND EMERGING ADULTS

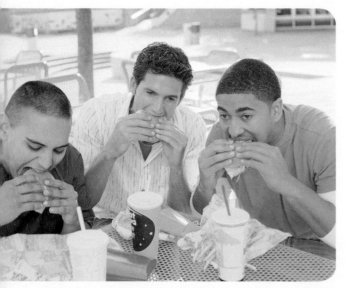

Why might it be easy to develop bad health habits in emerging and early adulthood?

athletics, peak performance often occurs in the early to mid-twenties. However, in recent years, some highly conditioned athletes—such as Dana Torres (Olympic swimming), and Tom Watson (golf)—have stretched the upper age limits of award-winning performances.

Not only do we reach our peak in physical performance during early adulthood, but it is also during this age period that we begin to decline in physical performance. Muscle tone and strength usually begin to show signs of decline around the age of 30. Sagging chins and protruding abdomens also may begin to appear for the first time. The lessening of physical abilities is a common complaint among the just-turned thirties.

HEALTH

Emerging adults have more than twice the mortality rate of adolescents (Park & others, 2006). As indicated in Figure 13.2, males are mainly responsible for the higher mortality rate of emerging adults.

Although emerging adults have a higher death rate than adolescents, emerging adults have few chronic health problems, and they have fewer colds and respiratory problems than when they were children (Rimsza & Kirk, 2005). Although most college students know what it takes to prevent illness and promote health, they don't fare very well when it comes to applying this information to themselves. In many cases, emerging adults are not as healthy as they seem (Fatusi & Hindin, 2010). A recent study revealed that college students from low-SES backgrounds engaged in lower levels of physical activity, ate more fast food and less fruits/vegetables, and used more unhealthy weight control methods than their higher-SES counterparts (VanKim & Laska, 2012).

A longitudinal study revealed that most bad health habits that were engaged in during adolescence increased in emerging adulthood (Harris & others, 2006). Inactivity, poor diet, obesity, substance abuse, inadequate reproductive health care, and use of health care facilities worsened in emerging adulthood. For example, when they were 12 to 18 years of age, only 5 percent of the study participants reported no weekly exercise, but when they became 19 to 26 years of age, 46 percent said they did not exercise during a typical week. Also, a recent study found that rates of being overweight or obese increased from 25.6 percent for college freshmen to 32 percent for college seniors (Nicoteri & Miskovsky, 2014).

In emerging and early adulthood, few individuals stop to think about how their personal lifestyles will affect their health later in their adult lives. As emerging adults, many of us develop a pattern of not eating breakfast, not eating regular meals, and relying on snacks as our main food source during the day, overeating to the point where we exceed the normal weight for our age, smoking moderately or excessively, drinking moderately or excessively, failing to exercise, and getting by with only a few hours of sleep at night (Cousineau, Goldstein, & Franco, 2005). These lifestyles are associated with poor health, which in turn diminishes life satisfaction (Luo & others, 2014). In the Berkeley Longitudinal Study—in which individuals were evaluated over a period of 40 years—physical health at age 30 predicted life satisfaction at age 70, more so for men than for women (Mussen, Honzik, & Eichorn, 1982).

One study explored links between health behavior and life satisfaction in more than 17,000 individuals 17 to 30 years of age in 21 countries (Grant, Wardle, & Steptoe, 2009). The young adults' life satisfaction was positively related to not smoking, exercising regularly, using sun protection, eating fruit, and limiting fat intake, but was not related to alcohol consumption and fiber intake.

The health profile of emerging and young adults can be improved by reducing the incidence of certain health-impairing lifestyles, such as overeating, and by engaging in health-improving lifestyles that include good eating habits, regular exercise, abstaining from drugs, and getting adequate sleep (Blake, Munoz, & Volpe, 2014; Sussman & Arnett, 2014). For example, a recent study of college students found that regularly engaging in moderate or vigorous physical activity was linked to adequate daily fruit and vegetable consumption, healthy body mass index, not smoking, being less depressed, having a lower incidence of binge drinking, being less likely to have multiple sex partners, and getting adequate sleep (Dinger, Brittain, & Hutchinson, 2014). A recent study found a bidirectional link between sleep quality/duration and adjustment (depression, stress, and self-esteem) (Tavernier & Willoughby, 2014).

Emerging adults are not the only ones who are getting inadequate sleep. Many adults in their late twenties and thirties don't get enough either (Brimah & others, 2013). A recent statement by the American Academy of Sleep Medicine and Sleep Research Society (Luyster & others, 2012) emphasized that chronic sleep deprivation may contribute to cardiovascular disease and a shortened life span, and also result in cognitive and motor impairment that increase the risk of motor vehicle crashes and work-related accidents.

The average American adult gets just under seven hours of sleep a night. How much sleep do adults need to function optimally the next day? An increasing number of experts note that eight hours of sleep or more per night are necessary for optimal performance the next day. These experts argue that many adults have become sleep deprived (Brimah & others, 2013). Work pressures, school pressures, family obligations, and social obligations often lead to long hours of wakefulness and irregular sleep/wake schedules.

Professional guidelines for adolescents recommend annual preventive visits with screening and guidance for health-related behaviors. However, a large-scale survey revealed that only 38 percent of adolescents had seen a doctor for preventive care in the previous 12 months, and few were given guidance for health-related behaviors (Irwin & others, 2009). Of special concern is the low use of health services by older adolescent males (Hoover & others, 2010). A recent study examined the delivery of preventive health care services to emerging adults 18 to 26 years of age (Lau & others, 2013). In this study, rates of preventive services utilized by emerging adults were generally low. Females were more likely to receive health care services than males were.

EATING AND WEIGHT

In Chapters 7 and 9, we discussed aspects of overweight children's lives, and in Chapter 11 we examined the eating disorders of anorexia nervosa and bulimia nervosa in adolescence. Now we will turn our attention to obesity and the extensive preoccupation that many young adults have with dieting.

Obesity   Obesity is not only a problem for many children and adolescents but also a serious and pervasive problem for many adults (Schiff, 2015; Wardlaw & others, 2015). A national survey found that 27 percent of U.S. 20- to 39-year-olds were obese (National Center for Health Statistics, 2011). A recent Gallup poll (2013a) reported that 29.1 percent of 30- to 44-year-olds are obese, the highest rate in the poll's history. Also, a recent analysis predicted that 42 percent of U.S. adults will be obese in 2030 (Finkelstein & others, 2012).

An international comparison of 33 developed countries revealed that the United States had the highest percentage of obese adults (OECD, 2010). Figure 13.3 shows the developed countries with the highest and lowest percentages of obese adults.

Being overweight or obese is linked to increased risk of hypertension, diabetes, and cardiovascular disease (Lynch, Elmore, & Kotecki, 2015; Wenger, 2014). Overweight and obesity also are associated with mental health problems. For example, a meta-analysis revealed that overweight women were more likely to be depressed than women who were not overweight, but no significant difference was found for men (de Wit & others, 2010).

What factors determine whether or not a person becomes obese? Possible influences include both heredity and environmental conditions, and dieting.

Heredity   Until recently, the genetic component of obesity was underestimated by scientists. Some individuals inherit a tendency to be overweight (Heath, 2014). Researchers have documented that animals can be inbred to have a propensity for obesity (Brown & others, 2011). Further, identical human twins have similar weights, even when they are reared apart (Collaku & others, 2004).

I'LL HAVE A MONSTER TRIPLE BURGER WITH CHEESE AND GIANT FRIES...OH AND A DIET COLA, I'VE GOT TO WATCH MY WEIGHT!

menu

COLA

© www.CartoonStock.com

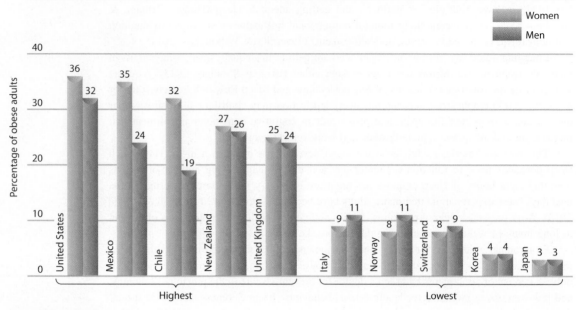

FIGURE **13.3**

COUNTRIES WITH THE HIGHEST AND LOWEST PERCENTAGES OF OBESE ADULTS IN 33 DEVELOPED COUNTRIES

Source: OECD (2010), *Obesity and the Economics of Prevention—Fit Not Fat.* Paris: OECD.

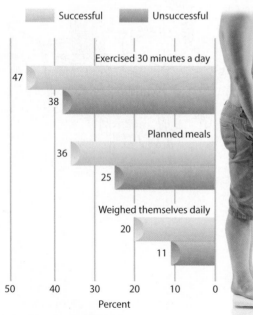

FIGURE **13.4**

COMPARISON OF STRATEGIES USED BY SUCCESSFUL AND UNSUCCESSFUL DIETERS

Environmental Factors Environmental factors play an important role in obesity (Thompson & Manore, 2013; Willett, 2013). The human genome has not changed markedly in the last century, yet obesity has noticeably increased. The obesity rate has doubled in the United States since 1900. This dramatic increase in obesity likely is due to greater availability of food (especially food high in fat), greater reliance on energy-saving devices, and declining physical activity. One study found that in 2000, U.S. women ate 335 more calories a day and men 168 more calories a day than they did in the early 1970s (National Center for Health Statistics, 2004).

Sociocultural factors are involved in obesity, which is six times more prevalent among women with low incomes than among women with high incomes. Americans also are more obese than Europeans and people in many other areas of the world (OECD, 2010).

Dieting Ironically, although obesity is on the rise, dieting has become an obsession with many Americans (Blake, 2015; Donatelle, 2015). Although many Americans regularly embark on a diet, few are successful in keeping weight off over the long term and many dieters risk becoming fatter (Bombak, 2014). A research review of the long-term outcomes of calorie-restricting diets revealed that overall one-third to two-thirds of dieters regain more weight than they lost on their diets (Mann & others, 2007). However, some individuals do lose weight and maintain the loss (Aguiar & others, 2014; Hinderliter & others, 2014). How often this occurs and whether some diet programs work better than others are still open questions.

What we *do* know about losing weight is that the most effective programs include exercise (Chatzigeorgiou & others, 2014; Ryan & others, 2014; Unick & others, 2013). A research review concluded that adults who engaged in diet-plus-exercise programs lost more weight than those who relied on diet-only programs (Wu & others, 2009). A study of approximately 2,000 U.S. adults found that exercising 30 minutes a day, planning meals, and weighing themselves daily were the main strategies used by successful dieters as compared with unsuccessful dieters (Kruger, Blanck, & Gillespie, 2006) (see Figure 13.4). Another study also revealed that daily weigh-ins are linked to maintaining weight loss (Wing & others, 2007).

REGULAR EXERCISE

One of the main reasons health experts want people to exercise is that it helps to prevent chronic disorders such as heart disease and diabetes (Thompson & Manore, 2015). Many health experts recommend that young adults engage in 30 minutes or more of aerobic exercise daily. **Aerobic exercise** is sustained exercise—jogging, swimming, or cycling, for example— that stimulates heart and lung activity. Most health experts recommend that you raise your heart rate to at least 60 percent of your maximum heart rate. Only about one-fifth of adults, however, achieve these recommended levels of physical activity.

A national poll in the United States found that 51.6 percent of individuals 18 years of age and older exercised for 30 or more minutes 3 or more days a week (Gallup, 2013b). In this survey, young adults 18 to 29 years of age (56.8 percent) were the most likely to exercise of all adult age groups. Also in this survey, men were more likely to exercise than women.

Researchers have found that exercise benefits not only physical health, but mental health as well. In particular, exercise improves self-concept and reduces anxiety and depression (Behrman & Ebemeier, 2014; Henchoz & others, 2014). Meta-analyses have shown that exercise can be as effective in reducing depression as psychotherapy (Richardson & others, 2005). A recent daily diary study found that on days when emerging adult (18 to 25 years of age) college students engaged in more physical activity they also reported greater satisfaction with life (Maher & others, 2013).

Here are some helpful strategies for making exercise part of your life:

- *Reduce screen time.* Heavy screen viewing (TV, Internet, and so on) is linked to poor health and obesity. A recent study revealed that compared with individuals who watch no TV, watching TV 6 hours a day reduces life expectancy by 4.8 years (Veerman & others, 2012). Replace some of your screen time with exercise.

- *Chart your progress.* Systematically recording your exercise workouts will help you to chart your progress. This strategy is especially helpful over the long term.

- *Get rid of excuses.* People make up all kinds of excuses for not exercising. A typical excuse is "I don't have enough time." You likely do have enough time to exercise 30 minutes per day.

- *Imagine the alternative.* Ask yourself whether you are too busy to take care of your own health. What will your life be like if you lose your health?

SUBSTANCE ABUSE

In Chapter 11, we explored substance abuse in adolescence. Fortunately, by the time individuals reach their mid-twenties, many have reduced their use of alcohol and drugs. That is the conclusion reached by Jerald Bachman and his colleagues (2002) in a longitudinal analysis of more than 38,000 individuals who were evaluated from the time they were high school seniors through their twenties. As in adolescence, male college students and young adults are more likely to take drugs than their female counterparts (Johnston & others, 2008). One study revealed that only 20 percent of college students reported abstaining from alcohol (Huang & others, 2009).

Let's take a closer look at alcohol consumption and nicotine use by young adults and consider how this activity may become **addiction,** which is a behavior pattern characterized by an overwhelming involvement with a drug and a preoccupation with securing its supply.

Alcohol   Two problems associated with excessive alcohol consumption are binge drinking and alcoholism.

developmental **connection**
Health
Do adolescents exercise more or less than children do? Chapter 11, p. 351

What are your exercise goals? What are some strategies for incorporating exercise into your life?

aerobic exercise Sustained exercise (such as jogging, swimming, or cycling) that stimulates heart and lung activity.

addiction A pattern of behavior characterized by an overwhelming involvement with using a drug and a preoccupation with securing its supply.

What kinds of problems are associated with binge drinking in college?

Binge Drinking   Heavy binge drinking often occurs in college, and it can take its toll on students (Kinney, 2012). Chronic binge drinking is more common among college men, especially those who live in fraternity houses (Chen & Jacobson, 2012; Johnston & others, 2013; Schulenberg & others, 2000).

In 2012, 37.4 percent of U.S. college students reported having had five or more drinks in a row at least once in the last two weeks (Johnston & others, 2013). The term *extreme binge drinking* describes individuals who had 10 or more drinks in a row. In 2010 approximately 13 percent of college students reported drinking this heavily (Johnston & others, 2011). While drinking rates among college students have remained high, drinking, including binge drinking, has declined in recent years. For example, binge drinking declined by 4 percent from 2007 to 2012 (Johnston & others, 2013).

In a national survey of drinking patterns on 140 campuses, almost half of the binge drinkers reported problems that included absence from classes, physical injuries, troubles with police, and unprotected sex (Wechsler & others, 2002). For example, binge-drinking college students were 11 times as likely to fall behind in school, 10 times as likely to drive after drinking, and twice as likely to have unprotected sex as college students who did not engage in binge drinking. Further, in a recent study, college men who frequently engaged in binge drinking had vascular changes in blood flow that are a precursor for developing atherosclerosis (hardening of the arteries) and other cardiovascular problems such as having a heart attack or a stroke (Goslawski & others, 2013).

Drinking alcohol before going out—called *pregaming*—has become common among college students (Ahmed & others, 2014; Hummer & others, 2013; Silvestri & others, 2013). One study revealed that almost two-thirds of students on one campus had pregamed at least once during a two-week period (DeJong, DeRicco, & Schneider, 2010). Another recent study found that two-thirds of 18- to 24-year-old women on one college pregamed (Read, Merrill, & Bytschkow, 2010). Drinking games, in which the goal is to become intoxicated, also have become common on college campuses (Cameron & others, 2010). Higher levels of alcohol use have been consistently linked to higher rates of sexual risk taking, such as engaging in casual sex, having sex without using contraception, and sexual assaults (Khan & others, 2012).

When does binge drinking peak during development? A longitudinal study revealed that binge drinking peaks at about 21 to 22 years of age and then declines through the remainder of the twenties (Bachman & others, 2002) (see Figure 13.5). Recent data from the Monitoring the Future study at the University of Michigan also indicate that binge drinking peaks at 21 to 22 years of age (39 percent reported that they had engaged in binge drinking at least once in the last 2 weeks) (Johnston & others, 2013).

Alcoholism   *Alcoholism* is a disorder that involves long-term, repeated, uncontrolled, compulsive, and excessive use of alcoholic beverages and impairs the drinker's health and social

FIGURE **13.5**

BINGE DRINKING IN THE ADOLESCENCE—EARLY ADULTHOOD TRANSITION. Note that the percentage of individuals engaging in binge drinking peaked at 21 or 22 years of age and then declined gradually through the remainder of the twenties. Binge drinking was defined as having five or more alcoholic drinks in a row in the past two weeks.

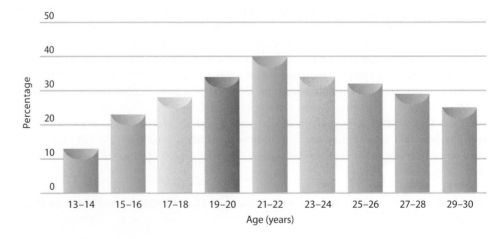

relationships. One in nine individuals who drink will become an alcoholic. Those who do are disproportionately related to alcoholics (Gordh, Brkic, & Soderpalm, 2011). Family studies consistently reveal a high frequency of alcoholism in the first-degree relatives of alcoholics (Lee & others, 2013). An estimated 50 to 60 percent of individuals who become alcoholics are believed to have a genetic predisposition for it.

Researchers have found a genetic influence on alcoholism (Novo-Veleiro & others, 2014; Ulloa & others, 2014). Researchers also have documented that environmental factors play a role in alcoholism (O'Malley, 2014). For example, family studies indicate that many individuals who suffer from alcoholism do not have close relatives who are addicted to alcohol (McCutcheon & others, 2012). Large cultural variations in alcohol use also underscore the environment's role in alcoholism. For example, Orthodox Jews and Mormons have especially low rates of alcohol use and alcoholism.

About one-third of alcoholics recover, whether or not they are ever in a treatment program. This figure was found in a long-term study of 700 individuals over 50 years and has consistently been found by other researchers as well (Vaillant, 1992). There is a "one-third rule" for alcoholism: By age 65, one-third of alcoholics are dead or in terrible shape, one-third are abstinent or drinking socially, and one-third are still trying to beat their addiction.

Cigarette Smoking and Nicotine Converging evidence from a number of studies underscores the dangers of smoking or being around those who smoke (American Cancer Society, 2014). For example, smoking is linked to 30 percent of cancer deaths, 21 percent of heart disease deaths, and 82 percent of chronic pulmonary disease deaths. Secondhand smoke is implicated in as many as 9,000 lung cancer deaths a year. As we saw in Chapter 7, "Physical and Cognitive Development in Early Childhood," children of smokers are at risk for a number of health problems, especially asthma (Carlsson & others, 2013; Hur, Liang, & Lin, 2014; Jarosinska & others, 2014).

Fewer people smoke today than in the past, and almost half of all living adults who ever smoked have quit. In the United States, the prevalence of smoking in individuals 18 years of age and older dropped from 42 percent in 1965 to 18 percent (20 percent of males, 14.5 percent of females) in 2012 (Centers for Disease Control and Prevention, 2014). However, more than 50 million Americans still smoke cigarettes today. Cigarette smoking accounts for approximately 450,000 deaths, or 1 in 5 deaths, annually in the United States (Centers for Disease Control and Prevention, 2014).

Most adult smokers would like to quit, but their addiction to nicotine often makes quitting a challenge (Mennecke & others, 2014). Nicotine, the active drug in cigarettes, is a stimulant that increases the smoker's energy and alertness, a pleasurable and reinforcing experience (Swan & others, 2013). Nicotine also stimulates neurotransmitters (especially dopamine) that have a calming or pain-reducing effect (Di Ciano, Grandy, & Le Foll, 2014).

"There's no shooting—we just make you keep smoking."
© Michael Shaw/The New Yorker Collection/ www.cartoonbank.com

developmental **connection**

Health

Many individuals who smoke in emerging adulthood and early adulthood began smoking during adolescence. Chapter 11, p. 353

Review *Connect* Reflect

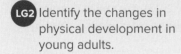 Identify the changes in physical development in young adults.

Review

- When does physical performance peak and then slow down in adulthood?
- What characterizes health in emerging and early adulthood?
- What are some important things to know about eating and weight?
- What are the benefits of exercise?
- How extensive is substance abuse in young adults? What effects does it have on their lives?

Connect

- Problems with weight in adulthood are often preceded by problems with weight

earlier in life. What are some of the influences on children's eating and exercise behavior in early childhood that you learned about in Chapter 7?

Reflect *Your Own Personal Journey of Life*

- What is (or was) your life like from age 18 to 25? Do Arnett's five characteristics of emerging adulthood accurately describe your own experience during this period?

3 Sexuality (LG3) Discuss sexuality in young adults.

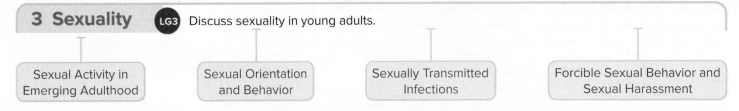

| Sexual Activity in Emerging Adulthood | Sexual Orientation and Behavior | Sexually Transmitted Infections | Forcible Sexual Behavior and Sexual Harassment |

We do not need sex for everyday survival the way we need food and water, but we do need it for the survival of the species. In Chapter 11, we looked at how adolescents develop a sexual identity and become sexually active. What happens to their sexuality during adulthood? Let's examine the sexual activity of Americans and their sexual orientation, as well as some of the problems that can be associated with sexual activity.

SEXUAL ACTIVITY IN EMERGING ADULTHOOD

At the beginning of emerging adulthood (age 18), surveys indicate that slightly more than 60 percent of individuals have experienced sexual intercourse, but by the end of emerging adulthood (age 25), most individuals have had sexual intercourse (Lefkowitz & Gillen, 2006). Also, the average age of marriage in the United States is currently 28 for males and 26 for females (Copen & others, 2012). Thus, emerging adulthood is a time frame during which most individuals are both sexually active and unmarried (Lefkowitz & Gillen, 2006).

Uncertainty characterizes many emerging adults' sexual relationships. Consider a recent study of emerging adult daters and cohabitors that found nearly half reported a reconciliation (a breakup followed by a reunion) (Halpern-Meekin & others, 2013). One study of 18- to 26-year-olds revealed that perceived relationship commitment, though not formal relationship commitment (usually indexed by marriage), was linked to sexual enjoyment (Galinsky & Sonenstein, 2013).

Casual sex is more common in emerging adulthood than in the late twenties (Fielder & others, 2014; Lyons & others, 2013). A recent trend has involved "hooking up" to have non-relationship sex (from kissing to intercourse) (Katz & Schneider, 2013; Olmstead & others, 2014; Vrangalova, 2014). A recent study revealed that 20 percent of first-year college women on one large university campus engaged in at least one hook-up over the course of the school year (Fielder & others, 2013). In this study, impulsivity, sensation seeking, and alcohol use were among the predictors of a higher likelihood of hooking up. In addition to hooking up, another type of casual sex that has recently increased in emerging adults is "friends with benefits," which involves a relationship formed by the integration of friendship and sexual intimacy without an explicit commitment characteristic of an exclusive romantic relationship (Owen, Fincham, & Manthos, 2013).

What are some predictors of risky heterosexual behavior in emerging adults, such as engaging in casual and unprotected sexual intercourse? Some research findings indicate the following (Lefkowitz & Gillen, 2006):

- Sexual risk factors increase in emerging adulthood, with males engaging in more of these risk factors than females (Mahalik & others, 2013). For example, males have more casual sexual partners while females report being more selective about their choice of a sexual partner.
- Individuals who became sexually active in adolescence engage in more risky sexual behaviors in emerging adulthood than do their counterparts who delayed their sexual debuts until emerging adulthood (Capaldi & others, 2002).
- Emerging adults who were enrolled in college or who had graduated from college reported having fewer casual sex partners than those without a high school diploma (Lyons & others, 2013).

Approximately 60 percent of emerging adults have had sexual intercourse with only one individual in the past year, but compared with young adults in their late twenties and thirties, emerging adults are more likely to have had sexual intercourse with two or more individuals. Although emerging adults have sexual intercourse with more individuals than

developmental connection

Sexuality

Having intercourse in early adolescence is a risk factor in development. Chapter 11, p. 346

young adults, they have sex less frequently. Approximately 25 percent of emerging adults report having sexual intercourse only a couple of times a year or not at all (Michael & others, 1994).

SEXUAL ORIENTATION AND BEHAVIOR

A national study of sexual behavior in the United States among adults 25 to 44 years of age found that 98 percent of the women and 97 percent of the men said that they had ever engaged in vaginal intercourse (Chandra & others, 2011). Also in this study, 89 percent of the women and 90 percent of the men reported that they had ever had oral sex with an opposite-sex partner, and 36 percent of the women and 44 percent of the men stated that they had ever had anal sex with an opposite-sex partner.

Detailed information about various aspects of sexual activity in adults of different ages comes from the 1994 Sex in America survey. In this study Robert Michael and his colleagues (1994) interviewed more than 3,000 people from 18 to 59 years of age who were randomly selected, in sharp contrast with earlier samples that were based on unrepresentative groups of volunteers.

Heterosexual Attitudes and Behavior   Here are some of the key findings from the 1994 Sex in America survey:

- Americans tend to fall into three categories: one-third have sex twice a week or more, one-third a few times a month, and one-third a few times a year or not at all.
- Married (and cohabiting) couples have sex more often than noncohabiting couples (see Figure 13.6).
- Most Americans do not engage in kinky sexual acts. When asked about their favorite sexual acts, the vast majority (96 percent) said that vaginal sex was "very" or "somewhat" appealing. Oral sex was in third place, after an activity that many have not labeled a sexual act—watching a partner undress.
- Adultery is clearly the exception rather than the rule. Nearly 75 percent of the married men and 85 percent of the married women indicated that they have never been unfaithful.
- Men think about sex far more often than women do—54 percent of the men said they think about it every day or several times a day, whereas 67 percent of the women said they think about it only a few times a week or a few times a month.

In sum, one of the most powerful messages in the 1994 survey was that Americans' sexual lives are more conservative than was previously believed. Although 17 percent of the men and 3 percent of the women reported having had sex with at least 21 partners, the overall impression from the survey was that sexual behavior is ruled by marriage and monogamy for most Americans.

How extensive are gender differences in sexuality? A meta-analysis revealed that men reported having slightly more sexual experience and more permissive attitudes than women for most aspects of sexuality (Petersen & Hyde, 2010). For the following factors, stronger differences were found: Men indicated that they engaged more in masturbation, pornography use, and casual sex, and they held more permissive attitudes about casual sex than their female counterparts. A recent analysis (Sprecher, Treger, & Sakaluk, 2013) of almost 8,000 emerging adults found that males had stronger permissive attitudes, especially about sex in casual relationships, than the "slightly more" permissive attitudes in the meta-analysis (Petersen & Hyde, 2010) just described. In the more recent study, African American males had more permissive sexual attitudes than non-Latino White, Latino, and Asian males, while there were no ethnic differences found among females (Sprecher, Treger, & Sakaluk, 2013).

Given all of the media and public attention to the negative aspects of sexuality—such as adolescent pregnancy, sexually transmitted infections, rape, and so on—it is important to underscore that research has strongly supported the role of sexual activity in well-being (Brody, 2010; King, 2014). For example, in a Swedish study, frequency of sexual intercourse was strongly related to life satisfaction for both men and women (Brody & Costa, 2009).

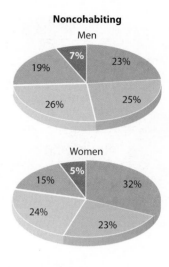

Noncohabiting

Men

23% 25% 26% 19% 7%

Women

32% 23% 24% 15% 5%

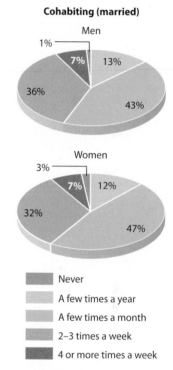

Cohabiting (married)

Men

13% 43% 36% 7% 1%

Women

12% 47% 32% 7% 3%

- Never
- A few times a year
- A few times a month
- 2–3 times a week
- 4 or more times a week

FIGURE **13.6**

THE SEX IN AMERICA SURVEY. The percentages show noncohabiting and cohabiting (married) males' and females' responses to the survey question "How often have you had sex in the past year?" (Michael & others, 1994). *What was one feature of the Sex in America survey that made it superior to most surveys of sexual behavior?*

What likely determines an individual's sexual orientation?

Sources of Sexual Orientation In the Sex in America survey, 2.7 percent of the men and 1.3 percent of the women reported having had same-sex relations in the past year (Michael & others, 1994). Why are some individuals lesbian, gay, or bisexual (LGB) and others heterosexual? Speculation about this question has been extensive (Crooks & Baur, 2014).

Until the end of the nineteenth century, it was generally believed that people were either heterosexual or homosexual. Today, sexual orientation is generally seen not as an either/or proposition but as a continuum ranging from exclusive male-female relations to exclusive same-sex relations (King, 2014). Some individuals are bisexual, being sexually attracted to people of both sexes.

People sometimes think that bisexuality is simply a stepping-stone to homosexuality, while others view it as a sexual orientation itself or as an indicator of sexual fluidity (King, 2014). Evidence supports the notion that bisexuality is a stable orientation that involves attraction to both sexes (Lippa, 2013; Mock & Eibach, 2012).

Compared with men, women are more likely to change their sexual patterns and desires (Diamond, 2008; Knight & Hope, 2012; Mock & Eibach, 2012). Women are more likely than men to have sexual experiences with same- and opposite-sex partners, even if they identify themselves strongly as being heterosexual or lesbian (King, 2014). Also, women are more likely than men to identify themselves as bisexual (Gates, 2011).

All people, regardless of their sexual orientation, have similar physiological responses during sexual arousal and seem to be aroused by the same types of tactile stimulation. Investigators typically find no differences between LGBs and heterosexuals in a wide range of attitudes, behaviors, and adjustments (Fingerhut & Peplau, 2013).

Recently, researchers have explored the possible biological basis of same-sex relations. The results of hormone studies have been inconsistent. If gays are given male sex hormones (androgens), their sexual orientation doesn't change. Their sexual desire merely increases. A very early prenatal critical period might influence sexual orientation (Hines, 2013). If this critical-period hypothesis turns out to be correct, it would explain why clinicians have found that sexual orientation is difficult, if not impossible, to modify.

An individual's sexual orientation—same-sex, heterosexual, or bisexual—is most likely determined by a combination of genetic, hormonal, cognitive, and environmental factors (Hyde & DeLamater, 2014; King, 2014). Most experts on same-sex relations point out that no single factor alone causes sexual orientation and that the relative weight of each factor can vary from one individual to the next.

Researchers have examined the role of genes in sexual orientation by using twins to estimate the genetic and environmental contributions to sexual orientation. A recent Swedish study of almost 4,000 twins demonstrated that only about 35 percent of the variation in homosexual behavior in men and 19 percent in women were explained by genetic differences (Langstrom & others, 2010). This result indicates that although genes likely play a role in sexual orientation, their influence is not as strong in explaining sexuality as it is for other characteristics such as intelligence (King, 2014).

developmental **connection**

Research Methods

A twin study compares the behavioral similarity of identical twins with that of fraternal twins. Chapter 2, p. 64

STI	Description/cause	Incidence	Treatment
Gonorrhea	Commonly called the "drip" or "clap." Caused by the bacterium *Neisseria gonorrhoeae*. Spread by contact between infected moist membranes (genital, oral-genital, or anal-genital) of two individuals. Characterized by discharge from penis or vagina and painful urination. Can lead to infertility.	500,000 cases annually in U.S.	Penicillin, other antibiotics
Syphilis	Caused by the bacterium *Treponema pallidum*. Characterized by the appearance of a sore where syphilis entered the body. The sore can be on the external genitals, vagina, or anus. Later, a skin rash breaks out on palms of hands and bottom of feet. If not treated, can eventually lead to paralysis or even death.	100,000 cases annually in U.S.	Penicillin
Chlamydia	A common STI named for the bacterium *Chlamydia trachomatis*, an organism that spreads by sexual contact and infects the genital organs of both sexes. A special concern is that females with chlamydia may become infertile. It is recommended that adolescent and young adult females have an annual screening for this STI.	About 3 million people in U.S. annually.	Antibiotics
Genital herpes	Caused by a family of viruses with different strains. Involves an eruption of sores and blisters. Spread by sexual contact.	One of five U.S. adults	No known cure but antiviral medications can shorten outbreaks
AIDS	Caused by a virus, the human immunodeficiency virus (HIV), which destroys the body's immune system. Semen and blood are the main vehicles of transmission. Common symptoms include fevers, night sweats, weight loss, chronic fatigue, and swollen lymph nodes.	More than 300,000 cumulative cases of HIV virus in U.S. 25–34-year-olds; epidemic incidence in sub-Saharan countries	New treatments have slowed the progression from HIV to AIDS; no cure
Genital warts	Caused by the human papillomavirus (HPV), which does not always produce symptoms. Usually appear as small, hard painless bumps in the vaginal area, or around the anus. Very contagious. Certain high-risk types of this virus cause cervical cancer and other genital cancers. May recur despite treatment. A new HPV preventive vaccine, Gardasil, has been approved for girls and women 9–26 years of age.	About 5.5 million new cases annually; considered the most common STI in the U.S.	A topical drug, freezing, or surgery

FIGURE **13.7**
SEXUALLY TRANSMITTED INFECTIONS

Attitudes and Behavior of Lesbians and Gays Many gender differences that appear in heterosexual relationships also occur in same-sex relationships (Diamond & Savin-Williams, 2015; Savin-Williams, 2015; Savin-Williams & Cohen, 2015). For example, like heterosexual women, lesbians have fewer sexual partners than gay men, and lesbians have less permissive attitudes about casual sex outside a primary relationship than gay men do (Fingerhut & Peplau, 2013).

A special concern involving sexual minority individuals are the hate crimes and stigma-related experiences they encounter (Clark, 2014). In one study, approximately 20 percent of sexual minority adults reported having experienced a person or property crime related to their sexual orientation, and about 50 percent said they had experienced verbal harassment (Herek, 2009).

SEXUALLY TRANSMITTED INFECTIONS

Sexually transmitted infections (STIs) are diseases that are primarily spread through sexual contact—intercourse as well as oral-genital and anal-genital sex. STIs affect about one in six U.S. adults (National Center for Health Statistics, 2014). Among the most prevalent STIs are bacterial infections (such as gonorrhea, syphilis, and chlamydia) and STIs caused by viruses—genital herpes, genital warts, and HIV, which can lead to AIDS. Figure 13.7 describes several sexually transmitted infections.

No single STI has had a greater impact on sexual behavior, or created more public fear in the last several decades, than infection with the human immunodeficiency virus (HIV). HIV is a sexually transmitted infection that destroys the body's immune system. Once a person is infected with HIV, the virus breaks down and overpowers the immune system, which

sexually transmitted infections (STIs) Diseases that are contracted primarily through sexual activity.

leads to acquired immune deficiency syndrome (AIDS). An individual sick with AIDS has such a weakened immune system that a common cold can be life threatening.

In 2010, 1.2 million people in the United States were living with an HIV infection (National Center for Health Statistics, 2013). In 2010, male-male sexual contact continued to be the most frequent AIDS transmission category. A recent study of U.S. 18- to 29-year-olds found that men having sex with men had a greater risk of contracting HIV during risky sex than men having sex only with women (Centers for Disease Control and Prevention, 2012).

Because of education and the development of more effective drug treatments, deaths due to HIV/AIDS have begun to decline in the United States (National Center for Health Statistics, 2013). To read about the background and work of one individual who counsels HIV/AIDS patients, see *Connecting with Careers*.

Globally, the total number of individuals living with HIV was 34 million at the end of 2010, with 22 million of these individuals with HIV living in sub-Saharan Africa. Approximately half of all new HIV infections around the world occur in the 15- to 24-year-old age category. The good news is that global rates of HIV infection fell nearly 25 percent from 2001 to 2009 with substantial decreases in India and South Africa (UNAIDS, 2011). In one study, only 49 percent of 15- to 24-year-old females in low- and middle-income countries knew that using a condom helps to prevent HIV infection, compared with 74 percent of young males (UNAIDS, 2011).

What are some effective strategies for protecting against HIV and other sexually transmitted infections? They include the following:

- *Know your risk status and that of your partner.* Anyone who has had previous sexual activity with another person might have contracted an STI without being aware of it. Spend time getting to know a prospective partner before you have sex. Use this time to inform the other person of your STI status and inquire about your partner's. Remember that many people lie about their STI status.

- *Obtain medical examinations.* Many experts recommend that couples who want to begin a sexual relationship have a medical checkup to rule out STIs before they engage in sex. If cost is an issue, contact your campus health service or a public health clinic.

- *Have protected, not unprotected, sex.* When used correctly, latex condoms help to prevent many STIs from being transmitted. Condoms are most effective in preventing gonorrhea, syphilis, chlamydia, and HIV. They are less effective against the spread of herpes.

- *Do not have sex with multiple partners.* One of the best predictors of getting an STI is having sex with multiple partners. Having more than one sex partner elevates the likelihood that you will encounter an infected partner.

FORCIBLE SEXUAL BEHAVIOR AND SEXUAL HARASSMENT

Too often, sex involves the exercise of power. Here, we will briefly look at three of the problems that may result: two types of rape and sexual harassment.

Rape   **Rape** is forcible sexual intercourse with a person who does not give consent. Legal definitions of rape differ from state to state. For example, in some states husbands are not prohibited from forcing their wives to have intercourse, although this has been challenged in several of those states.

Because victims may be reluctant to suffer the consequences of reporting rape, the actual incidence is not easily determined (Cleere & Lynn, 2013; Krebs, 2014). Nearly 200,000 rapes are reported each year in the United States. A recent study of college women who had been raped revealed that only 11.5 percent of them reported the rape to authorities and of those for which the rape involved drugs and/or alcohol, only 2.7 percent of the rapes were reported (Wolitzky-Taylor & others, 2011).

Although most victims of rape are women, rape of men does occur (Bullock & Beckson, 2011). Men in prisons are especially vulnerable to rape, usually by heterosexual males who use rape as a means of establishing their dominance and power (Barth, 2012).

Why does rape of women occur so often in the United States? Among the causes given are that males are socialized to be sexually aggressive, to regard women as inferior beings, and to view their own pleasure as the most important objective in sexual relations (Davies, Gilston, & Rogers, 2012; Rudman, Fetterolf, & Sanchez, 2013). Researchers have found that male rapists share the following characteristics: aggression enhances their sense of power or masculinity; they are angry at women in general; and they want to hurt and humiliate their victims (Yarber, Sayad, & Strong, 2013). A recent study revealed that a higher level of men's sexual narcissism (assessed by these factors: sexual exploitation, sexual entitlement, low sexual empathy, and sexual skill) was linked to a greater likelihood that they would engage in sexual aggression (Widman & McNulty, 2010). A recent study also revealed that regardless of whether or not the victim was using substances, sexual assault was more likely to occur when the offender was using substances (Brecklin & Ullman, 2010).

Rape is a traumatic experience for the victims and those close to them (Littleton, 2014). As victims strive to get their lives back to normal, they may experience depression, fear, anxiety, increased substance use, and suicidal thoughts for months or years (Bryan & others, 2013). Many victims make changes in their lives—such as moving to a new apartment or refusing to go out at night. Recovery depends on the victim's coping abilities, psychological adjustment prior to the assault, and social support. Parents, a partner, and others close to the victim can provide important support for recovery, as can mental health professionals (Ahrens & Aldana, 2012; Resick & others, 2012).

An increasing concern is **date or acquaintance rape,** which is coercive sexual activity directed at someone with whom the perpetrator is at least casually acquainted (Sabina & Ho, 2014; Turchik & Hassija, 2014). In one survey, two-thirds of female college freshmen reported having been date raped or having experienced an attempted date rape at least once (Watts & Zimmerman, 2002). About two-thirds of college men admit that they fondle women against their will, and half admit to forcing sexual activity.

A number of colleges and universities describe the red zone as a period of time early in the first year of college when women are at especially high risk for unwanted sexual experiences. One study revealed that first-year women were more at risk for unwanted sexual

What are some characteristics of acquaintance rape in colleges and universities?

rape Forcible sexual intercourse with a person who does not consent to it.

date or acquaintance rape Coercive sexual activity directed at someone with whom the perpetrator is at least casually acquainted.

How Prevalent Are Sexual Assaults on College Campuses?

A major study that focused on campus sexual assault involved a phone survey of 4,446 women attending two- or four-year colleges (Fisher, Cullen, & Turner, 2000). Sexual victimization was measured in a two-stage process. First, a series of screening questions were asked to determine whether the respondent had experienced an act that might possibly be a victimization. Second, if the respondent answered "yes," she was asked detailed questions about the incident, such as the type of unwanted contact and the means of coercion. In addition, respondents were asked about other aspects of their lives, including their lifestyles, routine activities, living arrangements, and prior sexual victimization.

Slightly less than 3 percent said that they had experienced either a rape or an attempted rape during the current academic year. About 1 in 10 college women said that they had experienced rape in their lifetime. Unwanted or uninvited sexual contacts were widespread, with more than one-third of the college women reporting these incidents. As shown in Figure 13.8, in this study, most women (about 9 out of 10) knew the person who had sexually victimized them. Most of the women attempted to take protective actions against their assailants but were reluctant to report the victimization to the police for a number of reasons (such as embarrassment, not clearly understanding the legal definition of rape, or not wanting to define someone they knew who had victimized them as a rapist). Several factors were associated with sexual victimization: living on campus, being unmarried, getting drunk frequently, and experiencing prior sexual victimization. The majority of rapes occurred in living quarters.

In addition, the researchers in this study examined a form of sexual victimization that has been studied infrequently: stalking. Thirteen percent of the female students said they had been stalked since the school year began. As with other sexual victimizations, 80 percent knew their stalkers, who most often were boyfriends (42 percent) or classmates (24 percent). Stalking incidents lasted an average of 60 days.

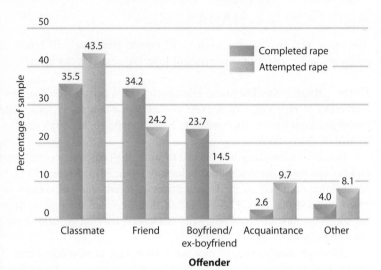

FIGURE **13.8**

RELATIONSHIP BETWEEN VICTIM AND OFFENDER IN COMPLETED AND ATTEMPTED RAPES OF COLLEGE WOMEN. In a phone survey of college women, slightly less than 3 percent of the women said they had experienced a rape or attempted rape during the academic year (Fisher, Cullen, & Turner, 2000). The percentages shown here indicate the relationship between the victim and the offender. *What were some possible advantages and disadvantages of using a phone survey rather than face-to-face interviews to conduct this study?*

Given the prevalence of sexual assault on college campuses and the frequency with which those assaults involve perpetrators the victims know, it is clear that more research needs to be dedicated to effective intervention strategies for young men and women. In the past, too often the responsibility of prevention was placed on the would-be victim's behavior. While those sorts of strategies are not unhelpful, prevention strategies that target the behavior of the would-be rapist might get closer to the root of the problem.

experiences, especially early in the fall term, than second-year women (Kimble & others, 2008). Exactly how prevalent are sexual assaults on college campuses? To find out, see *Connecting Through Research*.

Sexual Harassment   Sexual harassment is a manifestation of power of one person over another. It takes many forms, ranging from inappropriate sexual remarks and physical contact (patting, brushing against another person's body) to blatant propositions and sexual assaults. Millions of women experience sexual harassment each year in work and educational settings (Cantalupo, 2014). Sexual harassment of men by women also occurs but to a far lesser extent than sexual harassment of women by men.

In a survey of 2,000 college women, 62 percent reported having experienced sexual harassment while attending college (American Association of University Women, 2006). Most of the college women said that the sexual harassment involved noncontact forms such as crude jokes, remarks, and gestures. However, almost one-third said that the sexual harassment was physical in nature. Sexual harassment can result in serious psychological consequences for the victim. The elimination of this type of exploitation requires the establishment of work and academic environments that provide women and men with equal opportunities to develop a career and obtain an education in a climate free of sexual harassment (Nielsen & Einarsen, 2012).

Review Connect Reflect

LG3 Discuss sexuality in young adults.

Review

- What characterizes the sexual activity of emerging adults?
- What is the nature of heterosexuality and same-sex sexual orientation?
- What are sexually transmitted infections? What are some important things to know about AIDS?
- What is rape? What is date or acquaintance rape? What are the effects of forcible sexual behavior and sexual harassment?

Connect

- As you learned in this section, sexual assault is connected with aggression in males. In Chapter 8, what was identified as one way in which children learn to behave aggressively?

Reflect *Your Own Personal Journey of Life*

- How would you describe your sexual experiences during emerging adulthood? How similar or dissimilar are they to the way sexuality in emerging adulthood was described in this section?

4 Cognitive Development

LG4 Characterize cognitive changes in early adulthood.

Cognitive Stages

Creativity

Are there changes in cognitive performance during early adulthood? To explore the nature of cognition during this period of development, we will focus on issues related to cognitive stages and creative thinking.

COGNITIVE STAGES

Are young adults more advanced in their thinking than adolescents are? Let's examine how Jean Piaget and others have answered this intriguing question.

Piaget's View Piaget concluded that an adolescent and an adult think qualitatively in the same way. That is, Piaget argued that at approximately 11 to 15 years of age, adolescents enter the formal operational stage, which is characterized by more logical, abstract, and idealistic thinking than the concrete operational thinking of 7- to 11-year-olds. Piaget did stress that young adults are more quantitatively advanced in their thinking in the sense that they have more knowledge than adolescents. He also reasoned, as do information-processing psychologists, that adults especially increase their knowledge in a specific area, such as a physicist's understanding of physics or a financial analyst's knowledge about finance. According to Piaget, however, formal operational thought is the final stage in cognitive development, and it characterizes adults as well as adolescents.

What are some ways that young adults might think differently from adolescents?

developmental **connection**

Cognitive Theory

Adolescent cognition also includes adolescent egocentrism. Chapter 11, p. 358

Some developmentalists theorize it is not until adulthood that many individuals consolidate their formal operational thinking. That is, they may begin to plan and hypothesize about intellectual problems in adolescence, but they become more systematic and sophisticated at this process as young adults. Nonetheless, even many adults do not think in formal operational ways (Keating, 2004).

Is There a Fifth, Postformal Stage? Some theorists have pieced together these descriptions of adult thinking and have proposed that young adults move into a new qualitative stage of cognitive development, postformal thought (Sinnott, 2003). **Postformal thought** is:

- *Reflective, relativistic, and contextual.* As young adults engage in solving problems, they might think deeply about many aspects of work, politics, relationships, and other areas of life (Labouvie-Vief, 1986). They find that what might be the best solution to a problem at work (with a boss or co-worker) might not be the best solution at home (with a romantic partner). Thus, postformal thought holds that the correct answer to a problem requires reflective thinking and may vary from one situation to another. Some psychologists argue that reflective thinking continues to increase and becomes more internal and less contextual in middle age (Labouvie-Vief, Gruhn, & Studer, 2010; Mascalo & Fischer, 2010).

- *Provisional.* Many young adults also become more skeptical about the truth and seem unwilling to accept an answer as final. Thus, they come to see the search for truth as an ongoing and perhaps never-ending process.

- *Realistic.* Young adults understand that thinking can't always be abstract. In many instances, it must be realistic and pragmatic.

- *Recognized as being influenced by emotion.* Emerging and young adults are more likely than adolescents to understand that their thinking is influenced by emotions (Labouvie-Vief, 2009; Labouvie-Vief, Gruhn, & Studer, 2010). However, too often negative emotions produce thinking that is distorted and self-serving at this point in development.

developmental **connection**

Cognitive Theory

Links between cognition and emotion are increasingly being studied. Chapter 1, p. 13

One effort to assess postformal thinking is the 10-item Complex Postformal Thought Questionnaire (Sinnott & Johnson, 1997). Figure 13.9 presents the questionnaire and gives you an opportunity to evaluate your thinking at the postformal level. Researchers have found that the questionnaire items reflect three main categories of postformal thinking: (1) Taking into account multiple aspects of a problem or situation; (2) Making a subjective choice in a particular problem situation; and (3) Perceiving underlying complexities in a situation (Cartwright & others, 2009).

How strong is the evidence for a fifth, postformal stage of cognitive development? Researchers have found that young adults are more likely to engage in postformal thinking than adolescents are (Commons & Bresette, 2006). But critics argue that research has yet to document that postformal thought is a qualitatively more advanced stage than formal operational thought.

developmental **connection**

Cognitive Theory

Some developmental psychologists believe that wisdom advances through adulthood. Chapter 18, p. 547

CREATIVITY

Early adulthood is a time of great creativity for some people. At the age of 30, Thomas Edison invented the phonograph, Hans Christian Andersen wrote his first volume of fairy tales, and Mozart composed *The Marriage of Figaro*. One early study of creativity found that individuals' most creative products were generated in their thirties and that 80 percent of the most important creative contributions were completed by age 50 (Lehman, 1960).

More recently, researchers have found that creativity does peak in adulthood and then decline, but that the peak often occurs in the forties. However, qualifying any conclusion about age and creative accomplishments are (1) the magnitude of the decline in productivity,

postformal thought Thinking that is reflective, relativistic, contextual, provisional, realistic, and influenced by emotions.

Respond to each of the items below in terms of how well they characterize your thinking from 1 = Not True (of Self) to 7 = Very True (of Self).	Not True 1	2	3	4	5	6	Very True 7
1. I see the paradoxes in life.							
2. I see more than one method that can be used to reach a goal.							
3. I am aware that I can decide which reality to experience at a particular time; but I know that reality is really multi-level and more complicated.							
4. There are many "right" ways to define any life experience; I must make a final decision on how I define the problems of life.							
5. I am aware that sometimes "succeeding" in the everyday world means finding a concrete answer to one of life's problems; but sometimes it means finding a correct path that would carry me through any problems of this type.							
6. Almost all problems can be solved by logic, but this may require different types of "logics."							
7. I tend to see several causes connected with any event.							
8. I see that a given dilemma always has several good solutions.							
9. I realize that I often have several goals in mind, or that life seems to have several goals in mind for me. So I go toward more than one in following my path in life.							
10. I can see the hidden logic in others' solutions to the problem of life, even if I don't agree with their solutions and follow my own path.							

FIGURE 13.9

COMPLEX POSTFORMAL THOUGHT QUESTIONNAIRE. After you have responded to the items, total your score, which can range from 10 to 70. The higher your score, the more likely you are to engage in postformal thinking.

(2) contrasts across creative domains, and (3) individual differences in lifetime output (Simonton, 1996).

Even though a decline in creative contributions is often found in the fifties and later, the decline is not as great as is commonly thought. An impressive array of creative accomplishments can occur in late adulthood. One of the most remarkable examples of creative accomplishment in late adulthood can be found in the life of Henri Chevreul. After a distinguished career as a physicist, Chevreul switched fields in his nineties to become a pioneer in gerontological research. He published his last research paper just a year prior to his death at the age of 103!

Any consideration of decline in creativity with age requires attention to the field of creativity involved (Jones, Reedy, & Weinberg, 2014; Kozbelt, 2014; McKay & Kaufman, 2014). In such fields as philosophy and history, older adults often show as much creativity as they did when they were in their thirties and forties. By contrast, in such fields as lyric poetry, abstract math, and theoretical physics, the peak of creativity is often reached in the twenties or thirties.

There also is extensive individual variation in the lifetime output of creative individuals. Typically, the most productive creators in any field are far more prolific than their least productive counterparts. The contrast is so extreme that the top 10 percent of creative producers frequently account for 50 percent of the creative output in a particular field. For instance, only 16 composers account for half of the music regularly performed in the classical repertoire.

Can you make yourself more creative? To read about strategies for becoming more creative, see *Connecting Development to Life*.

developmental **connection**

Creativity

What strategies are likely to enhance children's creative thinking? Chapter 9, p. 284

Flow and Other Strategies for Living a More Creative Life

Mihaly Csikszentmihalyi (pronounced ME-high CHICK-sent-me-high-ee) has studied the nature of creativity for a number of decades and has recommended a number of strategies for becoming more creative (Csikszentmihalyi, 1995, 2014). In one project, Csikszentmihalyi (1995) interviewed 90 leading figures in art, business, government, education, and science to learn how creativity works. He discovered that creative people regularly experience a state he calls flow, a heightened state of pleasure experienced when we are engaged in mental and physical challenges that absorb us. Csikszentmihalyi (2000) points out that everyone is capable of achieving flow. Based on his interviews with some of the most creative people in the world, the first step toward a more creative life is cultivating your curiosity and interest. How can you do this? Here are some ideas:

- Try to be surprised by something every day. Maybe it is something you see, hear, or read about. Become absorbed in a lecture or a book. Be open to what the world is telling you. Life is a stream of experiences. Swim widely and deeply in it, and your life will be richer.
- Try to surprise at least one person every day. In a lot of things you do, you have to be predictable and patterned. Do something different for a change. Ask a question you normally would not ask. Invite someone to go to a show or a museum you never have visited.
- Write down each day what surprised you and how you surprised others. Most creative people keep a diary, notes, or lab records to ensure that their experience is not fleeting or forgotten. Start with a specific task. Each evening record the most surprising event that occurred that day and your most surprising action. After a few days, reread your notes and reflect on your past experiences. After a few

weeks, you might see a pattern of interest emerging in your notes, one that might suggest an area you can explore in greater depth.
- When something sparks your interest, follow it. Usually when something captures your attention, it is short-lived—an idea, a song, a flower. Too often we are too busy to explore the idea, song, or flower further. Or we think these areas are none of our business because we are not experts about them. Yet the world is our business. We can't know which part of it is best suited to our interests until we make a serious effort to learn as much about as many aspects of it as possible.
- Wake up in the morning with a specific goal to look forward to. Creative people wake up eager to start the day. Why? Not necessarily because they are cheerful, enthusiastic types but because they know that there is something meaningful to accomplish each day, and they can't wait to get started.
- Spend time in settings that stimulate your creativity. In Csikszentmihalyi's (1995) research, he gave people an electronic pager and beeped them randomly at different times of the day. When he asked them how they felt, they reported the highest levels of creativity when walking, driving, or swimming. I (your author) do my most creative thinking when I'm jogging. These activities are semiautomatic in that they take a certain amount of attention while leaving some time free to make connections among ideas.

Mihaly Csikszentmihalyi, in the setting where he gets his most creative ideas. *When and where do you get your most creative thoughts?*

Can the strategies for stimulating creative thinking in children found in the Connecting Development to Life *interlude in Chapter 9 also be used by adults? How do the strategies discussed in Chapter 9 compare with those discussed here?*

Review Connect Reflect

 LG4 Characterize cognitive changes in early adulthood.

Review
- What changes in cognitive development in young adults have been proposed?
- Does creativity decline in adulthood? How can people lead more creative lives?

Connect
- As discussed in this section, postformal thought is characterized in part by an understanding that emotions and subjective factors influence thinking.

Why are adolescents not typically capable of this kind of awareness?

Reflect *Your Own Personal Journey of Life*
- If you are in emerging adulthood, what do you think are the most important cognitive changes that have taken place so far in the transition period? If you are older, reflect on your emerging adult years and describe some of the cognitive changes that occurred during this time.

5 Careers and Work **LG5** Explain the key dimensions of career and work in early adulthood.

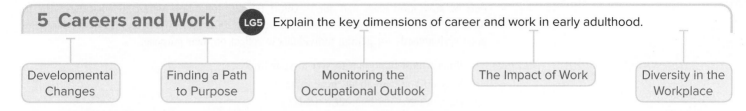

| Developmental Changes | Finding a Path to Purpose | Monitoring the Occupational Outlook | The Impact of Work | Diversity in the Workplace |

Earning a living, choosing an occupation, establishing a career, and developing in a career—these are important themes of early adulthood. What are some of the factors that go into choosing a job or career, and how does work typically affect the lives of young adults?

DEVELOPMENTAL CHANGES

Many children have idealistic fantasies about what they want to be when they grow up. For example, many young children want to be superheroes, sports stars, or movie actors. In the high school years, they often have begun to think about careers from a somewhat less idealistic perspective. In their late teens and early twenties, their career decision making has usually turned more serious as they explore different career possibilities and zero in on the career they want to enter. In college, this often means choosing a major or specialization that is designed to lead to work in a particular field. By their early and mid-twenties, many individuals have completed their education or training and entered a full-time occupation. From the mid-twenties through the remainder of early adulthood, individuals often seek to establish their emerging career in a particular field. They may work hard to move up the career ladder and improve their financial standing.

"Did you think the ladder of success would be straight up?"
© Joseph Farris/The New Yorker Collection/www.cartoonbank.com

Phyllis Moen (2009a) recently described the career mystique—an ingrained cultural belief that engaging in hard work for long hours through adulthood will lead to status, security, and happiness. That is, many individuals envision a career path that will enable them to fulfill the American dream of upward mobility by climbing occupational ladders. However, the lockstep career mystique has never been a reality for many individuals, especially ethnic minority individuals, women, and poorly educated adults. Further, the career mystique has increasingly become a myth for many individuals in middle-income occupations as global outsourcing of jobs and the 2007–2009 recession have threatened the job security of millions of Americans.

FINDING A PATH TO PURPOSE

William Damon (2008) proposed in his book *The Path to Purpose: Helping Our Children Find Their Calling in Life* that purpose is a missing ingredient in many adolescents' and emerging adults' achievement and career development. Too many youth drift aimlessly through their high school and college years, Damon says, engaging in behavior that places them at risk for not fulfilling their potential and not finding a life pursuit that energizes them.

In interviews with 12- to 22-year-olds, Damon found that only about 20 percent had a clear vision of where they wanted to go in life, what they wanted to achieve, and why. The largest percentage—about 60 percent—had engaged in some potentially purposeful activities, such as service learning or fruitful discussions with a career counselor—but they still did not have a real commitment or any reasonable plans for reaching their goals. And slightly more than 20 percent expressed no aspirations and in some instances said they didn't see any reason to have aspirations.

Damon concludes that most teachers and parents communicate the importance of studying hard and getting good grades, but rarely discuss the purpose of academic achievement. Damon emphasizes that too often students focus

Hari Prabhakar (*in rear*) at a screening camp in India that he created as part of his Tribal India Health Foundation. Hari reflects William Damon's concept of finding a path to purpose. His ambition is to become an international health expert. Hari graduated from Johns Hopkins University in 2006 with a double major in public health and writing. A top student (3.9 GPA), he took the initiative to pursue a number of activities outside the classroom, in the health field. As he made the transition from high school to college, Hari created the Tribal India Health Foundation (www.tihf.org), which provides assistance in bringing low-cost health care to rural areas in India. Juggling his roles as a student and as the foundation's director, Hari spent about 15 hours a week leading Tribal India Health throughout his four undergraduate years. In describing his work, Hari said (Johns Hopkins University, 2006):

"I have found it very challenging to coordinate the international operation. . . . It takes a lot of work, and there's not a lot of free time. But it's worth it when I visit our patients and see how they and the community are getting better." (Prabhakar, 2007)
Sources: Johns Hopkins University (2006); Prabhakar (2007).

only on short-term goals and don't explore the big, long-term picture of what they want to do in life. These interview questions that Damon (2008, p. 135) has used in his research are good springboards for getting individuals to reflect on their purpose:

- What's most important to you in your life?
- Why do you care about those things?
- Do you have any long-term goals?
- Why are these goals important to you?
- What does it mean to have a good life?
- What does it mean to be a good person?
- If you were looking back on your life now, how would you like to be remembered?

A recent study found that discussing such questions involving their values and life goals improved college students' goal direction (Bundick, 2011).

developmental **connection**

Work

The middle-aged worker faces a number of challenges in the twenty-first century. Chapter 15, p. 476

MONITORING THE OCCUPATIONAL OUTLOOK

As you explore the type of work you are likely to enjoy and in which you can succeed, it is important to be knowledgeable about different fields and companies. Occupations may have many job openings one year but few in another year as economic conditions change. Thus, it is critical to keep up with the occupational outlook in various fields. An excellent source for doing this is the U.S. government's *Occupational Outlook Handbook,* which is revised every two years.

According to the 2012–2013 handbook, service industries, especially health services, professional and business services, and education, are projected to account for the greatest numbers of new jobs in the next decade (Occupational Outlook Handbook, 2012). Projected job growth varies widely by educational requirements. Jobs that require a college degree are expected to grow the fastest. Most of the highest-paying occupations require a college degree.

THE IMPACT OF WORK

Work defines people in fundamental ways (Highhouse & Schmitt, 2013; Motowidlo & Kell, 2013; Parker, 2014). It is an important influence on their financial standing, housing, the way they spend their time, where they live, their friendships, and their health (Allen, 2013; Blustein, 2013). Some people define their identity through their work. Work also creates a structure and rhythm to life that is often missed when individuals do not work for an extended period. During periods when they are unable to work, many individuals experience emotional distress and low self-esteem.

Most individuals spend about one-third of their time at work. In one survey, 35 percent of Americans worked 40 hours a week, but 18 percent worked 51 hours or more per week (Center for Survey Research at the University of Connecticut, 2000). Only 10 percent worked less than 30 hours a week.

A trend in the U.S. workforce is the disappearing long-term career for an increasing number of adults, especially men in private-sector jobs (Hollister, 2011). Among the reasons for the disappearance of many long-term jobs is the dramatic increase in technology and availability of cheaper labor in other countries.

Many young and older adults are working at a series of jobs that often last for a short time (Greenhaus, 2013; Greenhaus & Callanan, 2013). Early careers are especially unstable as some young workers move from "survival jobs" to "career jobs" as they seek a job that matches their personal interests/goals (Mortimer, 2012). A study of more than 1,100 individuals from 18 to 31 years of age revealed that maintaining a high aspiration and certainty over career goals better insulated individuals against unemployment in the severe economic recession that began in 2007 (Vuolo, Staff, & Mortimer, 2012).

An important consideration regarding work is how stressful it is (Demsky, Ellis, & Fritz, 2014; Sonnentag & Frese, 2013). A national survey of U.S. adults revealed that 55 percent indicated they were less productive because of stress (American Psychological Association, 2007). In this study, 52 percent reported that they considered or made a career decision, such as looking for a new job,

What are some characteristics of work settings linked with employees' stress?

declining a promotion, or quitting a job, because of stress in the workplace (American Psychological Association, 2007). In this survey, main sources of stress included low salaries (44 percent), lack of advancement opportunities (42 percent), uncertain job expectations (40 percent), and long hours (39 percent). A recent study revealed that stressors at work were linked to arterial hypertension in employees (Lamy & others, 2014).

Many adults have changing expectations about work, yet employers often aren't meeting their expectations (Hall & Mirvis, 2013; Richardson & Schaeffer, 2013). For example, current policies and practices were designed for male breadwinners and an industrial economy, making these policies and practices out of step with a workforce of women and men, and of single-parent and dual earners. Many workers today want flexibility and greater control over their work schedules, yet most employers offer little flexibility, even though policies like flextime may be "on the books."

Work During College   The percentage of full-time U.S. college students who also held jobs increased from 34 percent in 1970 to 47 percent in 2008, then declined to 41 percent in 2011 (down from a peak of 52 percent in 2000) (National Center for Education Statistics, 2013). In this recent survey, 74 percent of part-time U.S. college students were employed, down from 81 percent in 2008.

Working can help offset some of the costs of schooling, but working also can restrict students' opportunities to learn. For those who identified themselves primarily as students, one national study found that as the number of hours worked per week increased, their grades suffered (National Center for Education Statistics, 2002) (see Figure 13.10). Thus, college students need to carefully examine whether the number of hours they work is having a negative impact on their college success.

Of course, jobs also can contribute to your education. More than 1,000 colleges in the United States offer *cooperative (co-op) programs,* which are paid apprenticeships in a field that you are interested in pursuing. (You may not be permitted to participate in a co-op program until your junior year.) Other useful opportunities for working while going to college include internships and part-time or summer jobs relevant to your field of study. Participating in these work experiences can help you land the job you want after you graduate.

Unemployment   Unemployment rates in the United States have remained high in recent years, and global unemployment is increasing. Unemployment produces stress regardless of whether the job loss is temporary, cyclical, or permanent (Jalles & Andresen, 2014; Kalousova & Burgard, 2014). Economic problems that led to the recession at the end of the first decade of the twenty-first century produced unusually high unemployment rates. Researchers have found that unemployment is related to physical problems (such as heart attack and stroke), emotional problems (such as depression and anxiety), marital difficulties, and homicide (Backhans & Hemmingsson, 2012; Freyer-Adam & others, 2011). A recent study revealed that 90 or more days of unemployment was associated with subsequent cardiovascular disease across an 8-year follow-up period (Lundin & others, 2014). A 15-year longitudinal study of more than 24,000 adults found that life satisfaction dropped considerably following unemployment and increased after becoming reemployed but did not completely return to the life satisfaction level previous to being unemployed (Lucas & others, 2004). A recent research review concluded that unemployment was associated with an increased mortality risk for individuals in the early and middle stages of their careers, but the increase was less pronounced for those who became unemployed late in

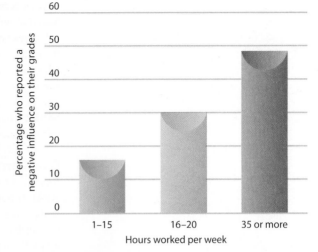

FIGURE 13.10

THE RELATION OF HOURS WORKED PER WEEK IN COLLEGE TO GRADES. Among students working to pay for school expenses, 16 percent of those working 1 to 15 hours per week reported that working negatively influenced their grades (National Center for Education Statistics, 2002). Thirty percent of college students who worked 16 to 20 hours a week said the same, as did 48 percent who worked 35 hours or more per week.

The economic recession that hit in 2007 resulted in millions of Americans losing their jobs, such as the individuals in line here waiting to apply for unemployment benefits in June 2009 in Chicago. *What are some of the potential negative outcomes of the stress caused by job loss?*

their careers (Roelfs & others, 2011). And a recent study found that involuntary job loss was linked to an increase in attempted suicide and suicide (Milner & others, 2014).

Stress caused by unemployment comes not only from a loss of income and the resulting financial hardships but also from decreased self-esteem (Howe & others, 2012). Individuals who cope best with unemployment have financial resources to rely on, often savings or the earnings of other family members. The support of understanding, adaptable family members also helps individuals cope with unemployment. Job counseling and self-help groups can provide emotional support during the job search as well as practical advice on finding job opportunities, writing résumés, and answering questions in job interviews (van Hooft, 2014).

Dual-Earner Couples Dual-earner couples may face special challenges finding a balance between work and family life (Allen, 2013; Richardson & Schaeffer, 2013; Shimazu & others, 2014). If both partners are working, who cleans the house or calls the repairman or takes care of the other endless details involved in maintaining a home? If the couple has children, who is responsible for making sure that the children get to school or to piano practice on time, who writes the notes to approve field trips or meets the teacher or makes the dental appointments?

Although single-earner married families still make up a sizeable minority of families, the proportion of two-earner couples has increased considerably in recent decades. As more U.S. women took jobs outside the home, the division of responsibility for work and family changed in three ways: (1) U.S. men are taking increased responsibility for maintaining the home; (2) U.S. women are taking increased responsibility for breadwinning; (3) U.S. men are showing greater interest in their families and parenting.

Many jobs have been designed for single earners, usually male breadwinners, without regard to family responsibilities or the realities of people's lives (Richardson & Schaeffer, 2013). Consequently, many dual-earner couples engage in a range of adaptive strategies to coordinate their work and manage the family side of the work-family equation (Moen, 2009a, b). Researchers have found that even though couples may strive for gender equality in dual-earner families, gender inequalities persist (Cunningham, 2009). For example, women still do not earn as much as men in the same jobs, and this inequity means that gender divisions in how much time each partner spends in paid work, homemaking, and caring for children continue. Thus, dual-earner career decisions often are made in favor of men's greater earning power, with women spending more time than men taking care of the home and caring for children (Moen, 2009b).

DIVERSITY IN THE WORKPLACE

The workplace is becoming increasingly diverse (Hebl & Avery, 2013). Whereas at one time few women were employed outside the home, in developed countries women have increasingly entered the labor force. A recent projection indicates that women's share of the U.S. labor force will increase faster than men's share through 2020 (Occupational Outlook Handbook, 2012). In the United States, more than one-fourth of today's lawyers, physicians, computer scientists, and chemists are women.

Ethnic diversity also is increasing in the workplace in every developed country except France. In the United States, between 1980 and 2004 the percentage of Latinos and Asian Americans more than doubled in the workplace, a trend that is continuing (Occupational Outlook Handbook, 2012). Latinos are projected to constitute a larger percentage of the labor force than African Americans by 2020, growing from 13 percent in 2006 to 18.6 percent in 2020 (Occupational Outlook Handbook, 2012). The increasing diversity in the workplace requires a sensitivity to cultural differences and an appreciation of the cultural values that workers bring to a job (Hebl & Avery, 2013).

Despite the increasing diversity in the workplace, women and ethnic minorities experience difficulty in breaking through the glass ceiling that prevents them from being promoted to higher rungs on the corporate ladder. This invisible barrier to career advancement prevents women and ethnic minorities from holding managerial or executive jobs regardless of their accomplishments and merits (Schueller-Weidekamm & Kautzky-Willer, 2012).

How has the diversity of the workplace increased in recent years?

Review Connect Reflect

LG5 Explain the key dimensions of career and work in early adulthood.

Review
- What are some developmental changes in careers and work?
- What does Damon argue is missing in many individuals' career pursuits?
- Which occupational areas are likely to offer the greatest increase in jobs in the next decade?
- What are some important things to know about work?
- What characterizes diversity in the workplace?

Connect
- How might what you learned about gender in Chapter 10 relate to what you learned in this section about how gender affects work opportunities and work environments?

Reflect *Your Own Personal Journey of Life*
- If you are an emerging adult, what careers do you want to pursue? How much education will they require? If you are older, how satisfied are you with your career choices as an emerging adult and young adult? Explain.

topical connections *looking forward*

At some point in middle age, more time stretches behind us than ahead of us. Midlife is changing—entered later and lasting longer—for many people. Middle adulthood is a time of declining physical skills and expanding responsibility, as well as balancing work and relationships. For many individuals, cognitive abilities peak in middle age, although some aspects of information processing, such as perceptual speed and memory, decline. Work continues to be central to people's lives in middle adulthood. Middle age also is when individuals become more interested in understanding the meaning of life.

reach your **learning goals**

Physical and Cognitive Development in Early Adulthood

1 The Transition from Adolescence to Adulthood

LG1 Describe the transition from adolescence to adulthood.

Becoming an Adult

- Emerging adulthood is the term given to the transition from adolescence to adulthood. This period ranges from about 18 to 25 years of age, and it is characterized by experimentation and exploration. There is both continuity and change in the transition from adolescence to adulthood. Two criteria for adult status are economic independence and taking responsibility for the consequences of one's actions.

The Transition from High School to College

- The transition from high school to college can have both positive and negative aspects. Although students may feel more grown up and be intellectually challenged by academic work, for many the transition involves a focus on the stressful move from being the oldest and most powerful group of students to being the youngest and least powerful. U.S. college students today report experiencing more stress and depression than college students in the past.

2 Physical Development

 LG2 Identify the changes in physical development in young adults.

Physical Performance and Development

- Peak physical performance is often reached between 19 and 26 years of age. Toward the latter part of early adulthood, a detectable slowdown in physical performance is apparent for most individuals.

Health

- Emerging adults have more than twice the mortality rate of adolescents, with males being mainly responsible for the increase. Despite their higher mortality rate, emerging adults in general have few chronic health problems. Many emerging adults develop bad health habits that can impair their health later in life.

Eating and Weight

- Obesity is a serious problem, with about 33 percent of Americans overweight enough to be at increased health risk. Heredity, leptin, set point, and environmental factors are involved in obesity. Most diets don't work over the long term. For those that do, exercise is usually an important component.

Regular Exercise

- Both moderate and intense exercise produce important physical and psychological gains.

Substance Abuse

- By the mid-twenties, a reduction in alcohol and drug use often takes place. Binge drinking among college students is still a major concern and can cause students to miss classes, have trouble with police, and engage in unprotected sex. Alcoholism is a disorder that impairs an individual's health and social relationships. Fewer young adults are smoking cigarettes now than in past decades. Most adult smokers would like to quit but their addiction to nicotine makes quitting a challenge.

3 Sexuality

 LG3 Discuss sexuality in young adults.

Sexual Activity in Emerging Adulthood

- Emerging adulthood is a time during which most individuals are sexually active and become married. Emerging adults have sexual intercourse with more individuals than young adults, but they have sex less frequently. Also, casual sex is more common in emerging adulthood than young adulthood.

Sexual Orientation and Behavior

- In the 1994 Sex in America survey, American adults' sexual lives were portrayed as more conservative than was previously believed. An individual's sexual preference likely is the result of a combination of genetic, hormonal, cognitive, and environmental factors.

Sexually Transmitted Infections

- Also called STIs, sexually transmitted infections are contracted primarily through sexual contact. The STI that has received the most attention in the last several decades is infection with HIV, which can lead to AIDS (acquired immune deficiency syndrome). A person with AIDS has a weakened immune system—even a cold can be life threatening.

Forcible Sexual Behavior and Sexual Harassment

- Rape is forcible sexual intercourse with a person who does not give consent. Date or acquaintance rape involves coercive sexual activity directed at someone with whom the perpetrator is at least casually acquainted. Sexual harassment occurs when one person uses his or her power over another individual in a sexual manner, which can result in serious psychological consequences for the victim.

4 Cognitive Development

LG4 Characterize cognitive changes in early adulthood.

Cognitive Stages

- Formal operational thought is Piaget's final cognitive stage, beginning at about age 11 to 15. According to Piaget, although adults are quantitatively more knowledgeable than adolescents, adults do not enter a new, qualitatively different stage. However, some have proposed that young adults move into a qualitatively higher stage of postformal thought that is more reflective, relativistic, and contextual; provisional; realistic; and recognized as being influenced by emotion.

Creativity

- Creativity peaks in adulthood, often in the forties, and then declines. However, there is extensive individual variation in lifetime creative output. Csikszentmihalyi proposed that the first step toward living a creative life is to cultivate curiosity and interest.

5 Careers and Work

 LG5 Explain the key dimensions of career and work in early adulthood.

Developmental Changes

Finding a Path to Purpose

Monitoring the Occupational Outlook

The Impact of Work

Diversity in the Workplace

- Many young children have idealistic fantasies about a career. In the late teens and early twenties, their career thinking has usually turned more serious. By their early to mid-twenties, many individuals have completed their education or training and started in a career. In the remainder of early adulthood, they seek to establish their emerging career and start moving up the career ladder. Many individuals believe in the career mystique but recently this has become a myth for increasing numbers of Americans.

- Damon argues that too many individuals have not found a path to purpose in their career development. He concludes that too often individuals focus on short-term goals and don't explore the big, long-term picture of what they want to do with their lives.

- Jobs that require a college education are expected to be the fastest-growing and highest-paying occupational sector in the United States over the next decade. Education, health care, business, and professional services are projected to account for most of the new jobs.

- Work defines people in fundamental ways and is a key aspect of their identity. Most individuals spend about one-third of their adult life at work. Eighty percent of part-time U.S. college students work while going to college. Working during college can have positive or negative outcomes. Unemployment produces stress regardless of whether the job loss is temporary, cyclical, or permanent. The increasing number of women who work in careers outside the home has led to new work-related issues. Because of dual-earner households, there has been a considerable increase in the time men spend in household work and child care.

- The U.S. workplace has become increasingly diverse. Women have become a larger proportion of the workforce in recent years. Latinos are projected to represent a larger percentage of the U.S. workforce than African Americans by 2020.

key **terms**

emerging adulthood 402
aerobic exercise 409
addiction 409

sexually transmitted infections (STIs) 415

rape 417
date or acquaintance rape 417

postformal thought 420

key **people**

Jeffrey Arnett 402
Joseph Allen 403
Claudia Allen 403

Jerald Bachman 409
Robert Michael 413

Jean Piaget 419
Mihaly Csikszentmihalyi 422

Phyllis Moen 423
William Damon 423

chapter 14

SOCIOEMOTIONAL DEVELOPMENT IN EARLY ADULTHOOD

chapter outline

1 Stability and Change from Childhood to Adulthood

Learning Goal 1 Describe stability and change in temperament, and summarize adult attachment styles.

Temperament
Attachment

2 Attraction, Love, and Close Relationships

Learning Goal 2 Identify some key aspects of attraction, love, and close relationships.

Attraction
The Faces of Love
Falling Out of Love

3 Adult Lifestyles

Learning Goal 3 Characterize adult lifestyles.

Single Adults
Cohabiting Adults
Married Adults
Divorced Adults
Remarried Adults
Gay and Lesbian Adults

4 Marriage and the Family

Learning Goal 4 Discuss making marriage work, parenting, and divorce.

Making Marriage Work
Becoming a Parent
Dealing with Divorce

Commitment is an important issue in a romantic relationship for most individuals. Consider Gwenna, who decides that it is time to have a talk with Greg about his commitment to their relationship (Lerner, 1989, pp. 44–45):

She shared her perspective on both the strengths and weaknesses of their relationship and what her hopes were for the future. She asked Greg to do the same. Unlike earlier conversations, this one was conducted without her pursuing him, pressuring him, or diagnosing his problems with women. At the same time, she asked Greg some clear questions, which exposed his vagueness.

"How will you know when you are ready to make a commitment? What specifically would you need to change or be different than it is today?"

"I don't know," was Greg's response. When questioned further, the best he could come up with was that he'd just feel it.

"How much more time do you need to make a decision one way or another?"

"I'm not sure," Greg replied. "Maybe a couple of years, but I really can't answer a question like that. I can't predict my feelings."

And so it went.

Gwenna really loved this man, but two years (and maybe longer) was longer than she could comfortably wait. So, after much thought she told Greg that she would wait till fall (about ten months), and that she would move on if he couldn't commit himself to marriage by then. She was open about her wish to marry and have a family with him, but she was equally clear that her first priority was a mutually committed relationship. If Greg was not at that point by fall, then she would end the relationship—painful though it would be.

During the waiting period, Gwenna was able to not pursue him and not get distant or otherwise reactive to his expressions of ambivalence and doubt. In this way she gave Greg emotional space to struggle with his dilemma and the relationship had its best chance of succeeding. Her bottom-line position ("a decision by fall") was not a threat or an attempt to rope Greg in, but rather a clear statement of what was acceptable to her.

When fall arrived, Greg told Gwenna he needed another six months to make up his mind. Gwenna deliberated a while and decided she could live with that. But when the six months were up, Greg was uncertain and asked for more time. It was then that Gwenna took the painful but ultimately empowering step of ending their relationship.

topical connections *looking **back***

A key aspect of socioemotional development in adolescence is an increased interest in identity; many of the key changes in identity, though, take place in emerging adulthood. Seeking autonomy in healthy ways while still being securely attached to parents are important aspects of parent-adolescent relationships. Adolescents also are motivated to spend more time with peers, friendships become more intimate, and romantic relationships begin to play a more important role in adolescents' lives.

preview

Love is of central importance in each of our lives, as it is in Gwenna and Greg's lives. Shortly, we will discuss the many faces of love, as well as marriage and the family, the diversity of adult lifestyles, and the role of gender in relationships. To begin, though, we will return to an issue we initially considered in Chapter 1: stability and change.

1 Stability and Change from Childhood to Adulthood

LG1 Describe stability and change in temperament, and summarize adult attachment styles.

Temperament   Attachment

To what extent is temperament in childhood linked to temperament in adulthood?

developmental **connection**

Temperament

Among the main temperament categories are Chess and Thomas' easy and difficult; Kagan's inhibition; and Rothbart and Bates' effortful control (self-regulation). Chapter 6, p. 172

For adults, socioemotional development revolves around adaptively integrating our emotional experiences into enjoyable relationships with others on a daily basis. Young adults like Gwenna and Greg face choices and challenges in adopting lifestyles that will be emotionally satisfying, predictable, and manageable for them. They do not come to these tasks as blank slates, but do their decisions and actions simply reflect the persons they had become by the end of adolescence?

Current research shows that the first 20 years of life are not meaningless in predicting an adult's socioemotional landscape (Cicchetti & Toth, 2015; Thompson, 2015). And there is also every reason to believe that experiences in the early adult years are important in determining what the individual will be like later in adulthood. A common finding is that the smaller the time intervals over which we measure socioemotional characteristics, the more similar an individual will look from one measurement to the next. Thus, if we measure an individual's self-esteem at the age of 20 and then again at the age of 30, we will probably find more stability than if we measured the individual's self-esteem at the age of 10 and then again at the age of 30.

In trying to understand the young adult's socioemotional development, it would be misleading to look at an adult's life only in the present tense, ignoring the unfolding of social relationships and emotions. So, too, it would be a mistake to search only through a 30-year-old's first 5 to 10 years of life in trying to understand why he or she is having difficulty in a close relationship.

TEMPERAMENT

How stable is temperament? Recall that *temperament* is an individual's behavioral style and characteristic emotional responses. In early adulthood, most individuals show fewer emotional mood swings than they did in adolescence, and they become more responsible and engage in less risk-taking behavior (Charles & Luong, 2011). Along with these signs of a general change in temperament, researchers also find links between some dimensions of childhood temperament and adult personality (Shiner & DeYoung, 2013). For example, in one longitudinal study, children who were highly active at age 4 were likely to be very outgoing at age 23 (Franz, 1996).

Are other aspects of temperament in childhood linked with adjustment in adulthood? In Chapter 6, we saw that researchers have proposed various ways of describing and classifying types and dimensions of personality. Research has linked several of these types and dimensions during childhood with characteristics of adult personality (Shiner & DeYoung, 2013; Zentner & Shiner, 2012). For example:

- *Easy and difficult temperaments.* In one longitudinal study, children who had an easy temperament at 3 to 5 years of age were likely to be well adjusted as young adults (Chess & Thomas, 1987). In contrast, many children who had a difficult temperament at 3 to 5 years of age were not well adjusted as young adults.

	Initial Temperament Trait: Inhibition	
	Child A	**Child B**
Intervening Context		
Caregivers	Caregivers (parents) who are sensitive and accepting, and let child set his or her own pace.	Caregivers who use inappropriate "low-level control" and attempt to force the child into new situations.
Physical Environment	Presence of "stimulus shelters" or "defensible spaces" that the children can retreat to when there is too much stimulation.	Child continually encounters noisy, chaotic environments that allow no escape from stimulation.
Peers	Peer groups with other inhibited children with common interests, so the child feels accepted.	Peer groups consist of athletic extroverts, so the child feels rejected.
Schools	School is "undermanned," so inhibited children are more likely to be tolerated and feel they can make a contribution.	School is "overmanned," so inhibited children are less likely to be tolerated and more likely to feel undervalued.
Personality Outcomes		
	As an adult, individual is closer to extraversion (outgoing, sociable) and is emotionally stable.	As an adult, individual is closer to introversion and has more emotional problems.

FIGURE **14.1**

TEMPERAMENT IN CHILDHOOD, PERSONALITY IN ADULTHOOD, AND INTERVENING CONTEXTS. Varying experiences with caregivers, the physical environment, peers, and schools can modify links between temperament in childhood and personality in adulthood. The example given here is for inhibition.

- *Inhibition.* Individuals who had an inhibited temperament in childhood are less likely than other adults to be assertive or experience social support, and more likely to delay entering a stable job track (Lengua & Wachs, 2012; Wachs, 2000).

- *Ability to control one's emotions.* In one longitudinal study, when 3-year-old children showed good control of their emotions and were resilient in the face of stress, they were likely to continue to handle emotions effectively as adults (Block, 1993). By contrast, when 3-year-olds had low emotional control and were not very resilient, they were likely to show problems in these areas as young adults.

In sum, these studies reveal some continuity between certain aspects of temperament in childhood and adjustment in early adulthood (Rothbart, 2011). However, as Theodore Wachs (1994, 2000) has proposed, links between temperament in childhood and personality in adulthood might vary depending on the intervening contexts in individuals' experience. For example, Figure 14.1 describes contexts in which an infant who displayed an inhibited temperament might develop a relatively sociable adult personality.

ATTACHMENT

Like temperament, attachment appears during infancy and plays an important part in socioemotional development (Thompson, 2015). We discussed its role in infancy and adolescence (see Chapters 6 and 12). How do these earlier patterns of attachment and adults' attachment styles influence the lives of adults?

Although relationships with romantic partners differ from those with parents, romantic partners fulfill some of the same needs for adults as parents do for their children. Recall from Chapter 6 that *securely attached* infants are defined as those who use the caregiver as a secure base from which to explore the environment. Similarly, adults may count on their romantic partners to be a secure base to which they can return and obtain comfort and security in stressful times (Shaver & Mikulincer, 2013; Zayas & Hazan, 2014).

Do adult attachment patterns with partners reflect childhood and adolescent attachment patterns with parents? In a widely cited retrospective study, Cindy Hazan and Phillip Shaver

developmental **connection**

Attachment

Secure and insecure attachment have been proposed as important aspects of infants' and adolescents' socioemotional development. Chapter 6, p. 180; Chapter 12, p. 379

How are attachment patterns in childhood linked to relationships in emerging and early adulthood?

(1987) revealed that young adults who were securely attached in their romantic relationships were more likely to describe their early relationship with their parents as securely attached. Also, in a longitudinal study, infants who were securely attached at 1 year of age were securely attached 20 years later in their adult romantic relationships (Steele & others, 1998). Further, a longitudinal study revealed that securely attached infants were in more stable romantic relationships in adulthood than their insecurely attached counterparts (Salvatore & others, 2011). A recent study found that insecure attachment to parents and peers at age 14 predicted a more anxious romantic attachment style at 22 years of age (Pascuzzo, Cyr, & Moss, 2013). However, in another study links between early attachment styles and later attachment styles were lessened by stressful and disruptive experiences such as the death of a parent or instability of caregiving (Lewis, Feiring, & Rosenthal, 2000).

Recall from our discussion in Chapter 6, "Socioemotional Development in Infancy," that consistently positive caregiving over a number of years is likely an important factor in connecting early attachment with functioning later in development. For example, a longitudinal study revealed that changes in attachment security/insecurity from infancy to adulthood were linked to stresses and supports in socioemotional contexts (Van Ryzin, Carlson, & Sroufe, 2011). The study just described (Van Ryzin, Carlson, & Sroufe, 2011) reflects an increasingly accepted view of the nature of attachment and its influence on development. That is, it is important to recognize that attachment security in infancy does not always by itself produce long-term positive outcomes, but rather is linked to later outcomes through connections with the way children, adolescents, and adults subsequently experience various social contexts as they develop. Recall from our discussion in Chapter 6 that the Van Ryzin, Carlson, and Sroufe (2011) study reflects a *developmental cascade model,* which involves connections across domains over time that influence developmental pathways and outcomes (Cicchetti & Toth, 2015; Groh & others, 2014; Zayas & Hazan, 2014). Also recall from Chapter 6 that some studies have recently found support for gene-environment interactions in linking infant attachment to adult attachment, while others have not found these gene-environment links (Fraley & others, 2013; Hefferman & Fraley, 2014; Raby & others, 2013).

Following is a description of the widely used measure of adult attachment created by Hazan and Shaver (1987, p. 515):

Read each paragraph and then place a check mark next to the description that best describes you:

1. I find it relatively easy to get close to others and I am comfortable depending on them and having them depend on me. I don't worry about being abandoned or about someone getting too close to me.

2. I am somewhat uncomfortable being close to others. I find it difficult to trust them completely and to allow myself to depend on them. I get nervous when anyone gets too close to me and it bothers me when someone tries to be more intimate with me than I feel comfortable with.

3. I find that others are reluctant to get as close as I would like. I often worry that my partner doesn't really love me or won't want to stay with me. I want to get very close to my partner, and this sometimes scares people away.

These items correspond to three attachment styles—secure attachment (option 1 above) and two insecure attachment styles (avoidant—option 2 above, and anxious—option 3 above):

- **Secure attachment style.** Securely attached adults have positive views of relationships, find it easy to get close to others, and are not overly concerned with or stressed out about their romantic relationships. These adults tend to enjoy sexuality in the context of a committed relationship and are less likely than others to have one-night stands.

- **Avoidant attachment style.** Avoidant individuals are hesitant about getting involved in romantic relationships and once they are in a relationship tend to distance themselves from their partner.

- **Anxious attachment style.** These individuals demand closeness, are less trusting, and are more emotional, jealous, and possessive.

The majority of adults (about 60 to 80 percent) describe themselves as securely attached, and not surprisingly adults prefer having a securely attached partner (Zeifman & Hazan, 2008).

Researchers are studying links between adults' current attachment styles and many aspects of their lives (Craparo & others, 2014; Zayas & Hazan, 2014). For example, securely attached adults are more satisfied with their close relationships than insecurely attached adults, and the relationships of securely attached adults are more likely to be characterized by trust, commitment, and longevity.

The following studies have confirmed the importance of adult attachment styles in people's lives:

- Attachment-anxious individuals showed strong ambivalence toward a romantic partner (Mikulincer & others, 2010).

- A national survey indicated that insecure attachment in adults was associated with the development of disease and chronic illness, especially cardiovascular system problems such as high blood pressure, heart attack, and stroke (McWilliams & Bailey, 2010).

- Attachment-anxious and attachment-avoidant adults had higher levels of depressive and anxious symptoms than attachment-secure adults (Jinyao & others, 2012).

- Adults with avoidant and anxious attachment patterns had a lower level of sexual satisfaction than their counterparts with a secure attachment pattern (Brassard & others, 2012).

- In two longitudinal studies of newlywed marriages, spouses were more likely to engage in infidelity when either they or their partner had a highly anxious attachment style (Russell, Baker, & McNulty, 2013).

Leading experts Mario Mikulincer and Phillip Shaver (2007; Shaver & Mikulincer, 2013) reached the following conclusions about the benefits of secure attachment. Individuals who are securely attached have a well-integrated sense of self-acceptance, self-esteem, and self-efficacy. They have the ability to control their emotions, are optimistic, and are resilient. Facing stress and adversity, they activate cognitive representations of security, are mindful of what is happening around them, and mobilize effective coping strategies.

If you have an insecure attachment style, are you stuck with it and does it doom you to have problematic relationships? Attachment categories are somewhat stable in adulthood, but adults do have the capacity to change their attachment thinking and behavior. Although attachment insecurities are linked to relationship problems, attachment style makes only a moderate-size contribution to relationship functioning because other factors contribute to relationship satisfaction and success. Later in the chapter, we will discuss such factors in our coverage of marital relationships.

secure attachment style An attachment style that describes adults who have positive views of relationships, find it easy to get close to others, and are not overly concerned or stressed out about their romantic relationships.

avoidant attachment style An attachment style that describes adults who are hesitant about getting involved in romantic relationships and once in a relationship tend to distance themselves from their partner.

anxious attachment style An attachment style that describes adults who demand closeness, are less trusting, and are more emotional, jealous, and possessive.

What are some key dimensions of attachment in adulthood, and how are they related to relationship patterns and well-being?

Review Connect Reflect

LG1 Describe stability and change in temperament, and summarize adult attachment styles.

Review

- How stable is temperament from childhood to adulthood?
- What attachment styles characterize adults, and how are they linked to relationship outcomes?

Connect

- In Chapter 12, what behaviors were linked to insecure attachment in adolescence?

Reflect *Your Own Personal Journey of Life*

- What is your attachment style? How do you think it affects your relationships?

2 Attraction, Love, and Close Relationships

LG2 Identify some key aspects of attraction, love, and close relationships.

| Attraction | The Faces of Love | Falling Out of Love |

These are the themes of our exploration of close relationships: how these relationships get started, the faces of love, and falling out of love.

ATTRACTION

What attracts people like Gwenna and Greg to each other and motivates them to spend more time together? How important are first impressions, personality traits, and physical attraction in determining the relationships we form?

First Impressions   When we first meet someone, typically the new acquaintance quickly makes an impression (King, 2014). That first impression can have lasting effects (Uleman & Kressel, 2013). How fast do we make these initial impressions of others? In one study, judgments made after just a 100-millisecond exposure time to unfamiliar faces was sufficient for individuals to form an impression (Willis & Todorov, 2006).

Are first impressions accurate? Numerous studies have found that immediate impressions can be accurate. Based on very little evidence, such as that provided by photographs, very brief interactions, or video clips, individuals can accurately detect a person's romantic interest in them (Place & others, 2012), tendency to be violent (Stillman, Maner, & Baumeister, 2010), and sexual orientation (Stern & others, 2013).

Familiarity and Similarity   Although first impressions may contribute to whether a relationship will develop, of course there is much more involved in whether a relationship will endure. Familiarity may breed contempt, as the old saying goes, but researchers have found that familiarity is an important condition for a close relationship to develop. For the most part, friends and lovers are people who have been around each other for a long time; they may have grown up together, gone to high school or college together, worked together, or gone to the same social events (Anderson & Sabatelli, 2011).

Another old saying, "Birds of a feather flock together," also helps to explain attraction. Overall, our friends and lovers are much more like us than unlike us (Guerrero, Andersen, & Afifi, 2011). Friends and lovers tend to have similar attitudes, values, lifestyles, and physical attractiveness. For some characteristics, though, opposites may attract. An introvert may wish to be with an extravert, or someone with little money may wish to associate with someone who is wealthy, for example.

(*Left*) Manti Te'o; (*Right*) Michelle Przbyksi and Andy Lalinde.

Why are people attracted to others who have similar attitudes, values, and lifestyles? **Consensual validation** is one reason. Our own attitudes and values are supported when someone else's attitudes and values are similar to ours—their attitudes and values validate ours. Another reason similarity matters is that people tend to shy away from the unknown. We often prefer to be around people whose attitudes and values we can predict. And similarity implies that we will enjoy doing things with another person who likes the same things and has similar attitudes.

Recently, attraction has not only taken place in person but also over the Internet (Bateson & others, 2012; Cacioppo & others, 2013). More than 16 million individuals in the United States and 14 million in China have tried online matchmaking (Masters, 2008).

Is looking for love online likely to work out? It didn't work out so well in 2012 for Notre Dame linebacker Manti Te'o, whose online girlfriend turned out to be a "catfish," someone who fakes an identity on line. Connecting online for love did turn out positively for two Columbia graduate students, Michelle Przbyksi and Andy Lalinde (Steinberg, 2011). They only lived several blocks away from each other, so soon after they communicated online through Datemyschool.com, an online dating site exclusively for college students, they met in person, really hit it off, applied for a marriage license 10 days later, and eventually got married.

However, a recent editorial by Samantha Nickalls (2012) in *The Tower,* the student newspaper at Arcadia University in Philadelphia, argued that online dating sites might be okay for people in their thirties and older but not for college students. She commented:

> The dating pool of our age is huge. Huge. After all, marriage is not on most people's minds when they're in college, but dating (or perhaps just hooking up) most certainly is. A college campus, in fact, is like living a dating service because the majority of people are looking for the same thing you are. As long as you put yourself out there, flirt a bit, and be friendly, chances are that people will notice.

Some critics argue that online romantic relationships lose the interpersonal connection while others emphasize that the Internet may benefit shy or anxious individuals who find it difficult to meet potential partners in person (Holmes, Little, & Welsh, 2009). One problem with online matchmaking is that many individuals misrepresent their characteristics,

consensual validation An explanation of why individuals are attracted to people who are similar to them. Our own attitudes and behavior are supported and validated when someone else's attitudes and behavior are similar to our own.

This is DEFINATELY the last time I arrange a date over the internet...

© Fran Orford, www.francartoons.com

such as how old they are, how attractive they are, and their occupation. Despite such dishonesty, some researchers have found that romantic relationships initiated on the Internet are more likely than relationships established in person to last for more than two years (Bargh & McKenna, 2004). And a national study of more than 19,000 individuals found that more than one-third of marriages now begin online (Cacioppo & others, 2013). Also in this study, marriages that began online were slightly less likely to break up and were characterized by slightly higher marital satisfaction than those that started in traditional offline contexts.

What do you think? Is searching online for romantic relationships a good idea? What are some cautions that should be taken if you pursue an online romantic relationship?

Physical Attractiveness   As important as familiarity and similarity may be, they do not explain the spark that often ignites a romantic relationship: physical attractiveness. How important is physical attractiveness in relationships? Psychologists do not consider the link between physical beauty and attraction to be as clear-cut as many advertising agencies would like us to believe. For example, psychologists have determined that men and women differ on the importance of good looks when they seek an intimate partner. Women tend to rate as most important such traits as considerateness, honesty, dependability, kindness, understanding, and earning prospects; men prefer good looks, cooking skills, and frugality (Buss & Barnes, 1986; Eastwick & Finkel, 2008). And a recent study found that partner physical attractiveness played a larger role in predicting husbands' marital satisfaction than in predicting wives' marital satisfaction (Meltzer & others, 2014).

Complicating research about the role of physical attraction is changing standards of what is deemed attractive. The criteria for beauty can differ, not just across cultures, but over time within cultures as well. In the 1950s, the ideal of female beauty in the United States was typified by the well-rounded figure of Marilyn Monroe. Today, Monroe's 135-pound, 5-foot, 5-inch physique might be regarded as a bit overweight. The current ideal physique for both men and women is neither pleasingly plump nor extremely slender.

The force of similarity also operates at a physical level. We usually seek out someone at our own level of attractiveness in physical characteristics as well as social attributes. Research validates the **matching hypothesis,** which states that although we may prefer a more attractive person in the abstract, in the real world we end up choosing someone who is close to our own level of attractiveness.

Love is a canvas furnished by nature and embroidered by imagination.

—VOLTAIRE
French Essayist, 18th Century

THE FACES OF LOVE

Once we are initially attracted to another person, other opportunities exist that may deepen the relationship to love. Love refers to a vast and complex territory of human behavior, spanning a range of relationships that includes friendship, romantic love, affectionate love, and consummate love (Berscheid, 2010). In most of these types of love, one recurring theme is intimacy (Sternberg & Sternberg, 2013).

Intimacy   Self-disclosure and the sharing of private thoughts are hallmarks of intimacy (Prager, 2013). As we discussed in Chapter 12, adolescents have an increased need for intimacy. At the same time, they are engaged in the essential tasks of developing an identity and establishing their independence from their parents. Juggling the competing demands of intimacy, identity, and independence also becomes a central task of adulthood.

Erikson's Stage: Intimacy Versus Isolation   Recall from our discussion in Chapter 12 that Erik Erikson (1968) argues that identity versus identity confusion—pursuing who we are, what we are all about, and where we are going in life—is the most important issue to be negotiated in adolescence. In early adulthood, according to Erikson, after individuals are well on their way to establishing stable and successful identities, they enter the sixth developmental stage, which is intimacy versus isolation. Erikson describes intimacy as finding oneself

matching hypothesis States that although we prefer a more attractive person in the abstract, in the real world we end up choosing someone who is close to our own level of attractiveness.

How is adult friendship different among female friends, male friends, and cross-gender friends?

while losing oneself in another person, and it requires a commitment to another person. If a person fails to develop an intimate relationship in early adulthood, according to Erikson, isolation results.

One study confirmed Erikson's theory that identity development in adolescence is a precursor to intimacy in romantic relationships during emerging adulthood (Beyers & Seiffge-Krenke, 2010). And a meta-analysis revealed a positive link between identity development and intimacy, with the connection being stronger for men than for women (Arseth & others, 2009).

Friendship   Increasingly researchers are finding that friendship plays an important role in development throughout the human life span (Blieszner & Roberto, 2012). Most U.S. men and women have a best friend—92 percent of women and 88 percent of men have a best friend of the same sex (Blieszner, 2009). Many friendships are long-lasting, as 65 percent of U.S. adults have known their best friend for at least 10 years and only 15 percent have known their best friend for less than 5 years. Adulthood brings opportunities for new friendships as individuals move to new locations and may establish new friendships in their neighborhood or at work (Blieszner, 2009).

Gender Differences in Friendships   As in the childhood and adolescent years, there are gender differences in adult friendship (Blieszner & Roberto, 2012). Compared with men, women have more close friends and their friendships involve more self-disclosure and exchange of mutual support (Dow & Wood, 2006). Women are more likely to listen at length to what a friend has to say and be sympathetic, and women have been labeled as "talking companions" because talk is so central to their relationship (Gouldner & Strong, 1987). Women's friendships tend to be characterized not only by depth but also by breadth: Women share many aspects of their experiences, thoughts, and feelings (Helgeson, 2012). When female friends get together, they like to talk, but male friends are more likely to engage in activities, especially outdoors. Thus, the adult male pattern of friendship often involves keeping one's distance while sharing useful information. Men are less likely than women to talk about their weaknesses with their friends, and men seek practical solutions to their problems rather than sympathy (Tannen, 1990). Also, adult male friendships are more competitive than those of women (Helgeson, 2012).

Friendships Between Women and Men   What about female-male friendship? Cross-gender friendships are more common among adults than children but less common than same-gender friendships in adulthood (Blieszner, 2009). Cross-gender friendships can provide both opportunities and problems (Helgeson, 2012). The opportunities involve learning more about common feelings and interests and shared characteristics, as well as acquiring knowledge and understanding of beliefs and activities that historically have been typical of the other gender.

developmental **connection**

Erikson's Theory

Erikson's adolescence stage is identity versus identity confusion and his middle adulthood stage is generativity versus stagnation. Chapter 12, p. 372; Chapter 16, p. 486

We are what we love.

—**ERIK ERIKSON**

Danish-Born American Psychoanalyst and Author, 20th Century

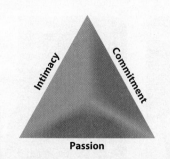

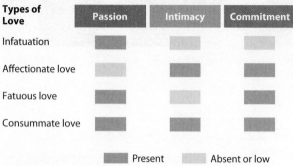

Types of Love	Passion	Intimacy	Commitment
Infatuation	■	□	□
Affectionate love	□	■	■
Fatuous love	■	□	■
Consummate love	■	■	■

■ Present   □ Absent or low

FIGURE 14.2

STERNBERG'S TRIANGLE OF LOVE. Sternberg identified three dimensions of love: passion, intimacy, and commitment. Various combinations of these dimensions result in infatuation, affectionate love, fatuous love, and consummate love.

romantic love Also called passionate love, or eros, romantic love has strong sexual and infatuation components and often predominates early in a love relationship.

affectionate love In this type of love, also called companionate love, an individual desires to have the other person near and has a deep, caring affection for the other person.

Problems can arise in cross-gender friendships because of different expectations. One problem that can plague an adult cross-gender friendship is unclear sexual boundaries, which can produce tension and confusion.

Romantic Love   Some friendships evolve into **romantic love,** which is also called passionate love or eros. Romantic love has strong components of sexuality and infatuation, and it often predominates in the early part of a love relationship (Berscheid, 2010). A meta-analysis found that males show higher avoidance and lower anxiety about romantic love than females (Del Giudice, 2011).

A complex intermingling of different emotions goes into romantic love—including such emotions as passion, fear, anger, sexual desire, joy, and jealousy (Del Giudice, 2011). Well-known love researcher Ellen Berscheid (1988) says that sexual desire is the most important ingredient of romantic love. Obviously, some of these emotions are a source of anguish, which can lead to other issues such as depression. Indeed, a recent study revealed that a heightened state of romantic love in young adults was linked to stronger depression and anxiety symptoms but better sleep quality (Bajoghli & others, 2014).

Affectionate Love   Love is more than just passion (Berscheid, 2010). **Affectionate love,** also called *companionate love,* is the type of love that occurs when someone desires to have the other person near and has a deep, caring affection for the person. The early stages of love have more romantic love ingredients—but as love matures, passion tends to give way to affection (Sternberg & Sternberg, 2013).

Consummate Love   So far we have discussed two forms of love: romantic (or passionate) and affectionate (or companionate). According to Robert J. Sternberg (1988), these are not the only forms of love. Sternberg proposed a triarchic theory of love in which love can be thought of as a triangle with three main dimensions—passion, intimacy, and commitment. Passion, as described earlier in the romantic love section, is physical and sexual attraction to another. Intimacy relates to the emotional feelings of warmth, closeness, and sharing in a relationship. Commitment is the cognitive appraisal of the relationship and the intent to maintain the relationship even in the face of problems.

In Sternberg's theory, the strongest, fullest form of love is *consummate love,* which involves all three dimensions (see Figure 14.2). If passion is the only ingredient in a relationship (with intimacy and commitment low or absent), we are merely *infatuated.* An affair or a fling in which there is little intimacy and even less commitment is an example. A relationship marked by intimacy and commitment but low or lacking in passion is called *affectionate love,* a pattern often found among couples who have been married for many years. If passion and commitment are present but intimacy is not, Sternberg calls the relationship *fatuous love,* as when one person worships another from a distance. But if couples share all three dimensions—passion, intimacy, and commitment—they experience consummate love (Sternberg & Sternberg, 2013).

FALLING OUT OF LOVE

The collapse of a close relationship may feel tragic. In the long run, however, as was the case for Gwenna, our happiness and personal development may benefit from ending a close relationship.

In particular, ending a relationship may be wise if you are obsessed with someone who repeatedly betrays your trust; if you are involved with someone who is draining you emotionally or financially or both; or if you are desperately in love with someone who does not return your feelings.

Being in love when love is not returned can lead to depression, obsessive thoughts, sexual dysfunction, health problems, inability to work effectively, difficulty in making new friends, and self-condemnation (Sbarra, 2012). Thinking clearly in such relationships is often difficult because our thoughts are so colored by arousing emotions (Guerrero, Andersen, &

What Are the Positive Outcomes to the Breakup of a Romantic Relationship?

Studies of romantic breakups have mainly focused on their negative aspects (Kato, 2005; Moreau & others, 2011; Simon & Barrett, 2010). Few studies have explored the possibility that a romantic breakup might lead to positive changes.

One study assessed the personal growth that can follow the breakup of a romantic relationship (Tashiro & Frazier, 2003). The participants were 92 undergraduate students who had experienced a relationship breakup in the past nine months. They were asked to describe "what positive changes, if any, have happened as a result of your breakup that might serve to improve your future romantic relationships" (p. 118).

Self-reported positive growth was common following a romantic breakup. Changes were categorized as personal, relational, and environmental. The most commonly reported types of growth were personal changes, which included feeling stronger and more self-confident, more independent, and better off emotionally. Relational positive changes included gaining relational wisdom, and environmental positive changes included having better friendships because of the breakup. Figure 14.3 provides examples of these positive changes. Women were more likely to report positive growth than men were.

Change category	Exemplars of frequently mentioned responses
Personal positives	1. "I am more self-confident." 2. "Through breaking up I found I could handle more on my own." 3. "I didn't always have to be the strong one, it's okay to cry or be upset without having to take care of him."
Relational positives	1. "Better communication." 2. "I learned many relationship skills that I can apply in the future (for example, the importance of saying you're sorry)." 3. "I know not to jump into a relationship too quickly."
Environmental positives	1. "I rely on my friends more. I forgot how important friends are when I was with him." 2. "Concentrate on school more: I can put so much more time and effort toward school." 3. "I believe friends' and family's opinions count—will seek them out in future relationships."

FIGURE 14.3

EXAMPLES OF POSITIVE CHANGES IN THE AFTERMATH OF A ROMANTIC BREAKUP

Afifi, 2011). A study of unmarried relationship dissolution in 18- to 35-year-olds revealed that experiencing a breakup was linked to an increase in psychological stress and a decrease in life satisfaction (Rhoades & others, 2011).

Are there any positive outcomes to the breakup of a romantic relationship? To find out, see *Connecting Through Research*.

Review *Connect* Reflect

 LG2 Identify some key aspects of attraction, love, and close relationships.

Review
- What attracts someone to another person?
- What are some different types of love?
- What characterizes falling out of love?

Connect
- Describe how dating in adolescence differs from dating in early adulthood.

Reflect *Your Own Personal Journey of Life*
- Think about your own experiences with love. Based on those experiences, what advice about love would you give to someone else?

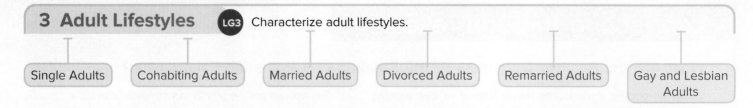
A striking social change in recent decades has been the decreased stigma attached to individuals who do not maintain what were long considered conventional families. Adults today choose many lifestyles and form many types of families (Klinenberg, 2013). They live alone, cohabit, marry, divorce, or live with someone of the same sex.

In his book, *The Marriage-Go-Round,* sociologist Andrew Cherlin (2009) concluded that the United States has more marriages and remarriages, more divorces, and more short-term cohabiting (living together) relationships than most countries. Combined, these lifestyles create more turnover and movement in and out of relationships in the United States than in virtually any other country. Let's explore these varying relationship lifestyles.

SINGLE ADULTS

Recent decades have seen a dramatic rise in the percentage of single (unmarried) adults. Data from 2009 indicate that for the first time in history the proportion of individuals 25 to 34 years of age who had never been married (46 percent) exceeded those who were married at the time of the census (45 percent) (U.S. Census Bureau, 2010). The increasing number of single adults is the result of rising rates of cohabitation and a trend toward postponing marriage. The United States has a lower percentage of single adults than do many other countries such as Great Britain, Germany, and Japan. Also, the fastest growth in the number of people adopting a single adult lifestyle is occurring in rapidly developing countries such as China, India, and Brazil (Klinenberg, 2012, 2013).

Even when single adults enjoy their lifestyles and are highly competent individuals, they often are stereotyped (Schwartz & Scott, 2012). Stereotypes associated with being single range from the "swinging single" to the "desperately lonely, suicidal" single. Of course, most single adults are somewhere between these extremes.

Common challenges faced by single adults may include forming intimate relationships with other adults, confronting loneliness, and finding a niche in a society that is marriage-oriented. Bella DePaulo (2006, 2011) argues that society has a widespread bias against unmarried adults that is seen in everything from missed perks in jobs to deep social and financial prejudices.

Advantages of being single include having time to make decisions about one's life course, time to develop personal resources to meet goals, freedom to make autonomous decisions and pursue one's own schedule and interests, opportunities to explore new places and try out new things, and privacy. Compared with married adults, single adults are more likely to spend time with friends and neighbors, dine in restaurants, and attend art classes and lectures (Klinenberg, 2012, 2013). Once adults reach the age of 30, they may face increasing pressure to settle down and get married. This is when many single adults make a conscious decision to marry or to remain single.

A nationally representative U.S. survey of more than 5,000 single adults 21 years and older not in a committed relationship revealed that men are more interested in love, marriage, and children than their counterparts were in earlier generations (Match.com, 2011). In this study, today's women desire more independence in their relationships than their mothers did. Across every age group, more women than men reported wanting to pursue their own interests, have personal space, have their own bank account, have regular nights out with girlfriends, and take vacations on their own. In a second national survey, many single adults reported that they were looking for love but not marriage (Match.com, 2012). In this survey, almost 40 percent of the single adults were uncertain about whether they wanted to get married, 34 percent said they did want to marry, and 27 percent said they didn't want to get married.

COHABITING ADULTS

Cohabitation refers to living together in a sexual relationship without being married. Cohabitation has undergone considerable changes in recent years (Rose-Greenland & Smock, 2013; Smock & Gupta, 2013). As indicated in Figure 14.4, there has been a dramatic increase in the number of cohabiting U.S. couples since 1970, with more than 60 percent cohabiting prior to getting married (The National Marriage Project, 2011). And the upward trend shows no sign of letting up, having risen from 3.8 million cohabiting couples in 2000 to 7.5 million cohabiting couples in 2010 (U.S. Census Bureau, 2010). Cohabitation rates are even higher in some countries—in Sweden, for example, cohabitation before marriage is virtually universal (Stokes & Raley, 2009).

A recent national study of women in the United States found the following statistics regarding cohabitation based on interviews conducted between 2006 and 2010 (Copen, Daniels, & Mosher, 2012):

- Length of cohabitation is increasing—an average of 22 months in 2010 compared with 13 months in 1995.

- After three years of cohabiting, 40 percent of women got married, 32 percent continued to live with their partner, and 27 percent had moved out of the cohabiting relationship.

- Education is linked to cohabitation rates—70 percent of women who did not have a high school diploma cohabited in their first union, compared with 47 percent of women who had a bachelor's degree or higher. For women who cohabited in their twenties to forties, among those with higher education the cohabitation was more likely to result in marriage (53 percent) than it was for their counterparts who had not graduated from high school (30 percent).

Some couples view their cohabitation not as a precursor to marriage but as an ongoing lifestyle (Klinenberg, 2013; Schwartz & Scott, 2012). These couples do not want the official aspects of marriage. A recent study revealed that young adults' main reasons for cohabiting are to spend time together, share expenses, and evaluate compatibility (Huang & others, 2011). In this study, gender differences emerged regarding perceived drawbacks of cohabiting: men were more concerned about their loss of freedom while women were more concerned about delays in getting married.

Couples who cohabit face certain problems (Urquia, O'Campo, & Ray, 2013). Disapproval by parents and other family members can place emotional strain on the cohabiting couple. Some cohabiting couples have difficulty purchasing and owning property jointly. Legal rights involving the dissolution of the relationship are less clear than in a divorce.

If a couple lives together before they marry, does cohabiting help or harm their chances of having a stable and happy marriage? The majority of studies have found lower rates of marital satisfaction and higher rates of divorce in couples who lived together before getting married (Copen & others, 2012; Whitehead & Popenoe, 2003). However, recent research indicates that the link between premarital cohabitation and marital instability in first marriages has weakened in recent cohorts (Copen & others, 2012; Smock & Gupta, 2013).

What might explain the possibility that cohabiting is linked with divorce more than not cohabiting? The most frequently given explanation is that the less traditional lifestyle of cohabitation may attract less conventional individuals who are not great believers in marriage in the first place. An alternative explanation is that the experience of cohabiting changes people's attitudes and habits in ways that increase their likelihood of divorce.

Recent research has provided clarification of cohabitation outcomes. One meta-analysis found that the link between cohabitation and marital instability did not hold up when only cohabitation with the eventual marital partner was examined, indicating that these cohabitors may attach more long-term positive meaning to living together (Jose, O'Leary, & Moyer, 2010). Another study also revealed that for first marriages, cohabiting with the spouse without first being engaged was linked to more negative interaction and a higher probability of divorce than cohabiting after engagement (Stanley & others, 2006). In contrast, premarital cohabitation prior to a second marriage placed couples at risk for divorce regardless of whether they were engaged. A recent study also found that the marriage of couples who were cohabiting but not engaged was less likely to survive to the 10- to 15-year mark than the marriage of their counterparts who were engaged when they cohabited (Copen & others, 2012). Also, one analysis

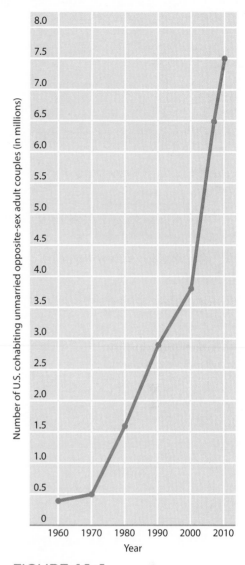

FIGURE **14.4**

THE INCREASE IN COHABITATION IN THE UNITED STATES. Since 1970, there has been a dramatic increase in the number of unmarried adults living together in the United States.

What are some potential advantages and disadvantages of cohabitation?

indicated that cohabiting does not have a negative effect on marriage if the couple did not have any previous live-in lovers and did not have children prior to the marriage (Cherlin, 2009). And a recent study concluded that the risk of marital dissolution between cohabitors was much smaller when they cohabited in their mid-twenties and later (Kuperberg, 2014).

MARRIED ADULTS

Until about 1930, stable marriage was widely accepted as the endpoint of adult development. In the last 70 to 80 years, however, personal fulfillment both inside and outside marriage has emerged as a goal that competes with marital stability. The changing norm of male-female equality in marriage and increasingly high expectations for what a marital relationship should be has produced marital relationships that are more fragile and intense than they were for earlier generations (Lavner & Bradbury, 2012). A recent study of 502 newlyweds found that nearly all couples had optimistic forecasts of how their marriage would change over the next four years (Lavner, Karney, & Bradbury, 2013). Despite their optimistic forecasts, their marital satisfaction declined across this time frame. Wives with the most optimistic forecasts showed the steepest declines in marital satisfaction.

Some characteristics of marital partners predict whether the marriage will last longer. Two such characteristics are education and ethnicity. In a recent interview study with more than 22,000 women, both women and men with a bachelor's degree were found to be more likely to delay marriage but also more likely to eventually get married and stay married for more than 20 years (Copen & others, 2012). Also in this study, Asian American women were the most likely of all ethnic groups to be in a first marriage that lasted at least 20 years—70 percent were in a first marriage that lasted this long compared with 54 percent for non-Latino White women, 53 percent for Latino women, and 37 percent for African American women.

Marital Trends In recent years, marriage rates in the United States have declined. In a recent year (2011), the marriage rate was 6.2 per 1,000 individuals, down from 8.2 in 2000 (National Center for Vital Statistics, 2013). In 2012, 48.6 percent of Americans were married, down from 72 percent in 1960 (U.S. Census Bureau, 2013).

More adults are remaining single longer, with 27 percent of U.S. adults currently having never married (Pew Research Center, 2010). In 2011, the U.S. average age for a first marriage climbed to 28.7 years for men and 26.5 years for women, higher than at any other point in history (Pew Research Center, 2011). In 1980, the average age for a first marriage in the United States was 24 years for men and 21 years for women. In addition, the increase in cohabitation and a slight decline in the percentage of divorced individuals who remarry contribute to the decline in marriage rates in the United States (Copen & others, 2012).

Despite the decline in marriage rates, the United States is still a marrying society. In 2010, by 40 years of age, 77 percent of individuals had ever been married, although this figure is substantially below the figure of 93 percent in the 1960s (Pew Research Center, 2011). In a recent national poll, more than 40 percent of Americans under 30 predicted that marriage was headed for extinction, yet only 5 percent of those young adults said they didn't want to get married (Pew Research Center, 2010). These findings may reflect marriage's role as a way to show friends and family that you have a successful social life (Cherlin, 2009).

Is there a best age to get married? Marriages in adolescence are more likely to end in divorce than marriages in adulthood (Copen & others, 2012). However, researchers have not been able to pin down a specific age or age span for getting married in adulthood that is most likely to result in a successful marriage (Furstenberg, 2007).

How happy are people who do marry? The average duration of a marriage in the United States is currently just over nine years. As indicated in Figure 14.5, the percentage of married individuals in the United States who said their marriages were "very happy" declined from the 1970s through the early 1990s before approaching a plateau (Popenoe, 2009). Notice in Figure 14.5 that married men consistently report being happier than married women.

Cross-Cultural Comparisons Many aspects of marriage vary across cultures. For example, as part of China's efforts to control population growth, a 1981 law sets the minimum age for marriage at 22 years for males, 20 for females.

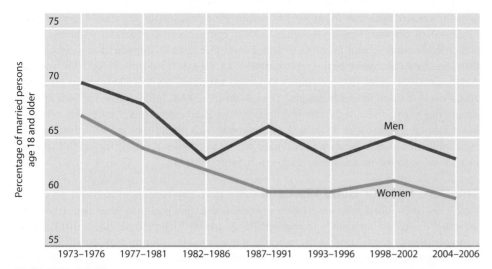

FIGURE 14.5

PERCENTAGE OF MARRIED PERSONS AGE 18 AND OLDER WITH "VERY HAPPY" MARRIAGES

The traits that people look for in a marriage partner vary around the world. In one large-scale study of 9,474 adults from 37 cultures on six continents and five islands, people varied most regarding how much they valued chastity—desiring a marital partner with no previous experience in sexual intercourse (Buss & others, 1990). Chastity was the most important characteristic in selecting a marital partner in China, India, Indonesia, Iran, Taiwan, and the Palestinian Arab culture. Adults from Ireland and Japan placed moderate importance on chastity. In contrast, adults in Sweden, Finland, Norway, the Netherlands, and Germany generally said that chastity was not important in selecting a marital partner.

Domesticity is also valued in some cultures and not in others. In this study, adults from the Zulu culture in South Africa, Estonia, and Colombia placed a high value on housekeeping skills in their marital preferences. By contrast, adults in the United States, Canada, and all western European countries except Spain said that housekeeping skill was not an important trait in their partner.

Religion plays an important role in marriage in many cultures. For example, Islam stresses the honor of the male and the purity of the female. It also emphasizes the woman's role in child-bearing, child rearing, educating children, and instilling the Islamic faith in their children. In India, a majority of marriages continue to be arranged. However, as more women have entered the workforce in India and moved from rural areas to cities, these Indian women increasingly resist an arranged marriage. In one study conducted in a small village in India, elopement (also called love marriages there) recently became more common than arranged marriages (Allendorf, 2013).

International comparisons of marriage also reveal that individuals in Scandinavian countries marry later than Americans, whereas their counterparts in many African, Asian, and Latin American countries marry younger (Waite, 2009). In Denmark, for example, almost 80 percent of the women and 90 percent of the men aged 20 to 24 have never been married. In Hungary, less than 40 percent of the women and 70 percent of the men in this age bracket have never been married. In Scandinavian countries, cohabitation is popular among young adults; however, most Scandinavians eventually marry. In Sweden, women delay marriage until they are about 31, men until they are 33. Some countries, such as Hungary, encourage early marriage and childbearing to offset declines in the population. Like Scandinavian countries, Japan has a high proportion of unmarried young people. However, rather than cohabiting as the Scandinavians do, unmarried Japanese young adults live at home longer with their parents before marrying.

Premarital Education Premarital education occurs in a group and focuses on relationship advice. Might premarital education improve the quality of a marriage and possibly reduce the chances that the marriage will end in divorce? Researchers have found that it can (Markman & others, 2013; Owen & others, 2011). For example, a survey of more than 3,000 adults revealed that premarital education was linked to a higher level of marital satisfaction and

(a)

(b)

(c)

(*a*) In Scandinavian countries, cohabitation is popular; only a small percentage of 20- to 24-year-olds are married. (*b*) Islam stresses male honor and female purity. (*c*) Japanese young adults live at home longer with their parents before marrying than young adults in most other countries.

commitment to a spouse, a lower level of destructive marital conflict, and a 31 percent lower likelihood of divorce (Stanley & others, 2006). The premarital education programs in the study ranged from several hours to 20 hours, with a median of 8 hours. It is recommended that premarital education begin approximately six months to a year before the wedding. Another study revealed that individuals in second marriages are less likely to get premarital education than those in first marriages (Doss & others, 2009). In this study, for both first and second marriages, individuals who received premarital education had a lower risk of subsequent marital distress and divorce. A recent study also found that the effectiveness of a premarital education program was enhanced when the couples had a better level of communication prior to the intervention (Markman & others, 2013).

The Benefits of a Good Marriage   Are there any benefits to having a good marriage? Yes. Individuals who are happily married live longer, healthier lives than those who are either divorced or unhappily married (Miller & others, 2013; Shor & others, 2012; Proulx & Snyder-Rivas, 2013). One study indicated that the longer women were married, the less likely they were to develop a chronic health condition and that the longer men were married, the lower their risk of developing a disease (Dupre & Meadows, 2007). One study of U.S. adults 50 years and older also revealed that a lower portion of adult life spent in marriage was linked to an increased likelihood of dying at an earlier age (Henretta, 2010). And a recent large-scale analysis of data from a number of studies indicated that being married benefitted the longevity of men more than women (Rendall & others, 2011). Further, an unhappy marriage can shorten a person's life by an average of four years (Gove, Style, & Hughes, 1990).

What are the reasons for these benefits of a happy marriage? People in happy marriages likely feel less physically and emotionally stressed, which puts less wear and tear on a person's body. Such wear and tear can lead to physical ailments such as high blood pressure and heart disease, as well as psychological problems such as anxiety, depression, and substance abuse.

DIVORCED ADULTS

Divorce has become an epidemic in the United States (Braver & Lamb, 2013). However, the divorce rate declined in recent decades after peaking at 5.1 divorces per 1,000 people in 1981 and had declined to 3.6 divorces per 1,000 people in 2011 (National Center for Vital Statistics, 2013). In 2000, the divorce rate was 4.0 divorces per 1,000 people. The 2011 figure (3.6) compares with a marriage rate of 6.8 per 1,000 people. Although the U.S. divorce rate has dropped, it continues to be one of the highest divorce rates in the world. Russia has the highest divorce rate (4.7 divorces per 1,000 people) (UNSTAT, 2011). In the United States, nearly half of first marriages will break up within 20 years (Copen & others, 2012).

Although U.S. divorce rates have increased in all socioeconomic groups, some groups have a higher incidence of divorce (Amato, 2010; Repetti, Flook, & Sperling, 2011). Youthful marriage, low educational level, low income, not having a religious affiliation, having parents who are divorced, and having a baby before marriage are factors that are associated with increases in divorce (Hoelter, 2009). And the following characteristics of one's partner increase the likelihood of divorce: alcoholism, psychological problems, domestic violence, infidelity, and inadequate division of household labor (Hoelter, 2009).

Earlier, we indicated that researchers have not been able to pin down a specific age that is the best time to marry so that the marriage is unlikely to end in a divorce. However, if a divorce is going to occur, it usually takes place early in a marriage; most occur in the fifth to tenth year of marriage based on U.S. data (National Center for Health Statistics, 2000) (see Figure 14.6). A recent study also found that divorce peaked in Finland at approximately five to seven years of marriage, after which the rate of divorce gradually declined (Kulu, 2014). This timing may reflect an effort by partners in troubled marriages to stay in the marriage and try to work things out. If after several years these efforts don't improve the relationship, they may then seek a divorce.

Both partners experience challenges after a marriage dissolves (Breslau & others, 2011). Divorced adults have higher rates of depression, anxiety, physical illnesses, suicide, motor vehicle accidents, alcoholism, and mortality (Braver & Lamb, 2013). Both divorced women and divorced men complain of loneliness, diminished self-esteem, anxiety about the unknowns in their lives, and difficulty in forming satisfactory new intimate relationships (Hetherington,

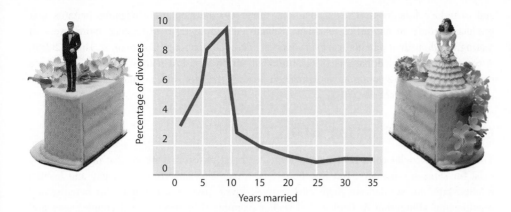

FIGURE **14.6**

THE DIVORCE RATE IN RELATION TO NUMBER OF YEARS MARRIED. Shown here is the percentage of divorces as a function of how long couples have been married. Notice that most divorces occur in the early years of marriage, peaking in the fifth to tenth years of marriage.

2006). One study revealed that following marital dissolution, both men and women were more likely to experience an episode of depression than individuals who remained with a spouse over a two-year period (Rotermann, 2007). And a Swedish study found that divorced adults were more likely to smoke daily than married or cohabiting adults (Lindstrom, 2010).

There are gender differences in the process and outcomes of divorce (Braver & Lamb, 2013). Women are more likely to sense that something is wrong with the marriage and are more likely to seek a divorce than are men. Women also show better emotional adjustment and are more likely to perceive divorce as getting a "second chance" to increase their happiness, improve their social lives, and see better work opportunities. However, divorce typically has a more negative economic impact on women that it does on men.

Despite all of these stresses and challenges, many people do cope effectively with divorce. Later in this chapter, we consider the varied paths people take after a divorce and suggested strategies for coping.

REMARRIED ADULTS

Men remarry after a divorce sooner than women do, and men with higher incomes are more likely to remarry than their counterparts with lower incomes. Remarriage occurs sooner for partners who initiate a divorce (especially in the first several years after divorce and for older women) than those who do not (Sweeney, 2009, 2010). Recent data indicate that the remarriage rate in the United States has recently declined, going from 50 of every 1,000 divorced or widowed Americans in 1990 to 29 of every 1,000 in 2011 (U.S. Census Bureau, 2013). One reason for the decline is the dramatic increase in cohabitation in recent years.

Evidence regarding the benefits of remarriage is mixed. Remarried families are more likely to be unstable than first marriages, with divorce more likely to occur, especially in the first several years of the remarried family, than in first marriages (Waite, 2009). Adults who remarry have a lower level of mental health (higher rates of depression, for example) than adults in first marriages, but remarriage often improves the financial status of remarried adults, especially women (Waite, 2009). Researchers have found that remarried adults' marital relationship is more egalitarian and more likely to be characterized by shared decision making than first marriages (Waite, 2009). Remarried wives also report that they have more influence on financial matters in their new family than do wives in first marriages (Waite, 2009).

Stepfamilies come in many sizes and forms (DeGenova & others, 2011; Scarf, 2013; Seccombe, 2012). The custodial and noncustodial parents and stepparents all might have been married and divorced, in some cases more than once. These parents might be caring for children from prior marriages and have a large network of relatives. Approximately 50 percent of remarried women bear children within their newly formed union, although the presence of stepchildren from a prior marriage reduces the likelihood of childbearing with the new husband (Waite, 2009). And some remarried individuals are more adult-focused, responding more to the concerns of their partner, while others are more child-focused, responding more to the concerns of the children (Anderson & Greene, 2011).

As indicated earlier, remarried adults often find it difficult to stay remarried. Why? For one thing, many remarry not for love but for financial reasons, for help in rearing children,

developmental **connection**

Family and Peers

Children in divorced families have more adjustment problems than children in never-divorced, intact families, but a majority of children in divorced families do not have adjustment problems. Chapter 8, p. 252

and to reduce loneliness. They also might carry into the stepfamily negative patterns that produced failure in an earlier marriage. Remarried couples also experience more stress in rearing children than parents in never-divorced families (Ganong, Coleman, & Hans, 2006). A recent study revealed that a positive attitude about divorce, low marital quality, and divorce proneness were more common for remarried persons than for their counterparts in first marriages (Whitton & others, 2013).

GAY AND LESBIAN ADULTS

The legal and social context of marriage creates barriers to breaking up that do not usually exist for same-sex partners. But in other ways, researchers have found that gay and lesbian relationships are similar—in their satisfactions, loves, joys, and conflicts—to heterosexual relationships (Fingerhut & Peplau, 2013). For example, like heterosexual couples, gay and lesbian couples need to find the balance of romantic love, affection, autonomy, and equality that is acceptable to both partners (Kurdek, 2006).

Lesbian couples especially place a high priority on equality in their relationships (Fingerhut & Peplau, 2013). One study of couples revealed that over the course of 10 years of cohabitation, partners in gay and lesbian relationships showed a higher average level of relationship quality than heterosexual couples (Kurdek, 2007).

It is estimated that of same-sex couples in the United States, lesbian couples are approximately five times more likely to be raising children than are gay couples (Miller & Price, 2013). An increasing number of same-sex couples are adopting children (Farr & Patterson, 2013). The percentage of same-sex couples who have adopted children nearly doubled from 10 percent in 2000 to 19 percent in 2009 (DiBennardo & Gates, 2014; Gates, 2013). Recall from Chapter 8 that recent research indicated lesbian and gay couples shared child care more than heterosexual couples, with lesbian couples being the most supportive and gay couples the least supportive (Farr & Patterson, 2013).

There are numerous misconceptions about gay and lesbian couples (Fingerhut & Peplau, 2013). Contrary to stereotypes, one partner is masculine and the other feminine in only a small percentage of gay and lesbian couples. Only a small segment of the gay population has a large number of sexual partners, and this is uncommon among lesbians. Furthermore, researchers have found that gays and lesbians prefer long-term, committed relationships (Fingerhut & Peplau, 2013). About half of committed gay couples do have an open relationship that allows the possibility of sex (but not affectionate love) outside the relationship. Lesbian couples usually do not have this type of open relationship.

A special concern is the stigma, prejudice, and discrimination that lesbian, gay, and bisexual individuals experience because of widespread social devaluation of same-sex relationships (Balsam & Hughes, 2013). However, one study indicated that many individuals in these relationships saw stigma as bringing them closer together and strengthening their relationship (Frost, 2011).

---

developmental **connection**

Parenting

Researchers have found few differences between children who are being raised by gay and lesbian parents and children who are being raised by heterosexual parents. Chapter 8, p. 254

Review Connect Reflect

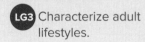 Characterize adult lifestyles.

Review

- What are characteristics of the lives of single adults?
- What are key features of the lives of cohabiting adults?
- What are current marital trends?
- How does divorce affect adults?
- What are the lives of remarried parents like?
- How are gay and lesbian couples like or unlike heterosexual couples?

Connect

- What did you learn in Chapter 8 about the effects of divorce and remarriage on the children in those families?

Reflect *Your Own Personal Journey of Life*

- Which type of lifestyle are you living today? What do you think are the advantages and disadvantages of this lifestyle for you? If you could have a different lifestyle, which one would you choose? Why?

Making Marriage Work	Becoming a Parent	Dealing with Divorce

Whatever lifestyles young adults choose, their choices will bring certain challenges. Because many choose the lifestyle of marriage, we'll consider some of the challenges in marriage and how to make it work. We also examine some challenges in parenting and trends in childbearing. Given the statistics about divorce rates in the previous section, we'll then consider how to deal with divorce.

MAKING MARRIAGE WORK

John Gottman (1994, 2006, 2011; Gottman & Silver, 1999) has been studying married couples' lives since the early 1970s. He uses many methods to analyze what makes marriages work. Gottman interviews couples about the history of their marriage, their philosophy about marriage, and how they view their parents' marriages. He videotapes them talking to each other about how their day went and evaluates what they say about the good and bad times in their marriages. Gottman also uses physiological measures to record their heart rate, blood flow, blood pressure, and immune functioning moment by moment. He checks back with the couples every year to see how their marriage is faring. Gottman's research represents the most extensive assessment of marital relationships available. Currently, he and his colleagues are following 700 couples in seven studies.

Gottman argues that it is important to realize that love is not something magical and that through knowledge and effort couples can improve their relationship. In his research, Gottman has identified seven main practices that help marriages succeed:

John Gottman, who has conducted extensive research on what makes marriages work.

> Unlike most approaches to helping couples, mine is based on knowing what makes marriages succeed rather than fail.
>
> —**JOHN GOTTMAN**
> *Contemporary Psychologist, University of Washington*

- *Establish love maps.* Individuals in successful marriages have personal insights and detailed maps of each other's life and world. They aren't psychological strangers. In good marriages, partners are willing to share their feelings with each other. They use these "love maps" to express not only their understanding of each other but also their fondness and admiration.

- *Nurture fondness and admiration.* In successful marriages, partners sing each other's praises. More than 90 percent of the time, when couples put a positive spin on their marriage's history, the marriage is likely to have a positive future.

- *Turn toward each other instead of away.* In good marriages, spouses are adept at turning toward each other regularly. They see each other as friends. This friendship doesn't keep arguments from occurring, but it can prevent differences from overwhelming the relationship. In these good marriages, spouses respect each other and appreciate each other's point of view despite disagreements.

- *Let your partner influence you.* Bad marriages often involve one spouse who is unwilling to share power with the other. Although power-mongering is more common in husbands, some wives also show this trait. A willingness to share power and to respect the other person's view is a prerequisite to compromising. One study revealed that equality in decision making was one of the main factors that predicted positive marriage quality (Amato, 2007).

- *Solve solvable conflicts.* Two types of problems occur in marriage: (1) perpetual and (2) solvable. Perpetual problems are the type that do not go away and may include disagreements about whether to have children and how often to have sex. Solvable problems can be worked out and may include such things as not helping each other reduce daily stresses and not being verbally affectionate. Unfortunately, more than two-thirds of marital problems fall into the perpetual category. Fortunately, marital therapists have found that couples often don't have to solve their perpetual problems for the marriage to work. In his research, Gottman has found that to resolve conflicts, couples should start out with a soft rather than a harsh approach, try to make and

What makes marriages work? What are the benefits of having a good marriage?

receive "repair attempts," regulate their emotions, compromise, and be tolerant of each other's faults. Conflict resolution is not about one person making changes; it is about negotiating and accommodating each other.

- *Overcome gridlock.* One partner wants the other to attend church; the other is an atheist. One partner is a homebody; the other wants to go out and socialize a lot. Such problems often produce gridlock. Gottman believes the key to ending gridlock is not to solve the problem but to move from gridlock to dialogue and be patient.

- *Create shared meaning.* The more partners can speak candidly and respectfully with each other, the more likely it is that they will create shared meaning in their marriage. This also includes sharing goals with one's spouse and working together to achieve each other's goals.

In addition to Gottman's view, other experts on marriage argue that such factors as forgiveness and commitment are important aspects of a successful marriage (Fincham, Stanley, & Beach, 2007). These factors function as self-repair processes in healthy relationships. For example, spouses may have a heated argument that has the potential to harm their relationship (Amato, 2007). After calming down, they may forgive each other and repair the damage.

Spouses with a strong commitment to each other may in times of conflict sacrifice their personal self-interest for the benefit of the marriage. Commitment especially becomes important when a couple is not happily married and can help them get through hard times with the hope that the future will involve positive changes in the relationship.

For remarried couples, strategies for coping with the stress of living in a stepfamily include the following (Visher & Visher, 1989):

- *Have realistic expectations.* Allow time for loving relationships to develop, and look at the complexity of the stepfamily as a challenge to overcome.

- *Develop new positive relationships within the family.* Create new traditions and ways of dealing with difficult circumstances. Allocation of time is especially important because so many people are involved. The remarried couple needs to allot time alone for each other.

BECOMING A PARENT

For many young adults, parental roles are well planned, coordinated with other roles in life, and developed with the individual's economic situation in mind. For others, the discovery that they are about to become parents is a startling surprise. In either event, the prospective parents may have mixed emotions and romantic illusions about having a child (Carl, 2012; Florsheim, 2014).

Parenting Myths and Reality   The needs and expectations of parents have stimulated many myths about parenting (Williams, Sawyer, & Wahlstrom, 2012). These parenting myths include the following:

- The birth of a child will save a failing marriage.
- As a possession or extension of the parent, the child will think, feel, and behave as the parent did in his or her childhood.
- Having a child gives the parents a "second chance" to achieve what they should have achieved.
- Parenting is instinctual and requires no training.

Parenting requires a number of interpersonal skills and imposes emotional demands, yet there is little in the way of formal education for this task. Most parents learn parenting practices from their own parents—some they accept, some they discard. Unfortunately, when methods of parents are passed on from one generation to the next, both desirable and undesirable practices are perpetuated. Adding to the reality of the task of parenting, husbands and wives may bring different parenting practices to the marriage. The parents, then, may struggle with each other about who has a better way to interact with a child.

Parent educators seek to help individuals to become better parents. To read about the work of one parent educator, see *Connecting with Careers.*

> We never know the love of our parents until we have become parents.
>
> —**Henry Ward Beecher**
> *American Clergyman, 19th Century*

What are some parenting myths?

Janis Keyser, Parent Educator

Janis Keyser is a parent educator who teaches in the Department of Early Childhood Education at Cabrillo College in California. In addition to teaching college classes and conducting parenting workshops, she also has coauthored a book with Laura Davis (1997): *Becoming the Parent You Want to Be: A Sourcebook of Strategies for the First Five Years.*

Keyser also writes as an expert on the iVillage Web site (www.ivillage.com/pregnancy-parenting), and she co-authors a nationally syndicated parenting column, "Growing Up, Growing Together." Keyser is the mother of three, stepmother of five, grandmother of twelve, and great-grandmother of six.

Janis Keyser (*right*), conducting a parenting workshop.

Trends in Childbearing   Like marriage, the age at which individuals have children has been increasing (Lauer & Lauer, 2012). In 2008, the average age at which women gave birth for the first time was 25 years of age, up from 21 years of age in 2001 (U.S. Census Bureau, 2011).

As the use of birth control has become common, many individuals consciously choose when they will have children and how many children they will rear. The number of one-child families is increasing, for example, and U.S. women overall are having fewer children. These childbearing changes are creating several trends:

- By giving birth to fewer children and reducing the demands of child care, women free up a significant portion of their life spans for other endeavors.
- Men are apt to invest a greater amount of time in fathering.
- Parental care is often supplemented by institutional care (child care, for example).

As more women show an increased interest in developing a career, they are not only marrying later but also having fewer children and having them later in life. What are some of the advantages of having children early or late? Some of the advantages of having children early (in the twenties) are that the parents are likely to have more physical energy (for example, they can cope better with such matters as getting up in the middle of the night with infants and waiting up until adolescents come home at night); the mother is likely to have fewer medical problems with pregnancy and childbirth; and the parents may be less likely to build up expectations for their children, as do many couples who have waited many years to have children.

There are also advantages to having children later (in the thirties): The parents will have had more time to consider their goals in life, such as what they want from their family and career roles; the parents will be more mature and will be able to benefit from their life experiences to engage in more competent parenting; and the parents will be better established in their careers and have more income for child-rearing expenses.

DEALING WITH DIVORCE

If a marriage doesn't work, what happens after divorce? Psychologically, one of the most common characteristics of divorced adults is difficulty trusting someone else in a romantic relationship. Following a divorce, though, people's lives can take diverse turns (Ben-Zur, 2012; Smith & others, 2012). In E. Mavis Hetherington's research, men and women took six common pathways in exiting divorce (Hetherington & Kelly, 2002, pp. 98–108):

- *The enhancers.* Accounting for 20 percent of the divorced group, most were females who "grew more competent, well-adjusted, and self-fulfilled" following their divorce (p. 98). They were competent in multiple areas of life, showing a remarkable ability to

developmental connection

Parenting

For most families, an authoritative parenting style is linked to more positive behavior on the part of children than authoritarian, indulgent, and neglectful styles. Chapter 8, p. 245

Coping and Adapting in the Aftermath of Divorce

Hetherington recommends the following strategies for divorced adults (Hetherington & Kelly, 2002):

- Think of divorce as a chance to grow personally and to develop more positive relationships.
- Make decisions carefully. The consequences of your decision making regarding work, lovers, and children may last a lifetime.
- Focus more on the future than the past. Think about what is most important for you going forward in your life, set some challenging goals, and plan how to reach them.
- Use your strengths and resources to cope with difficulties.
- Don't expect to be successful and happy in everything you do. "The road to a more satisfying life is bumpy and will have many detours" (p. 109).

- Remember that "you are never trapped by one pathway. Most of those who were categorized as defeated immediately after divorce gradually moved on to a better life, but moving onward usually requires some effort" (p. 109).

Look back again at the six common pathways for exiting divorce that Hetherington proposes. Consider how someone on each of those pathways might particularly benefit from employing one or another of these strategies.

What are some diverse pathways individuals' lives can take following a divorce?

bounce back from stressful circumstances and to create something meaningful out of problems.

- *The good-enoughs.* The largest group of divorced individuals, they were described as average people coping with divorce. They showed some strengths and some weaknesses, some successes and some failures. When they experienced a problem, they tried to solve it. Many of them attended night classes, found new friends, developed active social lives, and were motivated to get higher-paying jobs. However, they were not as good at planning and were less persistent than the enhancers. Good-enough women usually married men who educationally and economically were similar to their first husbands, often going into a new marriage that was not much of an improvement over the first one.
- *The seekers.* These individuals were motivated to find new mates as soon as possible. "At one year post-divorce, 40 percent of the men and 38 percent of the women had been classified as seekers. But as people found new partners or remarried, or became more secure or satisfied in their single life, this category shrank and came to be predominated by men" (p. 102).
- *The libertines.* People in this category often spent more time in singles bars and had more casual sex than their counterparts in the other divorce categories. However, by the end of the first year post-divorce, they often grew disillusioned with their sensation-seeking lifestyle and wanted a stable relationship.
- *The competent loners.* These individuals, who made up only about 10 percent of the divorced group, were "well-adjusted, self-sufficient, and socially skilled." They had a successful career, an active social life, and a wide range of interests. However, "unlike enhancers, competent loners had little interest in sharing their lives with anyone else" (p. 105).
- *The defeated.* Some of these individuals had problems before their divorce, and these problems increased after the breakup when "the added stress of a failed marriage was more than they could handle. Others had difficulty coping because divorce cost them a spouse who had supported them, or in the case of a drinking problem, restricted them" (p. 106).

To read about some guidelines for coping and adapting in the aftermath of divorce, see *Connecting Development to Life.*

Review
- What makes a marriage work?
- What are some current trends in childbearing?
- What paths do people take after a divorce?

Connect
- In this section you read about some of the advantages of having children early or late in one's life. What did you learn about maternal age in Chapter 3?

Reflect *Your Own Personal Journey of Life*
- What do you think would be the best age to have children? Why?

---

topical connections *looking forward*

Middle adulthood is a time when individuals experience Erikson's seventh life-span stage, generativity versus stagnation. In this stage, it is important for middle-aged adults to contribute in meaningful ways to the next generation. In Levinson's theory, one of the key conflicts of middle age involves coping with the young-old polarity in life. Midlife crises are not as common as believed by many; however, when they occur, negative life events usually are involved. A number of longitudinal studies of stability and change in adult development have been conducted, and recently it has been argued that stability peaks in middle adulthood. Affectionate love increases in middle age. Many middle-aged adults become grandparents. Middle-aged women especially play an important role in connecting generations.

---

reach your **learning goals**

Socioemotional Development in Early Adulthood

1 Stability and Change from Childhood to Adulthood

 LG1 Describe stability and change in temperament, and summarize adult attachment styles.

> Temperament

- Links between childhood temperament and adult personality can vary, depending on contexts in an individual's experience. A high activity level in early childhood is linked with being an outgoing young adult. Young adults show fewer mood swings, are more responsible, and engage in less risk taking than adolescents. In some cases, certain dimensions of temperament in childhood are linked with adjustment problems in early adulthood.

> Attachment

- Three adult attachment styles are secure attachment, avoidant attachment, and anxious attachment. Attachment styles in early adulthood are linked with a number of relationship patterns and developmental outcomes. For example, securely attached adults often show more positive relationship patterns than insecurely attached adults. Also, adults with avoidant and anxious attachment styles tend to be more depressed and have more relationship problems than securely attached adults.

2 Attraction, Love, and Close Relationships

LG2 Identify some key aspects of attraction, love, and close relationships.

Attraction

- First impressions can be enduring. Familiarity precedes a close relationship. We like to associate with people who are similar to us. The principles of consensual validation and matching can explain this. Similarity in personality attributes may be especially important in a relationship's success. The criteria for physical attractiveness vary across cultures and historical time.

The Faces of Love

- The different types of love include friendship, romantic love, affectionate love, and consummate love. Friendship plays an important role in adult development, especially in providing emotional support. Romantic love, also called passionate love, includes passion, sexuality, and a mixture of emotions, not all of which are positive. Affectionate love, also called companionate love, usually becomes more important as relationships mature. Shaver proposed a developmental model of love and Sternberg a triarchic model of love (with dimensions of passion, intimacy, and commitment).

Falling Out of Love

- The collapse of a close relationship can be traumatic, but for some individuals it results in happiness and personal development. For most individuals, falling out of love is painful and emotionally intense.

3 Adult Lifestyles

LG3 Characterize adult lifestyles.

Single Adults

- Being single has become an increasingly prominent lifestyle. Autonomy is one of its advantages. Intimacy, loneliness, and finding a positive identity in a marriage-oriented society are challenges faced by single adults.

Cohabiting Adults

- Cohabitation is an increasingly popular lifestyle, but researchers have found it is often linked to negative marital outcomes, although this link depends on the timing of cohabitation. Negative marital outcomes are more likely when cohabitation occurs prior to becoming engaged.

Married Adults

- The age at which individuals marry in the United States is increasing. Despite a decline in marriage rates, a large percentage of Americans still marry. The benefits of marriage include better physical and mental health and a longer life.

Divorced Adults

- The U.S. divorce rate increased dramatically in the middle of the twentieth century but began to decline in the 1980s. Divorce is complex and emotional. Both divorced men and women can experience loneliness, anxiety, and difficulty in forming new relationships.

Remarried Adults

- When adults remarry, they tend to do so rather quickly, with men remarrying sooner than women. Remarriage confers some benefits on adults but also some problems. Remarried families are less stable than families in first marriages, and remarried adults have a lower level of mental health than adults in first marriages, although remarriage improves adults' (especially women's) financial status. Stepfamilies come in many sizes and forms.

Gay and Lesbian Adults

- One of the most striking findings about gay and lesbian couples is how similar their relationships are to heterosexual couples' relationships.

4 Marriage and the Family

LG4 Discuss making marriage work, parenting, and divorce.

Making Marriage Work

- Gottman's research indicates that happily married couples establish love maps, nurture fondness and admiration, turn toward each other, accept the influence of the partner, solve solvable conflicts, overcome gridlock, and create shared meaning.

Becoming a Parent

- Families are becoming smaller, and many women are delaying childbirth until they have become well established in a career. There are some advantages to having children earlier in adulthood and some advantages to having them later.

Dealing with Divorce

- Hetherington identified six pathways taken by people after divorce: enhancers, good-enoughs, seekers, libertines, competent loners, and the defeated. About 20 percent became better adjusted and more competent after the divorce.

key terms

key people

section eight

Generations will depend on the ability of every procreating individual to face his children.

—Erik Erikson
American Psychologist, 20th Century

Middle Adulthood

In middle adulthood, what we have been forms what we will be. For some of us, middle age is a foggy place, a time when we need to discover what we are running from and to and why. We compare our life with what we vowed to make it. In middle age, more time stretches behind us than before us, and some evaluations, however reluctant, have to be made. As the young-old polarity greets us with a special force, we need to join the daring of youth with the discipline of age in a way that does justice to both. As middle-aged adults, we come to sense that the generations of living things pass in a short while and, like runners, hand on the torch of life. Section 8 consists of two chapters: "Physical and Cognitive Development in Middle Adulthood" (Chapter 15) and "Socioemotional Development in Middle Adulthood" (Chapter 16).

PHYSICAL AND COGNITIVE DEVELOPMENT IN MIDDLE ADULTHOOD

chapter outline

1 The Nature of Middle Adulthood

Learning Goal 1 Explain how midlife is changing, and define middle adulthood.

Changing Midlife
Defining Middle Adulthood

2 Physical Development

Learning Goal 2 Discuss physical changes in middle adulthood.

Physical Changes
Health, Disease, Stress, and Control
Mortality Rates
Sexuality

3 Cognitive Development

Learning Goal 3 Identify cognitive changes in middle adulthood.

Intelligence
Information Processing

4 Careers, Work, and Leisure

Learning Goal 4 Characterize career development, work, and leisure in middle adulthood.

Work in Midlife
Career Challenges and Changes
Leisure

5 Religion, Spirituality, and Meaning in Life

Learning Goal 5 Explain the roles of religion, spirituality, and meaning in life during middle adulthood.

Religion, Spirituality, and Adult Lives
Religion, Spirituality, and Health
Meaning in Life

O ur perception of time depends on where we are in the life span. We are more concerned about time at some points in life than others. The rock group Pink Floyd, in their song "Time", described how when people are young life seems longer and time passes slower, but when we get older, time seems to fly by so quickly.

In middle adulthood as well as late adulthood, individuals increasingly think about time-left-to-live instead of time-since-birth (Kotter-Gruhn & Smith, 2011; Setterson, 2009). Middle-aged adults begin to look back to where they have been, reflecting on what they have done with the time they have had. They look toward the future more in terms of how much time remains to accomplish what they hope to do with their lives. Older adults look backwards even more than middle-aged adults, not surprising given the shorter future in the life that they have. Also not surprisingly, given the many years they still have to live, emerging adults and young adults are more likely to look forward in time than backwards in time.

Another aspect of time perception in middle age is the topic of whether time seems to speed by much faster as we get older. Talk to just about any middle-aged person and he or she will tell you that time does indeed fly by much faster than it did when they were younger. Why might this be? One view is that for 10 year olds, one year makes up 10 percent of their life so far and for 20 year olds it makes up 5 percent of their life. However, for 50 year olds, one year comprises just one-fiftieth of the their life, and thus the one year seems to fly by more quickly since it makes up a much smaller portion of the time they have lived. A second view is that as middle age sets in, we begin to think more about the shrinking time we have left to live. Because of the fewer years we have left, we wish time would slow down but because it doesn't we perceive time to be flying by even faster. A common comment by someone who has reached 60 is, "Where did my 50s go? It seems like only yesterday I was 50 and now I'm 60." A third view is that new experiences slow down our perception of time while repeat experiences make time seem to go faster. Younger people are more likely to have new experiences and all of these new experiences slow down their perception of time. By contrast, as middle age is reached, more experiences are ones people already have had and thus they perceive time to be speeding by.

topical connections *looking back*

Emerging adulthood, which occurs at approximately 18 to 25 years of age, is characterized by experimentation and exploration. Peak physical performance often occurs from about 19 to 26 years of age, but toward the latter part of early adulthood, a slowdown in physical performance is often apparent. Emerging adults have sexual intercourse with more individuals than young adults, but have sex less frequently. Thinking becomes more pragmatic and reflective in early adulthood than adolescence. Career development is an important aspect of early adulthood, and work becomes a more central aspect of most young adults' lives.

preview

When young adults look forward in time to what their lives might be like as middle-aged adults, too often they anticipate that things will go downhill. However, like all periods of the human life span, for most individuals there usually are positive and negative features of middle age. In this first chapter on middle adulthood, we will discuss physical changes; cognitive changes; changes in careers, work, and leisure; as well as the importance of religion and meaning in life during middle adulthood. To begin, though, we will explore how middle age is changing.

1 The Nature of Middle Adulthood

LG1 Explain how midlife is changing, and define middle adulthood.

Changing Midlife

Defining Middle Adulthood

Is midlife experienced the same way today as it was 100 years ago? Is it different from what it was like just 25 years ago? How can middle adulthood be defined, and what are some of its main characteristics?

CHANGING MIDLIFE

Many of today's 50-year-olds are in better shape, more alert, and more productive than their 40-year-old counterparts from a generation or two earlier. As more people lead healthier lifestyles and medical discoveries help to slow down the aging process, the boundaries of middle age are being pushed upward. It looks like middle age is starting later and lasting longer for increasing numbers of active, healthy, and productive people. A current saying is "60 is the new 40," implying that many 60-year-olds today are living a life that is as active, productive, and healthy as earlier generations did in their forties.

Questions such as, "To which age group do you belong?" and "How old do you feel?" reflect the concept of age identity. A consistent finding is that as adults become older their age identity is younger than their chronological age (Setterson & Trauten, 2009; Westerhof, 2009). One study found that almost half of the individuals 65 to 69 years of age considered themselves middle-aged (National Council on Aging, 2000). Another study discovered a similar pattern: Half of the 60- to 75-year-olds viewed themselves as being middle-aged (Lachman, Maier, & Budner, 2000). And a recent British survey of people over 50 years of age revealed that they perceived middle age to begin at 53 (Beneden Health, 2013). In this study, respondents said that being middle-aged is characterized by enjoying afternoon naps, groaning when you bend down, and preferring a quiet night in rather than a night out. Also, some individuals consider the upper boundary of midlife as the age at which they make the transition from work to retirement.

When Carl Jung studied midlife transitions early in the twentieth century, he referred to midlife as the afternoon of life (Jung, 1933). Midlife serves as an important preparation for late adulthood, "the evening of life" (Lachman, 2004, p. 306). But "midlife" came much earlier in Jung's time. In 1900 the average life expectancy was only 47 years of age; only 3 percent of the population lived past 65. Today, the average life expectancy is 78, and 12 percent of the U.S. population is older than 65. As a much greater percentage of the population lives to an older age, the midpoint of life and what constitutes middle age or middle adulthood are getting harder to pin down (Cohen, 2012).

In a recent book, *In Our Prime: The Invention of Middle Age*, Patricia Cohen (2012) describes how middle age wasn't thought of as a separate developmental period until the mid-1800s and the term

How is midlife changing?

midlife wasn't in a dictionary until 1895. In Cohen's analysis, advances in health and more people living to older ages especially fueled the emergence of thinking about middle age. People today take longer to grow up and longer to die than in past centuries.

Compared with previous decades and centuries, an increasing percentage of the population is made up of middle-aged and older adults. In the past, the age structure of the population could be represented by a pyramid, with the largest percentage of the population in the childhood years. Today, the percentages of people at different ages in the life span are more similar, creating what is called the "rectangularization" of the age distribution (a vertical rectangle) (Himes, 2009). The rectangularization has been created by health advances that promote longevity, low fertility rates, and the aging of the baby-boom cohort (Moen, 2007).

The portrait of midlife described so far here suggests that for too long the negative aspects of this developmental period have been overdrawn. However, as will be seen in the following sections, it is important not to go too far in describing midlife positively. Many physical aspects decline in middle adulthood, and increased rates of health problems such as obesity need to be considered in taking a balanced perspective on this age period.

DEFINING MIDDLE ADULTHOOD

Although the age boundaries are not set in stone, we will consider **middle adulthood** to be the developmental period that begins at approximately 40 to 45 years of age and extends to about 60 to 65 years of age. For many people, middle adulthood is a time of declining physical skills and expanding responsibility; a period in which people become more conscious of the young-old polarity and the shrinking amount of time left in life; a point when individuals seek to transmit something meaningful to the next generation; and a time when people reach and maintain satisfaction in their careers. In sum, middle adulthood involves "balancing work and relationship responsibilities in the midst of the physical and psychological changes associated with aging" (Lachman, 2004, p. 305).

In midlife, as in other age periods, individuals make choices—selecting what to do, deciding how to invest time and resources, and evaluating what aspects of their lives they need to change. In midlife, "a serious accident, loss, or illness" may be a "wake-up call" and produce "a major restructuring of time and a reassessment" of life's priorities (Lachman, 2004, p. 310). And with an absence of seniority protections, many middle-aged adults experience unexpected job loss and/or are strongly encouraged to take early retirement packages (Sweet, Moen, & Meiksins, 2007).

The concept of gains (growth) and losses (decline) is an important one in life-span development (Dixon & others, 2013). Middle adulthood is the age period in which gains and losses as well as biological and sociocultural factors balance each other (Baltes, Lindenberger, & Staudinger, 2006). Although biological functioning declines in middle adulthood, sociocultural supports such as education, career, and relationships may peak in middle adulthood (Willis & Schaie, 2005).

Remember from our discussion in Chapter 1 that individuals have not only a chronological age but also biological, psychological, and social ages. Some experts conclude that compared with earlier and later periods, middle age is influenced more heavily by sociocultural factors (Willis & Martin, 2005).

For many healthy adults, middle age is lasting longer than it did for previous generations. Indeed, an increasing number of experts on middle adulthood describe the age period of 55 to 65 as *late midlife* (Deeg, 2005). Compared with earlier midlife, late midlife is more likely to be characterized by "the death of a parent, the last child leaving the parental home, becoming a grandparent, the preparation for retirement, and in most cases actual retirement. Many people in this age range experience their first confrontation with health problems" (Deeg, 2005). Overall, then, although gains and losses may balance each other in early midlife, losses may begin to outnumber gains for many individuals in late midlife (Baltes, Lindenberger, & Staudinger, 2006).

Keep in mind, though, that midlife is characterized by individual variations (Ailshire & Burgard, 2012; Schaie, 2013). As life-span expert Gilbert Brim (1992) commented, middle adulthood is full of changes, twists, and turns; the path is not fixed. People move in and out of states of success and failure.

developmental **connection**

Life-Span Perspective

There are four types of age: chronological, biological, psychological, and social. Chapter 1, p. 16

middle adulthood The developmental period that begins at approximately 40 to 45 years of age and extends to about 60 to 65 years of age.

2 Physical Development   **LG2** Discuss physical changes in middle adulthood.

Physical Changes   Health, Disease, Stress, and Control   Mortality Rates   Sexuality

What physical changes characterize middle adulthood? How healthy are middle-aged adults? What are the main causes of death in middle age? How sexually active are individuals in middle adulthood?

PHYSICAL CHANGES

Unlike the rather dramatic physical changes that occur in early adolescence and the sometimes abrupt decline in old age, midlife physical changes are usually more gradual. Although everyone experiences some physical change due to aging in middle adulthood, the rates of this aging vary considerably from one individual to another. Genetic makeup and lifestyle factors play important roles in determining whether chronic disease will appear and when. Middle age is a window through which we can glimpse later life while there is still time to engage in prevention and to influence some of the course of aging (Bertrand, Kranz Graham, & Lachman, 2013; Lachman, 2004). Let's now explore some of the physical changes of middle age.

Visible Signs   The most visible signs of physical changes in middle adulthood involve physical appearance. The first outwardly noticeable signs of aging usually are apparent by the forties or fifties. The skin begins to wrinkle and sag because of a loss of fat and collagen in underlying tissues (Pageon & others, 2014). Small, localized areas of pigmentation in the skin produce age spots, especially in areas that are exposed to sunlight, such as the hands and face. Hair becomes thinner and grayer due to a lower replacement rate and a decline in melanin production. Fingernails and toenails develop ridges and become thicker and more brittle. A recent twin study found that twins who had been smoking longer were more likely to have sagging facial skin and wrinkles, especially in the middle and lower portion of the face (Okada & others, 2013).

Since a youthful appearance is valued in many cultures, individuals whose hair is graying, whose skin is wrinkling, whose body is sagging, and whose teeth are yellowing may strive to make themselves look younger. Undergoing cosmetic surgery, dyeing hair, purchasing wigs, enrolling in weight reduction programs, participating in exercise regimens, and taking heavy doses of vitamins are common in middle age. Baby boomers have shown a strong interest in plastic surgery and Botox, which may reflect their desire to slow down the aging process (Chen & Dashtipour, 2013; Jiang & others, 2014).

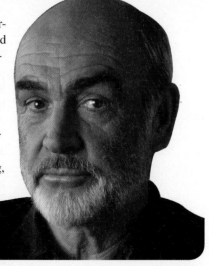

Height and Weight   Individuals lose height in middle age, and many gain weight (Paoli & others, 2014; Winett & others, 2014). On average, men from 30 to

Famous actor Sean Connery as a young adult in his twenties (*top*) and as a middle-aged adult in his fifties (*bottom*). *What are some of the most outwardly noticeable signs of aging in middle adulthood?*

50 years of age lose about one inch in height, then may lose another inch from 50 to 70 years of age (Hoyer & Roodin, 2009). The height loss for women can be as much as 2 inches from 25 to 75 years of age. Note that there are large variations in the extent to which individuals become shorter with aging. The decrease in height is due to bone loss in the vertebrae. On average, body fat accounts for about 10 percent of body weight in adolescence; it makes up 20 percent or more in middle age.

Obesity increases from early to middle adulthood. In a recent national U.S. survey, in 2011–2012 39.5 percent of U.S. adults 40 to 59 years of age were classified as obese compared with 30.3 percent of younger adults (Centers for Disease Control and Prevention, 2013). Being overweight is a critical health problem in middle adulthood (Simon & others, 2011). For example, obesity increases the probability that an individual will suffer a number of other ailments, among them hypertension (abnormally high blood pressure), diabetes, and digestive disorders (Nag & Ghosh, 2014; Nezu & others, 2013). A large-scale study found that being overweight or obese in middle age increases an individual's risk of dying earlier (Adams & others, 2006). More than 500,000 50- to 71-year-olds completed surveys about their height and weight, and the researchers examined the participants' death records across a 10-year period. Those who were overweight (defined as a body mass index, which takes into account height and weight, of 25 or more) at age 50 had a 20 to 40 percent higher risk of earlier death, whereas those who were obese (a body mass index of 30 or more) at age 50 had a 100 to 200 percent higher risk of premature death.

Strength, Joints, and Bones   As we saw in Chapter 13, maximum physical strength often is attained during the twenties. The term *sarcopenia* is given to age-related loss of muscle mass and strength (Sayer & others, 2013). Muscle loss with age occurs at a rate of approximately 1 to 2 percent per year after age 50 (Marcell, 2003). A loss of strength especially occurs in the back and legs. Researchers are seeking to identify genes that are linked to the development of sarcopenia (Tan & others, 2012). Obesity is a risk factor for sarcopenia (Parr, Coffey, & Hawley, 2013). Recently, researchers have increasingly used the term "sarcopenic obesity" to describe individuals who have sarcopenia and are obese (Scott & others, 2014). A recent study found that sarcopenic obesity was linked to hypertension (Park & others, 2013). And a research review concluded that weight management and resistance training were the best strategies to slow down the decline of muscle mass and muscle strength (Rolland & others, 2011).

Peak functioning of the body's joints also usually occurs in the twenties. The cushions for the movement of bones (such as tendons and ligaments) become less efficient in middle adulthood, a time when many individuals experience joint stiffness and more difficulty in movement.

Maximum bone density occurs by the mid- to late thirties, after which there is a progressive loss of bone. The rate of this bone loss begins slowly but accelerates with further aging (Baron, 2012). Women lose bone mass twice as fast as men do. By the end of midlife, bones break more easily and heal more slowly (Rachner, Khosia, & Hofbauer, 2011).

Vision and Hearing   *Accommodation* of the eye—the ability to focus and maintain an image on the retina—experiences its sharpest decline between 40 and 59 years of age. In particular, middle-aged individuals begin to have difficulty viewing close objects.

The eye's blood supply also diminishes, although usually not until the fifties or sixties. The reduced blood supply may decrease the visual field's size and account for an increase in the eye's blind spot. At 60 years of age, the retina receives only one-third as much light as it did at 20 years of age, mostly because of the reduced size of the pupil (Scialfa & Kline, 2007).

Hearing also can start to decline by age 40. Auditory assessments indicate that hearing loss occurs in up to 50 percent of individuals 50 years and older (Fowler & Leigh-Paffenroth, 2007). Sensitivity to high pitches usually declines first; the ability to hear low-pitched sounds does not seem to decline much in middle adulthood. Men usually lose their sensitivity to high-pitched sounds sooner than women do. However, this gender difference might be due to men's greater exposure to noise in occupations such as mining, automobile work, and so on.

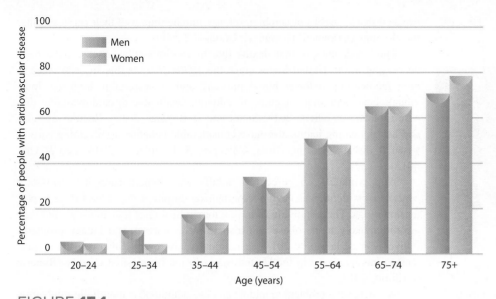

FIGURE **15.1**

THE RELATION OF AGE AND GENDER TO CARDIOVASCULAR DISEASE. Notice the sharp increase in cardiovascular disease in middle age.

Researchers are identifying new possibilities for improving the vision and hearing of people as they age. One strategy involves better control of glare or background noise (Natalizia & others, 2010). Laser surgery and implantation of intraocular lenses have become routine procedures for correcting vision in middle-aged adults (Fang, Wang, & He, 2013). In addition, recent advances in hearing aids have dramatically improved hearing for many individuals (Banerjee, 2011).

Cardiovascular System   Midlife is a time when high blood pressure and high cholesterol often take adults by surprise. Cardiovascular disease increases considerably in middle age (Hwang & others, 2014; Siegler & others, 2013; Wang & others, 2014), as indicated in Figure 15.1.

The level of cholesterol in the blood increases during the adult years and in midlife begins to accumulate on the artery walls, increasing the risk of cardiovascular disease (Emery & others, 2013). The type of cholesterol in the blood, however, influences its effect (Chan & others, 2013; Wang & others, 2014). Cholesterol comes in two forms: LDL (low-density lipoprotein) and HDL (high-density lipoprotein). LDL is often referred to as "bad" cholesterol because when the level of LDL is too high, it sticks to the lining of blood vessels, which can lead to atherosclerosis (hardening of the arteries) (Wenger, 2014). HDL is often referred to as "good" cholesterol because when it is high and LDL is low, the risk of cardiovascular disease is lower (Karavia & others, 2014; Li & others, 2013).

High blood pressure (hypertension), too, often begins to appear for many individuals in their forties and fifties (Roberie & Elliott, 2012; Tzourio, Laurent, & Debette, 2014). At menopause, a woman's blood pressure rises sharply and usually remains above that of a man through life's later years (Taler, 2009). A recent study found that uncontrolled hypertension can damage the brain's structure and function as early as the late thirties and early forties (Maillard & others, 2012). In this study, structural damage to the brain's white matter (axons) and decreased volume of gray matter (cell bodies and dendrites) occurred for individuals who had hypertension (top number above 140 and bottom number above 90). And a recent study revealed that hypertension in middle age was linked to risk of cognitive impairment in late adulthood (23 years later) (Virta & others, 2013).

Exercise, weight control, and a diet rich in fruits, vegetables, and whole grains can often help to stave off many cardiovascular problems in middle age (Cuenca-Garcia & others, 2014; Santilli & others, 2013). For example, although cholesterol levels are influenced by heredity, LDL can be reduced and HDL increased by eating food that is low in saturated fat and cholesterol and by exercising regularly (Logan, 2011). One study of postmenopausal women

Members of the Masai tribe in Kenya, Africa, can stay on a treadmill for a long time because of their active lives. The extremely low incidence of heart disease in the Masai tribe is likely linked to their energetic lifestyle.

What characterizes metabolic syndrome?

revealed that 12 weeks of aerobic exercise training improved their cardiovascular functioning (O'Donnell, Kirwan, & Goodman, 2009).

The good news is that deaths due to cardiovascular disease have been decreasing in the United States since the 1970s. Why is this so? Advances in drug medication to lower blood pressure and cholesterol in high-risk individuals have been major factors in reducing deaths due to cardiovascular disease (Karavia & others, 2014; Sandesara & Bogarat, 2013). Regular exercise and healthy eating habits also have considerable benefits in preventing cardiovascular disease (Cozma Dima, Cojocaru, & Postolache, 2014; Lee & Ory, 2013).

Approximately 15 percent of adults with hypertension have *resistant hypertension,* defined as having hypertension despite using at least three hypertension drugs. These individuals have a longer history of hypertension, and they are more likely to be obese and also to have diabetes and kidney problems (Oliveras & de la Sierra, 2014). A national study revealed that resistant hypertension has increased in the United States in the twenty-first century (Roberie & Elliott, 2012).

An increasing problem in middle and late adulthood is **metabolic syndrome,** a condition characterized by hypertension, obesity, and insulin resistance (Samson & Garber, 2014). Researchers have found that chronic stress exposure is linked to metabolic syndrome (Fabre & others, 2013). Metabolic syndrome often leads to the development of diabetes and cardiovascular disease (Landsberg & others, 2013; Scuteri & others, 2014). Weight loss and exercise are strongly recommended as part of the treatment of metabolic syndrome (Samson & Garber, 2014; Vissers & others, 2013). Several recent studies have provided information about risk factors for metabolic syndrome:

- A meta-analysis revealed that metabolic syndrome was an important risk factor for any cause of death (Wu, Liu, & Ho, 2010).
- Of four indices of obesity (body mass index, waist circumference, waist hip ratio, and waist height ratio, waist circumference was the best predictor of metabolic syndrome (Bener & others, 2013).
- Individuals with metabolic syndrome who were physically active reduced their risk of developing cardiovascular disease (Broekhuizen & others, 2011).

Does your fitness level during early adulthood have much impact on your risk of cardiovascular disease in middle age? To find out, see *Connecting Through Research.*

Lungs   There is little change in lung capacity through most of middle adulthood for many individuals. However, at about age 55, the proteins in lung tissue become less elastic. This change, combined with a gradual stiffening of the chest wall, decreases the lungs' capacity to shuttle oxygen from the air people breathe to the blood in their veins. The lung capacity of individuals who are smokers drops precipitously in middle age, but if the individuals quit smoking, their lung capacity improves, although not to the level of individuals who have never smoked.

Exercise is linked to better lung functioning and a lower risk of developing lung cancer. In a recent study, more than 17,000 men were given a cardiovascular fitness assessment at 50 years of age (Lakoski & others, 2013). Subsequent analysis of Medicare claims and deaths found that the risk of being diagnosed with lung cancer was reduced by 68 percent for men who were the most fit compared with those who were the least fit.

Research also has found that low cognitive ability in early adulthood is linked to reduced lung functioning in middle age (Carroll & others, 2011). And reduced lung functioning is related to lower cognitive ability later in development (Shipley & others, 2007). Such links between reduced lung functioning and cognitive ability are likely related to the influence of pulmonary functioning on brain structure and function, which in turn affects cognition (MacDonald, DeCarlo, & Dixon, 2011).

metabolic syndrome A condition characterized by hypertension, obesity, and insulin resistance. Metabolic syndrome often leads to the onset of diabetes and cardiovascular disease.

How Does Physical Fitness in Young Adults Predict Cardiovascular Health in Middle Age?

One longitudinal study was the first large-scale observational study to examine the role of physical fitness on healthy young adults' development of risk factors for heart disease (Carnethon & others, 2003). Previous studies had focused on the relationship between fitness and death from heart disease and stroke.

The study involved 4,487 men and women in four cities (Birmingham, Alabama; Chicago, Illinois; Minneapolis, Minnesota; and Oakland, California). Initial assessments were made when the participants were 18 to 30 years of age and follow-up assessments were conducted 2, 5, 7, 10, and 15 years later. Cardiorespiratory fitness was measured with an exercise treadmill test, which consisted of up to nine two-minute stages of progressive difficulty.

How might physical fitness in early adulthood be linked to health in middle adulthood?

Poor cardiorespiratory fitness in young men and women, determined by the duration of their treadmill exercise test, was associated with their risk of developing hypertension, diabetes, and metabolic syndrome in middle age. Improved fitness over seven years was related to a reduced risk of developing diabetes and metabolic syndrome.

This research reinforces the importance of establishing good health habits early in life. Staying fit when you are younger not only improves your health at that point in your life but also increases the likelihood that you will remain healthy as you get older.

How might physical fitness in early adulthood be linked to health in middle adulthood?

Sleep　The average American adult gets just under seven hours of sleep a night. How much sleep do adults need to function optimally the next day? An increasing number of experts note that eight hours of sleep or more per night are necessary for optimal performance the next day. These experts argue that many adults have become sleep deprived (McKenna & others, 2013). Work pressures, school pressures, family obligations, and social obligations often lead to long hours of wakefulness and irregular sleep/wake schedules (Soderstrom & others, 2012). Habitual sleep deprivation is linked to morbidity, especially among people with cardiovascular disease (Grandner & others, 2013).

Some aspects of sleep become more problematic in middle age (Green & others, 2012). The total number of hours slept usually remains the same as in early adulthood, but beginning in the forties, wakeful periods are more frequent and there is less of the deepest type of sleep. The amount of time spent lying awake in bed at night begins to increase in middle age, and this can produce a feeling of being less rested in the morning. Sleep-disordered breathing and restless legs syndrome become more prevalent in middle age (Polo-Kantola, 2011). A recent study also found that middle-aged adults who slept less than six hours a night on average had an increased risk of developing stroke symptoms (Ruiter & others, 2012). And a recent study revealed that sleep deprivation was associated with less effective immune system functioning (Wilder-Smith & others, 2013). A recent research review concluded that sleep deprivation is linked to problems in long-term memory consolidation (Abel & others, 2013). Also, sleep problems in midlife are more common among individuals who use a higher number of prescription and nonprescription drugs, are obese, have cardiovascular disease, or are depressed (Loponen & others, 2010).

HEALTH, DISEASE, STRESS, AND CONTROL

In middle adulthood, the frequency of accidents declines and individuals are less susceptible to colds and allergies than in childhood, adolescence, or early adulthood. Indeed, many individuals live through middle adulthood without having a disease or persistent health problem.

However, disease and persistent health problems become more common in middle adulthood for some individuals.

Chronic disorders are characterized by a slow onset and a long duration (Hoyt & Stanton, 2012; Ory & others, 2013). Chronic disorders are rare in early adulthood, increase in middle adulthood, and become common in late adulthood. Overall, arthritis is the leading chronic disorder in middle age, followed by hypertension, but the frequency of chronic disorders in middle age varies by gender. Men have a higher incidence of fatal chronic conditions (such as coronary heart disease, cancer, and stroke); women have a higher incidence of nonfatal ones (such as arthritis, varicose veins, and bursitis).

Stress and Disease   Stress is increasingly identified as a factor in many diseases (Schwarzer & Luszczynska, 2013). The cumulative effect of stress often takes a toll on the health of individuals by the time they reach middle age. David Almeida and his colleagues (2011) conclude that chronic stress or prolonged exposure to stressors can have damaging effects on physical functioning, including an unhealthy overproduction of corticosteroids such as cortisol. Chronic stress can interfere with immune functioning, and this stress is linked to disease not only through the immune system but also through cardiovascular factors (Emery & others, 2013; Stowell, Robles, & Kane, 2013). A recent study discovered that chronic stress accelerated pancreatic cancer growth (Kim-Fuchs & others, 2014). Also, a recent study of middle-aged adults found that when they had a high level of allostatic load (wearing down of the body's systems in response to high stress levels), their episodic memory and executive function was harmed (Karlamangia & others, 2014). And a recent study of occupationally active 44- to 58-year-olds revealed that perceived stress symptoms in midlife were linked to self-care disability and mobility limitations 28 years later (Kulmala & others, 2013).

The Immune System and Stress   The immune system keeps us healthy by recognizing foreign materials such as bacteria, viruses, and tumors and then destroying them (Stowell, Robles, & Kane, 2013). Immune system functioning becomes less effective with normal aging (Dougall & others, 2013; Evers & others, 2014).

The immune system's machinery consists of billions of white blood cells located in the circulatory system. The number of white blood cells and their effectiveness in killing foreign viruses or bacteria are related to stress levels. When a person is under stress, viruses and bacteria are more likely to multiply and cause disease. One study in young and middle-aged adults revealed that persistently unemployed individuals had lower natural killer (NK) cell levels than their previously unemployed counterparts who became reemployed (Cohen & others, 2007). NK cells are a type of white blood cell that is more likely to be present in low-stress circumstances (see Figure 15.2). Lower levels of NK cells in stressful situations indicate a weakened immune system. One study indicated aerobic fitness was related to the presence of a lower level of senescent T cells (prematurely aging cells that result from persistent immune activation) (Spielmann & others, 2011).

Chronic stressors are linked to a downturn in immune system functioning in a number of contexts, including worries about living next to a damaged nuclear reactor, failures in close relationships (divorce, separation, and marital distress), depression, loneliness, and burdensome caregiving for a family member with progressive illness (Fagundes, Glaser, & Kiecolt-Glaser, 2013; Fagundes & others, 2013; Jaremka & others, 2013a, b; Jaremka & others, 2014a).

Sheldon Cohen and his colleagues have conducted a number of studies on immunity and susceptibility to infectious disease (Cohen & Janicki-Deverts, 2012; Cohen & others, 2012, 2013; Cohen & Shachar, 2012). They have found that that factors such as stress, emotion, and lack of social support compromise people's immune system functioning in ways that alter their bodies' ability to fight off disease.

Stress and the Cardiovascular System   Stress and negative emotions can affect the development and course of cardiovascular disease by altering underlying physiological processes (Emery & others, 2013; Lamy & others, 2014). Sometimes, though, the link

developmental **connection**

Stress

Recently, a variation of hormonal stress theory has emphasized a decline in immune system functioning as an important contributor to lower resistance to stress in older adults. Chapter 17, p. 517

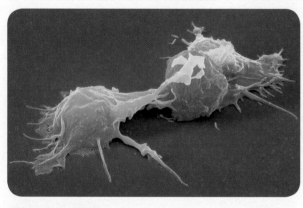

FIGURE **15.2**

NK CELLS AND CANCER. Two natural killer (NK) cells (*yellow*) are shown attacking a leukemia cell (*red*). Notice the blisters that the leukemia cell has developed to defend itself. Nonetheless, the NK cells are surrounding the leukemia cell and are about to destroy it.

chronic disorders Disorders that are characterized by slow onset and long duration. They are rare in early adulthood, increase during middle adulthood, and become common in late adulthood.

between stress and cardiovascular disease is indirect. For example, people who live in a chronically stressed condition, such as persistent poverty, are more likely to take up smoking, start overeating, and avoid exercising (Sowah, Busse, & Amoroso, 2013). All of these stress-related behaviors are linked with the development of cardiovascular disease (Sultan-Taieb & others, 2013).

Control Although many diseases increase in middle age, having a sense of control is linked to many aspects of health and well-being (Bertrand, Kranz Graham, & Lachman, 2013). Researchers have found that having a sense of control peaks in midlife and then declines in late adulthood (Lachman, 2006; Lachman, Rosnick, & Rocke, 2009). However, in any adult age period, there is a wide range of individual differences in beliefs about control. Margie Lachman and her colleagues (2011) argue that having a sense of control in middle age is one of the most important modifiable factors in delaying the onset of diseases in middle adulthood and reducing the frequency of diseases in late adulthood.

MORTALITY RATES

Infectious disease was the main cause of death until the middle of the twentieth century. As infectious disease rates declined and more individuals lived through middle age, rates of chronic disorders increased (Keiley-Moore, 2009). Chronic diseases are now the main causes of death for individuals in middle adulthood.

In middle age, many deaths are caused by a single, readily identifiable condition, whereas in old age, death is more likely to result from the combined effects of several chronic conditions (Pizza & others, 2011). For many years heart disease was the leading cause of death in middle adulthood, followed by cancer; however, since 2005 more individuals 45 to 64 years of age in the United States died of cancer, followed by cardiovascular disease (Kochanek & others, 2011). The gap between cancer and the second leading cause of death widens as individuals age from 45 to 54 and 55 to 64 years of age (Heron, 2013). Men have higher mortality rates than women for all of the leading causes of death (Kochanek & others, 2011).

SEXUALITY

What kinds of changes characterize the sexuality of women and men as they go through middle age? **Climacteric** is a term that is used to describe the midlife transition in which fertility declines. Let's explore the substantial differences in the climacteric experienced by women and men.

Menopause **Menopause** is the time in middle age, usually during the late forties or early fifties, when a woman's menstrual periods cease. The average age at which U.S. women have their last period is 51 (Wise, 2006). However, there is a large variation in the age at which menopause occurs—from 39 to 59 years of age. Later menopause is linked with increased risk of breast cancer (Mishra & others, 2009).

Recall from Chapter 11, "Physical and Cognitive Development in Adolescence," that the timing of menarche, a girl's first menstruation, has significantly decreased since the mid-nineteenth century, occurring as much as four years earlier in some countries (Susman & Dorn, 2013). Has there been a similar earlier onset in the occurrence of menopause? No, there hasn't been a corresponding change in menopause, and there is little or no correlation between ages at menarche and the onset of menopause (Gosden, 2007).

Perimenopause is the transitional period from normal menstrual periods to no menstrual periods at all, which often takes up to 10 years. Perimenopause usually occurs during the forties but can occur in the thirties (Martins & others, 2014). One study of 30- to 50-year-old women found that depressed feelings, headaches, moodiness, and palpitations were the perimenopausal symptoms that these women most frequently discussed with health-care providers (Lyndaker & Hulton, 2004). A recent research review found increased evidence that effective use of menopausal hormone replacement therapy is not linked to cardiovascular disease problems during perimenopause (Valdiviezo, Lawson, & Ouyang, 2013). Lifestyle factors such as whether women are overweight, smoke, drink heavily, or exercise regularly

climacteric The midlife transition during which fertility declines.

menopause Cessation of a woman's menstrual periods, usually during the late forties or early fifties.

Researchers have found that almost 50 percent of Canadian and American women have occasional hot flashes during the menopausal transition, but only one in seven Japanese women do (Lock, 1998). *What factors might account for these variations?*

during perimenopause influence aspects of their future health such as whether they develop cardiovascular disease or chronic illnesses (ESHRE Capri Workshop Group, 2011; Kagitani & others, 2014).

In menopause, production of estrogen by the ovaries declines dramatically, and this decline produces uncomfortable symptoms in some women—"hot flashes," nausea, fatigue, and rapid heartbeat, for example (Brockie & others, 2014). However, cross-cultural studies reveal variations in the menopause experience (Lerner-Geva & others, 2010; Sievert & Obermeyer, 2012). For example, hot flashes are uncommon in Mayan women (Beyene, 1986). Asian women report fewer hot flashes than women in Western societies (Payer, 1991). It is difficult to determine the extent to which these cross-cultural variations are due to genetic, dietary, reproductive, or cultural factors.

Menopause overall is not the negative experience for most women that it was once thought to be (Henderson, 2011). Most women do not have severe physical or psychological problems related to menopause. For example, a recent research review concluded that there is no clear evidence that depressive disorders occur more often during menopause than at other times in a woman's reproductive life (Judd, Hickey, & Bryant, 2012).

However, the loss of fertility is an important marker for women—it means that they have to make final decisions about having children. Women in their thirties who have never had children sometimes speak about being "up against the biological clock" because they cannot postpone choices about having children much longer.

Until recently, hormone replacement therapy was often prescribed as treatment for unpleasant side effects of menopause. *Hormone replacement therapy (HRT)* augments the declining levels of reproductive hormone production by the ovaries (Terry & Tehranifar, 2013). HRT can consist of various forms of estrogen, usually in combination with a progestin. A study of HRT's effects was halted as evidence emerged that participants who were receiving HRT faced an increased risk of stroke (National Institutes of Health, 2004). Since the link between HRT and increased risk of stroke was reported, there has been a 50 percent or more reduction in the use of HRT (Pines, Sturdee, & Maclennan, 2012). However, recent research has found a reduction of cardiovascular disease and minimal risks with HRT when it is initiated before 60 years of age and/or within 10 years of menopause and continued for six years or more (Hodis & others, 2012). Further evidence indicates that when women start HRT in their fifties and continue its use for 5 to 30 years, there is an increase in 1.5 quality life years for the women (Hodis & Mack, 2014). Also, a recent meta-analysis concluded that HRT was linked to decreased lung cancer in females, especially nonsmoking females and females with BMI less than 25 kg/m (Yao & others, 2013).

The National Institutes of Health recommends that women who have not had a hysterectomy and who are currently taking hormones consult with their doctor to determine whether they should continue the treatment. If they are taking HRT for short-term relief of menopausal symptoms, the benefits may outweigh the risks (Santen & others, 2014). Many middle-aged women are seeking alternatives to HRT such as regular exercise, dietary supplements, herbal remedies, relaxation therapy, acupuncture, and nonsteroidal medications (Al-Safi & Santoro, 2014; Buhling & others, 2014; Velders & Diel, 2013; Ward-Ritacco & others, 2014). A recent study revealed that in sedentary women, aerobic training for 6 months decreased menopausal symptoms, especially night sweats, mood swings, and irritability (Moilanen & others, 2012). Another recent study found that yoga improved the quality of life of menopausal women (Reed & others, 2014).

Hormonal Changes in Middle-Aged Men   Do men go through anything like the menopause that women experience? That is, is there a male menopause? During middle adulthood, most men do not lose their capacity to father children, although there usually is a modest decline in their sexual hormone level and activity (Blumel & others, 2014). They experience hormonal changes in their fifties and sixties, but nothing like the dramatic drop in estrogen that women experience. Testosterone production begins to decline about 1 percent a year during middle adulthood, and sperm count usually declines slowly, but men do not lose their fertility in middle age. The term *male hypogonadism* is used to describe a condition in which the body does not produce enough testosterone (Mayo Clinic, 2013).

	Percentage Engaging in Sex				
Age Groups	Not at all	A few times per year	A few times per month	2–3 times a week	4 or more times a week
Men					
18–24	15	21	24	28	12
25–29	7	15	31	36	11
30–39	8	15	37	23	6
40–49	9	18	40	27	6
50–59	11	22	43	20	3
Women					
18–24	11	16	2	9	12
25–29	5	10	38	37	10
30–39	9	16	6	33	6
40–49	15	16	44	20	5
50–59	30	22	35	12	2

FIGURE 15.3

THE SEX IN AMERICA SURVEY: FREQUENCY OF SEX AT DIFFERENT POINTS IN ADULT DEVELOPMENT. *Why do you think the frequency of sex declines as men and women get older?*

Recently, there has been a dramatic surge of interest in *testosterone replacement therapy (TRT)* (Kaplan & Hu, 2013; Rahnema & others, 2014; Ullah, Riche, & Koch, 2014). For many decades, it was thought that TRT increased the risk of prostate cancer, but recent research reviews indicate that is not the case, at least when taken for one year or less (Cui & others, 2014; Khera & others, 2014). It is now accepted that TRT can improve sexual functioning, muscle strength, and bone health (Isidori & others, 2014; Mayo Clinic, 2013). Two recent studies found that TRT improved older men's sexual function as well as their mood (Miner & others, 2013; Okada & others, 2014). Further, a recent study found that a higher testosterone level was linked to better episodic memory in middle-aged males (Panizzon & others, 2014). However, a recent research review concluded that the benefit-risk ratio for older adult men is uncertain (Isidori & others, 2014). Men who have prostate cancer or breast cancer should not take TRT, and men who are at risk for blood clotting (those who have atrial fibrillation, for example) also should not use TRT (Osterberg, Bernie, & Ramasamy, 2014).

Erectile dysfunction (ED) (difficulty attaining or maintaining penile erection) affects approximately 50 percent of men 40 to 70 years of age (Berookhim & Bar-Charma, 2011). Low testosterone levels can contribute to erectile dysfunction. Smoking, diabetes, hypertension, elevated cholesterol levels, obesity, and lack of exercise also are associated with erectile problems in middle-aged men (Asian & others, 2014; Tanik & others, 2014; Weinberg & others, 2013). The main treatment for men with erectile dysfunction has not focused on TRT but on Viagra and similar drugs such as Levitra and Cialis (Kim & others, 2014; Kirby, Creanga, & Stecher, 2013; McMahon, 2014). Viagra works by allowing increased blood flow into the penis, which produces an erection. Its success rate is in the 60 to 85 percent range (Claes & others, 2010).

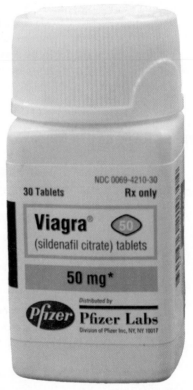

Sexual Attitudes and Behavior Although the ability of men and women to function sexually shows little biological decline in middle adulthood, sexual activity usually occurs less frequently in midlife than in early adulthood (Waite, Das, & Laumann, 2009). Figure 15.3 shows the age trends in frequency of sex from the Sex in America survey (described in Chapter 13). The frequency of having sex was greatest for individuals aged 25 to 29 years old (47 percent had sex twice a week or more) and dropped off for individuals in their fifties (23 percent of 50- to 59-year-old males said they had sex twice a week or more, and only 14 percent of the females in this age group reported this frequency) (Michael & others, 1994). Note, though, that the Sex in America survey may underestimate the frequency of sexual activity of middle-aged adults because the data were collected prior to the widespread use of erectile dysfunction drugs such as Viagra. Other research indicates that middle-aged men want sex, think about it more, and masturbate more often than middle-aged women (Stones & Stones, 2007). For many other forms of sexual behavior, such as kissing and hugging, sexual

erectile dysfunction (ED) The inability to adequately achieve and maintain an erection to attain satisfactory sexual performance.

touching, and oral sex, male and female middle-aged adults report similar frequency of engagement (Stones & Stones, 2007).

If middle-aged adults have sex less frequently than they did in early adulthood, does it mean they are less satisfied with their sex life? In a Canadian study of 40- to 64-year-olds, only 30 percent reported that their sexual life was less satisfying than it had been when they were in their twenties (Wright, 2006).

Living with a spouse or partner makes all the difference in whether people engage in sexual activity, especially for women over 40 years of age. In one study conducted as part of the Midlife in the United States Study (MIDUS), 95 percent of women in their forties with partners said that they had been sexually active in the last six months, compared with only 53 percent of those without partners (Brim, 1999). By their fifties, 88 percent of women living with a partner have been sexually active in the last six months, but only 37 percent of those who are neither married nor living with someone say they have had sex in the last six months.

A large-scale study of U.S. adults 40 to 80 years of age found that premature ejaculation (26 percent) and erectile difficulties (22 percent) were the most common sexual problems of older men while lack of sexual interest (33 percent) and lubrication difficulties (21 percent) were the most common sexual problems of older women (Laumann & others, 2009).

A person's health in middle age is a key factor in sexual activity (Field & others, 2013). One study found that how often individuals have sexual intercourse, the quality of their sexual life, and their interest in sex were linked to how physically healthy they were (Lindau & Gavrilova, 2010). And a recent study of aging adults 55 years and older revealed that how sexually active they were was associated with their physical and mental health (Bach & others, 2013).

Review Connect Reflect

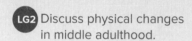 Discuss physical changes in middle adulthood.

Review
- What are some key physical changes in middle adulthood?
- How would you characterize health and disease in middle adulthood?
- What are the main causes of death in middle age?
- What are the sexual lives of middle-aged adults like?

Connect
- In this section, you read that the production of estrogen by the ovaries declines dramatically in menopause. What did you learn about estrogen's role in puberty in Chapter 11?

Reflect Your Own Personal Journey of Life
- If you are a young or middle-aged adult, what can you do at this point in your life to optimize your health in middle age? If you are an older adult, what could you have done differently to optimize your health in middle age?

3 Cognitive Development

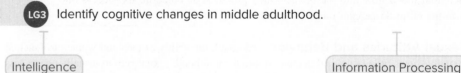 Identify cognitive changes in middle adulthood.

Intelligence | Information Processing

We have seen that middle-aged adults may not see as well, run as fast, or be as healthy as they were in their twenties and thirties. But what about their cognitive skills? Do these skills decline as we enter and move through middle adulthood? To answer this question, we will explore the possibility of cognitive changes in intelligence and information processing.

INTELLIGENCE

Our exploration of possible changes in intelligence in middle adulthood focuses on the concepts of fluid and crystallized intelligence, the Seattle Longitudinal Study, and cohort effects.

Fluid and Crystallized Intelligence   John Horn argues that some abilities begin to decline in middle age while others increase (Horn & Donaldson, 1980). Horn maintains that **crystallized intelligence,** an individual's accumulated information and verbal skills, continues to increase in middle adulthood, whereas **fluid intelligence,** one's ability to reason abstractly, begins to decline in middle adulthood (see Figure 15.4).

Horn's data were collected in a cross-sectional manner. Remember from Chapter 1 that a cross-sectional study assesses individuals of different ages at the same point in time. For example, a cross-sectional study might assess the intelligence of different groups of 40-, 50-, and 60-year-olds in a single evaluation, such as in 1980. The 40-year-olds in the study would have been born in 1940 and the 60-year-olds in 1920—different eras that offered different economic and educational opportunities. The 60-year-olds likely had fewer educational opportunities as they grew up. Thus, if we find differences between 40- and 60-year-olds on intelligence tests when they are assessed cross-sectionally, these differences might be due to cohort effects related to educational differences rather than to age.

By contrast, remember from Chapter 1 that in a longitudinal study, the same individuals are studied over a period of time. Thus, a longitudinal study of intelligence in middle adulthood might consist of giving the same intelligence test to the same individuals when they are 40, 50, and 60 years of age. As we see next, whether data on intelligence are collected cross-sectionally or longitudinally can make a difference in what is found about changes in crystallized and fluid intelligence and about intellectual decline (Abrams, 2009; Schaie, 2011a, b, 2013).

The Seattle Longitudinal Study   The Seattle Longitudinal Study that involves extensive evaluation of intellectual abilities during adulthood was initiated by K. Warner Schaie (1994, 1996, 2005, 2010, 2011a, b, 2013). Participants have been assessed at seven-year intervals since 1956: 1963, 1970, 1977, 1984, 1991, 1998, 2005, and 2012. Five hundred individuals initially were tested in 1956. New waves of participants are added periodically. The main focus in the Seattle Longitudinal Study has been on individual change and stability in intelligence, and the study is regarded as one of the most thorough examinations of how people develop and change as they go through adulthood.

The main mental abilities tested in this study are:

- Verbal comprehension (ability to understand ideas expressed in words)
- Verbal memory (ability to encode and recall meaningful language units, such as a list of words)
- Number (ability to perform simple mathematical computations such as addition, subtraction, and multiplication)
- Spatial orientation (ability to visualize and mentally rotate stimuli in two- and three-dimensional space)
- Inductive reasoning (ability to recognize and understand patterns and relationships in a problem and to use this understanding to solve other instances of the problem)
- Perceptual speed (ability to quickly and accurately make simple discriminations in visual stimuli)

As shown in Figure 15.5, the highest level of functioning for four of the six intellectual abilities occurred in the middle adulthood years (Schaie, 2013). For both women and men, peak performance on verbal ability, verbal memory, inductive reasoning, and spatial orientation was attained in middle age. For only two of the six abilities—number and perceptual speed—were there declines in middle age. Perceptual speed showed the earliest decline, actually beginning in early adulthood. Interestingly, in terms of John Horn's ideas that were discussed earlier, for the participants in the Seattle Longitudinal Study, middle age was a time of peak performance for some aspects of both crystallized intelligence (verbal ability) and fluid intelligence (spatial orientation and inductive reasoning).

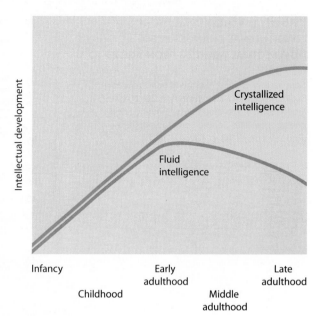

FIGURE 15.4

FLUID AND CRYSTALLIZED INTELLECTUAL DEVELOPMENT ACROSS THE LIFE SPAN. According to Horn, crystallized intelligence (based on cumulative learning experiences) increases throughout the life span, but fluid intelligence (the ability to perceive and manipulate information) steadily declines from middle adulthood onward.

developmental **connection**

Cognitive Theory

A fifth, postformal stage of cognitive development has been proposed to describe cognitive advances in early adulthood. Chapter 13, p. 420

crystallized intelligence Accumulated information and verbal skills, which increase in middle adulthood, according to Horn.

fluid intelligence The ability to reason abstractly, which begins to decline from middle adulthood onward, according to Horn.

FIGURE **15.5**

**LONGITUDINAL CHANGES IN SIX
INTELLECTUAL ABILITIES FROM AGE 25 TO
AGE 95.**

Source: K.W. Schaie: "Longitudinal Changes in
Six Intellectual Abilities from Age 25 to Age 95"
Figure 5.7a, in Developmental Influences on
Intelligence: The Seattle Longitudinal Study,
(2nd rev edit.) 2013, p. 162.

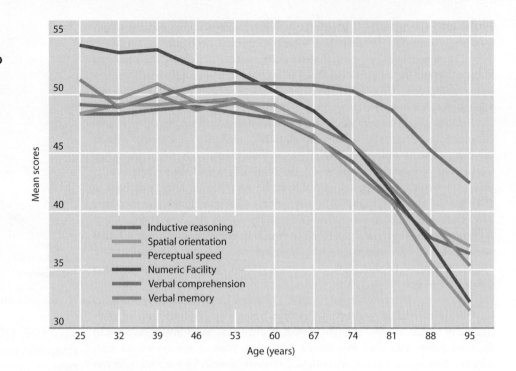

When Schaie (1994) assessed intellectual abilities both cross-sectionally and longitudinally, he found declines to be more likely in the cross-sectional than in the longitudinal assessments. For example, as shown in Figure 15.6, when assessed cross-sectionally, inductive reasoning showed a consistent decline during middle adulthood. In contrast, when assessed longitudinally, inductive reasoning increased until toward the end of middle adulthood when it began to show a slight decline. In Schaie's (2008, 2009, 2010, 2011a, b, 2013) view, it is in middle adulthood, not early adulthood, that people reach a peak in many intellectual skills.

In further analysis, Schaie (2007) examined generational differences in parents and their children over a seven-year time frame from 60 to 67 years of age. That is, parents were assessed when they were 60 to 67 years of age; and when their children reached 60 to 67 years of age, they also were assessed. Higher levels of cognitive functioning occurred for the second generation in inductive reasoning, verbal memory, and spatial orientation, whereas the first generation scored higher on numeric ability. Noteworthy was the finding that the parent generation showed cognitive decline from 60 to 67 years of age, but their offspring showed stability or modest increases in cognitive functioning across the same age range.

Such differences across generations involve cohort effects. In one analysis, Schaie (2011b) concluded that the advances in cognitive functioning in middle age that have occurred in recent decades are likely due to factors such as educational attainment, occupational structures (increases of workers in professional occupations and work complexity), health care and lifestyles, immigration, and social interventions in poverty. The impressive gains in cognitive functioning in recent cohorts have been documented more clearly for fluid intelligence than for crystallized intelligence (Schaie, 2011b).

The results from Schaie's study that have been described so far focus on average cognitive stability or change for all participants across the middle adulthood years. Schaie and Sherry Willis (Schaie, 2005; Willis & Schaie, 2005) examined individual differences for the participants in the Seattle study and found substantial individual variations. They classified participants as "decliners," "stable," or "gainers" for three categories—number ability, delayed recall (a verbal memory task), and word fluency—from 46 to 60 years of age. The largest percentage of decline (31 percent) or gain (16 percent) occurred for delayed recall; the largest percentage with stable scores (79 percent) occurred for numerical ability. Word fluency declined for 20 percent of the individuals from 46 to 60 years of age.

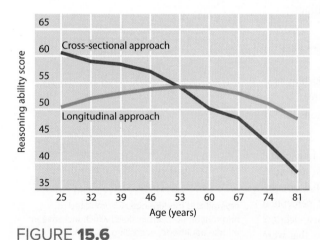

FIGURE **15.6**

**CROSS-SECTIONAL AND LONGITUDINAL COMPARISONS
OF INTELLECTUAL CHANGE IN MIDDLE ADULTHOOD.** *Why
do you think reasoning ability peaks during middle adulthood?*

Might the individual variations in cognitive trajectories in midlife be linked to cognitive impairment in late adulthood? In Willis and Schaie's analysis, cognitively normal and impaired older adults did not differ on measures of vocabulary, spatial orientation, and numerical ability in middle adulthood. However, declines in memory (immediate recall and delayed recall), word fluency, and perceptual speed in middle adulthood were linked to neuropsychologists' ratings of the individuals' cognitive impairment in late adulthood.

Some researchers disagree with Schaie that middle adulthood is the time when the level of functioning in a number of cognitive domains is maintained or even increases (Finch, 2009). For example, Timothy Salthouse (2009, 2012) recently has argued that cross-sectional research on aging and cognitive functioning should not be dismissed and that this research indicates reasoning, memory, spatial visualization, and processing speed begin declining in early adulthood and show further decline in the fifties. Salthouse (2009, 2012) agrees that cognitive functioning involving accumulated knowledge, such as vocabulary and general information, does not show early age-related decline but rather continues to increase at least until 60 years of age.

K. Warner Schaie (*right*) is one of the leading pioneers in the field of life-span development. He is shown here with two older adults who are actively using their cognitive skills. Schaie's research represents one of the most thorough examinations of how individuals develop and change as they go through the adult years.

Salthouse (2009, 2012) has emphasized that a lower level of cognitive functioning in early and middle adulthood is likely due to age-related neurobiological decline. Cross-sectional studies have shown that the following neurobiological factors decline during the twenties and thirties: regional brain volume, cortical thickness, synaptic density, some aspects of myelination, the functioning of some aspects of neurotransmitters such as dopamine and serotonin, blood flow in the cerebral cortex, and the accumulation of tangles in neurons (Del Tredici & Braak, 2008; Finch, 2009; Hsu & others, 2008; Pieperhoff & others, 2008).

Schaie (2009, 2010, 2011a, b, 2013) continues to emphasize that longitudinal studies hold the key to determining age-related changes in cognitive functioning and that middle age is the time during which many cognitive skills actually peak. In the next decade, expanding research on age-related neurobiological changes and their possible links to cognitive skills should further refine our knowledge about age-related cognitive functioning in the adult years (Fletcher & Rapp, 2013; Hansen & others, 2014; Klaassen & others, 2014).

INFORMATION PROCESSING

As we saw in our discussion of theories of development (Chapter 1) and of cognitive development from infancy through adolescence (Chapters 5, 7, 9, and 11), the information-processing approach provides another way of examining cognitive abilities. Among the information-processing changes that take place in middle adulthood are those involved in speed of processing information, memory, expertise, and practical problem-solving skills.

Speed of Information Processing   As we saw in Schaie's (1994, 1996, 2011a, b, 2013) Seattle Longitudinal Study, perceptual speed begins declining in early adulthood and continues to decline in middle adulthood. A common way to assess speed of information is through a reaction-time task, in which individuals simply press a button as soon as they see a light appear. Middle-aged adults are slower to push the button when the light appears than young adults are. However, keep in mind that the decline is not dramatic—under 1 second in most investigations.

A current interest focuses on possible causes for the decline in speed of processing information in adults (Salthouse, 2009, 2012). The causes may occur at different levels of analysis, such as cognitive ("maintaining goals, switching between tasks, or preserving internal representations despite distraction"), neuroanatomical ("changes in specific brain regions, such as the prefrontal cortex"), and neurochemical ("changes in neurotransmitter systems" such as dopamine) (Hartley, 2006, p. 201).

Memory   In Schaie's (1994, 1996) Seattle Longitudinal Study, verbal memory peaked during the fifties. However, in some other studies verbal memory has shown a decline in

developmental **connection**

Memory

Some types of memory decline more than others in older adults. Chapter 18, p. 543

middle age, especially when assessed in cross-sectional studies (Salthouse, 2009, 2012). For example, in several studies in which people were asked to remember lists of words, numbers, or meaningful prose, younger adults outperformed middle-aged adults (Salthouse & Skovronek, 1992). Although there still is some controversy about whether memory declines during middle adulthood, most experts conclude that it does decline at some point during this period of adult development (Lundervold, Wollschlager, & Wehling, 2014; McCabe & Loaiza, 2012; Salthouse, 2012). However, some experts argue that studies that have concluded there is a decline in memory during middle age often have compared young adults in their twenties with older middle-aged adults in their late fifties and even have included some individuals in their sixties (Schaie, 2000). In this view, memory decline is either nonexistent or minimal in the early part of middle age but does occur in the latter part of middle age or in late adulthood.

Cognitive aging expert Denise Park (2001) argues that starting in late middle age, more time is needed to learn new information. The slowdown in learning new information has been linked to changes in *working memory,* the mental "workbench" where individuals manipulate and assemble information when making decisions, solving problems, and comprehending written and spoken language (Baddeley, 2007, 2012). In this view, in late middle age working memory capacity becomes more limited. Think of this situation as an overcrowded desk with many items in disarray. As a result of the overcrowding and disarray, long-term memory becomes less reliable, more time is needed to enter new information into long-term storage, and more time is required to retrieve the information. Thus, Park concludes that much of the blame for declining memory in late middle age is a result of information overload that builds up as we go through the adult years.

Memory decline is more likely to occur when individuals don't use effective memory strategies, such as organization and imagery (Small & others, 2012). By organizing lists of phone numbers into different categories, or imagining the phone numbers as representing different objects around the house, many individuals can improve their memory in middle adulthood.

Expertise   Because it takes so long to attain, expertise often shows up more in middle adulthood than in early adulthood (Charness & Krampe, 2008). Recall from Chapter 9 that expertise involves having extensive, highly organized knowledge and understanding of a particular domain. Developing expertise and becoming an "expert" in a field usually is the result of many years of experience, learning, and effort.

Strategies that distinguish experts from novices include these:

- Experts are more likely to rely on their accumulated experience to solve problems.
- Experts often process information automatically and analyze it more efficiently when solving a problem in their domain than novices do.
- Experts have better strategies and shortcuts to solving problems in their domain than novices do.
- Experts are more creative and flexible in solving problems in their domain than novices are.

Practical Problem Solving   Everyday problem solving is another important aspect of cognition (Allaire, 2012; Margrett & Deshpande-Kamat, 2009). Nancy Denney (1986, 1990) observed circumstances such as how young and middle-aged adults handled a landlord who would not fix their stove and what they did if a bank failed to deposit a check. She found that the ability to solve such practical problems improved through the forties and fifties as individuals accumulated practical experience.

However, since Denney's research other studies on everyday problem-solving and decision-making effectiveness across the adult years have been conducted (Allaire, 2012; Margrett & Deshpande-Kamat, 2009). A recent analysis of research found no evidence for significant changes in everyday cognition from 20 to 75 years of age (Salthouse, 2012). One possible explanation for the lack of any decline in everyday cognition is the increase in accumulated knowledge individuals possess as they grow older (Allaire, 2012).

developmental **connection**

Memory

Working memory plays an important role in many aspects of children's cognitive and language development. Chapter 9, p. 280

developmental **connection**

Information Processing

One study found that 10- and 11-year-old children who were experienced chess players ("experts") remembered more about chess pieces than college students who were not chess players ("novices"). Chapter 9, p. 281

4 Careers, Work, and Leisure

LG4 Characterize career development, work, and leisure in middle adulthood.

Work in Midlife   Career Challenges and Changes   Leisure

What are some issues that workers face in midlife? What role does leisure play in the lives of middle-aged adults?

WORK IN MIDLIFE

The role of work, whether one works in a full-time career, a part-time job, as a volunteer, or a homemaker, is central during middle adulthood. Many middle-aged adults reach their peak in position and earnings. However, they may also be saddled with multiple financial burdens including rent or mortgage, child care, medical bills, home repairs, college tuition, loans to family members, or bills from nursing homes.

In the United States, approximately 80 percent of individuals 40 to 59 years of age are employed. In the 51-to-59 age group, slightly less than 25 percent do not work. More than half of this age group say that a health condition or an impairment limits the type of paid work that they do (Sterns & Huyck, 2001). Also, a recent study found that difficulty managing different job demands was associated with poor health in middle-aged adults (Nabe-Nielsen & others, 2014).

Do middle-aged workers perform their work as competently as younger adults? Age-related declines occur in some occupations, such as air traffic controllers and professional athletes, but for most jobs, no differences have been found in the work performance of young adults and middle-aged adults (Sturman, 2003; Salthouse, 2012).

However, leading Finnish researcher Clas-Hakan Nygard (2013) concludes from his longitudinal research that the ability to work effectively peaks during middle age because of increased motivation, work experience, employer loyalty, and better strategic thinking. Nygard also has found that the quality of work done by employees in middle age is linked to how much their work is appreciated and how well they get along with their immediate supervisors. And Nygard and his colleagues discovered that work ability in middle age was linked to mortality and disability 28 years later (von Bonsdorff & others, 2011, 2012).

For many people, midlife is a time of evaluation, assessment, and reflection in terms of the work they are doing now and what they want to do in the future (Moen, 2009). Among the work issues that some people face in midlife are recognizing limitations in career progress, deciding whether to change jobs or careers, determining how and when to rebalance family and work, and planning for retirement (Sterns & Huyck, 2001).

Couples increasingly have both spouses in the workforce who are expecting to retire. Historically retirement has been a male transition, but today far more couples are planning two retirements—his and hers (Moen, 2009; Moen, Kelly, & Magennis, 2008).

developmental connection

Work

Work defines people in fundamental ways, influencing their financial standing, housing, the way they spend their time, where they live, their friendships, and their health. Chapter 13, p. 424

What characterizes work in middle adulthood?

HAGAR © 1987 King FEATURES SYNDICATE.

Sigmund Freud once commented that the two things adults need to do well to adapt to society's demands are to work and to love. To his list we add "to play." In our fast-paced society, it is all too easy to get caught up in the frenzied, hectic pace of our achievement-oriented work world and ignore leisure and play. Imagine your life as a middle-aged adult. *What would be the ideal mix of work and leisure? What leisure activities do you want to enjoy as a middle-aged adult?*

leisure The pleasant times after work when individuals are free to pursue activities and interests of their own choosing.

religion An organized set of beliefs, practices, rituals, and symbols that increases an individual's connection to a sacred or transcendent other (God, higher power, or higher truth).

religiousness The degree to which an individual is affiliated with an organized religion, participates in prescribed rituals and practices, feels a sense of connection with its beliefs, and is involved in a community of believers.

The recent economic downturn and recession in the United States has forced some middle-aged individuals into premature retirement because of job loss and fear of not being able to reenter the work force (Cahill, Giandrea, & Quinn, 2014). Such premature retirement also may result in accumulating insufficient financial resources to cover an increasingly long retirement period (de Wind & others, 2014; Lusardi, Mitchell, & Curto, 2012).

CAREER CHALLENGES AND CHANGES

Middle-aged workers face several important challenges in the twenty-first century (Brand, 2014). These include the globalization of work, rapid developments in information technologies, downsizing of organizations, early retirement, and concerns about pensions and health care.

Globalization has replaced what was once a primarily White male workforce with employees of different ethnic and national backgrounds. To improve profits, many companies are restructuring, downsizing, and outsourcing jobs. One of the outcomes of these changes is to offer incentives to middle-aged employees to retire early—in their fifties, or in some cases even forties, rather than their sixties.

The decline in defined-benefit pensions and increased uncertainty about the fate of health insurance are decreasing the sense of personal control among middle-aged workers. As a consequence, many are delaying retirement.

Some midlife career changes are self-motivated; others are the consequence of losing one's job (Brand, 2014). Some individuals in middle age decide that they don't want to spend the rest of their lives doing the same kind of work they have been doing (Hoyer & Roodin, 2009). One aspect of middle adulthood involves adjusting idealistic hopes to accommodate realistic possibilities in light of how much time individuals have before they retire and how fast they are reaching their occupational goals (Levinson, 1978). If individuals perceive that they are behind schedule, if their goals are unrealistic, they don't like the work they are doing, or their job has become too stressful, they could become motivated to change jobs.

A final point to make about career development in middle adulthood is that cognitive factors earlier in development are linked to occupational attainment in middle age. In one study, task persistence at 13 years of age was related to occupational success in middle age (Andersson & Bergman, 2011).

LEISURE

As adults, not only must we learn how to work well, but we also need to learn how to relax and enjoy leisure (Eriksson Sorman & others, 2014). **Leisure** refers to the pleasant times after work when individuals are free to pursue activities and interests of their own choosing—hobbies, sports, or reading, for example. In one analysis of research on what U.S. adults regret the most, not engaging in more leisure was one of the top six regrets (Roese & Summerville, 2005).

Leisure can be an especially important aspect of middle adulthood (Nicolaisen, Thorsen, & Eriksen, 2012). By middle adulthood, more money is available to many individuals, and there may be more free time and paid vacations. In short, midlife changes may produce expanded opportunities for leisure.

In one study, 12,338 men 35 to 57 years of age were assessed each year for five years regarding whether or not they took vacations (Gump & Matthews, 2000). Then the researchers examined the medical and death records over nine years for men who lived for at least a year after the last vacation survey. Compared with those who never took vacations, men who went on annual vacations were 21 percent less likely to die over the nine years and 32 percent less likely to die of coronary heart disease. And a recent Finnish study found that engaging in little leisure-time activity in middle age was linked to risk of cognitive impairment in late adulthood (23 years later) (Virta & others, 2013).

Adults at midlife need to begin preparing psychologically for retirement. Constructive and fulfilling leisure activities in middle adulthood are an important part of this preparation. If an adult develops leisure activities that can be continued into retirement, the transition from work to retirement can be less stressful.

Review Connect Reflect

 LG4 Characterize career development, work, and leisure in middle adulthood.

Review
- What are some issues that workers face in midlife?
- What career challenges and changes might people experience in middle adulthood?
- What characterizes leisure in middle age?

Connect
- In this section you learned about the leisure time of adults in middle age.

What did you learn about cultural differences and leisure time in adolescence in Chapter 12?

Reflect *Your Own Personal Journey of Life*
- What do you want your work life and leisure to be like in middle age? If you are middle-aged, what are your work life and leisure activities like? If you are an older adult, what were they like in middle age?

5 Religion, Spirituality, and Meaning in Life

LG5 Explain the roles of religion, spirituality, and meaning in life during middle adulthood.

| Religion, Spirituality, and Adult Lives | Religion, Spirituality, and Health | Meaning in Life |

What roles do religion and spirituality play in our development as adults? Is the meaning of life an important theme for many middle-aged adults?

RELIGION, SPIRITUALITY, AND ADULT LIVES

Can religion be distinguished from spirituality? Recent analysis by Pamela King and her colleagues (2011) provides the following distinctions:

- **Religion** is an organized set of beliefs, practices, rituals, and symbols that increases an individual's connection to a sacred or transcendent other (God, higher power, or ultimate truth).
- **Religiousness** refers to the degree of affiliation with an organized religion, participation in its prescribed rituals and practices, connection with its beliefs, and involvement in a community of believers.

What roles do religion and spirituality play in the lives of middle-aged adults?

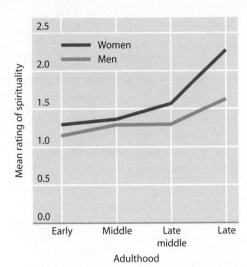

FIGURE **15.7**

LEVEL OF SPIRITUALITY IN FOUR ADULT AGE PERIODS. In a longitudinal study, the spirituality of individuals in four different adult age periods—early (thirties), middle (forties), late middle (mid-fifties/early sixties), and late (late sixties/early seventies) adulthood—was assessed (Wink & Dillon, 2002). Based on responses to open-ended questions in interviews, the spirituality of the individuals was coded on a 5-point scale with 5 being the highest level of spirituality and 1 the lowest.

- - - - - - - - - - - ➡

developmental **connection**

Religion

Religion and spirituality play important roles in the lives of many older adults. Chapter 18, p. 563

When more time stretches behind than stretches before one, some assessments, however reluctantly and incompletely, begin to be made.

—**JAMES BALDWIN**

American Novelist, 20th Century

spirituality Experiencing something beyond oneself in a transcendent manner and living in a way that benefits others and society.

meaning-making coping Involves drawing on beliefs, values, and goals to change the meaning of a stressful situation, especially in times of chronic stress such as when a loved one dies.

- **Spirituality** involves experiencing something beyond oneself in a transcendent manner and living in a way that benefits others and society.

In thinking about religion, spirituality, and adult development, it is important to consider the role of individual differences. Religion and spirituality are powerful influences for some adults but hold little or no significance for others (McCullough & others, 2005). Further, the influence of religion and spirituality in people's lives may change as they develop (Sapp, 2010). In John Clausen's (1993) longitudinal investigation, some individuals who had been strongly religious in their early adult years became less so in middle age, while others became more religious in middle age.

In the MacArthur Foundation Study of Midlife Development, more than 70 percent of U.S. middle-aged adults described themselves as religious and said that spirituality was a major part of their lives (Brim, 1999). In a longitudinal study of individuals from their early thirties through their late sixties and early seventies, a significant increase in spirituality occurred between late middle adulthood (mid-fifties/early sixties) and late adulthood (Wink & Dillon, 2002) (see Figure 15.7). And a recent survey found that 77 percent of 30- to 49-year-olds and 84 percent of 50- to 64-year-olds reported having a religious affiliation (compared with 67 percent of 18- to 29-year-olds and 90 percent of 90-year-old and over adults) (Pew Research, 2012).

Women have consistently shown a stronger interest in religion and spirituality than men have. In the longitudinal study just described, the spirituality of women increased more than men in the second half of life (Wink & Dillon, 2002).

RELIGION, SPIRITUALITY, AND HEALTH

How might religion influence physical health? Some cults and religious sects encourage behaviors that can be damaging to health, such as ignoring sound medical advice (Manca, 2013; Williams & Sternthal, 2007). For individuals in the religious mainstream, researchers increasingly are finding that spirituality/religion is positively linked to health (Krause & Hayward, 2014; McCullough & Willoughby, 2009). Researchers have found that religious commitment helps to moderate blood pressure and reduce hypertension, and that religious attendance is linked to a reduction in hypertension (Gillum & Ingram, 2007). And in an analysis of a number of studies, adults with a higher level of spirituality/religion had an 18 percent reduction in mortality (Lucchetti, Lucchetti, & Koenig, 2011). In this analysis, a high level of spirituality/religion had a stronger link to longevity than 60 percent of 25 other health interventions (such as eating fruits and vegetables and taking statin drugs for cardiovascular disease). In *Connecting Development to Life,* we explore links between religion, spirituality, and coping.

In sum, various dimensions of religion and coping can help some individuals cope more effectively with challenges in their lives (Olson & others, 2012; Park, 2010, 2012a, b; 2013; Park & Slattery, 2013). Religious counselors often advise people about mental health and coping. To read about the work of one religious counselor, see *Connecting with Careers.*

MEANING IN LIFE

Austrian psychiatrist Viktor Frankl's mother, father, brother, and wife died in the concentration camps and gas chambers in Auschwitz, Poland. Frankl survived the concentration camp and went on to write about meaning in life. In his book *Man's Search for Meaning,* Frankl (1984) emphasized each person's uniqueness and the finiteness of life. He argued that examining the finiteness of our existence and the certainty of death adds meaning to life. If life were not finite, said Frankl, we could spend our life doing just about whatever we pleased because time would continue forever.

Frankl said that the three most distinct human qualities are spirituality, freedom, and responsibility. Spirituality, in his view, does not have a religious underpinning. Rather, it refers to a human being's uniqueness of spirit, philosophy, and mind. Frankl proposed that people need to ask themselves questions such as why they exist, what they want from life, and what the meaning of their life might be.

Religion, Spirituality, and Coping

What is the connection between religion, spirituality, and the ability to cope with stress? Researchers are increasingly finding that religion and spirituality are related to well-being (Masters & Hooker, 2013; Pirutinsky, 2013). A recent study revealed that highly religious individuals were less likely than their moderately religious, somewhat religious, and non-religious counterparts to be psychologically distressed (Park, 2013). Also, in a study of 850 medically ill patients admitted to an acute-care hospital, religious coping was related to low rates of depression (Koenig & others, 1992).

Religious coping is often beneficial during times of high stress (Pargament & others, 2013). For example, in one study individuals were divided into those who were experiencing high stress and those with low stress (Manton, 1989). In the high-stress group, spiritual support was significantly related to low rates of depression and high levels of self-esteem. No such links were found in the low-stress group. One study revealed that when religion was an important aspect of people's lives, they frequently prayed, had positive religious core beliefs, worried less, were less anxious, and had a lower level of depressive symptoms (Rosmarin, Krumrei, & Andersson, 2009).

How is religion linked to the ability to cope with stress?

A recent interest in linking religion and coping focuses on **meaning-making coping,** which involves drawing on beliefs, values, and goals to change the meaning of a stressful situation, especially in times of chronic stress such as when a loved one dies. In Crystal Park's (2005, 2007, 2010, 2013) view, religious individuals experience more disruption of their beliefs, values, and goals immediately after the death of a loved one than individuals who are not religious. Eventually, though, individuals who are religious often show better adjustment to the loss. Initially, religion is linked with more depressed feelings about a loved one's death. Over time, however, as religious individuals search for meaning in their loss, the depressed feelings lessen. Thus, religion can serve as a meaning system through which bereaved individuals are able to reframe their loss and even find avenues of personal growth.

If religion is linked to the ability to cope with stress better and if stress is linked to disease (as indicated earlier in the chapter), what then can be concluded about a possible indirect link between religion and disease?

It is in middle adulthood that individuals begin to be faced with death more often, especially the deaths of parents and other older relatives. Also faced with less time in their life, many individuals in middle age begin to ask and evaluate the questions that Frankl proposed (Cohen, 2009). And, as indicated in *Connecting Development to Life,* meaning-making coping is especially helpful in times of chronic stress and loss.

connecting with careers

Gabriel Dy-Liacco, University Professor and Pastoral Counselor

Gabriel Dy-Liacco currently is a professor in religious and pastoral counseling at Regent University in Virginia Beach, Virginia. He obtained his Ph.D. in pastoral counseling from Loyola College in Maryland and has worked as a psychotherapist in mental health settings such as a substance-abuse program, military family center, psychiatric clinic, and community mental health center. Earlier in his career he was a pastoral counselor at the Pastoral Counseling and Consultation Centers of Greater Washington, DC, and taught at Loyola University in Maryland. As a pastoral counselor, he works with adolescents and adults in the aspects of their lives that they show the most concern about—psychological, spiritual, or the interface of both. Having lived in Peru, Japan, and the Philippines, he brings considerable multicultural experience to teaching and counseling settings.

What characterizes the search for meaning in life?

Having a sense of meaning in life can lead to clearer guidelines for living one's life and enhanced motivation to take care of oneself and reach goals. A higher level of meaning in life also is linked to a higher level of psychological well-being and physical health (Park, 2012b).

Roy Baumeister and Kathleen Vohs (2002, pp. 610–611) argue that the quest for a meaningful life can be understood in terms of four main needs for meaning that guide how people try to make sense of their lives:

- *Need for purpose.* "Present events draw meaning from their connection with future events." Purposes can be divided into (1) goals and (2) fulfillments. Life can be oriented toward a future anticipated state, such as living happily ever after or being in love.
- *Need for values.* This "can lend a sense of goodness or positive characterization of life and justify certain courses of action. Values enable people to decide whether certain acts are right or wrong." Frankl's (1984) view of meaning in life emphasized value as the main form of meaning that people need.
- *Need for a sense of efficacy.* This involves the "belief that one can make a difference. A life that had purposes and values but no efficacy would be tragic. The person might know what is desirable but could not do anything with that knowledge." With a sense of efficacy, people believe that they can control their environment, which has positive physical and mental health benefits (Bandura, 2012).
- *Need for self-worth.* Most individuals want to be "good, worthy persons. Self-worth can be pursued individually."

Researchers are increasingly studying the factors involved in a person's exploration of meaning in life and whether developing a sense of meaning in life is linked to positive developmental outcomes. Research indicates that many individuals state that religion played an important role in increasing their exploration of meaning in life (Krause, 2008, 2009). Studies also suggest that individuals who have found a sense of meaning in life are more physically healthy, happier, and experience less depression than their counterparts who report that they have not discovered meaning in life (Debats, 1990; Krause, 2004, 2009).

Review *Connect* Reflect

 Explain the roles of religion, spirituality, and meaning in life during middle adulthood.

Review
- What are some characteristics of religion and spirituality in middle-aged individuals?
- How are religion and spirituality linked to physical and mental health?
- What role does meaning in life play in middle adulthood?

Connect
- In this section, you read about religion and spirituality and middle adulthood. In Chapter 12, what did you learn about the role of religion in adolescents' lives?

Reflect *Your Own Personal Journey of Life*
- How important is finding a meaning in life to you at this point in your development? What do you think the most important aspects of meaning in life are?

topical connections *looking forward*

In Chapter 17, you will read about biological views on why people age and what people can do to possibly slow down the aging process. You also will learn about the factors that influence life expectancy and what the lives of centenarians—people who live to be 100 or older—are like. The many physical changes that occur in late adulthood, including those involving the brain, also will be described in Chapter 17. In Chapter 18, you will learn about numerous cognitive changes in older adults, as well as the influences of work and retirement, mental health, and religion in their lives.

reach your **learning goals**

Physical and Cognitive Development in Middle Adulthood

1 The Nature of Middle Adulthood

LG1 Explain how midlife is changing, and define middle adulthood.

Changing Midlife

- As more people live to an older age, what we think of as middle age seems to be occurring later. A major reason developmentalists are beginning to study middle age is the dramatic increase in the number of individuals entering this period of the life span.

Defining Middle Adulthood

- Middle age involves extensive individual variation. With this variation in mind, we will consider middle adulthood to be entered at about 40 to 45 years of age and exited at approximately 60 to 65 years of age. Middle adulthood is the age period in which gains and losses as well as biological and sociocultural factors balance each other. Some experts conclude that sociocultural factors influence development in midlife more than biological factors do.

2 Physical Development

LG2 Discuss physical changes in middle adulthood.

Physical Changes

- The physical changes of midlife are usually gradual. Genetic and lifestyle factors play important roles in whether chronic diseases will appear and when. Among the physical changes of middle adulthood are changes in physical appearance (wrinkles, age spots); height (decrease) and weight (increase); strength, joints, and bones; vision and hearing; cardiovascular system; lungs; and sleep.

Health, Disease, Stress, and Control

- In middle age, the frequency of accidents declines and individuals are less susceptible to colds and allergies. Chronic disorders rarely appear in early adulthood, increase in middle adulthood, and become more common in late adulthood. Arthritis is the leading chronic disorder in middle age, followed by hypertension. Men have more fatal chronic disorders, women more nonfatal ones in middle age. Immune system functioning declines with age. Emotional stress likely is an important factor contributing to cardiovascular disease. People who live in a chronically stressed condition are more likely to smoke, overeat, and not exercise. All of these stress-related behaviors are linked with cardiovascular disease. Having a sense of control peaks in middle adulthood and is linked to many aspects of health and disease.

Mortality Rates

- In middle adulthood, chronic diseases are the main causes of death. Until recently, cardiovascular disease was the leading cause of death in middle age, but now cancer is the leading cause of death in this age group.

Sexuality

- Climacteric is the midlife transition in which fertility declines. The vast majority of women do not have serious physical or psychological problems related to menopause, which usually takes place in the late forties or early fifties, but menopause is an important marker because it signals the end of childbearing capability. Hormone replacement therapy (HRT) augments the declining levels of reproductive hormone production by the ovaries. HRT consists of various forms of estrogen, usually combined with progestin. Recent evidence of risks associated with HRT suggests that its long-term use should be seriously evaluated. Men do not experience an inability to father children in middle age, although their testosterone levels decline. A male menopause, like the dramatic decline in estrogen in women, does not occur. Sexual behavior occurs less frequently in middle adulthood than in early adulthood. Nonetheless, a majority of middle-aged adults show a moderate or strong interest in sex.

3 Cognitive Development

 LG3 Identify cognitive changes in middle adulthood.

Intelligence

- Horn argued that crystallized intelligence (accumulated information and verbal skills) continues to increase in middle adulthood, whereas fluid intelligence (ability to reason abstractly) begins to decline. Schaie and Willis found that longitudinal assessments of intellectual abilities are less likely than cross-sectional assessments to find declines in middle adulthood and are more likely to find improvements. The highest level of four intellectual abilities (vocabulary, verbal memory, inductive reasoning, and spatial orientation) occurred in middle age. Recent analysis shows considerable individual variation in intellectual abilities across middle adulthood and indicates that variations in some abilities are more predictive of cognitive impairment in late adulthood than others. Salthouse argues that decline in a number of cognitive functions begins in early adulthood and continues through the fifties. Declines have recently been identified in some aspects of neurobiological functioning that may be linked to age-related changes in cognitive functioning.

Information Processing

- Speed of information processing, often assessed through reaction time, continues to decline in middle adulthood. Although Schaie found that verbal memory increased in middle age, some researchers have found that memory declines in middle age. Working memory declines in late middle age. Memory is more likely to decline in middle age when individuals don't use effective strategies. Expertise involves having an extensive, highly organized knowledge and an understanding of a particular domain. Expertise often increases in middle adulthood. Practical problem solving remains stable in early and middle adulthood but declines in late adulthood.

4 Careers, Work, and Leisure

 LG4 Characterize career development, work, and leisure in middle adulthood.

Work in Midlife

- For many people, midlife is a time of reflection, assessment, and evaluation of their current work and what they plan to do in the future. One important issue is whether individuals will continue to do the type of work they currently do or change jobs or careers.

Career Challenges and Changes

- Today's middle-aged workers face challenges such as the globalization of work, rapid developments in information technologies, downsizing of organizations, pressure to take early retirement, and concerns about pensions and health care. Midlife job or career changes can be self-motivated or forced on individuals.

Leisure

- We not only need to learn to work well, but we also need to learn to enjoy leisure. Midlife may be an especially important time for leisure because of the physical changes that occur and because of a desire to prepare for an active retirement.

5 Religion, Spirituality, and Meaning in Life

 LG5 Explain the roles of religion, spirituality, and meaning in life during middle adulthood.

Religion, Spirituality, and Adult Lives

- Religion and spirituality are important dimensions of many Americans' lives. Women show a stronger interest in religion and spirituality than men do. It is important to consider individual differences in religious and spiritual interest.

Religion, Spirituality, and Health

- In some cases, religion and spirituality can be negatively linked to physical health, as when cults or religious sects discourage individuals from obtaining medical care. In mainstream religions, researchers are increasingly finding that religion is positively related to health. Religion and spirituality can enhance coping for some individuals.

Meaning in Life

- Frankl argues that examining the finiteness of our existence leads to exploration of meaning in life. Faced with the death of older relatives and less time to live themselves, many middle-aged individuals increasingly examine life's meaning. Baumeister and Vohs argue that a quest for a meaningful life involves fulfilling four main needs: purpose, values, efficacy, and self-worth.

key **terms**

middle adulthood 460
metabolic syndrome 464
chronic disorders 466
climacteric 467

menopause 467
erectile dysfunction (ED) 469
crystallized intelligence 471
fluid intelligence 471

leisure 476
religion 476
religiousness 476
spirituality 478

meaning-making
  coping 478

key **people**

Gilbert Brim 460
David Almeida 466
Sheldon Cohen 466
Margie Lachman 467
John Horn 471

K. Warner Schaie 471
Sherry Willis 472
Timothy Salthouse 473
Denise Park 474
Nancy Denney 474

Clas-Hakan Nygard 475
Pamela King 477
John Clausen 478
Viktor Frankl 478
Crystal Park 479

Roy Baumeister 480
Kathleen Vohs 480

chapter 16

SOCIOEMOTIONAL DEVELOPMENT IN MIDDLE ADULTHOOD

chapter **outline**

1 Personality Theories and Adult Development

Learning Goal 1 Describe personality theories and socioemotional development in middle adulthood.

Stages of Adulthood
The Life-Events Approach
Stress and Personal Control in Midlife
Contexts of Midlife Development

2 Stability and Change

Learning Goal 2 Discuss stability and change in development during middle adulthood, as reflected in longitudinal studies.

Longitudinal Studies
Conclusions

3 Close Relationships

Learning Goal 3 Identify some important aspects of close relationships in middle adulthood.

Love and Marriage at Midlife
The Empty Nest and Its Refilling
Sibling Relationships and Friendships
Grandparenting
Intergenerational Relationships

Forty-five-year-old Sarah feels tired, depressed, and angry when she looks back on the way her life has gone. She became pregnant when she was 17 and married Ben, the baby's father. They stayed together for three years after their son was born, and then Ben left her for another woman. Sarah went to work as a salesclerk to make ends meet. Eight years later, she married Alan, who had two children from a previous marriage. Sarah stopped working for several years to care for the children. Then, like Ben, Alan started seeing someone else. Sarah found out about it from a friend. Nevertheless, Sarah stayed with Alan for another year. Finally, he was gone so much that she could not take it anymore and decided to divorce him. Sarah went back to work again as a salesclerk; she has been in the same position for 16 years now. During those 16 years, she dated a number of men, but the relationships never seemed to work out. Her son never finished high school and has drug problems. Her father died last year, and Sarah is trying to help her mother financially, although she can barely pay her own bills. Sarah looks in the mirror and does not like what she sees. She sees her past as a shambles, and her future does not look rosy, either.

Forty-five-year-old Wanda feels energetic, happy, and satisfied. As a young woman, she graduated from college and worked for three years as a high school math teacher. She married Andy, who had just finished law school. One year later, they had their first child, Josh. Wanda stayed home with Josh for two years, and then returned to her job as a math teacher. Even during her pregnancy, Wanda stayed active and exercised regularly, playing tennis almost every day. After her pregnancy, she kept up her exercise habits. Wanda and Andy had another child, Wendy. Now, as they move into their middle-age years, their children are both off at college, and Wanda and Andy are enjoying spending more time with each other. Last weekend, they visited Josh at his college, and the weekend before they visited Wendy at hers. Wanda continued working as a high school math teacher until six years ago. She had developed computer skills as part of her job and had taken some computer courses at a nearby college. She resigned her math teaching job and took a job with a computer company, where she has already worked her way into management. Wanda looks in the mirror and likes what she sees. She sees her past as enjoyable, although not without hills and valleys, and she looks toward the future with enthusiasm.

topical connections *looking back*

Emerging adulthood, which occurs from approximately 18 to 25 years of age, is a transitional period between adolescence and early adulthood—a time when individuals intensely explore their identity and experience instability in different contexts. A secure attachment style benefits young adults. Love and possibly marriage become central aspects of many young adults' socioemotional development. Searching for a balance between the need for independence and freedom and the need for intimacy and commitment characterizes the lives of many young adults. Many young adults not only are marrying later or not at all but are having children later than in past decades, and many choose to cohabit with a romantic partner.

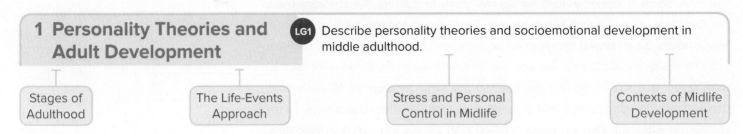

preview

As with Sarah and Wanda, there are individual variations in the way people experience middle age. To begin the chapter, we will examine personality theories and development in middle age, including ideas about individual variation. Then we will turn our attention to the ways in which individuals change or stay the same as they go through the adult years. Finally we will explore a number of aspects of close relationships during middle adulthood.

1 Personality Theories and Adult Development

LG1 Describe personality theories and socioemotional development in middle adulthood.

Stages of Adulthood

The Life-Events Approach

Stress and Personal Control in Midlife

Contexts of Midlife Development

The generations of living things pass in a short time, and like runners, hand on the torch of life.

—LUCRETIUS
Roman Poet, 1st Century B.C.

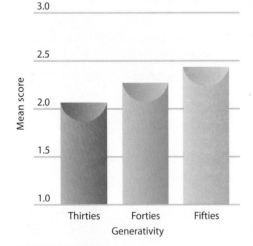

FIGURE 16.1

CHANGES IN GENERATIVITY FROM THE THIRTIES THROUGH THE FIFTIES. Generativity increased in Smith College women as they aged from their thirties through their fifties (Stewart, Ostrove, & Helson, 2001). The women rated themselves on a 3-point scale indicating the extent to which they thought the statements about generativity were descriptive of their lives. Higher scores reflect greater generativity.

What is the best way to conceptualize middle age? Is it a stage or a crisis? How extensively is middle age influenced by life events? Do middle-aged adults experience stress and personal control differently from adults at other life stages? Is personality linked with contexts such as the point in history when individuals go through midlife, their culture, and their gender?

STAGES OF ADULTHOOD

Adult stage theories have been plentiful, and they have contributed to the view that midlife brings a crisis in development. Two prominent theories that define stages of adult development are Erik Erikson's life-span view and Daniel Levinson's seasons of a man's life.

Erikson's Stage of Generativity Versus Stagnation Erikson (1968) proposed that middle-aged adults face a significant issue—generativity versus stagnation, which is the name Erikson gave to the seventh stage in his life-span theory. Generativity encompasses adults' desire to leave legacies of themselves to the next generation (Busch & Hofer, 2012; Tabuchi & others, 2014). Through these legacies adults achieve a kind of immortality. By contrast, stagnation (sometimes called "self-absorption") develops when individuals sense that they have done nothing for the next generation.

Middle-aged adults can develop generativity in a number of ways (Kotre, 1984). Through biological generativity, adults have offspring. Through parental generativity, adults nurture and guide children. Through work generativity, adults develop skills that are passed down to others. And through cultural generativity, adults create, renovate, or conserve some aspect of culture that ultimately survives.

Adults promote and guide the next generation by parenting, teaching, leading, and doing things that benefit the community. One of the participants in a study of aging said: "From twenty to thirty I learned how to get along with my wife. From thirty to forty I learned how to be a success at my job, and at forty to fifty I worried less about myself and more about the children" (Vaillant, 2002, p. 114). Generative adults commit themselves to the continuation and improvement of society as a whole through their connection to the next generation. Generative adults develop a positive legacy of the self and then offer it as a gift to the next generation.

Does research support Erikson's theory that generativity is an important dimension of middle age? Yes, it does (Newton & Stewart, 2012). In George Vaillant's (2002) longitudinal studies of aging, generativity (defined in this study as "taking care of the next generation") in middle age was more strongly related than intimacy to whether individuals would have an enduring and happy marriage at 75 to 80 years of age.

Other research also supports Erikson's (1968) view on the importance of generativity in middle adulthood. In one study, Carol Ryff (1984) examined the views of women and men at different ages and found that middle-aged adults especially were concerned about generativity. In a longitudinal study of Smith College women, the desire for generativity increased as the participants aged from their thirties to their fifties (Stewart, Ostrove, & Helson, 2001) (see Figure 16.1).

Levinson's Seasons of a Man's Life In *The Seasons of a Man's Life* (1978), clinical psychologist Daniel Levinson reported the results of extensive interviews with 40 middle-aged men. The interviews were conducted with hourly workers, business executives, academic biologists, and novelists. Levinson bolstered his conclusions with information from the biographies of famous men and the development of memorable characters in literature. Although Levinson's major interest focused on midlife change, he described a number of stages and transitions during the period from 17 to 65 years of age, as shown in Figure 16.2. Levinson emphasizes that developmental tasks must be mastered at each stage.

At the end of one's teens, according to Levinson, a transition from dependence to independence should occur. This transition is marked by the formation of a dream—an image of the kind of life the youth wants to have, especially in terms of a career and marriage. Levinson sees the twenties as a novice phase of adult development. It is a time of reasonably free experimentation and of testing the dream in the real world. In early adulthood, the two major tasks to be mastered are exploring the possibilities for adult living and developing a stable life structure.

From about the ages of 28 to 33, a man goes through a transition period in which he must face the more serious question of determining his goals. During his thirties, he usually focuses on family and career development. In the later years of this period, he enters a phase of Becoming One's Own Man (or BOOM, as Levinson calls it). By age 40, he has reached a stable point in his career, has outgrown his earlier, more tenuous attempts at learning to become an adult, and now must look forward to the kind of life he will lead as a middle-aged adult.

According to Levinson, the transition to middle adulthood lasts about five years (ages 40 to 45) and requires the adult male to come to grips with four major conflicts that have existed in his life since adolescence: (1) being young versus being old, (2) being destructive versus being constructive, (3) being masculine versus being feminine, and (4) being attached to others versus being separated from them. Seventy to 80 percent of the men Levinson interviewed found the midlife transition tumultuous and psychologically painful, as many aspects of their lives came into question. According to Levinson, the success of the midlife transition rests on how effectively the individual reduces the polarities and accepts each of them as an integral part of his being.

Because Levinson interviewed middle-aged men, we can consider the data about middle adulthood more valid than the data about early adulthood. When individuals are asked to remember information about earlier parts of their lives, they may distort and forget things. The original Levinson data included no women, although Levinson (1996) reported that his stages, transitions, and the crisis of middle age hold for women as well as men. Levinson's work included no statistical analysis. However, the quality and quantity of the Levinson biographies make them outstanding examples of the clinical tradition.

How Pervasive Are Midlife Crises? Levinson (1978) views midlife as a crisis, arguing that the middle-aged adult is suspended between the past and the future, trying to cope with this gap that threatens life's continuity. George Vaillant (1977) has a different view. Vaillant's study—called the "Grant Study"—involved Harvard University men in their early thirties and in their late forties who initially had been interviewed as undergraduates. He concludes that just as adolescence is a time for detecting parental flaws and discovering the truth about childhood, the forties are a decade of reassessing and recording the truth about the adolescent and adulthood years. However, whereas Levinson sees midlife as a crisis, Vaillant maintains that only a minority of adults experience a midlife crisis:

> Just as pop psychologists have reveled in the not-so-common high drama of adolescent turmoil, just so the popular press, sensing good copy, has made all too much of the midlife crisis. The term *midlife crisis* brings to mind some variation of the renegade minister who leaves behind four children and the congregation that loved him in order to drive off in a magenta Porsche with a 25-year-old striptease artiste. . . . As with adolescent turmoil, midlife crises are much rarer in community samples than in clinical samples. (pp. 222–223)

Late adult transition: Age 60 to 65

Era of late adulthood: 60 to ?

Middle adult transition: Age 40 to 45

Culminating life structure for middle adulthood: 55 to 60

Age 50 transition: 50 to 55

Entry life structure for middle adulthood: 45 to 50

Early adult transition: Age 17 to 22

Culminating life structure for early adulthood: 33 to 40

Age 30 transition: 28 to 33

Entry life structure for early adulthood: 22 to 28

FIGURE **16.2**

LEVINSON'S PERIODS OF ADULT DEVELOPMENT. According to Daniel Levinson, adulthood for men has three main stages that are surrounded by transition periods. Specific tasks and challenges are associated with each stage.

developmental **connection**

Personality

Erikson's early adulthood stage is intimacy versus isolation and his late adulthood stage is integrity versus despair. Chapter 14, p. 438; Chapter 19, p. 569

Midlife crises are greatly exaggerated in America.

—**GEORGE VAILLANT**

Contemporary Psychologist, Harvard University

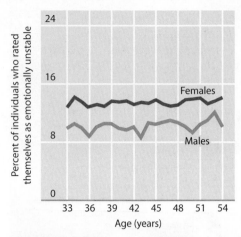

FIGURE 16.3

EMOTIONAL INSTABILITY AND AGE. In one longitudinal study, the emotional instability of individuals was assessed from age 33 to age 54 (McCrae & Costa, 1990). No significant increase in emotional instability occurred during the middle-aged years.

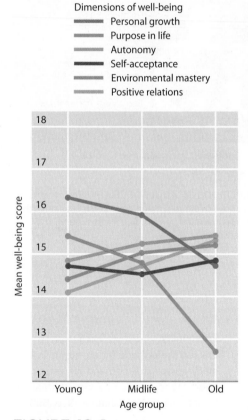

FIGURE 16.4

AGE AND WELL-BEING. In one study, six dimensions of well-being (self-acceptance, positive relations, personal growth, purpose in life, environmental mastery, and autonomy) were assessed in three different age groups of individuals (young adults, middle-aged adults, and older adults) (Keyes & Ryff, 1998). An increase or little change in most of the dimensions of well-being occurred during middle adulthood.

Thus, for most people midlife is not a crisis (Pudrovska, 2009). As we saw in Chapter 15, many cognitive skills, such as vocabulary, verbal memory, and inductive reasoning, peak in midlife, and many individuals reach the height of their career success in midlife. Further, feelings of general well-being and life satisfaction tend to be reported as high by people in middle adulthood (Martin, Grunendahl, & Martin, 2001).

A number of research studies have documented that midlife is not characterized by pervasive crises:

- One study found that 26 percent of middle-aged U.S. adults said they had experienced a midlife crisis, but most attributed the crisis to negative life events rather than aging (Wethington, Kessler, & Pixley, 2004).

- A longitudinal study of more than 2,000 individuals found few midlife crises (McCrae & Costa, 1990; Siegler & Costa, 1999). In this study, the emotional instability of individuals did not significantly increase during their middle-aged years (see Figure 16.3).

- A study of individuals described as young adults (average age 19), middle-aged adults (average age 46), and older adults (average age 73) found that their ability to master their environment, autonomy, and personal relations improved during middle age (Keyes & Ryff, 1998) (see Figure 16.4).

Adult development experts are virtually unanimous in their belief that midlife crises have been exaggerated (Brim, Ryff, & Kessler, 2004; Lachman, 2004; Pudrovska, 2009; Wethington, Kessler, & Pixley, 2004). In sum:

- The stage theories place too much emphasis on crises in development, especially midlife crises.

- There often is considerable individual variation in the way people experience the stages, a topic that we will turn to next.

Individual Variations   Stage theories focus on the universals of adult personality development as they try to pin down stages that all individuals go through in their adult lives. These theories do not adequately address individual variations in adult development. One extensive study of a random sample of 500 men at midlife, for example, found extensive individual variation among men (Farrell & Rosenberg, 1981). In the individual variations view, middle-aged adults interpret, shape, alter, and give meaning to their lives.

Some individuals may experience a midlife crisis in some contexts of their lives but not others (Lachman, 2004). For example, turmoil and stress may characterize a person's life at work even while things are going smoothly at home.

Researchers have found that in one-third of the cases in which individuals have reported going through a midlife crisis, the "crisis is triggered by life events such as a job loss, financial problems, or illness" (Lachman, 2004, p. 315). Let's now explore the role of life events in midlife development.

THE LIFE-EVENTS APPROACH

Age-related stages represent one major way to examine adult personality development. A second major way to conceptualize adult personality development is to focus on life events (Luhmann & others, 2012; Schwarzer & Luszezynska, 2013). In the early version of the life-events approach, life events were viewed as taxing circumstances for individuals, forcing them to change their personality (Holmes & Rahe, 1967). Events such as the death of a spouse, divorce, marriage, and so on were believed to involve varying degrees of stress, and therefore likely to influence the individual's development.

Today's life-events approach is more sophisticated. In the **contemporary life-events approach,** how life events influence the individual's development depends not only on the life event itself but also on mediating factors (such as physical health and family supports), the individual's adaptation to the life event (such as appraisal of the threat and coping strategies), the life-stage context, and the sociohistorical context (see Figure 16.5).

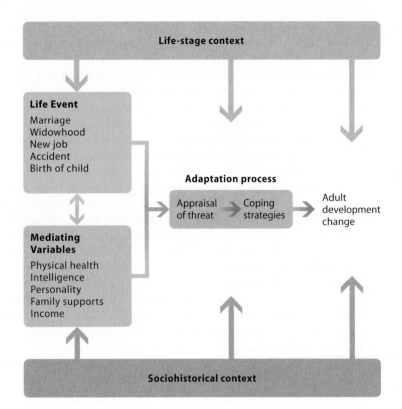

FIGURE **16.5**

A CONTEMPORARY LIFE-EVENTS FRAMEWORK FOR INTERPRETING ADULT DEVELOPMENTAL CHANGE. According to the contemporary life-events approach, the influence of a life event depends on the event itself, on mediating variables, on the life-stage and sociohistorical context, and on the individual's appraisal of the event and coping strategies.

For example, if individuals are in poor health and have little family support, life events are likely to be more stressful. And a divorce may be more stressful after many years of marriage when adults are in their fifties than when they have been married only several years and are in their twenties, a finding indicating that the life-stage context of an event makes a difference. The sociohistorical context also makes a difference. For example, adults may be able to cope more effectively with divorce today than in the 1950s because divorce has become more commonplace and accepted in today's society. Whatever the context or mediating variables, however, one individual may perceive a life event as highly stressful, whereas another individual may perceive the same event as a challenge.

Although the life-events approach offers valuable insights for understanding adult development, it has its drawbacks. One drawback is that the life-events approach places too much emphasis on change. It does not adequately recognize the stability that, at least to some degree, characterizes adult development.

Another drawback is that it may not be life's major events that are the primary sources of stress, but our daily experiences (Almeida & others, 2011; Hamilton & Julian, 2014; Jacob & others, 2014). Enduring a boring but tense job or living in poverty does not show up on scales of major life events. Yet the everyday pounding from these conditions can add up to a highly stressful life and eventually lead to illness. Greater insight into the source of life's stresses might come from focusing more on daily hassles and daily uplifts (McIntosh, Gillanders, & Rodgers, 2010). Researchers have found that young and middle-aged adults experience a greater daily frequency of stressors than older adults (Almeida & Horn, 2004). In one study, healthy older adult women 63 to 93 years of age reported their daily experiences over the course of one week (Charles & others, 2010). In this study, the older a woman was, the fewer stressors and less frequent negative affect she reported. Also, in recent research, greater emotional reactivity to daily stressors was linked to increased risk of reporting a chronic physical health condition and anxiety/mood disorders 10 years later (Charles & others, 2013; Piazza & others, 2013). Further, a recent study found that daily stressors were linked to cortisol secretion (cortisol is the body's primary stress hormone) in older adults who were experiencing depression and anxiety (Vasiliadis, Forget, & Preville, 2013). And a recent study of adults (mean age = 57 years) revealed that higher levels of daily stressors were associated with increased cortisol output, especially if the stressors included arguments and other problems at home (Stawski & others, 2013).

contemporary life-events approach Approach emphasizing that how a life event influences the individual's development depends not only on the life event, but also on mediating factors, the individual's adaptation to the life event, the life-stage context, and the sociohistorical context.

Daily Hassles	Percentage of Times Checked
Concerns about weight	52.4
Health of family member	48.1
Rising prices of common goods	43.7
Home maintenance	42.8
Too many things to do	38.6
Misplacing or losing things	38.1
Yardwork/outside home maintenance	38.1
Property, investment, or taxes	37.6
Crime	37.1
Physical appearance	35.9

Daily Uplifts	
Relating well with your spouse or lover	76.3
Relating well with friends	74.4
Completing a task	73.3
Feeling healthy	72.7
Getting enough sleep	69.7
Eating out	68.4
Meeting your responsibilities	68.1
Visiting, phoning, or writing someone	67.7
Spending time with family	66.7
Home (inside) pleasing to you	65.5

FIGURE 16.6

THE TEN MOST FREQUENT DAILY HASSLES AND UPLIFTS OF MIDDLE-AGED ADULTS OVER A NINE-MONTH PERIOD. *How do these hassles and uplifts compare with your own?*

developmental **connection**

Stress

Adolescence has been characterized too negatively, dating from Hall's storm and stress view of adolescents. Chapter 11, p. 340

fight-or-flight The view that when men experience stress, they are more likely to engage in a fight-or-flight pattern, as reflected in being aggressive, withdrawing from social contact, or drinking alcohol.

tend-and-befriend Taylor's view that when women experience stress, they are likely to engage in a tend-and-befriend pattern, seeking social alliances with others, especially female friends.

One study found that the daily hassles most frequently reported by college students were wasting time, concerns about meeting high standards, and being lonely (Kanner & others, 1981). Among the uplifts reported most frequently by the college students were entertainment, getting along well with friends, and completing a task. In this same study, the daily hassles reported most often by middle-aged adults were concerns about weight and the health of a family member, while their most frequently reported daily uplifts involved relating well with a spouse or lover, or a friend (see Figure 16.6). And the middle-aged adults were more likely than the college students to report that their daily hassles involved economic concerns (rising prices and taxes, for example).

The manner in which different stressors affect health varies—life events often produce prolonged arousal whereas daily stressors are linked to spikes in arousal (Piazza & others, 2010). Consider caring for a spouse who has Alzheimer disease. In this case, a life event (spouse diagnosed with an incurable disease) produces chronic stress for the caregiver, which also is linked to the daily stressors involved in caring for the individual.

Critics of the daily hassles approach argue that some of the same problems involved with life-events scales occur when daily hassles are assessed. For example, knowing about an adult's daily hassles tells us nothing about physical changes, about how the individual copes with hassles, or about how the individual perceives hassles.

STRESS AND PERSONAL CONTROL IN MIDLIFE

As we have seen, there is conclusive evidence that midlife is not a time when a majority of adults experience a tumultuous crisis, but if they do experience a midlife crisis it is often linked to stressful life events. Do middle-aged adults experience stress differently from young adults and older adults?

Stress, Personal Control, and Age   One study using daily diaries over a one-week period found that both young and middle-aged adults had more days that were stressful and that were characterized by multiple stresses than older adults (Almeida & Horn, 2004). In this study, although young adults experienced daily stressors more frequently than middle-aged adults, middle-aged adults experienced more "overload" stressors that involved juggling too many activities at once. Another study also revealed that middle-aged and older adults showed a smaller increase in psychological distress to interpersonal stressors than did younger adults, and middle-aged adults were less physically reactive to work stressors than were younger adults (Neupert, Almeida, & Charles, 2007).

To what extent do middle-aged adults perceive that they can control what happens to them? As you read in Chapter 15, researchers have found that on average a sense of personal control peaks in midlife and then declines (Lachman, 2006). In one study, approximately 80 percent of the young adults (25 to 39 years of age), 71 percent of the middle-aged adults (40 to 59 years of age), and 62 percent of the older adults (60 to 75 years of age) reported that they were often in control of their lives (Lachman & Firth, 2004). However, some aspects of personal control increase with age while others decrease (Lachman, Neupert, & Agrigoroaei, 2011). For example, middle-aged adults feel a greater sense of control over their finances, work, and marriage than younger adults but less control over their sex life and their children (Lachman & Firth, 2004).

Stress and Gender   Women and men differ in the way they experience and respond to stressors (Almeida & others, 2011). Women are more vulnerable to social stressors such as those involving romance, family, and work. For example, women experience higher levels of stress than men do when things go wrong in romantic and marital relationships. Women also are more likely than men to become depressed when they encounter stressful life events such as divorce or the death of a friend. A recent study of more than 2,800 adults 50 years and older in Taiwan also found that women were more susceptible to depressive symptoms when they felt constant stress from finances, increasing stress from jobs, and fluctuating stress in family relationships (Lin & others, 2011).

When men face stress, they are more likely to respond in a **fight-or-flight** manner—to become aggressive, withdraw from social contact, or drink alcohol. By contrast, according to Shelley Taylor and her colleagues (2011a, b, c; Taylor & others, 2000), when women experience stress, they are more likely to engage in a **tend-and-befriend** pattern, seeking social alliances with others, especially friends. Taylor argues that when women experience stress an influx of the hormone *oxytocin*, which is linked to nurturing in animals, is released.

CONTEXTS OF MIDLIFE DEVELOPMENT

Both Sarah and Wanda, whose stories appeared at the beginning of this chapter, are working mothers. In almost every other way, however, their lives could scarcely be more different. Why? Part of the answer might lie in the different contexts of their lives. The contemporary life-events approach (like Bronfenbrenner's theory, discussed in Chapter 1) highlights the importance of the complex setting of our lives—of everything from our income and family supports to our sociohistorical circumstances. Let's examine how three aspects of the contexts of life influence development during middle adulthood: historical contexts (cohort effects), gender, and culture.

Historical Contexts (Cohort Effects)   Some developmentalists conclude that changing historical times and different social expectations influence how different cohorts—groups of individuals born in the same year or time period—move through the life span (Schaie, 2010, 2013). Bernice Neugarten (1986) argues that our values, attitudes, expectations, and behaviors are influenced by the period in which we live. For example, individuals born during the difficult times of the Great Depression may have a different outlook on life from those born during the optimistic 1950s, says Neugarten.

Neugarten (1986) holds that the social environment of a particular age group can alter its **social clock**—the timetable on which individuals are expected to accomplish life's tasks, such as getting married, having children, or establishing themselves in a career. Social clocks provide guides for our lives; individuals whose lives are not synchronized with these social clocks find life to be more stressful than those who are on schedule, says Neugarten. For example, the fact that Sarah's pregnancy occurred when she was a teenager probably increased the stressfulness of that pregnancy. Neugarten argues that today there is much less agreement than in the past on the right age or sequence for the occurrence of major life events such as having children or retiring. Indeed, one study found that between the late 1950s and the late 1970s, there was a dramatic decline in adults' beliefs that there is a "best age" for major life events and achievements (Passuth, Maines, & Neugarten, 1984) (see Figure 16.7).

Gender Contexts   Critics say that the stage theories of adult development have a male bias. For example, the central focus of stage theories is on career choice and work achievement, which historically have dominated men's life choices and life chances more than women's. The stage theories do not adequately address women's concerns about relationships, interdependence, and caring (Gilligan, 1982). The adult stage theories have also placed little importance on childbearing and child rearing. Women's family roles are complex and often have a higher salience in their lives than in men's lives. The role demands that women experience in balancing career and family are usually not experienced as intensely by men.

Should midlife and the years beyond be feared by women as a time of declining youth and opportunity? Or is middle adulthood a new prime of life, a time for renewal, for shedding preoccupations with a youthful appearance and body, and for seeking new challenges, valuing maturity, and enjoying change?

How do women and men differ in the way they experience and respond to stressors?

developmental **connection**

Research Methods

Cohort effects have also been described as normative, history-graded influences. Chapter 1, p. 32

Critics say the stage theories of adult development reflect a male bias by emphasizing career choice and achievement, and that they do not adequately address women's concerns about relationships, interdependence, and caring. The stage theories assume a normative sequence of development, but as women's roles have become more varied and complex, determining what is normative is difficult. *What kinds of changes have taken place in the lives of middle-aged women in recent years?*

social clock The timetable according to which individuals are expected to accomplish life's tasks, such as getting married, having children, or establishing themselves in a career.

Late '50s Study

Late '70s Study

Activity/event	Appropriate age range	Percent who agree (late '50s study)		Percent who agree (late '70s study)	
		Men	Women	Men	Women
Best age for a man to marry	20–25	80	90	42	42
Best age for a woman to marry	19–24	85	90	44	36
When most people should become grandparents	45–50	84	79	64	57
Best age for most people to finish school and go to work	20–22	86	82	36	38
When most men should be settled on a career	24–26	74	64	24	26
When most men hold their top jobs	45–50	71	58	38	31
When most people should be ready to retire	60–65	83	86	66	41
When a man has the most responsibilities	35–50	79	75	49	50
When a man accomplishes most	40–50	82	71	46	41
The prime of life for a man	35–50	86	80	59	66
When a woman has the most responsibilities	25–40	93	91	59	53
When a woman accomplishes the most	30–45	94	92	57	48

FIGURE 16.7

INDIVIDUALS' CONCEPTIONS OF THE BEST AGE FOR MAJOR LIFE EVENTS AND ACHIEVEMENTS: LATE 1950S AND LATE 1970S. *What do you think is the best age to experience each of these major life events and accomplishments?*

Gusii dancers perform on habitat day in Nairobi, Kenya. Movement from one status to another in the Gusii culture is due primarily to life events, not age. The Gusii do not have a clearly labeled midlife transition.

In one study, the early fifties were indeed a new prime of life for many women (Mitchell & Helson, 1990). In this sample of 700 women aged 26 to 80, women in their early fifties most often described their lives as "first-rate." Conditions that distinguished the lives of women in their early fifties from those of women in other age periods included more "empty nests," better health, higher income, and more concern for parents. Women in their early fifties showed confidence, involvement, security, and breadth of personality.

In sum, the view that midlife is a negative age period for women is stereotypical, as so many perceptions of age periods are. Midlife is a diversified, heterogeneous period for women, just as it is for men.

Cultural Contexts In many cultures, especially nonindustrialized cultures, the concept of middle age is not very clear, or in some cases is absent. It is common in nonindustrialized societies to describe individuals as young or old but not as middle-aged (Grambs, 1989). Some cultures have no words for "adolescent," "young adult," or "middle-aged adult."

Consider the Gusii culture, located in the African country of Kenya. The Gusii divide the life course differently for females and males (LeVine, 1979): females: (1) infant, (2) uncircumcised girl, (3) circumcised girl, (4) married woman, and (5) female elder; males: (1) infant, (2) uncircumcised boy, (3) circumcised boy warrior, and (4) male elder. Thus, movement from one status to the next is due primarily to life events, not age, in the Gusii culture.

Although the Gusii do not have a clearly labeled midlife transition, some of the Gusii adults do reassess their lives around the age of 40. At this time, these Gusii adults examine their current status and the limited time they have remaining in their lives. Their physical strength is decreasing, and they know they cannot farm their land forever, so they seek spiritual powers by becoming ritual practitioners or healers. As in the American culture, however, a midlife crisis in the Gusii culture is the exception rather than the rule.

Review *Connect* Reflect

LG1 Describe personality theories and socioemotional development in middle adulthood.

Review

- What are some theories of adult stages of development?
- What is the life-events approach?
- How do middle-aged adults experience stress and personal control differently from young and older adults?
- How do contexts influence midlife development?

Connect

- In this section, you read that some researchers criticize the stage theories

of adult development as having a male bias. What did you learn about gender bias in research in Chapter 1?

Reflect *Your Own Personal Journey of Life*

- Which approach makes more sense—adult stage or life events—in explaining your own development as you go through adulthood? Or do you think both approaches should be considered in understanding your adult development? Explain your answer.

---

2 Stability and Change

LG2 Discuss stability and change in development during middle adulthood, as reflected in longitudinal studies.

Longitudinal Studies	Conclusions

Sarah's adult life, described in the chapter opening, has followed a painful path. Were her sorrows an inevitable result of how she learned to cope with problems earlier in life? Is it possible for her, in middle age, to change her coping strategies or how she relates to other people?

LONGITUDINAL STUDIES

We will examine four longitudinal studies that can help us understand the extent to which there is stability or change in adult development: Costa and McCrae's Baltimore Study, the Berkeley Longitudinal Studies, Helson's Mills College Study, and Vaillant's studies.

Costa and McCrae's Baltimore Study   A major, ongoing study of adult personality development is being conducted by Paul Costa and Robert McCrae (1998; McCrae & Costa, 2003, 2006). They focus on what are called the **Big Five factors of personality,** which are openness to experience, conscientiousness, extraversion, agreeableness, and neuroticism (emotional stability); these personality factors are described in Figure 16.8. (Notice that if you create an acronym from these factor names, you will get the word OCEAN.) A number of research studies point toward these factors as important dimensions of personality (Hill & others, 2012; Hill, Nickel & Roberts, 2014; Mike & others, 2014; Roberts & others, 2014).

Big Five factors of personality Emotional stability (neuroticism), extraversion, openness to experience, agreeableness, and conscientiousness.

Openness	**C**onscientiousness	**E**xtraversion	**A**greeableness	**N**euroticism (emotional stability)
• Imaginative or practical	• Organized or disorganized	• Sociable or retiring	• Softhearted or ruthless	• Calm or anxious
• Interested in variety or routine	• Careful or careless	• Fun-loving or somber	• Trusting or suspicious	• Secure or insecure
• Independent or conforming	• Disciplined or impulsive	• Affectionate or reserved	• Helpful or uncooperative	• Self-satisfied or self-pitying

FIGURE **16.8**

THE BIG FIVE FACTORS OF PERSONALITY. Each of the broad supertraits encompasses more narrow traits and characteristics. Use the acronym OCEAN to remember the Big Five personality factors: openness, conscientiousness, extraversion, agreeableness, and neuroticism.

Using their five-factor personality test, Costa and McCrae (1995, 2000) studied approximately 1,000 college-educated men and women ages 20 to 96, assessing the same individuals over many years. Data collection began in the 1950s and is ongoing. Costa and McCrae concluded that considerable stability occurs in the five personality factors—emotional stability, extraversion, openness, agreeableness, and conscientiousness. However, more recent research indicates greater developmental changes in the five personality factors in adulthood (Kranz Graham & Lachman, 2013; Lucas & Donnellan, 2011; Soto & others, 2011). For example, a recent study found that emotional stability, extraversion, openness, and agreeableness were lower in early adulthood, peaked between 40 and 60 years of age, and decreased in late adulthood, while conscientiousness showed a continuous increase from early adulthood to late adulthood (Specht, Egloff, & Schukle, 2011). Most research studies indicate that the greatest change occurs in early adulthood (Hill, Allemand, & Roberts, 2014: Lucas & Donnellan, 2011; Roberts, Donnellan, & Hill, 2013).

Further evidence for the importance of the Big Five factors indicates that they are related to such important aspects of a person's life as health, intelligence, achievement and work, relationships, and happiness (Quoidbach, Gilbert, & Wilson, 2013; McCrae, Gaines, & Wellington, 2013; Soto, 2014). Researchers also have found that personality stability or changes in a positive direction (lower neuroticism, for example) are associated with better health and more competent cognitive functioning (Kranz Graham & Lachman, 2013; Turiano & others, 2012). The following research reflects such connections of personality traits to other aspects of people's lives:

- Across a 10-year period, four of the five factors (the exception being openness) predicted outcomes involving physical health, blood pressure, and number of days limited at work or home due to physical health problems (Turiano & others, 2012). Individuals high on neuroticism report more health complaints (Carver & Connor-Smith, 2010).

- A study found that conscientiousness was related to college students' grade point averages (Noftle & Robins, 2007).

- A meta-analysis revealed that openness was linked to pursuing entrepreneurial goals such as starting a new business, and to success in those pursuits (Zhao, Seibert, & Lumpkin, 2010).

- Individuals high on agreeableness were more likely to have satisfying romantic relationships (Donnellan, Larsen-Rife, & Conger, 2005).

Berkeley Longitudinal Studies   In the Berkeley Longitudinal Studies, more than 500 children and their parents were initially studied in the late 1920s and early 1930s. The book *Present and Past in Middle Life* (Eichorn & others, 1981) profiles these individuals as they became middle-aged. The results from early adolescence through a portion of midlife did not support either extreme in the debate over whether personality is characterized by stability or change. Some characteristics were more stable than others, however. The most stable characteristics were the degree to which individuals were intellectually oriented, self-confident, and open to new experiences. The characteristics that changed the most included the extent to which the individuals were nurturant or hostile and whether or not they had good self-control.

John Clausen (1993), one of the researchers in the Berkeley Longitudinal Studies, stresses that too much attention has been given to discontinuities for all members of the human species, as exemplified in the adult stage theories. He points out that some people experience recurrent crises and undergo substantial changes over the life course, whereas others have more stable, continuous lives entailing very little change.

Helson's Mills College Study   Another longitudinal investigation of adult personality development was conducted by Ravenna Helson and her colleagues (George, Helson, & John, 2011; Helson, 1997; Helson & Wink, 1992; Stewart, Ostrove, & Helson, 2001). They initially studied 132 women who were seniors at Mills College in California in the late 1950s and then studied them again when they were in their thirties, forties, and fifties. Helson and her colleagues distinguished three main groups among the Mills women: family-oriented, career-oriented (whether or not they also wanted families), and those who followed neither path (women without children who pursued only low-level work).

Based on their study of middle-aged women, Ravenna Helson and her colleagues described the women as experiencing a midlife consciousness rather than a midlife crisis. *What were some other findings in the Mills College study?*

During their early forties, many of the women shared the concerns that stage theorists such as Levinson found in men: concern for young and old, introspectiveness, interest in roots, and awareness of limitations and death. However, the researchers in the Mills College Study concluded that rather than being in a midlife crisis, the women were experiencing *midlife consciousness*. The researchers also discovered that commitment to the tasks of early adulthood—whether to a career or family (or both)—helped women learn to control their impulses, develop interpersonal skills, become independent, and work hard to achieve goals. Women who did not commit themselves to one of these lifestyle patterns faced fewer challenges and did not develop as fully as the other women (Rosenfeld & Stark, 1987).

In the Mills College Study, some women moved toward becoming "pillars of society" in their early forties to early fifties. Menopause, caring for aging parents, and an empty nest were not associated with an increase in responsibility and self-control (Helson & Wink, 1992). And as you read earlier, in a recent study that assessed the Mills College women from their twenties to their seventies, the Big Five factors were linked to changing historical circumstances in the women's lives (George, Helson, & John, 2011).

George Vaillant's Studies

Longitudinal studies by George Vaillant help us explore a question that differs somewhat from the topics examined by the studies described so far: Does personality at middle age predict what a person's life will be like in late adulthood? Vaillant (2002) has conducted three longitudinal studies of adult development and aging: (1) a sample of 268 socially advantaged Harvard graduates born about 1920 (called the Grant Study); (2) a sample of 456 socially disadvantaged inner-city men born about 1930; and (3) a sample of 90 middle-SES, intellectually gifted women born about 1910. These individuals have been assessed numerous times (in most cases, every two years), beginning in the 1920s to 1940s and continuing today for those still living. The main assessments involve extensive interviews with the participants, their parents, and teachers.

Vaillant categorized 75- to 80-year-olds as "happy-well," "sad-sick," or "dead." He used data collected from these individuals when they were 50 years of age to predict which categories they were likely to end up in at 75 to 80 years of age. Alcohol abuse and smoking at age 50 were the best predictors of which individuals would be dead at 75 to 80 years of age. Other factors at age 50 that were linked with being in the "happy-well" category at 75 to 80 years of age included getting regular exercise, avoiding being overweight, being well educated, having a stable marriage, being future-oriented, being thankful and forgiving, empathizing with others, being active with other people, and having good coping skills.

Wealth and income at age 50 were not linked with being in the "happy-well" category at 75 to 80 years of age. Generativity in middle age (defined as "taking care of the next generation") was more strongly related than intimacy to whether individuals would have an enduring and happy marriage at 75 to 80 years of age (Vaillant, 2002).

The results for one of Vaillant's studies, the Grant Study of Harvard men, are shown in Figure 16.9. Note that when individuals at 50 years of age were not heavy smokers, did not abuse alcohol, had a stable marriage, exercised, maintained a normal weight, and had good coping skills, they were more likely to be alive and happy at 75 to 80 years of age.

CONCLUSIONS

What can be concluded about stability and change in regard to personality development during the adult years? According to a research review by leading researchers Brent Roberts and Daniel Mroczek (2008), there is increasing evidence that personality traits continue to change during the adult years, even into late adulthood. However, in a meta-analysis of 92 longitudinal studies,

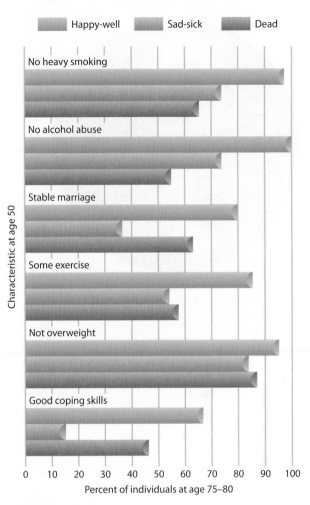

FIGURE 16.9

LINKS BETWEEN CHARACTERISTICS AT AGE 50 AND HEALTH AND HAPPINESS AT AGE 75 TO 80. In a longitudinal study, the characteristics shown above at age 50 were related to whether individuals were happy-well, sad-sick, or dead at age 75 to 80 (Vaillant, 2002).

developmental **connection**

Life-Span Perspective

The extent to which development is characterized by stability and/or change is one of the key issues in the study of life-span development. Chapter 1, p. 18

At age 55, actor Jack Nicholson said, "I feel exactly the same as I've always felt: a slightly reined-in voracious beast." Nicholson felt his personality had not changed much. Some others might think they have changed more. *How much does personality change and how does it stay the same through adulthood?*

- - - - - - - - - ➤

developmental **connection**

Personality

The Big Five factors are linked to longevity. Chapter 19, p. 575

the greatest change in personality traits occurred in early adulthood—from about 20 to 40 years of age (Roberts, Walton, & Viechtbauer, 2006).

Thus, people show more stability in their personality when they reach midlife than they did when they were younger adults (Roberts, Donnellan, & Hill, 2013). These findings support what is called a *cumulative personality model of personality development,* which states that with time and age people become more adept at interacting with their environment in ways that promote increased stability of personality (Caspi & Roberts, 2001).

This does not mean that change is absent throughout middle and late adulthood. Ample evidence shows that social contexts, new experiences, and sociohistorical changes can affect personality development, but the changes in middle and late adulthood are usually not as great as those in early adulthood (Mroczek, Spiro, & Griffin, 2006; Quoidbach, Gilbert, & Wilson, 2013). In general, changes in personality traits across adulthood also occur in a positive direction. Over time, "people become more confident, warm, responsible, and calm" (Roberts & Mroczek, 2008, p. 33). Such positive changes equate with becoming more socially mature.

In sum, recent research contradicts the old view that stability of personality begins to set in at about 30 years of age (Bertrand, Kranz Graham, & Lachman, 2013; Donnellan, Hill, & Roberts, 2014; Quoidbach, Gilbert, & Wilson, 2013; Shanahan & others, 2014). Although there are some consistent developmental changes in the personality traits of large numbers of people, at the individual level people can show unique patterns of personality traits—and these patterns often reflect life experiences related to themes of their particular developmental period (Roberts & Mroczek, 2008). For example, researchers have found that individuals who are in a stable marriage and a solid career track become more socially dominant, conscientious, and emotionally stable as they go through early adulthood (Roberts & Wood, 2006). And for some of these individuals there is greater change in their personality traits than for other individuals (McAdams & Olson, 2010; Roberts & Mroczek, 2008; Roberts, Donnellan, & Hill, 2013).

What do people perceive about stability and change in their personality earlier in life and the extent to which their personality will change or be stable in the future? A recent study asked more than 7,000 adults from 18 to 68 years of age (mean age = 40 years) to describe how much their personality had changed in the past and to predict how much it would change in the next 10 years (Quoidbach, Gilbert, & Wilson, 2013). Young adults, middle-aged adults, and older adults all thought that they had changed a great deal in the past but would hardly change at all in the future. In other analyses that included actual assessment of personality traits using a measure of the Big Five factors, the researchers found that the adults were reasonably good at estimating any changes in their personality over the prior decade but that they significantly underestimated how much their personality would change in the next 10 years. These researchers found that the older adults became, the less they perceived that they had changed in the past or would change in the future.

Review Connect Reflect

 Discuss stability and change in development during middle adulthood, as reflected in longitudinal studies.

Review
- Identify four longitudinal studies and describe their results.
- What conclusions can be reached about stability and change in development during middle adulthood?

Connect
- This section discussed four different longitudinal studies. What are the pros and cons of using a longitudinal study to collect data (as discussed in Chapter 1)?

Reflect *Your Own Personal Journey of Life*
- How much stability and change have characterized your life so far? How much stability and change do you predict will characterize your future development as an adult? Explain.

| Love and Marriage at Midlife | The Empty Nest and Its Refilling | Sibling Relationships and Friendships | Grandparenting | Intergenerational Relationships |

There is a consensus among middle-aged Americans that a major component of well-being involves positive relationships with others, especially parents, spouse, and offspring (Blieszner & Roberto, 2012; Markus & others, 2004). To begin our examination of midlife relationships, let's explore love and marriage in middle-aged adults.

LOVE AND MARRIAGE AT MIDLIFE

Remember from Chapter 14 that two major forms of love are romantic love and affectionate love. The fires of romantic love are strong in early adulthood. Affectionate, or companionate, love increases during middle adulthood. That is, physical attraction, romance, and passion are more important in new relationships, especially in early adulthood. Security, loyalty, and mutual emotional interest become more important as relationships mature, especially in middle adulthood.

What characterizes marriage in middle adulthood?

One study revealed that marital satisfaction increased in middle age (Gorchoff, John, & Helson, 2008). Some of the marriages that were difficult and rocky during early adulthood improved during middle adulthood. Although the partners may have lived through a great deal of turmoil, they eventually discovered a deep and solid foundation on which to anchor their relationship. In middle adulthood, marital partners may have fewer financial worries, less housework and chores, and more time with each other. Middle-aged partners are more likely to view their marriage as positive if they engage in mutual activities.

Most individuals in midlife who are married voice considerable satisfaction with being married. In a large-scale study of individuals in middle adulthood, 72 percent of those who were married said their marriage was either "excellent" or "very good" (Brim, 1999). Possibly by middle age, many of the worst marriages already have dissolved. However, a recent study revealed that married and partnered middle-aged adults were more likely to view their relationships with ambivalence or indifference than their late adulthood counterparts (Windsor & Butterworth, 2010).

Divorce in middle adulthood may be more positive in some ways, more negative in others, than divorce in early adulthood. On one hand, for mature individuals, the perils of divorce can be fewer and less intense than for younger individuals. They have more resources, and they can simplify their lives by disposing of possessions, such as a large home, which they no longer need. Their children are adults and may be able to cope with their parents' divorce more effectively. The partners may have gained a better understanding of themselves and may be searching for changes that could include ending a poor marriage. One study found that women who initiated a divorce in midlife were characterized more by self-focused growth and optimism than were women whose husbands initiated the divorce (Sakraida, 2005).

What are some ways that divorce might be more positive or more negative in middle adulthood than in early adulthood?

On the other hand, the emotional and time commitment to marriage that has existed for so many years may not be lightly given up. Many midlife individuals perceive a divorce as a failure during what could have been the best years of their lives. The divorcer might see the situation as an escape from an untenable relationship, but the divorced partner usually sees it as betrayal, the ending of a relationship that had been built up over many years and that involved a great deal of commitment and trust. Also, divorce may lower the economic standing of some middle-aged and older women who have a limited number of options (Mitchell, 2007). These women may lack the necessary education, skills, and employment experience to maintain a standard of living that is as high as it was when they were married. Further, a recent study found that women who became divorced from 40 to 59 years of age reported being more lonely following the divorce than men who became divorced in this age period (Nicolaisen & Thorsen, 2014). In sum, divorce in midlife may have positive outcomes for some individuals and negative outcomes for others (Pudrovska, 2009).

A survey by AARP (2004) of 1,148 40- to 79-year-olds who were divorced at least once in their forties, fifties, or sixties found that staying married because of their children was by far the main reason many people took so long to become divorced. Despite the worry and stress involved in going through a divorce, three out of four of the divorcees said they had made the right decision to dissolve their marriage and reported a positive outlook on life. Sixty-six percent of the divorced women said they had initiated the divorce, compared with only 41 percent of the divorced men. The divorced women were much more afraid of having financial problems (44 percent) than were the divorced men (11 percent). Following are the main reasons the middle-aged and older adult women cited for their divorce: (1) verbal, physical, or emotional abuse (23 percent); (2) alcohol or drug abuse (18 percent); and (3) cheating (17 percent). The main reasons the middle-aged and older men cited for their divorce were (1) no obvious problems, just fell out of love (17 percent); (2) cheating (14 percent); and (3) different values, lifestyles (14 percent).

THE EMPTY NEST AND ITS REFILLING

An important event in a family is the launching of a child into adult life. Parents undergo adjustments as a result of the child's absence. Students usually think that their parents suffer from their absence. In fact, parents who live vicariously through their children might experience the **empty nest syndrome,** which includes a decline in marital satisfaction after children leave the home. For most parents, however, marital satisfaction does not decline after children have left home but rather increases during the years after child rearing (Fingerman & Baker, 2006). With their children gone, marital partners have time to pursue career interests and to spend with each other. A recent study revealed that the transition to an empty nest increased marital satisfaction and this increase was linked to an increase in the quality of time—but not the quantity of time—spent with partners (Gorchoff, John, & Helson, 2008).

In today's uncertain economic climate, the refilling of the empty nest is becoming a common occurrence as adult children return home after several years of college, after graduating from college, or to save money after taking a full-time job (Merrill, 2009). Young adults also may move in with their parents after an unsuccessful career or a divorce. And some individuals don't leave home at all until their middle to late twenties because they cannot support themselves financially. Numerous labels have been applied to these young adults who return to their parents' homes to live, including "boomerang kids" and "B2B" (or Back-to-Bedroom) (Furman, 2005).

The middle generation has always provided support for the younger generation, even after the nest is bare. Through loans and monetary gifts for education, and through emotional support, the middle generation has helped the younger generation. Adult children appreciate the financial and emotional support their parents provide them at a time when they often feel considerable stress about their career, work, and lifestyle. And parents feel good that they can provide this support. A recent study of 40- to 60-year-old parents revealed that they provided financial, practical, and emotional support on average every few weeks to each of their children over 18 years of age (Fingerman & others, 2009).

However, as with most family living arrangements, there are both pluses and minuses when adult children return home. A common complaint voiced by both adult children and their parents is a loss of privacy. The adult children complain that their parents restrict their independence, cramp their sex lives, reduce their music listening, and treat them as children rather than adults. Parents often complain that their quiet home has become noisy, that they stay up late worrying when their adult children will come home, that meals are difficult to plan because of conflicting schedules, that their relationship as a married couple has been invaded, and that they have to shoulder too much responsibility for their adult children. In sum, when adult children return home to live, there is a disequilibrium in family life that requires considerable adaptation by parents and their adult children. To read about strategies that young adults and their parents can use to get along better, see *Connecting Development to Life*.

empty nest syndrome A decrease in marital satisfaction that occurs after children leave home, because parents derive considerable satisfaction from their children.

Strategies for Parents and Their Young Adult Children

When adult children ask to return home to live, parents and their adult children should agree beforehand on the conditions and expectations. For example, they might discuss and agree on whether young adults will pay rent, wash their own clothes, cook their own meals, do any household chores, pay their phone bills, come and go as they please, be sexually active or drink alcohol at home, and so on. If these conditions aren't negotiated at the beginning, conflict often results because the expectations of parents and young adult children will likely be violated.

Parents need to treat young adult children more like adults than children and to let go of much of their parenting role. Parents should interact with young adult children not as dependent children who need to be closely monitored and protected but rather as adults who are capable of responsible, mature behavior. Adult children have the right to choose how much they sleep and eat, how they dress, whom they choose as friends and lovers, what career they pursue, and how they spend their money. However, if the young adult children act in ways that interfere with their parents' lifestyles, parents need to say so. The discussion should focus not on the young adult children's choices but on how their activities are unacceptable while living together in the same home.

Some parents don't let go of their young adult children when they should. They engage in "permaparenting," which can impede not only their adult children's movement toward independence and responsibility but also their own postparenting lives. "Helicopter parents" is another label that describes parents who hover too closely in their effort to

What are some strategies that can help parents and their young adult children get along better?

ensure that their children succeed in college and adult life (Paul, 2003). Although well intentioned, this intrusiveness by parents can slow the process by which their children become responsible adults.

When they move back home, young adult children need to think about how they will need to change their behavior to make the living arrangement work. Elina Furman (2005) provides some good recommendations in *Boomerang Nation: How to Survive Living with Your Parents . . . the Second Time Around.* She recommends that when young adult children move back home they expect to make adjustments. And as recommended earlier, she urges young adults to sit down with their parents and negotiate the ground rules for living at home before they actually move back. Furman also recommends that young adults set a deadline for how long they will live at home and then stay focused on their goals (whether they want to save enough money to pay off their debts, save enough to start a business or buy their own home, finish graduate school, and so on). Too often young adults spend the money they save by moving home on luxuries such as shopping binges, nights on the town, expensive clothes, and unnecessary travel, further delaying their ability to move out of their parents' home.

Children who leave college and return to live at home with their parents are on the cusp of young adulthood, a time called emerging adulthood (as described in Chapter 12). What characterizes individuals' identity development during this time?

SIBLING RELATIONSHIPS AND FRIENDSHIPS

Sibling relationships persist over the entire life span for most adults (Whiteman, McHale, & Soli, 2011). Eighty-five percent of today's adults have at least one living sibling. Sibling relationships in adulthood may be extremely close, apathetic, or highly rivalrous (Bedford, 2009). The majority of sibling relationships in adulthood are close (Cicirelli, 2009). Those siblings who are psychologically close to each other in adulthood tended to be that way in childhood. It is rare for sibling closeness to develop for the first time in adulthood (Dunn, 1984, 2007). One study revealed that adult siblings often provide practical and emotional support to each other (Voorpostel & Blieszner, 2008). Another study revealed that men who had poor sibling relationships in childhood were more likely to develop depression by age 50 than men who had more positive sibling relationships as children (Waldinger, Vaillant, & Orav, 2007).

developmental **connection**

Family and Peers

Many siblings have mixed feelings about each other. Chapter 8, p. 250

Friendships are as important in middle adulthood as they were in early adulthood (Blieszner & Roberto, 2012). It takes time to develop intimate friendships, so friendships that have endured over the adult years are often deeper than those that are newly formed in middle adulthood.

GRANDPARENTING

The increase in longevity is influencing the nature of grandparenting (Monserud, 2011). In 1900 only 4 percent of 10-year-old children had four living grandparents, but in 2000 that figure had risen to more than 40 percent. And in 1990 only about 20 percent of people who were 30 years of age had living grandparents, a figure that is projected to increase to 80 percent in 2020 (Hagestad & Uhlenberg, 2007). Further increases in longevity are likely to support this trend in the future, although the current trend in delaying childbearing is likely to undermine it (Szinovacz, 2009).

Grandparents play important roles in the lives of many grandchildren (Bangerter & Waldron, 2014; Hadfield, 2014; Newton & Stewart, 2012). Many adults become grandparents for the first time during middle age. Researchers have consistently found that grandmothers have more contact with grandchildren than do grandfathers (Watson, Randolph, & Lyons, 2005). Perhaps women tend to define their role as grandmothers as part of their responsibility for maintaining ties between family members across generations. Men may have fewer expectations about the grandfather role and see it as more voluntary.

Grandparent Roles and Styles   What is the meaning of the grandparent role? Three prominent meanings are attached to being a grandparent (Neugarten & Weinstein, 1964). For some older adults, being a grandparent is a source of biological reward and continuity. For others, being a grandparent is a source of emotional self-fulfillment, generating feelings of companionship and satisfaction that may have been missing in earlier adult-child relationships. And for yet others, being a grandparent is a remote role. A recent study revealed that grandparenting can provide a sense of purpose and a feeling of being valued during middle and late adulthood when generative needs are strong (Thiele & Whelan, 2008).

The grandparent role may have different functions in different families, in different ethnic groups and cultures, and in different situations (Watson, Randolph, & Lyons, 2005). For example, in one study of White, African American, and Mexican American grandparents and grandchildren, the Mexican American grandparents saw their grandchildren most frequently, provided the most support for the grandchildren and their parents, and had the most satisfying relationships with their grandchildren (Bengtson, 1985). And in a study of three generations of families in Chicago, grandmothers had closer relationships with their children and grandchildren and gave more personal advice than grandfathers did (Hagestad, 1985).

The diversity of grandparenting also was apparent in an early investigation of how grandparents interacted with their grandchildren (Neugarten & Weinstein, 1964). Three styles were dominant—formal, fun-seeking, and distant. In the formal style, the grandparent performed what was considered to be a proper and prescribed role. These grandparents showed a strong interest in their grandchildren but were careful not to give child-rearing advice. In the fun-seeking style, the grandparent was informal and playful. Grandchildren were a source of leisure activity; mutual satisfaction was emphasized. A substantial portion of grandparents were distant figures. In the distant-figure style, the grandparent was benevolent but interaction was infrequent. Grandparents who were over the age of 65 were more likely to display a formal style of interaction; those under 65 were more likely to display a fun-seeking style. Because the grandparent role links three generations—grandparents, parents, and grandchildren—the grandparent role is often mediated by parents at least until grandchildren become adults (Szinovacz, 2009).

The Changing Profile of Grandparents   In 2009, 7.8 million children lived with at least one grandparent, a 64 percent increase since 1981 when 4.7 million children were living with at least one grandparent (U.S. Census Bureau, 2011). Divorce, adolescent pregnancies, and drug use by parents are the main reasons that grandparents are thrust back into the "parenting" role they thought

What are some grandparents' roles and styles?

they had shed. One study revealed that grandparent involvement was linked with better adjustment in single-parent and stepparent families than in two-parent biological families (Attar-Schwartz & others, 2009).

Less than 20 percent of grandparents whose grandchildren move in with them are 65 years old or older. Almost half of the grandchildren who move in with grandparents are raised by a single grandmother. These families are mainly African American (53 percent). When both grandparents are raising grandchildren, the families are overwhelmingly non-Latino White.

A majority of the grandparents living with their children contributed to the family income and provided child care while parents worked. Only about 10 percent of the grandparents who move in with their children and grandchildren are in poverty. Almost half of the grandparents who move in with their children are immigrants. Partly because women live longer than men, more grandmothers than grandfathers live with their children. About 70 percent of the grandparents who move in with their children are grandmothers.

Grandparents who are full-time caregivers for grandchildren are at elevated risk for health problems, depression, and stress (Silverstein, 2009). A recent review concluded that grandparents raising grandchildren are especially at risk for developing depression (Hadfield, 2014). Caring for grandchildren is linked with these problems in part because full-time grandparent caregivers are often characterized by low-income, minority status, and by not being married (Minkler & Fuller-Thompson, 2005). Grandparents who are part-time caregivers are less likely to have the negative health portrait that full-time grandparent caregivers have. In a recent study of part-time grandparent caregivers, few negative effects on grandparents were found (Hughes & others, 2007).

In some cases, divorce may increase children's contact with grandparents, as when grandparents assume a stronger caregiving role; in others, a custodial parent may try to restrict grandparents' time with children. One recent study revealed that when children's relationship with their father deteriorated after a divorce, their relationships with their paternal grandparents also were distant, negative, or nonexistent (Ahrons, 2007).

As divorce and remarriage have become more common, a special concern of grandparents is visitation privileges with their grandchildren (Kivnik & Sinclair, 2007). In the last two decades, more states have passed laws giving grandparents the right to petition a court for visitation privileges with their grandchildren, even if a parent objects. Whether such forced visitation rights for grandparents are in the child's best interest is still being debated.

INTERGENERATIONAL RELATIONSHIPS

Family is important to most people. When 21,000 adults aged 40 to 79 in 21 countries were asked, "When you think of who you are, you think mainly of _____," 63 percent said "family," 9 percent said "religion," and 8 percent said "work" (HSBC Insurance, 2007). In this study, in all 21 countries, middle-aged and older adults expressed a strong feeling of responsibility between generations in their family, with the strongest intergenerational ties indicated in Saudi Arabia, India, and Turkey. More than 80 percent of the middle-aged and older adults reported that adults have a duty to care for their parents (and parents-in-law) in time of need later in life.

Adults in midlife play important roles in the lives of the young and the old (Birditt & Wardjiman, 2012; Fingerman & others, 2014; Fingerman & Birditt, 2011; Fingerman, Sechrist, & Birditt, 2013). Middle-aged adults share their experience and transmit values to the younger generation. They may be launching children and experiencing the empty nest, adjusting to having grown children return home, or becoming grandparents. They also may be giving or receiving financial assistance, caring for a widowed or sick parent, or adapting to being the oldest generation after both parents have died.

Middle-aged adults have been described as the "sandwich," "squeezed," or "overload" generation because of the responsibilities they have for their adolescent and young adult children as well as their aging parents (Etaugh & Bridges, 2010; Pudrovska, 2009). However, an alternative view is that in the United States, a "sandwich" generation, in which the middle generation cares for both grown children and aging parents simultaneously, occurs less often than a "pivot"

Middle-aged and older adults around the world show a strong sense of family responsibility. A recent study of middle-aged and older adults in 21 countries revealed the strongest intergenerational ties in Saudi Arabia.

What is the nature of intergenerational relationships?

generation, in which the middle generation alternates attention between the demands of grown children and aging parents (Birditt & Wardjiman, 2012; Fingerman & Birditt, 2011; Fingerman, Sechrist, & Birditt, 2013).

Many middle-aged adults experience considerable stress when their parents become very ill and die. One survey found that when adults enter midlife, 41 percent have both parents alive, but that 77 percent leave midlife with no parents alive (Bumpass & Aquilino, 1994). By middle age, more than 40 percent of adult children (most of them daughters) provide care for aging parents or parents-in-law (Blieszner & Roberto, 2012; National Alliance for Caregiving, 2009). However, two recent studies revealed that middle-aged parents are more likely to provide support to their grown children than to their parents (Fingerman & others, 2011a, 2012). When middle-aged adults have a parent with a disability, their support for that parent increases (Fingerman & others, 2011b). This support might involve locating a nursing home and monitoring its quality, procuring medical services, arranging public service assistance, and handling finances. In some cases, adult children provide direct assistance with daily living, including such activities as eating, bathing, and dressing. Even less severely impaired older adults may need help with shopping, housework, transportation, home maintenance, and bill paying.

Some researchers have found that relationships between aging parents and their children are usually characterized by ambivalence (Birditt, Fingerman, & Zarit, 2010; Birditt & Wardjiman, 2012; Fingerman & Birditt, 2011; Fingerman & others, 2011a; Fingerman, Sechrist, & Birditt, 2013; Pitzer, Fingerman, & Lefkowitz, 2014). Perceptions include love, reciprocal help, and shared values on the positive side and isolation, family conflicts and problems, abuse, neglect, and caregiver stress on the negative side. A recent study found that middle-aged adults positively supported family responsibility to emerging adult children but were more ambivalent about providing care for aging parents, viewing it as both a joy and a burden (Igarashi & others, 2013). However, a recent study in the Netherlands revealed that affection and support, reflecting solidarity, were more prevalent than ambivalence in intergenerational relationships (Hogerbrugge & Komter, 2012).

With each new generation, personality characteristics, attitudes, and values are replicated or changed. As older family members die, their biological, intellectual, emotional, and personal legacies are carried on in the next generation. Their children become the oldest generation and their grandchildren the second generation. As adult children become middle-aged, they often develop more positive perceptions of their parents (Field, 1999). Both similarity and dissimilarity across generations are found. For example, similarity between parents and an adult child is most noticeable in religion and politics, least in gender roles, lifestyle, and work orientation.

The following studies provide further evidence of the importance of intergenerational relationships in development:

- The motivation of adult children to provide social support to their older parents was linked with earlier family experiences (Silverstein & others, 2002). Children who spent more time in shared activities with their parents and received more financial support from them earlier in their lives provided more support to their parents as they became older.
- Children of divorced parents were disproportionately likely to end their own marriage than were children from intact, never-divorced families, although the transmission of divorce across generations has declined in recent years (Wolfinger, 2011).
- Parents who smoked early and often, and who persisted in becoming regular smokers, were more likely to have adolescents who became smokers (Chassin & others, 2008).
- Safe, stable, and supportive/trusting relationships with intimate partners and between mothers and children were linked to breaking the intergenerational cycle of abuse in families (Jaffee & others, 2013).

How Do Mothers' and Daughters' Descriptions of Enjoyable Visits Differ at Different Points in Adult Development?

Karen Fingerman (2000) studied 48 pairs of older adult mothers (mean age, 76 years) and their middle-aged daughters (mean age, 46 years), and 44 pairs of middle-aged mothers (mean age, 47 years) and their young adult daughters (mean age, 21 years). Interviewers asked participants (p. 98):

> Think about the last time you had a particularly enjoyable visit with your daughter/mother. By visit, I mean a time when you got together, went to the other's house (or your daughter came home from college), or talked on the phone. Tell a little about what went on. Please provide as much information as you can about the visit, what happened, and why it was particularly enjoyable.

Transcriptions of descriptions of the visits were coded, and the results for the coded categories were summarized as follows (Fingerman, 2000, pp. 100–102):

• *Investment and connection.* Mothers in both age groups were more invested in their relationships with their daughters than their daughters were with them.

• *Family.* Older mothers and daughters were more likely than younger pairs to describe the larger kin network, such as the daughter's children, siblings, father, husband, or the family in general. By contrast, younger pairs "were more likely to stick to their own relationship and to discuss situations in which the two of them had enjoyed a special event."

• *Nurturance.* "Young adult daughters and older adult mothers were more likely to report pleasure from having the other party help them in some way than were middle-aged women."

• *Interacting.* Younger mothers tended to focus on activities in which they enjoyed their daughters' emergence as young adults. "Younger daughters derived pleasure from having their mothers around as sounding boards, whereas older daughters" enjoyed the link to the past that their mothers represented.

• *Negative comments.* Mothers and daughters in the older pairs "were more likely to say something negative than were younger mothers and daughters," although these comments were still infrequent.

In sum, mothers' and daughters' perceptions of their visits reflected a combination of individual developmental needs. Although the focus of mothers' and daughters' relationships may change, in general mothers were more invested in relationships with their daughters than the reverse throughout adulthood.

Gender differences also characterize intergenerational relationships (Etaugh & Bridges, 2010). Women have an especially important role in maintaining family relationships across generations. Women's relationships across generations are typically closer than other family bonds (Merrill, 2009). In one study, mothers and their daughters had much closer relationships during their adult years than mothers and sons, fathers and daughters, and fathers and sons (Rossi, 1989). Also in this study, married men were more involved with their wives' kin than with their own. Also, a recent study revealed that mothers' intergenerational ties were more influential for grandparent-grandchild relationships than fathers' (Monserud, 2008). To further explore intergenerational relationships, see the *Connecting Through Research* interlude.

When adults immigrate into another country, intergenerational stress may increase (Lin & others, 2014). In the last several decades, increasing numbers of Mexicans have immigrated into the United States, and their numbers are expected to increase. The pattern of immigration usually involves separation from the extended family (Parra-Cardona & others, 2006). It may also involve separation of immediate family members, with the husband coming first and then later bringing his wife and children. Those who were initially isolated, especially the wife, experience considerable stress due to relocation and the absence of family and friends. Within several years, a social network is usually established in the ethnic neighborhood.

As soon as some stability in their lives is achieved, Mexican families may sponsor the immigration of extended family members, such as a maternal or paternal sister or mother who provides child care and enables the mother to go to work. In some cases, the older generation remains behind and joins their grown children in old age. The accessibility of Mexico facilitates visits to and from the village for vacations or at a time of crisis, such as when an adolescent runs away from home.

What are three levels of acculturation that characterize many Mexican American families?

Karen Fingerman, Professor, Department of Human Development and Family Sciences, and Researcher on Families and Aging

Dr. Karen Fingerman is a leading expert on aging, families, and socio-emotional development. She currently is a Professor in the Department of Human Development and Family Sciences within the School of Human Ecology at the University of Texas at Austin. Prior to coming to UT-Austin, she was the Berner Hanley Professor of Gerontology at Purdue University. Dr. Fingerman obtained her Ph.D. from the University of Michigan and did post-doctoral work at Stanford University. She has published numerous articles on the positive and negative aspects of relationships involving mothers and daughters, grandparents and grand-children, friends, and acquaintances, and peripheral social ties. The National Institute of Aging, the Brookdale Foundation, and the MacArthur Transitions to Adulthood group have funded her research. Dr. Fingerman has received the Springer Award for Early Career Achievement in Research on Adult Development and Aging from the American Psychological Association, as well as the Margaret Baltes Award for Early Career Achievement in Behavioral and Social Gerontology from the Gerontological Association of America.

Dr. Karen Fingerman, leading expert on aging, families, and socioemotional development. Also you can use the following from what was in the previous Connecting with Careers on p. 528 of LSD 14th: *For more information on what professors and researchers do, see page 41 in the Careers in Life-Span Development appendix.*

The discrepancies between acculturation levels can give rise to conflicting expectations within Mexican American families (Sarkisian, Gerena, & Gerstel, 2006; Simpkins, Vest, & Price, 2011). The immigrant parents' model of child rearing may be out of phase with the dominant culture's model, which may cause reverberations through the family's generations, as discussed in earlier chapters. For example, parents and grandparents may be especially resistant to the demands for autonomy and dating made by adolescent daughters (Wilkinson-Lee & others, 2006). And in recent years an increasing number of female youth have left their Mexican American homes to further their education, an event that is often stressful for families with strong ties to Mexican values.

Karen Fingerman has conducted research on intergenerational relations and development in midlife. To read about her work, see the *Connecting with Careers* profile.

Review Connect Reflect

 LG3 Identify some important aspects of close relationships in middle adulthood.

Review

- How can love and marriage at midlife be characterized?
- What is the empty nest? How has it been refilling?
- What are sibling relationships and friendships like in middle adulthood?
- What is the nature of grandparenting?
- What are relationships across generations like?

Connect

- In this section, you read about divorce in middle adulthood. In Chapter 14, what did you learn was one of the most common characteristics of divorced adults?

Reflect *Your Own Personal Journey of Life*

- What was or is the nature of your relationship with your grandparents? What are intergenerational relationships like in your family?

topical connections *looking forward*

Erikson's eighth and final stage of development—integrity versus despair—occurs in late adulthood. In this stage, individuals engage in a life review. Being active is linked with life satisfaction in late adulthood. Older adults become more selective about their social networks and choose to spend more time with emotionally rewarding relationships and less time with peripheral relationships. Older adults also experience more positive emotions and fewer negative emotions than younger adults. The personality traits of conscientiousness and agreeableness also increase in late adulthood. Because of losses (declines in physical or cognitive skills, for example), older adults often have to use accommodative strategies to reach their goals.

reach your **learning goals**

Socioemotional Development in Middle Adulthood

1 Personality Theories and Adult Development

 LG1 Describe personality theories and socioemotional development in middle adulthood.

Stages of Adulthood

- Erikson says that the seventh stage of the human life span, generativity versus stagnation, occurs in middle adulthood. Four types of generativity are biological, parental, work, and cultural. In Levinson's theory, developmental tasks must be mastered at different points in development, and changes in middle age focus on four conflicts: being young versus being old, being destructive versus being constructive, being masculine versus being feminine, and being attached to others versus being separated from them. Levinson asserted that a majority of Americans, especially men, experience a midlife crisis. Research, however, indicates that midlife crises are not pervasive. There is considerable individual variation in development during middle adulthood.

The Life-Events Approach

- According to the early version of the life-events approach, life events produce taxing circumstances that create stress. In the contemporary version of the life-events approach, how life events influence the individual's development depends not only on the life event but also on mediating factors, adaptation to the event, the life-stage context, and the sociohistorical context.

Stress and Personal Control in Midlife

- Researchers have found that young and middle-aged adults experience more stressful days and more multiple stressors than do older adults. On average, a sense of personal control decreases as adults become older—however, some aspects of personal control increase. Women and men differ in the way they experience and respond to stressors. Women are more likely to respond to stress in a tend-and-befriend manner, men in a flight-or-fight manner.

Contexts of Midlife Development

- Neugarten argues that the social environment of a particular cohort can alter its social clock—the timetable according to which individuals are expected to accomplish life's tasks. Critics say that the adult stage theories are male biased because they place too much emphasis on achievement and careers and do not adequately address women's concerns about relationships. Midlife is a heterogeneous period for women, as it is for men. For some women, midlife is the prime of their lives. Many cultures do not have a clear concept of middle age. In many nonindustrialized societies, a woman's status improves in middle age.

2 Stability and Change

 LG2 Discuss stability and change in development during middle adulthood, as reflected in longitudinal studies.

Longitudinal Studies

- In Costa and McCrae's Baltimore Study, the Big Five personality factors—openness to experience, conscientiousness, extraversion, agreeableness, and neuroticism—showed considerable stability. However, researchers recently have found that the greatest change in personality occurs in early adulthood, with positive aspects of the factors peaking in middle age.

The Big Five factors are linked to important aspects of a person's life, such as health and work. In the Berkeley Longitudinal Studies, extremes in the stability-change argument were not supported. The most stable characteristics were intellectual orientation, self-confidence, and openness to new experiences. The characteristics that changed the most were nurturance, hostility, and self-control. Helson's Mills College Study of women distinguished family-oriented and career-oriented women, and those who followed neither path. In their early forties, women experienced many of the concerns that Levinson described for men. However, rather than a midlife crisis, women experienced midlife consciousness. George Vaillant's research revealed links between a number of characteristics at age 50 and health and well-being at 75 to 80 years of age.

Conclusions

- The cumulative personality model states that with time and age personality becomes more stable. Changes in personality traits occur more in early adulthood than middle and late adulthood, but a number of aspects of personality do continue to change after early adulthood. Change in personality traits across adulthood occurs in a positive direction, reflecting social maturity. At the individual level, changes in personality are often linked to life experiences related to a particular developmental period. Some people change more than others.

3 Close Relationships

LG3 Identify some important aspects of close relationships in middle adulthood.

Love and Marriage at Midlife

- Affectionate love increases in midlife, especially in marriages that have endured many years. A majority of middle-aged adults who are married say that their marriage is very good or excellent. Researchers recently have found that the perils of divorce in midlife can be fewer and less intense than those for divorcing young adults.

The Empty Nest and Its Refilling

- Rather than decreasing marital satisfaction as once thought, the empty nest increases it for most parents. Following an unsuccessful career or a divorce, an increasing number of young adults are returning home to live with their parents. Some young adults do not leave home until their middle to late twenties because they are unable to support themselves financially.

Sibling Relationships and Friendships

Grandparenting

- Sibling relationships continue throughout life. Some are close; others are distant. Friendships continue to be important in middle age.

- There are different grandparent roles and styles. Grandmothers spend more time with grandchildren than grandfathers, and the grandmother role involves greater expectations for maintaining ties across generations than the grandfather role. The profile of grandparents is changing because of such factors as divorce and remarriage. An increasing number of U.S. grandchildren live with their grandparents.

Intergenerational Relationships

- Family members usually maintain contact across generations. Mothers and daughters have the closest relationships. The middle-aged generation, which has been called the "sandwich" or "squeezed" generation, plays an important role in linking generations.

key **terms**

key **people**

To be seventy years young is sometimes far more cheerful and hopeful than to be forty years old.

—**OLIVER WENDELL HOLMES, SR.**
American Physician, 19th Century

Late Adulthood

The rhythm and meaning of human development eventually wend their way to late adulthood, when each of us stands alone at the heart of the earth and suddenly it is evening. We shed the leaves of youth and are stripped by the winds of time down to the truth. We learn that life is lived forward but understood backward. We trace the connection between the end and the beginning of life and try to figure out what this whole show is about before it is out. Ultimately, we come to know that we are what survives of us. Section 9 contains three chapters: "Physical Development in Late Adulthood (Chapter 17), "Cognitive Development in Late Adulthood" (Chapter 18), and "Socioemotional Development in Late Adulthood" (Chapter 19).

chapter 17

PHYSICAL DEVELOPMENT IN LATE ADULTHOOD

chapter outline

1 Longevity

Learning Goal 1 Characterize longevity and discuss the biological theories of aging.

Life Expectancy and Life Span
The Young-Old and the Oldest-Old
Biological Theories of Aging

2 The Course of Physical Development in Late Adulthood

Learning Goal 2 Describe how a person's brain and body change in late adulthood.

The Aging Brain
Sleep
The Immune System
Physical Appearance and Movement
Sensory Development
The Circulatory and Respiratory Systems
Sexuality

3 Health

Learning Goal 3 Identify health problems in older adults and describe how they can be treated.

Health Problems
Substance Use and Abuse
Exercise, Nutrition, and Weight
Health Treatment

Jonathan Swift said, "No wise man ever wished to be younger." Without a doubt, a 70-year-old body does not work as well as it once did. It is also true that an individual's fear of aging is often greater than need be. As more individuals live to a ripe *and* active old age, our image of aging is changing. Although on average a 75-year-old's joints should be stiffening, people can practice not to be average. For example, a 75-year-old man might *choose* to train for and run a marathon; an 80-year-old woman whose capacity for work is undiminished might *choose* to make and sell children's toys.

Consider Mary "May" Segal, who was diagnosed with cardiovascular problems about the time she retired at the age of 65. Her heart complications spurred her to begin an exercise program that involved climbing the steps at Duke University's football stadium in Durham, North Carolina. May turned 100 years of age in 2013 and has continued a regular exercise regimen for the last 35 years. When May was 78, she began exercising at the newly opened Duke University Health and Fitness Center. She still goes to the Center regularly, starting just after 9 a.m. May's exercise regimen includes a swim, four laps walking around a track, and a 30-minute workout on a NuStep machine that involves a combination of leg exercise that is much like climbing stairs and arm exercise that is similar to cross-country skiing. May's exercise

May Segal engaging in her exercise routine on her 100th birthday at the Duke University Health and Fitness Center.

speed is slower than it was when she was younger, and she now has to use a walker when she does her four laps around the track. In addition, she has reduced the number of days she works out to three per week.

As an indication of May's motivation, resilience, and persistence, when she was 94 she fell and broke her hip, which for elderly adults can be a difficult setback with a prolonged recovery period. Her doctor told her she would never walk again, but May did recover and has continued her regular exercise program.

topical connections *looking back*

As more individuals are living healthier lives and medical discoveries are slowing down the aging process, middle age appears to be starting later and lasting longer. Increasingly, early middle age (40–54) is distinguished from late middle age (55–65). However, middle age is a time of declining physical skills—such as loss of height, impaired vision and hearing, and reduced cardiovascular functioning. Sleep also becomes more problematic. Sexual changes occur as women enter menopause, many middle-aged men begin to experience erectile dysfunction, and couples engage less frequently in sexual intercourse.

preview

The story of May Segal's physical development and well-being raises some truly fascinating questions about life-span development, which we will explore in this chapter. They include: Why do we age, and what, if anything, can we do to slow down the process? How long can we live? What chance do we have of living to be 100? How does the body change in old age? Can certain eating habits and exercise patterns help us live longer? How can we enhance older adults' quality of life?

---

1 Longevity (LG1) Characterize longevity and discuss the biological theories of aging.

| Life Expectancy and Life Span | The Young-Old and the Oldest-Old | Biological Theories of Aging |

In his 80s, Nobel-winning chemist Linus Pauling argued that vitamin C slows the aging process. Aging researcher Roy Walford fasted two days a week because he believed calorie restriction slows the aging process. What do we really know about longevity?

LIFE EXPECTANCY AND LIFE SPAN

We are no longer a youthful society. The proportion of individuals at different ages has become increasingly similar. Since the beginning of recorded history, **life span,** the maximum number of years an individual can live, has remained at approximately 120 to 125 years of age. But since 1900, improvements in medicine, nutrition, exercise, and lifestyle have increased our life expectancy by an average of 30 years. Keep in mind that it is not just improvements in the health and well-being of adults that have contributed to increased longevity but also the substantial reduction in infant deaths in recent decades.

Recall from Chapter 1 that **life expectancy** is the number of years that the average person born in a particular year will probably live. The average life expectancy of individuals born today in the United States is 78.7 years (Hoyert & Xu, 2012). Sixty-five-year-olds in the United States today can expect to live an average of 18.6 more years (19.9 for females, 17.2 for males) (U.S. Census Bureau, 2011). Older adults who are 100 years of age can only expect to live an average of 2.3 years longer (U.S. Census Bureau, 2011).

Life Expectancy   How does the United States fare in life expectancy, compared with other countries around the world? We do considerably better than some and somewhat worse than others. In 2011, Monaco had the highest estimated life expectancy at birth (90 years), followed by Macau (a region of China near Hong Kong), Japan, and Singapore (84 years) (Central Intelligence Agency, 2012). Of 221 countries, the United States ranked fiftieth at 78 years. The lowest estimated life expectancy in 2011 occurred in the African countries of Chad, Guinea-Bissau, South Africa, and Swaziland (49 years). Differences in life expectancies across countries are due to such factors as health conditions and medical care throughout the life span.

Life expectancy also differs for various ethnic groups within the United States and for men and women (Hoyert & Xu, 2012). For example, the life expectancy of African Americans (75) in the United States is 6 years lower than the life expectancy for Latinos (81) and 4 years lower than for non-Latino Whites (79) (Centers for Disease Control and Prevention, 2012a). Latino women have a life expectancy of 84 and non-Latino White women have a life expectancy of 81, followed by African American women (78), non-Latino White men (76 years), and African American men (72 years) (Hoyert & Xu, 2012).

In 2011, the overall life expectancy for women was 81.1 years of age, and for men it was 76.3 years of age (Hoyert & Xu, 2012). Beginning in the mid-thirties, women outnumber men; this gap widens during the remainder of the adult years. By the time adults are 75 years of age, more than 61 percent of the population is female; for those 85 and over, the figure is almost 70 percent female. Why can women expect to live longer than men? Social factors

---

Each of us stands alone at the heart of the earth, pierced through by a ray of sunshine: And suddenly it is evening.

—**SALVATORE QUASIMODO**
Italian Poet, 20th Century

developmental **connection**

Life Expectancy

In the twentieth century alone, life expectancy in the United States increased by 30 years. Chapter 1, p. 5

life span The maximum number of years an individual can live. The life span of human beings is about 120 to 125 years of age.

life expectancy The number of years that will probably be lived by the average person born in a particular year.

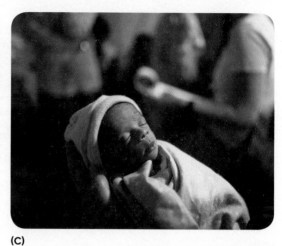

(a)   (b)   (c)

(*a*) People in Monaco, a very wealthy country with virtually no poverty and superb health care, have the highest life expectancy in the world (90 years); (*b*) Life expectancy in Russia is only 66 years of age, likely due to high rates of alcohol consumption and tobacco use; and (*c*) Haiti, a country with high rates of poverty where many newborns have a low birth weight, has a life expectancy of 63.

such as health attitudes, habits, lifestyles, and occupation are probably important (Saint Onge, 2009). Men are more likely than women to die from most of the leading causes of death in the United States, including cancer of the respiratory system, motor vehicle accidents, cirrhosis of the liver, emphysema, and coronary heart disease (Robine, 2011). These causes of death are associated with lifestyle. For example, the sex difference in deaths due to lung cancer and emphysema occurs because men are heavier smokers than women.

The sex difference in longevity also is influenced by biological factors (Gems, 2014; Regan & Partridge, 2014; Soerensen, 2012). In virtually all species, females outlive males. Women have more resistance to infections and degenerative diseases (Pan & Chang, 2012). For example, the female's estrogen production helps to protect her from arteriosclerosis (hardening of the arteries). And the additional X chromosome that women carry in comparison with men may be associated with the production of more antibodies to fight off disease. The sex difference in mortality is still present but less pronounced than in the past. In 1979, the sex difference in longevity favored women by 7.8 years but in 2011 the difference was down to 4.8 years (Hoyert & Xu, 2012).

Among various groups, the longest average longevity in the United States belongs to Seventh Day Adventists, who have a life expectancy of 88 years. One reason for their longevity is that their religious beliefs include positive lifestyle choices such as a vegetarian diet.

What about your own life expectancy? What is the likelihood that you will live to be 100? To evaluate this possibility, see Figure 17.1.

Centenarians   In industrialized countries, the number of centenarians (individuals 100 years and older) is increasing at a rate of approximately 7 percent each year (Perls, 2007). In the United States, there were only 15,000 centenarians in 1980, a number that rose to 72,000 in 2010 and is projected to reach 600,000 by 2050 (U.S. Census Bureau, 2011). The United States has the most centenarians, followed by Japan, China, and England/Wales (Hall, 2008). It is estimated that there are about 60 to 70 supercentenarians (individuals 110 years or older) in the United States and about 300 to 450 worldwide (Perls, 2007).

Three major studies of centenarians are the New England Centenarian Study, the Georgia Centenarian Study, and the Chinese Longitudinal Healthy Longevity Survey. The New England Centenarian Study (NECS) began in 1994 under the direction of Thomas Perls and his colleagues (Perls, 2007, 2009; Sebastiani & others, 2012, 2013; Sebastiani & Perls, 2012; Terry & others, 2008). Many people expect that "the older you get, the sicker you get." However, in the NECS, this is not true for a majority of centenarians. The researchers have found that chronic high-mortality diseases are markedly delayed for many years in centenarians, with many not experiencing disability until near the end of their lives (Sebastiani & Perls, 2012). A recent NECS study of centenarians from 100 to 119 years of age found that the older the age group (110 to 119—referred to as *supercentenarians*—compared with

Decide how each item applies to you and add or subtract the appropriate number of years from your basic life expectancy.

1. Family history
___ Add five years if two or more of your grandparents lived to 80 or beyond.
___ Subtract four years if any parent, grandparent, sister, or brother died of a heart attack or stroke before 50.
___ Subtract two years if anyone died from these diseases before 60.
___ Subtract three years for each case of diabetes, thyroid disorder, breast cancer, cancer of the digestive system, asthma, or chronic bronchitis among parents or grandparents.

2. Marital status
___ If you are married, add four years.
___ If you are over 25 and not married, subtract one year for every unmarried decade.

3. Economic status
___ Add two years if your family income is over $60,000 per year.
___ Subtract three years if you have been poor for the greater part of your life.

4. Physique
___ Subtract one year for every 10 pounds you are overweight.
___ For each inch your girth measurement exceeds your chest measurement deduct two years.
___ Add three years if you are over 40 and not overweight.

5. Exercise
___ Add three years if you exercise regularly and moderately (jogging three times a week).
___ Add five years if you exercise regularly and vigorously (long-distance running three times a week).
___ Subtract three years if your job is sedentary.
___ Add three years if your job is active.

6. Alcohol
___ Add two years if you are a light drinker (one to three drinks a day).
___ Subtract five to ten years if you are a heavy drinker (more than four drinks per day).
___ Subtract one year if you are a teetotaler.

7. Smoking
___ Subtract eight years if you smoke two or more packs of cigarettes per day.
___ Subtract two years if you smoke one to two packs per day.
___ Subtract two years if you smoke less than one pack.
___ Subtract two years if you regularly smoke a pipe or cigars.

8. Disposition
___ Add two years if you are a reasoned, practical person.
___ Subtract two years if you are aggressive, intense, and competitive.
___ Add one to five years if you are basically happy and content with life.
___ Subtract one to five years if you are often unhappy, worried, and often feel guilty.

9. Education
___ Subtract two years if you have less than a high school education.
___ Add one year if you attended four years of school beyond high school.
___ Add three years if you attended five or more years beyond high school.

10. Environment
___ Add four years if you have lived most of your life in a rural environment.
___ Subtract two years if you have lived most of your life in an urban environment.

11. Sleep
___ Subtract five years if you sleep more than nine hours a day.

12. Temperature
___ Add two years if your home's thermostat is set at no more than 68° F.

13. Health care
___ Add three years if you have regular medical checkups and regular dental care.
___ Subtract two years if you are frequently ill.

___ **Your Life Expectancy Total**

FIGURE **17.1**

CAN YOU LIVE TO BE 100? This test gives you a rough guide for predicting your longevity. The basic life expectancy for men is age 75, and for women it is 81. Write down your basic life expectancy. If you are in your fifties or sixties, you should add ten years to the basic figure because you have already proved yourself to be a durable individual. If you are over age 60 and active, you can even add another two years.

developmental **connection**

Heredity

Scientists are increasing their search for genes that are linked to how long people are likely to live. Chapter 2, p. 53

100 to 104, for example), the later the onset of diseases such as cancer and cardiovascular disease, as well as functional decline (Andersen & others, 2012). Perls refers to this process of staving off high-mortality chronic diseases until much later ages than usual as the *compression of morbidity*.

Among the factors in the NECS that are associated with living to be 100 are longevity genes and the ability to cope effectively with stress. The researchers also have discovered a strong genetic component of living to be 100 that consists of many genetic links that each have modest effects but as a group can have a strong influence (Sebastiani & Perls, 2012). For example, a recent meta-analysis of five studies in the United States, Europe, and Japan concluded that when their influence is combined, approximately 130 genes "do a relatively good job" of differentiating centenarians from non-centenarians (Sebastiani & others, 2013). These genes play roles in Alzheimer disease, diabetes, cardiovascular disease, cancer, and various biological processes. Other characteristics of centenarians in the New England Centenarian study include the following: few of the centenarians are obese, habitual smoking is rare, and only a small percentage (less than 15 percent) have had significant changes in their thinking skills (disproving the belief that most centenarians likely would develop Alzheimer disease).

Three participants in the New England Centenarian Study: (left) Agnes Fenton, who lives in Englewood, New Jersey, is 107 years of age and says she doesn't feel any older than when she was 15. She still cooks her own meals and her only health complaint is arthritis in her right hand. (Center) Louis Charpentier, who lives in the Boston area, is 99 years of age and every day carves wooden figures in his basement shop. Louis says is memory is still terrific. (Right) Edythe Kirchmaier, who lives in the New York City area, is Facebook's oldest user at 105 years of age. As of July, 2014, Edythe had more than 51,000 followers on Facebook! She volunteers every week at her favorite charity, still drives her car, and frequently uses the Internet to look up information and facts.

In addition to the New England Centenarian study, another major ongoing study is the Georgia Centenarian study conducted by Leonard Poon and his colleagues (Cho, Martin, & Poon, 2012; Dai & others, 2013; Haslam & others, 2014; Hensley & others, 2012; Johnson & others, 2013; Martin & others, 2014; Mitchell & others, 2013; Poon & others, 2010, 2012; Randall & others, 2011, 2012). In a review, Poon and his colleagues (2010) concluded that social dynamics involving life events (experiencing a higher number of negative life events is linked to lower self-rated health), personality (conscientiousness is positively associated with higher levels of physical and mental health), cognition (cognitive measures are better predictors of mental health than physical health), and socioeconomic resources and support systems (social, economic, and personal resources are related to mental and physical health) contribute to the health and quality of life of older adults, including centenarians.

Yet another major study is the Chinese Longitudinal Healthy Longevity Survey, which includes older adults, some of whom are centenarians (Feng, Li, & others, 2012; Feng, Wang, & Jones, 2013; Feng, Wang, & others, 2012; Luo & Waite, 2014; Wang, Chen, & Han, 2014; Zeng & Shen, 2010). In one investigation involving this sample, Chinese centenarians showed better coping and adjustment (greater personal tenacity, optimism, coping with negative moods, secure relationships, and personal control) than their Chinese counterparts in their nineties, eighties, or seventies (Zeng & Shen, 2010). In this study, 94- to 98-year-olds with better resilience had a 43 percent higher likelihood of becoming a centenarian than their same-aged counterparts who were less resilient.

How do centenarians view their lives? What are their opinions about why they have been able to live so long?

- Elza Wynn concluded that he has been able to live so long because he made up his mind to do so. He says he was thinking about dying when he was 77, but decided to wait awhile (Segerberg, 1982).
- Ruth Climer was a physical education teacher for many years and later competed in the Senior Olympics. To live to be 100, she says, it is important to stay focused on what is good now and not give in to negative thoughts. Ruth also thinks staying busy and always moving forward are keys to longevity (O'Dell, 2013).
- Billy Red Fox thinks that being active and not worrying are important keys to living to be 100. At 95, he switched jobs to become a public relations representative. Even at 100, he travels 11 months of the year making public appearances and talking with older adults (Segerberg, 1982).
- Simo Radulovich thinks living to an old age requires having a sense of humor, living moderately, and sleeping well. He still engages in exercise games with his friends every day and says he never has been afraid of anything but always had confidence that he could get through the tough times (O'Dell, 2013).
- Mary Butler says that finding something to laugh about every day helps her live longer. She thinks a good laugh is better than a dose of medicine anytime (Segerberg, 1982).

(a) Frenchwoman Jeanne Louise Calment, shown here celebrating her 117th birthday, is the oldest documented living person. She lived to be 122 years of age. (b) Simo Radulovich, 103 years of age in 2013, says that the best thing about living past 100 is being able to enjoy family and friends. He and his wife have been married more than 60 years.

developmental **connection**

Nature and Nurture

The nature-nurture issue is a key aspect of understanding development throughout the human life span. Chapter 1, p. 17; Chapter 2, p. 68

- Duran Baez remarried at 50 and went on to have 15 more children. At 100 years of age, he was asked if he had any ambitions he had not yet realized. Duran replied, "No" (Segerberg, 1982).
- Jeanne Louise Calment, the world's longest-living person who died at 122, attributed her longevity to a number of things:

Don't worry about things you can't do anything about. Enjoy an occasional glass of port wine and a diet rich in olive oil. Laugh often. Regarding her ability to live so long, she once said that God must have forgotten about her. On her 120th birthday, an interviewer asked her what kind of future she anticipated. Jeanne Louise replied, "A very short one." Becoming accustomed to the media attention she got, at 117 she stated, "I wait for death . . . and journalists." She walked, biked, and exercised regularly. Jeanne Louise began taking fencing lessons at 85 and rode a bicycle until she was 100.

What chance do you have of living to be 100? Genes play an important role in surviving to an extreme old age (Hu & others, 2014). As we saw in Chapter 2, "Biological Beginnings," the search for longevity genes has recently intensified (Morris & others, 2014; Moskalev & others, 2014). But there are additional factors at work, such as family history, health (weight, diet, smoking, and exercise), education, personality, stress, and lifestyle. Remember from Chapter 2 that in the epigenetic approach, there is increasing interest in determining gene × environment (G × E) interactions that influence development (Miller & others, 2013; Moore, 2013; Moskalev & others, 2014).

To further examine the factors that are involved in living to a very old age, let's journey to the island of Okinawa in the East China Sea where individuals live longer than anywhere else in the world. In Okinawa, there are 34.7 centenarians for every 100,000 inhabitants, the highest ratio in the world. In comparison, the United States has about 10 centenarians for every 100,000 residents. The life expectancy in Okinawa is 81.2 years (86 for women, 78 for men), also one of the highest in the world.

What is responsible for such longevity in Okinawa? Some possible explanations include the following (Bendjilali & others, 2014; Willcox, Scapagnini, & Willcox, 2014; Willcox & Willcox, 2014; Willcox, Willcox, & Suzuki, 2002; Willcox & others, 2007, 2008):

- *Diet.* Okinawans eat very healthy food, heavy on grains, fish, and vegetables, light on meat, eggs, and dairy products. This diet actually produces mild caloric restriction (10 to 15 percent) (Willcox & Willcox, 2014). The risk of dying from cancer is far lower among Okinawans than among Japanese and Americans (see Figure 17.2). About 100,000 Okinawans moved to Brazil and quickly adopted the eating regimen of their new home, one heavy on red meat. The result: The life expectancy of the Brazilian Okinawans is now 17 years lower than Okinawa's 81 years!

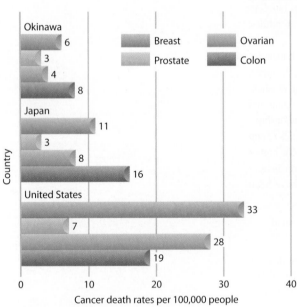

FIGURE 17.2

RISKS OF DYING FROM CANCER IN OKINAWA, JAPAN, AND THE UNITED STATES. The risk of dying from different forms of cancer is lower in Okinawa than in the United States and Japan (Willcox, Willcox, & Suzuki, 2002). Okinawans eat lots of tofu and soy products, which are rich in flavonoids (substances that are believed to lower the risk of breast and prostate cancer). They also consume large amounts of fish, especially tuna, mackerel, and salmon, which reduce the risk of breast cancer.

- *Low-stress lifestyle.* The easygoing lifestyle in Okinawa more closely resembles that of a laid-back South Sea island than that of the high-stress world on the Japanese mainland.
- *Caring community.* Okinawans look out for each other and do not isolate or ignore their older adults. If older adults need help, they don't hesitate to ask a neighbor. Such support and caring is likely responsible for Okinawa having the lowest suicide rate among older women in East Asia, an area noted for its high suicide rate among older women.
- *Activity.* Many older adults in Okinawa are physically vigorous, engaging in activities such as taking walks and working in their gardens. Many older Okinawans also continue working at their jobs.
- *Spirituality.* Many older adults in Okinawa find a sense of purpose in spiritual practice. Prayer is commonplace and believed to ease the mind of stress and problems.

Teru Kingjo, 88, continues to work as a weaver on Okinawa Island, Japan. She, like many Okinawans, believes that having a sense of purpose helps people to live longer.

THE YOUNG-OLD AND THE OLDEST-OLD

Do you want to live to be 100, or 90? As we discussed in Chapter 1, these ages are part of late adulthood, which begins in the sixties and extends to approximately 120 to 125 years of age. This is the longest span of any period of human development—50 to 60 years. Increasingly, a distinction is being made between the *young-old* (65 to 84 years of age) and *oldest-old* (85 years and older). An increased interest in successful aging is producing a portrayal of the oldest-old that is more optimistic than past stereotypes (Andersen & others, 2012; Jeste & others, 2013). Interventions such as cataract surgery and a variety of rehabilitation strategies are improving the functioning of the oldest-old. And there is cause for optimism in the development of new regimens of prevention and intervention, such as engaging in regular exercise (Buchman & others, 2012; Haltiwanger, 2013).

Many experts on aging prefer to talk about such categories as the young-old and oldest-old in terms of *function* rather than age. Remember from Chapter 1 that we described age not only in terms of chronological age but also in terms of biological age, psychological age, and social age. Thus, in terms of *functional age*—the person's actual ability to function—an 85-year-old might well be more biologically and psychologically fit than a 65-year-old.

Still, there are some significant differences between adults in their sixties or seventies and adults who are 85 and older. As we discussed in Chapter 1, Paul Baltes and his colleagues (Baltes, 2003; Scheibe, Freund, & Baltes, 2007) argue that the oldest-old (85 and over) face a number of problems, including sizable losses in cognitive potential and ability to learn; an increase in chronic stress; a substantial prevalence of physical and mental disabilities; high levels of frailty; increased loneliness; and the difficulty of dying with dignity at older ages. He contrasts the problems of the oldest-old with the increase in successful aging of adults in their sixties and seventies. Compared with the oldest-old, the young-old have a substantial potential for physical and cognitive fitness, higher levels of emotional well-being, and more effective strategies for mastering the gains and losses of old age.

The oldest-old today are mostly female, and the majority of these women are widowed and live alone if they are not institutionalized. The majority also are hospitalized at some time in the last years of life, and the majority die alone in a hospital or institution. Their needs, capacities, and resources are often different from those of older adults in their sixties and seventies (Scheibe, Freund, & Baltes, 2007).

Despite the negative portrait of the oldest-old by Baltes and his colleagues, they are a heterogeneous, diversified group. In the New England Centenarian Study, 15 percent of the individuals 100 years and older were living independently at home, 35 percent with family members or in assisted living, and 50 percent in nursing homes (Perls, 2007).

A significant number of the oldest-old have cognitive impairments, but many do not (Mall & others, 2014; Tarnanas & others, 2014). Almost one-fourth of the oldest-old are institutionalized, and many report some limitation of activity or difficulties in caring for themselves. However, more than three-fourths are not institutionalized. The majority of older adults aged 80 and over continue to live in the community. More than one-third of older

> To me old age is always fifteen years older than I am.
>
> **—BERNARD BARUCH**
> *American Statesman, 20th Century*

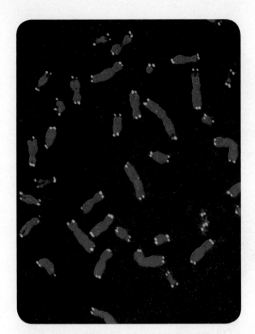

FIGURE **17.3**

TELOMERES AND AGING. The photograph shows actual telomeres lighting up the tips of chromosomes.

adults 80 and over who live in the community report that their health is excellent or good; 40 percent say that they have no activity limitations (Suzman & others, 1992). Less than 50 percent of U.S. 85- to 89-year-olds have a disability (Siegler, Bosworth, & Poon, 2003), and a substantial subgroup of the oldest-old are robust and active. The oldest-old who have aged successfully have often been unnoticed and unstudied.

BIOLOGICAL THEORIES OF AGING

Even if we stay remarkably healthy, we begin to age at some point. In fact, some life-span experts argue that biological aging begins at birth (Schaie, 2000). What are the biological explanations of aging? Intriguing explanations of why we age are provided by five biological theories: evolutionary theory, cellular clock theory, free-radical theory, mitochondrial theory, and hormonal stress theory.

Evolutionary Theory   Recall from Chapter 2 the view that the benefits conferred by evolutionary selection decrease with age (Baltes, 2003). In the **evolutionary theory of aging,** natural selection has not eliminated many harmful conditions and nonadaptive characteristics in older adults (Gems, 2014; Le Couteur & Simpson, 2011; Shokhirev & Johnson, 2014). Why? Because natural selection is linked to reproductive fitness, which is present only in the earlier part of adulthood. For example, consider Alzheimer disease, an irreversible brain disorder that does not appear until late middle adulthood or late adulthood. In evolutionary theory, if Alzheimer disease occurred earlier in development, it might have been eliminated many centuries ago.

Cellular Clock Theory   **Cellular clock theory** is Leonard Hayflick's (1977) theory that cells can divide a maximum of about 75 to 80 times, and that as we age our cells become less capable of dividing. Hayflick found that cells extracted from adults in their fifties to seventies divided fewer than 75 to 80 times. Based on the ways cells divide, Hayflick places the upper limit of the human life-span potential at about 120 to 125 years of age.

In the last decade, scientists have tried to fill in a gap in cellular clock theory (Ding & others, 2014; Zhao & others, 2014). Hayflick did not know why cells die. The answer may lie at the tips of chromosomes, at telomeres, which are DNA sequences that cap chromosomes (Harari & others, 2013; Zhang & others, 2014).

Each time a cell divides, the telomeres become shorter and shorter (see Figure 17.3). After about 70 or 80 replications, the telomeres are dramatically reduced, and the cell no longer can reproduce. One study revealed that healthy centenarians had longer telomeres than unhealthy centenarians (Terry & others, 2008). And recent studies even have found that shorter telomere length is linked to having worse social relationships, being less optimistic, and showing greater hostility (Uchino & others, 2012; Zalli & others, 2014).

Injecting the enzyme telomerase into human cells grown in the laboratory has been found to substantially extend the life of the cells beyond the approximately 70 to 80 normal cell divisions (Harrison, 2012). However, telomerase is present in approximately 85 to 90 percent of cancerous cells and thus may not produce healthy life extension of cells (Bertorelle & others, 2014; Fakhoury, Nimmo, & Autexier, 2007). To capitalize on the high presence of telomerase in cancerous cells, researchers currently are investigating telomerase-related gene therapies that inhibit telomerase and lead to the death of cancerous cells while keeping healthy cells alive (Christodoulidou & others, 2013; Londono-Vallejo & Wellinger, 2012). A recent focus of these gene therapies is on stem cells and their renewal (Hoffmeyer & others, 2012). Telomeres and telomerase are increasingly thought to be key components of the stem cell regeneration process, providing a possible avenue to restrain cancer and delay aging (Gunes & Rudolph, 2013; Shay, Reddel, & Wright, 2012).

Free-Radical Theory   A second microbiological theory of aging is **free-radical theory,** which states that people age because when cells metabolize energy, the by-products include unstable oxygen molecules known as *free radicals*. The free radicals ricochet around the cells, damaging DNA and other cellular structures (Bachschmid & others, 2013;

evolutionary theory of aging This theory states that natural selection has not eliminated many harmful conditions and nonadaptive characteristics in older adults; thus, the benefits conferred by evolution decline with age because natural selection is linked to reproductive fitness.

cellular clock theory Leonard Hayflick's theory that the maximum number of times that human cells can divide is about 75 to 80. As we age, our cells have less capacity to divide.

free-radical theory A microbiological theory of aging that states that people age because normal metabolic processes within their cells produce unstable oxygen molecules known as free radicals. These molecules ricochet around inside cells, damaging DNA and other cellular structures.

da Cruz & others, 2014). The damage can lead to a range of disorders, including cancer and arthritis (Kolovou & others, 2014; Tezil & Basaga, 2014). Overeating is linked with an increase in free radicals, and researchers recently have found that calorie restriction—a diet restricted in calories but adequate in proteins, vitamins, and minerals—reduces the oxidative damage created by free radicals (Cerqueira & others, 2012; Kowaltowski, 2011). In addition to diet, researchers also are exploring the role that exercise might play in reducing oxidative damage in cells (Sarifakioglu & others, 2014). A recent study of obese men found that endurance exercise reduced their oxidative damage (Samjoo & others, 2013).

Mitochondrial Theory   There is increasing interest in the role that *mitochondria*—tiny bodies within cells that supply essential energy for function, growth, and repair—might play in aging (Arnsburg & Kirstein-Miles, 2014; Shih & Donmez, 2013) (see Figure 17.4). **Mitochondrial theory** states that aging is due to the decay of mitochondria. It appears that this decay is primarily caused by oxidative damage and loss of critical micronutrients supplied by the cell (Christian & Shadel, 2014; Romano & others, 2014; Valcarcel-Ares & others, 2014).

How does this damage and loss of nutrients occur? Among the by-products of mitochondrial energy production are the free radicals we just described. According to the mitochondrial theory, the damage caused by free radicals initiates a self-perpetuating cycle in which oxidative damage impairs mitochondrial function, which results in the generation of even greater amounts of free radicals. The result is that over time the affected mitochondria become so inefficient that they cannot generate enough energy to meet cellular needs (Schulz & others, 2014; Schiavi & Ventura, 2014).

Defects in mitochondria are linked with cardiovascular disease, neurodegenerative diseases such as Alzheimer disease, Parkinson disease, and decline in liver functioning (Fabian & others, 2014; Edeas & Weissig, 2013). Mitochondria likely play important roles in neuronal plasticity (Dorszewska, 2013). However, it is not known whether the defects in mitochondria cause aging or are merely accompaniments of the aging process (Brand, 2011).

Hormonal Stress Theory   Cellular clock, free-radical, and mitochondrial theories attempt to explain aging at the cellular level. In contrast, **hormonal stress theory** argues that aging in the body's hormonal system can lower resistance to stress and increase the likelihood of disease (Finch & Seeman, 1999).

When faced with external challenges such as stressful situations, the human body adapts by altering internal physiological processes (Almeida & others, 2011). This process of adaptation and adjustment is referred to as *allostasis*. Allostasis is adaptive in the short term; however, continuous accommodation of physiological systems in response to stressors may result in *allostatic load*, a wearing down of body systems due to constant activity (Tomiyama & others, 2012).

Normally, when people experience stressors, the body responds by releasing certain hormones. As people age, the hormones stimulated by stress remain at elevated levels longer than they did when people were younger (Finch, 2011). These prolonged, elevated levels of stress-related hormones are associated with increased risks for many diseases, including cardiovascular disease, cancer, diabetes, and hypertension (Steptoe & Kivimaki, 2012). Researchers are exploring stress buffering strategies, including exercise, in an effort to find ways to attenuate some of the negative effects of stress on the aging process (Bauer & others, 2013).

Recently, a variation of hormonal stress theory has emphasized the role of a decline in immune system functioning with aging (Mate, Madrid, & la Fuente, 2014; Solana & others, 2012). Aging contributes to immune system deficits that give rise to infectious diseases in older adults (Badowski & others, 2014; Stowell, Robles, & Kane, 2013). The extended duration of stress and diminished restorative processes in older adults may accelerate the effects of aging on immunity.

Which of these biological theories best explains aging? That question has not yet been answered. It might turn out that more than one—or perhaps all—of these biological processes contribute to aging (Miller, 2009).

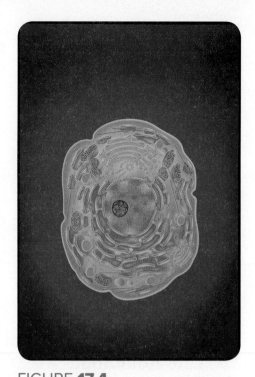

FIGURE **17.4**

MITOCHONDRIA. This color-coded illustration of a typical cell shows mitochondria in green. The illustration also includes the nucleus (pink) with its DNA (brown). *In what ways might changes in mitochondria be involved in aging?*

mitochondrial theory The theory that aging is caused by the decay of mitochondria, tiny cellular bodies that supply energy for function, growth, and repair.

hormonal stress theory The theory that aging in the body's hormonal system can decrease resistance to stress and increase the likelihood of disease.

Review
- What is the difference between life span and life expectancy? What characterizes centenarians? What sex differences exist in longevity?
- How can the differences between the young-old and oldest-old be summarized?
- What are the five main biological theories of aging?

Connect
- Go back to Figure 17.1 and see if you can link any of the items listed with research

or theories you read about in this section or in earlier chapters (for example, item 2 states "If you are married, add four years," and in Chapter 14 we read that "Individuals who are happily married live longer, healthier lives than either divorced individuals or those who are unhappily married").

Reflect *Your Own Personal Journey of Life*
- To what age do you think you will live? Why? To what age would you like to live?

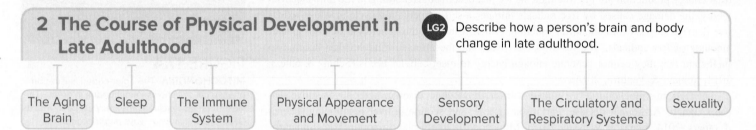

2 The Course of Physical Development in Late Adulthood

LG2 Describe how a person's brain and body change in late adulthood.

| The Aging Brain | Sleep | The Immune System | Physical Appearance and Movement | Sensory Development | The Circulatory and Respiratory Systems | Sexuality |

The physical decline that accompanies aging usually occurs slowly, and sometimes lost function can even be restored. We'll examine the main physical changes behind the losses of late adulthood and describe ways that older adults can age successfully.

THE AGING BRAIN

How does the brain change during late adulthood? Does it retain plasticity?

The Shrinking, Slowing Brain On average, the brain loses 5 to 10 percent of its weight between the ages of 20 and 90. Brain volume also decreases (Fjell & Walhovd, 2010). A recent study found a decrease in total brain volume and volume in key brain structures such as the frontal lobes and hippocampus from 22 to 88 years of age (Sherwood & others, 2011). Another study found that the volume of the brain was 15 percent less in older adults than younger adults (Shan & others, 2005). And in one analysis it was concluded that in healthy aging the decrease in brain volume is due mainly to shrinkage of neurons, lower numbers of synapses, and reduced length of axons but only to a minor extent attributable to neuron loss (Fjell & Walhovd, 2010).

Some areas of the brain shrink more than others (Raz & others, 2010). The prefrontal cortex is one area that shrinks the most with aging, and recent research has linked this shrinkage with a decrease in cognitive functioning and slower motor behavior in older adults (Jellinger & Attems, 2013; Rosano & others, 2012). The sensory regions of the brain—such as the primary visual cortex, primary motor cortex, and somatosensory cortex—are less vulnerable to the aging process (Rodrique & Kennedy, 2011).

A general slowing of function in the brain and spinal cord begins in middle adulthood and accelerates in late adulthood (Rosano & others, 2012). Both physical coordination and intellectual performance are affected. For example, after age 70 many adults no longer show a knee jerk reflex, and by age 90 most reflexes are much slower (Spence, 1989). The slowing of the brain can impair the performance of older adults on intelligence tests and various cognitive tasks, especially those that are timed (Lu & others, 2011). For example, a neuroimaging

developmental connection

Brain Development

Substantial growth in the prefrontal cortex occurs throughout infancy, childhood, and adolescence. Chapter 4, p. 107; Chapter 7, p. 216; Chapter 9, p. 268; Chapter 11, p. 344

study revealed that older adults were more likely to be characterized by slower processing in the prefrontal cortex during retrieval of information on a cognitive task than were younger adults (Rypma, Eldreth, & Rebbechi, 2007).

Historically, as in the research just discussed, much of the focus on links between brain functioning and aging has been on volume of brain structures and regions. Today, increased emphasis is being given to changes in myelination and neural networks. Recent research indicates that demyelination (a deterioration in the myelin sheath that encases axons, which is associated with information processing) of the brain occurs with aging in older adults (Callaghan & others, 2014; Rodrique & Kennedy, 2011).

Aging has also been linked to a reduction in synaptic functioning and the production of some neurotransmitters, including acetylcholine, dopamine, and gamma-aminobutyric acid (GABA) (Juraska & Lowry, 2012; Marcello & others, 2012). Reductions in acetylcholine have been linked to small declines in memory functioning and to the severe memory loss associated with Alzheimer disease, which will be further discussed in Chapter 18 (Merad & others, 2014). Normal age-related reductions in dopamine may cause problems in planning and carrying out motor activities (Balarajah & Cavanna, 2013). Severe reductions in the production of dopamine have been linked with age-related diseases characterized by a loss of motor control, such as Parkinson disease (Park & others, 2014). GABA helps to control the preciseness of the signal sent from one neuron to another, decreasing "noise," and its production decreases with aging (Hoshino, 2013).

The Adapting Brain   The story of the aging brain is far from being limited to loss and decline in functioning. The aging brain has remarkable adaptive capabilities (Cai & others, 2014; Karatsoreos & McEwen, 2013). Even in late adulthood, the brain loses only a portion of its ability to function, and the activities older adults engage in can influence the brain's development (Ansado & others, 2013; Kraft, 2012). For example, in one fMRI study, higher levels of aerobic fitness were linked with greater volume in the hippocampus, which translates into better memory (Erickson & others, 2009).

Can adults, even aging adults, generate new neurons? Researchers have found that **neurogenesis,** the generation of new neurons, does occur in lower mammalian species, such as mice. Also, research indicates that exercise and an enriched, complex environment can generate new brain cells in rats and mice, and that stress reduces their survival rate (Kuipers & others, 2013; Ramirez-Rodriquez & others, 2014) (see Figure 17.5). And one study revealed that coping with stress stimulated hippocampal neurogenesis in adult monkeys (Lyons & others, 2010). Researchers also have discovered that if rats are cognitively challenged to learn something, new brain cells survive longer (Shors, 2009).

It also is now accepted that neurogenesis can occur in human adults (Goritz & Frisen, 2012; Ruan & others, 2014). However, researchers have documented neurogenesis in only two brain regions: the hippocampus, which is involved in memory, and the olfactory bulb, which is involved in smell (Brus, Keller, & Levy, 2013; Huart, Rombaux, & Hummel, 2013;

neurogenesis The generation of new neurons.

developmental **connection**

Brain Development

At the peak of neurogenesis in prenatal development, it is estimated that as many as 200,000 neurons are being generated every minute. Chapter 3, p. 78

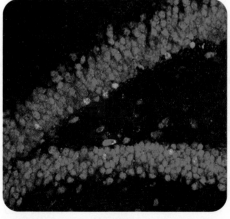
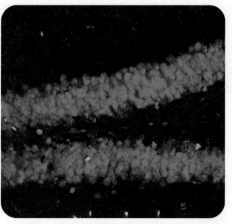

Exercise   **Enriched Environment**

FIGURE **17.5**

GENERATING NEW NERVE CELLS IN ADULT MICE. Researchers have found that exercise (running) and an enriched environment (a larger cage and many toys) can cause brain cells in adult mice to divide and form new brain cells (Kempermann, van Praag, & Gage, 2000). Cells were labeled with a chemical marker that becomes integrated into the DNA of dividing cells (red). Four weeks later, they were also labeled to mark neurons (nerve cells). As shown here, both the running mice and the mice in an enriched environment had many cells that were still dividing (red) and others that had differentiated into new nerve cells (orange).

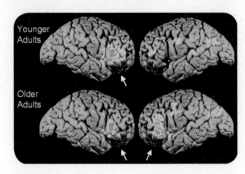

FIGURE 17.6

THE DECREASE IN BRAIN LATERALIZATION IN OLDER ADULTS. Younger adults primarily used the right prefrontal region of the brain (*top left photo*) during a recall memory task, whereas older adults used both the left and right prefrontal regions (*bottom two photos*).

developmental **connection**

Language

Speech and grammar are highly lateralized, strongly depending on activity in the left hemisphere. Chapter 4, p. 106

Left Hemisphere **Right Hemisphere**

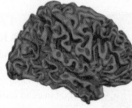

FIGURE 17.7

INDIVIDUAL DIFFERENCES IN HEMISPHERIC SPECIALIZATION IN OLDER ADULTS. On tough questions—such as "Are 'zombies' and 'unicorns' living or nonliving?"—the red patches indicate that T. Boone Pickens (who was tested at age 80) was relying mainly on the left hemisphere of his brain to make a decision. Most older adults show a stronger bilateral activation, using both hemispheres more equally than Pickens, whose lateralization was more characteristic of younger adults.

Mobley & others, 2014; Rolando & Taylor, 2014). It also is not known what functions these new brain cells perform, and at this point researchers have documented that they last for only several weeks (Nelson, 2006). Researchers currently are studying factors that might inhibit or promote neurogenesis, including various drugs, stress, and exercise (Gregoire & others, 2014; Schoenfeld & Gould, 2013). They also are examining how the grafting of neural stem cells to various regions of the brain, such as the hippocampus, might increase neurogenesis (Farioli-Vecchioli & others, 2014; He & others, 2013). Interest also is being directed to the possible role neurogenesis might play in neurodegenerative diseases, such as Alzheimer disease, Parkinson disease, and Huntington disease (Benarroch, 2013; Wang & Jin, 2014).

Dendritic growth can occur in human adults, possibly even in older adults (Eliasieh, Liets, & Chalupa, 2007). Recall from Chapter 4, "Physical Development in Infancy," that dendrites are the receiving portion of the neuron. One study compared the brains of adults at various ages (Coleman, 1986). From the forties through the seventies, the growth of dendrites increased. However, among people in their nineties dendritic growth no longer occurred. This dendritic growth might compensate for the possible loss of neurons through the seventies but not during the nineties. Lack of dendritic growth in older adults could be due to a lack of environmental stimulation and activity. Further research is needed to clarify precisely how dendrites change during aging.

Changes in lateralization may provide one type of adaptation in aging adults (Zhu, Zacks, & Slade, 2010). Recall that lateralization is the specialization of function in one hemisphere of the brain or the other. Using neuroimaging techniques, researchers found that brain activity in the prefrontal cortex is lateralized less in older adults than in younger adults when they are engaging in cognitive tasks (Angel & others, 2011; Cabeza, 2002; Manenti, Cotelli, & Miniussi, 2011; Rossi & others, 2005). For example, Figure 17.6 shows that when younger adults are given the task of recognizing words they have previously seen, they process the information primarily in the right hemisphere; older adults are more likely to use both hemispheres (Madden & others, 1999). The decrease in lateralization in older adults likely plays a compensatory role in the aging brain. That is, using both hemispheres may improve the cognitive functioning of older adults.

Of course, there are individual differences in how the brain changes in older adults (Nyberg & Backman, 2011). Consider highly successful business executive 85-year-old T. Boone Pickens, who continues to lead a very active lifestyle, regularly exercising and engaging in cognitively complex work. Pickens underwent an fMRI in cognitive neuroscientist Denise Park's laboratory, during which he was presented with various cognitive tasks. Instead of both hemispheres being active, his left hemisphere was dominant, just as is the case for most younger adults (Helman, 2008). Indeed, as the cognitive tasks became more complex, Pickens was more likely to use the left hemisphere of his brain (see Figure 17.7). Further indication of variation in the link between brain lateralization and cognitive processing was found in a recent study (Manenti, Cotelli, & Miniussi, 2010). Older adults who performed better on memory tasks showed less asymmetry in the prefrontal cortex than their counterparts who performed more poorly on the tasks.

Does staying intellectually challenged affect one's quality of life and longevity? To read further about aging and the brain, see *Connecting Through Research*.

SLEEP

Fifty percent or more of older adults complain of having difficulty sleeping, which can have detrimental effects on their lives (Farajinia & others, 2014; Neikrug & Ancoli-Israel, 2010). A recent study revealed that sleep time and sleep efficiency declined in older adults (Moraes & others, 2014). Poor sleep is a risk factor for falls, obesity, a lower level of cognitive functioning, and earlier death (Boelens, Hekman, & Verkerke, 2013; Xiao & others, 2013). For example, researchers found that spending more time in sleep benefitted older adults' memory (Aly & Moscovitch, 2010). Also, a recent research review indicated that improving older adults' sleep through behavioral and pharmaceutical treatments may enhance their cognitive skills (Pace-Schott & Spencer, 2011). Further, a recent study revealed poor quality of sleep in individuals with mild cognitive impairment, which in some cases is a

Does Staying Intellectually Challenged Affect One's Quality of Life and Longevity?

The Nun Study, directed by David Snowdon, is an intriguing ongoing investigation of aging in 678 nuns, many of whom live in a convent in Mankato, Minnesota (Snowdon, 2003; Pakhomov & Hemmy, 2014; Tyas & others, 2007). Each of the 678 nuns agreed to participate in annual assessments of her cognitive and physical functioning. They also agreed to donate their brains for scientific research when they die, and they are the largest group of brain donors in the world. Examination of the nuns' donated brains, as well as others', has led neuroscientists to believe that the brain has a remarkable capacity to change and grow, even in old age. The Sisters of Notre Dame in Mankato lead intellectually challenging lives, and brain researchers believe this contributes to their quality of life as older adults and possibly increases their longevity.

(a) (b)

(*a*) Sister Marcella Zachman (*left*) finally stopped teaching at age 97. Now, at 99, she helps ailing nuns exercise their brains by quizzing them on vocabulary or playing a card game called Skip-Bo, at which she deliberately loses. Sister Mary Esther Boor (*right*), also 99 years of age, is a former teacher who stays alert by doing puzzles and volunteering to work the front desk. (*b*) A technician holds the brain of a deceased Mankato nun. The nuns donate their brains for research that explores the effects of stimulation on brain growth.

Findings from the Nun Study so far include the following:

- Idea density, a measure of linguistic ability assessed through autobiographies early in the adult years (age 22), was linked with higher brain weight, fewer incidences of mild cognitive impairment, and fewer characteristics of Alzheimer disease in 75- to 95-year-old nuns (Riley & others, 2005).
- Positive emotions early in adulthood were linked to longevity (Danner, Snowdon, & Friesen, 2001). Handwritten autobiographies from 180 nuns, composed when they were 22 years of age, were scored for emotional content. The nuns whose early writings had higher scores for positive emotional content were more likely to still be alive at 75 to 95 years of age than their counterparts whose early writings were characterized by negative emotional content.

- Sisters who had taught for most of their lives showed more moderate declines in intellectual skills than those who had spent most of their lives in service-based tasks, which supports the notion that stimulating the brain with intellectual activity keeps neurons healthy and alive (Snowdon, 2002).

This and other research provides hope that scientists will discover ways to tap into the brain's capacity to adapt in order to prevent and treat brain diseases (Wirth & others, 2014). For example, scientists might learn more effective ways to improve older adults' cognitive functioning, reduce Alzheimer disease, and help older adults recover from strokes (Kalladka & Muir, 2014; Wen & others, 2014). Even when areas of the brain are permanently damaged by stroke, new message routes can be created to get around the blockage or to resume the function of that area, indicating that the brain does adapt.

precursor for Alzheimer disease (Hita-Yanez, Atienza, & Cantero, 2013). And a recent study found that sleep duration of more than 7 hours per night in older adults was linked to longer telomere length, which was similar to the telomere length of middle-aged adults (Cribbet & others, 2014).

Many of the sleep problems of older adults are associated with health problems (Reyes & others, 2013; Rothman & Mattson, 2012). Strategies to help older adults sleep better at night include avoiding caffeine, avoiding over-the-counter sleep remedies, staying physically active during the day, staying mentally active, and limiting naps (Morin, Savard, & Ouellet, 2013). A recent study revealed that regular exercise improves the sleep profile of older adults (Lira & others, 2011).

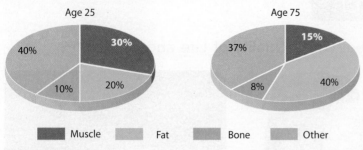

Percentage of total weight

Age 25   Age 75

Muscle   Fat   Bone   Other

FIGURE **17.8**

CHANGES IN BODY COMPOSITION OF BONE, MUSCLE, AND FAT FROM 25 TO 75 YEARS OF AGE. Notice the decrease in bone and muscle and the increase in fat from 25 to 75 years of age.

developmental **connection**

Biological Processes

On average, men lose 1 to 2 inches in height from 30 to 70 years of age and women can lose an much as 2 inches in height from age 25 to 75. Chapter 15, p. 461

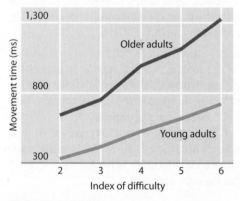

FIGURE **17.9**

MOVEMENT AND AGING. Older adults take longer to move than young adults, and this change occurs across a range of movement difficulty (Ketcham & Stelmach, 2001).

THE IMMUNE SYSTEM

Declining function of the body's immune system with aging is well documented (Cavanaugh, Weyand, & Goronzy, 2012; Stowell, Robles, & Kane, 2013). As indicated earlier in our discussion of hormonal stress theory, the extended duration of stress and diminished restorative processes in older adults may accelerate the effects of aging on immunity (Solana & others, 2012). Also, malnutrition involving low levels of protein is linked to a decrease in T cells that destroy infected cells and hence to deterioration in the immune system (Hughes & others, 2009). Exercise can improve immune system functioning (Spielmann & others, 2011). Because of the decline in the functioning of the immune system that accompanies aging, vaccination against influenza is especially important in older adults (Parodi & others, 2011).

PHYSICAL APPEARANCE AND MOVEMENT

In late adulthood, the changes in physical appearance that began occurring during middle age (as discussed in Chapter 15) become more pronounced. Wrinkles and age spots are the most noticeable changes.

We also become shorter as we get older. As we saw in Chapter 15, both men and women become shorter in late adulthood because of bone loss in their vertebrae (Hoyer & Roodin, 2009).

Our weight usually drops after we reach 60 years of age. This likely occurs because of muscle loss, which also gives our bodies a "sagging" look (Evans, 2010). Figure 17.8 shows the declining percentage of muscle and bone from age 25 to age 75, and the corresponding increase in the percentage of fat. A recent study found that long-term aerobic exercise was linked with greater muscle strength in 65- to 86-year-olds (Crane, Macneil, & Tarnopsolsky, 2013).

Older adults move more slowly than young adults, and this slowing occurs for movements with a wide range of difficulty (Davis & others, 2013) (see Figure 17.9). Adequate mobility is an important aspect of maintaining an independent and active lifestyle in late adulthood (Clark & others, 2011). Recent research indicates that obesity contributes to mobility limitation in older adults (Murphy & others, 2014; Vincent, Raiser, & Vincent, 2012). The good news is that regular walking decreases the onset of physical disability and reduces functional limitations in older adults (Mullen & others, 2012; Newman & others, 2006). Also, one study found that a combined program of physical activity and weight loss was linked to preserving mobility in older, obese adults in poor cardiovascular health (Rejeski & others, 2011).

SENSORY DEVELOPMENT

Seeing, hearing, and other aspects of sensory functioning are linked with our ability to perform everyday activities (Hochberg & others, 2012; Schneider & others, 2011). This link was documented in a study of more than 500 adults, 70 to 102 years of age, in which sensory acuity, especially visual capacity, was related to whether and how well older adults bathed and groomed themselves, completed household chores, engaged in intellectual activities, and watched TV (Marsiske, Klumb, & Baltes, 1997). How do vision, hearing, taste, smell, touch, and sensitivity to pain change in late adulthood?

Vision   With aging, visual acuity, color vision, and depth perception decline. Several diseases of the eye also may emerge in aging adults.

Visual Acuity   In late adulthood, the decline in vision that began for most adults in early or middle adulthood becomes more pronounced (Polat & others, 2012). Visual processing speed declines in older adults (Owsley, 2011). Night driving is especially difficult, to some extent because of diminishing sensitivity to contrasts and reduced tolerance for glare (Gruber & others, 2013). Dark adaptation is slower—that is, older individuals take longer to recover their vision when going from a well-lighted room to semidarkness. The area of the visual field becomes smaller, a change suggesting that the intensity of a stimulus in the peripheral area of the visual field needs to be increased if the stimulus is to be seen. Events taking place away from the center of the visual field might not be detected (West & others, 2010).

This visual decline often can be traced to a reduction in the quality or intensity of light reaching the retina (Nag & Wadhwa, 2012). At 60 years of age, the retina receives only about one-third as much light as it did at 20 years of age (Scialfa & Kline, 2007). In extreme old age, these changes might be accompanied by degenerative changes in the retina, causing severe difficulty in seeing. Large-print books and magnifiers might be needed in such cases.

An extensive study of visual changes in adults found that the age of older adults was a significant factor in how extensively their visual functioning differed from that of younger adults (Brabyn & others, 2001). Beyond 75, and more so beyond age 85, older adults showed significantly worse performance on a number of visual tasks in comparison with young adults and older adults in their sixties and early seventies. The greatest decline in visual perception beyond 75, and especially beyond 85, involved glare. The older adults, especially those 85 and older, fared much worse in being able to see clearly when glare was present, and they took much longer to recover from glare than younger adults did (see Figure 17.10). For example, whereas young adults recover vision following glare in less than 10 seconds, 50 percent of 90-year-olds have not recovered vision after 1.5 minutes.

Recent research has shown that sensory decline in older adults is linked to a decline in cognitive functioning. One study of individuals in their seventies revealed that visual decline was related to slower speed of processing information, which in turn was associated with greater cognitive decline (Clay & others, 2009). And a recent study found that hearing loss was associated with a reduction in cognitive functioning in older adults (Lin, 2011).

Color Vision   Color vision also may decline with age in older adults as a result of the yellowing of the lens of the eye (Scialfa & Kline, 2007). This decline is most likely to occur in the green-blue-violet part of the color spectrum. As a result, older adults may have trouble accurately matching closely related colors such as navy socks and black socks.

Depth Perception   As with many types of perception, depth perception changes little after infancy until adults become older. Depth perception typically declines in late adulthood, which can make it difficult for the older adult to determine how close or far away or how high or low something is (Bian & Anderson, 2008). A decline in depth perception can make steps or street curbs difficult to manage.

Diseases of the Eye   Three diseases that can impair the vision of older adults are cataracts, glaucoma, and macular degeneration:

- **Cataracts** involve a thickening of the lens of the eye that causes vision to become cloudy, opaque, and distorted (Leuschen & others, 2013). By age 70, approximately 30 percent of individuals experience a partial loss of vision due to cataracts. Initially, cataracts can be treated by glasses; if they worsen, the cloudy lens should be surgically removed and replaced with an artificial one (Chung & others, 2009; Michalska-Malecka & others, 2013). Diabetes is a risk factor for the development of cataracts (Olafsdottir, Andersson, & Stefansson, 2012).
- **Glaucoma** involves damage to the optic nerve because of the pressure created by a buildup of fluid in the eye (Akpek & Smith, 2013). Approximately 1 percent of individuals in their seventies and 10 percent of those in their nineties have glaucoma, which can be treated with eye drops. If left untreated, glaucoma can ultimately destroy a person's vision.

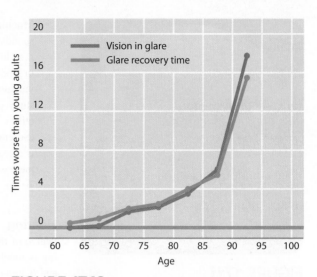

FIGURE 17.10

RATES OF DECLINE IN VISUAL FUNCTIONING RELATED TO GLARE IN ADULTS OF DIFFERENT AGES. Older adults, especially those 85 and older, fare much worse than younger adults in being able to see clearly when glare is present, and their recovery from glare is much slower. These data were collected from a random sample of community-dwelling older adults living in Marin County, California. For each age, the graph shows the factor by which the group's median performance was worse than normative values for young adults.

developmental **connection**

Perception

The visual cliff was used to determine whether infants have depth perception. Chapter 4, p. 128

cataracts A thickening of the lens of the eye that causes vision to become cloudy, opaque, and distorted.

glaucoma Damage to the optic nerve because of the pressure created by a buildup of fluid in the eye.

FIGURE 17.11

MACULAR DEGENERATION. This simulation of the effect of macular degeneration shows how individuals with this eye disease can see their peripheral field of vision but can't clearly see what is in their central visual field.

• **Macular degeneration** involves deterioration of the macula of the retina, which corresponds to the focal center of the visual field. Individuals with macular degeneration may have relatively normal peripheral vision but be unable to see clearly what is right in front of them (Taylor, 2012) (see Figure 17.11). This condition affects 1 in 25 individuals from 66 to 74 years of age and 1 in 6 of those 75 years old and older. One study revealed that cigarette smoking contributes to macular degeneration (Schmidt & others, 2006). If the disease is detected early, it can be treated with laser surgery (Sorensen & Kemp, 2010). However, macular degeneration is difficult to treat and thus is a leading cause of blindness in older adults (Cacho & others, 2010). Also, there is increased interest in using stem-cell-based therapy for macular degeneration (Eveleth, 2013).

Hearing For hearing as for vision, the age of older adults is important in determining the degree of decline (Pacala & Yeuh, 2012) (see Figure 17.12). The decline in vision and hearing is much greater in individuals 75 years and older than in individuals 65 to 74 years of age (Charness & Bosman, 1992).

Hearing impairment usually does not become much of an impediment until late adulthood (Li-Korotky, 2012). Only 19 percent of individuals from 45 to 54 years of age experience some type of hearing problem (Harris, 1975). By contrast, a recent national survey revealed that 63 percent of adults 70 years and older had a hearing loss defined as an inability to hear sounds at frequencies higher than 25 dB with their better ear (Lin & others, 2011). In this study, hearing aids were used by 40 percent of those with moderate hearing loss.

Older adults often don't recognize that they have a hearing problem, deny that they have one, or accept it as a part of growing old (Pacala & Yeuh, 2012). A recent study across 10 years also found that poor nutrition and a lifetime of smoking were linked to more rapid onset of hearing difficulties in older adults (Heine & others, 2013).

Hearing loss in older adults is linked to declines in activities of daily living, cognitive functioning, and language, as indicated by the results of the following research. One study found that severity of age-related hearing loss was linked to impaired activities of daily living (Gopinath & others, 2012). Another study revealed that hearing loss was associated with a reduction in cognitive functioning in older adults (Lin, 2011).

Smell and Taste Most older adults lose some of their sense of smell or taste, or both (Murphy, 2009). These losses often begin around 60 years of age (Hawkes, 2006). A majority of individuals age 80 and older experience a significant reduction in smell (Lafreniere & Mann, 2009). Researchers have found that older adults show a greater decline in their sense of smell than in their sense of taste (Schiffman, 2007). Smell and taste decline less in healthy older adults than in their less healthy counterparts.

Touch and Pain Changes in touch and pain sensitivity are also associated with aging (Arneric & others, 2014; Kemp & others, 2014; Mantyh, 2014). One study found that with aging, individuals could detect touch less in the lower extremities (ankles, knees, and so

Perceptual System	65 to 74 years	75 years and older
Vision	There is a loss of acuity even with corrective lenses. Less transmission of light occurs through the retina (half as much as in young adults). Greater susceptibility to glare occurs. Color discrimination ability decreases.	There is a significant loss of visual acuity and color discrimination, and a decrease in the size of the perceived visual field. In late old age, people are at significant risk for visual dysfunction from cataracts and glaucoma.
Hearing	There is a significant loss of hearing at high frequencies and some loss at middle frequencies. These losses can be helped by a hearing aid. There is greater susceptibility to masking of what is heard by noise.	There is a significant loss at high and middle frequencies. A hearing aid is more likely to be needed than in young-old age.

FIGURE 17.12

VISION AND HEARING DECLINE IN LATE ADULTHOOD

on) than in the upper extremities (wrists, shoulders, and so on) (Corso, 1977). For most older adults, a decline in touch sensitivity is not problematic (Hoyer & Roodin, 2009). And one study revealed that older adults who are blind retain a high level of touch sensitivity, which likely is linked to their use of active touch in their daily lives (Legge & others, 2008).

An estimated 60 to 75 percent of older adults report at least some persistent pain (Molton & Terrill, 2014). The most frequent pain complaints of older adults are back pain (40 percent), peripheral neuropathic pain (35 percent), and chronic joint pain (15 to 25 percent) (Denard & others, 2010). The presence of pain increases with age in older adults, and women are more likely to report having pain than are men (Tsang & others, 2008). Older adults are less sensitive to pain than are younger adults (Harkins, Price, & Martinelli, 1986). However, when older adults experience pain they may be less tolerant of it than are younger adults (Farrell, 2012).

Researchers have found that older adults experience a decrease in brain volume related to pain processing and this decline is most pronounced in the prefrontal cortex and hippocampus and less pronounced in the brain stem (Farrell, 2012). Other physical changes in pain processing occur in the somatosensory pathways (Yezierski, 2012). Although decreased sensitivity to pain can help older adults cope with disease and injury, it can also mask injuries and illnesses that need to be treated.

Perceptual Motor Coupling   As we saw in Chapter 4, perception and action are coupled in infants and children. Perception and action are coupled throughout the human life span. Driving a car illustrates the coupling of perceptual and motor skills. The decline in perceptual-motor skills in late adulthood makes driving a car difficult for many older adults (Dawson & others, 2010; Stavrinos & others, 2013). Drivers over the age of 65 are involved in more traffic accidents than middle-aged adults because of mistakes such as improper turns, not yielding the right of way, and not obeying traffic signs; their younger counterparts are more likely to have accidents because they are speeding (Sterns, Barrett, & Alexander, 1985; Lavalliere & others, 2011). Older adults can compensate for declines in perceptual-motor skills by driving shorter distances, choosing less congested routes, and driving only in daylight.

A recent extensive research review evaluated the effectiveness of two types of interventions in improving older adults' driving: cognitive training and exercise (Ross, Schmidt, & Ball, 2013):

- *Cognitive training.* Cognitive training programs have shown some success in older adults, including improving their driving safety and making driving less difficult. In one study conducted by Karlene Ball and her colleagues (2010), training designed to enhance speed of processing produced more than a 40 percent reduction in at-fault crashes over a six-year period.

- *Education.* Results are mixed with regard to educational interventions that seek to improve older adults' driving ability and to reduce their involvement in traffic accidents (Gaines & others, 2011).

THE CIRCULATORY AND RESPIRATORY SYSTEMS

Cardiovascular disorders increase in late adulthood (Emery, Anderson, & Goodwin, 2013; Veronica & Esther, 2012). In one analysis, 57 percent of 80-year-old men and 60 percent of 81-year-old women had hypertension, and 32 percent of the men and 31 percent of the women had experienced a stroke (Aronow, 2007).

Today, most experts on aging recommend that consistent blood pressures above 120/80 should be treated to reduce the risk of heart attack, stroke, or kidney disease (Krakoff, 2008). A rise in blood pressure with age can be linked to illness, obesity, stiffening of blood vessels, stress, or lack of exercise (Fiocco & others, 2013). The longer any of these factors persist, the higher the individual's blood pressure gets. A recent national analysis found that resistant hypertension (hypertension that cannot be controlled with at least four antihypertensive agents) is increasing in the United States, likely because of increases in obesity and the

macular degeneration A disease that involves deterioration of the macula of the retina, which corresponds to the focal center of the visual field.

developmental connection

Sexuality

Older adults may express their sexuality differently from younger adults, focusing on touching and caressing in their sexual relationship when sexual intercourse becomes difficult. Chapter 19, p. 581

What are some characteristics of sexuality in older adults? How does sexuality change during late adulthood?

growing percentage of older adults in the population (Roberie & Elliott, 2012). Resistant hypertension is more common in the elderly (Strunk & Mayer, 2013).

Various drugs, a healthy diet, and exercise can reduce the risk of cardiovascular disease in many older adults (Tselepis, 2014). One study revealed that diminished exercise capacity and lack of walking were the best predictors of earlier death in older adults with heart problems (Reibis & others, 2010).

In the respiratory system, lung capacity drops 40 percent between the ages of 20 and 80, even when disease is not present (Fozard, 1992). Lungs lose elasticity, the chest shrinks, and the diaphragm weakens (Lalley, 2013). The good news, though, is that older adults can improve lung functioning with diaphragm-strengthening exercises. Severe impairments in lung functioning and death can result from smoking (Wilhelmsen & others, 2011).

SEXUALITY

In the absence of two circumstances—disease and the belief that old people are or should be asexual—sexuality can be lifelong (Corona & others, 2013; Marshall, 2012). Aging, however, does induce some changes in human sexual performance, more so in males than in females (Gray & Garcia, 2012).

Orgasm becomes less frequent in males with age, occurring in every second to third attempt rather than every time. More direct stimulation usually is needed to produce an erection. From 65 to 80 years of age, approximately one out of four men have serious problems getting and/or keeping erections, and after 80 years of age the percentage rises to one out of two men (Butler & Lewis, 2002). However, with recent advances in erectile dysfunction medications such as Viagra, an increasing number of older men, especially the young-old, are able to have an erection (Kim & others, 2014; Kirby, Creanga, & Strecher, 2013). Also, recent research suggests that declining levels of serum testosterone, which is linked to erectile dysfunction, can be treated with testosterone replacement therapy to improve sexual functioning in males (Celik & Yucel, 2014). However, the benefit-risk ratio of testosterone replacement therapy is uncertain for older males (Isidori & others, 2014).

An interview study of more than 3,000 adults 57 to 85 years of age revealed that many older adults are sexually active as long as they are healthy (Lindau & others, 2007). Sexual activity did decline through the later years of life: 73 percent of people 57 to 64 years old, 53 percent of people 65 to 74 years old, and 26 percent of adults 75 to 85 years old reported that they were sexually active. Even in the sexually active oldest group (75 to 85), more than 50 percent said they still have sex at least two to three times a month. Fifty-eight percent of sexually active 65- to 74-year-olds and 31 percent of 75- to 85-year-olds said they engage in oral sex. As with middle-aged and younger adults, older adults who did not have a partner were far less likely to be sexually active than those who had a partner. For older adults with a partner who reported not having sex, the main reason was poor health, especially the male partner's physical health.

A large-scale study of individuals from 57 to 85 years of age revealed that sexual activity, a good-quality sexual life, and interest in sex were positively related to health in middle and late adulthood (Lindau & Gavrilova, 2010). Also in this study, these aspects of sexuality were higher for aging males than aging women, and this gap widened with age. Further, sexually active life expectancy was longer for men than women, but men lost more years of sexually active life due to poor health than women did.

As indicated in Figure 17.13, sexual activity with a partner declined from the last part of middle adulthood through late adulthood, with a lower rate of sexual activity with a partner for women than men. Indeed, a challenge for a sexually interested older woman is not having a partner. At 70 years of age, approximately 70 percent of women don't have a partner compared with only about 35 percent of men. Many older women's husbands have died, and many older men are in relationships with younger women.

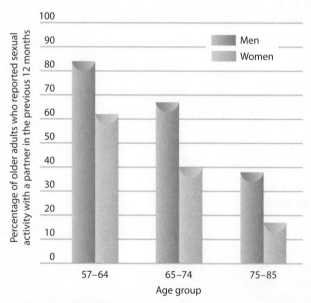

FIGURE **17.13**

SEXUAL ACTIVITY IN OLDER ADULTS WITH A PARTNER

Review *Connect* Reflect

LG2 Describe how a person's brain and body change in late adulthood.

Review

- How much plasticity and adaptability does the aging brain have?
- What characterizes older adults' sleep?
- How does the immune system change with aging?
- What changes in physical appearance and movement characterize late adulthood?
- How do vision, hearing, smell and taste, touch, and sensitivity to pain change in older adults?
- How do the circulatory and respiratory systems change in older adults?
- What is the nature of sexuality in late adulthood?

Connect

- Many of the declines in the functioning of individuals in late adulthood start occurring in middle adulthood. Which declines in functioning occur mainly in late adulthood?

Reflect *Your Own Personal Journey of Life*

- If you could interview the Mankato nuns, what questions would you want to ask them to help you improve your understanding of successful aging?

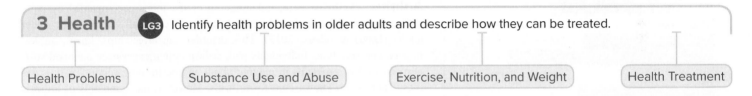

3 Health **LG3** Identify health problems in older adults and describe how they can be treated.

| Health Problems | Substance Use and Abuse | Exercise, Nutrition, and Weight | Health Treatment |

How healthy are older adults? What types of health problems do they have, and what can be done to maintain or improve their health and ability to function in everyday life?

HEALTH PROBLEMS

As we age, we become more susceptible to disease or illness. The majority of adults who are still alive at 80 years of age or older are likely to have some type of impairment. Chronic diseases (those with a slow onset and a long duration) are rare in early adulthood, increase in middle adulthood, and become more common in late adulthood (Hirsch & Sirois, 2014; Tinetti & others, 2011). As indicated in Figure 17.14, 84 percent of U.S. adults 65 years of age and older have one or more chronic conditions, and 62 percent have two or more chronic conditions (Partnership for Solutions, 2002).

As shown in Figure 17.15, arthritis is the most common chronic disorder in late adulthood, followed by hypertension. Older women have a higher incidence of arthritis and hypertension and are more likely to have visual problems, but are less likely to have hearing problems, than older men are.

Although adults over the age of 65 often have a physical impairment, many of them can still carry on their everyday activities or work. Chronic conditions associated with the greatest limitations on work are heart conditions (52 percent), diabetes (34 percent), asthma (27 percent), and arthritis (27 percent). Conflict in relationships has been linked with greater decline in older adults with diabetes or hypertension (Seeman & Chen, 2002). Low income is also strongly related to health problems in late adulthood (Ferraro, 2006). Approximately three times as many poor as non-poor older adults report

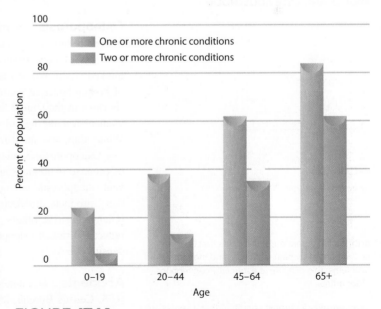

FIGURE **17.14**

PERCENT OF U.S. POPULATION WITH CHRONIC CONDITIONS ACROSS AGE GROUPS

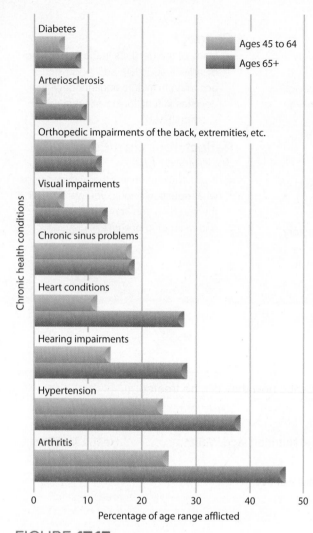

FIGURE 17.15

THE MOST PREVALENT CHRONIC CONDITIONS IN MIDDLE AND LATE ADULTHOOD

arthritis Inflammation of the joints that is accompanied by pain, stiffness, and movement problems; this disease is especially common in older adults.

osteoporosis A chronic condition that involves an extensive loss of bone tissue and is the main reason many older adults walk with a marked stoop.

that their activities are limited by chronic disorders. Recent studies document links between low socioeconomic status and health problems (Bayer & others, 2013; Granados, 2013). One study revealed that frailty increased for low-income older adults, regardless of their ethnicity (Szanton & others, 2010).

Causes of Death in Older Adults   Nearly 60 percent of U.S. adults 65 to 74 years old die of cancer or cardiovascular disease (Murphy, Xu, & Kochanek, 2012). As we saw in Chapter 15, cancer recently replaced cardiovascular disease as the leading cause of death in U.S. middle-aged adults. However, cardiovascular disease is the leading cause of death in U.S. 65- to 74-year-olds (Hoyert & Xu, 2012). And in the 75 to 84 and 85 and over age groups, cardiovascular disease also is the leading cause of death (Hoyert & Xu, 2012). As individuals age through the late adult years, the older they are the more likely they are to die of cardiovascular disease rather than cancer.

Ethnicity is linked with the death rates of older adults (U.S. Census Bureau, 2013). Among ethnic groups in the United States, African Americans have high death rates for stroke, heart disease, lung cancer, and female breast cancer. Asian Americans and Latinos have low death rates for these diseases. In the last decade, death rates for most diseases in African Americans, Latinos, and Asian Americans have decreased. However, death rates for most diseases remain high for African Americans (U.S. Census Bureau, 2013).

Arthritis   Arthritis is an inflammation of the joints accompanied by pain, stiffness, and movement problems. Arthritis is especially common in older adults (Davis & others, 2013). This disorder can affect hips, knees, ankles, fingers, and vertebrae. Individuals with arthritis often experience pain and stiffness, as well as problems in moving about and performing routine daily activities. There is no known cure for arthritis. However, the symptoms of arthritis can be reduced by drugs such as aspirin, range-of-motion exercises for the afflicted joints, weight reduction, and in extreme cases, replacement of the crippled joint with a prosthesis (Xu & others, 2013). Recent research has documented the benefits of exercise in older adults with arthritis (Oiestad & others, 2013). For example, a high-intensity, 16-week strength-training program significantly increased the strength and reduced the pain of arthritis patients (Flint-Wagner & others, 2009).

Osteoporosis   Normal aging brings some loss of bone tissue, but in some instances loss of bone tissue can become severe (Rothman & others, 2014). **Osteoporosis** involves an extensive loss of bone tissue. Osteoporosis is the main reason many older adults walk with a marked stoop. Women are especially vulnerable to osteoporosis, which is the leading cause of broken bones in women (Davis & others, 2013). Approximately 80 percent of osteoporosis cases in the United States occur in females, 20 percent in males. Almost two-thirds of all women over the age of 60 are affected by osteoporosis. It is more common in non-Latina White, thin, and small-framed women.

Osteoporosis is related to deficiencies in calcium, vitamin D, and estrogen, and to lack of exercise (Christianson & Shen, 2013; Kitchin, 2013; Welch & Hardcastle, 2014). To prevent osteoporosis, young and middle-aged women should eat foods rich in calcium (such as dairy products, broccoli, turnip greens, and kale), exercise regularly, and avoid smoking (Giangregorio & others, 2014; Hsu & others, 2014). Drugs such as Fosamax can be used to reduce the risk of osteoporosis (Iolascon & others, 2013). Aging women should also get bone density checks.

Accidents   Unintended injuries are the ninth leading cause of death among older adults (U.S. Census Bureau, 2013). Injuries resulting from a fall at home or a traffic accident in which an older adult is a driver or an older pedestrian is hit by a vehicle are common (Verghese & others, 2010). Falls are the leading cause of injury deaths among adults who are 65 years and older (National Center for Health Statistics, 2013). Each year, approximately

200,000 adults over the age of 65 (most of them women) fracture a hip in a fall. Half of these older adults die within 12 months, frequently from pneumonia. Two-thirds of older adults who experience a fall are likely to fall again in the next six months.

SUBSTANCE USE AND ABUSE

In many cases, older adults are taking multiple medications, which can increase the risks associated with consuming alcohol or other drugs. For example, when combined with tranquilizers or sedatives, alcohol use can impair breathing, produce excessive sedation, and be fatal.

How extensive is substance abuse in older adults? A national survey found that in 2010 the percentage of individuals who engaged in binge drinking (defined as four or more drinks for women and five or more drinks for men on one occasion in the past 30 days) declined considerably in the middle and late adulthood years (Centers for Disease Control and Prevention, 2012b) (see Figure 17.16). However, the frequency of binge drinking in the past 30 days was highest among older adults (5.5 episodes).

Despite the decline in the percentage of individuals who engage in binge drinking in late adulthood, the Substance Abuse and Mental Health Services Administration (2003) has identified substance abuse among older adults as the "invisible epidemic" in the United States. The belief is that substance abuse often goes undetected in older adults, and there is concern about older adults who abuse not only illicit drugs but prescription drugs as well (Wu & Blazer, 2011). Too often, screening questionnaires are not appropriate for older adults, and the consequences of alcohol abuse—such as depression, inadequate nutrition, congestive heart failure, and frequent falls—may erroneously be attributed to other medical or psychological conditions (Hoyer & Roodin, 2009). Because of the dramatic increase in the number of older adults anticipated over the twenty-first century, substance abuse is likely to characterize an increasing number of older adults (Atkinson, Ryan, & Turner, 2001).

Late-onset alcoholism is the label used to describe the onset of alcoholism after the age of 65. Late-onset alcoholism is often related to loneliness, loss of a spouse, or a disabling condition.

Researchers have found a protective effect of moderate alcohol use in older adults (Holahan & others, 2012; Smigielski, Bielecki, & Drygas, 2013; O'Keefe & others, 2014). One study revealed better physical and mental health, and increased longevity in older adults who drank moderately compared with those who drank heavily or did not drink at all (Rozzini, Ranhoff, & Trabucchi, 2007). Benefits of moderate drinking include better physical and mental performance, greater openness to social contacts, and ability to assert mastery over one's life.

Researchers have especially found that moderate drinking of red wine is linked to better health and increased longevity (Khurana & others, 2013; O'Keefe & others, 2014). Explanations of the benefits of red wine center on its role in lowering stress and reducing the risk of coronary heart disease (Carrizzo & others, 2013). Evidence is increasing that a chemical in the skin of red wine grapes—resveratrol—plays a key role in red wine's health benefits (Flamini & others, 2013; Pallauf & others, 2013). One study found that red wine, but not white, killed several lines of cancer cells (Wallenborg & others, 2009). Scientists are exploring how resveratrol, as well as calorie restriction, increases SIRT1, an enzyme that is involved in DNA repair and aging (Barger, 2013).

EXERCISE, NUTRITION, AND WEIGHT

Can exercise slow the aging process? Can eating a nutritious but calorie-reduced diet increase longevity? Let's examine how exercise, nutrition, and weight control might influence how healthily we age.

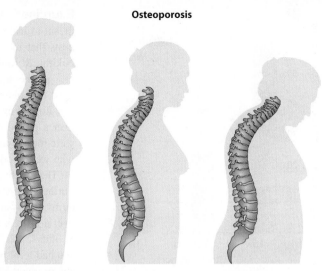

Osteoporosis

What characterizes osteoporosis? What factors contribute to osteoporosis?

Age Group	Percent	Drinks Per Occasion	Frequency
18–24	28	9	4.2
25–34	28	8	4.2
35–44	19	8	4.1
45–64	13	7	4.7
65 & over	4	5	5.5

FIGURE **17.16**

BINGE DRINKING THROUGH THE LIFE SPAN. *Note:* Percent refers to percent of individuals in a particular age group who engaged in binge drinking on an occasion in the past 30 days (4 or more drinks for women, 5 or more for men). Drinks per occasion reflects the intensity of the binge drinking. Frequency indicates the number of occasions in which binge drinking occurred in the past 30 days.
Source: After data presented by the Centers for Disease Control and Prevention, 2012b, Table 1.

What might explain the finding that drinking red wine in moderation is linked to better health and increased longevity?

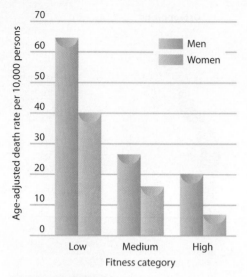

FIGURE **17.17**

PHYSICAL FITNESS AND MORTALITY. In this study of middle-aged and older adults, being moderately fit or highly fit meant that individuals were less likely to die over a period of eight years than their less fit (sedentary) counterparts (Blair & others, 1989).

- - - - - - - - - →

developmental **connection**

Health

Being physically fit and cognitively fit are key aspects of successful aging. Chapter 19, p. 588

FIGURE **17.18**

THE JOGGING HOG EXPERIMENT. Jogging hogs reveal the dramatic effects of exercise on health. In one investigation, a group of hogs was trained to run approximately 100 miles per week (Bloor & White, 1983). Then the researchers narrowed the arteries that supplied blood to the hogs' hearts. The hearts of the jogging hogs developed extensive alternate pathways for blood supply, and 42 percent of the threatened heart tissue was salvaged, compared with only 17 percent in a control group of non-jogging hogs.

Exercise Although we may be in the evening of our lives in late adulthood, we are not meant to live out our remaining years passively. Everything we know about older adults suggests that the more active they are, the healthier and happier they are likely to be (Freund, Nikitin, & Riediger, 2013).

In one study, exercise literally made the difference between life and death for middle-aged and older adults. More than 10,000 men and women were divided into categories of low fitness, medium fitness, and high fitness (Blair & others, 1989). Then they were studied over a period of eight years. As shown in Figure 17.17, sedentary participants (low fitness) were more than twice as likely to die during the eight-year time span of the study than those who were moderately fit and more than three times as likely to die as those who were highly fit. The positive effects of being physically fit occurred for both men and women in this study. Further, one study revealed that 60-year-old and older adults who were in the lowest fifth in terms of physical fitness as determined by a treadmill test were four times more likely to die over a 12-year period than their counterparts who were in the top fifth of physical fitness (Sui & others, 2007). A longitudinal study found that men who exercised regularly at 72 years of age had a 30 percent higher probability of still being alive at 90 years of age than their sedentary counterparts (Yates & others, 2008). And a study of more than 11,000 women found that low cardiorespiratory fitness was a significant predictor of death (Farrell & others, 2010).

Setting exercise goals and then carrying out an exercise plan not only are important in young adults but older adults as well. For example, a recent study of elderly women revealed that those who had set exercise-related personal goals were four times more likely to report high exercise activity eight years later (Saajanaho & others, 2014).

Gerontologists increasingly recommend strength training in addition to aerobic activity and stretching for older adults (Kennis & others, 2013; Machado-Vidotti & others, 2014; Nascimento Dda & others, 2014). The average person's lean body mass declines with age—about 6.6 pounds of lean muscle are lost each decade during the adult years. The rate of loss accelerates after age 45. Resistance exercises can preserve and possibly increase muscle mass in older adults (Forbes, Little, & Candow, 2012; Nascimento Dda & others, 2014).

Exercise is an excellent way to maintain health (Nagamatsu & others, 2014; Park, Han, & Kang, 2014; Siegler & others, 2013a, b; Vrantsidis & others, 2014). The current recommendations for older adults' physical activity are 2 hours and 30 minutes of moderate-intensity aerobic activity (brisk walking, for example) per week and muscle-strengthening activities on 2 or more days a week (Centers for Disease Control and Prevention, 2014). In the recent recommendations, even greater benefits can be attained with 5 hours of moderate intensity aerobic activity per week.

Researchers continue to document the positive effects of exercise in older adults. Exercise helps people to live independent lives with dignity in late adulthood (Caprara & others, 2013). At 80, 90, and even 100 years of age, exercise can help prevent older adults from falling down or even being institutionalized. Being physically fit means being able to do the things you want to do, whether you are young or old. More about research on exercise's positive benefits for health is shown in Figure 17.18.

Researchers who study exercise and aging have made the following discoveries:

- *Exercise is linked to increased longevity.* A recent study of older adults found that total daily physical activity was linked to increased longevity across a four-year period (Buchman & others, 2012). In a longitudinal study of Chinese women, those who exercised regularly were less likely to die over approximately a six-year period (Matthews & others, 2007). And in one analysis, energy expenditure by older adults during exercise that burns up at least 1,000 calories a week was estimated to increase life expectancy by about 30 percent, while burning up 2,000 calories a week in exercise was estimated to increase life expectancy by about 50 percent (Lee & Skerrett, 2001).

- *Exercise is related to prevention of common chronic diseases.* Exercise can reduce the risk of developing cardiovascular disease, type 2 diabetes, osteoporosis, stroke, and breast cancer (O'Keefe, Schnohr, & Lavie, 2013). For example, a recent study of older adults found that a higher lifetime physical activity level reduced age-related decline in cardiovascular and respiratory functions (Bailey & others, 2013).

- *Exercise is associated with improvement in the treatment of many diseases.* When exercise is used as part of the treatment, individuals with these diseases show improvement in symptoms: arthritis, pulmonary disease, congestive heart failure, coronary artery disease, hypertension, type 2 diabetes, obesity, and Alzheimer disease (Meikle & others, 2013; Oiestad & others, 2013; Vigorito & Giallauria, 2014).

- *Exercise improves older adults' cellular functioning.* Researchers increasingly are finding that exercise improves cellular functioning in older adults (Gielen & others, 2011). For example, researchers recently have found that aerobic exercise is linked to greater telomere length in older adults (Denham & others, 2013; Mason & others, 2013). And a recent study found that aerobic exercise increased proteins related to mitochondrial functioning in older adults (Konopka & others, 2014).

- *Exercise improves immune system functioning in older adults* (Moro-Garcia & others, 2014; Simpson & others, 2012). One study revealed that following exercise, a number of components of immune system functioning in older adult women improved (Sakamoto & others, 2009).

- *Exercise can optimize body composition and reduce the decline in motor skills as aging occurs.* Exercise can increase muscle mass and bone mass, as well as decrease bone fragility (Hewitt & others, 2014; Hsu & others, 2014; Olesen & others, 2014). One study found that participation in exercise activities was linked to a delay in the onset and progression of frailty (Peterson & others, 2009). And a recent study of elderly women revealed that a five-week Pilates class was associated with improved balance and strength in elderly women one year later (Bird & Fell, 2014). Increasingly, whole-body vibration training is being used with older adults to improve their balance control and muscle strength (Cristi & others, 2013; Ritzmann & others, 2014). Whole-body vibration training involves a person standing, or lying down on a machine with a vibrating platform. The machine's vibrations force muscles to rapidly contract and relax.

- *Exercise reduces the likelihood that older adults will develop mental health problems and can be effective in the treatment of mental health problems.* For example, exercise reduces the likelihood that older adults will develop depression and can be effective in treating depression in older adults (Park, Han, & Kang, 2014; Villaverde Gutierrez & others, 2012; Wang & others, 2014).

- *Exercise can reduce the negative effects of stress in older adults* (Moreira & others, 2014; Schoenfeld & others, 2013). A recent study revealed that older adults with a high level of stress who engaged in aerobic exercise had a lower cortisol level than their high-stress counterparts who did not engage in aerobic exercise (Heaney, Carroll, & Phillips, 2014).

- *Exercise is linked to improved brain, cognitive, and affective functioning in older adults.* Older adults who exercise show better brain functioning and process information more effectively than older adults who don't exercise (Nagamatsu & others, 2014; Kirk-Sanchez & McGough, 2014; Voss & others, 2013). A recent research review concluded that more active and physically fit older adults can allocate more attentional resources in interacting with the environment and process information more quickly (Gomez-Pinilla & Hillman, 2013).

As an example of exercise's influence on cognition, a study of older adults revealed that exercise increased the size of the hippocampus and improved memory (Erickson & others, 2011). Regarding affect, a recent study found that moderate-intensity exercise was associated with an increase in positive affect and a decrease in negative affect (Hogan, Mata, & Carstensen, 2013).

Despite the extensive documentation of exercise's power to improve older adults' health and quality of life, a national survey revealed that older adults have increased their exercise levels only slightly in recent years (Centers for Disease Control and Prevention, 2008) (see Figure 17.19). Possible explanations of older adults' failure to substantially increase their exercise focus on such factors as chronic illnesses, life crises (such as a spouse's death) that disrupt exercise schedules, embarrassment at being around others who are in better shape

Johnny Kelley, finishing one of the many Boston Marathons he ran as an older adult. In 1991, he ran his sixtieth Boston Marathon and, in 2000, he was named "Runner of the Century" by *Runner's World* magazine. At 70 years of age, Kelley was still running 50 miles a week. At that point in his life, Kelley said, "I'm afraid to stop running. I feel so good. I want to stay alive." He lived 27 more years and died at age 97 in 2004.

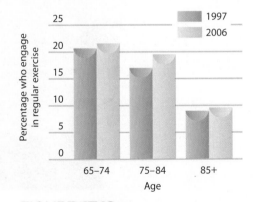

FIGURE **17.19**

REGULAR EXERCISE BY U.S. OLDER ADULTS: 1997 TO 2006

(especially if they haven't exercised much earlier in life), and the "why bother?" factor (not believing that exercise will improve their lives much) (Painter, 2008). But as we have seen, it is never too late to begin exercising, and older adults can significantly benefit from regular exercise (Guirado & others, 2012).

Nutrition and Weight   Three aspects of nutrition are especially important in older adults: (1) getting adequate nutrition, (2) avoiding overweight and obesity, and (3) the role of calorie restriction in improving health and extending life.

Healthy Nutrition   Eating a healthy, balanced diet and taking appropriate vitamins are important in helping older adults maintain their health. One change in eating behavior that can occur in older adults is a decrease in snacking between meals, which contributes to harmful weight loss, especially in women. Among the strategies for increasing weight gain in these women are the use of taste enhancers and calorie supplements between meals.

Overweight and Obesity   A recent national survey found that 35.4 percent of U.S. adults 60 years of age and older were obese in 2011–2012 (Ogden & others, 2013). In this recent survey, 32 percent of men and 38.1 percent of U.S. adults 60 years of age and older were obese. A recent large-scale study found a substantial link between being overweight/obese and having a higher mortality risk (Masters & others, 2013). However, some recent studies have reported that overweight adults live longer than normal-weight adults or that being overweight is not a risk factor for earlier death, especially in older adults (Berraho & others, 2010; Chang & others, 2012; Flicker & others, 2010). A recent study found that older adults whose overweight status was stable did not have a higher mortality risk but that those with a trajectory of increasing obesity from the fifties onward did have a higher mortality risk (Zheng, Tumin, & Qian, 2013).

A magazine article even mentioned that chubby might be the new healthy (Kolata, 2007). It's not clear why a few extra pounds that place someone in the overweight category might be linked to longevity. Possibly for some older adults, such as those recovering from surgery or those who develop pneumonia, the extra pounds may be protective. Some researchers argue that studies revealing a link between being overweight and living longer is likely due to inclusion of participants who have preexisting diseases (sometimes labeled "reverse causality") or sarcopenia (loss of lean body mass) (Greenberg, 2006).

Despite the several studies that have found a link between being overweight and living longer, the majority of studies have revealed that being overweight is a risk factor for an earlier death (de Hollander & others, 2012; Katzmarzyk & others, 2012; Masters & others, 2013; Preston & Stokes, 2011; Rizzuto & Fratiglioni, 2014). For example, a recent study of 70- to 75-year-olds revealed that a higher body mass index (BMI) was associated with all-cause mortality risk, with the greatest risk occurring for death due to cardiovascular disease (de Hollander & others, 2012). Obesity is linked to the acceleration of diseases in many older adults (Anton & others, 2013; Perez & others, 2013; Winett & others, 2014).

Researchers also consistently find that when individuals are overweight and fit, they have a much better health profile and greater longevity than those who are overweight and not fit (Masters & others, 2013; Matheson, King, & Everett, 2012). Some leading researchers now conclude that inactivity and low cardiorespiratory fitness are greater threats to health and longevity than being overweight (McAuley & Blair, 2011).

Calorie Restriction   Some studies have shown that calorie restriction in laboratory animals (such as rats and roundworms) can increase the animals' longevity (Fontana & Hu, 2014; Vera & others, 2013). And researchers have found that chronic problems such as cardiovascular, kidney, and liver disease appear at a later age when calories are restricted (Robertson & Mitchell, 2013; Yan & others, 2013). In addition, some recent research indicates that calorie restriction may provide neuroprotection for an aging central nervous system (Willette & others, 2012). One study revealed that after older adults engaged in calorie restriction for three months, their verbal memory improved (Witte & others, 2009).

What characterizes the current controversy about longevity and being overweight?

No one knows for certain how calorie restriction works to increase the life span of animals. Some scientists suggest that it might lower the level of free radicals and reduce oxidative stress in cells (Stankovic & others, 2013). For example, one study found that calorie restriction slowed the age-related increase in oxidative stress (Ward & others, 2005).

Others argue that calorie restriction might trigger a state of emergency called "survival mode" in which the body eliminates all unnecessary functions to focus only on staying alive. This survival mode likely is the result of evolution in which calorie restriction allowed animals to survive periods of famine, and thus the genes remain in the genomes of animal and human species today (Chen & Guarente, 2007).

However, a 25-year longitudinal study conducted by the National Institute of Aging casts some doubt on whether a calorie-restricted diet will increase longevity (Mattison & others, 2012). In this study, monkeys who were fed 30 percent fewer calories did not live longer than a control group of monkeys. The researchers concluded that genes and diet composition are likely better predictors of longevity than calorie restriction per se. The results in the National Institute of Aging study contrast with an ongoing study at the Wisconsin National Primate Research Center, which has reported a 30 percent improved survival rate for calorie-restricted monkeys (Colman & others, 2009). Thus, an appropriate conclusion at this time is that further research is needed to definitively answer the question as to whether calorie restriction increased longevity, especially in humans.

Whether similar very-low-calorie diets can stretch the human life span is not known (Stein & others, 2012). In some instances, the animals in these studies ate 40 percent less than normal. In humans, a typical level of calorie restriction involves a 30 percent decrease, which translates to about 1,120 calories a day for the average woman and 1,540 for the average man.

Do underweight women and men live longer? One study revealed that women who were 20 pounds or more underweight lived longer even after controlling for smoking, hypertension, alcohol intake, and other factors (Wandell, Carlsson, & Theobald, 2009). In this study, underweight men did not live longer when various factors were controlled.

The Controversy Over Vitamins and Aging   For years, most experts on aging and health argued that a balanced diet was all that was needed for successful aging; vitamin supplements were not recommended. However, recent research suggests the possibility that some vitamin supplements—mainly a group called "antioxidants," which includes vitamin C, vitamin E, and beta-carotene—help to slow the aging process and improve the health of older adults.

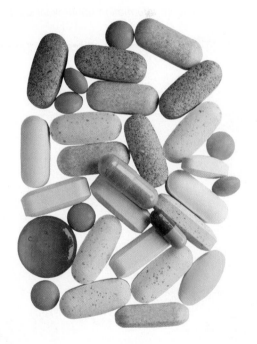

The theory is that antioxidants counteract the cell damage caused by free radicals, which are produced both by the body's own metabolism and by environmental factors such as smoking, pollution, and bad chemicals in the diet (Gandhi & Abramov, 2012). When free radicals cause damage (oxidation) in one cell, a chain reaction of damage follows. Antioxidants are theorized to act much like a fire extinguisher, helping to neutralize free-radical activity and reduce oxidative stress (Da Costa, Badawi, & El-Sohemy, 2012).

What have research studies found about the role of antioxidants in health? Recent research reviews have not supported the belief that antioxidant vitamin supplements can reduce the incidence of cancer and cardiovascular disease (Chen & others, 2012; Moyer, 2013; Potter, 2014). However, a recent meta-analysis of seven studies concluded that dietary intakes (not vitamin supplements) of vitamin E, C, and beta-carotene were linked to a reduced risk of Alzheimer disease (Li, Shen, & Ji, 2012).

There still are many uncertainties about the role of antioxidant vitamins in health (Otaegui-Arrazola & others, 2014). For example, it is unclear which vitamins should be taken, how large a dose should be taken, what the restraints are, and so on. Critics also argue that the key experimental studies documenting the effectiveness of the vitamins in slowing the aging process have not been conducted. The studies in this area thus far have been so-called population studies that are correlational rather than experimental in nature. Other factors—such as exercise, better health practices, and good nutritional habits—might be responsible for the positive findings about vitamins and aging rather than vitamins per se. Also, the free-radical theory is a theory and not a fact, and is only one of a number of theories about why we age.

HEALTH TREATMENT

The increase in the aging population is predicted to dramatically escalate health care costs over the foreseeable future. As older adults live longer, disease management programs will need to be expanded to handle the chronic disorders of older adults. The increasing demand for health services among the expanding population of older adults is likely to bring shortages

Sarah Kagan, Geriatric Nurse

Sarah Kagan is a professor of nursing at the University of Pennsylvania School of Nursing. She provides nursing consultation to patients, their families, nurses, and physicians regarding the complex needs of older adults related to their hospitalization. She also consults on research and the management of patients who have head and neck cancers. Kagan teaches in the undergraduate nursing program, where she directs a course on "Nursing Care in the Older Adult." In 2003, she was awarded a MacArthur Fellowship for her work in the field of nursing.

In Kagan's own words:

I'm lucky to be doing what I love—caring for older adults and families—and learning from them so that I can share this knowledge and develop or investigate better ways of caring. My special interests in the care of older adults who have cancer allow me the intimate privilege of being with patients at the best and worst times of their lives. That intimacy acts as a beacon—it reminds me of the value I and nursing as a profession contribute to society and the rewards offered in return (Kagan, 2008, p. 1).

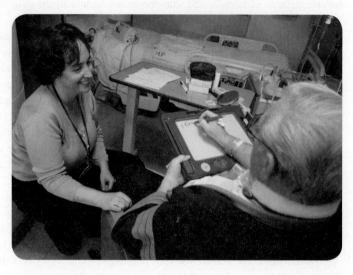

Sarah Kagan with a patient.

For more information about what geriatric nurses do, see page 43 in the Careers in Life-Span Development appendix.

of many types of health care professionals, including geriatric nurses, doctors, and health care aides (Bardach & Rowles, 2012).

What is the quality of health treatment that older adults in the United States receive? A study of older adults with health problems revealed that they receive the recommended medical care they need only half the time (Wenger & others, 2003). The researchers examined the medical records of 372 frail older adults who had been treated by two managed-care organizations over the course of one year. Then they documented the medical care each patient received and judged it using standard indicators of quality. For example, many older adults with an unsteady gait didn't get the help they need, such as physical therapy to improve their walking ability. Clearly, the quality of health treatment provided to older adults needs to be significantly improved.

Geriatric nurses can be especially helpful in treating the health care problems of older adults. To read about the work of one geriatric nurse, see *Connecting with Careers*.

The development of alternative home and community-based care has decreased the percentage of older adults who live in nursing homes (Katz & others, 2009). Still, as older adults age, their probability of being in a nursing home increases (see Figure 17.20). The quality of nursing homes and other extended-care facilities for older adults varies enormously and is a source of continuing concern (Hunt, Corazzini, & Anderson, 2014; Shah & others, 2012). More than one-third of these facilities are seriously deficient. They fail federally mandated inspections because they do not meet the minimum standards for physicians, pharmacists, and various rehabilitation specialists (occupational and physical therapists). Further concerns focus on the patient's right to privacy, access to medical information, safety, and lifestyle freedom within the individual's range of mental and physical capabilities.

Because of the inadequate quality of many nursing homes and the escalating costs for nursing home care, many specialists in the health problems of the aged stress that home health care, elder-care centers, and preventive medicine clinics

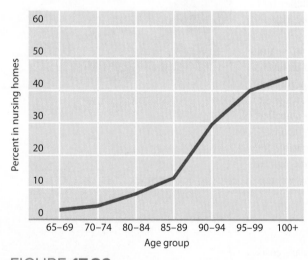

FIGURE 17.20

PERCENTAGE OF U.S. OLDER ADULTS OF DIFFERENT AGES IN NURSING HOMES

Health Care Providers and Older Adults

The attitudes of both the health care provider and the older adult are important aspects of the older adult's health care (Agrali & Akyar, 2014). Unfortunately, health care providers too often share society's stereotypes and negative attitudes toward older adults (Eymard & Douglas, 2012). In a health care setting, these attitudes can take the form of avoidance, dislike, and begrudged tolerance rather than positive, hopeful treatment. Health care personnel are more likely to be interested in treating younger persons, who more often have acute problems with a higher prognosis for successful recovery. They often are less motivated to treat older persons, who are more likely to have chronic problems with a lower prognosis for successful recovery.

Not only are physicians less responsive to older patients, but older patients often take a less active role in medical encounters with health care personnel than do younger patients. Older adults should be encouraged to take a more active role in their own health care.

The demand for home-care aides is predicted to increase dramatically in the next several decades because of the likely doubling of the 65-year-and-older population and older adults' preference for remaining out of nursing homes (Moos, 2007). Not only is it important to significantly increase the number of health care professionals available to treat older adults, but it is also very important that they not harbor negative stereotypes of older adults and that they show very positive attitudes toward them.

---

are good alternatives (Berenson & others, 2012; Kilgore, 2014). They are potentially less expensive than hospitals and nursing homes. They also are less likely to engender the feelings of depersonalization and dependency that occur so often in residents of institutions. Currently, there is an increased demand for, but shortage of, home-care workers because of the increase in population of older adults and their preference to stay out of nursing homes (Moos, 2007).

In a classic study, Judith Rodin and Ellen Langer (1977) found that an important factor related to health, and even survival, in a nursing home is the patient's feelings of control and self-determination. A group of elderly nursing home residents were encouraged to make more day-to-day choices and thus feel they had more responsibility for control over their lives. They began to decide such matters as what they ate, when their visitors could come, what movies they saw, and who could come to their rooms. A similar group in the same nursing home was told by the administrator how caring the nursing home was and how much the staff wanted to help, but these residents were given no opportunity to take more control over their lives. Eighteen months later, the residents who had been given responsibility and control were more alert and active, and said they were happier, than the residents who were only encouraged to feel that the staff would try to satisfy their needs. And the "responsible" or "self-control" group had significantly better improvement in their health than did the "dependent" group. Even more important was the finding that after 18 months only half as many nursing home residents in the "responsibility" group had died as in the "dependent" group (see Figure 17.21). Perceived control over one's environment, then, can literally be a matter of life or death.

Rodin's research shows that simply giving nursing home residents options for control can change their behavior and improve their health. To read further about health care providers and older adults, see *Connecting Development to Life*.

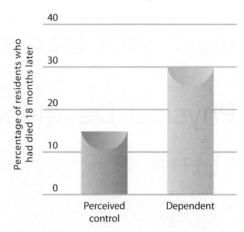

FIGURE 17.21

PERCEIVED CONTROL AND MORTALITY. In the study by Rodin and Langer (1977), nursing home residents who were encouraged to feel more in control of their lives were more likely to be alive 18 months later than those who were treated as being more dependent on the nursing home staff.

Review

- What are some common health problems in older adults? What are the main causes of death in older adults?
- What characterizes substance abuse in late adulthood?
- How do exercise, nutrition, and weight influence development in late adulthood?
- What are some options and issues in the health treatment of older adults?

Connect

- In this section, we learned that older adults fare better when they are given more responsibility and control in various aspects of their lives. At what other age stages is giving individuals more responsibility and control particularly important for their development? In what way(s)?

Reflect *Your Own Personal Journey of Life*

- What changes in your lifestyle now might help you age more successfully when you become an older adult?

---

topical **connections** *looking forward*

Eventually, the human life span ends with death. Compared with younger adults and children, most older adults are closer to death and more likely to know that they will die gradually over a period of time rather than suddenly. Physical impairments—such as cardiovascular disease and cancer—are the most likely reasons older adults will die. Actual death is sometimes difficult to determine and involves which portions of the brain are no longer functioning. Care for the dying often involves providing comfort and managing pain.

---

reach your **learning goals**

Physical Development in Late Adulthood

1 Longevity

Life Expectancy and Life Span

The Young-Old and the Oldest-Old

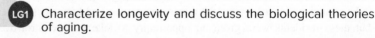 **LG1** Characterize longevity and discuss the biological theories of aging.

- Life expectancy refers to the number of years that will probably be lived by an average person born in a particular year. Life span is the maximum number of years an individual can live. Life expectancy has dramatically increased; life span has not. An increasing number of individuals live to be 100 or older. Genetics, health, and coping well with stress can contribute to becoming a centenarian. On the average, females live about six years longer than males do. The sex difference is likely due to biological and social factors.

- In terms of chronological age, the young-old have been described as being 65 to 84 years of age and the oldest-old as 85 years and older. Many experts on aging prefer to describe the young-old, old-old, and oldest-old in terms of functional age rather than chronological age. This view accounts for the fact that some 85-year-olds are more biologically and psychologically fit than some 65-year-olds. However, those 85 and older face significant problems, whereas those in their sixties and seventies are experiencing an increase in successful aging.

Biological Theories of Aging

- Five biological theories are evolutionary theory, cellular clock theory, free-radical theory, mitochondrial theory, and hormonal stress theory. The evolutionary theory of aging proposes that natural selection has not eliminated many harmful conditions and nonadaptive characteristics in older adults; thus, the benefits conferred by evolution decline with age because natural selection is linked to reproductive fitness. Hayflick proposed the cellular clock theory, which states that cells can divide a maximum of about 75 to 80 times, and that as we age, our cells become less capable of dividing. Telomeres are likely to be involved in explaining why cells lose their capacity to divide. According to free-radical theory, people age because unstable oxygen molecules called free radicals are produced in the cells and damage cellular structures. According to mitochondrial theory, aging is due to the decay of mitochondria, which are tiny cellular bodies that supply energy for function, growth, and repair. According to hormonal stress theory, aging in the body's hormonal system can lower resilience to stress and increase the likelihood of disease.

2 The Course of Physical Development in Late Adulthood

 LG2 Describe how a person's brain and body change in late adulthood.

The Aging Brain

- The brain loses weight and volume with age, and there is a general slowing of function in the central nervous system that begins in middle adulthood and increases in late adulthood. However, researchers have recently found that older adults can generate new neurons, and at least through the seventies, new dendrites. The aging brain retains considerable plasticity and adaptiveness. For example, it may compensate for losses in some regions of the brain by shifting responsibilities to other regions. A decrease in lateralization may reflect this kind of compensation, or it may reflect an age-related decline in the specialization of function.

Sleep

- Approximately 50 percent of older adults complain of having difficulty sleeping. Poor sleep can result in earlier death and lower cognitive functioning. Many sleep problems among older adults are linked to health conditions.

The Immune System

- Declines in immune system functioning with aging are well documented. Exercise can improve immune system functioning.

Physical Appearance and Movement

- The most obvious signs of aging are wrinkled skin and age spots on the skin. People get shorter as they age, and their weight often decreases after age 60 because of loss of muscle. The movement of older adults slows across a wide range of movement tasks.

Sensory Development

- Declines in visual acuity, color vision, and depth perception usually occur with age, especially after age 75. The yellowing of the eye's lens with age reduces color differentiation. The ability to see the periphery of a visual field also declines in older adults. Significant declines in visual functioning related to glare characterize adults 75 years and older and are prevalent among those 85 and older. Three diseases that can impair the vision of older adults are cataracts, glaucoma, and macular degeneration. Hearing decline can begin in middle age but usually does not become much of an impediment until late adulthood. Hearing aids (for conductive hearing loss) and cochlear implants (for neurosensory hearing loss) can diminish hearing problems for many older adults. Smell and taste can decline, although the decline is minimal in healthy older adults. Changes in touch sensitivity are associated with aging, although this does not present a problem for most older adults. Sensitivity to pain decreases in late adulthood. As with infants and children, perceptual motor coupling characterizes older adults; driving a vehicle is an example of this coupling.

The Circulatory and Respiratory Systems

- Cardiovascular disorders increase in late adulthood. Consistent high blood pressure should be treated to reduce the risk of stroke, heart attack, and kidney disease. Lung capacity does drop with age, but older adults can improve lung functioning with diaphragm-strengthening exercises.

Sexuality

- Aging in late adulthood does include some changes in sexual performance, more so for males than females. Nonetheless, there are no known age limits to sexual activity.

3 Health

LG3 Identify health problems in older adults and describe how they can be treated.

Health Problems

- As we age, our probability of disease or illness increases. Chronic disorders are rare in early adulthood, increase in middle adulthood, and become more common in late adulthood. The most common chronic disorder in late adulthood is arthritis. Nearly three-fourths of older adults die of cancer, heart disease, or stroke. Osteoporosis is the main reason many older adults walk with a stoop; women are especially vulnerable to this condition. Accidents are usually more debilitating to older than to younger adults.

Substance Use and Abuse

- The percentage of older adults who engage in binge drinking declines compared with earlier in adulthood, but moderate drinking of red wine can bring health benefits. Abuse of illicit and prescription drugs is a growing problem in the United States, although it is more difficult to detect in older adults than in younger adults.

Exercise, Nutrition, and Weight

- The physical benefits of exercise have been demonstrated in older adults. Aerobic exercise and weight lifting are both recommended if the adults are physically capable of them. It is important for older adults to eat healthy foods and take appropriate vitamins. Current controversy involves whether overweight adults live longer than normal-weight adults. Being overweight is linked to health problems, and being obese predicts earlier death. Calorie restriction in animals can increase the animals' life span, but whether this works with humans is not known. In humans, there has been recent controversy about whether being overweight is associated with an increased mortality rate in older adults. Most nutritional experts recommend a well-balanced, low-fat diet for older adults but do not recommend an extremely low-calorie diet. Controversy surrounds the question of whether vitamin supplements—especially the antioxidants vitamin C, vitamin E, and beta-carotene—can slow the aging process and improve older adults' health. Recent research reviews concluded that taking antioxidant vitamin supplements does not reduce the risk of cancer and cardiovascular disease.

Health Treatment

- Although only 3 percent of adults over 65 reside in nursing homes, 23 percent of adults 85 and over do. The quality of nursing homes varies enormously. Alternatives to nursing homes are being proposed. Simply giving nursing home residents options for control can change their behavior and improve their health. The attitudes of both the health care provider and the older adult patient are important aspects of the older adult's health care. Too often health care personnel share society's negative view of older adults.

key terms

life span 510
life expectancy 510
evolutionary theory of aging 516
cellular clock theory 516

free-radical theory 516
mitochondrial theory 517
hormonal stress theory 517

neurogenesis 519
cataracts 523
glaucoma 523

macular degeneration 525
arthritis 528
osteoporosis 528

key people

Leonard Hayflick 516

Judith Rodin 535

Ellen Langer 535

chapter 18

COGNITIVE DEVELOPMENT IN LATE ADULTHOOD

chapter outline

In 2010, 90-year-old Helen Small completed her master's degree at the University of Texas at Dallas (UT-Dallas). The topic of her master's degree research project was romantic relationships in late adulthood. Helen said she had interviewed only one individual who was older than she was at the time—a 92-year-old man.

I (your author, John Santrock) first met Helen when she took my undergraduate course in life-span development in 2006. After the first test, Helen stopped showing up and I wondered what had happened to her. It turns out that she had broken her shoulder when she tripped over a curb while hurrying to class. The next semester, she took my class again and did a great job in it, even though for the first several months she had to take notes with her left hand (she's right-handed) because of her lingering shoulder problem.

Helen Small with the author of your text, John Santrock, in his undergraduate course on life-span development at the University of Texas at Dallas in spring 2012. Helen now returns each semester to talk with students in the class about cognitive aging. This past semester, I had to reschedule the date of the topic because Helen had other work commitments the day it was originally scheduled.

Helen grew up during the Great Depression and first went to college in 1938 at the University of Akron but attended for only one year. She got married and her marriage lasted 62 years. After her husband's death, Helen went back to college in 2002, first at Brookhaven Community College and then at UT-Dallas. When I interviewed her recently, she told me that she had promised her mother that she would finish college. Her most important advice for college students, "Finish college and be persistent. When you make a commitment, always see it through. Don't quit. Go after what you want in life."

Helen not only is cognitively fit, she also is physically fit. She works out three times a week for about an hour each time—aerobically on a treadmill for about 30 minutes and then on six different weight machines.

What struck me most about Helen when she took my undergraduate course in life-span development was how appreciative she was of the opportunity to learn and how tenaciously she pursued studying and doing well in the course. Helen was quite popular with the younger students and was a terrific role model for them.

topical connections *looking back*

Most individuals reach the peak of their cognitive functioning in middle adulthood. However, some cognitive processes increase while others decline in middle age. For example, vocabulary peaks and speed of processing decreases in middle age. Expertise also typically increases during this age period. For many people, midlife is a time when individuals reflect and evaluate their current work and what they plan to do in the future. Many middle-aged adults increasingly examine life's meaning.

After her graduation, I asked her what she planned to do during the next few years and she responded, "I've got to figure out what I'm going to do with the rest of my life." Helen now comes each semester to my course in life-span development when we are discussing cognitive aging. She wows the class and has been an inspiration to all who come in contact with her.

What has Helen done over the last several years to stay cognitively fit? She has worked as a public ambassador both for Dr. Denise Park's Center for Vital Longevity at UT-Dallas and the Perot Science Museum. She also wrote her first book: *Why Not? My Seventy Year Plan for a College Degree* (Small, 2011). It's a wonderful, motivating invitation to live your life fully and reach your potential no matter what your age.

preview

Helen Small leads a very active cognitive life as an older adult. Just how well older adults can and do function cognitively is an important question we will explore in this chapter. We also will examine aspects of language development, work and retirement, mental health, and religion.

Helen Small published her first book, *Why Not? My Seventy Year Plan for a College Degree*, in 2011 at the age of 91.

1 Cognitive Functioning in Older Adults

LG1 Describe the cognitive functioning of older adults.

| Multidimensionality and Multidirectionality | Education, Work, and Health | Use It or Lose It | Training Cognitive Skills | Cognitive Neuroscience and Aging |

At age 76, Anna Mary Robertson Moses, better known as Grandma Moses, took up painting and became internationally famous, staging 15 one-woman shows throughout Europe. At age 89, Arthur Rubinstein gave one of his best performances at New York's Carnegie Hall. When Pablo Casals was 95, a reporter asked him, "Mr. Casals, you are the greatest cellist who ever lived. Why do you still practice six hours a day?" Mr. Casals replied, "Because I feel like I am making progress" (Canfield & Hansen, 1995).

MULTIDIMENSIONALITY AND MULTIDIRECTIONALITY

In thinking about the nature of cognitive change in adulthood, it is important to consider that cognition is a multidimensional concept (Dixon & others, 2013). It is also important to consider that, although some dimensions of cognition might decline as we age, others might remain stable or even improve.

Cognitive Mechanics and Cognitive Pragmatics Paul Baltes (2003; Baltes, Lindenberger, & Staudinger, 2006) clarified the distinction between those aspects of the aging mind that show decline and those that remain stable or even improve:

- **Cognitive mechanics** are the "hardware" of the mind and reflect the neurophysiological architecture of the brain that was developed through evolution. Cognitive mechanics consist of these components: speed and accuracy of the processes involved in sensory input, attention, visual and motor memory, discrimination, comparison, and categorization. Because of the strong influence of biology, heredity, and health on cognitive mechanics,

developmental **connection**

Intelligence

Fluid intelligence is the ability to reason abstractly; crystallized intelligence is an individual's accumulated information and verbal skills. Chapter 15, p. 471

cognitive mechanics The "hardware" of the mind, reflecting the neurophysiological architecture of the brain. Cognitive mechanics involve the speed and accuracy of the processes involving sensory input, visual and motor memory, discrimination, comparison, and categorization.

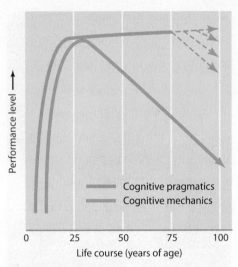

FIGURE **18.1**

THEORIZED AGE CHANGES IN COGNITIVE MECHANICS AND COGNITIVE PRAGMATICS.
Baltes argues that cognitive mechanics decline during aging, whereas cognitive pragmatics do not decline for many people until they become very old. Cognitive mechanics have a biological/genetic foundation; cognitive pragmatics have an experiential/cultural foundation. The broken lines from 75 to 100 years of age indicate possible individual variations in cognitive pragmatics.

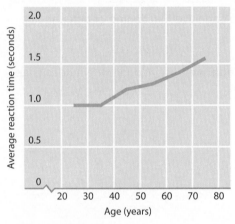

FIGURE **18.2**

THE RELATION OF AGE TO REACTION TIME.
In one study, the average reaction time began to slow in the forties, and this decline accelerated in the sixties and seventies (Salthouse, 1994). The task used to assess reaction time required individuals to match numbers with symbols on a computer screen.

developmental **connection**

Attention

Young children make progress in many aspects of attention, including sustained attention and executive attention. Chapter 7, p. 214

---

their decline with aging is likely. Some researchers conclude that the decline in cognitive mechanics may begin as soon as early midlife (Salthouse, 2013a, b).

- **Cognitive pragmatics** are the culture-based "software programs" of the mind. Cognitive pragmatics include reading and writing skills, language comprehension, educational qualifications, professional skills, and also the type of knowledge about the self and life skills that help us to master or cope with life. Because of the strong influence of culture on cognitive pragmatics, their improvement into old age is possible. Thus, although cognitive mechanics may decline in old age, cognitive pragmatics may actually improve, at least until individuals become very old (see Figure 18.1).

The distinction between cognitive mechanics and cognitive pragmatics is similar to the one between fluid (mechanics) and crystallized (pragmatics) intelligence that was described in Chapter 15. Indeed, the similarity is so strong that some experts now describe cognitive aging patterns in terms of *fluid mechanics* and *crystallized pragmatics* (Lovden & Lindenberger, 2007).

What factors are most likely to contribute to the decline in fluid mechanics in late adulthood? Among the most likely candidates are declines in processing speed and working memory capacity, and suppression of irrelevant information (inhibition) (Lovden & Lindenberger, 2007).

Now that we have examined the distinction between fluid mechanics and crystallized pragmatics, let's explore some of the more specific cognitive processes that reflect these two general domains, beginning with speed of processing.

Speed of Processing   It is now well accepted that the speed of processing information declines in late adulthood (Hoogendam & others, 2014; Robitaille & others, 2013; Salthouse, 2012, 2013a, b). Figure 18.2 illustrates this decline through the results of a study that measured reaction times in adults.

Although speed of processing information slows down in late adulthood, there is considerable individual variation in this ability. Accumulated knowledge may compensate to some degree for slower processing speed in older adults.

The decline in processing speed in older adults is likely due to a decline in functioning of the brain and central nervous system (Finch, 2009, 2011; Nilsson & others, 2014; Papp & others, 2014). Health and exercise may influence the extent to which processing speed declines (Ellis & others, 2014). For example, one study found that following six months of aerobic exercise older adults showed improvement on reaction time tasks (Kramer & others, 1999).

Attention   Changes in attention are important aspects of cognitive aging (Pierce & Andersen, 2014; Sylvain-Roy, Lungu, & Belleville, 2014). Researchers have found that older adults are less able to ignore distracting information than younger adults, and this distractibility becomes more pronounced as attentional demands increase (Mund, Bell, & Buchner, 2010). Recent research indicates that the greater distractibility of older adults is associated with less effective functioning in neural networks running through the frontal and parietal lobes of the brain, which are involved in cognitive control (Campbell & others, 2012). Also, a recent research review concluded that more active and physically fit older adults are better able to allocate attention when interacting with the environment (Gomez-Pinilla & Hillman, 2013). And a recent study revealed that older adults who participated in 20 one-hour video game training sessions with a commercially available program (Lumosity) showed a significant reduction in distraction and increased alertness (Mayas & others, 2014). The Lumosity program sessions focus on problem solving, mental calculation, working memory, and attention.

In Chapter 7, "Physical and Cognitive Development in Early Childhood," you read about two types of attention—sustained and executive. Here we will discuss those two types of attention in older adults as well as two other types of attention: selective and divided attention.

- **Selective attention** involves focusing on a specific aspect of experience that is relevant while ignoring others that are irrelevant. An example of selective attention is the ability to focus on one voice among many in a crowded room or a noisy restaurant. Another is making a decision about which stimuli to attend to when making a left turn at an intersection. Generally, older adults are less adept at selective attention than younger adults are (Ben-David & others, 2014; Caban-Holt & others, 2012; Quigley &

Muller, 2014). In a recent study, 10 weeks of speed of processing training improved the selective attention of older adults (O'Brien & others, 2013).

- **Divided attention** involves concentrating on more than one activity at the same time. When the two competing tasks are reasonably easy, age differences among adults are minimal or nonexistent. However, the more difficult the competing tasks are, the less effectively older adults divide attention than younger adults (Bucur & Madden, 2007).

- **Sustained attention** is focused and extended engagement with an object, task, event, or some other aspect of the environment. Sometimes sustained attention is referred to as *vigilance*. On tests of simple vigilance and sustained attention, older adults usually perform as well as younger adults. However, on complex vigilance tasks, older adults' performance usually drops (Bucur & Madden, 2007). And a recent study of older adults found that the greater the variability in their sustained attention (vigilance), the more likely they were to experience falls (O'Halloran & others, 2011).

- **Executive attention** involves planning of actions, allocating attention to goals, detecting and compensating for errors, monitoring progress on tasks, and dealing with novel or difficult circumstances. One study found that older adults had deficiencies in executive attention (Mahoney & others, 2010). In this study, a lower level of executive attention in older adults was linked to low blood pressure, which likely is related to reduced blood flow to the brain's frontal lobes.

What are some developmental changes in attention in late adulthood?

Memory The main dimensions of memory and aging that have been studied include explicit and implicit memory, episodic memory, semantic memory, cognitive resources (such as working memory and perceptual speed), source memory, prospective memory, and non-cognitive influences such as health, education, and socioeconomic factors.

Explicit and Implicit Memory Researchers have found that aging is linked with a decline in explicit memory (Kim & Giovanello, 2011; Ward, Berry, & Shanks, 2014). **Explicit memory** is memory of facts and experiences that individuals consciously know and can state. Explicit memory also is sometimes called declarative memory. Examples of explicit memory include being at a grocery store and remembering what you wanted to buy, being able to name the capital of Illinois, or recounting the events in a movie you have seen. **Implicit memory** is memory without conscious recollection; it involves skills and routine procedures that are automatically performed. Examples of implicit memory include driving a car, swinging a golf club, or typing on a computer keyboard without having to consciously think about how to perform these tasks.

Implicit memory is less likely to be adversely affected by aging than explicit memory is (Norman, Holmin, & Bartholomew, 2011; Nyberg & others, 2012). Thus, older adults are more likely to forget what items they wanted to buy at a grocery store (unless they write them down on a list and take it with them) than they are to forget how to drive a car. Their perceptual speed might be slower in driving the car, but they remember how to do it.

Episodic Memory and Semantic Memory Episodic and semantic memory are viewed as forms of explicit memory. **Episodic memory** is the retention of information about the where and when of life's happenings. For example, what was the color of the walls in your bedroom when you were a child, what was your first date like, what were you doing when you heard that airplanes had struck the World Trade Center, and what did you eat for breakfast this morning?

Younger adults have better episodic memory than older adults have, both for real and imagined events (Friedman, 2013; McDonough & Gallo, 2013). A study of 18- to 94-year-olds revealed that increased age was linked to increased difficulty in retrieving episodic information, facts, and events (Siedlecki, 2007). Also, older adults think that they can remember older events better than more recent events, typically reporting that they can remember what happened to them years ago but can't remember what they did yesterday. However, researchers consistently have found that, contrary to such self-reports, in older adults the older the memory, the less accurate it is. This has been documented in studies of memory for high school classmates, foreign languages learned in school over the life span, names of grade school teachers, and autobiographical facts kept in diaries (Smith, 1996).

cognitive pragmatics The culture-based "software programs" of the mind. Cognitive pragmatics include reading and writing skills, language comprehension, educational qualifications, professional skills, and also the type of knowledge about the self and life skills that help us to master or cope with life.

selective attention Focusing on a specific aspect of experience that is relevant while ignoring others that are irrelevant.

divided attention Concentrating on more than one activity at the same time.

sustained attention Focused and extended engagement with an object, task, event, or other aspect of the environment.

executive attention Aspects of thinking that include planning actions, allocating attention to goals, detecting and compensating for errors, monitoring progress on tasks, and dealing with novel or difficult circumstances.

explicit memory Memory of facts and experiences that individuals consciously know and can state.

implicit memory Memory without conscious recollection; involves skills and routine procedures that are automatically performed.

episodic memory The retention of information about the where and when of life's happenings.

Semantic memory is a person's knowledge about the world. It includes a person's fields of expertise, such as knowledge of chess for a skilled chess player; general academic knowledge of the sort learned in school, such as knowledge of geometry; and "everyday knowledge" about the meanings of words, famous individuals, important places, and common things, such as what day is Valentine's Day. Semantic memory appears to be independent of an individual's personal identity with the past. For example, you can access a fact—such as "Lima is the capital of Peru"—and not have the foggiest idea of when and where you learned it.

Does semantic memory decline with age? Among the tasks that researchers often use to assess semantic memory are those involving vocabulary, general knowledge, and word identification (Miotto & others, 2013). Older adults do often take longer to retrieve semantic information, but usually they can ultimately retrieve it. However, the ability to retrieve very specific information (such as names) usually declines in older adults (Luo & Craik, 2008). For the most part, episodic memory declines more than semantic memory in older adults (Kuo & others, 2014; Ofen & Shing, 2013; Small & others, 2012b).

Although many aspects of semantic memory are reasonably well preserved in late adulthood, a common memory problem for older adults is the *tip-of-the-tongue (TOT) phenomenon,* in which individuals can't quite retrieve familiar information but have the feeling that they should be able to retrieve it (Bucur & Madden, 2007). Researchers have found that older adults are more likely to experience TOT states than younger adults are (Bucur & Madden, 2007; Salthouse & Mandell, 2013). A recent study of older adults found that the most commonly reported errors in memory over the last 24 hours were those involving tip-of-the-tongue (Ossher, Flegal, & Lustig, 2013).

Cognitive Resources: Working Memory and Perceptual Speed   One view of memory suggests that a limited number of cognitive resources can be devoted to any cognitive task. Two important cognitive resource mechanisms are working memory and perceptual speed (Baddeley, 2012; Nilsson & others, 2014; Salthouse, 2013a, b). Recall from Chapters 9 and 15 that *working memory* is closely linked to short-term memory but places more emphasis on memory as a place for mental work. Working memory is like a mental "workbench" that allows children and adults to manipulate and assemble information when making decisions, solving problems, and comprehending written and spoken language (Baddeley, 2007, 2010, 2012). Researchers have found declines in working memory during late adulthood (Cansino & others, 2013; Ko & others, 2014; Peich, Husain, & Bays, 2013). A recent study revealed that working memory continued to decline from 65 to 89 years of age (Elliott & others, 2011). Another recent study found that multitasking especially produced a disruption in older adults' working memory, likely because of an interruption in retrieving information (Clapp & others, 2011). And in yet another recent study, verbal and visual working memory declined at similar rates during aging (Kumar & Priyadarshi, 2013). Further, a recent study found that visually encoded working memory was linked to older adults' mobility (Kawagoe & Sekiyama, 2014). Explanations of the decline in working memory in older adults often focus on their less efficient inhibition in preventing irrelevant information from entering working memory and their increased distractibility (Lustig & Hasher, 2009; Yi & Friedman, 2014).

Is there plasticity in the working memory of older adults? A recent experimental study revealed that moderate exercise resulted in faster reaction time on a working memory task in older adults (Hogan, Mata, & Carstensen, 2013). Another study found that cognitive training improved older adults' working memory (Borella & others, 2013). Also, in a recent study, strategy training improved the working memory of older adults (Bailey, Dunlosky, & Hertzog, 2014). Thus, there appears to be some plasticity in the working memory of older adults.

Perceptual speed is a cognitive resource that involves the ability to perform simple perceptual-motor tasks such as deciding whether pairs of two-digit or two-letter strings are the same or different or determining the time required to step on the brakes when the car directly ahead stops. Perceptual speed shows considerable decline in late adulthood and is strongly linked with declines in working memory (Dirk, 2012; Hoogendam & others, 2014; Salthouse, 2013a). A recent study revealed that age-related slowing in processing speed was linked to a breakdown in myelin in the brain (Lu & others, 2013). Another recent study found that 10 hours of visual speed of processing training was effective in improving older adults' speed of processing, attention, and executive function (Wolinksy & others, 2013).

semantic memory A person's knowledge about the world—including one's fields of expertise, general academic knowledge of the sort learned in school, and "everyday knowledge."

Source Memory **Source memory** is the ability to remember where one learned something. Failures of source memory increase with age in the adult years and they can create awkward situations, as when an older adult forgets who told a joke and retells it to the source (Davidson & others, 2013; El Haj & Allain, 2012). A recent study revealed that self-referenced encoding improved the source memory of older adults (Leshikar & Duarte, 2014).

Lynn Hasher (2003, p. 1301) argues that age differences are substantial in many studies of memory, such as source memory, when individuals are asked "for a piece of information that just doesn't matter much. But if you ask for information that is important, old people do every bit as well as young adults . . . young people have mental resources to burn. As people get older, they get more selective in how they use their resources."

Prospective Memory **Prospective memory** involves remembering to do something in the future, such as remembering to take your medicine or remembering to do an errand. In a recent study, prospective memory played an important role in older adults' successful management of the medications they needed to take (Woods & others, 2014). Although some researchers have found a decline in prospective memory with age (Kelly & others, 2013; Smith & Hunt, 2014), a number of studies show that whether there is a decline depends on such factors as the nature of the task, what is being assessed, and the context of the assessment (Einstein & McDaniel, 2005; Mullet & others, 2013; Scullin, Bugg, & McDaniel, 2012). For example, age-related deficits occur more often in prospective memory tasks that are time-based (such as remembering to call someone next Friday) than those that are event-based (remembering to tell your friend to read a particular book the next time you see her). Further, declines in prospective memory occur more often in laboratories than in real-life settings (Bisiacchi, Tarantino, & Ciccola, 2008). Indeed, in some real-life settings, such as keeping appointments, older adults' prospective memory is better than younger adults' (Luo & Craik, 2008).

Conclusions About Memory and Aging Most, but not all, aspects of memory decline during late adulthood (Kuo & others, 2014; Nyberg & others, 2012; Schaie, 2013). The decline occurs primarily in explicit, episodic, and working memory, not in semantic memory or implicit memory. A decline in perceptual speed is associated with memory decline (Salthouse, 2013a, b). Successful aging does not mean eliminating memory decline altogether, but it does mean reducing the decline and adapting to it. As we will see later in this chapter, older adults can use certain strategies to reduce memory decline.

Does the time of day when an older adult's or a younger adult's memory is tested affect the results? To find out, read *Connecting Through Research*.

Executive Function We discussed executive function in a number of chapters earlier in the text. Recall that *executive function* is an umbrella-like concept that consists of a number of higher-level cognitive processes linked to the development of the brain's prefrontal cortex (Diamond, 2013). Executive function involves managing one's thoughts to engage in goal-directed behavior and to exercise self-control.

How does executive function change in late adulthood? In Chapter 17, "Physical Development in Late Adulthood," you read that the prefrontal cortex is one area of the brain that especially shrinks with aging, and recent research has linked this shrinkage with a decrease in working memory and other cognitive activities in older adults (Callaghan & others, 2014; Toepper & others, 2014; Yuan & Raz, 2014). A recent study found that dysregulation of signaling by the neurotransmitter GABA may play a role in impaired working memory in older adults (Banuelos & others, 2014).

Aspects of working memory that especially decline in older adults involve (1) updating memory representations that are relevant for the task at hand and (2) replacing old, no longer relevant information (Friedman & others, 2008). Older adults also are less effective at engaging in cognitive control than when they were younger (Campbell & others, 2012). For example, in terms of cognitive flexibility, older adults don't perform as well as younger adults at switching back and forth between tasks or mental sets (Luszcz, 2011). And in terms of cognitive inhibition, older adults are less effective than younger adults at inhibiting dominant or automatic responses (Coxon & others, 2012).

Although in general aspects of executive function decline in late adulthood, there is considerable variability in executive function among older adults. For example, some older

This older woman has forgotten where she put the keys to her car. *What type of memory is involved in this situation?*

Prospective memory involves remembering to do something in the future. This woman is keeping track of what she plans to buy when she goes to a grocery store the next day.

developmental **connection**

Cognitive Processes

Executive function is increasingly recognized as an important concept in development. Chapter 7, p. 216; Chapter 9, 282; Chapter 11, p. 359

source memory The ability to remember where one learned something.

prospective memory Remembering to do something in the future.

Does the Time of Day an Older Adult's or a Younger Adult's Memory Is Tested Affect the Results?

Certain testing conditions may show exaggerated memory declines in older adults (Borella & others, 2011; Yoon & others, 2010). Most researchers conduct their studies in the afternoon, a convenient time for researchers and undergraduate participants. Traditional-age college students in their late teens and early twenties are often more alert and function more optimally in the afternoon, but approximately 75 percent of older adults are "morning persons" who perform best early in the day (Helmuth, 2003).

Lynn Hasher and her colleagues (2001) tested the memory of college students 18 to 32 years of age and community volunteers 58 to 78 years of age in the late afternoon (about 4 p.m. to 5 p.m.) and in the morning (about 8 a.m. to 9 a.m.). Regardless of the time of day, the younger college students performed better than the older adults on the memory tests, which involved recognizing sentences from a story and memorizing lists of words. However, when the participants took the memory test in the morning rather than the late afternoon, the age difference in performance decreased considerably (see Figure 18.3).

In another study, the memory performance of older adults also was poorer in the evening (Hogan & others, 2009). In this study, the older adults' performance on cognitive tasks was more variable than that of the younger adults, especially during their non-optimal time of day—the evening.

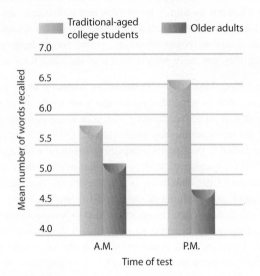

FIGURE **18.3**

MEMORY, AGE, AND TIME OF DAY TESTED (A.M. OR P.M.). In one study, traditional-aged college students performed better than older adults in both the a.m. and the p.m. Note, however, that the memory of the older adults was better when they were tested in the morning than in the afternoon, whereas the memory of the traditional-aged college students was not as good in the morning as it was in the afternoon (Hasher & others, 2001).

adults have a better working memory and are more cognitively flexible than other older adults (Kayama & others, 2014; Kelly & others, 2014; Peltz, Gratton, & Fabiani, 2011). And there is increasing research evidence that aerobic exercise improves executive function in older adults (Guiney & Machado, 2013). For example, a recent study found that more physically fit older adults had greater cognitive flexibility than their less physically fit counterparts (Berryman & others, 2013). Also, in a recent meta-analysis, tai chi participation was associated with better executive function in older adults (Wayne & others, 2014). And in a recent study, executive functions of inhibitory control, mental set shifting, and attentional flexibility predicted functional mobility over a one-year period in older adults (Gothe & others, 2014).

Executive function increasingly is thought to be involved not only in cognitive performance but also in emotion regulation, adaptation to life's challenges, motivation, and social functioning (Forte & others, 2013; Luszcz, 2011). Research on these aspects of executive function has only recently begun. A recent study revealed that executive function impairment was associated with increased risk of falls and fall-related injuries in older adults (Muir & others, 2013).

Some critics argue that not much benefit is derived from placing various cognitive processes under the broader concept of executive function. Although we have described a number of components of executive function here—working memory, cognitive inhibition, cognitive flexibility, and so on—a consensus has not been reached on what the components are, how they are connected, and how they develop. That said, the concept of executive function is not likely to go away any time soon, and further research, especially meta-analyses, should provide a clearer picture of executive function and how it develops through the life span (Luszcz, 2011).

Decision Making Despite declines in many aspects of memory, such as working memory and long-term memory, many older adults preserve decision-making skills reasonably well (Healey & Hasher, 2009). However, some researchers have found negative changes in decision making in older adults (Eppinger & others, 2014). One recent study revealed that compared with younger adults, older adults were far more inconsistent in their choices (Tymula & others, 2013). Also, in some cases, age-related decreases in memory will impair decision making (Brand & Markowitsch, 2010). One study revealed that a reduction in effective decision making in risky situations during late adulthood was linked to declines in memory and processing speed (Henninger, Madden, & Huettel, 2010). However, older adults often perform well when decision making is not constrained by time pressures, when the decision is meaningful for them, and when the decisions do not involve high risks (Boyle & others, 2012; Yoon, Cole, & Lee, 2009).

Wisdom Does wisdom, like good wine, improve with age? What is this thing we call "wisdom"? A recent research review found 24 definitions of wisdom, although there was significant overlap in the definitions (Bangen, Meeks, & Jest, 2013). In this review, the following subcomponents of wisdom were commonly cited: knowledge of life, prosocial values, self-understanding, acknowledgment of uncertainty, emotional balance, tolerance, openness, spirituality, and sense of humor.

Thus, while there is still some disagreement regarding how wisdom should be defined, following is the definition of wisdom that has been used by leading expert Paul Baltes and his colleagues (Baltes & Kunzmann, 2007; Baltes & Smith, 2008): **Wisdom** is expert knowledge about the practical aspects of life that permits excellent judgment about important matters. This practical knowledge involves exceptional insight into human development and life matters, good judgment, and an understanding of how to cope with difficult life problems. Thus, wisdom, more than standard conceptions of intelligence, focuses on life's pragmatic concerns and human conditions (Ferrari & Weststrate, 2013; Jeste & Oswald, 2014; Staudinger & Gluck, 2011; Thomas & Kunzmann, 2014; Webster, Westerhof, & Bohlmeijer, 2014).

In regard to wisdom, research by Baltes and his colleagues (Baltes & Kunzmann, 2007; Baltes & Smith, 2008) yielded the following findings:

- High levels of wisdom are rare. Few people, including older adults, attain a high level of wisdom. That only a small percentage of adults show wisdom supports the contention that it requires experience, practice, or complex skills.

- The time frame of late adolescence and early adulthood is the main age window for wisdom to emerge (Staudinger & Dorner, 2007; Staudinger & Gluck, 2011). No further advances in wisdom have been found for middle-aged and older adults beyond the level they attained as young adults.

- Factors other than age are critical for wisdom to develop to a high level. For example, certain life experiences, such as being trained and working in a field concerned with difficult life problems and having wisdom-enhancing mentors, contribute to higher levels of wisdom. Also, people higher in wisdom have values that are more likely to consider the welfare of others than to focus solely on their own happiness.

- Personality-related factors, such as openness to experience, generativity, and creativity, are better predictors of wisdom than cognitive factors such as intelligence.

EDUCATION, WORK, AND HEALTH

Education, work, and health are three important influences on the cognitive functioning of older adults. They are also three of the most important factors involved in understanding why cohort effects need to be taken into account in studying the cognitive functioning of older adults. Indeed, cohort effects are very important considerations in the study of cognitive aging (Hofer, Rast, & Piccinin, 2012; Schaie, 2013).

Education Successive generations in America's twentieth century were better educated, and this trend continues in the twenty-first century (Lachman & others, 2010; Schaie, 2013). Not only were today's older adults more likely to go to college when they were young adults than were their parents or grandparents, but more older adults are returning to college today

It is always in season for the old to learn.

—AESCHYLUS
Greek Playwright, 5th Century B.C.

Older adults might not be as quick with their thoughts or behavior as younger people, but wisdom may be an entirely different matter. This older woman shares the wisdom of her experience with a classroom of children. *How is wisdom described by life-span developmentalists?*

wisdom Expert knowledge about the practical aspects of life that permits excellent judgment about important matters.

How are education, work, and health linked to cognitive functioning in older adults?

to further their education than in past generations. Educational experiences are positively correlated with scores on intelligence tests and information-processing tasks, such as memory exercises (Muniz-Terrera & others, 2013; Steffener & others, 2014). One study revealed that older adults with less education had lower cognitive abilities than those with more education (Lachman & others, 2010). However, for older adults with less education, frequently engaging in cognitive activities improved their episodic memory. Also, a recent study found that older adults with a higher level of education had better cognitive functioning (Rapp & others, 2014).

Work Successive generations have also had work experiences that included a stronger emphasis on cognitively oriented labor. Our great-grandfathers and grandfathers were more likely to be manual laborers than were our fathers, who are more likely to be involved in cognitively oriented occupations. As the industrial society continues to be replaced by the information society, younger generations will have more experience in jobs that require considerable cognitive investment. The increased emphasis on complex information processing in jobs likely enhances an individual's intellectual abilities (Kristjuhan & Taidre, 2010).

In one study, substantive complex work was linked with higher intellectual functioning in older adults (Schooler, Mulatu, & Oates, 1999). Another study revealed that a higher level of cognitive stimulation at work and outside work was linked to improved cognitive functioning over a 10-year period in both young and older adults (Marquie & others, 2010). And a recent study of middle-aged and older adults found that employment gaps involving unemployment or sickness were associated with a higher risk of cognitive impairment (Leist & others, 2013).

Health Successive generations have also been healthier in late adulthood as better treatments for a variety of illnesses (such as hypertension) have been developed. Many of these illnesses, such as stroke and heart disease, have a negative impact on intellectual performance (Chuang & others, 2014; Ganguli & others, 2014; Joosten & others, 2013). Hypertension has been linked to lower cognitive performance in a number of studies, not only in older adults but also in young and middle-aged adults (Virta & others, 2013). And, as we will see later in this chapter, Alzheimer disease has a devastating effect on older adults' physical and cognitive functioning (Hayden & others, 2014; Smits & others, 2014). Researchers also have found age-related cognitive decline in adults with mood disorders such as depression (Mackin & others, 2014; van den Kommer & others, 2013). Thus, some of the decline in intellectual performance found for older adults is likely due to health-related factors rather than to age per se (Korten & others, 2014; Morra & others, 2013).

K. Warner Schaie (1994) concluded that although some diseases—such as hypertension and diabetes—are linked to cognitive drop-offs, they do not directly cause mental decline. Rather, the lifestyles of the individuals with the diseases might be the culprits. For example, poor eating habits, inactivity, and stress are related to both physical and mental decline (Annweiler & others, 2012; Kraft, 2012). For example, a recent study of older adults found that a higher level of stress was linked to an accelerated decline of cognitive functioning (Aggarwal & others, 2014).

In his most recent account of links between health and cognitive factors, Schaie (2013) concluded that the association may be reciprocal. That is, a healthy body facilitates cognitive competence, and cognitive competence facilitates the maintenance of physical health.

A number of research studies have found that exercise is linked to improved cognitive functioning in older adults (Kirk-Sanchez & McGough, 2014; Leon & others, 2014; Small & others, 2012a). A recent research review concluded that physical exercise is a promising non-pharmaceutical intervention to prevent or reduce age-related cognitive decline (Bherer, Erickson, & Liu-Ambrose, 2013). Also recall from Chapter 17 that a recent research review concluded that exercise's influence on cognition occurs through changes in molecular events associated with the management of energy metabolism and synaptic plasticity (Gomez-Pinilla & Hillman, 2013). And remember that earlier in the chapter we discussed a study that revealed a program involving moderate exercise increased the working memory of older adults (Hogan, Mata, & Carstensen, 2013). Here are the results of four other studies linking physical exercise and cognitive development in older adults:

- In a study of healthy 60- to 75-year-olds, those who engaged in a physical training program showed improved concentration three months later (Linde & Alfermann, 2014).

- Community-dwelling women 65 years of age and older did not have cognitive impairment or physical limitations when they were initially assessed (Yaffe & others, 2001). Six to eight years later, the women with higher physical activity when they were initially assessed were less likely to experience cognitive decline.
- A higher level of cardiorespiratory fitness in older adults was linked to better performance on a cognitive task through recruitment of neural circuits in the prefrontal and parietal regions of the brain (Prakash & others, 2011).
- A recent study found that 6 months of dance intervention was linked to improved cognitive functioning in elderly adults (Kattenstroth & others, 2013).

A final aspect of health that is important to consider in cognitive functioning in older adults is *terminal decline*. This concept emphasizes that changes in cognitive functioning may be linked more to distance from death or cognition-related pathology than to distance from birth (Burns & others, 2014; Hulur & others, 2013; Wilson & others, 2012). A recent study revealed that on average, a faster rate of cognitive decline occurred on average about 7.7 years prior to death and varied across individuals (Muniz-Terrera & others, 2013). Another recent study found that a recent cohort that died in the 2000s had a steeper terminal decline in cognition than the cohort that preceded it in the 1990s (Hulur & others, 2013). The researchers concluded that this result occurred because of recent increases in "manufacturing" survival by keeping very ill and frail older adults alive through medical advances.

USE IT OR LOSE IT

Changes in cognitive activity patterns might result in disuse and consequent atrophy of cognitive skills (de Frias & Dixon, 2014; Gordon, 2013). This concept is captured by the phrase "use it or lose it." Mental activities that likely benefit the maintenance of cognitive skills in older adults include activities such as reading books, doing crossword puzzles, and going to lectures and concerts. "Use it or lose it" also is a significant component of the engagement model of cognitive optimization that emphasizes how intellectual and social engagement can buffer age-related declines in intellectual development (Park & Bischof, 2011; Park & others, 2014; Park & Reuter-Lorenz, 2009; Stine-Morrow & Basak, 2011). The following studies support the "use it or lose it" concept and the engagement model of cognitive optimization:

- In the Victoria Longitudinal Study, when middle-aged and older adults participated in intellectually engaging activities it served to buffer them against cognitive decline (Hultsch & others, 1999). Further analyses of the participants in this study revealed that engagement in cognitively complex activities was linked to faster and more consistent processing speed (Bielak & others, 2007). And in the most recent analysis of these older adults over a 12-year period, those who reduced their cognitive lifestyle activities (such as using a computer, playing bridge) subsequently showed decline in cognitive functioning in verbal speed, episodic memory, and semantic memory (Small & others, 2012a). The decline in cognitive functioning was linked to subsequent lower engagement in social activities.
- In a longitudinal study of 801 Catholic priests 65 years and older, those who regularly read books, did crossword puzzles, or otherwise exercised their minds were 47 percent less likely to develop Alzheimer disease than the priests who rarely engaged in these activities (Wilson & others, 2002).
- Reading daily was linked to increased longevity for men in their seventies (Jacobs & others, 2008).
- At the beginning of a longitudinal study, 75- to 85-year-olds indicated how often they participated in six activities—reading, writing, doing crossword puzzles, playing card or board games, having group discussions, and playing music—on a daily basis (Hall & others, 2009). Across the five years of the study, the point at which memory loss accelerated was assessed and it was found that for each additional activity the older adult engaged in, the onset of rapid memory loss was delayed by 0.18 years. For older adults who participated in 11 activities per week compared with their counterparts who engaged in only 4 activities per week, the point at which accelerated memory decline occurred was delayed by 1.29 years.

developmental **connection**

Health

Exercise is linked to increased longevity and the prevention of common chronic diseases. Chapter 17, p. 529

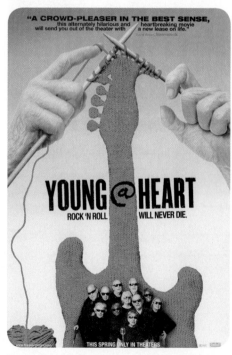

The Young@Heart chorus—whose average age is 80. Young@Heart became a hit documentary in 2008. The documentary displays the singing talents, energy, and optimism of a remarkable group of older adults, who clearly are on the "use it" side of "use it or lose it."

TRAINING COGNITIVE SKILLS

If older adults are losing cognitive skills, can they be retrained? An increasing number of research studies indicate that this is possible to some degree (Bailey, Dunlosky, & Hertzog, 2014; Boron, Willis, & Schaie, 2007; Mayas & others, 2014; Willis & Caskie, 2013). Two key conclusions can be derived from research in this area: (1) training can improve the cognitive skills of many older adults, but (2) there is some loss in plasticity in late adulthood, especially in those who are 85 years and older (Baltes, Lindenberger, & Staudinger, 2006). Let's now examine the results of several cognitive training studies involving older adults.

In an extensive study by Sherry Willis and her colleagues (2006), older adults were randomly assigned to one of four groups: training in (1) reasoning, (2) memory, (3) speed of processing, or (4) a control group that received no training. Each type of training showed an immediate effect in its domain—reasoning training improved reasoning, memory training improved memory, and speed of processing training improved speed of processing. However, the training effects did not transfer across cognitive domains, such that speed of processing training did not benefit the older adults' memory or reasoning, for example. The older adults who were given reasoning training did have less difficulty in the activities of daily living than a control group who did not receive this training. The activities of daily living that were assessed included how independently the older adults were able to prepare meals, do housework, do finances, go shopping, and engage in health maintenance. Each intervention maintained its effects on the specific targeted ability across the five years of the study. However, neither memory nor speed of processing training benefited the older adults' activities of daily living.

Another study had older adults participate in a 20-week activity called Senior Odyssey, a team-based program involving creative problem solving that is derived from the Odyssey of the Mind program for children and emerging adults (Stine-Morrow & others, 2007). In a field experiment, compared with a control group who did not experience Senior Odyssey, the Senior Odyssey participants showed improved processing speed, somewhat improved creative thinking, and increased mindfulness. *Mindfulness* involves generating new ideas, being open to new information, and being aware of multiple perspectives (Langer, 2000, 2007).

And yet another study of 60- to 90-year-olds found that sustained engagement in cognitively demanding, novel activities improved the older adults' episodic memory (Park & others, 2014). To produce this result, the older adults spent an average of 16.5 hours a week for three months learning how to quilt or how to use digital photography.

To what extent can training improve cognitive functioning of older adults?

As we discussed earlier in the chapter, researchers are also finding that improving the physical fitness of older adults can improve their cognitive functioning (Gomez-Pinilla & Hillman, 2013; Kirk-Sanchez & McGough, 2014). A research review revealed that aerobic fitness training improved planning, scheduling, working memory, resistance to distraction, and processing involving multiple tasks in older adults (Colcombe & Kramer, 2003).

Recent meta-examinations of four longitudinal observational studies (Long Beach Longitudinal Study; Origins of Variance in the Oldest-old [Octo-Twin] Study in Sweden; Seattle Longitudinal Study; and Victoria Longitudinal Study in Canada) of older adults' naturalistic cognitive activities found that changes in cognitive activity predicted cognitive outcomes as long as two decades later (Brown & others, 2012; Lindwall & others, 2012; Mitchell & others, 2012; Rebok & others, 2014). However, the studies provided no support for the concept that engaging in cognitive activity at an earlier point in development improved older adults' ability to later withstand cognitive decline. On a positive note, when older adults continued to increase their engagement in cognitive and physical activities, they were better able to maintain their cognitive functioning in late adulthood.

The Stanford Center for Longevity (2011) recently reported information based on a consensus of leading scientists in the field of aging. One of their concerns is the misinformation given to the public touting products to improve the functioning of the mind for which there is no scientific evidence. Nutritional supplements, games, and software products have all been advertised as "magic bullets" to slow the decline of mental functioning and improve the mental ability of older adults. Some of the claims are reasonable but not scientifically tested, while others are unrealistic and implausible. A research review of dietary supplements and cognitive aging did indicate that ginkgo biloba was linked with improvements in some aspects of attention in older adults and that omega-3 polyunsaturated fatty acids (fish oil) was related to reduced risk of age-related cognitive decline (Gorby, Brownawell, & Falk, 2010). In this research review, there was no evidence of cognitive improvements in aging adults who took supplements containing ginseng and glucose. Also, a recent experimental study with 50- to 75-year-old females found that those who took fish oil for 26 weeks had improved executive function and beneficial effects on a number of areas of brain functioning compared with their female counterparts who took a placebo pill (Witte & others, 2014). Overall, though, research has not provided consistent plausible evidence that dietary supplements can accomplish major cognitive goals in aging adults over a number of years. However, some software-based cognitive training games have been found to improve older adults' cognitive functioning (Hertzog & others, 2009; Lange & others, 2010; Nouchi & others, 2013). For example, a recent study of 60- to 85-year-olds found that a multitasking video game that simulates day-to-day driving experiences (NeuroRacer) improved cognitive control skills, such as sustained attention and working memory, after training on the video game and six months later (Anguera & others, 2013). Nonetheless, the training games may improve cognitive skills in a laboratory setting but not generalize to gains in the real world.

In sum, some improvements in the cognitive vitality of older adults can be accomplished through cognitive and fitness training (Brown & others, 2012; Mitchell & others, 2012; Rebok & others, 2014; Wolinsky & others, 2013). However, benefits have not been observed in all studies (Salthouse, 2007, 2013a, b). An important finding in the recent meta-analysis of four longitudinal studies was that older adults were better able to maintain their cognitive functioning over a prolonged period of time when increasing their engagement in cognitive and physical activities (Rebok & others, 2014). Further research is needed to determine more precisely which cognitive improvements occur in older adults as a result of training (Salthouse, 2013a, b).

COGNITIVE NEUROSCIENCE AND AGING

On several occasions in this chapter and in Chapter 17, we have discussed that certain regions of the brain are involved in links between aging and cognitive functioning. In this section, we further explore the substantial increase in interest in the brain's role in aging and cognitive functioning. The field of *cognitive neuroscience* has emerged as the major discipline that explores the links between brain activity and cognitive functioning (Banuelos & others, 2014; Fletcher & Rapp, 2013; Reuter-Lorenz, 2013; Yuan & Raz, 2014). This field especially relies on brain-imaging techniques, such as fMRI, PET, and DTI (diffusion tensor imaging) to reveal the areas of the brain that are activated when individuals engage in certain cognitive activities (Leshikar & Duarte, 2014; Toepper & others, 2014). For example, as an older adult is asked to encode and then retrieve verbal materials or images of scenes, the older adult's brain activity will be monitored by an fMRI brain scan.

Changes in the brain can influence cognitive functioning, and changes in cognitive functioning can influence the brain. For example, aging of the brain's prefrontal cortex may produce a decline in working memory (Reuter-Lorenz, 2013; Takeuchi & others, 2012; Toepper & others, 2014). And when older adults do not regularly use their working memory (recall the section on "Use It or Lose It"), neural connections in the prefrontal lobe may atrophy. Further, cognitive interventions that activate older adults' working memory may increase these neural connections.

Although in its infancy as a field, the cognitive neuroscience of aging is beginning to uncover some important links between aging, the brain, and cognitive functioning (Antonenko & Floel, 2014; Ash & Rapp, 2014; Callaghan & others, 2014; Reuter-Lorenz, 2013; Steffener & others, 2014). These include the following:

- Neural circuits in specific regions of the brain's prefrontal cortex decline, and this decline is linked to poorer performance by older adults on complex reasoning, working memory, and episodic memory tasks (Grady & others, 2006) (see Figure 18.4).
- Recall from Chapter 17 that older adults are more likely than younger adults to use both hemispheres of the brain to compensate for aging

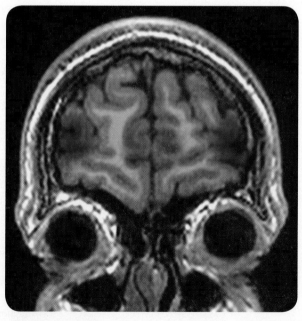

FIGURE **18.4**

THE PREFRONTAL CORTEX. Advances in neuroimaging are allowing researchers to make significant progress in connecting changes in the brain with cognitive development. Shown here is an fMRI of the brain's prefrontal cortex. *What links have been found between the prefrontal cortex, aging, and cognitive development?*

declines in attention, memory, and language (Dennis & Cabeza, 2008; Davis & others, 2012). Two recent neuroimaging studies revealed that older adults showed better memory performance when both hemispheres of the brain were active in processing information (Angel & others, 2011; Manenti, Cotelli, & Miniussi, 2011).

- Functioning of the hippocampus declines to a lesser degree than the functioning of the frontal lobes in older adults (Antonenko & Floel, 2014). In K. Warner Schaie's (2013) recent research, individuals whose memory and executive function declined in middle age had more hippocampal atrophy in late adulthood, but those whose memory and executive function improved in middle age did not show a decline in hippocampal functioning in late adulthood.

- Patterns of neural decline with aging are larger for retrieval than encoding (Gutchess & others, 2005).

- Compared with younger adults, older adults often show greater activity in the frontal and parietal lobes of the brain on simple tasks but as attentional demands increase, older adults display less effective functioning in the frontal and parietal lobes of the brain that involve cognitive control (Campbell & others, 2012).

- Younger adults have better connectivity between brain regions than older adults do (Antonenko & Floel, 2014; Goh, 2011; Waring, Addis, & Kensinger, 2013). For example, one study revealed that younger adults had more connections between brain activations in frontal, occipital, and hippocampal regions than older adults during a difficult encoding task (Leshikar & others, 2010).

- An increasing number of cognitive and physical fitness training studies include brain-imaging techniques such as fMRI to assess the results of such training on brain function (Bherer, Erickson, & Liu-Ambrose, 2013; Kirk-Sanchez & McGough, 2014). In one study, older adults who walked one hour a day three days a week for six months showed increased volume in the frontal and temporal lobes of the brain (Colcombe & others, 2006).

Denise Park and Patricia Reuter-Lorenz (2009) proposed a neurocognitive scaffolding view of connections between the aging brain and cognition. In this view, increased activation in the prefrontal cortex with aging reflects an adaptive brain that is compensating for declining neural structures and function and declines in various aspects of cognition, including working memory and long-term memory. Scaffolding involves the use of complementary neural circuits to protect cognitive functioning in an aging brain. Among the factors that can strengthen brain scaffolding are cognitive engagement and exercise.

developmental **connection**

Brain Development

The activities older adults engage in can influence the brain's development. Chapter 17, p. 531

Review *Connect* Reflect

LG1 Describe the cognitive functioning of older adults.

Review

- How is cognition multidimensional and multidirectional in older adults? What changes in cognitive processing take place in aging adults?
- How do education, work, and health affect cognition in aging adults?
- What is the concept of "use it or lose it"?
- To what extent can older adults' cognitive skills be retrained?
- What characterizes the cognitive neuroscience of aging?

Connect

- The term *scaffolding* was used in this section to describe the use of complementary neural circuits to protect cognitive functioning in an aging brain. How has the term *scaffolding* been used elsewhere in the text?

Reflect *Your Own Personal Journey of Life*

- Can you think of older adults who have made significant contributions in late adulthood other than those we mentioned in the chapter? Spend some time reading about these individuals and evaluate how their intellectual interests contributed to their life satisfaction as older adults. What did you learn from their lives that might benefit your cognitive development and life satisfaction as an older adult?

Most research on language development has focused on infancy and childhood. It is generally thought that for most of adulthood individuals maintain their language skills (Thornton & Light, 2006). The vocabulary of individuals often continues to increase throughout most of the adult years, at least until late adulthood (Schaie, 2013; Singh-Manoux & others, 2012). Many older adults maintain or improve their word knowledge and word meaning (Burke & Shafto, 2004).

In late adulthood, however, some decrements in language may appear (Antonenko & others, 2013; Obler, 2009). Among the most common language-related complaints reported by older adults are difficulty in retrieving words to use in conversation and problems understanding spoken language in certain contexts (Clark-Cotton, Williams, & Goral, 2007). This often involves the *tip-of-the-tongue phenomenon,* in which individuals are confident that they can remember something but just can't quite seem to retrieve it from memory, which we discussed earlier in the section on memory and aging (Ossher, Flegal, & Lustig, 2013). Older adults also report that in less than ideal listening conditions they can have difficulty in understanding speech. This difficulty is most likely to occur when speech is rapid, competing stimuli are present (a noisy room, for example), and when they can't see their conversation partner (in a telephone conversation, for example). The difficulty in understanding speech may be due to hearing loss (Benichov & others, 2012). In general, though, most language skills decline little among older adults if they are healthy (Clark-Cotton & others, 2007).

Some aspects of the phonological skills of older adults are different from those of younger adults (Clark-Cotton & others, 2007; Mattys & Scharenborg, 2014; Singh-Manoux & others, 2012). Older adults' speech is typically lower in volume, slower, less precisely articulated, and less fluent (more pauses, fillers, repetition, and corrections). Despite these age differences, most older adults' speech skills are adequate for everyday communication.

Researchers have found conflicting information about changes in *discourse* (extended verbal expression in speech or writing) with aging. "Some (researchers) have reported increased elaborateness, while others have reported less varied and less complex syntax" (Obler, 2009, p. 459). One aspect of discourse where age differences have been found involves retelling a story or giving instructions for completing a task. When engaging in this type of discourse, older adults are more likely than younger adults to omit key elements, creating discourse that is less fluent and more difficult to follow (Clark-Cotton & others, 2007). A recent study found that when retelling a story, older adults were more likely than younger adults to compress discourse and less likely to improve the cohesiveness of their narratives (Saling, Laroo, & Saling, 2012).

Nonlanguage factors may be responsible for some of the declines in language skills that do occur in older adults (Obler, 2009). Slower information-processing speed and a decline in working memory, especially in being able to keep information in mind while processing, likely contribute to decreased language efficiency in older adults (Salthouse, 2013a; Stine-Morrow, 2007).

Language does change among individuals with Alzheimer disease, which we will discuss later in the chapter (Ferris & Farlow, 2013; Obler, 2009). Word-finding/generating difficulties are one of the earliest symptoms of Alzheimer disease (Haugrud, Crossley, & Vrbancic, 2011). Individuals with Alzheimer disease especially have difficulty on tests of semantic verbal fluency, in which they have to say as many words as possible in a category (fruits or animals, for example) in a given time, typically one minute (Pakhomov, Hemmy, & Lim, 2012; Weakley & Schmitter-Edgecombe, 2014). Most individuals with the disease do retain much of their ability to produce well-formed sentences until the late stages of the disease. Nonetheless, they do make more grammatical errors than older adults without the disease (Huang, Meyer, & Federmeier, 2012; Kail, Lemaire, & Lecacheur, 2012).

Recently, interest has been generated in the possibility that bilingualism may delay the onset of Alzheimer disease (Fischer & Schweizer, 2014). A recent study found that the onset of Alzheimer disease occurred 4.5 years later in bilingual older adults (Alladi & others, 2013). Another recent study revealed that the onset of symptoms and first office visit for Alzheimer disease occurred several years later for bilingual than for monolingual older adults (Bialystok & others, 2014). It is not yet clear why this advantage occurs for bilingual older adults, but one possible explanation is better executive function.

Review
- What are the main changes in language development in older adults?

Connect
- In this section, we learned that some aspects of the phonological skills of older adults are different from those of younger adults. By what age are children typically capable of producing all the vowel sounds and most of the consonant sounds of their language (discussed in Chapter 7)?

Reflect *Your Own Personal Journey of Life*
- What might you be able to do as an older adult to preserve or even enhance your language skills?

---

3 Work and Retirement

 LG3 Discuss aging and adaptation to work and retirement.

| Work | Retirement in the United States and Other Countries | Adjustment to Retirement |

What percentage of older adults continue to work? How productive are they? Who adjusts best to retirement? What is the changing pattern of retirement in the United States and around the world? Let's look at the answers to these and other questions.

developmental **connection**

Work

In the United States, approximately 80 percent of individuals 40 to 59 years of age are employed. Chapter 15, p. 475

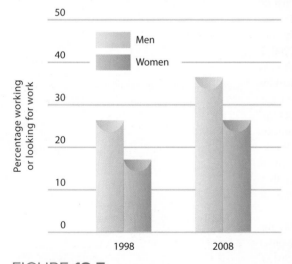

FIGURE **18.5**

PERCENTAGE OF 65- TO 69-YEAR-OLD U.S. MEN AND WOMEN WORKING OR LOOKING FOR WORK IN 1998 AND 2008

WORK

The percentage of older U.S. adult men who are still working or returning to work has been increasing since the early 1990s. As more women have entered the workforce, the percentage of older adult women still working also has increased. Figure 18.5 shows the increase in the percentage of men and women 65 to 69 years old who were still working or looking for work from 1998 to 2008 (U.S. Bureau of Labor Statistics, 2008).

Since the mid-1990s, a significant shift has occurred in the percentage of older adults working part-time or full-time (U.S. Bureau of Labor Statistics, 2008). As shown in Figure 18.6, after 1995, of the adults 65 and older in the workforce, those engaging in full-time work rose substantially and those working part-time decreased considerably. This significant rise in full-time employment likely reflects the increasing number of older adults who realize that they may not have adequate money to fund their retirement (Rix, 2011). For the first time since data were first collected in 1981, in 2011, more than 1 in 9 U.S. men over the age of 75 were working (U.S. Bureau of Labor Statistics, 2012). In 2011, about 1 in 20 U.S. women over the age of 75 were working. Also, older adults are increasingly seeking some type of bridge employment that permits a gradual rather than a sudden movement out of the work context (Bowen, Noack, & Staudinger, 2011).

A recent survey revealed that 47 percent of Americans 50 years and older now expect to retire later than they previously envisioned (Associated Press-NORC Center for Public Affairs Research, 2013). In this survey, 78 percent of the workers said that they were planning to retire later because of financial reasons, with many citing that they had less retirement savings than they did before the recent recession.

Cognitive ability is one of the best predictors of job performance in older adults. And older workers have lower rates of absenteeism, fewer accidents, and higher job satisfaction than their younger counterparts (Warr, 2004). Thus, the older worker can be of considerable value to a company, above and beyond the older worker's cognitive competence. Changes in federal law now allow individuals over the age of 65 to continue working (Shore & Goldberg, 2005). Also, remember from our discussion earlier in this chapter that substantively complex work is linked with a higher level of intellectual functioning (Schooler, 2007). Further, a recent study found that working in an occupation with a high level of mental demands was linked to higher levels of cognitive functioning before retirement and a slower rate of cognitive decline after retirement (Fisher & others, 2014). In sum, a cognitively stimulating work context promotes successful aging (Bowen, Noack, & Staudinger, 2011).

Several recent studies also have found that older adults who work have better physical profiles that those who retire. For example, a recent study found that physical functioning declined faster in retirement than in full-time work for employees 65 years of age and older, with the difference not explained by absence of chronic diseases and lifestyle risks (Stenholm & others, 2014). Another study revealed that retirement increased the risk of having a heart attack in older adults (Olesen & others, 2014).

In sum, age affects many aspects of work. Nonetheless, many studies of work and aging—such as evaluation of hiring and performance—have yielded inconsistent results. Important contextual factors—such as age composition of departments or applicant pools, occupations, and jobs—all affect decisions about older workers. It also is important to recognize that age-ist stereotypes of workers and of tasks can limit older workers' career opportunities and can encourage early retirement or other forms of downsizing that adversely affect older workers (Finkelstein & Farrell, 2007). A recent study of older workers found that self-evaluation of one's skills and values, being positive about change, and participating in a supportive work environment were linked to adaptive competence in work (Unson & Richardson, 2013).

FIGURE 18.6

PERCENTAGE OF U.S. ADULTS 65 YEARS AND OLDER IN THE LABOR FORCE WHO ARE WORKING FULL-TIME OR PART-TIME

RETIREMENT IN THE UNITED STATES AND IN OTHER COUNTRIES

At what age do most people retire in the United States? Do many people return to the workforce at some point after they have retired? What is retirement like in other countries?

Retirement in the United States   The option to retire is a late-twentieth-century phenomenon in the United States (Higo & Williamson, 2009). It exists largely because of the 1935 implementation of the Social Security system, which gives benefits to older workers when they retire. On average, today's workers will spend 10 to 15 percent of their lives in retirement. A survey revealed that as baby boomers move into their sixties, they expect to retire later than either their parents or their grandparents (Frey, 2007). In 2011, in the United States, the average age of retirement was 64 for men and 62 for women (Munnell, 2011).

In the past, when most people reached an accepted retirement age, such as some point in their sixties, retirement meant a one-way exit from full-time work to full-time leisure. Leading expert Phyllis Moen (2007) described how today, when people reach their sixties, the life path they follow is less clear:

- some individuals don't retire, continuing in their career jobs
- some retire from their career work and then take up a new and different job
- some retire from career jobs but do volunteer work
- some retire from a post-retirement job and go on to yet another job
- some move in and out of the workforce, so they never really have a "career" job from which they retire
- some individuals who are in poor health move to a disability status and eventually into retirement
- some who are laid off define it as "retirement."

Ninety-two-year-old Russell "Bob" Harrell (right) puts in 12-hour days at Sieco Consulting Engineers in Columbus, Indiana. A highway and bridge engineer, he designs and plans roads. James Rice (age 48), a vice president of client services at Sieco, says that Bob wants to learn something new every day and that he has learned many life lessons from being around him. Harrell says he is not planning to retire. *What are some variations in work and retirement in older adults?*

The night hath not yet come: We are not quite cut off from labor by the failing of light; some work remains for us to do and dare.

—**HENRY WADSWORTH LONGFELLOW**
American Poet, 19th Century

Approximately 7 million retired Americans return to work after they have retired (Putnam Investments, 2006). When retired adults return to the labor force, it occurs on average four years after retirement (Hardy, 2006). In many instances, the jobs pay much less than their pre-retirement jobs. In one study of older adults who returned to work, approximately two-thirds said they were happy they had done so, while about one-third indicated they were forced to go back to work to meet financial needs (Putnam Investments, 2006).

Just as the life path after individuals reach retirement age may vary, so do the reasons for working. For example, some older adults who reach retirement age work for financial reasons, others to stay busy, and yet others to "give back" (Moen, 2007).

Work and Retirement in Other Countries What characterizes work and retirement in other countries? One analysis concluded that Italy has the earliest average retirement age (59) for men and women (OECD, 2010). In this analysis, Norway and Iceland had the oldest average retirement age (67) for men and women.

A large-scale study of 21,000 individuals aged 40 to 79 in 21 countries examined patterns of work and retirement (HSBC Insurance, 2007). On average, 33 percent of individuals in their sixties and 11 percent in their seventies were still in some kind of paid employment. In this study, 19 percent of those in their seventies in the United States were still working. A substantial percentage of individuals expect to continue working as long as possible before retiring (HSBC Insurance, 2007).

In the study of work and retirement in 21 countries, Japanese retirees missed the work slightly more than they expected and the money considerably less than they expected (HSBC Insurance, 2007). U.S. retirees missed both the work and the money slightly less than they expected. German retirees were the least likely to miss the work, Turkish and Chinese retirees the most likely to miss it. Regarding money, Japanese and Chinese retirees were the least likely to miss it, Turkish retirees the most likely to miss it.

Early retirement policies were introduced by many companies in the 1970s and 1980s with the intention of making room for younger workers (Coe & others, 2012). However, the recent survey indicated that an increasing number of adults are beginning to reject the early retirement option as they hear about people who retired and then regretted it. In the 21-country study, on average only 12 percent of individuals in their forties and fifties expected to take early retirement while 16 percent in their sixties and seventies had taken early retirement. Only in Germany, South Korea, and Hong Kong did a higher percentage of individuals expect to take earlier retirement than in the past.

In the study of work and retirement in 21 countries, what were some variations across countries regarding the extent to which retirees missed work and money?

ADJUSTMENT TO RETIREMENT

Retirement is a process, not an event (Wang, 2012). Much of the research on retirement has been cross-sectional rather than longitudinal and has focused on men rather than women. One study found that men had higher morale when they had retired within the last two years compared with men who had been retired for longer periods of time (Kim & Moen, 2002). Another study revealed that retired married and remarried women reported being more satisfied with their lives and in better health than retired women who were widowed, separated, divorced, or had never been married (Price & Joo, 2005). Yet another study indicated that women spend less time planning for retirement than men do (Jacobs-Lawson, Hershey, & Neukam, 2005). And a recent study revealed that higher levels of financial assets and job satisfaction were more strongly linked to men's higher psychological well-being in retirement, while preretirement social contacts were more strongly related to women's psychological well-being in retirement (Kubicek & others, 2010).

Older adults who adjust best to retirement are healthy, have adequate income, are active, are better educated, have an extended social network including both friends and family, and usually were satisfied with their lives before they retired (Damman, Henkens, & Kalmijn, 2014; Jokela & others, 2010). Older adults with inadequate income and poor health, and who must adjust to other stress that occurs at the same time as retirement, such as the death of a spouse, have the most difficult time adjusting to retirement (Reichstadt & others, 2007).

The U.S. retirement system is in transition (Butrica, Smith, & Iams, 2012; Kramer, 2012). The recent economic downturn, high unemployment rate, and potential changes in Social Security and health insurance coverage for retired individuals in the United States have made having enough money for retirement an even greater concern (Bosworth, 2012). A 2012 survey indicated that confidence in having enough money to live comfortably in retirement dropped to 14 percent (Helman, Copeland, & VanDerhei, 2012). In this survey, the percent of workers who reported that they expect to retire after the age of 65 grew to 37 percent (compared to 11 percent in 1991). With regard to retirement income, the two main worries of individuals as they approach retirement are: (1) drawing retirement income from savings, and (2) paying for health care expenses (Yakoboski, 2011).

Flexibility is also a key factor in whether individuals adjust well to retirement (Wang, 2012). When people retire, they no longer have the structured environment they had when they were working, so they need to be flexible and discover and pursue their own interests. Cultivating interests and friends unrelated to work improves adaptation to retirement.

Planning ahead and then successfully carrying out the plan are important aspects of adjusting well in retirement (Adams & Rau, 2011). A special concern in retirement planning involves women, who are likely to live longer than men, more likely to live alone, and tend to have lower retirement income (less likely to remarry and more likely to be widowed) (Moen, 2007; Prickett & Angel, 2011).

It is important not only to plan financially for retirement but also to consider other aspects of your life (Shultz & Wang, 2011). In addition to financial planning, individuals need to ask questions about retirement such as these: What am I going to do with my leisure time? How am I going to stay physically fit? What am I going to do socially? What am I going to do to keep my mind active?

What are some keys to adjusting effectively in retirement?

Review Connect Reflect

 LG3 Discuss aging and adaptation to work and retirement.

Review
- What characterizes the work of older adults?
- Compare retirement in the United States with retirement in other countries.
- How can individuals adjust effectively to retirement?

Connect
- In Chapter 12, you learned that U.S. adolescents spend much more time in unstructured leisure activities than East Asian adolescents do. How might establishing challenging lifelong leisure activities as an adolescent benefit an individual at retirement age?

Reflect *Your Own Personal Journey of Life*
- At what age would you like to retire? Or would you prefer to continue working as an older adult as long as you are healthy?

4 Mental Health **LG4** Describe mental health problems in older adults.

| Depression | Dementia, Alzheimer Disease, and Other Afflictions | Fear of Victimization, Crime, and Elder Maltreatment |

Although a substantial portion of the population can now look forward to a longer life, that life may unfortunately be hampered by a mental disorder in old age (Knight & Kellough, 2013). This prospect is both troubling to the individual and costly to society. Mental disorders make individuals increasingly dependent on the help and care of others. The cost of caring for older adults with mental health disorders is estimated to be more than $40 billion per year in the United States. More important than the loss in dollars, though, is the loss of human potential and the suffering involved for individuals and their families. Although

What characterizes depression in older adults?

developmental **connection**

Gender

One reason that females have higher rates of depression is that they ruminate more in their depressed mood and amplify it more than males do. Chapter 12, p. 391

major depression A mood disorder in which the individual is deeply unhappy, demoralized, self-derogatory, and bored. The person does not feel well, loses stamina easily, has poor appetite, and is listless and unmotivated. Major depression is so widespread that it has been called the "common cold" of mental disorders.

dementia A global term for any neurological disorder in which the primary symptoms involve a deterioration of mental functioning.

Alzheimer disease A progressive, irreversible brain disorder characterized by a gradual deterioration of memory, reasoning, language, and eventually, physical function.

mental disorders in older adults are a major concern, it is important to understand that older adults do not have a higher incidence of mental disorders than younger adults do (Busse & Blazer, 1996).

DEPRESSION

Major depression is a mood disorder in which the individual is deeply unhappy, demoralized, self-derogatory, and bored. The person does not feel well, loses stamina easily, has a poor appetite, and is listless and unmotivated. Major depression has been called the "common cold" of mental disorders. However, a review concluded that depression is less common among older adults than younger adults (Fiske, Wetherell, & Gatz, 2009). More than half of the cases of depression in older adults represent the first time in their lives that these individuals have developed depression (Fiske, Wetherell, & Gatz, 2009).

One study found that the lower frequency of depressive symptoms in older adults compared with middle-aged adults was linked to fewer economic hardships, fewer negative social interchanges, and increased religiosity (Schieman, van Gundy, & Taylor, 2004). Other research indicates that older adults who engage in regular exercise, especially aerobic exercise, are less likely to be depressed, whereas those who are in poor health and experiencing pain are more likely to be depressed (Cimpean & Drake, 2011). Depressive symptoms increase among the oldest-old (85 years and older), and this increase is associated with a higher percentage of women in the group, more physical disability, greater cognitive impairment, and lower socioeconomic status (Hybels & Blazer, 2004).

In the childhood, adolescent, and early adulthood years, females show higher rates of depression than males do (Nolen-Hoeksema, 2011). Does this gender difference hold for middle-aged and older adults? A longitudinal study found more depression in women than men at 50 and 60 years of age, but not at 80 years of age (Barefoot & others, 2001). Men showed increases in depressive symptoms from 60 to 80, but women did not. In this cohort, men may have undergone more profound role shifts after 60 years of age because they were more likely than women to have retired from active involvement in the work world. Thus, the absence of a gender difference in depression in older adults may be cohort-specific and may not hold as women who have entered the workforce in greater numbers are assessed in late adulthood.

Among the most common predictors of depression in older adults are earlier depressive symptoms, poor health, disability, losses such as the death of a spouse, and low social support (Bland, 2012; Saint Onge, Krueger, & Rogers, 2014). Insomnia is often overlooked as a risk factor for depression in older adults (Fiske, Wetherell, & Gatz, 2009). Curtailment of daily activities is a common pathway to late-life depression (Fiske, Wetherell, & Gatz, 2009). Often accompanying this curtailment of activity is an increase in self-critical thinking that exacerbates depression. A recent meta-analysis found that the following living arrangements were linked to risk for depression in older adults: living alone, in a nursing home, or in an institutionalized setting (Xiu-Ying & others, 2012).

Depression is a treatable condition, not only in young adults but in older adults as well (Kohen & others, 2011; Piazza & Charles, 2012). Unfortunately, as many as 80 percent of older adults with depressive symptoms receive no treatment at all. Combinations of medications and psychotherapy produce significant improvement in almost four out of five older adults with depression (Koenig & Blazer, 1996). Further, exercise can reduce depression in older adults. For example, a recent study of older adults found that even light-intensity exercise was linked to a lower level of depression (Loprinzi, 2013). Also, engagement in valued activities and religious/spiritual involvement can reduce depressive symptoms (Fiske, Wetherell, & Gatz, 2009). Life review/reminiscence therapy, which we will discuss further in Chapter 19, is underutilized in the treatment of depression in older adults (Fiske, Wetherell, & Gatz, 2009).

Major depression can result not only in sadness but also in suicidal tendencies (Bergman-Levy & others, 2011). Nearly 25 percent of individuals who commit suicide in the United States are 65 years of age or older (Church, Siegel, & Fowler, 1988). The older adult most likely to commit suicide is a male who lives alone, has lost his spouse, and is experiencing failing health (Ruckenhauser, Yazdani, & Ravaglia, 2007).

DEMENTIA, ALZHEIMER DISEASE, AND OTHER AFFLICTIONS

Among the most debilitating of mental disorders in older adults are the dementias (Clare & others, 2012). In recent years, extensive attention has been focused on the most common dementia, Alzheimer disease.

Dementia **Dementia** is a global term for any neurological disorder in which the primary symptoms involve a deterioration of mental functioning. Individuals with dementia often lose the ability to care for themselves and can become unable to recognize familiar surroundings and people—including family members (McMillan & others, 2014; Valkanova & Ebmeier, 2014; Ziso & Larner, 2013). It is estimated that 23 percent of women and 17 percent of men 85 years and older are at risk for developing dementia (Alzheimer's Association, 2013). However, these estimates may be high because of the Alzheimer's Association's lobbying efforts to increase funding for research and treatment facilities. Dementia is a broad category, and it is important that every effort is made to determine the specific cause of deteriorating mental functioning (Velayudhan & others, 2014).

Alzheimer Disease One form of dementia is **Alzheimer disease**—a progressive, irreversible brain disorder that is characterized by a gradual deterioration of memory, reasoning, language, and eventually, physical function. In 2013, an estimated 5.2 million adults in the United States had Alzheimer disease, and it is projected that 10 million baby boomers will develop Alzheimer disease in their lifetime (Alzheimer's Association, 2013). Figure 18.7 shows the estimated risks for developing Alzheimer disease at different ages for women and men (Alzheimer's Association, 2010). Women are more likely than men to develop Alzheimer disease because they live longer than men and their longer life expectancy increases the number of years during which they can develop it. It is estimated that Alzheimer disease triples the health care costs of Americans 65 years of age and older (Alzheimer's Association, 2013). Because of the increasing prevalence of Alzheimer disease, researchers have stepped up their efforts to discover the causes of the disease and to find more effective ways to treat it (Grill & Monsell, 2014; Wilhelmus & others, 2014; Wisse & others, 2014; Zlater & others, 2014).

Causes Alzheimer disease involves a deficiency in the important brain messenger chemical acetylcholine, which plays an important role in memory (Jiang & others, 2014; Mesulam, 2013; Nardone & others, 2014). Also, as Alzheimer disease progresses, the brain shrinks and deteriorates (see Figure 18.8). This deterioration is characterized by the formation of *amyloid plaques* (dense deposits of protein that accumulate in the blood vessels) and *neurofibrillary tangles* (twisted fibers that build up in neurons) (Mungas & others, 2014; Taher & others, 2014; Wisnewski & Goni, 2014). Neurofibrillary tangles consist mainly of a protein called *tau* (Avila & others, 2014; Pooler, Noble, & Hanger, 2014). Currently, there is considerable research interest in the roles that amyloid and tau play in Alzheimer disease (Tian & others, 2014; Vromman & others, 2013).

There also is increasing interest in the role that oxidative stress might play in Alzheimer disease (Luque-Contreras & others, 2014; Meras-Rios & others, 2014; Pohanka, 2013). Oxidative stress occurs when the body's antioxidant defenses don't cope with free radical attacks and oxidation in the body. Recall from Chapter 17 that free radical theory is a major theory of aging.

Although scientists are not certain what causes Alzheimer disease, age is an important risk factor and genes also are likely to play an important role (Feng & others, 2014; Tang & others, 2014). The number of individuals with Alzheimer disease doubles every five years after the age of 65. A gene called *apolipoprotein E (ApoE)* is linked to increasing presence of plaques and tangles in the brain. Special attention has focused on an allele (an alternative form of a gene) labeled ApoE4, an allele that is a strong risk factor for Alzheimer disease (Argyri & others, 2014; Dorey & others, 2014; Osorio & others, 2014). In K. Warner Schaie's (2013) recent research, individuals who had the ApoE4 allele showed more cognitive decline beginning in middle age. A recent study found that the ApoE4 gene created a cascade of molecular signaling that causes blood vessels to become more porous, allowing toxic substances to leak into the brain and damage neurons (Bell & others, 2012).

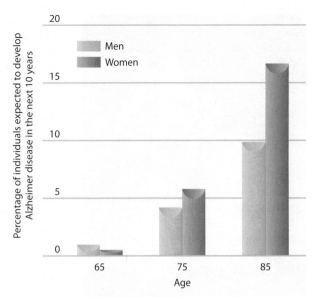

FIGURE **18.7**

ESTIMATED RISKS FOR DEVELOPING ALZHEIMER DISEASE AT DIFFERENT AGES FOR WOMEN AND MEN
Source: Alzheimer's Association (2010).

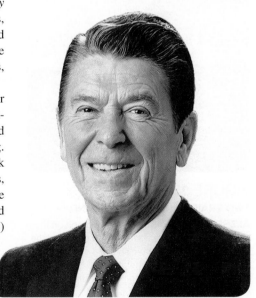

Former president Ronald Reagan was diagnosed with Alzheimer disease at age 83.

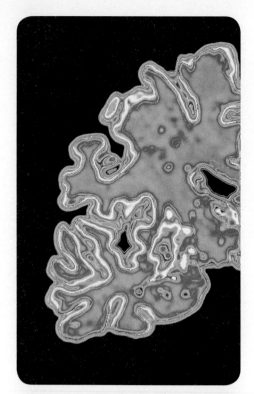

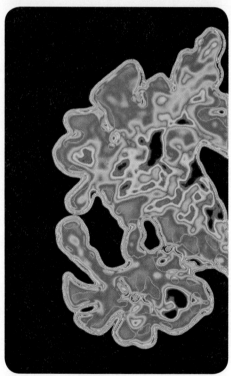

FIGURE 18.8

TWO BRAINS: NORMAL AGING AND ALZHEIMER DISEASE. The photograph on the top shows a slice of a normal aging brain and the photograph on the bottom shows a slice of a brain ravaged by Alzheimer disease. Notice the deterioration and shrinking in the Alzheimer disease brain.

Despite links between the presence of the ApoE4 gene and Alzheimer disease, less than 50 percent of the individuals who are carriers of the ApoE4 gene develop dementia in old age. Advances as a result of the Human Genome Project have recently resulted in identification of other genes that are risk factors for Alzheimer disease, although they are not as strongly linked to the disease as the ApoE4 gene (Lillenes & others, 2013).

Although individuals with a family history of Alzheimer disease are at greater risk, the disease is complex and likely caused by a number of factors, including lifestyles (Jiang & others, 2013). Researchers are finding that healthy lifestyle factors may lower the risk of Alzheimer disease or delay the onset of the disease (Suehs & others, 2014). For example, older adults with Alzheimer disease are more likely to have cardiovascular disease than are individuals who do not have Alzheimer disease (Murr & others, 2014; Wang & others, 2013). Recently, more cardiac risk factors have been implicated in Alzheimer disease—obesity, smoking, atherosclerosis, high cholesterol, lipids, and permanent atrial fibrillation (Dublin & others, 2014; Grammas & others, 2014). One of the best strategies for intervening in the lives of people who are at risk for Alzheimer disease is to improve their cardiac functioning through diet, drugs, and exercise (Tavassoli & others, 2013). One study of older adults found that those who exercised three or more times a week were less likely to develop Alzheimer disease over a six-year period than those who exercised less (Larson & others, 2006).

Early Detection and Drug Treatment   *Mild cognitive impairment (MCI)* represents a potential transitional state between the cognitive changes of normal aging and very early stages of Alzheimer disease and other dementias. MCI is increasingly recognized as a risk factor for Alzheimer disease. Estimates indicate that as many as 10 to 20 percent of individuals 65 years of age and older have MCI (Alzheimer's Association, 2013). Many individuals with MCI do not go on to develop Alzheimer disease, but MCI is a risk factor for Alzheimer disease. A recent study revealed that individuals with mild cognitive impairment who developed Alzheimer disease had at least one copy of the ApoE4 gene (Alegret & others, 2014). In this study, the extent of memory impairment was the key factor that was linked to the speed of decline from mild cognitive impairment to Alzheimer disease.

Distinguishing between individuals who merely have age-associated declines in memory and those with MCI is difficult, as is predicting which individuals with MCI will subsequently develop Alzheimer disease (Poil & others, 2013; Richens & others, 2014). A research review concluded that fMRI measurement of neuron loss in the medial temporal lobe is a predictor of memory loss and eventually dementia (Vellas & Aisen, 2010). Further, another study revealed that amyloid beta—a protein fragment that forms plaques in the brain—was present in the spinal fluid of approximately 75 percent of the individuals with mild cognitive impairment (De Meyer & others, 2010). Every one of the older adults with mild cognitive impairment who had the amyloid beta in their spinal fluid developed Alzheimer disease within five years.

Drug Treatment of Alzheimer Disease   Several drugs called cholinerase inhibitors have been approved by the U.S. Food and Drug Administration to treat Alzheimer disease. They are designed to improve memory and other cognitive functions by increasing levels of acetylcholine in the brain (Honig & Boyd, 2013; Reale & others, 2014). A recent research review concluded that cholinesterase inhibitors do not reduce progression to dementia (Masoodi, 2013). Keep in mind, though, that the drugs used to treat Alzheimer disease only slow the downward progression of the disease; they do not address its cause (Alves & others, 2012). Also, no drugs have yet been approved by the Federal Drug Administration for the treatment of MCI (Alzheimer's Association, 2010).

Caring for Individuals with Alzheimer Disease   A special concern is caring for Alzheimer patients (Kamiya & others, 2014). Health-care professionals emphasize that the family can be an important support system for the Alzheimer patient, but this support can have costs for the family, who can become emotionally and physically drained by the extensive care required for a person with Alzheimer disease (Carling-Jenkins & others, 2012; Ornstein & others, 2014). A recent study compared family members' perception of caring for someone with Alzheimer disease, cancer, or schizophrenia (Papastavrou & others, 2012). In this study, the highest perceived burden was reported for Alzheimer disease.

Respite care (services that provide temporary relief for those who are caring for individuals with disabilities, illnesses, or the elderly) has been developed to help people who have

Jan Weaver, Director of the Alzheimer's Association of Dallas

Dr. Weaver joined the Alzheimer's Association, Greater Dallas Chapter, as director of services and education in 1999. Prior to that time, she served as associate director of education for the Texas Institute for Research and Education on Aging and director of the National Academy for Teaching and Learning About Aging at the University of North Texas. As a gerontologist, Weaver plans and develops services and educational programs that address patterns of human development related to aging. Among the services that Weaver supervises at the Alzheimer's Association are a resource center and helpline, a family assistance program, a care program, support groups, referrals and information, educational conferences, and community seminars.

Weaver recognizes that people of all ages should have an informed and balanced view of older adults that helps them perceive aging as a process of growth and fulfillment rather than a process of decline and dependency. Weaver earned her Ph.D. in sociology, with an emphasis in gerontology, from the University of Texas in 1996.

Jan Weaver giving a lecture on Alzheimer disease.

to meet the day-to-day needs of Alzheimer patients. This type of care provides an important break from the burden of providing chronic care (de la Cuesta-Benjumea, 2011).

There are many career opportunities for working with individuals who have Alzheimer disease. To read about the work of a director of an Alzheimer association, see *Connecting with Careers.*

Parkinson Disease Another type of dementia is **Parkinson disease,** a chronic, progressive disease characterized by muscle tremors, slowing of movement, and partial facial paralysis. Parkinson disease is triggered by degeneration of dopamine-producing neurons in the brain (Catalan & others, 2013). Dopamine is a neurotransmitter that is necessary for normal brain functioning. Why these neurons degenerate is not known.

The main treatment for Parkinson disease involves administering drugs that enhance the effect of dopamine (dopamine agonists) in the disease's earlier stages and later administering the drug L-dopa, which is converted by the brain into dopamine (Mestre & others, 2014). However, it is difficult to determine the correct level of dosage of L-dopa and it loses efficacy over time (Nomoto & others, 2009).

Another treatment for advanced Parkinson disease is deep brain stimulation (DBS), which involves implantation of electrodes within the brain (Kim & others, 2014; Pollack, 2013). The electrodes are then stimulated by a pacemaker-like device. Recent studies indicated that deep brain stimulation may provide benefits for individuals with Parkinson disease (Vedam-Mai & others, 2014). Other recent studies indicate that certain types of dance, such as the tango, can improve the movement skills of individuals with Parkinson disease (Kaski & others, 2014; Ransmayr, 2011). Stem cell transplantation and gene therapy also offer hope for treating the disease (Badger & others, 2014; Wyse, Dunbar, & Rossignol, 2014).

Muhammad Ali, one of the world's leading sports figures, has Parkinson disease.

FEAR OF VICTIMIZATION, CRIME, AND ELDER MALTREATMENT

Some of the physical decline and limitations that characterize development in late adulthood contribute to a sense of vulnerability and fear among older adults. For some older adults, fear of crime may become a deterrent to travel, attendance at social events, and the pursuit of an active lifestyle. Almost one-fourth of older adults say they have a basic fear of being the victim of a crime. However, in reality, possibly because of the precautions they take, older

Parkinson disease A chronic, progressive disease characterized by muscle tremors, slowing of movement, and partial facial paralysis.

Meeting the Mental Health Needs of Older Adults

Older adults receive disproportionately fewer mental health services than young or middle-aged adults (Moak, 2011). One estimate is that only 2.7 percent of all clinical services provided by psychologists go to older adults, although individuals aged 65 and over make up more than 11 percent of the population. Psychotherapy can be expensive. Although reduced fees and sometimes no fee can be arranged in public hospitals for older adults from low-income backgrounds, many older adults who need psychotherapy do not get it (Knight & others, 2006). It has been said that psychotherapists like to work with young, attractive, verbal, intelligent, and successful clients (called YAVISes) rather than those who are quiet, ugly, old, institutionalized, and different (called QUOIDs). Psychotherapists have been accused of failing to see older adults because they perceive that older adults have a poor prognosis for therapy success; they do not feel they have adequate training to treat older adults, who may have special problems requiring special treatment; and they may have stereotypes that label older adults as low-status and unworthy recipients of treatment (Virnig & others, 2004).

How can we better meet the mental health needs of older adults? First, mental health professionals must be encouraged to include greater numbers of older adults in their client lists, and older adults must be convinced that they can benefit from therapy (Baskin & others, 2011; Knight & Kellough, 2013). Second, we must make mental health care affordable. For example, Medicare continues to fall short of providing many mental health services for older adults, especially for those in need of long-term care (Knight & Lee, 2007).

Margaret Gatz (*right*) has been a crusader for better mental health treatment of older adults. She believes that mental health professionals need to be encouraged to include greater numbers of older adults in their client lists and that we need to better educate the elderly about how they can benefit from therapy. *What are some common mechanisms of change that can be used to improve the mental health of older adults?*

Earlier in this chapter, we discussed stereotypes and ageism with regard to older adults in the workforce. How are those concepts related to what you just read in this interlude?

---

adults are less likely than younger adults to be the victim of a crime. However, the crimes committed against older adults are likely to be serious offenses such as armed robbery. Older adults are also victims of nonviolent crimes such as fraud, vandalism, purse snatching, and harassment (Navarro & others, 2013). Estimates of the incidence of crimes against older adults may be low because older adults may not report crimes, fearing retribution from criminals or believing the criminal justice system cannot help them.

How often does elder abuse occur? A research review indicated that 6 percent of older adults reported experiencing significant abuse in the last month (Cooper, Selwood, & Livingston, 2008). In this study, 16 percent of home-care staff admitted to significant psychological abuse of older adults. Elder maltreatment may be perpetrated by anyone, but it is primarily carried out by family members (Dakin & Pearlmutter, 2009; Yan, 2014). As with child maltreatment, elder maltreatment can involve neglect, psychological abuse, or physical abuse (Burnes, Rizzo, & Courtney, 2014; Castle, Ferguson-Rome, & Teresi, 2014; Sooryanarayana, Choo, & Hairi, 2013). Older adults are most often abused by their spouses. A special concern is the burden older women carry in facing possible physical violence. In the research review described above, 5.6 percent of older adult couples said they had experienced physical violence in their relationship in the last month.

Older adults also can experience institutional abuse, which involves mistreatment of older adults living in facilities such as nursing homes, hospitals, or long-term care centers (Charpentier & Soulieres, 2013). Institutional abuse of older adults include the staff engaging in rough handling, hitting, or slapping patients, inappropriate treatment, and psychological abuse, such as social isolation and threats.

Maltreated older adults, as well as older adults who are depressed, have a dementia, or have another mental disorder, may need mental health treatment (Cisler & others, 2012). To read about this topic, see *Connecting Development to Life*.

Review *Connect* Reflect

LG4 Describe mental health problems in older adults.

Review

- What is the nature of depression in older adults?
- What are dementia, Alzheimer disease, and Parkinson disease like in older adults?
- How extensive is fear of victimization, crime, and maltreatment in older adults?

Connect

- We also discussed depression in adolescence in Chapter 12. What are some differences in how depression is characterized in adolescence as opposed to late adulthood?

Reflect *Your Own Personal Journey of Life*

- Have any older adults in your family background experienced mental health problems as adults? If so, what were these mental health problems? If they have experienced mental health problems, what were the likely causes of the problems?

5 Religion and Spirituality

LG5 Explain the role of religion and spirituality in the lives of older adults.

In Chapter 15, we discussed religion, spirituality, and meaning in life with a special focus on middle age, including links between religion/spirituality and health. Here we will continue our exploration of religion and spirituality by considering their importance in the lives of many older adults.

In many societies around the world, older adults are the spiritual leaders in their churches and communities. For example, in the Catholic Church more popes have been elected in their eighties than in any other 10-year period of the human life span.

The religious patterns of older adults have increasingly been studied (George & others, 2013; Krause, 2012; Sun & others, 2012). A longitudinal study found that religious service attendance was stable in middle adulthood, increased in late adulthood, then declined later in the older adult years (Hayward & Krause, 2013b). A research review concluded that individuals with a stronger spiritual/religious orientation were more likely to live longer (Lucchetti, Lucchetti, & Koenig. 2011). Also, in one study, religious attendance at least weekly compared with never was linked to a lower risk of mortality (Gillum & others, 2008). Another study revealed that African American and Caribbean Black older adults reported higher levels of religious participation, religious coping, and spirituality than non-Latino White older adults (Taylor, Chatters, & Jackson, 2007). And in one study, older adults who reported having a higher level of spirituality had more resilience in the face of stressful and difficult circumstances (Vahia & others, 2011b).

Individuals over 65 years of age are more likely than younger people to say that religious faith is the most significant influence in their lives, that they try to put religious faith into practice, and that they attend religious services (Gallup & Bezilla, 1992). A recent study of more than 500 African Americans 55 to 105 years of age revealed that they had a strong identification with religious institutions and high levels of attendance and participation in religious activities (Williams, Keigher, & Williams, 2012). And a Pew poll found that belief in God was higher in older adulthood than in any other age period (Pew Forum on Religion and Public Life, 2008).

Is religion related to a sense of well-being and life satisfaction in old age? In one study, older adults' self-esteem was highest when they had a strong religious commitment and lowest when they had little religious commitment (Krause, 1995). In another study, older adults who derived a sense of meaning in life from religion had higher levels of life satisfaction, self-esteem, and optimism (Krause, 2003). And a recent study found that older adults who had a higher level of religious identification were less likely to be depressed (Ysseldyk, Haslam, & Haslam, 2013).

During late adulthood, many individuals increasingly engage in prayer. *How might this be linked with longevity?*

developmental connection

Religion and Spirituality

Meaning-making coping involves drawing on beliefs, values, and goals to change the meaning of a stressful situation, especially in times of chronic stress, such as when a loved one dies. Chapter 15, p. 477

Religion and spirituality can meet some important psychological needs in older adults, helping them to face impending death, to find and maintain a sense of meaningfulness in life, and to accept the inevitable losses of old age (George & others, 2013; Koenig, 2004). Socially, the religious community can serve many functions for older adults, such as social activities, social support, and the opportunity to assume teaching and leadership roles (Krause, 2012). A recent study revealed that over a period of seven years, older adults who attended church regularly increased the amount of emotional support they gave and received but decreased the amount of tangible support they gave and received (Hayward & Krause, 2013a).

Review *Connect* Reflect

 Explain the role of religion and spirituality in the lives of older adults.

Review
- What are some characteristics of religion and spirituality in older adults?

Connect
- We just learned that prayer and meditation may reduce stress and dampen the body's production of stress hormones. Why is this especially important in the aging process?

Reflect *Your Own Personal Journey of Life*
- Do you think you will become more or less religious as an older adult than you are now? Explain.

---

topical connections *looking forward*

In Chapter 19, you will read about a number of theories that seek to explain older adults' socioemotional development, including Erikson's final stage (integrity versus despair). Older adults become more selective than middle-aged adults about the people they want to spend time with. There is considerable diversity in older adults' lifestyles, and an increasing number of older adults cohabit. Social support is especially important in older adults' lives and is linked to their physical and mental health. An important aspect of late adulthood is not dwelling too extensively on the negative aspects of aging but rather pursuing the key dimensions of successful aging.

reach your **learning goals**

Cognitive Development in Late Adulthood

1 Cognitive Functioning in Older Adults

 Describe the cognitive functioning of older adults.

Multidimensionality and Multidirectionality

- Cognitive mechanics (the neurophysiological architecture, including the brain) are more likely to decline in older adults than are cognitive pragmatics (the culture-based software of the mind). Speed of processing declines in older adults. Older adults' attention declines more on complex than simple tasks. Regarding memory, in late adulthood, explicit memory declines more than implicit memory; episodic memory declines more than semantic memory; working memory also declines. Components of executive function—such as cognitive control and working memory—decline in late adulthood. Decision making is reasonably well preserved in older adults. Wisdom is expert knowledge about the practical aspects of life that permits excellent judgment about important matters. Baltes and his colleagues have found that high levels of wisdom are rare, the time frame of late adolescence and early adulthood is the main window for wisdom to emerge, factors other than age are critical for wisdom to develop, and personality-related factors are better predictors of wisdom than cognitive factors such as intelligence.

Education, Work, and Health

- Successive generations of Americans have been better educated. Education is positively correlated with scores on intelligence tests. Older adults may return to college for a number of reasons. Successive generations have had work experiences that include a stronger emphasis on cognitively oriented labor. The increased emphasis on information processing in jobs likely enhances an individual's intellectual abilities. Poor health is related to decreased performance on intelligence tests by older adults. Exercise is linked to higher cognitive functioning in older adults.

Use It or Lose It

- Researchers are finding that older adults who engage in cognitive activities, especially challenging ones, have higher cognitive functioning than those who don't use their cognitive skills.

Training Cognitive Skills

- Two main conclusions can be derived from research on training cognitive skills in older adults: (1) training can improve the cognitive skills of many older adults, and (2) there is some loss in plasticity in late adulthood.

Cognitive Neuroscience and Aging

- There has been considerable recent interest in the cognitive neuroscience of aging that focuses on links among aging, the brain, and cognitive functioning. This field especially relies on fMRI and PET scans to assess brain functioning while individuals are engaging in cognitive tasks. One of the most consistent findings in this field is a decline in the functioning of specific regions in the prefrontal cortex in older adults and links between this decline and poorer performance on tasks involving complex reasoning, working memory, and episodic memory.

2 Language Development

 **LG2** Characterize changes in language in older adults.

- For many individuals, knowledge of words and word meanings continues unchanged or may even improve in late adulthood. However, some decline in language skills may occur in retrieval of words for use in conversation, comprehension of speech, phonological skills, and some aspects of discourse. These changes in language skills in older adults likely occur as a consequence of declines in hearing or memory, in a reduced speed of processing information, or as a result of disease.

3 Work and Retirement

LG3 Discuss aging and adaptation to work and retirement.

Work

- Today, the percentage of men over 65 who continue to work full-time is less than at the beginning of the twentieth century. An important change in older adults' work patterns is the increase in part-time work. Some individuals continue a life of strong work productivity throughout late adulthood.

Retirement in the United States and in Other Countries

- A retirement option for older workers is a late-twentieth-century phenomenon in the United States. Americans are more likely to continue working in their seventies than are workers in other countries.

Adjustment to Retirement

- The pathways individuals follow when they reach retirement age today are less clear than in the past. Those who adjust best to retirement are individuals who are healthy, have adequate income, are active, are better educated, have an extended social network of friends and family, and are satisfied with their lives before they retire.

4 Mental Health

 LG4 Describe mental health problems in older adults.

Depression

Dementia, Alzheimer Disease, and Other Afflictions

Fear of Victimization, Crime, and Elder Maltreatment

- Depression has been called the "common cold" of mental disorders. However, a majority of older adults with depressive symptoms never receive mental health treatment.

- Dementia is a global term for any neurological disorder in which the primary symptoms involve a deterioration of mental functioning. Alzheimer disease is by far the most common dementia. This progressive, irreversible disorder is characterized by gradual deterioration of memory, reasoning, language, and eventually physical functioning. Special efforts are being made to discover the causes of Alzheimer disease and effective treatments for it. The increase in amyloid plaques and neurofibrillary tangles in Alzheimer patients may hold important keys to improving our understanding of the disease. Alzheimer disease is characterized by a deficiency in acetylcholine that affects memory. Also, in Alzheimer disease the brain shrinks and deteriorates as plaques and tangles form. Important concerns are the financial implications of caring for Alzheimer patients and the burdens placed on caregivers. In addition to Alzheimer disease, another type of dementia is Parkinson disease.

- Some of the physical decline and limitations that characterize development in late adulthood contribute to a sense of vulnerability and fear among older adults. Almost one-fourth of older adults say they have a basic fear of being the victim of a crime. Older women are more likely than older men to be victimized or abused.

5 Religion and Spirituality

LG5 Explain the role of religion and spirituality in the lives of older adults.

- Many older adults are spiritual leaders in their church and community. Religious interest increases in old age and is related to a sense of well-being in the elderly.

key terms

cognitive mechanics 541
cognitive pragmatics 543
selective attention 543
divided attention 543
sustained attention 543

executive attention 543
explicit memory 543
implicit memory 543
episodic memory 543
semantic memory 544

source memory 545
prospective memory 545
wisdom 547
major depression 558
dementia 558

Alzheimer disease 558
Parkinson disease 561

key people

Paul Baltes 541
Lynn Hasher 545

K. Warner Schaie 548
Sherry Willis 550

Phyllis Moen 555

chapter 19

SOCIOEMOTIONAL DEVELOPMENT IN LATE ADULTHOOD

chapter outline

Bob Cousy was a star player on Boston Celtics teams that won numerous National Basketball Association championships. In recognition of his athletic accomplishments, Cousy was honored by ESPN as one of the top 100 athletes of the twentieth century. After he retired from basketball, he became a college basketball coach and then into his seventies was a broadcaster of Boston Celtics basketball games. Now in his eighties, Cousy has retired from broadcasting but continues to play golf and tennis on a regular basis. He has a number of positive social relationships, including a marriage of more than 50 years, children and grandchildren, and many friends.

Bob Cousy as a Boston Celtics star when he was a young adult (*left*) and as an older adult (*right*). *What are some changes he has made in his life as an older adult?*

As is the case with many famous people, Cousy's awards reveal little about his personal life and contributions. Two examples illustrate his humanitarian efforts to help others (McClellan, 2004). First, when Cousy played for the Boston Celtics, his African American teammate, Chuck Cooper, was refused a room on a road trip because of his race. Cousy expressed anger to his coach about the situation and then accompanied an appreciative Cooper on a train back to Boston. Second, the Bob Cousy Humanitarian Fund "honors individuals who have given their lives to using the game of basketball as a medium to help others" (p. 4). The Humanitarian Fund reflects Cousy's motivation to care for others, be appreciative and give something back, and make the world less self-centered.

topical connections *looking back*

Middle adulthood is a time when individuals become more conscious of the young-old polarity in life and the shrinking amount of time left in their lives. And it is a time when individuals seek to transmit something meaningful to the next generation. The concept of midlife crisis has been exaggerated; when people do experience this crisis, it often is linked to negative life events. Stability of personality peaks in middle adulthood, and marital satisfaction often increases at this time. Many middle-aged adults become grandparents and the middle-aged generation plays a key role in intergenerational relationships, with middle-aged women especially connecting generations.

preview

Bob Cousy's life as an older adult reflects some of the themes of socioemotional development in older adults that we will discuss in this chapter. These include the important role that being active plays in life satisfaction, the need to adapt to changing skills, and the ways in which close relationships with friends and family contribute to an emotionally fulfilling life.

1 Theories of Socioemotional Development

LG1 Discuss four theories of socioemotional development and aging.

- Erikson's Theory
- Activity Theory
- Socioemotional Selectivity Theory
- Selective Optimization with Compensation Theory

We will explore four main theories that focus on socioemotional development in late adulthood: Erikson's theory, activity theory, socioemotional selectivity theory, and selective optimization with compensation theory.

ERIKSON'S THEORY

We initially discussed Erik Erikson's (1968) eight stages of the human life span in Chapter 1, and as we explored different periods of development in this book, we examined the stages in more detail. Here we will discuss his final stage.

Integrity Versus Despair   **Integrity versus despair** is Erikson's eighth and final stage of development, which individuals experience during late adulthood. This stage involves reflecting on the past and either piecing together a positive review or concluding that one's life has not been well spent. Through many different routes, the older adult may have developed a positive outlook in each of the preceding periods. If so, retrospective glances and reminiscences will reveal a picture of a life well spent, and the older adult will be satisfied (integrity). But if the older adult resolved one or more of the earlier stages in a negative way (being socially isolated in early adulthood or stagnating in middle adulthood, for example), retrospective glances about the total worth of his or her life might be negative (despair). Figure 19.1 portrays how positive resolutions of Erikson's eight stages can culminate in wisdom and integrity for older adults.

Life Review   Life review is prominent in Erikson's final stage of integrity versus despair. Life review involves looking back at one's life experiences, evaluating them, interpreting them, and often reinterpreting them (George, 2010; Wu & others, 2012). A leading expert on aging, Robert Butler, provided this perspective on life review: ". . . there are chances for pain, anger, guilt, and grief, but there are also opportunities for resolution and celebration, for affirmation and hope, for reconciliation and personal growth" (Butler, 2007, p. 72).

Butler (2007) states that the life review is set in motion by looking forward to death. Sometimes the life review proceeds quietly; at other times it is intense, requiring considerable work to achieve some sense of personality integration. The life review may be observed initially in stray and insignificant thoughts about oneself and one's life history. These thoughts may continue to emerge in brief intermittent spurts or become essentially continuous. One 76-year-old man commented, "My life is in the back of my mind. It can't be any other way. Thoughts of the past play on me. Sometimes I play with them, encouraging and savoring them; at other times I dismiss them."

Life reviews can include sociocultural dimensions, such as culture, ethnicity, and gender. Life reviews also can include interpersonal, relationship dimensions, including sharing and intimacy with family members or a friend (Korte & others, 2014; Randall, 2013). And life reviews can include personal dimensions, which might involve the creation and discovery of

developmental **connection**

Erikson's Theory

Erikson's other two adult stages are intimacy versus isolation (early adulthood) and generativity versus stagnation (middle adulthood). Chapter 14, p. 438; Chapter 16, p. 486

What characterizes a life review in late adulthood?

integrity versus despair Erikson's eighth and final stage of development, which individuals experience in late adulthood. This involves reflecting on the past and either piecing together a positive review or concluding that one's life has not been well spent.

FIGURE 19.1

ERIKSON'S VIEW OF HOW POSITIVE RESOLUTION OF THE EIGHT STAGES OF THE HUMAN LIFE SPAN CAN CULMINATE IN WISDOM AND INTEGRITY IN OLD AGE. In Erikson's view, each stage of life is associated with a particular psychosocial conflict and a particular resolution. In this chart, Erikson describes how the issue from each of the earlier stages can mature into the many facets of integrity and wisdom in old age.

Conflict and Resolution	Culmination in Old Age
Old age Integrity vs. despair: wisdom	Existential identity; a sense of integrity strong enough to withstand physical disintegration.
Middle adulthood Generativity vs. stagnation: care	Caring for others, and empathy and concern.
Early adulthood Intimacy vs. isolation: love	Sense of complexity of relationships; value of tenderness and loving freely.
Adolescence Identity vs. confusion: fidelity	Sense of complexity of life; merger of sensory, logical, and aesthetic perception.
School age Industry vs. inferiority: competence	Humility; acceptance of the course of one's life and unfulfilled hopes.
Early childhood Initiative vs. guilt: purpose	Humor; empathy; resilience.
Toddlerhood Autonomy vs. shame: will	Acceptance of the cycle of life, from integration to disintegration.
Infancy Basic trust vs. mistrust: hope	Appreciation of interdependence and relatedness.

meaning and coherence. These personal dimensions might unfold in such a way that the pieces do or don't make sense to the older adult. The life review might result in increased meaning in life and mastery, but it also might revive bitterness and negative thoughts (Korte, Westerhof, & Bohlmeijer, 2012). In the final analysis, each person's life review is to some degree unique.

One aspect of life review involves identifying and reflecting on not only the positive aspects of one's life but also on regrets as part of developing mature levels of wisdom and self-understanding (Choi & Jun, 2009). The hope is that by examining not only the positive aspects of one's life, but also what one has regretted doing (or not doing), a more accurate vision of the complexity of one's life and possibly increased life satisfaction will be attained (King & Hicks, 2007).

When working with older clients, some clinicians use *reminiscence therapy,* which involves discussing past activities and experiences with another individual or group (Blake, 2013; Klever, 2013). The therapy may include the use of photographs, familiar items, and video/audio recordings. Researchers have found that reminiscence therapy improves the mood of older adults, including those with dementia (Subramaniam & Woods, 2012). A recent meta-analysis of 128 studies found that through reminiscence therapy clients attained a higher sense of integrity (based on Erikson's concept of integrity versus despair) (Pinquart & Forstmeier, 2012). Smaller effects occurred for purpose in life, preparing for death, mastery, positive well-being, social integration, and cognitive performance. The largest improvements were made for depressive symptoms in depressed individuals and persons with chronic physical disease. One recent study with elderly institutionalized adults found that 8 weeks of group reminiscence therapy resulted in increased self-esteem, life satisfaction, and psychological well-being, and reduced depression (Melendez-Moral & others, 2013).

ACTIVITY THEORY

Activity theory states that the more active and involved older adults are, the more likely they are to be satisfied with their lives. Researchers have found strong support for activity theory, beginning in the 1960s and continuing into the twenty-first century (Bielak & others, 2014; Morrow-Howell & others, 2014; Neugarten, Havighurst, & Tobin, 1968; Phillips, Wojcicki, & McAuley, 2013; Solberg & others, 2014). These researchers have found that when older adults are active, energetic, and productive, they age more successfully and are happier than if they disengage from society. A recent study found that older adults were happiest when

Should adults stay active or become more disengaged as they become older? Explain.

activity theory The theory that the more active and involved older adults are, the more likely they are to be satisfied with their lives.

they combined effortful social, physical, cognitive, and household activities with restful activities (Oerlemans, Bakker, & Veenhoven, 2011). Another recent study of Canadian older adults revealed that those who were more physically active had higher life satisfaction and greater social interaction than their physically inactive counterparts (Azagba & Sharaf, 2014).

Activity theory suggests that many individuals will achieve greater life satisfaction if they continue their middle-adulthood roles into late adulthood. If these roles are stripped from them (as in early retirement), it is important for them to find substitute roles that keep them active and involved.

SOCIOEMOTIONAL SELECTIVITY THEORY

Socioemotional selectivity theory states that older adults become more selective about their social networks. Because they place a high value on emotional satisfaction, older adults spend more time with familiar individuals with whom they have had rewarding relationships. Developed by Laura Carstensen (1998, 2006, 2008, 2009; Carstensen & others, 2011), this theory states that older adults deliberately withdraw from social contact with individuals peripheral to their lives while maintaining or increasing contact with close friends and family members with whom they have had enjoyable relationships. This selective narrowing of social interaction maximizes positive emotional experiences and minimizes emotional risks as individuals become older.

Socioemotional selectivity theory challenges the stereotype that the majority of older adults are in emotional despair because of their social isolation (Carstensen & Fried, 2012). Rather, older adults consciously choose to decrease the total number of their social contacts in favor of spending increasing time in emotionally rewarding moments with friends and family. That is, they systematically refine their social networks so that available social partners satisfy their emotional needs.

Is there research evidence to support life-span differences in the composition of social networks? Researchers have found that older adults have far smaller social networks than younger adults (Charles & Carstensen, 2010; Wrzus & others, 2013). In one study of individuals 69 to 104 years of age, the oldest participants had fewer peripheral social contacts than the relatively younger participants but about the same number of close emotional relationships (Lang & Carstensen, 1994). In a recent study of individuals from 18 to 94 years of age, with increasing age in adulthood, they had fewer peripheral social contacts but retained close relationships with people who provided them with emotional support (English & Carstensen, 2014b).

Socioemotional selectivity theory also focuses on the types of goals that individuals are motivated to achieve (Biggs, Carstensen, & Hogan, 2012; Carstensen & others, 2011). It states that two important classes of goals are (1) knowledge-related and (2) emotional. This theory emphasizes that the trajectory of motivation for knowledge-related goals starts relatively high in the early years of life, peaking in adolescence and early adulthood, and then declines during middle and late adulthood (see Figure 19.2). The emotion trajectory is high during infancy and early childhood, declines from middle childhood through early adulthood, and increases in middle and late adulthood.

One of the main reasons given for these changing trajectories in knowledge-related and emotion-related goals involves the perception of time (Carstensen, 2006; Carstensen & others, 2011). When time is perceived as open-ended, as it is when individuals are younger, people are more strongly motivated to pursue information, even at the cost of emotional satisfaction. But as older adults perceive that they have less time left in their lives, they are motivated to spend more time pursuing emotional satisfaction (Kaszniak & Menchola, 2012). Are older adults more emotionally satisfied than younger adults? To read further about how emotion changes across the life span, see the *Connecting Through Research* interlude.

In general, compared with younger adults, the feelings of older adults mellow. Emotional life is on a more even keel, with fewer highs and lows. It may be that although older adults have less extreme joy, they have more contentment, especially when they are connected in

Laura Carstensen (*right*), in a caring relationship with an older woman. Her theory of socioemotional selectivity is gaining recognition as an important perspective on aging.

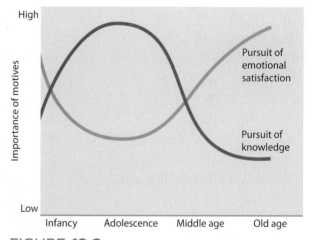

FIGURE **19.2**

IDEALIZED MODEL OF SOCIOEMOTIONAL SELECTIVITY THROUGH THE LIFE SPAN. In Carstensen's theory of socioemotional selectivity, the motivation to reach knowledge-related and emotion-related goals changes across the life span.

socioemotional selectivity theory The theory that older adults become more selective about their social networks. Because they place a high value on emotional satisfaction, older adults often spend more time with familiar individuals with whom they have had rewarding relationships.

connecting through research

How Do Emotions Change Across Adulthood?

One study examined emotional changes across adulthood in 2,727 persons from 25 to 74 years of age in the United States (Mroczek & Kolarz, 1998). Participants completed a survey that assessed the frequency of their positive and negative emotions over a 30-day time frame. Two six-item scales were created: one for positive emotion, the other for negative emotion. Participants rated each of the following items on a scale ranging from 1 (none of the time) to 5 (all of the time):

Positive Affect	Negative Affect
1. Cheerful	1. So sad nothing could cheer you up
2. In good spirits	2. Nervous
3. Extremely happy	3. Restless or fidgety
4. Calm or peaceful	4. Hopeless
5. Satisfied	5. That everything was an effort
6. Full of life	6. Worthless

Thus, scores could range from 6 to 30 for positive affect and for negative affect.

Overall, older adults reported experiencing more positive emotion and less negative emotion than younger adults, and the increase in positive emotion with age in adults occurred at an accelerating rate (see

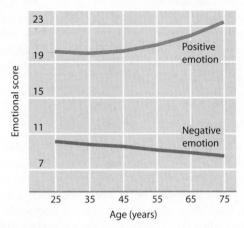

FIGURE **19.3**

CHANGES IN POSITIVE AND NEGATIVE EMOTION ACROSS THE ADULT YEARS. Positive and negative scores had a possible range of 6 to 30 with higher scores reflecting positive emotion and lower scores negative emotion. Positive emotion increased in middle adulthood and late adulthood while negative emotion declined.

Figure 19.3). In sum, researchers have found that the emotional life of older adults is more positive than was once believed (Carstensen & others, 2011).

positive ways with friends and family. Compared with younger adults, older adults react less to negative circumstances, are better at ignoring irrelevant negative information, and remember more positive than negative information (Mather, 2012).

One study revealed that positive emotion increased and negative emotion (except for sadness) decreased from 50 years of age through the mid-eighties (Stone & others, 2010). In this study, a pronounced decline in anger occurred from the early twenties and sadness was essentially unchanged from the early twenties through the mid-eighties. Another study found that aging was linked to more positive overall well-being and greater emotional stability (Carstensen & others, 2011). In this study, adults who experienced more positive than negative emotions were more likely to remain alive over a 13-year period. Other research also indicates that happier people live longer (Frey, 2011). A recent study of individuals from 22 to 93 years of age explored emotional experiences in the mornings and evenings (English & Carstensen, 2014a). Older adults reported experiencing more positive emotions than younger adults at both times of the day. Thus, the emotional life of older adults is more positive than stereotypes suggest (Lynchard & Radvansky, 2012; Carstensen & Fried, 2012; Yeung, Wong, & Lok, 2011).

SELECTIVE OPTIMIZATION WITH COMPENSATION THEORY

Selective optimization with compensation theory states that successful aging depends on three main factors: selection, optimization, and compensation (SOC). The theory describes how people can produce new resources and allocate them effectively to the tasks they want to master (Freund, Nikitin, & Riediger, 2013; Riediger, Li, & Lindenberger, 2006; Staudinger & Jacobs, 2010). *Selection* is based on the concept that older adults have a reduced capacity and loss of functioning, which require a reduction in performance in most life domains.

selective optimization with compensation theory The theory that successful aging is related to three main factors: selection, optimization, and compensation.

Strategies for Effectively Engaging in Selective Optimization with Compensation

What are some good strategies that aging adults can engage in to attain selective optimization with compensation? According to Paul Baltes and his colleagues (Baltes, Lindenberger, & Staudinger, 2006; Freund & Baltes, 2002), these strategies are likely to be effective:

Selection Strategies

- Focus on the most important goal at a particular time.
- Think about what you want in life and commit yourself to one or two major goals.
- To reach a particular goal, you may need to abandon other goals.

Optimization Strategies

- Keep working on what you have planned until you are successful.
- Persevere and keep trying until you reach your goal.

- When you want to achieve something, you may need to be patient until the right moment arrives.

Compensation Strategies

- When things don't go the way they used to, search for other ways to achieve what you want.
- If things don't go well for you, be willing to let others help you.
- When things don't go as well as in the past, keep trying other ways until you can achieve results that are similar to what you accomplished earlier in your life.

How might you revise these guidelines to include the use of new technologies?

Optimization suggests that it is possible to maintain performance in some areas through continued practice and the use of new technologies. *Compensation* becomes relevant when life tasks require a level of capacity beyond the current level of the older adult's performance potential. Older adults especially need to compensate in circumstances involving high mental or physical demands, such as when thinking about and memorizing new material in a very short period of time, reacting quickly when driving a car, or running fast. When older adults develop an illness, the need for compensation is obvious.

Selective optimization with compensation theory was proposed by Paul Baltes and his colleagues (Baltes, 2003; Baltes, Lindenberger, & Staudinger, 2006). They describe the life of the late Arthur Rubinstein to illustrate their theory. When he was interviewed at 80 years of age, Rubinstein said that three factors were responsible for his ability to maintain his status as an admired concert pianist into old age. First, he mastered the weakness of old age by reducing the scope of his performances and playing fewer pieces (which reflects selection). Second, he spent more time at practice than earlier in his life (which reflects optimization). Third, he used special strategies, such as slowing down before fast segments, thus creating the image of faster playing (which reflects compensation).

The process of selective optimization with compensation is likely to be effective whenever people pursue successful outcomes (Hutchinson & Nimrod, 2012; Freund, Nikitin, & Riediger, 2013; Staudinger & Jacobs, 2010). What makes SOC attractive to researchers who study aging is that it makes explicit how individuals can manage and adapt to losses. By using SOC, older adults can continue to live satisfying lives, although in a more restricted manner.

Loss is a common dimension of old age, although there are wide variations in the nature of the losses involved. Because of these individual variations, the specific form of selection, optimization, and compensation will likely vary, depending on the person's life history, pattern of interests, values, health, skills, and resources. To read about some strategies for effectively engaging in selective optimization with compensation, see *Connecting Development to Life*.

In Baltes' view (2003; Baltes, Lindenberger, & Staudinger, 2006), the selection of domains and life priorities is an important aspect of development. Life goals and priorities likely vary across the life course for most people. For many individuals, it is not just the sheer attainment of goals, but rather the attainment of *meaningful* goals, that makes life satisfying.

A cross-sectional study by Ursula Staudinger (1996) assessed the personal life investments of 25- to 105-year-olds (see Figure 19.4). From 25 to 34 years of age, participants said that they personally invested more time in work, friends, family, and independence, in that order. From 35 to 54 and 55 to 65 years of age, family became more important than friends

developmental **connection**

Life-Span Perspective

Baltes proposed eight main characteristics of the life-span perspective, one of which is that development involves growth, maintenance, and regulation of loss. Chapter 1, p. 5

25 to 34 Years	35 to 54 Years	55 to 65 Years	70 to 84 Years	85 to105 Years
Work	Family	Family	Family	Health
Friends	Work	Health	Health	Family
Family	Friends	Friends	Cognitive fitness	Thinking about life
Independence	Cognitive fitness	Cognitive fitness	Friends	Cognitive fitness

FIGURE 19.4

DEGREE OF PERSONAL LIFE INVESTMENT AT DIFFERENT POINTS IN LIFE. Shown here are the top four domains of personal life investment at different points in life. The highest degree of investment is listed at the top (for example, work was the highest personal investment from 25 to 34 years of age, family from 35 to 84, and health from 85 to 105).

to them in terms of their personal investment. Little changed in the rank ordering of persons 70 to 84 years old, but for participants 85 to 105 years old, health became the most important personal investment. Thinking about life showed up for the first time on the most important list for those who were 85 to 105 years old.

One point to note about the study just described is the demarcation of late adulthood into the subcategories of 70 to 84 and 85 to 105 years of age. This fits with our comments on a number of occasions in this book that researchers increasingly recognize the importance of comparing older adults of different ages rather than studying them as one age group.

Review Connect Reflect

 LG1 Discuss four theories of socioemotional development and aging.

Review

- What is Erikson's theory of late adulthood?
- What is activity theory?
- What is socioemotional selectivity theory?
- What is selective optimization with compensation theory?

Connect

- How does the life reflection of older adults differ from the life reflection of

individuals in middle adulthood who are approaching retirement age?

Reflect *Your Own Personal Journey of Life*

- Which of the four theories best describes the lives of older adults you know? Explain.

2 Personality, the Self, and Society

 LG2 Describe links between personality and mortality, and identify changes in the self and society in late adulthood.

Personality	The Self and Society	Older Adults in Society

Do some personality traits change in late adulthood? Is personality linked to mortality in older adults? Do self-perceptions and self-control change in late adulthood? How are older adults perceived and treated by society? We will explore these and other topics in the next few pages.

PERSONALITY

We described the Big Five factors of personality in Chapter 16, "Socioemotional Development in Middle Adulthood." Researchers have found that several of the Big Five factors of personality continue to change in late adulthood (Roberts, Donnellan, & Hill, 2013). For example, in one study conscientiousness continued to increase in late adulthood (Roberts, Walton, & Bogg, 2005) and in another study older adults were more conscientious and agreeable than middle-aged and younger adults (Allemand, Zimprich, & Hendriks, 2008).

Might certain personality traits be related to how long older adults live? Researchers have found that some personality traits are associated with the mortality of older adults (Roberts, Donnellan, & Hill, 2013). A longitudinal study of more than 1,200 individuals across seven decades revealed that a higher score on the Big Five personality factor of conscientiousness predicted a lower risk of earlier death from childhood through late adulthood (Martin, Friedman, & Schwartz, 2007). A higher level of conscientiousness has been linked to living a longer life than the other four factors (Hill & others, 2011; Iwasa & others, 2008; Wilson & others, 2004).

Following are the results of three other studies of the Big Five factors in older adults:

- The transition into late adulthood was characterized by increases in these aspects of conscientiousness: impulse control, reliability, and conventionality (Jackson & others, 2009).
- Perceived social support predicted increased conscientiousness in older adults (Hill & others, 2014).
- More severe depression in older adults was associated with higher neuroticism and lower extraversion and conscientiousness (Koorevaar & others, 2013).
- Elevated neuroticism, lower conscientiousness, and lower openness were related to an increased risk of older adults' developing Alzheimer disease across a period of six years (Duberstein & others, 2011).

Affect and outlook on life are also linked to mortality in older adults (Carstensen & others, 2011). Older adults characterized by negative affect don't live as long as those who display more positive affect, and optimistic older adults who have a positive outlook on life live longer than their counterparts who are more pessimistic and have a negative outlook on life (Mosing & others, 2012).

developmental **connection**

Personality

The Big Five factors of personality are openness, conscientiousness, extraversion, agreeableness, and neuroticism. Chapter 16, p. 493

THE SELF AND SOCIETY

Our exploration of the self focuses on changes in self-esteem, possible selves, self-acceptance, and self-control. In Chapter 12, we described how self-esteem drops in adolescence, especially for girls. How does self-esteem change during the adult years?

Self-Esteem In the cross-sectional study of self-esteem described in Chapter 12, researchers studied a very large, diverse sample of more than 300,000 individuals from 9 to 90 years of age (Robins & others, 2002). About two-thirds of the participants were from the United States. The individuals were asked to respond to the item "I have high self-esteem" on the following five-point scale:

1	2	3	4	5
Strongly Disagree				**Strongly Agree**

Self-esteem increased in the twenties, leveled off in the thirties and forties, rose considerably in the fifties and sixties, and then dropped significantly in the seventies and eighties (see Figure 19.5). Throughout most of the adult years, the self-esteem of males was higher than the self-esteem of females. However, in the seventies and eighties, the self-esteem of males and females converged.

Why might self-esteem decline in older adults? Explanations include deteriorating physical health and negative societal attitudes toward older adults, although these factors were not examined in the large-scale study just described. Researchers have found that in late

FIGURE **19.5**

SELF-ESTEEM ACROSS THE LIFE SPAN. One cross-sectional study found that self-esteem was high in childhood, dropped in adolescence, increased through early and middle adulthood, then dropped in the seventies and eighties (Robins & others, 2002). More than 300,000 individuals were asked the extent to which they have high self-esteem on a five-point scale, with 5 being "Strongly Agree" and 1 being "Strongly Disagree."

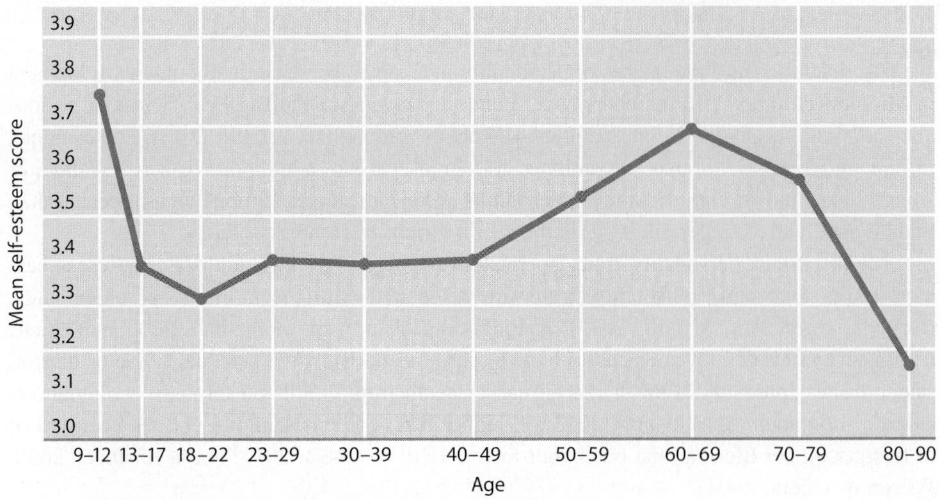

I am the family face;

Flesh perishes,

I live on,

Projecting trait and trace

Through time to times anon,

And leaping from place to place

Over oblivion.

—THOMAS HARDY

English Novelist and Poet, 19th Century

adulthood, being widowed, institutionalized, or physically impaired, having a low religious commitment, and experiencing a decline in health are linked to low self-esteem (Giarrusso & Bengtson, 2007).

Although older adults may derive self-esteem from earlier successes in some domains, such as work and family, some aspects of their lives require continued support for self-esteem (Smith, 2009). For example, older adults' self-esteem benefits when they are told they are nice and accepted by others. A recent study revealed that older adults had higher self-esteem when they had a youthful identity and more positive personal experiences (Westerhof, Whitbourne, & Freeman, 2012). And another recent study also found that older adults with higher self-esteem were more likely to be characterized by successful aging factors (Cha, Seo, & Sok, 2012).

Possible Selves   Possible selves are what individuals might become, what they would like to become, and what they are afraid of becoming (Bolkan & Hooker, 2012; Markus & Nurius, 1987). Acceptance of ideal and future selves decreases and acceptance of past selves increases in older adults (Ryff, 1991).

One study of older adults (mean age of 81) revealed that hope-related activities were associated with more positive affect and a higher probability of survival over a 10-year period (Hoppmann & others, 2007). Also in this study, hoped-for selves were linked to more likely participation in these domains. Another study of older adults 70 to 100-plus years found that over time 72 percent of the older adults added new domains of hope and 53 percent added new fears (Smith & Freund, 2002). In this study, hopes and fears about health were reported more often than ones related to family and social relationships. Also, when some individuals are middle-aged adults, their possible selves center on attaining hoped-for selves, such as acquiring material possessions, but in late adulthood they become more concerned with maintaining what they have acquired and preventing or avoiding health problems and dependency (Smith, 2009).

Self-Control   Although older adults are aware of age-related losses, most are able to maintain a sense of self-control (Lewis, Todd, & Xu, 2011). A survey across a range of 21 developed and developing countries revealed that a majority of adults in their sixties and seventies reported being in control of their lives (HSBC Insurance, 2007). In developed countries such as Denmark, the United States, and Great Britain, adults in their sixties and seventies reported having more control over their lives than did their counterparts in their forties and fifties. Older adults in Denmark reported the highest perceptions of control.

Self-control plays an important role in older adults' engagement in healthy activities. A recent study of 65- to 92-year-olds found that self-control was linked to better outcomes for well-being and depression following a six-week program of yoga (Bonura & Tennenbaum, 2014). Another recent study revealed that self-control was a key factor in older adults' physical activity levels (Franke & others, 2014).

possible selves What individuals might become, what they would like to become, and what they are afraid of becoming.

Researchers also have studied how people self-regulate their behavior in specific areas of their lives (Bertrand, Graham, & Lachman, 2013; Bolkan & Hooker, 2012). One study examined individuals from 13 to 90 years of age. For the oldest group (60 to 90 years of age), control was lowest in the physical domain; for the youngest group (13 to 18 years of age), it was lowest in the social domain (Bradley & Webb, 1976). Other researchers have found a decline in perceived control of cognitive functioning in older adults (Bertrand & Lachman, 2003).

OLDER ADULTS IN SOCIETY

Does society negatively stereotype older adults? What are some social policy issues in an aging society?

Stereotyping Older Adults   Social participation by older adults is often discouraged by **ageism,** which is prejudice against others because of their age, especially prejudice against older adults (Jonson, 2013; Lawler & others, 2014). Older adults are often perceived as incapable of thinking clearly, learning new things, enjoying sex, contributing to the community, or holding responsible jobs. Many older adults face painful discrimination and might be too polite or timid to attack it. Because of their age, older adults might not be hired for new jobs or might be eased out of old ones; they might be shunned socially; and they might be edged out of their family life. A recent study revealed that perceiving themselves as different (self-differentiation) from others in their age group was effective in reducing the impact of negative information on older adults' self-evaluation (Weiss, Sassenberg, & Freund, 2013).

The personal consequences of negative stereotyping about aging can be serious (Band-Winterstein, 2014; Malinen & Johnston, 2013; Rippon & others, 2014). A physician (60 years old himself) told an 80-year-old patient: "Well, of course, you are tired. You just need to slow down. Don't try to do so much. After all, you are very old." Many older adults accept this type of advice even though it is rooted in age stereotyping rather than medical records.

Ageism is widespread (Anderson & others, 2013). One study found that men were more likely to negatively stereotype older adults than were women (Rupp, Vodanovich, & Crede, 2005). Research indicates that the most frequent form is disrespect for older adults, followed by assumptions about ailments or frailty caused by age (Palmore, 2004). However, the increased number of adults living to an older age has led to active efforts to improve society's image of older adults, obtain better living conditions for older adults, and increase their political clout.

Nonetheless, there are considerable variations in stereotyping of older adults in different countries. A recent study of European countries found that older adults were perceived as more competent in countries such as Denmark in which they engaged in paid or volunteer work, and perceived as less competent in countries such as Poland in which they were less likely to participate in paid or volunteer work (Bowen & Skirbekk, 2013).

Policy Issues in an Aging Society   The aging society and older persons' status in this society raise policy issues related to the well-being of older adults (Fisher & others, 2013; Greenlund & others, 2012). These include the status of the economy, the provision of health care, supports for families who care for older adults, and generational inequity, each of which we consider in turn.

Status of the Economy   An important issue involving the economy and aging is concern that the U.S. economy cannot bear the burden of so many older persons, who by reason of their age alone are usually consumers rather than producers. However, not all persons 65 and over are nonworkers, and not all persons 18 to 64 are workers. Thus, it is incorrect to simply describe older adults as consumers and younger adults as producers. However, the recent economic crisis has placed considerable burdens on many older adults, who have seen their nongovernment retirement funds drop precipitously (Strand, 2010). Especially bothersome is the low rate of savings among U.S. adults, which further exacerbated the financial problems of older adults in the recent economic downturn (Gould & Hertel-Fernandez, 2010). As indicated in Chapter 18, recent surveys indicate that Americans' confidence in their ability to retire comfortably has reached all-time lows in recent years (Helman, Copeland, & VanDerhei, 2012).

ageism Prejudice against others because of their age, especially prejudice against older adults.

What are some concerns about health care for older adults?

Health Care   An aging society also brings with it various problems involving health care (Siegler & others, 2013a, b). Escalating health care costs are currently the focus of considerable concern (Alzheimer's Association, 2013). One factor that contributes to rising health care costs is the increasing number of older adults. Older adults have more illnesses than younger adults, despite the fact that many older adults report that their health is good. Older adults see doctors more often, are hospitalized more often, and have longer hospital stays. Approximately one-third of the total health bill of the United States is for the care of adults 65 and over, who comprise only 12 percent of the population. The health care needs of older adults are reflected in Medicare and Medicaid (Hansen, 2012; Lee, 2013). Of interest is the fact that until the Affordable Care Act was recently enacted, the United States was the only developed country that did not have a national health care system. Older adults themselves still pay about one-third of their total health care costs. Thus, older adults as well as younger adults are adversely affected by rising medical costs (McDonough, 2012).

A special concern is that while many of the health problems of older adults are chronic rather than acute, the medical system is still based on a "cure" rather than a "care" model. Chronic illness is long-term, often lifelong, and requires long-term, if not lifelong, management (Cadogan, Phillips, & Ziminski, 2014; Harris, Pan, & Mukhtar, 2010). Chronic illness often follows a pattern of an acute period that may require hospitalization, followed by a longer period of remission, and then repetitions of this pattern. The patient's home, rather than the hospital, often becomes the location for managing the patient's chronic illness. In a home-based system, a new type of cooperative relationship between doctors, nurses, patients, family members, and other service providers needs to be developed (Kamp, Wellman, & Russell, 2010). Health care personnel need to be trained and be available to provide home services (Irish, 2011).

Eldercare   **Eldercare** is the physical and emotional caretaking of older members of the family, whether that care involves day-to-day physical assistance or responsibility for arranging and overseeing such care. An important issue involving eldercare is how it can best be provided (Trukeschitz & others, 2013; Zacher, Jimmieson & Winter, 2012). With so many women in the labor market, who will replace them as caregivers? An added problem is that many caregivers are in their sixties, and many of them are ill themselves. They may find it especially stressful to be responsible for the care of relatives who are in their eighties or nineties.

Generational Inequity   Yet another policy issue involving aging is **generational inequity,** the view that our aging society is being unfair to its younger members because older adults pile up advantages by receiving an inequitably large allocation of resources. Some authors have argued that generational inequity produces intergenerational conflict and divisiveness in the society at large (Longman, 1987). The generational equity issue raises questions about whether the young should be required to pay for the old (Auerbach & Lee, 2011; Daniels, 2012; Williamson, 2011). This concern has especially increased with the enactment of the government's Affordable Care Act in which healthy younger adults, who use the health care system far less than older adults, nonetheless are required to sign up for the health care program or pay a penalty.

Income   Many older adults are understandably concerned about their income (Ehnes, 2012; Tse & others, 2014). Of special concern are older adults who are poor (Reno & Veghte, 2011). Researchers have found that poverty in late adulthood is linked to an increase in physical and mental health problems (Cagney & others, 2014; Sztramko & others, 2014). Poverty also is linked to lower levels of physical and cognitive fitness in older adults (Johnson & others, 2011). And one study revealed that low SES increased the risk of earlier death in older adults (Krueger & Chang, 2008).

Census data suggest that the overall number of older people living in poverty has declined since the 1960s, but in 2012, 9.1 percent of older adults in the United States still were living in poverty (U.S. Census Bureau, 2013). In 2010, U.S. women 65 years and older (10.7 percent) were much more likely to live in poverty than their male counterparts (6.2 percent) (U.S. Census Bureau, 2012). Nineteen percent of single, divorced, or widowed women

eldercare Physical and emotional caretaking for older members of the family, whether by giving day-to-day physical assistance or by being responsible for overseeing such care.

generational inequity The view that our aging society is being unfair to its younger members because older adults pile up advantages by receiving inequitably large allocations of resources.

65 years and older lived in poverty. There is a special concern about poverty among older women and considerable discussion about the role of Social Security in providing a broad economic safety net for them (Jokinen-Gordon, 2012; Soneji & King, 2012).

Poverty rates among older adults who belong to ethnic minorities are two to three times higher than the rate for non-Latino Whites. Combining gender and ethnicity, 41 percent of older Latinas and 31 percent of African American women lived in poverty in 2010 (U.S. Census Bureau, 2011). Also, the oldest-old are the age subgroup of older adults most likely to be living in poverty.

However, it is not just individuals in low-income, poverty conditions who harbor fears of not having enough money in their older adult years. A recent study of older adults found that the 2008 U.S. recession reduced their wealth and increased their feelings of depression and use of antidepressant drugs (McInerney, Mellor, & Nicolas, 2013).

Living Arrangements   One stereotype of older adults is that they are often residents in institutions—hospitals, mental hospitals, nursing homes, and so on. However, nearly 95 percent of older adults live in the community. Almost two-thirds of older adults live with family members—their spouse, a child, or a sibling, for example—and almost one-third live alone. The older people become, the greater are their odds for living alone. Half of older women 75 years and older live alone. The majority of older adults living alone are widowed, encompassing three times as many women as men (U.S. Census Bureau, 2012). Older adults who live alone often report being more lonely than their counterparts who live with someone (Kirkevold & others, 2013). However, as with younger adults, living alone as an older adult does not necessarily mean being lonely. Older adults who can sustain themselves while living alone often have good health and few disabilities, and they may have regular social exchanges with relatives, friends, and neighbors.

Technology   The Internet plays an increasingly important role in providing access to information and communication for adults as well as youth (Berner & others, 2014; Bers & Kazakoff, 2013; Schmidt, Wahl, & Plischke, 2014). A longitudinal study revealed that Internet use by older adults reduced their likelihood of being depressed by one-third (Cotten & others, 2014).

How well are older adults keeping up with changes in technology? Older adults are less likely to have a computer in their home and less likely to use the Internet than younger adults, but older adults are the fastest-growing segment of Internet users (Czaja & others, 2006). A 2013 national survey conducted by the Pew Research Center found that 59 percent of U.S. older adults reported that they use the Internet (in 2000, only 13 percent of older adults said they use the Internet) (Smith, 2014). This survey identified two distinct groups of older adults who use the Internet: (1) those who are younger, more highly educated, and more affluent; and (2) those who are older, less affluent, and have significant health or disability challenges. The same survey found that once older adults begin using the Internet, it becomes an integral part of their daily lives. Among those 65 years and older who use the Internet, 71 percent report going online every day or almost every day (compared with 88 percent of 18- to 29-year-olds, 84 percent of 30- to 49-year-olds, and 79 percent of 50- to 64-year-olds). At approximately 75 years of age, Internet use drops off considerably.

Increasing numbers of older adults use e-mail to communicate with relatives. As with children and younger adults, cautions about verifying the accuracy of information—especially on topics involving health care—on the Internet should always be kept in mind (Miller & Bell, 2012).

Links between older adults' use of technology and their cognitive development also are being studied. One study found that frequent computer use was linked to higher performance on cognitive tasks in older adults (Tun & Lachman, 2010). And researchers are examining the role that video games could play in maintaining or improving older adults' cognitive skills (McDougall & House, 2012). For example, a research study found that a lengthy 40-hour video game training program improved older adults' attention and memory (Smith & others, 2009). And a recent study revealed that a brain training game that elderly adults played about 15 minutes a day for 4 weeks improved their executive function and speed of processing information (Nouchi & others, 2012).

Are older adults keeping up with changes in technology?

3 Families and Social Relationships

LG3 Characterize the families and social relationships of aging adults.

Lifestyle Diversity | Attachment | Older Adult Parents and Their Adult Children | Great-Grandparenting | Friendship | Social Support and Social Integration | Altruism and Volunteering

What are some adaptations that many married older adults need to make?

Are the close relationships of older adults different from those of younger adults? What are the lifestyles of older adults like? What characterizes the relationships of older adult parents and their adult children? Is the role of great-grandparents different from the role of grandparents? What do friendships and social networks contribute to the lives of older adults? What types of social support do older adults need and want? How might older adults' altruism and volunteerism contribute to positive outcomes?

LIFESTYLE DIVERSITY

The lifestyles of older adults are changing. Formerly, the later years of life were likely to consist of marriage for men and widowhood for women. With demographic shifts toward marital dissolution characterized by divorce, one-third of adults can now expect to marry, divorce, and remarry during their lifetime. Let's now explore some of the diverse lifestyles of older adults, beginning with those who are married or partnered.

Married Older Adults In 2012, 58 percent of U.S. adults over 65 years of age were married (U.S. Census Bureau, 2012). Older men (72 percent) were far more likely to be married than older women (45 percent). In 2012, 27 percent of U.S. adults over 65 years of age were widowed (U.S. Census Bureau, 2012). There were more than four times as many widows (8.5 million) as widowers (2.1 million).

The time from retirement until death is sometimes referred to as the "final stage in the marriage process." The portrait of marriage in the lives of older adults is a positive one for many couples (Piazza & Charles, 2012; Strout & Howard, 2012). Individuals who are in a marriage or a partnership in late adulthood are usually happier, are less distressed, and live longer than those who are single (Peek, 2009). A recent study of octogenarians revealed that marital satisfaction helped to insulate their happiness from the effects of daily fluctuations in perceived health (Waldinger & Schulz, 2010). Also, a longitudinal study of adults 75 years of age and older revealed that individuals who were married were less likely to die during a seven-year time span (Rasulo, Christensen, & Tomassini, 2005). And a recent study found that marital satisfaction in older adults was linked to whether an individual was depressed or not (Walker & others, 2013).

Retirement alters a couple's lifestyle, requiring adaptation (Price & Nesteruk, 2010). The greatest changes occur in the traditional family structure in which the husband works and the wife is a homemaker. The husband may not know what to do with his time, and his wife may feel uneasy having him around the house so much of the day. In traditional families, both partners may need to move toward more expressive roles. The husband must adjust from being the provider outside of the home to being a helper around the house; the wife must change from being the only homemaker to being a partner who shares and delegates household duties. Marital happiness of older adults is also affected by each partner's ability to deal with personal challenges, including aging, illness, and the prospect of widowhood.

In late adulthood, married individuals are more likely to find themselves having to care for a sick partner with a limiting health condition (Blieszner & Roberto, 2012). The stress of caring for a spouse who has a chronic disease can place demands on intimacy.

Divorced and Remarried Older Adults

An increasing number of older adults are divorced. In 1980, only 5 percent of older adults were divorced, but by 2012, 14 percent of women and 12 percent of men 65 years and older in the United States were divorced or separated (U.S. Census Bureau, 2012). Many of these individuals were divorced or separated before entering late adulthood. The majority of divorced older adults are women, due to their greater longevity. Men are more likely than women to remarry, thus removing themselves from the pool of divorced older adults (Peek, 2009). Divorce is far less common among older adults than younger adults, likely reflecting cohort effects rather than age effects since divorce was somewhat rare when current cohorts of older adults were young (Peek, 2009).

There are social, financial, and physical consequences of divorce for older adults (Butrica & Smith, 2012; Piazza & Charles, 2012). Divorce can weaken kinship ties when it occurs in later life, especially in the case of older men. Divorced older women are less likely to have adequate financial resources than married older women, and older adults who are divorced have more health problems than those who are not (Bennett, 2006).

Rising divorce rates, increased longevity, and better health have led to an increase in remarriage by older adults (Ganong & Coleman, 2006). What happens when an older adult who is divorced or widowed wants to remarry or does remarry? Some older adults perceive negative social pressure about their decision to remarry. These negative sanctions range from raised eyebrows to rejection by adult children. However, the majority of adult children support the decision of their older adult parents to remarry. A recent analysis revealed that divorce rates were 2.5 times higher for middle-aged and older adults who had remarried than for those in first marriages (Brown & Lin, 2012).

Researchers have found that remarried parents and stepparents provide less support to adult stepchildren than parents in first marriages (White, 1994). A recent study revealed relatively weak ties between older adults and their stepchildren (Noel-Miller, 2013). In this study, older stepparents' social contact with their stepchildren was mainly linked to the stepparent continuing to be married to the stepchildren's biological parent. When divorce occurred in an older adult stepfamily, the divorced stepparent's frequency of contact with stepchildren dropped abruptly.

Cohabiting Older Adults

An increasing number of older adults cohabit (Noel-Miller, 2011). In 1960, hardly any older adults cohabited (Chevan, 1996). From 2000 to 2010, cohabitation in adults 50 years and older increased from 1.2 million to 2.5 million (Brown, Bulanda, & Lee, 2012). Still, only a small percentage of older adults cohabit—in 2010, 3 percent of older adults were cohabiting (Mykyta & Macartney, 2012). It is expected that the number of

developmental **connection**

Marriage

The benefits of a happy marriage include less physical and emotional stress, which puts less wear and tear on the body. Chapter 14, p. 446

cohabiting older adults will increase further as the large cohort of baby boomers become 65 years of age and older and bring their historically more nontraditional values about love, sex, and relationships to late adulthood. In many cases, the cohabiting is more for companionship than for love. In other cases, such as when one partner faces the potential for expensive care, a couple may decide to maintain their assets separately and thus not marry. One study found that older adults who cohabited had a more positive, stable relationship than younger adults who cohabited, although older adults were less likely to have plans to marry their partner (King & Scott, 2005).

Does cohabiting affect an individual's health? A study of more than 8,000 51- to 61-year-old adults revealed that the health of couples who cohabited did not differ from the health of married couples (Waite, 2005). However, another study of individuals 50 years of age and older found that those who cohabited were more depressed than their married counterparts (Brown, Bulanda, & Lee, 2005). And a recent study indicated that cohabiting older adults were less likely to receive partner care than married older adults (Noel-Miller, 2011).

ATTACHMENT

There has been far less research on attachment in aging adults than on attachment in children, adolescents, and young adults. A recent research review on attachment in older adults reached the following conclusions (Van Assche & others, 2013):

- Older adults have fewer attachment relationships than younger adults (Cicirelli, 2010).
- With increasing age, attachment anxiety decreases (Chopik, Edelstein, & Fraley, 2013).
- In late adulthood, attachment security is associated with greater psychological and physical well-being than attachment anxiety (Bodner & Cohen-Fridel, 2010).
- Insecure attachment is linked to more perceived negative caregiver burden in caring for patients with Alzheimer disease (Karantzas, Evans, & Foddy, 2010).

A recent large-scale study examined attachment anxiety and avoidance in individuals from 18 to 70 years of age (Chopik, Edelstein, & Fraley, 2013). In this study, attachment anxiety was highest among adults in their mid-twenties and lowest among middle-aged and older adults. Developmental changes in avoidant attachment were not as strong as in anxious attachment, although anxious attachment was highest for middle-aged adults and lowest for young adults and older adults. Also in this study, partnered adults showed lower levels of attachment anxiety and avoidance than single adults.

OLDER ADULT PARENTS AND THEIR ADULT CHILDREN

Parent-child relationships in later life differ from those earlier in the life span (Antonucci, Birditt, & Ajrouch, 2013; Bangerter & others, 2014; Birditt & Wardjiman, 2012; Fingerman & Birditt, 2011; Fingerman & others, 2011a, b; Fingerman, Sechrist, & Birditt, 2013; Kim & others, 2014). They are influenced by a lengthy joint history and extensive shared experiences and memories.

Approximately 80 percent of older adults have living children, many of whom are middle-aged. About 10 percent of older adults have children who are 65 years or older. Adult children are an important part of the aging parent's social network. Researchers have found that older adults with children have more contacts with relatives than those without children (Johnson & Troll, 1992).

Increasingly, diversity characterizes the lifestyles of older adult parents and their adult children. Divorce, remarriage, cohabitation, and nonmarital childbearing are more common in the history of older adults today than in the past.

Gender plays an important role in relationships involving older adult parents and their children (Ward-Griffin & others, 2007). Adult daughters are more likely than adult sons to be involved in the lives of their aging parents. For example, adult daughters are three times more likely than are adult sons to give parents assistance with daily living activities (Dwyer & Coward, 1991).

As discussed in Chapter 16, "Socioemotional Development in Middle Adulthood," middle-aged adults are more likely to provide support if their parents have a disability (Antonucci, Birditt, & Ajrouch, 2013). A valuable service that adult children can perform is to coordinate and monitor services for an aging parent who becomes disabled (Jones & others, 2011). Even less severely impaired older adults may need help with shopping, housework, transportation, home maintenance, and bill paying.

As discussed in Chapter 16, some researchers have found that relationships between aging parents and their children are usually characterized by ambivalence (Bangerter & others, 2014; Fingerman & Birditt, 2011; Fingerman, Sechrist, & Birditt, 2013). Perceptions include love, reciprocal help, and shared values on the positive side and isolation, family conflicts and problems, abuse, neglect, and caregiver stress on the negative side. A study of adult children's relationships with their older adult parents revealed that ambivalence was likely to be present when relationships involved in-laws, those in poor health, and adult children with poor parental relationships in early life (Wilson, Shuey, & Elder, 2003). A recent study, though, revealed that affection and support, reflecting solidarity, were more prevalent than ambivalence in intergenerational relationships (Hogerbrugge & Komter, 2012).

At the beginning of the twentieth century, the three-generation family was common, but now the four-generation family is common as well. Thus, an increasing number of grandparents are also great-grandparents. The four-generation family shown here is the Jordans—author John Santrock's mother-in-law, daughter, granddaughter, and wife.

GREAT-GRANDPARENTING

Because of increased longevity, more grandparents today than in the past are also great-grandparents. At the turn of the twentieth century, the three-generation family was common, but now the four-generation family is common. One contribution of great-grandparents is to transmit family history by telling their children, grandchildren, and great-grandchildren where the family came from, what their members achieved, what they endured, and how their lives changed over the years (Harris, 2002).

There has been little research on great-grandparenting. One study examined the relationship between young adults and their grandparents and great-grandparents (Roberto & Skoglund, 1996). The young adults interacted with, and participated in more activities with, their grandparents than with their great-grandparents. They also perceived their grandparents as having a more defined role and being more influential in their lives than their great-grandparents.

FRIENDSHIP

In early adulthood, friendship networks expand as new social connections are made away from home. In late adulthood, new friendships are less likely to be forged, although some adults do seek out new friendships, especially following the death of a spouse (Zettel-Watson & Rook, 2009).

Aging expert Laura Carstensen (1998) concluded that people choose close friends over new friends as they grow older. And as long as they have several close people in their network, they seem content, says Carstensen. Supporting Carstensen's view, in one study older adults said they experienced less intense positive emotions with new friends and more intense positive emotions with established friends (Charles & Piazza, 2007) (see Figure 19.6).

In one study of married older adults, women were more depressed than men if they did not have a best friend, and women who did have a friend reported lower levels of depression (Antonucci, Lansford, & Akiyama, 2001). Similarly, women who did not have a best friend were less satisfied with life than women who did have a best friend.

The following studies document the importance of friendship in older adults:

- In late adulthood, friendships were more important than family relationships in predicting mental health (Fiori, Antonucci, & Cortina, 2006). For example, older adults

developmental **connection**

Family and Peers

It takes time to develop intimate friendships, so friendships that have endured over the adult years are often deeper than those that have just been formed in middle adulthood. Chapter 16, p. 499

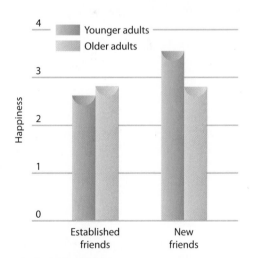

FIGURE **19.6**

HAPPINESS OF YOUNGER ADULTS AND OLDER ADULTS WITH NEW AND ESTABLISHED FRIENDS. *Note:* The happiness scale ranged from 0 to 6, with participants rating how intensely they experienced happiness (0 = not at all, 6 = extremely intense). Older adults' mean age was 71; younger adults' mean age was 23.

What are some characteristics of older adults' friendships?

whose social contacts were mainly restricted to their family members were more likely to have depressive symptoms. Friends likely provide emotional intimacy and companionship, as well as integration into the community (Antonucci, Akiyama, & Sherman, 2007).

- Activities with friends increased positive affect and life satisfaction in older adults (Huxhold, Miche, & Schuz, 2014).
- Older adults who had close ties with friends were less likely to die across a seven-year age span (Rasulo, Christensen, & Tomassini, 2005). The findings were stronger for women than men.

SOCIAL SUPPORT AND SOCIAL INTEGRATION

Social support and social integration play important roles in the physical and mental health of older adults (Antonucci, Birditt, & Ajrouch, 2013; Li, Ji, & Chen, 2014; Utz & others, 2014).

Social Support In the **convoy model of social relations,** individuals go through life embedded in a personal network of individuals to whom they give and from whom they receive social support (Antonucci, Birditt, & Ajrouch, 2013). For older adults, social support is related to their physical and mental health (Cheng, Lee, & Chow, 2010; Li, Ji, & Chen, 2014). It is linked with a reduction in symptoms of disease, with the ability to meet one's own health care needs, and reduced mortality (Rook & others, 2007). A higher level of social support also is related to a lower probability of an older adult being institutionalized and depressed (Herd & others, 2011; Richardson & others, 2011). Further, a recent study revealed that older adults who experienced a higher level of social support showed later cognitive decline than their counterparts with a lower level of social support (Dickinson & others, 2011).

Social support for older adults can be provided by different adults (Antonucci, Birditt, & Ajrouch, 2013). Older adults who are married are less likely to need formal social supports, such as home nursing care, adult day care, and home-delivered meals, than are nonmarried older adults. Families play important roles in social support for older adults, but friends also can provide invaluable resources for social support (Blieszner & Roberto, 2012). Also, social support for older adults may vary across cultures. For example, in the United States, the focal support person for an older adult is most likely to be a daughter, whereas in Japan it is most likely to be a daughter-in-law.

Social Integration Social integration also plays an important role in the lives of many older adults (Antonucci, Birditt, & Ajrouch, 2013; Fingerman, Brown, & Blieszner, 2011; Hawkley & Cacioppo, 2012; Stephens, Breheny, & Mansvelt, 2014). Remember from our earlier discussion of socioemotional selectivity theory that many older adults choose to have fewer peripheral social contacts and more emotionally positive contacts with friends and family (Carstensen & others, 2011). Thus, a decrease in the overall social activity of many older adults may reflect their greater interest in spending more time in the small circle of friends and family members where they are less likely to have negative emotional experiences. Researchers have found that older adults tend to report being less lonely than younger adults and less lonely than would be expected based on their circumstances (Schnittker, 2007). Their reports of feeling less lonely than younger adults likely reflect their more selective social networks and greater acceptance of solitude in their lives (Antonucci, Birditt, & Ajrouch, 2013).

Following are the findings of a number of recent research studies on loneliness in older adults:

- The most consistent factor that predicted loneliness in older adults at 70, 78, and 85 years of age was not being married (Stessman & others, 2014).

convoy model of social relations Model in which individuals go through life embedded in a personal network of individuals to whom they give and from whom they receive support.

- For 60- to 80-year-olds, the partner's death was a stronger indicator of loneliness for men than for women (Nicolaisen & Thorsen, 2014).

- Increased use of the Internet by older adults was associated with making it easier to meet new people, feeling less isolated, and feeling more connected with friends and family (Cotten, Anderson, & McCullough, 2013).

- As older adults increased the number of different types of social activities in which they participated, self-perception of their health improved, they felt less lonely, and they were more satisfied with life (Gilmour, 2012).

Recently, researchers also have explored the extent to which loneliness and social isolation are linked to various outcomes in elderly adults (Gerst-Emerson, Shovali, & Markides, 2014; Newall & Menec, 2014; Skingley, 2013). Both loneliness and social isolation are associated with increased health problems and mortality (Cohen-Mansfield & Perach, 2014; Luo & others, 2012). However, a recent study found that social isolation was a better predictor of mortality than loneliness (Steptoe & others, 2013). Another recent study of elderly adults revealed that both loneliness and social isolation were associated with decreases in cognitive functioning four years later (Shankar & others, 2013).

ALTRUISM AND VOLUNTEERING

Are older adults more altruistic than younger adults? In a recent investigation, older adults' strategies were more likely to be aimed at contributing to the public good while younger adults' strategies were more likely to focus on optimizing personal financial gain (Freund & Blanchard-Fields, 2014).

A common perception is that older adults need to be given help rather than give help themselves. A recent national survey found that 24.1 percent of U.S. adults 65 years and older engaged in volunteering in 2013 (U.S. Bureau of Labor Statistics, 2013). In this survey, the highest percentage of volunteering occurred between 35 and 44 years of age (30.6 percent). However, older adults are more likely than any other age group to volunteer more than 100 hours annually (Burr, 2009). Almost 50 percent of the volunteering efforts of older adults are for services provided by religious organizations (Burr, 2009).

Might volunteering improve the well-being and life-satisfaction of older adults? Researchers have found that when older adults engage in altruistic behavior and volunteering they benefit from these activities (Klinedinst & Resnick, 2014; Pilkington, Windsor, & Crisp, 2012). For example, in a recent study, older adults who volunteered more than 200 hours in the previous 12 months were more likely to show an increase in psychological well-being and physical exercise than their older adult counterparts who did not engage in volunteer activities (Sneed & Cohen, 2013). Among the reasons for the positive outcomes of volunteering are its provision of constructive activities and productive roles, social integration, and enhanced meaningfulness (Tan & others, 2007).

Might giving help as an older adult even be linked to longevity? One study followed 423 older adult couples for five years (Brown & others, 2003). At the beginning of the study, the couples were asked about the extent to which they had given or received emotional or practical help in the past year. Five years later, those who said they had helped others were half as likely to have died. One possible reason for this finding is that helping others may reduce the output of stress hormones, which improves cardiovascular health and strengthens the immune system. A 12-year longitudinal study revealed that older adults who had persistently low or declining feelings of usefulness to others had an increased risk of earlier death (Gruenewald & others, 2009). A recent study also revealed that older adults who volunteered for other-oriented reasons had a decreased mortality risk but those who volunteered for self-oriented reasons had a mortality risk similar to nonvolunteers (Konrath & others, 2012). And in a recent meta-analysis, older adults who engaged in organizational volunteering had a lower mortality risk than those who did not (Okun, Yeung, & Brown, 2013).

Ninety-eight-year-old volunteer Iva Broadus plays cards with 10-year-old DeAngela Williams in Dallas, Texas. Iva recently was recognized as the oldest volunteer in the Big Sister program in the United States. Iva says that card-playing helps to keep her memory and thinking skills sharp and can help DeAngela's as well.

developmental **connection**

Community and Culture

Service learning is linked with numerous positive outcomes in youth. Chapter 11, p. 365

Review Connect Reflect

LG3 Characterize the families and social relationships of aging adults.

Review

- How would you profile the diversity of adult lifestyles?
- How does attachment change in older adults?
- What characterizes the relationships of older adult parents and their adult children?
- Is the role of great-grandparents different from the role of grandparents?
- What are friendships of older adults like?
- What roles do social support and social integration play in late adulthood?
- How are altruism and volunteerism linked to positive outcomes in older adults?

Connect

- In this section, you read that a low level of social integration is linked with coronary heart disease in older adults. What did you learn about heart disease and stress in middle adulthood in Chapter 15?

Reflect *Your Own Personal Journey of Life*

- If you are an emerging or young adult, what is the nature of the relationship of your parents with their parents and grandparents (if they are alive)? If you are a middle-aged adult, how would you characterize your relationship with your parents (if they are still alive)?

4 Ethnicity, Gender, and Culture

LG4 Summarize how ethnicity, gender, and culture are linked with aging.

Ethnicity Gender Culture

How is ethnicity linked to aging? Do gender roles change in late adulthood? What are the social aspects of aging in different cultures?

ETHNICITY

Of special concern are ethnic minority older adults, especially African Americans and Latinos, who are overrepresented in poverty statistics (Jackson, Govia, & Sellers, 2011). Consider Harry, a 72-year-old African American who lives in a run-down hotel in Los Angeles. He suffers from arthritis and uses a walker. He has not been able to work for years, and government payments are barely enough to meet his needs.

Comparative information about African Americans, Latinos, and Whites indicates a possible double jeopardy for elderly ethnic minority individuals. They face problems related to both ageism and racism (Hatzfeld, Laveist, & Gaston-Johansson, 2012). Both the wealth and the health of ethnic minority older adults decrease more rapidly than for elderly non-Latino Whites (Yee & Chiriboga, 2007). Older ethnic minority individuals are more likely to become ill but less likely to receive treatment (Shenson & others, 2012). They also are more likely to have a history of less education, higher levels of unemployment, worse housing conditions, and shorter life expectancies than their non-Latino White counterparts (Gee, Walsemann, & Brondolo, 2012). And many ethnic minority workers never enjoy the Social Security and Medicare benefits to which their earnings contribute, because they die before reaching the age of eligibility for benefits (Jackson, Govia, & Sellers, 2011).

Despite the stress and discrimination older ethnic minority individuals face, many of these older adults have developed coping mechanisms that allow them to survive in the dominant non-Latino White world. Extension of family networks helps older minority-group individuals cope with the bare essentials of living and gives them a sense of being loved (Karasik & Hamon, 2007). Churches in African American and Latino communities provide avenues for meaningful social participation, feelings of power, and a sense of internal satisfaction (Hill & others, 2006). And residential concentrations of ethnic minority groups give their older members a sense of belonging. Thus, it always is important to consider individual variations in the lives of aging minorities. To read about one individual who is providing help for aging minorities, see *Connecting with Careers.*

A special concern is the stress faced by older African American women, many of whom view religion as a source of strength to help them cope. *What are some other characteristics of being female, a member of an ethnic minority, and old?*

Dr. Norma Thomas has worked for more than three decades in the field of aging. She obtained her undergraduate degree in social work from Pennsylvania State University and her doctoral degree in social work from the University of Pennsylvania. Thomas' activities are varied. Earlier in her career, as a social work practitioner, she provided services to older adults of color in an effort to improve their lives. She currently is a professor and academic administrator at Widener University in Chester, Pennsylvania, a fellow of the Institute of Aging at the University of Pennsylvania, and the chief executive officer and cofounder of the Center on Ethnic and Minority Aging (CEMA). CEMA was formed to provide research, consultation, training, and services to benefit aging individuals of color, their families, and their communities. Thomas has created numerous community service events that benefit older adults of color, especially African Americans and Latinos. She has also been a consultant to various national, regional, and state agencies in her effort to improve the lives of aging adults of color.

Norma Thomas.

For more information about what professors and social workers do, see pages 41 and 42 in the Careers in Life-Span Development appendix.

GENDER

Do our gender roles change when we become older adults? Some developmentalists conclude that femininity decreases in women and that masculinity decreases in men when they reach late adulthood (Gutmann, 1975). The evidence suggests that older men do become more feminine—nurturant, sensitive, and so on—but it appears that older women do not necessarily become more masculine—assertive, dominant, and so on (Turner, 1982). Keep in mind that cohort effects are especially important to consider in areas such as gender roles. As sociohistorical changes take place and are considered more frequently in life-span investigations, what were once perceived to be age effects may turn out to be cohort effects (Schaie, 2013).

A possible double jeopardy also faces many women—the burden of both ageism and sexism (Meyer & Parker, 2011). Not only is it important to be concerned about older women's double jeopardy of ageism and sexism, but special attention also needs to be devoted to female ethnic minority older adults (Jackson, Govia, & Sellers, 2011). They face what could be described as triple jeopardy—ageism, sexism, and racism (Hinze, Lin, & Andersson, 2012). Older women in ethnic minority groups have faced considerable stress in their lives. In dealing with this stress, they have shown remarkable adaptability, resilience, responsibility, and coping skills.

CULTURE

What promotes a good old age in most cultures? One analysis indicated that three factors are important in living the "good life" as an older adult: health, security, and kinship/support (Fry, 2007).

Another important question is: What factors are associated with whether older adults are accorded a position of high status in a culture? In one view, seven factors are most likely to predict high status for older adults in a culture (Sangree, 1989):

- Older persons have valuable knowledge.
- Older persons control key family/community resources.

Cultures vary in the prestige they give to older adults. In the Navajo culture, older adults are especially treated with respect because of their wisdom and extensive life experiences. *What are some other factors that are linked with respect for older adults in a culture?*

- Older persons are permitted to engage in useful and valued functions as long as possible.
- There is role continuity throughout the life span.
- Age-related role changes involve greater responsibility, authority, and advisory capacity.
- The extended family is a common family arrangement in the culture, and the older person is integrated into the extended family.
- In general, respect for older adults is greater in collectivistic cultures (such as China and Japan) than in individualistic cultures (such as the United States). However, some researchers are finding that this collectivistic/individualistic difference in respect for older adults is not as strong as it used to be, and that in some cases older adults in individualistic cultures receive considerable respect (Antonucci, Vandewater, & Lansford, 2000).

Review *Connect* Reflect

LG4 Summarize how ethnicity, gender, and culture are linked with aging.

Review
- How does ethnicity modify the experience of aging?
- Do gender roles change in late adulthood? Explain.
- How is aging experienced in different cultures?

Connect
- In this section, you read that ethnic minorities face additional challenges in aging. What did you learn about ethnicity and life expectancy in Chapter 17?

Reflect *Your Own Personal Journey of Life*
- How would you describe the experiences of the older adults in your family background that were influenced by their ethnicity, gender, and culture?

5 Successful Aging

LG5 Explain how to age successfully.

developmental **connection**

Health

Regular exercise is linked to increased longevity and prevention of many chronic diseases. Chapter 17, p. 530

For too long, the positive dimensions of late adulthood were ignored (Cheng, 2014; Cosco & others, 2014; Hodge & others, 2014; Johnson & Mutchler, 2014; Lamb, 2014). Throughout this book, we have called attention to the positive aspects of aging. There are many robust, healthy older adults. With a proper diet, an active lifestyle, mental stimulation and flexibility, positive coping skills, good social relationships and support, and the absence of disease, many abilities can be maintained or in some cases even improved as we get older (Antonucci, Birditt, & Ajrouch, 2013). Even when individuals develop a disease, improvements in medicine mean that increasing numbers of older adults can continue to lead active, constructive lives (Siegler & others, 2013a, b). A recent Canadian study found that the predicted self-rated probability of aging successfully was 41 percent for those 65 to 74, 33 percent for those 75 to 84, and 22 percent for those 85+ years of age (Meng & D'Arcy, 2014). In this study, being younger, married, a regular drinker, in better health (self-perceived), and satisfied with life were associated with successful aging. Presence of disease was linked to a significant decline in successful aging.

Being active is especially important to successful aging (Parisi & others, 2014; Solberg & others, 2013). Older adults who exercise regularly, attend meetings, participate in church activities, and go on trips are more satisfied with their lives than their counterparts who disengage from society (Berchicci & others, 2014). Older adults who engage in challenging cognitive activities are more likely to retain their cognitive skills for a longer period of time (Kirk-Sanchez & McGough, 2014; Park & others, 2014; Rebok & others, 2014). Older adults who are emotionally selective, optimize their choices, and compensate effectively for losses increase their chances of aging successfully (English & Carstensen, 2014a; Freund, Nikitin, & Riediger, 2013).

Successful aging also involves perceived control over the environment (Bertrand, Graham, & Lachman, 2013; Milte & others, 2014). In Chapter 17, we described how perceived control over the environment had a positive effect on nursing home residents' health and longevity. In recent years, the term *self-efficacy* has often been used to describe perceived control over the environment and the ability to produce positive outcomes (Bandura, 2010,

2012). Researchers have found that many older adults are quite effective in maintaining a sense of control and have a positive view of themselves (Bertrand, Graham, & Lachman, 2013; Park, Elavsky, & Koo, 2014). For example, a study of centenarians found that many were very happy and that self-efficacy and an optimistic attitude were linked to their happiness (Jopp & Rott, 2006). And one study revealed that maximizing psychological resources (self-efficacy and optimism) was linked to a higher quality of life for older adults (Bowling & Lliffe, 2011). Examining the positive aspects of aging is an important trend in life-span development that is likely to benefit future generations of older adults (Freund, Nikitin, & Riediger, 2013; Hodge & others, 2014). And a very important agenda is to continue to improve our understanding of how people can live longer, healthier, more productive and satisfying lives (Nagamatsu & others, 2014; Park, Han, & Kang, 2014).

Review *Connect* Reflect

LG5 Explain how to age successfully.

Review
- What factors are linked with aging successfully?

Connect
- In this section, you read that self-efficacy and an optimistic attitude are linked to the happiness of centenarians. In Chapter 17, what factors were identified as playing important roles in helping people survive to extreme old age?

Reflect *Your Own Personal Journey of Life*
- How might your ability to age successfully as an older adult be related to what you are doing in your life now?

topical **connections** *looking forward*

In death, dying, and grieving, dying individuals and those close to them experience intense emotions. The dying individual doesn't go through a set sequence of stages, but at various points may show denial, anger, or acceptance. It is important for family and friends to communicate effectively with a dying person. In coping with the death of another person, grief may be experienced as emotional numbness, separation anxiety, despair, sadness, or loneliness. In some cases, grief may last for years. Among the most difficult losses are the death of a child or a spouse. Social support benefits widows and widowers.

reach your **learning goals**

Socioemotional Development in Late Adulthood

1 Theories of Socioemotional Development

LG1 Discuss four theories of socioemotional development and aging.

Erikson's Theory

- Erikson's eighth and final stage of development, which individuals experience in late adulthood, involves reflecting on the past and either integrating it positively or concluding that one's life has not been well spent. Life review is an important theme in Erikson's stage of integrity versus despair.

| Activity Theory |

- Activity theory states that the more active and involved older adults are, the more likely they are to be satisfied with their lives. This theory has been strongly supported by research.

| Socioemotional Selectivity Theory |

- Socioemotional selectivity theory states that older adults become more selective about their social networks. Because they place a high value on emotional satisfaction, they are motivated to spend more time with familiar individuals with whom they have had rewarding relationships. Knowledge-related and emotion-related goals change across the life span, with emotion-related goals being more important when individuals get older.

| Selective Optimization with Compensation Theory |

- Selective optimization with compensation theory states that successful aging is linked with three main factors: (1) selection of performance domains, (2) optimization of existing capacities, and (3) compensation for deficits. These are especially likely to be relevant when loss occurs.

2 Personality, the Self, and Society Describe links between personality and mortality, and identify changes in the self and society in late adulthood.

| Personality |

- The personality traits of conscientiousness and agreeableness increase in late adulthood. Lower levels of conscientiousness, extraversion, and openness to experience, a higher level of neuroticism, negative affect, pessimism, and a negative outlook on life are related to earlier death in late adulthood.

| The Self and Society |

- In one large-scale study, self-esteem increased through most of adulthood but declined in the seventies and eighties. Further research is needed to verify these developmental changes in self-esteem. The stability of self-esteem declines in older adults. Possible selves are what individuals might become, what they would like to become, and what they are afraid of becoming. Possible selves change during late adulthood and are linked to engagement in various activities and longevity. Changes in types of self-acceptance occur through the adult years as acceptance of ideal and future selves decreases with age and acceptance of past selves increases. Most older adults effectively maintain a sense of self-control, although self-regulation may vary by domain. For example, older adults often show less self-regulation in the physical domain than younger adults.

| Older Adults in Society |

- Ageism is prejudice against others because of their age. Too many negative stereotypes of older adults continue to exist. Social policy issues in an aging society include the status of the economy and the continued viability of the Social Security system, the provision of health care, eldercare, and generational inequity. Of special concern are older adults who are in poverty. Poverty rates are especially high among older women who live alone and ethnic minority older adults. Most older adults live in the community rather than in institutions. Almost two-thirds of older adults live with family members. Older adults are less likely to have a computer in their home and less likely to use the Internet than younger adults, but they are the fastest-growing age segment of Internet users.

3 Families and Social Relationships Characterize the families and social relationships of aging adults.

| Lifestyle Diversity |

- Older adult men are more likely to be married than older adult women. Retirement alters a couple's lifestyle and requires adaptation. Married older adults are often happier than single older adults. There are social, financial, and physical consequences of divorce for older adults. More divorced older adults, increased longevity, and better health have led to an increase in remarriage by older adults. Some older adults perceive negative pressure about their decision to remarry after becoming widowed or divorced, although the majority of adult children support the decision of their older adult parents to remarry. An increasing number of older adults cohabit.

| Attachment |

- Older adults have fewer attachment relationships than younger adults; attachment anxiety decreases with increasing age; attachment security is linked to psychological and physical well-being in older adults; and insecure attachment is associated with a greater perceived negative caregiving burden in caring for Alzheimer disease patients.

| Older Adult Parents and Their Adult Children |

- Approximately 80 percent of older adults have living children, many of whom are middle-aged. Increasingly, diversity characterizes the relationships of older parents and their adult children. Adult daughters are more likely than adult sons to be involved in the lives of aging parents. An important task that adult children can perform is to coordinate and monitor services for an aging parent who becomes disabled. Ambivalence can characterize the relationships of adult children with their aging parents.

Great-Grandparenting

- Because of increased longevity, more grandparents today are also great-grandparents. One contribution of great-grandparents is knowledge of family history. One research study found that young adults have a more involved relationship with grandparents than with great-grandparents.

Friendship

Social Support and Social Integration

- There is more continuity than change in friendship for older adults.

- Social support is linked with improved physical and mental health in older adults. Older adults who participate in more organizations live longer than their counterparts who have low participation rates. Older adults often have fewer peripheral social ties but a strong motivation to spend time in relationships with close friends and family members that are emotionally rewarding.

Altruism and Volunteering

- Altruism is linked to having a longer life. Volunteering is associated with higher life satisfaction, less depression and anxiety, better physical health, and more positive emotions.

4 Ethnicity, Gender, and Culture

LG4 Summarize how ethnicity, gender, and culture are linked with aging.

Ethnicity

- Aging minorities cope with the double burden of ageism and racism. Nonetheless, there is considerable variation in the lives of aging minorities.

Gender

- There is stronger evidence that men become more feminine (nurturant, sensitive) as older adults than there is that women become more masculine (assertive). Older women face a double jeopardy of ageism and sexism.

Culture

- Historically, respect for older adults in China and Japan was high, but today their status is more variable. Factors that predict high status for the elderly across cultures range from their valuable knowledge to integration into the extended family.

5 Successful Aging

LG5 Explain how to age successfully.

- Increasingly, the positive aspects of older adulthood are being studied. Factors that are linked with successful aging include an active lifestyle, positive coping skills, good social relationships and support, and the absence of disease.

key **terms**

integrity versus despair 569
activity theory 570
socioemotional selectivity
  theory 571

selective optimization
  with compensation
  theory 572
possible selves 576

ageism 577
eldercare 578
generational
  inequity 578

convoy model of social
  relations 584

key **people**

Erik Erikson 569
Robert Butler 569

Laura Carstensen 571
Paul Baltes 573

Ursula Staudinger 573

section ten

Years following years steal something every day; At last they steal us from ourselves away.

—**ALEXANDER POPE**
English Poet, 18th Century

Endings

Our life ultimately ends—when we approach life's grave sustained and soothed with unfaltering trust or rave at the close of day; when at last years steal us from ourselves; and when we are linked to our children's children's children by an invisible cable that runs from age to age. This final section contains one chapter: "Death, Dying, and Grieving" (Chapter 20).

DEATH, DYING, AND GRIEVING

chapter **outline**

Paige Farley-Hackel and her best friend Ruth McCourt teamed up to take McCourt's 4-year-old daughter, Juliana, to Disneyland. They were originally booked on the same flight from Boston to Los Angeles, but McCourt decided to use her frequent flyer miles and go on a different airplane. Both their flights exploded 17 minutes apart after terrorists hijacked them, then rammed them into the twin towers of the World Trade Center in New York City on 9/11/2001.

Forty-five-year-old Ruth McCourt was a homemaker from New London, Connecticut, who had met Farley-Hackel at a day spa she used to own in Boston. McCourt gave up the business when she married, but the friendship between the two women lasted. They often traveled together and shared their passion for reading, cooking, and learning.

Forty-six-year-old Farley-Hackel was a writer, motivational speaker, and spiritual counselor who lived in Newton, Massachusetts. She was looking forward to the airing of the first few episodes of her new radio program, "Spiritually Speaking," and wanted to eventually be on *The Oprah Winfrey Show*, said her husband, Allan Hackel. Following 9/11, Oprah provided a memorial tribute to Farley-Hackel, McCourt, and Juliana.

topical **connections** *looking back*

In the United States, the leading cause of death in infancy is sudden infant death syndrome (SIDS). In early childhood, motor vehicle accidents are the leading cause of death, followed by cancer and cardiovascular disease. Injuries are the leading cause of death during middle and late childhood, and the most common cause of severe injury and death in this period is motor vehicle accidents, either as a pedestrian or as a passenger. The three leading causes of death in adolescence are accidents, homicide, and suicide. Emerging adults have more than twice the mortality rate of adolescents. For many years, heart disease was the leading cause of death in middle adulthood, followed by cancer; however, in 2005 more individuals 45 to 64 years of age in the United States died of cancer, followed by cardiovascular disease. Men have higher mortality rates than women for all of the leading causes of death. Nearly 60 percent of 65- to 74-year-old U.S. adults die of cancer or cardiovascular disease, with cancer now the leading cause of death. However, in the age groups of 75 to 84 and 85 and over, cardiovascular disease is the leading cause of death.

preview

In this final chapter of the book, we will explore many aspects of death and dying. Among the questions that we will ask are: What characterizes the death system and its cultural and historical contexts? How can death be defined? What are some links between development and death? How do people face their own death? How do individuals cope with the death of someone they love?

1 The Death System and Cultural Contexts

 LG1 Describe the death system and its cultural and historical contexts.

The Death System and Its Cultural Variations

Changing Historical Circumstances

Today in the United States, deaths of older adults account for approximately two-thirds of the 2 million deaths that occur each year. Thus, what we know about death, dying, and grieving mainly is based on information about older adults. Youthful death is far less common. What has changed historically in the United States is when, where, and how people die. And how we deal with death is part of our culture. Every culture has a death system, and variations in this death system occur across cultures.

developmental connection

Life Expectancy

The upper boundary of the human life span is 122 years of age (based on the oldest age documented). Chapter 1, p. 5

THE DEATH SYSTEM AND ITS CULTURAL VARIATIONS

Robert Kastenbaum (1932–2013) emphasizes that the *death system* in any culture comprises the following components (Kastenbaum 2009, 2012):

- *People.* Because death is inevitable, everyone is involved with death at some point, either their own death or the death of others. Some individuals have a more systematic role with death, such as those who work in the funeral industry and the clergy, as well as people who work in life-threatening contexts such as firefighters and police officers.

- *Places or contexts.* These include hospitals, funeral homes, cemeteries, hospices, battlefields, and memorials (such as the Vietnam Veterans Memorial wall in Washington, DC).

- *Times.* Death involves times or occasions, such as Memorial Day in the United States and the Day of the Dead in Mexico, which are times to honor those who have died. Also, anniversaries of disasters such as D-Day in World War II, 9/11/2001, and Hurricane Sandy in 2012, as well as the 2004 tsunami in Southeast Asia that took approximately 100,000 lives, are times when those who died are remembered in special ways such as ceremonies.

- *Objects.* Many objects in a culture are associated with death, including caskets, various black objects such as clothes, armbands, and hearses.

- *Symbols.* Symbols such as a skull and crossbones, as well as last rites in the Catholic religion and various religious ceremonies, are connected to death.

What are some cultural variations in the death system? To live a full life and die with glory was the prevailing goal of the ancient Greeks. Individuals are more conscious of death in times of war, famine, and plague. Whereas Americans are conditioned from early in life to live as though they were immortal, in much of the world this fiction cannot be maintained. Death crowds the streets of Calcutta in daily overdisplay, as it does in the impoverished villages of Africa's Sahel. By contrast, in the United States it is not uncommon to reach adulthood without having seen someone die.

A body lies in the flooded streets of New Orleans in the aftermath of Hurricane Katrina in 2005.

Most societies throughout history have had philosophical or religious beliefs about death, and most societies have a ritual that deals with death (Walter, 2012). Death may be seen as a punishment for one's sins, an act of atonement, or a judgment from a just God. For some, death means loneliness; for others, death is a quest for happiness. For still others, death represents redemption, a relief from the trials and tribulations of the earthly world. Some embrace death and welcome it; others abhor and fear it. For those who welcome it, death may be seen as the fitting end to a fulfilled life. From this perspective, how we depart from Earth is influenced by how we have lived.

In most societies, death is not viewed as the end of existence—after the biological body has died, the spiritual body is believed to live on. This religious perspective is favored by most Americans as well (Gowan, 2003). Cultural variations in attitudes toward death include belief in reincarnation, which is an important aspect of the Hindu and Buddhist religions (Bhuvaneswar & Stern, 2013). In the Gond culture of India, death is believed to be caused by magic and demons. The members of the Gond culture react angrily to death. In the Tanala culture of Madagascar, death is believed to be caused by natural forces. The members of the Tanala culture show a much more peaceful reaction to death than members of the Gond culture. Figure 20.1 shows a ritual associated with death in South Korea.

In many ways, we in the United States are death avoiders and death deniers (Norouzieh, 2005). This denial can take many forms, including our persistent search for a fountain of youth through diet, surgery, and other means, as well as the tendency of the funeral industry to gloss over death and fashion lifelike qualities in the dead.

FIGURE **20.1**

A RITUAL ASSOCIATED WITH DEATH. Family memorial day at the national cemetery in Seoul, South Korea.

CHANGING HISTORICAL CIRCUMSTANCES

One historical change involves the age group in which death most often occurs. Two hundred years ago, almost one of every two children died before the age of 10, and one parent died before children grew up. Today, death occurs most often among older adults (Carr, 2009). Life expectancy has increased from 47 years for a person born in 1900 to 78 years for someone born today (U.S. Census Bureau, 2013). In 1900, most people died at home, cared for by their family. As our population has aged and become more mobile, greater numbers of older adults die apart from their families (Carr, 2009). In the United States today, more than 80 percent of all deaths occur in institutions or hospitals. The care of a dying older person has shifted away from the family and minimized our exposure to death and its painful surroundings (Gold, 2011).

Review Connect Reflect

 Describe the death system and its cultural and historical contexts.

Review

- What characterizes the death system in a culture? What are some cultural variations in the death system?
- What are some changing sociohistorical circumstances regarding death?

Connect

- You just read about how changes in life expectancy over time have affected our experience of death. In earlier chapters, what did you learn about life expectancy and the age span that encompasses older adulthood?

Reflect *Your Own Personal Journey of Life*

- How extensively have death and dying been discussed in your family? Explain.

2 Defining Death and Life/Death Issues Evaluate issues in determining death and decisions regarding death.

Issues in Determining Death   Decisions Regarding Life, Death, and Health Care

Is there one point in the process of dying that is the point at which death takes place, or is there more of a gradual transition between life and death? What are some decisions individuals can make about life, death, and health care?

ISSUES IN DETERMINING DEATH

Thirty years ago, determining whether someone was dead was simpler than it is today. The end of certain biological functions, such as breathing and blood pressure, and the rigidity of the body (rigor mortis) were considered to be clear signs of death. In recent decades, defining death has become more complex (Goswami & others, 2013; Nair-Collins, Northrup, & Olcese, 2014; Taylor & others, 2014).

Brain death is a neurological definition of death, which states that a person is brain dead when all electrical activity of the brain has ceased for a specified period of time. A flat EEG (electroencephalogram) reading for a specified period of time is one criterion of brain death. The higher portions of the brain often die sooner than the lower portions. Because the brain's lower portions monitor heartbeat and respiration, individuals whose higher brain areas have died may continue to breathe and have a heartbeat (Binderman, Krakauer, & Solomon, 2012; MacDougall & others, 2014). The definition of brain death currently followed by most physicians includes the death of both the higher cortical functions and the lower brain stem functions (Sung & Greer, 2011).

Some medical experts argue that the criteria for death should include only higher cortical functioning. If the cortical death definition were adopted, then physicians could declare that a person is dead when there is no cortical functioning in that person, even though the lower brain stem is functioning. Supporters of the cortical death policy argue that the functions we associate with being human, such as intelligence and personality, are located in the higher cortical part of the brain. They believe that when these functions are lost, the "human being" is no longer alive.

DECISIONS REGARDING LIFE, DEATH, AND HEALTH CARE

In cases of catastrophic illness or accidents, patients might not be able to respond adequately to participate in decisions about their medical care. To prepare for this situation, some individuals make choices earlier.

Advance Care Planning *Advance care planning* refers the process of patients thinking about and communicating their preferences about end-of-life care (Abel & others, 2013; Harrison & McGee, 2014; Silveira, Witala, & Piette, 2014). For many patients in a coma, it is not clear what their wishes regarding termination of treatment might be if they still were conscious. A recent study found that advance care planning decreased life-sustaining treatment, increased hospice use, and decreased hospital use (Brinkman-Stoppelenburg, Rietjens, & van der Heide, 2014). Recognizing that some terminally ill patients might prefer to die rather than linger in a painful or vegetative state, the organization "Choice in Dying" created the *living will*, a legal document that reflects the patient's advance care planning. A recent study of older adults found that advance care planning was associated with improved quality of care at the end of life, including less in-hospital death and greater use of hospice care (Bischoff & others, 2013).

Physicians' concerns over malpractice suits and the efforts of people who support the living will concept have produced natural death legislation. Laws in all 50 states now accept

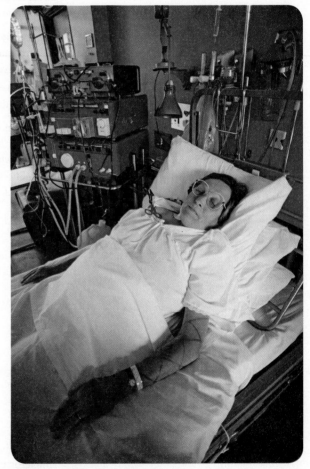

What are some issues in determining death?

brain death A neurological definition of death. A person is brain dead when all electrical activity of the brain has ceased for a specified period of time. A flat EEG recording is one criterion of brain death.

an *advance directive,* such as a living will. An advance directive states such preferences as whether life-sustaining procedures should or should not be used to prolong the life of an individual when death is imminent (Kovacs, Landzberg, & Goodlin, 2013). An advance directive must be signed while the individual still is able to think clearly (Quereshi & others, 2013). A study of end-of-life planning revealed that only 15 percent of patients 18 years of age and older had a living will (Clements, 2009). A recent research review concluded that physicians have a positive attitude toward advance directives (Coleman, 2013).

Recently, Physician Orders for Life-Sustaining Treatment (POLST), a document that is more specific than previous advance directives, was created (Buck & Fahlberg, 2014; Wenger & others, 2013). POLST translates treatment preferences into medical orders such as those involving cardiopulmonary resuscitation, extent of treatment, and artificial nutrition via a tube (Fromme & others, 2012). POLST involves the health care professional and the patient or surrogate conferring to determine and state the wishes of the patient. POLST is currently available or being considered in 34 states.

Euthanasia   Euthanasia ("easy death") is the act of painlessly ending the lives of individuals who are suffering from an incurable disease or severe disability (Augestad & others, 2013; Gormley-Fleming & Campbell, 2014). Sometimes euthanasia is called "mercy killing." Distinctions are made between two types of euthanasia: passive and active.

- **Passive euthanasia** occurs when a person is allowed to die by withholding available treatment, such as withdrawing a life-sustaining device. For example, this might involve turning off a respirator or a heart-lung machine.
- **Active euthanasia** occurs when death is deliberately induced, as when a lethal dose of a drug is injected.

Technological advances in life-support devices raise the issue of quality of life (Mishara & Weisstub, 2013). Nowhere was this more apparent than in the highly publicized case of Terri Schiavo, who suffered severe brain damage related to cardiac arrest and a lack of oxygen to the brain. She went into a coma and spent 15 years in a vegetative state. Across the 15 years, the question of whether passive euthanasia should be implemented or whether she should be kept in the vegetative state with the hope that her condition might change for the better was debated between family members and eventually at a number of levels in the judicial system. At one point toward the end of her life in the early spring of 2005, a court ordered that her feeding tube be removed. However, subsequent appeals led to its reinsertion twice. The feeding tube was removed a third and final time on March 18, 2005, and she died 13 days later.

Should individuals like Terri Schiavo be kept alive in a vegetative state? The trend is toward acceptance of passive euthanasia in the case of terminally ill patients (Seay, 2011).

The inflammatory argument that once equated this practice with suicide rarely is heard today. However, experts do not yet entirely agree on the precise boundaries or the exact mechanisms by which treatment decisions should be implemented (Miljkovic, Jones, & Miller, 2013). Can a comatose patient's life-support systems be disconnected when the patient has left no written instructions to that effect? Does the family of a comatose patient have the right to overrule the attending physician's decision to continue life-support systems? These questions have no simple or universally agreed-upon answers (Chambaere & others, 2012).

The most widely publicized cases of active euthanasia involve "assisted suicide." Jack Kevorkian, a Michigan physician, assisted a number of terminally ill patients in ending their lives. After a series of trials, Kevorkian was convicted of second-degree murder and given a 10- to 15-year sentence. He was released from prison at age 79 for good behavior in June 2007 and promised not to participate in any further assisted suicides. Kevorkian died in 2011 at the age of 83.

Assisted suicide is now legal in four European countries—The Netherlands, Belgium, Luxembourg, and most recently Switzerland (Steck & others, 2013). The United States government has no official policy on assisted suicide and leaves the decision up to each of the states. Currently, three states allow assisted suicide—Oregon, Washington, and

Terri Schiavo (*right*) shown with her mother. *What issues did the Terri Schiavo case raise?*

euthanasia The act of painlessly ending the lives of persons who are suffering from incurable diseases or severe disabilities; sometimes called "mercy killing."

passive euthanasia The withholding of available treatments, such as life-sustaining devices, in order to allow a person to die.

active euthanasia Death induced deliberately, as by injecting a lethal dose of a drug.

Montana. The manner in which assisted suicide is performed involves the physician giving the patient an overdose of muscle relaxants or sedatives, which causes a coma and then death. In states where assisted suicide is illegal, the crime is typically considered manslaughter or a felony. Canada has yet to approve assisted suicide but a recent study indicated that a majority of Canadians favored a change to Canada's Criminal Code that would make assisted suicide legal (Schafer, 2013).

A recent research review also revealed that the percentage of physician-assisted deaths ranged from 0.1 to 0.2 percent in the United States and Luxembourg to 1.8 to 2.9 percent in the Netherlands (Steck & others, 2013). In this review, the percentage of assisted suicide cases reported to authorities has increased in recent years and the individuals who die through assisted suicide are most likely to be males from 60 to 75 years of age.

Needed: Better Care for Dying Individuals   Death in America is often lonely, prolonged, and painful. Dying individuals often get too little or too much care. Scientific advances sometimes have made dying harder by delaying the inevitable. And even though painkillers are available, too many people experience severe pain during the last days and months of life (Meng & others, 2013). Many health care professionals have not been trained to provide adequate end-of-life care or to understand its importance. One study revealed that in many cases doctors don't give dying patients adequate information about how long they are likely to live or how various treatments will affect their lives (Harrington & Smith, 2008). For example, in this study of patients with advanced cancer, only 37 percent of doctors told patients how long they were likely to live.

Care providers are increasingly interested in helping individuals experience a "good death" (McIlfatrick & Hasson, 2014). One view is that a good death involves physical comfort, support from loved ones, acceptance, and appropriate medical care. For some individuals, a good death involves accepting one's impending death and not feeling like a burden to others (Carr, 2009).

Hospice is a program committed to making the end of life as free from pain, anxiety, and depression as possible (Guo & Jacelon, 2014; Sokol, 2013; Thomas, 2013). Traditionally, a hospital's goals have been to cure illness and prolong life. By contrast, hospice care emphasizes **palliative care,** which involves reducing pain and suffering and helping individuals die with dignity (Albrecht & others, 2013; Holloway & others, 2014; Kelley & others, 2014). However, U.S. hospitals recently have rapidly expanded their provision of palliative care. A recent study found that more than 85 percent of mid- to large-size U.S. hospitals have a palliative care team (Morrison, 2013). Hospice-care professionals work together to treat the dying person's symptoms, make the individual as comfortable as possible, show interest in the person and the person's family, and help everyone involved cope with death (Mah & others, 2013).

A primary hospice goal is to bring pain under control and to help dying patients face death in a psychologically healthy way (Hugel & others, 2014; Melia, 2014). The hospice also makes every effort to include the dying individual's family; it is believed that this strategy benefits not only the dying individual but family members as well, probably diminishing their guilt after the death (Kastenbaum, 2012).

The hospice movement has grown rapidly in the United States. More than 1,500 community groups are involved nationally in establishing hospice programs. Hospices are more likely to serve people with terminal cancer than those with other life-threatening conditions (Kastenbaum, 2012). Hospice advocates underscore that it is possible to control pain for almost any dying individual and to create an environment for the patient that is superior to that found in most hospitals (Hayslip, 1996). For hospice services to be covered by Medicare, a patient must be deemed by a physician to have six months or fewer to live. Also, some hospice providers require that the patient have a family caregiver in the home (or nearby) before agreeing to provide services for the patient.

Approximately 90 percent of hospice care is provided in patients' homes (Hayslip & Hansson, 2007). In some cases, home-based care is provided by community-based health care professionals or volunteers; in other cases, home-based care is provided by home health care agencies or the Visiting Nurse Associations. There is a rapidly growing need for competent home health aides in hospice and palliative care (Berta & others, 2013). Also, some hospice care is provided in free-standing, full-service hospice facilities and in hospice units in hospitals. To read about the work of a home hospice nurse, see *Connecting with Careers.*

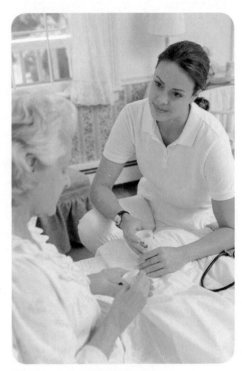

What characterizes hospice care?

hospice A program committed to making the end of life as free from pain, anxiety, and depression as possible. The goals of hospice contrast with those of a hospital, which are to cure disease and prolong life.

palliative care The type of care emphasized in a hospice, which involves reducing pain and suffering and helping individuals die with dignity.

Kathy McLaughlin, Home Hospice Nurse

Kathy McLaughlin is a home hospice nurse in Alexandria, Virginia. She provides care for individuals with terminal cancer, Alzheimer disease, and other diseases. There currently is a shortage of home hospice nurses in the United States.

McLaughlin says that she has seen too many people dying in pain, away from home, hooked up to needless machines. In her work as a home hospice nurse, she comments, "I know I'm making a difference. I just feel privileged to get the chance to meet this person who is not going to be around much longer. I want to enjoy the moment with this person. And I want them to enjoy the moment. They have great stories. They are better than novels." (McLaughlin, 2003, p. 1)

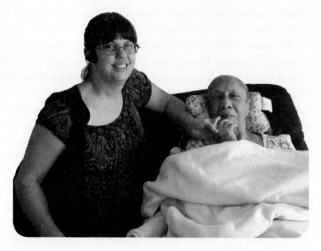

Kathy McLaughlin with her hospice patient Mary Monteiro.

Review Connect Reflect

 Evaluate issues in determining death and decisions regarding death.

Review

- What are some issues regarding the determination of death?
- What are some decisions to be made regarding life, death, and health care?

Connect

- In this section, you learned that one of the things that hospices try to provide

dying patients is adequate pain management. What did you learn about older adults in Chapter 17 that might help them deal with pain better than younger adults?

Reflect Your Own Personal Journey of Life

- Have you signed an advance directive (living will)? Why or why not?

---

3 A Developmental Perspective on Death

 Discuss death and attitudes about it at different points in development.

Causes of Death

Attitudes Toward Death at Different Points in the Life Span

Do the causes of death vary across the human life span? Do we have different expectations about death as we develop through the life span? What are our attitudes toward death at different points in our development?

CAUSES OF DEATH

Death can occur at any point in the human life span. Death can occur during prenatal development through miscarriages or stillborn births. Death can also occur during the birth process or in the first few days after birth, which usually happens because of a birth defect or because infants have not developed adequately to sustain life outside the uterus. In Chapter 4, "Physical Development in Infancy," we described *sudden infant death syndrome (SIDS),* in which infants stop breathing, usually during the night, and die without apparent cause (Rubens & Sarnat, 2013). SIDS currently is the leading cause of infant death in the United States, with the risk highest at 2 to 4 months of age (NICHD, 2013).

developmental connection

Conditions, Diseases, and Disorders
Nearly 3,000 deaths of infants a year in the United States are attributed to SIDS. Chapter 4, p. 111

In childhood, death occurs most often because of accidents or illness. Accidental death in childhood can be the consequence of events such as an automobile accident, drowning, poisoning, fire, or a fall from a high place. Major illnesses that cause death in children are heart disease, cancer, and birth defects.

Compared with childhood, death in adolescence is more likely to occur because of motor vehicle accidents, suicide, and homicide. Many motor vehicle accidents that cause death in adolescence are alcohol-related. We will examine suicide in greater depth shortly.

Older adults are more likely to die from chronic ailments such as heart disease and cancer, whereas younger adults are more likely to die from accidents. Older adults' diseases often incapacitate before they kill, which produces a course of dying that slowly leads to death. Of course, many young and middle-aged adults also die of heart disease, cancer, and other diseases.

ATTITUDES TOWARD DEATH AT DIFFERENT POINTS IN THE LIFE SPAN

The ages of children and adults influence the way they experience and think about death. A mature, adult-like conception of death includes an understanding that death is final and irreversible, that death represents the end of life, and that all living things die. Most researchers have found that as children grow, they develop a more mature approach to death (Hayslip & Hansson, 2003).

Childhood Even children 3 to 5 years of age have little or no idea of what death means. They may confuse death with sleep or ask in a puzzled way, "Why doesn't it move?" Preschool-aged children rarely get upset by the sight of a dead animal or by being told that a person has died. They believe that the dead can be brought back to life spontaneously by magic or by giving them food or medical treatment. Young children often believe that only people who want to die, or who are bad or careless, actually die. They also may blame themselves for the death of someone they know well, illogically reasoning that the event may have happened because they disobeyed the person who died.

Three- to nine-year-old children with their mother visiting their father's grave in Kenya. *What are some developmental changes in children's conceptions of death?*

Sometime in the middle and late childhood years, more realistic perceptions of death develop. In a review of research on children's conception of death, it was concluded that children probably do not view death as universal and irreversible until about 9 years of age (Cuddy-Casey & Orvaschel, 1997). Most children under 7 do not see death as likely. If they do, they tend to perceive it as reversible.

The death of a parent is especially difficult for children. When a child's parent dies, the child's school performance and peer relationships often worsen. For some children, as well as adults, a parent's death can be devastating and result in a hypersensitivity about death, including a fear of losing others close to the individual. In some cases, loss of a sibling can result in similar negative outcomes (Sood & others, 2006). However, a number of factors, such as the quality of the relationship and type of the death (whether due to an accident, long-standing illness, suicide, or murder, for example), can influence the individual's development following the death of a person close to the individual.

Most psychologists emphasize that honesty is the best strategy in discussing death with children. Treating the concept as unmentionable is thought to be an inappropriate strategy, yet most of us have grown up in a society in which death is rarely discussed.

In addition to honesty, the best response to a child's query about death might depend on the child's maturity level. For example, a preschool child requires a less elaborate explanation than an older child. Death can be explained to preschool children in simple physical and biological terms. Actually, what young children need more than elaborate explanations of death is reassurance that they are loved and will not be abandoned. Regardless of children's ages, adults should be sensitive and sympathetic, encouraging them to express their own feelings and ideas.

Adolescence Deaths of peers, friends, siblings, parents, grandparents, or great-grandparents bring death to the forefront of adolescents' lives. Adolescents develop more

We keep on thinking and rethinking death after we have passed through childhood's hour.

—ROBERT KASTENBAUM

Leading Expert on Death, Dying, and Grieving, 20th–21st Century

How might older adults' attitudes about death differ from those of younger adults?

abstract conceptions of death than children do. For example, adolescents describe death in terms of darkness, light, transition, or nothingness (Wenestam & Wass, 1987). They also develop religious and philosophical views about the nature of death and whether there is life after death.

Adulthood   There is no evidence that a special orientation toward death develops in early adulthood. An increase in consciousness about death accompanies individuals' awareness that they are aging, which usually intensifies in middle adulthood. In our discussion of middle adulthood, we indicated that midlife is a time when adults begin to think more about how much time is left in their lives. Researchers have found that middle-aged adults actually fear death more than do young adults or older adults (Kalish & Reynolds, 1976). Older adults, though, think about death more and talk about it more in conversation with others than do middle-aged and young adults. They also have more direct experience with death as their friends and relatives become ill and die (Hayslip & Hansson, 2003). Older adults are forced to examine the meanings of life and death more frequently than are younger adults.

In old age, one's own death may take on an appropriateness it lacked in earlier years. Some of the increased thinking and conversing about death, and an increased sense of integrity developed through a positive life review, may help older adults accept death. Older adults are less likely to have unfinished business than are younger adults. They usually do not have children who need to be guided to maturity, their spouses are more likely to be dead, and they are less likely to have work-related projects that require completion. Lacking such anticipations, death may be less emotionally painful to them. Even among older adults, however, attitudes toward death vary (Whitbourne & Meeks, 2011).

Review Connect Reflect

LG3 Discuss death and attitudes about it at different points in development.

Review

- What are some developmental changes in the causes of death?
- What are some attitudes about death at different points in development?

Connect

- In this section, you learned that children 3 to 5 years of age often believe that the dead can be brought back to life spontaneously by magic or by giving

them food or medical treatment. During which of Piaget's stages of development is a child's cognitive world dominated by egocentrism and magical beliefs?

Reflect *Your Own Personal Journey of Life*

- What is your current attitude about death? Has it changed since you were an adolescent? If so, how?

4 Facing One's Own Death

LG4 Explain the psychological aspects involved in facing one's own death and the contexts in which people die.

Kübler-Ross' Stages of Dying   Perceived Control and Denial   The Contexts in Which People Die

denial and isolation Kübler-Ross' first stage of dying, in which the dying person denies that she or he is really going to die.

anger Kübler-Ross' second stage of dying, in which the dying person's denial gives way to anger, resentment, rage, and envy.

Knowledge of death's inevitability permits us to establish priorities and structure our time accordingly. As we age, these priorities and structurings change in recognition of diminishing future time. Values concerning the most important uses of time also change. For example, when asked how they would spend their six remaining months of life, younger adults described such activities as traveling and accomplishing things they previously had not done; older adults described more inner-focused activities—contemplation and meditation, for example (Kalish & Reynolds, 1976).

602   CHAPTER 20   Death, Dying, and Grieving

Most dying individuals want an opportunity to make some decisions regarding their own life and death (Kastenbaum, 2012). Some individuals want to complete unfinished business; they want time to resolve problems and conflicts and to put their affairs in order.

One study examined the concerns of 36 dying individuals from 38 to 92 years of age with a mean age of 68 (Terry & others, 2006). The three areas of concern that consistently appeared were (1) privacy and autonomy, mainly in regard to their families; (2) inadequate information about physical changes and medication as they approached death; and (3) the motivation to shorten their life, which was indicated by all patients.

KÜBLER-ROSS' STAGES OF DYING

Might there be a sequence of stages we go through as we face death? Elisabeth Kübler-Ross (1969) divided the behavior and thinking of dying persons into five stages: denial and isolation, anger, bargaining, depression, and acceptance.

Denial and isolation is Kübler-Ross' first stage of dying, in which the person denies that death is really going to take place. The person may say, "No, it can't be me. It's not possible." This is a common reaction to terminal illness. However, denial is usually only a temporary defense. It is eventually replaced with increased awareness when the person is confronted with such matters as financial considerations, unfinished business, and worry about surviving family members.

Anger is Kübler-Ross' second stage of dying, in which the dying person recognizes that denial can no longer be maintained. Denial often gives way to anger, resentment, rage, and envy. The dying person's question is, "Why me?" At this point, the person becomes increasingly difficult to care for as anger may become displaced and projected onto physicians, nurses, family members, and even God. The realization of loss is great, and those who symbolize life, energy, and competent functioning are especially salient targets of the dying person's resentment and jealousy.

Bargaining is Kübler-Ross' third stage of dying, in which the person develops the hope that death can somehow be postponed or delayed. Some persons enter into a bargaining or negotiation—often with God—as they try to delay their death. Psychologically, the person is saying, "Yes, me, but . . ." In exchange for a few more days, weeks, or months of life, the person promises to lead a reformed life dedicated to God or to the service of others.

Depression is Kübler-Ross' fourth stage of dying, in which the dying person comes to accept the certainty of death. At this point, a period of depression or preparatory grief may appear. The dying person may become silent, refuse visitors, and spend much of the time crying or grieving. This behavior is normal and is an effort to disconnect the self from love objects. Attempts to cheer up the dying person at this stage should be discouraged, says Kübler-Ross, because the dying person has a need to contemplate impending death.

Acceptance is Kübler-Ross' fifth stage of dying, in which the person develops a sense of peace, an acceptance of his or her fate, and in many cases, a desire to be left alone. In this stage, feelings and physical pain may be virtually absent. Kübler-Ross describes this fifth stage as the end of the dying struggle, the final resting stage before death. A summary of Kübler-Ross' dying stages is presented in Figure 20.2.

What is the current evaluation of Kübler-Ross' theory? According to Robert Kastenbaum (2009, 2012), there are some problems with Kübler-Ross' approach:

- The existence of the five-stage sequence has not been demonstrated by either Kübler-Ross or independent research.
- The stage interpretation neglected the patients' situations, including relationship support, specific effects of illness, family obligations, and institutional climate in which they were interviewed.

However, Kübler-Ross' pioneering efforts were important in calling attention to those who are attempting to cope with life-threatening illnesses. She did much to encourage attention to the quality of life for dying persons and their families.

Because of the criticisms of Kübler-Ross' stages, some psychologists prefer to describe them not as stages but as potential reactions to dying. At any one moment, a number of emotions may wax and wane. Hope, disbelief, bewilderment, anger, and acceptance may

Sustained and soothed by an unfaltering trust, approach thy grave,
Like one who wraps the drapery of his couch
About him, and lies down to pleasant dreams.

—WILLIAM CULLEN BRYANT
American Poet, 19th Century

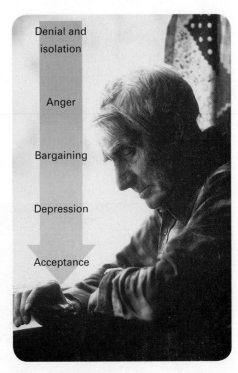

FIGURE **20.2**

KÜBLER-ROSS' STAGES OF DYING. According to Elisabeth Kübler-Ross, we go through five stages of dying: denial and isolation, anger, bargaining, depression, and acceptance. *Does everyone go through these stages, and do we go through them in the same order? Explain.*

bargaining Kübler-Ross' third stage of dying, in which the dying person develops the hope that death can somehow be postponed.

depression Kübler-Ross' fourth stage of dying, in which the dying person comes to accept the certainty of her or his death. A period of depression or preparatory grief may appear.

acceptance Kübler-Ross' fifth stage of dying, in which the dying person develops a sense of peace, an acceptance of her or his fate, and, in many cases, a desire to be left alone.

developmental connection

Religion

Religion can fulfill some important psychological needs in older adults, helping them face impending death and accept the inevitable losses in old age. Chapter 18, p. 563

Man is the only animal that finds his own existence a problem he has to solve and from which he cannot escape. In the same sense man is the only animal who knows he must die.

—ERICH FROMM
American Psychotherapist, 20th Century

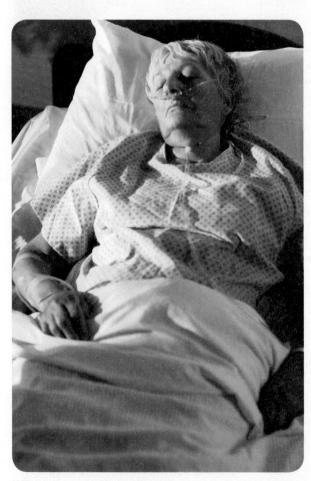

What are some positive and negative aspects of dying at home compared with dying in a hospital?

come and go as individuals try to make sense of what is happening to them (Renz & others, 2013).

In facing their own death, some individuals struggle until the end, desperately trying to hang on to their lives. Acceptance of death never comes for them. Some psychologists believe that the harder individuals fight to avoid the inevitable death they face and the more they deny it, the more difficulty they will have in dying peacefully and in a dignified way; other psychologists argue that not confronting death until the end may be adaptive for some individuals (Lifton, 1977).

The extent to which people have found meaning and purpose in their lives is linked with how they approach death (Dokken, 2013; Park, 2012). One study revealed that individuals with a chronic, life-threatening illness—congestive heart failure—were trying to find meaning in life (Park & others, 2008). In another study, individuals with less than three months to live who had found purpose and meaning in their lives felt the least despair in the final weeks, whereas dying individuals who saw no reason for living were the most distressed and wanted to hasten death (McClain, Rosenfeld, & Breitbart, 2003). In this and other studies, spirituality helped to buffer dying individuals from severe depression (Smith, McCullough, & Poll, 2003).

Do individuals become more spiritual as they get closer to death? A study of more than 100 patients with advanced congestive heart failure who were studied at two times six months apart found that as the patients perceived they were closer to death, they became more spiritual (Park, 2009).

PERCEIVED CONTROL AND DENIAL

Perceived control may work as an adaptive strategy for some older adults who face death. When individuals are led to believe they can influence and control events—such as prolonging their lives—they may become more alert and cheerful. Remember from Chapter 17 that giving nursing home residents options for control improved their attitudes and increased their longevity (Rodin & Langer, 1977).

Denial also may be a fruitful way for some individuals to approach death. It can be adaptive or maladaptive. Denial can be used to avoid the destructive impact of shock by delaying the necessity of dealing with one's death. Denial can insulate the individual from having to cope with intense feelings of anger and hurt; however, if denial keeps us from having a life-saving operation, it clearly is maladaptive. Denial is neither good nor bad; its adaptive qualities need to be evaluated on an individual basis.

THE CONTEXTS IN WHICH PEOPLE DIE

For dying individuals, the context in which they die is important (Hooyman & Kiyak, 2011). More than 50 percent of Americans die in hospitals and nearly 20 percent die in nursing homes. Some people spend their final days in isolation and fear (Clay, 1997). An increasing number of people choose to die in the humane atmosphere of a hospice. A recent Canadian study found that 71 percent of adults preferred to be at home if they were near death, 15 percent preferred to be in a hospice/palliative care facility, 7 percent preferred to be in a hospital, and only 2 percent preferred to be in a nursing home (Wilson & others, 2013).

Hospitals offer several important advantages to the dying individual; for example, professional staff members are readily available, and the medical technology present may prolong life. But a hospital may not be the best place for many people to die (Pantilat & Isaac, 2008). Most individuals say they would rather die at home (Jack & others, 2013; Jackson & others, 2010). Many feel, however, that they will be a burden at home, that there is limited space there, and that dying at home may alter relationships. Individuals who are facing death also worry about the competency of caregivers and availability of emergency medical treatment if they remain at home.

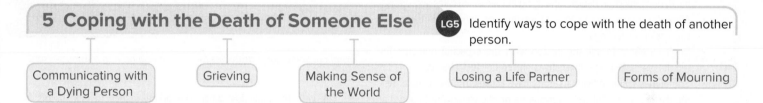

5 Coping with the Death of Someone Else **LG5** Identify ways to cope with the death of another person.

Communicating with a Dying Person | Grieving | Making Sense of the World | Losing a Life Partner | Forms of Mourning

Loss can come in many forms in our lives—divorce, a pet's death, loss of a job—but no loss is greater than that which comes through the death of someone we love and care for—a parent, sibling, spouse, relative, or friend. In the ratings of life's stresses that require the most adjustment, death of a spouse is given the highest number. How should we communicate with a dying individual? How do we cope with the death of someone we love?

COMMUNICATING WITH A DYING PERSON

Most psychologists argue that it is best for dying individuals to know that they are dying and that significant others know they are dying so they can interact and communicate with each other on the basis of this mutual knowledge (Banja, 2005). What are some of the advantages of this open awareness for the dying individual? First, dying individuals can close their lives in accord with their own ideas about proper dying. Second, they may be able to complete some plans and projects, can make arrangements for survivors, and can participate in decisions about a funeral and burial. Third, dying individuals have the opportunity to reminisce and to converse with people who have been important to them. And fourth, individuals who know they are dying have more understanding of what is happening within their bodies and what the medical staff is doing for them (Kalish, 1981).

In addition to keeping communication open, some experts reason that conversation should not focus on mental pathology or preparation for death but should focus on strengths of the individual and preparation for the remainder of life. Since external accomplishments are not possible, communication should be directed toward internal growth. Keep in mind also that important support for a dying individual may come not only from mental health professionals but also from nurses, physicians, a spouse, or intimate friends. In *Connecting Development to Life,* you can read further about effective ways to communicate with a dying person.

GRIEVING

Our exploration of grief focuses on dimensions of grieving, the dual-process model of coping with bereavement, and cultural diversity in healthy grieving.

connecting development to life

Effective Strategies for Communicating with a Dying Person

Effective strategies for communicating with a dying person include the following suggestions:

- Establish your presence, be at the same eye level; don't be afraid to touch the dying person—dying individuals are often starved for human touch.
- Eliminate distraction—for example, ask if it is okay to turn off the TV. Realize that excessive small talk can be a distraction.
- Dying individuals who are very frail often have little energy. If the dying person you are visiting is very frail, you may not want to visit for very long.
- Don't insist that the dying person feel acceptance about death if the dying person wants to deny the reality of the situation; on the other hand, don't insist on denial if the dying individual indicates acceptance.
- Allow the dying person to express guilt or anger; encourage the expression of feelings.
- Don't be afraid to ask the person what the expected outcome for the illness is. Discuss alternatives and unfinished business.
- Sometimes dying individuals don't have access to other people. Ask the dying person if there is anyone he or she would like to see that you can contact.
- Encourage the dying individual to reminisce, especially if you have memories in common.

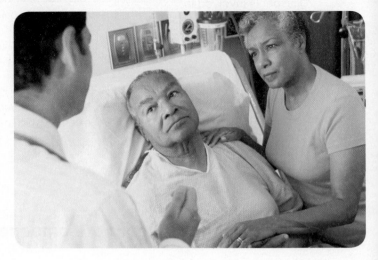

What are some good strategies for communicating with a dying person?

- Talk with the individual when she or he wishes to talk. If this is impossible, make an appointment and keep it.
- Express your regard for the dying individual. Don't be afraid to express love, and don't be afraid to say good-bye.

> Everyone can master grief
> but he who has it.
>
> —**WILLIAM SHAKESPEARE**
> *English Playwright, 17th Century*

grief The emotional numbness, disbelief, separation anxiety, despair, sadness, and loneliness that accompany the loss of someone we love.

Dimensions of Grieving **Grief** is the emotional numbness, disbelief, separation anxiety, despair, sadness, and loneliness that accompany the loss of someone we love. Grief is not a simple emotional state but rather a complex, evolving process with multiple dimensions (Barbosa, Sa, & Carlos-Roche, 2014; Romero, Ott, & Kelber, 2014). In this view, pining for the lost person is one important dimension. Pining or yearning reflects an intermittent, recurrent wish or need to recover the lost person. Another important dimension of grief is separation anxiety, which not only includes pining and preoccupation with thoughts of the deceased person but also focuses on places and things associated with the deceased, as well as crying or sighing (Root & Exline, 2014). Grief may also involve despair and sadness, which include a sense of hopelessness and defeat, depressive symptoms, apathy, loss of meaning for activities that used to involve the person who is gone, and growing desolation (Shear & Skritskaya, 2012).

These feelings occur repeatedly shortly after a loss (Shear, 2012a, b). As time passes, pining and protest over the loss tend to diminish, although episodes of depression and apathy may remain or increase. The sense of separation anxiety and loss may continue to the end of one's life, but most of us emerge from grief's tears, turning our attention once again to productive tasks and regaining a more positive view of life. The grieving process is more like a roller-coaster ride than an orderly progression of stages with clear-cut time frames. The ups and downs of grief often involve rapidly changing emotions, meeting the challenges of learning new skills, detecting personal weaknesses and limitations, creating new patterns of behavior, and forming new friendships and relationships (Feldon, 2003). For most individuals, grief becomes more manageable over time, with fewer abrupt highs and lows. But many grieving spouses report that even though time has brought some healing, they have never gotten over their loss. They have just learned to live with it. A recent study found that individuals in the early stages of spousal bereavement are at increased risk for distress in situations with special significance for the couple, such as the late spouse's birthday or a wedding anniversary (Carr & others, 2014).

Long-term grief is sometimes masked and can predispose individuals to become depressed and even suicidal (Miller, 2012). A recent study found that older adults who were bereaved had more dysregulated cortisol patterns, indicative of the intensity of their stress (Holland & others, 2014). Good family communication can help reduce the incidence of depression and suicidal thoughts. An estimated 80 to 90 percent of survivors experience normal or uncomplicated grief reactions that include sadness and even disbelief or considerable anguish. By six months after their loss, they accept it as a reality, are more optimistic about the future, and function competently in their everyday lives.

However, even six months after their loss, some individuals have difficulty moving on with their life, feeling numb or detached, believing their life is empty without the deceased, and feeling that the future has no meaning. This type of grief reaction has been referred to as *prolonged or complicated grief* (Herberman Mash, Fullerton, & Ursano, 2013; Prigerson & Maciejewski, 2014; Prigerson & others, 2011). It is estimated that approximately 7 to 10 percent of bereaved individuals have this prolonged or complicated grief (Maccalum & Bryant, 2013; Shear, Ghesquiere, & Glickman, 2013). Recently, this type of prolonged grief in which feelings of despair remain unresolved over an extended period of time has been labeled *complicated grief* or **prolonged grief disorder.** Complicated grief usually has negative consequences on physical and mental health (Marques & others, 2013). A person who loses someone on whom he or she was emotionally dependent is often at greatest risk for developing prolonged grief (Rodriquez Villar & others, 2012).

Complicated grief or prolonged grief disorder was recently considered for possible inclusion in DSM-V, the psychiatric classification system for mental health disorders (Bryant, 2012, 2013). Although it ended up not being included as a psychiatric disorder, it was described in an Appendix (American Psychiatric Association, 2013). The argument for not including complicated grief or prolonged grief as a psychiatric disorder was based on concerns that normal grieving would be turned into a medical condition.

Recently, there has been a substantial increase in research on complicated or prolonged grief (Hottensen, 2013; Supiano & Luptak, 2014). The following studies provide further information about this topic:

- Prolonged grief was more likely to occur when individuals had lost their spouse, lost a loved one unexpectedly, or spent time with the deceased every day in the last week of the person's life (Fujisawa & others, 2010).
- Adults with depression were more likely to also have complicated grief (Sung & others, 2011).
- Complicated grief was more likely to be present in older adults when the grief was in response to the death of a child or a spouse (Newsom & others, 2011).

Another type of grief is *disenfranchised grief,* which describes an individual's grief over a deceased person that is a socially ambiguous loss that can't be openly mourned or supported (Gill & Lowes, 2014; Spidell & others, 2011). Examples of disenfranchised grief include a relationship that isn't socially recognized such as an ex-spouse, a hidden loss such as an abortion, and circumstances of the death that are stigmatized such as death because of AIDS. Disenfranchised grief may intensify an individual's grief because the feelings cannot be publicly acknowledged. This type of grief may be hidden or repressed for many years, only to be reawakened by later deaths.

A death can sometimes bring out the best in people as they provide support and caring for the grieving person, or in some cases, a death can bring out the worst in people (Lightner & Hathaway, 1990). When death brings out the best, mourners feel recognized and consoled, touched by others' sympathy, and shored up by their kindness. Consider Jennifer Block's experience. After her husband died, her best friend encouraged her to get out and do things. The friend called Jennifer every day and took her out for ice cream, on walks, and to community events. Jennifer says that she will never forget her friend's support and caring.

Sometimes, however, friends may say and do the wrong things when someone dies (Lightner & Hathaway, 1990). Their grieving friend may feel slighted, insulted, disappointed, and alone when this happens. Perhaps a friend disappears from sight or makes an inappropriate or cruel

prolonged grief disorder Grief that involves enduring despair and remains unresolved over an extended period of time.

remark, such as "I thought you two were not getting along that well anyway." Consider Martha Cooper's experience. When her husband died, her friend told her to forget that part of her life because it was over. Martha was terribly disappointed at her friend's lack of empathy. As Martha remarked, you can't just forget about someone who was a part of your life for 45 years.

Dual-Process Model of Coping with Bereavement   The **dual-process model** of coping with bereavement has two main dimensions: (1) loss-oriented stressors, and (2) restoration-oriented stressors (Stroebe & Schut, 2010; Stroebe, Schut, & Boerner, 2010). Loss-oriented stressors focus on the deceased individual and can include grief work and both positive and negative reappraisals of the loss. A positive reappraisal of the loss might include acknowledging that death brought relief at the end of suffering, whereas a negative reappraisal might involve yearning for the loved one and ruminating about the death. Restoration-oriented stressors involve the secondary stressors that emerge as indirect outcomes of bereavement (Caserta & others, 2014). They can include a changing identity (such as from "wife" to "widow") and mastering skills (such as dealing with finances). Restoration rebuilds "shattered assumptions about the world and one's own place in it."

In the dual-process model, effective coping with bereavement often involves an oscillation between coping with loss and coping with restoration (Bennett, 2009; Shear, 2010). Earlier models often emphasized a sequence of coping with loss through such strategies as grief work as an initial phase, followed by restoration efforts. However, in the dual-process model, coping with loss and engaging in restoration can be carried out concurrently (Richardson, 2007). According to this model, the person coping with death might be involved in grief group therapy while settling the affairs of the loved one. Oscillation might occur in the short term during a particular day as well as across weeks, months, and even years. Although loss and restoration coping can occur concurrently, over time there often is an initial emphasis on coping with loss followed by greater emphasis on restoration (Milberg & others, 2008).

Coping and Type of Death   The impact of death on surviving individuals is strongly influenced by the circumstances under which the death occurred (Gold, 2011; Kristensen, Weisaeth, & Heir, 2012). Deaths that are sudden, untimely, violent, or traumatic are likely to have more intense and prolonged effects on surviving individuals and make the coping process more difficult for them (Maercker & Laior, 2012). Such deaths often are accompanied by post-traumatic stress disorder (PTSD) symptoms, such as intrusive thoughts, flashbacks, nightmares, sleep disturbance, problems in concentrating, and other difficulties (Nakajima & others, 2012). The death of a child can be especially devastating and extremely difficult for parents to cope with (Caeymaex & others, 2013; Lang & others, 2011).

Cultural Diversity in Healthy Grieving   Some approaches to grieving emphasize the importance of breaking bonds with the deceased and returning to autonomous lifestyles. People who persist in holding on to the deceased are believed to be in need of therapy. However, some doubt has been cast on whether this recommendation to break bonds is always the best therapeutic advice (Reisman, 2001).

Analyses of non-Western cultures suggest that beliefs about maintaining bonds with the deceased vary extensively. Maintenance of ties with the deceased is accepted and sustained in the religious rituals of Japan. Among the Hopi of Arizona, the deceased are forgotten as quickly as possible and life is carried on as usual. Their funeral ritual concludes with a break-off between mortals and spirits. The diversity of grieving is nowhere more clear than in two Muslim societies—one in Egypt, the other in Bali. In Egypt, the bereaved are encouraged to dwell at length on their grief, surrounded by others who relate similarly tragic accounts and express their own sorrow. By contrast, in Bali, the bereaved are encouraged to laugh and be joyful.

In sum, people grieve in a variety of ways (Bryant, 2012, 2013). The diverse grieving patterns are culturally embedded practices. Thus, there is no one right, ideal way to grieve. There are many different ways to feel about a deceased person and no set series of stages that the bereaved must pass through to become well adjusted. The stoic widower may need to cry out over his loss at times. The weeping widow may need to put her husband's wishes

How might grieving vary across individuals and cultures?

dual-process model A model of coping with bereavement that emphasizes oscillation between two dimensions: (1) loss-oriented stressors, and (2) restoration-oriented stressors.

aside as she becomes the financial manager of her estate. What is needed is an understanding that healthy coping with the death of a loved one involves growth, flexibility, and appropriateness within a cultural context.

MAKING SENSE OF THE WORLD

Not only do many individuals who face death search for meaning in life, so do many bereaved individuals (Carr, 2009; Park, 2010, 2012). One beneficial aspect of grieving is that it can stimulate people to try to make sense of their world (Alves & others, 2014). A common occurrence is to go over again and again all of the events that led up to the death. In the days and weeks after the death, the closest family members share experiences with each other, sometimes reminiscing over family experiences. In one study, women who became widowed in midlife were challenged by the crisis of their husband's death to examine meaningful directions for their lives (Danforth & Glass, 2001). Another study found that mourners who expressed positive themes of hope showed better adjustment than those who focused on negative themes of pain and suffering (Gamino & Sewell, 2004). And one study revealed that finding meaning in the death of a spouse was linked to a lower level of anger during bereavement (Kim, 2009).

When a death is caused by an accident or a disaster, the effort to make sense of it is pursued more vigorously. As added pieces of news come trickling in, they are integrated into the puzzle. The bereaved want to put the death into a perspective that they can understand—divine intervention, a curse from a neighboring tribe, a logical sequence of cause and effect, or whatever it may be. A study of more than 1,000 college students found that making sense was an important factor in their grieving of a violent loss by accident, homicide, or suicide (Currier, Holland, & Neimeyer, 2006).

These restaurant workers, who lost their jobs on 9/11/01, have made a bittersweet return by establishing a New York restaurant they call their own. Colors, named for the many nationalities and ethnic groups among its owners, is believed to be the city's first cooperative restaurant. World-famous restaurant Windows on the World was destroyed and 73 workers killed when the Twin Towers were destroyed by terrorists. The former Windows survivors at the new venture planned to split 60 percent of the profits between themselves and to donate the rest to a fund to open other cooperative restaurants.

LOSING A LIFE PARTNER

In 2010 in the United States, 13 percent of men and 40 percent of women age 65 and older were widowed (U.S. Census Bureau, 2012). Those left behind after the death of an intimate partner often suffer profound grief and often endure financial loss, loneliness, increased physical illness, and psychological disorders, including depression (Das, 2013; Lee, 2014; Naef & others, 2013). A study of widowed individuals 75 years and older found that loss of a spouse increases the likelihood of psychiatric visits and an earlier death (Moller & others, 2011). In another study, becoming widowed was associated with a 48 percent increase in risk of mortality (Sullivan & Fenelon, 2014). In this study, mortality risk increased for men if their wives' deaths were not expected but for women unexpected death of a husband mattered less in terms of their mortality risk. A recent study also revealed that widowed individuals who reported higher marital quality subsequently had more symptoms of depression after their spouse died (Schaan, 2013). In another recent study, widowed individuals, especially those in age-heterogamous unions (those comprising people of significantly different ages), had worse mental health than married persons but not worse physical health (Choi & Vasunilashorn, 2014).

Surviving spouses seek to cope with the loss of their spouse in various ways (Moss & Moss, 2014; Park, 2012). In one study, widowed individuals were more likely to intensify their religious and spiritual beliefs following the death of a spouse, and this increase was linked with a lower level of grief (Brown & others, 2004). Another study revealed that finding meaning in the death of a spouse was linked to a lower level of anger during bereavement (Kim, 2009). And a recent study revealed that widowed persons who did not expect to be reunited with their loved ones in the afterlife reported more depression, anger, and intrusive thoughts at 6 and 18 months after their loss (Carr & Sharp, 2014).

Many widows are lonely and benefit considerably from social support (de Vries & others, 2014; Utz, Caserta, & Lund, 2012). The poorer and less educated they are, the lonelier they tend to be. The bereaved are also at increased risk for many health problems (Mechakra-Tahiri & others, 2010). How might you expect widowhood to affect a woman's physical and mental health, for instance? The *Connecting Through Research* interlude examines how researchers have investigated the links between bereavement and health.

developmental **connection**

Stress

Meaning-making coping involves drawing on beliefs, values, and goals to change the meaning of a stressful situation, especially in times of chronic stress such as when a loved one dies. Chapter 15, p. 478

A widow with the photo of her husband who was recently killed in Afghanistan. *What are some factors that are related to the adjustment of a widow after the death of her husband?*

What Are Some Connections Between Marital Status and Length of Widowhood and Health in Women?

One three-year longitudinal study of more than 130,000 women aged 50 to 79 years in the United States as part of the Women's Health Initiative examined the effects of widowhood on physical and mental health, health behaviors, and health outcomes (Wilcox & others, 2003). Women were categorized as (1) remaining married, (2) transitioning from married to widowed, (3) remaining widowed, and (4) transitioning from widowed to married. Widows were further subdivided into the recently widowed (widowed for less than one year) and longer-term widowed (widowed for more than one year).

The following measures were used to assess the women's health:

- *Physical health.* Blood pressure was assessed after five minutes of quiet rest using the average of two readings with 30 seconds between the readings. Hypertension was defined as more than 140/90. Body mass index (BMI) was calculated and used to determine whether a woman was obese. A health survey assessed physical function and health status.
- *Mental health.* Depressive symptoms were assessed using a six-item depression scale, with participants rating the frequency of their depressed thoughts during the past week. The participants' self-report of antidepressant medicine use was also obtained. Information about social functioning and mental health was based on participants' responses on the Social Functioning Scale (Ware, Kosinski, & Dewey, 2000).

- *Health behaviors.* Dietary behaviors were assessed with a modified version of the National Cancer Institute—Health Habits and History Questionnaire. Participants also were asked if they smoked tobacco, and if so, how much. To assess physical activity, participants were asked how often they walked outside the home each week and the extent to which they engaged in strenuous or moderate exercise. To assess health care use, they were asked whether they had visited their doctor in the past year.
- *Health outcomes.* Cardiovascular disease and cancer occurrences were assessed annually and any overnight hospitalizations were noted.

At the beginning of the three-year study, married women reported better physical and mental health, and better health in general, than widowed women. Women who remained married over the three-year period of the study showed stability in mental health, recent widows experienced marked impairments in mental health, and longer-term widows showed stability or slight improvements in mental health. Both groups of widows (recent and longer-term) reported more unintentional weight loss across the three years.

The findings underscore the resilience of older women and their capacity to reestablish connections but also point to the need for services that strengthen social support for those who have difficulty making the transition from marriage to widowhood.

developmental **connection**

Community and Culture

For older adults, social support is linked with a reduction in the symptoms of disease and increased longevity. Chapter 19, p. 584

developmental **connection**

Religion

Religious participation is positively linked to health and longevity. Chapter 15, p. 478

Optimal adjustment after a death depends on several factors. A recent study found no differences between women and men in terms of bereavement effects on depressive symptoms (Sasson & Umberson, 2014). In this study, early long-term widowhood was associated with worse outcomes than late widowhood.

For both widows and widowers, social support helps them adjust to the death of a spouse (Antonucci, Birditt, & Ajrouch, 2013). The Widow-to-Widow program, begun in the 1960s, provides support for newly widowed women. Volunteer widows reach out to other widows, introducing them to others who may have similar problems, leading group discussions, and organizing social activities. The program has been adopted by the AARP and disseminated throughout the United States as the Widowed Persons Service. The model has since been adopted by numerous community organizations to provide support for those going through a difficult transition. Other widow support groups also are often beneficial in reducing bereaved spouses' depression (Maruyama & Atencio, 2008).

Researchers have found that religiosity and coping skills are related to well-being following the loss of a spouse in late adulthood (Leighton, 2008). Further, one study revealed that compared with continually married counterparts, adults aged 50 and older who experienced the death of a spouse reported a higher participation in volunteer work several years after the death (Li, 2007). The volunteer work helped to protect the spouses from depressive symptoms, and an increase in volunteer hours enhanced their self-efficacy. Another study also found that when older adults helped others following the death of a spouse, they experienced an accelerated decline in depressive symptoms (Brown & others, 2008).

(*Left*) A widow leading a funeral procession in the United States. (*Right*) A crowd gathered at a cremation ceremony in Bali, Indonesia, balancing decorative containers on their heads.

FORMS OF MOURNING

One decision facing the bereaved is what to do with the body. In the United States, in 2012, 42 percent of deaths were followed by cremation—a significant increase from a cremation rate of 14 percent in 1985 and 27 percent in 2000 (Cremation Association of North America, 2012). Based on current trends, the cremation percentage in the United States is expected to reach 60 percent in 2015. Cremation is more popular in the Pacific region of the United States, less popular in the South. Cremation also is more popular in Canada than in the United States and most popular of all in Japan and many other Asian countries.

The funeral is an important aspect of mourning in many cultures. In the United States, the trend is away from public funerals and displaying the dead body in an open casket and toward private funerals followed by a memorial ceremony (Callahan, 2009).

The funeral industry in the United States has been a focus of controversy in recent years. Funeral directors and their supporters argue that the funeral provides a form of closure to the relationship with the deceased, especially when there is an open casket. Their critics claim that funeral directors are just trying to make money and that embalming is grotesque. One way to avoid being exploited during bereavement is to purchase funeral arrangements in advance. However, in one survey only 24 percent of individuals 60 years of age and over had made any funeral arrangements (Kalish & Reynolds, 1976).

In some cultures, a ceremonial meal is shared after a death; in others, a black armband is worn by bereaved family members for one year following a death. Cultures vary in how they practice mourning. Two of those cultures are the Amish and traditional Judaism (Worthington, 1989).

The Amish are a conservative group with approximately 80,000 members in the United States, Ontario, and several small settlements in South and Central America. The Amish live in a family-oriented society in which family and community support are essential for survival. Today, they live at the same unhurried pace as that of their ancestors, using horses instead of cars and facing death with the same steadfast faith as their forebears. At the time of death, close neighbors assume the responsibility of notifying others of the death. The Amish community handles virtually all aspects of the funeral.

The funeral service is held in a barn in the warmer months and in a house during colder months. Calm acceptance of death, influenced by a deep religious faith, is an integral part of the Amish culture. Following the funeral, a high level of support is given to the bereaved family for at least a year. Visits to the family, special scrapbooks and handmade items for family members, new work projects started for the widow, and quilting days that combine fellowship and productivity are among the supports given to the bereaved

(*Top*) A funeral procession of horse-drawn buggies on their way to the burial of five young Amish girls who were murdered in October 2006. A remarkable aspect of their mourning involved the outpouring of support and forgiveness they gave to the widow of the murderer. (*Bottom*) Meeting in a Jewish graveyard.

family. A profound example of the Amish culture's religious faith and acceptance of death occurred after Charles Roberts shot and killed five Amish schoolgirls and then apparently took his own life in October 2006 in Bart Township, Pennsylvania. Soon after the murders and suicide, members of the Amish community visited his widow and offered their support and forgiveness.

The family and community also have specific and important roles in mourning in traditional Judaism. The program of mourning is divided into graduated time periods, each with its appropriate practices. The observance of these practices is required of the spouse and the immediate blood relatives of the deceased. The first period is aninut, the period between death and burial. The next two periods make up avelut, or mourning proper. The first of these is shivah, a period of seven days, which commences with the burial. It is followed by sheloshim, the 30-day period following the burial, including shivah. At the end of sheloshim, the mourning process is considered over for all but one's parents. For parents, mourning continues for 11 months, although observances are minimal.

The seven-day period of the shivah is especially important in traditional Judaism. The mourners, sitting together as a group through an extended period, have an opportunity to project their feelings to the group as a whole. Visits from others during shivah may help the mourners deal with feelings of guilt. After shivah, the mourners are encouraged to resume normal social interaction. In fact, it is customary for the mourners to walk together a short distance as a symbol of their return to society. In its entirety, the elaborate mourning system of traditional Judaism is designed to promote personal growth and to reintegrate bereaved individuals into the community.

Review Connect Reflect

 LG5 Identify ways to cope with the death of another person.

Review

- What are some strategies for communicating with a dying person?
- What is the nature of grieving?
- How is making sense of the world a beneficial outcome of grieving?
- What are some characteristics and outcomes of losing a life partner?
- What are some forms of mourning? What is the nature of the funeral?

Connect

- In this section, we learned that one advantage of knowing you are dying is

that you have the opportunity to reminisce. Which of Erikson's stages of development involves reflecting on the past and either piecing together a positive review or concluding that one's life has not been well spent?

Reflect Your Own Personal Journey of Life

- What are considered appropriate forms of mourning in the culture in which you live?

topical **connections** *looking back*

We have arrived at the end of this book. I hope this book and course have been a window to the life span of the human species and a window to your own personal journey in life.

Our study of the human life span has been long and complex. You have read about many physical, cognitive, and socioemotional changes that take place from conception through death. This is a good time to reflect on what you have learned. Which theories, studies, and ideas were especially interesting to you? What did you learn about your own development?

I wish you all the best in the remaining years of your journey through the human life span.

John W. Santrock

reach your **learning goals**

Death, Dying, and Grieving

1 The Death System and Cultural Contexts

 Describe the death system and its cultural and historical contexts.

The Death System and Its Cultural Variations

Changing Historical Circumstances

- In Kastenbaum's view, every culture has a death system that involves these components: people, places, times, objects, and symbols. Most cultures do not view death as the end of existence—spiritual life is thought to continue. Most societies throughout history have had philosophical or religious beliefs about death, and most societies have rituals that deal with death. The United States has been described as more of a death-denying and death-avoiding culture than most cultures.

- When, where, and why people die have changed historically. Today, death occurs most often among older adults. More than 80 percent of all deaths in the United States now occur in a hospital or other institution; our exposure to death in the family has been minimized.

2 Defining Death and Life/Death Issues

 Evaluate issues in determining death and decisions regarding death.

Issues in Determining Death

Decisions Regarding Life, Death, and Health Care

- Twenty-five years ago, determining whether someone was dead was simpler than it is today. Brain death is a neurological definition of death which states that a person is brain dead when all electrical activity of the brain has ceased for a specified period of time. Medical experts debate whether this should include the higher and lower brain functions or just the higher cortical functions. Currently, most physicians define brain death as the death of both the higher cortical functions and the lower brain stem functions.

- Decisions regarding life, death, and health care can involve whether to create a living will, to consider the possibility of euthanasia, and to arrange for hospice care. Living wills and advance directives are increasingly used. Euthanasia ("mercy killing") is the act of painlessly ending the life of a person who is suffering from an incurable disease or disability. Distinctions are made between active and passive euthanasia. Hospice care emphasizes reducing pain and suffering rather than prolonging life.

3 A Developmental Perspective on Death

 Discuss death and attitudes about it at different points in development.

Causes of Death

Attitudes Toward Death at Different Points in the Life Span

- Although death is more likely to occur in late adulthood, death can come at any point in development. In children and younger adults, death is more likely to occur because of accidents or illness; in older adults, death is more likely to occur because of chronic diseases such as heart disease or cancer.

- Infants do not have a concept of death. Preschool children also have little concept of death. Preschool children sometimes blame themselves for a person's death. In the elementary school years, children develop a more realistic orientation toward death. Most psychologists argue that honesty is the best strategy for helping children cope with death. Death may be glossed over in adolescence. Adolescents have more abstract, philosophical views of death than children do. Recent research indicates that rather than perceiving themselves as invulnerable, many adolescents believe they are likely to experience an early death. There is no evidence that a special orientation toward death emerges in early adulthood. Middle adulthood is a time when adults show a heightened consciousness about death and death anxiety. Older adults often show less death anxiety than middle-aged adults, but older adults experience and converse about death more. Attitudes about death may vary considerably among adults of any age.

4 Facing One's Own Death

 LG4 Explain the psychological aspects involved in facing one's own death and the contexts in which people die.

Kubler-Ross' Stages of Dying

Perceived Control and Denial

The Contexts in Which People Die

- Kübler-Ross proposed five stages of dying: denial and isolation, anger, bargaining, depression, and acceptance. Not all individuals go through the same sequence.

- Perceived control and denial may work together as an adaptive orientation for the dying individual. Denial can be adaptive or maladaptive, depending on the circumstances.

- The fact that most deaths in the United States occur in hospitals has advantages and disadvantages. Most individuals say they would rather die at home, but they are concerned that they will be a burden to family members and they worry about the lack of medical care.

5 Coping with the Death of Someone Else

 LG5 Identify ways to cope with the death of another person.

Communicating with a Dying Person

Grieving

Making Sense of the World

Losing a Life Partner

Forms of Mourning

- Most psychologists recommend an open communication system with the dying. Communication should not dwell on mental pathology or preparation for death but should emphasize the dying person's strengths.

- Grief is the emotional numbness, disbelief, separation anxiety, despair, sadness, and loneliness that accompany the loss of someone we love. Grief is multidimensional and in some cases may last for years. Prolonged grief involves enduring despair that is still unresolved after an extended period of time. In the dual-process model of coping with bereavement, oscillation occurs between two dimensions: (1) loss-oriented stressors, and (2) restoration-oriented stressors. Grief and coping vary with the type of death. There are cultural variations in grieving.

- The grieving process may stimulate individuals to strive to make sense out of their world. When a death is caused by an accident or disaster, the effort to make sense of it is pursued more vigorously.

- The death of an intimate partner often leads to profound grief. The bereaved are at risk for many health problems, although there are variations in the distress experienced by a surviving spouse. Social support benefits widows and widowers.

- Forms of mourning vary across cultures. Approximately two-thirds of corpses are disposed of by burial, one-third by cremation. An important aspect of mourning in many cultures is the funeral. In recent years, the funeral industry has been the focus of controversy. In some cultures, a ceremonial meal is shared after death.

key **terms**

brain death 597
euthanasia 598
passive euthanasia 598
active euthanasia 598

hospice 599
palliative care 599
denial and isolation 602
anger 602

bargaining 603
depression 603
acceptance 603
grief 606

prolonged grief disorder 607
dual-process model 608

key **people**

Robert Kastenbaum 595

Elisabeth Kübler-Ross 603

glossary

A

acceptance Kübler-Ross' fifth stage of dying, in which the dying person develops a sense of peace, an acceptance of her or his fate, and, in many cases, a desire to be left alone.

accommodation Piagetian concept of adjusting schemes to fit new information and experiences.

active euthanasia Death induced deliberately, as by injecting a lethal dose of a drug.

active (niche-picking) genotype-environment correlations Correlations that exist when children seek out environments they find compatible and stimulating.

activity theory The theory that the more active and involved older adults are, the more likely they are to be satisfied with their lives.

addiction A pattern of behavior characterized by an overwhelming involvement with using a drug and a preoccupation with securing its supply.

adolescent egocentrism The heightened self-consciousness of adolescents.

adoption study A study in which investigators seek to discover whether, in behavior and psychological characteristics, adopted children are more like their adoptive parents, who provided a home environment, or more like their biological parents, who contributed their heredity. Another form of the adoption study compares adoptive and biological siblings.

aerobic exercise Sustained exercise (such as jogging, swimming, or cycling) that stimulates heart and lung activity.

affectionate love In this type of love, also called companionate love, an individual desires to have the other person near and has a deep, caring affection for the other person.

affordances Opportunities for interaction offered by objects that fit within our capabilities to perform functional activities.

afterbirth The third stage of birth, when the placenta, umbilical cord, and other membranes are detached and expelled.

ageism Prejudice against others because of their age, especially prejudice against older adults.

Alzheimer disease A progressive, irreversible brain disorder characterized by a gradual deterioration of memory, reasoning, language, and eventually, physical function.

amnion The life-support system that is a bag or envelope that contains a clear fluid in which the developing embryo floats.

amygdala The region of the brain that is the seat of emotions.

androgyny The presence of positive masculine and feminine characteristics in the same individual.

anger Kübler-Ross' second stage of dying, in which the dying person's denial gives way to anger, resentment, rage, and envy.

anger cry A variation of the basic cry, with more excess air forced through the vocal cords.

animism The belief that inanimate objects have lifelike qualities and are capable of action.

anorexia nervosa An eating disorder that involves the relentless pursuit of thinness through starvation.

A-not-B error Error that occurs when infants make the mistake of selecting the familiar hiding place (A) rather than the new hiding place (B) of an object as they progress into substage 4 in Piaget's sensorimotor stage.

anxious attachment style An attachment style that describes adults who demand closeness, are less trusting, and are more emotional, jealous, and possessive.

Apgar Scale A widely used method of assessing the health of newborns at one and five minutes after birth. The Apgar Scale evaluates an infant's heart rate, respiratory effort, muscle tone, body color, and reflex irritability.

aphasia A loss or impairment of language ability caused by brain damage.

arthritis Inflammation of the joints that is accompanied by pain, stiffness, and movement problems; this disease is especially common in older adults.

Asperger syndrome A relatively mild autism spectrum disorder in which the child has relatively good verbal language skills, milder nonverbal language problems, and a restricted range of interests and relationships.

assimilation Piagetian concept of using existing schemes to deal with new information or experiences.

attachment A close emotional bond between two people.

attention The focusing of mental resources on select information.

attention deficit hyperactivity disorder (ADHD) A disability in which children consistently show one or more of the following characteristics: (1) inattention, (2) hyperactivity, and (3) impulsivity.

authoritarian parenting A restrictive, punitive style in which parents exhort the child to follow their directions and to respect their work and effort. The authoritarian parent places firm limits and controls on the child and allows little verbal exchange. Authoritarian parenting is associated with children's social incompetence.

authoritative parenting A parenting style in which parents encourage their children to be independent but still place limits and controls on their actions. Extensive verbal give-and-take is allowed, and parents are warm and nurturing toward the child. Authoritative parenting is associated with children's social competence.

autism spectrum disorders (ASD) Also called pervasive developmental disorders, they range from the severe disorder labeled autistic disorder to the milder disorder called Asperger syndrome. Children with these disorders are characterized by problems in social interaction, verbal and nonverbal communication, and repetitive behaviors.

autistic disorder A severe autism spectrum disorder that has its onset in the first three years of life and includes deficiencies in social relationships, abnormalities in communication, and restricted, repetitive, and stereotyped patterns of behavior.

autonomous morality In Piaget's theory, older children (about 10 years of age and older) become aware that rules and laws are created by people and that in judging an action one should consider the actor's intentions as well as the consequences.

average children Children who receive an average number of both positive and negative nominations from peers.

avoidant attachment style An attachment style that describes adults who are hesitant about getting involved in romantic relationships and once in a relationship tend to distance themselves from their partner.

B

bargaining Kübler-Ross' third stage of dying, in which the dying person develops the hope that death can somehow be postponed.

basic cry A rhythmic pattern usually consisting of a cry, a briefer silence, a shorter inspiratory whistle that is higher pitched than the main cry, and then a brief rest before the next cry.

Bayley Scales of Infant Development Scales developed by Nancy Bayley that are widely used to assess infant development. The current version has three components: a mental scale, a motor scale, and an infant behavior profile.

behavior genetics The field that seeks to discover the influence of heredity and environment on individual differences in human traits and development.

Big Five factors of personality Emotional stability (neuroticism), extraversion, openness to experience, agreeableness, and conscientiousness.

biological processes Changes in an individual's physical nature.

blastocyst The inner layer of cells that develops during the germinal period. These cells later develop into the embryo.

bonding The formation of a close connection, especially a physical bond, between parents and their newborn in the period shortly after birth.

brain death A neurological definition of death. A person is brain dead when all electrical activity of the brain has ceased for a specified period of time. A flat EEG recording is one criterion of brain death.

brainstorming A technique in which individuals are encouraged to come up with creative ideas in a group, play off each other's ideas, and say almost anything that comes to mind.

Brazelton Neonatal Behavioral Assessment Scale (NBAS) A measure that is used in the first month of life to assess the newborn's neurological development, reflexes, and reactions to people and objects.

breech position The baby's position in the uterus that causes the buttocks to be the first part to emerge from the vagina.

Broca's area An area in the brain's left frontal lobe that is involved in speech production.

Bronfenbrenner's ecological theory Bronfenbrenner's environmental systems theory that focuses on five environmental systems: microsystem, mesosystem, exosystem, macrosystem, and chronosystem.

bulimia nervosa An eating disorder in which the individual consistently follows a binge-and-purge pattern.

C

care perspective The moral perspective of Carol Gilligan, which views people in terms of their connectedness with others and emphasizes interpersonal communication, relationships with others, and concern for others.

case study An in-depth look at a single individual.

cataracts A thickening of the lens of the eye that causes vision to become cloudy, opaque, and distorted.

cellular clock theory Leonard Hayflick's theory that the maximum number of times that human cells can divide is about 75 to 80. As we age, our cells have less capacity to divide.

centration Focusing attention on one characteristic to the exclusion of all others.

cephalocaudal pattern Developmental sequence in which the earliest growth always occurs at the top—the head—with physical growth in size, weight, and feature differentiation gradually working from top to bottom.

cesarean delivery Surgical procedure in which the baby is removed from the mother's uterus through an incision made in her abdomen.

child-centered kindergarten Education that involves the whole child by considering both the child's physical, cognitive, and socioemotional development and the child's needs, interests, and learning styles.

child-directed speech Language spoken in a higher pitch than normal, with simple words and sentences.

chromosomes Threadlike structures that come in 23 pairs, with one member of each pair coming from each parent. Chromosomes contain the genetic substance DNA.

chronic disorders Disorders that are characterized by slow onset and long duration. They are rare in early adulthood, increase during middle adulthood, and become common in late adulthood.

climacteric The midlife transition during which fertility declines.

clique A small group of about 5 or 6 individuals that may form among adolescents who engage in similar activities.

cognitive control Effective control of thinking in a number of areas, including controlling attention, reducing interfering thoughts, and being cognitively flexible.

cognitive mechanics The "hardware" of the mind, reflecting the neurophysiological architecture of the brain. Cognitive mechanics involve the speed and accuracy of the processes involving sensory input, visual and motor memory, discrimination, comparison, and categorization.

cognitive pragmatics The culture-based "software programs" of the mind. Cognitive pragmatics include reading and writing skills, language comprehension, educational qualifications, professional skills, and also the type of knowledge about the self and life skills that help us to master or cope with life.

cognitive processes Changes in an individual's thought, intelligence, and language.

cohort effects Effects due to a person's time of birth, era, or generation rather than the person's actual age.

commitment Marcia's term for the part of identity development in which adolescents show a personal investment in identity.

concepts Cognitive groupings of similar objects, events, people, or ideas.

conscience An internal regulation of standards of right and wrong that involves integrating moral thought, feeling, and behavior.

consensual validation An explanation of why individuals are attracted to people who are similar to them. Our own attitudes and behavior are supported and validated when someone else's attitudes and behavior are similar to our own.

conservation In Piaget's theory, awareness that altering an object's or a substance's appearance does not change its basic properties.

constructive play Play that combines sensorimotor and repetitive activity with symbolic representation of ideas. Constructive play occurs when children engage in self-regulated creation or construction of a product or a solution.

constructivist approach A learner-centered approach that emphasizes the importance of individuals actively constructing their knowledge and understanding with guidance from the teacher.

contemporary life-events approach Approach emphasizing that how a life event influences the individual's development depends not only on the life event, but also on mediating factors, the individual's adaptation to the life event, the life-stage context, and the sociohistorical context.

continuity-discontinuity issue Debate about the extent to which development involves gradual, cumulative change (continuity) or distinct stages (discontinuity).

controversial children Children who are frequently nominated both as a best friend and as being disliked by their peers.

conventional reasoning The second, or intermediate, level in Kohlberg's theory of moral development. At this level, individuals abide by certain standards, but these are standards set by others such as parents or society.

convergent thinking Thinking that produces one correct answer and is characteristic of the kind of thinking tested by standardized intelligence tests.

convoy model of social relations Model in which individuals go through life embedded in a personal network of individuals to whom they give and from whom they receive support.

coordination of secondary circular reactions Piaget's fourth sensorimotor substage, which develops between 8 and 12 months of age. Actions become more outwardly directed, and infants coordinate schemes and act with intentionality.

coparenting Support parents provide for each other in jointly raising their children.

core knowledge approach States that infants are born with domain-specific innate knowledge systems.

corpus callosum The location where fibers connect the brain's left and right hemispheres.

correlation coefficient A number based on statistical analysis that is used to describe the degree of association between two variables.

correlational research Research that attempts to determine the strength of the relationship between two ormore events or characteristics.

creative thinking The ability to think in novel and unusual ways and to come up with unique solutions to problems.

crisis Marcia's term for a period of identity development during which the adolescent is exploring alternatives.

critical thinking Thinking reflectively and productively, as well as evaluating evidence.

cross-cultural studies Comparison of one culture with one or more other cultures. These provide information about the degree to which development is similar, or universal, across cultures, and the degree to which it is culture-specific.

cross-sectional approach A research strategy in which individuals of different ages are compared at one time.

crowd A larger group structure than a clique that is usually based on reputation; members may or may not spend much time together.

crystallized intelligence Accumulated information and verbal skills, which increase in middle adulthood, according to Horn.

cultural-familial intellectual disability Condition in which there is no evidence of organic brain damage but the individual's IQ generally is between 50 and 70.

culture The behavior patterns, beliefs, and all other products of a group that are passed on from generation to generation.

culture-fair tests Tests of intelligence that are designed to be free of cultural bias.

D

date or acquaintance rape Coercive sexual activity directed at someone with whom the perpetrator is at least casually acquainted.

deferred imitation   Imitation that occurs after a delay of hours or days.

dementia   A global term for any neurological disorder in which the primary symptoms involve a deterioration of mental functioning.

denial and isolation   Kübler-Ross' first stage of dying, in which the dying person denies that she or he is really going to die.

depression   Kübler-Ross' fourth stage of dying, in which the dying person comes to accept the certainty of her or his death. A period of depression or preparatory grief may appear.

descriptive research   Studies designed to observe and record behavior.

development   The pattern of change that begins at conception and continues through the life span. Most development involves growth, although it also includes decline brought on by aging and dying.

developmental cascade model   Involves connections across domains over time that influence developmental pathways and outcomes.

developmental quotient (DQ)   An overall score that combines subscores in motor, language, adaptive, and personal-social domains in the Gesell assessment of infants.

developmentally appropriate practice   Education that focuses on the typical developmental patterns of children (age-appropriateness) and the uniqueness of each child (individual-appropriateness).

difficult child   A child who tends to react negatively and cry frequently, engages in irregular daily routines, and is slow to accept change.

direct instruction approach   A structured, teacher-centered approach that is characterized by teacher direction and control, mastery of academic skills, high expectations for students' progress, maximum time spent on learning tasks, and efforts to keep negative affect to a minimum.

dishabituation   Recovery of a habituated response after a change in stimulation.

divergent thinking   Thinking that produces many answers to the same question and is characteristic of creativity.

divided attention   Concentrating on more than one activity at the same time.

DNA   A complex molecule that contains genetic information.

domain theory of moral development   Theory that identifies different domains of social knowledge and reasoning, including moral, social conventional, and personal domains. These domains arise from children's and adolescents' attempts to understand and deal with different forms of social experience.

doula   A caregiver who provides continuous physical, emotional, and educational support for the mother before, during, and after childbirth.

Down syndrome   A form of intellectual disability that is caused by the presence of an extra copy of chromosome 21.

dual-process model   A model of coping with bereavement that emphasizes oscillation between two dimensions: (1) loss-oriented stressors, and (2) restoration-oriented stressors.

dual-process model   A view of thinking in which decision making is influenced by two systems—one analytical and one experiential—that compete with each other.

dynamic systems theory   The perspective on motor development that seeks to explain how motor behaviors are assembled for perceiving and acting.

dyscalculia   Also known as developmental arithmetic disorder; a learning disability that involves difficulty in math computation.

dysgraphia   A learning disability that involves difficulty in handwriting.

dyslexia   A category of learning disabilities involving a severe impairment in the ability to read and spell.

E

easy child   A child who is generally in a positive mood, quickly establishes regular routines in infancy, and adapts easily to new experiences.

eclectic theoretical orientation   An orientation that does not follow any one theoretical approach but rather selects from each theory whatever is considered the best in it.

ecological view   The view that perception functions to bring organisms in contact with the environment and to increase adaptation.

egocentrism   The inability to distinguish between one's own perspective and someone else's (salient feature of the first substage of preoperational thought).

elaboration   An important strategy for remembering that involves engaging in more extensive processing of information.

eldercare   Physical and emotional caretaking for older members of the family, whether by giving day-to-day physical assistance or by being responsible for overseeing such care.

embryonic period   The period of prenatal development that occurs two to eight weeks after conception. During the embryonic period, the rate of cell differentiation intensifies, support systems for the cells form, and organs appear.

emerging adulthood   The transition from adolescence to adulthood (occurring from approximately 18 to 25 years of age), which is characterized by experimentation and exploration.

emotion   Feeling, or affect, that occurs when a person is in a state or interaction that is important to him or her. Emotion is characterized by behavior that reflects (expresses) the pleasantness or unpleasantness of the state a person is in or the transactions being experienced.

emotional and behavioral disorders   Serious, persistent problems that involve relationships, aggression, depression, fears associated with personal or school matters, as well as other inappropriate socioemotional characteristics.

empty nest syndrome   A decrease in marital satisfaction that occurs after children leave home, because parents derive considerable satisfaction from their children.

epigenetic view   Emphasizes that development is the result of an ongoing, bidirectional interchange between heredity and environment.

episodic memory   The retention of information about the where and when of life's happenings.

equilibration   A mechanism that Piaget proposed to explain how children shift from one stage of thought to the next.

erectile dysfunction (ED)   The inability to adequately achieve and maintain an erection to attain satisfactory sexual performance.

Erikson's theory   Includes eight stages of human development. Each stage consists of a unique developmental task that confronts individuals with a crisis that must be resolved.

ethnic gloss   Using an ethnic label such as African American or Latino in a superficial way that portrays an ethnic group as being more homogeneous than it really is.

ethnic identity   An enduring, basic aspect of the self that includes a sense of membership in an ethnic group and the attitudes and feelings related to that membership.

ethnicity   A characteristic based on cultural heritage, nationality characteristics, race, religion, and language.

ethology   Stresses that behavior is strongly influenced by biology, is tied to evolution, and is characterized by critical or sensitive periods.

euthanasia   The act of painlessly ending the lives of persons who are suffering from incurable diseases or severe disabilities; sometimes called "mercy killing."

evocative genotype-environment correlations   Correlations that exist when the child's genetically influenced characteristics elicit certain types of environments.

evolutionary psychology   Emphasizes the importance of adaptation, reproduction, and "survival of the fittest" in shaping behavior.

evolutionary theory of aging   This theory states that natural selection has not eliminated many harmful conditions and nonadaptive characteristics in older adults; thus, the benefits conferred by evolution decline with age because natural selection is linked to reproductive fitness.

executive attention   Aspects of thinking that include planning actions, allocating attention to goals, detecting and compensating for errors, monitoring progress on tasks, and dealing with novel or difficult circumstances.

executive function   An umbrella-like concept that consists of a number of higher-level cognitive processes linked to the development of the brain's prefrontal cortex. Executive function involves managing one's thoughts to engage in goal-directed behavior and self-control.

experiment   A carefully regulated procedure in which one or more of the factors believed to influence the behavior being studied are manipulated while all other factors are held constant.

explicit memory   Memory of facts and experiences that individuals consciously know and can state.

F

fast mapping   A process that helps to explain how young children learn the connection between a word and its referent so quickly.

fertilization A stage in reproduction when an egg and a sperm fuse to create a single cell, called a zygote.

fetal alcohol spectrum disorders (FASD) A cluster of abnormalities that appear in the offspring of mothers who drink alcohol heavily during pregnancy.

fetal period Lasting about seven months, the prenatal period between two months after conception and birth in typical pregnancies.

fight-or-flight The view that when men experience stress, they are more likely to engage in a fight-or-flight pattern, as reflected in being aggressive, withdrawing from social contact, or drinking alcohol.

fine motor skills Motor skills that involve more finely tuned movements, such as finger dexterity.

first habits and primary circular reactions Piaget's second sensorimotor substage, which develops between 1 and 4 months of age. In this substage, the infant coordinates sensation and two types of schemes: habits and primary circular reactions.

fluid intelligence The ability to reason abstractly, which begins to decline from middle adulthood onward, according to Horn.

fragile X syndrome A genetic disorder involving an abnormality in the X chromosome, which becomes constricted and often breaks.

free-radical theory A microbiological theory of aging that states that people age because normal metabolic processes within their cells produce unstable oxygen molecules known as free radicals. These molecules ricochet around inside cells, damaging DNA and other cellular structures.

fuzzy trace theory States that memory is best understood by considering two types of memory representations: (1) verbatim memory trace, and (2) gist. In this theory, older children's better memory is attributed to the fuzzy traces created by extracting the gist of information.

G

games Activities engaged in for pleasure that include rules and often involve competition with one or more individuals.

gender The characteristics of people as males or females.

gender identity The sense of being male or female, which most children acquire by the time they are 3 years old.

gender role A set of expectations that prescribes how females or males should think, act, and feel.

gender schema theory The theory that gender typing emerges as children develop gender schemas of their culture's gender-appropriate and gender-inappropriate behavior.

gender stereotypes Broad categories that reflect our impressions and beliefs about females and males.

gender typing Acquisition of a traditional masculine or feminine role.

gene x environment (G × E) interaction The interaction of a specific measured variation in the DNA and a specific measured aspect of the environment.

generational inequity The view that our aging society is being unfair to its younger members because older adults pile up advantages by receiving inequitably large allocations of resources.

genes Units of hereditary information composed of DNA. Genes help cells to reproduce themselves and help manufacture the proteins that maintain life.

genotype A person's genetic heritage; the actual genetic material.

germinal period The period of prenatal development that takes place in the first two weeks after conception. It includes the creation of the zygote, continued cell division, and the attachment of the zygote to the uterine wall.

gifted Having above-average intelligence (an IQ of 130 or higher) and/or superior talent for something.

glaucoma Damage to the optic nerve because of the pressure created by a buildup of fluid in the eye.

goodness of fit Refers to the match between a child's temperament and the environmental demands with which the child must cope.

grasping reflex A neonatal reflex that occurs when something touches the infant's palms. The infant responds by grasping tightly.

grief The emotional numbness, disbelief, separation anxiety, despair, sadness, and loneliness that accompany the loss of someone we love.

gross motor skills Motor skills that involve large-muscle activities, such as walking.

growth hormone deficiency Absence or deficiency of growth hormone produced by the pituitary gland to stimulate the body to grow.

H

habituation Decreased responsiveness to a stimulus after repeated presentations of the stimulus.

heteronomous morality Kohlberg's first stage of preconventional reasoning in which moral thinking is tied to punishment.

heteronomous morality The first stage of moral development in Piaget's theory, occurring from approximately 4 to 7 years of age. Justice and rules are conceived of as unchangeable properties of the world, removed from the control of people.

hormonal stress theory The theory that aging in the body's hormonal system can decrease resistance to stress and increase the likelihood of disease.

hormones Powerful chemical substances secreted by the endocrine glands and carried through the body by the bloodstream.

hospice A program committed to making the end of life as free from pain, anxiety, and depression as possible. The goals of hospice contrast with those of a hospital, which are to cure disease and prolong life.

hypotheses Specific assumptions and predictions that can be tested to determine their accuracy.

hypothetical-deductive reasoning Piaget's formal operational concept that adolescents have the cognitive ability to develop hypotheses, or best guesses, about ways to solve problems.

I

identity achievement Marcia's term for the status of individuals who have undergone a crisis and have made a commitment.

identity diffusion Marcia's term for the status of individuals who have not yet experienced a crisis (explored meaningful alternatives) or made any commitments.

identity foreclosure Marcia's term for the status of individuals who have made a commitment but have not experienced a crisis.

identity moratorium Marcia's term for the status of individuals who are in the midst of a crisis, but their commitments are either absent or vaguely defined.

imaginary audience Adolescents' belief that others are as interested in them as they themselves are, as well as attention-getting behavior motivated by a desire to be noticed, visible, and "on stage."

immanent justice The concept that if a rule is broken, punishment will be meted out immediately.

implicit memory Memory without conscious recollection; involves skills and routine procedures that are automatically performed.

inclusion Educating a child with special education needs full-time in the regular classroom.

individual differences The stable, consistent ways in which people differ from each other.

individualism, instrumental purpose, and exchange Kohlberg's second stage of preconventional reasoning, in which individuals pursue their own interests but also let others do the same.

individualized education plan (IEP) A written statement that spells out a program specifically tailored to a child with a disability.

indulgent parenting A style of parenting in which parents are highly involved with their children but place few demands or controls on them. Indulgent parenting is associated with children's social incompetence, especially a lack of self-control.

infinite generativity The ability to produce an endless number of meaningful sentences using a finite set of words and rules.

information-processing theory Emphasizes that individuals manipulate information, monitor it, and strategize about it. Central to this theory are the processes of memory and thinking.

insecure avoidant babies Babies who show insecurity by avoiding the caregiver.

insecure disorganized babies Babies who show insecurity by being disorganized and disoriented.

insecure resistant babies Babies who often cling to the caregiver, then resist the caregiver by fighting against the closeness, perhaps by kicking or pushing away.

integrity versus despair Erikson's eighth and final stage of development, which individuals experience in late adulthood. This involves reflecting on the past and either piecing together a positive review or concluding that one's life has not been well spent.

intellectual disability A condition of limited mental ability in which the individual (1) has a low IQ, usually below 70 on a traditional intelligence test, (2) has difficulty adapting to the demands of everyday life, and (3) first exhibits these characteristics by age 18.

intelligence Problem-solving skills and the ability to learn from and adapt to the experiences of everyday life.

intelligence quotient (IQ) A person's mental age divided by chronological age, multiplied by 100.

intermodal perception The ability to relate and integrate information from two or more sensory modalities, such as vision and hearing.

internalization of schemes Piaget's sixth and final sensorimotor substage, which develops between 18 and 24 months of age. In this substage, the infant develops the ability to use primitive symbols.

intimacy in friendships Self-disclosure and the sharing of private thoughts.

intuitive thought substage Piaget's second substage of preoperational thought, in which children begin to use primitive reasoning and want to know the answers to all sorts of questions (between 4 and 7 years of age).

J

joint attention Process that occurs when individuals focus on the same object and are able to track another's behavior, one individual directs another's attention, and reciprocal interaction takes place.

justice perspective A moral perspective that focuses on the rights of the individual and in which individuals independently make moral decisions.

juvenile delinquent An adolescent who breaks the law or engages in behavior that is considered illegal.

K

kangaroo care Treatment for preterm infants that involves skin-to-skin contact.

Klinefelter syndrome A chromosomal disorder in which males have an extra X chromosome, making them XXY instead of XY.

kwashiorkor A condition caused by severe protein deficiency in which the child's abdomen and feet become swollen with water; usually appears between 1 and 3 years of age.

L

laboratory A controlled setting in which many of the complex factors of the "real world" are removed.

language A form of communication, whether spoken, written, or signed, that is based on a system of symbols. Language consists of the words used by a community and the rules for varying and combining them.

language acquisition device (LAD) Chomsky's term that describes a biological endowment enabling the child to detect the features and rules of language, including phonology, syntax, and semantics.

lateralization Specialization of function in one hemisphere of the cerebral cortex or the other.

learning disability Difficulty in understanding or using spoken or written language or in doing mathematics. To be classified as a learning disability, the learning problem is not primarily the result of visual, hearing, or motor disabilities; intellectual disability; emotional disorders; or due to environmental, cultural, or economic disadvantage.

least restrictive environment (LRE) A setting that is as similar as possible to the one in which children who do not have a disability are educated.

leisure The pleasant times after work when individuals are free to pursue activities and interests of their own choosing.

life expectancy The number of years that will probably be lived by the average person born in a particular year.

life span The maximum number of years an individual can live. The life span of human beings is about 120 to 125 years of age.

life-span perspective The perspective that development is lifelong, multidimensional, multidirectional, plastic, multidisciplinary, and contextual; involves growth, maintenance, and regulation; and is constructed through biological, sociocultural, and individual factors working together.

limbic system A lower, subcortical system in the brain that is the seat of emotions and experience of rewards. This system is almost completely developed in early adolescence.

longitudinal approach A research strategy in which the same individuals are studied over a period of time, usually several years or more.

long-term memory A relatively permanent type of memory that holds huge amounts of information for a long period of time.

low birth weight infants An infant that weighs less than 5½ pounds at birth.

M

macular degeneration A disease that involves deterioration of the macula of the retina, which corresponds to the focal center of the visual field.

major depression A mood disorder in which the individual is deeply unhappy, demoralized, self-derogatory, and bored. The person does not feel well, loses stamina easily, has poor appetite, and is listless and unmotivated. Major depression is so widespread that it has been called the "common cold" of mental disorders.

marasmus A wasting away of body tissues in the infant's first year, caused by severe protein-calorie deficiency.

matching hypothesis States that although we prefer a more attractive person in the abstract, in the real world we end up choosing someone who is close to our own level of attractiveness.

meaning-making coping Involves drawing on beliefs, values, and goals to change the meaning of a stressful situation, especially in times of chronic stress such as when a loved one dies.

meiosis A specialized form of cell division that occurs to form eggs and sperm (also known as gametes).

memory A central feature of cognitive development, pertaining to all situations in which an individual retains information over time.

menarche A girl's first menstruation.

menopause Cessation of a woman's menstrual periods, usually during the late forties or early fifties.

mental age (MA) Binet's measure of an individual's level of mental development, compared with that of others.

metabolic syndrome A condition characterized by hypertension, obesity, and insulin resistance. Metabolic syndrome often leads to the onset of diabetes and cardiovascular disease.

metacognition Cognition about cognition, or knowing about knowing.

metalinguistic awareness Refers to knowledge about language, such as understanding what a preposition is or being able to discuss the sounds of a language.

middle adulthood The developmental period that begins at approximately 40 to 45 years of age and extends to about 60 to 65 years of age.

mindfulness Being alert, mentally present, and cognitively flexible while going through life's everyday activities and tasks.

mindset The cognitive view, either fixed or growth, that individuals develop for themselves.

mitochondrial theory The theory that aging is caused by the decay of mitochondria, tiny cellular bodies that supply energy for function, growth, and repair.

mitosis Cellular reproduction in which the cell's nucleus duplicates itself with two new cells being formed, each containing the same DNA as the parent cell, arranged in the same 23 pairs of chromosomes.

Montessori approach An educational philosophy in which children are given considerable freedom and spontaneity in choosing activities and are allowed to move from one activity to another as they desire.

moral development Development that involves thoughts, feelings, and behaviors regarding rules and conventions about what people should do in their interactions with other people.

Moro reflex A neonatal startle response that occurs in reaction to a sudden, intense noise or movement. When startled, the newborn arches its back, throws its head back, and flings out its arms and legs. Then the newborn rapidly pulls its arms and legs close to the center of the body.

morphology Units of meaning involved in word formation.

mutual interpersonal expectations, relationships, and interpersonal conformity Kohlberg's third stage of moral development. At this stage, individuals value trust, caring, and loyalty to others as a basis of moral judgments.

myelination The process by which the nerve cells are covered and insulated with a layer of fat cells, which increases the speed at which information travels through the nervous system.

N

narcissism A self-centered and self-concerned approach toward others.

natural childbirth This method attempts to reduce the mother's pain by decreasing her fear through education about childbirth and relaxation techniques during delivery.

naturalistic observation Studies that involve observing behavior in real-world settings.

nature-nurture issue Debate about whether development is primarily influenced by nature or

nurture. Nature refers to an organism's biological inheritance, nurture to its environmental experiences.

neglected children Children who are infrequently nominated as a best friend but are not disliked by their peers.

neglectful parenting A style of parenting in which the parent is uninvolved in the child's life; it is associated with children's social incompetence, especially a lack of self-control.

Neonatal Intensive Care Unit Neurobehavioral Scale (NNNS) An "offspring" of the NBAS, the NNNS provides an assessment of the newborn's behavior, neurological and stress responses, and regulatory capacities.

neo-Piagetians Developmentalists who argue that Piaget got some things right but that his theory needs considerable revision. They have elaborated on Piaget's theory, giving more emphasis to information processing, strategies, and precise cognitive steps.

neuroconstructivist view Perspective holding that biological processes and environmental conditions influence the brain's development; the brain has plasticity and is context dependent; and development of the brain and cognitive development are closely linked.

neurogenesis The generation of new neurons.

neurons Nerve cells, which handle information processing at the cellular level in the brain.

nonnormative life events Unusual occurrences that have a major impact on an individual's life.

nonshared environmental experiences The child's own unique experiences, both within the family and outside the family, that are not shared with another sibling. Thus, experiences occurring within the family can be part of the "nonshared environment."

normal distribution A symmetrical distribution with most scores falling in the middle of the possible range of scores and a few scores appearing toward the extremes of the range.

normative age-graded influences Influences that are similar for individuals in a particular age group.

normative history-graded influences Influences that are common to people of a particular generation because of historical circumstances.

O

object permanence The Piagetian term for understanding that objects and events continue to exist even when they cannot directly be seen, heard, or touched.

operations In Piaget's theory, these are reversible mental actions that allow children to do mentally what they formerly did physically.

organic intellectual disability A genetic disorder or condition involving brain damage that is linked to a low level of intellectual functioning.

organization Piaget's concept of grouping isolated behaviors and thoughts into a higher-order, more smoothly functioning cognitive system.

organogenesis Organ formation that takes place during the first two months of prenatal development.

osteoporosis A chronic condition that involves an extensive loss of bone tissue and is the main reason many older adults walk with a marked stoop.

P

pain cry A sudden appearance of a long, initial loud cry without preliminary moaning, followed by breath holding.

palliative care The type of care emphasized in a hospice, which involves reducing pain and suffering and helping individuals die with dignity.

Parkinson disease A chronic, progressive disease characterized by muscle tremors, slowing of movement, and partial facial paralysis.

passive euthanasia The withholding of available treatments, such as life-sustaining devices, in order to allow a person to die.

passive genotype-environment correlations Correlations that exist when the natural parents, who are genetically related to the child, provide a rearing environment for the child.

perception The interpretation of what is sensed.

personal fable The part of adolescent egocentrism that involves an adolescent's sense of uniqueness and invincibility (or invulnerability).

perspective taking The social cognitive process involved in assuming the perspective of others and understanding their thoughts and feelings.

phenotype The way an individual's genotype is expressed in observed and measurable characteristics.

phenylketonuria (PKU) A genetic disorder in which an individual cannot properly metabolize an amino acid called phenylalanine. PKU is now easily detected but, if left untreated, results in intellectual disability and hyperactivity.

phonics approach The idea that reading instruction should teach the basic rules for translating written symbols into sounds.

phonology The sound system of the language, including the sounds that are used and how they may be combined.

Piaget's theory Theory stating that children actively construct their understanding of the world and go through four stages of cognitive development.

placenta A life-support system that consists of a disk-shaped group of tissues in which small blood vessels from the mother and offspring intertwine.

popular children Children who are frequently nominated as a best friend and are rarely disliked by their peers.

possible selves What individuals might become, what they would like to become, and what they are afraid of becoming.

postconventional reasoning The highest level in Kohlberg's theory of moral development. At this level, the individual recognizes alternative moral courses, explores the options, and then decides on a personal moral code.

postformal thought Thinking that is reflective, relativistic, contextual, provisional, realistic, and influenced by emotions.

postpartum depression Characteristic of women who have such strong feelings of sadness,

anxiety, or despair that they have trouble coping with daily tasks in the postpartum period.

postpartum period The period after childbirth when the mother adjusts, both physically and psychologically, to the process of childbirth. This period lasts for about six weeks or until her body has completed its adjustment and returned to a near prepregnant state.

practice play Play that involves repetition of behavior when new skills are being learned or when physical or mental mastery and coordination of skills are required for games or sports.

pragmatics The appropriate use of language in different contexts.

preconventional reasoning The lowest level in Kohlberg's theory of moral development. The individual's moral reasoning is controlled primarily by external rewards and punishment.

preoperational stage Piaget's second stage, lasting from about 2 to 7 years of age, during which children begin to represent the world with words, images, and drawings, and symbolic thought goes beyond simple connections of sensory information and physical action; stable concepts are formed, mental reasoning emerges, egocentrism is present, and magical beliefs are constructed.

prepared childbirth Developed by French obstetrician Ferdinand Lamaze, this childbirth strategy is similar to natural childbirth but includes a special breathing technique to control pushing in the final stages of labor and a more detailed anatomy and physiology course.

pretense/symbolic play Play in which the child transforms the physical environment into a symbol.

preterm infants Those born before the completion of 37 weeks of gestation (the time between fertilization and birth).

primary circular reaction A scheme based on the attempt to reproduce an event that initially occurred by chance.

primary emotions Emotions that are present in humans and other animals and emerge early in life; examples are joy, anger, sadness, fear, and disgust.

Project Head Start A government-funded program that is designed to provide children from low-income families with the opportunity to acquire the skills and experiences important for school success.

prolonged grief disorder Grief that involves enduring despair and remains unresolved over an extended period of time.

prospective memory Remembering to do something in the future.

proximodistal pattern Developmental sequence in which growth starts at the center of the body and moves toward the extremities.

psychoanalytic theories Theories that describe development as primarily unconscious and heavily colored by emotion. Behavior is merely a surface characteristic, and the symbolic workings of the mind have to be analyzed to understand behavior. Early experiences with parents are emphasized.

psychoanalytic theory of gender A theory deriving from Freud's view that the preschool child develops a sexual attraction to the opposite-sex parent, by approximately 5 or 6 years of age renounces this attraction because of anxious feelings, and subsequently identifies with the same-sex parent, unconsciously adopting the same-sex parent's characteristics.

puberty A period of rapid physical maturation, occurring primarily in early adolescence, that involves hormonal and bodily changes.

R

rape Forcible sexual intercourse with a person who does not consent to it.

reciprocal socialization Socialization that is bidirectional; children socialize parents, just as parents socialize children.

reflexes Built-in reactions to stimuli that govern the newborn's movements, which are automatic and beyond the newborn's control.

reflexive smile A smile that does not occur in response to external stimuli. It happens during the first month after birth, usually during sleep.

rejected children Children who are infrequently nominated as a best friend and are actively disliked by their peers.

religion An organized set of beliefs, practices, rituals, and symbols that increases an individual's connection to a sacred or transcendent other (God, higher power, or higher truth).

religiousness The degree to which an individual is affiliated with an organized religion, participates in prescribed rituals and practices, feels a sense of connection with its beliefs, and is involved in a community of believers.

rite of passage A ceremony or ritual that marks an individual's transition from one status to another. Most rites of passage focus on the transition to adult status.

romantic love Also called passionate love, or eros, romantic love has strong sexual and infatuation components and often predominates early in a love relationship.

rooting reflex A newborn's built-in reaction that occurs when the infant's cheek is stroked or the side of the mouth is touched. In response, the infant turns his or her head toward the side that was touched, in an apparent effort to find something to suck.

S

scaffolding Practice in which parents time interactions so that infants experience turn taking with the parents.

schemes In Piaget's theory, actions or mental representations that organize knowledge.

scientific method An approach that can be used to obtain accurate information. It includes the following steps: (1) conceptualize the problem, (2) collect data, (3) draw conclusions, and (4) revise research conclusions and theory.

secondary circular reactions Piaget's third sensorimotor substage, which develops between 4 and 8 months of age. In this substage, the infant becomes more object-oriented, moving beyond preoccupation with the self.

secure attachment style An attachment style that describes adults who have positive views of relationships, find it easy to get close to others, and are not overly concerned or stressed out about their romantic relationships.

securely attached babies Babies who use the caregiver as a secure base from which to explore the environment.

selective attention Focusing on a specific aspect of experience that is relevant while ignoring others that are irrelevant.

selective optimization with compensation theory The theory that successful aging is related to three main factors: selection, optimization, and compensation.

self-concept Domain-specific evaluations of the self.

self-conscious emotions Emotions that require self-awareness, especially consciousness and a sense of "me"; examples include jealousy, empathy, and embarrassment.

self-efficacy The belief that one can master a situation and produce favorable outcomes.

self-esteem The global evaluative dimension of the self. Self-esteem is also referred to as self-worth or self-image.

self-understanding The child's cognitive representation of self, the substance and content of the child's self-conceptions.

semantic memory A person's knowledge about the world—including one's fields of expertise, general academic knowledge of the sort learned in school, and "everyday knowledge."

semantics The meaning of words and sentences.

sensation The product of the interaction between information and the sensory receptors—the eyes, ears, tongue, nostrils, and skin.

sensorimotor play Behavior engaged in by infants that lets them derive pleasure from exercising their existing sensorimotor schemas.

sensorimotor stage The first of Piaget's stages, which lasts from birth to about 2 years of age; infants construct an understanding of the world by coordinating sensory experiences with motoric actions.

separation protest An infant's distressed crying when the caregiver leaves.

seriation The concrete operation that involves ordering stimuli along a quantitative dimension (such as length).

service learning A form of education that promotes social responsibility and service to the community.

sexually transmitted infections (STIs) Infections that are contracted primarily through sexual contact, including oral-genital and anal-genital contact.

shape constancy The recognition that an object's shape remains the same even though its orientation to us changes.

shared environmental experiences Siblings' common environmental experiences, such as their parents' personalities and intellectual orientation, the family's socioeconomic status, and the neighborhood in which they live.

short-term memory The memory component in which individuals retain information for up to 30 seconds, assuming there is no rehearsal of the information.

sickle-cell anemia A genetic disorder that affects the red blood cells and occurs most often in people of African descent.

simple reflexes Piaget's first sensorimotor substage, which corresponds to the first month after birth. In this substage, sensation and action are coordinated primarily through reflexive behaviors.

size constancy The recognition that an object remains the same even though the retinal image of the object changes as you move toward or away from the object.

slow-to-warm-up child A child who has a low activity level, is somewhat negative, and displays a low intensity of mood.

small for date infants Also called small for gestational age infants, these infants' birth weights are below normal when the length of pregnancy is considered. Small for date infants may be preterm or full term.

social cognitive theory The view of psychologists who emphasize behavior, environment, and cognition as the key factors in development.

social cognitive theory of gender A theory emphasizing that children's gender development occurs through the observation and imitation of gender behavior and through the rewards and punishments children experience for gender-appropriate and gender-inappropriate behavior.

social constructivist approach An approach that emphasizes the social contexts of learning and asserts that knowledge is mutually built and constructed. Vygotsky's theory reflects this approach.

social contract or utility and individual rights The fifth Kohlberg stage. At this stage, individuals reason that values, rights, and principles undergird or transcend the law.

social conventional reasoning Thoughts about social consensus and convention, in contrast with moral reasoning, which stresses ethical issues.

social play Play that involves social interactions with peers.

social policy A national government's course of action designed to promote the welfare of its citizens.

social referencing "Reading" emotional cues in others to help determine how to act in a particular situation.

social role theory A theory that gender differences result from the contrasting roles of men and women.

social smile A smile in response to an external stimulus, which early in development is typically a face.

social systems morality The fourth stage in Kohlberg's theory of moral development, in which moral judgments are based on understanding the social order, law, justice, and duty.

socioeconomic status (SES) Refers to the grouping of people with similar occupational, educational, and economic characteristics.

socioemotional processes Changes in an individual's relationships with other people, emotions, and personality.

socioemotional selectivity theory The theory that older adults become more selective about their social networks. Because they place a high value on emotional satisfaction, older adults often spend more time with familiar individuals with whom they have had rewarding relationships.

source memory The ability to remember where one learned something.

spirituality Experiencing something beyond oneself in a transcendent manner and living in a way that benefits others and society.

stability-change issue Debate about whether we become older renditions of our early experience (stability) or whether we develop into someone different from who we were at an earlier point in development (change).

standardized test A test with uniform procedures for administration and scoring. Many standardized tests allow a person's performance to be compared with the performance of other individuals.

Strange Situation An observational measure of infant attachment that requires the infant to move through a series of introductions, separations, and reunions with the caregiver and an adult stranger in a prescribed order.

stranger anxiety An infant's fear and wariness of strangers; it tends to appear during the second half of the first year of life.

strategies Deliberate mental activities that improve the processing of information.

sucking reflex A newborn's built-in reaction to automatically suck an object placed in its mouth. The sucking reflex enables the infant to get nourishment before he or she has associated a nipple with food and also serves as a self-soothing or self-regulating mechanism.

sudden infant death syndrome (SIDS) A condition that occurs when an infant stops breathing, usually during the night, and suddenly dies without an apparent cause.

sustained attention Focused and extended engagement with an object, task, event, or other aspect of the environment.

symbolic function substage Piaget's first substage of preoperational thought, in which the child gains the ability to mentally represent an object that is not present (between about 2 and 4 years of age).

syntax The ways words are combined to form acceptable phrases and sentences.

T

telegraphic speech The use of short and precise words without grammatical markers such as articles, auxiliary verbs, and other connectives.

temperament Involves individual differences in behavioral styles, emotions, and characteristic ways of responding.

teratogen From the Greek word *tera*, meaning "monster." Any agent that causes a birth defect. The field of study that investigates the causes of birth defects is called teratology.

tertiary circular reactions, novelty, and curiosity Piaget's fifth sensorimotor substage, which develops between 12 and 18 months of age. In this substage, infants become intrigued by the many properties of objects and by the many things that they can make happen to objects.

theory An interrelated, coherent set of ideas that helps to explain phenomena and facilitate predictions.

theory of mind Awareness of one's own mental processes and the mental processes of others.

top-dog phenomenon The circumstance of moving from the top position in elementary school to the lowest position in middle or junior high school.

transitivity The ability to logically combine relations to understand certain conclusions.

triarchic theory of intelligence Sternberg's theory that intelligence consists of analytical intelligence, creative intelligence, and practical intelligence.

trophoblast The outer layer of cells that develops in the germinal period. These cells provide nutrition and support for the embryo.

Turner syndrome A chromosome disorder in females in which either an X chromosome is missing, making the person XO instead of XX, or the second X chromosome is partially deleted.

twin study A study in which the behavioral similarity of identical twins is compared with the behavioral similarity of fraternal twins.

U

umbilical cord A life-support system containing two arteries and one vein that connects the baby to the placenta.

universal ethical principles The sixth and highest stage in Kohlberg's theory of moral development, in which individuals develop a moral standard based on universal human rights.

visual preference method A method used to determine whether infants can distinguish one stimulus from another by measuring the length of time they attend to different stimuli.

V

Vygotsky's theory A sociocultural cognitive theory that emphasizes how culture and social interaction guide cognitive development.

W

Wernicke's area An area in the brain's left hemisphere that is involved in language comprehension.

whole-language approach An approach to reading instruction based on the idea that instruction should parallel children's natural language learning. Reading materials should be whole and meaningful.

wisdom Expert knowledge about the practical aspects of life that permits excellent judgment about important matters.

working memory A mental "workbench" where individuals manipulate and assemble information when making decisions, solving problems, and comprehending written and spoken language.

X

XYY syndrome A chromosomal disorder in which males have an extra Y chromosome.

Z

zone of proximal development (ZPD) Vygotsky's term for tasks that are too difficult for children to master alone but can be mastered with the assistance of adults or more-skilled children.

zygote A single cell formed through fertilization.

references

A

AARP (2004). *The divorce experience: A study of divorce at midlife and beyond.* Washington, DC: AARP.

Abbasi, M., & others (2010). The effect of hypnosis on pain relief during labor and childbirth in Iranian pregnant women. *International Journal of Clinical and Experimental Hypnosis, 57,* 174–183.

Abbott, L. C., & Winzer-Serhan, U. H. (2012). Smoking during pregnancy: Lessons learned from epidemiological studies and experimental studies using animals. *Critical Reviews in Toxicology, 42,* 279–303.

ABC News (2005, December 12). Larry Page and Sergey Brin. Retrieved September 16, 2007, from http://abcnews.go.com?Entertainment/12/8/05

Abdulle, A., Al-Junaibi, A., & Nagelkerke, N. (2014). High blood pressure and its association with body weight among children and adolescents in the United Arab Emirates. *PLoS One, 9*(1), e85129.

Abel, J., Pring, A., Rich, A., Malik, T., & Verne, J. (2013). The impact of advance care planning of place of death, a hospice retrospective cohort study. *BMJ Supportive and Palliative Care, 3,* 168–173.

Abel, T., Havekes, R., Saletin, J. M., & Walker, M. P. (2013). Sleep, plasticity, and memory from molecules to whole-brain networks. *Current Biology, 23,* R774–R788.

Abrams, L. (2009). Exploring the generality of retest effects: Commentary on "When does age-related cognitive decline begin?" *Neurobiology of Aging, 30,* 525–527.

Abyzov, A., & others (2013). Analysis of variable retroduplications in human populations suggests coupling of retrotransposition to cell division. *Genome Research, 23,* 2042–2052.

Accornero, V. H., Anthony, J. C., Morrow, C. E., Xue, L., & Bandstra, E. S. (2006). Prenatal cocaine exposure: An examination of childhood externalizing and internalizing behavior problems at age 7 years. *Epidemiology, Psychiatry, and Society, 15,* 20–29.

Achieve, Inc. (2005). *An action agenda for improving America's high schools.* Washington, DC: Author.

Ackerman, J. P., Riggins, T., & Black, M. M. (2010). A review of the effects of prenatal cocaine exposure among school-aged children. *Pediatrics, 125,* 554–565.

Adams, G. A., & Rau, B. L. (2011). Putting off tomorrow to do what you want today: Planning for retirement. *American Psychologist, 66,* 180–192.

Adams, K. F., & others (2006). Overweight, obesity, and mortality in a large prospective cohort of persons 50 to 71 years old. *New England Journal of Medicine, 355,* 763–768.

Adamson, L., & Frick, J. (2003). The still face: A history of a shared experimental paradigm. *Infancy, 4,* 451–473.

Adkins, D. E., Daw, J. K., McClay, J. L., & van den Oord, E. J. (2012). The influence of five monoamine genes on trajectories of depressive symptoms across adolescence and young adulthood. *Development and Psychopathology, 24,* 267–285.

Administration for Children & Families (2008). *Statistical fact sheet fiscal year 2008.* Washington, DC: Author.

Adolph, K. E. (1997). Learning in the development of infant locomotion. *Monographs of the Society for Research in Child Development, 62*(3, Serial No. 251).

Adolph, K. E., & Berger, S. E. (2005). Physical and motor development. In M. H. Bornstein & M. E. Lamb (Eds.), *Developmental psychology* (5th ed.). Mahwah, NJ: Erlbaum.

Adolph, K. E., & Berger, S. E. (2013). Development of the motor system. In H. Pashler, T. Crane, M. Kinsbourne, F. Ferreira, & R. Zemel (Eds.), *The encyclopedia of the mind.* Thousand Oaks, CA: Sage.

Adolph, K. E., Karasik, L. B., & Tamis-LeMonda, C. S. (2010). Moving between cultures: Cross-cultural research on motor development. In M. Bornstein & L. R. Cote (Eds.), *Handbook of cross-cultural developmental science: Vol. 1. Domains of development across cultures.* Clifton, NJ : Psychology Press.

Adolph, K. E., & Kretch, K. S. (2014, in press). Gibson's theory of perceptual learning. In H. Keller (Ed.), *International encyclopedia of social and behavioral sciences* (2nd ed.). New York: Oxford University Press.

Adolph, K. E., Kretch, K. S., & LoBue, V. (2014). Fear of height in infants? *Current Directions in Psychological Science, 23,* 60–66.

Adolph, K. E., & Robinson, S. R. R. (2015, in press). Motor development. In R. Lerner (Ed.), *Handbook of Child Psychology and Developmental Science* (7th Ed.). New York: Wiley.

Adolph, K. E., Vereijken, B., & Shrout, P. E. (2003). What changes in infant walking and why? *Child Development, 74,* 475–497.

Adolph, K. E., & others (2012). How do you learn to walk? Thousands of steps and dozens of falls per day. *Psychological Science, 23*(11), 1387–1394.

Agency for Healthcare Research and Quality (2007). *Evidence report/Technology assessment Number 153: Breastfeeding and maternal and health outcomes in developed countries.* Rockville, MD: U.S. Department of Health and Human Services.

Aggarwal, N. T., & others (2014, in press). Perceived stress and change in cognitive function among adults 65 years and older. *Psychosomatic Medicine.*

Agrali, H., & Akyar, I. (2014, in press). Older diabetic patients' attitudes and beliefs about health and illness. *Journal of Clinical Nursing.*

Agras, W. S., Hammer, L. D., McNicholas, F., & Karemer, H. C. (2004). Risk factors for childhood overweight: A prospective study from birth to 9.5 years. *Journal of Pediatrics, 145,* 20–25.

Agras, W. S., & others (2004). Report of the National Institutes of Health workshop on overcoming barriers to treatment research in anorexia nervosa. *International Journal of Eating Disorders, 35,* 509–521.

Aguiar, E. J., & others (2014, in press). Efficacy of interventions that include diet, aerobic and resistance training component for type 2 diabetes prevention: A systematic review and meta-analysis. *International Journal of Behavioral Nutrition and Physical Activity.*

Ahern, E. C., & Lamb, M. E. (2014, in press). Research-based child investigative interviewing. *Community Care Inform.*

Ahluwalia, I. B., Tessaro, I., Grumer-Strawn, L. M., MacGowan, C., & Benton-Davis, S. (2000). Georgia's breastfeeding promotion program for low-income women. *Pediatrics, 105,* E-85–E-87.

Ahmed, R., Hustad, J. T., Lasalle, L., & Bosari, B. (2014, in press). Hospitalizations for students with an alcohol-related sanction: Gender and pregaming as risk factors. *Journal of American College Health.*

Ahmed, S., & others (2011). Community kangaroo mother care: Implementation and potential for neonatal survival and health in very low-income settings. *Journal of Perinatology, 31,* 361–367.

Ahrens, C. E., & Aldana, E. (2012). The ties that bind: Understanding the impact of sexual assault disclosure on survivors' relationships with friends, family, and partners. *Journal of Trauma & Dissociation, 13,* 226–243.

Ahrons, C. (2004). *We're still family.* New York: HarperCollins.

Ahrons, C. (2007). Family ties after divorce: Long-term implications for children. *Family Process, 46,* 53–65.

Ailshire, J. A., & Burgard, S. A. (2012). Family relationships and troubled sleep among U.S. adults: Examining the influences of contact frequency and relationship quality. *Journal of Health and Social Behavior, 53,* 248–262.

Ainsworth, M. D. S. (1979). Infant-mother attachment. *American Psychologist, 34,* 932–937.

Akbari, A., & others (2011). Parity and breastfeeding are preventive measures against breast cancer in Iranian women. *Breast Cancer, 18,* 51–55.

Akhtar, N., & Herold, K. (2008). Pragmatic development. In M. M. Haith & J. B. Benson (Eds.), *Encyclopedia of infant and early childhood development.* Oxford, UK: Elsevier.

Akpek, E. K., & Smith, R. A. (2013). Current treatment strategies for age-related ocular conditions. *American Journal of Managed Care, 19*(5, Suppl.), S76–S84.

Aksglaede, L., & others (2013). 47, XXY Klinefelter syndrome: Clinical characteristics and age-specific recommendations for medical management. *American Journal of Medical Genetics C: Seminars in Medical Genetics, 163,* 55–63.

Alberga, A. S., & others (2012). Healthy eating, aerobic and resistance training in youth (HEARTY): Study rationale, design, and methods. *Contemporary Clinical Trials, 33,* 839–847.

Alberico, S., & others (2014). The role of gestational diabetes, pre-pregnancy body mass index, and gestational weight gain on the risk of newborn macrosoma: Results from a prospective multicenter study. *BMC Pregnancy and Childbirth, 14*(1), 23.

Albert, D., & Steinberg, L. (2011a). Judgment and decision making in adolescence. *Journal of Research on Adolescence, 21,* 211–224.

Albert, D., & Steinberg, L. (2011b). Peer influences on adolescent risk behavior. In M. Bardo, D. Fishbein, & R. Milich (Eds.), *Inhibitory control and drug abuse prevention: From research to translation.* New York: Springer.

Alberts, E., Elkind, D., & Ginsberg, S. (2007). The personal fable and risk taking in early adolescence. *Journal of Youth and Adolescence, 36,* 71–76.

Albrecht, J. S., & others (2013). Quality of hospice care for individuals with dementia. *Journal of the American Geriatrics Society, 61,* 1060–1065.

Alegret, M., & others (2014, in press). Cognitive, genetic, and brain perfusion factors associated with four-year incidence of Alzheimer's disease from mild cognitive impairment. *Journal of Alzheimer's Disease.*

Alkayed, K., Al Hmood, A., & Madanat, F. (2013). Prognostic effect of blood transfusion in children with acute lymphoblastic leukemia, *Blood Research, 48,* 133–148.

Alladi, S., & others (2013). Bilingualism delays age of onset of dementia, independent of education and immigration status. *Neurology, 81,* 1938–1944.

Allaire, J. C. (2012). Everyday cognition. In S. K. Whitbourne & M. Sliwinski (Eds.), *Wiley-Blackwell handbook of adult development and aging.* New York: Wiley.

Allemand, M., Zimprich, D., & Hendriks, A. A. J. (2008). Age differences in five personality domains across the life span. *Developmental Psychology, 44,* 758–770.

Allen, J. P., & others (2009, April). *Portrait of the secure teen as an adult.* Paper presented at the meeting of the Society for Research in Child Development, Denver.

Allen, J., & Allen, C. (2009). *Escaping the endless adolescence.* New York: Ballantine.

Allen, J. P., Chango, J., Szwedo, D., & Schad, M. (2014). Long-term sequalae of subclinical depressive symptoms in early adolescence. *Development and Psychopathology, 26,* 171–180.

Allen, J. P., & Miga, E. M. (2010). Attachment in adolescence: A move to the level of emotion regulation. *Journal of Social and Personal Relationships, 27,* 226–234.

Allen, T. D. (2013). The work-family role interface: A synthesis of the research from industrial and organizational psychology. In I. B. Weiner & others (Eds.), *Handbook of psychology* (2nd ed., Vol. 12). New York: Wiley.

Allendorf, K. (2013). Schemas of marital change: From arranged marriages to eloping for love. *Journal of Marriage and the Family, 75,* 453–469.

Allington, R. L. (2015). *What really matters for middle school readers.* Upper Saddle River, NJ: Pearson.

Allor, J., & Al Otaiba, S. A. (2013). In B. G. Cook & M. G. Tankersley (Eds.), *Research-based practices in special education.* Upper Saddle River, NJ: Pearson.

Almeida, D. M., & Horn, M. C. (2004). Is daily life more stressful during middle adulthood? In C. D. Ryff & R. C. Kessler (Eds.), *A portrait of midlife in the United States.* Chicago: University of Chicago Press.

Almeida, D. M., Piazza, J. R., Stawski, R. S., & Klein, L. C. (2011). The speedometer of life: Stress, health, and aging. In K. W. Schaie & S. L. Willis (Eds.), *Handbook of the psychology of aging* (7th ed.). New York: Elsevier.

Almquist, Y.B., & Brannstrom, L. (2014). Childhood peer status and the clustering of social, economic, and health-related circumstances in adulthood. *Social Science & Medicine, 105,* 67–75.

Al-Safi, Z. A., & Santoro, N. (2014, in press). Menopausal hormone therapy and menopausal symptoms. *Fertility and Sterility.*

Alsaker, F. D., & Valanover, S. (2012). The Bernese Program Against Victimization in Kindergarten and Elementary School. *New Directions in Youth Development, 133,* 15–28.

Alvarez, O., & others (2012). Effect of hydroxyurea treatment on renal function parameters: Results from the multi-center placebo controlled Baby HUG clinical trial for infants with sickle cell anemia. *Pediatric Blood and Cancer, 59*(4), 668–674.

Alves, D., & others (2014). Innovative moments in grief therapy: The meaning reconstruction approach and the processes of self-narrative performance. *Psychotherapy Research, 24,* 25–41.

Alves, L., Correia, A. S., Miguel, R., Alegria, P., & Bugalho, P. (2012). Alzheimer's disease: A clinical practice-oriented review. *Frontiers in Neurology, 3,* 63.

Aly, M., & Moscovitch, M. (2010). The effects of sleep on episodic memory in older and younger adults. *Memory, 18,* 327–334.

Alzheimer's Association (2010). 2010 Alzheimer's disease facts and figures. *Alzheimer's Disease & Dementia, 6,* 158–194.

Alzheimer's Association (2013). *2013 Alzheimer's disease facts and figures.* Chicago: Alzheimer's Association.

Amabile, T. M. (1993). Commentary. In D. Goleman, P. Kaufman, & M. Ray, *The creative spirit.* New York: Plume.

Amato, P. R. (2007). Transformative processes in marriage: Some thoughts from a sociologist. *Journal of Marriage and the Family, 69,* 305–309.

Amato, P. R. (2010). Research on divorce: Continuing trends and new developments. *Journal of Marriage and the Family, 72,* 650–666.

Amato, P. R., & Booth, A. (1996). A prospective study of divorce and parent-child relationships, *Journal of Marriage and the Family, 58,* 356–365.

Amato, P. R., & Dorius, C. (2010). Fathers, children, and divorce. In M. E. Lamb (Ed.), *The role of the father in child development* (5th ed.) New York: Wiley.

Ambrose, D., Sternberg, R. J., & Sriraman, B. (2012). Considering the effects of dogmatism on giftedness and talent development. In D. Ambrose, R. J. Sternberg, & B. Sriraman (Eds.), *Confronting dogmatism in gifted education.* New York: Taylor & Francis.

American Academy of Pediatrics: Section on Breastfeeding (2012). Breastfeeding and the use of human milk. *Pediatrics, 129,* e827–e841.

American Academy of Pediatrics & Reiff, M. I. (2011). *ADHD: What every parent needs to know* (2nd ed.). Washington, DC: Author.

American Academy of Pediatrics Task Force on Infant Positioning and SIDS (2000). Changing concepts of sudden infant death syndrome. *Pediatrics, 105,* 650–656.

American Association of University Women (2006). *Drawing the line: Sexual harassment on campus.* Washington, DC: American Association of University Women.

American Cancer Society (2014). *Information and resources for cancer.* Retrieved March 20, 2014, from http:www.cancer.org

American College Health Association (2008). American College Health Association National College Health Assessment, Spring 2007. *Journal of American College Health, 56,* 469–479.

American Pregnancy Association (2014). *Mercury levels in fish.* Retrieved February 1, 2014, from www.americanpregnancy.org/pregnancyhealth/fishmercury.htm

American Psychiatric Association (2013). *Diagnostic and statistical manual of mental disorders, 5th edition (DSM-V).* Washington, DC: Author.

American Psychological Association (2003). *Psychology: Scientific problem solvers.* Washington, DC: Author.

American Psychological Association (2007). *Stress in America.* Washington, DC: Author.

Amso, D., & Johnson, S. P. (2010). Building object knowledge from perceptual input. In B. Hood & L. Santos (Eds.), *The origins of object knowledge.* New York: Oxford University Press.

Amsterdam, B. K. (1968). *Mirror behavior in children under two years of age.* Unpublished doctoral dissertation. University of North Carolina, Chapel Hill.

Anderman, E. M. (2012). Adolescence. In K. L. Harris, S. Graham, & T. Urdan (Eds.), *APA educational psychology handbook.* Washington, DC: American Psychological Association.

Andersen, S. L., Sebastiani, P., Dworkis, D. A., Feldman, L., & Perls, T. T. (2012). Health span approximates life span among many supercentenarians: Compression of morbidity at the approximate limit of life span. *Journals of Gerontology A: Biological Sciences and Medical Sciences, 67A,* 395–405.

Anderson, A. L., & Thomason, M. E. (2013). Functional plasticity before the cradle: A review of neural functional imaging in the human fetus. *Neuroscience and Biobehavioral Review, 37*(9 Pt B), 2220–2232.

Anderson, E. R., & Greene, S. M. (2011). "My child and I are a package deal": Balancing adult and child concerns in repartnering after divorce. *Journal of Family Psychology, 25,* 741–750.

Anderson, E., Greene, S. M., Hetherington, E. M., & Clingempeel, W. G. (1999). The dynamics of parental remarriage. In E. M. Hetherington (Ed.), *Coping with divorce, single parenting, and remarriage.* Mahwah, NJ: Erlbaum.

Anderson, K. A., Richardson, V. E., Fields, N. L., & Harootyan, R. A. (2013). Inclusion or exclusion? Exploring barriers to employment for low-income older adults. *Journal of Gerontological Social Work, 56,* 318–334.

Anderson, M. L., & Finlay, B. L. (2014). Allocating structure to function: The strong links between neuroplasticity and natural selection. *Frontiers in Human Neuroscience, 7,* 918.

Anderson, P. J., & others (2011). Attention problems in a representative sample of extremely preterm/extremely low birth weight children. *Developmental Neuropsychology, 36,* 57–73.

Anderson, S. A., & Sabatelli, R. M. (2011). *Family interaction* (5th ed.). Upper Saddle River, NJ: Pearson.

Andersson, H., & Bergman, L. R. (2011). The role of task persistence in young adolescence for successful educational and occupational attainment in middle adulthood. *Developmental Psychology, 47,* 950–960.

Andersson, U. (2010). The contribution of working memory capacity to foreign language comprehension in children. *Memory, 18,* 458–472.

Angel, L., Fay, S., Bouazzaoui, B., & Isingrini, M. (2011). Two hemispheres for better memory in old age: Role of executive functioning. *Journal of Cognitive Neuroscience, 23*(12), 3767–3777.

Anguera, J. A., & others (2013). Video game training enhances cognitive control in older adults. *Nature, 501,* 97–101.

Annweiler, C., Montero-Odasso, M., Bartha, R., & Beauchet, O. (2012). Nutrient biomarker patterns, cognitive function, and MRI measures of brain aging. *Neurology, 78,* 1281.

Ansado, J., & others (2013). Coping with task demand in aging using neural compensation and neural reserve triggers primarily intra-hemispheric-based neurofunctional reorganization. *Neuroscience Research, 75,* 295–304.

Anspaugh, D., & Ezell, G. (2013). *Teaching today's health* (10th ed.). Upper Saddle River, NJ: Pearson.

Antai-Otong, D. (2003). Suicide: Life span considerations. *Nursing Clinics of North America, 38,* 137–150.

Anton, S. D., Karabetian, C., Naugle, K., & Buford, T. W. (2013). Obesity and diabetes as accelerators of functional decline: Can lifestyle interventions maintain functional status in high risk older adults? *Experimental Gerontology, 48,* 888–897.

Antonenko, D., & Floel, A. (2014). Healthy aging by staying selectively connected: A mini-review. *Gerontology, 60*(1), 3–9.

Antonenko, D., & others (2013). Functional and structural syntax networks in aging. *Neuroimage, 83,* 513–523.

Antonucci, R., & others (2012). Use of non-steroidal anti-inflammatory drugs in pregnancy: Impact on the fetus and newborn. *Current Drug Metabolism, 13*(4), 474–490.

Antonucci, T. C., Ajrouch, K., & Birditt, K. (2014). The convoy model: Explaining social relations from a multidisciplinary perspective. *Gerontologist, 54,* 82–92.

Antonucci, T. C., Akiyama, H., & Sherman, A. M. (2007). Social networks, support, and integration. In J. E. Birren (Ed.), *Encyclopedia of gerontology* (2nd ed.). San Diego: Academic Press.

Antonucci, T. C., Birditt, K., & Ajrouch, K. (2013). Social relationships and aging. In I.B Weiner & others (Eds.), *Handbook of psychology* (2nd ed., Vol. 6). New York: Wiley.

Antonucci, T. C., Lansford, J. E., & Akiyama, H. (2001). The impact of positive and negative aspects of marital relationships and friendships on the well-being of older adults. In J. P. Reinhardt (Ed.), *Negative and positive support.* Mahwah, NJ: Erlbaum.

Antonucci, T. C., Vandewater, E. A., & Lansford, J. E. (2000). Adulthood and aging: Social processes and development. In A. Kazdin (Ed.), *Encyclopedia of psychology.* Washington, DC & New York: American Psychological Association and Oxford University Press.

Anyaegbu, E., & Dharnidharka, V. R. (2014). Hypertension in the teenagers. *Pediatric Clinics of North America, 61,* 131–151.

Apperly, I. A. (2012). EPS prize lecture. "What is theory of mind": Concepts, cognitive processes, and individual differences. *Quarterly Journal of Experimental Psychology, 65*(5), 825–839.

Arabi, M., Frongillo, E. A., Avula, R., & Mangasaryan, N. (2012). Infant and young child feeding in developing countries. *Child Development, 83,* 32–45.

Arbib, M. A. (2012). *How the brain got language.* New York: Oxford University Press.

Argyri, L., & others (2014, in press). Molecular basis for increased risk for late-onset Alzheimer's disease due to the naturally occurring Leu28Pro mutation in apolipoprotein E4. *Journal of Biological Chemistry.*

Ariceli, G., Castro, J., Cesena, J., & Toro, J. (2005). Anorexia nervosa in male adolescents: Body image, eating attitudes, and psychological traits. *Journal of Adolescent Health, 36,* 221–226.

Arneric, S. P., Laird, J. M., Chappell, A. S., & Kennedy, J. D. (2014). Tailoring chronic pain treatments for the elderly: Are we prepared for the challenge? *Drug Discovery Today, 19*(1), 8–17.

Arnett, J. J. (2004). *Emerging adulthood.* New York: Oxford University Press.

Arnett, J. J. (2006). Emerging adulthood: Understanding the new way of coming of age. In J. J. Arnett & J. L. Tanner (Eds.), *Emerging adults in America.* Washington, DC: American Psychological Association.

Arnett, J. J. (2007). Socialization in emerging adulthood. In J. E. Grusec & P. D. Hastings (Eds.), *Handbook of socialization.* New York: Guilford.

Arnett, J. J. (2010). Oh, grow up! Generational grumbling and the new life stage of emerging adulthood—Commentary on Trzesniewski & Donnellan (2010). *Perspectives on Psychological Science, 5,* 89–92.

Arnett, J. J. (Ed.) (2012). *Adolescent psychology around the world.* New York: Psychology Press.

Arnett, J. J., & Fishel, E. (2013). *When will my grown-up kid grow up?* New York: Workman.

Arnold, A. (2012, April). *Reframing sexual differentiation in the brain.* Paper presented at the Gender Development Research conference, San Francisco.

Arnold, K., & others (2013). Fetal alcohol spectrum disorders: Knowledge and screening practices of university hospital medical students and residents. *Journal of Population Therapeutics and Clinical Pharmacology, 20,* e18–e25.

Arnsburg, K., & Kirstein-Miles, J. (2014). Interrelation between protein synthesis, proteostasis, and life span. *Current Genomics, 15,* 66–75.

Aronow, W. S. (2007). Cardiovascular system. In J. E. Birren (ed.), *Encyclopedia of gerontology* (2nd ed.). San Diego: Academic Press.

Aronson, E. (1986, August). *Teaching students things they think they already know about: The case of prejudice and desegregation.* Paper presented at the meeting of the American Psychological Association, Washington, DC.

Arseth, A., Kroger, J., Martinussen, M., & Marcia, J. E. (2009). Meta-analytic studies of identity status and the relational issues of attachment and intimacy. *Identity, 9,* 1–32.

Arterberry, M. E. (2008). Perceptual development. In M. E. Haith & J. B. Benson (Eds.), *Encyclopedia of infant and early childhood development.* Oxford, UK: Elsevier.

Asbury, K., & Plomin, R. (2014). *G is for genes: The impact of genetics on education and achievement.* New York: Wiley.

Asero, P., & others (2014, in press). Relevance of genetic investigation in male infertility. *Journal of Endocrinological Investigation.*

Ash, J. A., & Rapp, P. R. (2014 in press). A quantitative neural network approach to understanding aging phenotypes. *Aging Research Reviews.*

Asheer, S., & others (2014). Engaging pregnant and parenting teens: Early challenges and lessons learned from the evaluation of adolescent pregnancy prevention approaches. *Journal of Adolescent Health, 5*(3, Suppl.), S84–S91.

Asian, Y., & others (2014, in press). The impact of metabolic syndrome on serum total testosterone level in patients with erectile dysfunction. *Aging Male.*

Aslan, A., Zellner, M., & Bauml, K. H. (2010). Working memory capacity predicts listwise directed forgetting in adults and children. *Memory, 18*(4), 442–450.

Aslin, R. N. (2012). Infant eyes: A window on cognitive development. *Infancy, 17,* 126–140.

Aslin, R. N., Jusczyk, P. W., & Pisoni, D. B. (1998). Speech and auditory processing during infancy: Constraints on and precursors to language. In W. Damon (Ed.), *Handbook of child psychology* (5th ed., Vol. 2). New York: Wiley.

Aspen Institute (2013). *Two generations, one future.* Washington, DC: Aspen Institute.

Associated Press–NORC Center for Public Affairs Research (2013). *Survey on later-life work.* Chicago: NORC Center for Public Affairs, University of Chicago.

Astington, J. W., & Hughes, C. (2013). Theory of mind: Self-reflection and social understanding. In P. D. Zelazo (Ed.), *Handbook of developmental psychology.* New York: Oxford University Press.

Atkinson, J., & Braddick, O. (2013). Visual development. In P. D. Zelazo (Ed.), *Oxford handbook of developmental psychology.* New York: Oxford University Press.

Atkinson, R. M., Ryan, S. C., & Turner, J. A. (2001). Variation among aging alcoholic patients in treatment. *American Journal of Geriatric Psychiatry, 9,* 275–282.

Attar-Schwartz, S., Tan, J. P., Buchanan, A., Flouri, E., & Griggs, J. (2009). Grandparenting and adolescent development in two-parent biological, lone-parent, and step-families. *Journal of Family Psychology, 23,* 67–75.

Auerbach, A. J., & Lee, R. (2011). Welfare and generational equity in sustainable unfunded pension systems. *Journal of Public Economics, 95,* 16–27.

Augestad, L. A., Rand-Hendriksen, K., Staverm, K., & Kristiansen, I. S. (2013). Time trade-off and attitudes toward euthanasia: Implications of using 'death' as an anchor in health state valuation. *Quality of Life Research, 22*(4), 705–714.

Autism Research Institute (2013). *DSM-V: What changes may mean.* Retrieved May 7, 2013 from www.autism.com/index.php/news_dsmV

Avery, M. D. (2013). Current resources for evidence-based practice, May/June 2013. *Journal of Midwifery and Women's Health, 58,* 339–345.

Avila, J., & others (2014, in press). Sources of extracellular tau and its signaling. *Journal of Alzheimer's Disease.*

Ayoub, C., Vallotton, C. D., & Mastergeorge, A. M. (2011). Developmental pathways to integrated social skills: The role of parenting and early intervention. *Child Development, 82,* 583–600.

Azagba, S., & Sharaf, M. F. (2014). Physical inactivity among older Canadian adults. *Journal of Physical Activity and Health, 11*(1), 99–108.

Azmitia, M., Syed, M., & Radmacher, K. A. (2014, in press). Finding your niche: Identity and emotional support in emerging adults' adjustment to the transition to college. *Journal of Research in Adolescence.*

B

Babbar, S., Parks-Savage, A. C., & Chauhan, S. P. (2012). Yoga during pregnancy. *American Journal of Perinatology, 29*(6), 459–464.

Bach, L. E., Mortimer, J. A., Vandeweerd, C., & Corvin, J. (2013). The association of physical and mental health with sexual activity in older adults in a retirement community. *Journal of Sexual Medicine, 10*(11), 2671–2678.

Bachman, J. G., & others (2002). *The decline of substance abuse in young adulthood.* Mahwah, NJ: Erlbaum.

Bachman, J. G., & others (2008). *The education-drug use connection.* Clifton, NJ: Psychology Press.

Bachschmid, M. M., & others (2013). Vascular aging: Chronic oxidative stress and impairment of redox signaling—consequences for vascular homeostatis and disease. *Annals of Medicine, 45*(1), 17–36.

Backhans, M. C., & Hemmingsson, T. (2012). Unemployment and mental health—Who is (not) affected? *European Journal of Public Health, 22,* 429–433.

Badaly, D. (2013). Peer similarity and influence for weight-related outcomes in adolescence: A meta-analytic review. *Clinical Psychology Review, 33,* 1218–1236.

Baddeley, A. D. (1990). *Human memory: Theory and practice.* Boston: Allyn & Bacon.

Baddeley, A. D. (2001). *Is working memory still working?* Paper presented at the meeting of the American Psychological Association, San Francisco.

Baddeley, A. D. (2007). *Working memory, thought, and action.* New York: Oxford University Press.

Baddeley, A. D. (2010). Working memory. *Current Biology, 20,* 136–140.

Baddeley, A. D. (2012). Working memory: Theories, models, and controversies. *Annual Review of Psychology* (Vol. 63). Palo Alto, CA: Annual Reviews.

Badger, J. L., & others (2014). Parkinson's disease in a dish—using stem cells as a molecular tool. *Neuropharmacology, 76* Pt. A, 88–96.

Badowski, M., & others (2014, in press). The influence of intrinsic and extrinsic factors on immune system aging. *Immunobiology.*

Baer, J., & Kaufman, J. C. (2013). *Being creative inside and outside the classroom.* The Netherlands: Sense Publishers.

Bahrick, L. E. (2010). Intermodal perception and selective attention to intersensory redundancy: Implications for social development and autism. In J. G. Bremner & T. D. Wachs (Eds.), *Wiley-Blackwell handbook of infant development* (2nd ed.). New York: Wiley.

Bahrick, L. E., & Hollich, G. (2008). Intermodal perception. In M. M. Haith & J. B. Benson (Eds.), *Encyclopedia of infant and early childhood development.* Oxford, UK: Elsevier.

Bailey, D. M., & others (2013). Elevated aerobic fitness sustained throughout the adult lifespan is associated with improved cerebral hemodynamics. *Stroke, 44*(11), 3235–3238.

Bailey, H. R., Dunlosky, J., & Hertzog, C. (2014, in press). Does strategy training reduce age-related deficits in working memory? *Gerontology.*

Baillargeon, R. (1995). The object concept revisited: New directions in the investigation of infants' physical knowledge. In C. E. Granrud (Ed.), *Visual perception and cognition in infancy.* Hillsdale, NJ: Erlbaum.

Baillargeon, R. (2004). The acquisition of physical knowledge in infancy: A summary in eight lessons. In U. Goswami (Ed.), *Blackwell handbook of childhood cognitive development.* Malden, MA: Blackwell.

Baillargeon, R. (2008). Innate ideas revisited: For a principle of persistence in infants' physical reasoning. *Perspectives on Psychological Science, 3,* 2–13.

Baillargeon, R. (2014). Cognitive development in infancy. *Annual Review of Psychology* (Vol. 65). Palo Alto, CA: Annual Reviews.

Baillargeon, R., & Carey, S. (2012). Core cognition and beyond: The acquisition of physical and numerical knowledge. In S. Pauen & M. Bornstein (Eds.), *Early childhood development and later outcome.* New York: Cambridge University Press.

Baillargeon, R., & DeVos, J. (1991). Object permanence in young children: Further evidence. *Child Development, 62,* 1227–1246.

Baillargeon, R., Li, J., Gertner, Y., & Wu, D. (2011). How do infants reason about physical events? In U. Goswami (Ed.), *Wiley-Blackwell handbook of childhood cognitive development* (2nd ed.). New York: Wiley.

Baillargeon, R., & others (2012). Object individuation and physical reasoning in infancy: An integrative account. *Language, Learning, and Development, 8,* 4–46.

Bajoghli, H., & others (2014, in press). "I love you more than I can stand!"—romantic love, symptoms of depression and anxiety, and sleep complaints are related among young adults. *International Journal of Psychiatry in Clinical Practice.*

Bakeman, R., & Brown, J. V. (1980). Early interaction: Consequences for social and mental development at three years. *Child Development, 51,* 437–447.

Baker, J. H., Thorton, L. M., Lichtenstein, P., & Bulik, C. M. (2012). Pubertal development predicts eating behaviors in adolescents. *International Journal of Eating Disorders, 45*(7), 819–826.

Baker, J. K., Fenning, R. M., & Crnic, K. A. (2011). Emotion socialization by mothers and fathers: Coherence among behaviors and associations with parent attitudes and children's competence. *Social Development, 20,* 412–430.

Baker, R. K., Pettigrew, T. L., & Poulin-Dubois, D. (2014). Infants' ability to associate motion paths with object kinds. *Infant Behavior and Development, 37,* 119–129.

Bakermans-Kranenburg, M. J., & van IJzendoorn, M. H. (2011). Differential susceptibility to rearing environment depending on dopamine-related genes: New evidence and a meta-analysis. *Development and Psychopathology, 23,* 39–52.

Balarajah, S., & Cavanna, A. E. (2013). The pathophysiology of impulse control disorders in Parkinson disease. *Behavioral Neurology, 26*(4), 237–244.

Baldwin, S. A., Christian, S., Berkeljon, A., & Shadish, W. R. (2012). The effects of family therapies for adolescent delinquency and substance abuse: A meta-analysis. *Journal of Marital and Family Therapy, 38,* 281–304.

Ball, J. W., Bindler, R. C., & Cowen, K. J. (2014, in press). *Child health nursing* (3rd ed.). Upper Saddle River, NJ: Pearson.

Ball, K., Edwards, J. D., Ross, L. A., & McGwin, G. (2010). Effects of cognitive training interventions with older adults: a randomized controlled trial. *Journal of the American Geriatrics Society, 55,* 1–10.

Balsa, A. I., Giuliano, L. M., & French, M. T. (2011). The effects of alcohol use on academic achievement in high school. *Economics of Education Review, 30,* 1–15.

Balsam, K., & Hughes, T. (2013). Sexual orientation, victimization, and hate crimes. In C. J. Patterson & A. R. D'Augelli (Eds.), *Handbook of psychology and sexual orientation.* New York: Oxford University Press.

Baltes, P. B. (1987). Theoretical propositions of life-span developmental psychology: On the dynamics between growth and decline. *Developmental Psychology, 23,* 611–626.

Baltes, P. B. (2003). On the incomplete architecture of human ontogeny: Selection, optimization, and compensation as foundation for developmental theory. In U. M. Staudinger & U. Lindenberger (Eds.), *Understanding human development.* Boston: Kluwer.

Baltes, P. B. (2006). *Facing our limits. The very old and the future of aging.* Unpublished manuscript, Max Planck Institute, Berlin.

Baltes, P. B., & Kunzmann, U. (2007). Wisdom and aging: The road toward excellence in mind and character. In D. C. Park & N. Schwarz (Eds.), *Cognitive aging: A primer* (2nd ed.). Philadelphia: Psychology Press.

Baltes, P. B., Lindenberger, U., & Staudinger, U. (2006). Life-span theory in developmental psychology. In W. Damon & R. Lerner (Eds.), *Handbook of child psychology* (6th ed.), New York: Wiley.

Baltes, P. B., Reuter-Lorenz, P., & Rösler, F. (Eds.) (2011). *Lifespan development and the brain.* New York: Cambridge University Press.

Baltes, P. B., & Smith, J. (2003). New frontiers in the future of aging: From successful aging of the young old to the dilemmas of the fourth age. *Gerontology, 49,* 123–135.

Baltes, P. B., & Smith, J. (2008). The fascination of wisdom: Its nature, ontogeny, and function. *Perspectives in Psychological Sciences, 3,* 56–64.

Bamaca-Colbert, M., Umana-Taylor, A. J., Espinosa-Hernandez, G., & Brown, A. M. (2012). Behavioral autonomy expectations among Mexican-origin mother-daughter dyads: An examination of within-group variability. *Journal of Adolescence, 35,* 691–700.

Bandura, A. (1986). *Social foundations of thought and action: A social cognitive theory.* Englewood Cliffs, NJ: Prentice Hall.

Bandura, A. (1998, August). *Swimming against the mainstream: Accentuating the positive aspects of humanity.* Paper presented at the meeting of the American Psychological Association, San Francisco.

Bandura, A. (2001). Social cognitive theory. *Annual Review of Psychology* (Vol. 52). Palo Alto, CA: Annual Reviews.

Bandura, A. (2004, May). *Toward a psychology of human agency.* Paper presented at the meeting of the American Psychological Society, Chicago.

Bandura, A. (2008). Reconstrual of free will from the agentic perspective of social cognitive theory. In J. Baer, J. C. Kaufman, & R. F. Baumeister (Eds.), *Are we free? Psychology and free will.* Oxford, UK: Oxford University Press.

Bandura, A. (2009). Social and policy impact of social cognitive theory. In M. Mark, S. Donaldson & B. Campbell (Eds.), *Social psychology and program/policy evaluation.* New York: Guilford.

Bandura, A. (2010a). Self-efficacy. In D. Matsumoto (Ed.), *Cambridge dictionary of psychology.* New York: Cambridge University Press.

Bandura, A. (2010b). Vicarious learning. In D. Matsumoto (Ed.), *Cambridge dictionary of psychology.* New York: Cambridge University Press.

Bandura, A. (2012). Social cognitive theory. *Annual Review of Clinical Psychology* (Vol. 8). Palo Alto, CA: Annual Reviews.

Band-Winterstein, T. (2014, in press). Health care provision for older persons: The interplay between ageism and elder neglect. *Journal of Applied Gerontology.*

Banerjee, S. (2011). Hearing aids in the real world: Use of multimemory and multivolume controls. *Journal of the American Academy of Audiology, 22,* 359–374.

Bangen, K. J., Meeks, T. W., & Jeste, D. V. (2013). Defining and assessing wisdom: A review of the literature. *American Journal of Geriatric Psychiatry, 21,* 1254–1266.

Bangerter, L. R., Kim, K., Birditt, K. S., & Fingerman, K. L. (2014, in press). Perceptions of giving and support and depressive symptoms in late life. *Gerontologist.*

Bangerter, L. R., & Waldron, V. R. (2014). Turning points in long-distance grandparent-grandchild relationships. *Journal of Aging Studies, 29,* 88–97.

Banja, J. (2005). Talking to the dying. *Case Manager, 16,* 37–39.

Bank, L., Burraston, B., & Snyder, J. (2004). Sibling conflict and ineffective parenting as predictors of adolescent boys' antisocial behavior and peer difficulties: Additive and interactive effects. *Journal of Research on Adolescence. 14,* 99–125.

Banks, J. A. (2014). *Introduction to multicultural education* (5th ed.) Upper Saddle River, NJ: Pearson.

Banuelos, C., & others (2014). Prefrontal cortical GABAergic dysfunction contributes to age-related working memory impairment. *Journal of Neuroscience, 34,* 3457–3466.

Barakat, R., Pelaez, M., Montejo, R., Refoyo, I., & Coteron, J. (2014, in press). Exercise throughout pregnancy does not cause preterm delivery: A randomized, controlled trial. *Journal of Physical Activity and Health.*

Barbosa, V., Sa, M., & Carlos Rocha, J. (2014). Randomised controlled trial of cognitive narrative intervention for complicated grief in widowhood. *Aging and Mental Health, 18,* 354–362.

Barclay, L., & others (2012). The professionalizing of breast feeding—where are we a decade on? *Midwifery, 28*(3), 281–290.

Bardach, S. H., & Rowles, G. D. (2012). Geriatric education in the health professions: Are we making progress? *Gerontologist, 52*(5), 607–618.

Barefoot, J. C., Mortensen, E. L., Helms, J., Avlund, K., & Schroll, M. (2001). A longitudinal study of gender differences in depressive symptoms from age 50 to 80. *Psychology and Aging, 16,* 342–345.

Barger, J. L. (2013). An adipocentric perspective of resveratrol as a calorie restriction mimetic. *Annals of the New York Academy of Sciences, 1290,* 122–129.

Bargh, J. A., & McKenna, K. Y. A. (2004). The Internet and social life. *Annual Review of Psychology* (Vol. 55). Palo Alto, CA: Annual Reviews.

Barker, R., & Wright, H. F. (1951). *One boy's day.* New York: Harper & Row.

Barnett, J. E., & Francis, A. L. (2012). Using higher order thinking questions to foster critical thinking: A classroom study. *Educational Psychology, 32,* 201–211.

Barnett, W. S., & others (2006). *Educational effectiveness of the Tools of the Mind curriculum: A randomized trial.* New Brunswick, NJ: National Institute of Early Education Research, Rutgers University.

Baron, C. (2012). Using the gradient of human cortical bone properties to determine age-related bone changes via ultrasonic guided waves. *Ultrasound in Medicine and Biology, 38,* 972–981.

Baron, N. S. (1992). *Growing up with language.* Reading, MA: Addison-Wesley.

Baron-Cohen, S. (2008). Autism, hypersystematizing, and truth. *Quarterly Journal of Experimental Psychology, 61,* 64–75.

Baron-Cohen, S. (2011). The empathizing-systematizing (E-S) theory of autism: A cognitive developmental account. In U. Goswami (Ed.), *Wiley-Blackwell handbook of childhood cognitive development* (2nd ed.). New York: Wiley.

Baron-Cohen, S., Golan, O., Chapman, E., & Granader, Y. (2007). Transported to a world of emotion. *The Psychologist, 20,* 76–77.

Barrett, T. M., Traupman, E., & Needham, A. (2008). Infants' visual anticipation of object structure in grasp planning. *Infant Behavior and Development, 31,* 1–9.

Bartel, M. A., Weinstein, J. R., & Schaffer, D. V. (2012). Directed evolution of novel adeno-associated viruses for therapeutic gene delivery. *Gene Therapy, 19*(6), 694–700.

Barth, T. (2012). Relationships and sexuality of imprisoned men in the German penal system—a survey of inmates in a Berlin prison. *International Journal of Law and Psychiatry, 35,* 153–158.

Bartlett, J. D., & others (2014, in press). An ecological analysis of infant neglect by adolescent mothers. *Child Abuse and Neglect.*

Bartsch, K., & Wellman, H. M. (1995). *Children talk about the mind.* New York: Oxford University Press.

Bascandziev, I., & Harris, P. L. (2011). The role of testimony in young children's solution of a gravity-driven invisible displacement task. *Cognitive Development, 25,* 233–246.

Basilio, C. D., & others (2014, in press). The Mexican-American Biculturalism Scale: Bicultural comfort, ease, and advantage for adolescents and adults. *Psychological Assessment.*

Baskin, F., & others (2011). Coalitions on mental health and aging: Lessons learned for policy and practice. *Journal of Aging and Social Policy, 23,* 323–332.

Bassil, K. L., & others (2014, in press). Impact of late preterm and early term infants on Canadian Neonatal Intensive Care Units. *American Journal of Perinatology.*

Bates, E. (1990). Language about me and you: Pronomial reference and the emerging concept of self. In D. Cicchetti & M. Beeghly (Eds.), *The self in transition: Infancy to childhood.* Chicago: University of Chicago Press.

Bates, J. E. (2012a). Behavioral regulation as a product of temperament and environment. In S. L. Olson & A. J. Sameroff (Eds.), *Biopsychosocial regulatory processes in the development of childhood behavioral problems.* New York: Cambridge University Press.

Bates, J. E. (2012b). Temperament as a tool in promoting early childhood development. In S. L. Odom, E. P. Pungello, & N. Gardner-Neblett (Eds.), *Infants, toddlers, and families in poverty.* New York: Guilford University Press.

Bateson, D. J., Weisberg, E., McCaffery, K. J., & Luscombe, G. M. (2012). When online becomes Online: Attitudes to safer sex practices in older and younger women using an Australian internet dating service. *Sexual Health, 9,* 152–159.

Bauer, M. E., & others (2013). Psychoneuroendocrine interventions aimed at attenuating immunosenescence. *Biogerontology. 14*(1), 9–20.

Bauer, P. J. (2009a). Learning and memory: Like a horse and carriage. In A. Woodward & A. Needham (Eds.), *Learning and the infant mind.* New York: Oxford University Press.

Bauer, P. J. (2009b). Neurodevelopmental changes in infancy and beyond: implications for learning and memory. In O. A. Barbarin & B. H. Wasik (Eds.), *Handbook of child development and early education.* New York: Guilford.

Bauer, P. J. (2013). Memory. In P. D. Zelazo (Ed.), *Oxford handbook of developmental psychology.* New York: Oxford University Press.

Bauer, P. J., & Fivush, R. (Eds.) (2014). *Wiley-Blackwell handbook of children's memory.* New York: Wiley.

Bauer, P. J., Wenner, J. A., Dropik, P. I., & Wewerka, S. S. (2000). Parameters of remembering and forgetting in the transition from infancy to early childhood. *Monographs of the Society for Research in Child Development, 65*(4, Serial No. 263).

Bauer, P., & Zelazo, P. D. (2013). X. NIH Toolbox Cognition Battery (CB): Summary, conclusions, and implications for cognitive development. *Monographs of the Society for Research in Child Development, 78,* 133–146.

Bauer, R. M., & Dunn, C. B. (2013). Research methods in neuropsychology. In I. B. Weiner & others (Eds.), *Handbook of psychology* (2nd ed., Vol. 2). New York: Wiley.

Bauman, K. E., & others (2002). Influence of a family program on adolescent smoking and drinking prevalence. *Prevention Science, 3,* 35–42.

Bauman, R. W. (2015, in press). *Microbiology with diseases by body system* (4th ed.). Upper Saddle River, NJ: Pearson.

Baumeister, R. F., Campbell, J. D., Krueger, J. I., & Vohs, K. D. (2003). Does high self-esteem cause better performance, interpersonal success, happiness, or healthier lifestyles? *Psychological Science in the Public Interest, 4*(1), 1–44.

Baumeister, R. F., & Vohs, K. D. (2002). The pursuit of meaningfulness in life. In C. R. Snyder & S. J. Lopez (Eds.), *Handbook of positive psychology.* New York: Oxford University Press.

Baumrind, D. (1971). Current patterns of parental authority. *Developmental Psychology Monographs, 4*(1, Pt. 2).

Baumrind, D. (1999, November). Unpublished review of J. W. Santrock's *Child development* (9th ed.). New York: McGraw-Hill.

Baumrind, D. (2012). Authoritative parenting revisited: History and current status. In R. Larzelere, A. S. Morris, & A. W. Harist (Eds.), *Authoritative parenting.* Washington, DC: American Psychological Association.

Baumrind, D., Larzelere, R. E., & Cowan, P. A. (2002). Ordinary physical punishment: is it harmful? Comment on Gershoff. *Psychological Bulletin, 128,* 590–595.

Baumrind, D., Larzelere, R. E., & Owens, E. B. (2010). Effects of preschool parents' power assertive patterns and practices on adolescent development. *Parenting, 10,* 157–201.

Bauserman, R. (2002). Child adjustment in joint-custody versus sole-custody arrangements: A meta-analytical review. *Journal of Family Psychology, 16,* 91–102.

Bayer, R., Fairchild, A. L., Hopper, K., & Nathanson, C. A. (2013). Public health. Confronting the sorry state of U.S. health. *Science, 341,* 962–963.

Bayley, N. (1969). *Manual for the Bayley Scales of Infant Development.* New York: Psychological Corporation.

Bayley, N. (2006). *Bayley Scales of Infant and Toddler Development* (3rd ed.). San Antonio: Harcourt Assessment.

Beach, S. R. H., & Whisman, M. A. (2013). Genetics and epigenetics in family context: Introduction to the special section. *Journal of Family Psychology, 27,* 1–2.

Bearman, S. K., Presnall, K., Martinez, E., & Stice, E. (2006). The skinny on body dissatisfaction: A longitudinal study of adolescent girls and boys. *Journal of Youth and Adolescence, 35,* 217–229.

Beaty, J. J., & Pratt, L. (2015, in press). *Early literacy in preschool and kindergarten* (4th ed.). Upper Saddle River, NJ: Pearson.

Beauchamp, G., & Mennella, J. A. (2009). Early flavor learning and its impact on later feeding behavior. *Journal of Pediatric Gastroenterology and Nutrition, 48*(1, Suppl.), S25–S30.

Beaver, K. M., Vaughn, M. G., Wright, J. P., & Delisi, M. (2012). An interaction between perceived stress and 5HTTLPR genotype in the prediction of stable depressive symptomatology. *American Journal of Orthopsychiatry, 82,* 260–266.

Bechtold, A. G., Bushnell, E. W., & Salapatek, P. (1979, April.) *Infants' visual localization of visual and auditory targets.* Paper presented at the meeting of the Society for Research in Child Development, San Francisco.

Beckmann, M. M., & Stock, O. M. (2013). Antenatal perineal massage for reducing perineal trauma. *Cochrane Database of Systematic Reviews, 4,* CD005123.

Bedford, V. H. (2009). Sibling relationships: Adulthood. In D. Carr (Ed.), *Encyclopedia of the life course and human development.* Boston: Gale Cengage.

Bednar, R. L., Wells, M. G., & Peterson, S. R. (1995). *Self-esteem* (2nd ed.). Washington, DC: American Psychological Association.

Beeghly, M., & others. (2006). Prenatal cocaine exposure and children's language functioning at 6 and 9.5 years: Moderating effects of child age, birthweight, and gender. *Journal of Pediatric Psychology, 31,* 98–115.

Beets, M. W., & Foley, J. T. (2008). Association of father involvement and neighborhood quality with kindergartners' physical activity: A multilevel structural equation model. *American Journal of Health Promotion, 22*(3), 195–203.

Beets, M. W., & others (2014). From policy to practice: Strategies to meet physical activity standards in YMCA afterschool programs. *American Journal of Preventive Medicine, 46,* 281–288.

Behrens, H. (2012). Grammatical categories. In E. L. Bavin (Ed.), *Cambridge handbook of child language.* New York: Cambridge University Press.

Behrman, S., & Ebemeier, K. P. (2014). Can exercise prevent cognitive decline? *Practitioner, 258,* 17–21.

Bekman, S., & Aksu-Koc, A. (Eds.) (2012). *Perspectives on human development, family, and culture.* New York: Cambridge University Press.

Bell, A. F., Erickson, E. N., & Carter, C. S. (2014, in press). Beyond labor: The role of natural and synthetic oxytocin in the transition to motherhood. *Journal of Midwifery and Women's Health.*

Bell, L., & others (2013). Body mass index and waist circumference: Relationship to cardiovascular risk factors in children—Busselton Health Study 2005–2007. *Journal of Pediatrics and Child Health, 49*(11), 955–962.

Bell, M. A., & Cuevas, K. (2012). Using EEG to study cognitive development: Issues and practices. *Journal of Cognition and Development, 13,* 281–294.

Bell, M. A., & Cuevas, K. (2014). Psychobiology of executive function in early development. In J. A. Griffin, L. S. Freund, & P. McCardle (Eds.), *Executive function in preschool children.* Washington, DC: American Psychological Association.

Bell, M. A., Kraybill, J. H., & Diaz, A. (2014). Reactivity, regulation, and remembering: Associations between temperament and memory. In P. J. Bauer & R. Fivush (Eds.), *Handbook on the development of children's memory.* New York: Wiley.

Bell, M. A., Wolfe, C. D., & Adkins, D. R. (2007). Frontal lobe development during Infancy and childhood. In D. J., Coch, K. W., Fischer, & G. Dawson (Eds.), *Human behavior, learning, and the developing brain.* New York: Guilford.

Bell, R. D., & others (2012). Apolipoprotein E controls cerebrovascular integrity via cyclophilin A. *Nature, 485*(7399), 512–516.

Bell, S. M., & Ainsworth, M. D. S. (1972). Infant crying and maternal responsiveness. *Child Development, 43,* 1171–1190.

Belshaw, S. H., Siddique, J. A., Tanner, J., & Osho, G. S. (2012). The relationship between dating violence and suicidal behaviors in a national sample of adolescents. *Violence and Victims, 27,* 580–591.

Belsky, J. (1981). Early human experience: A family perspective. *Developmental Psychology, 17,* 3–23.

Belsky, J., & others. (2007). Are there long-term effects of early child care? *Child Development, 78,* 681–701.

Bem, S. I. (1977). On the utility of alternative procedures for assessing psychological androgyny. *Journal of Consulting and Clinical Psychology, 45,* 196–205.

Benarroch, E. E. (2013). Adult neurogenesis in the dentate gyrus: General concepts and potential implications. *Neurology, 81*(16), 1443–1452.

Ben-David, B. M., Tewari, A., Shakuf, V., & van Lieshout, P. H. (2014). Stroop effects in Alzheimer's disease: Selective attention speed of processing, or color-naming? A meta-analysis. *Journal of Alzheimer's Disease, 38*(4), 923–938.

Bender, H. L., & others (2007). Use of harsh discipline and developmental outcomes in adolescence. *Development and Psychopathology, 19,* 227–242.

Bendersky, M., & Sullivan, M. W. (2007). Basic methods in infant research. In A. Slater & M. Lewis (Eds.), *Introduction to infant development* (2nd ed.). New York: Oxford University Press.

Bendjilali, N., & others (2014, in press). Who are the Okinawans? Ancestry, genome diversity, and implications for the genetic study of human longevity from a geographically isolated population. *Journals of Gerontology A: Biological Sciences and Medical Sciences.*

Beneden Health (2013). *Middle age survey.* Unpublished data, Beneden Health, York, ENG.

Benediktsson, I., & others (2013). Comparing CenteringPregnancy to standard prenatal care plus prenatal education. *BMC Pregnancy and Childbirth* (Suppl.), S5.

Benenson, J. F., Apostolaris, N. H., & Parnass, J. (1997). Age and sex differences in dyadic and group interaction. *Developmental Psychology, 33,* 538–543.

Bener, A., & others (2013). Obesity index that better predicts metabolic syndrome: Body mass index, waist circumference, waist hip ratio, or waist height ratio. *Journal of Obesity, 2013,* 269038.

Bengtson, V. L. (1985). Diversity and symbolism in grandparental roles. In V. L. Bengtson & J. Robertson (Eds.), *Grandparenthood.* Newbury Park, CA: Sage.

Bengtsson, H., & Arvidsson, A. (2011). The impact of developing social perspective-taking skills on emotionality in middle and late childhood. *Social Development, 20,* 353–375.

Benichov, J., Cox, L. C., Tun, P. A., & Wingfield, A. (2012). Word recognition within a linguistic context: Effects of age, hearing acuity, verbal ability, and cognitive function. *Ear and Hearing, 33,* 250–256.

Benner, A. D., & Graham, S. (2013). The antecedents and consequences of racial/ethnic discrimination during adolescence: Does the source of discrimination matter? *Developmental Psychology, 49*(8), 1602–1613.

Bennett, K. M. (2006). Does marital status and marital status change predict physical health in older adults? *Psychological Medicine, 36,* 1313–1320.

Bennett, K. M. (2009). Widowhood. In D. Carr (Ed.), *Encyclopedia of the life course and human development.* Boston: Gale Cengage.

Bennett, S. A., Bagot, C. N., & Arya, R. (2012). Pregnancy loss and thrombophilia: The elusive link. *British Journal of Hematology, 157*(5), 529–542.

Bennetts, B. (2014). Update on molecular genetic testing methodologies. *Pathology, 46*(1, Suppl.), S38.

Benowitz-Fredericks, C. A., Garcia, K., Massey, M., Vassagar, B, & Borzekowski, D. L. (2012). Body image, eating disorders, and the relationship to adolescent media use. *Pediatric Clinics of North America, 59,* 693–704.

Benson, A. C., Torode, M. E., & Fiatarone Singh, M. A. (2008). The effects of high-intensity progressive resistance training on adiposity in children: A randomized controlled trial. *International Journal of Obesity, 32,* 1016–1027.

Benson, J. E., Sabbagh, M. A., Carlson, S. M., & Zelazo, P. D. (2014, in press). Individual differences in executive functioning predict preschoolers' improvement from theory-of-mind training. *Developmental Psychology.*

Ben-Zur, H. (2012). Loneliness, optimism, and well-being among married, divorced, and widowed individuals. *Journal of Psychology, 146,* 23–36.

Berchicci, M., Lucci, G., Perri, R. L., Spinelli, D., & Di Russo, F. (2014). Benefits of physical exercise on basic visuo-motor functions across age. *Frontiers in Aging Neuroscience, 6,* 48.

Berenson, J., Doty, M. M., Abram, M. K., & Shih, A. (2012). Achieving better quality of care for low-income populations: The roles of health insurance and the medical home in reducing health inequities. *Issues Brief, 11,* 1–18.

Bergen, D. (1988). Stages of play development. In D. Bergen (Ed.), *Play as a medium for learning and development.* Portsmouth, NH: Heinemann.

Berger, S. E., Chan, G., & Adolph, K. E. (2014, in press). What cruising infants understand about support for locomotion. *Infancy.*

Bergman-Levy, T., Barak, Y., Sigler, M., & Aizenberg, D. (2011). Suicide attempts and burden of physical illness among depressed elderly patients. *Archives of Gerontology and Geriatrics, 52,* 115–117.

Berk, L. E. (1994). Why children talk to themselves. *Scientific American, 271*(5), 78–83.

Berk, L. E., & Spuhl, S. T. (1995). Maternal interaction, private speech, and task performance in preschool children. *Early Childhood Research Quarterly, 10,* 145–169.

Berko Gleason, J. (2009). The development of language: An overview. In J. Berko Gleason & N. B. Ratner (Eds.), *The development of language* (7th ed.). Boston: Allyn & Bacon.

Berko, J. (1958). The child's learning of English morphology. *Word, 14,* 150–177.

Berlin, L. J. (2012). Leveraging attachment research to re-vision infant/toddler care for poor families. In S. L. Odom, E. P. Pungello, & N. Gardner-Nesblett (Eds.), *Infants, toddlers, and families in poverty.* New York: Guilford.

Berlin, L. J., & others (2009). Correlates and consequences of spanking and verbal punishment for low-income, White, African-American, and Mexican American toddlers. *Child Development, 80,* 1403–1420.

Berlyne, D. E. (1960). *Conflict, arousal, and curiosity.* New York: McGraw-Hill.

Berman, M. G., & others (2013). Dimensionality of brain networks linked to life-long individual differences in self-control. *Nature Communications, 4,* 1373.

Bernard, J. P., & others (2013). Combined screening for open spina bifida at 11–13 weeks using fetal biparietal diameter and maternal serum markers. *American Journal of Obstetrics and Gynecology, 209,* e1–e5.

Bernard, K., & Dozier, M. (2008). Adoption and foster placement. In M. M. Haith & J. B. Benson (Eds.), *Encyclopedia of infant and early childhood development.* Oxford, UK: Elsevier.

Bernard, K., & others (2012). Enhancing attachment organization among maltreated children: Results from a randomized clinical trial. *Child Development, 83,* 623–636.

Berndt, T. J., & Perry, T. B. (1990). Distinctive features and effects of early adolescent friendships. In R. Montemayor (Ed.), *Advances in adolescent research.* Greenwich, CT: JAI Press.

Berner, J., & others (2014, in press). Factors influencing Internet usage in older adults (65 years and above) living in rural and urban Sweden. *Health Informatics.*

Bernier, A., Carlson, S. M., Deschenes, M., & Matte-Gagne, C. (2011). Social precursors of preschoolers' executive functioning: A closer look at the early childrearing environment. *Developmental Science, 15,* 12–24.

Bernier, A., Carlson, S. M., & Whipple, N. (2010). From external regulation to self-regulation: Early parenting precursors of young children's executive functioning. *Child Development, 81,* 326–339.

Bernier, A., & others (2013). Sleep and cognition in preschool years: Specific links to executive functioning. *Child Development, 84*(5), 1542–1553.

Berninger, V., & Dunn, M. (2012). Brain and behavioral response to intervention for specific reading, writing, and math disabilities: What works for whom? In B. Wong, & D. Butler (Eds.), *Learning about LD* (4th ed.). New York: Elsevier.

Berninger, V. W., & O'Malley, M. M. (2011). Evidence-based diagnosis and treatment for specific learning disabilities involving impairments in written and/or oral language. *Journal of Learning Disabilities, 44,* 167–183.

Berookhim, B. M., & Bar-Charma, N. (2011). Medical implications of erectile dysfunction. *Medical Clinics of North America, 95,* 213–221.

Berraho, M., & others (2010). Body mass index, disability, and 13-year mortality in older French adults. *Journal of Aging and Health, 22,* 68–83.

Berry, J. W., Phinney, J. S., Kwak, K., & Sam, D. L. (2013). Introduction: Goals and research framework for studying immigrant youth. In J. W. Berry, & others (Eds.), *Immigrant youth in cultural transition.* New York: Psychology Press.

Berryman, N., & others (2013). Executive function, physical fitness, and mobility in well-functioning older adults. *Experimental Gerontology, 48,* 1402–1409.

Bers, M. U., & Kazakoff, E. R. (2013). Developmental technologies: Technology and human development. In I. B. Weiner & others (Eds.), *Handbook of aging* (2nd ed., Vol. 6). New York: Wiley.

Berscheid, E. (1988). Some comments on love's anatomy: Or, whatever happened to old-fashioned lust? In R. J. Sternberg (Ed.), *Anatomy of love.* New Haven, CT: Yale University Press.

Berscheid, E. (2010). Love in the fourth dimension. *Annual Review of Psychology* (Vol. 61). Palo Alto, CA: Annual Reviews.

Berta, W., Laporte, A., Deber, R., Baumann, A., & Gamble, B. (2013). The evolving role of health care aides in the long-term care and home and community care sectors in Canada. *Human Resources for Health 11*(1), 25.

Bertenthal, B. L. (2008). Perception and action. In M. M. Haith & J. B. Benson (Eds.), *Encyclopedia of infant and early childhood development*. Oxford, UK: Elsevier.

Bertenthal, B. I., Longo, M. R., & Kenny, S. (2007). Phenomenal permanence and the development of predictive tracking in infancy. *Child Development, 78,* 350–363.

Bertorelle, R., & others (2014). Telomeres, telomerase, and colorectal cancer. *World Journal of Gastroenterology, 20,* 1940–1950.

Bertrand, R., Graham, E. K., & Lachman, M. E. (2013). Personality development in adulthood and old age. In I. B. Weiner & others (Eds.), *Handbook of aging* (2nd ed., Vol. 6). New York: Wiley.

Bertrand, R. M., & Lachman, M. E. (2003). Personality development in adulthood and old age. In I. B. Weiner (Ed.), *Handbook of psychology* (2nd ed., Vol. 6). New York: Wiley.

Berwid, O. G., & Halperin, J. M. (2012). Emerging support for a role of exercise in attention-deficit/hyperactivity disorder intervention planning. *Current Psychiatry Reports, 14,* 543–551.

Best, J. R. (2010). Effects of physical activity on children's executive function: Contributions of experimental research on aerobic exercise. *Developmental Review, 30,* 331–351.

Betts, K. S., Williams, G. M., Najman, J. M., & Alati, R. (2014). Maternal depressive, anxious, and stress symptoms during pregnancy predict internalizing problems in adolescence. *Depression and Anxiety, 31,* 9–18.

Beuker, K. T., Rommelse, N.N, Donders, R., & Buitelaar, J. K. (2013). Development of early communication skills in the first two years of life. *Infant Behavior and Development, 36,* 71–83.

Bevan, D., Wittkowski, A., & Wells, A. (2013). A multiple-baseline study of the effects associated with metacognitive therapy in postpartum depression. *Journal of Midwifery and Women's Health, 58,* 69–75.

Beyene, Y. (1986). Cultural significance and physiological manifestations of menopause: A biocultural analysis. *Culture, Medicine and Psychiatry, 10,* 47–71.

Beyers, E., & Seiffge-Krenke, I. (2010). Does identity precede intimacy? Testing Erikson's theory on romantic development in emerging adults of the 21st century. *Journal of Adolescent Research, 25,* 387–415.

Bherer, L., Erickson, K. L., & Liu-Ambrose, T. (2013). A review of the effects of physical activity and exercise on cognitive and brain functions in older adults. *Journal of Aging Research, 2013,* 657508.

Bhuvaneswar, C. G., & Stern, T. A. (2013). Teaching cross-cultural aspects of mourning: A Hindu perspective on death and dying. *Palliative Support and Care, 11,* 79–84.

Bialystok, E. (1997). Effects of bilingualism and biliteracy on children's emerging concepts of print. *Developmental Psychology, 33,* 429–440.

Bialystok, E. (2001). *Bilingualism in development: Language, literacy, and cognition.* New York: Cambridge University Press.

Bialystok, E. (2007). Acquisition of literacy in preschool children. A framework for research. *Language Learning, 57,* 45–77.

Bialystok, E. (2010). Global-local and trail-making tasks by monolingual and bilingual children: Beyond inhibition. *Developmental Psychology, 46,* 93–105.

Bialystok, E. (2011, April). *Becoming bilingual: Emergence of cognitive outcomes of bilingualism in immersion education.* Paper presented at the meeting of the Society for Research in Child Development, Montreal.

Bialystok, E., & Craik, F. I. M. (2010). Cognitive and linguistic processing in the bilingual mind. *Current Directions in Psychological Science, 19,* 19–23.

Bialystok, E., Craik, F. I., Binns, M. A., Ossher, L., & Freedman, M. (2014). Effects of bilingualism on the age of onset and progression of MCI and AD: Evidence from executive function tests. *Neuropsychology, 28,* 290–304.

Bian, Z., & Anderson, G. J. (2008). Aging and the perceptual organization of 3-D scenes. *Psychology and Aging, 23,* 342–352.

Bibok, M. B., Carpendale, J. I., & Muller, U. (2009). Parental scaffolding and the development of executive function. *New Directions in Child and Adolescent Development, 123,* 17–24.

Biehle, S. N., & Mickelson, K. D. (2012). First-time parents' expectations about the division of childcare and play. *Journal of Family Psychology, 26,* 36–45.

Bielak, A. A., Cherbuin N., Bunce, D., & Anstey, K. J. (2014, in press). Preserved differentiation between physical activity and cognitive performance across young, middle, and older adulthood across eight years. *Journals of Gerontology B: Psychological Sciences and Social Sciences.*

Bielak, A. A. M., Hughes, T. F., Small, B. J., & Dixon, R. A. (2007). It's never too late to engage in lifestyle activities: Significant concurrent but not change relationships between lifestyle activities and cognitive speed. *Journals of Gerontology: Psychological Sciences and Social Sciences, 62B,* P331–P339.

Bierman, K. L., & Powers, C. J. (2009). Social skills training to improve peer relations. In K. H. Rubin, W. M. Bukowski, & B. Laursen (Eds.), *Handbook of peer interactions, relationships, and groups.* New York: Guilford.

Bierman, K. L., & others (2008). Executive functions and school readiness intervention: Impact, moderation, and mediation in the Head Start-REDI Program. *Development and Psychopathology, 20,* 821–843.

Bierman, K. L., & others (2014). Effects of Head Start REDI on children's outcomes one year later in different kindergarten contexts. *Child Development. 85*(1), 140–159.

Biggs, S., Carstensen, L. L., & Hogan, P. (2012). *Social capital, lifelong learning, and social innovation. Global population aging: Peril or promise?* Geneva, SWITZERLAND: World Economic Forum.

Binderman, C. D., Krakauer, E. L., & Solomon, M. Z. (2012). Time to revise the approach to cardiopulmonary resuscitation status. *JAMA, 307,* 917–918.

Bird, M. L., & Fell, J. (2014, in press). Pilates exercise has positive long term effects on the age-related decline in balance and strength in older, community dwelling men and women. *Journal of Aging and Physical Activity.*

Birditt, K. S., Fingerman, K. L., & Zarit, S. (2010). Adult children's problems and successes: Implications for intergenerational ambivalence. *Journals of Gerontology B: Psychological Sciences and Social Sciences, 65B,* 145–153.

Birditt, K. S., & Wardjiman, E. (2012a). Intergenerational relationships and aging. In S. K. Whitbourne & M. J. Sliwinski (Eds.), *Wiley-Blackwell handbook of adult development and aging.* New York: Wiley.

Birditt, K. S., & Wardjiman, E. (2012b). Partners and friends in adulthood. In S. K. Whitbourne & M. Sliwinski (Eds.), *Wiley-Blackwell handbook of adult development and aging.* New York: Wiley.

Birkeland, M. S., Melkevick, O., Holsen, I., & Wold, B. (2012). Trajectories of global self-esteem development during adolescence. *Journal of Adolescence, 35,* 43–54

Birman, B. F., & others. (2007). *State and local implementation of the "No Child Left Behind" act. Volume II—Teacher quality under "NCLB": Interim report.* Jessup, MD: U.S. Department of Education.

Bischoff, K. E., Sudore, R. Miao, Y., Boscardin, W. J., & Smith, A. K. (2013). Advance care planning and the quality of end-of-life care in older adults. *Journal of the American Geriatrics Society, 61,* 209–214.

Bisiacchi, P. S., Tarantino, V., & Ciccola, A. (2008). Aging and prospective memory: The role of working memory and monitoring processes. *Aging: Clinical and Experimental Research, 20,* 569–577.

Bisson, M., & others (2013). Maternal fitness at the onset of the second trimester of pregnancy: Correlates and relationship with infant birth weight. *Pediatric Obesity, 8*(6), 464–474.

Bjorklund, D. F. (2007). *Why youth is not wasted on the young.* Malden, MA: Blackwell.

Bjorklund, D. F. (2012). *Children's thinking* (5th ed.). Boston: Cengage.

Bjorklund, D. F. (2013). Cognitive development: An overview. In P. D. Zelazo (Ed.), *Oxford handbook of developmental psychology.* New York: Oxford University Press.

Bjorklund, D. F., & Pellegrini, A. D. (2002). *The origins of human nature.* New York: Oxford University Press.

Black, M. M., & Hurley, K. M. (2007). Helping children develop healthy eating habits. In R. E. Tremblay, R. G. Barr, R. D. Peters, & M. Boivin (Eds.), *Encyclopedia on early childhood development.* Retrieved March 19, 2008, from http://www.child-encyclopedia.com/documents/Black-HurleyANGxp_rev-Eating.pdf

Black, M. M., & Lozoff, B. (2008). Nutrition and diet. In M. M. Haith & J. B. Benson (Eds.), *Encyclopedia of infant and early childhood development.* Oxford, UK: Elsevier.

Black, R. E., & others (2013). Maternal and child undernutrition and overweight in low-income and middle-income countries. *Lancet, 382,* 427–451.

Blackwell, L. S., & Dweck, C. S. (2008). *The motivational impact of a computer-based program that teaches how the brain changes with learning.* Unpublished manuscript, Department of Psychology, Stanford University, Palo Alto, CA.

Blackwell, L. S., Trzesniewski, K. H., & Dweck, C. S. (2007). Implicit theories of intelligence predict achievement across an adolescent tradition: A longitudinal study and an intervention. *Child Development, 78,* 246–263.

Blaga, O. M., & others (2009). Structure and continuity of intellectual development in early childhood. *Intelligence, 37,* 106–113.

Blair, C., & Raver, C. C. (2012). Child development in the context of poverty: Experiential canalization of brain and behavior. *American Psychologist, 67,* 309–318.

Blair, C., & Raver, C. C. (2015, in press). School readiness and self-regulation: A developmental psychobiological approach. *Annual Review of Psychology* (Vol. 66). Palo Alto, CA: Annual Reviews.

Blair, C., Raver, C. C., & Berry, D. J. (2014). Two approaches estimating the effect of parenting on the development of executive function in early childhood. *Developmental Psychology, 50,* 554–565.

Blair, C., & Razza, R. P. (2007). Relating effortful control, executive functioning, and false belief understanding to emerging math and literacy ability in kindergarten. *Child Development, 78,* 647–663.

Blair, M., & Somerville, S. C. (2009). The importance of differentiation in young children's acquisition of expertise. *Cognition, 112,* 259–280.

Blair, S. N., & others (1989). Physical fitness and all-cause mortality: A prospective study of healthy men and women. *Journal of the American Medical Association, 262,* 2395–2401.

Blake, J. S. (2015). *Nutrition and you* (3rd ed.). Upper Saddle River, NJ: Pearson.

Blake, J. S., Munoz, K. D., & Volpe, S. (2014). *Nutrition: From science to you plus mastering nutrition with e-text* (2nd ed.). Upper Saddle River, NJ: Pearson.

Blake, M. (2013). Group reminiscence therapy for adults with dementia: A review. *British Journal of Community Nursing, 18,* 228–233.

Blakemore, J. E. O., Berenbaum, S. A., & Liben, L. S. (2009). *Gender development.* Clifton, NJ: Psychology Press.

Blakemore, S-J., & Mills, K. (2014). The social brain in adolescence. *Annual Review of Psychology* (Vol. 65). Palo Alto, CA: Annual Reviews.

Blanco, C., & others (2014, in press). Risk factors for anxiety disorders: Common and specific effects in a national sample. *Depression and Anxiety.*

Bland, P. (2012). Tackling anxiety and depression in older people in primary care. *Practitioner, 256,* 17–20.

Blandthorn, J., Forster, D. A., & Love, V. (2011). Neonatal and maternal outcomes following maternal use of buprenophine or methadone during pregnancy: Findings of a retrospective audit. *Women and Birth, 24,* 32–39.

Bleeker, F. E., Hopman, S. M., Merks, J. H., Aalfs, C. M., & Hennekam, R. C. (2014, in press). Brain tumors and syndromes in children. *Neuropediatrics.*

Blieszner, R. (2009). Friendship, adulthood. In D. Carr (Ed.), *Encyclpedia of the life course and human development.* Boston: Gale Cengage.

Blieszner, R., & Roberto, K. A. (2012a). Intergenerational relationships and aging. In S. K. Whitbourne & M. Sliwinski (Eds.), *Wiley-Blackwell handbook of adult development and aging.* New York: Wiley.

Blieszner, R., & Roberto, K. A. (2012b). Partner and friend relationships in adulthood. In S. K. Whitbourne & M. Sliwinski (Eds.), *Wiley-Blackwell handbook of adult development and aging.* New York: Wiley.

Block, J. (1993). Studying personality the long way. In D. Funder, R. D. Parke, C. Tomlinson-Keasey, & K. Widaman (Ed.), *Studying lives through time.* Washington, DC: American Psychological Association.

Bloom, B. (1985). *Developing talent in young people.* New York. Ballantine.

Bloom, L., Lifter, K., & Broughton, J. (1985). The convergence of early cognition and language in the second year of life. Problems in conceptualization and measurement. In M. Barren (Ed.), *Single word speech.* London: Wiley.

Bloom, P., & German, T. P. (2000). Two reasons to abandon the false belief task as a test of theory of mind. *Cognition, 77,* B25–B31.

Bloor, C., & White, F. (1983). *Unpublished manuscript.* La Jolla, CA: University of California at San Diego.

Blumel, J. E., Lavin, P., Vellejo, M. S., & Sarra, S. (2014, in press). Menopause or climacteric, just a semantic discussion or has it clinical implications? *Climacteric.*

Blustein, D. L. (2013). The psychology of working: A new perspective in a new era. In D. L. Blustein (Ed.), *Oxford handbook of the psychology of working.* New York: Oxford University Press.

Bodner, E., & Cohen-Fridel, S. (2010). Relations between attachment styles, ageism, and quality of life in late life. *International Psychogeriatrics, 22,* 1353–1361.

Bodrova, E., & Leong, D. J. (2007). *Tools of the mind* (2nd ed.). Geneva, Switzerland: International Bureau of Education. UNESCO.

Bodrova, E., Leong, D. J., & Akhutina, T. V. (2011). When everything new is well-forgotten old: Vygotsky/ Luria insights in the development of executive functions. *New Directions for Child and Adolescent Development, 133*(Fall), 11–28.

Boelens, C., Hekman, E. E., & Verkerke, G. J. (2013). Risk factors for falls of older citizens. *Technology and Health Care, 21,* 521–533.

Bogart, L. M., & others (2014). Peer victimization in the fifth grade and health in the tenth grade. *Pediatrics, 133,* 440–447.

Bohlin, G., & Hagekull, B. (2009). Socio-emotional development from infancy to young adulthood. *Scandinavian Journal of Psychology, 50,* 592–601.

Bolea-Alamanac, B., & others (2014, in press). Evidence-based guidelines for the pharmacological management of attention deficit hyperactivity disorder: Update on recommendations from the British Association of Psychopharmacology. *Journal of Psychopharmacology.*

Bolkan, C., & Hooker, K. (2012). Self-regulation and social cognition in adulthood: The gyroscope. In S. K. Whitbourne & M. J. Sliwinski (Eds.), *Wiley-Blackwell handbook of adult development and aging.* New York: Wiley.

Bombak, A. (2014). Obesity, health at every size, and public policy. *American Journal of Public Health, 104,* e60–e67.

Bonanno, R. A., & Hymel, S. (2013). Cyber bullying and internalizing difficulties: Above and beyond the impact of traditional forms of bullying. *Journal of Youth and Adolescence, 42,* 685–697.

Bonura, K. B., & Tenenbaum, G. (2014, in press). Effects of yoga on psychological health in older adults. *Journal of Physical Activity and Health.*

Booij, G. E. (2013). Morphological analysis. In B. Eeine & H. Narrog (Eds.), *Oxford handbook of linguistics.* New York: Oxford University Press.

Booth, A. (2006). Object function and categorization in infancy: Two mechanisms of facilitation. *Infancy, 10,* 145–169.

Booth, M. (2002). Arab adolescents facing the future: Enduring ideals and pressures to change. In B. B. Brown, R. W. Larson, & T. S. Saraswath (Eds.), *The world's youth.* New York: Cambridge University Press.

Booth-LaForce, C., & Kerns, K. A. (2009). Child-parent attachment relationships, peer relationships, and peer-group functioning. In K. H. Rubin, W. M. Bukowski, & B. Laursen (Eds.), *Handbook of peer interactions, relationships, and groups.* New York: Guilford.

Bor, W., McGee, T. R., & Fagan, A. A. (2004). Early risk factors for adolescent antisocial behavior: An Australian longitudinal study. *Australian and New Zealand Journal of Psychiatry, 38,* 365–372.

Boraska, V., & others (2014, in press). A genome-wide study of anorexia nervosa. *Molecular Psychiatry.*

Borella, E., Caretti, B., Zanoni, G., Zavagnin, M., & De Beni, R. (2013). Working memory training in old age: An examination of transfer and maintenance effects. *Archives of Clinical Neuropsychology, 28,* 331–347.

Borella, E., Ludwig, C., Dirck, J., & de Ribaupierre, A. (2011). The influence of time of testing on interference, working memory, processing speed, and vocabulary: Age differences in adulthood. *Experimental Aging Research, 37,* 76–107.

Borich, G. D. (2014). *Effective teaching methods* (8th ed.). Upper Saddle River, NJ: Pearson.

Bornstein, M. H. (1975). Qualities of color vision in infancy. *Journal of Experimental Child Psychology, 19,* 401–409.

Bornstein, M. H., Arterberry, M. E., & Mash, C. (2011). Perceptual development. In M. H. Bornstein & M. E. Lamb (Eds.), *Developmental psychology: An advanced textbook* (6th ed.). New York: Psychology Press.

Bornstein, M. H., Jager, J., & Steinberg, L. (2013). Adolescents, parents/friends/peers: A relationship model. In I. Weiner & others (Eds.), *Handbook of psychology* (2nd ed., Vol. 6). New York: Wiley.

Boron, J. B., Willis, S. L., & Schaie, K. W. (2007). Cognitive training gain as a predictor of mental status. *Journals of Gerontology B: Psychological Sciences and Social Sciences, 62B.* P45–P52.

Borrell, L. N., & Samuel, L. (2014, in press). Body mass index categories and mortality risk in U.S. adults: The effect of overweight and obesity on advancing death. *American Journal of Public Health.*

Borup, L., & others (2009). Acupuncture as pain relief during delivery: A randomized controlled trial. *Birth, 36,* 5–12.

Bosl, W., Tierney, A., Tager-Flusberg, H., & Nelson, C. (2011). EEG complexity as a biomarker for autism spectrum disorder risk. *BMC Medicine, 9,* 60.

Bosma, H. A., & Kunnen, E. S. (2001). Determinants and mechanisms in ego identity development: A review and synthesis. *Developmental Review, 21,* 39–66.

Bosworth, B. (2012, February). *Economic consequences of the great recession: Evidence from the Panel Study of Income Dynamics.* Chestnut Hill, MA: Center for Retirement Research at Boston College.

Botwinick, J. (1978). *Aging and behavior* (2nd ed.). New York: Springer.

Bouchard, T. J., Lykken, D. T., McGue, M., Segal, N. L., & Tellegen, A. (1990). Source of human psychological differences. The Minnesota Study of Twins Reared Apart. *Science, 250,* 223–228.

Boucher, J. (2012a). Putting theory of mind in its place: Psychological explanations of the socio-emotional-communicative impairments in autism spectrum disorder. *Autism, 16*(3), 226–246.

Boucher, J. (2012b). Research review: Structural language in autistic spectrum disorder—characteristics and causes. *Journal of Child Psychology and Psychiatry, 53,* 219–233.

Bowen, C. E., Noack, M. G., & Staudinger, U. M. (2011). Aging in the work context. In K. W. Schaie & S. L. Willis (Eds.), *Handbook of the psychology of aging* (7th ed.). New York: Elsevier.

Bowen, C. E., & Skirbekk, V. (2013). National stereotypes of older adults' competence are related to older adults' participation in paid and volunteer work. *Journals of Gerontology B:Psychological Sciences and Social Sciences, 68B,* 974–983.

Bower, T. G. R. (1966). Slant perception and shape constancy in infants. *Science, 151,* 832–834.

Bowlby, J. (1969). *Attachment and loss* (Vol. 1). London: Hogarth Press.

Bowlby, J. (1989). *Secure and insecure attachment.* New York: Basic Books.

Bowling, A., & Iliffe, S. (2011). Psychological approach to successful aging predicts future quality of life in older adults. *Health Quality and Life Outcomes, 9,* 13.

Bowman, N. A. (2010). The development of psychological well-being in first-year college students. *Journal of College Student Development, 51,* 180–200.

Boyer, K., & Diamond, A. (1992). Development of memory for temporal order in infants and young children. In A. Diamond (Ed.), *Development and neural bases of higher cognitive function.* New York: Academy of Sciences.

Boyle, J., & Cropley, M. (2004). Children's sleep: Problems and solutions. *Journal of Family Health Care, 14,* 61–63.

Boyle, P. A., Yu, L., Buchman, A. S., & Bennett, D. A. (2012). Risk aversion is associated with decision making among community-based older persons. *Frontiers in Psychology, 3,* 205.

Brabyn, J. A., Schneck, M. E., Haegerstrom-Portnoy, G., & Lott, L. (2001). The Smith-Keuttewell Institute (SKI) longitudinal study of vision function and its impact among the elderly. An overview. *Ophthalmology and Vision Science, 78,* 2464–2469.

Bradley, R. E., & Webb, R. (1976). Age-related differences in locus of control orientation in three behavior domains. *Human Development, 19,* 49–55.

Brainerd, C. J., & Reyna, V. E. (1993). Domains of fuzzy-trace theory. In M. L. Howe & R. Pasnak (Eds.), *Emerging themes in cognitive development.* New York: Springer.

Brainerd, C. J., & Reyna, V. E. (2014). Dual processes in memory development: Fuzzy-trace theory. In P. Bauer & R. Fivush (Eds.), *Wiley-Blackwell handbook of children's memory.* New York: Wiley.

Brand, J. (2014). Social consequences of job loss and unemployment. *Annual Review of Sociology* (Vol. 40). Palo Alto, CA: Annual Reviews.

Brand, M. (2011). Mitochondrial functioning and aging. In E. Masoro & S. Austad (Eds.), *Handbook of the biology of aging* (7th ed.). New York: Elsevier.

Brand, M., & Markowitsch, H. J. (2010). Mechanisms contributing to decision-making difficulties in late adulthood: Theoretical approaches, speculations, and empirical evidence. *Gerontology, 56,* 319–324.

Bransford, J., & others (2006). Learning theories in education. In P. A. Alexander & P. H. Winne (Eds.), *Handbook of educational psychology* (2nd ed.). Mahwah, NJ: Erlbaum.

Branum, A. M., Bailey, R., & Singer, B. J. (2013). Dietary supplement use and folate status during pregnancy in the United States. *Journal of Nutrition, 143*(4), 486–492.

Brassard, A., & others (2012). Romantic attachment insecurity predicts sexual dissatisfaction in couples seeking marital therapy. *Journal of Sexual and Marital Therapy, 38,* 245–262.

Braver, S. L., & Lamb, M. E. (2013). Marital dissolution. In G. W. Peterson & K. R. Bush (Eds.), *Handbook of marriage and the family* (3rd ed.). New York: Springer.

Brazelton, T. B. (2004). Preface: The Neonatal Intensive Care Unit Network Neurobehavioral Scale. *Pediatrics, 113*(Suppl.), S632–S633.

Brechwald, W. A., & Prinstein, M. J. (2011). Beyond homophily: A decade of advances in understanding peer influence processes. *Journal of Research on Adolescence, 21,* 166–179.

Brecklin, L. R., & Ullman, S. E. (2010). The roles of victim and offender substance use in sexual assault outcomes. *Journal of Interpersonal Violence, 25,* 1503–1522.

Bredekamp, S. (2014). *Effective practices in early childhood education* (2nd ed.). Upper Saddle River, NJ: Pearson.

Bremner, J. G., Slater, A. M., Johnson, S. P., Mason, U. C., & Spring, J. (2012). The effects of auditory information on 4-month-old infants' perception of trajectory continuity. *Child Development, 83*(3) 954–984.

Brendgen, M., Lamarche, V., Wanner, B., & Vitaro, F. (2010). Links between friendship relations and early adolescents' trajectories of depressed mood. *Developmental Psychology, 46,* 491–501.

Brent, R. L. (2009). Saving lives and changing family histories: Appropriate counseling of pregnant women and men and women of reproductive age concerning the risk of diagnostic radiation exposure during and before pregnancy. *American Journal of Obstetrics and Gynecology, 200,* 4–24.

Brent, R. L. (2011). The pulmonologist's role in caring for pregnant women with regard to reproductive risks of diagnostic radiological studies or radiation therapy. *Clinics in Chest Medicine, 32*(1), 33–42.

Breslau, J., & others (2011). A multinational study of mental disorders, marriage, and divorce. *Acta Psychiatrica Scandinavica, 124,* 474–486.

Bretherton, I. (2012). Afterword. In K. H. Brisch, *Treating attachment disorders* (2nd ed.). New York: Guilford.

Bretherton, I., Stolberg, U., & Kreye, M. (1981). Engaging strangers in proximal interaction: Infants' social initiative. *Developmental Psychology, 17,* 746–755.

Bridgett, D. J., Laake, L. M., Gartstein, M. A., & Dorn, D. (2013). Development of infant positive emotionality: The contribution of maternal characteristics and effects on subsequent parenting. *Infant and Child Development, 22*(4), 362–382.

Bril, B. (1999). Dires sur l'enfant selon les cultures. Etat des lieux et perspectives. In B. Brill, P. R. Dasen, C. Sabatier, & B. Krewer (Eds.), *Propos sur l'enfant et l'adolescent. Quels enfants pour quelles cultures?* Paris: L'Harmattan.

Brim, G. (1992, December 7). Commentary, *Newsweek,* p. 52.

Brim, G., Ryff, C. D., & Kessler, R. (Eds.) (2004). *How healthy we are: A national study of well-being in midlife.* Chicago: University of Chicago Press.

Brim, O. (1999). *The MacArthur Foundation study of midlife development.* Vero Beach, FL: MacArthur Foundation.

Brimah, P., & others (2013). Sleep duration and reported functional capacity among black and white U.S. adults. *Journal of Sleep Medicine, 9,* 605–609.

Brinkman-Stoppelenburg, A., Rietjens, J. A., & van der Heide, A. (2014, in press). The effects of advance care planning on end-of-life care: A systematic review. *Palliative Medicine.*

Brion, M., & others (2012). Sarcomeric gene mutations in sudden infant death syndrome (SIDS). *Forensic Science International, 219*(1), 278–281.

Britton, J. R., Britton, H. L., & Gronwaldt, V. (2006). Breastfeeding, sensitivity, and attachment. *Pediatrics, 118,* e1436–e1443.

Brockie, J., & others (2014, in press). EMAS position statement: Menopause for medical students. *Maturitas.*

Brodsky, J. L., Viner-Brown, S., & Handler, A. S. (2009). Changes in maternal cigarette smoking among pregnant WIC participants in Rhode Island. *Maternal and Child Health Journal, 13*(6), 822–831.

Brody, G. H., & others (2013). Supportive family environments, genes that confer sensitivity, and allostatic load among rural African American emerging adults: A prospective analysis. *Journal of Family Psychology, 27,* 22–29.

Brody, N. (2000). Intelligence. In A. Kazdin (Ed.), *Encyclopedia of psychology.* Washington, DC, & New York: American Psychological Association and Oxford University Press.

Brody, N. (2007). Does education influence intelligence? In P. C. Kyllonen, R. D. Roberts, & L. Stankov (Eds.), *Extending intelligence.* Mahwah, NJ: Erlbaum.

Brody, R. M., & Costa, R. M. (2009). Satisfaction (sexual, life, relationship, and mental health) is associated directly with penile-vaginal intercourse, but inversely related to other sexual behavior frequencies. *Journal of Sexual Medicine, 6,* 1947–1954.

Brody, S. (2010). The relative health benefits of different sexual activities. *Journal of Sexual Medicine, 7,* 1336–1361.

Brodzinsky, D. M., & Pinderhughes, E. (2002). Parenting and child development in adoptive families. In M. H. Bornstein (Ed.), *Handbook of parenting* (Vol. 1). Mahwah, NJ: Erlbaum.

Broekhuizen, L. N., & others (2011). Physical activity, metabolic syndrome, and coronary risk: The EPIC-Norfolk prospective population study. *European Journal of Cardiovascular Prevention and Rehabilitation,18,* 209–217.

Bronfenbrenner, U. (1986). Ecology of the family as a context for human development research perspectives. *Developmental Psychology, 22,* 723–742.

Bronfenbrenner, U. (2004). *Making human beings human.* Thousand Oaks, CA: Sage.

Bronfenbrenner, U., & Morris, P. (1998). The ecology of developmental processes. In W. Damon (Ed.), *Handbook of child psychology* (5th ed., Vol. 1). New York: Wiley.

Bronfenbrenner, U., & Morris, P. A. (2006). The ecology of human development. In W. Damon & R. Lerner (Eds.), *Handbook of child psychology* (6th ed.). New York: Wiley.

Broning, S., & others (2014). Implementing and evaluating the German adaptation of the "Strengthening Families Program 10–14"—a randomized-controlled multi-center study. *BMC Public Health, 14,* 83.

Bronstein, P. (2006). The family environment: Where gender role socialization begins. In J. Worell & C. D. Goodheart (Eds.), *Handbook of girls' and women's psychological health.* New York: Oxford University Press.

Brook, J. S., Brook, D. W., Gordon, A. S., Whiteman, M., & Cohen, P. (1990). The psychological etiology of adolescent drug use: A family interactional approach. *Genetic Psychology Monographs, 116*(2).

Brooker, R. J. (2015). *Genetics* (5th ed.). New York: McGraw-Hill.

Brooker, R. J., Widmaier, E. P., Grham, L., & Stiling, P. (2015). *Principles of biology.* New York: McGraw-Hill.

Brookhart, S. M., & Nitko, A. J. (2015). *Educational assessment of students* (7th ed.). Upper Saddle River, NJ: Pearson.

Brooks, J. G., & Brooks, M. G. (2001). *The case for constructivist classrooms* (2nd ed.). Upper Saddle River, NJ: Erlbaum.

Brooks, R., & Meltzoff, A. N. (2014). Gaze following: A mechanism for building social connections between infants and adults. In M. Mikulincer & P. R. Shaver (Eds.), *Mechanisms of social connection.* Washington, DC: American Psychological Association.

Brooks-Gunn, J. (2003). Do you believe in magic?: What we can expect from early childhood programs. *Social Policy Report, Society for Research in Child Development, XVII* (1), 1–13.

Brooks-Gunn, J., Han, W-J., & Waldfogel, J. (2010). First-year maternal employment and child development in the first seven years. *Monographs of the Society for Research in Child Development, 75*(2), 1–147.

Brooks-Gunn, J., & Warren, M. P. (1989). The psychological significance of secondary sexual characteristics in 9- to 11-year-old girls. *Child Development 59,* 161–169.

Brown, A. M., & Lindsey, D. T. (2013). Infant color vision and color preference: A tribute to David Teller. *Visual Neuroscience, 30,* 243–250.

Brown, B. B. (2011). Popularity in peer group perspective: The role of status in adolescent peer systems. In A. H. N. Cillessen, D. Schwartz, & L. Mayeux (Eds.), *Popularity in the peer system.* New York: Guilford.

Brown, B. B., & Bakken, J. P. (2011). Parenting and peer relationships: Invigorating research on family-peer linkages in adolescence. *Journal of Research on Adolescence, 21,* 153–165.

Brown, B. B., Bakken, J. P., Ameringer, S. W., & Mahon, S. D. (2008). A comprehensive conceptualization of the peer influence process in adolescence. In M. J. Prinstein & K. A. Dodge (Eds.), *Understanding peer influence in children and adolescents.* New York: Guilford.

Brown, B. B., & Larson, J. (2009). Peer relationships in adolescence. In R. M. Lerner & L. Steinberg (Eds.), *Handbook of adolescent development* (3rd ed.). New York: Wiley.

Brown, B. B., & Larson, R. W. (2002). The kaleidoscope of adolescence: Experiences of the world's youth at the beginning of the 21st century. In B. B. Brown, R. W. Larson, & T. S. Saraswathi (Eds.), *The world's youth.* New York: Cambridge University Press.

Brown, C. C., & others (2014). Genome-wide association and pharmacological profiling of 29 anticancer agents using lymphoblastoid cell lines. *Pharmacogenomics, 15,* 137–146.

Brown, C. L., & others (2012). Social activity and cognitive functioning over time: A coordinated analysis of four longitudinal studies. *Journal of Aging Research.* doi:10.1155/2012/287438

Brown, D. (2013). Morphological typology. In J. J. Song (Ed.), *Oxford handbook of linguistic typology.* New York: Oxford University Press.

Brown, H. L., & Graves, C. R. (2013). Smoking and marijuana in pregnancy. *Clinical Obstetrics and Gynecology, 56,* 107–113.

Brown, L. D., Feinberg, M., & Kan, M. L. (2012). Predicting engagement in a transition to parenthood program for couples. *Evaluation and Program Planning, 35,* 1–8.

Brown, L. F. Pridham, K. A., & Brown, R. (2014, in press). Sequential observation of infant regulated and dysregulated behavior following soothing and stimulating maternal behavior during feeding. *Journal for Specialists in Pediatric Nursing.*

Brown, L. M., Hansen, C. T., Huberty, A. F., & Castonquay, T. W. (2011). Traits of the metabolic syndrome after corpulent obesity in LAN, SHR, and DSS rats: Behavioral and metabolic interactions with adrenalectomy. *Physiology and Behavior, 103,* 98–103.

Brown, R. (1958). *Words and things.* Glencoe, IL: Free Press.

Brown, R. (1973). *A first language: The early stages.* Cambridge, MA: Harvard University Press.

Brown, S. L., Bulanda, J. R., & Lee, G. R. (2005). The significance of nonmarital cohabitation: Marital status and mental health benefits among middle-aged and older adults. *Journals of Gerontology B: Psychological Sciences and Social Sciences, 60B,* S21–S29.

Brown, S. L., Bulanda, J. R., & Lee, G. R. (2012). Transitions into and out of cohabitation in later life. *Journal of Marriage and the Family, 74,* 774–793.

Brown, S. L., & Lin, I-F. (2012). The gray divorce revolution: Rising divorce among middle-aged and older adults: 1990–2010. *Journals of Gerontology B: Psychological Sciences and Social Sciences, 67,* 731–741.

Brown, S. L., Nesse, R. M., House, J. S., & Utz, R. L. (2004). Religion and emotional compensation: Results from a prospective study of widowhood. *Personality and Social Psychology Bulletin, 30,* 1165–1174.

Brown, S. L., Nesse, R. M., Vinokur, A. D., & Smith, D. M. (2003). Providing social support may be more beneficial than receiving it: Results from a prospective study of mortality. *Psychological Science, 14,* 320–327.

Brown, W. H., & others (2009). Social and environmental factors associated with preschoolers' nonsedentary physical activity. *Child Development, 80,* 45–58.

Brownell, C. A., Lemerise, E. A., Pelphrey, K. A., & Roisman, G. I. (2015, in press). Measuring socioemotional behavior and development. In R. M. Lerner (Ed.), *Handbook of child psychology and developmental science* (7th ed.). New York: Wiley.

Brownell, C. A., Ramani, G. B., & Zerwas, S. (2006). Becoming a social partner with peers: Cooperation and social understanding in one- and two-year-olds. *Child Development, 77,* 803–821.

Brownell, C. A., Svetlova, M., Anderson, R., Nichols, S. R., & Drummond, J. (2013). Socialization of early prosocial behavior: Parents' talk about emotions is associated with sharing and helping in toddlers. *Infancy, 18,* 91–119.

Bruchmiller, K., Margraf, J., & Schneider, S. (2012). Is ADHD diagnosed in accord with diagnostic criteria? Overdiagnosis and influence of client gender on diagnosis. *Journal of Consulting and Clinical Psychology, 80,* 128–138.

Bruck, M., & Ceci, S. J. (1999). The suggestibility of children's memory. *Annual Review of Psychology* (Vol. 50). Palo Alto, CA: Annual Reviews.

Bruck, M., & Ceci, S. J. (2012). Forensic developmental psychology in the courtroom. In D. Faust & M. Ziskin (Eds.), *Coping with psychiatric and psychological testimony.* New York: Cambridge University Press.

Bruck, M., & Ceci, S. J. (2014, in press). Expert testimony in a child sex abuse case: Translating memory development research. *Memory.*

Brumariu, L. E., & Kerns, K. A. (2010). Parent-child attachment and internalizing symptomatology in childhood and adolescence: A review of empirical findings and future direction. *Development and Psychopathology, 22,* 177–203.

Brumariu, L. E., & Kerns, K. A. (2014, in press). Pathways to anxiety: Contributions to attachment history, temperament, peer competence, and ability to manage intense emotions. *Child Psychiatry and Human Development.*

Brumariu, L. E., Kerns, K. A., & Seibert, A. C. (2012). Mother-child attachment, emotion regulation, and anxiety symptoms in middle childhood. *Personal Relationships, 19*(3), 569–585.

Brummelman, E., & others (2014). "That's not beautiful—That's incredibly beautiful!" The adverse impact of inflated praise on children with low self-esteem. *Psychological Science, 25,* 728–735.

Brunell, P. A. (2014, in press). Measles in pregnancy is not kid's stuff. *Clinical Infectious Diseases.*

Brus, M., Keller, M., & Levy, F. (2013). Temporal features of adult neurogenesis: Differences and similarities across mammalian species. *Frontiers in Neuroscience, 7,* 135.

Bryan, C. J., McNaughton-Cassil, M., Osman, A., & Hernandez, A. M. (2013). The associations of physical and sexual assault with suicide risk in nonclinical military and undergraduate samples. *Suicide and Life-Threatening Behavior, 43,* 223–234.

Bryant, D. P., & others (2013). Instructional practices for improving student outcomes in solving arithmetic combinations. In B. G. Cook & M. G. Tankersley (Eds.), *Research-based practices in special education.* Upper Saddle River, NJ: Pearson.

Bryant, J. A. (Ed.) (2007). *The children's television community.* Mahwah, NJ: Erlbaum.

Bryant, J. B. (2012). Pragmatic development. In E. L. Bavin (Ed.), *Cambridge handbook of child language.* New York: Cambridge University Press.

Bryant, R. A. (2012). Grief as a psychiatric disorder. *British Journal of Psychiatry, 201,* 9–10.

Bryant, R. A. (2013). Is pathological grief lasting more than 12 months grief or depression? *Current Opinion in Psychiatry, 26,* 41–46.

Brynes, J. P. (2012). How neuroscience contributes to our understanding of learning and development in typically developing and special needs students. In K. R. Harris, S. Graham, & T. Urdan (Eds.), *APA educational psychology handbook.* Washington, DC: American Psychological Association.

Buchanan, S. L., & others (2012). Trends in morbidity associated with oxytocin use in labor in nulliparas at term. *Australian and New Zealand Journal of Obstetrics and Gynecology, 52,* 173–178.

Buchman, A. S., Yu, L., Boyle, P. A., Shah, R. C., & Bennett, D. A. (2012). Total daily physical activity and longevity in old age. *Archives of Internal Medicine, 172,* 444–446.

Buck, H. G., & Fahlberg, B. (2014). Using POLST to ensure patients' treatment preferences. *Nursing, 44,* 16–17.

Buckner, J. C., Mezzacappa, E., & Beardslee, M. R. (2009). Self-regulation and its relations to adaptive functioning in low income youths. *American Journal of Orthopsychiatry, 79,* 19–30.

Bucur, B., & Madden, D. J. (2007). Information processing/cognition. In J. E. Birren (Ed.), *Encyclopedia of gerontology* (2nd ed.). San Diego: Academic Press.

Budde, H., Voelcker-Rehage, C., Pietrabyk-Kendziorra, P., Ribeiro, P., & Tidow, G. (2008). Acute aerobic exercise improves attentional performance in adolescence. *Neuroscience Letters, 441,* 219–223.

Bugental, D., & Grusec, J. (2006). Socialization processes. In W. Damon & R. Lerner (Eds.), *Handbook of child psychology* (6th ed.). New York: Wiley.

Buhl, H. M., & Lanz, M. (2007). Emerging adulthood in Europe: Common traits and variability across five European countries. *Journal of Adolescent Research, 22,* 439–443.

Buhler, E., & others (2011). Differential diagnosis of autism spectrum disorder and attention deficit hyperactivity disorder by means of inhibitory control and 'theory of mind.' *Journal of Autism and Developmental Disorders, 41*(12), 1718–1726.

Buhling, K. J., & others (2014). The use of complementary and alternative medicine by women transitioning through menopause in Germany: Results of a survey of women aged 45–60 years. *Complementary Therapies in Medicine, 22,* 94–98.

Buhrmester, D. (1998). Need fulfillment. interpersonal competence, and the developmental contexts of early adolescent friendship. In W. M. Bukowski & A. F. Newcomb (Eds.), *The company they keep: Friendship in childhood and adolescence.* New York: Cambridge University Press.

Buist, K. L., Dekovic, M., & Prinzie, P. (2013). Sibling relationship quality and psychopathology of children and adolescents: A meta-analysis. *Clinical Psychology Review, 33,* 97–106.

Bukowski, R., & others (2008, January). *Folic acid and preterm birth.* Paper presented at the meeting of the Society for Maternal-Fetal Medicine, Dallas.

Bukowski, W. M., Buhrmester, D., & Underwood, M. K. (2011). Peer relations as a developmental context. In M. K. Underwood & L. M. Rosen (Eds.), *Social development.* New York: Guilford.

Bulf, H., & Valenza, E. (2013). Object-based visual attention in 8-month-old infants: Evidence from an eye-tracking study. *Developmental Psychology.* doi:10.1037/a0031310

Bulik, C. M., Berkman, N. D., Brownley, K. A., Sedway, J. A., & Lhor, K. N. (2007). Anorexia nervosa treatment: A systematic review of randomized controlled trials. *International Journal of Eating Disorders, 40,* 310–320.

Bullock, C. M., & Beckson, M. (2011). Male victims of sexual assault: Phenomenology, psychology, and physiology. *Journal of American Academy of Psychiatry and the Law, 39,* 197–205.

Bumpass, L., & Aquilino, W. (1994). *A social map of midlife: Family and work over the middle life course.* Center for Demography and Ecology, University of Wisconsin, Madison, WI.

Bumpus, M. F., Crouter, A. C., & McHale, S. M. (2001). Parental autonomy granting during adolescence: Gender differences in context. *Developmental Psychology, 37,* 163–173.

Bundick, M. J. (2011). The benefits of reflecting on and discussing purpose in life in emerging adulthood. *New Directions in Youth Development, 2011,* 89–103.

Buratti, S., Allwood, C. M., & Johansson, M. (2014). Stability in the metamemory realism of eyewitness confidence judgments. *Cognitive Processing, 15,* 39–53.

Burgess-Champoux, T. L., Larson, N., Neumark-Sztainer, D., Hannan, P. J., & Story, M. (2009). Are family meal patterns associated with overall diet quality during the transition from early to middle adolescence? *Journal of Nutrition Education and Behavior, 41,* 79–86.

Burke, D. M., Shafto, M. A. (2004). Aging and language production. *Current Directions in Psychological Science, 13,* 21–24.

Burnes, D. P., Rizzo, V. M., & Courtney, E. (2014, in press). Elder abuse and neglect risk alleviation in protective services. *Journal of Interpersonal Violence.*

Burnham, D., & Mattock, K. (2010). Auditory development. In J. G. Bremner & T. D. Wachs (Eds.), *Wiley-Blackwell handbook of infant development* (2nd ed.). New York: Wiley.

Burnham, M. M. (2014). Co-sleeping and self-soothing during infancy. In A. R. Wolfson & H. E. Montgomery-Downs (Eds.), *Oxford handbook of infant, child, and adolescent sleep and behavior.* New York: Oxford University Press.

Burns, C., Dunn, A., Brady, M., Starr, N., & Blosser, C. (2013). *Pediatric primary care* (5th ed.). New York: Elsevier.

Burns, R. A., Mitchell, P., Shaw, J., & Anstey, K. J. (2014). Trajectories of cognitive decline in the well-being of older women: The DYNOPTA project. *Psychology and Aging, 29,* 44–56.

Burr, J. (2009). Volunteering, later life. In D. Carr (Ed.), *Encyclopedia of the life course and human development.* Boston: Gale Cengage.

Burstyn, I., Kuhle, S., Allen, A. C., & Veugelers, P. (2012). The role of maternal smoking in effect of fetal growth restriction on poor scholastic achievement in elementary school. *International Journal of Environmental Research and Public Health, 9,* 408–420.

Burt, K. B., & Paysnick, A. A. (2012). Resilience in the transition to adulthood. *Development and Psychopathology, 24,* 493–505.

Burt, S. A. (2014, in press). Research review: The shared environment as a key source of variability in child and adolescent psychopathology. *Journal of Child Psychology and Psychiatry.*

Busch, H., & Hofer, J. (2012). Self-regulation and milestones of adult development: Intimacy and generativity. *Developmental Psychology, 48,* 282–293.

Bush, K. R., & Peterson, G. W. (2013). Parent-child relationships in diverse contexts. In G. W. Peterson & K. R. Bush (Eds.), *Handbook of marriage and the family* (3rd ed.). New York: Springer.

Bushnell, I. W. R. (2003). Newborn face recognition. In O. Pascalis & A. Slater (Eds.), *The development of face processing in infancy and early childhood.* New York: NOVA Science.

Buss, D. M. (1995). Psychological sex differences: Origins through sexual selection. *American Psychologist 50,* 164–168.

Buss, D. M. (2004). *Evolutionary psychology.* (2nd ed.). Boston: Allyn & Bacon.

Buss, D. M. (2008). *Evolutionary psychology* (3rd ed.). Boston: Allyn & Bacon.

Buss, D. M. (2012). *Evolutionary psychology* (4th ed.). Boston: Allyn & Bacon.

Buss, D. M., & Barnes, M. (1986). Preferences in human mate selection. *Journal of Personality and Social Psychology, 50,* 559–570.

Buss, D. M., & others. (1990). International preferences in selecting mates: A study of 37 cultures. *Journal of Cross-Cultural Psychology, 21,* 5–47.

Buss, K. A. (2011). Which fearful toddlers should we worry about? Context, fear regulation, and anxiety risk. *Developmental Psychology, 47,* 804–819.

Busse, E. W., & Blazer, D. G. (1996). *The American Psychiatric Press textbook of geriatric psychiatry* (2nd ed.). Washington, DC: American Psychiatric Press.

Bussey, K., & Bandura, A. (1999). Social cognitive theory of gender development and differentiation. *Psychological Review, 106,* 676–713.

Butler, R. N. (2007). Life review. In J. E. Birren (Ed.), *Encyclopedia of gerontology* (2nd ed.). San Diego: Academic Press.

Butler, R. N., & Lewis, M. (2002). *The new love and sex after 60.* New York: Ballantine.

Butrica, B. A., & Smith, K. E. (2012). The retirement prospects of divorced women. *Social Security Bulletin, 72,* 11–22.

Butrica, B. A., Smith, K. E., & Iams, H. M. (2012). This is not your parents' retirement: Comparing retirement income across generations. *Social Security Bulletin, 72,* 37–58.

Buttelmann, D., Over, H., Carpenter, M., & Tomasello, M. (2014). Eighteen-month-olds understand false beliefs in an unexpected-contents task. *Journal of Experimental Child Psychology, 119,* 120-126.

Butterworth, G. (2004). Joint visual attention in infancy. In G. Bremner & A. Slater (Eds.), *Theories of infant development.* Malden, MA: Blackwell.

Buttitta, M., Iliescu, C., Rousseau, A., & Guerrien, A. (2014, in press). Quality of life in overweight and obese children and adolescents : A literature review. *Quality of Life Research.*

Buzwell, S., & Rosenthal, D. (1996). Constructing a sexual self: Adolescents' sexual self-perceptions and sexual risk-taking. *Journal of Research on Adolescence, 6,* 489–513.

Byard, R. W. (2012a). Should infants and adults sleep in the same bed together? *Medical Journal of Australia, 196,* 10–11.

Byard, R. W. (2012b). The triple risk model for shared sleeping. *Journal of Pediatric Child Health, 48,* 947–948.

Byard, R. W. (2013). Breastfeeding and sudden infant death syndrome. *Journal of Pediatrics and Child Health, 49,* E353.

C

Caban-Holt, A., & others (2012). Age-expanded normative data for the Ruff 2&7 Selective Attention Test: Evaluating cognition in older males. *Clinical Neuropsychology, 26*(5), 751–768.

Cabeza, R. (2002). Hemispheric asymmetry reduction in older adults: The HAROLD model. *Psychology and Aging, 17,* 85–100.

Cabrera, N. J., Hofferth, S. L., & Chae, S. (2011). Patterns and predictors of father-infant engagement across race/ethnic groups. *Early Childhood Research Quarterly, 26,* 365–375.

Cacho, I., Dickinson, C. M., Smith, H. J., & Harper, P. A. (2010). Clinical impairment measures and reading performance in a large age-related macular degeneration group. *Optometry and Vision Science, 87*(5), 344–349.

Cacioppo, J. T., Cacioppo, S., Gonzaga, G. C., Ogburn, E. L., & VanderWheele, T. J. (2013). Marital satisfaction and break-ups differ across on-line and off-line meeting venues. *Proceedings of the National Academy of Sciences, 110*(25), 10135–10140.

Cadogan, M. P., Phillips, L. R., & Ziminski, C. E. (2014, in press). A perfect storm: Care transitions for vulnerable older adults discharged from the emergency department without a hospital admission. *Gerontologist.*

Caeymaex, L., & others (2013). Perceived role in end-of-life decision making in the NICU affects long-term parental grief response. *Archives of Disease in Childhood—Fetal and Neonatal Edition, 98*(1), F26–F31.

Cagney, K. A., Browning, C. R., Iveniuk, J., & English, N. (2014). The onset of depression during the great recession: Foreclosure and older adult mental health. *American Journal of Public Health, 104,* 498–505.

Cahill, K. E., Giandrea, M. D., & Quinn, J. F. (2014, in press). Retirement patterns and the macroeconomy, 1992–2010: The prevalence and determinants of bridge jobs, retirement, and reentry among three recent cohorts of older Americans. *Gerontologist.*

Cai, L., Chan, J. S., Yan, J. H., & Peng, K. (2014). Brain plasticity and motor practice in cognitive aging. *Frontiers in Aging Neuroscience, 6,* 31.

Cain, M. A., Bornick, P., & Whiteman, V. (2013). The maternal, fetal, and neonatal effects of cocaine exposure in pregnancy. *Clinical Obstetrics and Gynecology, 56,* 124–136.

Caldwell, B. A., & Redeker, N. S. (2014, in press). Maternal stress and psychological status and sleep in minority preschool children. *Public Health Nursing.*

Calkins, S. D., & Dollar, J. (2014). Caregiving influences on emotional regulation: Educational implications of a behavioral perspective. In R. Pekrun & L. Linnebrink-Garcia (Eds.), *International handbook of emotions in education.* New York: Routledge.

Callaghan, M. E., & others (2014, in press). Widespread age-related differences in the human brain microstructure revealed by quantitative magnetic resonance imaging. *Neurobiology of Aging.*

Callaghan, M. E., & others (2014, in press). Widespread age-related differences in the human brain microstructure revealed by quantitative magnetic resonance imaging. *Neurobiology of Aging.*

Callahan, D. (2009). Death, mourning, and medical practice. *Perspectives in Biological Medicine, 52,* 103–115.

Calvert, S. L., & Wartella, E. A. (2014). Children and electronic media. In E. T. Gershoff, R. S. Mistry, & D. A. Crosby (Eds.), *Societal contexts of child development.* New York: Oxford University Press.

Camacho, D. E., & Fuligni, A. J. (2014, in press). Extracurricular participation among adolescents from immigrant families. *Journal of Youth and Adolescence.*

Cameron, J. M., & others (2010). Drinking game participation among undergraduate students attending National Alcohol Screening Day. *Journal of American College Health, 58,* 499–506.

Campbell, F. A., Pungello, E. P., Miller-Johnson, S., Burchinal, M., & Ramey, C. T. (2001). The development of cognitive and academic abilities: Growth curves from an early childhood educational experiment. *Developmental Psychology, 37,* 231–243.

Campbell, F. A., & others (2012). Adult outcomes as a function of an early childhood educational program: An Abcedarian Project follow-up. *Developmental Psychology, 48,* 1033–1043.

Campbell, K. L., Grady, C. L., Ng, C., & Hasher, L. (2012). Age differences in the frontoparietal cognitive control network: Implications for distractibility. *Neuropsychologia, 50*(9), 2212–2223.

Campbell, L., Campbell, B., & Dickinson, D. (2004). *Teaching and learning through multiple intelligence* (3rd ed.). Boston Allyn & Bacon.

Campbell, L. A., Wan, J., Speck, P. M., & Hartig, M. T. (2014). Women, Infant, and Children (WIC) peer counselor contact with first time breastfeeding mothers. *Public Health Nursing, 31,* 3–9.

Campione-Barr, N. (2011). Sibling conflict. *Encyclopedia of Family Health.* Thousand Oaks, CA: Sage.

Campione-Barr, N., Greer, K. B., & Kruse, A. (2013). Differential associations between domains of sibling conflict and adolescent emotional adjustment. *Child Development, 84,* 938–954.

Campione-Barr, N., & Smetana, J. G. (2010). "Who said you could wear my sweater?" Adolescent siblings' conflicts and associations with relationship quality. *Child Development, 81,* 464–471.

Campos, J. J. (2005). Unpublished review of J. W. Santrock's *Life-span development* (10th ed.). New York: McGraw-Hill.

Canfield, J., & Hansen, M. V. (1995). *A second helping of chicken soup for the soul.* Deerfield Beach, FL: Health Communications.

Canfield, R. L., & Haith, M. M. (1991). Young infants' visual expectations for symmetric and asymmetric stimulus sequences. *Developmental Psychology, 27,* 198–208.

Cansino, S., & others (2013). The decline of verbal and visuospatial working memory across the life span. *Age, 35,* 2283–2302.

Cantalupo. N. C. (2014, in press). Institution-specific victimization surveys: Addressing legal and practical disincentives to gender-based violence reporting on college campuses. *Trauma, Violence, and Abuse.*

Capaldi, D. M., Stoolmiller, M., Clark, S., & Owen, L. D. (2002). Heterosexual risk behaviors in at-risk young men from early adolescence to young adulthood: Prevalence, prediction, and association with STD contraction. *Developmental Psychology, 38,* 394–406.

Caprara, M., & others (2013). Active aging promotion: Results from the vital aging program. *Current Gerontology and Geriatrics Research,* 2013: 817813.

Carl, J. D. (2012). *Short introduction to the U.S. Census.* Upper Saddle River, NJ: Pearson.

Carling-Jenkins, R., Torr, J., Iacono, T., & Bigby, C. (2012). Experiences of supporting people with Down syndrome and Alzheimer's disease in aged care and family environments. *Journal of Intellectual and Developmental Disability, 37,* 54–60.

Carlisle, J., Kenney, C., & Vereb, A. (2013). Vocabulary instruction for students with or at risk for learning disabilities: Promising approaches for learning words from text. In B. G. Cook & M. G. Tankersley (Eds.), *Research-based practices in special education.* Upper Saddle River, NJ: Pearson.

Carlson, M. D., Mendle, J., & Harden, K. P. (2014, in press). Early adverse environments and genetic influences on age at first sex: Evidence for gene x environment interaction. *Developmental Psychology.*

Carlson, S. M. (2010). Development of conscious control and imagination. In R. F. Baumeister, A. R. Mele, & K. D. Vohs (Eds.), *Free will and consciousness: how might they work?* New York: Oxford University Press.

Carlson, S. M. (2011). Introduction to the special issue: Executive function. *Journal of Experimental Child Psychology, 108,* 411–413.

Carlson, S. M., Claxton, L. J., & Moses, L. J. (2014, in press). The relation between executive function and theory of mind is more than skin deep. *Journal of Cognition and Development.*

Carlson, S. M., & White, R. (2011). Unpublished research. Minneapolis: Institute of Child Development, University of Minnesota.

Carlson, S. M., & White, R. (2013). Executive function and imagination. In M. Taylor (Ed.), *Handbook of imagination.* New York: Oxford University Press.

Carlson, S. M., White, R., & Davis-Unger, A. C. (2014, in press). Evidence for a relation between executive function and pretense representation in preschool children. *Cognitive Development.*

Carlson, S. M., Zelazo, P. D., & Faja, S. (2013). Executive function. In P. D. Zelazo (Ed.), *Oxford handbook of developmental psychology.* New York: Oxford University Press.

Carlsson, N., Johansson, A., Abrahamsson, A., & Andersson Gare, B. (2013). How to minimize children's environmental tobacco smoke exposure: An intervention in a clinical setting in high risk areas. *BMC Pediatrics, 13*(1), 76.

Carnethon, M. R., Gidding, S. S., Nehgme, R., Sidney, S., Jacobs, D. R., & Liu, K. (2003). Cardiorespiratory fitness in young adulthood and the development of cardiovascular disease risk factors. *Journal of the American Medical Association, 290,* 3092–3100.

Carpendale, J. I., & Chandler, M. J. (1996). On the distinction between false belief in understanding and subscribing to an interpretive theory of mind. *Child Development, 67,* 1686–1706.

Carpenter, J., Nagell, K., & Tomasello, M. (1998). Social cognition, joint attention, and communicative competence from 9 to 15 months of age. *Monographs of the Society for Research in Child Development. 70* (1, Serial No. 279).

Carpenter, M. (2011). Social cognition and social motivations in infancy. In U. Goswami (Ed.), *Wiley-Blackwell handbook of childhood cognitive development* (2nd ed.). New York: Wiley.

Carr, D. (2009). Death and dying. In D. Carr (Ed.), *Encyclopedia of the life course and human development.* Boston: Gale Cengage.

Carr, D., & Sharp, S. (2014). Do afterlife beliefs affect psychological adjustment to late-life spousal loss? *Journals of Gerontology B: Psychological Sciences and Social Sciences, 69B*(1), 103–112.

Carr, D., Sonnega, J., Nesse, R. M., & House, J. S. (2014). Do special occasions trigger psychological distress among older bereaved spouses? An empirical assessment of clinical wisdom. *Journals of Gerontology B: Psychological Sciences and Social Sciences, 69B,* 113–122.

Carrizzo, A., & others (2013). Antioxidant effects of resveratrol in cardiovascular, cerebral, and metabolic diseases. *Food and Chemical Toxicology, 61,* 215–226.

Carroll, D., & others (2011). Low cognitive ability in early adulthood is associated with reduced lung function in middle age: The Vietnam Experience Study. *Thorax, 66,* 884–888.

Carroll, J. L. (2013). *Sexuality now* (4th ed.). Boston: Cengage.

Carskadon, M. A. (2004). Sleep difficulties in young people. *Archives of Pediatric and Adolescent Medicine, 158,* 597–598.

Carskadon, M. A. (2005). Sleep and circadian rhythms in children and adolescents: Relevance for athletic performance of young people. *Clinical Sports Medicine, 24,* 319–328.

Carskadon, M. A. (2011a). Sleep in adolescents: The perfect storm. *Pediatric Clinics of North America, 58,* 637–647.

Carskadon, M. A. (2011b). Sleep's effects on cognition and learning in adolescence. *Progress in Brain Research, 190,* 137–143.

Carstensen, L. L. (1998). A life-span approach to social motivation. In J. Heckhausen & C. Dweck (Eds.), *Motivation and self-regulation across the life span.* New York: Cambridge University Press.

Carstensen, L. L. (2006). The influence of a sense of time on human development. *Science, 312,* 1913–1915.

Carstensen, L. L. (2008, May). *Long life in the 21st century.* Paper presented at the meeting of the Association of Psychological Science, Chicago.

Carstensen, L. L. (2009). *A long bright future.* New York: Random House.

Carstensen, L. L., & Fried, L. P. (2012). The meaning of old age. *Global population aging: Peril or promise?* Geneva, Switzerland: World Economic Forum.

Carstensen, L. L., & others (2011). Emotional experience improves with age: Evidence based on over 10 years of sampling. *Psychology and Aging, 26,* 21–33.

Carta, J. J., Greenwood, C., Baggett, K., Buzhardt, J., & Walker, D. (2012). Research-based approaches for individualizing caregiving and educational interventions for infants and toddlers in poverty. In S. L. Odom, E. P. Pungello, & N. Gardner-Neblett (Eds.), *Infants, toddlers, and families in poverty.* New York: Guilford.

Carter, C. S. (2014). Oxytocin pathways and the evolution of human behavior. *Annual Review of Psychology* (Vol. 65). Palo Alto, CA: Annual Reviews.

Cartwright, K. B., Galupo, M. P., Tyree, S. D., & Jennings, J. G. (2009). Reliability and validity of the Complex Postformal Thought Questionnaire: Assessing adults' cognitive development. *Journal of Adult Development, 16,* 183–189.

Cartwright, R., Agargun, M. Y., Kirkby, J., & Friedman, J. K. (2006). Relation of dreams to waking concerns. *Psychiatry Research, 141,* 261–270.

Carver, C. S., & Connor-Smith, J. (2010). Personality and coping. *Annual Review of Psychology* (Vol. 61). Palo Alto, CA: Annual Reviews.

Carver, K., Joyner, K., & Udry, J. R. (2003). National estimates of romantic relationships. *Annual Review of Psychology* (Vol. 54). Palo Alto, CA: Annual Reviews.

Case, R., & Mueller, M. R. (2001). Differentiation, integration, and covariance mapping as fundamental processes in cognitive and neurological growth. In J. L. McClelland & R. S. Slegler (Eds.), *Mechanisms of cognitive development.* Mahwah, NJ: Erlbaum.

Caserta, M., Utz, R., Lund, D., Swenson, K. L., & de Vries, B. (2014). Coping processes among bereaved spouses. *Death Studies, 38,* 145–155.

Casey, B. J. (2015, in press). The adolescent brain and self-control. *Annual Review of Psychology* (Vol. 66). Palo Alto, CA: Annual Reviews.

Casey, B. J., Jones, R. M., & Somerville, L. H. (2011). Braking and accelerating of the adolescent brain. *Journal of Research on Adolescence, 21,* 21–33.

Caspers, K. M., & others (2009). Association between the serotonin transporter polymorphism (5-HTTLPR) and adult unresolved attachment. *Developmental Psychology, 45,* 64–76.

Caspi, A., & Roberts, B. W. (2001). Personality development across the life course: The argument for change and continuity. *Psychological Inquiry, 12,* 49–66.

Caspi, A., & others (2003). Influence of life stress on depression: Moderation by a polymorphism in the 5-HTT gene. *Science, 301,* 386–389.

Cassidy, J., & others (2011). Enhancing infant attachment security: An examination of treatment efficacy and differential susceptibility. *Development and Psychopathology, 23,* 131–148.

Cassone, A. R. (2014, in press). Mindfulness training as an adjunct to evidence-based treatment for ADHD within families. *Journal of Attention Disorders.*

Castle, J., & others (2010). Parents' evaluation of adoption success: A follow-up study of intercountry and domestic adoptions. *American Journal of Orthopsychiatry, 79,* 522–531.

Castle, N., Ferguson-Rome, J. C., & Teresi, J. A. (2014, in press). Elder abuse in residential long-term care: An update to the 2003 National Research Council Report. *Journal of Applied Gerontology.*

Castrodale, V., & Rinehart, S. (2014). The golden hour: Improving the stabilization of the very low birth-weight infant. *Advances in Neonatal Care, 14,* 9–14.

Catalan, M. J., & others (2013). Levodopa infusion improves impulsivity and dopamine dysregulation syndrome in Parkinson's disease. *Movement Disorders, 28,* 2007–2010.

Catalano, R. F., & others (2012). Worldwide application of prevention science in adolescent health. *Lancet, 379,* 1653–1664.

Catarino, A., & others (2013, in press). Task-related functional connectivity in autism spectrum conditions: An EEG study using wavelet transform coherence. *Molecular Autism.*

Cavanagh, S. E. (2009). Puberty. In D. Carr (Ed.), *Encyclopedia of the life course and human development.* Boston: Gale Cengage.

Cavanaugh, M. M., Weyand, C. M., & Goronzy, J. J. (2012). Chronic inflammation and aging: DNA damage tips the balance. *Current Opinion in Immunology, 24*(4), 488–493.

Caylak, E. (2012). Biochemical and genetic analyses of childhood attention deficit/hyperactivity disorder. *American Journal of Medical Genetics B: Neuropsychiatric Genetics, 159B*(6), 613–627.

Ceci, S. J., & Gilstrap, L. L. (2000). Determinants of intelligence: Schooling and intelligence. In A. Kazdin (Ed.), *Encyclopedia of psychology.* Washington, DC, & New York: American Psychological Association and Oxford University Press.

Ceci, S. J., & Klemfuss, J. Z. (2010). Children's suggestibility: Knowns and unknowns. *The Advocate: Division 37 of APA, 33,* 3–7.

Cederborg, A-C., Alm, C., Da Silva Nises, D. L., & Lamb, M. E. (2014, in press). Investigative interviewing of alleged child abuse victims: Evaluation of a new training program for investigative interviewers. *Police Practice and Research.*

Celik, O., & Yucel, S. (2014). Testosterone replacement therapy: Should it be performed in erectile dysfunction? *Nephro-Urology Monthly, 5,* 858–861.

Center for Science in the Public Interest (2008). *Obesity on the kids' menu at top chains.* Retrieved October 2, 2008, from http://cspinet.org/new/200808041.html

Center for Survey Research at the University of Connecticut (2000). *Hours on the job.* Storrs: University of Connecticut, Center for Survey Research.

Centers for Disease Control and Prevention (2007). *Autism and developmental disabilities monitoring (ADDM) network.* Atlanta: Author.

Centers for Disease Control and Prevention (2008). *National Health Interview Study.* Atlanta: Author.

Centers for Disease Control and Prevention (2012). *Birth data.* Atlanta: Author.

Centers for Disease Control and Prevention (2012). *Breastfeeding report card, United States: Outcome indicators.* Retrieved August 14, 2013, from www.cdc.gov/breastfeeding/data/reportcard2.htm

Centers for Disease Control and Prevention (2012). *By the numbers full year 2011: Health measures from the National Health Interview Study, January–December 2011.* Atlanta: Author.

Centers for Disease Control and Prevention (2012). CDC estimates 1 in 88 children in the United States has been identified as having an autism spectrum disorder. *CDC Division of News & Electronic Media, 404.* Retrieved May 1, 2014, from http://www.cdc.gov/features/autismprevalence/

Centers for Disease Control and Prevention (2012). *Signs V. HIV infection, testing, and risk behaviors among youths—United States.* Atlanta: Author.

Centers for Disease Control and Prevention (2012, January 13). Vital signs: Binge drinking prevalence, frequency, and intensity among adults—United States, 2010. *Morbidity and Mortality Weekly Report (MMWR), 61*(1), 14–19.

Centers for Disease Control and Prevention (2013, October). Prevalence of obesity among adults: United States, 2011–2012. *NCHS Data Brief, 131,* 1–8.

Centers for Disease Control and Prevention (2014). *Body mass index for children and teens.* Atlanta: Author.

Centers for Disease Control and Prevention (2014). *Fast facts: Tobacco.* Retrieved March 20, 2014, from www.cdc.gov/tobacco/data_statistics/fact_sheets/fast_facts/

Centers for Disease Control and Prevention (2014). *How much physical activity do older adults need?* Atlanta: Author.

Centers for Disease Control and Prevention (2014). *Sexually transmitted disease surveillance.* Atlanta, GA: U.S. Department of Health and Human Services.

Central Intelligence Agency (2012). *The world factbook: Life expectancy at birth.* Washington, DC: CIA.

Cerqueira, F. M., Cunha, F. M., Laurindo, F. R., & Kowaltowski, A. J. (2012). Calorie restriction increases cerebral mitochondrial respiratory capacity in a NO mediated mechanism: Impact on neuronal survival. *Free Radical and Biological Medicine, 52,* 1236–1241.

Cha, N. H. Seo, E. J., & Sok, S. R. (2012). Factors influencing the successful aging of older Korean adults. *Contemporary Nurse, 41,* 78–87.

Chae, H. W., & others (2013). Final height and insulin-like growth factor-1 in children with medulloblastoma treated with growth hormone. *Child's Nervous System, 29*(10), 1459–1463.

Chambaere, K., & others (2012). Age-based disparities in end-of-life decisions in Belgium: A population-based death certificate survey. *BMC Public Health, 12,* 447.

Chan, C. H., & others (2014, in press). Sexual initiation and emotional/behavior problems in Taiwanese adolescents: A multivariate response profile analysis. *Archives of Sexual Behavior.*

Chan, H. C., & others (2013). Highly electronegative LDL from patients with ST-elevation myocardial infarction triggers platelet activation and aggregation. *Blood, 211,* 3632–3641.

Chance, P. (2014). *Learning and behavior* (7th ed.). Boston: Cengage.

Chandra, A., Mosher, W. D., Copen, C., & Sionean, C. (2011, March 3). Sexual behavior, sexual attraction, and sexual identity in the United States: Data from the 2006–2008 National Survey of Family Growth. *National Health Statistics Reports, 36,* 1–28.

Chandra-Mouli, V., Camacho, A. V., & Michaud, P. A. (2013). WHO guidelines on preventing early pregnancy and poor reproductive outcomes among adolescents in developing countries. *Journal of Adolescent Research, 52,* 517–522.

Chang, H. Y., & others (2014). Prenatal maternal depression is associated with low birth weight through shorter gestational age in term infants in Korea. *Early Human Development, 90,* 15–20.

Chang, S. H., Beason, T. S., Hunleth, J. M., & Colditz, G. A. (2012). A systematic review of body fat distribution and mortality in older people. *Maturitas, 72,* 175–191.

Chang, Y. K., Liu, S., Yu, H. H., & Lee, Y. H. (2012). Effect of acute exercise on executive function in children with attention deficit hyperactivity disorder. *Archives of Clinical Neuropsychology, 27,* 225–237.

Chang, Z., Lichtenstein, P., & Larsson, H. (2012). The effects of childhood ADHD symptoms on early-onset substance use: A Swedish twin study. *Journal of Abnormal Child Psychology, 40,* 425–435.

Chao, R. (2001). Extending research on the consequences of parenting style for Chinese Americans and European Americans. *Child Development, 72,* 1832–1843.

Chao, R. K. (2005, April). *The importance of Guan in describing control of immigrant Chinese.* Paper presented at the meeting of the Society for Research in Child Development, Atlanta.

Chao, R. K. (2007, March). *Research with Asian Americans: Looking back and moving forward.* Paper presented at the meeting of the Society for Research in Child Development, Boston.

Chao, R. K., & Otsuki-Clutter, M. (2011). Racial and ethnic differences: Sociocultural and contextual explanations. *Journal of Research on Adolescence, 21,* 47–60.

Chao, R., & Tseng, V. (2002). Parenting of Asians. In M. H. Bornstein (Ed.), *Handbook of parenting* (2nd ed., Vol. 4). Mahwah, NJ: Erlbaum.

Chaplin, J. E., & others (2012). Improvements in behavior and self-esteem following growth hormone treatment in short prepubertal children. *Hormone Research in Pediatrics, 75*(4), 291–303.

Chaplin, T. M., & Aldao, A. (2013). Gender differences in emotion expression in children: A meta-analytic review. *Psychological Bulletin, 139*(4), 735–765.

Charles, S. T., & Carstensen, L. L. (2010). *Social and emotional aging.* In S. Fiske & S. Taylor (Eds). *Annual Review of Psychology* (Vol. 61). Palo Alto, CA: Annual Reviews.

Charles, S. T., & Luong, G. (2011). Emotional experience across the life span. In K. L. Fingerman, C. A. Berg, J. Smith, & T. C. Antonucci (Eds.), *Handbook of life-span development.* New York: Springer.

Charles, S. T., & Piazza, J. R. (2007). Memories of social interactions: Age differences in emotion intensity. *Psychology and Aging, 22,* 300–309.

Charles, S. T., Piazza, J. R., Mogle, J., Sliwinski, M. J., & Almeida, D. M. (2013). The wear and tear of daily stressors on mental health. *Psychological Science, 24,* 733–741.

Charles, S. T., & others (2010). Fewer ups and downs: Daily stressors mediate age differences in negative affect. *Journals of Gerontology B: Psychological Sciences and Social Sciences, 65B,* 279–286.

Charlet, J., Schnekenburger, M., Brown, K. W., & Diederich, M. (2012). DNA demethylation increases sensitivity of neuroblastoma cells to chemotherapeutic drugs. *Biochemical Pharmacology, 83,* 858–865.

Charness, N., & Bosman, E. A. (1992). Human factors and aging. In F. I. M. Craik & T. A. Salthouse (Eds.), *The handbook of aging and cognition.* Hillsdale, NJ: Erlbaum.

Charness, N., & Krampe, R. T. (2008). Expertise and knowledge. In D. F. Alwin & S. M. Hofer (Eds.), *Handbook on cognitive aging.* Thousand Oaks, CA: Sage.

Charpentier, M., & Soulieres, M. (2013). Elder abuse and neglect in institutional settings: The resident's perspective. *Journal of Elder Abuse and Neglect, 25,* 339–354.

Chassin, L., & others (2008). Multiple trajectories of cigarette smoking and the intergenerational transmission of smoking: A multigenerational, longitudinal study of a midwestern community sample. *Health Psychology, 27,* 819–828.

Chaturvedi, S., & others (2014). Pharmacological interventions for hypertension in children. *Cochrane Database of Systematic Reviews, 2,* CD008117.

Chatzigeorgious, A., & others (2014, in press). Peripheral targets in obesity treatment: A comprehensive update. *Obesity Reviews.*

Chavarria, M. C., & others (2014, in press). Puberty in the corpus callosum. *Neuroscience.*

Chen, A. F., & others (2012). Free radical biology of the cardiology system. *Clinical Science, 123,* 73–91.

Chen, C., & Stevenson, H. W. (1989). Homework: A cross-cultural comparison. *Child Development, 60,* 551–561.

Chen, C. P., & others (2014). Prenatal diagnosis and molecular cytogenetic characterization of de novo pure partial trisomy 6p associated with microcephaly, craniosynostosis, and abnormal maternal serum biochemistry. *Gene, 536,* 425–429.

Chen, D., & Guarente, L. (2007). SIR2: A potential target for calorie restriction mimetics. *Trends in Molecular Medicine, 13,* 64–71.

Chen, G., & others (2014, in press). BMI, health behaviors, and quality of life in children and adolescents: A school-based study. *Pediatrics.*

Chen, J., & others (2014, in press). Genetic and environmental influences on depressive symptoms in Chinese children. *Behavior Genetics.*

Chen, J. J., & Dashtipour, K. (2013). Abo-, ino-, ona-, and rima-botulinum toxins in clinical therapy: A primer. *Pharmacotherapy, 33,* 304–318.

Chen, P., & Jacobson, K. C. (2012). Developmental trajectories of substance use from early adolescence to young adulthood: Gender and racial/ethnic differences. *Journal of Adolescent Health, 50,* 154–163.

Chen, X., Chung, J., Lechccier-Kimel, R., & French, D. (2011). Culture and social development. In P. K. Smith & C. H. Hart (Eds.), *Wiley-Blackwell perspectives on childhood social development* (2nd ed.). New York: Wiley.

Chen, X., Hastings, P. D., Rubin, K. H., Chen, H., Cen, G., & Stewart, S. L. (1998). Childrearing attitudes and behavioral inhibition in Chinese and Canadian toddlers: A cross-cultural study. *Developmental Psychology, 34,* 677–686.

Chen, Z. Y., & Liu, R. X. (2014). Comparing adolescent only children with those who have siblings on academic related outcomes and psychosocial adjustment. *Child Development Research,* Article ID: 578289.

Cheng, S. T. (2014). Defining successful aging: The need to distinguish pathways from outcomes. *International Psychogeriatrics, 26,* 527–531.

Cheng, S. T., Lee, C. K., & Chow, P. K. (2010). Social support and psychological well-being of nursing home residents in Hong Kong. *International Geriatrics, 22*(7), 1185–1190.

Cheng, Y., Lou, C., Gao, E., Emerson, M. R., & Zabin, L. S. (2012). The relationship between contact and unmarried adolescents' and young adults' traditional beliefs in three East Asian cities: A cross-cultural analysis. *Journal of Adolescent Health, 50*(3, Suppl.), S4–S11.

Cherlin, A. J. (2009). *The marriage-go-round.* New York: Random House.

Cherlin, A. J., & Furstenberg, F. F. (1994). Stepfamilies in the United States: A reconsideration. In J. Blake & J. Hagen (Eds.), *Annual Review of Sociology* (Vol. 20). Palo Alto, CA: Annual Reviews.

Chess, S., & Thomas, A. (1977). Temperamental individuality from childhood to adolescence. *Journal of Child Psychiatry, 16,* 218–226.

Chess, S., & Thomas, A. (1987). *Origins and evolution of behavior disorders.* Cambridge, MA: Harvard University Press.

Cheung, C., & Pomerantz, E. M. (2012). Why does parents' involvement in children's learning enhance children's achievement? The role of parent-oriented motivation. *Journal of Educational Psychology. 104*(3), 820–832.

Cheung, C. S., Pomerantz, E. M., & Dong, W. (2012). Does adolescents' disclosure to their parents matter for their academic adjustment? *Child Development, 84*(2), 693–710.

Chevan, A. (1996). As cheaply as one: Cohabitation in the older population. *Journal of Marriage and the Family, 58*(August), 656–667.

Chi, M. T. (1978). Knowledge structures and memory development. In R. S. Siegler (Ed.), *Children's thinking: What develops*? Hillsdale, NJ: Erlbaum.

Chick, C. F., & Reyna, V. F. (2012). A fuzzy trace theory of adolescent risk taking: Beyond self-control and sensation seeking. In V. F. Reyna & others (Ed.), *The adolescent brain.* Washington, DC: American Psychological Association.

Childers, J. B., & Tomasello, M. (2002). Two-year-olds learn novel nouns, verbs, and conventional actions from massed or distributed exposures. *Developmental Psychology, 38,* 967–978.

Cho, J., Martin, P., & Poon, L. W. (2012). The older they are, the less successful they become? Findings from the Georgia Centenarian Study. *Journal of Aging Research,* 2012: 695854.

Choi, K. H., & Vasunilashorn, S. (2014). Widowhood, age heterogamy, and health: The role of selection, marital quality, and health behaviors. *Journals of Gerontology B: Psychological Sciences and Social Sciences, 69,* 123–134.

Choi, N. G., & Jun, J. (2009). Life regrets and pride among low-income older adults: Relationships with depressive symptoms, current life stressors, and coping resources. *Aging and Mental Health, 13,* 213–225.

Choi, N. G., & Landeros, C. (2011). Wisdom from life's challenges: Qualitative interviews with low- and moderate-income older adults who were nominated as being wise. *Journal of Gerontological Social Work, 54,* 592–614.

Chomsky, N. (1957). *Syntactic structures.* The Hague: Mouton.

Chopik, W. J., Edelstein, R. S., & Fraley, R. C. (2013). From the cradle to the grave: Age differences in attachment from early adulthood to old age. *Journal of Personality, 81,* 171–183.

Christensen, L. B., Johnson, R. B., & Turner, L. A. (2015, in press). *Research methods* (12th ed.). Upper Saddle River, NJ: Pearson.

Christian, B. E., & Shadel, G. S. (2014). Aging: It's SIRTainly possible to restore mitochondrial dysfunction. *Current Biology, 24,* R206–R208.

Christianson, M. S., & Shen, W. (2013). Osteoporosis prevention and management: Nonpharmacologic and lifestyle options. *Clinical Obstetrics and Gynecology, 56,* 703–710.

Christie, J., Enz, B. J., Vukelilch, C., & Roskos, K. A. (2014). *Teaching language and literacy* (5th ed.). Upper Saddle River, NJ: Pearson.

Christodoulidou, A., & others (2013). The roles of telomerase in the generation of polyploidy during neoplastic cell growth. *Neoplasia, 15,* 156–168.

Chua, A. (2011). *Battle hymn of the tiger mom.* New York: Penguin.

Chuang, Y. F., & others (2014). Cardiovascular risks and brain function: A functional magnetic resonance imaging study of executive function in older adults. *Neurobiology of Aging, 35,* 1396–1403.

Chung, J. K., Park, S. H., Lee, W. J., & Lee, S. J. (2009). Bilateral cataract surgery: A controlled clinical trial. *Japan Journal of Ophthalmology, 53,* 107–113.

Church, D. K., Siegel, M. A., & Fowler, C. D. (1988). *Growing old in America.* Wylie, TX: Information Aids.

Cicchetti, D. (2011). Pathways to resilient functioning in maltreated children: From single to multilevel investigations. In D. Cicchetti & G. I. Roisman (Eds.), *The origins and organization of adaptation and maladaptation: Minnesota Symposia on Child Psychology* (Vol. 36). New York: Wiley.

Cicchetti, D. (2013). Developmental psychopathology. In P. Zelazo (Ed.), *Oxford handbook of developmental psychology.* New York: Oxford University Press.

Cicchetti, D., & Banny, A. (2014, in press). A developmental psychopathology perspective on child maltreatment. In M. Lewis & K. Rudolph (Eds.), *Handbook of developmental psychopathology.* New York: Springer.

Cicchetti, D., & Toth, S. L. (2006). Developmental psychopathology and preventive intervention. In W. Damon & R. Lerner (Eds.), *Handbook of child psychology,* (6th ed.). New York: Wiley.

Cicchetti, D., & Toth, S. L. (2015, in press). A multilevel perspective on child maltreatment. In R. M. Lerner (Ed.), *Handbook of child psychology and developmental science* (7th ed., Vol. 3). New York: Wiley.

Cicchetti, D., Toth, S. L., Nilsen, W. J., & Manley, J. T. (2014, in press). What do we know and why does it matter? The dissemination of evidence-based interventions for child maltreatment. In H. R. Schaeffer & K. Durkin (Eds.), *Blackwell handbook of developmental psychology in action.* New York: Blackwell.

Cicchetti, D., Toth, S. L., & Rogosch, F. A. (2005). *A prevention program for child maltreatment.* Unpublished manuscript, University of Rochester, Rochester, NY.

Cicirelli, V. (2009). Sibling relationships, later life. In D. Carr (Ed.), *Encyclopedia of the life course and human development.* Boston: Gale Cengage.

Cicirelli, V. G. (2010). Attachment relationships in old age. *Journal of Social and Personal Relationships, 27,* 191–199.

Cillessen, A. H. N., & Bellmore, A. D. (2011). Social skills and social competence in interactions with peers. In P. K. Smith & C. H. Hart (Eds.), *Wiley-Blackwell handbook of childhood social development* (2nd ed.). New York: Wiley.

Cillessen, A. H. N., & van den Berg, Y. H. M. (2012). Popularity and school adjustment. In A. M. Ryan & G. W. Ladd (Eds.), *Peer relationships and adjustment at school.* Charlotte, NC: Information Age Publishing.

Cimpean, D., & Drake, R. E. (2011). Treating co-morbid chronic medical conditions and anxiety/depression. *Epidemiology and Psychiatric Science, 20,* 141–150.

Cisler, J. M., Begle, A. M., Amstadter, A. B., & Acierno, R. (2012). Mistreatment and self-reported emotional symptoms: Results from the National Elder Mistreatment Study. *Journal of Elder Abuse and Neglect, 24,* 216–230.

Citkovitz, C., Schnyer, R. N., & Hoskins, I. A. (2011). Acupuncture during labor: Data are more promising than a recent review suggests. *BJOG, 118,* 101.

Claes, H. I., & others (2010). Understanding the effects of sildenafil treatment on erection maintenance and erection hardness. *Journal of Sexual Medicine, 7*(6), 2184–2191.

Clapp, W. C., Rubens, M. T., Sabharwal, J., & Gazzaley, A. (2011). Deficit switching between functional brain networks underlies the impact of multitasking on working memory in older adults. *Proceedings of the National Academy of Sciences U.S.A., 108,* 7212–7217.

Clare, L., & others (2012). Longitudinal trajectories of awareness and early-stage dementia. *Alzheimer Disease and Associated Disorders, 26,* 140–147.

Clark, B. (2008). *Growing up gifted* (7th ed.). Upper Saddle River, NJ: Prentice Hall.

Clark, D. J., & others (2011). Muscle performance and physical function are associated with voluntary rate of neuromuscular activation in older adults. *Journals of Gerontology A: Biological Sciences and Medical Sciences, 66A,* 115–121.

Clark, E. (1993). *The lexicon in acquisition.* New York: Cambridge University Press.

Clark, E. V. (2009). What shapes children's language? Child-directed speech and the process of acquisition. In V. C. M. Gathercole (Ed.), *Routes to language: Essays in honor of Melissa Bowerman.* New York: Psychology Press.

Clark, E. V. (2012). Lexical meaning. In E. L. Bavin (Ed.), *Cambridge handbook of child language.* New York: Cambridge University Press.

Clark, F. (2014). Discrimination against LGBT people triggers health concerns. *Lancet, 383,* 500–502.

Clark-Cotton, M. R., Williams, R. K., Goral, M., & Obler, L. K. (2007). Language and communication in aging. In J. E. Birren (Ed.), *Encyclopedia of gerontology* (2nd ed.). San Diego: Academic Press.

Clarke-Stewart, A. K., & Miner, J. L. (2008). Child and day care, effects of. In M. M. Haith & J. B. Benson (Eds.), *Encyclopedia of infant and early childhood development.* Oxford, UK: Elsevier.

Clarke-Stewart, A. K., & Parke, R. D. (2014). *Future families.* New York: Wiley.

Clarke-Stewart, A. K., & Parke, R. D. (2014). *Social development* (2nd ed.). New York: Wiley.

Class, Q. A., & others (2013). Maternal stress and infant mortality: The importance of the preconception period. *Psychological Science, 24*(7), 1309–1316.

Clausen, J. A. (1993). *American lives.* New York: Free Press.

Clay, O. J., & others (2009). Visual function and cognitive speed of processing mediate age-related decline in memory span and fluid intelligence. *Journal of Aging and Health, 21,* 547–566.

Clay, R. (2001, February). Fulfilling an unmet need. *Monitor on Psychology, 2.*

Clay, R. A. (1997, April). Helping dying patients let go of life in peace. *APA Monitor,* p. 42.

Clearfield, M. W., Diedrich, F. J., Smith, L. B., & Thelen, E. (2006). Young infants reach correctly in A-not-B tasks: On the development of stability and perseverance. *Infant Behavior and Development, 29,* 435–444.

Cleere, C., & Lynn, S. J. (2013). Acknowledged versus unacknowledged sexual assault among college students. *Journal of Interpersonal Violence, 28,* 2593–2611.

Clements, J. M. (2009). Patient perceptions on the use of advanced directives and life prolonging technology. *American Journal of Hospice and Palliative Care, 26,* 270–276.

Clifton, R. K., Morrongiello, B. A., Kulig, J. W., & Dowd, J. M. (1981). Developmental changes in auditory localization in infancy. In R. N. Aslin, J. R. Alberts, & M. R. Petersen (Eds.), *Development of perception* (Vol. 1). Orlando, FL: Academic Press.

Clifton, R. K., Muir, D. W., Ashmead, D. H., & Clarkson, M. G. (1993). Is visually guided reaching in early infancy a myth? *Child Development, 64,* 1099–1110.

Cluett, E. R., & Burns, E. (2009). Immersion in water in labour and birth. *Cochrane Database of Systematic Reviews,* CD000111.

Cnattingius, S., & others (2013). Maternal obesity and risk of preterm delivery. *Journal of the American Medical Association, 309,* 2362–2370.

Coe, N. B., von Gaudecker, H. M., Lindeboom, M., & Maurer, J. (2012). The effect of retirement on cognitive functioning. *Health Economics, 21,* 913–927.

CogMed (2013). *CogMed: Working memory is the engine of learning.* Upper Saddle River, NJ: Pearson.

Cohen, D. (2012). *How the child's mind develops* (2nd ed.). New York: Psychology Press.

Cohen, F., & others (2007). Immune function declines with unemployment and recovers after stressor termination. *Psychosomatic Medicine, 69,* 225–234.

Cohen, G. D. (2009). Creativity, later life. In D. Carr (Ed.), *Encyclopedia of the life course and human development.* Boston: Gale Cengage.

Cohen, G. L., & Prinstein, M. J. (2006). Peer contagion of aggression and health-risk behavior among adolescent males: An experimental investigation of effects on public conduct and private attitudes. *Child Development, 77,* 967–983.

Cohen, K. M., & Savin-Williams, R. C. (2013). Coming out to self and others: Unfolding of developmental milestones. In P. Levounis, J. Drescher, & M. Barber (Eds.), *Working with lesbian, gay, bisexual, and transgender people: Basic principles and case studies.* Arlington, VA: American Psychiatric Publishing.

Cohen, L. B. (2002, April). *Can infants really add and subtract?* Paper presented at the meeting of the International Conference on Infant Studies, Toronto.

Cohen, M. C., & Ramsey, D. A. (2014, in press). Shaken baby syndrome and forensic pathology. *Forensic Science and Medical Pathology.*

Cohen, P. (2012). *In our prime: The invention of middle age.* New York: Scribner.

Cohen, S., & Janicki-Deverts, D. (2012). Who's stressed? Distributions of psychological stress in the United States: Probability samples from 1983, 2006, and 2009. *Journal of Applied Social Psychology, 42,* 1320–1332.

Cohen, S., & others (2013). Association between telomere length and experimentally induced upper viral infection in healthy adults. *Journal of the American Medical Association, 309,* 699–705.

Cohen, S., & Shachar, I. (2012). Cytokines as regulators of proliferation and survival of healthy and malignant peripheral B cells. *Cytokine, 60,* 13–22.

Cohen, S., Janicki-Deverts, D., Crittenden, C. N., & Sneed, R. S. (2012). Personality and human immunity. In S. C. Segerstrom (Ed.), *Oxford handbook of psychoneuroimmunology.* New York: Oxford University Press.

Cohen-Mansfield, J., & Perach, R. (2014, in press). Interventions for alleviating loneliness among older adults: A critical review. *American Journal of Health Promotion.*

Cohen-Woods, S., Craig, I. W., & McGuffin, P. (2012). The current state of play on molecular genetics of depression. *Psychological Medicine, 43*(4), 673–687.

Coie, J. (2004). The impact of negative social experiences on the development of antisocial behavior. In J. B. Kupersmidt & K. A. Dodge (Eds.), *Children's peer relations: From development to intervention.* Washington, DC: American Psychological Association.

Colby, A., Koblberg, L., Gibbs, J., & Lieberman, M. (1983). A longitudinal study of moral judgment. *Monographs of the Society for Research in Child Development* (Serial No. 201).

Colcombe, S., & Kramer, A. F. (2003). Fitness effects on the cognitive function of older adults: A meta-analytic study. *Psychological Science, 14,* 125–130.

Colcombe, S. J., & others (2006). Aerobic exercise training increases brain volume in aging humans. *Journals of Gerontology: Medical Sciences, 61A,* 1166–1170.

Cole, P. M., & Tan, P. Z. (2007). Emotion socialization from a cultural perspective. In J. E. Grusec & P. D. Hastings (Eds.), *Handbook of socialization.* New York: Guilford.

Cole, P. M., Dennis, T. A., Smith-Simon, K. E., & Cohen, L. H. (2009). Preschoolers' emotion regulation strategy understanding: Relations with maternal socialization and child behavior. *Social Development, 18*(2), 324–352.

Cole, P. M., & Hall, S. E. (2012). Emotion dysregulation as a risk factor for psychopathology. In T. Beauchaine & S. Hinshaw (Eds.), *Developmental psychopathology.* New York: Wiley.

Coleman, A. M. (2013). Physicians' attitudes toward advance directives: A literature review of variables impacting on physicians' attitude toward advance directives. *American Journal of Hospice and Palliative Care, 30,* 696–706.

Coleman, M., Ganong, L., & Fine, M. (2004). Communication in stepfamilies. In A. L. Vangelisti (Ed.), *Handbook of family communication.* Mahwah, NJ: Erlbaum.

Coleman, P. D. (1986, August). *Regulation of dendritic extent: Human aging brain and Alzheimer's disease.* Paper presented at the meeting of the American Psychological Association, Washington, DC.

Coleman-Phox, K., Odouli, R., & Li, D. K. (2008). Use of a fan during sleep and the risk of sudden infant death syndrome. *Archives of Pediatric and Adolescent Medicine, 162,* 963–968.

Coley, R. L., Kull, M., Leventhal, T., & Lynch, A. D. (2014, in press). Profiles of housing and neighborhood contexts among low-income families: Links with children's well-being. *Citiscape.*

Coley, R. L., Votruba-Drzal, E., Miller, P. L., & Koury, A. (2013). Timing, extent, and type of child care and children's functioning in kindergarten. *Developmental Psychology, 49*(10), 1859–1873.

Coley, R. L., & others (2013). Sexual partner accumulation from adolescence through early adulthood: The role of family, peer, and school social norms. *Journal of Adolescent Health, 53,* 91–97.

Collaku, A., & others (2004). A genome-wide linkage scan for dietary energy and nutrient intakes. *American Journal of Clinical Nutrition, 79,* 881–886.

Collings, P. J., & others (2013). Physical activity intensity, sedentary time, and body composition in preschoolers. *American Journal of Clinical Nutrition, 97,* 1020–1028.

Collins, C., Duncanson, K., & Burrows, T. (2014, in press). A systematic review investigating associations between parenting styles and child feeding behaviors. *Journal of Human Nutrition and Dietetics.*

Collins, C. E., & others (2011). Parent diet modification, child activity, or both in obese children: An RCT. *Pediatrics, 127,* 619–627.

Collins, W. A., & van Dulmen, M. (2006). The significance of middle childhood peer competence for work and relationships in early childhood. In A. C. Huston & M. N. Ripke (Eds.), *Developmental contexts in middle childhood.* New York: Cambridge University Press.

Collins, W. A., Welsh, D. P., & Furman, W. (2009). Adolescent romantic relationships. *Annual Review of Psychology* (Vol. 60). Palo Alto, CA: Annual Reviews.

Colman, R. J., & others (2009). Caloric restriction delays disease onset and mortality in rhesus monkeys. *Science, 325,* 201–204.

Colonnesi, C., Stams, G. J., Koster, I., & Noom, M. J. (2010). The relation between pointing and language development: A meta-analysis. *Developmental Review, 30,* 352–366.

Columbo, J., Brez, C., & Curtindale, L. (2013). Infant perception and cognition. In I. B. Weiner & others (Eds.), *Handbook of psychology* (2nd ed., Vol. 6). New York: Wiley.

Columbo, J., Brez, C., & Curtindale, L. (2013). Infant perception and cognition. In I. B. Weiner & others (Eds.), *Handbook of psychology* (2nd ed., Vol. 6). New York: Wiley.

Comer, J. P. (1988). Educating poor minority children. *Scientific American, 259,* 42–48.

Comer, J. (2004). *Leave no child behind.* New Haven, CT: Yale University Press.

Comer, J. (2006). Child development: The under-weighted aspect of intelligence. In P. C. Kyllonen, R. D. Roberts, & L. Stankov (Eds.), *Extending intelligence.* Mahwah, NJ: Erlbaum.

Comer, J. (2010). Comer School Development Program. In J. Meece & J. Eccles (Eds.), *Handbook of research on schools, schooling, and human development.* New York: Routledge.

Committee on Injury, Violence, and Poison Prevention (2011). Child passenger safety. *Pediatrics, 127,* e1050–e1066.

Common Sense Media (2011). *Zero to eight: Children's media use in America.* Retrieved June 21, 2012, from www.commonsensemedia.org/research

Commoner, B. (2002). Unravelling the DNA myth: The spurious foundation of genetic engineering. *Harper's Magazine, 304,* 39–47.

Commons, M. L., & Bresette, L. M. (2006). Illuminating major creative scientific innovators with postformal stages. In C. Hoare (Ed.), *Handbook of adult development and learning.* New York: Oxford University Press.

Conde-Aguedelo, A., Belizan, J. M., & Diaz-Rossello, J. (2011). Kangaroo care to reduce morbidity and mortality in low birthweight infants. *Cochrane Database of Systematic Reviews,* March 16; (3) CD002771.

Condition of Education (2014). *Participation in education.* Washington, DC: U.S. Office of Education.

Conduct Problems Prevention Research Group. (2010). The difficulty of maintaining positive intervention effects: A look at disruptive behavior, deviant peer relations, and social skills during the middle school years. *Journal of Early Adolescence, 30*(4), 593–624.

Conduct Problems Prevention Research Group (2011). The effects of Fast Track preventive intervention on the development of conduct disorder across childhood. *Child Development, 82,* 331–345.

Conduct Problems Prevention Research Group (2013). Assessing findings from the Fast Track Study. *Journal of Experimental Criminology, 9,* 119–126.

Conduct Problems Prenvention Research Group (2014). Trajectories of risk for early sexual activity and early substance use in the Fast Track Prevention Program. *Prevention Science, 15*(1, Suppl.), S33–S46.

Cong, X., Ludington-Hoe, S. M., & Walsh, S. (2011). Randomized crossover trial of kangaroo care to reduce biobehavioral pain responses in preterm infants: A pilot study. *Biological Research for Nursing, 13,* 204–216.

Conger, R. D., & Chao, W. (1996). Adolescent depressed mood. In R. L. Simons (Ed.), *Understanding differences between divorced and intact families: Stress, interaction, and child outcome.* Thousand Oaks, CA: Sage.

Connell, A. M., Dishion, T. J., & Klostermann, S. (2012). Family checkup effects on adolescent arrest trajectories: Variation by developmental subtype. *Journal of Research on Adolescence, 22*(2), 367–380.

Connolly, J. A., & McIsaac, C. (2009). Romantic relationships in adolescence. In R. M. Lerner & L. Steinberg (Eds.), *Handbook of adolescent psychology* (3rd ed.), New York: Wiley.

Connolly, J. A., Nguyen, H. N., Pepler, D., Craig, W., & Jiang, D. (2013). Developmental trajectories of romantic stages and associations with problem behaviors during adolescence. *Journal of Adolescence, 36*(6), 1013–1024.

Conry-Murray, C., Kim, J. M., & Turiel, E. (2012, April). *U.S. and Korean children's judgments of gender norm violations.* Paper presented at the Gender Development Research conference, San Francisco.

Consoli, A., & others (2013). Suicidal behaviors in depressed adolescents: Role of perceived relationships in the family. *Child and Adolescent Psychiatry and Mental Health, 7*(1), 8.

Contant, T. L., Bass, J. E., & Carin, A. A. (2015, in press). *Teaching science through inquiry and investigation* (12th ed.). Upper Saddle River, NJ: Pearson.

Converse, A. K., Ahlers, E. O., Travers, B. G., Davidson, R. J. (2014). Tai chi training reduces self-report of inattention in healthy young adults. *Frontiers in Human Neuroscience, 8,* 13.

Cook, E. C., Buehler, C., & Blair, B. L. (2013). Adolescents' emotional reactivity across relationship contexts. *Developmental Psychology, 49*(2), 341–352.

Cook, M., & Birch, R. (1984). Infant perception of the shapes of tilted plane forms. *Infant Behavior and Development, 7,* 389–402.

Cooper, C., Selwood, A., & Livingston, G. (2008). The prevalence of elder abuse and neglect: A systematic review. *Age and Aging, 37,* 151–160.

Cooper, C. R. (2011). *Bridging multiple worlds.* New York: Oxford University Press.

Copen, C. E., Daniels, K., Vespa, J., & Mosher, W. D. (2012). First marriages in the United States: Data from the 2006-2010 National Survey of Family Growth. *National Health Statistics Report, 49,* 1–22.

Coplan, R. J., & Arbeau, K. A. (2009). Peer interactions and play in early childhood. In K. H. Rubin, W. M. Bukowski, & B. Laursen (Eds.), *Handbook of peer interactions, relationships, and groups.* New York: Guilford.

Cordier, S. (2008). Evidence for a role of paternal exposure in developmental toxicity. *Basic and Clinical Pharmacology and Toxicology, 102,* 176–181.

Cordova, D., Huang, S., Lally, M., Estrada, Y., & Prado, G. (2014, in press). Do parent-adolescent discrepancies in family functioning increase the risk of Hispanic adolescent HIV risk behaviors? *Family Process.*

Cornew, L., & others (2012). Atypical social referencing in infant siblings of children with autism spectrum disorders. *Journal of Autism and Developmental Disorders, 42*(12), 2611–2621.

Corona, G., Rastrelli, G., Maseroli, E., Forti, G., & Maggi, M. (2013). Sexual functioning of the aging male. *Best Practices & Research: Clinical Endocrinology and Metabolism, 27,* 581–601.

Corso, J. F. (1977). Auditory perception and communication. In J. E. Birren & K. W. Schaie (Eds.), *Handbook of the psychology of aging* (2nd ed.). New York: Van Nostrand Reinhold.

Cortes, E., Basra, R., & Kelleher, C. J. (2011). Waterbirth and pelvic floor injury: A retrospective study and postal survey using ICIQ modular long form questionnaires. *European Journal of Obstetrics, Gynecology, and Reproductive Biology, 155,* 27–30.

Cosco, T. D., & others (2014). Operational definitions of successful aging: A systematic review. *International Psychogeriatrics, 26,* 373–381.

Costa, P. T., & McCrae, R. R. (1995). Solid ground on the wetlands of personality. A reply to Black. *Psychological Bulletin, 117,* 216–220.

Costa, P. T., & McCrae, R. R. (1998). Personality assessment. In H. S. Friedman (Ed.), *Encyclopedia of mental health* (Vol. 3). San Diego: Academic Press.

Costa, P. T., & McCrae, R. R. (2000). Contemporary personality psychology. In C. E. Coffey and J. L. Cummings (Eds.), *Textbook of geriatric neuropsychiatry.* Washington, DC: American Psychiatric Press.

Costigan, S. A., Barnett, L., Plotnikoff, R. C., & Lubans, D. R. (2013). The health indicators associated with screen-based sedentary behavior among adolescent girls: A systematic review. *Journal of Adolescent Health, 52*(4), 382–392.

Costley, K. C. (2012). An overview of the life, central concepts, including classroom applications for Lev Vygotsky. *ERIC,* ED529565.

Cote, J., & Bynner, J. M. (2008). Changes in the transition to adulthood in the UK and Canada: The role of structure and aging in emerging adulthood. *Journal of Youth Studies, 11,* 251–258.

Cotten, S. R., Anderson, W. A., & McCullough, B. M. (2013). Impact of Internet use on loneliness and contact with others among older adults: Cross-sectional analysis. *Journal of Medical Internet Research, 15*(2), e39.

Cotten, S. R., Ford, G., Ford, S., & Hale, T. M. (2014, in press). Internet use and depression among retired older adults in the United States: A longitudinal analysis. *Journals of Gerontology B: Psychological Sciences and Social Sciences.*

Coubart, A., & others (2014). Dissociation between small and larger numerosities in newborn infants. *Developmental Science, 17,* 11–22.

Council of Economic Advisors (2000). *Teens and their parents in the 21st century: An examination of trends in teen behavior and the role of parent involvement.* Washington, DC: Author.

Courage, M. L., & Richards, J. E. (2008). Attention. In M. M. Haith & J. B. Benson (Eds.), *Encyclopedia of infant and early childhood development.* Oxford, UK: Elsevier.

Court, F., & others (2014, in press). Genome-wide parent-of-origin DNA methylation analysis reveals the intricacies of the human imprintome and suggests a germline methylation independent establishment of imprinting. *Genome Research.*

Cousineau, T. M., Goldstein, M., & Franco, D. L. (2005). A collaborative approach to nutrition education for college students. *Journal of American College Health, 53,* 79–84.

Cowan, C. P., & Cowan, P. A. (2000). *When partners become parents.* Mahwah, NJ: Erlbaum.

Cowan, M. K. (2015, in press). *Microbiology* (4th ed.). New York: McGraw-Hill.

Cowan, N. (2014). Short-term and working memory in childhood. In P. Bauer & R. Fivush (Eds.), *Wiley-Blackwell handbook of children's memory.* New York: Wiley.

Cowan, P., Cowan, C., Ablow, J., Johnson, V. K., & Measelle, J. (2005). *The family context of parenting in children's adaptation to elementary school.* Mahwah, NJ: Lawrence Erlbaum Associates.

Cowan, R., & Powell, D. (2014). The contributions of domain-general and numerical factors to third-grade arithmetic skills and mathematical learning disability. *Journal of Educational Psychology, 106,* 214–229.

Coxon, J. P., Van Impe, A., Wenderoth, N., & Swinnen, S. P. (2012). Aging and inhibitory control of action: Cortio-subthalamic connection strength predicts stopping performance. *Journal of Neuroscience, 32,* 8401–8412.

Coyne, S. M., Nelson, D. A., & Underwood, M. K. (2011). Aggression in children. In P. K. Smith & C. H. Hart (Eds.), *Wiley-Blackwell handbook of childhood social development* (2nd ed.). New York: Wiley.

Cozma Dima, C., Cojocaru, C. D., & Postolache, P. (2014, in press). Is exercise training effective for patients with chronic obstructive pulmonary disease and chronic ischemic heart disease? *Chest.*

Craft, C. S., & others (2014, in press). The extracellular matrix protein MAGP1 suppports thermogenesis and protects against obesity and diabetes through regulation of TGFB. *Diabetes.*

Crain, S. (2012). Sentence scope. In E. L. Bavin (Ed.), *Cambridge handbook of child language.* New York: Cambridge University Press.

Crane, J. D., Macneil, L. G., & Tarnopolsky, M. A. (2013). Long-term aerobic exercise is associated with greater muscle strength throughout the life span. *Journals of Gerontology A: Biological Sciences and Medical Sciences, 68,* 631–638.

Craparo, G., Gori, A., Petruccelli, I., Cannella, V., & Simonelli, C. (2014, in press). Intimate partner violence: Relationships between alexithymia, depression, attachment styles, and coping strategies of battered women. *Journal of Sexual Medicine.*

Crawford, D., & others (2010). The longitudinal influence of home and neighborhood environments on children's body mass index and physical activity over five years: The CLAN study. *International Journal of Obesity, 34,* 1177–1187.

Cremation Association of North America (2012). *Statistics about cremation trends.* Retrieved July 12, 2012, from www.cremationassociation.org/Media/CremationStatistics/tabid/95/Default.aspx

Cribbet, M. R., & others (2014). Cellular aging and restorative processes: Subjective sleep quality and duration moderate the association between age and telomere length in a sample of middle-aged and older adults. *Sleep, 37,* 65–70.

Cristi, C., & others (2014, in press). Whole-body vibration training increases physical fitness measures without alteration of inflammatory markers in older adults. *European Journal of Sport Science.*

Crocetti, E. Rabaglietta. E., & Sica, L. S. (2012). Personal identity in Italy. *New Directions in Child and Adolescent Development, 138,* 87–102.

Crockenberg, S. B. (1986). Are temperamental differences in babies associated with predictable differences in caregiving? In J. V. Lerner & R.M. Lerner (Eds.), *Temperament and social interaction during infancy and childhood.* San Francisco: Jossey-Bass.

Crone, E. A., & Dahl, R. E. (2012). Understanding adolescence as a period of social-affective engagement and goal flexibility. *Nature Reviews: Neuroscience, 13,* 636–650.

Crooks, R. L., & Baur, K. (2014). *Our sexuality* (12th ed.). Boston: Cengage.

Crosnoe, R. (2011). *Fitting in, standing out.* New York: Cambridge University Press.

Crosnoe, R., & Fuligni, A. J. (2012). Children from immigrant families: Introduction to the special section. *Child Development, 83,* 1471–1476.

Crosnoe, R., & Leventhal, T. (2014). School- and neighborhood-based interventions to improve the lives of disadvantaged children. In E. T. Gershoff, R. S. Mistry, & D. A. Crosby (Eds.), *The societal context of child development.* New York: Oxford University Press.

Crouter, A. C. (2006). Mothers and fathers at work. In A. Clarke-Stewart & J. Dunn (Eds.), *Families count.* New York: Cambridge University Press.

Crouter, A. C., & McHale, S. (2005). The long arm of the job revisited: Parenting in dual-earner families. In T. Luster & L. Okasagi (Eds.), *Parenting.* Mahwah, NJ: Erlbaum.

Crowley, K., Callahan, M. A., Tenenbaum, H. R., & Allen, E. (2001). Parents explain more to boys than to girls during shared scientific thinking. *Psychological Science. 12,* 258–261.

Crowley, S. J., & Carskadon, M. A. (2010). Modifications to weekend recovery sleep delay circadian phase in older adolescents. *Chronobiology International, 27,* 1469–1492.

Cruchaga, C., & others (2014). Rare encoding variants in the phospholipase D3 gene confer risk for Alzheimer's disease. *Nature, 505,* 550–554.

Cruz, J. E., Emery, R. E., & Turkheimer, E. (2012). Peer network drinking predicts increasing alcohol use from adolescence to early adulthood after controlling for genetic and shared environmental selection. *Developmental Psychology, 48*(5), 1390–1402.

Csikszentmihalyi, M. (1995). *Creativity.* New York: HarperCollins.

Csikszentmihalyi, M. (2000). Creativity: An overview. In A. Kazdin (Ed.), *Encyclopedia of psychology.* Washington, DC, & New York: American Psychological Association and Oxford University Press.

Csikszentmihalyi, M. (2014). The systems model of creativity and its applications. In D. K. Simonton (Ed.), *Wiley-Blackwell handbook of genius.* New York: Wiley.

Cubbin, C., Brindis, C. D., Jain, S., Santelli, J., & Braveman, P. (2010). Neighborhood poverty, aspirations and expectations, and initiation of sex. *Journal of Adolescent Health, 47,* 399–406.

Cuddy-Casey, M., & Orvaschel, H. (1997). Children's understanding of death in relation to child suicidality and homicidality. *Death Studies, 17,* 33–45.

Cuenca-Garcia, M., & others (2014). Dietary indices, cardiovascular risk factors, and mortality in middle-aged adults: Findings from the Aerobics Center Longitudinal Study. *Annals of Epidemiology, 24,* 297–303.

Cuevas, K., & others (2014, in press). What's mom got to do with it? Contributions of maternal executive function and caregiving to the development of executive function across early childhood. *Developmental Science.*

Cuevas, K., & Bell, K. A. (2014). Infant attention and early childhood executive function. *Child Development.*

Cuevas, K., Swingler, M. M., Bell, M. A., Maracovitch, S., & Calkins, S. D. (2012). Measures of frontal functioning and the emergence of inhibitory control processes at 10 months of age. *Developmental Cognitive Neuroscience, 2,* 235–243.

Cui, Y., Zong, H., Yan, H., & Zhang, Y. (2014, in press). The effect of testosterone replacement therapy on prostate cancer: A systematic review and meta-analysis. *Prostate Cancer and Prostatic Diseases.*

Culp, K. M. (2012). *An interesting career in psychological science: Research scientist at an education research organization.* Retrieved July 30, 2013, from www.apa.org/science/about/psa/2012/10/education-research.aspx

Cummings, E. M., & Davies, P. T. (2010). *Marital conflict and children: An emotional security perspective.* New York: Guilford.

Cummings, E. M., El-Sheikh, M., & Kouros, C. D. (2009). Children and violence: The role of children's regulation in the marital aggression-child adjustment link. *Clinical Child and Family Psychology Review, 12*(1), 3–15.

Cummings, E. M., & Schatz, J. N. (2012). Family conflict, emotional security, and child development: Translating research findings into a prevention program for community families. *Clinical Child and Family Psychology Review, 15,* 14–27.

Cummings, E. M., Bergman, K. N., & Kuznicki, K. A. (2014). Emerging methods for studying family systems. In S. McHale, P. Amato, & A. Booth (Eds.), *Emerging methods for family research.* New York: Springer.

Cummings, E. M., Braungart-Rieker, J. M., & Du Rocher-Schudlich, T. (2013). Emotion and personality development. In I. B. Weiner & others (Eds.), *Handbook of psychology* (2nd ed., Vol. 6). New York: Wiley.

Cummings, E. M., Koss, K. J., & Cheung, R. Y. M. (2015, in press). Interparental conflict and children's mental health: Emerging directions in emotional security theory. In C. R. Agnew & S. C. South (Eds.), *Interpersonal relationships and health.* New York: Oxford University Press.

Cummings, M. (2014). *Human heredity* (10th ed.). Boston: Cengage.

Cunningham, M. (2009). Housework. In D. Carr (Ed.), *Encyclopedia of the life course and human development.* Boston: Gale Cengage.

Cunningham, P. M. (2013). *Phonics they use: Words for reading and writing* (6th ed.). Boston: Allyn & Bacon.

Cunningham, S. A., Kramer, M. R., & Narayan, K. M. (2014). Incidence of child obesity in the United States. *New England Journal of Medicine, 370,* 403–411.

Curran, K., DuCette, J., Eisenstein, J., & Hyman, I. A. (2001, August). *Statistical analysis of the cross-cultural data: The third year.* Paper presented at the meeting of the American Psychological Association, San Francisco, CA.

Currie, C., & others (2012). Is obesity at individual and national level associated with lower age at menarche? Evidence from 34 countries in the Health Behavior in School-aged Children study. *Journal of Adolescent Health, 50,* 621–626.

Currier, J. M., Holland, J. M., & Neimeyer, R. A. (2006). Sense-making, grief, and the experience of violent loss: Toward a mediational model. *Death Studies, 30,* 403–428.

Cushner, K. H., McClelland, A., & Safford, P. (2015). *Human diversity in education* (8th ed.). New York: McGraw-Hill.

Cuzzolaro, M. (2014, in press). Eating and weight disorders: Studies on anorexia, bulimia, and obesity turns 19. *Eating and Weight Disorders.*

Cvencek, D., Meltzoff, A. N., & Greenwald, A. G. (2011). Math-gender stereotypes in elementary school children. *Child Development, 82,* 766–779.

Cypher, R. L. (2013). Collaborative approaches to prenatal care: Strategies of successful adolescent programs. *Journal of Perinatal and Neonatal Nursing, 27,* 134–144.

Czaja, S. J., & others (2006). Factors predicting the use of technology: Findings from the Center for Research and Education on Aging and Technology (CREATE). *Psychology and Aging, 21,* 333–352.

D

D'Apolito, K. (2013). Breastfeeding and substance abuse. *Clinical Obstetrics and Gynecology, 56,* 202–211.

D'Augelli, A. R. (1991). Gay men in college: Identity processes and adaptations. *Journal of College Student Development, 32,* 140–146.

Da Costa, L. A., Badawi, A., & El-Sohemy, A. (2012). Nutrigenetics and modulation of oxidative stress. *Annals of Nutrition and Metabolism* (3, Suppl.), S27–S36.

da Cruz, A. C., & others (2014). Oxidative stress and aging: Correlation with clinical parameters. *Aging: Clinical and Experimental Research, 26,* 7–12.

da Fonseca, E. B., Bittar, R. E., Damiao, R., & Zugiab, M. (2009). Prematurity prevention: The role of progesterone. *Current Opinion in Obstetrics and Gynecology, 21,* 142–147.

Dahl, R. E. (2004). Adolescent brain development: A period of vulnerability and opportunity. *Annals of the New York Academy of Sciences, 1021,* 1–122.

Dahlberg, U., & Aune, I. (2013). The woman's birth experience—the effect of interpersonal relationships and continuity of care. *Midwifery, 29*(4), 407–415.

Dahlen, H. G., Dowling, H., Tracy, M., Schmied, V., & Tracy, S. (2013). Maternal and perinatal outcomes amongst low risk women giving birth in water compared to six birth positions on land. A descriptive cross-sectional study in a birth center over 12 years. *Midwifery, 29,* 759–764.

Dai, T., & others (2013). Sources of variation on the mini-mental state examination in a population-based sample of centenarians. *Journal of the American Geriatrics Association, 61,* 1369–1376.

Dakin, E., & Pearlmutter, S. (2009). Older women's perceptions of elder maltreatment and ethical dilemmas in adult protective services: A cross-cultural, exploratory study. *Journal of Elder Abuse and Neglect, 21,* 15–57.

Dalley, J. W., & Roiser, J. P. (2012). Dopamine, serotonin, and impulsivity. *Neuroscience, 26,* 42–58.

Damman, M., Henkens, K., & Kalmijn, M. (2014, in press). Missing work after retirement: The role of life histories in the retirement adjustment process. *Gerontologist.*

Damon, W. (1988). *The moral child.* New York: Free Press.

Damon, W. (2008). *The path to purpose.* New York: Free Press.

Danforth, M. M., & Glass, J. C. (2001). Listen to my words, give meaning to my sorrow: A study in cognitive constructs in middle-aged bereaved widows. *Death Studies, 25,* 513–548.

Daniels, H. (2011). Vygotsky and psychology. In U. Goswami (Ed.), *Wiley-Blackwell handbook of childhood cognitive development* (2nd ed.). New York: Wiley.

Daniels, L. A., & others (2014, in press). Child eating behavior outcomes of an early feeding intervention to reduce risk indicators for child obesity: The NOURISH RCT. *Obesity.*

Daniels, N. (2012). Aging and intergenerational equity. *Global population aging: Peril or promise?* Geneva, Switzerland: World Economic Forum.

Danner, D., Snowdon, D., & Friesen, W. (2001). Positive emotions in early life and longevity: Findings from the Nun Study. *Journal of Personality and Social Psychology, 80*(5), 804–813.

Darcy, E. (2012). Gender issues in child and adolescent eating disorders. In J. Lock (Ed.), *Oxford handbook of child and adolescent eating disorders: Developmental perspectives.* New York: Oxford University Press.

Darwin, C. (1859). *On the origin of species.* London: John Murray.

Das, A. (2013). Spousal loss and health in late life: Moving beyong emotional trauma. *Journal of Aging Health, 25,* 221–242.

Dastani, Z., & others (2012). Novel loci for adiponectin levels and their influence on type 2 diabetes and metabolic traits: A multi-ethnic meta-analysis of 45,891 individuals. *PLoS One, 8*(3), e1002607.

Davalos, D. B., Yadon, C. A., & Tregellas, H. C. (2012). Untreated maternal depression and the potential risks to offspring: A review. *Archives of Women's Mental Health, 15,* 1–14.

Davanzo, R., & others (2013). Intermittent kangaroo mother care: A NICU proposal. *Journal of Human Lactation, 29,* 332–338.

Davidson, J. (2000). Giftedness. In A. Kazdin (Ed.), *Encyclopedia of psychology.* Washington, DC, & New York: American Psychological Association and Oxford University Press.

Davidson, P. S., & others (2013). Source memory in normal aging and Parkinson's disease. *Journal of Neuropsychology, 7,* 179–192.

Davidson, W. S., Jimenez, T. R., Onifade, E., & Hankins, S. S. (2010). Student experiences of the adolescent diversion project: A community-based exemplar in the pedagogy of service-learning. *American Journal of Community Psychology, 46,* 442–458.

Davies, G., & others (2011). Genome-wide association studies establish that human intelligence is highly heritable and polygenic. *Molecular Psychiatry, 16,* 996–1005.

Davies, J., & Brember, I. (1999). Reading and mathematics attainments and self-esteem in years 2 and 6—an eight-year cross-sectional study. *Educational Studies, 25,* 145–157.

Davies, M., Gilston, J., & Rogers, P. (2012). Examining the relationship between male rape myth acceptance, female rape myth acceptance, victim blame, homophobia, gender roles, and ambivalent sexism. *Journal of Interpersonal Violence. 27*(14), 2807–2823.

Davies, P. T., & Cicchetti, D. (2014, in press). How and why does the 5-HTTLPR gene moderate associations between maternal unresponsiveness and children's problems? *Child Development.*

Davis, A. E., Hyatt, G., & Arrasmith, D. (1998, February). "I Have a Dream" program. *Class One Evaluation Report.* Portland, OR: Northwest Regional Education Laboratory.

Davis, B. E., Moon, R. Y., Sachs, M. C., & Ottolinl, M. C. (1998). Effects of sleep position on infant motor development. *Pediatrics, 102,* 1135–1140.

Davis, C. F., Lazariu, V., & Sekhobo, J. P. (2010). Smoking cessation in the WIC program. *Maternal and Child Health Journal, 14*(3), 474–477.

Davis, C. L., & Cooper, S. (2011). Fitness, fatness, cognition, behavior, and academic achievement in overweight children: Do cross-sectional associations correspond to exercise trial outcomes? *Preventive Medicine, 52*(1, Suppl.), S65–S69.

Davis, C. L., & others (2011). Exercise improves executive functioning and alters neural activation in overweight children. *Health Psychology, 30,* 91–98.

Davis, C. L., & others (2012). Exercise dose and diabetes risk in overweight and obese children: A randomized controlled trial. *JAMA, 308,* 1103–1112.

Davis, L., & Keyser, J. (1997). *Becoming the parent you want to be: A sourcebook of strategies for the first five years.* New York: Broadway.

Davis, M. C., Burke, H. M., Zautra, A. J., & Stark, S. (2013). Arthritis and musculoskeletal conditions. In I. B. Weiner & others (Eds.), *Handbook of psychology* (2nd ed., Vol. 9). New York: Wiley.

Davis, S. W., Kragel, J. E., Madden, D. J., & Cabesa, R. (2012). The architecture of cross-hemispheric communication in the aging brain: Linking behavior to functional and structural connectivity. *Cerebral Cortex, 22,* 232–242.

Davison, K. K., Jurkowski, J. M., Li, K., Kranz, S., & Lawson, H. A. (2013). A childhood obesity intervention developed by families for families: Results from a pilot study. *International Journal of Behavioral Nutrition and Physical Activity, 10,* 3.

Davison, S. M., & others (2013). CHILE: An evidence-based preschool intervention for obesity prevention in Head Start. *Journal of School Health, 83,* 223–229.

Dawson, J. D., Uc, E. Y., Anderson, S. W., Johnson, A. M., & Rizzo, M. (2010). Neuropsychological predictors of driving errors in older adults. *Journal of the American Geriatric Society, 58*(6), 1090–1096.

Day, N. L., Goldschmidt, L., & Thomas, C. A. (2006). Prenatal marijuana exposure contributes to the prediction of marijuana use at age 14. *Addiction, 101,* 1313–1322.

Day, R. H., & McKenzie, B. E. (1973). Perceptual shape constancy in early infancy. *Perception, 2,* 315–320.

de Frias, C. M., & Dixon, R. A. (2014). Lifestyle engagement affects cognitive status differences and trajectories on executive functions in older adults. *Archives of Clinical Neuropsychology, 29,* 16–25.

De Giovanni, N., & Marchetti, D. (2012). Cocaine and its metabolites in the placenta: a systematic review of the literature. *Reproductive Toxicology, 33,* 1–14.

de Guzman, N. S., & Nishina, A. (2014). A longitudinal study of body dissatisfaction and pubertal timing in an ethnically diverse adolescent sample. *Body Image, 11,* 68–71.

de Haan, M., & Gunnar, M. R. (Eds.) (2009). *Handbook of developmental social neuroscience.* New York: Guilford.

de Hevia, M. D., & Spelke, E. S. (2010). Number-space mapping in human infants. *Psychological Science, 21,* 653–660.

de Hollander, E. L., & others (2012). The association between waist circumference and risk of mortality considering body mass index in 65- to 74-year-olds: A

meta-analysis of 29 cohorts involving more than 58,000 elderly persons. *International Journal of Epidemiology, 41*(3), 805–817.

de Jong Gierveld, J., & Merz, E-M. (2013). Parents' partnership decision making after divorce or widowhood: The role of (step) children. *Journal of Marriage and Family, 75,* 1098–1113.

de la Cuesta-Benjumea, C. (2011). Strategies for the relief of burden in advanced dementia care-giving. *Journal of Advanced Nursing, 67,* 1790–1799.

de Looze, M., & others (2014, in press). Parent-adolescent sexual communication and its association with adolescent sexual behaviors: A nationally representative analysis in the Netherlands. *Journal of Sexual Research.*

De Meyer, G., & others (2010). Diagnosis-independent Alzheimer disease biomarker signature in cognitively normal people. *Archives in Neurology, 67,* 949–956.

de Planell-Saguer, M., Lovinsky-Desir, S, & Miller, R. L. (2014, in press). Epigenetic regulation: The interface between prenatal and early-life exposure and asthma susceptibility. *Environmental and Molecular Mutagenesis.*

de Villiers, J., & de Villiers, P. (2013). Syntax acquisition. In P. D. Zelazo (Ed.), *Oxford handbook of developmental psychology.* New York: Oxford University Press.

de Vries, B., Utz, R., Caserta, M., & Lund, D. (2014). Friend and family contact and support in early widowhood. *Journals of Gerontology B: Psychological Sciences and Social Sciences, 69,* 75–84.

de Wind, A. W., & others (2014). Health, job characteristics, skills, and social and financial factors in relation to early retirement—results from a longitudinal study in the Netherlands. *Scandinavian Journal of Work, Environment, and Health, 40,* 186–194.

de Wit, L., & others. (2010). Depression and obesity: A meta-analysis of community-based studies. *Psychiatry Research, 178,* 230–235.

Deak, G., Krasno, A. M., Triesch, J., Lewis, J., & Sepeta, L. (2014, in press). Watch the hands: Infants can learn to follow gaze by seeing adults manipulate objects. *Developmental Science.*

Deary, I. J. (2012). Intelligence. *Annual Review of Intelligence* (Vol. 63). Palo Alto, CA: Annual Reviews.

Deater-Deckard, K. (2013). The social environment and the development of psychopathology. In P. D. Zelazo (Ed.), *Handbook of developmental psychology.* New York: Oxford University Press.

Debats, D. L. (1990). The Life Regard Index: Reliability and validity. *Psychological Reports, 67,* 27–34.

DeCasper, A. J., & Spence, M. J. (1986). Prenatal maternal speech influences newborn's perception of speech sounds. *Infant Behavior and Development, 9,* 133–150.

Dedon, P. C., & Begley, T. H. (2014, in press). A system of RNA modifications and biased codon use control cellular stress response at the level of transition. *Chemical Research in Toxicology.*

Deeg, D. J. H. (2005). The development of physical and mental health from late midlife to early old age. In S. L. Willis & Martin, M. (Eds.), *Middle adulthood.* Thousand Oaks, CA: Sage.

DeGenova, M. K., Rice, F. P., Stinnett, N., & Stinnett, N. L. (2011). *Intimate relationships, marriages, and families* (8th ed.). New York: McGraw-Hill.

DeJong, W., DeRicco, B., & Schneider, S. K. (2010). Pregaming: An exploratory study of strategic drinking by college students in Pennsylvania. *Journal of American College Health, 58,* 307–316.

Del Giudice, M. (2011). Sex differences in romantic attachment: A meta-analysis. *Personality and Social Psychology Bulletin, 37,* 193–214.

Del Tredici, K., & Braak, H. (2008). Neurofibrillary changes of the Alzheimer type in very elderly individuals: Neither inevitable nor benign. Commentary on no disease in the brain of a 115-year-old woman. *Neurobiology of Aging, 29,* 1133–1136.

DeLoache, J. S., Simcock, G., & Macari, S. (2007). Planes, trains, and automobiles—and tea sets: Extremely intense interests in very young children. *Developmental Psychology, 43,* 1579–1586.

DeMarie, D., & Lopez, L. (2014). Memory in school. In R. Fivush & P. Bauer (Eds.), *Wiley-Blackwell handbook of the development of children's memory.* New York: Wiley.

Dempster, F. N. (1981). Memory span: Sources of individual and developmental differences. *Psychological Bulletin, 80,* 63–100.

Demsky, C. A., Ellis, M. A., & Fritz, C. (2014, in press). Shrugging it off: Does psychological detachment from work mediate the relationship between workplace aggression and work-family conflict? *Journal of Occupational Health and Psychology.*

Denard, P. J., & others (2010). Back pain, neurogenic symptoms, and physical function in relation to spondylolisthesis among elderly men. *Spine Journal, 10,* 865–887.

Denham, J., & others (2013). Longer leukocyte telomeres are associated with ultra-endurance exercise independent of cardiovascular factors. *PLoS One, 8*(7), e69377.

Denham, S., & others (2011). Emotions and social development in childhood. In P. K. Smith & C. H. Hart (Eds.), *Wiley-Blackwell handbook of childhood social development* (2nd ed.). New York: Wiley.

Denham, S., & others (2012). Preschoolers' emotion knowledge: Self-regulatory foundations and predictors of school success. *Cognition and Emotion, 26*(4), 667–679.

Denham, S. A., Bassett, H. H., & Wyatt, T. (2007). The socialization of emotional competence. In J. E. Grusec & P. D. Hastings (Eds.), *Handbook of socialization.* New York: Guilford.

Denmark, F. L., Russo, N. F., Frieze, I. H., & Eschuzur, J. (1988). Guidelines for avoiding sexism in psychological research: A report of the ad hoc committee on nonsexist research. *American Psychologist. 43,* 582–585.

Denney, N. W. (1986, August). *Practical problem solving.* Paper presented at the meeting of the American Psychological Association, Washington, DC.

Denney, N. W. (1990). Adult age differences in traditional and practical problem solving. *Advances in Psychology, 72,* 329–349.

Dennis, N. A., & Cabeza, R. (2008). Neuroimaging of healthy cognitive aging. In F. I. M. Craik & T. A. Salthouse (Eds.), *Handbook of aging and cognition* (3rd ed.). Mahwah, NJ: Erlbaum.

Deodati, A., & Cianfarani, S. (2011). Impact of growth hormone therapy on adult height of children with idiopathic short stature: Systematic review. *British Medical Journal, 342,* c7157.

DePaulo, B. (2006). *Singled out.* New York: St. Martin's Press.

DePaulo, B. (2011). Living single: Lightening up those dark, dopey myths. In W. R. Cupach & B. H. Spitzberg (Eds.), *The dark side of close relationships.* New York: Routledge.

Derebail, V. K., & others (2014, in press). Sickle trait in African-American hemodialysis patients and higher erythropoiesis-stimulating agent dose. *Journal of the American Society of Nephrology.*

DeRosa, D. A., & Abruscato, J. (2015, in press). *Teaching children science* (8th ed.). Upper Saddle River, NJ: Pearson.

DeRose, L., & Brooks-Gunn, J. (2008). Pubertal development in early adolescence: Implications for affective processes. In N. B. Allen & L. Sheeber (Eds.), *Adolescent emotional development and the emergence of depressive disorders.* New York: Cambridge University Press.

Devaney, S. A., Palomaki, G. E., Scott, J. A., & Bianchi, D. W. (2011). Noninvasive fetal sex determination using cell-free fetal DNA: A systematic review and meta-analysis. *Journal of the American Medical Association, 306,* 627–636.

DeZolt, D. M., & Hull, S. H. (2001). Classroom and school climate. In J. Worell (Ed.), *Encyclopedia of women and gender.* San Diego: Academic Press.

Di Ciano, P., Grandy, D. K., & Le Foll, B. (2014). Dopamine D4 receptors in psychostimulant addiction. *Advances in Pharmacology, 69,* 301–321.

Di Ciommo, V., Forcella, E., & Cotugno, G. (2012). Living with phenylketonuria from the point of view of children, adolescents, and young adults: A qualitative study. *Journal of Developmental and Behavioral Pediatrics, 33,* 229–235.

Di Florio, A., & others (2014). Mood disorders and parity—a clue to the etiology of the postpartum trigger. *Journal of Affective Disorders, 152,* 334–349.

Diamond, A. (2013). Executive functions. *Annual Review of Psychology* (Vol. 64). Palo Alto, CA: Annual Reviews.

Diamond, A. D. (1985). Development of the ability to use recall to guide action, as indicated by infants' performance on A not B. *Child Development, 56,* 868–883.

Diamond, A., & Lee, K. (2011). Interventions shown to aid executive function development in children 4 to 12 years old. *Science, 333,* 959–964.

Diamond, A., Barnett, W. S., Thomas, J., & Munro, S. (2007). Preschool program improves cognitive control. *Science, 318,* 1387–1388.

Diamond, L. M. (2008). *Sexual fluidity: Understanding women's love and desire.* Cambridge, MA: Harvard University Press.

Diamond, L. M. (2013). Concepts of female sexual orientation. In C. Patterson & A. R. D'Augelli (Eds.), *The psychology sexual orientation.* New York: Cambridge University Press.

Diamond, L. M., & Savin-Williams, R. C. (2015, in press). Same-sex activity in adolescence: Multiple meanings and implications. In R. F. Fassinger & S. L. Morrow (Eds.), *Sex in the margins.* Washington, DC: American Psychological Association.

DiBennardo, R., & Gates, G. J. (2014, in press). Research note: U.S. Census same-sex couple data: Adjustments to reduce measurement error and empirical implications. *Population Research and Policy Review.*

Dickens, B. M. (2014). Ethical and legal aspects of noninvasive prenatal genetic diagnosis. *International Journal of Gynecology and Obstetrics, 124,* 181–184.

Dickinson, W. J., & others (2011). Change in stress and social support as predictors of cognitive decline in older adults with and without depression. *International Journal of Geriatric Psychiatry, 26,* 1267–1274.

Diego, M. A., Field, T., & Hernandez-Reif, M. (2008). Temperature increases in preterm infants during massage therapy. *Infant Behavior and Development, 31,* 149–152.

Diener, E. (2014). *Subjective well-being.* Retrieved January 23, 2014, from http://internal.psychology.illinois.edu/~ediener/SWLS.html

Diener, E., Emmons, R. A., Larson, R. J., & Griffin, S. (1985). The Satisfaction with Life Scale. *Journal of Personality Assessment, 49,* 71–75.

Dimmitt, C., & McCormick, C. B. (2012). Metacognition in education. In K. R. Harris, S. Graham, & T. Urdan (Eds.), *Handbook of educational psychology.* Washington, DC: American Psychological Association.

Ding, Z., & others (2014, in press). Estimating telomere length from whole genome sequence data. *Nucleic Acids Research.*

Dinger, M. K., Brittain, D. R., & Hutchinson, S. R. (2014). Associations between physical activity and health-related factors in a national sample of college students. *Journal of American College Health, 62,* 67–74.

Dionne, G., & others (2011). Associations between sleep-wake consolidation and language development: A developmental twin study. *Sleep, 34,* 987–995.

Dirk, J. (2012). Processing speed. In S. K. Whitbourne & M. Sliwinski (Eds.), *Wiley-Blackwell handbook of adulthood and aging.* New York: Wiley.

Dishion, T. J., & Piehler, T. F. (2009). Deviant by design: Peer contagion in development, interventions, and schools. In K. H. Rubin, W. M. Bukowski, & B. Laursen (Eds.), *Handbook of peer interactions, relationships, and groups.* New York: Guilford.

Diwadkar, V. A., & others (2013). Differences in cortico-striatal-cerebellar activation during working memory in syndromal and nonsyndromal children with prenatal exposure to alcohol. *Human Brain Mapping, 34,* 1931–1945.

Dixon, R. A., McFall, G. P., Whitehead, B. P., & Dolcos, S. (2013). Cognitive development in adulthood and aging. In I. B. Weiner & others (Eds.), *Handbook of psychology* (2nd ed., Vol. 6). New York: Wiley.

Dixon, S. V., Graber, J. A., & Brooks-Gunn, J. (2008). The roles of respect for parental authority and parenting practices in parent-child conflict among African American, Latino, and European American families. *Journal of Family Psychology, 22,* 1–10.

Doane, L. D., & Thurston, E. C. (2014). Associations among sleep, daily experiences, and loneliness in adolescence: Evidence of moderating and bidirectional pathways. *Journal of Adolescence, 37,* 145–154.

Dodge, K. A. (1983). Behavioral antecedents of peer social status. *Child Development, 54,* 1386–1399.

Dodge, K. A. (2011a). Context matters in child and family policy. *Child Development, 82,* 433–442.

Dodge, K. A. (2011b). Social information processing models of aggressive behavior. In M. Mikulincer & P. R. Shaver (Eds.), *Understanding and reducing aggression, violence, and their consequences.* Washington, DC: American Psychological Association.

Dodge, K. A., Godwin, J., & Conduct Problems Prevention Research Group (2013). Social-information-processing patterns mediate the impact of preventive intervention on adolescent antisocial behavior. *Psychological Science, 24,* 456–465.

Dodge, K. A., & McCourt, S. N. (2010). Translating models of antisocial behavioral development into efficacious intervention policy to prevent adolescent violence. *Developmental Psychobiology, 52,* 277–285.

Dodson, L. J., & Davies, A. P. C. (2014). Different challenges, different well-being: A comparison of psychological well-being across stepmothers and biological mothers and across four categories of stepmothers. *Journal of Divorce & Remarriage, 55,* 49–63.

Doherty, M. (2008). *Theory of mind.* Philadelphia: Psychology Press.

Dokken, D. (2013). Making meaning after the death of a child: Bereaved parents share their experiences. *Pediatric Nursing, 39,* 147–150.

Doll, C. A., & Broadie, K. (2014). Impaired activity-dependent neural circuit assembly and refinement in autism spectrum disorder genetic models. *Frontiers in Cellular Neuoroscience, 8,* 30.

Domsch, H., Lohaus, A., & Thomas, H. (2009). Prediction of childhood cognitive abilities from a set of early indicators of information processing capabilities. *Infant Behavior and Development, 32,* 91–102.

Donatelle, R. J. (2015). *Health* (11th ed.). Upper Saddle River, NJ: Pearson.

Dondi, M., Simion, F., & Caltran, G. (1999). Can newborns discriminate between their own cry and the cry of another newborn infant? *Developmental Psychology, 35*(2), 418–426.

Dong, B., Ma, J., Wang, H. J., & Wang, Z. Q. (2013). The association of overweight and obesity with blood pressure among Chinese children and adolescents. *Biomedical and Environmental Sciences, 26,* 437–444.

Donnellan, M. B., Hill, P. L., & Roberts, B. W. (2014, in press). Personality development across the life span: Current findings and future directions. In L. Cooper & M. Mikulincer (Eds.), *Handbook of personality and social psychology.* Washington, DC: American Psychological Association.

Donnellan, M. B., Larson-Rife, D., & Conger, R. D. (2005). Personality, family history, and competence in early adult romantic relationships. *Journal of Personality and Social Psychology, 88,* 562–576.

Donnerstein, E. (2012). Internet bullying. *Pediatric Clinics of North America, 59,* 623–633.

Doob, C. B. (2013). *Social inequality and social stratification in U.S. society.* Upper Saddle River, NJ: Pearson.

Dorey, E., Chang, N., Liu, Q. Y., Yang, Z., & Zhang, W. (2014, in press). Apoliloprotein E., amyloid-beta, and neuroinflammation in Alzheimer's disease. *Neuoroscience Bulletin.*

Dorszewska, J. (2013). Cell biology of normal brain aging: Synaptic plasticity-cell death. *Aging: Clinical and Experimental Research, 25,* 25–34.

Doss, B. D., Rhoades, G. K., Stanley, S. M., Markman, H. J., & Johnson, C. A. (2009). Differential use of premarital education in first and second marriages. *Journal of Family Psychology, 23,* 268–273.

Doty, R. L., & Shah, M. (2008). Taste and smell. In M. M. Haith & J. B. Benson (Eds.), *Encyclopedia of infant and early childhood development.* Oxford, UK: Elsevier.

Dougall, A. L., Biglan, C. W., Swanson, J. N., & Baum, A. (2013). Stress, coping, and immune function. In I. B. Weiner & others (Eds.), *Handbook of psychology* (2nd ed., Vol. 3). New York: Wiley.

Dow, B. J., & Wood, J. (Eds.) (2006). *The Sage handbook of gender and communication.* Thousand Oaks, CA: Sage.

Dowdy, S., & others (2013). Empower U: Effectiveness of an adolescent outreach and prevention program with sixth-grade boys and girls: A pilot study. *Journal of Pediatric Nursing, 28*(1), 77–84.

Dozier, M., Stovall-McClough, K. C., & Albus, K. E. (2009). Attachment and psychopathology in adulthood. In J. Cassidy & P. R. Shaver (Eds.), *Handbook of attachment* (2nd ed.). New York: Guilford.

Draghi-Lorenz, R. (2007, July). *Self-conscious emotions in young infants and the direct perception of self and others in interaction.* Paper presented at the meeting of the International Society for Research on Emotions, Sunshine Coast, Australia.

Drake, K. M., & others. (2012). Influence of sports, physical education, and active commuting to school on adolescent weight status. *Pediatrics, 130,* e296–e304.

Dreby, J. (2010). *Divided by borders.* Berkeley: University of California Press.

Drollette, E. S., & others (2014). Acute exercise facilitates brain function and cognition in children who need it most: An ERP study of individual differences in inhibitory control capacity. *Developmental Cognitive Neuroscience, 7,* 53–64.

Dryfoos, J. G. (1990). *Adolescents at risk: Prevalence or prevention.* New York: Oxford University Press.

Dryfoos, J., & Barkin, C. (2006). *Growing up in America today.* New York: Oxford University Press.

Duberstein, P. R., & others (2011). Personality and risk for Alzheimer's disease in adults 72 years of age and older: A 6-year follow-up. *Psychology and Aging, 26,* 351–362.

Dublin, S., & others (2014, in press). Neuropathologic changes associated with atrial fibrillation in a population-based autopsy cohort. *Journals of Gerontology A: Biological Sciences and Medical Sciences.*

Dubois, J., & others (2014, in press). The early development of brain white matter: A review of imaging studies in fetuses, newborns, and infants. *Neuroscience.*

Dubowitz, H. (2013). Neglect in children. *Pediatric Annals, 42,* 73–77.

Duchesne, S., Ratelle, C. F., & Feng, B. (2014, in press). Developmental trajectories of achievement goal orientations during the middle school transition: The contributions of emotional and behavioral dispositions. *Journal of Early Adolescence.*

Duggan, K. A., & Friedman, H. S. (2014). Lifetime biopsychosocial trajectories of the Terman gifted children: Health, well-being, and longevity. In D. K. Simonton (Ed.), *Wiley-Blackwell handbook of genius.* New York: Oxford University Press.

Duncan, G. J., & Magnuson, K. (2015, in press). The long reach of early childhood poverty. In W-J. Yeung & Y. Mui-Teng (Eds.), *Economic stress, human capital, and families in Asia: Research and policy challenges.* New York: Springer.

Duncan, G. J., Magnuson, K., & Votruba-Drzal, E. (2015, in press). Children and socioeconomic status. In M. H. Bornstein & T. Leventhal (Eds.), *Handbook of child psychology and developmental science* (7th ed., Vol. 4). New York: Wiley.

Dunn, D. W., & Kronenberger, W. G. (2013). Attention deficit. *Handbook of clinical psychology, 111,* 257–261.

Dunn, E. C., McLaughlin, K. A., Slopen, N., Rosand, J., & Smoller, J. W. (2013). Developmental timing of child maltreatment and symptoms of depression and suicidal ideation in young adulthood: Results from the National Longitudinal Study of Adolescent Health. *Depression and Anxiety, 30,* 955–964.

Dunn, J. (1984). Sibling studies and the developmental impact of critical incidents. In P. B. Baltes & O. G. Brim (Eds.), *Life-span development and behavior* (Vol. 6). Orlando, FL: Academic Press.

Dunn, J. (2007). Siblings and socialization. In J. E. Grusec & P. D. Hastings (Eds.), *Handbook of socialization.* New York: Guilford.

Dunn, J., & Kendrick, C. (1982). *Siblings.* Cambridge, MA: Harvard University Press.

Dunsmore, J. C., Booker, J. A., & Ollendick, T. H. (2013). Parental emotion coaching and child emotion regulation as protective factors for children with oppositional defiant disorder. *Social Development, 22*(3), 444–466.

Dupre, M. E., & Meadows, S. O. (2007). Disaggregating the effects of marital trajectories on health. *Journal of Family Issues, 28,* 623–652.

Durham, R., & Chapman, L. (2014). *Maternal-newborn nursing* (2nd ed.). Philadelphia: F. A. Davis.

Durrant, J. E. (2008). Physical punishment, culture, and rights: Current issues for professionals. *Journal of Developmental and Behavioral Pediatrics, 29,* 55–66.

Durrant, R., & Ellis, B. J. (2013). Evolutionary psychology. In I. B. Weiner & others (Eds.), *Handbook of psychology* (2nd ed., Vol. 3). New York: Wiley.

Durston, S., & others (2006). A shift from diffuse to focal cortical activity with development. *Developmental Science, 9,* 1–8.

Dvornyk, V., & Waqar-ul-Haq, H. (2012). Genetics of age at menarche: A systematic review. *Human Reproduction Update, 18,* 198–210.

Dweck, C. S. (2006). *Mindset.* New York: Random House.

Dweck, C. S. (2013). Social development. In P. Zelazo (Ed.), *Oxford handbook of developmental psychology.* New York: Oxford University Press.

Dweck, C. S. (2014, in press). Mindsets and social nature: Promoting change in the Middle East, the schoolyard, the racial divide, and willpower. *American Psychologist.*

Dweck, C. S., & Master, A. (2009). Self-theories and motivation: Students' beliefs about intelligence. In K. R. Wentzel & A. Wigfield (Eds.), *Handbook of motivation at school.* New York: Routledge.

Dworkin, S. L., & Santelli, J. (2007). Do abstinence-plus interventions reduce sexual risk behavior among youth? *PLoS Medicine, 4,* 1437–1439.

Dwyer, J. W., & Coward, R. T. (1991). A multivariate comparison of the involvement of adult sons versus daughters in the care of impaired parents. *Journal of Gerontology B: Psychological Sciences and Social Sciences, 46,* S259–S269.

Dykes, M. J., & Cassidy, J. (2011). Attachment and the processing of social information across the life span: Theory and evidence. *Psychological Bulletin, 137,* 19–46.

E

Eagan, K., Lozano, J. B., Hurtado, S., & Case, M. H. (2013). *The American freshman: National norms, Fall 2013.* Los Angeles: Higher Education Research Institute, UCLA.

Eagly, A. H. (2001). Social role theory of sex differences and similarities. In J. Worrell (Ed.), *Encyclopedia of women and gender.* San Diego: Academic Press.

Eagly, A. H., & Crowley, M. (1986). Gender and helping: A meta-analytic review of the social psychological literature. *Psychological Bulletin, 108,* 233–256.

Eagly, A. H., & Steffen, V. J. (1986). Gender and aggressive behavior: A meta-analytic review of the social psychological literature. *Psychological Bulletin. 100,* 309–330.

Eagly, A. H. (2010). Gender roles. In J. Levine & M. Hogg (Eds.), *Encyclopedia of group process and intergroup relations.* Thousand Oaks, CA: Sage.

Eagly, A. H. (2012). Women as leaders: Paths through the labyrinth. In M. C. Bligh & R. Riggio (Eds.), *When near is far and far is near: Exploring distance in leader-follower relationships.* New York: Wiley Blackwell.

Easterbrooks, M. A., Bartlett, J. D., Beeghly, M., & Thompson, R. A. (2013). Social and emotional development in infancy. In I. B. Weiner & others (Eds.), *Handbook of psychology* (2nd ed., Vol.6). New York: Wiley.

Eastwick, P. W., & Finkel, E. J. (2008). Sex differences in mate preferences revisited: Do people know what they initially desire in a romantic partner? *Journal of Personality and Social Psychology, 94,* 245–264.

Eaton, D. K., & others (2010, June 4). Youth risk behavior surveillance—United States, 2009. *MMWR Surveillance Summaries, 59*(5), 1–142.

Eaton, D. K., & others (2012). Youth risk behavior surveillance—United States 2011. *MMWR Surveillance Summaries, 61,* 1–162.

Eccles, J. S. (2007). Families, schools, and developing achievement-related motivations and engagement. In J. E. Grusec & P. D. Hastings (Eds.), *Handbook of socialization.* New York: Guilford.

Eccles, J. S. (2014). Gender and achievement choices. In E. T. Gershoff, R. S. Mistry, & D. A. Crosby (Eds.), *Societal contexts of child development.* New York: Oxford University Press.

Eccles, J. S., & Roeser, R. W. (2013). Schools as developmental contexts in adolescence. In I. B. Weiner & others (Eds.), *Handbook of psychology* (2nd ed., Vol. 6). New York: Wiley.

Echevarria, J. J., Richards-Tutor, C., & Vogt, M. J. (2015). *Response to intervention (RTI) and English learners: Using the SIOP model* (2nd ed.). Upper Saddle River, NJ: Pearson.

Eckerman, C., & Whitehead, H. (1999). How toddler peers generate coordinated action: A cross-cultural exploration. *Early Education & Development, 10,* 241–266.

Edeas, M., & Weissig, V. (2013). Targeting mitochondria: Strategies, innovations, and challenges: The future of medicine will come through mitochondria. *Mitochondrion, 13,* 1389–1390.

Ednick, M., & others. (2010). Sleep-related respiratory abnormalities and arousal pattern in achondroplasia during early infancy. *Journal of Pediatrics, 155,* 510–515.

Edwardson, C. L., & Gorely, T. (2010). Activity-related parenting practices and children's objectively measured physical activity. *Pediatric Exercise Science, 22,* 105–113.

Egan, S. K., & Perry, D. G. (2001). Gender identity: A multidimensional analysis with implications for psychosocial adjustment. *Developmental Psychology, 37,* 451–463.

Ehnes, J. (2012). Aging and financial (in)security. *Global population aging: Peril or promise?* Geneva, Switzerland: World Economic Forum.

Ehrlich, K. B., Dykas, M. J., & Cassidy, J. (2012). Tipping points in adolescent adjustment: Predicting social functioning from adolescents' conflict with parents and friends. *Journal of Family Psychology, 26,* 776–783.

Eichorn, D. H., Clausen, J. A., Haan, N., Honzik, M. P., & Mussen, P. H. (Eds.) (1981). *Present and past in middle life.* New York: Academic Press.

Eiferman, R. R. (1971). Social play in childhood. In R. Herron & B. Sutton-Smith (Eds.), *Child's play.* New York: Wiley.

Einstein, G. O., McDaniel, M. A. (2005). Prospective memory. *Current Directions in Psychological Science, 14,* 286–290.

Eisenberg, M. E., Bernat, D. H., Bearinger, L. H., & Resnick, M. D. (2008). Support for comprehensive sexuality education: Perspectives from parents of school-aged youth. *Journal of Adolescent Research, 42,* 352–359.

Eisenberg, M. E., Madsen, N., Oliphant, J. A., & Sieving, R. E. (2013). Barriers to providing sexuality education that teachers believe students need. *Journal of School Health, 83,* 335–342.

Eisenberg, N., & Morris, A. S. (2004). Moral cognitions and social responding in adolescence. In R. L. Lerner & L. Steinberg (Eds.), *Handbook of adolescent psychology* (2nd ed.). New York: Wiley.

Eisenberg, N., Morris, A. S., McDaniel, B., & Spinrad, T. L. (2009). Moral cognitions and prosocial responding in adolescence. In R. M. Lerner & L. Steinberg (Eds.), *Handbook of adolescent psychology* (3rd ed.). New York: Wiley.

Eisenberg, N., & Spinrad, T. L. (2014). Multidimensionality of prosocial behavior: Rethinking the conceptualization and development of prosocial behavior. In L. Padilla-Walker & G. Carlo (Eds.), *Prosocial behavior.* New York: Oxford University Press.

Eisenberg, N., Spinrad, T. L., & Eggum, N. D. (2010). Emotion-focused self-regulation and its relation to children's maladjustment. *Annual Review of Clinical Psychology* (Vol. 6). Palo Alto, CA: Annual Reviews.

Eisenberg, N., Spinrad, T. L., & Morris, A. S. (2013). Prosocial development. In P. D. Zelazo (Ed.), *Oxford handbook of developmental psychology.* New York: Oxford University Press.

Eisner, B., Pfeifer, C., Parker, C., & Hauf, P. (2013). Infants' perception of actions and situational constraints. *Journal of Experimental Child Psychology, 116,* 428–442.

Ekas, N. V., Lickenbrock, D. M., & Braungart-Rieker, J. M. (2014, in press). Developmental trajectories of emotion regulation across infancy: Do age and social partner influence temporal patterns? *Infancy.*

Ekin, A., & others (2014). Chromosomal and structural anomalies in fetuses with open neural tube defects. *Journal of Obstetrics and Gynecology, 34,* 156–159.

El Haj, M., & Allain, P. (2012). Relationship between source monitoring in episodic memory and executive function in normal aging. *Geriatrie et Psychologie Neuropsychiatrie du Viellissement, 10,* 197–205.

Elbourne, P. (2012). *Meaning.* New York: Oxford University Press.

Eliasieh, K., Liets, L. C., & Chalupa, L. M. (2007). Cellular reorganization in the human retina during normal aging. *Investigative Ophthalmology and Visual Science, 48,* 2824–2830.

Elkind, D. (1970, April 5). Erik Erikson's eight ages of man. *New York Times Magazine.*

Elkind, D. (1976). *Child development and education: A Piagetian perspective.* New York: Oxford University Press.

Elliott, E. M., & others (2011). Working memory in the oldest-old: Evidence from output serial position curves. *Memory and Cognition, 39*(8), 1423–1434.

Ellis, B. J., Shirtcliff, E. A., Boyce, W. T., Deardorff, J., & Essex, M. J. (2011). Quality of early family relationships and the timing and tempo of puberty: Effects depend on biological sensitivity to context. *Development and Psychopathology, 23,* 85–99.

Ellis, M. L., & others (2014, in press). Effects of cognitive speed of processing training among older adults with heart failure. *Journal of Aging and Health.*

Elsabbagh, M., & others (2012). Global prevalence of autism and other pervasive developmental disorders. *Autism Research, 5,* 160–179.

El-Sheikh, M. (2013). *Auburn University Child Sleep, Health, and Development Center.* Auburn, AL: Auburn University. *Society, 67,* 82–90.

El-Sheikh, M., & others (2013, in press). Economic adversity and children's sleep problems: Multiple indicators and moderation of health. *Health Psychology.* doi:10.1037/a0030413

El-Sheikh, M., Keiley, M., Erath, S. A., & Dyer, W. J. (2013). Marital conflict and growth in children's internalizing behavior: The role of autonomic nervous system activity. *Developmental Psychology, 49*(1), 92–108.

Emery, C. F., Anderson, D. R., & Goodwin, C. L. (2013). Coronary heart disease and hypertension. In I. B. Weiner & others (Eds.), *Handbook of psychology* (2nd ed., Vol. 9). New York: Wiley.

Emery, R. E. (2014). Families as systems: Some thoughts on methods and theory. In S. McHale, P. Amato, & A. Booth (Eds.), *Emerging methods in family research.* New York: Springer.

Emes, R. D., & Grant, S. G. N. (2013). Evolution of synapse complexity and diversity. *Annual Review of Neuroscience* (Vol. 35). Palo Alto, CA: Annual Reviews.

English, T., & Carstensen, L. L. (2014a). Emotional experience in the mornings and the evenings: Consideration of age differences in specific emotions by time of day. *Frontiers in Psychology, 5,* 185.

English, T., & Carstensen, L. L. (2014b). Selective narrowing of social networks across adulthood is associated with improved emotional experience in life. *International Journal of Behavioral Development, 38,* 195–202.

Ensembl Human (2010). *Explore the Homo sapiens genome.* Retrieved March 17, 2010, from www.ensembl.org/Homo_sapiens/index.html

Ensor, R., Spencer, D., & Hughes, C. (2011). You feel sad? Emotional understanding mediates effects of verbal ability and mother-child mutuality on prosocial behaviors: Findings from 2 to 4 years. *Social Development, 20,* 93–100.

Eppinger, B., Walter, M., Heekeren, H. R., & Li, S. C. (2013). Of goals and habits: Age-related and individual differences in goal-directed decision-making. *Frontiers in Neuroscience, 7,* 253.

Erickson, K. I., & others (2009). Aerobic fitness is associated with hippocampal volume in elderly humans. *Hippocampus, 19,* 1030–1039.

Erickson, K. I., & others (2011). Exercise training increases the size of the hippocampus and improves memory. *Proceedings of the National Academy of Sciences U.S.A., 108,* 3017–3022.

Erickson, S. J., & others (2013). Differential associations between maternal scaffolding and toddler emotion regulation in toddlers born preterm and full term. *Early Human Development, 89,* 699–704.

Ericson, N. (2001, June). *Addressing the problem of juvenile bullying.* Washington, DC: Office of Juvenile Justice and Delinquency Prevention, Office of Justice Programs, U.S. Department of Justice.

Ericsson, K. A. (2014). Creative genius: A view from the expert-performance approach. In D. K. Simonton (Ed.), *Wiley-Blackwell handbook of genius.* New York: Wiley.

Ericsson, K. A., Krampe, R., & Tesch-Romer, C. (1993). The role of deliberate practice in the acquisition of expert performance. *Psychological Review, 100,* 363–406.

Erikson, E. H. (1950). *Childhood and society.* New York: W. W. Norton.

Erikson, E. H. (1968). *Identity: Youth and crisis.* New York: W. W. Norton.

Eriksson Sorman, D., Sunderstrom, A., Ronnlund, M., Adolfsson, R., & Nilsson, L. G. (2014, in press). Leisure activity in old age and risk of dementia: A 15-year prospective study. *Journals of Gerontology B: Psychological Sciences and Social Sciences.*

Eriksson, U. J. (2009). Congenital malformations in diabetic pregnancy. *Seminar in Fetal and Neonatal Medicine.*

Erkut, S., & others (2013). Can sex education delay early sexual debut? *Journal of Early Adolescence, 33,* 482–497.

Escobar-Chaves, S. L., & Anderson, C. A. (2008). Media and risky behavior. *Future of Children, 18,* 147–180.

ESHRE Capri Workshop Group (2011). Perimenopausal risk factors and future health. *Human Reproduction Update, 17,* 706–717.

Espana-Romero, V., & others (2013). Objectively measured sedentary time, physical activity, and markers of body fat in preschool children. *Pediatric Exercise Science, 25,* 154–163.

Etaugh, C., & Bridges, J. S. (2010). *Women's lives* (2nd ed.). Boston: Allyn & Bacon.

Evans, G. W., & English, G. W. (2002). The environment of poverty. *Child Development, 73,* 1238–1248.

Evans, G. W., & Kim, P. (2007). Childhood poverty and health: Cumulative risk exposure and stress dysregulation. *Psychological Science, 18.* 953–957.

Evans, G. W., & Kim, P. (2013). Childhood poverty, chronic stress, self-regulation, and coping. *Child Development Perspectives, 7,* 43–48.

Evans, G. W., Li, D., & Sepanski Whipple, S. (2013). Cumulative risk and child development. *Psychological Bulletin, 139*, 1342–1396.

Evans, W. J. (2010). Skeletal muscle loss: Cachexia, sarcopenia, and inactivity. *American Journal of Clinical Nutrition, 91*, S1123–S1127.

Eveleth, D. D. (2013). Cell-based therapies for ocular disease. *Journal of Occupational and Pharmacological Therapeutics, 29*, 844–854.

Evers, A. W., & others (2014, in press). Does stress affect the joints? Daily stressors, stress vulnerability, immune and HPA axis activity, and short-term disease and symptom fluctuations in rheumatoid arthritis. *Annals of the Rheumatic Diseases*.

Eymard, A. S., & Douglas, D. H. (2012). Ageism among health care providers and interventions to improve their attitudes toward older adults: An integrative review. *Journal of Gerontological Nursing, 38*, 26–35.

Ezkurdia, L., & others (2014). The shrinking human protein coding complement: Are there fewer than 20,000 genes? *bioRxiv*, doi:10.1101/001909.

F

Fabbri, R., & others (2012). Cryopreservation of ovarian tissue in pediatric patients. *Obstetrics and Gynecology International*. doi:10.1155/2012/910698.

Fabian, S. G., & others (2014, in press). Mitochondrial biogenesis in health and disease. Molecular and therapeutic approaches. *Current Pharmaceutical Design*.

Fabiano, G. A., & others (2009). A meta-analysis of behavioral treatments for attention deficit/hyperactivity disorder. *Clinical Psychology Review, 29*, 129–140.

Fabre, B., & others (2013). Relationship between cortisol, life events, and metabolic syndrome in men. *Stress, 16*, 16–23.

Fabricius, W. V., Braver, S. L., Diaz, P., & Schenck, C. (2010). Custody and parenting time: Links to family relationships and well-being after divorce. In M. E. Lamb (Ed.), *The role of the father in child development* (5th ed.). New York: Wiley.

Fagan, J. F. (1992). Intelligence. A theoretical viewpoint. *Current Directions in Psychological Science, 1*, 82–86.

Fagan, J. F., Holland, C. R., & Wheeler, K. (2007). The prediction, from infancy, of adult IQ and achievement. *Intelligence, 35*, 225–231.

Fagot, B. I., Rogers, C. S., & Leinbach, M. D. (2000). Theories of gender socialization. In T. Eckes & H. M. Trautner (Eds.), *The developmental social psychology of gender*. Mahwah, NJ: Erlbaum.

Fagundes, C. P., & others (2013). Depressive symptoms enhance stress-induced inflammatory responses. *Brain, Behavior, and Immunity, 31*, 172–176.

Fagundes, C. P., Glaser, R., & Kiecolt-Glaser, J. K. (2013). Stressful early life experiences and immune dysregulation across the lifespan. *Brain, Behavior, and Immunity, 27*, 8–12.

Fakhoury, J., Nimmo, G. A., & Autexier, C. (2007). Harnessing telomerase in cancer therapeutics. *Anti-Cancer Agents in Medicinal Chemistry, 7*, 475–483.

Falbo, T., & Poston, D. L. (1993). The academic, personality, and physical outcomes of only children in China. *Child Development, 64*, 18–35.

Fall, A. M., & Roberts, G. (2012). High school dropouts: Interactions between social context, self perceptions, school engagement, and student dropout. *Journal of Adolescence, 35*(4), 787–798.

Fang, L., Wang, Y., & He, X. (2013). Theoretical analysis of wavefront aberration caused by treatment decentration and transition zone after custom myopic laser refractive surgery. *Journal of Cataract and Refractive Surgery, 39*, 1336–1347.

Fantz, R. L. (1963). *Pattern vision in newborn infants. Science, 140*, 286–297.

Farajinia, S., & others (2014). Aging of the suprochiasmatic clock. *Neuroscientist, 21*, 44–55.

Farioli-Vecchioli, S., & others (2014, in press). Running rescues defective adult neurogenesis by shortening the length of the cell cycle of neural stem and progenitor cells. *Stem Cells*.

Farr, R. H., & Patterson, C. J. (2013). Coparenting among lesbian, gay, and heterosexual couples: Associations with adopted children's outcomes. *Child Development, 84*, 1226–1240.

Farrell, M. J. (2012). Age-related changes in the structure and function of brain regions involved in pain processing. *Pain Medicine, 13*(2, Suppl.), S37–S43.

Farrell, M. P., & Rosenberg, S. D. (1981). *Men at mid-life*. Boston: Auburn House.

Farrell, S. W., Fitzgerald, S. J., McAuley, P., & Barlow, C. E. (2010). Cardiorespiratory fitness, adiposity, and all-cause mortality in women. *Medicine and Science in Sports and Exercise, 42*(11), 2006–2012.

Fasig, L. (2000). Toddlers' understanding of ownership: Implications for self-concept development. *Social Development, 9*, 370–382.

Fatusi, A. O., & Hindin, M. J. (2010). Adolescents and youths in developing countries: Health and development issues in context. *Journal of Adolescence, 33*, 499–508.

Fava, N. M., & Bay-Cheng, L. Y. (2012). Young women's adolescent experiences of oral sex: Relation of age of initiation to sexual motivation, sexual coercion, and psychological functioning. *Journal of Adolescence. 35*(5), 1191–1201.

Feeney, S., Moravcik, E., & Nolte, S. (2013). *Who am I in the lives of children?* (9th ed.). Upper Saddle River, NJ: Pearson.

Feinberg, M. E., Sakuma, K-L., Hostetler, M., & McHale, S. M. (2013). Enhancing sibling relationships to prevent adolescent problem behaviors: Theory, design, and feasibility *Siblings Are Special. Evaluation and Program Planning, 36*(1), 97–106.

Feldman, D. H. (2013). Cognitive development in childhood: A contemporary perspective. In I. B. Weiner & others (Eds.), *Handbook of psychology* (2nd ed., Vol. 6). New York: Wiley.

Feldman, H. M., & Reiff, M. I. (2014). Clinical practice: Attention deficit-hyperactivity disorder in children and adolescents. *New England Journal of Medicine, 370*, 838–846.

Feldman, R. (2007). Parent-infant synchrony. *Current Directions in Psychological Science, 16*, 340–345.

Feldman, R. (2012). Oxytocin and social affiliation in humans. *Hormones and Behavior, 61*, 380–391.

Feldman, R., Rosenthal, Z., & Eidelman, A. I. (2014). Maternal-preterm skin-to-skin contact enhances child physiologic organization and cognitive control across the first 10 years of life. *Biological Psychiatry, 75*, 56–64.

Feldman, S. S., & Elliott, G. R. (1990). Progress and promise of research on normal adolescent development. In S. S. Feldman & G. Elliott (Eds.), *At the threshold: The developing adolescent*. Cambridge, MA: Harvard University Press.

Feldman, S. S., & Rosenthal, D. A. (1999). *Factors influencing parents' and adolescents' evaluations of parents as sex communicators*. Unpublished manuscript, Stanford Center on Adolescence, Stanford University.

Feldman, S. S., Turner, R., & Araujo, K. (1999). Interpersonal context as an influence on sexual timetables of youths: Gender and ethnic effects. *Journal of Research on Adolescence, 9*, 25–52.

Feldon, J. M. (2003). Grief as a transformative experience: Weaving through different lifeworlds after a loved one has committed suicide. *International Journal of Mental Health Nursing, 12*, 74–85.

Feng, L., Wang, W. W., & Jones, K. (2013). A multilevel analysis of the role of the family and the state in self-rated health of elderly Chinese. *Health and Place, 23*, 148–156.

Feng, L., & others (2012). Tea drinking and cognitive function in oldest-old Chinese. *Journal of Nutrition, Health, and Aging, 16*, 754–758.

Feng, X., & others (2014, in press). Robust gene dysregulation in Alzheimer's disease brains. *Journal of Alzheimer's Disease*.

Feng, Z., Wang, W. W., Jones, K., & Li, Y. (2012). An exploratory multilevel analysis of income, income inequality, and self-rated health of the elderly in China. *Social Science and Medicine, 75*, 2481–2492.

Ferguson, C. J. (2013). Spanking, corporal punishment, and negative long-term outcomes: A meta-analytic review of longitudinal studies. *Clinical Psychology Review, 33*, 196–208.

Fergusson, D. M., Harwood, L. J., & Shannon, F. T. (1987). Breastfeeding and subsequent social adjustment in 6- to 8-year-old children. *Journal of Child Psychology and Psychiatry, 28*, 378–386.

Fergusson, D. M., McLeod, G. F., & Horwood, L. J. (2013). Childhood sexual abuse and adult developmental outcomes: Findings from a 30-year longitudinal study in New Zealand. *Child Abuse and Neglect, 37*, 664–674.

Ferrari, M., & Weststrate, N. (Eds.) (2013). *Personal wisdom*. New York: Springer.

Ferraro, K. F. (2006). Health and aging. In R. H. Binstock & L. K. George (Eds.), *Handbook of aging and the social sciences* (6th ed.). San Diego: Academic Press.

Ferris, S. H., & Farlow, M. (2013). Language impairment in Alzheimer's disease and benefits of acetylcholinesterase inhibitors. *Clinical Interventions in Aging, 8*, 1007–1114.

Field, D. (1999). A cross-cultural perspective on continuity and change in social relations in old age: Introduction to a special issue. *International Journal of Aging and Human Development, 48*, 257–262.

Field, N., & others (2013). Associations between health and sexual lifestyles in Britain: Findings from the third National Survey of Sexual Attitudes and Lifestyles (Natsal-3). *Lancet, 382*, 1830–1844.

Field, R. D., England, D. E., Andrews, C. Z., Martin, C. L., & Zosuls, K. M. (2012, April). *"I understand girls but not boys": Assessing gender-based relationship efficacy*. Paper presented at the Gender Development Research conference, San Francisco.

Field, T. M. (2001). Massage therapy facilitates weight gain in preterm infants. *Current Directions in Psychological Science, 10*, 51–55.

Field, T. M. (2007). *The amazing infant*. Malden, MA: Blackwell.

Field, T. M. (2010a). Postpartum depression effects on early interactions, parenting, and safety practices: A review. *Infant Behavior and Development, 33*, 1–6.

Field, T. M. (2010b). Pregnancy and labor massage. *European Review of Obstetrics and Gynecology, 5*, 177–181.

Field, T. M., Delgado, J., Diego, M., & Medina, L. (2013). Tai chi/yoga reduces prenatal depression and prematurity. *Journal of Bodywork and Movement Therapies,16*, 204–209.

Field, T. M., Diego, M., & Hernandez-Reif, M. (2008). Prematurity and potential predictors. *International Journal of Neuroscience, 118*, 277–289.

Field, T. M., Diego, M., & Hernandez-Reif, M. (2010). Preterm infant massage therapy research: A review. *Infant Behavior and Development, 33,* 115–124.

Field, T. M., Grizzle, N., Scafidi, F., & Schanberg, S. (1996). Massage and relaxation therapies effects on depressed adolescent mothers. *Adolescence, 31,* 903–911.

Field, T. M., Hernandez-Reif, M., Feijo, L., & Freedman, J. (2006). Prenatal, perinatal, and neonatal stimulation. *Infant Behavior & Development, 29,* 24–31.

Field, T. M., Hernandez-Reif, M., & Freedman, J. (2004, Fall). Stimulation programs for preterm infants. *SRCD Social Policy Reports, 28*(1), 1–20.

Field, T. M., Hernandez-Reif, M., Taylor, S., Quintino, O., & Burman, I. (1997). Labor pain is reduced by massage therapy. *Journal of Psychosomatic Obstetrics and Gynecology, 18,* 286–291.

Field, T. M., Quintino, O., Hernandez-Reif, M., & Koslosky, G. (1998). Adolescents with attention deficit hyperactivity disorder benefit from massage therapy. *Adolescence, 33,* 103–108.

Field, T. M., & others (1997). Brief report: Autistic children's attentiveness and responsivity improve after touch therapy. *Journal of Autism and Developmental Disorders, 27,* 333–338.

Field, T. M., & others (1998). Children with asthma have improved pulmonary functions after massage therapy. *Journal of Pediatrics, 132,* 854–858.

Field, T. M., & others (2004). Massage therapy by parents improves early growth and development. *Infant Behavior & Development, 27,* 435–442.

Field, T. M., & others (2008). Massage therapy reduces pain in pregnant women, alleviates prenatal depression in both parents and improves their relationships. *Journal of Bodywork and Movement Therapies, 12,* 146–150.

Field, T. M., & others (2012). Yoga and massage therapy reduce prenatal depression and prematurity. *Journal of Bodywork and Movement Therapies, 16,* 204–209.

Fielder, R. L., Walsh, J. L., Carey, K. B., & Carey, M. P. (2013). Predictors of sexual hookups: A theory-based, prospective study of first-year college women. *Archives of Sexual Behavior, 42,* 1425–1441.

Fielder, R. L., Walsh, J. L., Carey, K. B., & Carey, M. P. (2014). Sexual hookups and adverse health outcomes: A longitudinal study of first-year college women. *Journal of Sexual Research.*

Finch, C. E., & Seeman, T. E. (1999). Stress theories of aging. In V. L. Bengtson & K. W. Schaie (Eds.), *Handbook of theories of aging.* New York: Springer.

Finch, C. E. (2009). The neurobiology of middle-age has arrived. *Neurobiology of Aging, 30,* 515–520.

Finch, C. E. (2011). Inflammation and aging. In E. Masoro & S. Austad (Eds.), *Handbook of the biology of aging* (7th ed.). New York: Elsevier.

Fincham, F. D., Stanley, S. M., & Beach, S. R. H. (2007). Transformative processes in marriage: An analysis of emerging trends. *Journal of Marriage and the Family, 69,* 275–292.

Finer, L. B., & Philbin, J. M. (2013, in press). Sexual initiation, contraceptive use, and pregnancy among young adolescents. *Pediatrics, 131,* 886–891.

Finger, B., Hans, S. L., Bernstein, V. J., & Cox, S. M. (2009). Parent relationship quality and infant-mother attachment. *Attachment and Human Development, 11,* 285–306.

Fingerhut, A. W., & Peplau, L. A. (2013). Same-sex romantic relationships. In C. J. Patterson & A. R. D'Augelli (Eds.), *Handbook of psychology and sexual orientation.* New York: Oxford University Press.

Fingerman, K. L. (2000). Age and generational differences in mothers' and daughters' descriptions of enjoyable visits. *Journals of Gerontology B: Psychological and Social Sciences, 55,* P95–P106.

Fingerman, K. L., & Baker, B. (2006). Socioemotional aspects of aging. In J. Wilmouth & K. Ferraro (Eds.), *Perspectives in gerontology* (3rd ed.). New York: Springer.

Fingerman, K. L., & Birditt, K. S. (2011). Relationships between adults and their aging parents. In K. W. Schaie & S .L. Willis (Eds.), *Handbook of the psychology of aging* (7th ed.). New York: Elsevier.

Fingerman, K. L., Birditt, K. S., Nussbaum, J., & Schroeder, D. (2014, in press). Generational juggling: Midlife. In A. L. Vangelisti (Ed.), *Handbook of family communication* (2nd ed.). New York: Elsevier.

Fingerman, K. L., Brown, B. B., & Blieszner, R. (2011). Informal ties across the lifespan: Peers, consequential strangers, and people we encounter in daily life. In K. L. Fingerman, C. A. Berg, J. Smith, & T. C. Antonucci (Eds.), *Handbook of life-span development.* New York: Springer.

Fingerman, K. L., Cheng, Y. P., Tighe, L., Birditt, K. S., & Zarit, S. (2011b). Parent-child relationships in young adulthood. In A. Booth & others (Eds.), *Early adulthood in a family context.* New York: Springer.

Fingerman, K., Miller, L., Birditt, K., & Zarit, S. (2009). Giving to the good and needy: Parental support of grown children. *Journal of Marriage and the Family, 71,* 1220–1233.

Fingerman, K. L., Pillemer, K. A., Silverstein, M., & Suitor, J. J. (2012). The Baby Boomers' intergenerational relationships. *Gerontologist, 52,* 199–209.

Fingerman, K. L., Sechrist, J., & Birditt, K. (2013). Changing views on intergenerational ties. *Gerontology, 59,* 64–70.

Fingerman, K. L., & others (2011a). Who gets what and why: Help middle-aged adults provide to parents and grown children. *Journal of Gerontology B: Psychological Sciences and Social Sciences, 66,* 87–98.

Finkelstein, E. A., & others (2012). Obesity and severe obesity forecasts through 2030. *American Journal of Preventive Medicine, 42,* 563–570.

Finkelstein, L. M., & Farrell, S. K. (2007). An expanded view of age bias in the workplace. In K. S. Shultz & G. A. Adams (Eds.), *Aging and work in the 21st century.* Mahwah, NJ: Erlbaum.

Fiocco, A. J., & others (2013). The effects of an exercise and lifestyle intervention program on cardiovascular, metabolic factors, and cognitive performance in middle-aged adults with Type II diabetes: A pilot study. *Canadian Journal of Diabetes, 37,* 214–219.

Fiori, K. L., Antonucci, T. C., & Cortina, K. S. (2006). Social network typologies and mental health among older adults. *Journals of Gerontology B: Psychological Sciences and Social Sciences, 61,* P25–P32.

Fischer, C. E., & Schweizer, T. A. (2014, in press). How does speaking another language reduce the risk of dementia? *Expert Reviews of Neurotherapeutics.*

Fischer-Baum, S., & Rapp, B. (2014, in press). The analysis of perseverations in acquired dysgraphia reveals the internal structure of orthographic representations. *Cognitive Neuropsychology.*

Fischhoff, B., de Bruin, W., Parker, A. M., Millstein, S. G., & Halpern-Felsher, B. L. (2010). Adolescents' perceived risk of dying. *Journal of Adolescent Health, 46,* 265–269.

Fisher, B. S., Cullen, F. T., & Turner, M. G. (2000). *The sexual victimization of college women.* Washington, DC: National Institute of Justice.

Fisher, C. B., Busch-Rossnagel, N. A., Jopp, D. S., & Brown, J. L. (2013). Applied developmental science: Contributions and challenges for the 21st century. In I. B. Weiner & others (Eds.), *Handbook of psychology* (2nd ed., Vol. 6). New York: Wiley.

Fisher, G. G., & others (2014, in press). Mental work demands, retirement, and longitudinal trajectories of cognitive functioning. *Journal of Occupational Health Psychology.*

Fisher, K. R., Hirsh-Pasek, K., Newcombe, N., & Golinkoff, R. M. (2013). Taking shape: Supporting preschoolers' acquisition of geometric knowledge through guided play. *Child Development, 84*(6), 1872–1878.

Fisher, P. A. (2005, April). *Translational research on underlying mechanisms of risk among foster children: Implications for prevention science.* Paper presented at the meeting of the Society for Research in Child Development, Washington, DC.

Fiske, A., Wetherell, J. L., & Gatz, M. (2009). Depression in older adults. *Annual Review of Clinical Psychology* (Vol. 5). Palo Alto, CA: Annual Reviews.

Fitzgerald, A., Fitzgerald, N., & Aherne, C. (2012). Do peers matter? A review of peer and/or friends' influence on physical activity among American adolescents. *Journal of Adolescence, 35,* 941–958.

Fitzpatrick, K. K. (2012). Developmental considerations when treating anorexia nervosa in adolescents and young adults. In J. Lock (Ed.), *Oxford handbook of child and adolescent eating disorders: Developmental perspectives.* New York: Oxford University Press.

Fivush, R. (1993). Developmental perspectives on autobiographical recall. In G. S. Goodman & B. Bottoms (Eds.), *Child victims and child witnesses: Understanding and improving testimony.* New York: Guilford.

Fivush, R. (2011). The development of autobiographical memory. *Annual Review of Psychology* (Vol. 62). Palo Alto, CA: Annual Reviews.

Fivush, R., & Haden, C. A. (1997). Narrating and representing experience: Preschoolers' developing autobiographical accounts. In P. van den Broek, P. J. Bauer, & T. Bourg (Eds.), *Developmental spans in event representations and comprehension: Bridging fictional and actual events.* Mahwah, NJ: Erlbaum.

Fizke, E., Barthel, D., Peters, T., & Rakoczy, H. (2014). Executive function plays a role in coordinating different perspectives, particularly when one's own perspective is involved. *Cognition, 130,* 315–334.

Fjell, A. M., & Walhovd, K. B. (2010). Structural brain changes in aging: Courses, causes, and cognitive consequences. *Reviews in the Neurosciences, 21,* 187–222.

Flaherty, E. G., & others (2014). Evaluating children with fractures for child physical abuse. *Pediatrics, 133,* e477–e489.

Flamini, R., & others (2013). Advanced knowledge of three important classes of grap phenolics: Anthocyanins, stilbenes, and flavonols. *International Journal of Molecular Sciences, 14,* 19651–19669.

Flavell, J. H. (2004). Theory-of-mind development: Retrospect and prospect. *Merrill-Palmer Quarterly, 50,* 274–290.

Flavell, J. H., Friedrichs, A., & Hoyt, J. (1970). Developmental changes in memorization processes. *Cognitive Psychology, 1,* 324–340.

Flavell, J. H., Green, F. L., & Flavell, E. R. (1993). Children's understanding of the stream of consciousness. *Child Development, 64,* 95–120.

Flavell, J. H., Green, F. L., & Flavell, E. R. (1998). The mind has a mind of its own: Developing knowledge about mental uncontrollability. *Cognitive Development, 13,* 127–138.

Flavell, J. H., & Miller, P. H. (1998). Social cognition. In W. Damon (Ed.), *Handbook of child psychology* (5th ed.). New York: Wiley.

Flavell, J., Mumme, D., Green, F., & Flavell E. (1992). Young children's understanding of different types of beliefs. *Child Development, 63,* 960–977.

Fletcher, B. R., & Rapp, P. R. (2013). Normal neurocognitive aging. In I. B. Weiner & others (Eds.), *Handbook of psychology* (2nd ed., Vol. 3). New York: Wiley.

Flicek, P., & others (2013). Ensembl 2013. *Nucleic Acids Research, 41,* D48–D55.

Flicker, L., & others (2010). Body mass index and survival in men and women 70 to 75. *Journal of the American Geriatric Society, 58,* 234–241.

Flint, M. S., Baum, A., Chambers, W. H., & Jenkins, F. J. (2007). Induction of DNA damage, alteration of DNA repair, and transcriptional activation by stress hormones. *Psychoneuroendocrinology, 32,* 470–479.

Flint-Wagner, H. G., & others (2009). Assessment of a sixteen-week training program on strength, pain, and function in rheumatoid arthritis patients. *Journal of Clinical Rheumatology, 15,* 165–171.

Flom, R., & Pick, A. D. (2003). Verbal encouragement and joint attention in 18-month-old infants. *Infant Behavior and Development, 26,* 121–134.

Florsheim, P. (2014). *The young parenthood program.* New York: Oxford University Press.

Florsheim, P., Moore, D., & Edgington, C. (2003). Romantic relationships among pregnant and parenting adolescents. In P. Florsheim (Ed.), *Adolescent romantic relations and sexual behavior.* Mahwah, NJ: Erlbaum.

Flouri, E., Midouhas, E., & Joshi, H. (2014, in press). Family poverty and trajectories of children's emotional and behavioral problems: The moderating role of self-regulation and verbal cognitive ability. *Journal of Abnormal Child Psychology.*

Flynn, J. R. (1999). Searching for justice: The discovery of IQ gains over time. *American Psychologist, 54,* 5–20.

Flynn, J. R. (2007). The history of the American mind in the 20th century: a scenario to explain IQ gains over time and a case for the relevance of g. In P. C. Kyllonen, R. D. Roberts, & L. Stankov (Eds.), *Extending intelligence.* Mahwah, NJ: Erlbaum.

Flynn, J. R. (2011). Secular changes in intelligence. In R. J. Sternberg & S. B. Kaufman (Eds.), *Cambridge handbook of intelligence.* New York: Cambridge University Press.

Flynn, J. R. (2013). *Are we getting smarter?* New York: Cambridge University Press.

Fogel, A. (2010). *Infant development.* New York: Sloan.

Follari, L. (2015, in press). *Foundations and best practices in early childhood education* (3rd ed.). Upper Saddle River, NJ: Pearson.

Fontana, L., & Hu, F. B. (2014, in press). Optimal body weight for health and longevity: Bridging basic, clinical, and population research. *Aging Cell.*

Fontenot, H. B. (2007). Transition and adaptation to adoptive motherhood. *Journal of Obstetrics, Gynecologic, and Neonatal Nursing, 36,* 175–182.

Forbes, S. C., Little, J. P., & Candow, D. G. (2012). Exercise and nutritional interventions for improving aging and muscle health. *Endocrine, 42*(1), 29–38.

Ford, D. Y. (2012). Gifted and talented education: History, issues, and recommendations. In K. R. Harris, S. Graham, & T. Urdan (Eds.), *APA handbook of educational psychology.* Washington, DC: American Psychological Association.

Forget-Dubois, N., & others (2009). Early child language mediates the relation between home environment and school readiness. *Child Development, 80,* 736–749.

Forte, R., & others (2013). Executive function moderates the role of muscular fitness in determining functional mobility in older adults. *Aging: Clinical and Experimental Research, 25,* 291–298.

Fosco, G. M., Frank, J. L., & Dishion, T. J. (2012). Understanding the influence of deviant peers on problem behavior: Coercion and contagion in peer, family, and school environments. In S. R. Jimerson & others (Eds.), *Handbook of school violence and school safety.* New York: Routledge.

Fosco, G. M., Stormshak, E. A., Dishion, T. J., & Winter, C. (2012). Family relationships and parental monitoring during middle school as predictors of early adolescent problem behavior. *Journal of Clinical Child and Adolescent Psychology, 41,* 202–213.

Fowler, C. G., & Leigh-Paffenroth, W. B. (2007). Hearing. In J. E. Birren (Ed.), *Encyclopedia of gerontology* (2nd ed.). San Diego: Academic Press.

Fowler, M. G. (2014, in press). Efficacy and safety of an extended nevirapine regimen in infants of breastfeeding mothers with HIV-1 infection for prevention of HIV-1 transmission (HPTN 046): 18-month results of a randomized, double-blind, placebo-controlled trial. *Journal of Acquired Immune Deficiency Syndromes.*

Fox, B. J. (2014). *Phonics and word study for the teacher of reading* (11th ed.). Upper Saddle River, NJ: Pearson.

Fox, M. K., Pac, S., Devancy, B., & Jankowski, L. (2004). Feeding infants and toddlers study: What foods are infants and toddlers eating? *American Dietetic Association Journal, 104*(Suppl.), S22–S30.

Fox, M. K., & others (2010). Food consumption patterns of young preschoolers: Are they starting off on the right path? *Journal of the American Dietetic Association, 110*(Suppl 12), S52–S59.

Fox, N. A., Reeb-Sutherland, C., & Degnan, K. A. (2013). Personality and emotional development. In P. D. Zelazo (Eds.), *Handbook of developmental psychology.* New York: Oxford University Press.

Fozard, J. L. (1992, December 6). Commentary in "We can age successfully." *Parade Magazine,* pp. 14–15.

Fraley, R. C., Roisman, G. I. Booth-LaForce, C., Owen, M. T., & Holland, A. S. (2013). Interpersonal and genetic origins of adult attachment styles: A longitudinal study from infancy to early adulthood. *Journal of Personality and Social Psychology, 104,* 817–838.

Fraley, R. C., Roisman, G. I., & Haltigan, J. D. (2013). The legacy of early experiences in development: Formalizing alternative models of how early experiences are carried forward over time. *Developmental Psychology, 49*(1), 109–126.

Franchak, J. M., & Adolph, K. E. (2014, in press). Affordances as probabilistic functions: Implications for development, perception, and decisions for action. *Ecological Psychology.*

Francis, J., Fraser, G., & Marcia, J. E. (1989). *Cognitive and experimental factors in moratorium-achievement (MAMA) cycles.* Unpublished manuscript, Department of Psychology, Simon Fraser University, Burnaby, British Columbia.

Franco, P., & others (2010). Arousal from sleep mechanisms in infants. *Sleep Medicine, 11,* 603–614.

Frank, M. C., Vul, E., & Johnson, S. P. (2009). Development of infants' attention to faces during the first year. *Cognition, 110,* 160–170.

Franke, T., & others (2013). The secrets of highly active older adults. *Journal of Aging Studies, 27,* 398–409.

Frankl, V. (1984). *Man's search for meaning.* New York: Basic Books.

Franz, C. E. (1996). The implications of preschool tempo and motoric activity level for personality decades later. Reported in A. Caspi, Personality development across the life course, in W. Damon (Ed.), *Handbook of child psychology* (Vol. 3). New York: Wiley.

Frederikse, M., & others (2000). Sex differences in inferior lobule volume in schizophrenia. *American Journal of Psychiatry, 157,* 422–427.

Fredricks, J. A., & Eccles, J. S. (2010). Breadth of extracurricular participation and adolescent adjustment among African-American and European-American youth. *Journal of Research on Adolescence, 20,* 307–333.

Freeman, R. (2011). Reggio Emilia, Vygotsky, and family childcare: Four American providers describe their pedagogical practice. *Child Care in Practice, 17,* 227–246.

Freud, S. (1917). *A general introduction to psychoanalysis.* New York: Washington Square Press.

Freund, A. M., & Baltes, P. B. (2002). Life-management strategies of selection, optimization, and compensation: Measurement by self-report and construct validity. *Journal of Personality and Social Psychology, 82,* 642–662.

Freund, A. M., & Blanchard-Fields, F. (2014). Age-related differences in altruism across adulthood: Making personal financial gain versus contributing to the public good. *Developmental Psychology, 50*(4), 1125–1136.

Freund, A. M., Nikitin, J., & Riediger, M. (2013). Successful aging. In I. B. Weiner & others (Eds.), *Handbook of psychology* (2nd ed., Vol. 6). New York: Wiley.

Frey, B. S. (2011). Happy people live longer. *Science, 331,* 542–543.

Frey, W. H. (2007). *Mapping the growth of older America: Seniors and boomers in the early 21st century.* Washington, DC: The Brookings Institution.

Freyer-Adam, J., Gaertner, B., Tobschall, S., & John, U. (2011). Health risk factors and self-rated health among job-seekers. *BMC Public Health, 11,* 659.

Freytag. S., & others (2014). A network-based kernel machine test for the identification of risk pathways in genome-wide association studies. *Human Heredity, 76,* 64–75.

Fried, L. E., Williams, S., Cabral, H., & Hacker, K. (2013). Differences in risk factors for suicide attempts among 9th and 11th grade youth: A longitudinal perspective. *Journal of School Nursing, 29,* 113–122.

Friedman, D. (2013). The cognitive aging of episodic memory: A view based on the event-related brain potential. *Frontiers in Behavioral Neuroscience, 7,* 111.

Friedman, D., Nessler, D., Johnson, R., Ritter, W., & Bersick, M. (2008). Age-related changes in executive function: An event-related potential (ERP) investigation of task-switching. *Aging, Neuropsychology, and Cognition, 15,* 95–128.

Friedman, J. (2013). Twin separation. Retrieved February 14, 2013, from http://christinabaglivitinglof.com/twin-pregnancy/six-twin-experts-te. . .

Friedman, N. P., & others (2009). Individual differences in childhood sleep problems predict later cognitive control. *Sleep, 32,* 323–333.

Friedman, S. L., Melhuish, E., & Hill, C. (2010). Childcare research at the dawn of a new millennium: An update. In G. Bremner & T. Wachs (Eds.), *Wiley-Blackwell handbook of infant development* (2nd ed.). Oxford, UK: Wiley-Blackwell.

Friedman, W. J. (2014). Development of memory for the times of past events. In P. Bauer & R. Fivush (Eds.), *Wiley handbook of children's memory.* New York: Wiley.

Friend, M. (2014). *Special education* (4th ed.). Upper Saddle River, NJ: Pearson.

Friend, M., & Bursuck, W. D. (2015, in press). *Including students with special needs* (7th ed.). Upper Saddle River, NJ: Pearson.

Fromme, E. K., & others (2012). POLST registry do-not-resuscitate orders and other patient treatment preferences. *JAMA, 307,* 34–35.

Frost, D. M. (2011). Stigma and intimacy in same-sex relationships: A narrative approach. *Journal of Family Psychology, 25,* 1–10.

Fry, C. L. (2007). Comparative and cross-cultural studies. In J. E. Birren (Ed.), *Encyclopedia of gerontology* (2nd ed.). San Diego: Academic Press.

Fuglset, T. S., Endestad, T., Landro, N. I., & Ro, O. (2014, in press). Brain structure alterations associated with weight changes in young females with anorexia nervosa: A case series. *Neurocase.*

Fujisawa, D., & others (2010). Prevalence and determinants of complicated grief in general population. *Journal of Affective Disorders, 127,* 352–358.

Fujita, A., & others (2014, in press). A novel WTX mutation in a female patient with osteopathia striata with cranial sclerosis and hepatoblastoma. *American Journal of Medical Genetics A.*

Fuligni, A. J. (2012). Gaps, conflicts, and arguments between adolescents and their parents. *New Directions for Child and Adolescent Development, 135,* 105–110.

Fung, L. K., Quintin, E. M., Haas, B. W., & Reiss, A. L. (2012). Conceptualizing neurodevelopmental disorders through a mechanistic understanding of fragile X syndrome and Williams syndrome. *Current Opinion in Neurology, 25,* 112–124.

Furman, E. (2005). *Boomerang nation.* New York: Fireside.

Furman, W., Low, S., & Ho, M. J. (2009). Romantic experience and psychosocial adjustment in middle adolescence. *Journal of Clinical Child and Adolescent Psychology, 38,* 75–90.

Furstenberg, F. F. (2007). The future of marriage. In A. S. Skolnick & J. H. Skolnick (Eds.), *Family in transition* (14th ed.). Boston: Allyn & Bacon.

Furth, H. G., & Wachs, H. (1975). *Thinking goes to school.* New York: Oxford University Press.

Furukawa, S., Sameshima, H., & Ikenoue, T. (2014, in press). The impact of cesarean section on neonatal outcome of infants born at 23 weeks gestation. *Early Human Development.*

G

Gaias, L. M., & others (2012). Cross-cultural temperamental differences in infants, children, and adults in the United States of America and Finland, *53,* 119–128.

Gaiha, R., Kulkarni, V. S., Pandey, M. K., & Imai, K. S. (2012). On hunger and child mortality in India. *Journal of Asian and African Studies, 47,* 3–17.

Gaillard, A., & others (2014, in press). Predictors of postpartum depression: Prospective study of 264 women followed during pregnancy and postpartum. *Psychiatry Research.*

Gaines, J. M., Burke, K. L., Marx, K. A., Wagner, M., & Parrish, J. M. (2011). Enhancing older driver safety: A driving survey and evaluation of the CarFit program. *Journal of Safety Research, 42,* 351–358.

Gaither, S. E., Pauker, K., & Johnson, S. P. (2012). Biracial and monoracial infant own-race face perception: An eye tracking study. *Developmental Science, 15*(6), 775–782.

Galambos, N. L., Howard, A. L., & Maggs, J. L. (2011). Rise and fall of sleep quality with student experiences across the first year of the university. *Journal of Research on Adolescence, 21,* 342–349.

Galbally, M., Lewis, A. J., IJzendoorn, M., & Permezel, M. (2011). The role of oxytocin in mother-infant relations: A systematic review of human studies. *Harvard Review of Psychiatry, 19,* 1–14.

Galinsky, A. M., & Sonenstein, F. L. (2013). Relationship commitment, perceived equity, and sexual enjoyment among young adults in the United States. *Archives of Sexual Behavior, 42,* 93–104.

Galinsky, E. (2010). *Mind in the making.* New York: HarperCollins.

Galinsky, E., & David, J. (1988). *The preschool years: Family strategies that work—from experts and parents.* New York: Times Books.

Galland, B. C., Taylor, B. J., Edler, D. E., & Herbison, P. (2012). Normal sleep patterns in infants and children: A systematic review of observational studies. *Sleep Medicine Review, 16,* 213–222.

Galler, J. R., & others (2012). Infant malnutrition is associated with persisting attention deficits in middle childhood. *Journal of Nutrition, 142,* 788–794.

Galliano, D., & Bellver, J. (2013). Female obesity: Short- and long-term consequences on the offspring. *Gynecological Endocrinology, 28*(7), 626–631.

Galloway, J. C., & Thelen, E. (2004). Feet first: Object exploration in young infants. *Infant Behavior & Development, 27,* 107–112.

Gallup (2013a). *U.S. obesity rate climbing in 2013.* Washington, DC: Gallup.

Gallup (2013b). *No major change in Americans' exercise habits in 2013.* Washington, DC: Gallup.

Gallup, G. W., & Bezilla, R. (1992). *The religious life of young Americans.* Princeton, NJ: Gallup Institute.

Gamino, L. A., & Sewell, K. W. (2004). Meaning constructs as predictors of bereavement adjustment: A report from the Scott & White grief study. *Death Studies, 28,* 397–421.

Gandhi, S., & Abramov, A. Y. (2012). Mechanism of oxidative stress in neurodegeneration. *Oxidative Medicine and Cellular Longevity,* 428010.

Ganguli, M., & others (2014). Vascular risk factors and cognitive decline in a population sample. *Alzheimer Disease and Associated Disorders, 28,* 9–15.

Ganong, L., & Coleman, M. (2006). Obligations to stepparents acquired in later life: Relationship quality and acuity of needs. *Journals of Gerontology B: Psychological Sciences and Social Sciences, 61,* S80–S88.

Ganong, L., Coleman, M., & Hans, J. (2006). Divorce as prelude to stepfamily living and the consequences of re-divorce. In M. A. Fine & J. H. Harvey (Eds.), *Handbook of divorce and relationship dissolution.* Mahwah, NJ: Erlbaum.

Ganzewinkel, C. J., Anand, K. J., Kramer, B. W., & Andriessen, P. (2014, in press). Chronic pain in the newborn: Toward a definition. *Clinical Journal of Pain.*

Gao, W., & others (2014, in press). Development of human brain cortical network architecture during infancy. *Brain Structure and Function.*

Garcia-Hermoso, A., Saavedra, J. M., & Escalante, Y. (2013). Effects of exercise on resting blood pressure in obese children: A meta-analysis of randomized controlled trials. *Obesity Reviews, 14*(11), 919–928.

Gardner, H. (1983). *Frames of mind.* New York: Basic Books.

Gardner, H. (1993). *Multiple intelligences.* New York: Basic Books.

Gardner, H. (2002). The pursuit of excellence through education. In M. Ferrari (Ed.), *Learning from extraordinary minds.* Mahwah, NJ: Erlbaum.

Gardner, M. K. (2014). Theories of intelligence. In M. A. Bray & T. J., Kehle (Eds.), *Oxford handbook of school psychology.* New York: Oxford University Press.

Gardosi, J., & others (2013). Maternal and fetal risk factors for stillbirth: Population-based study. *British Medical Journal, 346,* f108.

Garfield, C. F., & others (2012). Trends in attention deficit hyperactivity disorder ambulatory diagnosis and medical treatment in the United States, 2000–2010. *Academic Pediatrics, 12,* 110–116.

Garofalo, R. (2010). Cytokines in human milk. *Journal of Pediatrics, 156*(Suppl. 2), S36–S40.

Garrison, M. M., Liekweg, K., & Christakis, D. A. (2011). Media use and child sleep: The impact of content, timing, and environment. *Pediatrics, 128,* 29–35.

Gartstein, M. A., Slobodskaya, H. R., Putnam, S. P., & Kirchhoff, C. (2014, in press). Cross-cultural evaluation of temperament development: Japan, United States of America, Poland, and Russia. *International Journal of Psychology and Psychological Therapy.*

Garvey, C. (2000). *Play* (enlarged ed.). Cambridge, MA: Harvard University Press.

Gates, C. J. (2011). *How many people are lesbian, gay, bisexual, and transgender?* Los Angeles: Williams Institute, UCLA.

Gates, G. J., (2013). Demographics and LGBT health. *Journal of Health and Human Behavior.*

Gates, W. (1998, July 20). Charity begins when I'm ready (interview). *Fortune.*

Gathwala, G., Singh, B., & Singh, J. (2010). Effect of kangaroo care on physical growth, breastfeeding, and its acceptability. *Tropical Doctor, 40,* 199–202.

Gauvain, M. (2008). Vygotsky's sociocultural theory. In M. M. Haith & J. B. Benson (Eds.), *Encyclopedia of infant and early childhood development.* Oxford, UK: Elsevier.

Gauvain, M. (2013). Sociocultural contexts of development. In P. D. Zelazo (Ed.), *Oxford handbook of developmental psychology.* New York: Oxford University Press.

Gawlick, S., & others (2014, in press). Prevalence of paternal perinatal depressiveness and its link to partnership satisfaction and birth concerns. *Archives of Women's Mental Health.*

Gee, C. C., Walsemann, K. M., & Brondolo, E. (2012). A life course perspective on how racism may be related to health inequities. *American Journal of Public Health, 102,* 967–974.

Gee, C. L., & Heyman, G. D. (2007). Children's evaluations of other people's self-descriptions. *Social Development, 16,* 800–818.

Geisinger, K. F. (2012). Norm- and criterion-referenced testing. In H. Cooper (Ed.), *APA handbook of research methods in psychology.* Washington, DC: American Psychological Association.

Gelman, R. (1969). Conservation acquisition: A problem of learning to attend to relevant attributes. *Journal of Experimental Child Psychology, 7,* 67–87.

Gelman, S. A. (2009). Learning from others: Children's construction of concepts. *Annual Review of Psychology* (Vol. 60). Palo Alto, CA: Annual Reviews.

Gelman, S. A. (2013). Concepts in development. In P. Zelazo (Ed.), *Oxford handbook of developmental psychology.* New York: Oxford University Press.

Gelman, S. A., & Kalish, C. W. (2006). Conceptual development. In W. Damon & R. Lerner (Eds.), *Handbook of child psychology* (6th ed.). New York: Wiley.

Gems, D. (2014). Evolution of sexually dimorphic longevity in humans. *Aging, 6,* 84–91.

Genesee, F., & Lindholm-Leary, K. (2012). The education of English language learners. In K. Harris, S. Graham, & T. Urdan (Eds.), *APA educational psychology handbook.* Washington, DC: American Psychological Association.

Gennetian, L. A., & Miller, C. (2002). Children and welfare reform: A view from an experimental welfare reform program in Minnesota. *Child Development, 73,* 601–620.

Gentile, D. A. (2011). The multiple dimensions of video game effects. *Child Development Perspectives, 5,* 75–81.

George, L. G., Helson, R., & John, O. P. (2011). The "CEO" of women's work lives: How big five conscientiousness, extraversion, and openness predict 50 years of work experiences in a changing sociocultural context. *Journal of Personality and Social Psychology, 101,* 812–830.

George, L. K. (2010). Still happy after all these years: Research frontiers on subjective well-being in later life. *Journals of Gerontology B: Psychological Sciences and Social Sciences, 65B,* 331–339.

George, L. K., & others (2013). Why gerontologists should care about empirical research on religion and health: Transdisciplinary perspectives. *Gerontologist, 53,* 898–906.

Gershoff, E. T. (2002). Corporal punishment by parents and associated child behaviors and experiences: A meta-analysis and theoretical review. *Psychological Bulletin, 128,* 539–579.

Gershoff, E. T. (2013). Spanking and development: We know enough now to stop hitting our children. *Child Development Perspectives, 7,* 133–137.

Gershoff, E. T., & Benner, A. D. (2014). Neighborhood and school contexts in the lives of children. In E. T. Gershoff, R. S. Mistry, & D. A. Crosby (Eds.), *The societal contexts of child development.* New York: Oxford University Press.

Gershoff, E. T., Lansford, J. E., Sexton, H. R., Davis-Kean, P., & Sameroff, A. (2012). Longitudinal links between spanking and children's externalizing behaviors in a national sample of White, Black, Hispanic, and Asian American families. *Child Development, 83,* 838–843.

Gershoff, E. T., Mistry, R. S., & Crosby, D. A. (Eds.) (2014). *Societal contexts of child development.* New York: Oxford University Press.

Gershoff, E. T., & others (2010). Parent discipline practices in an international sample: Associations with child behaviors and moderation by perceived normativeness. *Child Development, 81,* 487–502.

Gerson, S. A., & Woodward, A. L. (2014). The joint role of trained, untrained, and observed actions at the origins of goal recognition. *Infant Behavior and Development.*

Gerst-Emerson, K., Shovali, T. E., & Markides, K. S. (2014, in press). Loneliness among very old Mexican Americans: Findings from the Hispanic established populations epidemiologic studies of the elderly. *Archives of Gerontology and Geriatrics.*

Gerstenberg, F. X., Imhoff, R., Banse, R., & Schmitt, M. (2014). Discrepancies between implicit and explicit self-concepts of intelligence: Relations to modesty, narcissism, and achievement motivation. *Frontiers in Psychology, 5,* 85.

Gesell, A. (1934). *An atlas of infant behavior.* New Haven, CT: Yale University Press.

Gesell, A. L. (1934). *Infancy and human growth.* New York: Macmillan.

Gevensleben, H., & others (2014). Neurofeedback in ADHD: Further pieces of the puzzle. *Brain Topography, 27,* 20–32.

Gewirtz, J. (1977). Maternal responding and the conditioning of infant crying: Directions of influence within the attachment-acquisition process. In B. C. Etzel, J. M. LeBlanc, & D. M. Baer (Eds.), *New developments in behavioral research.* Hillsdale, NJ: Erlbaum.

Ghetti, S., & Alexander, K. W. (2004). "If it happened, I would remember it": Strategic use of event memorability in the rejection of false autobiographical events. *Child Development, 75,* 542–561.

Ghosh, S., Feingold, E., Chakaborty, S., & Dey, S. K. (2010). Telomere length is associated with types of chromosome 21 nondisjunction: A new insight into the maternal age effect on Down syndrome birth. *Human Genetics, 127,* 403–409.

Giangregorio, L. M., & others (2014, in press). Too fit to fracture: A consensus on future research priorities in osteoporosis and exercise. *Osteoporosis International.*

Giarrusso, R., & Bengtson, V. L. (2007). Self-esteem. In J. E. Birren (ed.), *Encyclopedia of gerontology* (2nd ed.). San Diego: Academic Press.

Gibbons, L., & others (2012). Inequities in the use of cesarean section deliveries in the world. *American Journal of Obstetrics and Gynecology, 206*(4), 331.e1–331.e19.

Gibbs, J. C. (2014). *Moral development and reality: Beyond the theories of Kohlberg and Hoffman* (3rd ed.). New York: Oxford University Press.

Gibbs, J. C., Basinger, K. S., Grime, R. L., & Snarey, J. R. (2007). Moral judgment development across cultures: Revisiting Kohlberg's universality claims. *Developmental Review, 27,* 443–500.

Gibson, E. J. (1969). *Principles of perceptual learning and development.* New York: Appleton-Century-Crofts.

Gibson, E. J. (1989). Exploratory behavior in the development of perceiving, acting, and the acquiring of knowledge. *Annual Review of Psychology* (Vol. 39). Palo Alto, CA: Annual Reviews.

Gibson, E. J. (2001). *Perceiving the affordances.* Mahwah, NJ: Erlbaum.

Gibson, E. J., & Walk, R. D. (1960). The "visual cliff." *Scientific American, 202,* 64–71.

Gibson, E. J., & others (1987). Detection of the traversability of surfaces by crawling and walking infants. *Journal of Experimental Psychology: Human Perception and Performance, 13,* 533–544.

Gibson, J. J. (1966). *The senses considered as perceptual systems.* Boston: Houghton Mifflin.

Gibson, J. J. (1979). *The ecological approach to visual perception.* Boston: Houghton Mifflin.

Giedd, J. N. (2012). The digital revolution and the adolescent brain. *Journal of Adolescent Health, 51,* 101–105.

Giedd, J. N., & others (2012). Anatomic magnetic resonance imaging of the developing child and adolescent brain. In V. F. Reyna & others (Eds.), *The adolescent brain.* Washington, DC: American Psychological Association.

Gielen, S., Sandri, M., Erbs, S., & Adams, V. (2011). Exercise-induced modulation of endothelial nitric oxide production. *Current Pharmaceutical Biotechnology, 12*(9), 1375–1384.

Gilbertson, S. L., & Graves, B. A. (2014, in press). Motivating parents to promote cardiovascular health in children. *Journal of Cardiovascular Nursing.*

Gill, P., & Lowes, L. (2014, in press). Renal transplant failure and disenfranchised grief: Participants' experiences in first year post-graft failure. *International Journal of Nursing Studies.*

Gillen-O'Neel, C., Huynh, V. W., & Fuligni, A. J. (2013). To study or to sleep? The academic costs of extra studying at the expense of sleep. *Child Development, 84*(1), 133–142.

Gilliam, M., & others (2011). Developmental trajectories of the corpus callosum in attention-deficit/hyperactivity disorder. *Biological Psychiatry, 69,* 839–846.

Gillig, P. M., & Sanders, R. D. (2011). Higher cortical functions: Attention and vigilance. *Innovations in Clinical Neuroscience, 8,* 43–46.

Gilligan, C. (1982). *In a different voice.* Cambridge, MA: Harvard University Press.

Gilligan, C. (1992, May). *Joining the resistance: Girls' development in adolescence.* Paper presented at the symposium on development and vulnerability in close relationships, Montreal, Quebec.

Gilligan, C. (1996). The centrality of relationships in psychological development: A puzzle, some evidence, and a theory. In G. G. Noam & K. W. Fischer (Eds.), *Development and vulnerability in close relationships.* Hillsdale, NJ: Erlbaum.

Gillum, R. F., & Ingram, D. D. (2007). Frequency of attendance at religious services, hypertension, and blood pressure: The Third National Health and Nutrition Examination Survey. *Psychosomatic Medicine, 68,* 382–385.

Gillum, R. F., King, D. E., Obisesan, T. O., & Koenig, H. G. (2008). Frequency of attendance at religious services and mortality in a U.S. national cohort. *Annals of Epidemiology, 18,* 124–129.

Gilmour, H. (2012). Social participation and the health and well-being of Canadian seniors. *Health Reports, 23,* 23–32.

Gimovsky, A., Khodak-Gelman, S., & Larsen, J. (2014). Making chorionic villus sampling painless for both the patient and the physician. *Journal of Ultrasound Medicine, 33,* 355–357.

Giorgis, C., & Glazer, J. I. (2013). *Literature for young children: Supporting emergent literacy, ages 0–8* (7th ed.). Boston: Allyn & Bacon.

Girls, Inc. (1991). *Truth, trusting, and technology: New research on preventing adolescent pregnancy.* Indianapolis: Author.

Glei, D. A. (1999). Measuring contraceptive use patterns among teenage and adult women. *Family Planning Perspectives, 31,* 73–80.

Glover, V. (2014). Maternal depression, anxiety, and stress during pregnancy and child outcome: What needs to be done. *Best Practice and Research: Clinical Obstetrics and Gynecology, 28,* 25–35.

Gluck, M. E., & others (2009). Maternal influence, not diabetic intrauterine environment, predicts children's energy intake. *Obesity, 17*(4), 772–777.

Goble, P. M., Martin, C. L., Hanish, L. D., & Fabes, R. A. (2012, April). *Defining preschool gender-typed activities.* Paper presented at the Gender Development Research conference, San Francisco.

Gogtay, N., & Thompson, P. M. (2010). Mapping gray matter development: Implications for typical development and vulnerability to psychopathology. *Brain and Cognition, 72,* 6–15.

Goh, J. O. (2011). Functional dedifferentiation and altered connectivity in older adults: Neural accounts of cognitive aging. *Aging and Disease, 2,* 30–48.

Gold, D. (2011). Death and dying. In R. H. Binstock & L. K. George (Eds.), *Handbook of aging and the social sciences* (7th ed.). New York: Elsevier.

Gold, M. S., Blum K., Oscar-Berman, M., & Braverman, E. R. (2014). Low dopamine function in attention deficit/hyperactivity disorder: Should genotyping signify early diagnosis in children? *Postgraduate Medicine, 126,* 153–177.

Goldberg, M. E., Gee, A., Ipata, A., Bisley, J., & Gottlieb, J. (2012). In G. R. Mangun, *Neuroscience of attention: Attentional control and selection.* New York: Oxford University Press.

Goldberg, W. A., & Lucas-Thompson, R. (2008). Maternal and paternal employment, effects of. In M. M. Haith & J. B. Benson (Eds.), *Encyclopedia of infant and early childhood development.* Oxford, UK: Elsevier.

Goldenberg, R. L., & Culhane, J. F. (2007). Low birth weight in the United States. *American Journal of Clinical Nutrition, 85*(Suppl.), S584–S590.

Goldfield, G. S. (2012). Making access to TV contingent on physical activity: Effects on liking and relative reinforcing value of TV and physical activity in overweight and obese children. *Journal of Behavioral Medicine, 35,* 1–7.

Goldin-Meadow, S. (2014a, in press). Language and the manual modality: How our hands help us talk and think. In N. J. Enfield & others (Eds.), *Cambridge handbook of linguistic anthropology.* New York: Cambridge University Press.

Goldin-Meadow, S. (2014b, in press). Widening the lens: What the manual modality reveals about language, learning, and cognition. *Philosophical Transactions of the Royal Society, Series B.*

Goldin-Meadow, S., & Alibali, M. W. A. (2013). Gesture's role in learning and development. In P. Zelazo (Ed.), *Oxford University handbook of developmental psychology.* New York: Oxford University Press.

Goldschmidt, L., Richardson, G. A., Willford, J., & Day, N. L. (2008). Prenatal marijuana exposure and intelligence test performance at age 6. *Journal of the American Academy of Child and Adolescent Psychiatry, 47,* 254–263.

Goldstein, M. H., King, A. P., & West, M. J. (2003). Social interaction shapes babbling: Testing parallels between birdsong and speech. *Proceedings of the National Academy of Sciences, 100*(13), 8030–8035.

Goldston, D. B., & others (2008). Cultural considerations in adolescent suicide prevention and psychosocial treatment. *American Psychologist, 63,* 14–31.

Golley, R. K., & others (2012). An index measuring adherence to complementary feeding guidelines has convergent validity as a measure of infant diet quality. *Journal of Nutrition, 142*(5), 901–908.

Golombok, S. (2011a). Children in new family forms. In R. Gross (Ed.), *Psychology* (6th ed.). London: Hodder Education.

Golombok, S. (2011b). Why I study lesbian families. In S. Ellis, V. Clarke, E. Peel, & D. Riggs (Eds.), *LGBTQ psychologies.* New York: Cambridge University Press.

Golombok, S., MacCallum, F., & Goodman, E. (2001). The "test-tube" generation: Parent-child relationships and the psychological well-being of in vitro fertilization children at adolescence. *Child Development, 72,* 599–608.

Golombok, S., & others (2008). Developmental trajectories of sex-typed behavior in boys and girls: A longitudinal general population study of children aged 2.5–8 years. *Child Development, 79,* 1583–1593.

Golombok, S., & others (2014, in press). Adoptive gay father families: Parent-child relationships and children's psychological adjustment. *Child Development.*

Golombok, S., & Tasker, F. (2010). Gay fathers. In M. E. Lamb (Ed.), *The role of the father in child development* (5th ed.). New York: Wiley.

Gomes, R. S., & others (2011). Primary versus secondary hypertension in children followed up at an outpatient tertiary unit. *Pediatric Nephrology, 26,* 441–447.

Gomez-Pinilla, F., & Hillman, C. (2013). The influence of exercise on cognitive abilities. *Comprehensive Physiology, 3,* 403–428.

Gonsalves, S. (2011). Connecting curriculum with community. *Education Digest, 76*(6), 56–59.

Gonzales-Barcala, F. J., & others (2013). Impact of parental smoking on childhood asthma. *Journal of Pediatrics, 89,* 294–299.

Gonzalez, A., Atkinson, L., & Fleming, A. S. (2009). Attachment and the comparative psychobiology of mothering. In M. de Haan & M. R. Gunnar (Eds.), *Developmental social neuroscience.* New York: Guilford.

Good, M., & Willoughby, T. (2008). Adolescence as a sensitive period for spiritual development. *Child Development Perspectives, 2,* 32–37.

Good, M., & Willoughby, T. (2010). Evaluating the direction of effects in the relationship between religious versus non-religious activities, academic success, and substance use. *Journal of Youth and Adolescence, 40*(6), 680–693.

Goodkind, S. (2014, in press). Single-sex public education for low-income youth of color: A critical theoretical review. *Sex Roles.*

Goodnough, L. T., & others (2011). How we treat: Transfusion medicine support of obstetric services. *Transfusion, 204,* e1–e12.

Goodvin, R., Meyer, S., Thompson, R. A., & Hayes, R. (2008). Self-understanding in early childhood: Associations with child attachment security and maternal negative affect. *Attachment and Human Development, 10,* 433–450.

Goodvin, R., Winer, A. C., & Thompson, R. A. (2014, in press). The individual child: Temperament, emotion, self, and personality. In M. Bornstein & M. E. Lamb (Eds.), *Developmental science* (7th ed.). New York: Psychology Press.

Gopalappa, C., Stover, J., Shaffer, N., & Mahy, M. (2014). The costs and benefits of Option B+ for the prevention of mother-to-child transmission of HIV. *AIDS, 28*(1, Suppl.), S5–S14.

Gopinath, B., & others (2012). Severity of age-related hearing loss is associated with impaired activities of daily living. *Age and Aging, 41,* 195–200.

Gopnik, A. (2010). Commentary in E. Galinsky (2010), *Mind in the making.* New York: Harper Collins.

Gorby, H. E., Brownawell, A. M., & Falk, M. C. (2010). Do specific dietary constituents and supplements affect mental energy? Review of the evidence. *Nutrition Reviews, 68,* 697–718.

Gorchoff, S. M., John, O. P., & Helson, R. (2008). Contextualizing change in marital satisfaction during middle age: An 18-year longitudinal study. *Psychological Science, 19,* 1194–1200.

Gordh, A. H., Brkic, S., & Soderpalm, B. (2011). Stress and consumption of alcohol in humans with a Type 1 family history of alcoholism in an experimental laboratory setting. *Pharmacology, Biochemistry, and Behavior, 99,* 696–703.

Gordon, I., Zagoory-Sharon, O., Leckman, J. F., & Feldman, R. (2010). Oxytocin and the development of parenting in humans. *Biological Psychiatry, 68,* 377–382.

Gordon, N. (2013). PS3-39: What are seniors doing to promote healthy aging? *Clinical Medicine and Research, 11,* 172.

Gordon-Larsen, P., Wang, H., & Popkin, B. M. (2014). Overweight dynamics in Chinese children and adults. *Obesity Reviews*(1, Suppl.), S37–S48.

Gorin, A. A., & others (2014). Steps to growing up healthy: A pediatric primary care based obesity prevention program for young children. *BMC Public Health, 14*(1), 72.

Goritz, C., & Frisen, J. (2012). Neural stem cells and neurogenesis in the adult. *Cell: Stem Cell, 10,* 657–659.

Gormley-Fleming, L., & Campbell, A. (2014). Rights of the child: To die? *British Journal of Nursing, 23,* 302–308.

Gortmaker, S. L., & Taveras, E. M. (2014). Who becomes obese during childhood—clues to prevention. *New England Journal of Medicine, 370,* 475–476.

Gosden, R. G. (2007). Menopause. In J. E. Birren (Ed.), *Encyclopedia of gerontology* (2nd ed.). San Diego: Academic Press.

Goslawski, M., & others (2013). Binge drinking impairs vascular function in young adults. *Journal of the American College of Cardiology, 62,* 201–207.

Gosmann, N. P., & others (2014, in press). Association between internalizing disorders and day-to-day activities of low energetic expenditure. *Child Psychiatry and Human Development.*

Gosselin, J. (2010). Individual and family factors related to psychosocial adjustment in stepmother families with adolescents. *Journal of Divorce and Remarriage, 51,* 108–123.

Goswami, S., & others (2013). Determination of brain death by apnea test adapted to extracorporeal cardiopulmonary resuscitation. *Journal of Cardiothoracic and Vascular Anesthesia, 27*(2), 312–314.

Gothe, N. P., & others (2014). Executive function processes predict mobility outcomes in older adults. *Journal of the American Geriatrics Society, 62,* 285–290.

Gottlieb, G. (2007). Probabilistic epigenesis. *Developmental Science, 10,* 1–11.

Gottlieb, G., Wahlsten, D., & Lickliter, R. (2006). The significance of biology for human development: A developmental psychobiological systems view. In W. Damon & R. Lerner (Eds.), *Handbook of child psychology* (6th ed.). New York: Wiley.

Gottman, J. M. (1994). *What predicts divorce?* Mahwah, NJ: Erlbaum.

Gottman, J. M. (2006, April, 29). Secrets of long term love. *New Scientist, 2549,* 40.

Gottman, J. M. (2011). *The science of trust.* New York: Norton.

Gottman, J. M. (2014). *Bringing home baby.* Retrieved February 16, 2014, from www.bbhonline.org/

Gottman, J. M. (2014). *Research on parenting.* Retrieved February 25, 2014, from www.gottman.com/parenting/research

Gottman, J. M., & Parker, J. G. (Eds.) (1987). *Conversations of friends.* New York: Cambridge University Press.

Gottman, J. M., Shapiro, A. F., Parthemer, J. (2004). Bringing baby home: A preventative intervention program for expectant couples. *International Journal of Childbirth Education, 19,* 28–30.

Gottman, J. M., & Silver, N. (1999). *The seven principles for making marriages work.* New York: Crown.

Gouin, K., & others (2011). Effects of cocaine use during pregnancy on low birthweight and preterm birth: Systematic review and metaanalyses. *American Journal of Obstetrics and Gynecology, 204*(4), 340.e1–340.e12.

Gould, E., & Hertel-Fernandez, A. (2010). Early retiree and near-elderly health insurance in a recession. *Journal of Aging and Social Policy, 22,* 172–187.

Gould, S. J. (1981). *The mismeasure of man.* New York: W. W. Norton.

Gouldner, H., & Strong, M. M. (1987). *Speaking of friendship.* New York: Greenwood Press.

Gove, W. R., Style, C. B., & Hughes, M. (1990). The effect of marriage on the well-being of adults. *Journal of Marriage and the Family, 11,* 4–35.

Gowan, D. E. (2003). Christian beliefs concerning death and life after death. In C. D. Bryant (Ed.), *Handbook of death and dying.* Thousand Oaks, CA: Sage.

Grabenhenrich, L. B., & others (2014, in press). Early-life determinants of asthma from birth to age 20 years: A German birth cohort study. *Journal of Allergy and Clinical Immunology.*

Graber, J. A., Brooks-Gunn, J., & Warren, M. P. (2006). Pubertal effects on adjustment in girls: Moving from demonstrating effects to identifying pathways. *Journal of Youth and Adolescence, 35,* 391–401.

Graber, J. A. (2013). Pubertal timing and the development of psychopathology in adolescence and beyond. *Hormones and Behavior, 64,* 262–269.

Graber, J. A., & Sontag, L. M. (2009). Internalizing problems during adolescence. In R. M. Lerner & L.

Steinberg (Eds.), *Handbook of adolescent psychology* (3rd ed.). New York: Wiley.

Graber, K. C., & Woods, A. M. (2013). *Physical education and activity for elementary classroom teachers.* New York: McGraw-Hill.

Grady, C. L., Springer, M. V., Hongwanishkul, D., McIntosh, A. R., & Winocur, G. (2006). Age-related changes in brain activity across the adult lifespan. *Journal of Cognitive Neuroscience, 18,* 227–241.

Grafenhain, M., Behne, T., Carpenter, M., & Tomasello, M. (2009). Young children's understanding of joint commitments. *Developmental Psychology, 45,* 1430–1443.

Graham, G. M., Holt-Hale, S., & Parker, M. A. (2013). *Children moving* (9th ed.). New York: McGraw-Hill.

Graham, S. (2005, February 16). Commentary in *USA TODAY,* p. 20.

Grambs, J. D. (1989). *Women over forty* (rev. ed.). New York: Springer.

Grammas, P., & others (2014, in press). A new paradigm for the treatment of Alzheimer's disease: Targeting vascular activation. *Journal of Alzheimer's Disease.*

Granados, J. A. (2013). Health at an advanced age: Social inequality and other factors potentially impacting longevity in nine high-income countries. *Maturitas, 74,* 137–147.

Grandner, M. A., Sands-Lincoln, M. R., Pak, V. M., & Garland, S. N. (2013). Sleep duration, cardiovascular disease, and proinflammatory biomarkers. *Nature Science: Sleep, 5,* 93–107.

Granger, R. C., Tseng, V., & Wilcox, B. L. (2014). Connecting research and policy. In E. T. Gershoff, R. S. Mistry, & D. A. Crosby (Eds.), *Societal contexts of child development.* New York: Oxford University Press.

Grant, J. (1993). *The state of the world's children.* New York: UNICEF and Oxford University Press.

Grant, N., Wardle, J., & Steptoe, A. (2009). The relationship between life satisfaction and health behavior: A cross-cultural analysis of young adults. *International Journal of Behavioral Medicine, 16,* 259–268.

Grant, T. M., & others (2013). The impact of prenatal alcohol exposure on addiction treatment. *Journal of Addiction Medicine, 7,* 87–95.

Graven, S. (2006). Sleep and brain development. *Clinical Perinatology, 33,* 693–706.

Gray, P. B., & Garcia, J. R. (2012). *Aging and human sexual behavior: Biocultural perspectives—a mini-review, 58*(5), 446–452.

Graziano, A. M., & Raulin, M. L. (2013). *Research methods* (8th ed.). Upper Saddle River, NJ: Pearson.

Gredler, M. E. (2012). Understanding Vygotsky for the classroom: Is it too late? *Educational Psychology Review, 24,* 113–131.

Green, J., Muir, H., & Maher, M. (2011). Child pedestrian casualties and deprivation. *Accidents: Analysis and Prevention, 43,* 714–723.

Green, M. J., Espie, C. A., Hunt, K., & Benzeval, M. (2012). The longitudinal course of insomnia symptoms: Inequalities by sex and occupational class among two different age cohorts followed for 20 years in the west of Scotland. *Sleep, 35,* 815–823.

Greenberg, J. A. (2006). Correcting biases in estimates of mortality attributable to obesity. *Obesity, 14,* 2071–2079.

Greenhaus, J., & Callanan, G. A. (2013). Career dynamics. In I. B. Weiner & others (Eds.), *Handbook of psychology* (2nd ed., Vol. 12). New York: Wiley.

Greenlund, K. J., & others (2012). Public health options for improving cardiovascular health among older Americans. *American Journal of Public Health, 102*(8), 1498–1507.

Greer, F. R., Sicherer, S. H., Burks, A. W., & the Committee on Nutrition and Section on Allergy and Immunology (2008). Effects of early nutritional interventions on the development of atopic disease in infants and children: The role of maternal dietary restriction, breast feeding, timing of introduction of complementary foods, and hydrolyzed formulas. *Pediatrics, 121,* 183–191.

Gregoire, C. A., & others (2014). Untangling the influence of voluntary running, environmental complexity, social housing, and stress on adult hippocampal neurogenesis. *PLoS One, 9*(1), e86237.

Gregorson, M., Kaufman, J. C., & Snyder, H. (Eds.) (2013). *Teaching creativity and teaching creatively.* New York: Springer.

Gregory, K. E., Dubois, N., & Steele, T. (2014). Nutritional and immunological considerations relevant to infant nutrition. *Journal of Perinatal and Neonatal Nursing.*

Griffiths, J. D., Marslen-Wilson, W. D., Stamatakis, E. A., & Tyler, L. K. (2013). Functional organization of the neural language system: Dorsal and ventral pathways are critical for syntax. *Cerebral Cortex, 23*(1), 139–147.

Grigorenko, E. (2000). Heritability and intelligence. In R. J. Sternberg (Ed.), *Handbook of intelligence.* New York: Cambridge University Press.

Grigorenko, E. L., & Takanishi, R. (Eds.) (2012). *Immigration, diversity, and education.* New York: Routledge.

Grigsby, T., & others (2014). Do adolescent drug use consequences predict externalizing and internalizing problems in emerging adulthood as well as traditional drug use measures in a Hispanic sample? *Addictive Behaviors, 39,* 644–651.

Grill, J. D., & Monsell, S. E. (2014). Choosing Alzheimer's disease prevention clinical trial populations. *Neurobiology of Aging, 35,* 466–471.

Groenman, A. P., & others (2013). Substance use disorders in adolescents with attention deficit hyperactivity disorder: A 4-year follow-up study. *Addiction. 108*(8), 1503–1511.

Groh, A. M., & others (2014, in press). Stability of attachment security from infancy to late adolescence. In C. Booth-LaForce & G. I. Roisman (Eds.), The adult attachment interview: Psychometrics, stability, and change from infancy, and developmental origins. *Monographs of the Society for Research in Child Development.*

Gross, J. J., Fredrickson, B. L., & Levenson, R. W. (1994). The psychophysiology of crying. *Psychophysiology, 31,* 460–468.

Grossmann, K., Grossmann, K. E., Spangler, G., Suess, G., & Unzner, L. (1985). Maternal sensitivity and newborns' orientation responses as related to quality of attachment in northern Germany. In L Bretherton & E. Waters (Eds.), Growing points of attachment theory and research. *Monographs of the Society for Research in Child Development, 50* (1–2, Serial No. 209).

Grotevant, H. D., & McDermott, J. M. (2014). Adoption: Biological and social processes linked to adaptation. *Annual Review of Psychology* (Vol. 65). Palo Alto, CA: Annual Reviews.

Grotevant, H. D., McRoy, R. G., Wrobel, G. M., & Ayers-Lopez, S. (2013). Contact between adoptive and birth families: Perspectives from the Minnesota/Texas Adoption Research Project. *Child Development Perspectives, 7*(3), 193–198.

Gruber, K. J., Cupito, S. H., & Dobson, C .F. (2013). Impact of doulas on healthy birth outcomes. *Journal of Perinatal Education, 22,* 49–58.

Gruber, N., Mosimann, U. P., Muri, R., & Nef. T. (2013). Vision and night driving abilities of elderly drivers. *Traffic Injury Prevention, 15,* 477–485.

Gruenewald, T. L., Karlamangia, A. S., Greendale, G. A., Singer, B. H., & Seeman, T. E. (2009). Increased mortality risk in older adults with persistently low or declining feelings of usefulness to others. *Journal of Aging and Health, 21,* 398–425.

Grusec, J. E. (2011). Socialization processes in the family: Social and emotional development. *Annual Review of Psychology* (Vol. 62). Palo Alto, CA: Annual Reviews.

Grusec, J. E., Chaparro, M. P., Johnston, M., & Sherman, A. (2013). Social development and social relationships in middle childhood. In I. B. Weiner & others (Eds.), *Handbook of psychology* (2nd ed., Vol. 6). New York: Wiley.

Grusec, J. E., Chaparro, M. P., Johnston, M., & Sherman, A. (2014). The development of moral behavior from a socialization perspective. In M. Killen & J. G. Smetana (Eds.), *Handbook of moral development* (2nd ed.). New York: Psychology Press.

Gueldner, B. A., & Merrell, K. W. (2014). Interventions with students with internalizing behavioral deficits. In M. A. Bray & T. J. Kehle (Eds.), *Oxford handbook of school psychology.* New York: Oxford University Press.

Guerrero, L. K., Andersen, P. A., & Afifi, W. A. (2011). *Close encounters: Communication in relationships* (3rd ed.). Thousand Oaks, CA: Sage.

Guffanti, G., & others (2013). Genome-wide association study implicates a novel RNA gene, the lincRNA AC068718.1, as a risk factor for post-traumatic stress disorder in women. *Psychoneuroendocrinology, 38,* 3029–3038.

Guido, C., & others (2014, in press). Human sperm anatomy and endocrinology in varicocele: Role of androgen receptor. *Reproduction.*

Guilford, J. P. (1967). *The structure of intellect.* New York: McGraw-Hill.

Guimard-Brunault, M., & others (2014, in press). Back to basics: Do children with autism spontaneously look at screen displaying a face or an object? *Autism Research and Treatment.*

Guiney, H., & Machado, L. (2013). Benefits of regular aerobic exercise for executive functioning in healthy populations. *Psychonomic Bulletin and Review, 20,* 73–86.

Guirado, G. N., & others (2012). Combined exercise training in asymptomatic elderly with controlled hypertension: Effects on functional capacity and cardiac diastolic function. *Medical Science Monitor, 28,* CR461–CR465.

Gump, B., & Matthews, K. (2000, March). *Annual vacations, health, and death.* Paper presented at the meeting of American Psychosomatic Society, Savannah, GA.

Gunderson, E. A., Ramirez, G., Beilock, S. L., & Levine, S. C. (2012). The role of parents and teachers in the development of gender-related attitudes. *Sex Roles, 66,* 153–166.

Gunes, C., & Rudolph, K. L. (2013). The role of telomeres in stem cells and cancer. *Cell, 152,* 390–393.

Gunnar, M. R., Fisher, P. A., & The Early Experience, Stress, and Prevention Network (2006). Bringing basic research on early experience and stress neurobiology to bear on preventive interventions for neglected and maltreated children. *Development and Psychopathology, 18,* 651–677.

Gunnar, M. R., & Herrera, A. M. (2013). The development of stress reactivity: A neurobiological perspective. In P. D. Zelazo (Ed.), *Oxford handbook of developmental psychology.* New York: Oxford University Press.

Gunnar, M. R., Malone, S., & Fisch, R. O. (1987). The psychobiology of stress and coping in the human neonate: Studies of the adrenocortical activity in response to stress in the first week of life. In T. Field, P. McCabe, & N. Scheiderman (Eds.), *Stress and coping*. Hillsdale, NJ: Erlbaum.

Gunning, T. G. (2013). *Creating literacy instruction for all children in grades pre-K to 4* (2nd ed.). Boston: Allyn & Bacon.

Guo, Q., & Jacelon, C. S. (2014, in press). An integrative review of dignity in end-of-life care. *Palliative Medicine.*

Guo, Z., & others (2014, in press). The impact of population structure on genomic prediction in stratified populations. *Theory of Applied Genetics.*

Gur, R. C., & others (1995). Sex differences in regional cerebral glucose metabolism during a resting state. *Science, 267,* 528–531.

Gurwitch, R. H., Silovsky, J. F., Schultz, S., Kees, M., & Burlingame, S. (2001). *Reactions and guidelines for children following trauma/disaster*. Norman, OK: Department of Pediatrics, University of Oklahoma Health Sciences Center.

Gustafsson, J-E. (2007). Schooling and intelligence. Effects of track of study on level and profile of cognitive abilities. In P. C. Kyllonen, R. D. Roberts, & L. Stankov (Eds.), *Extending intelligence*. Mahwah, NJ: Erlbaum.

Gutchess, A. H., & others (2005). Aging and the neural correlates of successful picture encoding: Frontal activations compensate for decreased medial-temporal activity. *Journal of Cognitive Neuroscience, 17,* 84–96.

Gutmann, D. L. (1975). Parenthood: A key to the comparative study of the life cycle. In N. Datan & L. Ginsberg (Eds.), *Life-span developmental psychology: Normative life crises*. New York: Academic Press.

Guttentag, C. L., & others (2014, in press). "My Baby and Me": Effects of an early, comprehensive parenting intervention on at-risk mothers and their children. *Developmental Psychology.*

Guttmannova, K., & others (2012). Examining explanatory mechanisms of the effects of early alcohol use on young adult alcohol competence. *Journal of Studies of Alcohol and Drugs, 73,* 379–390.

H

Hadfield, J. C. (2014, in press). The health of grandparents raising grandchildren: A literature review. *Journal of Gerontological Nursing.*

Hagen, J. W., & Lamb-Parker, F. G. (2008). Head Start. In M. M. Haith & J. B. Benson (Eds.), *Encyclopedia of infant and early childhood development*. Oxford, UK: Elsevier.

Hagestad, G. O. (1985). Continuity and connectedness. In V. L. Bengston & J. Robertson (Eds.), *Grandparenthood*. Newbury Park, CA: Sage.

Hagestad, G. O., & Uhlenberg, P. (2007). The impact of demographic changes on relations between age groups and generations: A comparative perspective. In K. W. Schaie & P. Uhlenberg (Eds.), *Demographic changes and the well-being of older persons*. New York: Springer.

Hagman, J. O., & Frank, G. K. W. (2012). Developmental concerns in psychopharmacological treatment of children and adolescents with eating disorders. In J. Lock (Ed.), *Oxford handbook of child and adolescent eating disorders: Developmental perspectives*. New York: Oxford University Press.

Haith, M. M., Hazen, C., & Goodman, G. S. (1988). Expectation and anticipation of dynamic visual events by 3.5-month-old babies. *Child Development, 59,* 467–479.

Hakuta, K. (2001, April). *Key policy milestones and directions in the education of English language learners*.

Paper prepared for the Rockefeller Symposium on educational equity, Washington, DC.

Hakuta, K. (2005, April). *Bilingualism at the intersection of research and public policy*. Paper presented at the meeting of the Society for Research in Child Development, Atlanta.

Hakuta, K., Butler, Y. G., & Witt, D. (2000). *How long does it take English learners to attain proficiency?* Berkeley, CA: The University of California Linguistic Minority Research Institute Policy Report 2000–1.

Hale, N., Picklesimer, A. H., Billings, D. L., & Covington-Kolb, S. (2014). The impact of Centering Pregnancy group prenatal care on postpartum family planning. *American Journal of Obstetrics and Gynecology, 210*(50), e1–e7.

Hall Haley, M., & Austin, T. Y. (2014). *Content-based second language teaching and learning* (2nd ed.). Upper Saddle River, NJ: Pearson.

Hall, C. B., & others (2009). Cognitive activities delay onset of memory decline in persons who develop dementia. *Neurology, 73,* 356–361.

Hall, D. T., & Mirvis, P. H. (2013). Redefining work, work identity, and career success. In D. L. Blustein (Ed.), *Oxford handbook of the psychology of working*. New York: Oxford University Press.

Hall, G. S. (1904). *Adolescence* (Vols. 1 & 2). Englewood Cliffs, NJ: Prentice Hall.

Hall, L. J. (2013). *Autism spectrum disorders* (2nd ed.). Upper Saddle River, NJ: Pearson.

Hall, S. S., & others (2014, in press). Using discrete trial training to identify specific learning impairments in boys with fragile X syndrome. *Journal of Autism and Developmental Disorders.*

Hall, W. J. (2008). Centenarians: Metaphor becomes reality. *Archives of Internal Medicine, 168,* 262–263.

Hallahan, D. P., Kaufmann, J. M., & Pullen, P. C. (2015). *Exceptional learners* (13th ed.). Upper Saddle River, NJ: Pearson.

Halonen, J., & Santrock, J. W. (2013). *Your guide to college success* (7th ed.). Boston: Cengage.

Halpern, D. F. (2012). *Sex differences in cognitive abilities* (2nd ed.). New York: Psychology Press.

Halpern, D. F., & others (2007). The science of sex differences in science and mathematics. *Psychological Science in the Public Interest, 8,* 1–51.

Halpern, D. F., & others (2011). The pseudoscience of single-sex schooling. *Science, 333,* 1706–1717.

Halpern-Meekin, S., Manning, W., Giordano, P. C., & Longmore, M. A. (2013). Relationship churning in emerging adulthood: On/off relationships and sex with an ex. *Journal of Adolescent Research, 28,* 166–188.

Halt, K., & Vainio, S. (2014, in press). Coordination of kidney organogenesis by Wnt signaling. *Pediatric Nephrology.*

Haltiwanger, E. P. (2013). Preventing falls. *Diabetes self-management, 30,* 10–12.

Hamilton, B. E., Martin, J. A., & Ventura, S. J. (2013). Births: Preliminary data for 2012. *National Vital Statistics Report*. Hyattsville, MD: National Center for Health Statistics.

Hamilton, J. L., & others (2014). Pubertal timing and vulnerabilities to depression in early adolescence: Differential pathways to depressive symptoms by sex. *Journal of Adolescence, 37,* 165–174.

Hamilton, L. D., & Julian, A. M. (2014, in press). The relationship between daily hassles and sexual function in men and women. *Journal of Sex and Marital Therapy.*

Hamlin, J. K. (2013). Moral judgment and action in preverbal infants and toddlers: Evidence for an innate moral core. *Current Directions in Psychological Science, 22,* 186–193.

Hamlin, J. K. (2014). The origins of human morality: Complex socio-moral evaluations by preverbal infants. In J. Decety & Y. Christen (Eds.), *New frontiers in social neuroscience*. New York: Springer.

Hammond, S. I., & others (2012). The effects of parental scaffolding on preschoolers' executive function. *Developmental Psychology, 48,* 271–281.

Han, J. J., Leichtman M. D., & Wang, Q. (1998). Autobiographical memory in Korean, Chinese, and American children. *Developmental Psychology, 34,* 701–713.

Han, W-J. (2009). Maternal employment. In D. Carr (Ed.), *Encyclopedia of the life course and human development*. Boston: Gale Cengage.

Handrinos, J., Cooper, P., Pauletti, R., & Perry, D. G. (2012, April). *Influences on girls' aggression toward gender-atypical boys*. Paper presented at the Gender Development Research conference, San Francisco.

Hanish, L. D., & Guerra, N. G. (2004). Aggressive victims, passive victims, and bullies: Developmental continuity or developmental change? *Merrill-Palmer Quarterly, 50,* 17–38.

Hansell, N. K., & others (2012). Genetic co-morbidity between neuroticism, anxiety/depression, and somatic distress in a sample of adolescent and young adult twins. *Psychological Medicine, 42,* 1249–1260.

Hansen, M. (2012). Confronting costs: Medicaid spending is at the top of many legislative lists. *State Legislatures, 38,* 30–32.

Hansen, M. L., Gunn, P. W., & Kaelber, D. C. (2007). Underdiagnosis of hypertension in children and adolescents. *Journal of the American Medical Association, 298,* 874–879.

Hansen, N. L., & others (2014, in press). Subclinical cognitive decline in middle age is associated with reduced task-induced deactivation of the brain's default mode network. *Human Brain Mapping.*

Haran, C., van Driel, M., Mitchell, B. L., & Brodribb, W. E. (2014). Clinical guidelines for postpartum women and infants in primary care—a systematic review. *BMC Pregnancy and Childbirth, 14*(1), 51.

Harari, Y., Romano, G. H., Ungar, L., & Kupiec, M. (2013). Nature vs. nurture: Interplay between the genetic control of telomere length and environmental factors. *Cell Cycle, 12,* 3465–3470.

Hardy, M. (2006). Older workers. In R. H. Binstock & L. K. George (Eds.), *Handbook of aging and the social sciences* (6th ed.). San Diego: Academic Press.

Hardy, S. A., & others (2014, in press). Moral identity as moral ideal self: Links to adolescent outcomes. *Developmental Psychology.*

Harkins, S. W., Price, D. D., & Martinelli, M. (1986). Effects of age on pain perception. *Journal of Gerontology, 41,* 58–63.

Harkness, S., & Super, E. M. (1995). Culture and parenting. In M. H. Bornstein (Ed.), *Handbook of parenting* (Vol. 3). Hillsdale, NJ: Erlbaum.

Harlow, H. F. (1958). The nature of love. *American Psychologist, 13,* 673–685.

Harold, G. T., & others (2013). The nature of nurture: Disentangling passive genotype-environment correlation from family relationship influences on children's externalizing problems. *Journal of Family Psychology, 27,* 12–21.

Harper, K. M., Tunc-Ozcan, E., Graf,, E. N., & Redel, E. E. (2014, in press). Intergenerational effects of prenatal ethanol on glucose tolerance and insulin responses. *Physiological Genomics.*

Harrington, S. E., & Smith, T. J. (2008). The role of chemotherapy at the end of life: "When is enough,

enough?" *Journal of the American Medical Association, 299*, 2667–2678.

Harris, C. D., Pan, L., & Mukhtar, Q. (2010). Changes in receiving preventive care services among U.S. adults with diabetes, 1997–2007. *Preventing Chronic Disease, 7*(3), A56.

Harris, G. (2002). *Grandparenting: How to meet its responsibilities.* Los Angeles: The Americas Group.

Harris, J. R. (1998). *The nurture assumption: Why children turn out the way they do: Parents matter less than you think and peers matter more.* New York: Free Press.

Harris, J. R. (2009). *The nurture assumption* (rev. ed.). New York: The Free Press.

Harris, J., Golinkoff, R. M., & Hirsh-Pasek, K. (2011). Lessons from the crib for the classroom: How children really learn vocabulary. In S. B. Neuman & D. K. Dickinson (Eds.), *Handbook of early literacy research* (Vol. 3). New York: Guilford.

Harris, K. M., Gorden-Larsen, P., Chantala, K., & Udry, J. R. (2006). Longitudinal trends in race/ethnic disparities in leading health indicators from adolescence to young adulthood. *Archives of Pediatrics and Adolescent Medicine, 160*, 74–81.

Harris, K. R., Graham, S., Brindle, M., & Sandmel, K. (2009). Metacognition and children's writing. In D. J. Hacker, J. Dunlosky, & A. Graesser (Eds.), *Handbook of metacognition in education.* New York: Elsevier.

Harris, L. (1975). *The myth and reality of aging in America.* Washington, DC: National Council on Aging.

Harris, P. L. (2006). Social cognition. In W. Damon & R. Lerner (Eds.), *Handbook of child psychology* (6th ed.). New York: Wiley.

Harrison, C. (2012). Aging: Telomerase gene therapy increases longevity. *Nature Reviews. Drug Discovery, 11*, 518.

Harrison, G. G., Hirschman, J. D., Owens, T. A., McNutt, S. W., & Sallack, L. E. (2014, in press). WIC infant and toddler feeding practices study: Protocol design and implementation. *American Journal of Clinical Nutrition.*

Harrison, K., & McGee, H. (2014). Advance care planning in practice. *BMJ Supportive and Palliative Care* (Suppl. 1), A87.

Hart, B., & Risley, T. R. (1995). *Meaningful differences in the everyday experience of young Americans.* Baltimore: Paul H. Brookes.

Hart, C. H., Yang, C., Charlesworth, R., & Burts, D. C. (2003, April). *Early childhood teachers' curriculum beliefs, classroom practices, and children's outcomes: What are the connections?* Paper presented at the biennial meeting of the Society for Research in Child Development, Tampa, FL.

Hart, C. N., Cairns, A., & Jelalian, E. (2011). Sleep and obesity in children and adolescents. *Pediatric Clinics of North America, 58*, 15–33.

Hart, D., & Karmel, M. P. (1996). Self-awareness and self-knowledge in humans, great apes, and monkeys. In A. Russori, K. Bard, & S. Parker (Eds.), *Reaching into thought.* New York: Cambridge University Press.

Hart, D., Matsuba, M. K., & Atkins, R. (2008). The moral and civic effects of learning to serve. In L. Nucci & D. Narvaez (Eds.), *Handbook of moral and character education.* Clinton, NJ: Psychology Press.

Hart, S., & Behrens, K. Y. (2013). Regulation of jealousy protest in the context of reunion following differential treatment. *Infancy 18*(6), 1076–1110.

Hart, S., & Carrington, H. (2002). Jealousy in 6-month-old infants: *Infancy, 3*, 395–402.

Harter, S. (2006). The self. In W. Damon & R. Lerner (Eds.), *Handbook of Child Psychology* (6th ed.). New York: Wiley.

Harter, S. (2012). *The construction of the self* (2nd ed.). New York: Wiley.

Harter, S. (2013). The development of self-esteem. In M. H. Kernis (Ed.), *Self-esteem issues and answers.* New York: Psychology Press.

Hartley, A. (2006). Changing role of the speed of processing construct in the cognitive psychology of human aging. In J. E. Birren & K. W. Schaie (Eds.), *Handbook of the psychology of aging* (6th ed.). San Diego: Academic Press.

Hartshorne, H., & May, M. S. (1928–1930). *Moral studies in the nature of character: Studies in the nature of character.* New York: Macmillan.

Hartup, W. W. (1983). The peer system. In P. H. Mussen (Ed.), *Handbook of child psychology* (4th ed., Vol. 4). New York: Wiley.

Hartup, W. W. (1996). The company they keep: Friendships and their developmental significance. *Child Development, 67*, 1–13.

Hartup, W. W. (2009). Critical issues and theoretical viewpoints. In K. H. Rubin, W. M. Bukowski, & B. Laursen (Eds.), *Handbook of peer interactions, relationships, and groups.* New York: Guilford.

Hasher, L. (2003, February 28). Commentary in "The wisdom of the wizened." *Science, 299*, 1300–1302.

Hasher, L., Chung, C., May, C. P., & Foong, N. (2001). Age, time of testing, and proactive interference. *Canadian Journal of Experimental Psychology, 56*, 200–207.

Hashim, H. A., Freddy, G., & Rosmatunisah, A. (2012). Relationships between negative affect and academic achievement among secondary school students: The mediating effects of habituated exercise. *Journal of Physical Activity and Health, 9*, 1012–1019.

Haslam, A., & others (2014). Vitamin D status is associated with grip strength in centenarians. *Journal of Nutrition in Gerontology and Geriatrics, 33*, 35–46.

Hastings, P. D., Utendale, W. T., & Sullivan, C. (2007). The socialization of prosocial development. In J. E. Grusec & P. D. Hastings (Eds.), *Handbook of socialization.* New York: Guilford.

Hatzfeld, J. J., Laveist, T. A., & Gaston-Johansson, F. G. (2012). Racial/ethnic disparities in the prevalence of selected chronic diseases among U.S. Air Force members, 2008. *Preventing Chronic Disease, 9*, E112.

Hauck, F. R., Signore, C., Fein, S. B., & Raju, T. N. (2008). Infant sleeping arrangements and practices during the first year of life. *Pediatrics, 122*(Suppl. 2), S113–S120.

Hauck, F. R., & others (2011). Breastfeeding and reduced risk of sudden infant death syndrome: A meta-analysis. *Pediatrics, 128*, 103–110.

Haugrud, N., Crossley, M., & Vrbancic, M. (2011). Clustering and switching strategies during verbal fluency performance differentiate Alzheimer's disease and healthy aging. *Journal of the International Alzheimer's Society, 17*, 1153–1157.

Hawkes, C. (2006). Olfaction in neurogenerative disorder. *Advances in Otorhinolaryngology, 63*, 133–151.

Hawkins, J. A., & Berndt, T. J. (1985, April). *Adjustment following the transition to junior high school.* Paper presented at the biennial meeting of the Society for Research in Child Development, Toronto.

Hawkley, L. C., & Cacioppo, J. T. (2012). Social connection and relationships in successful aging. In J. M. Rippe (Ed.), *Encyclopedia of lifestyle medicine and health.* Thousand Oaks, CA: Sage.

Hay, P. (2013). A systematic review of evidence for psychological treatments in eating disorders: 2005–2012. *International Journal of Eating Disorders, 46*, 462–469.

Hayatbakhsh, R., & others (2013). Early childhood predictors of early onset of smoking: A birth prospective study. *Addictive Behaviors, 38*, 2513–2519.

Hayden, K. M., & others (2014, in press). Pre-clinical phenotypes for Alzheimer disease: A latent profile approach. *American Journal of Geriatric Psychiatry.*

Haydon, A., & Halpern, G. T. (2010). Older romantic partners and depressive symptoms during adolescence. *Journal of Youth and Adolescence, 39*, 1240–1251.

Haydon, A. A., Herring, A. H., Prinstein, M. J., & Halpern, C. T. (2012). Beyond age at first sex: Patterns of emerging sexual behavior in adolescence and young adulthood. *Journal of Adolescent Health, 50*, 456–463.

Hayes, J. R., & Berninger, V. (2013). Cognitive processes in writing: A framework. In B. Arte, J. Dockrell, & V. Berninger (Eds.), *Writing development and instruction in children with hearing, speech, and language disorders.* New York: Oxford University Press.

Hayflick, L. (1977). The cellular basis for biological aging. In C. E. Finch & L. Hayflick (Eds.), *Handbook of the biology of aging.* New York: Van Nostrand.

Hayslip, B. (1996). Hospice. In J. E. Birren (Ed.), *Encyclopedia of gerontology* (Vol. 1). San Diego: Academic Press.

Hayslip, B., & Hansson, R. (2003). Death awareness and adjustment across the life span. In C. D. Bryant (Ed.), *Handbook of death and dying.* Thousand Oaks, CA: Sage.

Hayslip, B., & Hansson, R. O. (2007). Hospice. In J. E. Birren (Ed.), *Encyclopedia of gerontology* (2nd ed.). San Diego: Academic Press.

Hayward, R. D., & Krause, N. (2013a). Changes in church-based social support relationships during older adulthood. *Journals of Gerontology B: Psychological Sciences and Social Sciences, 68*, 85–96.

Hayward, R. D., & Krause, N. (2013b). Patterns of change in religious service attendance across the life course: Evidence from a 34-year longitudinal study. *Social Science Research, 42*, 1480–1489.

Hazan, C., & Shaver, P. R. (1987). Romantic love conceptualized as an attachment process. *Journal of Personality and Social Psychology, 52*, 522–524.

He, K., & others (2014, in press). ITIH family genes confer risk to schizophrenia and major depressive disorder in the Han Chinese population. *Progress in neuro-psychopharmacology and biological psychiatry.*

He, N., Wang, Z., Wang, Y., Shen, H., & Yin, M. (2013). ZY-1, a novel nicotinic analog, promotes proliferation and migration of adult hippocampal neural stem/progenitor cells. *Cellular and Molecular Neurobiology, 33*, 1149–1157.

Healey, M. K., & Hasher, L. (2009). Limitations to the deficit attenuation hypothesis: Aging and decision making. *Journal of Consumer Psychology, 19*, 17–22.

Heaney, J. L. J., Carroll, D., & Phillips, A. C. (2014). Physical activity, life events stress, cortisol, and DHEA in older adults: Preliminary findings that physical activity may buffer against the negative effects of stress. *Journal of Aging and Physical Activity.*

Heath, V. (2014, in press). Obesity: Genes and a hearty appetite conspire to increase childhood obesity risk. *Nature Reviews: Endocrinology.*

Hebl, M. R., & Avery, D. R. (2013). Diversity in organizations. In I. B. Weiner & others (Eds.), *Handbook of psychology* (2nd ed., Vol. 12). New York: Wiley.

Hefferman, M. E., & Fraley, R. C. (2014). How early experiences shape attraction, partner preferences, and attachment dynamics. In V. Zayas & C. Hazan (Eds.), *Bases of adult attachment.* New York: Springer.

Hegaard, H. K., & others (2008). Leisure time physical activity is associated with a reduced risk of preterm delivery. *American Journal of Obstetrics and Gynecology, 198*, e1–e5.

Heiman, G. W. (2014). *Basic statistics for the behavioral sciences* (7th ed.). Boston: Cengage.

Heiman, G. W. (2015, in press). *Behavioral sciences STAT* (2nd ed.). Boston: Cengage.

Heimann, M., & others (2006). Exploring the relation between memory, gestural communication, and the emergence of language in infancy: A longitudinal study. *Infant and Child Development, 15,* 233–249.

Heine, C., Browning, C., Cowlishaw, S., & Kendig, H. (2013). Trajectories of older adults' hearing difficulties: Examining the influence of health behaviors and social activity over ten years. *Geriatrics and Gerontology International, 13,* 911–918.

Hek, K., & others (2013). A genome-wide association study of depressive symptoms. *Biological Psychiatry, 73*(7), 667–678.

Helgeson, V. S. (2012). *Psychology of gender* (4th ed.). Upper Saddle River, NJ: Pearson.

Helman, C. (2008). Inside T. Boone Pickens' brain. *Forbes.* Retrieved June 15, 2008, from http://www.forbes.com/billionaires/forbes/2008/0630/076.html

Helman, R., Copeland, C., & VanDerhei, J. (2012). The 2012 Retirement Confidence Survey: Job insecurity, debt weigh on retirement confidence, savings. *EBRI Issue Brief, 369,* 5–32.

Helmuth, L. (2003). The wisdom of the wizened. *Science, 299,* 1300–1302.

Helson, R. (1997, August). *Personality change: When is it adult development?* Paper presented at the meeting of the American Psychological Association, Chicago.

Helson, R., & Wink, P. (1992). Personality change in women from the early 40s to early 50s. *Psychology and Aging, 7,* 46–55.

Helwig, C. C., & Turiel, E. (2011). Children's social and moral reasoning. In P. K. Smith & C. H. Hart (Eds.), *Wiley-Blackwell handbook of childhood social development* (2nd ed.). New York: Wiley.

Henchoz, Y., & others (2014, in press). Health impact of sport and exercise in emerging adult men: A prospective study. *Quality of Life Research.*

Henderson, J., & others (2014). Laboring women who used a birthing pool in obstetric units in Italy: Prospective observational study. *BMC Pregnancy and Childbirth, 14*(1), 17.

Henderson, V. W. (2011). Gonadal hormones and cognitive aging: A midlife perspective. *Women's Health, 7,* 81–93.

Hendricks-Munoz, K. D., & others (2013). Maternal and neonatal nurse perceived value of kangaroo mother care and maternal care partnership in the neonatal intensive care unit. *American Journal of Perinatology, 30,* 875–880.

Hendrie, G., Sohonopal, G., Lange, K., & Golley, R. (2013). Change in the family food environment is associated with positive dietary change in children. *International Journal of Behavioral Nutrition and Physical Activity, 10,* 4.

Henggeler, S. W., & Sheidow, L. J. (2012). Empirically supported family-based treatments for conduct disorder and delinquency in adolescents. *Journal of Marital and Family Therapy, 38,* 30–58.

Hennessey, B. A. (2011). Intrinsic motivation and creativity: Have we come full circle? In R. A. Beghetto & J. C. Kaufman (Eds.), *Nurturing creativity in the classroom.* New York: Cambridge University Press.

Henninger, D. E., Madden, D. J., & Huettel, S. A. (2010). Processing speed and memory mediate age-related differences in decision making. *Psychology and Aging, 25,* 262–270.

Henninger, M. L. (2013). *Teaching young children* (5th ed.). Upper Saddle River, NJ: Pearson.

Henretta, J. C. (2010). Lifetime marital history and mortality after age 50. *Journal of Aging and Health, 22*(8), 1198–1212.

Henriksen, T. B., & others (2004). Alcohol consumption at the time of conception and spontaneous abortion. *American Journal of Epidemiology, 160,* 661–667.

Hensley, B., & others (2012). Live events and personality predicting loneliness among centenarians: Findings from the Georgia Centenarian Study. *Journal of Psychology, 146,* 173–188.

Herberman Mash, H. B., Fullerton, C. S., & Ursano, R. J. (2013). Complicated grief and bereavement in young adults following close friend and sibling loss. *Depression and Anxiety, 30,* 1202–1210.

Herbers, J. E., & others (2011). Direct and indirect effects of parenting on academic functioning of young homeless children. *Early Education and Development, 22,* 77–104.

Herbers, J. E., & others (2014, in press). Trauma, adversity, and parent-child relationships among young children experiencing homelessness. *Journal of Abnormal Child Psychology.*

Herd, P., Robert, S. A., & House, J. S. (2011). Health disparities among older adults: Life course influences and policy solutions. In R. H. Binstock & L. K. George (Eds.), *Handbook of aging and the social sciences* (7th ed.). New York: Elsevier.

Herdt, G., & Polen-Petit, N. (2014). *Human sexuality.* New York: McGraw-Hill.

Herek, G. M. (2009). Hate crimes and stigma-related experiences among sexual minority adults in the United States: Prevalence estimates from a national probability sample. *Journal of Interpersonal Violence, 24,* 54–74.

Herman-Giddens, M. E. (2007). The decline in the age of menarche in the United States: Should we be concerned? *Journal of Adolescent Health, 40,* 201–203.

Hernandez, D. C., & Pressler, E. (2014, in press). Accumulation of childhood poverty on young adult overweight or obese status: Race/ethnicity and gender disparities. *Journal of Epidemiology and Community Health.*

Hernandez-Reif, M., Diego, M., & Field, T. (2007). Preterm infants show reduced stress behaviors and activity after 5 days of massage therapy. *Infant Behavior and Development, 30,* 557–561.

Heron, M. (2013, December 20). Deaths: Leading causes for 2010. *National Vital Statistics Reports, 62*(6), 1–96.

Herrera, S. G., & Murry, K. G. (2015, in press). Mastering ESL/EFL methods (3rd ed.). Upper Saddle River, NJ: Pearson.

Herting, M. M., Colby, J. B., Sowell, E. R., & Nagel, B. J. (2014). White matter connectivity and aerobic fitness in male adolescents. *Developmental Cognitive Neuroscience, 7,* 65–75.

Hertzog, C., Kramer, A. F., Wilson, R. S., & Lindenberger, U. (2009). Enrichment effects on adult cognitive development. *Psychological Perspectives in the Public Interest, 9,* 1–65.

Hetherington, E. M. (1993). An overview of the Virginia Longitudinal Study of Divorce and Remarriage with a focus on early adolescence. *Journal of Family Psychology, 7.* 39–56.

Hetherington, E. M. (2000). Divorce. In A. Kazdin (Ed.), *Encyclopedia of psychology.* Washington, DC, & New York: American Psychological Association and Oxford University Press.

Hetherington, E. M. (2006). The influence of conflict, marital problem solving, and parenting on children's adjustment in nondivorced, divorced, and remarried families. In A. Clarke-Stewart & J. Dunn (Eds.), *Families count.* New York: Oxford University Press.

Hetherington, E. M., & Kelly, J. (2002). *For better or for worse: Divorce reconsidered.* New York: Norton.

Hetherington, E. M., & Stanley-Hagan, M. (2002). Parenting in divorced and remarried families. In M. H. Bornstein (Ed.), *Handbook of parenting* (2nd ed., Vol. 3). Mahwah, NJ: Erlbaum.

Hewitt, J., & others (2014). Does progressive resistance and balance exercise reduce falls in residential aged care? Randomized controlled trial protocol for the SUNBEAM program. *Clinical Interventions in Aging, 9,* 369–376.

Hewlett, B. S. (1991). *Intimate fathers: The nature and context of Aka Pygmy.* Ann Arbor, MI: University of Michigan Press.

Hewlett, B. S. (2000). Culture, history, and sex: Anthropological perspectives on father involvement. *Marriage and Family Review, 29,* 324–340.

Hewlett, B. S., & MacFarlan, S. J. (2010). Fathers, roles in hunter-gatherer and other small-scale cultures. In M. E. Lamb (Ed.) *The role of the father in child development* (5th ed.). New York: Wiley.

Heyman, G. D., Fu, G., & Lee, K. (2013). Selective skepticism: American and Chinese children's reasoning about evaluative feedback. *Developmental Psychology, 49,* 543–553.

Heyman, G. D., & Legare, C. H. (2005). Children's evaluation of sources of information about traits. *Developmental Psychology, 41,* 636–647.

Higginbotham, B., & others (2012). Stepfathers and stepfamily education. *Journal of Divorce & Remarriage, 53,* 76–90.

High/Scope Resource (2005, Spring). The High/Scope Perry Preschool Study and the man who began it. *High/Scope Resource 9.* Ypsilanti, MI: High/Scope Press.

Highfield, R. (2008, April 30). *Harvard's baby brain research lab.* Retrieved January 24, 2009, from www.telegraph.co.uk/scienceandtechnology/science/sciencenews/3341166/Harvards-baby-brain-research-lab.html

Highhouse, S., & Schmitt, N. (2013). A snapshot in time: Industrial-organizational psychology today. In I. B. Weiner & others (Eds.), *Handbook of psychology* (2nd ed., Vol. 12). New York: Wiley.

Higo, M., & Williamson, J. B. (2009). Retirement. In D. Carr (Ed.), *Encyclopedia of the life course and human development.* Boston: Gale Cengage.

Hill, C. R., & Stafford, E. P. (1980). Parental care of children: Time diary estimate of quantity, predictability, and variety. *Journal of Human Resources, 15,* 219–239.

Hill, P. L., & others (2011). Conscientiousness and longevity: An examination of possible mediators. *Health Psychology, 30,* 536–541.

Hill, P. L., & others (2014). Perceived social support predicts increased conscientiousness during older adulthood. *Journals of Gerontology B: Psychological Sciences and Social Sciences.*

Hill, P. L., Allemand, M., & Roberts, B. W. (2014, in press). Stability of behavior: Implications for research. In R. Zinbarg (Ed.), *Encyclopedia of clinical psychology.* New York: Springer.

Hill, P. L., Nickel, L. B., & Roberts, B. W. (2014, in press). Are you in a healthy relationship? Linking conscientiousness to health via implementing and immunizing behaviors. *Journal of Personality.*

Hill, P. L., Turiano, N. A., Mroczek, D. K., & Roberts, B. W. (2012). Examining concurrent and longitudinal relations between personality traits and social well-being in adulthood. *Social Psychological and Personality Science, 3*(6), 698–705.

Hill, T. D., Burdette, A. M., Angel, J. L., & Angel, R. J. (2006). Religious attendance and cognitive functioning among older Mexican Americans. *Journals of Gerontology B: Psychological Sciences and Social Sciences, 61,* P3–P9.

Hillemeier, M. M., Morgan, P. L., Farkas, G., & Maczuga, S. A. (2013). Quality disparities in child care for at-risk children: Comparing Head Start and non-Head Start settings. *Journal of Maternal and Child Health, 17*(1), 180–188.

Hilliard, L. J., & others (2014, in press). Beyond the deficit model: Bullying and trajectories of character virtues in adolescence. *Journal of Youth and Adolescence.*

Himes, C. L. (2009). Age structure. In D. Carr (Ed.), *Encyclopedia of the life course and human development.* Boston: Gale Cengage.

Hinderliter, A. L., & others (2014, in press). The long-term effects of lifestyle change on blood pressure: One-year follow-up of the ENCORE study. *American Journal of Hypertension.*

Hindman, A. H., Skibbek, L. E., Miller, A., & Zimmerman, M. (2010). Ecological contexts and early learning: Contributions of child, family, and classroom factors during Head Start to literacy and mathematics growth through first grade. *Early Childhood Research Quarterly, 25,* 235–250.

Hines, M. (2013). Sex and sex differences. In P. D. Zelazo (Ed.), *Handbook of developmental psychology.* New York: Oxford University Press.

Hines, M., Lyseng-Williamson, K. A., & Deeks, E. D. (2013). 17 a-hydroxyprogesterone caproate (makena): A guide to its use in the prevention of preterm birth. *Clinical Drug Investigation, 33,* 223–227.

Hinkle, J. S., Tuckman, B. W., & Sampson, J. P. (1993). The psychology, physiology, and the creativity of middle school aerobic exercisers. *Elementary School Guidance & Counseling, 28,* 133–145.

Hinze, S. W., Lin, J., & Andersson, T. E. (2012). Can we capture the intersections? Older black women, education, and health. *Women's Health Issues, 22,* e91–e98.

Hirsch, B. J., & Rapkin, B. D. (1987). The transition to junior high school: A longitudinal study of self-esteem, psychological symptomatology, school life, and social support. *Child Development, 58,* 1235–1243.

Hirsch, J. K., & Sirois, F. M. (2014, in press). Hope and fatigue in chronic illness: The role of perceived stress. *Journal of Health Psychology.*

Hirsh-Pasek, K., & Golinkoff, R. M. (2014, in press). Early language and literacy: Six principles. In S. Gilford (Ed.), *Head Start teacher's guide.* New York: Teacher's College Press.

Hirsh-Pasek, K., Golinkoff, R. M., Singer, D., & Berk, L. (2009). *A mandate for playful learning in preschool: Presenting the evidence.* New York: Oxford University Press.

Hita-Yanez, E., Atienza, M., & Cantero, J. L. (2013). Polysomnographic and subjective sleep markers of mild cognitive impairment. *Sleep, 36,* 1327–1334.

Ho, C. (2013). Optimal duration of exclusive breastfeeding: Summaries of nursing care-related systematic reviews from the Cochrane Library. *International Journal of Evidence-Based Healthcare, 11,* 140–141.

Ho, G. W. (2014, in press). Acculturation and its implications on parenting for Chinese immigrants: A systematic review. *Journal of Transcultural Nursing.*

Ho, M., & others (2013). Impact of dietary and exercise interventions on weight change and metabolic outcomes in obese children and adolescents: A systematic review and meta-analysis of randomized trials. *JAMA Pediatrics, 167,* 759–768.

Hoare, E., & others (2014). Associations between obesogenic risk factors and depression among adolescents: A systematic review. *Obesity Reviews, 15,* 40–51.

Hochberg, C., & others (2012). Association of vision loss in glaucoma and age-related macular degeneration with IADL disability. *Investigative Ophthalmology and Visual Science, 53,* 3201–3206.

Hock, R. R. (2012). *Human sexuality* (3rd ed.). Upper Saddle River, NJ: Pearson.

Hodapp, R. M., Griffin, M. M., Burke, M., & Fisher, M. H. (2011). Intellectual disabilities. In R. J. Sternberg & S. B. Kaufman (Eds.), *Cambridge handbook of intelligence.* New York: Cambridge University Press.

Hodge, A. M., & others (2014). Dietary patterns as predictors of successful aging. *Journal of Nutrition, Health, and Aging, 18,* 221–227.

Hodis, H. N., Collins, P., Mack, W. J., & Schierbeck, L. L. (2012). The timing hypothesis for coronary heart disease prevention with hormone therapy: Past, present, and future in perspective. *Climacteric, 15,* 217–228.

Hodis, H. N., & Mack, W. J. (2014, in press). Hormone replacement therapy and the association with coronary heart disease and overall mortality: Clinical application of the timing hypothesis. *Journal of Steroid Biochemistry and Molecular Biology.*

Hoefnagels, M. (2015, in press). *Biology* (3rd ed.). New York: McGraw-Hill.

Hoelter, L. (2009). Divorce and separation. In D. Carr (Ed.), *Encyclopedia of the life course and human development.* Boston: Gale Cengage.

Hoeve, M., & others (2012). A meta-analysis of attachment to parents and delinquency. *Journal of Abnormal Child and Adolescent Psychology, 40*(5), 771–785.

Hofer, A., & others (2007). Sex differences in brain activation patterns during processing of positively and negatively balanced emotional stimuli. *Psychological Medicine, 37,* 109–119.

Hofer, S. M., Rast, P., & Piccinin, A. M. (2012). Methodological issues in research on adult development and aging. In S. K. Whitbourne & M. J. Sliwinski (Eds.), *Wiley-Blackwell handbook of adult development and aging.* New York: Wiley.

Hoff, E. (2014). *Language development* (5th ed.). Boston: Cengage.

Hoff, E., & Place, S. (2013). Bilingual language learners. In S. L. Odom, E. Pungello, & N. Gardner-Neblett (Eds.), *Re-visioning the beginning: Developmental and health science contributions to infant/toddler programs for children and families living in poverty.* New York: Guilford.

Hoff, E., Laursen, B., & Tardif, T. (2002). Socioeconomic status and parenting. In M. H. Bornstein (Ed.), *Handbook of parenting* (2nd ed.). Mahwah, NJ: Erlbaum.

Hofferth, S. L., & Reid, L. (2002). Early childbearing and children's achievement behavior over time. *Perspectives on Sexual and Reproductive Health, 34,* 41–49.

Hoffman, E., & Ewen, D. (2007). Supporting families, nurturing young children. *CLASP Policy Brief No. 9,* 1–11.

Hoffmeyer, K., & others (2012). Wnt/B-catenin signaling regulates telomerase in stem cells and cancer cells. *Science, 336,* 1549–1554.

Hogan, C. (2014). Socioeconomic factors affecting infant sleep-related deaths in St. Louis. *Public Health Nursing, 31,* 10–18.

Hogan, C. L., Mata, J., & Carstensen, L. L. (2013). Exercise holds immediate benefits for affect and cognition in younger and older adults. *Psychology and Aging, 28,* 587–594.

Hogan, M. J., & others (2009). Optimal time-of-day and consolidation of learning in younger and older adults. *Experimental Aging Research, 28,* 107–128.

Hogerbrugge, M. J., & Komter, A. E. (2012). Solidarity and ambivalence: Comparing two perspectives on intergenerational relations using longitudinal panel data. *Journals of Gerontology B: Psychological Sciences and Social Sciences, 67,* 372–383.

Holahan, C. J., & others (2012). Wine consumption and 20-year mortality among late-life moderate drinkers. *Journal of Studies in Alcohol and Drugs, 73,* 80–88.

Holden, G. W., Vittrup, B., & Rosen, L. H. (2011). Families, parenting, and discipline. In M. K. Underwood & L. H. Rosen (Eds.), *Social development.* New York: Guilford.

Holder, M. K., & Blaustein, J. D. (2014). Puberty and adolescence as a time of vulnerability to stressors that alter neurobehavioral processes. *Frontiers in Neuroscience, 35,* 89–110.

Holland, J. C., & others (2014, in press). Modifications in parent feeding practices and diet during family-based behavioral treatment improve child BMI. *Obesity.*

Holland, J. M., & others (2014). The unique impact of late-life bereavement and prolonged grief on diurnal cortisol. *Journals of Gerontology B: Psychological Sciences and Social Sciences, 69,* 4–11.

Hollister, M. (2011). Employment stability in the U.S. labor market: Rhetoric versus reality. *Annual Review of Sociology* (Vol. 37). Palo Alto, CA: Annual Reviews.

Holloway, R. G., & others (2014, in press). Palliative and end-of-life care in stroke: A statement for healthcare professionals from the American Heart Association/American Stroke Association. *Stroke.*

Holmes, L. B. (2011). Human teratogens: Update 2010. *Birth Defects Research A: Clinical and Molecular Teratology, 91,* 1–7.

Holmes, L. B., & Westgate, M. N. (2011). Inclusion and exclusion criteria for malformations in newborn infants exposed to potential teratogens. *Birth Defects Research, Part A: Clinical and Molecular Teratology, 91,* 807–812.

Holmes, R. M., Little, K. C., & Welsh, D. (2009). Dating and romantic relationships, adulthood. In D. Carr (Ed.), *Encyclopoedia of the life course and human development.* Boston: Gale Cengage.

Holmes, T. H., & Rahe, R. H. (1967). The social readjustment rating scale. *Journal of Psychosomatic Research, 11,* 213–218.

Holsen, I., Carlson Jones, D., & Skogbrott Birkeland, M. (2012). Body image satisfaction among Norwegian adolescents and young adults: A longitudinal study of the influence of interpersonal relationships and BMI. *Body Image, 9,* 201–208.

Holtz, P., & Appel, M. (2011). Internet use and video gaming predict problem behavior in early adolescence. *Journal of Adolescence, 17,* 37–44.

Honig, L. S., & Boyd, C. D. (2013). Treatment for Alzheimer's disease: Current management and experimental therapeutics. *Current Translational Geriatrics and Experimental Gerontology Reports, 2,* 174–181.

Hood, B. M. (1995). Gravity rules for 2- to 4-year-olds? *Cognitive Development, 10,* 577–598.

Hoogendam, Y. Y., & others (2014). *Patterns of cognitive functioning in aging: The Rotterdam Study, 29,* 133–140.

Hooper, S. R., & others (2008). Executive functions in young males with fragile X syndrome in comparison to mental age-matched controls: baseline findings from a longitudinal study. *Neuropsychology, 22,* 36–47.

Hoover, K. W., Tao, G., Berman, S., & Kent, C. K. (2010). Utilization of health services in physician offices and outpatient clinics by adolescents and young women in the United States: Implications for improving access to reproductive services. *Journal of Adolescent Health, 46,* 324–330.

Hooyman, N. R., & Kiyak, H. A. (2011). *Social gerontology* (9th ed.). Upper Saddle River, NJ: Pearson.

Hooyman, N., Kiyak, H. A., & Kawamoto, K. (2015, in press). *Aging matters.* Upper Saddle River, NJ: Pearson.

Hopkins, B. (1991). Facilitating early motor development: An intracultural study of West Indian mothers and their infants living in Britain. In J. K. Nugent, B. M. Lester, & T. B. Brazelton (Eds.), *The cultural context of infancy, Vol. 2: Multicultural and interdisciplinary approaches to parent relations.*

Hopkins, B., & Westra, T. (1990). Motor development, maternal expectations, and the role of handling. *Infant Behavior and Development, 13,* 117–122.

Hoppmann, C. A., Gerstorf, D., Smith, J., & Klumb, P. L. (2007). Linking possible selves and behavior: Do domain-specific hopes and fears translate into daily activities in very old age? *Journals of Gerontology B: Psychological Sciences and Social Sciences, 62,* P104–P111.

Horn, J. L., & Donaldson, G. (1980). Cognitive development II: Adulthood development of human abilities. In O. G. Brim & J. Kagan (Eds.), *Constancy and change in human development.* Cambridge, MA: Harvard University Press.

Horne, R. S., Franco, P., Adamson, T. M., Groswasser, J., & Kahn, A. (2002). Effects of body position on sleep and arousal characteristics in infants. *Early Human Development, 69,* 25–33.

Horner, G. (2014). Child neglect: Assessment and intervention. *Journal of Pediatric Health Care, 28,* 186–192.

Horowitz, E. K. (2013). *Becoming a second language teacher* (2nd ed.). Boston: Allyn & Bacon.

Hoshino, O. (2013). Ambient GABA responsible for age-related changes in multistable perception. *Neural Computation, 25,* 1164–1190.

Hospital for Sick Children, & others (2010). *The Hospital for Sick Children's handbook of pediatrics* (11th ed.). London: Elsevier.

Hostinar, C., Cicchetti, D., & Rogosch, F. A. (2014, in press). Oxytocin receptor gene (OXTR) polymorphism, perceived social support, and psychological symptoms in maltreated adolescents. *Development and Psychopathology.*

Hostinar, C. E., & Gunnar, M. R. (2013). The developmental psychobiology of stress and emotion in childhood. In I. B. Weiner & others (Eds.), *Handbook of psychology* (2nd ed., Vol. 6). New York: Wiley.

Hottensen, D. (2013). Bereavement: Caring for families and friends after a patient dies. *Omega, 67,* 121–126.

Houde, O., & others (2011). Functional magnetic resonance imaging study of Piaget's conservation-of-number task in preschool and school-age children: A neo-Piagetian approach. *Journal of Experimental Child Psychology, 110*(3), 332–346.

Houston, D., Golinkoff, R., Ma, W., & Hirsh-Pasek, I. (2014, in press). Word learning in infant- and adult-directed speech. *Language Learning and Development.*

Howard, A., & Rogers, A. N. (2014, in press). Role of translation factor 4G in lifespan regulation and age-related health. *Aging Research Reviews.*

Howe, G. W., Homberger, A. P., Weihs, K., Moreno, F., & Neiderhiser, J. M. (2012). Higher-order structure in the trajectories of depression and anxiety following sudden involuntary unemployment. *Journal of Abnormal Psychology, 121,* 325–338.

Howell, D. C. (2014). *Fundamental statistics for the behavioral sciences* (8th ed.). Boston: Cengage.

Howes, C. (2009). Friendship in early childhood. In K. H. Rubin, W. M. Bukowski, & B. Laursen (Eds.), *Handbook of peer interactions, relationships, and groups.* New York: Guilford.

Hoyer, W. J., & Roodin, P. A. (2009). *Adult development and aging* (6th ed.). New York: McGraw-Hill.

Hoyert, D. L., & Xu, J. X. (2012). Deaths: Preliminary data for 2011. *National Vital Statistics Reports, 61*(6), 1–52.

Hoyt, M. A., & Stanton, A. (2012). Adjustment to chronic illness. In A. Baum, T. A. Revenson, & J. Singer (Eds.), *Handbook of health psychology* (2nd ed.). New York: Psychology Press.

HSBC Insurance (2007). *The future of retirement: The new old age—global report.* London: HSBC.

Hsu, J. L., & others. (2008). Gender differences and age-related white matter changes of the human brain: A diffusion tensor imaging study. *NeuroImage, 39,* 566–577.

Hsu, W. L., Chen, C. Y., Tsao, J. Y., & Yang, R. S. (2014, in press). Balance control in elderly people with osteoporosis. *Journal of the Formosa Medical Association.*

Hu, J., & others (2014, in press). Tor-Sch9 deficiency catabolism of the ketone body-like acetic acid to promote trehalose accumulation and longevity. *Aging Cell.*

Hu, J. K., Wang, X., & Wang, P. (2014). Testing gene-gene interactions in genome-wide association studies. *Genetic Epidemiology, 38,* 123–134.

Huang, H. W., Meyer, A. M., & Federmeier, K. D. (2012). A "concrete view" of aging: Event-related potentials reveal age-related changes in basic integrated processes in language. *Neuropsychologia, 50,* 26–35.

Huang, J-H., DeJong, W., Towvim, L. G., & Schneider, S. K. (2009). Sociodemographic and psychobehavioral characteristics of U.S. college students who abstain from alcohol. *Journal of American College Health, 57,* 395–410.

Huang, K., & others (2014). MetaRef: A pan-genomic database for comparative and community microbial genomics. *Nucleic Acids Research, 42,* D618–D624.

Huang, P. M., Smock, P. J., Manning, W. D., & Bergstrom-Lynch, C. A. (2011). He says, she says: Gender and cohabitation. *Journal of Family Issues, 32,* 876–905.

Huang, Y., & Spelke, E. (2014, in press). Core knowledge and the emergence of symbols: The case of maps. *Journal of Cognition and Development.*

Huart, C., Rombaux, O. P., & Hummel, T. (2013). Plasticity of the human olfactory system: The olfactory bulb. *Molecules, 18,* 11586–11600.

Huebner, A. M., & Garrod, A. C. (1993). Moral reasoning among Tibetan monks: A study of Buddhist adolescents and young adults in Nepal. *Journal of Cross-Cultural Psychology, 24,* 167–185.

Huesmann, L. R., Dubow, E. F., Eron, L. D., & Boxer, P. (2006). Middle childhood family-contextual and personal factors as predictors of adult outcomes. In A. G. Huston & M. N. Ripke (Eds.), *Developmental contexts in middle childhood: Bridges to adolescence and adulthood.* New York: Cambridge University Press.

Huesmann, L. R., Moise-Titus, J., Podolski, C., & Eron, L. D. (2003). Longitudinal relations between children's exposure to TV violence and their aggressive and violent behavior in young adulthood: 1977–1992. *Developmental Psychology, 39,* 201–221.

Hugel, H., Gavin, C., Mitchell, C., & Edwards, D. (2014). Hospice at home services—the importance of integration and medical support. *BMJ Supportive and Palliative Care* (Suppl. 1), A90–A91.

Hughes, C., & Ensor, R. (2007). Executive function and theory of mind.: Predictive relations from ages 2 to 4. *Developmental Psychology, 43,* 1447–1459.

Hughes, C., & Ensor, R. (2009). How do families help or hinder the development of executive function? *New Directions in Child and Adolescent Psychiatry, 123,* 35–50.

Hughes, M. E., Waite, L. J., LaPierre, T. A., & Luo, Y. (2007). All in the family: The impact of caring for grandchildren on grandparents' health. *Journals of Gerontology B: Psychological Sciences and Social Sciences, 62,* S108–S119.

Hughes, S. M., & others (2009). Dendritic cell anergy results from endotoxemia in severe malnutrition. *Journal of Immunology, 183,* 2818–2826.

Huh, S. Y., Rifas-Shiman, S. L., Taveras, E. M., Oken, E., & Gillman, M. W. (2011). Timing of solid food introduction and risk of obesity in preschool children. *Pediatrics, 3,* e544–e551.

Hultsch, D. F., Hertzog, C., Small, B. J., & Dixon, R. A. (1999). Use it or lose it: Engaged lifestyle as a buffer of cognitive decline in aging? *Psychology and Aging, 14,* 245–263.

Hulur, G., Infuma, F. J., Ram, N., & Gerstorf, D. (2013). Cohorts based on decade of death: No evidence for secular trends favoring later cohorts in cognitive aging and terminal decline in the AHEAD study. *Psychology and Aging, 28,* 115–127.

Hummer, J. F., Napper, L. E., Ehret, P. E., & Labrie, J. W. (2013). Event-specific risk and ecological factors associated with prepartying among heavier drinking college students. *Addictive Behaviors, 38,* 1620–1628.

Hunt, S. R., Corazzini, K., & Anderson, R. A. (2014). Top nurse-management staffing and care quality in nursing homes. *Journal of Applied Gerontology, 33,* 51–74.

Hur, K., Liang, J., & Lin, S. Y. (2014). The role of secondhand smoke in allergic rhinitis: A systematic review. *International Forum of Allergy and Rhinology, 4,* 110–116.

Hurst, C. (2013). *Social inequality* (8th ed.). Upper Saddle River, NJ: Pearson.

Hurt, H., Brodsky, N. L., Roth, H., Malmud, F., & Giannetta, J. M. (2005). School performance of children with gestational cocaine exposure. *Neurotoxicology and Teratology, 27,* 203–211.

Hurt, T. R., Brody, G. H., McBride, V., Berkel, C., & Chen, Y. (2013). Elucidating parenting processes that influence alcohol use: A qualitative inquiry. *Journal of Adolescent Research, 28,* 3–30.

Hustedt, J. T., Friedman, A. H., & Barnett, W. S. (2012). Investments in early education: Resources at the federal and state levels. In R. C. Pianta (Ed.), *Handbook of early childhood education.* New York: Guilford.

Huston, A. C. (2012). How welfare and employment policies influence children's development. In V. Malholmes & R. King (Eds.), *Oxford handbook of poverty and child development.* New York: Oxford University Press.

Huston, A. C. (2014). Epilogue: The ecology of human development in the 21st century. In E. T. Gershoff, R. S. Mistry, & D. A. Crosby (Eds.), *Societal contexts of child development.* New York: Oxford University Press.

Huston, A. C., & Ripke, N. N. (2006). Experiences in middle and late childhood and children's development. In A. C. Huston & M. N. Ripke (Eds.), *Developmental contexts in middle childhood.* New York: Cambridge University Press.

Hutchinson, S. L., & Nimrod, G. (2012). Leisure as a resource for successful aging by older adults with chronic health conditions. *International Journal of Aging and Human Development, 74,* 41–65.

Hutson, J. R., & others (2013). Adverse placental effect of formic acid on hCG secretion is mitigated by folic acid. *Alcohol and Alcoholism, 48*(3), 283–287.

Huttenlocher, J., Haight, W., Bruk, A., Seltzer, M., & Lyons, T. (1991). Early vocabulary growth: Relation to language input and gender. *Developmental Psychology, 27,* 236–248.

Huttenlocher, P. R., & Dabholkar, A. S. (1997). Regional differences in synaptogenesis in human cerebral cortex. *Journal of Comparative Neurology, 37*(2), 167–178.

Huxhold, O., Miche, M., & Schuz, B. (2014, in press). Benefits of having friends in older ages: Differential effects of informal social activities on well-being in middle-aged and older adults. *Journals of Gerontology B: Psychological Sciences and Social Sciences.*

Hwang, A. C., & others (2014, in press). Predicting all-cause and cause-specific mortality by static and dynamic measurements of allostatic load: A 10-year population-based cohort study in Taiwan. *Journal of the American Medical Directors Association.*

Hybels, C. F., & Blazer, D. G. (2004). Epidemiology of the late-life mental disorders. *Clinical Geriatric Medicine, 19*, 663–696.

Hyde, D. C., & Spelke, E. S. (2012). Spatio-temporal dynamics of numerical processing: An ERP source localization study. *Human Brain Mapping, 33*, 2189–2203.

Hyde, J. S. (2014). Gender similarities and differences. *Annual Review of Psychology* (Vol. 66). Palo Alto, CA: Annual Reviews.

Hyde, J. S., & DeLamater, J. D. (2014). *Understanding human sexuality* (12th ed.). New York: McGraw-Hill.

Hyde, J. S., & Else-Quest, N. (2013). *Half the human experience* (8th ed.). Boston: Cengage.

Hyde, J. S., Lindberg, S. M., Linn, M. C., Ellis, A. B., & Williams, C. C. (2008). Gender similarities characterize math performance. *Science, 321*, 494–495.

Hyson, M. C., Copple, C., & Jones, J. (2006). Early childhood development and education. In W. Damon & R. Lerner (Eds.), *Handbook of child psychology* (6th ed.). New York: Wiley.

I

"I Have a Dream" Foundation (2013). *About us.* Retrieved August 22, 2013, from www.ihad.org

Ibrahim, R., & Eviatar, Z. (2012). The contribution of the two hemispheres to lexical decision in different languages. *Behavioral and Brain Functions, 8*, 3.

Ickovics, J. R., & others (2011). Effects of group prenatal care on psychosocial risk in pregnancy: Results from a randomized controlled trial. *Psychology and Health, 26*, 235–250.

Igarashi, H., Hooker, K., Coehlo, D. P., & Manoogian, M. M. (2013). "My nest is full": Intergenerational relationships at midlife. *Journal of Aging Studies, 27*, 102–112.

Impett, E. A., Schoolder, D., Tolman, L., Sorsoli, L., & Henson, J. M. (2008). Girls' relationship authenticity and self-esteem across adolescence, *Developmental Psychology, 44*, 722–733.

Insana, S. P., Williams, K. B., & Montgomery-Downs, H. E. (2013). Sleep disturbance and neurobehavioral performance among postpartum women. *Sleep, 36*, 73–81.

Insel, P. M., & Roth, W. T. (2014). *Connect core concepts in health* (13th ed.). New York: McGraw-Hill.

International Montessori Council (2006). Larry Page and Sergey Brin, founders of Google.com, credit their Montessori education for much of their success on prime-time television. Retrieved June 24, 2006, from http://www.Montessori.org/enews/Barbara_walters.html

Iolascon, G., & others (2013). Osteoporosis drugs in real-world clinical practice: An analysis of persistence. *Aging: Clinical and Experimental Research, 25*(1, Suppl.), S137–S141.

Iovannone, R. (2013). Teaching students with autism spectrum disorders. In B. G. Cook & M. G. Tankerslee (Ed.), *Research-based practices in special education.* Upper Saddle River, NJ: Pearson.

Ip, S., Chung, M., Raman, G., Trikaliinos, T. A., & Lau, J. (2009). A summary of the Agency for Healthcare Research and Quality's evidence report on breastfeeding in developed countries. *Breastfeeding Medicine, 4*(1, Suppl.), S17–S30.

Iqbal, M., & others (2012). Placental drug transporters and their role in fetal protection. *Placenta, 33*, 137–142.

Irish, C. (2011). Home health care: Helping to prevent and treat diabetes. *Caring, 30*, 28–32.

Irwin, C. E., Adams, S. H., Park, M. J., & Newacheck, P. W. (2009). Preventive care for adolescents: Few get visits and fewer get services. *Pediatrics, 123*, e365–e572.

Irwing, P., Booth, T., Nyborg, H., & Rushton, J. P. (2012). Are *g* and the general factor of personality (GFP) correlated? *Intelligence, 40*, 296–305.

Isaacs, B. (2012). *Understanding the Montessori approach: Early years education practice.* New York: Routledge.

Ishak, S., Franchak, J. M., & Adolph, K. E. (2014). Fear of height in infants. *Current Directions in Psychological Science, 23*, 60–66.

Isidori, A. M., & others (2014). A critical analysis of the role of testosterone in erectile function: From pathophysiology to treatment—a systematic analysis. *European Urology, 65*(1), 99–112.

Issel, L. M., & others (2011). A review of prenatal home-visiting effectiveness for improving birth outcomes. *Journal of Obstetrics, Gynecologic, and Neonatal Nursing, 40*, 157–165.

Ivanenko, A., & Larson, K. (2014, in press). Nighttime distractions: Fears, nightmares, and parasomnias. In A. R. Rolfson & H. E. Montgomery-Downs (Eds.), *Oxford handbook of infant, child, and adolescent sleep and behavior.* New York: Oxford University Press.

Iwasa, H., & others (2008). Personality and all-cause mortality among older adults dwelling in a Japanese community: A five-year population-based prospective cohort study. *American Journal of Geriatric Psychiatry, 16*, 399–405.

Iwata, S., & others (2012). Qualitative brain MRI at term and cognitive outcomes at 9 years after very preterm birth. *Pediatrics, 129*, e1138–1147.

Izard, C. E. (2009). Emotion theory and research: Highlights, unanswered questions, and emerging issues. *Annual Review of Psychology* (Vol. 60). Palo Alto, CA: Annual Reviews.

Izard, V., Dehaene-Lambertz, G., & Dehaene, S. (2008). Distinct cerebral pathways for object identity and number in human infants. *PLOS Biology, 6*, e11.

J

Jack, B. A., & others (2013). Supporting home care for the dying: An evaluation of healthcare professionals' perspectives of individually tailored hospice at home service. *Journal of Clinical Nursing, 22*, 2278–2286.

Jackson, A., Purkis, J., Burnham, E., Hundt, G. L., & Blaxter, L. (2010). Views of relatives, careers, and staff on end-of-life care pathways. *Emergency Nurse, 17*, 22–26.

Jackson, C. A., Henderson, M., Frank, J. W., & Haw, S. J. (2012). An overview of prevention of multiple risk behavior in adolescence and young adulthood. *Journal of Public Health, 34*(Suppl. 1), S31–S40.

Jackson, J. J., & others (2009). Not all conscientiousness scales change alike: A multimethod, multisample study of age differences in the facets of conscientiousness. *Journal of Personality and Social Psychology, 96*, 446–459.

Jackson, J. S., Govia, I. O., & Sellers, S. L. (2011). Racial and ethnic influences over the life course. In R. H. Binstock & L. K. George (Eds.), *Handbook of aging and the social sciences* (7th ed.). New York: Elsevier.

Jackson, L. A., & others (2012). The digital divide. In J. R. Levesque (Ed.), *Encyclopedia of adolescence.* New York: Springer.

Jackson, S. L. (2015, in press). *Research methods* (3rd ed.). Boston: Cengage.

Jacob, J. I. (2009). The socioemotional effects of non-maternal childcare on children in the USA: Critical review of recent studies. *Early Child Development and Care, 179*, 559–570.

Jacob, R., & others (2014). Daily hassles' role in health seeking behavior among low-income populations. *American Journal of Health Behavior, 38*, 297–306.

Jacobs, J. M., Hammerman-Rozenberg, R., Cohen, A., & Stressman, J. (2008). Reading daily predicts reduced mortality among men from a cohort of community dwelling 70-year-olds. *Journals of Gerontology B: Psychological Sciences and Social Sciences, 63*, S73–S80.

Jacobs-Lawson, J. M., Hershey, D. A., & Neukam, K. A. (2005). Gender differences in factors that influence time spent planning for retirement. *Journal of Women and Aging, 16*, 55–69.

Jaeggi, S. M., Berman, M. G., & Jonides, J. (2009). Training attentional processes. *Trends in Cognitive Science, 37*, 644–654.

Jaffee, S., & Hyde, J. S. (2000). Gender differences in moral orientation: A meta-analysis. *Psychological Bulletin, 126*, 703–726.

Jaffee, S. R., & others (2013). Safe, stable, nurturing relationships break the intergenerational cycle of abuse: A nationally representative cohort of children in the United Kingdom. *Journal of Adolescent Health, 53*(4, Suppl.), S4–S10.

Jahanfar, S., & Sharifah, H. (2013). Effects of restricted caffeine intake by mother on fetal, neonatal, and pregnancy outcome. *Cochrane Database of Systematic Reviews, 2*: CD006965.

Jalles, J. T., & Andresen, M. A. (2014, in press). Suicide and unemployment: A panel analysis of Canadian provinces. *Archives of Suicide Research.*

Jalongo, M. R. (2014). *Early childhood language arts* (6th ed.). Upper Saddle River, NJ: Pearson.

James, W. (1890/1950). *The principles of psychology.* New York: Dover.

Jansen, J., de Weerth, C., & Riksen-Walraven, J. M. (2008). Breastfeeding and the mother-infant relationship—A review. *Developmental Review, 28*, 503–521.

Janssen, I., & others (2005). Comparison of overweight and obesity prevalence in school-aged youth from 34 countries and their relationships with physical activity and dietary patterns. *Obesity Reviews, 6*, 123–132.

Jardri, R., & others (2012). Assessing fetal response to maternal speech using a noninvasive functional brain imaging technique. *International Journal of Developmental Neuroscience, 30*, 159–161.

Jaremka, L. M., Glaser, R., Malarkey, W. B., & Kiecolt-Glaser, J. K. (2013a). Marital distress prospectively predicts poorer cellular immune function. *Psychoneuroendocrinology, 38*(11), 2713–2719.

Jaremka, L. M., & others (2013b). Loneliness promotes inflammation during acute stress. *Psychological Science, 24*, 1089–1097.

Jaremka, L. M., & others (2014, in press). Pain, depression, and fatigue: Loneliness as a longitudinal risk factor. *Health Psychology.*

Jarosinka, D., Polanska, K., Woityniak, B., & Hanke, W. (2014, in press). Toward estimating the burden of disease attributable to second-hand smoke exposure in Polish children. *International Journal of Occupational Medicine and Environmental Health.*

Jellinger, K. A., & Attems, J. (2013). Neuropathological approaches to cerebral aging and neuroplasticity. *Dialogues in Clinical Neuroscience, 15,* 29–43.

Jenkins, J. M., & Astington, J. W. (1996). Cognitive factors and family structure associated with theory of mind development in young children. *Developmental Psychology, 32,* 70–78.

Jensen, W., Harward, S., & Bowen, J. M. (2014). Externalizing disorders in children and adolescents: Behaviorial excess and behavioral deficits. In M. A. Bray & T. J. Kehle (Eds.), *Oxford handbook of school psychology.* New York: Oxford University Press.

Jesse, D. E., & Kirkpatrick, M. K. (2013). Catching the spirit in cultural care: A midwifery exemplar. *Journal of Midwifery and Women's Health, 58,* 49–56.

Jeste, D. V., & Oswald, A. J. (2014, in press). Individual and societal wisdom: Explaining the paradox of human aging and high well-being. *Psychiatry.*

Jeste, D. V., & others (2013). Association between older and more successful aging: Critical role of resilience and depression. *American Journal of Psychiatry, 170,* 188–196.

Ji, B. T., & others (1997). Paternal cigarette smoking and the risk of childhood cancer among offspring of nonsmoking mothers. *Journal of the National Cancer Institute, 89,* 238–244.

Jia, R., & Schoppe-Sullivan, S. J. (2011). Relations between coparenting and father involvement in families with preschool-age children. *Developmental Psychology, 47,* 106–118.

Jiang, H. Y., & others (2014). Diffusion of two botulinum toxins type A on the forehead: Double-blinded, randomized, controlled study. *Dermatologic Surgery, 40,* 184–192.

Jiang, S., & others (2014, in press). M1 muscarinic acetylcholine receptor in Alzheimer's disease. *Neuroscience Bulletin.*

Jiang, T., Yu, J. T., Tian, Y., & Tan, L. (2013). Epidemiology and etiology of Alzheimer's disease: From genetic to non-genetic factors. *Current Alzheimer Research, 10,* 852–867.

Jiao, S., Ji, G., & Jing, Q. (1996). Cognitive development of Chinese urban only children and children with siblings. *Child Development, 67,* 387–395.

Jin, L., & others (2013). Placental concentrations of mercury, lead, cadmium, and arsenic and the risk of neural tube defects in a Chinese population. *Reproductive Toxicology, 35,* 25–31.

Jinyao, Y., & others (2012). Insecure attachment as a predictor of depressive and anxious symptomatology. *Depression and Anxiety, 29*(9), 789–796.

Jitendra, A., & Montague, M. (2013). Strategies for improving student outcomes in mathematical reasoning. In B. G. Cook & M. G. Tankersley (Eds.), *Research-based practices in special education.* Upper Saddle River, NJ: Pearson.

Joh, A. S., Jaswal, V. K., & Keen, R. (2011). Imagining a way out of the gravity bias: Preschoolers can visualize the solution to a spatial problem. *Child Development, 82,* 744–750.

Johns Hopkins University (2006, February 17). *Undergraduate honored for launching health program in India.* Baltimore: Johns Hopkins University News Releases.

Johnson, C. L., & Troll, L. E. (1992). Family functioning in late late life. *Journals of Gerontology, 47,* S66–S72.

Johnson, E. J., & others (2013). Relationship between serum and brain carotenoids, *a*-tocopherol, and retinol concentrations and cognitive performance in the oldest old from the Georgia Centenarian Study. *Journal of Aging Research.* doi:10.1155/2013/951786

Johnson, G. B. (2015, in press). *The living world* (8th ed.). New York: McGraw-Hill.

Johnson, J. S., & Newport, E. L. (1991). Critical period effects on universal properties of language: The status of subjacency in the acquisition of a second language. *Cognition, 39,* 215–258.

Johnson, K. J., & Mutchler, J. E. (2014). The emergence of positive gerontology: From disengagement to social involvement. *Gerontologist, 54,* 93–100.

Johnson, M. (2008, April 30). Commentary in R. Highfield, *Harvard's baby brain research lab.* Retrieved January 24, 2008, from www.telegraph.co.uk/scienceandtechnology/science/sciencenews/3341166/Harvards-baby-brain-research-lab.html

Johnson, M. H., Grossmann, T., & Cohen-Kadosh, K. (2009). Mapping functional brain development: Building a social brain through interactive specialization. *Developmental Psychology, 45,* 151–159.

Johnson, S. P. (2010). Perceptual completion in infancy. In S. P. Johnson (Ed.), *Neoconstructivism: The new science of cognitive development* (pp. 45–60). New York: Oxford University Press.

Johnson, S. P. (2011). A constructivist view of object perception in infancy. In L. M. Oakes, C. H. Cashon, M. Casasola, & D. H. Rakison (Eds.), *Infant perception and cognition.* New York: Oxford University Press.

Johnson, S. P. (2013). Object perception. In P. D. Zelazo (Ed.), *Handbook of developmental psychology.* New York: Oxford University Press.

Johnson, S. P., & Hannon, E. H. (2015, in press). Perceptual development. In R. M. Lerner (Ed.), *Handbook of child psychology and developmental science* (7th ed.). New York: Wiley.

Johnson, W., & Bouchard, T. J. (2014). Genetics of intellectual and personality traits associated with creative genius: Could geniuses be cosmobian dragon kings? In D. K. Simonton (Ed.), *Wiley-Blackwell handbook of genius.* New York: Wiley.

Johnson, W., Corley, J., Starr, J. M., & Deary, I. J. (2011). Psychological and physical health at age 70 in the Lothian Birth Cohort 1936: Links with early life IQ, SES, and current cognitive function and neighborhood environment. *Health Psychology, 30,* 1–11.

John-Steiner, V. (2007). Vygotsky on thinking and speaking. In H. Daniels, J. Wertsch, & M. Cole (Eds.), *The Cambridge companion to Vygotsky.* New York: Cambridge University Press.

Johnston, L. D., O'Malley, P. M., Bachman, J. G., & Schulenberg, J. E. (2008). *Monitoring the Future national survey results on drug use, 1975–2007, Volume II: College students and adults ages 19–45.* Bethesda, MD: National Institute on Drug Abuse.

Johnston, L. D., O'Malley, P. M., Bachman, J. G., & Schulenberg, J. E. (2008). *Monitoring the Future national survey results on drug use, 1975–2007, Volume 1: Secondary school students* (NIH Publication No. 08-6418A). Bethesda, MD: National Institute on Drug Abuse.

Johnston, L. D., O'Malley, P. M., Bachman, J. G., & Schulenberg, J. E. (2011). *Monitoring the Future national survey results on drug use, 1975–2010, Volume II: College students and adults ages 19–50.* Bethesda, MD: National Institute on Drug Abuse.

Johnston, L. D., O'Malley, P. M., Bachman, J. G., & Schulenberg, J. E. (2013). *Monitoring the Future national survey results on drug use, 1975–2012, Volume II: College students and adults ages 19–50.* Bethesda, MD: National Institute on Drug Abuse.

Johnston, L. D., O'Malley, P. M., Miech, R. A., Bachman, J. G., & Schulenberg, J. E. (2014). *Monitoring the Future national survey results on drug use, 1975–2013: Overview of key findings on adolescent drug use.* Ann Arbor: Institute of Social Research, University of Michigan.

Jokela, M., & others (2010). From midlife to early old age: Health trajectories associated with retirement. *Epidemiology, 21,* 284–290.

Jokinen-Gordon, H. (2012). Still penalized? Parity, age at first birth, and women's income in later life. *Journal of Women and Aging, 24,* 227–241.

Jolivette, K., & others (2013). Strategies to prevent problem behavior. In B. G. Cook & M. G. Tankersley (Eds.), *Research-based practices in special education.* Upper Saddle River, NJ: Pearson.

Jones, B. F., Reedy, E. J., & Weinberg, B. A. (2014). Age and scientific genius. In D. K. Simonton (Ed.), *Wiley-Blackwell handbook of genius.* New York: Wiley.

Jones, D., & others (2010). The impact of the Fast Track prevention trial on health services utilization by youth at risk for conduct problems. *Pediatrics, 125,* 130–136.

Jones, L., & others (2012). Pain management for women in labor: An overview of systematic reviews. *Cochrane Database of Systematic Reviews, 14*(3), CD009234.

Jones, M. D., & Galliher, R. V. (2007). Ethnic identity and psychosocial functioning in Navajo adolescents. *Journal of Research on Adolescence, 17,* 683–696.

Jones, M. C. (1965). Psychological correlates of somatic development. *Child Development, 36,* 899–911.

Jones, N. A. (2012). Delayed reactive cries demonstrate emotional and physiological dysregulation in newborns of depressed mothers. *Biological Psychology, 89,* 374–381.

Jones, P. S., & others (2011). Development of a caregiver empowerment model to promote positive outcomes. *Journal of Family Nursing, 17,* 11–28.

Jones, S. C., & Magee, C. A. (2014, in press). The role of family, friends, and peers in Australian adolescents' alcohol consumption. *Drug and Alcohol Review.*

Jonson, H. (2013). We will be different! Ageism and the temporal construction of old age. *Gerontologist, 53,* 194–204.

Jonson-Reid, M., Kohl, P. L., & Drake, B. (2012). Child and adolescent outcomes of chronic child maltreatment. *Pediatrics, 129,* 839–845.

Joosten, H., & others (2013). Cardiovascular risk profile and cognitive function in young, middle-aged, and elderly subjects. *Stroke, 44,* 1543–1549.

Jopp, D., & Rott, C. (2006). Adaptation in very old age: Exploring the role of resources and attitudes for centenarians' happiness. *Psychology and Aging, 21,* 266–280.

Jordan, C. H., & Zeigler-Hill, V. (2013). Secure and fragile forms of self-esteem. In V. Zeigler-Hill (Ed.), *Self-esteem.* New York: Psychology Press.

Jose, A., O'Leary, K. D., & Moyer, A. (2010). Does premarital cohabitation predict subsequent marital stability and marital quality? A meta-analysis. *Journal of Marriage and the Family, 72,* 105–116.

Joseph, J. (2006). *The missing gene.* New York: Algora.

Juang, L. P., Syed, M., & Cookston, J. T. (2012). Acculturation-based and everyday parent-adolescent conflict for Chinese American adolescents: Longitudinal trajectories and implications for mental health. *Journal of Family Psychology, 26,* 916–926.

Juang, L. P., & Umana-Taylor, A. J. (2012). Family conflict among Chinese- and Mexican-origin adolescents and their parents in the U.S.: An introduction. *New Directions in Child and Adolescent Development, 135,* 1–12.

Judd, F. K., Hickey, M., & Bryant, C. (2012). Depression and midlife: Are we overpathologising the menopause? *Journal of Affective Disorders, 136,* 199–211.

Julian, M. M. (2013). Age at adoption from institutional care as a window into the lasting effects of early experience. *Clinical Child and Family Psychology Review, 16*(2), 101–145.

Jung, C. (1933). *Modern man in search of a soul.* New York: Harcourt Brace.

Juraska, J. M., & Lowry, N. C. (2012), Neuroanatomical changes associated with cognitive aging. *Current Topics in Behavioral Neuroscience, 10,* 137–162.

Just, M. A., Keller, T. A., Malave, V. L., Kana, R. K., & Varma, S. (2012). Autism as a neural system disorder: A theory of frontal-posterior underconnectivity. *Neuroscience and Biobehavioral Reviews, 36,* 1292–1313.

K

Kadivar, H., & others (2014, in press). Adolescent views on comprehensive health risk assessment and counseling: Assessing gender differences. *Journal of Adolescent Health.*

Kaffashi, F., Scher, M. S., Ludington-Hoe, S. M., & Loparo, K. A. (2013). An analysis of kangaroo care intervention using neonatal EEG complexity: A preliminary study. *Clinical Neurophysiology, 124,* 238–246.

Kagan, J. (1987). Perspectives on infancy. In J. D. Osofsky (Ed.), *Handbook on infant development* (2nd ed.). New York: Wiley.

Kagan, J. (2002). Behavioral inhibition as a temperamental category. In R. J. Davidson, K. R. Scherer, & H. H. Goldsmith (Eds.), *Handbook of affective sciences.* New York: Oxford University Press.

Kagan, J. (2008). Fear and wariness. In M. M. Haith & J. B. Benson (Eds.), *Encyclopedia of infant and early childhood development.* Oxford, UK: Elsevier.

Kagan, J. (2010). Emotions and temperament. In M. H. Burnstein (Ed.), *Handbook of cultural developmental science.* New York: Psychology Press.

Kagan, J. (2013). Temperamental contributions to inhibited and uninhibited profiles. In P. D. Zelazo (Ed.), *Oxford handbook of developmental psychology.* New York: Oxford University Press.

Kagan, J. J., Kearsley, R. B., & Zelazo, P. R. (1978). *Infancy: Its place in human development.* Cambridge, MA: Harvard University Press.

Kagan, S. H. (2008). Faculty profile, University of Pennsylvania School of Nursing. Retrieved January 5, 2008, from www.nursing.upenn.edu/faculty/profile.asp

Kagitani, H., Asou, Y., Ishihara, N., Hoshide, S., & Kario, K. (2014). Hot flashes and blood pressure in middle-aged Japanese women. *American Journal of Hypertension, 27,* 503–507.

Kahn, J. A., & others (2008). Patterns and determinants of physical activity in U.S. adolescents. *Journal of Adolescent Health, 42,* 369–377.

Kahrs, B. A., Jung, W. P., & Lochman, J. J. (2013). Motor origins of tool use. *Child Development, 84*(3), 810–818.

Kail, M., Lemaire, P., & Lecacheur, M. (2012). Online grammaticality judgments in French young and older adults. *Experimental Aging Research, 38,* 186–207.

Kail, R. V. (2007). Longitudinal evidence that increases in processing speed and working memory enhance children's reasoning. *Psychological Science, 18,* 312–313.

Kalder, M., Knoblauch, K., Hrgovic, I., & Munstedt, K. (2011). Use of complementary and alternative medicine during pregnancy and delivery. *Archives of Gynecology and Obstetrics, 283*(3), 475–482.

Kalish, R. A. (1981). *Death, grief, and caring relationships,* Monterey, CA: Brooks/Cole.

Kalish, R. A., & Reynolds, D. K. (1976). *An overview of death and ethnicity.* Farmingdale, NY: Baywood.

Kalladka, D., & Muir, K. W. (2014). Brain repair: Cell therapy in stroke. *Stem Cells and Cloning, 7,* 31–44.

Kalousova, L., & Burgard, S. A. (2014). Unemployment, measured and perceived decline of economic resources: Contrasting three measures of recessionary hardships and their implications for adopting negative health behaviors. *Social Science and Medicine, 106,* 28–34.

Kamiya, M., Sakurai, T., Ogama, N., Maki, Y., & Toba, K. (2014). Factors associated with increased caregivers' burden in several cognitive stages of Alzheimer's disease. *Geriatrics and Gerontology International, 14*(2, Suppl.), S45–S55.

Kamp, B. J., Wellman, N. S., & Russell, C. (2010). Position of the American Dietetic Association, American Society for Nutrition, and Society for Nutrition Education: Food and nutrition programs for community-residing older adults. *Journal of Nutrition Education and Behavior, 42,* 72–82.

Kamphaus, R. W., & Mays, K. L. (2014). Assessment of internalizing behavioral deficits. In M. A. Bray & T. J. Kehle (Eds.), *Oxford handbook of school psychology.* New York: Oxford University Press.

Kan, P. F. (2014). Novel word retention in sequential bilingual children. *Journal of Child Language, 41,* 416–438.

Kancherla, V., Oakley, G. P., & Brent, R. L. (2014, in press). Urgent global opportunities to prevent birth defects. *Seminars in Fetal and Neonatal Medicine.*

Kang, H. K. (2014). Influence of culture and community perceptions on birth and perinatal care of immigrant women: Doulas' perspective. *Journal of Perinatal Education, 23,* 25–32.

Kanner, A. D., Coyne, J. C., Schaefer, C., & Lazarus, R. S. (1981). Comparison of two modes of stress measurement: Daily hassles and uplifts versus major life events. *Journal of Behavioral Medicine, 4,* 1–39.

Kantak, C., & others (2014, in press). Lab-on-a-chip technology: Impacting non-invasive prenatal diagnostics (NIPD) through miniaturization. *Lab on a Chip.*

Kantrowitz, B. (1991, Summer). The good, the bad, and the difference. *Newsweek,* pp. 48–50.

Kantowitz, B. H., Roediger, H. L., & Elmes, D. G. (2015, in press). *Experimental psychology* (10th ed.). Boston: Cengage.

Kaplan, A. L., & Hu, J. C. (2013). Use of testosterone replacement therapy in the United States and its effect on subsequent prostate cancer outcomes. *Urology, 82,* 321–326.

Kaplan, D. L., Jones, E. J., Olson, E. C., & Yunzal-Butler, C. B. (2013). Early age of first sex and health risk in an urban adolescent population. *Journal of School Health, 83,* 350–356.

Kapornai, K., & Vetro, A. (2008). Depression in children. *Current Opinion in Psychiatry, 21,* 1–7.

Kappeler, E. M., & Farb, A. F. (2014). Historical context for the creation of the Office of Adolescent Health and the Teen Pregnancy Prevention Program, *54*(3, Suppl.), S3–S9.

Kar, B. R., Rao, S. L., & Chandramouli, B. A. (2008). Cognitive development in children with chronic energy malnutrition. *Behavioral and Brain Functions, 4,* 31.

Karantzas, G. C., Evans, L., & Foddy, M. (2010). The role of attachment in current and future parent caregiving. *Journals of Gerontology B: Psychological Sciences and Social Sciences, 65B,* 573–580.

Karasik, R. J., & Hamon, R. R. (2007). Cultural diversity and aging families. In B. S. Trask & R. R. Hamon (Eds.), *Cultural diversity and families.* Thousand Oaks, CA: Sage.

Karatsoreos, I. N., & McEwen, B. S. (2013). Annual research review: The neurobiology and physiology of resilience and adaptation across the life course. *Journal of Child Psychology and Psychiatry, 54,* 337–347.

Karavia, E. A., & others (2014). HDL quality and functionality: What can proteins and genes predict? *Expert Review of Cardiovascular Therapy, 12,* 521–532.

Karlamangia, A. S., & others (2014). Biological correlates of adult cognition: Midlife in the United States (MIDUS). *Neurobiology of Aging, 35*(2), 387–394.

Karniol, R., Grosz, E., & Schorr, I. (2003). Caring, gender-role orientation, and volunteering. *Sex Roles, 49,* 11–19.

Karoly, L. A., & Bigelow, J. H. (2005). *The economics of investing in universal preschool education in California.* Santa Monica, CA: RAND Corporation.

Karreman, A., van Tuijl, C., van Aken, M. A., & Dekovic, M. (2008). Parenting, coparenting, and effortful control in preschoolers. *Journal of Family Psychology, 22,* 30–40.

Kaski, D., Allum, J. H., Bronstein, A. M., & Dominguez, R. O. (2014, in press). Applying anodal tDCS tango dancing in a patient with Parkinson's disease. *Neuroscience Letters.*

Kassahn, K. S., Scott, H. S., & Fletcher, J. M. (2014). Ensuring clinical validity—modernizing genetic testing services. *Pathology, 46*(1, Suppl.), S27–S28.

Kastenbaum, R. J. (2009). *Death, society, and human experience* (10th ed.). Boston: Allyn & Bacon.

Kastenbaum, R. J. (2012). *Death, society, and human experience* (11th ed.). Boston: Allyn & Bacon.

Kaszniak, A. W., & Menchola, M. (2012). Behavioral neuroscience of emotion in aging. *Current Topics in Behavioral Neuroscience, 10,* 51–56.

Kato, T. (2005). The relationship between coping with stress due to romantic break-ups and mental health. *Japanese Journal of Social Psychology, 20,* 171–180.

Kattenstroth, J. C., Kalisch, T., Holt, S., Tegenthoff, M., & Dinse, H. R. (2013). Six months of dance intervention enhances postural, sensorimotor, and cognitive performance in elderly without affecting cardio-respiratory functions. *Frontiers in Aging Neuroscience, 5,* 5.

Katz, J., & Schneider, M. E. (2013). Casual hookup sex during the first year of college: Prospective associations with attitudes about sex and love relationships. *Archives of Sexual Behavior, 42,* 1451–1462.

Katz, L. (1999). Curriculum disputes in early childhood education. *ERIC Clearinghouse on Elementary and Early Childhood Education,* Document EDO-PS-99–13.

Katz, P. R., Karuza, J., Intrator, O., & Mor, V. (2009). Nursing home physician specialists: A response to the workforce crisis in long-term care. *Annals of Internal Medicine, 150,* 411–413.

Katzmarzyk, P. T., & others (2012). Body mass index and risk of cardiovascular disease, cancer, and all-cause mortality. *Canadian Journal of Public Health, 103,* 147–151.

Kauffman, J. M., McGee, K., & Brigham, M. (2004). Enabling or disabling? Observations on changes in special education. *Phi Delta Kappan, 85,* 613–620.

Kaufman, J. C., & Sternberg, R. J. (2013). The creative mind. In C. Jones, M. Lorenzen, & R. F. Proctor (Eds.), *Handbook of psychology: Experimental psychology* (Vol. 4). New York: Wiley.

Kaur, A., & Phadke, S. R. (2012). Analysis of short stature cases referred for genetic evaluation. *Indian Journal of Pediatrics, 79*(12), 1597–1600.

Kavsek, M. (2004). Predicting IQ from infant visual habituation and dishabituation: A meta-analysis. *Journal of Applied Developmental Psychology, 25,* 369–393.

Kavsek, M. (2013). The comparator model of infant visual habituation and dishabituation: Recent insights. *Developmental Psychobiology, 55,* 793–808.

Kawabata, Y., Tseng, W. L., Murray-Close, D., & Crick, N. R. (2012). Developmental trajectories of Chinese children's relational and physical aggression: Associations with social-psychological adjustment problems. *Journal of Abnormal Child Psychology, 40*(7), 1087–1097.

Kawagoe, T., & Sekiyama, K. (2014, in press). Visually encoded working memory is closely associated with mobility in older adults. *Experimental Brain Research.*

Kayama, H., & others (2014). Effects of a Kinect-based exercise game on improving executive cognitive performance in community-dwelling elderly: Case control study. *Journal of Medical Internet Research, 16,* e61.

Kaynak, O., & others (2013). Relationships among parental monitoring and sensation seeking on the development of substance use disorder among college students. *Addictive Behaviors, 38,* 1457–1463.

Keating, D. P. (1990). Adolescent thinking. In S. S. Feldman & G. R. Elliott (Eds.), *At the threshold: The developing adolescent.* Cambridge, MA: Harvard University Press.

Keating, D. P. (2004). Cognitive and brain development. In R. Lerner & L. Steinberg (Ed.), *Handbook of adolescent psychology.* New York: Wiley.

Keating, D. P. (2009). Developmental science and giftedness: An integrated life-span framework. In F. D. Horowitz, R. F. Subotnik, & D. J. Matthews (Eds.), *The development of giftedness and talent across the life span.* Washington, DC: American Psychological Association.

Keen, R. (2005). Unpublished review of Santrock's *Topical approach to life-span development,* 3rd ed. New York: McGraw-Hill.

Keen, R. (2011). The development of problem solving in young children: A critical cognitive skill. *Annual Review of Psychology* (Vol. 62). Palo Alto, CA: Annual Reviews.

Keen, R., Lee, M-H., & Adolph, K. E. (2014, in press). Planning an action: A developmental progression in tool use. *Ecological Psychology.*

Kehle, T. J., & Bray, M. A. (2014). Individual differences. In M. A. Bray & T. J. Kehle (Eds.), *Oxford handbook of school psychology.* New York: Oxford University Press.

Keijsers, L., & Laird, R. D. (2010). Introduction to special issue: Careful conversations: Adolescents managing their parents' access to information. *Journal of Adolescence, 33,* 255–259.

Keiley-Moore, J. (2009). Chronic illness, adulthood and later life. In D. Carr (Ed.), *Encyclopedia of the life course and human development.* Boston: Gale Cengage.

Kell, H. J., & Lubinski, D. (2014). The study of mathematically precocious youth at maturity: Insights into elements of genius. In D. K. Simonton (Ed.), *Wiley-Blackwell handbook of genius.* New York: Wiley.

Keller, A., Ford, L., & Meacham, J. (1978). Dimensions of self concept in preschool children. *Developmental Psychology, 14,* 485–489.

Keller, H., Kartner, J., Borke, J., Yvosi, R., and Kleis, A. (2005). Parenting styles and the development of the categorical self: A longitudinal study on mirror self-recognition in Cameroonian Nso and German families. *International Journal of Behavioral Development, 29,* 496–504.

Kelley, A. S., & others (2014, in press). *Leveraging the Health and Retirement Study to Advance Palliative Care Research.*

Kelley, G. A., & Kelley, K. S. (2014, in press). Effects of exercise in the treatment of overweight and obese children and adolescents: A systematic review and analysis. *Journal of Obesity.*

Kellman, P. J., & Arterberry, M. E. (2006). Infant visual perception. In W. Damon & R. Lerner (Eds.), *Handbook of child psychology* (6th ed.). New York: Wiley.

Kellman, P. J., & Banks, M. S. (1998). Infant visual perception. In W. Damon (Ed.), *Handbook of child psychology* (5th ed., Vol. 2). New York: Wiley.

Kelly, A. J., Hertzog, C., Hayes, M. G., & Smith, A. D. (2013). The effects of age and focality on delay-execute prospective memory. *Neuropsychology, Development, and Cognition B: Aging, Neuropsychology, and Cognition, 20*(1), 101–124.

Kelly, D. J., & others (2005). Three-month-olds, but not newborns, prefer own-race faces. *Developmental Science, 8,* F31–F36.

Kelly, D. J., & others (2007). Cross-race preferences for same-race faces extend beyond the African versus Caucasian contrast in 3-month-old infants. *Infancy, 11,* 87–95.

Kelly, J. P., Borchert, J., & Teller, D. Y. (1997). The development of chromatic and achromatic sensitivity in infancy as tested with the sweep VEP. *Vision Research, 37,* 2057–2072.

Kelly, M. E., & others (2014). The impact of cognitive training and mental stimulation on cognitive and everyday functioning of healthy older adults: A systematic review and meta-analysis. *Aging Research Reviews, 15C,* 28–43.

Kelly, Y., & others (2013). Light drinking versus abstinence in pregnancy—behavioral and cognitive outcomes in 7-year-old children: A longitudinal cohort study. *BJOG, 120,* 1340–1347.

Keltner, K. W. (2013). *Tiger babies strike back.* New York: William Morrow.

Kemp, J., Despres, O., Pebayle, T., & Dufour, A. (2014). Age-related decrease in sensitivity to electrical stimulation is unrelated to skin conductance: An evoked potentials study. *Clinical Neurophysiology, 125,* 602–607.

Kempermann, G., van Praag, H., & Gage, F. H. (2000). Activity-dependent regulation of neuronal plasticity and self repair. *Progress in Brain Research 127,* 35–48.

Kendler, K. S., & others (2012). Genetic and familial environmental influences on the risk for drug abuse: A national Swedish adoption study. *Archives of General Psychiatry, 69*(7), 690–697.

Kendrick, K., Jutengren, G., & Stattin, H. (2012). The protective role of supportive friends against bullying perpetration and victimization. *Journal of Adolescence, 35*(4), 1069–1080.

Kennell, J. H. (2006) Randomized controlled trial of skin-to-skin contact from birth versus conventional incubator for physiological stabilization in 1200g to 2199 g newborns. *Acta Paediatica (Sweden), 95,* 15–16.

Kennell, J. H., & McGrath, S. K. (1999). Commentary: Practical and humanistic lessons from the Third World for perinatal caregivers everywhere. *Birth, 26,* 9–10.

Kennis, E., & others (2013). Long-term impact of strength training on muscle strength characteristics in older adults. *Archives of Physical Medicine and Rehabilitation, 94,* 2054–2060.

Kerns, K. A., & Seibert, A. C. (2012). Finding your way through the thicket: Promising approaches to assessing attachment in middle childhood. In E. Waters & B. Vaughn (Eds.), *Measuring attachment.* New York: Guilford.

Kerns, K. A., Siener, S., & Brumariu, L. E. (2011). Mother-child relationships, family context, and child characteristics as predictors of anxiety symptoms in middle childhood. *Development and Psychopathology, 23,* 593–604.

Ketcham, C. J., & Stelmach, G. E. (2001). Age-related declines in motor control. In J. E. Birren & K. W. Schale (Eds.), *Handbook of the psychology of aging* (5th ed.). San Diego: Academic Press.

Keyes, C. L. M., & Ryff, C. D. (1998). Generativity in adult lives: Social structure contours and quality of life consequences. In D. P. McAdams & E. de St. Aubin (Eds.), *Generativity and adult development: How and why we care for the next generation.* Washington, DC. American Psychological Association.

Khalessi, A., & Reich, S. M. (2013). A month of breastfeeding associated with greater adherence to pediatric nutrition guidelines. *Journal of Reproductive and Infant Psychology, 31,* 299–308.

Khan, M. R., Berger, A. T., Wells, B. E., & Cleland, C. M. (2012). Longitudinal associations between adolescent alcohol use and adult sexual risk behavior and sexually transmitted infection in the United States: Assessment of differences by race. *American Journal of Public Health, 102,* 867–876.

Khashan, A. S., Baker, P. N., & Kenny, L. C. (2010). Preterm birth and reduced birthweight in first and second teenage pregnancies: A register-based cohort study. *BMC Pregnancy and Childbirth, 10,* 36.

Khera, M., Crawford, D., Morales, A., Salonia, A., & Morgentaler, A. (2014). A new era of testosterone and prostate cancer: From physiology to clinical implications. *European Urology, 65*(1), 115–123.

Khurana, A., & others (2012). Early adolescent sexual debut: The mediating role of working memory ability, sensation seeking, and impulsivity. *Developmental Psychology, 48*(5), 1416–1428.

Khurana, S., & others (2013). Polyphenols: Benefits to the cardiovascular system in health and in aging. *Nutrients, 5,* 3779–3827.

Kiang, L., Andrews, K., Stein, G. L., Supple, A. J., & Gonzales, L. M. (2013). Socioeconomic stress and academic adjustment among Asian American adolescents: The protective role of family obligation. *Journal of Youth and Adolescence, 42,* 837–847.

Kiang, L., Witkow, M. R., & Champagne, M. C. (2013). Normative changes in ethnic and American identities and links with adjustment among Asian American adolescents. *Developmental Psychology, 17,* 1713–1722.

Kiblawi, Z. N., & others (2013). The effect of prenatal methamphetamine exposure on attention as assessed by continuous performance tests: Results from the Infant Development, Environment, and Lifestyle Study. *Journal of Developmental and Behavioral Pediatrics, 34,* 31–37.

Kidd, C., Piantadosi, S. T., & Aslin, R. N. (2012). The Goldilocks effect: Human infants allocate attention to visual sequences that are neither too simple nor too complex. *PLoS One, 7*(5), e36399.

Kielsmeier, J. (2011). The time is now. *Prevention Researcher, 18,* 3–7.

Kilbane, C. R., & Milman, N. B. (2014). *Teaching models.* Upper Saddle River, NJ: Pearson.

Kilgore, C. (2014). Why intermediate care services need to be refreshed. *Nursing Older People, 26,* 16–20.

Kilic, S., & others (2012). Environmental tobacco smoke exposure during intrauterine period promotes granulosa cell apoptosis: A prospective, randomized study. *Journal of Maternal-Fetal and Neonatal Medicine, 25*(10), 1904–1908.

Killen, M., & Smetana, J. G. (Eds.) (2014). *Handbook of moral development* (2nd ed.). New York: Psychology Press.

Kim, E. D., & others (2014). A return to normal erectile function with Tadalafil once daily after an incomplete response to as-needed PDE5 inhibitor therapy. *Journal of Sexual Medicine, 11*(3), 820–830.

Kim, H. I., & Johnson, S. P. (2014, in press). Detecting "infant-directedness" in face and voice. *Developmental Science.*

Kim, H. J., & others (2014, in press). Long-term cognitive outcome of bilateral subthalamic deep brain stimulation in Parkinson's disease. *Journal of Neurology.*

Kim, J. E., & Moen, P. (2002). Retirement transitions, gender, and psychological well-being: A life-course, ecological model. *Journals of Gerontology B: Psychological Sciences and Social Sciences, 57B,* P212–P222.

Kim, K., Zarit, S., Birditt, K. S., & Fingerman, K. L. (2014, in press). Discrepancy in reports of support exchanges between parents and adult offspring: Within- and between-family differences. *Journal of Family Psychology.*

Kim, K. H. (2010, May). Unpublished data. School of Education, College of William & Mary, Williamsburg, VA.

Kim, K. M., Vicenty, J., & Palmore, G. T. (2013). The potential of apolipoprotein E4 to act as a substrate for primary cultures of hippocampal neurons. *Biomaterials, 34,* 2694–2700.

Kim, S. H. (2009). The influence of finding meaning and worldview of accepting death on anger among bereaved older spouses. *Aging and Mental Health, 13,* 38–45.

Kim, S., Kochanska, G., Boldt, L. J., Nordling, J. K., & O'Bleness, J. J. (2014). Developmental trajectory from early responses to transgressions to future antisocial behavior: Evidence for the role of the parent-child relationship from two longitudinal studies. *Development and Psychopathology, 26,* 93–109.

Kim, S. M., Han, D. H., Trksak, G. H., & Lee, Y. S. (2014, in press). Gender differences in adolescent coping behaviors and suicidal ideation: Findings from a sample of 73,238 adolescents. *Anxiety, Stress, and Coping.*

Kim, S. Y., & Giovanello, K. S. (2011). The effects of attention on age-related relational memory deficits: Evidence from a novel attentional manipulation. *Psychology and Aging, 26,* 678–688.

Kim, S. Y., Wang, Y., Orozco-Lapray, D., Shen, Y., & Murtuza, M. (2013). Does "tiger parenting" exist? Parenting profiles of Chinese Americans and adolescent developmental outcomes. *Asian American Journal of Psychology, 4,* 7–18.

Kimble, M., Neacsiu, A. D., Flack, W. F., & Horner, J. (2008). Risk of unwanted sex for college women: Evidence for a red zone. *Journal of American College Health, 57,* 331–338.

Kim-Fuchs, C., & others (2014, in press). Chronic stress accelerates pancreatic cancer growth and invasion: A critical role for beta-adrenergic signaling in the pancreatic microenvironment. *Brain, Behavior, and Immunity.*

King, B. M., & Regan, P. (2014). *Human sexuality today* (8th ed.). Upper Saddle River, NJ: Pearson.

King, L. A. (2014). *Science of psychology* (3rd ed.). New York: McGraw-Hill.

King, L. A., & Hicks, J. A. (2007). Whatever happened to "What might have been?": Regrets, happiness, and maturity. *American Psychologist, 62,* 625–636.

King, P. E., Carr, A., & Boiter, C. (2011). Spirituality, religiosity, and youth thriving. In R. M. Lerner, J. V. Lerner, & J. B. Benson (Eds.), *Advances in child development and behavior: Positive youth development.* New York: Elsevier.

King, P. E., Ramos, J. S., & Clardy, C. E. (2013). Searching for the sacred: Religious and spiritual development among adolescents. In K. I. Pargament, J. Exline, & J. Jones (Eds.), *APA handbook of psychology, religion, and spirituality.* Washington, DC: American Psychological Association.

King, P. E., & Roeser, R. W. (2009). Religion and spirituality in adolescent development. In R. M. Lerner & L. Steinberg (Eds.), *Handbook of adolescent psychology* (3rd ed.). New York: Wiley.

King, V., & Scott, M. E. (2005). A comparison of cohabiting relationships among older and younger adults. *Journal of Marriage and the Family, 67,* 271–285.

Kinney, J. (2012). *Loosening the grip: A handbook of alcohol information* (10th ed.). New York: McGraw-Hill.

Kins, E., & Beyers, W. (2010). Failure to launch, failure to achieve criteria for adulthood? *Journal of Adolescent Research, 25,* 743–777.

Kirby, M., Creanga, D. L., & Stecher, V. J. (2013). Erectile function, erectile hardness, and tolerability in men treated with sildenafil 100 mg vs. 50 mg for erectile dysfunction. *International Journal of Clinical Practice, 67,* 1034–1039.

Kirk, R. E. (2013). Experimental design. In I. B. Weiner & others (Eds.), *Handbook of psychology* (2nd ed., Vol. 2). New York: Wiley.

Kirk, S. A., Gallagher, J. J., & Coleman, M. R. (2015). *Educating exceptional children* (14th ed.). Boston: Cengage.

Kirkevold, M., Moyle, W., Wilkinson, C., Meyer, J., & Haughe, S. (2013). Facing the challenge of adapting to life 'alone' in old age: The influence of losses. *Journal of Advanced Nursing, 69*(2), 394–403.

Kirkham, N. Z., Wagner, J. B., Swan, K. A., & Johnson, S. P. (2012). Sound support: Intermodal information facilitates infants' perception of an occluded trajectory. *Infant Behavior and Development, 35,* 174–178.

Kirkorian, H. L., Anderson, D. R., & Keen, R. (2012). Age differences in online processing of video: An eye movement study. *Child Development, 83,* 497–507.

Kirk-Sanchez, N. J., & McGough, E. L. (2014). Physical exercise and cognitive performance in the elderly: Current perspectives. *Clinical Interventions in Aging, 9,* 51–62.

Kisilevsky, B. S., & others (2003). Effects of experience on fetal voice recognition. *Psychological Science, 14,* 220–224.

Kisilevsky, B. S., & others (2009). Fetal sensitivity to properties of maternal speech and language. *Infant Behavior and Development, 32,* 59–71.

Kit, B. K., Simon, A. E., Brody, D. J., & Akinbami, L. J. (2013). U.S. prevalence and trends in tobacco smoke exposure among children and adolescents with asthma. *Pediatrics, 131,* 407–414.

Kitchin, B. (2013). Nutrition counseling for patients with osteoporosis: A personal approach. *Journal of Clinical Densitometry, 16,* 426–231.

Kitsantas, P., & Gaffney, K. F. (2010). Racial/ethnic disparities in infant mortality. *Journal of Perinatal Medicine, 38,* 87–94.

Kivnik, H. Q., & Sinclair, H. M. (2007). Grandparenthood. In J. E. Birren (Ed.), *Encyclopedia of gerontology* (2nd ed.). San Diego: Academic Press.

Klaassen, E. B., & others (2014). Working memory in middle aged males: Age-related brain activation changes and cognitive fatigue effects. *Biological Psychology, 96,* 134–143.

Klaczynski, P. (2001). The influence of analytic and heuristic processing on adolescent reasoning and decision making. *Child Development, 72,* 844–861.

Klahr, A. M., & Burt, S. A. (2014, in press). Elucidating the etiology of individual differences in parenting: A meta-analysis of behavioral genetic research. *Psychological Bulletin.*

Klaus, M., & Kennell, H. H. (1976). *Maternal-infant bonding.* St. Louis: Mosby.

Klein, S. (2012). *State of public school segregation in the United States, 2007–2010.* Washington, DC: Feminist Majority Foundation.

Kleinhaus, K., & others (2013). Prenatal stress and affective disorders in a population birth cohort. *Bipolar Disorders, 15,* 92–99.

Klever, S. (2013). Reminiscence therapy: Finding meaning in memories. *Nursing, 43,* 36–37.

Kliegman, R., Stanton, B., St. Geme, J., Schor, N., & Behrman, R. (2012). *Nelson textbook of pediatrics* (19th ed.). New York: Elsevier.

Klima, C., Norr, K., Conderheld, S., & Handler, A. (2009). Introduction of Centering Pregnancy in a public health clinic. *Journal of Midwifery and Women's Health, 54,* 27–34.

Klimstra, T. A., Hale, W. W., Raaijmakers, Q. A. W., Branje, S. J. T., & Meeus, W. H. H. (2010). Identity formation in adolescence: Change or stability? *Journal of Youth and Adolescence, 39,* 150–162.

Klinedinst, N. J., & Resnick, B. (2014). Volunteering and depressive symptoms among residents in a continuing care retirement community. *Journal of Gerontological Social Work, 57,* 52–71.

Klinenberg, E. (2012, February 4). Sunday Review: One's a crowd. *New York Times,* Retrieved from http://www.nytimes.com/2012/02/05/opinion/sunday/living-alone-means-being-social.html?_r=0

Klinenberg, E. (2013). *Going solo: The extraordinary rise and surprising appeal of living alone.* New York: Penguin.

Knight, B. G., Kaski, B., Shurgot, G. R., & Dave, J. (2006). Improving the mental health of older adults. In J. E. Birren & K. W. Schaie (Eds.), *Handbook of the psychology of aging* (6th ed.). San Diego: Academic Press.

Knight, B. B., & Kellough, J. (2013). Psychotherapy with older adults within a family context. In I. B. Weiner & others (Eds.), *Handbook of psychology* (2nd ed., Vol. 8). New York: Wiley.

Knight, B. G., & Lee, L. (2007). Mental health. In J. E. Birren (Ed.), *Encyclopedia of gerontology* (2nd ed.). San Diego: Academic Press.

Knight, C. P., & others (2014, in press). Trajectories of Mexican American and mainstream cultural values among Mexican American adolescents. *Journal of Youth and Adolescence.*

Knight, L. F., & Hope, D. A. M. (2012). Correlates of same-sex attractions and behaviors among self-identified heterosexual university students. *Archives of Sexual Behavior, 41,* 1199–1208.

Knox, M. (2010). On hitting children: A review of corporal punishment in the United States. *Journal of Pediatric Health Care, 24,* 103–107.

Ko, P. C., & others (2014, in press). Understanding age-related reductions in visual working memory capacity: Examining the stages of change detection. *Attention, Perception, and Psychophysics.*

Ko, S. H., Chen, C. H., Wang, H. H., & Su, Y. T. (2014, in press). Postpartum women's sleep quality and its predictors in Taiwan. *Journal of Nursing Scholarship.*

Ko, Y. L., Yang, C. L., Fang, C. L., Lee, M. Y., & Lin, P. C. (2013). Community-based postpartum exercise program. *Journal of Clinical Nursing, 22*(15–16), 2122–2131.

Kochanek, K. D., & others (2011). Deaths: Preliminary data 2009. *National Vital Statistics Reports, 59*(4), 1–51.

Kochanska, G., & Aksan, N. (2007). Conscience in childhood: Past, present, and future. *Merrill-Palmer Quarterly, 50,* 299–310.

Kochanska, G., Barry, R. A., Jimenez, N. B., Hollatz, A. L., & Woodard, J. (2009). Guilt and effortful control: Two mechanisms that prevent disruptive developmental trajectories. *Journal of Personality and Social Psychology, 97,* 322–333.

Kochanska, G., & Kim, S. (2012). Toward a new understanding of the legacy of early attachments for future antisocial trajectories: Evidence from two longitudinal studies. *Development and Psychopathology, 24*(3), 783–806.

Kochanska, G., & Kim, S. (2013). Early attachment organization with both parents and future behavior problems: From infancy to middle childhood. *Child Development, 84*(1), 283–296.

Kochanska, G., Koenig, J. L., Barry, R. A., Kim, S., & Yoon, J. E. (2010). Children's conscience during toddler and preschool years, moral self, and a competent, adaptive developmental trajectory. *Developmental Psychology, 46*, 1320–1322.

Koehler-Platten, K., Grow, L. L., Schulze, K. A., & Bertone, T. (2013). Using a lag reinforcement to increase phonemic variability in children with autistic spectrum disorders. *Analysis of Verbal Behavior, 29*, 71–83.

Koelblinger, C., & others (2013). Fetal magnetic resonance imaging of lymphangiomas. *Journal of Perinatal Medicine, 41*(4), 437–443.

Koenig, H. G. (2004). Religion, spirituality, and medicine: Research findings and implications for clinical practice. *Southern Medical Journal, 97*, 1194–2000.

Koenig, H. G., & Blazer, D. G. (1996). Depression. In J. E. Birren (Ed.), *Encyclopedia of gerontology* (Vol. 1). San Diego: Academic Press.

Koenig, H. G., & others (1992). Religious coping and depression in elderly hospitalized medically ill men. *American Journal of Psychiatry, 149*, 1693–1700.

Koenig, L. B., McGue, M., & Iacono, W. G. (2008). Stability and change in religiousness during emerging adulthood. *Developmental Psychology, 44*, 523–543.

Koh, H. (2014). The Teen Pregnancy Prevention Program: An evidence-based public health program model. *Journal of Adolescent Health, 54*(1, Suppl.), S1–S2.

Kohen, R., & others (2011). Response to psychosocial treatment in poststroke depression is associated with serotonin transporter polymorphisms. *Stroke, 42*, 2068–2070.

Kohlberg, L. (1958). *The development of modes of moral thinking and choice in the years 10 to 16.* Unpublished doctoral dissertation, University of Chicago.

Kohlberg, L. (1969). Stage and sequence: The cognitive-developmental approach to socialization. In D. A. Goslin (Ed.), *Handbook of socialization theory and research.* Chicago: Rand McNally.

Kohlberg, L. (1986). A current statement of some theoretical issues. In S. Modgil & C. Modgil (Eds.), *Lawrence Kohlberg.* Philadelphia: Falmer.

Kok, R., & others (2013). Attachment insecurity predicts child active resistance to parental requests in a compliance task. *Child Care Health and Development, 39*(2), 277–287.

Kokkevi, A., & others (2012). Multiple substance use and self-reported suicide attempts by adolescents in 16 countries. *European Child and Adolescent Psychiatry, 21*(8), 443–450.

Kolata, G. (2007, Nov 11). Chubby gets a second look. *New York Times,* p. D4.

Kollins, S. H., & Adcock, R. A. (2014, in press). ADHD, altered dopamine neurotransmission, and disrupted reinforcement processes: Implications for smoking and nicotine dependence. *Progress in Neuro-Psychopharmacology and Biological Psychiatry.*

Kolovou, G., & others (2014, in press). Aging mechanisms and associated lipid changes. *Current Vascular Pharmacology.*

Kong, A., & others (2012). Rate of *de novo* mutations and the importance of the father's age to disease risk. *Nature, 488*, 471–475.

Konopka, A. R., Suer, M. K., Wolff, C. A., & Harber, M. P. (2014). Markers of human skeletal muscle mitochondrial biogenesis and quality control: Effects of age and aerobic training. *Journals of Gerontology A: Biological Sciences and Medical Sciences, 69*, 371–388.

Konrath, S., Fuhrel-Forbis, A., Lou, A., & Brown, S. (2012). Motives for volunteering are associated with mortality risk in older adults. *Health Psychology, 31*, 87–96.

Koo, Y. J., & others (2012). Pregnancy outcomes according to increasing maternal age. *Taiwan Journal of Obstetrics and Gynecology, 51*, 60–65.

Koolschijn, P. C., Peper, J. S., & Crone, E. A. (2014). The influence of sex steroids on structural brain maturation in adolescence. *PLoS One, 9*(1), e83929.

Koorevaar, A. M., & others (2013). Big Five personality factors and depression diagnosis, severity, and age of onset in older adults. *Journal of Affective Disorders, 151*, 178–185.

Kopp, F., & Lindenberger, U. (2011). Effects of joint attention on long-term memory in 9-month-old infants: An event-related potentials study. *Developmental Science, 14*, 660–672.

Koppelman, K. L. (2014). *Understanding human differences* (4th ed.). Upper Saddle River, NJ: Pearson.

Koran, M. E., Hohman, T. J., Meda, S. A., & Thornton-Wells, T. A. (2014). Genetic interactions with inositol-related pathways are associated with longitudinal changes in ventricle size. *Journal of Alzheimer's Disease, 38*, 145–154.

Korat, O. (2009). The effect of maternal teaching talk on children's emergent literacy as a function of type of activity and maternal education level. *Journal of Applied Developmental Psychology, 30*, 34–42.

Koren, G., & Nordeng, H. (2012). Antidepressant use during pregnancy: The benefit-risk ratio. *American Journal of Obstetrics and Gynecology, 207*(3), 157–163.

Korte, J., Dorssaert, C. H., Westerhof, G. J., & Bohlmeijer, E. T. (2014). Life review in groups? An explorative analysis of social processes that facilitate or hinder the effectiveness of life review. *Aging and Mental Health, 18*, 376–384.

Korte, J., Westerhof, G. J., & Bohlmeijer, E. T. (2012). Mediating processes in an effective life-review intervention. *Psychology and Aging, 27*, 1172–1181.

Korten, N. C., & others (2014, in press). Heterogeneity of late-life depression: Relationship with cognitive functioning. *International Psychogeriatrics.*

Koss, K. J., & others (2011). Understanding children's emotional processes and behavioral strategies in the context of marital conflict. *Journal of Experimental Child Psychology, 109*, 336–352.

Koss, K. J., & others (2013). Patterns of children's adrenocortical reactivity to interparental conflict and associations with child adjustment: A growth mixture modeling approach. *Developmental Psychology, 49*(2), 317–326.

Koss, K. J., & others (2014, in press). Asymmetry in children's salivary cortisol and alpha-amylase in the context of marital conflict: Links to children's emotional security and adjustment. *Developmental Psychobiology.*

Kostelnik, M. J., Soderman, A. K., Whiren, A. P., & Rupiper, M. (2015, in press). *Developmentally appropriate curriculum* (6th ed.). Upper Saddle River, NJ: Pearson.

Kostovic, I., Judas, M., & Sedmak, G. (2011). Developmental history of the subplate zone, subplate neurons, and interstitial white matter neurons: Relevance for schizophrenia. *International Journal of Developmental Neuroscience, 29*(3), 193–205.

Kothandan, S. K. (2014, in press). School based interventions versus family based interventions in the treatment of childhood obesity—a systematic review. *Archives of Public Health.*

Kotovsky, L., & Baillargeon, R. (1994). Calibration-based reasoning about collision events in 11-month-old infants. *Cognition, 51*, 107–129.

Kotre, J. (1984). *Outliving the self: Generativity and the interpretation of lives.* Baltimore: Johns Hopkins University Press.

Kottak, C., & Kozaitis, K. (2012). *On being different* (4th ed.). New York: McGraw-Hill.

Kotter-Gruhn, D., & Smith, J. (2011). When time is running out: Changes in positive future perception and their relationships to changes in well-being in old age. *Psychology and Aging, 26*, 381–387.

Koulouglioti, C., & others (2014). The longitudinal association of young children's everyday routines to sleep duration. *Journal of Pediatric Health Care, 28*, 80–87.

Kovacs, A. H., Landzberg, M. J., & Goodlin, S. J. (2013). Advance care planning and end-of-life management of adult patients with congenital heart disease. *World Journal for Pediatric and Congenital Heart Surgery, 4*, 62–69.

Kowalski, R. M., Giumetti, G. W., Schroeder, A. N., & Lattanner, M. R. (2014, in press). Bullying in the digital age: A critical review and meta-analysis of cyberbullying research on youth. *Psychological Bulletin.*

Kowaltowski, A. J. (2011). Caloric restriction and redox state: Does this diet increase or decrease oxidant production? *Redox Report, 16*, 237–241.

Kozbelt, A. (2014). Musical creativity over the lifespan. In D. K. Simonton (Ed.), *Wiley-Blackwell handbook of genius.* New York: Wiley.

Kozhimmanil, K. B., & others (2013). Doula care, birth outcomes, and costs among Medicaid beneficiaries. *American Journal of Public Health, 103*(4), e113–e121.

Kozol, J. (2005). *The shame of the nation.* New York: Crown.

Kraft, E. (2012). Cognitive function, physical activity, and aging: Possible biological links and implications for multimodal interventions. *Neuropsychology, Development, and Cognition: Section B, Aging, Neuropsychology, Cognition, 19*, 248–263.

Kraft, J. M., & others (2012). Sex education and adolescent sexual behavior: Do community characteristics matter? *Contraception, 86*(3), 276–280.

Krafft, C. E., & others (2014). An eight month randomized controlled exercise trial alters brain activation during cognitive tasks in overweight children. *Obesity, 22*, 232–242.

Krakoff, L. R. (2008). Older patients need better guidelines for optimal treatment of high blood pressure: One size fits few. *Hypertension, 51*, 817–818.

Kramer, L. (2006, July 10). Commentary in "How your siblings make you who you are" by J. Kluger, *Time,* pp. 46–55.

Kramer, L., & Perozynski, L. (1999). Parental beliefs about managing sibling conflict. *Developmental Psychology, 35*, 489–499.

Kramer, L., & Radey, C. (1997). Improving sibling relationships among young children: A social skills training model. *Family Relations, 46*, 237–246.

Kramer, W. E. (2012). Large employers see scenarios under which they could move workers and retirees to exchanges. *Health Affairs, 31*, 299–305.

Kranz Graham, E., & Lachman, M. E. (2014, in preparation). *The associations between facet level personality and cognitive performance: What underlying characteristics drive trait level predictors across the adult lifespan?* Unpublished manuscript, Department of Psychology, Brandeis University, Waltham, MA.

Krause, N. (1995). Religiosity and self-esteem among older adults. *Journals of Gerontology B: Psychological Science, 50*, P236–P246.

Krause, N. (2003). Religious meaning and subjective well-being in late life. *Journals of Gerontology B: Psychological Social Sciences, 58*, S160–S170.

Krause, N. (2004). Stressors in highly valued roles, meaning in life, and the physical health status of older adults. *Journal of Gerontology: Social Sciences, 59,* S287–S297.

Krause, N. (2008). The social foundations of religious meaning in life. *Research on Aging, 30*(4), 395–427.

Krause, N. (2009). Deriving a sense of meaning in late life. In V. L. Bengtson, D. Gans, N. M. Putney, & M. Silverstein (Eds.), *Handbook of theories of aging.* New York: Springer.

Krause, N. (2012). Valuing the life experience of old adults and change in depressive symptoms: Exploring an overlooked benefit of involvement in religion. *Journal of Aging Health, 24,* 227–247.

Krause, N., & Hayward, R. D. (2014, in press). Religious involvement, practical wisdom, and self-rated health. *Journal of Aging and Health.*

Krebs, C. (2014, in press). Measuring sexual victimization: On what fronts is the jury still out and do we need it to come in? *Trauma, Violence, and Abuse.*

Kretch, K. S., & Adolph, K. E. (2013a). Cliff or step? Posture-specific learning at the edge of a drop-off. *Child Development, 84,* 226–240.

Kretch, K. S., & Adolph, K. E. (2013b). No bridge too high: Infants decide whether to cross based on bridge width, not drop-off height. *Developmental Science, 16,* 336–351.

Kretch, K. S., Franchak, J. M., & Adolph, K. E. (2014, in press). Crawling and walking infants see the world differently. *Child Development.*

Kreutzer, M., Leonard, C., & Flavell, J. H. (1975). An interview study of children's knowledge about memory. *Monographs of the Society for Research in Child Development, 40* (1, Serial No. 159).

Kriemler, S., & others (2011). Effect of school-based interventions on activity and fitness in children and adolescents: A review of reviews and systematic update. *British Journal of Sports Medicine, 45,* 923–930.

Kring, A. M. (2000). Gender and anger. In A. H. Fischer (Ed.), *Gender and emotion: Social psychological perspectives.* New York: Cambridge University Press.

Kristensen, P., Weisaeth, L., & Heir, T. (2012). Bereavement and mental health after sudden and violent losses: A review. *Psychiatry, 75,* 76–97.

Kristjuhan, U., & Taidre, E. (2010). Postponed aging in university teachers. *Rejuvenation Research, 13,* 356–358.

Kroger, J. (2012). The status of identity developments in identity research. In P. K. Kerig, M. S. Schulz, & S. T. Hauser (Eds.), *Adolescence and beyond.* New York: Oxford University Press.

Kroger, J., Martinussen, M., & Marcia, J. E. (2010). Identity change during adolescence and young adulthood: A meta-analysis. *Journal of Adolescence, 33,* 683–698.

Kronenberg, G., & others (2010). Impact of actin filament stabilization on adult hippocampal and olfactory bulb neurogenesis. *Journal of Neuoroscience, 30,* 3419–3431.

Krueger, J. I., Vohs, K. D., & Baumeister, R. F. (2008). Is the allure of self-esteem a mirage after all? *American Psychologist, 63,* 64.

Krueger, P. M., & Chang, V. W. (2008). Being poor and coping with stress: Health behaviors and the risk of death. *American Journal of Public Health, 98,* 889–896.

Kruger, J., Blanck, H. M., & Gillespie, C. (2006). Dietary and physical activity behaviors among adults successful at weight loss management. *International Journal of Behavioral Nutrition and Physical Activity, 3,* 17.

Krushkal, J., & others (2014, in press). Epigenetic analysis of neurocognitive development at 1 year of age in a community-based pregnancy cohort. *Behavior Genetics.*

Kubicek, B., Korunka C., Hoonakker, P., & Raymo, J. M. (2010). Work and family characteristics as predictors of early retirement in men and women. *Research on Aging, 32,* 467–498.

Kübler-Ross, E. (1969). *On death and dying.* New York: Macmillan.

Kuebli, J. (1994, March). Young children's understanding of everyday emotions. *Young Children, 49*(3), 36–47.

Kuhl, P. K. (1993). Infant speech perception: A window on psycholinguistic development. *International Journal of Psycholinguistics, 9,* 33–56.

Kuhl, P. K. (2000). A new view of language acquisition. *Proceedings of the National Academy of Science, 97*(22), 11850–11857.

Kuhl, P. K. (2007). Is speech learning "gated" by the social brain? *Developmental Science, 10,* 110–120.

Kuhl, P. K. (2009). Linking infant speech perception to language acquisition: Phonetic learning predicts language growth. In J. Colombo, P. McCardle, & L. Freund (Eds.), *Infant pathways to language.* New York: Psychology Press.

Kuhl, P. K. (2011). Social mechanisms in early language acquisition: Understanding integrated brain systems and supporting language. In J. Decety & J. Cacioppo (Eds.), *Handbook of social neuroscience.* New York: Oxford University Press.

Kuhl, P. K., & Damasio, A. (2012). Language. In E. R. Kandel & others (Eds.), *Principles of neural science* (5th ed.). New York: McGraw-Hill.

Kuhn, D. (1998). Afterword to Volume 2: Cognition, perception, and language. In W. Damon (Ed.), *Handbook of child psychology* (5th ed., Vol. 2). New York: Wiley.

Kuhn, D. (2009). Adolescent thinking. In R. M. Lerner & L. Steinberg (Eds.), *Handbook of adolescent psychology* (3rd ed.). New York: Wiley.

Kuhn, D. (2011). What is scientific thinking and how does it develop? In U. Goswami (Ed.), *Wiley-Blackwell handbook of childhood cognitive development* (2nd ed.). New York: Wiley Blackwell.

Kuhn, D. (2013). Reasoning. In P. D. Zelazo (Ed.), *Oxford handbook of developmental psychology.* New York: Oxford University Press.

Kuhn, D., Cheney, R., & Weinstock, M. (2000). The development of epistemological understanding. *Cognitive Development, 15,* 309–328.

Kuipers, S., Trentani, A., van der Zee, E. A., & den Boer, J. A. (2013). Chronic stress-induced changes in the rat brain: Role of sex differences and effect of long-term tianeptine treatment. *Neuropharmacology, 75C,* 426–436.

Kulkofsky, S., & Klemfuss, J. Z. (2008). What the stories children tell can tell about their memory: Narrative skill and young children's suggestibility. *Developmental Psychology, 44,* 1442–1456.

Kulmala, J., & others (2013). Perceived stress symptoms in midlife predict disability in old age: A 28-year prospective study. *Journals of Gerontology A: Biological Sciences and Medical Sciences, 68,* 984–991.

Kulu, H. (2014, in press). Marriage duration and divorce: The seven year itch or a lifelong itch? *Demography.*

Kumar, N., & Priyadarshi, B. (2013). Differential effect of aging on verbal and visuo-spatial working memory. *Aging and Disease, 12,* 170–177.

Kumar, R., & others (2014). Interactions between the FTO and GNB3 genes contribute to varied phenotypes in hypertension. *PLoS One, 8*(5), e63934.

Kunzweiler, C. (2007). Twin individuality. *Fresh ink: Essays from Boston College's first-year writing seminar, 9*(1), 2–3.

Kuo, L. J., & Anderson, R. C. (2012). Effects of early bilingualism on learning phonological regularities in a new language. *Journal of Experimental Child Psychology, 111,* 455–467.

Kuo, M. C., Kiu, I. P., Ting, K. H., & Chan, C. C. (2014). Age-related effects on perceptual and semantic encoding in memory. *Neuroscience, 261,* 95–106.

Kuperberg, A. (2014). Age at coresidence, premarital cohabitation, and marriage dissolution: 1985–2009. *Journal of Marriage and Family, 76,* 352–369.

Kurdek, L. A. (2006). Differences between partners from heterosexual, gay, and lesbian cohabiting couples. *Journal of Marriage and the Family, 68,* 509–528.

Kurdek, L. A. (2007). The allocation of household labor between partners in gay and lesbian couples. *Journal of Family Issues, 28,* 132–148.

L

Labouvie-Vief, G. (1986, August). *Modes of knowing and life-span cognition.* Paper presented at the meeting of the American Psychological Association, Washington, DC.

Labouvie-Vief, G. (2009). Cognition and equilibrium regulation in development and aging. In V. Bengtson & others (Eds.), *Handbook of theories of aging.* New York: Springer.

Labouvie-Vief, G., Gruhn, D., & Studer, J. (2010). Dynamic integration of emotion and cognition: Equilibrium regulation in development and aging. In M. E. Lamb, A. Freund, & R. M. Lerner (Eds.), *Handbook of life-span development* (Vol. 2). New York: Wiley.

Lacelle, C., Hebert, M., Lavoie, F., Vitaro, F., & Tremblay, R. E. (2012). Sexual health in women reporting a history of child sexual abuse. *Child Abuse and Neglect, 36,* 247–259.

Lachman, M. E. (2004). Development in midlife. *Annual Review of Psychology* (Vol. 55). Palo Alto, CA: Annual Reviews.

Lachman, M. E. (2006). Perceived control over aging-related declines. *Current Directions in Psychological Science, 15,* 282–286.

Lachman, M. E., Agrigoroaei, S., Murphy, C., & Tun, P. A. (2010). Frequent cognitive activity compensates for education differences in episodic memory. *American Journal of Geriatric Psychiatry, 18,* 4–10.

Lachman, M. E., & Firth, K. M. P. (2004). The adaptive value of feeling in control during midlife. In O. G. Brim, C. D. Ruff, & R. C. Kessler (Eds.), *How healthy are we?* Chicago: University of Chicago Press.

Lachman, M. E., Maier, H., & Budner, R. (2000). *A portrait of midlife.* Unpublished manuscript, Brandeis University, Waltham, MA.

Lachman, M. E., Neupert, S. D., & Agrigoroaei, S. (2011). The relevance of control beliefs for health and aging. In K. W. Schaie & S. L. Willis (Eds.), *Handbook of the psychology of aging* (7th ed.). New York: Elsevier.

Lachman, M. E., Rosnick, C., & Rocke, C. (2009). The rise and fall of control beliefs predict exercise behavior during and after an exercise intervention. *Journal of Aging and Physical Activity, 16,* 1–16.

Lacourse, E., & others (2014, in press). A longitudinal twin study of physical aggression during early childhood: Evidence for a developmentally dynamic gene. *Psychological Medicine.*

Ladd, G., Buhs, E., & Troop, W. (2004). School adjustment and social skills training. In P. K. Smith & C. H. Hart (Eds.), *Blackwell handbook of childhood social development.* Malden, MA: Blackwell.

LaFrance, M., Hecht, M. A., & Paluck, E. L. (2003). The contingent smile: A meta-analysis of sex differences in smiling. *Psychological Bulletin, 129,* 305–334.

Lafreniere, D., & Mann, N. (2009). Anosmia: Loss of smell in the elderly. *Otolaryngologic Clinics of North America, 42,* 123–131.

Lai, M-C., Lombardo, M. V., Chakrabarti, B., & Baron-Cohen, S. (2013). Subgrouping the autism "spectrum": Reflections on DSM-5. *PLoS Biology, 11*(4), e1001544.

Laible, D., & Karahuta, E. (2014). Prosocial behaviors in early childhood: Helping others, responding to the distress of others, and working with others. In L. Padilla-Walker & G. Carlo (Eds.), *Prosocial behavior.* New York: Oxford University Press.

Laible, D., & Thompson, R. A. (2007). Early socialization: A relationship perspective. In J. E. Grusec & P. D. Hastings (Eds.), *Handbook of socialization.* New York: Guilford.

Lakoski, S., & others (2013, June 2). *Exercise lowers cancer risk in middle-aged men.* Paper presented at the American Society of Clinical Oncology meeting, Chicago, IL.

Lalley, P. M. (2013). The aging respiratory system—pulmonary structure, function, and neural control. *Respiratory Physiology and Neurology, 187,* 199–210.

Lamb, M. E. (1994). Infant care practices and the application of knowledge. In C. B. Fisher & R. M. Lerner (Eds.), *Applied developmental psychology.* New York McGraw-Hill.

Lamb, M. E. (2000). The history of research on father involvement: An overview. *Marriage and Family Review, 29,* 23–42.

Lamb, M. E. (2013). Non-parental care and emotional development. In S. Pauen & M. Bornstein (Eds.), *Early childhood development and later outcomes.* New York: Cambridge University Press.

Lamb, M. E., Bornstein, M. H., & Teti, D. M. (2002). *Development in infancy* (4th ed.). Mahwah, NJ: Erlbaum.

Lamb, M. E., & Lewis, C. (2013). Father-child relationships. In C. S. Tamis-LeMonda & N. Cabrera (Eds.), *Handbook of father involvement* (2nd ed.). New York: Psychology Press.

Lamb, M. E., Malloy, L. C., Hershkowitz, I., & La Rooy, D. (2015, in press). Children and the law. In R. E. Lerner (Ed.), *Handbook of child psychology and developmental science* (7th ed.). New York: Wiley.

Lamb, S. (2014). Permanent personhood or meaningful decline? Toward a critical anthropology of successful aging. *Journal of Aging Studies, 29,* 41–52.

Lampard, A. M., Byrne, S. M., McLean, N., & Fursland, A. (2012). The Eating Disorder Inventory-2 perfectionism scale: Factor structure and associations with dietary restraint and weight and shape concern in eating disorders. *Eating Behaviors, 13,* 49–53.

Lamy, S., & others (2014, in press). Psychosocial and organizational work factors and incidence of arterial hypertension among female healthcare workers: Results of the Organisation des soins et santé des soignants cohort. *Journal of Hypertension.*

Lan, X., & others (2011). Investigating the links between the subcomponents of executive function and academic achievement: A cross-cultural analysis of Chinese and American preschoolers. *Journal of Experimental Child Psychology, 108,* 677–692.

Landau, B., Smith, L., & Jones, S. (1998). Object perception and object naming in early development. *Trends in Cognitive Science, 2,* 19–24.

Landrum, A. R., Mills, C. M., & Johnston, A. M. (2013). When do children trust the expert? Benevolence information influences children's trust more than expertise. *Developmental Science, 16,* 622–638.

Landsberg, L., & others (2013). Obesity-related hypertension: Pathogenesis, cardiovascular risk, and treatment—A position paper of the Obesity Society and the American Society of Hypertension. *Obesity, 21*(1), 8–24.

Lane, A., Harrison, M., & Murphy, N. (2014, in press). Screen time increases risk of overweight and obesity in active and inactive 9-year-old Irish children: A cross sectional analysis. *Journal of Physical Activity and Health.*

Lane, H. (1976). *The wild boy of Aveyron.* Cambridge, MA: Harvard University Press.

Lane, K. L., & others (2013). Strategies for decreasing aggressive, coercive behavior: A call for preventive efforts. In B. G. Cook & M. G. Tankersley (Eds.), *Research-based practices in special education.* Upper Saddle River, NJ: Pearson.

Lang, A., & others (2011). Perinatal loss and parental grief: The challenge of ambiguity and disenfranchised grief. *Omega, 63,* 183–196.

Lang, F. R., & Carstensen, L. L. (1994). Close emotional relationships in late life: Further support for proactive aging in the social domain. *Psychology and Aging, 9,* 315–324.

Langberg, J. M., Dvorsky, M. R., & Evans, S. W. (2013). What specific facets of executive function are associated with academic functioning in youth with attention-deficit/hyperactivity disorder? *Journal of Abnormal Child Psychology, 41,* 1145–1159.

Lange, B. S., & others (2010). The potential of virtual reality and gaming to assist successful aging with disability. *Physical Medicine and Rehabilitation Clinics of North America, 21,* 339–356.

Langellier, B. A., & others (2014). The new food package and breastfeeding outcomes among Women, Infants, and Children participants in Los Angeles County. *American Journal of Public Health, 104*(1, Suppl.), S112–S118.

Langer, E. J. (2000). Mindful learning. *Current Directions in Psychological Science, 9,* 220–223.

Langer, E. (2005). *On becoming an artist.* New York: Ballantine.

Langer, E. J. (2007, August). *Counterclockwise: Mindfulness and aging.* Paper presented at the meeting of the American Psychological Association, San Francisco.

Lango Allen, H., & others (2014, in press). Next generation sequencing of chromosomal rearrangements in patients with split-hand/split-foot malformation provides evidence for DYNC1L1 exonic enhancers of DLX5/6 expression in humans. *Journal of Medical Genetics.*

Langstrom, N., Rahman, Q., Carlstrom, E., & Lichtenstein, P. (2010). Genetic and environmental effects on same-sex sexual behaviour: A population study of twins in Sweden. *Archives of Sexual Behavior, 39,* 75–80.

Lansford, J. E. (2012). Divorce. In R. J. R. Levesque (Ed.), *Encyclopedia of adolescence.* New York: Springer.

Lansford, J. E. (2013). Single- and two-parent families. In J. Hattie & E. Anderman (Eds.), *International guide to student achievement.* New York: Routledge.

Lansford, J. E., & Deater-Deckard, K. (2012). Childrearing discipline and violence in developing countries. *Child Development, 83*(1), 62–75.

Lansford, J. E., Wager, L. B., Bates, J. E., Pettit, G. S., & Dodge, K. A. (2012). Forms of spanking and children's externalizing problems. *Family Relations, 61*(2), 224–236.

Lansford, J. E., & others (2005). Cultural normativeness as a moderator of the link between physical discipline and children's adjustment: A comparison of China, India, Italy, Kenya, Philippines, and Thailand. *Child Development, 76,* 1234–1246.

Lansford, J. E., & others (2010). Developmental precursors of number of sexual partners from ages 16 to 22. *Journal of Research on Adolescence, 20,* 651–677.

Lansford, J. E., & others (2011). Reciprocal relations between parents' physical discipline and children's externalizing behavior during middle childhood and adolescence. *Development and Psychopathology, 23,* 225–238.

Lansford, J. E., & others (2014, in press). Pathways of peer relationships from childhood to young adulthood. *Journal of Applied Developmental Psychology.*

Laopaiboon, M., & others (2009). Music during caesarean section under regional anaesthesia for improving maternal and infant outcomes. *Cochrane Database of Systematic Reviews,* CD006914.

Lapsley, D. K, & Yeager, D. (2013). Moral-character education. In I. B. Weiner & others (Eds.), *Handbook of psychology* (2nd ed., Vol. 7). New York: Wiley.

Larson, F. B., & others (2006). Exercise is associated with reduced risk for incident dementia among persons 65 years of age and older. *Annals of Internal Medicine, 144,* 73–81.

Larson, R. W. (2001). How U.S. children and adolescents spend their time: What it does (and doesn't) tell us about their development. *Current Directions in Psychological Science, 10,* 160–164.

Larson, R. W., & Angus, R. (2011). Adolescents' development of skills for agency in youth programs: Learning to think strategically. *Child Development, 82,* 277–294.

Larson, R. W., & Dawes, N. P. (2014, in press). How to cultivate adolescents' motivation: Effective strategies employed by the professional staff of American youth programs. In S. Joseph (Ed.), *Positive psychology in practice.* New York: Wiley.

Larson, R. W., Shernoff, D. J., & Bempechat, J. (2014, in press). A new paradigm for the science and practice of engaging young people. Engaging youth in schools: Evidence-based models to guide future innovations. In D. J. Shernoff & J. Empechat (Eds.), *NSSE Yearbook.* New York: Columbia Teachers College Record.

Larson, R. W., & Verma, S. (1999). How children and adolescents spend time across the world: Work, play, and developmental opportunities. *Psychological Bulletin, 125,* 701–736.

Larson, R. W., & Wilson, S. (2004). Adolescence across place and time; Globalization and the changing pathways to adulthood. In R. Lerner & L. Steinberg (Eds.), *Handbook of Adolescent Psychology.* New York: Wiley.

Larson, R., Wilson, S., & Rickman, A. (2009). Globalization, societal change, and adolescence across the world. In R. M. Lerner & L. Steinberg (Eds.), *Handbook of adolescent psychology* (3rd ed.). New York: Wiley.

Larzelere, R. E., & Kuhn, B. R. (2005). Comparing child outcomes of physical punishment and alternative disciplinary tactics: A meta-analysis. *Clinical Child and Family Psychology Review, 8,* 1–37.

Lau, J. S., Adams, S. H., Irwin, C. E., & Ozer, E. M. (2013). Receipt of preventive health services in young adults. *Journal of Adolescent Health, 52,* 42–49.

Laubjerg, M., & Petersson, B. (2011). Juvenile delinquency and psychiatric contact among adoptees compared to non-adoptees in Denmark: A nationwide register-based comparative study. *Nordic Journal of Psychiatry, 65,* 365–372.

Lauer, R. H., & Lauer, J. C. (2012). *Marriage and the family* (8th ed.). New York: McGraw-Hill.

Lauff, E., Ingels, S. J., & Christopher, E. M. (2014). *Educational longitudinal study of 2002 (ELS:2002): A first look at 2002 high school sophomores 10 years later.* NCES 2014-36. Washington, DC: U.S. Department of Education.

Laumann, E. O., Glasser, D. B., Neves, R. C., & Moreira, E. D. (2009). A population-based survey of sexual activity, sexual problems, and associated help-seeking behavior patterns in mature adults in the United

States of America. *International Journal of Impotence Research, 21,* 171–178.

Laurent, H. K., Ablow, J. C., & Measelle, J. (2012). Taking stress response out of the box: Stability, discontinuity, and temperament effects on HPA and SNS across social stressors in mother-infant dyads. *Developmental Psychology, 48,* 35–45.

Laursen, B., & Pursell, G. (2009). Conflict in peer relationships. In K. H. Rubin, W. M. Bukowski, & B. Laursen (Eds.), *Handbook of peer interactions, relationships, and groups.* New York: Guilford.

Lavalliere, M., & others (2011). Changing lanes in a simulator: Effects of aging on the control of the vehicle and visual inspection of mirrors and the blind spot. *Traffic Injury Prevention, 12,* 191–200.

Lavender, J. M., & others (2014, in press). Dimensions of emotion dysregulation in bulimia nervosa. *European Eating Disorders Review.*

Lavner, J. A., & Bradbury, T. N. (2012). Why do even satisfied newlyweds eventually go on to divorce? *Journal of Family Psychology, 26,* 1–10.

Lavner, J. A., Karney, B. R., & Bradbury, T. N. (2013). Newlyweds' optimistic forecasts of their marriage: For better or for worse? *Journal of Family Psychology, 27,* 531–540.

Lawler, M., Selby, P., Aapro, M. S., & Duffy, S. (2014). Ageism in cancer care. *British Medical Journal, 348,* g1614.

Lawrence, K. E., & others (2013). White matter microstructure in subjects with attention-deficit hyperactivity disorder and their siblings. *Journal of the American Academy of Child and Adolescent Psychiatry, 52,* 431–440.

Lawrence, R. A. (2012). Breastfeeding—a public health issue, not just a matter of choice. *Breastfeeding Medicine, 7,* 67–68.

Le Couteur, D. G., & Simpson, S. J. (2011). Adaptive senectitude: The prolongevity effects on aging. *Journals of Gerontology A: Biological Sciences and Medical Sciences, 66A,* 179–182.

Leaper, C. (2013). Gender development during childhood. In P. D. Zelazo (Ed.), *Oxford handbook of developmental psychology.* New York: Oxford University Press.

Leaper, C., & Bigler, R. S. (2011). Gender. In M. H. Underwood & L. H. Rosen (Eds.), *Social development.* New York: Guilford.

Ledesma, K. (2012). A place to call home. *Adoptive Families.* Retrieved from www.adoptivefamilies.com/articles.php?aid=2129

Lee, G. R. (2014). Current research on widowhood: Devastation and human resilience. *Journals of Gerontology B: Psychological Sciences and Social Sciences, 69,* 2–3.

Lee, I. M., & Skerrett, P. J. (2001). Physical activity and all-cause mortality: What is the dose-response relation? *Medical Science and Sports Exercise, 33*(6, Suppl.), S459–S471.

Lee, J. H., Jang, A. S., Park, S. W., Kim, D. J., & Park, C. S. (2014). Gene-gene interaction between CCR3 and Eotaxin genes: The relationship with blood eosinophilia in asthma. *Allergy, Asthma, and Immunology Research, 6,* 55–60.

Lee, J. S. (2013). Food insecurity and health costs: Research strategies using local, state, and national data sources for older adults. *Advances in Nursing, 4,* 42–50.

Lee, K., Cameron, C. A., Doucette, J., & Talwar, V. (2002). Phantoms and fabrications: Young children's detection of implausible lies. *Child Development, 73,* 1688–1702.

Lee, K., Quinn, P. C., Pascalis, O., & Slater, A. (2013). Development of face processing ability in childhood. In

P. D. Zelazo (Ed.), *Oxford handbook of developmental psychology.* New York: Oxford University Press.

Lee, K. Y., & others (2011). Effects of combined radiofrequency radiation exposure on the cell cycle and its regulatory proteins. *Bioelectromagnetics, 32,* 169–178.

Lee, S. H., Lee, B. C., Kim, J. W., Yi, J. S., & Choi, I. G. (2013). Association between alcoholism family history and alcohol screening scores among alcohol-dependent patients. *Clinical Psychopharmacology and Neuroscience, 11,* 89–95.

Lee, W-C., & Ory, M. G. (2013, in press). The engagement in physical activity for middle-aged and older adults with multiple chronic conditions: Findings from a community health assessment. *Journal of Aging Research.*

Lee, Y. H., & Song, G. G. (2014, in press). Genome-wide pathway analysis in attention-deficit/hyperactivity disorder. *Neurological Sciences.*

Leedy, P. D., & Ormrod, J. E. (2013). *Practical research* (10th ed.). Upper Saddle River, NJ: Pearson.

Leerkes, E. M. (2011). Maternal sensitivity during distressing tasks: A unique predictor of attachment security. *Infant Behavior and Development, 34,* 443–446.

Leerkes, E. M., Parade, S. H., & Gudmundson, J. A. (2011). Mothers' emotional reactions to crying pose risk for subsequent attachment insecurity. *Journal of Family Psychology, 25,* 635–643.

Lefkowitz, E. S., & Gillen, M. M. (2006). "Sex is just a normal part of life": Sexuality in emerging adulthood. In J. J. Arnett & J. L. Tanner (Eds.), *Emerging adults in America.* Washington, DC: American Psychological Association.

Legerstee, M. (1997). Contingency effects of people and objects on subsequent cognitive functioning in 3-month-old infants. *Social Development, 6,* 307–321.

Legge, G. E., Madison, C., Vaughn, B. N., Cheong, A. M., & Miller, J. C. (2008). Retention of high tactile acuity throughout the lifespan in blindness. *Perception and Psychophysics, 70,* 1471–1488.

Lehman, E. B., & others (2010). Long-term stability of young children's eyewitness accuracy, suggestibility, and resistance to misinformation. *Journal of Applied Developmental Psychology, 31,* 145–154.

Lehman, H. C. (1960). The age decrement in outstanding scientific creativity. *American Psychologist, 15,* 128–134.

Lehr, C. A., Hanson, A., Sinclair, M. F., & Christensen, S. I. (2003). Moving beyond dropout prevention towards school completion. *School Psychology Review, 32,* 342–364.

Leighton, S. (2008). Bereavement therapy with adolescents: Facilitating a process of spiritual growth. *Journal of Child and Adolescent Psychiatric Nursing, 21,* 24–34.

Leist, A. K., & others (2013). Time away from work predicts later cognitive function: Differences by activity during leave. *Annals of Epidemiology, 23,* 455–462.

Lempers, J. D., Flavell, E. R., & Flavell, J. H. (1977). The development in very young children of tacit knowledge concerning visual perception. *Genetic Psychology Monographs, 95,* 3–53.

Lengua, L., & Wachs, T. D. (2012). Temperament and risk: Resilient and vulnerable responses to adversity. In M. Zentner & R. Shiner (Eds.), *Handbook of temperament.* New York: Guilford.

Lenhart, A. (2012). Teens, smartphones, and texting: Texting volume is up while the frequency of voice calling is down. Retrieved May 2, 2013, from http://pewinternet.org/~/medai/Files/Reorts/2012/PIP_Teens_Smartphones_and-Texting.pdf

Lenhart, A., Purcell, K., Smith, A., & Zickuhr, K. (2010, February 3). *Social media and young adults.* Washington, DC: Pew Research Center.

Lennon, E. M., Gardner, J. M., Karmel, B. Z., & Flory, M. J. (2008). Bayley Scales of Infant Development. In M. M. Haith & J. B. Benson (Eds.), *Encyclopedia of infant and early childhood development.* Oxford, UK: Elsevier.

Lenoir, C. P., Mallet, E., & Calenda, E. (2000). Siblings of sudden infant death syndrome and near miss in about 30 families: Is there a genetic link? *Medical Hypotheses, 54,* 408–411.

Lenroot, R. K., & Giedd, J. N. (2006). Brain development in children and adolescents: Insights from anatomical magnetic resonance imaging. *Neuroscience and Biobehavioral Reviews, 30,* 718–729.

Leon, J., & others (2014, in press). A combination of physical and cognitive exercise improves reaction time in 61-84-years-old persons. *Journal of Aging and Physical Activity.*

Leone, J. E., Mullin, E. M., Maurer-Starks, S. S., & Rovito, M. J. (2014, in press). The Adolescent Body Image Satisfaction Scale (ABISS) for males: Exploratory factor analysis and implications for strength and conditioning professionals. *Journal of Strength and Conditioning Research.*

Leong, F. T. L., & others (2013). Ethnic minority psychology. In I. B. Weiner & others (Eds.), *Handbook of psychology* (2nd ed., Vol. 1). New York: Wiley.

Lepage, J. F., & others (2014, in press). Brain morphology in children with 47, XYY syndrome: A voxel- and surface-based morphometric study. *Genes, Brain, and Behavior.*

Lereya, S. T., Samara, M., & Wolke, D. (2013, in press). Parenting behavior and the risk of becoming victim and a bully/victim: A meta-analysis study. *Child Abuse and Neglect, 37*(12), 1091–1098.

Lerner, H. G. (1989). *The dance of intimacy.* New York: Harper & Row.

Lerner, J. V., & others (2013). Positive youth development: Processes, philosophies, and programs. In I. B. Weiner & others (Eds.), *Handbook of psychology* (2nd ed., Vol. 6). New York: Wiley.

Lerner, R. M., Boyd, M., & Du, D. (2008). Adolescent development. In I. B. Weiner & C. B. Craighead (Eds.), *Encyclopedia of psychology* (4th ed). Hoboken, NJ: Wiley.

Lerner-Geva, L., Boyko, V., Blumstein, T., & Benyamini, Y. (2010). The impact of education, cultural background, and lifestyle on symptoms of the menopausal transition: The Women's Health at Midlife Study. *Journal of Women's Health, 19,* 975–985.

Lesaux, N. K., & Siegel, L. S. (2003). The development of reading in children who speak English as a second language. *Developmental Psychology, 39,* 1005–1019.

Leshikar, E. D., Gutchess, A. H., Hebrank, A. C., Sutton, B. P., & Park, D. C. (2010). The impact of increased relational encoding demands in frontal and hippocampal function in older adults. *Cortex, 46,* 507–521.

Leshikar, E. D., & Duarte, A. (2014). Medial prefrontal cortex supports source memory for self-referenced materials in young and older adults. *Cognitive, Affective, and Behavioral Neuroscience, 14,* 236–252.

Lesley, C. (2005). *Burning fence: A western memoir of fatherhood.* New York: St. Martin's Press.

Lessow-Hurley, J. (2013). *Foundations of dual language instruction* (6th ed.). Boston: Allyn & Bacon.

Lester, B. M., & others (2002). The maternal lifestyle study: Effects of substance exposure during pregnancy on neurodevelopmental outcome in 1-month-old infants. *Pediatrics, 110,* 1182–1192.

Lester, B. M., & others (2011). Infant neurobehavioral development. *Seminars in Perinatology, 35,* 8–19.

Leuschen, J., & others (2013). Association of statin use with cataracts: A propensity score-matched analysis. *JAMA Ophthalmology, 131,* 1427–1431.

Levelt, W. J. M. (1989). *Speaking: From intention to articulation.* Cambridge, MA: MIT Press.

Lever-Duffy, J., & McDonald, J. (2015). *Teaching and learning with technology* (5th ed.). Upper Saddle River, NJ: Pearson.

Levin, J. A., Fox, J. A., & Forde, D. R. (2015). *Elementary statistics in social research* (12th ed.). Upper Saddle River, NJ: Pearson.

LeVine, S. (1979). *Mothers and wives: Gusii women of East Africa.* Chicago: University of Chicago Press.

Levine, T. P., & others (2008). Effects of prenatal cocaine exposure on special education in school-aged children. *Pediatrics, 122,* e83–e91.

Levinson, D. J. (1978). *The seasons of a man's life.* New York: Knopf.

Levinson, D. J. (1996). *Seasons of a woman's life.* New York: Alfred Knopf.

Levy, J. C. (2013). *Adaptive learning and the human condition.* Upper Saddle River, NJ: Pearson.

Lewis, A. C. (2007). Looking beyond NCLB. *Phi Delta Kappan, 88,* 483–484.

Lewis, M. (2005). Selfhood. In B. Hopkins (Ed.), *The Cambridge encyclopedia of child development.* Cambridge, UK: Cambridge University Press.

Lewis, M. (2007). Early emotional development. In A. Slater & M. Lewis (Eds.), *Introduction to infant development.* Malden, MA: Blackwell.

Lewis, M. (2008). The emergence of human emotions. In M. Lewis, J. M. Haviland Jones, & L. Feldman Barrett (Eds.), *Handbook of emotions* (3rd ed.). New York: Guilford.

Lewis, M. (2010). The emergence of consciousness and its role in human development. In W. F. Overton & R. M. Lerner (Eds.), *Handbook of life-span development* (2nd ed.). New York: Wiley.

Lewis, M. D. (2013). The development of emotion regulation: Integrating normative and individual differences through developmental neuroscience. In P. D. Zelazo (Ed.), *Handbook of developmental psychology.* New York: Oxford University Press.

Lewis, M., & Brooks-Gunn, J. (1979). *Social cognition and the acquisition of the self.* New York. Plenum.

Lewis, M., Feiring, C. & Rosenthal, S. (2000). Attachment over time. *Child Development, 71,* 707–720.

Lewis, M. D., Todd, R., & Xu, X. (2011). The development of emotion regulation: A neuropsychological perspective. In R. M. Lerner, W. F. Overton, A. M. Freund, & M. E. Lamb (Eds.), *Handbook of life-span development.* New York: Wiley.

Lewis, T. L., & Maurer, D. (2005). Multiple sensitive periods in human visual development: Evidence from visually deprived children. *Developmental Psychobiology, 46,* 163–183.

Lewis, T. L., & Maurer, D. (2009). Effects of early pattern deprivation on visual development. *Optometry and Vision Science, 86,* 640–646.

Lhila, A., & Long, S. (2011). What is driving the black-white difference in low birthweight in the U.S.? *Health Economics, 21,* 301–315.

Li, B. J., Jiang, Y. J., Yuan, F., & Ye, H. X. (2010). Exchange transfusion of least incompatible blood for severe hemolytic disease of the newborn due to anti-Rh17. *Transfusion Medicine, 20,* 66–69.

Li, C., Goran, M. I., Kaur, H., Nollen, N., & Ahluwalia, J. S. (2007). Developmental trajectories of overweight during childhood: Role of early life factors. *Obesity, 15,* 760–761.

Li, F. J., Shen, L., & Ji, H. F. (2012). Dietary intakes of vitamin E, vitamin C, and b-carotene, and risk of Alzheimer's disease: A meta-analysis. *Journal of Alzheimer's Disease, 31,* 753–758.

Li, H., Ji, Y., & Chen, T. (2014). The roles of different sources of social support on emotional well-being among Chinese elderly. *PLoS One, 9*(3), e90051.

Li, J., Olsen, J., Vestergaard, M., & Obel, C. (2011). Low Apgar scores and risk of childhood attention deficit hyperactivity disorder. *Journal of Pediatrics, 158,* 775–779.

Li, P. Q., & others (2014, in press). Development of noninvasive prenatal diagnosis of trisomy 21 by RT-MLPA with a new set of SNP markers. *Archives of Gynecology and Obstetrics.*

Li, W., Farkas, G., Duncan, G. J., Burchinal, M. R., & Vandell, D. L. (2013). Timing of high-quality child care and cognitive, language, and preacademic development. *Developmental Psychology, 49,* 1440–1451.

Li, X. P., & others (2013). The influence of statin-fibrate combination therapy on lipids profile and apolipoprotein A5 in patients with acute coronary syndrome. *Lipids in Health and Disease, 12,* 133.

Li, Y. (2007). Recovering from spousal bereavement in later life: Does volunteer participation play a role? *Journals of Gerontology: Psychological Sciences and Social Sciences, 62B,* S257–S266.

Li, Z., & others (2013). Maternal severe life events and risk of neural tube defects among rural Chinese. *Birth Defects Research A: Clinical and Molecular Teratology, 97,* 109–114.

Liang, Y. J., Xi, B., Song, A. Q., Liu, J. X., & Mi, J. (2012). Trends in general and abdominal obesity among Chinese children and adolescents, 1993–2009. *Pediatric Obesity, 7,* 355–364.

Liben, L. S. (1995). Psychology meets geography: Exploring the gender gap on the national geography bee. *Psychological Science Agenda, 8,* 8–9.

Liben, L. S., Bigler, R. S., & Hilliard, L. J. (2014). Gender development: From universality to individuality. In E. T. Gershoff, R. S. Mistry, & D. A. Crosby (Eds.), *Societal contexts of child development.* New York: Oxford University Press.

Libertus, K., & Needham, A. (2010). Teach to reach: The effects of active versus passive reading experiences on action and perception. *Vision Research, 50,* 2750–2757.

Libertus, K., & others (2013). Size matters: How age and reaching experiences shape infants' preferences for different sized objects. *Infant Behavior and Development, 36,* 189–198.

Lickliter, R. (2013). Biological development: Theoretical approaches, techniques, and key findings. In P. D. Zelazo (Ed.), *Oxford handbook of developmental psychology.* New York: Oxford University Press.

Lie, E., & Newcombe, N. (1999). Elementary school children's explicit and implicit memory for faces of preschool classmates. *Developmental Psychology, 35,* 102–112.

Lieven, E. (2008). Language development: overview. In M. M. Haith & J. B. Benson (Eds.), *Encyclopedia of infant and early childhood development.* Oxford, UK: Elsevier.

Lifton, R. J. (1977). The sense of immortality: On death and the continuity of life. In H. Feifel (Ed.), *New meanings of death.* New York: McGraw-Hill.

Lightner, C., & Hathaway, N. (1990). *Giving sorrow words.* New York: Warner.

Li-Korotky, H. S. (2012). Age-related hearing loss: Quality of care for quality of life. *Gerontologist, 52,* 265–271.

Lillard, A. (2006). Pretend play in toddlers. In C. A. Brownell & C. B. Kopp (Eds.), *Socioemotional development in the toddler year.* New York: Oxford University Press.

Lillard, A. S., & Kavanaugh, R. D. (2014, in press). The contribution of symbolic skills to the development of explicit theory of mind. *Child Development.*

Lillenes, M. S., & others (2013). Transient OGG1, APE1, PARP1, and Pol*B* expression in an Alzheimer's disease mouse model. *Mechanisms of Aging and Development, 34,* 467–477.

Lim, J. H., Park, S. Y., & Ryu, H. M. (2013). Non-invasive prenatal diagnosis of fetal trisomy 21 using cell-free fetal DNA in maternal blood. *Obstetrics and Gynecology Science, 56,* 58–66.

Lin, C. C., & others (2013). In utero exposure to environmental lead and manganese and neurodevelopment at 2 years of age. *Environmental Research, 123,* 52–57.

Lin, F. R. (2011). Hearing loss and cognition among older adults in the United States, *Journals of Gerontology A: Biological Sciences and Medical Sciences, 66,* 1131–1136.

Lin, F. R., Thorpe, R., Gordon-Salant, S., & Ferrucci, L. (2011). Hearing loss prevalence and risk factors among older adults in the United States. *Journals of Gerontology A: Biological Sciences and Medical Sciences, 66A*(5), 582–590.

Lin, H. W., Hsu, H. C., & Chang, M. C. (2011). Gender differences in the association between stress trajectories and depressive symptoms among middle aged and older adults in Taiwan. *Journal of Women and Aging, 23,* 233–345.

Lin, X., Bryant, C., Boldero, J., & Dow, B. (2014, in press). Older Chinese immigrants' relationships with their children: A literature review from a solidarity-conflict perspective. *Gerontologist.*

Lindau, S. T., & Gavrilova, N. (2010). Sex, health, and years of sexually active life gained due to good health: Evidence from two U.S. population based cross sectional surveys of aging. *British Medical Journal, 340,* c810.

Lindau, S. T., & others (2007). A study of sexuality and health among older adults in the United States. *New England Journal of Medicine, 357,* 762–774.

Lindberg, S. M., Hyde, J. S., Petersen, J. L., & Lin, M. C. (2010). New trends in gender and mathematics performance: A meta-analysis. *Psychological Bulletin, 136,* 1123–1135.

Lindblad, F., & Hjern, A. (2010). ADHD after fetal exposure to maternal smoking. *Nicotine and Tobacco Research, 12,* 408–415.

Linde, K., & Alfermann, D. (2014, in press). Single versus combined cognitive and physical activity effects on fluid cognitive abilities of healthy older adults: A 4-month randomized controlled trial with follow-up. *Journal of Aging and Physical Activity.*

Lindsay, M. K., & Burnett, E. (2013). The use of narcotics and street drugs during pregnancy. *Clinical Obstetrics and Gynecology, 56,* 133–141.

Lindstrom, M. (2010). Social capital, economic conditions, marital status, and daily smoking: A population-based study. *Public Health, 124,* 71–77.

Lindwall, M., & others (2012). Dynamic associations of change in physical activity and change in cognitive function: Coordinated analyses across four studies with up to 21 years of longitudinal data. *Journal of Aging Research.* doi:10.1155/2012/493598

Lippa, R. A. (2013). Men and women with bisexual identities show bisexual patterns of sexual attraction to male and female "swimsuit models." *Archives of Sexual Behavior, 42,* 187–196.

Lippman, L. A., & Keith, J. D. (2006). The demographics of spirituality among youth: International perspectives.

In E. Roehlkepartain, P. E. King, L. Wagener, & P. L. Benson (Eds.), *The handbook of spirituality in childhood and adolescence*. Thousand Oaks, CA: Sage.

Lipschitz, J. M., Yes, S., Weinstock, L. M., & Spirito, A. (2012). Adolescent and caregiver perception of family functioning: Relation to suicide ideation and attempts. *Psychiatry Research, 200,* 400–403.

Lipton, J., & Sahin, M. (2013). Fragile X syndrome therapeutics: Translation, meet translational medicine. *Neuron, 77,* 212–213.

Lipton, J., & Spelke, E. (2004). Discrimination of large and small numerosities by human infants. *Infancy, 5,* 271–290.

Lira, F. S., & others (2011). Exercise training improves sleep pattern and metabolic profile in elderly people in a time-dependent manner. *Lipids in Health and Disease, 10,* 1–6.

Lisha, N. E., & others (2014, in press). Evaluation of the psychometric properties of the Revised Inventory of the Dimensions of Emerging Adulthood (IDEA-R) in a sample of continuation high school students. *Evaluation and the Health Professions.*

Littleton, H. (2014, in press). Interpersonal violence on college campuses: Understanding risk factors and working to find solutions. *Trauma, Violence, and Abuse.*

Liu, G., & others (2014). Cardiovascular disease contributes to Alzheimer's disease: Evidence from large-scale genome-wide association studies. *Neurobiology of Aging, 35,* 786–792.

Liu, S., & others (2011). Similarity and difference in the processing of same- and other-race faces as revealed by eye-tracking in 4- to 9-month-old infants. *Journal of Experimental Child Psychology, 108,* 180–189.

Liu, Y. H., Chang, M. Y., & Chen, C. H. (2010). Effects of music therapy on labor pain and anxiety in Taiwanese first-time mothers. *Journal of Clinical Nursing, 19,* 1065–1072.

Lively, W., & Bromley, D. (1973). *Person perception in childhood and adolescence.* New York: Wiley.

Lleo, A., Moroni, L., Caliari, L., & Invernizzi, P. (2012). Autoimmunity and Turner's syndrome. *Autoimmunity Reviews, 11,* A538–A543.

Llewellyn, C. H., & others (2014, in press). Satiety mechanisms in genetic risk for obesity. *JAMA Pediatrics.*

Lloyd, J. W., & others (2015, in press). *Evidence-based reading instruction for ALL learners.* Upper Saddle River, NJ: Pearson.

Lock, J. (Ed.) (2012a). *Oxford handbook of child and adolescent eating disorders.* New York: Oxford University Press.

Lock, J. (2012b). Developmental translational research: Adolescence, brain circuitry, cognitive processes, and eating disorders. In J. Lock (Ed.), *Oxford handbook of child and adolescent eating disorders.* New York: Oxford University Press.

Lock, M. (1998). Menopause: Lessons from anthropology. *Psychosomatic Medicine, 60,* 410–419.

Loeber, R., & Burke, J. D. (2011). Developmental pathways in juvenile externalizing and internalizing problems. *Journal of Research on Adolescence, 21,* 34–46.

Logan, A. G. (2011). Hypertension in aging patients. *Expert Review of Cardiovascular Therapy, 9,* 113–120.

Logsdon, M. C., Wisner, K., & Hanusa, B. H. (2009). Does maternal role functioning improve with antidepressant treatment in women with postpartum depression? *Journal of Women's Health, 18,* 85–90.

Londono-Vallejo, J. A., & Wellinger, R. J. (2012). Telomeres and telomerase dance to the rhythm of the cell cycle. *Trends in Biochemical Science, 37*(9), 391–399.

Longman, P. (1987). *Born to pay: The new politics of aging in America.* Boston: Houghton Mifflin.

Loosli, S. V., Buschkuehl, M., Perrig, W. J., & Jaeggi, S. M. (2012). Working memory training improves reading processes in typically developing children. *Child Neuropsychology, 18,* 62–78.

Lopez, B. (2014, in press). Beyond modularization: The need of a socio-neuro-constructionist model of autism. *Journal of Autism and Developmental Disorders.*

Loponen, M., Hublin, C., Kalimo, R., Manttari, M., & Tenkanen, L. (2010). Joint effect of self-reported sleep problems and three components of the metabolic syndrome on risk of coronary heart disease. *Journal of Psychosomatic Research, 68,* 149–158.

Loprinzi, P. D. (2013). Objectively measured light and moderate-to-vigorous physical activity is associated with lower depression levels in older U.S. adults. *Aging and Mental Health, 17,* 801–805.

Lorenz, K. Z. (1965). *Evolution and the modification of behavior.* Chicago: University of Chicago Press.

Lovden, M., & Lindenberger, U. (2007). Intelligence. In J. E. Birren (Ed.), *Encyclopedia of gerontology* (2nd ed.). San Diego: Academic Press.

Love, J. M., Chazan-Cohen, R., Raikes, H., & Brooks-Gunn, J. (2013). What makes a difference: Early Head Start evaluation findings in a developmental context. *Monographs of the Society for Research in Child Development, 78,* 1–173.

Low, J., & Simpson, S. (2012). Effects of labeling on preschoolers' explicit false belief performance: Outcomes of cognitive flexibility or inhibitory control? *Child Development, 83*(3), 1072–1084.

Low, S., & others (2014). Engagement matters: Lessons from assessing classroom implementation of Steps to Respect: A bullying prevention program over a one-year period. *Prevention Science, 15*(2), 165–176.

Lowdermilk, D. L., Cashion, M. C., & Perry, S. E. (2014). *Maternity and women's health care: Text and simulation learning package (10th ed.).* New York: Elsevier.

Lowe, J. R., & others (2012). Association of maternal interaction with emotional regulation in 4- and 9-month old infants during the Still Face Paradigm. *Infant Behavior and Development, 35,* 295–302.

Lowe, K., & Dotterer, A. M. (2013). Parental monitoring, parental warmth, and minority youths' academic outcomes: Exploring the integrative model of parenting. *Journal of Youth and Adolescence, 42,* 1413–1425.

Lu, C. J., Yu, J. J., & Deng, J. W. (2012). Disease-syndrome combination clinical study of psoriasis: Present status, advantages, and prospects. *China Journal of Integrative Medicine, 18,* 166–171.

Lu, P. H., & others (2011). Age-related slowing in cognitive processing speed is associated with myelin integrity in a very healthy elderly sample. *Journal of Clinical and Experimental Neuropsychology, 33,* 1059–1068.

Lu, P. H., & others (2013). Myelin breakdown mediates age-related slowing in cognitive processing speed in healthy elderly men. *Brain and Cognition, 81*(1), 131–138.

Lucas, R. E., & Donnellan, M. B. (2011). Personality development across the life span: Longitudinal analyses with a national sample in Germany. *Journal of Personality and Social Psychology, 101,* 847–861.

Lucas, R. E., Clark, A. E., Yannis, G., & Diener, E. (2004). Unemployment alters the setpoint for life satisfaction. *Psychological Science, 15,* 8–13.

Lucchetti, G., Lucchetti, A. L., & Koenig, H. G. (2011). Impact of spirituality/religiosity on mortality: Comparison with other health interventions. *Explore, 7,* 234–238.

Lucovnik, M., & others (2011). Progestin treatment for the prevention of preterm births. *Acta Obstetrica et Gynecologica Scandinavica, 90,* 1057–1069.

Luders, E., & others (2004). Gender differences in cortical complexity. *Nature Neuroscience, 1,* 799–800.

Ludington-Hoe, S. M., & others (2006). Breast and infant temperatures with twins during kangaroo care. *Journal of Obstetric, Gynecologic, and Neonatal Nursing, 35,* 223–231.

Luhmann, M., Hofmann, W., Eid, M., & Lucas, R. E. (2012). Subjective well-being and adaptation to life events: A meta-analysis. *Journal of Personality and Social Psychology 102,* 592–615.

Luijk, M. P., & others (2011). Dopaminergic, serotonergic, and oxytonergic candidate genes associated with infant attachment security and disorganization? In search of main and interaction effects. *Journal of Child Psychology and Psychiatry, 52,* 1295–1307.

Luiselli, J. K. (Ed.) (2014). *Children and youth with autism spectrum disorder (ASD).* New York: Oxford University Press.

Lukowski, A. F., & Bauer, P. J. (2014). Long-term memory in infancy and early childhood. In P. J. Bauer & R. Fivush (Eds.), *Wiley-Blackwell handbook of children's memory.* New York: Wiley.

Lumpkin, A. (2014). *Introduction to physical education, exercise science, and sport studies* (9th ed.). New York: McGraw-Hill.

Luna, B., Padmanabhan, A., & Geier, C. (2014). The adaptive adolescent sensation-seeking period: Development of reward processing and its effect on cognitive control. In V. F. Reyna & V. Zayas (Eds.), *Neuroscience of decision making.* Washington, DC: American Psychological Association.

Lund, H. G., Reider, B. D., Whiting, A. B., & Prichard, J. R. (2010). Sleep patterns and predictors of disturbed sleep in a large population of college students. *Journal of Adolescent Health, 46,* 124–132.

Lundervold, A. J., Wollschlager, D., & Wehling, E. (2014, in press). Age and sex-related changes in episodic memory function in middle aged and older adults. *Scandinavian Journal of Psychology.*

Lundin, A., Falkstedt, D., Lundberg, I., & Hemmingsson, T. (2014). Unemployment and coronary heart disease among middle-aged men in Sweden: 39,243 men followed for 8 years. *Occupational and Environmental Medicine, 71,* 183–188.

Luo, J., & others (2014, in press). Risk patterns among college youth: Identification and implications for prevention and treatment. *Health Promotion Practice.*

Luo, L., & Craik, F. I. M. (2008). Aging and memory: A cognitive approach. *Canadian Journal of Psychology, 53,* 346–353.

Luo, Y., & Baillargeon, R. (2010). Toward a mentalistic account of early psychological reasoning. *Current Directions in Psychological Science, 19,* 301–307.

Luo, Y., & Waite, L. J. (2014, in press). Loneliness and mortality among older adults in China. *Journals of Gerontology B: Psychological Sciences and Social Sciences.*

Luo, Y., Hawkley, L. C., Waite, L. J., & Caccioppo, J. T. (2012). Loneliness, health, and mortality in old age: A national longitudinal study. *Social Science and Medicine, 74,* 907–914.

Luque-Contreras, D., & others (2014). Oxidative stress and metabolic syndrome: Cause or consequence of Alzheimer's disease. *Oxidative Medicine and Cellular Longevity, 2014:* 497802.

Luria, A., & Herzog, E. (1985, April). *Gender segregation across and within settings.* Paper presented at the biennial meeting of the Society for Research in Child Development, Toronto.

Lusardi, A., Mitchell, O. S., & Curto, V. (2012). *Financial sophistication in the older population.* Retrieved June 12, 2012, from www.pensionresearchcouncil.org/publications/document.php?fi...

Lusby, C. M., Goodman, S. H., Bell, M. A., & Newport, D. J. (2014, in press). Electroencephalogram patterns in infants of depressed mothers. *Developmental Psychobiology.*

Lushington, K., Pamula, Y., Martin, J., & Kennedy, J. D. (2014). Developmental changes in sleep: Infancy and preschool years. In A. R. Wolfson & E. Montgomery-Downs (Eds.), *Oxford handbook of infant, child, and adolescent sleep and behavior.* New York: Oxford University Press.

Lustig, C., & Hasher, L. (2009). Interference. In R. Schulz, L. Noelker, K. Rockwood, & R. Sprott (Eds.), *Encyclopedia of aging* (4th ed.). New York: Springer Publishing.

Luszcz, M. (2011). Executive functioning and cognitive aging. In K. W. Schaie & S. L. Willis (Eds.), *Handbook of the psychology of aging* (7th ed.). New York: Elsevier.

Luyster, F. S., & others (2012). Sleep: A health imperative. *Sleep, 35,* 727–734.

Lykken, D. (2001). *Happiness: What studies on twins show us about nature, nurture, and the happiness set point.* New York: Golden Books.

Lynch, A., Elmore, B., & Kotecki, J. (2015, in press). *Choosing health* (2nd ed.). Upper Saddle River, NJ: Pearson.

Lynch, E., Dezen, T., & Brown, N. (2012). *U.S. preterm birth rate shows five-year improvement.* Retrieved February 17, 2013, from www.marchofdimes.com/news/10894.html

Lynch, M. (2015). *Call to teach.* Upper Saddle River, NJ: Pearson.

Lynchard, N. A., & Radvansky, G. A. (2012). Age-related perspectives and emotion processing. *Psychology and Aging, 27*(4), 934–939.

Lyndaker, C., & Hulton, L. (2004). The influence of age on symptoms of perimenopause. *Journal of Obstetric, Gynecological, and Neonatal Nursing, 33,* 340–347.

Lyon, G. J., & Wang, K. (2012). Identifying disease mutations in genomic medicine settings: Current challenges and how to accelerate the process. *Genome Medicine, 4*(7), 58.

Lyon, T. D., & Flavell, J. H. (1993). Young children's understanding of forgetting over time. *Child Development, 64,* 789–800.

Lyons, D. M., & others (2010). Stress coping stimulates hippocampal neurogenesis in adult monkeys. *Proceedings of the National Academy of Sciences U.S.A., 107,* 14823–14827.

Lyons, H., Manning, W., Giordano, P., & Longmore, M. (2013). Predictors of heterosexual casual sex among young adults. *Archives of Sexual Behavior, 42,* 585–593.

M

Ma, L., & others (2014, in press). Empirical change in the prevalence of overweight and obesity in adolescents from 2007 to 2011 in Guangzhou, China. *European Journal of Pediatrics.*

Maalouf, F. T., & Brent, D. A. (2012). Child and adolescent depression intervention overview: What works for whom and how well? *Child and Adolescent Psychiatry Clinics of North America, 21,* 299–312.

Maccallum, F., & Bryant, R. A. (2013). A cognitive attachment model of prolonged grief: Integrating attachments, memory, and identity. *Clinical Psychology Review, 33,* 713–727.

Maccoby, E. E. (1998). *The two sexes: Growing up apart, coming together.* Cambridge, MA: Harvard University Press.

Maccoby, E. E. (2002). Gender and group processes. *Current Directions in Psychological Science, 11,* 54–58.

Maccoby, E. E., & Martin, J. A. (1983). Socialization in the context of the family: Parent-child interaction. In P. H. Mussen (Ed.), *Handbook of child psychology* (4th ed., Vol. 4). New York: Wiley.

MacDonald, S. W. S., DeCarlo, C. A., & Dixon, R. A. (2011). Linking biological and cognitive aging: Toward improving characterizations of developmental time. *Journals of Gerontology B: Psychological Sciences and Social Sciences, 66B*(1, Suppl.), i59–i70.

MacDougall, B. J., Robinson, J. D., Kappus, L., Sudikoff, S. N., & Greer, D. M. (2014, in press). Simulation-based training in brain death determination. *Neurocritical Care.*

MacFarlane, J. A. (1975). Olfaction in the development of social preferences in the human neonate. In *Parent-infant interaction.* Ciba Foundation Symposium No. 33. Amsterdam: Elsevier.

MacGeorge, E. L. (2003). Gender differences in attributions and emotions in helping contexts. *Sex Roles, 48,* 175–182.

Machado, B., & others (2014, in press). Risk factors and antecedent life events in the development of anorexia nervosa: A Portuguese case-control study. *European Eating Disorders Review.*

Machado-Vidotti, H. G., & others (2014). Cardiac autonomic responses during upper versus lower limb resistance exercise in healthy men. *Brazilian Journal of Physical Therapy, 18,* 1–18.

Mackin, R. S., & others (2014, in press). Association of age at depression onset with cognitive functioning in individuals with late-life depression and executive dysfunction. *American Journal of Geriatric Psychiatry.*

Madden, D. J., & others (1999). Aging and recognition memory: Changes in regional cerebral blood flow associated with components of reaction time distributions. *Journal of Cognitive Neuroscience, II,* 511–520.

Mader, S. S. (2014). *Inquiry into life* (14th ed.). New York: McGraw-Hill.

Mader, S. S., & Windelspecht, M. (2015). *Essentials of biology* (4th ed.). New York: McGraw-Hill.

Madill, A. (2012). Interviews and interviewing techniques. In H. Cooper (Ed.), *APA handbook of research methods in psychology.* Washington, DC: American Psychological Association.

Maercker, A., & Lalor, J. (2012). Diagnostic and clinical considerations in prolonged grief disorder. *Dialogues in Clinical Neuroscience, 14,* 167–176.

Mah, L., Grossman, D., Grief, C., & Rootenberg, M. (2013). Association between patient dignity and anxiety in geriatric palliative care. *Palliative Medicine, 27,* 478–479.

Mahalik, J. R., & others (2013). Changes in health risk behaviors for males and females from early adolescence through early adulthood. *Health Psychology, 32,* 685–694.

Maher, J. P., & others (2013). A daily analysis of physical activity and satisfaction with life in emerging adults. *Health Psychology, 32,* 647–656.

Mahn, H., & John-Steiner, V. (2013). Vygotsky and sociocultural approaches to teaching and learning. In I. B. Weiner & others (Eds.), *Handbook of psychology* (2nd ed., Vol. 7). New York: Wiley.

Maholmes, V., & King, R. B. (Eds.) (2012). *Oxford handbook of poverty and child development.* New York: Oxford University Press.

Mahoney, J. R., Verghese, J., Goldin, Y., Lipton, R., & Holtzer, R. (2010). Altering orienting and executive attention in older adults. *Journal of the International Neuropsychological Society, 16*(5), 877–889.

Maillard, P., & others (2012). Effects of systolic blood pressure on white-matter integrity in young adults in the

Framington Heart Study: A cross-sectional study. *Lancet Neurology, 11,* 1039–1047.

Major Depressive Disorder Working Group of the Psychiatric GWAS Consortium (2013). A mega-analysis of genome-wide association studies for major depressive disorder. *Molecular Psychiatry, 18*(4), 497–511.

Malamitsi-Puchner, A., & Boutsikou, T. (2006). Adolescent pregnancy and perinatal outcome. *Pediatric Endocrinology Review, 3*(1, Suppl.), S170–S171.

Malhomes, V. (2014). *Fostering resilience and well-being in children and families in poverty.* New York: Oxford University Press.

Malik, R., & others (2014, in press). Multilocus genetic risk score associates with ischemic stroke in case-control and prospective cohort studies. *Stroke.*

Malinen, S., & Johnston, L. (2013). Workplace ageism: Discovering hidden bias. *Experimental Aging Research, 39,* 445–465.

Mall, J. F., & others (2014). Cognition and psychopathology in nonagenarians and centenarians living in geriatric nursing homes in Switzerland: A focus on anosognosia. *Psychogeriatrics, 14,* 55–62.

Malloy, L. C., La Rooy, D. J., Lamb, M. A., & Katz, C. (2012). Developmentally sensitive interviewing for legal purposes. In M. E. Lamb, D. J. La Rooy, L. C. Malloy, & C. Katz (Eds.), *Children's testimony* (2nd ed.). New York: Wiley.

Maloy, R. W., Verock-O'Loughlin, R-E., Edwards, S. A., & Woolf, B. P. (2014). *Transforming learning with new technologies* (2nd ed.). Upper Saddle River, NJ: Pearson.

Manard, M., Carabin, D., Jasper, M., & Collette, F. (2014). Age-related decline in cognitive control: The role of fluid intelligence and processing sikoed. *BMC Neuroscience, 15*(1), 7.

Manca, T. (2013). Medicine and spiritual healing within a region of Canada: Preliminary findings concerning Christian Scientists' healthcare practices. *Journal of Religion and Health, 52,* 789–803.

Mandal, S., Abebe, F., & Chaudhary, J. (2014). –174G/C polymorphism in the interleukin-6 promoter is differently associated with prostate cancer incidence depending on race. *Genetics and Molecular Research, 13,* 139–151.

Mandara, J. (2006). The impact of family functioning on African American males' academic achievement: A review and clarification of the empirical literature. *Teachers College Record, 108,* 206–233.

Mandler, J. M. (2004). *The foundations of the mind: Origins of conceptual thought.* New York: Oxford University Press.

Mandler, J. M. (2009). Conceptual categorization. In D. H. Rakison & L. M. Oakes (Eds.), *Early category and concept development.* New York: Oxford University Press.

Mandler, J. M., & DeLoache, J. (2012). The beginnings of conceptual development. In S. Pauen & M. Bornstein (Eds.), *Early child development and later outcome.* New York: Cambridge University Press.

Mandler, J. M., & McDonough, L. (1993). Concept formation in infancy. *Cognitive Development, 8,* 291–318.

Manenti, R., Cotelli, M., & Miniussi, C. (2011). Successful physiological aging and episodic memory: A brain stimulation study. *Behavioral Brain Research, 216,* 153–158.

Mann, T., & others (2007). Medicare's search for effective obesity treatments. *American Psychologist, 62,* 220–233.

Manton, K. I. (1989). The stress buffering role of spiritual support: Cross-sectional and prospective investigations. *Journal for the Scientific Study of Religion, 28,* 310–323.

Mantyh, P. W. (2014). The neurobiology of skeletal pain. *European Journal of Neuroscience, 39,* 508–519.

Manuck, S. B., & McCaffery, J. M. (2014). Gene-environment interaction. *Annual Review of Psychology* (Vol. 65). Palo Alto, CA: Annual Reviews.

Maramara, L. A., He, W., & Ming, X. (2014, in press). Pre- and perinatal risk factors for autism spectrum disorder in a New Jersey cohort. *Journal of Child Neurology.*

Marcdante, K., & Kliegman, R. M. (2015, in press). *Nelson essentials of pediatrics* (7th ed.). New York: Elsevier.

Marceau, K., Dorn, L. D., & Susman, E. J. (2012). Stress and puberty-related hormone reactivity, negative emotionality, and parent-adolescent relationships. *Psychoneuroimmunology, 37*(8), 1286–1298.

Marcell, J. J. (2003). Sarcopenia: Causes, consequences, and preventions. *Journals of Gerontology A: Biological and Medical Sciences,* M911–M916.

Marcello, E., Epis, R., Saraceno, C., & Di Luca, M. (2012). Synaptic dysfunction in Alzheimer's disease. *Advances in Experimental Medicine and Biology, 970,* 573–601.

Marcia, J. E. (1980). Ego identity development. In J. Adelson (Ed.), *Handbook of adolescent psychology:* New York: Wiley.

Marcia, J. E. (1994). The empirical study of ego identity. In H. A. Bosma, T. L. G. Graafsma, H. D. Grotevant, & D. J. De Levita (Eds.), *Identity and development.* Newbury Park, CA: Sage.

Marcia, J. E. (2002). Identity and psychosocial development in adulthood. *Identity: An International Journal of Theory and Research, 2,* 7–28.

Marcotte, T. D., Bekman, N. M., Meyer, R. A., & Brown, S. A. (2012). High-risk driving behaviors among adolescent binge drinkers. *American Journal of Drug and Alcohol Abuse, 38*(4), 322–327.

Mares, M-L., & Pan, Z. (2013). Effects of *Sesame Street:* A meta-analysis of children's learning in 15 countries. *Journal of Applied Developmental Psychology, 34,* 140–151.

Margrett, J. A., & Deshpande-Kamat, N. (2009). Cognitive functioning and decline. In D. Carr (Ed.), *Encyclopedia of the life course and human development.* Boston: Gale Cengage.

Marie, C., & Trainor, L. J. (2013). Development of simultaneous pitch encoding: Infants show a high voice superiority effect. *Cerebral Cortex, 23*(3), 660–669.

Markant, J. C., & Thomas, K. M. (2013). Postnatal brain development. In P. D. Zelazo (Ed.), *Oxford handbook of developmental psychology.* New York: Oxford University Press.

Markham, C. M., & others (2010). Connectedness as a predictor of sexual and reproductive health outcomes for youth. *Journal of Adolescent Health, 46*(3, Suppl.), S23–S41.

Markham, K. B., Walker, H., Lynch, C. D., & Iams, J. D. (2014). Preterm birth rates in a prematurity prevention clinic after adoption of progestin prophylaxis. *Obstetrics and Gynecology, 123,* 34–39.

Markman, H. J., Rhoades, G. K., Stanley, S. M., & Peterson, K. M. (2013). A randomized clinical trial of the effectiveness of premarital intervention: Moderators of divorce outcomes. *Journal of Family Psychology, 27,* 165–172.

Marks, A. K., Godoy, C., & Garcia Coll, C. (2014). An ecological approach to understanding immigrant child and adolescent developmental competencies. In E. T. Gershoff, R. S. Mistry, & D. A. Crosby (Eds.), *Societal*

contexts of child development. New York: Oxford University Press.

Markus, H., & Nurius, P. (1987). Possible selves: The interface between motivation and self-concept. In K. M. Yardley & T. M. Honess (Eds.), *Self and identity.* New York: Wiley.

Markus, H. R., Ryff, C. D., Curhan, K., & Palmersheim, K. (2004). In their own words: Well-being among high school and college-educated adults. In G. Brim, C. D. Ryff, & R. Kessler (Eds.), *How healthy we are: A national study of well-being in midlife.* Chicago: University of Chicago Press.

Marmorstein, N. R., Iacono, W. G., & Legrand, L. (2014, in press). Obesity and depression in adolescence and beyond: Reciprocal risks. *International Journal of Obesity.*

Marques, L., & others (2013). Complicated grief symptoms in anxiety disorders: Prevalence and associated impairment. *Depression and Anxiety, 30,* 1211–1216.

Marquie, J. C., & others (2010). Higher mental stimulation at work is associated with improved cognitive functioning in both young and older workers. *Ergonomics, 53,* 1287–1301.

Marsh, H., Ellis, L., & Craven, R. (2002). How do preschool children feel about themselves? Unraveling measurement and multidimensional self-concept structure. *Developmental Psychology,* 38, 376–393.

Marsh, H. W., Martin, A. J., & Xu, M. (2012). Self-concept: Synergy of theory, mind, and application. In K. R. Harris, S. Graham, & T. Urdan (Eds.), *APA educational psychology handbook.* Washington, DC: American Psychological Association.

Marshall, B. L. (2012). Medicalization and the refashioning of age-related limits on sexuality. *Journal of Sexual Research, 49,* 337–343.

Marshall, S. K., Tilton-Weaver, L. C., & Bosdet, L. (2005). Information management: Considering adolescents' regulation of parental knowledge. *Journal of Adolescence, 28,* 633–647.

Marsiske, M., Klumb, P. L., & Baltes, M. M. (1997). Everyday activity patterns and sensory functioning in old age. *Psychology and Aging, 12,* 444–457.

Martin, C. L., & Ruble, D. N. (2010). Patterns of gender development. *Annual Review of Psychology* (Vol. 61). Palo Alto, CA: Annual Reviews.

Martin, C., & Evaldsson, A-C. (2012). Affordances for participation: Children's appropriation of rules in a Reggio Emilia school. *Mind, Culture, and Activity, 19,* 51–74.

Martin, C. L., & others (2013). The role of sex of peers and gender-typed activities in young children's peer affiliative networks: A longitudinal analysis of selection and influence. *Child Development, 84,* 921–937.

Martin, J. A., & others (2012). Births: Final data for 2010. *National Vital Statistics Reports, 61*(1).

Martin, J. A., & others (2013). Births: Final data for 2011. *National Vital Statistics Reports, 62*(1), 1–70.

Martin, L. R., Friedman, H. S., & Schwartz, J. E. (2007). Personality and mortality risk across the life span: The importance of conscientiousness as a biopsychosocial attribute. *Health Psychology, 26,* 428–436.

Martin, M., Grunendahl, M., & Martin, P. (2001). Age differences in stress, social resources, and well-being in middle and older age. *Journals of Gerontology: Psychological Sciences and Social Sciences.* 56B, P214–P222.

Martin, P., & others (2014). APOE *e*4, rated life experiences, and affect among centenarians. *Aging and Mental Health, 18,* 1740–1747.

Martins, W. P., & others (2014). Hormone therapy for female sexual function during perimenopause and postmenopause: A Cochrane review. *Climacteric, 17*(2), 133–135.

Maruyama, N. C., & Atencio, C. V. (2008). Evaluating a bereavement support group. *Palliative Support and Care, 6,* 43–49.

Mascalo, M. F., & Fischer, K. W. (2010). The dynamic development of thinking, feeling, and acting over the life span. In W. F. Overton & R. M. Lerner (Eds.), *Handbook of life-span development* (Vol. 1). New York: Wiley.

Mash, E. J., & Wolfe, D. A. (2013). Disorders of childhood and adolescence. In I. B. Weiner & others (Eds.), *Handbook of psychology* (2nd ed., Vol. 8). New York: Wiley.

Mason, C., & others (2013). Independent and combined effects of dietary weight loss and exercise on leukocyte telomere length in postmenopausal women. *Obesity, 21,* E549–E554.

Mason, K. A., Johnson, G. B., Losos, J. B., & Singer, S. (2015, in press). *Understanding biology.* New York: McGraw-Hill.

Mason, L., Harris, K. L., & Graham, S. (2013). Strategies for improving student outcomes in written expression. In B. G. Cook & M. G. Tankersley (Eds.), *Research-based practices in special education.* Upper Saddle River, NJ: Pearson.

Mason, M. J., Mennis, J., Linker, J., Bares, C., & Zaharakis, N. (2014). Peer attitudes effects on adolescent substance use: The moderating role of race and gender. *Prevention Science, 15,* 56–64.

Masoodi, N. (2013). Review: Cholinesterase inhibitors do not reduce progression to dementia from mild cognitive impairment. *Annals of Internal Medicine, 158,* JC2–JC3.

Masselli, G., & others (2011). MR imaging in the evaluation of placental abruption: Correlation with sonographic findings. *Radiology, 259*(1), 222–230.

Masten, A. S. (2006). Developmental psychopathology: Pathways to the future. *International Journal of Behavioral Development, 31,* 46–53.

Masten, A. S. (2009). Ordinary Magic: Lessons from research on resilience in human development. *Education Canada, 49*(3), 28–32.

Masten, A. S. (2011). Resilience in children threatened by extreme adversity: Frameworks for research, practice, and translational synergy. *Development and Psychopathology, 23,* 141–153.

Masten, A. S. (2012). Faculty profile: Ann Masten. *The Institute of Child Development further developments.* Minneapolis: School of Education.

Masten, A. S. (2013). Risk and resilience in development. In P. D. Zelazo (Ed.), *Oxford handbook of developmental psychology.* New York: Oxford University Press.

Masten, A. S. (2014a). Global perspectives on resilience in children and youth. *Child Development, 85,* 6–20.

Masten, A. S. (2014b, in press). *Ordinary magic: Resilience in development.* New York: Guilford.

Masten, A. S., Burt, K., & Coatsworth, J. D. (2006). Competence and psychopathology in development. In D. Cicchetti & D. Cohen (Eds.), *Developmental psychopathology: Risk, disorder, and psychopathology* (2nd ed., Vol. 3). New York: Wiley.

Masten, A. S., Liebkind, K., & Hernandez, D. J. (2012). *Realizing the potential of immigrant youth.* New York: Cambridge University Press.

Masten, A. S., & Narayan, A. J. (2012). Child development in the context of disaster, war, and psychopathology: The legacy of Norman Garmezy. *Annual Review of Psychology* (Vol. 63). Palo Alto, CA: Annual Reviews.

Masten, A. S., & Tellegen, A. (2012). Resilience in developmental psychology: Contributions of the Project Competence Longitudinal Study. *Development and Psychopathology, 24,* 345–361.

Masten, A. S., & others (2008). School success in motion: Protective factors for academic achievement in homeless and highly mobile children in Minneapolis. *Center for Urban and Regional Affairs Reporter, 38,* 3–12.

Masters, C. (2008, January 17). We just clicked. *Time magazine,* pp. 84–89.

Masters, K. S., & Hooker, S. A. (2013). Religion, spirituality, and health. In R. F. Paloutzian & C. L. Park (Eds.), *Handbook of the psychology of religion* (2nd ed.). New York: Guilford.

Masters, R. K., & others (2013). The impact of obesity on U.S. mortality levels: The importance of age and cohort factors in population estimates. *American Journal of Public Health, 103,* 1895–1901.

Matamura, M., & others (2014, in press). Associations between sleep habits and mental health status and suicidality in a longitudinal survey of monozygotic twin adolescents. *Journal of Sleep Research.*

Match.com (2011). The Match.com Singles in America Study. Retrieved February 7, 2011, from http://blog.match.com/singles-study.

Match.com (2012). *Singles in America 2012.* Retrieved June 10, 2012, from http://blog.match.com/singles-in-america/

Mate, I., Madrid, J. A., & la Fuente, M. D. (2014, in press). Chronobiology of the neuroimmunoendocrine system and aging. *Current Pharmaceutical Design.*

Mateus, V., Martins, C., Osorio, A., Martins, E. C., & Soares, I. (2013). Joint attention at 10 months of age in infant-mother dyads: Contrasting free-toy play with semi-structured toy-play. *Infant Behavior and Development, 36*(1), 176–179.

Mather, M. (2012). The emotion paradox in the human brain. *Annals of the New York Academy of Sciences, 1251,* 33–49.

Matheson, E. M., King, D. E., & Everett, C. J. (2012). Healthy lifestyle habits and mortality in overweight and obese individuals. *Journal of the American Board of Family Medicine, 25,* 9–15.

Matlow, J. N., Jubetsky, A., Aleksa, K., Berger, H., & Koren, G. (2013). The transfer of ethyl glucuronide across the dually perfused human placenta. *Placenta, 34*(4), 369–373.

Matos, A. P., Ferreira, J. A., & Haase, R. F. (2012). Television and aggression: A test of a mediated model with a sample of Portuguese students. *Journal of Social Psychology, 152,* 75–91.

Matsuba, M. K., Murazyn, T., & Hart, D. (2014). Moral identity and community. In M. Killen & J. G. Smetana (Eds.), *Handbook of moral development* (2nd ed.). New York: Psychology Press.

Matsuda, H., Yoshida, M., Wakamatsu, H., & Furuya, K. (2011). Fetal intraperitoneal injection of immunoglobulin diminishes alloimmune hemolysis. *Journal of Perinatology, 31,* 289–292.

Matthews, C. E., & others (2007). Influence of exercise, walking, cycling, and overall nonexercise physical activity on mortality in Chinese women. *American Journal of Epidemiology, 165,* 1343–1350.

Matthews, N. L., & others (2012). Does theory of mind performance differ in children with early-onset and regressive autism? *Developmental Science, 15,* 25–34.

Mattison, J. A., & others (2012). Impact of caloric restriction on health and survival in rhesus monkeys from the NIA study. *Nature, 489,* 318–321.

Mattys, S. L., & Scharenborg, O. (2014). Phoneme categorization and discrimination in younger and older adults: A comparative analysis of perceptual, lexical, and attentional factors. *Psychology and Aging, 29,* 150–162.

Maurer, D., & Lewis, T. L. (2013). Sensitive periods in visual development. In P. D. Zelazo (Ed.), *Oxford handbook of developmental psychology.* New York: Oxford University Press.

Maurer, D., Lewis, T. L., Brent, H. P., & Levin, A. V. (1999). Rapid improvement in the acuity of infants after visual input. *Science, 286,* 108–110.

Maurer, D., Mondloch, C. J., & Leis, T. L. (2007). Effects of early visual deprivation on perceptual and cognitive development. In C. von Hofsten & K. Rosander (Eds.), *Progress in Brain Research, 164,* 87–104.

Maurizio, S., & others (2013). Differential EMG biofeedback for children with ADHD: A control method for neurofeedback training with a case illustration. *Applied Psychophysiology and Biofeedback, 38,* 109–119.

Maxson, S. C. (2013). Behavioral genetics. In I. B. Weiner & others (Eds.), *Handbook of psychology* (2nd ed., Vol. 3). New York: Wiley.

Mayas, J., Parmentier, F. B., Andres, P., & Ballesteros, S. (2014). Plasticity of attentional functions in older adults after non-action video game training: A randomized controlled trial. *PloS One,* 9(3), e92269.

Mayer, K. D., & Zhang, L. (2009). Short- and long-term effects of cocaine abuse during pregnancy on heart development. *Therapeutic Advances in Cardiovascular Disease, 3,* 7–16.

Maynard, M., Carabin, D., Jaspar, M., & Collette, F. (2014). Age-related decline in cognitive control: The role of fluid intelligence and processing speed. *BMC Neuroscience, 15*(1), 7.

Mayo Clinic (2013). *Male hypogonadism.* Rochester, MN: Mayo Clinic.

Mayo Clinic (2014). *Pregnancy and fish: What's safe to eat?* Retrieved February 1, 2014, from www.mayoclinic.com/health/pregnancy-and-fish/PR00158

Mazzucato, V., & Schans, D. (2011). Transnational families and the well-being of children: Conceptual and methodological challenges. *Journal of Marriage and the Family, 73,* 704–712.

Mbugua Gitau, G., & others (2009). The influence of maternal age on the outcomes of pregnancy complicated by bleeding at less than 12 weeks. *Acta Obstetricia et Gynecologica Scandinavica, 88,* 116–118.

McAdams, D. P., & Olson, B. D. (2010). Personality development: Continuity and change over the life course. *Annual Review of Psychology* (Vol. 61). Palo Alto, CA: Annual Reviews.

McAuley, P. A., & Blair, S. N. (2011). Obesity paradoxes. *Journal of Sports Sciences, 29,* 773–782.

McBride Murry, V., Hill, N. E., Berkel, C. W., Witherspoon, D. P., & Bartz, D. (2015, in press). Children in diverse contexts. In R. M. Lerner (Ed.), *Handbook of child psychology and developmental science* (7th ed.). New York: Wiley.

McBride-Chang, C. (2004). *Children's literacy development.* New York: Oxford University Press.

McCabe, D. P., & Loaiza, V. M. (2012). Working memory. In S. K. Whitbourne & M. Sliwinski (Eds.), *Wiley-Blackwell handbook of adult development and aging.* New York: Wiley.

McCardle, P., Miller, B., Lee, J. R., & Tzeng, O. J. (2011). *Dyslexia across languages.* Baltimore: Brookes.

McCartney, K. (2003, July 16). Interview with Kathleen McCartney in A. Bucuvalas, "Child care and behavior," *HGSE News,* pp. 1–4. Cambridge, MA: Harvard Graduate School of Education.

McCartney, K., Dearing, E., Taylor, B. A., & Bub, K. L. (2007). Quality child care supports the achievement of low-income children: Direct and indirect pathways through caregiving and the home environment. *Journal of Applied Developmental Psychology, 28,* 411–426.

McCartney, K., & Yoshikawa, H. (Eds.) (2015, in press). *Framing the future for America's children: In honor of 40 years of the Children's Defense Fund.* Cambridge, MA: Harvard University Press.

McClain, C. S., Rosenfeld, B., & Breitbart, W. S. (2003, March). *The influence of spirituality on end-of-life despair in cancer patients close to death.* Paper presented at the meeting of American Psychosomatic Society, Phoenix.

McClellan, M. D. (2004, February 9). Captain Fantastic: The interview. *Celtic Nation,* pp. 1–9.

McClelland, K., Bowles, J., & Koopman, P. (2012). Male sex determination: Insights into molecular mechanisms. *Asian Journal of Andrology, 14,* 164–171.

McCormack, L. A., & others (2011). Weight-related teasing in a racially diverse sample of sixth-grade children. *Journal of the American Dietetic Association, 111,* 431–436.

McCormack, S. E., & others (2014, in press). Effects of exercise and lifestyle modification on fitness, insulin resistance, skeletal muscle oxidative phosphorylation and intramyocellular lipid content in obese children and adolescents. *Pediatric Obesity.*

McCormack, T., Hoerl, C., & Butterfill, C. (2012). *Tool use and causal cognition.* New York: Oxford University Press.

McCormick, C. B., Dimmitt, C., & Sullivan, F. R. (2013). Metacognition, learning, and instruction. In I. B. Weiner & others (Eds.), *Handbook of psychology* (2nd ed., Vol. 7). New York: Wiley.

McCoy, D. C., & Raver, C. C. (2011). Caregiver emotional expressiveness, child emotion regulation, and child behavior problems among Head Start families. *Social Development, 20,* 741–761.

McCoy, K. P., George, M. R., Cummings, E. M., & Davies, P. T. (2014, in press). Constructive and destructive marital conflict, parenting, and children's school and social adjustment. *Social Development.*

McCoy, M. L., & Keen, S. M. (2014, in press). *Child abuse and neglect* (2nd ed.). New York: Psychology Press.

McCrae, R. R., & Costa, P. T. (1990). *Personality in adulthood.* New York: Guilford.

McCrae, R. R., & Costa, P. T. (2003). *Personality in adulthood* (2nd ed.). New York: Guilford.

McCrae, R. R., & Costa, P. T. (2006). Cross-cultural perspectives on adult personality trait development. In D. K. Mroczek & T. D. Little (Eds.), *Handbook of personality development.* Mahwah, NJ: Erlbaum.

McCrae, R. R., Gaines, J. F., & Wellington, M. A. (2013). The five-factor model in fact and fiction. In I. B. Weiner & others (Eds.), *Handbook of psychology* (2nd ed., Vol. 5). New York: Wiley.

McCullough, M. E., & Willoughby, B. L. (2009). Religion, self-regulation, and self-control: Associations, explanations, and implications. *Psychological Bulletin, 135,* 69–93.

McCullough, M. E., Enders, C. K., Brion, S. L., & Jain, A. R. (2005). The varieties of religious development in adulthood: A longitudinal investigation of religion and rational choice. *Journal of Personality and Social Psychology, 89,* 78–89.

McCutcheon, V. V., & others (2012). Environmental influences predominate in remission from alcohol use disorder in young adult twins. *Psychological Medicine, 42*(11), 2421–2431.

McDonald, S., & others (2009). Preterm birth and low birth weight among in vitro fertilization singletons: a systematic review and meta-analyses. *European Journal of Obstetrics, Gynecology, and Reproductive Biology, 146*, 138–148.

McDonald, S. D., & others (2010). Preterm birth and low birth weight among in vitro fertilization twins: A systematic review and meta-analyses. *European Journal of Obstetrics, Gynecology, and Reproductive Biology, 148*, 105–113.

McDonough, I. M., & Gallo, D. A. (2013). Impaired retrieval monitoring for past and future autobiographical events in older adults. *Psychology and Aging, 28*, 457–466.

McDonough, J. E. (2012). The road ahead for the Affordable Care Act. *New England Journal of Medicine, 367*(3), 199–201.

McDougall, S., & House, B. (2012). Brain training in older adults: Evidence of transfer to memory span performance and pseudo-Matthew effects. *Neuropsychology, Development, and Cognition B: Aging, Neuroscience, and Cognition, 19*, 195–221.

McDuffie, A., Thurman, A. J., Hagerman, R. J., & Abbeduto, L. (2014, in press). Symptoms of autism in males with fragile X syndrome: A comparison to nonsyndromic ASD using current ADI-R scores. *Journal of Autism and Developmental Disorders.*

McElhaney, K. B., & Allen, J. P. (2012). Sociocultural perspectives on adolescent autonomy. In P. K. Kreig, M. S. Schulz, & S. T. Hauser (Eds.), *Adolescence and beyond.* New York: Oxford University Press.

McElvaney, R., Green, S., & Hogan, D. (2014). To tell or not to tell? Factors influencing young people's informal disclosures of child sexual abuse. *Journal of Interpersonal Violence, 29*, 928–947.

McElwain, N. L., & Booth-LaForce, C. (2006). Maternal sensitivity to infant distress and nondistress as predictors of infant-mother attachment security. *Journal of Family Psychology, 2*, 247–255.

McGarry, J., Kim, H., Sheng, X., Egger, M., & Baksh, L. (2009). Postpartum depression and help seeking behavior. *Journal of Midwifery and Women's Health, 54*, 50–56.

McGarvey, C., McDonnell, M., Hamilton, K., O'Regan, M., & Matthews, T. (2006). An eight-year study of risk factors for SIDS: Bed-sharing versus non-sharing. *Archives of Disease in Childhood, 91*, 318–323.

McHale, J., & Sullivan, M. (2008). Family systems. In M. Hersen & A. Gross (Eds.), *Handbook of Clinical Psychology* (Vol. 2). New York Wiley.

McHale, S. M., Updegraff, K. A., & Whiteman, S. D. (2013). Sibling relationships. In G. W. Peterson & K. R. Bush (Eds.), *Handbook of marriage and family* (3rd ed.). New York: Springer.

McIlfatrick, S., & Hasson, F. (2014). Evaluating an holistic assessment tool for palliative care practice. *Journal of Clinical Nursing, 23*, 1064–1075.

McInerney, M., Mellor, J. M., & Nicholas, L. H. (2013). Recession depression: Mental health effects of the 2008 stock market crash. *Journal of Health Economics, 32*, 1090–1104.

McIntosh, E., Gillanders, D., & Rodgers, S. (2010). Rumination, goal linking, daily hassles, and life events in major depression. *Clinical Psychology and Psychotherapy, 17*, 33–43.

McKay, A. S., & Kaufman, J. C. (2014). Literary geniuses: Their life, work, and death. In D. K. Simonton (Ed.), *Wiley-Blackwell handbook of genius.* New York: Wiley.

McKenna, L., Kodner, I. J., Healy, G. G., & Keune, J. D. (2013). Sleep deprivation: A call for institutional rules. *Surgery, 154*, 118–122.

McLaughlin, K. (2003, December 30). Commentary in K. Painter, "Nurse dispenses dignity for dying." *USA Today*, Section D, pp. 1–2.

McLaughlin, K. A., & others (2014, in press). Widespread reductions in cortical thickness following severe early-life deprivation: A neurodevelopmental pathway to attention-deficit/hyperactivity disorder. *Biological Psychiatry.*

McLoyd, V., Mistry, R. S., & Hardaway, C. R. (2013). Poverty and children's development: Familial processes as mediating influences. In E. T. Gershoff, R. S. Mistry, and D. A. Crosby (Eds.), *Societal contexts of child development.* New York: Oxford University Press.

McMahon, C. G. (2014). Erectile dysfunction. *International Medical Journal, 44*, 18–26.

McMahon, D. M., Liu, J., Zhang, H., Torres, M. E., & Best, R. G. (2013). Maternal obesity, folate intake, and neural tube defects in offspring. *Birth Defects A: Clinical and Molecular Teratology, 97*, 115–122.

McMillan, C. T., & others (2014, in press). The power of neuroimaging biomarkers for screening frontotemporal dementia. *Human Brain Mapping.*

McMillan, J. H. (2014). *Classroom assessment* (6th ed.). Upper Saddle River, NJ: Pearson.

McNeil, D. A., & others (2012). Getting more than they realized they needed: A qualitative study of women's experience of group prenatal care. *BMC Pregnancy and Childbirth, 12*, 17.

McNeil, D. A., & others (2013). A qualitative study of the experience of CenteringPregnancy group prenatal care for physicians. *BMC Pregnancy and Childbirth, 13*(1, Suppl.), S6.

McNicholas, F., & others (2014, in press). Medical, cognitive, and academic outcomes of very low birth weight infants at 10–14 years in Ireland. *Irish Journal of Medical Science.*

McRae, K., & others (2012). The development of emotion regulation: An fMRI study of cognitive reappraisal in children, adolescents, and adults. *Social Cognitive and Affective Neuroscience, 7*, 11–22.

McWilliams, L. A., & Bailey, S. J. (2010). Association between adult attachment rating and health conditions: Evidence from the National Comorbidity Survey replication. *Health Psychology, 29*, 446–453.

Meade, C. S., Kershaw, T. S., & Ickovics, J. R. (2008). The intergenerational cycle of teenage motherhood: An ecological approach. *Health Psychology, 27*, 419–429.

Mechakra-Tahiri, S. D., Zunzunegui, M. V., Preville, M., & Dube, M. (2010). Gender, social relationships and depressive disorders in adults aged 65 and over in Quebec. *Chronic Diseases in Canada, 30*, 56–65.

Meerlo, P., Sgoifo, A., & Suchecki, D. (2008). Restricted and disrupted sleep: Effects on autonomic function, neuroendocrine stress systems, and stress responsivity. *Sleep Medicine Review.*

Mehari, A., & others (2012). Mortality in adults with sickle-cell disease and pulmonary hypertension. *Journal of the American Medical Association, 307*, 1254–1256.

Meikle, J., Al-Sarraf, A., Li, M., Grierson, K., & Frohlich, J. (2013). Exercise in a healthy heart program: A cohort study. *Clinical Medicine Insights: Cardiology., 7*, 145–151.

Meins, E., & others (2013). Mind-mindedness and theory of mind: Mediating processes of language and perspectival symbolic play. *Child Development, 84*, 1777–1790.

Meisel, V., Servera, M., Garcia-Banda, G., Cardo, E., & Moreno, I. (2013). Neurofeedback and standard pharmacological intervention in ADHD: A randomized controlled trial with six-month follow-up. *Biological Psychology, 94*, 12–21.

Melendez-Moral, J. C., Charco-Ruiz, L., Mayordomo-Rodriquez, T., & Sales-Galan, A. (2013). Effects of a reminiscence program among institutionalized elderly adults. *Psicothema, 25*, 319–323.

Melia, K. M. (2014). When the body is past fixing: Caring for bodies, caring for people. *Journal of Clinical Nursing, 23*, 1616–1622.

Meltzer, A., McNulty, J. K., Jackson, G. L., & Karney, B. R. (2014). Sex differences in the implications of partner physical attractiveness for the trajectory of marital satisfaction. *Journal of Personality and Social Psychology, 106*, 418–428.

Meltzoff, A. N. (1988). Infant imitation and memory: Nine-month-old infants in immediate and deferred tests. *Child Development, 59*, 217–225.

Meltzoff, A. N. (2004). Imitation as a mechanism of social cognition: Origins of empathy, theory of mind, and the representation of action. In U. Goswami (Ed.), *Blackwell handbook of childhood cognitive development.* Malden, MA: Blackwell.

Meltzoff, A. N. (2005). Imitation. In B. Hopkins (Ed.), *Cambridge encyclopedia of child development.* Cambridge: Cambridge University Press.

Meltzoff, A. N. (2007). Infants' causal learning. In A. Gopnik & L. Schulz (Eds.), *Causal learning.* New York: Oxford University Press.

Meltzoff, A. N. (2008). Unpublished review of J. W. Santrock's *Life-Span development* (12th ed.). New York: McGraw-Hill.

Meltzoff, A. N. (2011). Social cognition and the origins of imitation, empathy, and theory of mind. In U. Goswami (Ed.), *Wiley-Blackwell handbook of childhood cognitive development* (2nd ed.). New York: Wiley.

Meltzoff, A. N., & Brooks, R. (2006). Eyes wide shut: The importance of eyes in infant gaze following and understanding of other minds. In R. Flom, K. Lee, & D. Muir (Eds.), *Gaze following: Its development and significance.* Mahwah, NJ: Erlbaum.

Meltzoff, A. N., & Moore, M. K. (1998). Object representation, identity, and the paradox of early permanence: Steps toward a new framework. *Infant Behavior and Development, 21*, 201–235.

Meltzoff, A. N., & Moore, M. K. (1999). A new foundation for cognitive development in infancy: The birth of the representational infant. In E. K. Skolnick, K. Nelson, S. A. Gelman, & P. H. Miller (Eds.), *Conceptual development,* Mahwah, NJ: Erlbaum.

Meltzoff, A. N., & Williamson, R. A. (2010). The importance of imitation for theories of social-cognitive development. In J. G. Bremner & T. D. Wachs (Eds.), *Wiley-Blackwell handbook of infant development* (2nd ed.). New York: Wiley.

Meltzoff, A. N., & Williamson, R. A. (2013). Imitation: Social, cognitive, and theoretical perspectives. In P. D. Zelazo (Ed.), *Oxford handbook of developmental psychology.* New York: Oxford University Press.

Meltzoff, A. N., Williamson, R. A., & Marshall, P. J. (2013). Developmental perspective on action science: Lessons from infant imitation and cognitive neuroscience. In W. Prinz & others (Eds.), *Action science.* Cambridge, MA: MIT Press.

Melzi, G., Schick, A. R., & Kennedy, J. L. (2011). Narrative elaboration and participation: Two dimensions of maternal elicitation style. *Child Development, 82*, 1282–1296.

Memari, A., Ziaee, V., Mirfaxeli, F., & Kordi, R. (2012). Investigation of autism comorbidities and associations in a school-based community sample. *Journal of Child and Adolescent Psychiatric Nursing, 25*, 84–90.

Menendez, S., Hidalgo, M. V., Jiminez, L., & Moreno, M. C. (2011). Father involvement and marital relationship during transition to parenthood: Differences between dual and single earners. *Spanish Journal of Psychology, 14*, 639–647.

Meng, H., Dobbs, D., Wang, S., & Hyer, K. (2013). Hospice use and public expenditures at the end of life in assisted living residents in a Florida Medicaid waiver program. *Journal of the American Geriatrics Society, 61*, 1777–1781.

Meng, X., & D'Arcy, C. (2014). Successful aging in Canada: Prevalence and predictors from a population-based sample of older adults. *Gerontology, 60*, 65–72.

Menn, L., & Stoel-Gammon, C. (2009). Phonological development: Learning sounds and sound patterns. In J. Berko Gleason (Ed.), *The development of language* (7th ed.). Boston: Allyn & Bacon.

Mennecke, A., & others (2014, in press). Physiological effects of cigarette smoking in the limbic system revealed by 3 tesla magnetic resonance spectroscopy. *Journal of Neural Transmission.*

Menon, R., & others (2011). Cigarette smoking induces oxidative stress and atopsis in normal fetal membranes. *Placenta, 32*, 317–322.

Menon, R., & others (2014, in press). Amniotic fluid metabolomic analysis in spontaneous preterm birth. *Reproductive Sciences.*

Menyuk, P., Liebergott, J., & Schultz, M. (1995). *Early language development in full-term and premature infants.* Hillsdale, NJ: Erlbaum.

Mepham, S. O., Bland, R. M., & Newell, M. L. (2011). Prevention of mother-to-child transmission of HIV in resource-rich and -poor settings. *BJOG, 118*, 202–218.

Merad, M., & others (2014, in press). Molecular interaction of acetylcholinesterase with carnosic acid derivaties: A neuroinformatics study. *CNS & Neurological Disorders Drug Targets.*

Meraz-Rios, M. A., & others (2014). Early onset Alzheimer's disease and oxidative stress. *Oxidative Medicine and Cellular Longevity, 2014:* 375968.

Meredith, N. V. (1978). Research between 1960 and 1970 on the standing height of young children in different parts of the world. In H. W. Reece & L. P. Lipsitt (Eds.), *Advances in child development and behavior* (Vol. 12). New York: Academic Press.

Merewood, A., & others (2007). Breastfeeding duration rates and factors affecting continued breastfeeding among infants born at an inner-city U.S. baby-friendly hospital. *Journal of Human Lactation, 23*, 157–164.

Merrill, D. M. (2009). Parent-child relationships: Later-life. In D. Carr (Ed.), *Encyclopedia of the life course and human development.* Boston: Gale Cengage.

Mersy, E., & others (2013). Noninvasive detection of fetal trisomy 21: Systematic review and report of quality and outcomes of diagnostic accuracy studies performed between 1997 and 2012. *Human Reproduction Update, 19*(4), 318–329.

Mesman, J., van Ijzendoorn, M. H., & Bakermans-Kranenburg, M. J. (2009). The many facets of the still-face paradigm: A review and meta analysis. *Developmental Review, 29*, 120–162.

Messiah, S. E., Miller, T. L., Lipshultz, S. E., & Bandstra, E. S. (2011). Potential latent effects of prenatal cocaine exposure on growth and the risk of cardiovascular and metabolic disease in childhood. *Progress in Pediatric Cardiology, 31*, 59–65.

Mestre, T. A., & others (2014, in press). Reluctance to start medication for Parkinson's disease: A mutual misunderstanding by patients and physicians. *Parkinsonism and Related Disorders.*

Mesulam, M. M. (2013). Cholinergic circuitry of the human nucleus basalis and its fate in Alzheimer's disease. *Journal of Comparative Neurology and Psychology, 521*, 4124–4144.

Metzger, A., & others (2013). Information management strategies with conversations about cigarette smoking: Parenting correlates and longitudinal associations with teen smoking. *Developmental Psychology, 49*, 1565–1578.

Meyer, M. H., & Parker, W. M. (2011). Gender, aging, and social policy. In R. H. Binstock & L. K. George (Eds.), *Handbook of aging and the social sciences* (7th ed.). New York: Elsevier.

Meyer, S. L., Weible, C. M., & Woeber, K. (2010). Perceptions and practice of waterbirth: A survey of Georgia midwives. *Journal of Midwifery and Women's Health, 55*, 55–59.

Meyer, U., & others (2014). Long-term effect of a school-based physical activity program (KISS) on fitness and adiposity in children: A cluster-randomized controlled trial. *PLoS One, 9*(2), e87929.

Michael, R. T., Gagnon, J. H., Laumann, E. O., & Kolata, G. (1994). *Sex in America.* Boston: Little, Brown.

Michalska-Malecka, K., & others (2013). Results of cataract surgery in the very elderly population. *Clinical Interventions in Aging, 8*, 1041–1046.

Mike, A., Harris, K., Roberts, B. W., & Jackson, J. J. (2014, in press). Conscientiousness: Lower-order structure, life course consequences, and development. In J. Wright (Ed.), *International encyclopedia of social and behavioral sciences* (2nd ed.). New York: Elsevier.

Mikulincer, M., & Shaver, P. R. (2007). *Attachment in adulthood.* New York: Guilford.

Mikulincer, M., Shaver, P. R., Bar-on, N., & ein-Dor, T. (2010). The pushes and pulls of close relationships: Attachment insecurities and relational ambivalence. *Journal of Personality and Social Psychology, 98*, 450–468.

Milan, S., & Acker, J. C. (2014, in press). Early attachment quality moderates eating disorder risk among adolescent girls. *Psychology and Health.*

Milberg, A., Olsson, E. C., Jakobsson, M., Olsson, M., & Friedrichsen, M. (2008). Family members' perceived needs for bereavement follow-up. *Journal of Pain and Symptom Management, 35*, 58–69.

Milburn, N. G., & others (2012). A family intervention to reduce sexual risk behavior, substance use, and delinquency among newly homeless youth. *Journal of Adolescent Health, 50*, 358–364.

Milesi, G., & others (2014, in press). Assessment of human hippocampal developmental neuroanatomy by means of ex-vivo 7T magnetic resonance imaging. *International Journal of Neuroscience.*

Miljkovic, M. D., Jones, B. L., & Miller, K. (2013). From the Euthanasia Society to Physicians Orders for Life-Sustaining Treatment: End-of-life care in the United States. *Cancer Journal, 19*, 438–443.

Miller, B. C., Benson, B., & Galbraith, K. A. (2001). Family relationships and adolescent pregnancy risk: A research synthesis. *Developmental Review, 21*, 1–38.

Miller, C. F., Lurye, L. E., Zusuls, K. M., & Ruble, D. N. (2009). Accessibility of gender stereotype domains: Developmental and gender differences in children. *Sex Roles, 60*, 870–881.

Miller, C., Martin, C. L., Fabes, R., & Hanish, D. (2013). Bringing the cognitive and social together: How gender detectives and gender enforcers shape children's gender development. In M. Banaji & S. Gelman (Eds.), *Navigating the social world: A developmental perspective.* New York: Oxford University Press.

Miller, C., & Price, J. (2013). *The number of children being raised by gay or lesbian parents.* Unpublished manuscript, Department of Economics, Brigham Young University, Provo, UT.

Miller, J. G., & Bland, C. G. (2014). A cultural perspective on moral development. In M. Killen & J. G. Smetana (Eds.), *Handbook of moral development* (2nd ed.). New York: Psychology Press.

Miller, L. M., & Bell, R. A. (2012). Online health information seeking: The influence of age, information trustworthiness, and search challenges. *Journal of Aging and Health, 24*, 525–541.

Miller, M., Loya, F., & Hinshaw, S. P. (2013). Executive functions in girls with and without ADHD: Developmental trajectories and associations with symptom change. *Journal of Child Psychology and Psychiatry, 54*, 1005–1015.

Miller, M. D. (2012). Complicated grief in late life. *Dialogues in Clinical Neuroscience 14*, 195–202.

Miller, P. H. (2010). *Theories of developmental psychology* (5th ed.). New York: Worth.

Miller, P. H. (2011). Piaget's theory: Past, present, and future. In U. Goswami (Ed.), *Wiley-Blackwell handbook of childhood cognitive development* (2nd ed.). New York: Wiley Blackwell.

Miller, P. H. (2014). The history of memory development research: Remembering our roots. In P. Bauer & R. Fivush (Eds.), *Wiley handbook on the development of children's memory.* New York: Wiley.

Miller, R. B., Hollist, C. S., Olsen, J., & Law, D. (2013). Marital quality and health over 20 years: A growth curve analysis. *Journal of Marriage and the Family, 75*, 667–680.

Miller, R., Wankerl, M., Stalder, T., Kirschbaum, C., & Alexander, N. (2013). The serotonin transporter gene-linked polymorphic region (5-HTTLPR) and cortisol stress reactivity: A meta-analysis. *Molecular Psychiatry, 18*, 1018–1024.

Miller, R. A. (2009). Cell stress and aging: New emphasis on multiplex resistance mechanisms. *Journals of Gerontology A: Biological Sciences and Medical Sciences, 64*, 179–182.

Miller, S., Malone, P., Dodge, K. A., & Conduct Problems Prevention Research Group (2010). Developmental trajectories of boys' and girls' delinquency: Sex differences and links to later adolescent outcomes. *Journal of Abnormal Child Psychology, 38*(7), 1021–1032.

Miller, S. A. (2012). *Theory of mind: Beyond the preschool years.* New York: Psychology Press.

Miller-Perrin, C. L., Perrin, R. D., & Kocur, J. L. (2009). Parental, physical, and psychological aggression: Psychological symptoms in young adults. *Child Abuse and Neglect, 33*, 1–11.

Mills, B., Reyna, V., & Estrada, S. (2008). Explaining contradictory relations between risk perception and risk taking. *Psychological Science, 19*, 429–433.

Mills, C. M. (2013). Knowing when to doubt: Developing a critical stance when learning from others. *Developmental Psychology, 114*, 63–76.

Mills, C. M., Elashi, F. B., & Archacki, M. A. (2011, March). *Evaluating sources of information and misinformation: Developmental and individual differences in the elementary school years.* Paper presented at the biennial meeting of the Society for Research in Child Development, Montreal.

Mills, C. M., & Landrum, A. R. (2012). Judging judges: How do children weigh the importance of capability for being a good decision maker? *British Journal of Developmental Psychology, 30*(3), 383–414.

Mills, D., & Mills, C. (2000). *Hungarian kindergarten curriculum translation.* London: Mills Production.

Mills-Koonce, W. R., Propper, C. B., & Barnett, M. (2012). Poor infant soothability and later insecure-ambivalent attachment: Developmental change in phenotypic markers of risk or two measures of the same construct? *Infant Behavior and Development, 35*, 215–235.

Milne, E., & others (2012). Parental prenatal smoking and risk of childhood acute lymphoblastic leukemia. *American Journal of Epidemiology, 175,* 43–53.

Milner, A., & others (2014, in press). The effects of involuntary job loss on suicide and suicide attempts among young adults: Evidence from a matched case-control study. *Australian and New Zealand Journal of Psychiatry.*

Milte, C. M., & others (2014, in press). Influence of health locus of control on recovery of function in recently hospitalized frail older adults. *Geriatrics and Gerontology International.*

Mindell, J. A., Sadeh, A., Kohyama, J., & How, T. H. (2010). Parental behaviors and sleep outcomes in infants and toddlers: A cross-cultural comparison. *Sleep Medicine, 11,* 393–399.

Mindell, J. A., Sadeh, A., Wiegand, B., How, T. H., & Goh, D. Y. (2010). Cross-cultural differences in infant and toddler sleep. *Sleep Medicine, 11,* 274–280.

Miner, M. M., Bhattacharya, R. K., Blick, G., Kushner, H., & Khera, M. (2013). 12-month observation of testosterone replacement effectiveness in a general population of men. *Postgraduate Medicine, 125,* 8–18.

Minkler, M., & Fuller-Thompson, E. (2005). African American grandparents raising grandchildren: A national study using the Census 2000 American Community Survey. *Journals of Gerontology B: Psychological Sciences and Social Sciences, 60,* S82–S92.

Minnes, S., & others (2010). The effects of prenatal cocaine exposure on problem behavior in children 4–10 years. *Neurotoxicology and Teratology, 32,* 443–451.

Minnesota Family Investment Program (2009). *Longitudinal study of early MFIP recipients.* Retrieved January 12, 2009, from http://www.dhs.state.mn.us/main/idcplg?IdcService=GET_DYNAMIC_CONVERSION&...

Minniti, F., & others (2014, in press). Breast-milk characteristics protecting against allergy. *Endocrine, Metabolic, and Immunder Disorders Drug Targets.*

Minsart, A. F., Buekens, P., Spiegelaere, M., & Englert, Y. (2013). Neonatal outcomes in obese mothers: A population-based analysis. *BMC Pregnancy and Childbirth, 13,* 36.

Miotto, E. C., & others (2013). Semantic strategy training increases memory performance and brain activity in patients with prefrontal cortex lesions. *Clinical Neurology and Neurosurgery, 115*(3), 309–316.

Mischel, W. (2004). Toward an integrative science of the person. *Annual Review of Psychology* (Vol. 55). Palo Alto, CA: Annual Reviews.

Mischel, W., Cantor, N., & Feldman, S. (1996). Principles of self-regulation: The nature of will power and self-control. In E. T. Higgins & A. W. Kruglanski (Eds.), *Social psychology.* New York: Guilford.

Mischel, W., & Moore, B. S. (1980). The role of ideation in voluntary delay for symbolically presented rewards. *Cognitive Therapy and Research, 4,* 211–221.

Mischel, W., & others (2011). 'Willpower' over the life span: Decomposing self-regulation. *Social Cognitive and Affective Neuroscience, 6,* 252–256.

Mishara, B. L., & Weisstub, D. N. (2013). Premises and evidence in the rhetoric of assisted suicide and euthanasia. *International Journal of Law and Psychiatry, 36,* 427–435.

Mishra, G. D., Cooper, R., Tom, S. E., & Kuh, D. (2009). Early life circumstances and their impact on menarche and menopause. *Women's Health, 5,* 175–190.

Mission, J. F., Marshall, N. E., & Caughey, A. B. (2013). Obesity in pregnancy: A big problem and getting bigger. *Obstetrical and Gynecological Survey, 68,* 389–399.

Mistry, J., Contreras, M., & Dutta, R. (2013). Culture and development. In I. B. Weiner & others (Eds.), *Handbook of psychology* (2nd ed., Vol. 6). New York: Wiley.

Mitchell, A. B., & Stewart, J. B. (2013). The efficacy of all-male academies: Insights from critical race theory (CRT). *Sex Roles, 69,* 382.

Mitchell, A. J., Yates, C., Williams, K., & Hall, R. W. (2013). Effects of daily kangaroo care on caradiorespiratory parameters in preterm infants. *Journal of Neonatal and Perinatal Medicine, 6,* 243–249.

Mitchell, B. A. (2007). Marriage and divorce. In J. E. Birren (Ed.), *Encyclopedia of gerontology* (2nd ed.). San Diego: Academic Press.

Mitchell, M. B., & others (2012). Cognitively stimulating activities: Effects on cognition across four studies with up to 21 years of longitudinal data. *Journal of Aging Research.* doi:10.1155/2012/461592

Mitchell, M. B., & others (2013). Norms for the Georgia Centenarian Study: Measures of verbal abstract reasoning, fluency, memory, and motor function. *Neuropsychology, Development, and Cognition B: Aging, Neuropsychology, and Cognition, 20,* 620–637.

Mitchell, V., & Helson, R. (1990). Women's prime of life: Is it the 50s? *Psychology of Women Quarterly, 14,* 451–470.

Miyake, K., Chen, S., & Campos, J. (1985). Infants' temperament, mothers' mode of interaction and attachment in Japan: An interim report. In I. Bretherton & F. Waters (Eds.), Growing points of attachment theory and research, *Monographs of the Society for Research in Child Development, 50* (1–2, Serial No. 109), 276–297.

Miyakoshi, K., & others (2013). Perinatal outcomes: Intravenous patient-controlled fentanyl versus no analgesia in labor. *Journal of Obstetrics and Gynecology Research, 39*(4), 783–789.

Mize, K. D., & Jones, N. A. (2012). Infant physiological and behavioral responses to loss of maternal attention to a social-rival. *International Journal of Psychophysiology, 83,* 16–23.

Mize, K. D., Pineda, M., Blau, A. K., Marsh, K., & Jones, N. A. (2014, in press). Infant physiological and behavioral responses to a jealousy provoking condition. *Infancy.*

MMWR (2006, June 9). *Youth risk behavior surveillance—United States 2005* (Vol. 255). Atlanta: Centers for Disease Control and Prevention.

Moak, G. S. (2011). Treatment of late-life mental disorders in primary care: We can do a better job. *Journal of Aging and Social Policy, 23,* 274–285.

Mobley, A. S., Rodriquez-Gil, D. J., Imamura, F., & Greer, C. A. (2014). Aging in the olfactory system. *Trends in Neuroscience, 37,* 37–44.

Mock, S. E., & Eibach, R. P. (2012). Stability and change in sexual orientation identity over a 10-year period in adulthood. *Archives of Sexual Behavior, 41,* 641–648.

Moen, P. (2007). Unpublished review of J. W. Santrock's *Life-span development* (12th ed.). New York: McGraw-Hill.

Moen, P. (2009a). Careers. In D. Carr (Ed.), *Encyclopedia of the life course and human development.* Boston: Gale Cengage.

Moen, P. (2009b). Dual-career couples. In D. Carr (Ed.), *Encyclopedia of the life course and human development.* Boston: Gale Cengage.

Moen, P., Kelly, E., and Magennis, R. (2008). Gender strategies: Social and institutional convoys, mystiques, and cycles of control. In M. C. Smith & T. G. Reio (Eds.), *Handbook of research on adult development and learning.* Mahwah: Erlbaum.

Moilanen, J. M., & others (2012). Effect of aerobic training on menopausal symptoms—a randomized controlled trial. *Menopause, 19,* 691–696.

Moise, K. J., & others (2013). Circulating cell-free DNA for the detection of RHD status and sex using reflex fetal identifiers. *Prenatal Diagnosis.*

Molina, B. S., & Pelham, W. E. (2014, in press). Attention-deficit/hyperactivity disorder and risk of substance use disorder: Developmental considerations, potential pathways, and opportunities for research. *Annual Review of Clinical Psychology* (Vol. 10). Palo Alto, CA: Annual Reviews.

Molina, B. S., & others (2013). Adolescent substance use in the multimodal treatment study of attention-deficit/hyperactivity disorder (ADH (MTA) as a function of childhood ADHD, random assignment to treatments, and subsequent medication. *Journal of the American Academy of Child and Adolescent Psychiatry, 52,* 250–263.

Molina, R. C., Roca, C. G., Zamorano, J. S., & Araya, E. G. (2010). Family planning and adolescent pregnancy. *Best Practices and Research: Clinical Obstetrics and Gynecology, 24,* 209–222.

Mollee, P. (2014, in press). New diagnostic strategies for assessment of amyloidosis and myeloma. *Pathology.*

Moller, J., Bjorkeenstam, E., Ljung, R., & Yngwe, M. A. (2011). Widowhood and the risk of psychiatric care, psychotropic medication, and all-cause mortality: A cohort of 658,022 elderly people in Sweden. *Aging and Mental Health, 15,* 259–266.

Molton, I. R., & Terrill, A. L. (2014). Overview of persistent pain in older adults. *American Psychologist, 69,* 197–207.

Monahan, K., & others (2014, in press). Integration of developmental neuroscience and contextual approaches to the study of adolescent psychopathology. In D. Cicchetti (Ed.), *Handbook of developmental psychopathology* (3rd ed.). New York: Wiley.

Money, K. M., & Stanwood, G. D. (2013). Developmental origins of brain disorders: Roles for dopamine. *Frontiers in Cellular Neuroscience, 7,* 260.

Monserud, M. A. (2008). Intergenerational relationships and affectual solidarity between grandparents and young adults. *Journal of Marriage and the Family, 70,* 182–195.

Monserud, M. A. (2011). Changes in grandchildren's adult role statuses and their relationships to grandparents. *Journal of Family Issues, 32,* 425–451.

Montagna, P., & Chokroverty, S. (2011). *Sleep disorders.* New York: Elsevier.

Monti, J. M., Hillman, C. H., & Cohen, N. J. (2012). Aerobic fitness enhances relational memory in preadolescent children: The FITKids randomized control trial. *Hippocampus, 22,* 1876–1882.

Montirosso, R., & others (2012). Level of NICU quality and developmental care and neurobehavioral performance in very preterm infants. *Pediatrics, 129*(5), e1129–e1137.

Montoya Arizabaleta, A. V., & others (2010). Aerobic exercise during pregnancy improves health-related quality of life: A randomized trial. *Journal of Physiotherapy, 56,* 253–258.

Moon, R. Y., & others (2012). Pacifier use and SIDS: Evidence for a consistently reduced risk. *Maternal and Child Health Journal, 16,* 609–614.

Moore, D. (2001). *The dependent gene.* New York: W. H. Freeman.

Moore, D. S. (2013). Behavioral genetics, genetics, and epigenetics. In P. D. Zelazo (Ed.), *Handbook of developmental psychology.* New York: Oxford University Press.

Moore, M. W., Brendel, P. C., & Fiez, J. A. (2014). Reading faces: Investigating the use of a novel face-based orthography in acquired alexia. *Brain and Language, 129C,* 7–13.

Moore, S. R., Harden, K. P., & Mendle, J. (2014, in press). Pubertal timing and adolescent sexual behavior in girls. *Developmental Psychology.*

Moos, B. (2007, July 4). Who'll care for aging boomers? Dallas Morning News, A1–A2.

Moraes, W., & others (2014, in press). Effects of aging on sleep structure throughout adulthood: A population-based study. *Sleep Medicine.*

Moran, S., & Gardner, H. (2006). Extraordinary achievements. In W. Damon & R. Lerner (Eds.), *Handbook of child psychology* (6th ed.). New York: Wiley.

Moran, S., & Gardner, H. (2007). Hill, skill, and will: Executive function from a multiple intelligences perspective. In L. Meltzer (ed.), *Executive function in education.* New York: Guilford.

Morasch, K. C., & Bell, M. A. (2012). Self-regulation of negative affect at 5 and 10 months. *Developmental Psychobiology, 54,* 215–221.

Morasch, K. C., Raj, V. R., & Bell, M. A. (2013). The development of cognitive control from infancy through childhood. In D. Reisberg (Ed.), *Oxford handbook of cognitive psychology.* New York: Oxford University Press.

Moreau, C., Beltzer, N., Bozon, M., Bajos, N., & the CSF Group (2011). Sexual risk taking following relationship break-ups. *European Journal of Contraception and Reproductive Health Care, 16,* 95–99.

Moreira, S. R., Lima, R. M., Silva, K. E., & Simoes, H. G. (2014). Combined exercise circuit session acutely attenuates stress-induced blood pressure reactivity in healthy adults. *Brazilian Journal of Physical Therapy, 18,* 38–46.

Morgan, S., Koren, G., & Bozzo, P. (2013). Is caffeine consumption safe during pregnancy? *Canadian Family Physician, 59,* 361–362.

Morin, C. M., Savard, J., & Ouellet, M-C. (2013). Nature and treatment of insomnia. In I. B. Weiner & others (Eds.), *Handbook of psychology* (2nd ed., Vol. 9). New York: Wiley.

Moro, M. R. (2014, in press). Parenthood in migration: How to face vulnerability. *Culture, Medicine, and Psychiatry.*

Moro-Garcia, M. A., & others (2014, in press). Frequence participation in high volume exercise throughout life is associated with a more differentiated adaptive immune response. *Brain, Behavior, and Immunity.*

Morra, L., Zade, D., McGlinchey, R. E., & Milberg, W. P. (2013). Normal aging and cognition: The unacknowledged contribution of cerebrovascular risk factors. *Neuropsychology, Development, and Cognition B: Aging, Neuropsychology, and Cognition, 20*(3), 271–297.

Morra, S., Gobbo, C., Marini, Z., & Sheese, R. (2008). *Cognitive development: Neo-Piagetian perspectives.* Mahwah, NJ: Erlbaum.

Morris, B. H., McGrath, A. C., Goldman, M. S., & Rottenberg, J. (2014). Parental depression confers greater perspective depression risk to females than males in emerging adulthood. *Child Psychiatry and Human Development, 45,* 78–89.

Morris, B. J., & others (2012). A 'snip' in time: What is the best age to circumcise? *BMC Pediatrics, 12,* 20.

Morris, B. J., & others (2014, in press). Genetic analysis of TOR complex gene variation with human longevity: A nested case-control study of American men of Japanese ancestry. *Journals of Gerontology A: Biological Sciences and Social Sciences.*

Morris, R. J., Thompson, K. C., & Morris, Y. P. (2013). Child psychotherapy. In I. B. Weiner & others (Eds.), *Handbook of psychology* (2nd ed., Vol. 8). New York: Wiley.

Morrison, G. S. (2014). *Fundamentals of early childhood education* (7th ed.). Upper Saddle River, NJ: Pearson.

Morrison, G. S. (2015, in press). *Early childhood education today* (13th ed.). Upper Saddle River, NJ: Pearson.

Morrison, R. S. (2013). Models of palliative care delivery in the United States. *Current Opinion in Supportive and Palliative Care, 7,* 201–206.

Morrison-Beedy, D., & others (2013). Reducing sexual risk behavior in adolescent girls: Results from a randomized trial. *Journal of Adolescent Health, 52,* 314–322.

Morrissey, T. W. (2009). Multiple child-care arrangements and young children's behavioral outcomes. *Child Development, 80,* 59–76.

Morrow, C. E., & others (2006). Learning disabilities and intellectual functioning in school-aged children with prenatal cocaine exposure. *Developmental Neuropsychology, 30,* 905–931.

Morrow-Howell, N., & others (2014, in press). An investigation of activity profiles of older adults. *Journals of Gerontology B: Psychological Sciences and Social Sciences.*

Mortensen, O., Torsheim, T., Melkevik, O., & Thuen, F. (2012). Adding a baby to the equation. Married and cohabiting women's relationship satisfaction in the transition to parenthood. *Family Process, 51,* 122–139.

Mortimer, J. T. (2012). The evolution, contributions, and prospects of Youth Development Study: An investigation in life course social psychology. *Social Psychology Quarterly, 75,* 5–27.

Mosing, M. A., & others (2012). Genetic influences on life span and its relationship to personality: A 16-year follow-up study of a sample of aging twins. *Psychosomatic Medicine, 74,* 16–22.

Moskalev, A. A., & others (2014, in press). Genetics and epigenetics of aging and longevity. *Cell Cycle.*

Moss, M. S., & Moss, S. Z. (2014). Widowhood in old age: Viewed in a family context. *Journal of Aging Studies, 29,* 98–106.

Motowidlo, S. J., & Kell, H. J. (2013). Job performance. In I. B. Weiner & others (Eds.), *Handbook of psychology* (2nd ed., Vol. 12). New York: Wiley.

Motti-Stefanidi, F., & Masten, A. S. (2014, in press). School success and school engagement in immigrant youth: A risk and resilience developmental perspective. *European Psychologist.*

Moulson, M. C., & Nelson, C. A. (2008). Neurological development. In M. M. Haith & J. B. Benson (Eds.), *Encyclopedia of infant and early childhood development.* Oxford, UK: Elsevier.

Moutsiana, C., & others (2014, in press). Making an effort to feel positive: Insecure attachment in infancy predicts the neural underpinnings of emotion regulation in adulthood. *Journal of Child Psychology and Psychiatry.*

Moyer, M. W. (2013). The myth of antioxidants. *Scientific American, 308*(2), 62–67.

Mparmpakas, D., & others (2013). Immune system function, stress, exercise, and nutrition profile can affect pregnancy outcome: Lessons from a Mediterranean cohort. *Experimental and Therapeutic Medicine, 5,* 411–418.

Mroczek, D. K., & Kolarz, C. M. (1998). The effect of age on positive and negative affect: A developmental perspective on happiness. *Journal of Personality and Social Psychology, 75,* 1333–1349.

Mroczek, D. K., Spiro, A., & Griffin, P. W. (2006). Personality and aging. In J. E. Birren & K. W. Schale

(Eds.), *Handbook of the psychology of aging* (6th ed.). San Diego: Academic Press.

Muir, S. W., & others (2013). Association of executive function impairment, history of falls, and physical performance in older adults: A cross-sectional population-based study in Eastern France. *Journal of Nutrition, Health, and Aging, 17,* 661–665.

Mullen, S. P., & others (2012). Physical activity and functional limitations in older adults: The influence of self-efficacy and functional performance. *Journals of Gerontology B: Psychological Sciences and Social Sciences, 67,* 354–361.

Muller, U., Zelazo, P. D., Lurye, L. E., & Lieberman, D. P. (2008). The effect of labeling on preschool children's performance in the Dimensional Change Card Sort task. *Cognitive Development, 23,* 395–408.

Mullet, H. G., & others (2013). Prospective memory and aging: Evidence for preserved spontaneous retrieval with exact but not related cues. *Psychology and Aging, 28,* 910–922.

Mund, I., Bell, R., & Buchner, A. (2010). Age differences in reading with distraction: Sensory or inhibitory deficits. *Psychology and Aging, 25,* 886–897.

Mundy, P., & others (2007). Individual differences and the development of joint attention in infancy. *Child Development, 78,* 938–954.

Mungas, D., & others (2014). A 2-process model for neuropathology and Alzheimer's disease. *Neurobiology of Aging, 35,* 301–308.

Muniz-Terra, G., & others (2013). Investigating terminal decline: Results from a UK population-based study of aging. *Psychology and Aging, 28,* 377–385.

Munnell, A. H. (2011). *What is the average retirement age?* (Issue Brief No.11-11). Chestnut Hill, MA: Center for Retirement Research, Boston College.

Murphy, C. (2009). The chemical senses and nutrition in older adults. *Journal of Nutrition for the Elderly, 27,* 247–265.

Murphy, D. A., Brecht, M. L., Huang, D., & Herbeck, D. M. (2012). Trajectories of delinquency from age 14 to 23 in the National Longitudinal Survey of Youth sample. *International Journal of Adolescence and Youth, 17,* 47–62.

Murphy, R. A., & others (2014, in press). Associations of BMI and adipose tissue area and density with incident mobility limitation and poor performance in older adults. *American Journal of Clinical Nutrition.*

Murphy, S. L., Xu, J., Kochanek, K. D. (2012, January 12). Deaths: Preliminary data for 2010. *National Vital Statistics Reports, 60*(4), Table 7, 54–58.

Murr, J., Carmichael, P.H., Julien, P., & Laurin, D. (2014, in press). Plasma oxidized low-density lipoprotein levels and risk of Alzheimer's disease. *Neurobiology of Aging.*

Murray, A. (2011). Montessori elementary philosophy reflects current motivation theories. *Montessori Life, 23,* 22–33.

Murray, S. S., & McKinney, E. S. (2014). *Foundations of maternal-newborn and women's health nursing—text and simulation learning package* (5th ed.). New York: Elsevier.

Mussen, P. H., Honzik, M., & Eichorn, D. (1982). Early adult antecedents of life satisfaction at age 70. *Journal of Gerontology, 37,* 316–322.

Myatchin, I., & Lagae, O. (2013, in press). Developmental changes in visuo-spatial working memory in normally developing children: Event-related potentials study. *Brain Development.*

Myers, D. G. (2010). *Psychology* (9th ed.). New York: Worth.

Myerson, J., Rank, M. R., Raines, F. Q., & Schnitzler, M. A. (1998). Race and general cognitive ability: The myth of diminishing returns in education. *Psychology Science, 9.*

Mykyta, L., & Macartney, S. (2012, June). Sharing a household. Composition and economic well-being: 2007–2010. *Current Population Report,* P60–P242. Washington, DC: U.S. Department of Commerce.

N

Nabe-Nielsen, K., & others (2014, in press). Demand-specific work ability, poor health, and working conditions in middle-aged full-time employees. *Applied Ergonomics.*

Nader, K. (2001). Treatment methods for childhood trauma. In J. P. Wilson, M. J. Friedman, & J. Lindy (Eds.), *Treating psychological trauma and PTSD.* New York: Guilford Press.

Naef, R., Ward, R., Mahrer-Imhof-R., & Grande, G. (2013). Characteristics of the bereavement experience of older persons after spousal loss: An integrative review. *International Journal of Nursing Studies, 50,* 1108–1121.

NAEYC (National Association for the Education of Young Children) (2009). *Developmentally appropriate practice in early childhood programs serving children from birth through age 8.* Washington, DC: Author.

Nag, T., & Ghosh, A. (2013). Cardiovascular disease risk factors in Asian Indian population: A systematic review. *Journal of Cardiovascular Disease Research, 4,* 222–228.

Nag, T. C., & Wadhwa, S. (2012). Ultrastructure of the human retina in aging and various pathological states. *Micron, 43,* 759–781.

Nagamatsu, L. S., & others (2014, in press). Exercise is medicine for the body and brain. *British Journal of Sports Medicine.*

Nagel, B. J., & others (2011). Altered white matter microstructure in children with attention-deficit/hyperactivity disorder. *Journal of the American Academy of Child and Adolescent Psychiatry, 50,* 283–292.

Naicker, K., Galambos, N. L., Zeng, Y., Senthilselvan, A., & Colman, I. (2013). Social, demographic, and health outcomes in the 10 years following adolescent depression. *Journal of Adolescent Health, 52,* 533–538.

Nair-Collins, M., Northrup, J., & Olcese, J. (2014, in press). Hypothalamic-pituitary function in brain death: A review. *Journal of Intensive Care Medicine.*

Najar, B., & others (2008). Effects of psychosocial stimulation on growth and development of severely malnourished children in a nutrition unit in Bangladesh. *European Journal of Clinical Nutrition, 63*(6), 725–731.

Najman, J. M., & others (2009). The impact of episodic and chronic poverty on child cognitive development. *Journal of Pediatrics, 154,* 284–289.

Najman, J. M., & others (2010). Timing and chronicity of family poverty and development of unhealthy behaviors in children: A longitudinal study. *Journal of Adolescent Health, 46,* 538–544.

Nakajima, S., Masaya, I., Akemi, S., & Takako, K. (2012). Complicated grief in those bereaved by violent death: The effects of post-traumatic stress disorder on complicated grief. *Dialogues in Clinical Neuroscience, 14,* 210–214.

Nanni, V., Uher, R., & Danese, A. (2012). Childhood maltreatment predicts unfavorable course of illness and treatment outcome in depression: A meta-analysis. *American Journal of Psychiatry, 169,* 141–151.

Nansel, T. R., & others (2001). Bullying behaviors among U.S. youth. *Journal of the American Medical Association, 285,* 2094–2100.

Nardone, R., & others (2014, in press). Dopamine differentially modulates central cholinergic circuits in patients with Alzheimer disease and CADASIL. *Journal of Neural Transmission.*

Narvaez, D. (2014, in press). *The neurobiology and development of human morality.* New York: Norton.

Narvaez, D., Panksepp, J., Schore, A. N., & Gleason, T. R. (Eds.) (2013). *Evolution, early experience, and human development.* New York: Oxford University Press.

Nascimento Dda, C., & others (2014). Sustained effect of resistance training on blood pressure and hand grip strength following a detraining period in elderly hypertensive women: A pilot study. *Clinical Interventions in Aging, 9,* 219–225.

Nash-Ditzel, S. (2010). Metacognitive reading strategies can improve comprehension. *Journal of College Reading and Learning, 40,* 45–63.

NASSPE (2012). *Single-sex schools/schools with single-sex classrooms/what's the difference.* Retrieved from www.singlesexschools.org/schools-schools.com

Natalizia, A., & others (2010). An overview of hearing impairment in older adults: Perspectives for rehabilitation with hearing aids. *European Review for Medical and Pharmaceutical Sciences, 14,* 223–229.

National Alliance for Caregiving (2009). *Caregiving in the United States 2009.* Retrieved June 29, 2012, from www.caregiving.org/pdf/research/Caregiving

National Assessment of Educational Progress (2012). *The nation's report card: 2012.* Washington, DC: U.S. Department of Education.

National Association for Gifted Children (2009). *State of the states in gifted education: 2008–2009.* Washington, DC: Author.

National Association for Sport and Physical Education (2002). *Active start: A statement of physical activity guidelines for children birth to five years.* Reston. VA: National Association for Sport and Physical Education Publications.

National Autism Association (2011). *All about autism.* Retrieved July 30, 2011, from http://www.nationalautismassociation.org/definitions.php

National Cancer Institute (2014). *Childhood cancer.* Rockville, MD: Author.

National Center for Education Statistics (2002). *Work during college.* Washington, DC: U.S. Office of Education.

National Center for Education Statistics (2009). *Comparative indicators of education in the United States and other G-8 countries: 2009.* Washington, DC: U.S. Department of Education.

National Center for Education Statistics (2012). Indicator A-33-3: Status dropout rates. *Digest of Education Statistics.* Washington, DC: U.S. Department of Education.

National Center for Education Statistics (2013, May). *Characteristics of postsecondary students.* Washington: U.S. Department of Education.

National Center for Education Statistics (2013). *The condition of education, 2013.* Washington, DC: U.S. Department of Education.

National Center for Health Statistics (2000). *Health United States 2000, with adolescent health chartbook.* Bethesda, MD: U.S. Department of Health and Human Services.

National Center for Health Statistics (2002). *Sexual behavior and selected health measures: Men and women 15–44 years of age, United States, 2002,* PHS 2003–1250. Atlanta: Centers for Disease Control and Prevention.

National Center for Health Statistics (2004). *Health United States.* Atlanta: Centers for Disease Control and Prevention.

National Center for Health Statistics (2011, March). *Adult obesity prevalence in the United States and Canada. NCHS Data Brief, No. 56.*

National Center for Health Statistics (2012). *Births.* Atlanta: Centers for Disease Control and Prevention.

National Center for Health Statistics (2013). *Death statistics.* Atlanta: Centers for Disease Control and Prevention.

National Center for Health Statistics (2014). *Death statistics.* Atlanta: Centers for Disease Control and Prevention.

National Center for Health Statistics (2014). *Sexually transmitted diseases.* Atlanta: Centers for Disease Control and Prevention.

National Center for Vital Statistics (2013). *Births, marriages, divorces, death: 2011.* Washington, DC: Author.

National Center on Shaken Baby Syndrome (2012). *Shaken baby syndrome.* Retrieved April, 20, 2011 from www.dontshake.org/

National Clearinghouse on Child Abuse and Neglect (2004). *What is child abuse and neglect?* Washington, DC: U.S. Department of Health and Human Services.

National Council on Aging (2000, March). *Myths and realities survey results.* Washington, DC: Author.

National Institute of Mental Health (2014). *Autism spectrum disorders (pervasive developmental disorders).* Retrieved February 27, 2014, from www.nimh.nih.gov/Publicat/autism.clm

National Institutes of Health (2008). Clinical trial.gov. Retrieved April 22, 2008.

National Institutes of Health. (2004). *Women's Health Initiative hormone therapy study.* Bethesda, MD: National Institutes of Health.

National Marriage Project (2011). *Unmarried cohabitation.* Retrieved June 9, 2012, from www.stateofourunions.org/2011/social_indicators.php

National Sleep Foundation (2006). *2006 Sleep in America poll.* Washington, DC: Author.

National Sleep Foundation. (2007). *2007 Sleep in America poll.* Washington, DC: Author.

National Sleep Foundation (2014). *Children's sleep habits.* Retrieved February 18, 2014, from www.sleepfoundation.org

National Vital Statistics Report (2004, March 7). *Deaths: Leading causes for 2002.* Atlanta: Centers for Disease Control and Prevention.

Navarro, A. E., Gassoumis, Z. D., & Wilber, K. H. (2013). Holding abusers accountable: An elder abuse forensic center increases criminal prosecution of financial exploitation. *Gerontologist, 53*(2), 303–312.

Neal, J. W., Neal, Z. P., & Cappella, E. (2014, in press). I know who my friends are, but do you? Predictors of self-reported and peer-inferred relationships. *Child Development.*

Needham, A. (2009). Learning in infants' object perception, object-directed action, and tool use. In A. Needham & A. Woodward (Eds.), *Learning and the infant mind.* New York: Oxford University Press.

Needham, A., Barrett, T., & Peterman, K. (2002). A pick-me-up for infants' exploratory skills: Early simulated experiences reaching for objects using 'sticky mittens' enhances young infants' object exploration skills. *Infant Behavior and Development, 25,* 279–295.

Neikrug, A. B., & Ancoli-Israel, S. (2010). Sleep disorders in the older adult: A mini-review. *Gerontology, 56,* 181–189.

Nelson, A. M. (2012). A comprehensive review of the evidence and current recommendations related to pacifier use. *Journal of Pediatric Nursing, 27,* 690–699.

Nelson, C. A. (2003). Neural development and lifelong plasticity. In R. M. Lerner, F. Jacobs, & D. Wertlieb (Eds.), *Handbook of applied developmental science* (Vol. 1). Thousand Oaks, CA: Sage.

Nelson, C. A. (2006). Unpublished review of J. W. Santrock's *Topical approach to life-span development,* 4th ed. New York: McGraw-Hill.

Nelson, C. A. (2007). A developmental cognitive neuroscience approach to the study of atypical development: A model system involving infants of diabetic mothers. In D. Coch, G. Dawson, & K. W. Fischer (Eds.), *Human behavior, learning, and the developing brain.* New York: Guilford.

Nelson, C. A. (2013). Brain development and behavior. In A. M. Rudolph, C. Rudolph, L. First, G. Lister, & A. A. Gershon (Eds.), *Rudolph's pediatrics* (22nd ed.). New York: McGraw-Hill.

Nelson, C. A. (2013a). The effects of early psychosocial deprivation. In M. Woodhead & J. Oates (Eds.), *Early childhood in focus 7: Developing brains.* Great Britain: The Open University.

Nelson, C.A (2013b). Some thoughts on the development and neural bases of face processing. In M. Banaji & S. Gelman (Eds.), *The development of social cognition.* New York: Oxford University Press.

Nelson, C. A., Fox, N. A., & Zeanah, C. H. (2014). *Romania's abandoned children.* Cambridge, MA : Harvard University Press.

Nelson, C. A., Thomas, K. M., & de Haan, M. (2006). Neural bases of cognitive development. In W. Damon & R. Lerner, (Eds.), *Handbook of child psychology* (6th ed.). New York: Wiley.

Nelson, J. A., & others (2012). Maternal expressive style and children's emotional development. *Infant and Child Development, 3,* 267–286.

Nelson, J. A., & others (2013). Preschool-aged children's understanding of gratitude: Relations with emotion and mental state knowledge. *British Journal of Developmental Psychology, 31,* 42–56.

Nelson, J. L., Palonsky, S. B., & McCarthy, M. R. (2013). *Critical issues in education* (8th ed.). New York: McGraw-Hill.

Nelson, K. (1999). Levels and modes of representation: Issues for the theory of conceptual change and development. In E. K. Skolnick, K. Nelson, S. A. Gelman, & P. H. Miller (Eds.), *Conceptual development.* Mahwah, NJ: Erlbaum.

Nelson, K. (2013). Introduction to the special issue. *Cognitive Development, 28,* 175–177.

Nelson, L. J., & others (2007). "If you want me to treat you like an adult, start acting like one!" Comparing the criteria that emerging adults and their parents have for adulthood. *Journal of Family Psychology, 21,* 665–674.

Nelson, S. K., Kushlev, K., English, T., Dunn, E. W., & Lyubomirsky, S. (2013). In defense of parenthood: Children associated with more joy than misery. *Psychological Science, 24,* 3–10.

Nelson, S. K., Kushley, K., & Lyubomirsky, S. (2014, in press). The pains and pleasures of parenting: When, why, and how is parenthood associated with more or less well-being? *Psychological Bulletin.*

Neugarten, B. L. (1986). The aging society. In A. Pifer & L. Bronte (Eds.), *Our aging society: Paradox and promise.* New York: W. W. Norton.

Neugarten, B. L. (1988, August). *Policy issues for an aging society.* Paper presented at the meeting of the American Psychological Association. Atlanta.

Neugarten, B. L., Havighurst, R. J., & Tobin, S. S. (1968). Personality and patterns of aging. In B. L.

Neugarten (Ed.), *Middle age and aging.* Chicago: University of Chicago Press.

Neugarten, B. L., & Weinstein, K. K. (1964). The changing American grandparent. *Journal of Marriage and the Family, 26,* 199–204.

Neupert, S. D., Almeida, D. M., & Charles, S. T. (2007). Age differences in reactivity to daily stressors: The role of personal control. *Journals of Gerontology: Psychological Sciences and Social Sciences, 62B,* P316–P225.

Nevarez, M. D., & others (2010). Associations of early life risk factors with infant sleep duration. *Academic Pediatrics, 10,* 187–193.

Neville, H. J. (2006). Different profiles of plasticity within human cognition. In Y. Munakata & M. H. Johnson (Eds.), *Attention and Performance XXI: Processes of change in brain and cognitive development.* Oxford. UK: Oxford University Press.

Newall, N. E., & Menec, V. H. (2014, in press). Targeting socially isolated older adults: A process evaluation of the Senior Center Without Walls social and educational program. *Journal of Applied Gerontology.*

Newcombe, N. (2008). The development of implicit and explicit memory. In N. Cowan & M. Courage (Eds.), *The development of memory in childhood.* Philadelphia: Psychology Press.

Newell, K., Scully, D. M., McDonald, P. V., & Baillargeon, R. (1989). Task constraints and infant grip configurations. *Developmental Psychobiology, 22,* 817–832.

Newman, A. B., & others (2006). Association of long-distance corridor walk performance with mortality, cardiovascular disease, mobility limitation, and disability. *Journal of the American Medical Association, 295,* 2018–2026.

Newsom, R. S., Boelen, P. A., Hofman, A., & Tiemeier, H. (2011). The prevalence and characteristics of complicated grief in older adults. *Journal of Affective Disorders, 132,* 231–238.

Newton, N. J., & Stewart, A. J. (2012). Personality development in adulthood. In S. K. Whitbourne & M. Sliwinski (Eds.), *Wiley-Blackwell handbook of adult development and aging.* New York: Wiley.

Nezu, A. M., Raggio, G., Evans, A. N., & Zezu, C. M. (2013). Diabetes mellitus. In I. B. Weiner & others (Eds.), *Handbook of psychology* (2nd ed., Vol. 9). New York: Wiley.

Ng, F. F., Pomerantz, E. M., & Deng C. (2014). Why are Chinese parents more psychologically controlling than American parents? "My child is my report card." *Child Development, 85,* 355–369.

Ng, F. F., Pomerantz, E. M., & Lam, S. (2013). European American and Chinese parents' beliefs about children's schoolwork: Considering indigenous Chinese nations. *International Journal of Behavioral Development, 37,* 387–394.

Nguyen, T. V., & others (2013). Testosterone-related cortical maturation across childhood and adolescence. *Cerebral Cortex, 23*(6), 1424–1432.

NICHD (2013). *SIDS facts.* Retrieved October 17, 2013, from http://www.nichd.nih/gov/sids

NICHD Early Child Care Research Network (2000). Factors associated with fathers' caregiving activities and sensitivity with young children. *Developmental Psychology, 14,* 200–219.

NICHD Early Child Care Research Network (2001). Nonmaternal care and family factors in early development: An overview of the NICHD study of Early Child Care. *Journal of Applied Developmental Psychology, 22,* 457–492.

NICHD Early Child Care Research Network (2002). Structure → Process → Outcome: Direct and indirect

effects of child care quality on young children's development. *Psychological Science, 13,* 199–206.

NICHD Early Child Care Research Network (2003). Does amount of time spent in child care predict socioemotional adjustment during the transition to kindergarten? *Child Development, 74,* 976–1005.

NICHD Early Child Care Research Network (2004). Type of child care and children's development at 54 months. *Early Childhood Research Quarterly, 19,* 203–230.

NICHD Early Child Care Research Network (2005). *Child care and development.* New York: Guilford.

NICHD Early Child Care Research Network (2005). Duration and developmental timing of poverty and children's cognitive and social development from birth through third grade. *Child Development, 76,* 795–810.

NICHD Early Child Care Research Network (2005). Predicting individual differences in attention, memory, and planning in first graders from experiences at home, child care, and school. *Developmental Psychology, 41,* 99–114.

NICHD Early Child Care Research Network (2006). Infant-mother attachment classification: Risk and protection in relation to changing maternal caregiving quality. *Developmental Psychology, 42,* 38–58.

NICHD Early Child Care Research Network (2009). Family-peer linkages: The mediational role of attentional processes. *Social Development, 18*(4), 875–895.

NICHD Early Child Care Research Network (2010). Testing a series of causal propositions relating time spent in child care to children's externalizing behavior. *Developmental Psychology, 46*(1), 1–17.

Nickalls, S. (2012, March 9). Why college students shouldn't online date. *The Tower.* Philadelphia: Arcadia University. Retrieved February 27, 2013, from http://tower.arcadia.edu/?p=754

Nicolaisen, M., & Thorsen, K. (2014). Loneliness among men and women—a five-year follow-up study. *Aging and Mental Health, 18,* 194–206.

Nicolaisen, M., Thorsen, K., & Eriksen, S. H. (2012). Jump into the void? Factors related to a preferred retirement age: Gender, social interests, and leisure activities. *International Journal of Aging and Human Development, 75,* 239–271.

Nicoteri, J. A., & Miskovsky, M. J. (2014, in press). Revisiting the freshman "15": Assessing body mass index in the first college year and beyond. *Journal of the American Association of Nurse Practitioners.*

Nielsen, M. B., & Einarsen, S. (2012). Prospective relationships between workplace sexual harassment and psychological distress. *Occupational Medicine, 62,* 226–228.

Nieto, A. M., & Yoshikawa, H. (2014). Beyond families and schools: Future directions in practice and policy for children in immigrant families. In E. T. Gershoff, R. S. Mistry, & D. A. Crosby (Eds.), *Societal contexts of child development.* New York: Oxford University Press.

Nijmeijer, J. S., & others (2014, in press). Quantitative linkage for autism spectrum disorders symptoms in attention-deficit/hyperactivity disorder: Significant locus on chromosome 7Q11. *Journal of Autism and Developmental Disorders.*

Nilsson, J., Thomas, A. J., O'Brien, J. T., & Gallagher, P. (2014). White matter and cognitive decline in aging: A focus on processing speed and variability. *Journal of the International Neuropsychological Society, 20,* 262–267.

Nisbett, R. E. (2003). *The geography of thought.* New York: Free Press.

Nisbett, R. E., & others (2012). Intelligence: New findings and theoretical developments. *American Psychologist, 67*(2), 130–159.

Nixon, S. A., Rubincam, C., Casale, M., & Flicker, S. (2011). Is 80% a passing grade? Meanings attached to condom use in an abstinence-plus HIV prevention programme in South Africa. *AIDS Care, 23*, 213–220.

Noddings, N. (2007). *When school reform goes wrong.* New York: Teachers College Press.

Noel-Miller, C. M. (2011). Partner caregiving in older cohabiting couples. *Journals of Gerontology B: Psychological Sciences and Social Sciences, 66B*, 341–353.

Noel-Miller, C. M. (2013). Former stepparents' contact with their stepchildren after midlife. *Journals of Gerontology B: Psychological Sciences and Social Sciences, 68*, 409–419.

Noftle, E. E., & Robins, R. W. (2007). Personality predictors of academic outcomes: Big five correlates of GPA and SAT scores. *Journal of Personality and Social Psychology, 93*, 116–130.

Nogueira, M., & others (2014, in press). Early-age clinical and developmental features associated with substance use disorders in attention-deficit/hyperactivity disorder in adults. *Comprehensive Psychiatry.*

Nolen-Hoeksema, S. (2011). *Abnormal psychology* (5th ed.). New York: McGraw-Hill.

Nomoto, M., & others (2009). Inter- and intra-individual variation in L-dopa pharmacokinetics in the treatment of Parkinson's disease. *Parkinsonism and Related Disorders, 15*(1, Suppl.), S21–S24.

Norman, J. F., Holmin, J. S., & Bartholomew, A. N. (2011). Visual memories for perceived length are well preserved in older adults. *Vision Research, 51*, 2057–2062.

Norouzieh, K. (2005). Case management of the dying child. *Case Manager, 16*, 54–57.

Nottelmann, E. D., & others (1987). Gonadal and adrenal hormone correlates of adjustment in early adolescence. In R. M. Lerner & T. T. Foch (Eds.), *Biological-psychological interactions in early adolescence.* Hillsdale, NJ: Erlbaum.

Nouchi, R., & others (2012). Brain training game improves executive functions and processing speed in the elderly: A randomized controlled trial. *PLoS One, 7*(1), e29676.

Nouchi, R., & others (2013). Brain training game boosts executive functions, working memory, and processing speed in young adults: A randomized controlled trial. *PLoS, 8*(2), e55518.

Novick, G., & others (2013). Group prenatal care: Model fidelity and outcomes. *American Journal of Obstetrics and Gynecology, 209*(2), 112.e1–112.e6.

Novo-Veleiro, I., & others (2014, in press). A genetic variant in the microRNA-146a gene is associated with susceptibility to alcohol disorders. *European Psychiatry.*

Nucci, L. (2006). Education for moral development. In M. Killen & J. Smetana (Eds.), *Handbook of moral development.* Mahwah, NJ: Erlbaum.

Nudo, R. J., & McNeal, D. (2013). Plasticity of cerebral functions. *Handbook of Clinical Neurology, 110*, 13–21.

Nyberg, L., & Backman, L. (2011). Influences of biological and self-initiated factors on brain and cognition in adulthood and aging. In P. B. Baltes, P. A. Reuter-Lorenz, & F. Rosler (Eds.), *Lifespan development and the brain.* New York: Cambridge University Press.

Nyberg, L., Lovden, M., Rilund, K., Lindenberger, U., & Backman, L. (2012). Memory aging and brain maintenance. *Current Trends in Cognitive Science, 16*, 292–305.

Nygard, C-H. (2013). *The ability to work peaks in middle age.* Interview. Retrieved September 15, 2013, from http://researchandstudy.uta.fi/2013/09/12/the-ability-to-work-peaks-in-middle-age/

O

O'Brien, E. J., Bartoletti, M., & Leitzel, J. D. (2013). Self-esteem, psychopathology, and psychotherapy. In M. H. Kernis (Ed.), *Self-esteem issues and answers.* New York: Psychology Press.

O'Brien, J. L., & others (2013). Cognitive training and selective attention in the aging brain: An electrophysiological study. *Clinical Neurophysiology, 124*, 2198–2208.

O'Brien, M., & Moss, P. (2010). Fathers, work, and family policies in Europe. In M. E. Lamb (Ed.), *The father's role in child development* (5th ed.). New York: Wiley.

O'Brien, M., & others (2011). Longitudinal associations between children's understanding of emotions and theory of mind. *Cognition and Emotion, 25*, 1074–1086.

O'Brien, M., & others (2013). Women's work and child care: Perspectives and prospects. In E. T. Gershoff, R. S. Mistry, & D. A. Crosby (Eds.), *Societal contexts of child development.* New York: Oxford University Press.

O'Callaghan, F. V., & others (2010). The link between sleep problems in infancy and early childhood and attention problems at 5 and 14 years: Evidence from a birth cohort study. *Early Human Development, 86*, 419–424.

O'Dell, C. (2013). *Centenarians' secrets. What you can learn from people who've lived 100-plus years.* Retrieved February 20, 2013, from www.caring.com/articles/centenarians-secrets

O'Donnell, A. M. (2011). Constructivism. In K. R. Harris, S. Graham, & T. Urdan (Eds.), *APA educational psychology handbook.* Washington, DC: American Psychological Association.

O'Donnell, E., Kirwan, L. D., & Goodman, J. M. (2009). Aerobic exercise training in healthy postmenopausal women: Effects of hormone therapy. *Menopause, 16*, 770–776.

O'Halloran, A. M., & others (2011). Falls and fall efficacy: The role of sustained attention in older adults. *BMC Geriatrics, 11*, 85.

O'Hara, M. W., & McCabe, F. (2013). Postpartum depression: Current status and future directions. *Annual Review of Clinical Psychology* (Vol. 9). Palo Alto, CA: Annual Reviews.

O'Hara, R. E., Gibbons, F. X., Weng, C. Y., Gerrard, M., & Simons, R. L. (2012). Perceived racial discrimination as a barrier to college enrollment for African Americans. *Personality and Social Psychology Bulletin, 38*, 77–89.

O'Keefe, J. H., Bhatti, S. K., Baiwa, A., Dinicolantonio, J. J., & Lavie, C. J. (2014). Alcohol and cardiovascular health: The dose does make the poison . . . or the remedy. *Mayo Clinic Proceedings, 89*, 382–393.

O'Keefe, J. H., Schnohr, P., & Lavie, C. J. (2013). The dose of running that best confers longevity. *Heart, 99*, 588–590.

O'Keeffe, L. M., Greene, R. A., & Kearney, P. M. (2014, in press). The effect of moderate gestational alcohol consumption during pregnancy on speech and language outcomes in children: A systematic review. *Systematic Reviews.*

O'Malley, P. M. (2014). A review of studies of drinking patterns in the United States since 1940. *Journal of Studies on Alcohol and Drugs, 75*(17, Suppl.), S18–S25.

O'Neill, S., & others (2013). Cesarean section and subsequent ectopic pregnancy: A systematic review and meta-analysis. *BJOG, 120*(6), 671–680.

O'Reilly, M. F., & others (2014). Naturalistic approaches to social skills training and development. In J. K. Luiselli (Ed.), *Children and youth with autism spectrum disorder.* New York: Oxford University Press.

Oakes, L. M. (2012). Advances in eye-tracking in infancy research. *Infancy, 17*, 1–8.

Oakes, L. M., Kannass, K. N., & Shaddy, D. J. (2002). Developmental changes in endogenous control of attention: The role of target familiarity on infants' distraction latency. *Child Development, 73*, 1644–1655.

Oates, J., & Abraham, S. (2010). *Llewellyn-Jones fundamentals of obstetrics and gynecology* (9th ed.). New York: Elsevier.

Obler, L. K. (2009). Development in the older years. In Berko Gleason (Ed.), *The development of language* (7th ed.). Boston: Allyn & Bacon.

Obradovic, J. (2010). Effortful control and adaptive functioning of homeless children: Variable- and person-focused analyses. *Journal of Applied Developmental Psychology, 39*, 90–102.

Occupational Outlook Handbook (2012). Washington, DC: U.S. Department of Labor, Bureau of Labor Statistics.

Ochs, E., & Schieffelin, B. (2008). Language socialization and language acquisition. In P. A. Duff & N. H. Hornberger (Eds.), *Encyclopedia of language and education.* New York: Springer.

Odom, S., Boyd, B., Hall, L. J., & Hume, K. A. (2014). Comprehensive treatment models for children and youth with autism. In F. R. Volkmar & others (Eds.), *Handbook of autism and pervasive developmental disorders.* New York: Wiley.

OECD (2010). *Aging and employment status.* Paris, France: OECD.

OECD (2010). *Obesity and the economics of prevention—Fit not fat.* Paris: OECD.

Oerlemans, W. G., Bakker, A. B., & Veenhoven, R. (2011). Finding the key to happy aging: A day reconstruction study of happiness. *Journals of Gerontology B: Psychological Sciences and Social Sciences, 66*, 665–674.

Ofen, N., & Shing, Y. L. (2013). From perception to memory: Changes in memory systems across the lifespan. *Neuroscience and Biobehavioral Reviews, 37*, 2258–2267.

Offer, D., Ostrov E., Howard, K. I., & Atkinson, R. (1988). *The teenage world: Adolescents' self-image in ten countries.* New York: Plenum.

Ogbuanu, I. U., & others (2014, in press). Maternal, fetal, and neonatal outcomes associated with measles during pregnancy: Namibia, 2009–2010. *Clinical Infectious Diseases.*

Ogden, C. L., Carroll, M. D., Kit, B. K., & Flegal, K. M. (2012, January). Prevalence of obesity in the United States, 2009–2010. *NCHS Data Brief*, 1–9.

Ogden, C. L., Carroll, M. D., Kit, B. K., & Flegal, K. M. (2013, October). Prevalence of obesity among adults: United States, 2011–2012. *NCHS Data Brief, No. 131*, 1–7.

Ogden, C. L., Carroll, M. D., Kit, B. K., & Flegal, K. M. (2014). Prevalence of childhood and adult obesity in the United States, 2011–2012. *Journal of the American Medical Association, 311*, 308–314.

Ogden, C. L., Carroll, M. D., Kit, B. K., & Flegal, K. M. (2014). Prevalence of childhood obesity in the United States, 2011–2012. *Journal of the American Medical Association, 311*, 806–814.

Ogolsky, B. G., Lloyd, S. A., & Cate, R. M. (Eds.) (2013). *The developmental course of romantic relationships.* New York: Psychology Press.

Oiestad, B. E., & others (2013). Efficacy of strength and aerobic exercise on patient-reported outcomes and structural changes in patients with knee osteoarthritis: Study protocol for a randomized trial. *BMC Musculoskeletal Disorders, 14*(1), 266.

Okada, H. C., Alleyne, B., Varghai, K., Kinder, K., & Guyuron, B. (2013). Facial changes caused by smoking:

A comparison between smoking and non-smoking identical twins. *Plastic and Reconstructive Surgery, 132*(5), 1085–1092.

Okada, K., & others (2014, in press). Comprehensive evaluation of androgen replacement therapy in aging Japanese men with late-onset hypogonadism. *Aging Male.*

Okun, M. A., Yeung, E. W., & Brown, S. (2013). Volunteering by older adults and risk of mortality: A meta-analysis. *Psychology and Aging, 28,* 564–577.

Okun, N., & others (2014). Pregnancy outcomes after assisted human reproduction. *Journal of Obstetrics and Gynecology Canada.*

Olafsdottir, E., Andersson, D. K., & Stefansson, E. (2012). The prevalence of cataract in a population of with and without type 2 diabetes mellitus. *Acta Ophthalmologica, 90,* 334–340.

Olds, D. L., & others (2004). Effects of home visits by paraprofessionals and nurses: Age 4 follow-up of a randomized trial. *Pediatrics, 114,* 1560–1568.

Olds, D. L., & others (2007). Effects of nurse home visiting on maternal and child functioning: Age 9 follow-up of a randomized trial. *Pediatrics, 120,* e832–e845.

Olds, D. L., & others (2014, in press). Effects of home visits by paraprofessionals and by nurses on children: Follow-up of a randomized trial age 6 and 9 years. *JAMA Pediatrics.*

Olesen, J., & others (2014, in press). Exercise training, but not resveratrol, improve metabolic and inflammatory status in skeletal muscle of aged men. *Journal of Physiology.*

Olesen, K., Rugulies, R., Rod, N. H., & Bonde, J. P. (2014). Does retirement reduce the risk of myocardial infarction? A prospective registry linkage study of 617,511 Danish workers. *International Journal of Epidemiology, 43,* 160–167.

Oliveras, A., & de la Sierra, A. (2014). Resistant hypertension: Patient characteristics, risk factors, co-morbidities, and outcomes. *Journal of Human Hypertension, 28*(4), 213–217.

Olmstead, S. B., Roberson, P. N., Pasley, K., & Fincham, F. D. (2014, in press). Hooking up and risk behaviors among first semester college men: What is the role of precollege experience? *Journal of Sexual Research.*

Olson, B. H., Haider, S. J., Vangjel, L., Bolton, T. A., & Gold, J. G. (2010a). A quasi-experimental evaluation of a breastfeeding support program for low income women in Michigan. *Maternal and Child Health Journal, 14*(1), 86–93.

Olson, B. H., Horodynski, M. A., Brophy-Herb, H., & Iwanski, K. C. (2010b). Health professionals' perspectives on the infant feeding practices of low income mothers. *Maternal and Child Health Journal, 14*(1), 75–85.

Olson, M. M., Trevino, D. B., Geske, J. A., & Vanderpool, H. (2012). Religious coping and mental health outcomes: An exploratory study of socioeconomically disadvantaged patients. *Explore, 8,* 172–176.

Olszewski-Kubilius, P., & Thomson, D. (2013). Gifted education programs and procedures. In I. B. Weiner & others (Eds.), *Handbook of psychology* (2nd ed., Vol. 7). New York: Wiley.

Olweus, D. (2003). Prevalence estimation of school bullying with the Olweus bully/victim questionnaire. *Aggressive Behavior, 29*(3), 239–269.

Olweus, D. (2013). School bullying: Development and some important challenges. *Annual Review of Clinical Psychology* (Vol. 9). Palo Alto, CA: Annual Reviews.

Opfer, J. E., & Gelman, S. A. (2011). Development of the animate-inanimate distinction. In U. Goswami (Ed.), *Wiley-Blackwell handbook of childhood cognitive development* (2nd ed.). New York: Wiley.

Ophir, E., Nass, C., & Wagner, A. D. (2009). Cognitive control in media multitaskers. *Proceedings of the National Academy of Sciences USA, 106,* 15583–15587.

Oppenheimer, C. W., Hankin, B. L., Young, J. F., & Smolen, A. (2013). Youth genetic vulnerability to maternal depressive symptoms: 5-HTTLPR as moderator of intergenerational transmission effects in a multiwave prospective study. *Depression and Anxiety, 30*(3), 190–196.

Ornstein, K., & others (2013). The differential impact of unique behavioral and psychological symptoms for the dementia caregiver: How and why do patients' individual symptom clusters impact caregiver depressive symptoms? *American Journal of Geriatric Psychiatry, 21,* 1277–1286.

Ornstein, P. A., Coffman, J. L., & Grammer, J. K. (2007, April). *Teachers' memory-relevant conversations and children's memory performance.* Paper presented at the biennial meeting of the Society for Research in Child Development, Boston.

Ornstein, P. A., Coffman, J. L., & Grammer, J. K. (2009). Learning to remember. In O. A. Barbarin & B. H. Wasik (Eds.), *Handbook of child development and early education.* New York: Guilford.

Ornstein, P. A., Coffman, J. L., Grammer, J. K., San Souci, P. P., & McCall, L. E. (2010). Linking the classroom context and the development of children's memory skills. In J. Meece & J. Eccles (Eds.), *Handbook of research on schools, schooling, and human development.* New York: Routledge.

Orsi, C. M., Hale, D. E., & Lynch, J. L. (2011). Pediatric obesity epidemiology. *Current Opinion in Endocrinology, Diabetes, and Obesity, 18,* 14–22.

Ory, M. G., & others (2013). National study of chronic disease self-management: Six-month outcome findings. *Journal of Aging and Health, 25,* 1258–1274.

Osorio, R. S., & others (2014). Imaging and cerebrospinal fluid biomarkers in the search for Alzheimer's disease mechanisms. *Neurogenerative Diseases, 13,* 163–165.

Ossher, L., Flegal, K. E., & Lustig, C. (2013). Everyday memory errors in older adults. *Neuropsychology, Development, and Cognition, B: Aging, Neuroscience, and Cognition, 20,* 220–244.

Ostchega, Y., & others (2009). Trends of elevated blood pressure among children and adolescents: Data from the National Health and Nutrition Examination Survey, 1988–2006. *American Journal of Hypertension, 22,* 59–67.

Osterberg, E. C., Bernie, A. M., & Ramasamy, R. (2014). Risk of replacement testosterone therapy in men. *Indian Journal of Urology, 30,* 2–7.

Otaegui-Arrazola, A., & others (2014). Diet, cognition, and Alzheimer's disease: Food for thought. *European Journal of Nutrition, 53,* 1–23.

Otsuka, Y., & others (2012). Perception of mooney faces by young infants: The role of local feature visibility, contrast polarity, and motion. *Journal of Experimental Child Psychology, 111,* 164–179.

Oturai, G., Kolling, T., & Knopf, M. (2013). Relations between 18-month-olds' gaze pattern and target action performance: A deferred imitation study using eye tracking. *Infant Behavior and Development, 36,* 736–748.

Owen, J., Fincham, F. D., & Manthos, M. (2013). Friendship after a friends with benefits relationship: Deception, psychological functioning, and social connectedness. *Archives of Sexual Behavior, 42*(8), 1443–1449.

Owen, J. J., Rhoades, G. K., Stanley, S. M., & Markman, H. J. (2011). The role of leaders' working alliance in premarital education. *Journal of Family Psychology, 25,* 49–57.

Owens, J., & Mindell, J. (2011). *Sleep in children and adolescents.* New York: Elsevier.

Owsley, C. (2011). Aging and vision. *Vision Research, 51,* 1610–1622.

P

Pacala, J. T., & Yeuh, B. (2012). Hearing defects in the older patient: "I didn't notice anything." *JAMA, 307,* 1185–1194.

Pace-Schott, E. F., & Spencer, R. M. (2011). Age-related changes in the cognitive function of sleep. *Progress in Brain Research, 191,* 75–89.

Padilla-Walker, L., & Carlo, G. (Eds.) (2014). *Prosocial behavior.* New York: Oxford University Press.

Page, K. A., Romero, A., Buchanan, T. A., & Xiang, A. H. (2014, in press). Gestational diabetes mellitus, maternal obesity, and adiposity in offspring. *Journal of Pediatraics.*

Pageon, H., & others (2014). Skin aging by glycation: Lessons from the reconstructed skin model. *Clinical Chemistry and Laboratory Medicine, 52*(1), 169–174.

Painter, K. (2008, June 16). Older, wiser, but less active. *USA Today,* p. 4D.

Pakhomov, S. V., & Hemmy, L. S. (2014, in press). A computational linguistic measure of clustering behavior on semantic verbal fluency task predicts risk of future dementia in the Nun Study. *Cortex.*

Pakhomov, S. V., Hemmy, L. S., & Lim, K. O. (2012). Automated semantic indices related to cognitive function and rate of cognitive decline. *Neuropsychologia, 50*(9), 2165–2175.

Palermo, T. M. (2014). A brief history of child and adolescent sleep research: Key contributions in psychology. In A. R. Wolfson & E. Montgomery-Downs (Eds.), *Oxford handbook of infant, child, and adolescent sleep and behavior.* New York: Oxford University Press.

Pallauf, K., Giller, K., Huebbe, P., & Rimbach, G. (2013). Nutrition and healthy aging: Calorie restriction or polyphenol-rich "MediterrAsian" diet? *Oxidative Medicine and Cellular Longevity.* doi:10.1155/2013/707421

Palmore, E. B. (2004). Research note: Ageism in Canada and the United States. *Journal of Cross Cultural Gerontology, 19,* 41–46.

Pan, B. A., Rowe, M. L., Singer, J. D., & Snow, C. E. (2005). Maternal correlates of growth in toddler vocabulary production in low-income families. *Child Development, 76,* 763–782.

Pan, B. A., & Uccelli, P. (2009). Semantic development. In J. Berko Gleason & N. Rather (Eds.), *The development of language* (7th ed.). Boston: Allyn & Bacon.

Pan, Z., & Chang, C. (2012). Gender and the regulation of longevity: Implications for autoimmunity. *Autoimmunity Reviews, 11,* A393–A403.

Panizzon, M. S., & others (2014, in press). Interaction of APOE genotype and testosterone on episodic memory in middle-aged men. *Neurobiology of Aging.*

Pantilat, S. Z., & Isaac, M. (2008). End-of-life care for the hospitalized patient. *Medical Clinics of North America, 92,* 349–370.

Paoli, A., & others (2014, in press). Effects of high-intensity circuit training, low-intensity circuit training, and endurance training on blood pressure and lipoproteins in middle-aged overweight men. *Lipids in Health and Disease.*

Papasavva, T. E., & others (2013). A minimal set of SNPs for the noninvasive prenatal diagnosis of b-thalassaemia. *Annals of Human Genetics, 77*(2), 115–124.

Papastavrou, E., Charlalambous, A., Tsangari, H., & Karayiannis, G. (2012). The burdensome and depressive experience of caring: What cancer, schizophrenia, and Alzheimer's disease caregivers have in common. *Cancer Nursing, 35,* 187–194.

Papp, K. V., & others (2014, in press). Processing speed in normal aging: Effects of white matter hyperintensities and hippocampal volume loss. *Neuropsychology, Development, and Cognition, Section B: Aging, Neuropsychology, and Cognition.*

Parens, E., & Johnston, J. (2009). Facts, values, and attention-deficit hyperactivity disorder (ADHD): An update on the controversies. *Child and Adolescent Psychiatry and Mental Health, 3,* 1.

Parfitt, Y., Pike, A., & Ayers, S. (2014, in press). Infant developmental outcomes: A family systems perspective. *Infant and Child Development.*

Pargament, K. I., Falb, M. D., Ano, G., & Wachholtz, A. B. (2013). The religious dimensions of coping. In R. F. Paloutzian & C. L. Park (Eds.), *Handbook of the psychology of religion* (2nd ed.). New York: Guilford.

Parish-Morris, J., Golinkoff, R. M., & Hirsh-Pasek, K. (2013). From coo to code: A brief story of language development. In P. D. Zelazo (Ed.), *Handbook of developmental psychology.* New York: Oxford University Press.

Parisi, J. M., & others (2014). The association between lifestyle activities and late-life depressive symptoms. *Activities, Adaptation, and Aging, 38,* 1–10.

Park, C. H., Elavsky, S., & Koo, K. M. (2014). Factors influencing physical activity in older adults, *Journal of Exercise Rehabilitation, 10,* 45–52.

Park, C. J., Yelland, G. W., Taffe, J. R., & Gray, K. M. (2012). Morphological and syntactic skills in language samples of pre-school aged children with autism: Atypical development? *International Journal of Speech and Language Pathology, 14,* 95–108.

Park, C. L. (2005). Religion as a meaning-making system. *Psychology of Religion Newsletter, 30*(2), 1–9.

Park, C. L. (2007). Religiousness/spirituality and health: A meaning systems perspective. *Journal of Behavioral Medicine, 30,* 319–328.

Park, C. L. (2009). Meaning making in cancer survivorship. In P. T. P. Wong & P. S. Fry (Eds.), *The human quest for meaning* (2nd ed.). New York: Psychology Press.

Park, C. L. (2010). Making sense out of the meaning literature: An integrative review of meaning making and its effect on adjustment to stressful life events. *Psychological Bulletin, 136,* 257–301.

Park, C. L. (2012a). Meaning making in cancer survivorship. In P. T. P. Wong (Ed.), *Handbook of meaning* (2nd ed.). Thousand Oaks, CA: Sage.

Park, C. L. (2012b). Meaning, spirituality, and growth: Protective and resilience factors in health and illness. In A. S. Baum, T. A. Revenson, & J. E. Singer (Eds.), *Handbook of health psychology* (2nd ed.). New York: Sage.

Park, C. L. (2013). Religion and meaning. In R. F. Paloutzian & C. L. Park (Eds.), *Handbook of the psychology of religion* (2nd ed.). New York: Guilford.

Park, C. L., Malone, M. R., Suresh, D. P., Bliss, D., & Rosen, R. I. (2008). Coping, meaning in life, and the quality of life in congestive heart failure patients. *Quality of Life Research, 17,* 21–26.

Park, C. L., & Slattery, J. M. (2013). Religion, spirituality, and mental health. In R. F. Paloutzian & C. L. Park (Eds.), *Handbook of the psychology of religion* (2nd ed.). New York: Guilford.

Park, D. (2001). Commentary in R. Restak, *The secret life of the brain.* Washington, DC: Joseph Henry Press.

Park, D. C., & Bischof, G. N. (2011). Neuroplasticity, aging, and cognitive function. In K. W. Schaie & S. L. Willis (Eds.), *Handbook of the psychology of aging* (7th ed.). New York: Elsevier.

Park, D. C., & Reuter-Lorenz, P. (2009). The adaptive brain: Aging and neurocognitive scaffolding. *Annual Review of Psychology* (Vol. 60). Palo Alto, CA: Annual Reviews.

Park, D. C., & others (2014). The impact of sustained engagement on cognitive function in older adults: The Synapse Project. *Psychological Science, 25,* 103–112.

Park, E. M., Meltzer-Brody, S., & Stickgold, R. (2013). Poor sleep maintenance and subjective sleep quality are associated with postpartum depression symptom severity. *Archives of Women's Mental Health, 16*(6), 539–547.

Park, J., Lewis, M. M., Huang, X., & Latash, M. L. (2014). Dopaminergic modulation of motor coordination in Parkinson's disease. *Parkinsonism and Related Disorders, 20,* 64–68.

Park, M. J., Mulye, T. P., Adams, S. H., Brindis, C. D., & Irwin, C. E. (2006). The health status of young adults in the United States. *Journal of Adolescent Health, 39,* 305–317.

Park, N. S., & others (2013). Typologies of religiousness/spirituality: Implications for health and well-being. *Journal of Religion and Health, 52,* 828–839.

Park, S. H., Han, K. S., & Kang, C. B. (2014, in press). Effects of exercise programs on depressive symptoms, quality of life, and self-esteem in older people: A systematic review of randomized controlled trials. *Applied Nursing Research.*

Park, S. H., & others (2013). Sarcopenic obesity as an independent risk factor of hypertension. *Journal of the American Society of Hypertension, 7*(6), 420–425.

Parkay, F. W. (2013). *Becoming a teacher* (9th ed.). Upper Saddle River, NJ: Pearson.

Parke, R. D. (2013). *Future families: Diverse forms, rich possibilities.* New York: Wiley Blackwell.

Parke, R. D., & Burlel, R. (2006). Socialization in the family Ethnic and ecological perspectives. In W. Damon & R. Lerner (Eds.), *Handbook of child psychology* (6th ed.). New York: Wiley.

Parke, R. D., & Clarke-Stewart, A. K. (2011). *Social development.* New York: Wiley.

Parker, S. K. (2014). Work design for our times: Going beyond intrinsic motivation. *Annual Review of Psychology* (Vol. 65). Palo Alto, CA: Annual Reviews.

Parkinson, P. (2010). Changing policies regarding separated fathers in Australia. In M. E. Lamb (Ed.), *The role of the father in child development* (5th ed.). New York: Wiley.

Parodi, V., de Florentiis, D., Martini, M., & Ansaldi, F. (2011). Inactivated influenza vaccines: Recent progress and implications for the elderly. *Drugs and Aging, 28,* 93–106.

Parr, E. B., Coffey, V. G., & Hawley, J. A. (2013). 'Sarcobesity': A medical conundrum. *Maturitas, 74,* 109–113.

Parra-Cardona, J. R., Bulock, L. A., Imig, D. R., Villarruel, F. A., & Gold, S. J. (2006). "trabajando duro todos los dias": Learning from the life experiences of Mexican-origin migrant families. *Family Relations, 55,* 361–375.

Parrett, A.L., & others (2011). Adiposity and aerobic fitness are associated with metabolic disease risk in children. *Applied Physiology, Nutrition, and Metabolism, 36,* 72–79.

Parrillo, V. N. (2014). *Strangers to these shores* (11th ed.). Upper Saddle River, NJ: Pearson.

Parrott, A.C., & others (2014). MDMA and heightened cortisol: A neurohormonal perspective on the pregnancy outcomes of mothers who used 'Ecstasy' during pregnancy. *Human Psychopharmacology, 29,* 1–7.

Partnership for Solutions (2002). *Multiple chronic conditions: Complications in care and treatment.* Baltimore: Johns Hopkins University.

Pascuzzo, K., Cyr, C., & Moss, E. (2013). Longitudinal association between adolescent attachment, adult romantic attachment, and emotion regulation strategies. *Attachment and Human Development, 15,* 83–103.

Pasley, K., & Moorefield, B. S. (2004). Step-families. In M. Coleman & L. Ganong (Eds.), *Handbook of contemporary families.* Thousand Oaks, CA: Sage.

Passini, S. (2012). The delinquency-drug relationship: The influence of social reputation and moral disengagement. *Addictive Behaviors, 37,* 577–579.

Passuth, P. M., Maines, D. R., & Neugarten, B. L. (1984). *Age norms and age constraints twenty years later.* Paper presented at the annual meeting of the Midwest Sociological Society, Chicago.

Pathman, T., & St. Jacques, P. L. (2014). Locating events in personal time: Time in autobiography. In P. Bauer & R. Fivush (Eds.), *Wiley-Blackwell handbook of children's memory.* New York: Wiley.

Patterson, C. J. (2013a). Family lives of gay and lesbian adults. In G. W. Peterson & K. R. Bush (Eds.), *Handbook of marriage and the family* (3rd ed.). New York: Springer.

Patterson, C. J. (2014, in press). Sexual minority youth and youth with sexual minority parents. In A. Ben Arieh & others (Eds.), *Handbook of child research.* Thousand Oaks, CA: Sage.

Patterson, C. J., & D'Augelli, A. R. (Eds.) (2013). *The psychology of sexual orientation.* New York: Cambridge University Press.

Patterson, C. J., & Farr, R. H. (2014, in press). Children of lesbian and gay parents: Reflections on the research-policy interface. In H. R. Schaffer & K. Durkin (Eds.), *Blackwell handbook of developmental psychology in action.* New York: Wiley.

Patton, G. C., & others (2011). Overweight and obesity between adolescence and early adulthood: A 10-year prospective study. *Journal of Adolescent Health, 45,* 275–280.

Paul, K. H., & Olson, C. M. (2013). Moving beyond quantity of participation in process evaluation of an intervention to prevent excessive pregnancy weight gain. *International Journal of Behavioral Nutrition and Physical Activity, 10,* 23.

Paul, P. (2003, Sept/Oct). The PermaParent trap. *Psychology Today, 36*(5), 40–53.

Paulhus, D. L. (2008). Birth order. In M. M. Haith & J. B. Benson (Eds.), *Encyclopedia of infant and early childhood development.* Oxford, UK: Elsevier.

Paus, T., & others (2007). Morphological properties of the action-observation cortical network in adolescents with low and high resistance to peer influence. *Social Neuroscience 3*(3), 303–316.

Payer, L. (1991). The menopause in various cultures. In H. Burger & M. Boulet (Eds.), *A portrait of the menopause.* Park Ridge, NJ: Parthenon.

Pea, R., & others (2012). Media use, face-to-face communication, media multitasking, and social well-being among 8- to 12-year-old girls. *Developmental Psychology, 48,* 327–336.

Pearlman, E. (2013). Twin psychological development. Retrieved February 14, 2013 from http://christinabaglivitinglof.com/twin-pregnancy/six-twin-experts-te ...

Pearson, R. M., & others (2013). Maternal depression during pregnancy and the postnatal period: Risk and possible mechanisms for offspring depression at age 18 years. *JAMA Psychiatry, 70,* 1312–1319.

Pechorro, P., & others (2014, in press). Age of crime onset and psychopathic traits in female juvenile delinquents. *International Journal of Offender Therapy and Comparative Criminology.*

Pedersen, W., & Mastekaasa, A. (2011). Conduct disorder symptoms and subsequent pregnancy, childbirth, and abortion: A population-based longitudinal study of adolescents. *Journal of Adolescence, 34,* 1025–1033.

Peek, M. K. (2009). Marriage in later life. In D. Carr (Ed.), *Encyclopedia of the life course and human development.* Boston: Gale Cengage.

Peets, K., Hodges, E. V. E., & Salmivalli, C. (2011). Actualization of social cognitions into aggressive behavior toward disliked targets. *Social Development, 20,* 233–250.

Peich, M. C., Husain, M., & Bays, P. M. (2013). Age-related decline of precision and binding in visual working memory. *Psychology and Aging, 28,* 729–743.

Pelaez, M., Virues-Ortega, J., & Gewirtz, J. L. (2012). Acquisition of social referencing via discrimination training in infants. *Journal of Applied Behavior Analysis, 45,* 23–36.

Pelton, S. L., & Leibovitz, E. (2009). Recent advances in otitis media. *Pediatric Infectious Disease Journal, 28* (Suppl. 10), S133–S137.

Peltz, C. B., Gratton, G., & Fabiani, M. (2011). Age-related changes in electrophysiological and neuropsychological indices of working memory, attention control, and cognitive flexibility. *Frontiers in Psychology, 2,* 190.

Penela, E. C., & others (2012). Maternal caregiving moderates the relation between temperamental fear and social behavior with peers. *Infancy, 17*(6), 715–730.

Peng, P., & Fuchs, D. (2014, in press). A meta-analysis of working memory deficits in children with learning difficulties: Is there a difference between the verbal domain and numerical domain? *Journal of Learning Disabilities.*

Pennell, A., Salo-Coombs, V., Hering, A., Spielman, F., & Fecho, K. (2011). Anesthesia and analgesia-related preferences and outcomes of women who have birth plans. *Journal of Midwifery and Women's Health, 56,* 376–381.

Pereira-Lancha, L. L., Campos-Ferraz, P. L., & Junior, L. A. H. (2012). Obesity: Considerations about etiology, metabolism, and the use of experimental models. *Diabetes, Metabolic Syndrome, and Obesity, 5,* 75–87.

Perez, M. V., & others (2013). Risk factors for atrial fibrillation and their population burden in postmenopausal women: The Women's Health Initiative Observational Study. *Heart, 99,* 1173–1178.

Perkins, S. C., Finegood, E. D., & Swain, J. E. (2013). Poverty and language development: Roles of parenting and stress. *Innovations in Clinical Neuroscience, 10,* 10–19.

Perlman, L. (2008, July 22). Am I an I or We? *Twins,* pp.1–2.

Perls, T. T. (2007). Centenarians. In J. E. Birren (Ed.), *Encyclopedia of gerontology* (2nd ed.). San Diego: Academic Press.

Perls, T. T. (2009). Health and disease in 85 year olds: Baseline findings from the Newcastle 85+ cohort study. *British Medical Journal, 339,* b4904.

Perry, D. (2012, April). *The intrapsychics of gender.* Paper presented at the Gender Development Research conference, San Francisco.

Perry, N. B., & others (2012). The relation between maternal emotional support and child physiological regulation across the preschool years. *Developmental Psychobiology, 55*(4), 382–394.

Perry, N. B., & others (2013). *Early cardiac vagal regulation predicts the trajectory of externalizing behaviors across the preschool periods.* Unpublished manuscript, University of North Carolina—Greensboro.

Persky, H. R., Dane, M. C., & Jin, Y. (2003). *The nation's report card: Writing 2002.* Washington, DC: U.S. Department of Education.

Pesce, Crova, L., Cereatti, L., Casella, R., & Bellucci, M. (2009). Physical activity and mental performance in preadolescents: Effects of acute exercise on free-recall memory.

Peskin, H. (1967). Pubertal onset and ego functioning. *Journal of Abnormal Psychology, 72,* 1–15.

Pessia, E., & others (2012). Mammalian X chromosome inactivation evolved as a dosage-compensation mechanism for dosage-sensitive genes on the X chromosome. *Proceedings of the National Academy of Sciences USA, 109,* 5346–5351.

Peters, K. F., & Petrill, S. A. (2011). Comparison of background, needs, and expectations for genetic counseling of adults with experience with Down syndrome, Marfan syndrome, and neurofibromatosis. *American Journal of Medical Genetics A, 155,* 684–696.

Petersen, I. T., & others (2012). Interaction between serotonin transporter polymorphism (5-HTTLPR) and stressful life events in adolescents' trajectories of anxious/depressed symptoms. *Developmental Psychology, 48*(5), 1463–1475.

Petersen, J. L., & Hyde, J. S. (2010). A meta-analytic review of research on gender differences in sexuality, 1973–2007. *Psychological Bulletin, 136,* 21–38.

Peterson, C. C., Garnett, M., Kelly, A., & Attwood, T. (2009). Everyday social and conversation applications of theory-of-mind understanding by children with autism spectrum disorders or typical development. *European Child and Adolescent Psychiatry, 18,* 105–115.

Peterson, C. C., Wellman, H. M., & Slaughter, V. (2012). The mind behind the message: Advancing theory-of-mind scales for typically developing children, and those with deafness, autism, or Asperger syndrome. *Child Development, 83,* 469–485.

Petrick-Steward, E. (2012). *Beginning writers in the zone of proximal development.* New York: Psychology Press.

Pew Forum on Religion and Public Life (2008). *U.S. religious landscape study.* Washington, DC: Pew Research Center.

Pew Research Center (2010). *The decline of marriage and rise of new families.* Washington, DC: Author.

Pew Research Center (2010). *Millennials: Confident, connected, open to change.* Washington, DC: Pew Research Center.

Pew Research Center (2011, December). *Barely half of U.S. adults are married—a record low.* Washington, DC: Pew Research Center.

Pew Research Center (2012). *Religion and Public Life Project.* Washington, DC: Pew Research.

Pfefferbaum, B., Newman, E., & Nelson, S.D. (2014). Mental health interventions for children exposed to disasters and terrorism. *Journal of Child and Adolescent Psychopharmacology, 24,* 24–31.

Pfeifer, M., Goldsmith, H. H., Davidson, R. J., & Rickman, M. (2002). Continuity and change in inhibited and uninhibited children. *Child Development, 73,* 1474–1485.

Pfeiffer, U. J., Vogeley, K., & Schilbach, L. (2013). From gaze cueing to dual eye-tracking: Novel approaches to investigate the neural correlates of gaze in social interaction. *Neuroscience and Biobehavioral Reviews, 37,* 2516–2528.

Phillips, D. A., & Lowenstein, A. (2011). Early care, education, and development. *Annual Review of Psychology* (Vol. 62). Palo Alto, CA: Annual Reviews.

Phillips, S. M., Wojcicki, T. R., & McAuley, E. (2013). Physical activity and quality of life in older adults: An 18-month panel analysis. *Quality of Life Research, 22,* 1647–1654.

Phinney, J. S. (2008). Bridging identities and disciplines: Advances and challenges in understanding multiple identities. In M. Azmitia, M. Syed, & K. Radmacher (Eds.), *The intersections of personal and social identities. New Directions for Child and Adolescent Development, 120,* 97–109.

Phinney, J. S., Berry, J. W., Sam, D. L., & Vedder, P. (2013a). Understanding immigrant youth: Conclusions and implications. In J. W. Berry & others (Eds.), *Immigrant youth in transition.* New York: Psychology Press.

Phinney, J. S., Berry, J. W., Vedder, P., & Liebkind, K. (2013b). Acculturation experience: Attitudes, identities, and behaviors of immigrant youth. In J. W. Berry & others (Eds.), *Immigrant youth in cultural transition.* New York: Psychology Press.

Phinney, J. S., & Ong, A. D. (2007). Ethnic identity in immigrant families. In J. E. Lansford, K. Deater-Deckard, & M. H. Bornstein (Eds.), *Immigrant families in contemporary society.* New York: Guilford.

Piaget, J. (1932). *The moral judgment of the child.* New York: Harcourt Brace Jovanovich.

Piaget, J. (1952). *The origins of intelligence in children,* (M. Cook, Trans.). New York: International Universities Press.

Piaget, J. (1954). *The construction of reality in the child.* New York: Basic Books.

Piaget, J. (1962). *Play, dreams, and imitation.* New York: W. W. Norton.

Piaget, J., & Inhelder, B. (1969). *The child's conception of space* (F. J. Langdon & J. L. Lunzer, Trans.). New York: W. W. Norton.

Piazza, J. R., Almeida, D. M., Dmitrieva, N. O., & Klein, L. C. (2010). Frontiers in the use of biomarkers of health in research on stress and aging. *Journals of Gerontology B: Psychological Sciences and Social Sciences, 65B,* 513–525.

Piazza, J. R., & Charles, S. T. (2012). Affective disorders and age: The view through a developmental lens. In S. K. Whitbourne & M. J. Sliwinski (Eds.), *Wiley-Blackwell handbook of adult development and aging.* New York: Wiley.

Piazza, J. R., Charles, S. T., Sliwinski, M. J., Mogle, J., & Almeida, D. M. (2013). Affective reactivity to daily stressors and long-term risk of reporting chronic physical health condition. *Annals of Behavior Medicine, 45,* 110–120.

Pieperhoff, P., & others (2008). Deformation field morphometry reveals age-related structural differences between the brains of adults up to 51 years. *Journal of Neuroscience, 28,* 828–842.

Pierce, R. S., & Anderson, G. J. (2014). The effects of age and workload on 3D spatial attention in dual-task driving. *Accident Analysis and Prevention, 67C,* 96–104.

Pilkington, P. D., Windsor, T. D., & Crisp, D. A. (2012). Volunteering and subjective well-being in midlife and older adults: The role of supportive social networks. *Journals of Gerontology B: Psychological Sciences and Social Sciences, 67,* 249–260.

Pines, A., Sturdee, D. W., & Maclennan, A. H. (2012). Quality of life and the role of menopausal hormone therapy. *Climacteric, 15,* 213–216.

Ping, H., & Hagopian, W. (2006). Environmental factors in the development of type 1 diabetes. *Reviews in Endocrine and Metabolic Disorders, 7,* 149–162.

Pinninti, S. G., & Kimberlin, D. W. (2013). Neonatal herpes simplex virus infections. *Pediatric Clinics of North America, 60,* 351–365.

Pinquart, M., Feubner, C., & Ahnert, L. (2013). Meta-analytic evidence for stability of attachments from infancy to early adulthood. *Attachment and Human Development, 15,* 189–218.

Pinquart, M., & Forstmeier, S. (2012). Effects of reminiscence interventions on psychosocial outcomes: A meta-analysis. *Aging and Mental Health, 16,* 541–558.

Pinsker, J. E. (2012). Turner syndrome: Updating the paradigm of clinical care. *Journal of Clinical Endocrinology and Metabolism. 97*(6), E994–1003

Piper, B. J., & others (2011). Abnormalities in parentally rated executive function in methamphetamine/polysubstance exposed children. *Pharmacology, Biochemistry, and Behavior, 98,* 432–439.

Pirutinsky, S. (2013). Is the connection between religion and psychological functioning due to religion's social value? A failure to replicate. *Journal of Religion and Health, 52,* 782–784.

Pitzer, L. M., Fingerman, K. L., & Lefkowitz, E. S. (2014, in press). Support and negativity in the adult parent tie: Development of the Parent Adult Relationship Questionnaire (PARQ). *International Journal of Aging and Human Development.*

Pizza, V., & others (2011). Neuroinflam-aging and neurodegenerative diseases: An overview. *CNS & Neurological Disorders Drug Targets, 10,* 621–634.

Place, S. S., Todd, P. M., Zhuang, J., Penke, L., & Asendorf, J. B. (2012). Judging romantic interest of others from thin slices is a cross-cultural ability. *Evolution & Human Behavior, 335*(5), 547–550.

Platt, B., Kadosh, K. C., & Lau, J. Y. (2013). The role of peer rejection in adolescent depression. *Depression and Anxiety, 30,* 809–821.

Plomin, R. (1999). Genetics and general cognitive ability. *Nature, 402*(Suppl.), C25–C29.

Plomin, R. (2004). Genetics and developmental psychology. *Merrill-Palmer Quarterly, 50,* 341–352.

Plomin, R., DeFries, J. C., McClearn, G. E., & McGuffin, P. (2009). *Behavioral genetics* (5th ed.). New York: W. H. Freeman.

Plucker, J. (2010, July 19). Commentary in P. Bronson & A. Merryman, The creativity crisis. *Newsweek,* 45–46.

Pohanka, M. (2013). Alzheimer's disease and oxidative stress: A link to etiology? A review. *Current Medicinal Chemistry, 21,* 356–364.

Poil, S. S., & others (2013). Integrative EEG biomarkers predict progression in Alzheimer's disease at the MCI stage. *Frontiers in Aging Neuroscience, 5,* 58.

Polat, U., & others (2012). Training the brain to overcome the effect of aging on the human eye. *Science Reports, 2,* 278.

Pollack, P. (2013). Deep brain stimulation for Parkinson's disease—patient selection. *Handbook of Clinical Neurology, 116C,* 97–105.

Pollack, W. (1999). *Real boys.* New York: Owl Books.

Polo-Kantola, P. (2011). Sleep problems in midlife and beyond. *Maturitas, 68,* 224–232.

Pomerantz, E. M. (2013). *Center for Parent-Child Studies.* Retrieved July 20, 2013, from http://labs.psychology.illinois.edu/cpcs/

Pomerantz, E. M., Cheung, C. S., & Qin, L. (2012). Relatedness between children and parents: Implications for motivation. In R. Ryan (Ed.), *Oxford handbook of motivation.* New York: Oxford University Press.

Pomerantz, E. M., & Kempner, S. G. (2013). Mothers' daily person and process praise: Implications for children's intelligence and motivation. *Developmental Psychology, 49,* 2040–2046.

Pomerantz, E. M., Kim, E. M., & Cheung, C. S. (2012). Parents' involvement in children's learning. In K. R. Harris & others (Eds.), *APA educational psychology handbook.* Washington, DC: American Psychological Association.

Pontifex, M. B., Saliba, B. J., Raine, L. B., Picchietti, D. L., & Hillman, C. H. (2013). Exercise improves behavioral, neurocognitive, and scholastic performance in children with attention-deficit/hyperactivity disorder. *Journal of Pediatrics, 162,* 543–551.

Pooler, A. M., Noble, W., & Hanger, D. P. (2014). A role for tau at the synapse in Alzheimer's disease pathogenesis. *Neuropharmacology, 76, Pt. A,* 1–8.

Poon, L. W., & others (2010). Understanding centenarians' psychosocial dynamics and their contributions to health and quality of life. *Current Gerontology and Geriatrics Research.* doi:10.1155/2010/680657

Poon, L. W., & others (2012). Understanding dementia prevalence among centenarians. *Journals of Gerontology A: Biological Sciences and Medical Sciences, 67,* 358–365.

Popenoe, D. (2009). *The state of our unions 2008. Updates of social indicators: Tables and charts.* Piscataway, NJ: The National Marriage Project.

Posada, G., & Kaloustian, G. (2010). Parent-infant interaction. In J. G. Bremner & T. D. Wachs (Eds.), *Wiley-Blackwell handbook of infant development* (2nd ed.). New York: Wiley.

Posner, J., Park, C., & Wang, Z. (2014, in press). Connecting the dots: A review of resting connectivity MRI studies in attention-deficit/hyperactivity disorder. *Neuropsychology Review.*

Posner, M. I., & Rothbart, M. K. (2007). *Educating the human brain.* Washington, DC: American Psychological Association.

Potapova, N. V., Gartstein, M. A., & Bridgett, D. J. (2014). Paternal influences on infant temperament: Effects of father internalizing problems, parent-related stress, and temperament. *Infant Behavior and Development, 37,* 105–110.

Potochnick, S. (2014). How states can reduce the dropout rate for undocumented immigrant youth: The effects of in-state resident tuition policies. *Social Science Research, 45,* 18–32.

Potochnick, S., Perreira, K. M., & Fuligni, A. (2012). Fitting in: The roles of social acceptance and discrimination in shaping the daily psychological well-being of Latino youth. *Social Science Quarterly, 93,* 173–190.

Potter, J. D. (2014, in press). The failure of cancer chemoprevention. *Carcinogenesis.*

Potthast, N., Neuner, F., & Catani, C. (2014, in press). The contribution of emotional maltreatment to alcohol dependence in a treatment-seeking sample. *Addictive Behaviors.*

Poulin, F., Kiesner, J., Pedersen, S., & Dishion, T. J. (2011). A short-term longitudinal analysis of friendship selection on early adolescent substance use. *Journal of Adolescence, 34,* 249–256.

Poulin, F., & Pedersen, S. (2007). Developmental changes in gender composition of friendship networks in adolescent girls and boys. *Developmental Psychology, 43,* 1484–1496.

Powell, B., Cooper, G., Hoffman, K., & Marvin, B. (2014). *The circle of security intervention.* New York: Guilford.

Powell, S. A. (2015, in press). *Your introduction to education* (3rd ed.). Upper Saddle River, NJ: Pearson.

Powell, S. D. (2015). *Your introduction to education* (3rd ed.). Upper Saddle River, NJ: Pearson.

Power, T. G. (2011). Social play. In P. K. Smith & C. H. Hart (Eds.), *Wiley-Blackwell handbook of childhood social development* (2nd ed.). New York: Wiley.

Powers, C. J., & Bierman, K. L. (2013). The multifaceted impact of peer relations on aggressive-disruptive behavior in early elementary school. *Developmental Psychology, 49*(6), 1174–1186.

Prabhakar, H. (2007). Hopkins interactive guest blog: The public health experience at Johns Hopkins. Retrieved January 31, 2008, from http://hopkins.typepad.com/guest/2007/03/the_public_heal.html

Prado, E. L., & others (2014, in press). Extending the Developmental Milestones Checklist for use in a different context in sub-Saharan Africa. *Acta Pediatrica.*

Prager, K. J. (2013). *The dilemmas of intimacy.* New York: Taylor & Francis.

Prakash, R. S., & others (2011). Cardiovascular fitness and attentional control in the aging brain. *Frontiers in Human Neuroscience, 4*(229), 1–12.

Prameela, K. K. (2011). Breastfeeding—anti-viral potential and relevance to the influenza virus pandemic. *Medical Journal of Malaysia, 66,* 166–169.

Pratt, C., & Bryant, P. E. (1990). Young children understand that looking leads to knowing (so long as they are looking in a single barrel). *Child Development, 61,* 973–982.

Prendergast, C., & Gidding, S. S. (2014, in press). Cardiovascular risk in children and adolescents with type 2 diabetes mellitus. *Current Diabetes Reports.*

Pressley, M. (2003). Psychology of literacy and literacy instruction. In I. B. Weiner (Ed.), *Handbook of psychology.* New York: Wiley.

Pressley, M. (2007). An interview with Michael Pressley by Terri Flowerday and Michael Shaughnessy. *Educational Psychology Review, 19,* 1–12.

Pressley, M., Mohan, L., Fingeret, L., Reffitt, K., & Raphael-Bogaert, L. R. (2007). Writing instruction in engaging and effective elementary settings. In S. Graham. C. A. MacArthur, & J. Fitzgerald (Eds.), *Best practices in writing instruction.* New York: Guilford.

Pressley, M., Raphael, L., Gallagher, D., & DiBella, J. (2004). Providence–St. Mel School: How a school that works for African-American students works. *Journal of Educational Psychology, 96,* 216–235.

Pressley, M., & others (2003). *Motivating primary-grades teachers.* New York: Guilford.

Preston, S. H., & Stokes, A. (2011). Contribution of obesity to international differences in life expectancy. *American Journal of Public Health, 101,* 2137–2143.

Price, C. A., & Joo, E. (2005). Exploring the relationship between marital status and women's retirement satisfaction. *International Journal of Aging and Human Development, 61,* 37–55.

Price, C. A., & Nesteruk, O. (2010). Creating retirement paths: Examples from the lives of women. *Journal of Women and Aging, 22,* 136–149.

Prickett, K. C., & Angel, J. L. (2011). The new health care law: How will women near retirement fare? *Women's Health Issues, 21,* 331–337.

Prigerson, H. G., & Maciejewski, P. K. (2014). Predicting prolonged grief disorder: Caregiver prodrome turns bereaved survivor syndrome. Commentary on Thomas et al. *Journal of Pain and Symptom Management, 47,* 516–517.

Prigerson, H. G., & others (2011). Prolonged grief disorder: Psychometric validation of criteria for proposed for DSM-V and ICD-11. *PLOS Medicine, 6*(8), e1000121.

Principe, G., Greenhoot, A. F., & Ceci, S. J. (2014, in press). Young children's eyewitness memory. In D. S. Lindsay & T. Perfect (Eds.), *Sage handbook of applied memory.* Thousand Oaks, CA: Sage.

Prinstein, M. J. (2007). Moderators of peer contagion: A longitudinal examination of depression socialization between adolescents and their best friends. *Journal of Clinical Child and Adolescent Psychology, 36,* 159–170.

Prinstein, M. J., & Dodge, K. A. (2008). Current issues in peer influence. In M. J. Prinstein & K. A. Dodge (Eds.), *Understanding peer influence in children and adolescents*. New York: Guilford.

Proulx, C. M., & Snyder-Rivas, L. A. (2013). The longitudinal association between marital happiness, problems, and self-rated health. *Journal of Family Psychology, 27,* 194–202.

Pryor, J. H., DeAngelo, L., Blake, L. P. (2011). *The American freshman: National norms for fall 2011*. Los Angeles: Higher Education Research Institute, UCLA.

Psychster Inc (2010) *Psychology of social media*. Retrieved February 21, 2013, from www.psychster.com

Puccini, D., & Liszkowski, U. (2012). 15-month-old infants fast map words but not representational gestures of multimodal labels. *Frontiers in Psychology, 3,* 101.

Pudrovska, T. (2009). Midlife crises and transitions. In D. Carr (Ed.), *Encyclopedia of the life course and human development*. Boston: Gale Cengage.

Pufal, M. A., & others (2012). Prevalence of overweight in children of obese patients: A dietary overview. *Obesity Surgery, 22*(8), 1220–1224.

Puhl, R. M., & King, K. M. (2013). Weight discrimination and bullying. *Best Practice and Research: Clinical Endocrinology and Metabolism, 27,* 117–127.

Puma, M., & others (2010). *Head Start impact study. Final report*. Washington, DC: Administration for Children & Families.

Purtell, K. M., & McLoyd, V. C. (2013). Parents' participation in a work-based anti-poverty program can enhance their children's future orientation: Understanding pathways of influence. *Journal of Youth and Adolescence, 42*(6), 777–791.

Putallaz, M., & others (2007). Overt and relational aggression and victimization: Multiple perspectives within the school setting. *Journal of School Psychology, 45,* 523–547.

Putnam Investments (2006). *Survey of the working retired*. Franklin, MA: Putnam Investments.

Puzzanchera, C., & Robson, C. (2014, February). Delinquency cases in juvenile court, 2010. *Juvenile Offenders and Victims: National Report Series*, Washington, DC: U.S. Department of Justice.

Q

Qin, J. B., & others (2014). Risk factors for congenital syphilis and adverse pregnancy outcomes in offspring of women with syphilis in Shenzhen, China: A prospective nested case-control study. *Sexually Transmitted Diseases, 41,* 13–23.

Quereshi, A. I., & others (2013). Impact of advanced healthcare directives on treatment decisions by physicians in patients with acute stroke. *Critical Care Medicine, 41,* 1468–1475.

Quigley, C., & Muller, M. M. (2014). Feature-selective attention in healthy old age: A selective decline in selective attention. *Journal of Neuroscience, 34,* 2471–2476.

Quinlan-Davidson, M., & others (2014). Suicide among young people in America. *Journal of Adolescent Health, 54,* 262–268.

Quinn, P. C. (2014, in press). What do infants know about cats, dogs, and people? Development of a "like-people" representation for nonhuman animals. In L. Esposito & others (Eds.), *Social neuroscience of human-animal interaction*. New York: Elsevier.

Quinn, P. C., & others (2013). On the developmental origins of differential responding to social category information. In M. R. Banaji & S. A. Gelman (Eds.), *Navigating the social world: What infants, children,*

and other species can teach us. New York: Oxford University Press.

Quoidbach, J., Gilbert, D., & Wilson, T. D. (2013). The end of history illusion. *Science, 339,* 96–98.

R

Raby, K. L., Cicchetti, D., Carlson, E. A., Egeland, B., & Collins, A. W. (2013). Genetic contributions to continuity and change in attachment security: A prospective, longitudinal investigation from infancy to young adulthood. *Journal of Child Psychology and Psychiatry, 54*(11), 1223–1230.

Raby, K. L., & Roisman, G. I. (2014, in press). Gene-environment interplay and risk and resilience during childhood. In R. E. Tremblay & others (Eds.), *Encyclopedia on early childhood development*. Montreal, Quebec: Centre for Excellence for Early Childhood Development.

Rachner, T. D., Khosia, S., & Hofbauer, L. C. (2011). Osteoporosis: Now and the future. *Lancet, 377,* 1276–1287.

Rahnema, C. D., & others (2014, in press). Anabolic steroid-induced hypogonadism: Diagnosis and treatment. *Fertility and Sterility*.

Raikes, H. A., Virmani, E. A., Thompson, R. A., & Hatton, H. (2013). Declines in peer conflict from preschool through first grade: Influences from early attachment and social information processing. *Attachment and Human Development, 15*(1), 65–82.

Raikes, H., & others (2006). Mother-child bookreading in low-income families: Correlates and outcomes during the first three years of life. *Child Development, 77,* 924–953.

Raj, T., & others (2014, in press). CD33: Increased inclusion of exon 2 implicates the Ig V0set domain in Alzheimer's disease susceptibility. *Human Molecular Genetics*.

Rajaraman, P., & others (2011). Early life exposure to diagnostic radiation and ultrasound scans and risk of childhood cancer: Case-control study. *British Medical Journal, 342,* d472.

Rakison, D. H., & Lawson, C. A. (2013). Categorization. In P. Zelazo (Ed.), *Oxford handbook of developmental psychology*. New York: Oxford University Press.

Rakoczy, H. (2012). Do infants have a theory of mind? *British Journal of Developmental Psychology, 30,* 59–74.

Ram, K. T., & others (2008). Duration of lactation is associated with lower prevalence of the metabolic syndrome in midlife—SWAN, the study of women's health across the nation. *American Journal of Obstetrics and Gynecology, 198,* e1–e6.

Ram, N., Shikyo, M., Lunkenheimer, E. S., Doerksen, S., & Conroy, D. (2014). Families as coordinated symbiotic systems: Making use of nonlinear dynamic models. In S. McHale, P. Amato, & A. Booth (Eds.), *Emerging methods in family research*. New York: Springer.

Ramchandani, P. G., & others (2013). Do early father-infant interactions predict the onset of externalizing behaviors in young children? Findings from a longitudinal cohort study. *Journal of Child Psychology and Psychiatry, 54,* 56–64.

Ramey, C. T., & Campbell, F. A. (1984). Preventive education for high-risk children: Cognitive consequences of the Carolina Abecedarian Project. *American Journal of Mental Deficiency, 88,* 515–532.

Ramey, C. T., & Ramey, S. L. (1998). Early prevention and early experience. *American Psychologist, 53,* 109–120.

Ramey, C.T., Ramey, S. L., & Lanzi, R. G. (2001). Intelligence and experience. In R. J. Sternberg & E. I.

Grigorenko (Eds.), *Environmental effects on cognitive development*. Mahwah, NJ: Erlbaum.

Ramey, S. L. (2005). Human developmental science serving children and families: Contributions of the NICHD study of early child care. In NICHD Early Child Care Research Network (Eds.), *Child care and development*. New York: Guilford.

Ramirez-Rodriquez, G., & others (2014). Environmental enrichment induces neuroplastic changes in middle age female BalbC mice and increases the hippocampal levels of BDNF, p-Akt, and p-MAPK1/2. *Neuroscience*.

Ramus, F. (2014, in press). Neuroimaging sheds new light on the phonological deficit in dyslexia. *Trends in Cognitive Science*.

Rancourt, D., Chouskas-Bradley, S., Cohen, G. L., & Prinstein, M. J. (2014, in press). An experimental examination of peers' influence on adolescent girls' intent to engage in madaptive weight-related behaviors. *International Journal of Eating Disorders*.

Randall, G. K., Martin, P., Bishop, A. J., Johnson, M. A., & Poon, L. W. (2012). Social resources and change in functional health: Comparing three age groups. *International Journal of Aging and Human Development, 75,* 1–29.

Randall, G. K., Martin, P., Bishop, A. J., Poon, L. W., & Johnson, M. A. (2011). Age differences and changes in resources essential to aging well: A comparison of sexagenarians, octogenarians, and centenarians. *Current Gerontology and Geriatrics Research*. doi:10.1155/2011/357896

Randall, W. L. (2013). The importance of being ironic: Narrative openness and personal resilience in later life. *Gerontologist, 53*(1), 9–16.

Ransmayr, G. (2011). Physical, occupational, speech, and swallowing therapies and exercise in Parkinson's disease. *Journal of Neural Transmission, 118,* 773–781.

Rapp, S. R., & others (2013). Educational attainment, MRI changes, and cognitive function in older postmenopausal women from the Women's Health Initiative Memory Study. *International Journal of Psychiatry in Medicine, 46,* 121–143.

Rasulo, D., Christensen, K., & Tomassini, C. (2005). The influence of social relations on mortality in later life: A study on elderly Danish twins. *Gerontologist, 45,* 601–608.

Rathunde, K., & Csiksentmihalyi, M. (2006). The developing person: An experiential perspective. In W. Damon & R. Lerner (Eds.), Handbook of child psychology (6th ed.). New York: Wiley.

Ratner, N. B. (2013). Why talk with children matters: Clinical implications of infant- and child-directed speech research. *Seminars in Speech and Language, 34,* 203–214.

Rauner, A., Mess, F., & Woll, A. (2013). The relationship between physical activity, physical fitness, and overweight in adolescents: A systematic review of studies published in or after 2000. *BMC Pediatrics, 13,* 19.

Raven, P. H., Johnson, G. B., Mason, K. A., Loscos, J., & Singer, S. (2014). *Biology* (10th ed.). New York: McGraw-Hill.

Raver, C. C., & others (2011). CSRP's impact on low-income preschoolers' preacademic skills: Self-regulation as a mediating mechanism. *Child Development, 82,* 362–378.

Raver, C. C., & others (2012). Testing models of children's self-regulation within educational contexts: Implications for measurement. *Advances in Child Development and Behavior, 42,* 245–270.

Raver, C. C., & others (2013). Predicting individual differences in low-income children's executive control from early to middle childhood. *Developmental Science, 16,* 394–408.

Raz, N., Ghisletta, P., Rodrique, K. M., Kennedy, K. M., & Lindenberger, U. (2010). Trajectories of brain aging in middle-aged and older adults: Regional and individual differences. *Neuroimage, 51*(2), 501–511.

Raznahan, A., & others (2014). Longitudinal four-dimensional mapping of subcortical anatomy in human development. *Proceedings of the National Academy of Sciences USA, 111,* 1592–1597.

Razza, R. A., Martin, A., & Brooks-Gunn, J. (2012). The implications of early attentional regulational for school success among low-income children. *Journal of Applied Developmental Psychology, 33,* 311–319.

Read, J. P., Merrill, J. E., & Bytschkow, K. (2010). Before the party starts: Risk factors and reasons for "pregaming" in college students. *Journal of American College Health, 58,* 461–472.

Reale, M. A., & others (2014, in press). Selective acetyl- and butyrylcholinesterase inhibitors reduce amyloid-B ex vivo activation of peripheral chemo-cytokines from Alzheimer's disease subjects: Exploring the cholinergic anti-inflammatory pathway. *Current Alzheimer Research.*

Realini, J. P., Buzi, R. S., Smith, P. B., & Martinez, M. (2010). Evaluation of "big decisions": An abstinence-plus sexuality. *Journal of Sex and Marital Therapy, 36,* 313–326.

Rebok, G. W., & others (2014, in press). Ten-year effects of the Advanced Cognitive Training for Independent and Vital Elderly Cognitive Training Trial on cognition and everyday functioning in older adults. *Journal of the American Geriatrics Society.*

Redford, L., Corral, S., Bradley, C., & Fisher, H. L. (2013). The prevalence and impact of child maltreatment and other types of victimization in the UK: Findings from a population survey of caregivers, children, and young people and young adults. *Child Abuse and Neglect, 37,* 801–813.

Redshaw, M., & Henderson, J. (2013). Fathers' engagement in pregnancy and childbirth: Evdience from a national survey. *BMC Pregnancy and Childbirth, 13,* 70.

Reed, S. D., & others (2014, in press). Menopausal quality of life: RCT of yoga, exercise, and omega-3 supplements. *American Journal of Obstetrics and Gynecology.*

Reese, B. M., Haydon, A. A., Herring, A. H., & Halpern, C. T. (2013). The association between sequences of sexual initiation and the likelihood of teenage pregnancy. *Journal of Adolescent Health, 52,* 228–233.

Reeve, C. L., & Charles, J. E. (2008). Survey of opinions on the primacy of g and social consequences of ability testing: A comparison of expert and non-expert views. *Intelligence, 36,* 681–688.

Regalado, M., Sareen, H., Inkelas, M., Wissow, L. S., & Halfon, N. (2004). Parents' discipline of young children: Results from the National Survey of Early Childhood Health. *Pediatrics, 113,* 1952–1958.

Regan, J. C., & Partridge, L. (2013). Gender and longevity: Why do men die earlier than women? Comparative and experimental evidence. *Best Practices in Research. Clinical Endocrinology and Metabolism, 27,* 467–479.

Regev, R. H., & others (2003). Excess mortality and morbidity among small-for-gestational-age premature infants: A population-based study. *Journal of Pediatrics, 143,* 186–191.

Reibis, R. K., Treszi, A., Wegscheider, K., Ehrlich, B., Dissmann, R., & Voller, H. (2010). Exercise capacity is the most powerful predictor of 2-year mortality in patients with left ventricular systolic dysfunction. *Herz, 35,* 104–110.

Reichstadt, J., Depp, C. A., Palinkas, L. A., Folsom, D. P., & Jeste, D. V. (2007). Building blocks of successful aging: A focus group study of older adults' perceived

contributors to successful aging. *American Journal of Geriatric Psychiatry, 15,* 194–201.

Reid, P. T., & Zalk, S. R. (2001). Academic environments: Gender and ethnicity in U.S. higher education. In J. Worell (Ed.), *Encyclopedia of women and gender.* San Diego: Academic Press.

Reijmerink, N. E., & others (2011). Toll-like receptors and microbial exposure: Gene-gene and gene-environment interaction in the development of atopy. *European Respiratory Journal, 128,* 948–955.

Reijntjes, A., & others (2013). Costs and benefits of bullying in the context of the peer group: A three-wave longitudinal analysis. *Journal of Abnormal Psychology, 41,* 1217–1219.

Reilly, D. (2012). Gender, culture, and sex-typed cognitive abilities. *PLoS One, 7*(7), e39904.

Reilly, D., & Neumann, D. L. (2013). Gender-role differences in spatial ability: A meta-analytic review. *Sex Roles, 68,* 521–535.

Reindollar, R. H., & Goldman, M. B. (2012). Gonadotropin therapy: A 20th century relic. *Fertility and Sterility, 97,* 813–818.

Reis, S. M., & Renzulli, J. S. (2014). Challenging gifted and talented learners with a continuum of research-based intervention strategies. In M. A. Bray & T. J. Kehle (Eds.), *Oxford handbook of school psychology.* New York: Oxford University Press.

Reisman, A. S. (2001). Death of a spouse: Basic assumptions and continuation of bonds. *Death Studies, 25,* 445–460.

Rejeski, W. J., & others (2011). Translating weight loss and physical activity programs into the community to preserve mobility in older, obese adults in poor cardiovascular health. *Archives of Internal Medicine, 171*(10), 880–886.

Rendall, M. S., Weden, M. M., Faveault, M. M., & Waldron, H. (2011). The protective effect of marriage for survival: A review and update. *Demography, 48,* 481–506.

Rengasamy, M., & others (2013). The bi-directional relationship between parent-adolescent conflict and treatment outcome for treatment-resistant adolescent depression. *Journal of the American Academy of Child and Adolescent Psychiatry, 52,* 370–377.

Reno, V. P., & Veghte, B. (2011). Economic status of the aged in the United States. In R. H. Binstock & L. K. George (Eds.), *Handbook of aging and the social sciences* (7th ed.). New York: Elsevier.

Renz, M., & others (2013). Dying is a transition. *American Journal of Hospice and Palliative Care, 30,* 283–290.

Renzetti, C. M., & Kennedy-Bergen, R. M. (2015, in press). *Understanding diversity.* Upper Saddle River, NJ: Pearson.

Repacholi, B. M., & Gopnik, A. (1997). Early reasoning about desires: Evidence from 14- and 18-month-olds. *Developmental Psychology, 33,* 12–21.

Repetti, R., Flook, L., & Sperling, J. (2011). Family influences in development across the life span. In K. L. Fingerman, C. A. Berg, J. Smith, & T. C. Antonucci (Eds.), *Handbook of life-span development.* New York: Springer.

Reproductive Endocrinology and Infertility Committee & others (2012). Advanced reproductive age and fertility. *Journal of Obstetrics and Gynecology Canada.*

Resick, P. A., & others (2012). Long-term consequences of cognitive-behavioral treatments for posttraumatic stress disorder among female rape survivors. *Journal of Consulting and Clinical Psychology, 80,* 201–210.

Reuter-Lorenz, P. A. (2013). Aging and cognitive neuroimaging: A fertile union. *Perspectives on Psychological Science, 8,* 68–77.

Reutzel, D. R., & Cooter, R. B. (2015, in press). *Teaching children to read* (7th ed.). Upper Saddle River, NJ: Pearson.

Reyes, S., Algarin, C., Burnout, D., & Peirano, P. (2013). Sleep/wake patterns and physical performance in older adults. *Aging: Clinical and Experimental Research, 25,* 175–181.

Reyna, V. F. (2004). How people make decisions that involve risk: A dual-process approach. *Current Directions in Psychological Science, 13,* 60–66.

Reyna, V. F., Chapman, S. B., Dougherty, M. R., & Confrey, J. (Eds.) (2012). *The adolescent brain.* Washington, DC: American Psychological Association.

Reyna, V., & Farley, F. (2006). Risk and rationality on adolescent decision-making: Implications for theory, practice, and public policy. *Psychological Science in the Public Interest, 7,* 1–44.

Reyna, V. F., & Rivers, S. E. (2008). Current theories of risk and rational decision making. *Developmental Review, 28,* 1–11.

Reyna, V. F., & Zayas, V. (Eds.) (2014). *Neuroscience of risky decision making.* Washington, DC: American Psychological Association.

Reyna, V. F., & others (2011). Neurobiological and memory models of risky decision making in adolescents versus young adults. *Journal of Experimental Psychology: Learning, Memory, and Cognition, 37,* 1125–1142.

Reynolds, E. H. (2014). The neurology of folic acid deficiency. *Handbook of Clinical Neurology, 120,* 927–943.

Reznick, J. S. (2013). Research design and methods: Toward a cumulative developmental science. In P. D. Zelazo (Ed.), *Oxford handbook of developmental psychology.* New York: Oxford University Press.

Reznick, J. S. (2014). Working memory in infancy. In P. Bauer & R. Fivush (Eds.), *Wiley-Blackwell handbook of children's memory.* New York: Wiley.

Rhoades, G. K., Kamp Dusch, C. M., Atkins, D. C., Stanley, S. M., & Markman, H. J. (2011). Breaking up is hard to do: The impact of unmarried relationship dissolution on mental health and life satisfaction. *Journal of Family Psychology 25,* 366–374.

Rhodes, A. E., & others (2012). Child maltreatment and onset of emergency department presentations for suicide-related behaviors. *Child Abuse and Neglect, 36,* 542–551.

Richards, J. E. (2009). Attention to the brain in infancy. In S. Johnson (Ed.), *Neuroconstructivism: The new science of cognitive development.* New York: Oxford University Press.

Richards, J. E. (2010). Infant attention, arousal, and the brain. In L. M. Oaks, C. H. Cashon, M. Casaola, & D. H. Rakison (Eds.), *Infant perception and cognition.* New York: Oxford University Press.

Richards, J. E. (2013). Cortical sources of ERP in the prosaccade and antisaccade task using realistic source models. *Frontiers in Systems Neuroscience, 7,* 27.

Richards, J. E., Reynolds, G. D., & Courage, M. I. (2010). The neural bases of infant attention. *Current Directions in Psychological Science, 19,* 41–46.

Richardson, C. R., & others (2005). Integrating physical activity into mental health services for persons with serious mental illness. *Psychiatric Services, 56,* 324–331.

Richardson, G. A., Goldschmidt, L., Leech, S., & Willford, J. (2011). Prenatal cocaine exposure: Effects on mother- and teacher-rated behavior problems and growth in school-aged children. *Neurotoxicology and Teratology, 33,* 69–77.

Richardson, G. A., Goldschmidt, L., & Willford, J. (2008). The effects of prenatal cocaine use on infant development. *Neurotoxicology and Teratology, 30,* 96–106.

Richardson, M. S., & Schaeffer, C. (2013). From work and family to a dual model of working. In D. L. Blustein (Ed.), *Oxford handbook of the psychology of working*. New York: Oxford University Press.

Richardson, T. M., & others (2011). Depression and its correlates among older adults accessing social services. *Journal of Nursing Care Quality, 59,* 321–326.

Richardson, V. E. (2007). A dual process model of grief counseling: Findings from the Changing Lives of Older Couples (CLOC) study. *Journal of Gerontological Social Work, 48,* 311–329.

Richens, J. L., Morgan, K., & O'Shea, P. (2014, in press). Reverse engineering of Alzheimer's disease based on biomarker pathways analysis. *Neurobiology of Aging.*

Rideout, V., Foehr, U. G., & Roberts, D. P. (2010). *Generation M: Media in the lives of 8- to 18-year-olds.* Menlo Park, CA: Kaiser Family Foundation.

Riediger, M., Li, S-C., & Lindenberger, U. (2006). Selection, optimization, and compensation as developmental mechanisms of adaptive resource allocation: Review and preview. In J. E. Birren & K. W. Schaie (Eds.), *Handbook of the psychology of aging* (6th ed.). San Diego: Academic Press.

Riesch, S. K., & others (2013). Modifiable family factors among treatment-seeking families of children with high body mass index: Report of a pilot study. *Journal of Pediatric Health Care, 27*(4), 254–266.

Riggins, T. (2012). Building blocks of recollection. In S. Ghetti & P. J. Bauer (Eds.), *Origins and development of recollection.* New York: Oxford University Press.

Righi, G., & others (2014, in press). Infants' experience-dependent processing of male and female faces: Insights from eye tracking and event-related potentials. *Developmental Cognitive Neuroscience.*

Riley, K. P., Snowdon, D. A., Derosiers, M. F., & Markesbery, W. R. (2005). Early life linguistic ability, late life cognitive function, and neuropathology: Findings from the Nun Study. *Neurobiology of Aging, 26,* 341–347.

Riley, M., & Bluhm, B. (2012). High blood pressure in children and adolescents. *American Family Physician, 85,* 693–700.

Rimsza, M. E., & Kirk, G. M. (2005). Common medical problems of the college student. *Pediatric Clinics of North America, 52,* 9–24.

Rippon, I., & others (2014, in press). Perceived age discrimination in older adults. *Age and Aging.*

Ritzmann, R., Kramer, A., Bernhardt, S., & Gollhofer, A. (2014). Whole body vibration training—improving balance control and muscle endurance. *PLoS One, 9*(2), e89905.

Riva Crugnola, C., Ierardi, E., Gazzotti, S., & Albizzati, A. (2014). Motherhood in adolescent mothers: Maternal attachment, mother-infant styles of interaction, and emotion regulation at three months. *Infant Behavior and Development, 37,* 44–56.

Rivas-Drake, D., & others (2014a, in press). Ethnic and racial identity revisited: An integrated conceptualization. *Child Development.*

Rivas-Drake, D., & others (2014b, in press). Feeling good, happy, and proud: A meta-analysis of positive ethnic-racial affect and adjustment. *Child Development.*

Rix, S. (2011). Employment and aging. In R. H. Binstock & L. K. George (Eds.), *Handbook of aging and the social sciences* (7th ed.). New York: Elsevier.

Rizzo, M. S. (1999, May 8), Genetic counseling combines science with a human touch. *Kansas City Star,* p. 3.

Rizzuto, D., & Fratiglioni, L. (2014, in press). Lifestyle factors related to mortality and survival: A mini-review. *Gerontology.*

Roane, B. M., & Taylor, D. J. (2014). Pediatric insomnia. In A.R. Wolfson & H. E. Montgomery-Downs

(Eds.), *Oxford handbook of infant, child, and adolescent sleep and behavior.* New York: Oxford University Press.

Robbers, S., & others (2012). Childhood problem behavior and parental divorce: Evidence for gene-environment interaction. *Social Psychiatry and Psychiatric Epidemiology, 47*(10), 1539–1548.

Roberie, D. R., & Elliott, W. J. (2012). What is the prevalence of resistant hypertension in the United States? *Current Opinion in Cardiology, 27,* 386–391.

Roberto, K. A., & Skoglund, R. R. (1996). Interactions with grandparents and great grandparents: A comparison of activities, influences, and relationships. *International Journal of Aging and Human Development, 43,* 107–117.

Roberts, B. W., Donnellan, M. B., & Hill, P. L. (2013). Personality trait development in adulthood: Findings and implications. In I. B. Weiner & others (Eds.), *Handbook of psychology* (2nd ed., Vol. 5). New York: Wiley.

Roberts, B. W., Edmonds, G., & Grijalva, E. (2010). It is developmental me, not generation me: Developmental changes are more important than generational changes in narcissism—Commentary on Trzesniewski & Donnellan (2010). *Perspectives on Psychological Science,* 97–102.

Roberts, B. W., & Mroczek, D. (2008). Personality trait change in adulthood. *Current Directions in Psychological Science, 17,* 31–35.

Roberts, B. W., Walton, K. E., & Bogg, T. (2005). Conscientiousness and health across the life course. *Review of General Psychology, 9,* 156–168.

Roberts, B. W., Walton, K. E., & Viechtbauer, W. (2006). Patterns of mean-level change in personality traits across the life course. A meta-analysis of longitudinal studies. *Psychological Bulletin, 132,* 1–25.

Roberts, B. W., & Wood, D. (2006). Personality development in the context of the neo-socioanalytic model of personality. In D. Mroczek & T. Little (Eds.), *Handbook of personality development.* Mahwah, NJ: Erlbaum.

Roberts, B. W., & others (2014, in press). What is conscientiousness and how can it be assessed? *Developmental Psychology.*

Roberts, D. F., & Foehr, U. G. (2008). Trends in media use. *Future of Children, 18*(1), 11–37.

Robertson, L. T., & Mitchell, J. R. (2013). Benefits of short-term dietary restriction in mammals. *Experimental Gerontology, 48,* 1043–1048.

Robine, J. M. (2011). The weaker sex. *Aging: Clinical and Experimental Research, 23,* 80–83.

Robins, R. W., Trzesniewski, K. H., Tracey, J. L., Potter, J., & Gosling, S. D. (2002). Age differences in self-esteem from age 9 to 90. *Psychology and Aging, 17,* 423–434.

Robinson-Zanartu, C., Doerr, P., & Portman, J. (2015). *Teaching 21 thinking skills for the 21st century.* Upper Saddle River, NJ: Pearson.

Robitaille, A., & others (2013). Longitudinal mediation of processing speed on age-related change in memory and fluid intelligence. *Psychology and Aging, 28,* 887–901.

Rochan, P. A., & others (2014, in press). Demographic characteristics and healthcare use of centenarians: A population-based cohort study. *Journal of the American Geriatrics Society.*

Rochlen, A. B., McKelley, R. A., Suizzo, M-A., & Scaringi, V. (2008). Predictors of relationship satisfaction, psychological well-being, and life-satisfaction among stay-at-home fathers. *Psychology of Men and Masculinity, 9,* 17–28.

Rode, S. S., Chang, P., Fisch, R. O., & Sroufe, L. A. (1981). Attachment patterns of infants separated at birth. *Developmental Psychology, 17,* 188–191.

Rodgers, C. (2013). Why kangaroo care should be standard for all newborns. *Journal of Midwifery and Women's Health, 58,* 249–252.

Rodin, J., & Langer, E. J. (1977). Long term effects of a control-relevant intervention with the institutionalized aged. *Journal of Personality and Social Psychology, 35,* 397–402.

Rodkey, E. N., & Pillai Riddell, R. (2014). The infancy of infant pain research: The experimental origins of infant pain denial. *Journal of Pain, 14,* 338–350.

Rodkin, P. C., & Ryan, A. M. (2012). Child and adolescent peer relationships in educational context. In K. R. Harris, S. Graham, & T. Urdan (Eds.), *APA handbook of educational psychology.* Washington, DC: American Psychological Association.

Rodriguez, E. T., & others (2009). The formative role of home literacy experiences across the first three years of life in children from low-income families. *Journal of Applied Developmental Psychology, 30*(6), 677–694.

Rodrique, K. M., & Kennedy, K. M. (2011). The cognitive consequences of structural changes to the aging brain. In K. W. Schaie & S. L.Willis (Eds.), *Handbook of the psychology of aging* (7th ed.). New York: Elsevier.

Rodriquez Villar, S., & others (2012). Prolonged grief disorder in the next of kin of adult patients who die during or after admission to intensive care. *Chest, 141,* 1635–1636.

Roelfs, D. J., Shor, E., Davidson, K. W., & Schwartz, J. E. (2011). Losing life and livelihood: A systematic review and meta-analysis of unemployment and all-cause mortality. *Social Science & Medicine, 72,* 840–854.

Roese, N. J., & Summerville, A. (2005). What we regret most ... and why. *Personality and Social Psychology Bulletin, 31,* 1273–1285.

Roeser, R. W., & Zelazo, P. D. (2012). Contemplative science, education and child development. *Child Development Perspectives, 6,* 143–145.

Rognum, I. J., & others (2014). Serotonin metabolites in the cerebrospinal fluid in sudden infant death syndrome. *Journal of Neuropathology and Experimental Neurology, 73,* 115–122.

Rogoff, B. (2003). *The cultural nature of human development.* New York: Oxford University Press.

Rohde, C., & others (2014, in press). Unrestricted fruits and vegetables in the PKU diet: A 1-year follow-up. *European Journal of Clinical Nutrition.*

Roisman, G. I., & Fraley, R. C. (2012). A behavior-genetic study of the legacy of early caregiving experiences: Academic skills, social competence, and externalizing behavior in kindergarten. *Child Development, 83,* 728–742.

Roisman, G. I., & Groh, A. M. (2011). Attachment theory and research in developmental psychology: An overview and appreciative critique. In M. K. Underwood & L. H. Rosen (Eds.), *Social development.* New York: Wiley.

Rolando, C., & Taylor, V. (2014). Neural stem cell of the hippocampus: Development, physiology regulation, and dysfunction in disease. *Current Topics in Developmental Biology, 107,* 183–206.

Rolland, Y., & others (2011). Treatment strategies for sarcopenia and frailty. *Medical Clinics of North America, 95,* 427–438.

Romano, A. D., Greco, E., Vendemiale, G., & Serviddio, G. (2014, in press). Bioenergetics and mitochondrial dysfunction in aging: Recent insights for a therapeutical approach. *Current Pharmaceutical Design.*

Romero, M. M., Ott, C. H., & Kelber, S. T. (2014). Predictors of grief in bereaved family caregivers of persons with Alzheimer's disease. A prospective study. *Death Studies, 38,* 395–403.

Romo, L. F., Mireles-Rios, R., & Lopez-Tello, G. (2014). Latina mothers' and daughters' expectations for autonomy at age 15 (La Quinceanera). *Journal of Adolescent Research, 29*(2), 279–294.

Ronald, A., & Hoekstra, R. A. (2011). Autism spectrum disorders and autistic traits: A decade of new twin studies. *American Journal of Medical Genetics B: Neuropsychiatric Genetics, 156*, 255–274.

Ronfard, S., & Harris, P. L. (2014). When will Little Red Riding Hood become scared? Children's attribution of mental states to a story character. *Developmental Psychology, 50*(1), 283–292.

Rook, K. S., Mavandadi, S., Sorkin, D. H., & Zettel, L. A. (2007). Optimizing social relationships as a resource for health and well-being in later life. In C. M. Aldwin, C. L. Park, & A. Spiro (Eds.), *Handbook of health psychology and aging.* New York: Guilford.

Root, B. L., & Exline, J. J. (2014). The role of continuing bonds in coping with grief: Overview and future directions. *Death Studies, 38*, 1–8.

Rosano, C., & others (2012). Slower gait, slower information processing, and smaller prefrontal area in older adults. *Age and Aging, 41*, 58–64.

Rose, A. J., & others (2012). How girls and boys expect disclosure about problems will make them feel: Implications for friendship. *Child Development, 83*, 844–863.

Rose, A. J., Carlson, W., & Waller, E. M. (2007). Prospective associations of co-rumination with friendship and emotional adjustment: Considering the socioemotional trade-offs of co-rumination. *Developmental Psychology, 43*, 1019–1031.

Rose, S. A., Feldman, J. F., Jankowski, J. J., & Van Rossem, R. (2012). Information processing from infancy to 11 years: Continuities and prediction of IQ. *Intelligence, 40*, 445–457.

Rose-Greenland, F., & Smock, P. J. (2013). Living together unmarried: What do we know about cohabiting families? In G. W. Peterson & K. R. Bush (Eds.), *Handbook of marriage and the family* (3rd ed.). New York: Springer.

Rosenblith, J. F. (1992). *In the beginning* (2nd ed.). Newbury Park, CA: Sage.

Rosenfeld, A., & Stark, E. (1987, May). The prime of our lives. *Psychology Today.* pp. 62–72.

Rosengard, C. (2009). Confronting the intendedness of adolescent rapid repeat pregnancy. *Journal of Adolescent Health, 44*, 5–6.

Rosenstein, D., & Oster, H. (1988). Differential facial responses to four basic tastes in newborns. *Child Development, 59*, 1555–1568.

Rosmarin, D. H., Krumrei, E. J., & Andersson, G. (2009). Religion as a predictor of psychological distress in two religious communities. *Cognitive Behavior Therapy, 38*, 54–64.

Rosnow, R. L., & Rosenthal, R. (2013). *Beginning psychological research* (7th ed.). Boston: Cengage.

Ross, A. H., & Juarez, C. A. (2014, in press). A brief history of fatal child maltreatment and neglect. *Forensic Science, Medicine, and Pathology.*

Ross, H. A., & others (2014, in press). Harmonization of growth hormone measurement results: The empirical approach. *Clinical Chemica Acta.*

Ross, J. L., & others (2012). Behavioral and social phenotypes in boys with 47, XYY syndrome or 47, XXY Klinefelter syndrome. *Pediatrics, 129*, 769–778.

Ross, L. A., Schmidt, E. L., & Ball, K. (2013). Interventions to maintain mobility: What works? *Accident Analysis and Prevention, 61*, 167–196.

Rossi, A. S. (1989). A life-course approach to gender, aging, and intergenerational relations. In K. W. Schaie & C. Schooler (Eds.), *Social structure and aging.* Hillsdale, NJ: Erlbaum.

Rossi, S., & others (2005). Age-related functional changes of prefrontal cortex in long-term memory: A repetitive transcranial magnetic stimulation study. *Journal of Neuroscience, 24*, 7939–7944.

Rote, W. M., & others (2012). Associations between observed mother-adolescent interactions and adolescent information management. *Journal of Research on Adolescence, 22*, 206–214.

Rotermann, M. (2007). Marital breakdown and subsequent depression. *Health Reports, 18*, 33–44.

Roth, J., Brooks-Gunn, J., Murray, L., & Foster, W. (1998). Promoting healthy adolescents: Synthesis of youth development program evaluations. *Journal of Research on Adolescence, 8*, 423–459.

Rothbart, M. K. (2004). Temperament and the pursuit of an integrated developmental psychology. *Merrill-Palmer Quarterly, 50*, 492–505.

Rothbart, M. K. (2007). Temperament, development, and personality. *Current Directions in Psychological Science, 16*, 207–212.

Rothbart, M. K. (2011). *Becoming who we are.* New York: Guilford.

Rothbart, M. K., & Bates, J. E. (2006). Temperament. In W. Damon & R. Lerner (Eds.), *Handbook of child psychology* (6th ed.). New York: Wiley.

Rothbart, M. K., & Gartstein, M. A. (2008). Temperament. In M. M. Haith & J. B. Benson (Eds.), *Encyclopedia of infant and early childhood development.* Oxford, UK: Elsevier.

Rothbaum, F., Poll, M., Azuma, H., Miyake, K., & Welsz, J. (2000). The development of close relationships in Japan and the United States: Paths of symbiotic harmony and generative tension. *Child Development, 71*, 1121–1142.

Rothman, M. S., Miller, P. D., Lewiecki, E. M., & Bilezikian, J. P. (2014, in press). Bone density testing: Science, the media, and patient care. *Current Osteoporosis Reports.*

Rothman, S. M., & Mattson, M. P. (2012). Sleep disturbances in Alzheimer's and Parkinson's diseases. *Neuromolecular Medicine, 14*(3), 194–204.

Roubinov, D. S., Luecken, L. J., Crnic, K. A., & Gonzales, N. A. (2014). Postnatal depression in Mexican American fathers: Demographic, cultural, and familial predictors. *Journal of Affective Disorders, 152*, 360–368.

Rousssotte, F. F. (2011). Abnormal brain activation during working memory in children with prenatal exposure to drugs of abuse: The effects of methamphetamine, alcohol, and polydrug exposure. *NeuroImage, 54*, 3067–3075.

Rovee-Collier, C. (1987). Learning and memory in children. In J. D. Osofsky (Ed.), *Handbook of infant development* (2nd ed.). New York: Wiley.

Rovee-Collier, C. (2004). Infant learning and memory. In U. Goswami (Ed.), *Blackwell handbook of childhood cognitive development.* Malden, MA: Blackwell.

Rovee-Collier, C. (2007). The development of infant memory. In N. Cowan & M. Courage (Eds.), *The development of memory in childhood.* Philadelphia: Psychology Press.

Rovee-Collier, C. (2008). The development of infant memory. In N. Cowan & M. Courage (Eds.), *The development of memory in childhood.* Philadelphia: Psychology Press.

Rovee-Collier, C., & Barr, R. (2010). Infant learning and memory. In U. J. G. Bremner & T. D. Wachs (Ed.), *Wiley-Blackwell handbook of infant development* (2nd ed.). New York: Wiley.

Rowe, M., & Goldin-Meadow, S. A. (2009). Differences in early gesture explain SES disparities in child vocabulary size at school entry. *Science, 323*, 951–953.

Roza, S. J., & others (2010). Maternal folic acid supplement use in early pregnancy and child behavioural problems: The Generation R study. *British Journal of Nutrition, 103*, 445–452.

Rozzini, R., Ranhoff, A., & Trabucchi, M. (2007). Alcoholic beverage and long-term mortality in elderly people living at home. *Journals of Gerontology: Biological Sciences and Medical Sciences, 62A*, M1313–M1314.

Ruan, L., & others (2014). Neurogenesis in neurological and psychiatric diseases and brain injury: From bench to bedside. *Progress in Neurobiology, 115C*, 116–137.

Rubens, D., & Sarnat, H. B. (2013). Sudden infant death syndrome: An update and new perspectives of etiology. *Handbook of Clinical Neurology, 112*, 867–874.

Rubin, K. H., Bowker, J. C., McDonald, K. L., & Menzer, M. (2013). Peer relationships in childhood. In P. D. Zelazo (Ed.), *Oxford handbook of developmental psychology.* New York: Oxford University Press.

Rubin, K. H., Bukowski, W., & Parker, J. G. (1998). Peer interactions, relationships, and groups. In N. Eisenberg (Ed.), *Handbook of child psychology* (5th ed., Vol. 3). New York: Wiley.

Rubin, K. H., Bukowski, W., & Parker, J. (2006). Peer interactions, relationships, and groups. In W. Damon & R. Lerner (Eds.), *Handbook of child psychology* (6th ed.). New York: Wiley.

Ruble, D. (1983). The development of social comparison processes and their role in achievement-related self-socialization. In E. Higgins, D. Ruble, & W. Hartup (Eds.), *Social cognitive development: A social-cultural perspective.* New York: Cambridge University Press.

Ruckenhauser, G., Yazdani, F., & Ravaglia, G. (2007). Suicide in old age: Illness or autonomous decision of the will? *Archives of Gerontology and Geriatrics, 44*(6, Suppl.), S355–S358.

Rudang, R., Mellstrom, D., Clark, E., Ohlsson, C., & Lorentzon, M. (2012). Advancing maternal age is associated with lower bone mineral density in young adult male offspring. *Osteoporosis International, 23*, 475–482.

Rudman, L. A., Fetterolf, J. C., & Sanchez, D. T. (2013). What motivates the sexual double standard? More support for male versus female control theory. *Personality and Social Psychology Bulletin, 39*, 250–263.

Rueda, M. R., & Posner, M. I. (2013). Development of attentional networks. In P. D. Zelazo (Ed.), *Oxford handbook of developmental psychology.* New York: Oxford University Press.

Rueda, M. R., Posner, M. I., & Rothbart, M. K. (2005). The development of executive attention: Contributions to the emergence of self-regulation. *Developmental Neuropsychology, 28*, 573–594.

Ruiter, M., & others (2012, June 11). *Short sleep predicts stroke symptoms in persons of normal weight.* Paper presented at the annual meeting of the Associated Professional Sleep Societies (APSS), Boston.

Rumberger, R. W. (1983). Dropping out of high school: The influence of race, sex, and family background. *American Educational Research Journal, 20*, 194–220.

Rupp, D. E., Vodanovich, S. J., & Crede, M. (2005). The multidimensional nature of ageism: Construct validity and group differences. *Journal of Social Psychology, 145*, 335–362.

Russell, S. T., Crockett, L. J., & Chao, R. K. (2010). *Asian American parenting and parent-adolescent relationships.* New York: Springer.

Russell, V. M., Baker, L. R., & McNulty, J. K. (2013). Attachment insecurity and infidelity in marriage: Do studies of dating relationships inform us about marriage? *Journal of Family Psychology, 27*, 242–251.

Rutter, J., & Thapar, A. (2014). Genetics of autism spectrum disorders. In F. R. Volkmar & others (Eds.), *Handbook of autism and pervasive developmental disorders.* New York: Wiley.

Ruzek, E., Burchinal, M., Farkas, G., & Duncan, G. J. (2014, in press). The quality of toddler child care and cognitive skills at 24 months: Propensity score analysis results from the ECLS-B. *Early Child Research Quarterly.*

Ryan, A. S., & others (2014, in press). Aerobic exercise and weight loss reduce vascular markers of inflammation and improve insulin sensitivity in obese women. *Journal of the American Geriatrics Society.*

Ryff, C. D. (1984). Personality development from the inside: The subjective experience of change in adulthood and aging. In P. B. Baltes & O. G. Brim (Eds.), *Life-span development and behavior.* New York: Academic Press.

Ryff, C. D. (1991). Possible selves in adulthood and old age: A tale of shifting horizons. *Psychology and Aging, 6,* 286–295.

Rypma, B., Eldreth, D. A., & Rebbechi, D. (2007). Age-related differences in activation-performance relations in delayed-response tasks: A multiple component analyses. *Cortex, 43,* 65–76.

S

Saajanaho, M., & others (2014, in press). Older women's personal goals and exercise activity: An eight-year follow-up. *Journal of Aging and Physical Activity.*

Saarento, S., Boulton, A. J., & Salmivalli, C. (2014, in press). Reducing bullying and victimization: Student- and classroom-level mechanisms of change. *Journal of Abnormal Child Psychology.*

Saarinen, S., & others (2014, in press). Visuospatial working memory in 7- to 12-year-old children with disruptive behavior disorders. *Child Psychiatry and Human Development.*

Saarni, C. (1999). *The development of emotional competence.* New York: Guilford.

Saarni, C., Campos, J., Camras, L. A., & Witherington, D. (2006). Emotional development. In W. Damon & R. Lerner (Eds.), *Handbook of child psychology* (6th ed.). New York: Wiley.

Sabbagh, M. A., Xu, F., Carlson, S. M., Moses, L. J., & Lee, K. (2006). The development of executive functioning and theory of mind: A comparison of Chinese and U.S. preschoolers. *Psychological Science, 17,* 74–81.

Sabina, C., & Ho, L. Y. (2014, in press). Campus and college victim responses to sexual assault and dating violence: Disclosure, service utilization, and service provision. *Trauma, Violence, and Abuse.*

Sacrey, L. A., Germani, T., Bryson, S. E., & Zwaigenbaum, L. (2014). Reaching and grasping in autism spectrum disorder: A review of recent literature. *Frontiers in Neurology, 5,* 6.

Sadeh, A. (2007). Consequences of sleep loss or sleep disruption in children. *Sleep Medicine, 2,* 513–520.

Sadeh, A. (2008). Sleep. In M. M. Haith & J. B. Benson (Eds.), *Encyclopedia of infant and early childhood development.* Oxford, UK: Elsevier.

Sadker, D. M., & Zittleman, K. (2012). *Teachers, schools, and society* (3rd ed.). New York: McGraw-Hill.

Sagiv, S. K., Epstein, J. N., Bellinger, D. C., & Korrick, S. A. (2012). Pre- and postnatal risk factors for ADHD in a nonclinical pediatric population. *Journal of Attention Disorders, 17*(1), 47–57.

Saifer, S. (2007, August 29). *Tools of the Mind—A Vygotskian-inspired early childhood curriculum.* Paper presented at the 17th Annual Conference of the European Early Childhood Education Research Association, Prague.

Saint Onge, J. M. (2009). Mortality. In D. Carr (Ed.), *Encyclopedia of the life course and human development.* Boston: Gale Cengage.

Saint-Onge, J. M., Krueger, K. M., & Rogers, R. G. (2014, in press). The relationship between major depression and nonsuicide mortality for U.S. adults: The importance of health behaviors. *Journals of Gerontology B: Psychological Sciences and Social Sciences.*

Sakamoto, Y., & others (2009). Effect of exercise, aging, and functional capacity on acute secretory immunoglobulin A response in elderly people over 75 years of age. *Geriatrics and Gerontology International, 9,* 81–88.

Sakraida, T. J. (2005). Divorce transition differences of midlife women. *Issues in Mental Health Nursing, 26,* 225–249.

Salama, R. H., & others (2013). Clinical and biochemical effects of environmental tobacco smoking on pregnancy outcome. *Indian Journal of Clinical Biochemistry, 28,* 368–373.

Sale, A., Berardi, N., & Maffei, L. (2014). Environment and brain plasticity: Towards an endogenous pharmacotherapy. *Physiological Reviews, 94,* 189–234.

Saling, L. L., Laroo, N., & Saling, M. M. (2012). When more is less: Failure to compress discourse with re-telling in normal aging. *Acta Psychologica, 139,* 220–224.

Salmivalli, C., & Peets, K. (2009). Bullies, victims, and bully-victim relationships in middle childhood and adolescence. In K. H. Rubin, W. M. Bukowski, & B. Laursen (Eds.), *Handbook of peer interactions, relationships, and groups.* New York: Guilford.

Salmivalli, C., Peets, K., & Hodges, E. V. E. (2011). Bullying. In P. K. Smith & C. H. Hart (Eds.), *Wiley-Blackwell handbook of childhood social development* (2nd ed.). New York: Wiley.

Salthouse, T. A. (1994). The nature of influence of speed on adult age differences in cognition. *Developmental Psychology, 30,* 240–259.

Salthouse, T. A. (2007). Reaction time. In J. E. Birren (Ed.), *Encyclopedia of gerontology* (2nd ed.). San Diego: Academic Press.

Salthouse, T. A. (2009). When does age-related cognitive decline begin? *Neurobiology of Aging, 30,* 507–514.

Salthouse, T. A. (2012). Consequences of age-related cognitive declines. *Annual Review of Psychology* (Vol. 63). Palo Alto, CA: Annual Reviews.

Salthouse, T. A. (2013). Executive functioning. In D. C. Park & N. Schwartz (Eds.), *Cognitive aging* (2nd ed.). New York: Psychology Press.

Salthouse, T. A. (2013). Within cohort age differences in cognitive functioning. *Psychological Science.*

Salthouse, T. A., & Mandell, A. R. (2013). Do age-related increases in tip-of-the-tongue experiences signify episodic memory deficits? *Psychological Science, 24,* 2489–2497.

Salthouse, T. A., & Skovronek, E. (1992). Within-context assessment of working memory. *Journal of Gerontology, 47,* P110–P117.

Salvatore, J. E., Kuo, S. I., Steele, R. D., Simpson, J. A., & Collins, W. A. (2011). Recovering from conflict in romantic relationships: A developmental perspective. *Psychological Science, 22,* 376–383.

Sameroff, A. J. (2009). The transactional model. In A. J. Sameroff (Ed.), *The transactional model of development: How children and contexts shape each other.* Washington, DC: American Psychological Association.

Sameroff, A. J. (2012). Conceptual issues in studying the development of self-regulation. In S. L. Olson & A. J. Sameroff (Eds.), *Biopsychosocial regulatory processes in the development of childhood behavioral problems.* New York: Cambridge University Press.

Samhan, Y. M., El-Sabae, H. H., Khafagy, H. F., & Maher, M. A. (2013). A pilot study to compare epidural identification and catheterization using a saline-filled syringe versus a continuous hydrostatic pressure system. *Journal of Anesthesia, 27*(4), 607–610.

Samjoo, I. A., & others (2013). The effect of endurance exercise on both skeletal muscle and systemic oxidative stress in previously sedentary obese men. *Nutrition and Diabetes, 3,* e88.

Samson, S. L., & Garber, A. J. (2014). Metabolic syndrome. *Endocrinology and Metabolism Clinics of North America, 43,* 1–23.

Sanbonmatsu, D. M., Strayer, D. L., Medeiros-Ward, N., & Watson, J. M. (2013). Who multi-tasks and why? Multi-tasking ability, perceived multi-tasking ability, impulsivity, and sensation seeking. *PLoS One, 8*(1), e54402.

Sanchez, C. E., Richards, J. E., & Almli, C. R. (2012). Neurodevelopmental MRI brain templates from 2 weeks to 4 years of age. *Developmental Psychobiology, 54,* 77–91.

Sandesara, P., & Bogart, D. B. (2013). Almost everyone over 50 should be put on a statin to reduce the risk of cardiovascular disease: A protagonist view. *Missouri Medicine, 110*(4), 332–338.

Sangree, W. H. (1989). Age and power: Life-course trajectories and age structuring of power relations in East and West Africa. In D. I. Kertzer & K. W. Schaie (Eds.), *Age structuring in comparative perspective.* Hillsdale, NJ: Erlbaum.

Sankupellay, M., & others (2011). Characteristics of sleep EEG power spectra in healthy infants in the first two years of life. *Clinical Neurophysiology, 122,* 236–243.

Sanson, A., & Rothbart, M. K. (1995). Child temperament and parenting. In M. H. Bornstein (Ed.), *Handbook of parenting* (Vol. 4). Hillsdale, NJ: Erlbaum.

Santen, R. J., Stuenkel, C. A., Burger, H. G., & Manson, J. E. (2014, in press). Competency in menopause management: Whither goest the internist? *Journal of Women's Health.*

Santilli, F., & others (2013). Effects of high-amount-high-intensity exercise on in vivo platelet activation: Modulation by lipid peroxidation and AGE/RAGE axis. *Thrombosis and Hemostasis, 110*(6), 1232–1240.

Santrock, J. W., Sitterle, K. A., & Warshak, R. A. (1988). Parent-child relationships in stepfather families. In P. Bronstein & C. P. Cowan (Eds.), *Fatherhood today: Men's changing roles in the family.* New York: Wiley.

Sapp, S. (2010). What have religion and spirituality to do with aging? Three approaches. *Gerontologist, 50,* 271–275.

Sarchiapone, M., & others (2014). Hours of sleep in adolescents and its association with anxiety, emotional concerns, and suicidal ideation. *Sleep Medicine, 15,* 248–254.

Sarifakioglu, B., & others (2014, in press). Effects of a 12-week combined exercise therapy on oxidative stress in female fibromyalgia patients. *Rheumatology International.*

Sarkisian, N., Gerena, M., & Gerstel, N. (2006). Extended family ties among Mexicans, Puerto Ricans, and Whites: Superintegration or disintegration? *Family Relations, 55,* 330–334.

Sarlos, P., & others (2014). Susceptibility to ulcerative colitis in Hungarian patients determined by gene-gene interaction. *World Journal of Gastroenterology.*

Saroglou, V. (2013). Religion, spirituality, and altruism. In K. I. Pargament, J. Exline, & J. Jones (Eds.), *Handbook of psychology, religion, and spirituality.* Washington, DC: American Psychological Association.

Sasson, I., & Umberson, D. J. (2014). Widowhood and depression: New light on gender differences, selection, and psychological adjustment. *Journals of Gerontology B: Psychological Sciences and Social Sciences, 69,* 135–145.

Sauber-Schatz, E. K., & others (2014). Vital signs: Restraint use and motor vehicle occupant death rates among children aged 0–12—United States, 2002–2011. *MMWR Morbidity and Mortality Weekly Reports, 63*(5), 113–118.

Saunders, T. J. (2014, in press). The health impact of sedentary behavior in children and youth. *Applied Physiology, Nutrition, and Metabolism.*

Sauter, D., McDonald, N. M., Grangi, D., & Messinger, D. S. (2014, in press). Nonverbal expressions of positive emotions. In M. Tugade, & others (Eds.), *Handbook of positive emotions.* New York: Guilford.

Savin-Williams, R. C. (2015, in press). The new sexual-minority teenager. In D. A. Powell & J. S. Kaufman (Eds.), *The meaning of sexual identity in the 21st century.* New York: Cambridge.

Savin-Williams, R. C., & Cohen, K. (2015, in press). Gay, lesbian, and bisexual youth. In J. D. Wright (Ed.), *International encyclopedia of the social and behavioral sciences* (2nd ed.). New York: Oxford University Press.

Sayer, A. A., & others (2013). New horizons in the pathogenesis, diagnosis, and management of sarcopenia. *Age and Aging, 42*(2), 145–150.

Sbarra, D. A. (2012). Marital dissolution and physical health outcomes: A review of mechanisms. *The science of the couple. The Ontario Symposium* (Vol.12). New York: Psychology Press.

Scarf, M. (2013). The remarriage blueprint. New York: Scribner.

Scarr, S. (1993). Biological and cultural diversity: The legacy of Darwin for development. *Child Development, 64,* 1333–1353.

Schaan, B. (2013). Widowhood and depression among older Europeans—the role of gender, caregiving, marital quality, and regional context. *Journals of Gerontology B: Psychological Sciences and Social Sciences, 68,* 431–442.

Schaefer, R. T. (2013). *Race and ethnicity in the United States* (7th ed.). Upper Saddle River, NJ: Pearson.

Schaefer, R. T. (2015, in press). *Racial and ethnic groups* (14th ed.). Upper Saddle River, NJ: Pearson.

Schafer, A. (2013). Physician assisted suicide: The great Canadian euthanasia debate. *International Journal of Law and Psychiatry, 36,* 522–531.

Schaffer, H. R. (1996). *Social development.* Cambridge, MA: Blackwell.

Schaffer, M. A., Goodhue, A., Stennes, K., & Lanigan, C. (2012). Evaluation of a public health nurse visiting program for pregnant and parenting teens. *Public Health Nursing, 29,* 218–231.

Schaie, K. W. (1994). The life course of adult intellectual abilities. *American Psychologist, 49,* 304–313.

Schaie, K. W. (1996). *Intellectual development in adulthood: The Seattle Longitudinal Study.* New York: Cambridge University Press.

Schaie, K.W. (2000). Unpublished review of J. W. Santrock's *Life-span development,* 8th ed. New York: McGraw-Hill.

Schaie, K. W. (2005). *Developmental influences on adult intelligence: The Seattle Longitudinal Study.* New York: Oxford University Press.

Schaie, K. W. (2007). Generational differences: Age-period cohort. In J. E. Birren (Ed.), *Encyclopedia of gerontology* (2nd ed.). San Diego: Academic Press.

Schaie, K. W. (2008). Historical processes and patterns of cognitive aging. In S. M. Hofer & D. F. Alwin (Eds.),

Handbook on cognitive aging: An interdisciplinary perspective. Thousand Oaks, CA: Sage.

Schaie, K. W. (2009). "When does age-related cognitive decline begin?" Salthouse again reifies the "cross-sectional fallacy." *Neurobiology of Aging, 30,* 528–529.

Schaie, K. W. (2010). Adult intellectual abilities. *Corsini encyclopedia of psychology.* New York: Wiley.

Schaie, K. W. (2011a). *Developmental influences on adult intellectual development.* New York: Oxford University Press.

Schaie, K. W. (2011b). Historical influences on aging and behavior. In K. W. Schaie & S. L. Willis (Eds.), *Handbook of the psychology of aging* (7th ed.). New York: Elsevier.

Schaie, K. W. (2013). *The Seattle Longitudinal Study: Developmental influences on adult intellectual development* (2nd Ed.). New York: Oxford University Press.

Schaie, K. W., & Willis, S. L. (2014, in press). The Seattle Longitudinal Study of Adulthood Cognitive Development. *Bulletin of the International Society for the Study of Behavioral Development.*

Schattschneider, C., Fletcher, J. M., Francis, D. J., Carlson, C. D., & Foorman, B. R. (2004). Kindergarten prediction of reading skills: A longitudinal comparative analysis. *Journal of Educational Psychology, 96,* 265–282.

Scheerings, M. S., Cobham, V. E., & McDermott, B. (2014). Policy and administrative issues for large-scale clinical interventions following disasters. *Journal of Child and Adolescent Psychopharmacology, 24,* 39–46.

Scheibe, S., Freund, A. M., & Baltes, P. B. (2007). Toward a psychology of life-longings: The optimal (utopian) life. *Developmental Psychology, 43,* 778–795.

Scher, A., & Harel, J. (2008). Separation and stranger anxiety. In M. M. Haith & J. B. Benson (Eds.), *Encyclopedia of infant and early childhood development.* Oxford, UK: Elsevier.

Schiavi, A., & Ventura, N. (2014, in press). The interplay between mitochondria and autophagy and its role in the aging process. *Experimental Gerontology.*

Schieffelin, B. (2005). *The give and take of everyday life.* Tucson, AZ: Fenestra.

Schieman, S., van Gundy, K., & Taylor, J. (2004). The relationship between age and depressive symptoms: A test of competing explanatory and suppression influences. *Journal of Aging Health, 14,* 260–285.

Schiff, W. J. (2015). *Nutrition essentials.* New York: McGraw-Hill.

Schiffman, S. S. (2007). Smell and taste. In J. E. Birren (ed.), *Encyclopedia of gerontology* (2nd ed.). San Diego: Academic Press.

Schilling, E. A., Aseltine, R. H., Glanovsky, J. L., James, A., & Jacobs, D. (2009). Adolescent alcohol use, suicidal ideation, and suicide attempts. *Journal of Adolescent Health, 44,* 335–341.

Schlam, T. R., Wilson, N. L., Shoda, Y., Mischel, W., & Ayduk, O. (2013). Preschoolers' delay of gratification predicts their body mass 30 years later. *Journal of Pediatrics, 162,* 90–93.

Schlegel, M. (2000). All work and play. *Monitor on Psychology 31*(11), 50–51.

Schmidt, L. I., Wahl, H. W., & Plischke, H. (2014). Older adults' performance in technology-based tasks: Cognitive ability and beyond. *Journal of Gerontological Nursing, 40,* 18–24.

Schmidt, S., & others (2006). Cigarette smoking strongly modifies the association of LOC387715 and age related macular degeneration. *American Journal of Human Genetics, 78,* 852–864.

Schneider, E., & others (2014, in press). Widespread differences in cortex DNA methylation of the "language gene" CNTNAP2 between humans and chimpanzees. *Epigenetics.*

Schneider, J. M., & others (2011). Dual sensory impairment in older age. *Journal of Aging and Health, 23,* 1309–1324.

Schneider, W. (2011). Memory development in childhood. In U. Goswami (Ed.), *Wiley-Blackwell handbook of childhood cognitive development* (2nd ed.). New York: Wiley-Blackwell.

Schnittker, J. (2007). Look (closely) at all the lonely people: Age and social psychology of social support. *Journal of Aging and Health, 19,* 659–682.

Schoeneberger, J. (2012). Longitudinal attendance patterns: Developing high school dropouts. *Clearinghouse, 85,* 7–14.

Schoenfeld, T. J., & Gould, E. (2013). Differential effects of stress and gludocorticoids on adult neurogenesis. *Current Topics in Behavioral Neuroscience, 15,* 139–164.

Schoenfeld, T. J., & others (2013). Physical exercise prevents stress-induced activation of granule neurons and enhances local inhibitory mechanisms in the dentate gyrus. *Journal of Neuroscience, 33,* 7770–7777.

Schoffstall, C. L., & Cohen, R. (2011). Cyber aggression: The relation between online offenders and offline social competence. *Social Development, 20*(3), 587–604.

Schooler, C. (2007). Use it—and keep it, longer, probably: A reply to Salthouse (2006). *Perspectives on Psychological Science, 2,* 24–29.

Schooler, C., Mulatu, S., & Oates, G. (1999). The continuing effects of substantively complex work on the intellectual functioning of older workers. *Psychology and Aging, 14,* 483–506.

Schoon, I., Jones, E., Cheng, H., & Maughan, B. (2012). Family hardship, family instability, and cognitive development. *Journal of Epidemiology and Community Health, 66*(8), 716–722.

Schueller-Weidekamm, C., & Kautzky-Willer, A. (2012). Challenges of work-life balance for women physicians/mothers working in leadership positions. *Gender Medicine, 9*(4), 244–250.

Schulenberg, J., O'Malley, P. M., Bachman, J. G., & Johnson, L. D. (2000). "Spread your wings and fly": The course of health and well-being during the transition to young adulthood. In L. Crockett & R. Silbereisen (Eds.), *Negotiating adolescence in times of social change.* New York: Cambridge University Press.

Schulenberg, J. E., & Zarrett, N. R. (2006). Mental health during emerging adulthood: Continuity and discontinuity in courses, causes, and functions. In J. J. Arnett & J. L. Tanner (Eds.), *Emerging adults in America.* Washington, DC: American Psychological Association.

Schulz, E., Wenzel, P., Munzel, T., & Daiber, A. (2014). Mitochondrial redox signaling: Interaction of mitochondrial reactive oxygen species with other sources of oxidative stress. *Antioxidants and Redox Signaling, 20*(2), 308–324.

Schunk, D. H. (2012). *Learning theories: An educational perspective* (5th ed.). Upper Saddle River, NJ: Prentice Hall.

Schunk, D. H., & Zimmerman, B. J. (2013). Self-regulation and learning. In I. B. Weiner & others (Eds.), *Handbook of psychology* (2nd ed., Vol. 7). New York: Wiley.

Schuurmans, C., & Kurrasch, D. (2013). Neurodevelopmental consequences of maternal distress: What do we really know? *Clinical Genetic, 83,* 108–117.

Schwalbe, C. S., Gearing, R. E., MacKenzie, M. J., Brewer, K. B., & Ibrahim, R. (2012). A meta-analysis of experimental studies of diversion programs for juvenile defenders. *Clinical Psychology Review, 32,* 26–33.

Schwartz, D., Kelly, B. M., Duong, M., & Badaly, D. (2010). Contextual perspective on intervention and prevention efforts for bully/victim problems. In E. M. Vernberg & B. K. Biggs (Eds.), *Preventing and treating bullying and victimization*. New York: Oxford University Press.

Schwartz, D., & others (2014, in press). Peer victimization during middle childhood as a lead indicator of internalizing problems and diagnostic outcomes in late adolescence. *Journal of Clinical Child and Adolescent Psychology*.

Schwartz, M. A., & Scott, B. M. (2012). *Marriages and families, census update* (6th ed.). Upper Saddle River, NJ: Pearson.

Schwartz, S. J., Cano, M. A., & Zamboanga, B. L. (2014, in press). The identity development of immigrant children and youth. In C. Suarez-Orozco, M. Abo-Zena, & A. K. Marks (Eds.), *The development of immigrant-origin children*. New York: New York University Press.

Schwartz, S. J., Donnellan, M. B., Ravert, R. D., Luyckx, K., & Zamboanga, B. L. (2013). Identity development, personality, and well-being in adolescence and emerging adulthood: Theory, research, and recent advances. In I. B. Weiner & others (Eds.), *Handbook of psychology* (2nd ed., Vol. 6). New York: Wiley.

Schwartz, S. J., Zamboanga, B. L., Meca, A., & Ritchie, R. A. (2012). Identity around the world: An overview. *New Directions in Child and Adolescent Development, 138,* 1–18.

Schwartz, S. J., & others (2014, in press). Identity. In J. J. Arnett (Ed.), *Oxford handbook of emerging adulthood*. New York: Oxford University Press.

Schwartz, S. J., & others (2014, in press). What have we learned since Schwartz (2001)? A reappraisal of the field. In K. McLean & M. Syed (Eds.), *Oxford handbook of identity development*. New York: Oxford University Press.

Schwartz, S. J., & others (2015a, in press). The identity dynamics of acculturation and multiculturalism: Situating acculturation in context. In V. Benet-Martinez & Y.Y Hong (Eds.), *Oxford handbook of multicultural identity*. New York: Oxford University Press.

Schwartz, S. J., & others (2015b, in press). Personal, ethnic, and cultural identity in urban youth: Links with risk and resilience. In G. Creasey & P. Jarvis (Eds.), *Adolescent development and school achievement in urban communities*. New York: Routledge.

Schwarz, B., Stutz, M., & Ledermann, T. (2012). Perceived interparental conflict and early adolescents' friendships: The role of attachment security and emotion regulation. *Journal of Youth and Adolescence, 41,* 1240–1252.

Schwarzer, R., & Luszczynska, A. (2013). Stressful life events. In I. B. Weiner & others (Eds.), *Handbook of psychology* (2nd ed., Vol. 9). New York: Wiley.

Schweinhart, L. J., & others (2005). *Lifetime effects: The High/Scope Perry Preschool Study through age 40*. Ypsilanti, MI: High/Scope Press.

Scialfa, C. T., & Kline, D. W. (2007). Vision. In J. E. Birren (Ed.), *Encyclopedia of gerontology* (2nd ed.). San Diego: Academic Press.

Sciberras, E., Ukoumunne, O. C., & Efron, D. (2011). Predictors of parent-reported attention-deficit/hyperactivity disorder in children aged 6-7 years: A national longitudinal study. *Journal of Abnormal Child Psychology, 39,* 1025–1034.

Science Daily (2008, January 15). Human gene count tumbles again, p. 1.

Scott, D., & others (2014, in press). Sarcopenic obesity and dynamic obesity: 5-year associations with falls risk in middle-aged and older adults. *Obesity*.

Scourfield, J., Van den Bree, M., Martin, N., & McGuffin, P. (2004). Conduct problems in children and adolescents: A twin study. *Archives of General Psychiatry, 61,* 489–496.

Scullin, M. K., Bugg, J. M., & McDaniel, M. A. (2012). Whoops, I did it again: Commission errors in prospective memory. *Psychology of Aging, 27,* 46–53.

Scuteri, A., & others (2014, in press). Metabolic syndrome across Europe: Different clusters of risk factors. *European Journal of Preventive Cardiology*.

Search Institute (2010). *Teen voice*. Minneapolis: Search Institute.

Seay, G. (2011). Euthanasia and common sense: A reply to Garcia. *Journal of Medical Philosophy, 36,* 321–327.

Sebastiani, P., & Perls, T. T. (2012). The genetics of extreme longevity: Lessons from the New England Centenarian study. *Frontiers in Genetics, 30*(3), 277.

Sebastiani, P., & others (2012). Whole genome sequences of a male and female supercentenarian, ages greater than 114 years. *Frontiers in Genetics, 2,* 90.

Sebastiani, P., & others (2013). Meta-analysis of genetic variants associated with human exceptional longevity. *Aging, 5,* 653–661.

Seccombe, K. (2012). *Exploring marriages and families*. Upper Saddle River, NJ: Pearson.

Seeman, T. E., & Chen, X. (2002). Risk and protective factors for physical functioning in older adults with and without chronic conditions: MacArthur Studies of Successful Aging. *Journal of Gerontology: Social Sciences, 57B,* S135–S144.

Segerberg, O. (1982). *Living to be 100: 1,200 who did and how they did it*. New York: Charles Scribner's Sons.

Seiter, L. N., & Nelson, L. J. (2011). An examination of emerging adulthood in college students and nonstudents in India. *Journal of Adolescent Research, 26,* 506–536.

Sekhobo, J. P., Edmunds, L. S., Reynolds, D. K., Dalenius, K., & Sharma, A. (2010). Trends in the prevalence of obesity and overweight among children enrolled in the New York State WIC program, 2002–2007. *Public Health Reports, 125,* 218–224.

Selman, R. L. (1980). *The growth of interpersonal understanding*. New York: Academic Press.

Sen, B. (2010). The relationship between frequency of family dinner and adolescent problem behaviors after adjusting for other characteristics. *Journal of Adolescence, 33,* 187–196.

Senechal, M., & Lefevre, J. A. (2014, in press). Continuity and change in the home literacy environment as predictors of growth in vocabulary and reading. *Child Development*.

Sengpiel, V., & others (2013). Maternal caffeine intake during pregnancy is associated with birth weight but not gestational length: Results from a large prospective observational cohort study. *BMC Medicine, 11,* 42.

Senter, L., Sackoff, J., Landi, K., & Boyd, L. (2010). Studying sudden and unexpected deaths in a time of changing death certification and investigation practices: Evaluating sleep-related risk factors for infant death in New York City. *Maternal and Child Health, 15*(2), 242–248.

Serhan, N., Eg, E., Ayranci, U., & Kosgeroglu, N. (2013). Prevalence of postpartum depression in mothers and fathers and its correlates. *Journal of Clinical Nursing, 22,* 279–284.

Serra, M. J., & Metcalfe, J. (2010). Effective implementation of metacognition. In D. J. Hacker, J. Dunlosky, & A. C. Graesser (Eds.), *Handbook of metacognition and education*. New York: Psychology Press.

Sethna, V., Murray, L., & Ramchandani, P. G. (2012). Depressed fathers' speech to their 3-month-old infants: A study of cognitive and mentalizing features in paternal speech. *Psychological Medicine, 42*(11), 2361–2371.

Setterson, R. A. (2009). Neugarten, Bernice. In D. Carr (Ed.), *Encyclopedia of the life course and human development*. Boston: Gale Cengage.

Setterson, R. A., & Trauten, M. E. (2009). The new terrain of old age: Hallmarks, freedoms, and risks. In V. L. Bengtson, D. Gans, N. M. Putney, & M. Silverstein (Eds.), *Handbook of theories of aging*. New York: Springer.

Shah, M. K., & Austin, K. R. (2014, in press). Do home visiting services received during pregnancy improve birth outcomes? Findings from Virginia PRAMS 2007–2008. *Public Health Nursing*.

Shah, R., & others (2012). Prenatal methamphetamine exposure and short-term maternal and infant medical outcomes. *American Journal of Perinatology, 29*(5), 391–400.

Shah, S. M., Carey, I. M., Harris, T., Dewilde, S., & Cook, D. G. (2012). Quality of prescribing in care homes and the community in England and Wales. *British Journal of General Practice, 62,* 329–336.

Shamah, T., & Villalpando, S. (2006). The role of enriched foods in infant and child nutrition. *British Journal of Nutrition, 96*(1, Suppl.), S73–S77.

Shan, Z. Y., Liu, J. Z., Sahgal, V., Wang, B., & Yue, G. H. (2005). Selective atrophy of left hemisphere and frontal lobe of the brain in older men. *Journals of Gerontology A: Biological Sciences and Medical Sciences, 60,* A165–A174.

Shanahan, M. J., Hill, P. L., Roberts, B. W., Eccles, J., & Friedman, H. S. (2014, in press). Conscientiousness, health, and aging: The life course of personality model. *Developmental Psychology*.

Shankar, A., Hamer, M., McMunn, A., & Steptoe, A. (2013). Social isolation and loneliness: Relationships with cognitive function during 4 years of follow-up in the English Longitudinal Study of Aging. *Psychosomatic Aging, 75,* 161–170.

Shankaran, S., & others (2010). Prenatal cocaine exposure and BMI and blood pressure at 9 years of age. *Journal of Hypertension, 28,* 1166–1175.

Shapiro, A. F., & Gottman, J. M. (2005). Effects on marriage of a psycho-education intervention with couples undergoing the transition to parenthood, evaluation at 1 year post-intervention. *Journal of Family Communication, 5,* 1–24.

Sharma, N., Classen, J., & Cohen, L. G. (2013). Neural plasticity and its contribution to functional recovery. *Handbook of Clinical Psychology, 110,* 3–12.

Shatz, M., & Gelman, R. (1973). The development of communication skills: Modifications in the speech of young children as a function of the listener. *Monographs of the Society for Research in Child Development, 38* (Serial No. 152).

Shaver, P. R., & Mikulincer, M. (2013). Attachment-related contributions to the study of psychopathology. In P. Luyten & others (Eds.), *Handbook of contemporary psychodynamic approaches to psychopathology*. New York: Guilford.

Shaw, P., & others (2007). Attention-deficit/hyperactivity disorder is characterized by a delay in cortical maturation. *Proceedings of the National Academy of Sciences, 104*(49), 19649–19654.

Shay, J. W., Reddel, R. R., & Wright, W. E. (2012). Cancer and telomeres—an ALTernative to telomerase. *Science, 336,* 1388–1390.

Shaywitz, B. A., Lyon, G. R., & Shaywitz, S. E. (2006). The role of functional magnetic resonance imaging in understanding reading and dyslexia. *Developmental Neuropsychology, 30,* 613–632.

Shaywitz, S. E., Gruen, J. R., & Shaywitz, B. A. (2007). Management of dyslexia, its rationale and underlying neurobiology. *Pediatric Clinics of North America, 54,* 609–623.

Shear, M. K. (2010). Exploring the role of experiential avoidance from the perspective of attachment theory and the dual process model. *Omega, 61,* 357–369.

Shear, M. K. (2012a). Getting straight about grief. *Depression and Anxiety, 29,* 461–464.

Shear, M. K. (2012b). Grief and mourning gone awry: Pathway and course of complicated grief. *Dialogues in Clinical Neuroscience, 14,* 119–128.

Shear, M. K., Ghesquiere, A., & Glickman, K. (2013). Bereavement and complicated grief. *Current Psychiatric Reports, 15*(11), 406.

Shear, M. K., & Skritskaya, N. A. (2012). Bereavement and anxiety. *Current Psychiatry Reports, 14,* 169–175.

Shebloski, B., Conger, K. J., & Widaman, K. F. (2005). Reciprocal links among differential parenting, perceived partiality, and self worth: A three-wave longitudinal study. *Journal of Family Psychology, 19,* 633–642.

Sheftall, A. H., Mathias, C. W., Furr, R. M., & Dougherty, D. M. (2013). Adolescent attachment security, family functioning, and suicide attempts. *Attachment and Human Development, 15,* 368–383.

Shek, D. T. (2012). Spirituality as a positive youth development construct: A conceptual review. *Scientific World Journal, No.* 458953.

Shenson, D., & others (2012). Developing an integrated strategy to reduce ethnic and racial disparities in the delivery of clinical preventive services for older Americans. *American Journal of Public Health, 102*(8), e44–e50.

Sherwood, C. C., & others (2011). Aging of the cerebral cortex differs between humans and chimpanzees. *Proceedings of the National Academy of Sciences U.S.A., 108,* 13029–13034.

Shibata, Y., & others (2012). Extrachromosomal microDNAs and chromosomal microdeletions in normal tissues. *Science, 336,* 82–86.

Shih, J., & Donmez, G. (2013). Mitochondrial sirtuins as therapeutic targets for age-related disorders. *Genes and Cancer, 4,* 91–96.

Shimazu, A., & others (2014). Work-to-family conflict and family-to-work conflict among Japanese dual-earner couples with preschool children: A spillover-crossover perspective. *Journal of Occupational Health, 55,* 234–243.

Shin, K. O., & others (2014). Exercise training improves cardiac autonomic nervous system activity in type 1 diabetic children. *Journal of Physical Therapy Science, 26,* 111–115.

Shin, S. H., Hong, H. G., & Hazen, A. L. (2010). Childhood sexual abuse and adolescence substance use: A latent class analysis. *Drug and Alcohol Dependence, 109,* 226–235.

Shiner, R. L., & DeYoung, C. G. (2013). The structure of temperament and personality: A developmental approach. In P. D. Zelazo (Ed.), *Oxford handbook of developmental psychology.* New York: Oxford University Press.

Shipley, B.A., Der, G., Taylor, M. D., & Deary, I. J. (2007). Association between mortality and cognitive change over 7 years in a large representative sample of UK residents. *Psychosomatic Medicine, 69,* 640–650.

Shirai, N., & Imura, T. (2014). Looking away before moving forward: Changes in optic-flow perception precede locomotor development. *Psychological Science, 25,* 485–493.

Shokhirev, M. N., & Johnson, A. A. (2014). Effects of extrinsic mortality on the evolution of aging: A stochastic modeling approach. *PLoS One, 9*(1), e86602.

Shor, E., Roelfs, D. J., Bugyi, P., & Schwartz, J. E. (2012). Meta-analysis of marital dissolution and mortality: Reevaluating the intersection of gender and age. *Social Science and Medicine, 75,* 46–59.

Shore, L. M., & Goldberg, C. B. (2005). Age discrimination in the work place. In R. L. Dipobye & A. Colella (Eds.), *Discrimination at work.* Mahwah, NJ: Erlbaum.

Shors, T. J. (2009). Saving new brain cells. *Scientific American, 300,* 46–52.

Shuai, L., Chan, R. C., & Wang, Y. (2011). Executive function profile of Chinese boys with attention-deficit hyperactivity disorder: Different subtypes and comorbidity. *Archives of Clinical Neuropsychology, 26,* 120–132.

Shuaib, A. A., Frass, K. A., Al-Harazi, A. H., & Ghanem, N. S. (2011). Pregnancy outcomes of mothers aged 17 years or less. *Saudi Medical Journal, 32,* 166–170.

Shukla, D. K., Keehn, B., Smylie, D. M., & Muller, R. A. (2011). Microstructural abnormalities of short-distance white matter tracts in autism spectrum disorders. *Neuropsychologia, 49,* 1378–1382.

Shultz, K. S., & Wang, M. (2011). Psychological perspectives on the changing nature of retirement. *American Psychologist, 66,* 170–179.

Shuman, V., & Scherer, K. (2014). Concepts and structure of emotions. In R. Pekrun & L. Linnenbrink-Garcia (Eds.), *International handbook of emotions in education.* New York: Routledge.

Shwalb, D. W., Shwalb, B. J., & Lamb, M. E. (2013). *Fathers in cultural context.* New York: Routledge.

Siedlecki, K. L. (2007). Investigating the structure and age invariance of episodic memory across the adult life span. *Psychology and Aging, 22,* 251–268.

Siegel, D. H. (2013). Open adoption: Adoptive parents' reactions two decades later. *Social Work, 58,* 43–52.

Siegel, R. S., & Brandon, A. R. (2014). Adolescents, pregnancy, and mental health. *Journal of Pediatric and Adolescent Gynecology, 27*(3), 138–150.

Siegler, I. C., Bosworth, H. B., Davey, A., & Elias, M. F. (2013). Disease, health, and aging in the first decade of the 21st century. In I. B. Weiner & others (Eds.), *Handbook of psychology* (2nd ed., Vol. 6). New York: Wiley.

Siegler, I. C., Bosworth, H. B., & Poon, L. W. (2003). Disease, health, and aging. In I. B. Weiner (Ed.), *Handbook of psychology* (Vol. VI). New York: Wiley.

Siegler, I. C., & Costa, P. T. (1999, August). *Personality change and continuity in midlife: UNC Alumni Heart Study.* Paper presented at the meeting of the American Psychological Association, Boston.

Siegler, I. C., Elias, M. F., Brummett, B. H., & Bosworth, H. B. (2013). Adult development and aging. In I. B. Weiner & others (Eds.), *Handbook of psychology* (2nd ed., Vol. 9). New York: Wiley.

Siegler, R. S. (2006). Microgenetic analysis of learning. In W. Damon & R. Lerner (Eds.), *Handbook of child psychology* (6th ed.). New York: Wiley.

Siegler, R. S. (2012). From theory to application and back: Following in the giant footsteps of David Klahr. In S. M. Carver & J. Shrager (Eds.), *The journey from child to scientist: Integrating cognitive development and the education sciences.* Thousand Oaks, CA: Sage.

Siegler, R. S. (2013). How do people become experts? In J. Staszewski (Ed.), *Expertise and skill acquisition: The impact of William C. Chase.* New York: Taylor & Francis.

Siegler, R. S., Fazio, L. K., Bailey, D. H., & Zhou, X. (2013). Fractions: The new frontier for theories of numerical development. *Trends in Cognitive Science, 17,* 13–19.

Siegler, R. S., & Mu, Y. (2008). Chinese children excel on novel mathematics problems even before elementary school. *Psychological Science, 19,* 759–763.

Siegler, R. S., & Thompson, C. A. (2014). Numerical landmarks are useful—except when they're not. *Journal of Experimental Child Psychology, 120,* 39–58.

Siener, S., & Kerns, K. A. (2012). Emotion regulation and depressive symptoms in preadolescence. *Child Psychiatry and Human Development, 43,* 414–430.

Sievert, L. L., & Obermeyer, C. M. (2012). Symptom clusters at midlife: A four-country comparison of checklist and qualitative responses. *Menopause, 19,* 133–144.

Silva, C. (2005, October 31). When the dynamo talks, city listens. *Boston Globe,* pp. B1, B4.

Silveira, M. J., Witala, W., & Piette, J. (2014, in press). Advance directive completion by elderly Americans: A decade of change. *Journal of the American Geriatrics Society.*

Silverstein, M. (2009). Caregiving. In D. Carr (Ed.), *Encyclopedia of the life course and human development.* Boston: Gale Cengage.

Silverstein, M., Conroy, S. J., Wang, H., Giarrusso, R., & Bengtson, V. L. (2002). Reciprocity in parent-child relation over the adult life course. *Journals of Gerontology: Psychological Sciences and Social Sciences, 57B,* S3–S13.

Silvestri, M. M., Cameron, J. M., Borsari, B., & Correia, C. J. (2013). Examining alcohol and alcohol-free versions of a simulated drinking game procedure. *Journal of Studies on Alcohol and Drugs, 74,* 329–336.

Sim, M. P. Y., & Lamb, M. E. (2014, in press). Children's disclosure about sexual abuse: How motivational factors affect linguistic categories related to deception detection. *Psychology, Crime, and Law.*

Simkin, P., & Bolding, A. (2004). Update on nonpharmacological approaches to relieve labor pain and prevent suffering. *Journal of Midwifery and Women's Health, 49,* 489–504.

Simmons, D. (2011). Diabetes and obesity in pregnancy. *Best Practice and Research, Clinical Obstetrics and Gynecology, 25,* 25–36.

Simmons, E. S., Lanter, E., & Lyons, M. (2014). Supporting mainstream educational success. In F. R. Volkmer & others (Eds.), *Handbook of autism and pervasive developmental disorders.* New York: Wiley.

Simmons, R. G., & Blyth, D. A. (1987). *Moving into adolescence.* Hawthorne, NY: Aldine.

Simon, E. J. (2015, in press). *Biology.* Upper Saddle River, NJ: Pearson.

Simon, G. E., & others (2011). Obesity, depression, and health service costs among middle-aged women. *Journal of General Internal Medicine, 26,* 1284–1290.

Simon, R. W., & Barrett, A. E. (2010). Nonmarital romantic relationships and mental health in early adulthood: Does the association differ for women and men? *Journal of Health and Social Behavior, 51,* 168–182.

Simonetti, G. D., & others (2011). Determinants of blood pressure in preschool children: the role of parental smoking. *Circulation, 123,* 292–298.

Simonton, D. K. (1996). Creativity. In J. E. Birren (Ed.), *Encyclopedia of aging.* San Diego: Academic Press.

Simpkins, S. D., Delgado, M. Y., Price, C. D., Quach, A., & Starbuck, E. (2013). Socioeconomic status, ethnicity, culture, and immigration: Examining the potential mechanisms underlying Mexican-origin adolescents' organized activity participation. *Developmental Psychology, 49*(4), 706–721.

Simpkins, S. D., Fredricks, J. A., Davis-Kean, P. E., & Eccles, J. S. (2006). Healthy mind, healthy habits: The influence of activity involvement in middle childhood. In A. C. Huston & M. N. Ripke (Eds.), *Developmental contexts in middle childhood.* New York: Cambridge University Press.

Simpkins, S. D., Vest, A. E., & Price, C. D. (2011). Intergenerational continuity and discontinuity in

Mexican-origin youths' participation in organized activities: Insights from mixed-methods. *Journal of Family Psychology, 25,* 814–824.

Simpson, E. A., & others (2014, in press). The development of facial identity discrimination through learned attention. *Developmental Biology.*

Simpson, H. B., & others (2013). Treatment of obsessive-compulsive disorder complicated by comorbid eating disorders. *Cognitive Behavior Therapy, 42,* 64–76.

Simpson, R. J., & others (2012). Exercise and the aging immune system. *Aging Research and Reviews, 1,* 404–420.

Singer, D., Golinkoff, R. M., & Hirsh-Pasek, K. (Eds.) (2006). *Play = learning: How play motivates and enhances children's cognitive and social-emotional growth.* New York: Oxford University Press.

Singer, T. (2012). The past, present, and future of social neuroscience: A European perspective. *Neuroimage, 61*(2), 437–449.

Singh-Manoux, A., & others (2012). Timing and onset of cognitive decline: Results from Whitehall II prospective cohort study. *British Medical Journal, 344,* d7622.

Sinnott, J. D. (2003). Postformal thought and adult development: Living in balance. In J. Demick & C. Andreoletti (Eds.), *Handbook of adult development.* New York: Kluwer.

Sinnott, J. D., & Johnson, L. (1997). Brief report: Complex formal thought in skilled research administrators. *Journal of Adult Development, 4,* 45–53.

Sirard, J. R., & others (2013). Physical activity and screen time in adolescents and their friends. *American Journal of Preventive Medicine, 44,* 48–55.

Sirsch, U., Dreher, E., Mayr, E., & Willinger, U. (2009). What does it take to be an adult in Australia? Views of adulthood in Australian adolescents, emerging adults and adults. *Journal of Adolescent Research, 24,* 275–292.

Skingley, A. (2013). Older people, isolation, and loneliness: Implications for community nursing. *British Journal of Community Nursing, 18,* 84–90.

Skinner, B. F. (1938). *The behavior of organisms: An experimental analysis.* New York: Appleton-Century-Crofts.

Skinner, B. F. (1957). *Verbal behavior.* New York: Appleton-Century-Crofts.

Slatcher, R. B., & Trentacosta, C. J. (2012). Influences of parent and child negative emotionality on young children's everyday behaviors. *Emotion, 12*(5), 932–942.

Slater, A. M., Bremner, J. G., Johnson, S. P., & Hayes, R. (2011). The role of perceptual processes in infant addition/subtraction events. In L. M. Oakes, C. H. Cashon, M. Casasola, & D. H. Rakison (Eds.), *Early perceptual and cognitive development.* New York: Oxford University Press.

Slater, A., Field, T., & Hernandez-Reif, M. (2007). The development of the senses. In A. Slater & M. Lewis (Eds.), *Introduction to infant development* (2nd ed.). New York: Oxford University Press.

Slater, A. M., Morison, V., & Somers, M. (1988). Orientation discrimination and cortical function in the human newborn. *Perception, 17,* 597–602.

Sleet, D. A., & Mercy, J. A. (2003). Promotion of safety, security, and well-being. In M. H. Bornstein, L. Davidson, C. L. M. Keyes, & K. A. Moore (Eds.), *Well-being.* Mahwah, NJ: Erlbaum.

Slobin, D. (1972, July). Children and language: They learn the same way around the world. *Psychology Today,* 71–76.

Smaldino, S. E., Lowther, D. L., Russell, J. W., & Mims, C. (2015). *Instructional technology and media for learning* (11th ed.). Upper Saddle River, NJ: Pearson,

Small, B. J., Dixon, R. A., McArdle, J. J., & Grimm, K. J. (2012a). Do changes in lifestyle engagement moderate cognitive decline in normal aging? Evidence from the Victoria Longitudinal Study. *Neuropsychology, 26,* 144–155.

Small, B. J., Rawson, K. S., Eisel, S., & McEvoy, C. L. (2012). *Memory and aging.* In S. K. Whitbourne & M. Sliwinski (Eds.), *Wiley-Blackwell handbook of adulthood and aging.* New York: Wiley.

Small, H. (2011). *Why not? My seventy year plan for a college degree.* Franklin, TN: Carpenter's Son Publishing.

Smetana, J. G. (2011a). *Adolescents, families, and social development: How adolescents construct their worlds.* New York: Wiley-Blackwell.

Smetana, J. G. (2011b). Adolescents' social reasoning and relationships with parents: Conflicts and coordinations within and across domains. In E. Amsel & J. Smetana (Eds.), *Adolescent vulnerabilities and opportunities: Constructivist and developmental perspectives.* New York: Cambridge University Press.

Smetana, J. G. (2013). Moral development: The social domain theory view. In P. D. Zelazo (Ed.), *Handbook of developmental psychology.* New York: Oxford University Press.

Smetana, J., Jambon, M., & Ball, C. (2014). The social domain approach to children's moral and social judgments. In M. Killen & J. Smetana (Eds.), *Handbook of moral development* (2nd ed.). New York: Oxford University Press.

Smigielski, J., Bielecki, W., & Drygas, W. (2013). Health and lifestyle-related determinants of survival rate in the male residents of the city of Lodz. *International Journal of Occupational Medicine and Environmental Health, 26,* 337–348.

Smith, A. D. (1996). Memory. In J. E. Birren (Ed.), *Encyclopedia of gerontology* (Vol. 2). San Diego: Academic Press.

Smith, A. (2014, April 3). *Older adults and technology use.* Washington, DC: Pew Research Center.

Smith, A., Chein, J., & Steinberg, L. (2014, in press). Impact of socio-emotional context, brain development, and pubertal maturation on adolescent decision making. *Hormones and Behavior.*

Smith, C., & Denton, M. (2005). *Soul searching: The religious and spiritual lives of American teenagers.* New York: Oxford University Press.

Smith, C. A., Levett, K. M., Collins, C. T., & Jones, L. (2012). Massage, reflexology, and other manual methods for pain management. *Cochrane Database of Systematic Reviews, 15*(2), CD009290.

Smith, D. D., & Tyler, N. C. (2014). *Introduction to contemporary special education.* Upper Saddle River, NJ: Pearson.

Smith, G. E., & others (2009). A cognitive training program based on principles of brain plasticity: Results from the improvement in memory with plasticity-based adaptive cognitive training (IMPACT) study. *Journal of the American Geriatrics Society, 57,* 594–603.

Smith, J. (2009). Self. In D. Carr (Ed.), *Encyclopedia of the life course and human development.* Boston: Gale Cengage.

Smith, J., & Freund, A. M. (2002). The dynamics of possible selves in old age. *Journals of Gerontology B: Psychological Sciences and Social Sciences, 57,* P492–P500.

Smith, L. E., & Howard, K. S. (2008). Continuity of paternal social support and depressive symptoms among new mothers. *Journal of Family Psychology, 22,* 763–773.

Smith, P. H., Hornish, G. G., Leonard, K. E., & Cornelius, J. R. (2012). Women ending marriage to a

problem drinking partner decrease their own risk for problem drinking. *Addiction, 108*(8), 145–146.

Smith, P. K., & Pellegrini, A. (2013). Learning through play. In R. E. Tremblay & others (Eds.), *Encyclopedia of early childhood development.* Montreal: Centre of Excellence for Early Childhood Development.

Smith, R. A., & Davis, S. F. (2013). *Psychologist as detective* (6th ed.). Upper Saddle River, NJ: Pearson.

Smith, R. E., & Hunt, R. R. (2014). Prospective memory in young and older adults: The effects of task importance and ongoing task load. *Neuropsychology, Development, and Cognition B: Aging, Neuropsychology, and Cognition, 21,* 411–431.

Smith, R. L., Rose, A. J., & Schwartz-Mette, R. A. (2010). Relational and overt aggression in childhood and adolescence: Clarifying mean-level gender differences and associations with peer acceptance. *Social Development, 19,* 243–269.

Smith, T. B., McCullough, M. E., & Poll, J. (2003). Religiousness and depression. Evidence for a main effect and the moderating influence of stressful life events. *Psychological Bulletin, 129,* 614–636.

Smits, L. L., & others (2014, in press). Regional atrophy is associated with impairment in distinct cognitive domains in Alzheimer's disease. *Alzheimer's and Dementia.*

Smock, P. J., & Gupta, S. (2013). Cohabitation in contemporary North America. In A. Booth, A. C. Crouter, & N. S. Landale (Eds.), *Just living together.* New York: Psychology Press.

Snarey, J. (1987, June). A question of morality. *Psychology Today,* pp. 6–8.

Sneed, R. S., & Cohen, S. (2013). A prospective study of volunteerism and hypertension risk in older adults. *Psychology and Aging, 28,* 578–586.

Snow, C. E., & Kang, J. Y. (2006). Becoming bilingual, biliterate, and bicultural. In W. Damon & R. Lerner (Eds.), *Handbook of child psychology* (6th ed.). New York: Wiley.

Snowdon, D. A. (2002). *Aging with grace: What the Nun Study teaches us about leading longer, healthier, and more meaningful lives.* New York: Bantam.

Snowdon, D. A. (2003). Healthy aging and dementia: Findings from the Nun Study. *Annals of Internal Medicine, 139,* 450–454.

Soares, N. S., & Patel, D. R. (2012). Office screening and early identification of children with autism. *Pediatric Clinics of North America, 59,* 89–102.

Soderstrom, M., & others (2012). Insufficient sleep predicts clinical burnout. *Journal of Occupational Health Psychology, 17,* 175–183.

Soerensen, M. (2012). Genetic variation and human longevity. *Danish Medical Journal, 59,* B4454.

Sokol, B. W., Snjezana, H., & Muller, U. (2010). Social understanding and self-regulation: From perspective-taking to theory-of-mind. In B. Sokol, U. Muller, J. Carpendale, A. Young, & G. Iarocci (Eds.), *Self- and social regulation.* New York: Oxford University Press.

Sokol, E. W. (2013). National plan to address Alzheimer's disease offers hope for new home care and hospice provisions. *Caring, 32,* 24–27.

Solana, R., & others (2012). Innate immunosenescence: Effect of aging on cells and receptors of the innate immune system in humans. *Seminars in Immunology, 24,* 331–341.

Solberg, P. A., Halvari, H., Ommundsen, Y., & Hopkins, W. G. (2014). A one-year follow-up of effects of exercise programs on well-being in older adults. *Journal of Aging and Physical Activity, 22,* 52–64.

Soller, B. (2014). Caught in a bad romance: Adolescent romantic relationships and mental health. *Journal of Health and Social Behavior, 55,* 56–72.

Solmeyer, A. R., McHale, S. M., Killoren, S. E., & Updegraff, K. A. (2011). Coparenting around siblings' differential treatment in Mexican-origin families. *Developmental Psychology, 25,* 251–260.

Solomon, E., Martin, C., Martin, D. W., & Berg, L. R. (2015, in press). *Biology* (10th ed.). Boston: Cengage.

Soneji, S., & King, G. (2012). Statistical security for social security. *Demography, 49*(3), 1037–1060.

Song, A. V., & Halpern-Felsher, B. L. (2010). Predictive relationship between adolescent oral and vaginal sex: Results from a prospective, longitudinal study. *Archives of Pediatric and Adolescent Medicine,165,* 243–249.

Song, J. J. (Ed.) (2013). *Oxford handbook of linguistic typology.* New York: Oxford University Press.

Sonnentag, S., & Frese, M. (2013). Stress in organizations. In I. B. Weiner & others (Eds.), *Handbook of psychology* (2nd ed., Vol. 12). New York: Wiley.

Sood, A. B., Razdan, A., Weller, E. B., & Weller, R. A. (2006). Children's reactions to parental and sibling death. *Current Psychiatry Reports, 8,* 115–120.

Sooryanarayana, R., Choo, W. Y., & Hairi, N. N. (2013). A review of the prevalence and measurement of elderly abuse in the community. *Trauma, Violence, and Abuse, 14,* 316–325.

Sophian, C. (1985). Perseveration and infants' search: A comparison of two- and three-location tasks. *Developmental Psychology, 21,* 187–194.

Sorensen, K., & others (2012). Recent secular trends in pubertal timing: Implications for evaluation and diagnosis of precocious puberty. *Hormone Research in Pediatrics, 77,* 137–145.

Sorensen, T. L., & Kemp, H. (2010). Ranibizumab treatment in patients with neovascular age-related macular degeneration and very low vision. *Acta Ophthalmologica, 89*(1), e97.

Sorte, J., Daeschel, I., & Amador, C. (2014). *Nutrition, health, and safety for young children* (2nd ed.). Upper Saddle River, NJ: Pearson.

Soska, K. C., & Adolph, K. E. (2014). Perception-action development from infants to adults: Perceiving affordances for reaching through openings. *Journal of Experimental Child Psychology, 117,* 92–105.

Soter, A. O. (2013). *Grammar, usage, and punctuation.* Boston: Allyn & Bacon.

Soto, C. J. (2014, in press). Is happiness good for your personality? Concurrent and prospective relations of the Big Five with subjective well-being. *Journal of Personality.*

Soto, C. J., John, O. P., Gosling, S. D., & Potter, J. (2011). Age differences in personality traits from 10 to 65: Big Five domains and facets in a large cross-sectional sample. *Journal of Personality and Social Psychology, 100,* 333–348.

Sowah, L. A., Busse, S., & Amoroso, A. (2013). HIV, tobacco use, and poverty: A potential cause of disparities in health status by race and social status. *Journal of Health Care for the Poor and Underserved, 24,* 1215–1225.

Sowell, E. R., & others (2004). Longitudinal mapping of cortical thickness and brain growth in children. *Journal of Neuroscience, 24,* 8223–8231.

Spangler, G., Johann, M., Ronai, Z., & Zimmermann, P. (2009). Genetic and environmental influence on attachment disorganization. *Journal of Child Psychology and Psychiatry, 50,* 952–961.

Specht, J., Egloff, B., & Schukle, S. C. (2011). Stability and change of personality across the life course: The impact of age and major life events on mean-level and rank-order stability of the Big Five. *Journal of Personality and Social Psychology, 101,* 862–882.

Spelke, E. S. (1979). Perceiving bimodally specified events in infancy. *Developmental Psychology, 5,* 626–636.

Spelke, E. S. (1991). Physical knowledge in infancy: Reflections on Piaget's theory. In S. Carey & R. Gelman (Eds.), *The epigenesis of mind: Essays on biology and cognition.* Hillsdale, NJ: Erlbaum.

Spelke, E. S. (2000). Core knowledge. *American Psychologist, 55,* 1233–1243.

Spelke, E. S. (2003). Developing knowledge of space: Core systems and new combinations. In S. M. Kosslyn & A. Galaburda (Eds.), *Languages of the brain.* Cambridge, MA: Harvard University Press.

Spelke, E. S. (2011). Natural number and natural geometry. In E. Brannon & S. Dehaene (Eds.), *Space, time, and number in the brain.* New York: Oxford University Press.

Spelke, E. S. (2013). Developmental sources of social divisions. *Neurosciences and the human person: New perspectives on human activities.* Unpublished manuscript, Department of Psychology, Harvard University, Cambridge, MA.

Spelke, E. S., Breinlinger, K., Macomber, J., & Jacobson, K. (1992). Origins of knowledge. *Psychological Review, 99,* 605–632.

Spelke, E. S., & Hespos, S. J. (2001). Continuity, competence, and the object concept. In E. Dupoux (Ed.), *Language, brain, and behavior.* Cambridge, MA: Bradford/MIT Press.

Spelke, E. S., & Kinzler, K. D. (2007). Core knowledge. *Developmental Science 10,* 89–96.

Spelke, E. S., & Owsley, C. J. (1979). Intermodal exploration and knowledge in infancy. *Infant Behavior and Development, 2,* 13–28.

Spence, A. P. (1989). *Biology of human aging.* Englewood Cliffs, NJ: Prentice Hall.

Spence, J. T., & Helmreich, R. (1978). *Masculinity and femininity: Their psychological dimensions.* Austin: University of Texas Press.

Sperling, R. A., Richmond, A. S., Ramsay, C. M., & Klapp, M. (2012). The measurement and predictive ability of metacognition in middle school learners. *Journal of Educational Research, 105,* 1–7.

Spidell, S., & others (2011). Grief in healthcare chaplains: An investigation of disenfranchised grief. *Journal of Health Care Chaplaincy, 17,* 75–86.

Spieker, S. J., & others (2012). Relational aggression in middle childhood: Predictors and adolescent outcomes. *Social Development, 21,* 354–375.

Spielmann, G., & others (2011). Aerobic fitness is associated with lower proportions of senescent blood T cells in man. *Brain, Behavior, and Immunity, 25,* 1521–1529.

Sprecher, S., Treger, S., & Sakaluk, J. K. (2013). Premarital sexual standards and sociosexuality: Gender, ethnicity, and cohort differences. *Archives of Sexual Behavior, 42,* 1395–1405.

Spring, J. (2014). *American education* (16th ed.). New York: McGraw-Hill.

Squier, W. (2014, in press). "Shaken baby syndrome" and forensic psychology. *Forensic Science and Medical Pathology.*

Sroufe, L. A., Coffino, B., & Carlson, E. A. (2010). Conceptualizing the role of early experience: Lessons from the Minnesota Longitudinal Study. *Developmental Review, 30,* 36–51.

Sroufe, L. A., Egeland, B., Carlson, E., & Collins, W. A. (2005). The place of early attachment in developmental context. In K. E. Grossman, K. Grossman, & E. Waters (Eds.), *The power of longitudinal attachment research. From infancy and childhood to adulthood.* New York: Guilford.

Sroufe, L. A., Waters, E., & Matas, L. (1974). Contextual determinants of infant affectional response. In M. Lewis & L. Rosenblum (Eds.), *Origins of fear.* New York: Wiley.

Stadler, Z. K., Scharder, K. A., Vijai, J., Robson, M. E., & Offit, K. (2014, in press). Cancer genomics and inherited risk. *Journal of Clinical Oncology.*

Stamatakis, E., & other (2013). Type-specific screen time associations with cardiovascular risk markers in children. *American Journal of Preventive Medicine, 44,* 481–488.

Stanford Center for Longevity (2011). *Experts consensus on brain health.* Retrieved April 30, 2011, from http://longevity.stanford.edu/mymind/cognitiveagingstatement

Stanford University Medical Center (2012). *Growth hormone deficiency.* Palo Alto, CA: Author.

Stangor, C. (2015, in press). *Research methods for the behavioral sciences* (5th ed.). Boston: Cengage.

Stankovic, M., & others (2013). Effects of caloric restriction on oxidative stress parameters. *General Physiology and Biophysics, 32,* 277–283.

Stanley, S. M., Amato, P. R., Johnson, C. A., & Markman, H. J. (2006). Premarital education, marital quality, and marital stability: Findings from a large, household survey. *Journal of Family Psychology, 20,* 117–126.

Starr, C., Evers, C., & Start, L. (2015, in press). *Biology* (9th ed.). Boston: Cengage.

Starr, L. R., & others (2012). Love hurts (in more ways than one): Specificity of psychological symptoms as predictors and consequences of romantic activity among early adolescent girls. *Journal of Clinical Psychology, 68*(4), 373–381.

Staszewski, J. (Ed.) (2013). *Expertise and skill acquisition: The impact of William C. Chase.* New York: Taylor & Francis.

Staudinger, U. M. (1996). Psychologische Produktivitat und Selbstenfaltung im Alter. In M. M. Baltes & L. Montada (Eds.), *Produktives Leben im Alter.* Frankfurt: Campus.

Staudinger, U. M., & Dorner, J. (2007). Wisdom. In J. E. Birren (Ed.), *Encyclopedia of gerontology* (2nd ed.). San Diego: Academic Press.

Staudinger, U. M., & Gluck, J. (2011). Psychological wisdom research. *Annual Review of Psychology* (Vol. 62). Palo Alto, CA: Annual Reviews.

Staudinger, U. M., & Jacobs, C. B. (2010). Life-span perspectives on positive personality development in adulthood and old age. In R. M. Lerner, W. F. Overton, A. M. Freund, & M. E. Lamb (Eds.), *Handbook of life-span development.* New York: Wiley.

Stavrinos, D., & others (2013). Impact of distracted driving on safety and traffic flow. *Accident Analysis and Prevention, 61,* 63–70.

Stawski, R. S., Cichy, K. E., Piazza, J. R., & Almei da, D. M. (2013). Associations among daily stressors and salivary cortisol: Findings from the National Study of Daily Experiences. *Psychoneuroendocrinology, 38*(11), 2654–2465.

Steck, N., & others (2013). Euthanasia and assisted suicide in selected European countries and U.S. states: Systematic literature review. *Medical Care, 51,* 938–944.

Steele, J., Waters, E., Crowell, J., & Treboux, D. (1998, June). *Self-report measures of attachment: Secure bonds to other attachment measures and attachment theory.* Paper presented at the meeting of the International Society for the Study of Personal Relationships, Saratoga Springs, NY.

Steffener, J., Barulli, D., Habeck, C., & Stern, Y. (2014). Neuroimaging explanations of age-related differences in task performance. *Frontiers in Aging Neuroscience, 6,* 46.

Steiger, A. E., Allemand, M., Robins, R. W., & Fend, H. A. (2014). Low and decreasing self-esteem during adolescence predict adult depression two decades later. *Journal of Personality and Social Psychology, 106,* 325–338.

Stein, A. D. (2014, in press). Overweight children: A growing problem. *Journal of Pediatrics.*

Stein, P. K., & others (2012). Caloric restriction may reverse age-related autonomic decline in humans. *Aging Cell, 11*(4), 644–650.

Steinberg, L. (2011). Adolescent risk-taking: A social neuroscience perspective. In E. Amsel & J. Smetana (Eds.), *Adolescent vulnerabilities and opportunities: Constructivist developmental perspectives.* New York: Cambridge University Press.

Steinberg, L. (2015a, in press). How should the science of adolescent brain pathology inform legal policy? In J. Bhabba (Ed.), *Coming of age.* Philadelphia: University of Pennsylvania Press.

Steinberg, L. (2015b, in press). The neural underpinnings of adolescent risk-taking: The roles of reward-seeking, impulse control, and peers. In G. Oettigen & P. Gollwitzer (Eds.), *Self-regulation in adolescence.* New York: Cambridge University Press.

Steinberg, L. D., & Silk, J. S. (2002). Parenting adolescents. In M. Bornstein (Ed.), *Handbook of parenting* (2nd ed., Vol. I). Mahwah, NJ: Erlbaum.

Steinberg, S. (2011, June 11). New dating site helps college students find love. *CNN Living.* Retrieved February 27, 2013, from www.cnn.com/2011/LIVING/06/22date.my.school/index.html

Steiner, J. E. (1979). Human facial expressions in response to taste and smell stimulation. In H. Reese & L. Lipsitt (Eds.), *Advances in child behavior and behavior, 13,* 257–295.

Steiner, N. J., & others (2014, in press). In-school neurofeedback training for ADHD: Sustained improvements from a randomized controlled trial. *Pediatrics.*

Stenholm, S., & others (2014, in press). Age-related trajectories of physical functioning in work and retirement: The role of sociodemographic factors, lifestyles, and disease. *Journal of Epidemiology and Community Health.*

Stephens, C., Breheny, M., & Mansvelt, J. (2014, in press). Healthy aging from the perspective of older people: A capabilities approach to resilience. *Psychology and Health.*

Steptoe, A., & Kivimaki, M. (2012). Stress and cardiovascular disease. *Nature Reviews. Cardiology, 9,* 360–370.

Steptoe, A., Shankar, A., Demakakos, P., & Wardle, J. (2013). Social isolation, loneliness, and all-cause mortality in older men and women. *Proceedings of the National Academy of Sciences, 110,* 5797–5801.

Sterin, J. C. (2014). *Mass media revolution,* (2nd ed.). Upper Saddle River, NJ: Pearson.

Stern, C., West, T. V., Jost, J. T., & Rule, N. Q. (2013). The politics of gaydar: Ideological differences in the use of gendered cues in categorizing sexual orientation. *Journal of Personality and Social Psychology, 104,* 520–541.

Stern, D. N. (2010). A new look at parent-infant interaction: Infant arousal dynamics. In B. M. Lester & J. D. Sparrow (Eds.), *Nurturing children and families: Building on the legacy of T. Berry Brazelton.* New York: Wiley.

Stern, D. N., Beebe, B., Jaffe, J., & Bennett, S. L. (1977). The infant's stimulus world during social interaction: A study of caregiver behaviors with particular reference to repetition and timing. In H. R. Schaffer (Ed.), *Studies in mother-infant interaction.* London: Academic Press.

Sternberg, K., & Sternberg, R. J. (2013). Love. In H. Pashler (Ed.), *Encyclopedia of the mind.* Thousand Oaks, CA: Sage.

Sternberg, R. J. (1986). *Intelligence applied.* San Diego. Harcourt Brace Jovanovich.

Sternberg, R. J. (1988). *The triangle of love.* New York: Basic Books.

Sternberg, R. J. (2004). Individual differences in cognitive development. In U. Goswami (Ed.), *Blackwell handbook of childhood cognitive development.* Malden, MA: Blackwell.

Sternberg, R. J. (2010). Human intelligence. In V. S. Ramachandran (Ed.), *Encyclopedia of human behavior* (2nd ed.). New York: Elsevier.

Sternberg, R. J. (2011). Individual differences in cognitive development. In U. Goswami (Ed.), *Wiley-Blackwell handbook of childhood cognitive development* (2nd ed.). Malden, MA: Blackwell.

Sternberg, R. J. (2012). Human intelligence. In V. S. Ramachandran (Ed.), *Encyclopedia of human behavior* (2nd ed.). New York: Elsevier.

Sternberg, R. J. (2013). Contemporary theories of intelligence. In I. B. Weiner & others (Eds.), *Handbook of psychology* (2nd ed., Vol. 7). New York: Wiley.

Sternberg, R. J. (2014a). Human intelligence: Historical and conceptual perspectives. In J. Wright (Ed.), *Encyclopedia of social and behavioral sciences* (2nd ed.). New York: Elsevier.

Sternberg, R. J. (2014b). Multiple intelligences in the new age of thinking. In S. Goldstein & J. Naglieri (Eds.), *Evolutionary theory.* New York: Springer.

Sternberg, R. J., & Bridges, S. L. (2014). Varieties of genius. In D. K. Simonton (Ed.), *Wiley-Blackwell handbook of genius.* New York: Wiley.

Sterns, H. L., Barrett, G. V., & Alexander, R. A. (1985). Accidents and the aging individual. In J. E. Birren & K. W. Schaie (Eds.), *Handbook of the psychology of aging.* New York: Van Nostrand Reinhold.

Sterns, H., & Huyck, M. H. (2001) The role of work in midlife. In M. Lachman (Ed.), *Handbook of midlife development.* New York: Wiley.

Stessman, J., & others (2014, in press). Loneliness, health, and longevity. *Journals of Gerontology B: Psychological Sciences and Social Sciences.*

Steur, F. B., Applefield, J. M., & Smith, R. (1971). Televised aggression and interpersonal aggression of preschool children. *Journal of Experimental Child Psychology, 11,* 442–447.

Stevens, C., & Bavelier, D. (2012). The role of selective attention on academic foundations: A cognitive neuroscience perspective. *Developmental Cognitive Neuroscience, 15*(1, Suppl.), S30–S48.

Stevenson, H. W. (1995). Mathematics achievements of American students: First in the world by the year 2000. In C. A. Nelson (Ed.), *Basic and applied perspectives on learning, cognition, and development.* Minneapolis: University of Minnesota Press.

Stevenson, H. W. (2000). Middle childhood: Education and schooling. In A. Kazdin (Ed.), *Encyclopedia of psychology.* Washington, DC, & New York: American Psychological Association and Oxford University Press.

Stevenson, H. W., Hofer, B. K., & Randel, B. (1999). *Middle childhood: Education and schooling.* Unpublished manuscript, Dept. of Psychology, University of Michigan, Ann Arbor.

Stevenson, H. W., Lee, S., & Stigler, J. W. (1986). Mathematics achievement of Chinese, Japanese, and American children. *Science, 231,* 693–699.

Stevenson, H. W., & Newman, R. S. (1986). Long-term prediction of achievement and attitudes in mathematics and reading. *Child Development, 57,* 646–659.

Stevenson, H. W., & Zusho, A. (2002). Adolescence in China and Japan: Adapting to a changing environment. In B. B. Brown, R. W. Larson, & T. S. Saraswathi (Eds.), *The world's youth.* New York: Cambridge University Press.

Stevenson, H. W., & others (1990). Contexts of achievement. *Monographs of the Society for Research in Child Development, 55* (Serial No. 221).

Stewart, A. D., & others (2012). Body image, shape, and volumetric assessments using 3D whole body laser scanning and 2D digital photography in females with a diagnosed eating disorder: Preliminary novel findings. *British Journal of Psychology, 103,* 183–202.

Stewart, A. J., Ostrove, J. M., & Helson, R. (2001). Middle aging in women: Patterns of personality change from the 30s to the 50s. *Journal of Adult Development. 8,* 23–37.

Stiggins, R. (2008). *Introduction to student involved assessment for learning* (5th ed.). Upper Saddle River, NJ: Prentice Hall.

Stikes, R., & Barbier, D. (2013). Applying the plan-do-study-act model to increase the use of kangaroo care. *Journal of Nursing Management, 21,* 70–78.

Stiles-Shields, C., Hoste, R. R., Doyle, P. M., & Le Grange, D. (2012). A review of family-based treatment for adolescents with eating disorders. *Reviews on Recent Clinical Trials, 7,* 133–140.

Stillman, T. F., Maner, J. K., & Baumeister, R. F. (2010). Thin slice of violence: Distinguishing violent from nonviolent sex offenders at a glance. *Evolution of Human Behavior, 31,* 298–303.

Stine-Morrow, E. A.L. (2007). The Dumbledore hypothesis of cognitive aging. *Current Directions in Psychological Science, 16,* 295–299.

Stine-Morrow, E. A. L., & Basak, C. (2011). Cognitive interventions. In K. W. Schaie & S. L. Willis (Eds.), *Handbook of the psychology of aging* (7th ed.). New York: Elsevier.

Stine-Morrow, E. A. L., Parisi, J. M., Morrow, D. G., Greene, J., & Park, D. C. (2007). An engagement model of cognitive optimization through adulthood. *Journals of Gerontology B: Psychological Sciences and Social Sciences, 62,* P62–P69.

Stipek, D. (2005, February 16). Commentary in *USA TODAY,* p. 10.

Stokes, C. E., & Raley, R. K. (2009). Cohabitation. In D. Carr (Ed.), *Encyclopedia of the life course and human development.* Boston: Gale Cengage.

Stone, A. A., Schwartz, J. E., Broderick, J. E., & Deaton, A. (2010). A snapshot of the age distribution of psychological well-being in the United States. *Proceedings of the National Academy of Sciences U.S.A., 107,* 9985–9990.

Stones, M., & Stones, L. (2007). Sexuality, sensuality, and intimacy. In J. E. Birren (Ed.), *Encyclopedia of gerontology* (2nd ed.). San Diego: Academic Press.

Stovitz, S. D., & others (2014). Stage 1 treatment of pediatric overweight and obesity: A pilot and feasibility randomized controlled trial. *Child Obesity, 10,* 50–57.

Stowell, J. R., Robles, T., & Kane, H. S. (2013). Psychoneuroimmunology: Mechanisms, individual differences, and interventions. In I. B. Weiner & others (Eds.), *Handbook of psychology* (2nd ed., Vol. 9). New York: Wiley.

Strand, A. (2010). Low levels of retirement resources in the near-elderly time period and future participation in means-tested programs. *Social Security Bulletin, 70,* 1–21.

Strathearn, L., Iyenger, U., Fonagy, P., Kim, S. (2012). Maternal oxytocin response during mother-infant interaction: Associations with adult temperament. *Hormones and Behavior, 61,* 429–435.

Strauss, M. A., Sugarman, D. B., & Giles-Sims, J. (1997). Spanking by parents and subsequent anti-social behavior in children. *Archives of Pediatrics and Adolescent Medicine, 151,* 761–767.

Stroebe, M., & Schut, H. (2010). The dual process model of coping with bereavement: A decade on. *Omega, 61,* 273–289.

Stroebe, M., Schut, H., & Boerner, K. (2010). Continuing bonds in adaptation to bereavement: Toward theoretical integration. *Clinical Psychology Review, 30,* 259–268.

Strout, K. A., & Howard, E. (2012). The six dimensions of wellness and cognition in aging adults. *Journal of Holistic Nursing, 30*(3), 195–204.

Strunk, A. D., & Mayer, S. D. (2013). Resistant hypertension in the elderly: Optimizing outcomes while avoiding adverse effects. *Consultant Pharmacologist, 28,* 307–312.

Stuebe, A. M., & Schwartz, E. G. (2010). The risks and benefits of infant feeding practices for women and their children. *Journal of Perinatology, 30,* 155–162.

Sturman, M. C. (2003). Searching for the inverted U-shaped relationship between time and performance: Meta-analyses of the experience/performance, tenure/performance, and age-performance relationships. *Journal of Management, 29,* 609–640.

Su, Y., & others (2013). Identification of novel human glioblastoma-specific transcripts by serial analysis of gene expression data mining. *Cancer Biomarkers, 13,* 367–375.

Suarez, L., & others (2011). Maternal smoking, passive tobacco smoke, and neural tube defects. *Birth Defects Research A: Clinical and Molecular Teratology, 91,* 29–33.

Subramaniam, P., & Woods, B. (2012). The impact of individual reminiscence therapy for people with dementia: Systematic review. *Expert Review of Neurotherapeutics, 12,* 545–555.

Substance Abuse and Mental Health Services Administration (2003). *Aging and substance abuse.* Washington, DC: U.S. Department of Health and Human Services.

Sudfeld, C. R., & others (2013). Herpes simplex virus type 2 cross-sectional seroprevalence and the estimated rate of neonatal infections among a cohort of rural Malawian female adolescents. *Sexually Transmitted Diseases, 89,* 561–567.

Sue, D., Sue, D. W., Sue, D. M., & Sue, S. (2014). *Essentials of understanding abnormal psychology* (2nd ed.). Boston: Cengage.

Sue, D., Sue, D. W., Sue, S., & Sue, D. M. (2013). *Understanding abnormal behavior* (10th ed.). Boston: Cengage.

Suehs, B. T., & others (2014). Household members of persons with Alzheimer's disease: Health conditions, healthcare resource use, and healthcare costs. *Journal of the American Geriatrics Society, 62,* 435–441.

Sugden, N. A., Mohamed-Ali, M. I., & Moulson, M. C. (2014). I spy with my little eye: Typical, daily exposure to faces documented from a first-person infant perspective. *Developmental Psychobiology, 56,* 249–261.

Sugita, Y. (2004). Experience in early infancy is indispensable for color perception. *Current Biology, 14,* 1267–1271.

Sui, X., & others (2007). Cardiorespiratory fitness and adiposity as mortality predictors in older adults. *Journal of the American Medical Association, 298,* 2507–2516.

Sullivan, A. R., & Fenelon, A. (2014). Patterns of widowhood mortality. *Journals of Gerontology B: Psychological Sciences and Social Sciences, 69,* 53–62.

Sullivan, H. S. (1953). *The interpersonal theory of psychiatry.* New York: W. W. Norton.

Sullivan, K., & Sullivan, A. (1980). Adolescent-parent separation. *Developmental Psychology, 16,* 93–99.

Sultan-Taieb, H., Chastang, J. F., Mansouri, M., & Niedhammer, I. (2013). The annual costs of cardiovascular diseases and mental disorders attributable to job strain in France. *BMC Public Health, 13,* 748.

Sun, F., & others (2012). Predicting the trajectories of depressive symptoms among southern community-dwelling older adults: The role of religiosity. *Aging and Mental Health, 16,* 189–198.

Sun, S. S., & others (2008). Childhood obesity predicts adult metabolic syndrome: The Fels Longitudinal Study. *Journal of Pediatrics, 152,* 191–200.

Sun, Y., Tao, F., Hao, J., & Wan, Y. (2010). The mediating effects of stress and coping on depression among adolescents in China. *Journal of Child and Adolescent Psychiatric Nursing, 23,* 173–180.

Sung, G., & Greer, D. (2011). The case for simplifying brain death criteria. *Neurology, 76,* 113–114.

Sung, S. C., & others (2011). Complicated grief among individuals with major depression: Prevalence, comorbidity, and associated features. *Journal of Affective Disorders, 134,* 453–458.

Super, C., & Harkness, S. (1997). The cultural structuring of child development. In J. W. Berry, Y. H. Poortinga, & J. Pandey (Eds.), *Handbook of cross-cultural psychology: Theory and method* (Vol. 2). Boston: Allyn & Bacon.

Supiano, K. P., & Luptak, M. (2014, in press). Complicated grief in older adults: A randomized controlled trial of complicated grief group therapy. *Gerontologist.*

Susman, E. J., & Dorn, L. D. (2013). Puberty: Its role in development. In I. B. Weiner & others (Eds.), *Handbook of psychology* (2nd ed., Vol. 6). New York: Wiley.

Sussman, S., & Arnett, J. J. (2014, in press). Emerging adulthood: Developmental period facilitative of the addictions. *Evaluation and the Health Professions.*

Sutcliffe, K., & others (2012). Comparing midwife-led and doctor-led maternity care: A systematic review of reviews. *Journal of Advanced Nursing, 68*(11), 2376–2386.

Suzman, R. M., Harris, T., Hadley, E. C., Kovar, M. G., & Weindruch, R. (1992). The robust oldest old: Optimistic perspectives for increasing healthy life expectancy. In R. M. Suzman, D. P. Willis, & K. G. Manton (Eds.), *The oldest old.* New York: Oxford University Press.

Swamy, G. K., Ostbye, T., & Skjaerven, R. (2008). Association of preterm birth with long-term survival, reproduction, and next generation preterm birth. *Journal of the American Medical Association, 299,* 1429–1436.

Swan, G., & others (2013). Tobacco dependence. In I. B. Weiner & others (Eds.), *Handbook of psychology* (2nd ed.). New York: Wiley.

Swanson, A., Ramos, E., & Snyder, H. (2014, in press). Next generation sequencing is the impetus for the next generation of laboratory-based genetic counselors. *Journal of Genetic Counseling.*

Swanson, H. L. (2014). Learning disabilities. In M. A. Bray & T. J. Kehle (Eds.), *Oxford handbook of school psychology.* New York: Oxford University Press.

Sweeney, M. M. (2009). Remarriage. In D. Carr (Ed.), *Encyclopedia of the life course and human development.* Boston: Gale Cengage.

Sweeney, M. M. (2010). Remarriage and stepfamilies: Strategic sites for family scholarship in the 21st century. *Journal of Marriage and the Family, 72,* 667–684.

Sweet, S., Moen, P., & Meiksins, P. (2007). Dual earners in double jeopardy: Preparing for job loss in the new risk economy. In B. A. Rubin (Ed.), *Research in the sociology of work.* New York: Elsevier.

Swing, E. L., Gentile, D. A., Anderson, C. A., & Walsh, D. A. (2010). Television and video game exposure and the development of attention problems. *Pediatrics, 126,* 214–221.

Syed, M. (2013). Assessment of ethnic identity and acculturation. In K. Geisinger (Ed.), *APA handbook of testing and assessment in psychology.* Washington, DC: American Psychological Association.

Syed, M., & Juang, L. P. (2014, in press). Ethnic identity, ethnic coherence, and psychological functioning: Testing basic assumptions of the developmental model. *Cultural Diversity and Ethnic Minority Psychology.*

Sykes, C. J. (1995). *Dumbing down our kids: Why America's children feel good about themselves but can't read, write, or add.* New York: St. Martin's Press.

Sylvain-Roy, S., Lungu, O., & Belleville, S. (2014, in press). Normal aging of the attentional control functions that underlie working memory. *Journals of Gerontology B: Psychological Sciences and Social Sciences.*

Symon, B., & Bammann, M. (2012). Feeding in the first year of life—emerging benefits of introducing comple-mentary solids from 4 months. *Australian Family Physician, 41,* 226–229.

Szanton, S. L., Seplaki, C. L., Thorpe, R. J., Allen, J. K., & Fried, L. P. (2010). Socioeconomic status is associated with frailty: The Women's Health and Aging Studies. *Journal of Epidemiology and Community Health, 64,* 63–67.

Szinovacz, M. E. (2009). Grandparenthood. In D. Carr (Ed.), *Encyclopedia of the life course and human development.* Boston: Gale Cengage.

Sztramko, R., & others (2014). Demographics, health-care utilization, and substance use profiles of older adults in Canada's lowest income neighborhood. *Canadian Geriatrics Journal, 17,* 5–11.

T

Tabuchi, M., Nakagawa, T., Miura, A., & Gondo, Y. (2014, in press). Generativity and interaction between the old and young: The role of perceived respect and perceived rejection. *Gerontologist.*

Taher, N., & others (2014). Amyloid-*b* alters the DNA methylation status of cell-fate genes in an Alzheimer's disease model. *Journal of Alzheimer's Disease, 38,* 831–844.

Taige, N. M., & others (2007). Antenatal maternal stress and long-term effects on child neurodevelopment: How and why? *Journal of Child Psychology and Psychiatry, 48,* 245–261.

Takasaki, N., & others (2014). A heterozygous mutation of GALNTL5 affects male infertility with impairment of sperm motility. *Proceedings of the National Academy of Sciences USA, 11,* 1120–1125.

Takayanagi, T., & others (2013). Cognitive outcome of very low birth weight infants at 6 years of age. *Pediatrics International, 55*(5), 594–598.

Takeuchi, H., & others (2012). Neural correlates of the differences between working memory speed and simple sensorimotor speed: An fMRI study. *PLoS One, 7*(1), e30579.

Taler, S. J. (2009). Hypertension in women. *Current Hypertension Reports, 11,* 23–28.

Tamis-LeMonda, C. S., & Song, L. (2013). Parent-infant communicative interactions in cultural context. In R. M. Lerner (Ed.), *Handbook of psychology* (Vol. 6). New York: Wiley.

Tan, E. J., Xue, Q. L., Li, T., Carlson, M. C., & Fried, L. P. (2007). Volunteering: A physical activity intervention for older adults—The Experience Corps program in Baltimore. *Journal of Urban Health, 83,* 954–969.

Tan, L. J., & others (2012). Molecular genetic studies of gene identification for sarcopenia. *Human Genetics, 131,* 1–31.

Tan, P. Z., Armstrong, L. M., & Cole, P. M. (2013). Relations between temperament and anger regulation over early childhood. *Social Development, 22,* 755–772.

Tando, T., & others (2014, in press). Developmental changes in frontal lobe function during a verbal fluency task: A multi-channel near-infrared spectroscopy study. *Brain and Development.*

Tandon, S. D., & others (2011). Preventing perinatal depression in low-income home visiting clients: A randomized controlled trial. *Journal of Consulting and Clinical Psychology, 79,* 707–712.

Tang, M., & others (2014). GSK-3/CREB pathway involved in the gx-50's effect on Alzheimer's disease. *Neuropharmacology, 81C,* 256–266.

Tang, Y., & Posner, M. I. (2009). Attention training and attention state training. *Trends in Cognitive Science, 13,* 222–227.

Tanik, S., & others (2014). Cardiometabolic risk factors in patients with erectile dysfunction. *Scientific World Journal,* 892091.

Tannen, D. (1990). *You just don't understand: Women and men in conversation.* New York: Ballantine.

Tarnanas, I., & others (2014, in press). Can a novel computerized cognitive screening test provide additional information for early detection of Alzheimer's disease? *Alzheimer's and Dementia.*

Tarokh, L., & Carskadon, M. A. (2010). Developmental changes in the human sleep EEG during early adolescence. *Sleep, 33,* 801–809.

Tashiro, T., & Frazier, P. (2003). "I'll never be in a relationship like that again": *Personal Relationships, 10,* 113–128.

Tasker, F. L., and Golombok, S. (1997). *Growing up in a lesbian family: Effects on child development.* New York: Guilford.

Tavassoli, N., & others (2013). Factors associated with the undertreatment of atrial fibrillation in geriatric outpatients with Alzheimer's disease. *American Journal of Cardiovascular Drugs, 13*(6), 425–433.

Tavernier, R., & Willoughby, T. (2014). Bidirectional associations between sleep (quality and duration) and psychological functioning across the university years. *Developmental Psychology,* 1395–1405.

Taverno Ross, S., Dowda, M., Saunders, R., & Pate, R. (2013). Double dose: The cumulative effect of TV viewing at home and in preschool on children's activity patterns and weight status. *Pediatric Exercise Science, 25,* 262–272.

Taylor, A. (2012). Introduction to the issue regarding research on age related macular degeneration. *Molecular Aspects of Medicine, 33*(4), 291–294.

Taylor, C. A., Manganello, J. A., Lee, S. J., & Rice, J. C. (2010). Mothers' spanking of 3-year-old children and subsequent risk of children's aggressive behavior. *Pediatrics, 125,* e1057–e1065.

Taylor, R. D., & Lopez, E. I. (2005). Family management practice, school achievement, and problem behavior in African American adolescents: Mediating processes. *Applied Developmental Psychology, 26,* 39–49.

Taylor, R. J., Chatters, L. M., & Jackson, J. S. (2007). Religious and spiritual involvement among older African Americans, Caribbean Blacks, and non-Hispanic Whites: Findings from the National Survey of American Life. *Journals of Gerontology: Psychological and Social Sciences* (Vol. 62b), S238–S250.

Taylor, S. E. (2011a). *Health psychology* (8th ed.). New York: McGraw-Hill.

Taylor, S. E. (2011b). Tend and befriend theory. In A. M. van Lange, A. W. Kruglanski, & E. T. Higgins (Eds.), *Handbook of theories of social psychology.* Thousand Oaks, CA: Sage.

Taylor, S. E. (2011c). Affiliation and stress. In S. S. Folkman (Ed.), *Oxford handbook of stress, health, and coping.* New York: Oxford University Press.

Taylor, S. E., & others (2000). Biobehavioral responses to stress in females: Tend-and-befriend, not fight-or-flight. *Psychological Review, 107,* 411–429.

Taylor, T., & others (2014). Computerized tomography (CT) angiography for confirmation of the clinical diagnosis of brain death. *Cochrane Database of Systematic Reviews, 3,* CD009694.

te Velde, S. J., & others (2012). Energy balance-related behaviors associated with overweight and obesity in preschool children: A systematic review of prospective studies. *Obesity Reviews, 13*(1, Suppl.), S56–S74.

Telkemeyer, S., & others (2011). Acoustic processing of temporally modulated sounds in infants: Evidence from a combined near-infrared spectroscopy and EEG study. *Frontiers in Psychology, 2,* 62.

Telzer, E. H., Fuligni, A. J., Lieberman, M. D., & Galvan, A. (2013). Meaningful family relationships: Neurocognitive buffers of adolescent risk taking. *Journal of Cognitive Neuroscience, 25,* 374–387.

Templeton, S., & Gehsmann, K. (2014). *Teaching reading and writing.* Upper Saddle River, NJ: Pearson.

Tenenbaum, H., & May, D. (2014). Gender in parent-child relationships. In P. Leman & H. Tenenbaum (Eds.), *Gender and development.* New York: Psychology Press.

Tenthani, L., & others (2014). Retention in care under universal antiretroviral therapy for HIV-infected pregnancy and breastfeeding women ('Option B+') in Malawi, *AIDS, 28,* 589–598.

Terman, L. (1925). *Genetic studies of genius. Vol. 1: Mental and physical traits of a thousand gifted children.* Stanford, CA: Stanford University Press.

Terry, D. F., Nolan, V. G., Andersen, S. L., Perls, T. T., & Cawthon, R. (2008). Association of longer telomeres with better health in centenarians. *Journals of Gerontology A: Biological Sciences and Medical Sciences, 63,* 809–812.

Terry, M. B., & Tehranifar, P. (2013). Hormone replacement therapy and breast cancer risk: More evidence of risk stratification? *Journal of the National Cancer Institute, 105*(18), 1342–1343.

Terry, W., Olson, L. G., Wilss, L., & Boulton-Lewis, G. (2006). Experience of dying: Concerns of dying patients and of carers. *Internal Medicine Journal, 36,* 338–346.

Teti, D. M., Kim, B. R., Mayer, G., & Countermine, M. (2010). Maternal availability at bedtime predicts infant sleep quality. *Journal of Family Psychology, 24,* 307–315.

Teunissen, H. A., & others (2014, in press). An experimental study of the effects of peer drinking norms on adolescents' drinker prototypes. *Addictive Behaviors.*

Tezil, T., & Basaga, H. (2014, in press). Modulation of death cell in age-related diseases. *Current Pharmaceutical Design.*

Thagard, P. (2014). Artistic genius and creative cognition. In D. K. Simonton (Ed.), *Wiley-Blackwell handbook of genius.* New York: Wiley.

Thapar, A., Collishaw, S., Pine, D. S., & Thapar, A. K. (2012). Depression in adolescence. *Lancet, 379,* 1056–1067.

Tharp, R. G. (1994). Intergroup differences among Native Americans in socialization and child cognition: An erthogenetic analysis. In P. M. Greenfield & R. Cocking (Eds.), *Cross-cultural roots of minority child development.* Mahwah, NJ: Erlbaum.

The, N. S., & others (2010). Association of adolescent obesity with risk of severe obesity in adulthood. *Journal of the American Medical Association, 304,* 2042–2047.

Thelen, E. (2000). Perception and motor development. In A. Kazdin (Ed.), *Encyclopedia of psychology.* Washington, DC, & New York: American Psychological Association and Oxford University Press.

Thelen, E., & Smith, L. B. (1998). Dynamic systems theory. In W. Damon & R. Lerner (Eds.), *Handbook of child psychology* (5th ed., Vol. 1.). New York: Wiley.

Thelen, E., & Smith, L. B. (2006). Dynamic development of action and thought. In W. Damon & R. Lerner (Eds.), *Handbook of child psychology* (6th ed.). New York: Wiley.

Thelen, E., & others (1993). The transition to reaching: Mapping intention and intrinsic dynamics. *Child Development, 64,* 1058–1098.

Theurer, W. M., & Bhavsar, A. K. (2013). Prevention of unintentional childhood injury. *American Family Physician, 87,* 502–509.

Thiele, D. M., & Whelan, T. A. (2008). The relationship between grandparent satisfaction, meaning, and generativity. *International Journal of Aging and Human Development, 66,* 21–48.

Thomas, A., & Chess, S. (1991). Temperament in adolescence and its functional significance. In R. M. Lerner, A. C. Petersen, & J. Brooks-Gunn (Eds.), *Encyclopedia of adolescence* (Vol. 2). New York: Garland.

Thomas, M. S. C., & Johnson, M. H. (2008). New advances in understanding sensitive periods in brain development. *Current Directions in Psychological Science, 17,* 1–5.

Thomas, S. A. (2013). Effective pain management of older adult hospice patients with cancer. *Home Healthcare Nurse, 31,* 242–247.

Thomas, S., & Kunzmann, U. (2014, in press). Age differences in wisdom-related knowledge: Does the age relevance of the task matter? *Journals of Gerontology B: Psychological Sciences and Social Sciences.*

Thomason, M. E., & Thompson, P. M. (2011). Diffusion imaging, white matter, and psychopathology. *Annual Review of Clinical Psychology* (Vol. 7). Palo Alto, CA: Annual Reviews.

Thompson, J., & Manore, M. (2015). *Nutrition* (4th ed.). Upper Saddle River, NJ: Pearson.

Thompson, J., Manore, M., & Vaughan, L. (2014). *Science of nutrition* (3rd ed.). Upper Saddle River, NJ: Pearson.

Thompson, M. P., Kuruwita, C., & Foster, E. M. (2009). Transitions in suicide risk in a nationally representative sample of adolescents. *Journal of Adolescent Health, 44,* 458–463.

Thompson, R. A. (2006). The development of the person. In W. Damon & R. Lerner (Eds.), *Handbook of child psychology* (6th ed.). New York: Wiley.

Thompson, R. A. (2009). Early foundations: Conscience and the development of moral character. In D. Narvaez & D. Lapsley (Eds.), *Moral self, identity and character: Prospects for a new field of study.* New York: Cambridge University Press.

Thompson, R. A. (2011). The emotionate child. In D. Cicchetti & G. I. Roissman (Eds.), *The origins and organization of adaptation and maladaptation. Minnesota Symposium on Child Psychology* (Vol. 36). New York: Wiley.

Thompson, R. A. (2012). Whither the preoperational child? Toward a life-span moral development theory. *Child Development Perspectives, 6,* 423–429.

Thompson, R. A. (2013). Attachment and its development: Precis and prospect. In P. Zelazo (Ed.),

Oxford handbook of developmental psychology. New York: Oxford University Press.

Thompson, R. A. (2014). Conscience development in early childhood. In M. Killen & J. G. Smetana (Eds.), *Handbook of moral development* (2nd ed.). New York: Psychology Press.

Thompson, R. A. (2014, in press). Early attachment and later development: New questions. In J. Cassidy & P. R. Shaver (Eds.), *Handbook of attachment* (3rd ed.). New York: Guilford.

Thompson, R. A. (2014). Why are relationships important to children's well-being? In A. Ben-Arieh, I. Frones, F. Cases, & J. Korbin (Eds.), *Handbook of child well-being*. New York: Springer.

Thompson, R. A. (2015, in press). Relationships, regulation, and development. In R. M. Lerner (Ed.), *Handbook of child psychology and developmental science* (7th ed.). New York: Wiley.

Thompson, R. A., Meyer, S. C., & McGinley, M. (2006). Understanding values in relationships: The development of conscience. In M. Killen & J. Smetana (Eds.), *Handbook of moral development*. Mahwah, NJ: Erlbaum.

Thompson, R. A., & Newton, E. K. (2013). Baby altruists? Examining the complexity of prosocial motivation in young children. *Infancy, 18,* 120–133.

Thompson, R. A., & Virmani, E. A. (2010). Self and personality. In M. H. Bornstein (Ed.), *Handbook of cultural developmental science*. New York: Psychology Press.

Thompson, R. A., Winer, A. C., & Goodvin, R. (2014, in press). The individual child: Temperament, emotion, self, and personality. In M. H. Bornstein & M. E. Lamb (Eds.), *Developmental science* (6th ed.). New York: Psychology Press.

Thompson, R. A., & others (2009, April). *Parent-child relationships, conversation, and developing emotion regulation.* Paper presented at the meeting of the Society for Research in Child Development, Denver.

Thompson, R., & others (2012). Suicidal ideation in adolescence: Examining the role of recent adverse experiences. *Journal of Adolescence, 35,* 175–186.

Thompson, W. E., & Bynum, J. E. (2013). *Juvenile delinquency* (9th ed.). Upper Saddle River, NJ: Pearson.

Thornberg, R., & Jungert, T. (2014). School bullying and mechanisms of moral disengagement. *Aggressive Behavior, 40,* 99–108.

Thornton, R., & Light, L. C. (2006). Aging and language. In J. E. Birren & K. W. Schaie (Eds.), *Handbook of the psychology of aging* (6th ed.). San Diego: Academic Press.

Tian, T., Zhang, B., Jia, Y., & Li, Z. (2014, in press). Promise and challenge: The lens model as a biomarker for early diagnosis of Alzheimer's disease. *Disease Markers.*

Tikotzky, L., Sadeh, A., & Glickman-Gavrieli, T. (2010). Infant sleep and paternal involvement in infant caregiving during the first 6 months of life. *Journal of Pediatric Psychology, 36*(1), 36–46.

Tikotzky, L., & Shaashua, L. (2012). Infant sleep and early parental sleep-related cognitions predict sleep in pre-school children. *Sleep Medicine, 13,* 185–192.

Tilton-Weaver, L. C., Burk, W. J., Kerr, M., & Stattin, H. (2013). Can parental monitoring and peer management reduce the selection or influence of delinquent peers? Testing the question using a dynamic social network approach. *Developmental Psychology, 49,* 2057–2070.

Tilton-Weaver, L. C., & Marshall, S. K. (2008). Adolescents' agency in information management. In M. Kerr, H. Stattin, & R. C. M. Engels (Eds.), *What can parents do? New insights into the role of parents in adolescent problem behavior.* New York: Wiley.

Timmermans, S., & others (2011). Individual accumulation of heterogeneous risks explains inequalities within deprived neighborhoods. *European Journal of Epidemiology, 26*(2), 165–180.

Tinetti, M. E., & others (2011). Effect of chronic disease-related symptoms and impairments on universal outcomes in older adults. *Journal of the American Geriatric Society, 59,* 1618–1627.

Tinloy, J., & others (2014). Exercise during pregnancy and risk of late term birth, cesarean delivery, and hospitalizations. *Women's Health Issues, 24,* e99–e104.

Toepper, M., & others (2014). The impact of age on load-related dorsolateral prefrontal cortex. *Frontiers in Aging Neuroscience, 6,* 9.

Tolani, N., & Brooks-Gunn, J. (2008). Family support, international trends. In M. M. Haith & J. B. Benson (Eds.), *Encyclopedia of infant and early childhood development.* Oxford, UK: Elsevier.

Tomasello, M. (2003). *Constructing a language: A usage-based theory of language acquisition.* Cambridge, MA: Harvard University Press.

Tomasello, M. (2006). Acquiring linguistic constructions. In W. Damon & R. Lerner (Eds.), *Handbook of child psychology* (6th ed.). New York: Wiley.

Tomasello, M. (2011). Language development. In U. Goswami (Ed.), *Wiley-Blackwell handbook of childhood cognitive development* (2nd ed.). New York: Wiley.

Tomasello, M. (2014). *A natural history of human thinking.* Cambridge, MA: Harvard University Press.

Tomasello, M., & Hamann, K. (2012). Collaboration in young children. *Quarterly Journal of Experimental Psychology, 65,* 1–12.

Tomiyama, A. J., & others (2012). Does cellular aging relate to patterns of allostasis? An examination of basal and stress reactive HPA axis activity and telomere length. *Physiology and Behavior, 106,* 40–45.

Tompkins, G. E. (2013). *Language arts* (8th ed.). Boston: Allyn & Bacon.

Tompkins, G. E. (2015, in press). *Literacy in the early grades* (4th ed.). Upper Saddle River, NJ: Pearson.

Tong, X., Deacon, S. H., & Cain, K. (2014). Morphological and syntactic awareness in poor comprehenders: Another piece of the puzzle. *Journal of Learning Disabilities, 47,* 22–33.

Torres, J. M. (2013). Breast milk and labor support: Lactation consultants' and doulas' strategies for navigating the medical context of maternity care. *Sociology of Health and Illness, 35*(6), 924–938.

Toth, S. L., Gravener-Davis, J. A., Guild, D. J., & Cicchetti, D. (2014, in press). Relational interventions for child maltreatment: Past, present, and future perspectives. *Development and Psychopathology.*

Toure, K., & others (2012). Positioning women's and children's health in African union policy-making: A policy analysis. *Global Health, 8,* 3.

Trainor, L. J., & He, C. (2013). Auditory and musical development. In P. D. Zelazo (Ed.), *Handbook of developmental psychology.* New York: Oxford University Press.

Traskowski, M., Yang, J., Visscher, P. M., & Plomin, R. (2013). DNA evidence for strong genetic stability and increasing heritability of intelligence from age 7 to 12. *Molecular Psychiatry, 43,* 267–273.

Trautner, H. M., & others (2005). Rigidity and flexibility of gender stereotypes in children: Developmental or differential? *Infant and Child Development, 14,* 365–381.

Trehub, S. E., Schneider, B. A., Thorpe, L. A., & Judge, P. (1991). Observational measures of auditory sensitivity in early infancy. *Developmental Psychology, 27,* 40–49.

Tremblay, M. S., & others (2012). Canadian sedentary behavior guidelines for the early years (0–4 years). *Applied Physiology, Nutrition, and Metabolism, 37,* 370–380.

Triche, E. W., & Hossain, N. (2007). Environmental factors implicated in the causation of adverse pregnancy outcome. *Seminars in Perinatology, 31,* 240–242.

Trickett, P. K., & Negriff, S. (2011). Child maltreatment and social relationships. In M. H. Underwood & L. H. Rosen (Eds.), *Social development.* New York: Guilford.

Trickett, P. K., Negriff, S., Ji, J., & Peckins, M. (2011). Child maltreatment and adolescent development. *Journal of Research on Adolescence, 21,* 3–20.

Trimble, J. E. (1988, August). *The enculturation of contemporary psychology.* Paper presented at the meeting of the American Psychological Association, New Orleans.

Trommsdorff, G. (2012). A social change and human development perspective on the value of children. In S. Bekman & A. Aksu-Koc (Eds.), *Perspectives on human development, families, and culture.* New York: Cambridge University Press.

Tronick, E. (2010). Infants and mothers: Self- and mutual regulation and meaning making. In B. M. Lester & J. D. Sparrow (Eds.), *Nurturing children and families: Building on the legacy of T. Berry Brazelton.* New York: Wiley.

Troop-Gordon, W., & Ladd, G. W. (2014, in press). Teachers' victimization-related beliefs and strategies: Associations with students' aggressive behavior and peer victimization. *Journal of Abnormal Child Psychology.*

Trost, S. G., Fees, B., & Dzewaltowski, D. (2008). Feasibility and efficacy of "move and learn" physical activity curriculum in preschool children. *Journal of Physical Activity and Health, 5,* 88–103.

Trucco, E. M., & others (2014, in press). Early adolescent alcohol use in context: How neighborhoods, parents, and peers impact youth. *Development and Psychopathology.*

Trueswell, J. C., Median, T. N., Hafri, A., & Gleitman, L. R. (2013). Propose but verify: Fast mapping meets cross-situational word learning. *Cognitive Psychology, 66,* 126–156.

Truglio, R. T., & Kotler, J. A. (2014). Language, literacy, and media: What's the word on *Sesame Street*? In E. T. Gershoff, R. S. Mistry, & D. A. Crosby (Eds.), *Societal contexts of child development.* New York: Oxford University Press.

Trukeschitz, B., Schenider, U., Muhlmann, R., & Ponocny, I. (2013). Informal eldercare and work-related strain. *Journals of Gerontology B: Psychological Sciences and Social Sciences, 68,* 257–267.

Trzesniewski, K. H., & Donnellan, M. B. (2010). Rethinking "generation me": A study of cohort effects from 1976–2006. *Perspectives on Psychological Science, 5,* 58–75.

Trzesniewski, K. H., Donnellan, M. B., & Robins, R. W. (2008). Do today's young people really think they are so extraordinary? An examination of secular trends in narcissism and self-enhancement. *Psychological Science, 19,* 181–188.

Trzesniewski, K. H., & others (2006). Adolescent low self-esteem is a risk factor for adult poor health, criminal behavior, and limited economic prospects. *Developmental Psychology, 42,* 381–390.

Trzesniewski, M., Donnellan, M. B., & Robins, R. W. (2008). Is "Generation Me" really more narcissistic than previous generations? *Journal of Personality, 76,* 903–918.

Trzesniewski, M., Donnellan, M. B., & Robins, R. W. (2013). Development of self-esteem. In V. Zeigler-Hill (Ed.), *Self-esteem.* New York: Psychology Press.

Tsang, A., & others (2008). Common persistent pain conditions in developed and developing countries: Gender and age differences and comorbidity with depression-anxiety disorders. *Journal of Pain, 9,* 883–891.

Tse, M., & others (2014). Health supplement consumption behavior in the older population: An exploratory study. *Frontiers in Public Health, 2,* 11.

Tselepis, A. D. (2014). Cilostazol-based triple antiplatelet therapy in the era of generic clopidogrel and new potent antiplatelet agents. *Current Medical Research and Opinion, 30,* 51–54.

Tsitsika, A. K., & others (2014). Bullying behaviors in children and adolescents: "An ongoing story." *Frontiers in Public Health, 2,* 7.

Tun, P. A., & Lachman, M. E. (2010). The association between computer use and cognition across adulthood: Use it so you won't lose it? *Psychology and Aging, 25*(3), 560–568.

Turchik, J. A., & Hassija, C. M. (2014, in press). Female sexual victimization among college students: Assault severity, health risk behaviors, and sexual functioning. *Journal of Interpersonal Violence.*

Turiano, N. A., & others (2012). Personality trait level and change as predictors of health outcomes: Findings of a national study of Americans (MIDUS). *Journals of Gerontology B: Psychological Sciences and Social Sciences, 67,* 4–12.

Turiel, E. (2014). Morality: Epistemology, development, and social judgments. In M. Killen & J. G. Smetana (Eds.), *Handbook of moral development* (2nd ed.). New York: Psychology Press.

Turkeltaub, P. E., Gareau, L., Flowers, D. L., Zeffiro, T. A., & Eden, G. F. (2003). Development of neural mechanisms for reading. *Nature Neuroscience, 6,* 767–773.

Turnbull, A., Rutherford-Turnbull, H., Wehmeyer, M. L., & Shogren, K. A. (2013). *Exceptional lives* (7th ed.). Upper Saddle River, NJ: Pearson.

Turner, B. F. (1982). Sex-related differences in aging. In B. B. Wolman (Ed.), *Handbook of developmental psychology.* Englewood Cliffs, NJ: Prentice Hall.

Turner, B. J., Navuluri, N., Winkler, P., Vale, S., & Finley, E. (2014, in press). A qualitative study of family healthy lifestyle behaviors of Mexican-American and Mexican immigrant fathers and mothers. *Journal of the Academy of Nutrition and Dietetics.*

Twenge, J. M., Konrath, S., Foster, J. D., Campbell, W. K., & Bushman, B. J. (2008a). Egos inflating over time: A cross-temporal meta-analysis of the Narcissistic Personality Inventory. *Journal of Personality, 76,* 875–902.

Twenge, J. M., Konrath, S., Foster, J. D., Campbell, W. K., & Bushman, B. J. (2008b). Further evidence of an increase in narcissism among college students. *Journal of Personality, 76,* 919–928.

Tyas, S. L., & others (2007). Transitions to mild cognitive impairments, dementia, and death: Findings from the Nun Study. *American Journal of Epidemiology, 165,* 1231–1238.

Tymula, A., & others (2013). Like cognitive function, decision making across the life span shows profound age-related changes. *Proceedings of the National Academy of Sciences, 110,* 17143–17148.

Tzourio, C., Laurent, S., & Debette, S. (2014, in press). Is hypertension associated with an accelerated aging in the brain? *Hypertension.*

U

Ubell, C. (1992, December 6). We can age successfully. *Parade,* pp. 14–15.

Uchino, B. N., & others (2012). Social relationships and health: Is feeling positive, negative, or both (ambivalent) about your social ties related to telomeres? *Health Psychology, 31*(6), 789–796.

Ueno, M., & others (2011). The organization of wariness of heights in experienced crawlers. *Infancy, 17,* 376–392.

Uher, R., & Rutter, M. (2012). Classification of feeding and eating disorders: Review of evidence and proposals for ICD-11. *World Psychiatry, 11,* 80–92.

Uleman, J. S., & Kressel, L. M. (2013). A brief history of theory and research in impression formation. In D. E. Carlston (Ed.), *Oxford handbook of social cognition.* New York: Oxford University Press.

Ullah, M. I., Riche, D. M., & Koch, C. A. (2014). Transdermal testosterone replacement therapy in men. *Drug Design, Development, and Therapy, 8,* 101–112.

Ulloa, A. E., & others (2014, in press). Association between copy number variation losses and alcohol dependence across African American and European American ethnic groups. *Alcoholism: Clinical and Experimental Research.*

Umana-Taylor, A. J., & Updegraff, K. A. (2013). Latino families in the United States. In G. W. Patterson & K. R. Bush (Eds.), *Handbook of marriage and the family* (3rd ed.). New York: Springer.

Umana-Taylor, A. J., Wong, J. J., Gonzalez, N. A., & Dumka, L. E. (2012). Ethnic identity and gender as moderators of the association between discrimination and academic adjustment among Mexican-origin adolescents. *Journal of Adolescence, 35*(4), 773–786.

Umana-Taylor, A. J., & others (2014, in press). Ethnic and racial identity revisited: An integrated conceptualization. *Child Development.*

UNAIDS (2011). *AIDS at 30: Nations at a crossroads.* Geneva, Switzerland: United Nations.

Underwood, M. (2004). Sticks and stones and social exclusion: Aggression among boys and girls. In P. K. Smith & C. H. Hart (Eds.), *Blackwell handbook of childhood social development.* Malden, MA: Blackwell.

Underwood, M. K. (2011). Aggression. In M. K. Underwood & L. H. Rosen (Eds.), *Social development.* New York: Wiley.

Undheim, A. M. (2013). Involvement in bullying as predictor of suicidal ideation among 12- to 15-year-old Norwegian adolescents. *European Child and Adolescent Psychiatry, 22,* 357–265.

Ungar, L., Altmann, A., & Greicius, M. D. (2014, in press). Apolipoprotein E, gender, and Alzheimer's disease: An overlooked, but potent and promising interaction. *Brain Imaging and Behavior.*

UNICEF (2004). *The state of the world's children 2004.* Geneva Switzerland: UNICEF.

UNICEF (2007). *The state of the world's children 2007.* Geneva, Switzerland: UNICEF.

UNICEF (2011). *The state of the world's children 2011.* Geneva, Switzerland: UNICEF. Switzerland.

UNICEF (2013). *The state of the world's children 2013.* Geneva, Switzerland: UNICEF.

UNICEF (2014). *The state of the world's children 2014.* Geneva, Switzerland: UNICEF.

Unick, J. L., & others (2013). The long-term effectiveness of a lifestyle intervention in severely obese individuals. *American Journal of Medicine, 126,* 236–242.

United Nations (2002). *Improving the quality of life of girls.* New York: United Nations.

Unson, C., & Richardson, M. (2013). Insights into the experiences of older workers and change: Through the lens of selection, optimization, and compensation. *Gerontologist, 53,* 484–494.

UNSTAT (2011). *Marriages and crude marriage rates.* Retrieved September 4, 2013, from http://unstats.un.org/unsd/demographic/products/dyb/dyb2011/Table23.pdf

Urquia, M. L., O'Campo, P. J., & Ray, J. G. (2013). Marital status, duration of cohabitation, and psychological well-being among childbearing women: A Canadian nationwide study. *American Journal of Public Health, 103,* e8–e15.

Ursache, U. A., Blair, C., Stifter, C., & Voegtline, K. (2013). Emotional reactivity and regulation in infancy interact to predict executive functioning in early childhood. *Developmental Psychology, 49*(1), 127–137.

U.S. Bureau of Labor Statistics (2008). *Employment of older workers.* Washington, DC: Author.

U.S. Bureau of Labor Statistics (2012). *Employment of older workers.* Washington, DC: Author.

U.S. Bureau of Labor Statistics (2013). *Volunteering in the United States 2013.* Washington, DC: Author.

U.S. Census Bureau (2010). *People.* Washington, DC: Author.

U.S. Census Bureau (2011). Census Bureau reports 64 percent increase in the number of children living with a grandparent over the last two decades. Retrieved September 2, 2011, from www.census.gov/prod/2011pubs/p.70-126.pdf

U.S. Census Bureau (2011, May 8). *Mother's Day: May 8, 2011.* Retrieved August 28, 2011, from www.census/gov/newsroom/releases/archives/facts_for_features_special_editions/cb

U.S. Census Bureau (2011, September). Income, poverty, and health insurance coverage in the United States: 2010. *Current Population Survey, Annual Social and Economic Supplement,* P60–239.

U.S. Census Bureau (2012). *Death statistics.* Washington, DC: Author.

U.S. Census Bureau (2012). *Families and living arrangements 2012.* Washington, DC: Author.

U.S. Census Bureau (2012). *Profile American: Facts for features. Father's Day: June 17, 2012.* Washington, DC: Author.

U.S. Census Bureau (2013). *Births, deaths, marriages, divorces.* Washington, DC: Author.

U.S. Census Bureau (2013). *People.* Washington, DC: Author.

U.S. Census Bureau (2013). *Poverty.* Washington, DC: Author.

U.S. Department of Energy (2001). *The human genome project.* Washington, DC: Author.

U.S. Department of Health and Human Services (2010). *Child maltreatment 2009.* Washington, DC: Author.

U.S. Department of Health and Human Services (2014). *Folic acid.* Retrieved February 1, 2014, from www.cdc.gov/ncbddd/folicacid/

Utz, R. L., Caserta, M., & Lund, D. (2012). Grief, depressive symptoms, and physical health among recently bereaved spouses. *Gerontologist, 52,* 460–471.

Utz, R. L., & others (2014). Feeling lonely versus being alone: Loneliness and social support among recently bereaved persons. *Journals of Gerontology B: Psychological Sciences and Social Sciences, 69,* 85–94.

V

Vahia, I. V., & others (2011). Psychological protective factors across the lifespan: Implications for psychiatry. *Psychiatric Clinics of North America, 34,* 231–248.

Vaillant, G. E. (1977). *Adaptation of life.* Boston: Little, Brown.

Vaillant, G. E. (1992). Is there a natural history of addiction? In C. P. O'Brien & J. H. Jaffe (Eds.), *Addictive states.* Cambridge, MA: Harvard University Press.

Vaillant, G. E. (2002). *Aging well.* Boston: Little, Brown.

Vaish, A., Carpenter, M., & Tomasello, M. (2010). Young children selectively avoid helping people with harmful intentions. *Child Development, 81,* 1661–1669.

Valcarel-Ares, M. N., & others (2014, in press). Mitochondrial dysfunction promotes and aggravates the inflammatory response in normal human synoviocytes. *Rheumatology.*

Valdiviezo, C., Lawson, S., & Ouyang, P. (2013). An update on menopausal hormone replacement therapy in women and cardiovascular disease. *Current Opinion in Endocrinology, Diabetes, and Obesity, 20,* 148–155.

Valente, T. W., & others (2013). A comparison of peer influence measures as predictors of smoking among predominately Hispanic/Latino high school adolescents. *Journal of Adolescent Health, 52,* 358–364.

Valenzuela, C. F., Morton, R. A., Diaz, M. R., & Topper, L. (2012). Does moderate drinking harm the fetal brain? Insights from animal models. *Trends in Neuroscience, 35*(5), 284–292.

Valkanova, V., & Ebmeier, K. P. (2014, in press). Neuroimaging in dementia. *Maturitas.*

Van Assche, L., & others (2013). Attachment in old age: Theoretical assumptions, empirical findings, and implications for clinical practice. *Clinical Psychology Review, 33,* 67–81.

van de Weijer-Bergsma, E., Formsa, A. R., de Bruin, E., & Bogels, S. M. (2012). The effectiveness of mindfulness training on behavioral problems and attentional functioning in adolescents with ADHD. *Journal of Child and Family Studies, 21,* 775–787.

van den Boom, D. C. (1989). Neonatal irritability and the development of attachment. In G. A. Kohnstamm, J. E. Bates, & M. K. Rothbart (Eds.), *Temperament in childhood.* New York: Wiley.

van den Dries, L., Juffer, F., van IJzendoorn, M. H., & Bakersman-Kranenburg, M. J. (2010). Infants' physical and cognitive development after international adoption from foster care or institutions in China. *Journal of Developmental and Behavioral Pediatrics, 31,* 144–150.

van den Kommer, T. N., & others (2013). Depression and cognition: How do they interrelate in old age? *American Journal of Geriatric Psychiatry, 21,* 398–410.

van Dijk, M., Hunnius, S., & van Geert, P. (2012). The dynamics of feeding during the introduction to solid food. *Infant Behavior and Development, 35,* 226–239.

van Geel, M., Vedder, P., & Tanilon, J. (2014, in press). Relationship between peer victimization, cyberbullying, and suicide in children and adolescents: A meta-analysis. *JAMA Pediatrics.*

van Goethem, A. A. J., & others (2012). The role of adolescents' morality and identity in volunteering: Age and gender differences in the process model. *Journal of Adolescence, 35,* 509–520.

Van Hecke, V., & others (2012). Infant responding to joint attention, executive processes, and self-regulation in preschool children. *Infant Development and Behavior, 35,* 303–311.

van Hooft, E. A. (2014). Motivating and hindering factors during the reemployment process: The added value of employment counselors' assessment. *Journal of Occupational Health Psychology, 19,* 1–17.

van IJzendoorn, M. H., & Kroonenberg, P. M. (1988). Cross-cultural patterns of attachment: A meta-analysis of the Strange Situation. *Child Development, 59,* 147–156.

Van Norstrand, D. W., & others (2012). Connexin43 mutation causes heterogeneous gap junction loss and sudden infant death. *Circulation, 125,* 474–481.

Van Ryzin, M. J., Carlson, E. A., & Sroufe, L. A. (2011). Attachment discontinuity in a high-risk sample. *Attachment and Human Development, 13,* 381–401.

Van Ryzin, M. J., Johnson, A. B., Leve, L. D., & Kim, H. K. (2011). The number of sexual partners and health-risking sexual behavior: Prediction from high school entry to high school exit. *Archives of Sexual Behavior, 40,* 939–949.

Vandell, D. L., & others (2010). Do effects of early childcare extend to age 15 years? From the NICHD Study of Early Child Care and Youth Development. *Child Development, 81,* 737–756.

Vanderwert, R. E., & Nelson, C. A. (2014). The use of near-infrared spectroscopy in the study of typical and atypical development. *Neuroimage, 85,* 264–271.

Vanhalst, J., Luyckx, K., Raes, F., & Goossens, L. (2012). Loneliness and depression symptoms: The mediating and moderating role of uncontrollable ruminative thoughts. *Journal of Psychology, 146,* 259–276.

VanKim, N. A., & Laska, M. N. (2012). Socioeconomic disparities in emerging adult weight and weight behaviors. *American Journal of Health Behavior, 3*(4), 433–445.

Varner, M. W., & others (2014). Association between stillbirth and illicit drug use and smoking during pregnancy. *Obstetrics and Gynecology, 123,* 113–125.

Vasiliadis, H. M., Forget, H., & Preville, M. (2013). The association between self-reported daily hassles and cortisol levels in depression and anxiety in community living older adults. *International Journal of Geriatric Psychiatry, 28,* 991–997.

Vaughan, C. A., & Halpern, C. T. (2010). Gender differences in depressive symptoms during adolescence: The contributions of weight-related concerns and behaviors. *Journal of Research on Adolescence, 20,* 389–419.

Vaughn, B. E., Elmore-Staton, L., Shin, N., & el-Sheikh, M. (2014, in press). Sleep as a support for social competence, peer relations, and cognitive functioning in preschool children. *Behavioral Sleep Medicine.*

Vaughn, S. R., & Bos, C. S. (2015, in press). *Strategies for teaching students with learning and behavior problems* (9th ed.). Upper Saddle River, NJ: Pearson.

Vaughn, S. R., Bos, C. S., & Schumm, J. S. (2014). *Teaching students who are exceptional, diverse, and at risk in the general education classroom* (6th ed.). Upper Saddle River, NJ: Pearson.

Vazsonyi, A. T., & Huang, L. (2010). Where self-control comes from: On the development of self-control and its relationship to deviance over time. *Developmental Psychology, 46,* 245–257.

Vedam-Mai, V., & others (2014). Increased precursor cell proliferation after deep brain stimulation for Parkinson's disease: A human study. *PLoS One, 9*(3), e88770.

Veerman, J. L., & others (2012). Television viewing time and reduced life expectancy: A life table analysis. *British Journal of Sports Medicine, 46,* 927–930.

Velayudhan, L., & others (2014, in press). Review of brief cognitive tests for patients with suspected dementia. *International Psychogeriatrics.*

Velders, M., & Diel, P. (2013). How sex hormones promote skeletal muscle regeneration. *Sports Medicine, 43*(11), 1089–1100.

Velez, C. E., Wolchik, S. A., Tein, J. Y., & Sandler, I. (2011). Protecting children from the consequences of divorce: A longitudinal study of the effects of parenting on children's coping responses. *Child Development, 82,* 244–257.

Vellas, B., & Aisen, P. S. (2010). Editorial: Early Alzheimer's trials: New developments. *Journal of Nutrition, Health, and Aging, 14,* 293.

Venners, S. A., & others (2004). Paternal smoking and pregnancy loss: A prospective study using a biomarker of pregnancy. *American Journal of Epidemiology, 159,* 993–1001.

Ventura, S. J., & Hamilton, B. E. (2011, February). U.S. teenage birth rate resumes decline. *NCHS Data Brief, 58,* 1–3.

Vera, E., & others (2013). Telomerase reverse transcriptase synergizes with calorie restriction to increase health span and extend mouse longevity. *PLoS One, 8*(1), e53760.

Verghese, J., Ambrose, A. F., Lipton, R. B., & Wang, C. (2010). Neurological gait abnormalities and risk of falls in older adults. *Journal of Neurology, 257,* 392–398.

Verhoef, M., van den Eijnden, R. J., Koning, I. M., & Vollebergh, W. A. (2014, in press). Age at menarche and adolescent alcohol use. *Journal of Youth and Adolescence.*

Verly, M., & others (2014). Altered functional connectivity of the language network in ASD: Role of classical language areas and cerebellum. *Neuroimage Clinical, 4,* 374–382.

Veronica, G., & Esther, R. R. (2012). Aging, metabolic syndrome, and the heart. *Aging and Disease, 3,* 269–279.

Vetter, N. C., & others (2014, in press). Ongoing development of social cognition in adolescence. *Child Neuropsychology.*

Viachantoni, A. (2012). Financial inequality and gender in older people. *Maturitas, 72*(2), 104–107.

Vigorito, C., & Giallauria, F. (2014). Effects of exercise on cardiovascular performance in the elderly. *Frontiers in Physiology, 5,* 51.

Vihman, M. M. (2014). *Phonological development* (2nd ed.). New York: Wiley.

Villaverde Gutierrez, C., & others (2012). Influence of exercise on mood in postmenopausal women. *Journal of Clinical Nursing, 21,* 923–928.

Vincent, H. K., Raiser, S. N., & Vincent, K. R. (2012). The aging musculoskeletal system and obesity-related considerations with exercise. *Aging Research and Reviews, 11,* 361–373.

Vinik, J., Almas, A., & Grusec, J. (2011). Mothers' knowledge of what distresses and comforts their children predicts children's coping, empathy, and prosocial behavior. *Parenting: Science and Practice, 11,* 56–71.

Virnig, B., & others (2004). Does Medicare managed care provide equal treatment for mental illness across race? *Archives of General Psychiatry, 61,* 201–205.

Virta, J. J., & others (2013). Midlife cardiovascular risk factors and late cognitive impairment. *European Journal of Epidemiology, 28,* 405–416.

Visher, E., & Visher, J. (1989). Parenting coalitions after remarriage: Dynamics and therapeutic guidelines. *Family Relations, 38,* 65–70.

Vissers, D., & others (2013). The effect of exercise on visceral adipose tissue in overweight adults: A systematic review and meta-analysis. *PLoS One, 8*(2), e56415.

Vitaro, F., Boivin, M., & Bukowski, W. M. (2009). The role of friendship in child and adolescent psychological development. In K. H. Rubin, W. M. Bukowski, & B. Laursen (Eds.), *Handbook of peer interaction, relationships, and groups.* New York: Guilford.

Vittrup, B., Holden, G. W., & Buck, M. (2006). Attitudes predict the use of physical punishment: A prospective study of the emergence of disciplinary practices. *Pediatrics, 117,* 2055–2064.

Vlatkovic, I. B., & others (2014, in press). Prenatal diagnosis of sex chromosome aneuploidies and disorders of sex development—A retrospective analysis of 11-year data. *Journal of Perinatal Medicine.*

Volbrecht, M. M., & Goldsmith, H. H. (2010). Early temperamental and family predictors of shyness and anxiety. *Developmental Psychology, 46,* 1192–1205.

Volkmar, F. R., Riechow, B., Westphal, A., & Mandell, D. S. (2014). Autism and autism spectrum diagnostic concepts. In F. R. Volkmar & others (Eds.), *Handbook of autism and pervasive developmental disorders.* New York: Wiley.

Volpe, E. M., Hardie, T. L., Cerulli, C., Sommers, M. S., & Morrison-Beedy, D. (2013). What's age got to do with it? Partner age difference, power, intimate partner violence, and sexual risk in urban adolescents. *Journal of Interpersonal Violence, 28,* 2068–2087.

Volpe, R. J., & Chafouleas, S. M. (2014). Assessment of externalizing behavior deficits. In M. A. Bray & T. J. Kehle (Eds.), *Oxford handbook of school psychology.* New York: Oxford University Press.

von Bonsdorff, M. B., & others (2011). Work ability in midlife as a predictor of mortality and disability in later life: A 28-year prospective follow-up study. *Canadian Medical Association Journal, 183,* E235-E242.

von Bonsdorff, M. B., & others (2012). Work ability as a determinant of old age disability severity: Evidence from the 28-year Finnish longitudinal study on municipal employees. *Aging: Clinical and Experimental Research, 24,* 354–360.

Von Korff, L., & Grotevant, H. D. (2011). Contact in adoption and adoptive family identity formation: The mediating role of family conversation. *Journal of Family Psychology, 25,* 393–401.

Von Polier, G. G., Vioet, T. D., & Herpertz-Dahlmann, B. (2012). ADHD and delinquency—A developmental perspective. *Behavioral Sciences and the Law, 30,* 121–139.

Vong, K-I. (2012). Play—A multimodal manifestation in kindergarten education in China. *Early Years: An International Journal of Research and Development, 32*(1), 35–48.

Voorpostel, M., & Blieszner, R. (2008). Intergenerational solidarity and support between adult siblings. *Journal of Marriage and the Family, 70,* 157–167.

Voss, M. W., Vivar, C., Kramer, A. F., & van Praag, H. (2013). Bridging animal and human models of exercise-induced brain plasticity. *Trends in Cognitive Science, 17,* 525–544.

Votavova, H., & others (2012). Deregulation of gene expression induced by environmental tobacco smoke exposure in pregnancy. *Nicotine and Tobacco Research, 14*(9), 1073–1082.

Votruba-Drzal, E., Coley, R. L., & Chase-Lansdale, P. L. (2004). Child care and low-income children's development: Direct and moderated effects. *Child Development, 75,* 296–312.

Vozzola, E. C. (2014). *Moral development: Theory and applications.* New York: Psychology Press.

Vrangalova, Z. (2014, in press). Does casual sex harm college students' well-being? A longitudinal investigation of the role of motivation. *Archives of Sexual Behavior.*

Vrangalova, Z., & Savin-Williams, R. C. (2012). Mostly heterosexual and mostly gay/lesbian: New sexual orientation identities and the sexual orientation continuum. *Archives of Sexual Behavior, 41*(1), 85–101.

Vrantsidis, F., & others (2014). Living Longer Living Stronger: A community-delivered strength training program improving function and quality of life. *Australasian Journal of Aging, 33,* 22–25.

Vromman, A., & others (2013). β-amyloid context intensifies vascular smooth muscle cells' induced-inflammatory response and de-differentiation. *Aging Cell, 13*(3), 358–369.

Vuolo, M., Staff, J., & Mortimer, J. T. (2012). Weathering the great recession: Psychological and behavioral trajectories in the transition from school to work. *Developmental Psychology, 48,* 1759–1773.

Vurpillot, E. (1968). The development of scanning strategies and their relation to visual differentiation. *Journal of Experimental Child Psychology, 6,* 632–650.

Vygotsky, L. S. (1962). *Thought and language.* Cambridge, MA: MIT Press.

W

Waber, D. P. (2010). *Rethinking learning disabilities.* New York: Guilford Press.

Wachs, T. D. (1994). Fit, context and the transition between temperament and personality. In C. Halverson, G. Kohnstamm, & R. Martin (Eds.), *The developing structure of personality from infancy to adulthood.* Hillsdale, NJ: Erlbaum.

Wachs, T. D. (2000). *Necessary but not sufficient.* Washington, DC: American Psychological Association.

Wagner, L., & Hoff, E. (2013). Language development. In I. B. Weiner & others (Eds.), *Handbook of psychology* (2nd ed.). New York: Wiley.

Waite, L. J. (2005, June). *The case for marriage.* Paper presented at the ninth annual Smart Marriages conference, Dallas.

Waite, L. J. (2009). Marriage. In D. Carr (Ed.), *Encyclopedia of the life course and human development.* Boston: Gale Cengage.

Waite, L. J., Das, A., & Laumann, E. O. (2009). Sexual activity, later life. In D. Carr (Ed.), *Encyclopedia of the life course and human development.* Boston: Gale Cengage.

Walden, T. (1991). Infant social referencing. In J. Garber & K. Dodge (Eds.), *The development of emotional regulation and dysregulation.* New York: Cambridge University Press.

Waldenstrom, U., & others (2014). Adverse pregnancy outcomes related to advanced maternal age compared with smoking and being overweight. *Obstetrics and Gynecology, 123,* 104–112.

Waldinger, R. J., & Schulz, M. C. (2010). What's love got to do with it? Social functioning, perceived health, and daily happiness in married octogenarians. *Psychology and Aging, 25,* 422–431.

Waldinger, R. J., Vaillant, G. E., & Orav, E. J. (2007). Childhood sibling relationships as a predictor of major depression in adulthood: A 30-year prospective study. *American Journal of Psychiatry, 164,* 949–954.

Walker, L. (1982). The sequentiality of Kohlberg's stages of moral development. *Child Development, 53,* 1130–1136.

Walker, L. H. M., & Syed, M. (2013). Integrating identities: Ethnic and academic identities among diverse college students. *Teachers College Record, 115*(8), 1–24.

Walker, L. J. (2002). In W. Damon (Ed.), *Bringing in a new era of character education.* Stanford, CA: Hoover Press.

Walker, L. J. (2004). Progress and prospects in the psychology of moral development. *Merrill-Palmer Quarterly, 50,* 546–557.

Walker, L. J. (2014, in press). Exemplars' moral behavior is self-regarding. *New Directions for Child and Adolescent Development.*

Walker, L. J. (2014). Moral personality, motivation, and identity. In M. Killen & J. G. Smetana (Eds.), *Handbook of moral development* (2nd ed.). New York: Taylor & Frances.

Walker, L. J. (2014). Prosocial exemplarity in adolescence and adulthood. In L. Padilla-Walker & G. Carlo (Eds.), *Prosocial behavior.* New York: Oxford University Press.

Walker, L. J., & Frimer, J. A. (2009). Moral personality exemplified. In D. Narváez & D. K. Lapsley (Eds.),

Personality, identity and character: Explorations in moral psychology (pp. 232–255). New York: Cambridge University Press.

Walker, R., & others (2013). Marital satisfaction in older couples: The role of satisfaction with social networks and psychological well-being. *International Journal of Aging and Human Development, 76,* 123–139.

Walker, S. (2006). Unpublished review of J. W. Santrock's *Topical approach to life-span development* (3rd ed.). New York: McGraw-Hill.

Wallenborg, K., & others (2009). Red wine triggers cell death and thiroredoxin reductase inhibition: Effects beyond resveratrol and SIRT 1. *Experimental Cell Research, 315,* 1360–1371.

Waller, E. M., & Rose, A. J. (2010). Adjustment trade-offs of co-rumination in mother-adolescent relationships. *Journal of Adolescence, 33,* 487–497.

Wallerstein, J. S. (2008). Divorce. In M. M. Haith & J. B. Benson (Eds.), *Encyclopedia of infant and early childhood development.* Oxford, UK: Elsevier.

Walsh, L. V. (2013). Historical reflection on health promotion within midwifery care in the United States. *Journal of Midwifery and Women's Health, 58,* 253–256.

Walsh, R. (2011). Lifestyle and mental health. *American Psychologist, 66,* 79–92.

Walter, T. (2012). Why different countries manage death differently: A comparative analysis of modern urban societies. *British Journal of Sociology, 63,* 123–145.

Wan, G. W. Y., & Leung, P. W. L. (2010). Factors accounting for youth suicide attempt in Hong Kong: A model building. *Journal of Adolescence, 33,* 575–582.

Wandell, P. E., Carlsson, A. C., & Theobald, H. (2009). The association between BMI value and long-term mortality. *International Journal of Obesity, 33,* 577–582.

Wang, B., & Jin, K. (2014, in press). Current perspectives on the link between neuroinflammation and neurogenesis. *Metabolic Brain Disease.*

Wang, B., & others (2014). The impact of youth, family, peer, and neighborhood risk factors on developmental trajectories of risk involvement from early through middle adolescence. *Social Science Medicine, 106,* 43–52.

Wang, F., & others (2014, in press). The effects of tai chi on depression, anxiety, and psychological well-being: A systematic review and meta-analysis. *International Journal of Behavioral Medicine.*

Wang, H. M., Chen, T. C., Jiang, S. Q., Liu, Y. J., & Tian, J. W. (2014, in press). Association of conventional risk factors for cardiovascular disease with IMT in middle-aged and elderly Chinese. *International Journal of Cardiovascular Imaging.*

Wang, J., Chen, T., & Han, B. (2014). Does co-residence with adult children associate with better psychological well-being among the oldest old in China? *Aging and Mental Health, 18,* 232–239.

Wang, J., & others (2013). Unintended effect of cardiovascular drugs on the pathogenesis of Alzheimer's disease. *PLoS One, 8*(6), e65232.

Wang, M. (2012). Retirement: An adult developmental perspective. In S. K. Whitbourne & M. Sliwinski (Eds.), *Wiley-Blackwell handbook of adulthood and aging.* New York: Wiley.

Wang, R., Li, J., Fang, H., Tian, M., & Liu, J. (2012). Individual differences in holistic processing predict face recognition ability. *Psychological Science, 23,* 169–177.

Wang, W. C., & others (2013). Hydroxyurea is associated with lower costs of care of young children with sickle cell anemia. *Pediatrics, 132,* 677–683.

Ward, E. V., Berry, C. J., & Shanks, D. R. (2013). Age effects on explicit and implicit memory. *Frontiers in Psychology, 4,* 639.

Ward, W. F., & others (2005). Effects of age and caloric restriction on lipid peroxidation: Measurement of oxidative stress by F2-isoprostane levels. *Journals of Gerontology A: Biological Sciences and Medical Sciences, 60,* 847–851.

Ward-Griffin, C., Oudshoorn, A., Clark, K., & Bol, N. (2007). Mother-adult daughter relationships within dementia care: A critical analysis. *Journal of Family Nursing, 13,* 13–32.

Wardlaw, G. M., & Smith, A. M. (2015, in press). *Contemporary nutrition* (4th ed.). New York: McGraw-Hill.

Wardlaw, G. M., Smith, A. M., & Collene, A. L. (2015, in press). *Contemporary nutrition* (4th ed.). New York: McGraw-Hill.

Ward-Ritacco, C. L., & others (2014, in press). Adiposity, physical activity, and muscle quality are independently related to physical function performance in middle-aged postmenopausal women. *Menopause.*

Ware, J. E., Kosinski, M., Dewey, J. E. (2000). *How to score Version 2 of the SF-36 Health Survey.* Boston: QualityMetric.

Waring, J. D., Addis, D. R., & Kensinger, E. A. (2013). Effects of aging on neural connectivity underlying selective memory for emotional scenes. *Neurobiology of Aging, 34*(2), 451–467.

Warr, P. (2004). Work, well-being, and mental health. In J. Baring, E. K. Kelloway, & M. R. Frone (Eds.), *Handbook of work stress.* Thousand Oaks, CA. Sage.

Warrier, V., Baron-Cohen, S., & Chakrabarti, B. (2014, in press). Genetic variations in GABRB3 is associated with Asperger syndrome and multiple endophenotypes relevant to autism. *Molecular Autism.*

Warshak, R. A. (2007, January). Personal communication, Department of Psychology, University of Texas at Dallas, Richardson.

Warshak, R. A. (2014). Social science and parenting plans for young children: A consensus report. *Psychology, Public Policy, and the Law, 20,* 46–67.

Watamura, S. E., Phillips, D. A., Morrissey, D. A., McCartney, T. W., & Bub, K. (2011). Double jeopardy: Poorer social-emotional outcomes for children in the NICHD SECCYD who experience home and child-care environments that convey risk. *Child Development, 82,* 48–65.

Waters, S. F., West, T. V., & Mendes, W. B. (2014, in press). Stress contagion: Physiological covariation between mothers and infants. *Psychological Science.*

Watson, D. (2012). Objective tests as instruments of psychological theory and research. In H. Cooper (Ed.), *APA handbook of research methods in psychology.* Washington, DC: American Psychological Association.

Watson, G. L., Arcona, A. P., Antonuccio, D. O., & Healy, D. (2014). Shooting the messenger: The case of ADHD. *Journal of Contemporary Psychotherapy, 44,* 43–52.

Watson, J. A., Randolph, S. M., & Lyons, J. L. (2005). African-American grandmothers as health educators in the family. *International Journal of Aging and Human Development, 60,* 343–356.

Watson, J. B. (1928). *Psychological care of infant and child.* New York: W. W. Norton.

Watts, C., & Zimmerman, C. (2002). Violence against women: Global scope and magnitude. *Lancet, 359,* 1232–1237.

Waxman, S. (2013). Building a better bridge. In M. Banaji, S. Gelman, & S. Lehr (Eds.), *Navigating the social world: The early years.* New York: Oxford University Press.

Waxman, S., & others (2014, in press). Are nouns learned before verbs? Infants provide insight into a longstanding debate. *Child Development Perspectives.*

Wayne, A. (2011). Commentary in interview: Childhood cancers in transition. Retrieved April 12, 2011, from http://home.ccr.cancer.gov/connections/2010/Vol4_No2/clinic2.asp

Wayne, P. M., & others (2014, in press). Effects of tai chi on cognitive performance in older adults: Systematic review and meta-analysis. *Journal of the American Geriatrics Society.*

Weakley, A., & Schmitter-Edgecombe, M. (2014, in press). Analysis of verbal fluency ability in Alzheimer's disease: The role of clustering, switching, and semantic proximities. *Archives of Clinical Neuropsychology.*

Webb, L. D., Metha, A., & Jordan, K. F. (2013). *Foundations of American education* (7th ed.). Upper Saddle River, NJ: Pearson.

Webb, M. S., Passmore, D., Cline, G., & Maguire, D. (2014, in press). Ethical issues related to caring for low birth weight infants. *Nursing Ethics.*

Weber, M. A., Risdon, R. S., Ashworth, M. T., Malone, M. T., & Sebire, N. J. (2012). Autopsy findings of co-sleeping-associated sudden unexpected death in infancy: Relationship between pathological features and asphyxial mode of death. *Journal of Pediatric and Child Health, 48,* 335–341.

Webster, J. D., Westerhof, G. J., & Bohlmeijer, E. T. (2014). Wisdom and mental health across the lifespan. *Journals of Gerontology B: Psychological Sciences and Social Sciences, 69,* 209–218.

Wechsler, H., & others (2002). Trends in college binge drinking during a period of increased prevention efforts: Findings from four Harvard School of Public Health college alcohol study surveys, 1993–2001. *Journal of American College Health, 50,* 203–217.

Wehby, G. L., & others (2011). The impact of maternal smoking during pregnancy on early child neurodevelopment. *Journal of Human Capital, 5,* 207–254.

Wei, R., & others (2013). Dynamic expression of microRNAs during the differentiation of human embryonic stem cells into insulin-producing cells. *Gene, 518*(2), 246–255.

Wei, Y., & others (2014, in press). Paternally induced transgenerational inheritance of susceptibility to diabetes in mammals. *Proceedings of the National Academy of Sciences U.S.A.*

Weikert, D. P. (1993). Long-term positive effects in the Perry Preschool Head Start Program. Unpublished data, High Scope Foundation, Ypsilanti, MI.

Weinberg, A. E., & others (2013). Diabetes severity, metabolic syndrome, and the risk of erectile dysfunction. *Journal of Sexual Medicine, 10*(12), 3102–3109.

Weiner, C. P., & Buhimschi, C. (2009). *Drugs for pregnant and lactating women* (2nd ed.). London: Elsevier.

Weinraub, M., & others (2012). Patterns of developmental change in infants' nighttime sleep awakenings from 6 to 36 months of age. *Developmental Psychology, 48*(6), 1511–1528.

Weisleder, A., & Fernald, A. (2014, in press). Talking to children matters: Early language experience strengthens processing and builds vocabulary. *Psychological Science.*

Weisman, O., Zagoory-Sharon, O., & Feldman, R. (2014). Oxytocin administration, salivary testosterone, and father-infant social behavior. *Progress in Neuro-Psychopharmacology and Biological Psychiatry, 49,* 47–52.

Weisner, T. S., & Duncan, G. J. (2014). The world isn't linear or additive or decontextualized: Pluralism and mixed methods in understanding the effects of antipoverty programs on children and parenting. In E. T. Gershoff, R. S. Mistry, & D. A. Crosby (Eds.), *The societal contexts of child development.* New York; Oxford University Press.

Weiss, D., Sassenberg, K., & Freund, A. M. (2013). When feeling different pays off: How older adults can counteract negative age-related information. *Psychology and Aging, 28,* 1140–1146.

Weiss, L. A., & others (2008). Association between microdeletion and microduplication at 16p11.2 and autism. *New England Journal of Medicine, 358,* 667–675.

Weissman, P., & Hendrick, J. (2014). *The whole child: Developmental education for the early years* (10th ed.). Upper Saddle River, NJ: Pearson.

Welch, A. A., & Hardcastle, A. C. (2014, in press). The effects of flavonoids on bone. *Current Osteoporosis Reports.*

Wellman, H. M. (2011). Developing a theory of mind. In U. Goswami (Ed.), *Wiley-Blackwell handbook of childhood cognitive development* (2nd ed.). New York: Wiley.

Wellman, H. M., Cross, D., & Watson, J. (2001). Meta-analysis of theory-of-mind development: The truth about false belief. *Child Development, 72,* 655–684.

Wellman, H. M., & Woolley, J. D. (1990). From simple desires to ordinary beliefs: The early development of everyday psychology. *Cognition, 35,* 245–275.

Wells, E. M., & others (2011). Body burdens of mercury, lead, selenium, and copper among Baltimore newborns. *Environmental Research, 111,* 411–417.

Wen, X., & others (2014). In vivo monitoring of neural stem cells after transplantation in acute cerebral infarction with dual-modal MR imaging and optical imaging. *Biomaterials, 35,* 4627–4635.

Wenestam, C. G., & Wass, H. (1987). Swedish and U.S. children's thinking about death: A qualitative study and cross-cultural comparison. *Death Studies, 11,* 99–121.

Wenger, N. K. (2014, in press). Prevention of cardiovascular diseases: Highlights for the clinician of the 2013 American College of Cardiology/American Heart Association guidelines. *Clinical Cardiology.*

Wenger, N. S., & others. (2003). The quality of medical care provided to vulnerable community-dwelling older patients. *Annals of Internal Medicine, 139,* 740–747.

Wenger, N. S., & others (2013). Implementation of Physician Orders for Life Sustaining Treatment in nursing homes in California: Evaluation of a novel statewide dissemination mechanism. *Journal of General Internal Medicine, 28,* 51–57.

Wentzel, K. R. (1997). Student motivation in middle school: The role of perceived pedagogical caring. *Journal of Educational Psychology, 89,* 411–419.

Wentzel, K. R. (2013). School adjustment. In I. B. Weiner & others (Eds.), *Handbook of psychology* (2nd ed., Vol. 7). New York: Wiley.

Wentzel, K. R., & Asher, S. R. (1995). The academic lives of neglected, rejected, popular and controversial children. *Child Development. 66,* 754–763.

Wentzel, K. R., Barry, C. M., & Caldwell, K. A. (2004). Friendships in middle schools: Influences on motivation and school adjustment. *Journal of Educational Psychology, 96,* 195–203.

Werker, J. F., & Gervain, J. (2013). Speech perception in infancy: A foundation of language acquisition. In P. D. Zelazo (Ed.), *Handbook of developmental psychology.* New York: Oxford University Press.

Werner, A., Uldbjerg, N., Zachariae, R., Wu, C. S., & Nohr, E. A. (2013). Antenatal hypnosis training and childbirth experience: A randomized controlled trial. *Birth, 40,* 272–280.

Werner, N. E., & others (2014, in press). Maternal social coaching quality interrupts the development of relational aggression during early childhood. *Social Development.*

West, K., Mathews, B., & Kerns, K. A. (2013). Mother-child attachment and cognitive performance in middle childhood: An examination of mediating mechanisms. *Early Childhood Research Quarterly, 28,* 259–270.

West, S. K., & others (2010). Older drivers and failure to stop at red lights. *Journals of Gerontology A: Biological Sciences and Medical Sciences, 65A,* 179–183.

Westerhof, G. J. (2009). Age identity. In D. Carr (Ed.), *Encyclopedia of the life course and human development.* Boston: Gale Cengage.

Westerhof, G. J., Whitbourne, S. K., & Freeman, G. P. (2012). The aging self in a cultural context: The relation of conceptions of aging to identity processes and self-esteem in the United States and the Netherlands. *Journals of Gerontology B: Psychological Sciences and Social Sciences, 67,* 52–60.

Westerman, G., Thomas, M. S. C., & Karmiloff-Smith, A. (2011). Neuroconstructivism. In U. Goswami (Ed.), *Wiley-Blackwell handbook of childhood cognitive development* (2nd ed.). New York: Wiley.

Wethington, E., Kessler, R. C., & Pixley, J. E. (2004). Turning points in adulthood. In O. G. Brim, C. D. Ryff, & R. C. Kessler (Eds.), *How healthy are we?* Chicago: University of Chicago Press.

Whaley, L. (2013). Syntactic typology. In J. J. Song (Ed.), *Oxford handbook of linguistic typology.* New York: Oxford University Press.

Whaley, S. E., Jiang, L., Gomez, J., & Jenks, E. (2011). Literacy promotion for families participating in the Women, Infants, and Children program. *Pediatrics, 127,* 454–461.

Whaley, S. E., Ritchie, L. D., Spector, P., & Gomez, J. (2013). Revised WIC food package improves diets of WIC families. *Journal of Nutrition and Education Behavior, 44*(3), 204–209.

Wheeden, A., & others (1993). Massage effects on cocaine-exposed preterm neonates. *Journal of Developmental and Behavioral Pediatrics, 14,* 318–322.

Wheeler, J. J., Mayton, M. R., & Carter, S. L. (2015, in press). *Methods of teaching students with autism spectrum disorders.* Upper Saddle River, NJ: Pearson.

Whitbourne, S. K., & Meeks, S. (2011). Psychopathology, bereavement, and aging. In K. W. Schaie & S. L. Willis (Eds.), *Handbook of the psychology of aging* (7th ed.). New York: Elsevier.

White, E., Slane, J. D., Klump, K. L., Burt, S. A., & Pivarnik, J. (2014, in press). Sex differences in genetic and environmental influences on percent body fatness and physical activity. *Journal of Physical Activity and Health.*

White, J. W. (2001). Aggression and gender. In J. Worell (Ed.), *Encyclopedia of gender and women.* San Diego: Academic Press.

White, K., Yeager, V. A., Menachemi, N., & Scarinci, I. C. (2014, in press). Impact of Alabama's immigration law on access to health care among Latina immigrants and children: Implications for national reform. *American Journal of Public Health.*

White, L. (1994). Stepfamilies over the life course: Social support. In A. Booth and J. Dunne (Eds.), *Stepfamilies: Who benefits and who does not.* Hillsdale, NJ: Erlbaum.

White, R., & Kramer-Albers, E. M. (2014). Axon-glia interaction and membrane traffic in myelin formation. *Frontiers in Cellular Neuroscience, 7,* 284.

Whitehead, B. D., & Popenoe, D. (2003). *The state of our unions.* Piscataway, NJ: The National Marriage Project, Rutgers University.

Whiteman, S. D., McHale, S. M., & Soli, A. (2011). Theoretical perspectives on sibling relationships. *Journal of Family Theory and Review, 3,* 124–139.

Whitton, S. W., Stanley, S. M., Markman, H. W., & Johnson, C. A. (2013). Attitudes toward divorce, commitment, and divorce proneness in first marriages and remarriages, *75,* 276–287.

Wickelgren, I. (1999). Nurture helps to mold able minds. *Science, 283,* 1832–1834.

Widman, L., & McNulty, J. K. (2010). Sexual narcissism and the perpetration of sexual aggression. *Archives of Sexual Behavior, 39,* 939–946.

Widman, L., & others (2014, in press). Sexual communication between early adolescents and their dating partners, parents, and best friends. *Journal of Sexual Research.*

Widom, C. S., Czaja, S. J., Bentley, T., & Johnson, M. S. (2012). A prospective investigation of physical health outcomes in abused and neglected children: New findings from a 30-year follow-up. *American Journal of Public Health, 102*(6), 1135–1144.

Wiecko, F. M. (2014). Late-onset offending: Fact or fiction. *International Journal of Offender Therapy and Comparative Criminology, 58,* 107–129.

Wilcox, S., & others (2003). The effects of widowhood on physical and mental health, health behaviors, and health outcomes: The women's health initiative. *Health Psychology, 22,* 513–522.

Wilczynski, S. M., & others (2014). Evidence-based practice and autism spectrum disorders. In M. A. Bray & T. J. Kehle (Eds.), *Oxford handbook of school psychology.* New York: Oxford University Press.

Wilder-Smith, A., Mustafa, F. B., Earnest, A., Gen, L., & Macary, P. A. (2013). Impact of partial sleep deprivation on immune markers. *Sleep Medicine, 14*(10), 1031–1034.

Wilhelms, E. A., & Reyna, V. F. (2013). Fuzzy trace theory and medical decisions by minors: Differences in reasoning between adolescents and adults. *Journal of Medicine and Philosophy, 38,* 268–282.

Wilhelmsen, L., & others (2011). Factors associated with reaching 90 years of age: A study of men born in 1913 in Gothenberg, Sweden. *Journal of Internal Medicine, 269,* 441–451.

Wilhelmus, M. M., de Jager, M., Bakker, E. N., & Drukarch, B. (2014, in press). Tissue transglutaminase in Alzheimer's disease: Involvement in pathogenesis and its potential as a therapeutic target. *Journal of Alzheimer's Disease.*

Wilkinson-Lee, A. M., Russell, S. T., Lee, F. C.H., & The Latina/o Teen Pregnancy Prevention Workgroup (2006). Practitioners' perspectives on cultural sensitivity in Latina pregnancy prevention. *Family Relations, 55,* 376–389.

Willcox, B. J., & Willcox, M. D. (2014). Caloric restriction, caloric restriction mimetics, and healthy aging in Okinawa: Controversies and clinical implications. *Current Opinion in Clinical Nutrition and Metabolic Care, 17,* 51–58.

Willcox, B. J., Willcox, M. D., & Suzuki, M. (2002). *The Okinawa Program.* New York: Crown.

Willcox, D. C., Scapagnini, G., & Willcox, B. J. (2014, in press). Healthy aging diets other than Mediterranean: A focus on the Okinawan diet. *Mechanisms of Aging and Development.*

Willcox, D. C., Willcox, B. J., He, Q., Wang, N. C., & Suzuki, M. (2008). They really are that old: A validation study of centenarian prevalence in Okinawa. *Journals of Gerontology A: Biological Sciences and Medical Sciences, 63,* 338–349.

Willcox, D. C., Willcox, B. J., Sokolovsky, J., & Sakihara, S. (2007). The cultural context of "successful aging" among older women weavers in a Northern Okinawan village: The role of productive activity. *Journal of Cross Cultural Gerontology, 22,* 137–165.

Willett, W. (2013). The current evidence on healthy eating. *Annual Review of Nutrition* (Vol. 34). Palo Alto, CA: Annual Reviews.

Willette, A. A., & others (2012). Calorie restriction reduces the influence of glucoregulatory dysfunction on regional brain volume in aged rhesus monkeys. *Diabetes, 61,* 1036–1042.

Willey, J., Sherwood, L., & Woolverton, C. (2014). *Prescott's microbiology* (9th ed.). New York: McGraw-Hill.

Williams, B. K., Sawyer, S. C., & Wahlstrom, C. M. (2012). *Marriages, families, and intimate relationships* (2nd ed.). Upper Saddle River, NJ: Pearson.

Williams, D. R., & Sternthal, M. J. (2007). Spirituality, religion, and health: Evidence and research directions. *Medical Journal of Australia, 186*(Suppl.), S47–S50.

Williams, G. L., Keigher, S., & Williams, A. V. (2012). Spiritual well-being among older African Americans in a midwestern city. *Journal of Religion and Health, 51*(2), 355–370.

Williams, J., & others (2014). Is there a place for extended assessments in addressing child sexual abuse allegations? How sensitivity and specificity impact professional perspectives. *Journal of Child Sexual Abuse, 23,* 179–197.

Williams, J. L., Aiyer, S. M., Durkee, M. I., & Tolan, P. H. (2014, in press). The protective role of ethnic identity for urban adolescent males facing multiple stressors. *Journal of Youth and Adolescence.*

Williamson, J. B. (2011). The future of retirement security. In R. H. Binstock & L. K. George (Eds.), *Handbook of aging and the social sciences* (7th ed.). New York: Elsevier.

Williamson, R. A., Donohue, M. R., & Tully, E. C. (2013). Learning how to help others: Two-year-olds' social learning of a prosocial act. *Journal of Experimental Child Psychology, 114,* 543–550.

Willis, J., & Todorov, A. (2006). First impressions: Making up your mind after a 100-ms exposure to a face. *Psychological Science, 17,* 592–598.

Willis, S. L., & Caskie, G. (2013). Reasoning training in the ACTIVE study: Who benefits. *Journal of Aging and Health, 25,* 8.

Willis, S. L., & Martin, M. (2005). Preface. In S. C. Willis & M. Martin (Eds.), *Middle adulthood.* Thousand Oaks, CA: Sage.

Willis, S. L., & Schaie, K. W. (2005). Cognitive trajectory in midlife and cognitive functioning in old age. In S. K. Wills & M. Martin (Eds.), *Middle adulthood.* Thousand Oaks, CA: Sage.

Willis, S. L., & Schaie, K. W. (2006). A co-constructionist view of the third age: The case of cognition. *Annual Review of Gerontology and Geriatrics* (Vol. 26). Palo Alto, CA: Annual Reviews.

Willis, S. L., & others (2006). Long-term effects of cognitive training on everyday functional outcomes in older adults. *Journal of the American Medical Association, 296,* 2805–2814.

Willoughby, K. A., Desrocher, M., Levine, B., & Rovet, J. F. (2012). Episodic and semantic autobiographical memory and everyday memory during late childhood and early adolescence. *Frontiers in Psychology, 3,* 53.

Wilson, A. E., Shuey, K. M., & Elder, G. H. (2003). Ambivalence in relationships of adult children to aging parents and in-laws. *Journal of Marriage and the Family, 65,* 1055–1072.

Wilson, D., & Hockenberry, M. (2012). *Wong's clinical manual of pediatric nursing* (7th ed.). New York: Elsevier.

Wilson, D. M., & others (2013). The preferred place of the last days: Results of a representative population-based public survey. *Journal of Palliative Medicine, 16,* 502–508.

Wilson, K. R., Havighurst, S. S., & Harley, A. E. (2012). Tuning in to kids: An effectiveness trial of a parenting program targeting emotion socialization of preschoolers. *Journal of Family Psychology, 26,* 56–65.

Wilson, R. S., Mendes de Leon, C. F., Bienas, J. L., Evans, D. A., & Bennett, D. A. (2004). Personality and mortality in old age. *Journal of Gerontology Psychological Sciences and Social Sciences, 59,* P110–P116.

Wilson, R. S., & others (2002). Participation in cognitively stimulating activities and risk of incident Alzheimer disease. *Journal of the American Medical Association, 287,* 742–748.

Wilson, R. S., & others (2012). Terminal dedifferentiation of cognitive abilities. *Neurology, 78,* 1116–1122.

Windle, M. (2012). Longitudinal data analysis. In H. Cooper (Ed.), *APA handbook of research methods in psychology.* Washington, DC: American Psychological Association.

Windsor, T. D., & Butterworth, P. (2010). Supportive, aversive, ambivalent, and indifferent partner evaluations in midlife and young-old adulthood. *Journals of Gerontology B: Psychological Sciences and Social Sciences, 65B,* 287–295.

Winett, R. A., & others (2014). Developing a new treatment paradigm for disease prevention and healthy aging. *Translational Behavioral Medicine, 4,* 117–123.

Wing, R., & others (2007). "STOP Regain": Are there negative effects of daily weighing? *Journal of Consulting and Clinical Psychology, 75,* 652–656.

Wink, P., & Dillon, M. (2002). Spiritual development across the adult life course. Findings from a longitudinal study. *Journal of Adult Development, 9,* 79–94.

Winner, E. (1996). *Gifted children: Myths and realities.* New York: Basic Books.

Winner, E. (2006). Development in the arts. In W. Damon & R. Lerner (Eds.), *Handbook of child psychology* (6th ed.). New York: Wiley.

Winner, E. (2009). Toward broadening our understanding of giftedness: The spatial domain. In F. D. Horowitz, R. F. Subotnik, & D. J. Matthews (Eds.), *The development of giftedness and talent across the life span.* Washington, DC: American Psychological.

Winner, E. (2014). Child prodigies and adult genius: A weak link. In D. K. Simonton (Ed.), *Wiley-Blackwell handbook of genius.* New York: Wiley.

Winner, F. (1986, August.). Where pelicans kiss seals. *Psychology Today,* pp. 24–35.

Winsler, A., Carlton, M. P., & Barry, M. J. (2000). Age-related changes in preschool children's systematic use of private speech in a natural setting. *Journal of Child Language, 27,* 665–687.

Winsper, C., Lereya, T., Zanarini, M., & Wolke, D. (2012). Involvement in bullying and suicide-related behavior at 11 years: A prospective birth cohort study. *Journal of the Academy of Child and Adolescent Psychiatry, 51,* 271–282.

Wirth, M., & others (2014, in press). Neuroprotective pathways: Lifestyle activity, brain pathology, and cognition in cognitively normal older adults. *Neurobiology of Aging.*

Wise, P. M. (2006). Aging of the female reproductive system. In E. J. Masoro & S. N. Austad (Eds.), *Handbook of the biology of aging* (6th ed.). San Diego: Academic Press.

Wisniwski, T., & Goni, F. (2014). Immunotherapy for Alzheimer's disease. *Biochemical Pharmacology, 88,* 499–507.

Wisse, L. E., & others (2014, in press). Hippocampal subfield volumes at 7T in early Alzheimer's disease and normal aging. *Neurobiology of Aging.*

Wit, J. M., Kiess, W., & Mullis, P. (2011). Genetic evaluation of short stature: Best practices and research. *Clinical Endocrinology and Metabolism, 25,* 1–17.

Witherington, D. C., Campos, J. J., Harriger, J. A., Bryan, C., & Margett, T. E. (2010). Emotion and its development in infancy. In J. G. Bremner & T. D. Wachs (Eds.), *Wiley-Blackwell handbook of infant development* (2nd ed.). New York: Wiley.

Witkin, H. A., & others (1976). Criminality in XYY and XXY men. *Science, 193,* 547–555.

Witt, W. P., & others (2014). Maternal stressful life events prior to conception and the impact on infant birth in the United States. *American Journal of Public Health, 104*(1, Suppl.), S81–S89.

Witte, A. V., Fobker, M., Gellner, R., Knecht, S., & Fioel, A. (2009). Caloric restriction improves memory in elderly humans. *Proceedings of the National Academy of Sciences U.S.A., 106,* 1255–1260.

Witte, A. V., & others (2014, in press). Long-chain omega-3 fatty acids improve brain function and structure in older adults. *Cerebral Cortex.*

Wittig, S. L., & Spatz, D. L. (2008). Induced lactation: Gaining a better understanding. *MCN, The Journal of Maternal Child Nursing, 33,* 76–81.

Wojtowicz, A., & others (2011). Aspirin resistance may be associated with adverse pregnancy outcomes. *Neuroendocrinology Letters, 32,* 334–339.

Wolfinger, N. H. (2011). More evidence for trends in the intergenerational transmission of divorce: A completed cohort approach using data from the general social survey. *Demography, 48,* 581–592.

Wolinsky, F. D., Vander Weg, M. W., Howren, M. B., Jones, M. P., & Dotson, M. M. (2013). A randomized controlled trial of cognitive training using a visual speed of processing intervention in middle aged and older adults. *PLoS One,8*(5), e61624.

Wolitzky-Taylor, K. B., & others (2011). Reporting rape in a national sample of college women. *American Journal of College Health, 59,* 582–587.

Wolke, D., Schreier, A., Zanarini, M. C., & Winsper, C. (2012). Bullied by peers in childhood and borderline personality symptoms at 11 years of age: A prospective study. *Journal of Child Psychology and Psychiatry, 53*(8), 846–855.

Wong, C. G., & Stevens, M. C. (2012). The effects of stimulant medication on working memory functional connectivity in attention-deficit/hyperactivity disorder. *Biological Psychiatry, 71,* 458–466.

Wong, F., & others (2013). Cerebrovascular control is altered in healthy term infants when they sleep prone. *Sleep, 36,* 1911–1918.

Wong, M. M., & Brower, K. J. (2012). The prospective relationship between sleep problems and suicidal behavior in the National Longitudinal Study of Adolescent Health, *Journal of Psychiatric Research, 46,* 953–959.

Wong, S. S., Sugimoto-Matsuda, J. J., Chang, J. Y., & Hishinuma, E. S. (2012). Ethnic differences in risk factors for suicide among American high school students, 2009: The vulnerability of multiracial and Pacific Islander adolescents. *Archives of Suicide Research, 16,* 159–173.

Woods, S. P., & others (2014, in press). Event-based prospective memory is independently associated with self-report of medication management in older adults. *Aging and Mental Health.*

Woodward, A. L., & Markman, E. M. (1998). Early word learning. In D. Kuhn & R. S. Siegler (Eds.), *Handbook of child psychology* (5th ed., Vol. 2). New York: Wiley.

Woodward, A., Markman, E., & Fitzsimmons, C. (1994). Rapid word learning in 13- and 18-month-olds. *Developmental Psychology, 30,* 553–556.

Woolett, L. A. (2011). Review: Transport of maternal cholesterol to the fetal circulation. *Placenta, 32*(2, Suppl.), S18–S21.

Woolverton, C., Prescott, L. M., Harley, J. P., & Klein, D. A. (2014). *Prescott's microbiology* (9th ed.). New York: McGraw-Hill.

World Health Organization (2000, February 2). *Adolescent health behavior in 28 countries.* Geneva, Switzerland: World Health Organization.

Worthington, E. L. (1989). Religious faith across the life span: Implications for counseling and research. *Counseling Psychologist, 17,* 555–612.

Wright, J. (2006, March 16). Boomers in the bedroom: Sexual attitudes and behaviours in the boomer generation. Ipsos Reid survey. Retrieved February 28, 2009, from http://www.ipsos-na.com

Wright, M. F., & Li, Y. (2013). The association between cyber victimization and subsequent cyber aggression: The moderating effect of peer rejection. *Journal of Youth and Adolescence, 42,* 662–674.

Wrzus, C., Hanel, M., Wagner, J., & Neyer, F. J. (2013). Social network changes and life events across the life span: A meta-analysis. *Psychological Bulletin, 139*(1), 53–80.

Wu, L. F., Chuo, L. J., & Wu, S. T. (2012). The effect of group instrumental reminiscence therapy in older single veterans who live in a veterans home in Taiwan. *International Journal of Geriatric Psychiatry, 27,* 107–108.

Wu, L. T., & Blazer, D. G. (2011). Illicit and nonmedical drug use among older adults: A review. *Journal of Aging and Health, 23,* 481–504.

Wu, T., Gao, X., Chen, M., & van Dam, R. M. (2009). Long-term effectiveness of diet-plus-exercise interventions vs. diet-only interventions for weight loss: A meta-analysis. *Obesity Review, 10,* 313–323.

Wu, T. W., & others (2014, in press). Maintenance of whole-body therapeutic hypothermia during patient transport and magnetic resonance imaging. *Pediatric Radiology.*

Wu, W. S., Liu, Z., & Ho, S. C. (2010). Metabolic syndrome and all-cause mortality: A meta-analysis of prospective cohort studies. *European Journal of Epidemiology, 25,* 375–384.

Wuest, D. A., & Fisette, J. L. (2015). *Foundations of physical education, exercise science, and sport* (18th ed.). New York: McGraw-Hill.

Wynn, K. (1992). Addition and subtraction by human infants. *Nature, 358,* 749–570.

Wyse, R. D., Dunbar, G. L., & Rossignol, J. (2014). Use of genetically modified mesenchymal stem cells to treat neurodegenerative diseases. *International Journal of Molecular Sciences, 15,* 1719–1745.

X

Xiao, O., & others (2013). A large prospective investigation of sleep duration, weight change, and obesity in the NIH-AARP Diet and Health Study cohort. *American Journal of Epidemiology, 178,* 1600–1610.

Xiao, W. S., Quinn, P. C., Pascalis, O., & Lee, K. (2014, in press). Own- and other-race face scanning in infants: Implications for perceptual narrowing. *Developmental Psychobiology.*

Xie, Q., & Young, M. E. (1999). Integrated child development in rural China. *Education: The World Bank.* Washington, DC: The World Bank.

Xiu-Ying, H., & others (2012). Living arrangements and risk for late life depression: A meta-analysis of published literature. *International Journal of Psychiatry in Medicine, 43,* 19–34.

Xu, F., Spelke, E., & Goddard, S. (2005). Number sense in human infants. *Developmental Science, 8,* 88–101.

Xu, H., & others (2013). The function of BMP4 during neurogenesis in the adult hippocampus in Alzheimer's disease. *Aging Research and Reviews, 12*(1), 157–164.

Xue, F., Holzman, C., Rahbar, M. H., Trosko, K., & Fischer, L. (2007). Maternal fish consumption, mercury levels, and risk of preterm delivery. *Environmental Health Perspectives, 115,* 42–47.

Y

Yaffe, K., Barnes, D., Nevitt, M., Lui, L., & Covinsky, K. (2001). A prospective study of physical activity and cognitive decline in elderly women. *Archives of Internal Medicine, 161,* 1703–1708.

Yakoboski, P. J. (2011). Worries and plans as individuals approach retirement. *Benefits Quarterly, 27,* 34–37.

Yan, C. F., Hung, Y. C., Gau, M. L., & Lin, K. C. (2014, in press). Effects of stability ball exercise program on low back pain and daily life interference during pregnancy. *Midwifery.*

Yan, E. (2014, in press). Abuse of older persons with dementia by family caregivers: Results of a 6-month prospective study in Hong Kong. *International Journal of Geriatric Psychiatry.*

Yan, L., & others (2013). Calorie restriction can reverse, as well as prevent, aging cardiomyopathy. *Age, 35,* 2177–2182.

Yang, S. J., & others (2013). Differences in predictors of traditional and cyber-bullying: A 2-year longitudinal study in Korean school children. *European Child and Adolescent Psychiatry, 22,* 309–318.

Yang, Y. (2008). Social inequalities in happiness in the United States, 1972–2004: An age-period-cohort analysis. *American Sociological Review, 73,* 204–226.

Yanof, J. A. (2013). Play technique in psychodynamic psychotherapy. *Child and Adolescent Psychiatric Clinics of North America, 22,* 261–282.

Yao, Y., Gu, X., Zhu, J., Yuan, D., & Song, Y. (2013). Hormone replacement therapy in females can decrease the risk of lung cancer: A meta-analysis. *PLoS One, 8*(8), e71236.

Yap, M. B., Pilkington, P. D., Ryan, S. M., & Jorm, A. F. (2014). Parental factors associated with depression and anxiety in young people: A systematic review and meta-anslysis. *Journal of Affective Disorders, 156,* 8–23.

Yap, Q. J., & others (2013). Tracking cerebral white matter changes across the lifespan: Insights from diffusion tensor imaging studies. *Journal of Neural Transmission, 120,* 1369–1395.

Yarber, W., Sayad, B., & Strong, B. (2013). *Human sexuality* (8th ed.). New York: McGraw-Hill.

Yates, D. (2014). Myelination: Switching modes of myelination. *Nature Reviews Neuroscience, 15,* 66–67.

Yates, L. B., Djuousse, L., Kurth, T., Buring, J. E., & Gaziano, J. M. (2008). Exceptional longevity in men: Modifiable factors associated with survival and function to age 90 years. *Archives of Internal Medicine, 168,* 284–290.

Yee, B. W. K., & Chiriboga, D. A. (2007). Issues of diversity in health psychology and aging. In C. M. Aldwin, C. L. Park, & A. Spiro (Eds.), *Handbook of health psychology and aging.* New York: Guilford.

Yen, C. F., & others (2014, in press). Association between school bullying levels/types and mental health problems among Taiwanese adolescents. *Comprehensive Psychiatry.*

Yeung, D. Y., Wong, C. K., & Lok, D. P. (2011). Emotion regulation mediates age differences in emotions. *Aging and Mental Health, 15,* 414–418.

Yeung, W-J., & Mui-Teng, Y. (Eds.) (2015, in press). *Economic stress, human capital, and families in Asia: Research and policy challenges.* New York: Springer.

Yezierski, R. P. (2012). The effects of age on pain sensitivity: Preclinical studies. *Pain Medicine, 13*(2, Suppl.), S27–S36.

Yi, Y., & Friedman, D. (2014). Age-related differences in working memory: ERPs reveal age-related delays in selection- and inhibition-related processes. *Neuropsychology, Development, and Cognition B: Aging, Neuropsychology, and Cognition, 21,* 483–513.

Yin, R. K. (2012). Case study methods. In H. Cooper (Ed.), *APA handbook of research methods in psychology.* Washington, DC: American Psychological Association.

Yochum, C., & others (2014). Prenatal cigarette smoke exposure causes hyperactivity and aggressive behavior: Role of catecgikanubes and BDNF. *Experimental Neurology, 254C,* 145–152.

Yokoyama, A., & others (2013). Trends in gastrectomy and ADH1B and ALDH2 genotypes in Japanese alcoholic men and their gene-gastrectomy, gene-gene, and gene-age interactions. *Alcohol and Alcoholism, 48,* 146–152.

Yonker, J. E., Schnabelrauch, C. A., & DeHaan, L. G. (2012). The relationship between spirituality and religiosity on psychological outcomes in adolescents and emerging adults: A meta-analytic review. *Journal of Adolescence, 35,* 299–314.

Yoon, C., Cole, C. A., & Lee, M. P. (2009). Consumer decision making and aging: Current knowledge and future directions. *Journal of Consumer Psychology, 19,* 2–16.

Yoon, C., May, C. P., Goldstein, D., & Hasher, L. (2010). Aging, circadian arousal patterns and cognition. In D. Park and N. Schwarz (Eds.), *Cognitive aging: A primer* (2nd ed.). Psychology Press.

Yoshikawa, H. (2012). *Immigrants raising citizens: Undocumented parents and their young children.* New York: Russell Sage.

Young, B. J., Furman, W., & Laursen, B. (2014). Models of change and continuity in romantic experiences. In F. D. Fincham & M. Cui (Eds.), *Romantic relationships in emerging adulthood.* New York: Cambridge University Press.

Young, K. T. (1990). American conceptions of infant development from 1955 to 1984: What the experts are telling parents. *Child Development, 61,* 17–28.

Youniss, J., McLellan, J. A., & Yates, M. (1999). Religion, community service, and identity in American youth. *Journal of Adolescence, 22,* 243–253.

Youth Risk Behavior Survey (2011). *Trends in the prevalence of suicide-related behaviors: National YRB, 1991–2011.* Retrieved June 6, 2012, from www.cdc.gov/yrbss

Ysseldyk, R., Haslam, S. A., & Haslam, C. (2013). Abide with me: Religious group identification among older adults promotes health and well-being by maintaining multiple group memberships. *Aging and Mental Health, 17,* 869–879.

Yu, B., & others (2013). Association of genome-wide variation with highly sensitive cardiac troponin-T levels in European Americans and blacks: A meta-analysis from the atherosclerosis risk in communities and cardiovascular health studies. *Circulation: Cardiovascular Genetics, 6*(1), 82–88.

Yu, C. Y., & others (2012). Prenatal predictors for father-infant attachment after childbirth. *Journal of Clinical Nursing, 21*(11–12), 1577–1583.

Yu, R., Branje, S., Keijsers, L., Koot, H. M., & Meeus, W. (2013). Pals, problems, and personality: The moderating role of personality in the longitudinal association between adolescents' and best friends' delinquency. *Journal of Personality, 81,* 499–509.

Yu, R., Ryan, L. H., Schaie, K. W., & Willis, S. L. (2014, in press). Using multi-level modeling to understand factors associated with cognition in older adults: The Seattle Longitudinal Study. *Journal of Nursing and Health.*

Yuan, P., & Raz, N. (2014). Prefrontal cortex and executive functions in healthy adults: A meta-analysis of structural neuroimaging studies. *Neuroscience and Biobehavioral Reviews, 42C,* 180–192.

Yudkin, D., Hayward, B., Aladjem, M. I., Kumari, D., & Usdin, K. (2014, in press). Chromosome fragility and the abnormal replication of the FMR1 locus in fragile X syndrome. *Human Molecular Genetics.*

Yun, K., & others (2014). Effects of maternal-child home visitation on pregnancy spacing for first-time Latina mothers. *American Journal of Public Health, 104*(1, Suppl.), S152–S158.

Z

Zacher, H., Jimmieson, N. L., & Winter, G. (2012). Eldercare demands, mental health, and work performance: The moderating role of satisfaction with eldercare tasks. *Journal of Occupational Health Psychology, 17*(1), 52–64.

Zachrisson, H. D., Lekhal, R., Dearing, E., & Toppelberg, C. O. (2013). Little evidence that time in child care causes externalizing problems during early childhood in Norway. *Child Development, 84,* 1152–1170.

Zalli, A., & others (2014, in press). Shorter telomeres with high telomerase activity are associated with raised allostatic load and impoverished psychosocial resources. *Proceedings of the National Academy of Sciences U.S.A.*

Zamuner, T., Fais, L., & Werker, J. F. (2014, in press). Infants track words in early word-object associations. *Developmental Science.*

Zanella, S., & others (2014). When norepinephrine becomes a driver of breathing irregularities: How intermittent hypoxia fundamentally alters the modulatory response of the respiratory network. *Journal of Neuroscience, 34,* 36–50.

Zannas, A. S., & others (2012). Stressful life events, perceived stress, and 12-month course of geriatric depression: Direct effects and moderation by the 5-HTTLPR and COMT Val158Met polymorphisms. *Stress, 15*(4), 425–434.

Zayas, V., & Hazan, C. (Eds.) (2014). *Bases of adult attachment.* New York: Springer.

Zeifman, D., & Hazan, C. (2008). Pair bonds as attachments: Reevaluating the evidence. In J. Cassidy & P. R. Shaver (Eds.), *Handbook of attachment* (2nd ed.). New York: Guilford.

Zeisel, S. H. (2011). The supply of choline is important for fetal progenitor cells. *Seminars in Cell and Developmental Biology, 22,* 624–628.

Zelazo, P. D. (2013). Developmental psychology: A new synthesis. In P. D. Zelazo (Ed.), *Handbook of developmental psychology.* New York: Wiley.

Zelazo, P. D., & Lyons, K. E. (2012). The potential benefits of mindfulness training in early childhood: A developmental social cognitive neuroscience perspective. *Child Development Perspectives, 6,* 154–160.

Zelazo, P. D., & Muller, U. (2011). Executive function in typical and atypical children. In U. Goswami (Ed.), *Wiley-Blackwell handbook of childhood cognitive development* (2nd ed.). New York: Wiley.

Zeng, Y., & Shen, K. (2010). Resilience significantly contributes to exceptional longevity. *Current Gerontology and Geriatrics Research.* doi: 10.1155/2010/525693

Zentner, M., & Shiner, R. L. (Eds.) (2012). Fifty years of progress in temperament research: A synthesis of major themes, findings, challenges, and a look forward. In M. Zentner & R. Shiner (Eds.), *Handbook of temperament.* New York: Guilford.

Zeskind, P. S., Klein, L., & Marshall, T. R. (1992). Adults' perceptions of experimental modifications of durations and expiratory sounds in infant crying. *Developmental Psychology, 28,* 1153–1162.

Zettel-Watson, L., & Rook, K. S. (2009). Friendship, later life. In D. Carr (Ed.), *Encyclopedia of the life course and human development.* Boston: Gale Cengage.

Zetterqvist, M., Lundh, L. G., & Svedin, C. G. (2013). A comparison of adolescents engaging in self-injurious behaviors with and without suicidal intent: Self-reported experiences of adverse life events and trauma symptoms. *Journal of Youth and Adolescence, 42,* 1257–1272.

Zhai, F., Raver, C. C., & Jones, S. (2012). Quality of subsequent schools and impacts of early interventions: Evidence from a randomized controlled trial in Head Start settings. *Children and Youth Services Review, 34*(5), 946–954.

Zhang, L., Zhang, X. H., Liang, M. Y., & Ren, M. H. (2010). Prenatal cytogenetic diagnosis study of 2782 cases of high-risk pregnant women. *China Medicine (English), 123,* 423–430.

Zhang, W. G., & others (2014, in press). Select aging biomarkers based on telomere length and chronological age to build a biological age equation. *Age.*

Zhang, Y. X., Zhang, Z. C., & Xie, L. (2014, in press). Distribution curve of waist-to-height ratio and its association with blood pressure among children and adolescents: Study in a large population in an eastern coastal province, China. *European Journal of Pediatrics.*

Zhao, H., Seibert, S. E., & Lumpkin, G. T. (2010). The relationship of personality to entrepreneurial intentions and performance: A meta-analytic review. *Journal of Management, 36,* 381–404.

Zhao, J., & others (2014). Association of plasma glucose, insulin, and cardiovascular risk factors in overweight and obese children. *Saudi Medical Journal, 35,* 132–137.

Zhao, M., Kong, L., & Qu, H. (2014, in press). A systems biology approach to identify intelligence quotient score-related genomic regions and pathways relevant to potential therapeutic targets. *Scientific Reports.*

Zhao, X., & others (2014). An obesity genetic risk score is associated with metabolic syndrome in Chinese children. *Gene, 535,* 299–302.

Zhao, Z., Pan, X., Liu, L., & Liu, N. (2014, in press). Telomere length maintenance, shortening, and lengthening. *Journal of Cellular Physiology.*

Zheng, H., Tumin, D., & Qian, Z. (2013). Obesity and mortality risk: New findings from body mass index trajectories. *American Journal of Epidemiology, 178,* 1591–1599.

Zhou, P., Su, Y. E., Crain, S., Gao, L., & Zhan, L. (2012). Children's use of phonological information in ambiguity resolution: A view from Mandarin Chinese. *Journal of Child Language, 39*(4), 687–730.

Zhou, Q. (2013). Commentary in S. Smith, Children of "tiger parents" develop more aggression and depression, research shows. Retrieved July 20, 2013, from www.cbsnews.com/news/children-of-tiger-parents-develop-more-aggression-and-depression-research-shows/

Zhou, Q., & others (2012). Asset and protective factors for Asian American children's mental health adjustment. *Child Development Perspectives, 6,* 312–319.

Zhu, D. C., Zacks, R. T., & Slade, J. M. (2010). Brain activation during interference resolution in young and older adults: An fMRI study. *Neuroimage, 50,* 810–817.

Ziegler-Hill, V. (2013). The current state of research concerning self-esteem. In V. Ziegler-Hill (Ed.), *Self-esteem.* New York: Psychology Press.

Zielinksi, A. E., Rochette, L. M., & Smith, G. A. (2012). Stair-related injuries to young children treated in U.S. emergency departments, 1999–2008. *Pediatrics, 129,* 721–729.

Zielinski, D. S. (2009). Child maltreatment and adult socioeconomic well-being. *Child Abuse and Neglect, 33,* 666–678.

Ziemer, C. J., Plumert, J. M., & Pick, A. D. (2012). To grasp or not to grasp: Infants' actions toward objects and pictures. *Infancy, 17*(5), 479–497.

Zigler, E., Gilliam, W. S., & Barnett, W. S. (Eds.) (2011). *The pre-K debates: Controversies and Issues.* Baltimore: Brookes.

Zigler, E. F., Gilliam, W. S., & Jones, S. M. (2006). *A vision for universal preschool education.* New York: Cambridge University Press.

Zigler, E. F., & Styfco, S. J. (1994). Head Start: Criticisms in a constructive context. *American Psychologist, 49,* 127–132.

Zigler, E. F., & Styfco, S. J. (2010). *The hidden history of Head Start.* New York: Oxford University Press.

Ziol-Guest, K. M. (2009). Child custody and support. In D. Carr (Ed.), *Encyclopedia of the life course and human development.* Boston: Gale Cengage.

Ziso, B., & Larner, A. (2013). CODEX (Cognitive Disorders Examination) for the detection of dementia and mild cognitive impairment: Diagnostic utility. *Journal of Neurology, Neurosurgery, and Psychiatry, 84,* e2.

Zlatar, Z. Z., & others (2014, in press). Increased hippocampal blood flow in sedentary older adults at genetic risk for Alzheimer's disease. *Journal of Alzheimer's Disease.*

Zollner, H. S., Fuchs, K. A., & Fegert, J. M. (2014, in press). Prevention of sexual abuse: Improved information is crucial. *Child and Adolescent Psychiatry and Mental Health.*

Zozuls, K., Martin, C., England, D., Andrews, N., & Borders, A. (2012, April). *"I don't want to talk to them because I don't know how to": The role of relationship efficacy in children's gender-related intergroup processes.* Paper presented at the Gender Development Research conference, San Francisco.

Zulauf, C. A., Sprich, S. E., Safren, S. A., & Wilens, T. E. (2014, in press). The complicated relationship between attention-deficit/hyperactivity disorder and substance use disorders. *Current Psychiatry Reports.*

credits

TEXT CREDITS

Chapter 1

Page 5: Figure 1.1: John Santrock, *Life-Span Development*, 14/e, fig. 1.1. Copyright © 2013 McGraw-Hill Companies. Used with permission; p. 14: © Robert Weber/The New Yorker Collection/The Cartoon Bank; p. 31: fig. 1.19: John Santrock, *Children*, 9/e, fig. 2.12. Copyright © 2007 McGraw-Hill Companies. Used with permission.

Chapter 2

Page 52: Figure 2.3: John Santrock, *Psychology*, 7/e. Copyright © 2003 McGraw-Hill Companies. Used with permission; p. 66: fig. 2.11: John Santrock, *Children*, 9/e, fig. 3.10. Copyright © 2007 McGraw-Hill Companies. Used with permission.

Chapter 3

Page 77: Figure 3.3: John Santrock, *Children*, 9/e, fig. 4.3. Copyright © 2007 McGraw-Hill Companies. Used with permission; p. 92: fig. 3.7: John Santrock, *Children*, 10/e. Copyright © McGraw-Hill Companies. Used with permission; p. 96: fig. 3.11: John Santrock, *Child Development*, 10/e, fig. 4.11. Copyright © 2004 McGraw-Hill Companies. Used with permission.

Chapter 4

Page 105: Figure 4.1: John Santrock, *Children*, 9/e, fig. 6.1. Copyright © 2007 McGraw-Hill Companies. Used with permission; p. 107: fig. 4.6: John Santrock, *Child Development*, 10/e, fig. 5.2. Copyright © 2004 McGraw-Hill Companies. Used with permission; p. 108: fig. 4.8: John Santrock, *Child Development*, 11/e, fig. 5.11. Copyright © 2007 McGraw-Hill Companies. Used with permission; p. 110: fig. 4.11: John Santrock, *Child Development*, 11/e, fig. 5.13. Copyright © 2007 McGraw-Hill Companies. Used with permission; p. 113: fig. 4.12: John Santrock, *Child Development*, 10/e, fig. 5.11. Copyright © 2004 McGraw-Hill Companies. Used with permission.

Chapter 5

Page 136: Figure 5.2: J. Piaget, *The Origins of Intelligence in Children*, 1952. New York International Universities Press, pp. 27, 159, 225, 273, 339; p. 149: fig. 5.10: DeLoache; Simcock; Mecari, "Planes, Trains and Automobiles," *Developmental Psychology*, vol. 43, pp. 1579–1586. Copyright © 2007 by the American Psychological Association; p. 157(top): fig. 5.14: John Santrock, *Children*, 9/e fig. 7.11. Copyright © 2007 McGraw-Hill Companies. Used with permission; p. 157 (bottom): fig. 5.15: John Santrock, *A. Topical Approach to Life Span Development*, 4/e, fig. 10.2. Copyright © 2008 McGraw-Hill Companies. Used with permission; p. 159: fig. 5.18: Hart and Risley (1995), *Meaningful Differences in the Everyday Experiences of Young American Children*, Baltimore: Paul H. Brookes Publishing Co. Used with permission of Paul H. Brookes Publishing Co.

Chapter 6

Page 177: Figure 6.4: John Santrock, *Life-Span Development*, 4/e. Copyright © 1999 McGraw-Hill Companies. Used with permission; p. 186: fig. 6.9: Jay Belsky, "Early Human Experience: A Family Perspective," *in Developmental Psychology*, vol. 17, pp. 3–23. Copyright © 1981 by the American Psychological Association.

Chapter 7

Page 207: Figure 7.5: John Santrock, *Psychology*, 7/e. Copyright © 2003 McGraw-Hill Companies. Used with permission; p. 208: © 1989 Lee Lorenz/The New Yorker Collection/The Cartoon Bank. Used with permission; p. 207: fig.7.5: "The Symbolic Drawings of Young Children," reprinted courtesy of D. Wolf and J. Nove. Used with permission of Dennie Palmer Wolf, Annenberg Institute, Brown University; p. 212: fig. 7.10: Elena Bodrova; Deborah J. Leong, "Tools of the Mind." Used with permission; p. 214: fig. 7.12: John Santrock, *Children*, 7/e. Copyright © 2003 McGraw-Hill Companies. Used with permission; p. 215: Maggie Bruck, Text from *Annual Review of Psychology*, vol. 50, 1999. Copyright © 1999 by Maggie Bruck. Used with permission; p. 219: fig. 7.17: After Joseph Jastrow, 1900; p. 222: fig. 7.18: Jean Berko, 1958, "The Child's Learning of English Morphology," in *Word*, vol. 14, p. 154. Used courtesy of Jean Berko Gleason; p. 244: fig. 7.19: Excerpted from NAEYC, "Developmentally Appropriate Practice in Early Childhood Programs Serving Children from Birth Through Age 8," Position statement, (Washington, DC: NAEYC, 2009). Copyright © 2009 NAEYC. Reprinted with permission. Full text of this position statement is available at http://www.naeyc.org/positionstatements/ppp.

Chapter 8

Page 241: © Edward Koren/The New Yorker Collection/The Cartoon Bank. Used by permission; p. 243: fig. 8.1: John Santrock, *Child Development*, 10/e, fig. 13.3. Copyright © 2004 McGraw-Hill Companies. Used with permission.

Chapter 9

Page 269: Figure 9.1: John Santrock, *Children*, 9/e fig. 9.3. Copyright © 2007 McGraw-Hill Companies. Used with permission; p. 275: fig. 9.5: Shaw et al (2007) "Attention Deficit/Hyperactivity Disorder is Characterized by a Delay in Cortical Maturation," *Proceedings of the National Academy of Science*, vol. 104, p. 1950, fig. 2. Copyright © 2007 National Academy of Sciences, USA. Used with permission; p. 283: © Sam Gross/The New Yorker Collection/The Cartoon Bank. Used with permission; p. 284: © Sidney Harris/ScienceCartoonsPlus.com. Used with permission; p. 288: © Donald Reilly/The New Yorker Collection/The Cartoon Bank. Used by permission; p. 290: fig. 9.13: Ulric Neisser, *The Increase in IQ Scores from 1932 to 1997*. Copyright © by the executors to the Estate of Urlic Neisser. All rights Reserved. Used with permission; p. 292: fig. 9.14: From *Raven's Progressive Matrices*. Copyright © 1998 by NCS Pearson, Inc. All rights reserved. Used with permission.

Chapter 10

Page 316: Figure 10.3: John Santrock, *A Topical Approach to Life-Span Development*, 3/e, fig. 12.4. Copyright © 2007 McGraw-Hill Companies. Used with permission; p. 316: © Joel Pett. Author rights reserved; p. 318: fig. 10.4: Sandra Bem, adapted from *The Bem Sex-Role Inventory*, 1971, 1981. Mind Garden, Inc.

Chapter 11

Page 342: ZITS © ZITS Partnership, Dist. By King Features. Used by permission; p. 345: fig. 11.4: John Santrock, *Essentials of Life-Span Development*, 1/e. Copyright © 2008 McGraw-Hill Companies. Used with permission; p. 346: fig. 11.5: John Santrock, *Adolescence*, 15e, fig. 6.1. Copyright 2014 © McGraw-Hill Companies. Used with permission; p. 348: fig. 11.6: John Santrock, *Adolescence*, 15e, fig. 6.5. Copyright © McGraw-Hill Companies. Used with permission; p. 353: fig. 11.8: John Santrock, *Adolescence*, 15e, fig. 13.4. Copyright © McGraw-Hill Companies. Used with permission; p. 357: © Edward Koren/The New Yorker Collection/www.cartoonbank.com.

Chapter 12

Page 393: Figure 12.8: D.B. Goldston et al., "Cultural Considerations in Adolescent Suicide Prevention and Psychological Treatment," in *American Psychologist*, vol. 63, pp. 14–31. Copyright © 2008 American Psychological Association.

Chapter 13

Page 404: Figure 13.1: "The American College Health Association National College Health Assessment," in *Journal of American College Health*, vol. 57, no. 5, 2009, Table 17, p. 487. Used with permission of American College of Health Association; p. 407: © www.CartoonStock.com. Used with permission; p. 408: fig. 13.3: John Santrock, *A Topical Life-Span Development*, 6/e, p. 138. Copyright © McGraw-Hill Companies. Used with permission; p. 408: fig. 13.4: J. Kruger, H.M. Blank, and G. Gillespie, "Comparisons of Strategies in Successful and Unsuccessful Dieters," from "Dietary and Physical Activity Behaviors Among Adults Successful at Weight Loss Management," in *International Journal of Behavioral Nutrition and Physical Activity*, vol. 3, p. 17, 2006. Bio Medical Central; p. 411: © Michael Shaw/The New Yorker Collection/www.cartoonbank.com; p. 415: fig. 13.7: John Santrock, *Children*, 9/e, fig. 15.8. Copyright © 2007 McGraw-Hill Companies. Used with permission; p. 421: fig. 13.9: John Santrock, *Adolescence*, 14/e, fig. 3.5. Copyright © 2012 McGraw-Hill Companies. Used by permission; p. 423: © Joseph Farris/The New Yorker Collection/www.cartoonbank.com.

Chapter 14

Page 438: Copyright © Fran Orford, www.francartoons.com; p. 443: fig. 14.4: U.S. Bureau of the Census, Washington, DC; p. 452: E. Mavis Hetherington and John Kelly, excerpt from *For Better or for Worse: Divorce Reconsidered,* pp. 98–108. W.W. Norton, 2002.

Chapter 15

Page 472: Figure 15.6: John Santrock, *Life-Span Development,* 8/e. Copyright © 2002 McGraw-Hill Companies. Used by permission; p. 478: HAGGAR © 1987 by King Features Syndicate, Inc. World rights reserved. Used with permission.

Chapter 16

Page 488: Figure 16.3: John Santrock, *A Topical Approach to Life-Span Development,* 3/e, fig. 11.12. Copyright © 2007 McGraw-Hill Companies. Used with permission; p. 493: fig. 16.8: John Santrock, *Psychology,* 7/e, fig. 12.11. Copyright © 2003 McGraw-Hill Companies. Used with permission; p. 488: fig. 16.4: Nansel et al., 2001. "Bullying Behaviors Among U.S. Youth," *Journal of the American Medical Association,* Vol. 285, pp. 2094–2100.

Chapter 17

Page 512: Figure 17.1: Richard Schultz, *The Psychology of Death Dying and Bereavement.* Copyright © 1978 McGraw-Hill Companies. Used with permission; p. 534: fig. 17.20: John Santrock, *A Topical Approach to Life-Span Development,* 4/e, fig. 4.6. Copyright © 2008 McGraw-Hill Companies. Used with permission.

Chapter 18

Page 554: Figure 18.6: John Santrock, *A Topical Approach to Life-Span Development,* 6/e, fig. 16.11. Copyright © 2008 McGraw-Hill Companies. Used with permission; p. 555: fig. 18.7: John Santrock, *A Tropical Approach to Life-Span Development,* 6/e, fig. 16.12. Copyright © 2008 McGraw-Hill Companies. Used with permission.

Chapter 19

Page 572: Figure 19.3: D. Mroczwk and C.M. Kolarz, *Journal of Personality and Social Psychology,* vol. 75, pp. 1333–1349. Copyright © 1998 American Psychological Association.

Photo Research by Jen Blankenship

Contents

Page iv(top): © Randy M. Ury/Corbis; p. iv(bottom): © MedicalRF.com/Getty Images RF; p. v: © Jamie Grill/Brand X Pictures/Getty Images RF; p. vi: © Ariel Skelley/Corbis; p. vii(top): © Ariel Skelley/Corbis; p. vii(bottom): © Comstock Images/Getty Images RF; p. viii: © Jupiter Images/Comstock/Getty Images RF; p. ix: © Tomas Rodriguez/Corbis RF; p. x: © Rod Porteous/Robert Harding World Imagery/Corbis; p. xi: © Hans Neleman/Getty Images.

About the Author Photo Courtesy of Dr. John Santrock

Expert Consultants

Page xiii(Schaie): Courtesy of Dr. K. Warner Schaie; p. xiii(Deater-Deckard): Courtesy of Dr. Kirby Deater-Deckard and Keirsten Deater-Deckard; p. xiv(Miller): Courtesy of Dr. Patricia Miller; p. xiv(Schulenberg): Courtesy of Dr. John Schulenberg; p. xiv(Reuter-Lorenz): Courtesy of Dr. Patricia Reuter-Lorenz; p. xiv(Johnson): Courtesy of UCLA News Service; p. xiv(Rose): Courtesy of Dr. Amanda Rose, photo by Anastasia Pottinger; p. xv(Thompson): Courtesy of Dr. Ross Thompson; p. xv(Edwards): Courtesy of Dr. Jerri Edwards, photography courtesy of Rosa Diaz; p. xv(Carr): Courtesy of Dr. Deborah Carr, photography courtesy of Myra Klarman.

Chapter 1

Opener: © Randy M. Ury/Corbis; p. 2: © Jay Reilly/Upper Cut Images/Getty Images; p. 3(Kaczynski, adult): © Seanna O'Sullivan; p. 3(Kaczynski, teen): © WBBM-TV/AFP/Getty Images; p. 3(Walker, adult): © AP Images; p. 3(Walker, child): Courtesy of Alice Walker; 1.1(tortoise): © Digital Vision/PunchStock RF; 1.1(mouse): © Redmond Durrell/Alamy RF; p. 5: Margaret M. and Paul B. Baltes Foundation; p. 6: © Walter Hodges/Corbis; p. 7(top): © Adam Hunger/Reuters/Landov; p. 7(bottom): © Comstock Images/Jupiter Images/Alamy RF; p. 8 (top): Courtesy of Luis Vargas; p. 8(bottom): © Robert Maust/Photo Agora; p. 9(top left): © Nancy Agostini; p. 9(top right): Naser Siddique/UNICEF Bangladesh; p. 9(bottom): Courtesy of the Children's Defense Fund and Marian Wright Edelman; p. 10: © Dawn Villella Photography; p. 13: © iStockphoto.com/leva; 1.8(left to right): © Brand X Pictures/PunchStock RF; Courtesy of John Santrock; © Laurence Mouton/Photoalto/PictureQuest RF; © Digital Vision RF; © SW Productions/Getty Images RF; © Blue Moon Stock/Alamy Images RF; © Kristi J. Black/Corbis RF; © Ronnie Kaufman/Blend Images LLC RF; p. 15: © Jetta Productions/Blend Images/Getty Images; p. 17(top left): © Jay Syverson/Corbis; p. 17(top right): © Owaki-Kulla Corbis; p. 17(bottom): © Rubberball/PictureQuest RF; p. 20(top): © Bettmann/Corbis; p. 20 (bottom): © Jon Erikson/The Image Works; p. 21: © Yves de Braine/Black Star/Stock Photo; 1.13(left to right): © Stockbyte/Getty Images RF; © BananaStock/PunchStock RF; © image100/Corbis RF; © Jose Pelaez/Corbis RF; p. 23: A.R. Lauria/Dr. Michael Cole, Laboratory of Human Cognition, University of California, San Diego; p. 24(top): © AP Images; p. 24(bottom): © Linda A Cicero/Stanford News Service; p. 25: © Nina Leen/Time Life Pictures/Getty Images; p. 26: Courtesy of Cornell University; p. 28: © Philadelphia Inquirer/MCT/Landov Images; p. 29: © Bettmann/Corbis; 1.18: Dr. Susan Tapert, University of California, San Diego; 1.19: © Digital Vision/PunchStock RF; p. 33(top left): George Grantham Bain Collection, Library of Congress, Reproduction Number #LC-USZ62-63966; p. 33(top right): © Jamie Grill/Blend Images/Corbis RF; p. 33 (bottom): © Mark Bowden/E+/Getty Images RF;

p. 34: © The McGraw-Hill Companies, Inc./Mark Dierker, photographer; p. 36: Courtesy of Dr. Pam Reid; p. 37(left): © Anthony Cassidy/The Image Bank/Getty Images; p. 37(right): © PunchStock/Digital Vision RF.

Chapter 2

Opener: © MedicalRF.com/Getty Images RF; p. 46: © China Tourism Press/The Image Bank/Getty Images; p. 48: © Frans Lemmens/Corbis; 2.1: © Alan and Sandy Carey/Photodisc/Getty Images RF; p. 50: Courtesy of Dr. Gilda Morelli; 2.4: © Don W. Fawcett/Science Source; 2.5: © CMSP/Custom Medical Stock Photo-All rights reserved; p. 55: © James Shaffer/PhotoEdit; p. 58: Courtesy of Holly Ishmael Welsh; p. 59: © Jacques Pavlovsky/Sygma/Corbis; 2.8: © Du Cane Medical Imaging Ltd./Science Source; p. 63: © Don Mason/Blend Images/Corbis; p. 64: © Myrleen Pearson/PhotoEdit; p. 66: © Duomo/Corbis; p. 69: © Francisco Romero/E+/Getty Images RF.

Chapter 3

Opener: © Steve Allen/The Image Bank/Getty Images; p. 73: Courtesy of John Santrock; 3.3(top to bottom): © David Spears/PhotoTake, Inc.; © Neil Bromhall/Science Source; © Brand X Pictures/PunchStock RF; p. 78: © Bill Hughes/AP Images; 3.4: © Claude Edelmann/Science Source; p. 80: Streissguth, AP, Landesman-Dwyer S, Martin, JC, & Smith, DW (1980). "Teratogenic effects of alcohol in humans and laboratory animals," *Science,* 209, 353–361; p. 81: © Chuck Nacke/Alamy; p. 82: © Sergey Guneev/RIA Novosti; p. 83: © Betty Press/Woodfin Camp & Associates; p. 85(top): © Ryan Pyle/Ryan Pyle/Corbis; p. 85(bottom): © Tracy Frankel/The Image Bank/Getty Images; p. 86: © Jose Luis Pelaez Inc./Blend Images/Getty Images RF; p. 87: © Jonathan Nourok/Getty Images; p. 88: © Viviane Moos/Corbis; p. 89(top): Courtesy of Linda Pugh; p. 89(bottom): © Barros & Barros/Stockbyte/Getty Images RF; p. 90: Courtesy of Dr. Holly Beckwith; p. 92: © Diether Endlicher/AP Images; p. 93: © casenbina/E+/Getty Images RF; p. 94: Courtesy of Dr. Tiffany Field; p. 96: Courtesy of Dr. Diane Sanford; p. 97: © Howard Grey/Getty Images RF.

Chapter 4

Opener: © Jamie Grill/Brand X Pictures/Getty Images RF; p. 102: © Image Source/Getty Images RF; p. 103 (top): © Wendy Stone/Corbis; p. 103(bottom): © Dave Bartruff/Corbis; 4.2: Courtesy of Vanessa Vogel Farley; 4.3: © Dr. Patricia Kuhl, Institute for Learning and Brain Sciences, University of Washington; 4.4: © A. Glauberman/Science Source; 4.5: © ER Productions/Getty Images RF; 4.8: Courtesy of Dr. Harry T. Chugani, Children's Hospital of Michigan; 4.9: Courtesy of The Rehbein Family; p. 111: © Maria Teijeiro/Cultura/Getty Images RF; p. 114: © Blend Images/Getty Images RF; p. 115: © USDA Food and Nutrition Service, Supplemental Nutrition Assistance Program; p. 116: Courtesy Brazelton Touchpoints Center; p. 117(top): Courtesy of Dr. David Thelen; p. 117(bottom): © Harry Bartlett/The Image Bank/Getty Images; 4.12(top): © Petit Format/Photo Researchers; 4.12(bottom): © Stockbyte/PunchStock RF; 4.13: © Dr. Karen Adolph, New York University; 4.14(left to right): © Barbara Penoyar/Getty Images RF; © Digital

© Paul Chesley/The Image Bank/Getty Images; p. 378: © BananaStock/PunchStock RF; p. 379(top): © Stockbyte/Getty Images RF; p. 379 (bottom): © BananaStock/PunchStock RF; 12.3: © BananaStock/PunchStock RF; p. 381: © SW Productions/Getty Images RF; p. 382(top): © Image Source/Corbis RF; p. 382(bottom): © Jose Luis Pelaez Inc./Blend Images/Getty Images RF; p. 383: © Digital Vision/Getty Images RF; p. 385: © AFP/Getty Images; p. 386: © Daniel Laine/Gamma Rapho; p. 387(top): © Caroline Woodham/Photographer's Choice RF/Getty Images RF; p. 387(bottom): © Blend Images/TIPS Images RF; p. 388: © Digital Vision/Alamy RF; p. 390: © Chuck Savage/Corbis; p. 391: Courtesy of Dr. Rodney Hammond; p. 392: © BananaStock/PunchStock RF; p. 394(top): © BananaStock/PunchStock RF; p. 394(bottom): © Purestock/Getty Images RF.

Chapter 13

Opener: © Jupiter Images/Comstock/Getty Images RF; p. 400: © LWA/Taxi/Getty Images; p. 401: © Cosima Scavolini/LaPresse/Zumapress.com/Newscom; p. 403: © Hero Images/Corbis RF; p. 404: © Stockbyte/PunchStock RF; p. 405: Courtesy of Grace Leaf; p. 406: © BananaStock/Jupiter Images RF; 13.4: © iStockphoto.com/Ljupco; p. 409: © Randy M. Ury/Corbis; p. 410: © Joe Raedle/Newsmakers/Getty Images; p. 414(left to right): © PhotoAlto/PunchStock RF; © 2009 JupiterImages Corporation RF; © 2009 JupiterImages Corporation RF; p. 416: Courtesy of Dr. Patricia D. Hawkins; p. 417: © Creasource/Corbis; p. 419: © Yuri Arcurs/Alamy RF; p. 422: Courtesy of Dr. Mihaly Csikszentmihalyi; p. 423: Courtesy of Hari Prabhakar; p. 424: © Image Source/JupiterImages RF; p. 425: © Scott Olson/Getty Images; p. 426: © Ryan McVay/Getty Images RF.

Chapter 14

Opener: © Ariel Skelley/Blend Images/Corbis RF; p. 432(top): © Heide Benser/Corbis; p. 432(bottom): © LWA-Sharie Kennedy/Corbis; p. 434(left): © Runstudio/Taxi Japan/Getty Images; p. 434(right): © Jade/Blend Images/Getty Images RF; p. 435: © MM Productions/Corbis RF; p. 437(left): © John Biever/Sports Illustrated/Getty Images; p. Courtesy of Michelle and Andres Lalinde; p. 439(left to right): © Stockdisc/PunchStock RF; © BananaStock Ltd RF; © Ingram Publishing/age fotostock RF; p. 443: © Image Source/Corbis RF; p. 445(a): © Mats Widen/Getty Images RF; p. 445(b): © Image Source/age fotostock RF; p. 445(c): © BLOOMimage/Getty Images RF; 14.6: © Digital Vision/Getty Images RF; p. 449(top): Courtesy of The Gottman Institute, www.gottman.com; p. 449(bottom): © Ranald Mackechnie/The Image Bank/Getty Images; p. 450: © Ryan McVay/Getty Images RF; p. 451: Courtesy of Janis Keyser; p. 452: © Tony Freeman/PhotoEdit.

Chapter 15

Opener: © Tomas Rodriguez/Corbis RF; p. 457: © Digital Vision/Getty Images RF; p. 459: © ColorBlind/Getty Images RF; p. 461(top): © Bettmann/Corbis; p. 461(bottom): © Matthew Mendelsohn/Corbis; p. 464(top): Courtesy of The Family of Dr. George V. Mann; p. 464(bottom): © Ryan McVay/Getty Images RF; p. 465: © Michael DeYoung/Blend Images/Getty Images RF; 15.2: © Eye of Science/Science Source; p. 468: © Blue Moon Stock/PunchStock RF; p. 469: © McGraw-Hill Companies, Suzie Ross, Photographer; p. 473: Courtesy of Dr. K. Warner Schaie; p. 475: © Brand X Pictures/PunchStock RF; p. 476: © Digital Vision/Getty Images RF; p. 477: © Erik S. Lesser/Corbis; p. 479: © PunchStock RF; p. 480: © Michael Prince/Corbis.

Chapter 16

Opener: © Peter Correz/The Image Bank/Getty Images; 16.2(top to bottom): © Amos Morgan/Getty Images RF; © Corbis RF; © Thomas Northcut/Getty Images RF; p. 491(top): © altrendo images/Getty Images; p. 491(bottom): © Corbis RF; 16.7(top): © Corbis RF; © H. Armstrong Roberts/Retrofile/Getty Images; p. 492 © Betty Press/Woodfin Camp & Associates; p.494: © Francine Fleischer/Corbis; p. 496: © Noel Vasquez/Stringer/Getty Images; p. 497(top): © Digital Vision/Getty Images RF; p. 497(bottom): © Stock4B/Getty Images; p. 499: © Tom Grill/Corbis RF; p. 500: © Jose Luis Pelaez, Inc./Corbis; p. 501: © Reza/National Geographic/Getty Images; p. 502: © Ron Levine/Photolibrary/Getty Images; p. 503: © Steve Casimiro/The Image Bank/Getty Images; p. 504: Courtesy of Dr. Karen Fingerman.

Chapter 17

Opener: © Rod Porteous/Robert Harding World Imagery/Corbis; p. 508: © Ariel Skelley/Blend Images/Getty Images; p. 509: © Jill Knight/The News & Observer/AP Images; p. 511(a): © Christophe Ena/AP Images; p. 511(b): © Anatoly Semekhin/ITAR-TASS/Newscom; p. 511(c): © Chip Somodevilla/Getty Images; P. 513(left to right): © Carmine Galasson/The Record/MCT/Newscom; Courtesy of the New England Centenarian Study, Boston University; © Isaac Hernandez; p. 514(a): © Jean Pierre Fizet/Sygma/Corbis; p. 514(b): Courtesy of The Radulovich Family; p. 515: © Ana Nance Photography/Redux; 17.3: Courtesy of Dr. Jerry Shay; 17.4: © J. Bavosi/Science Source; 17.5: Courtesy of Dr. Fred Gage, The Salk Institute for Biological Studies; 17.6: Courtesy of Dr. Roberto Cabeza; p. 521: © James Balog; 17.11: © Cordelia Molloy/Science Source; p. 526: © Image Source/Photodisc/Getty Images RF; p. 529: © Norbert Schaefer/Corbis; 17.18: Courtesy of Maxine Bloor; p. 531: © Charles Krupa/AP Images; p. 532: © Sherrie Nickol/Citizen Stock/Corbis RF; p. 533: © Stockbyte RF; p. 534: © Jacqueline Larma/AP Images; p. 535: © jonya/E+/Getty Images RF.

Chapter 18

Opener: © Jonathan Kirn/The Image Bank/Getty Images; p. 540: Courtesy of Dr. John Santrock; p. 541: Courtesy of Helen Small; p. 543: © Digital Vision/Getty Images RF; p. 545(top): © Clarissa Leahy/The Image Bank/Getty Images; p. 545 (bottom): © DAJ/Getty Images RF; p. 547: © Elizabeth Crews; p. 548(top to bottom): © Silverstock/Getty Images RF; © Blend Images/Getty Images RF; © Tom Grill/Corbis RF; p. 549: © Fox Searchlight/Photofest; p. 550: © Blend Images/Alamy RF; 18.4: Courtesy of Dr. Sam Gilbert, Institute of Cognitive Neuroscience, UK; p. 555: © Greg Sailor; p. 556: © Chuck Savage/Corbis; p. 557: © Bronwyn Kidd/Getty Images RF; p. 558: © G. Baden/Corbis; p. 559: © Bettmann/Corbis; 18.8: © Alfred Pasieka/Science Source; p. 561(top): Courtesy of Jan Weaver DeCrescenzo; p. 561 (bottom): © AP Images; p. 562: Courtesy of Dr. Margaret Gatz; p. 563: © Bryan F. Peterson/Corbis.

Chapter 19

Opener: © George Shelley/Corbis; p. 568(left): © Hy Peskin/Sports Illustrated/Getty Images; p. 568(right): © Jesse D Garrabrant/NBAE/Getty Images; p. 569: © Owen Franken/Corbis; p. 570: © Chuck Savage/Corbis; p. 571: Courtesy of Dr. Laura Carstensen; 19.4(left to right): © Eyewire/Getty Images RF; © Photodisc/Getty Images RF; © Digital Stock/Corbis RF; © Hoby Finn/Getty Images RF; © Corbis RF; p. 578: © Fuse/Getty Images RF; p. 579: © Peter Dazeley/Photographer's Choice/Getty Images; p. 580: © Thinkstock/Stockbyte/Getty Images RF; p. 583: Courtesy of Dr. John Santrock; p. 584: © Terry Vine/Blend Images/Getty Images RF; p. 585: © Dallas Morning News, photographer Jim Mahoney; p. 586: © Gabriela Hasbun/Getty Images; p. 587(top): Courtesy of Dr. Norma Thomas; p. 587(bottom): © Alison Wright/Corbis.

Chapter 20

Opener: © Hans Neleman/Getty Images; p. 593: © Fuse/Getty Images RF; p. 596: © Robert Galbraith/Reuters/Corbis; 20.1: © Ahn Young-joon/AP Images; p. 597: © Dario Mitidieri/Getty Images; p.598: © Handout Courtesy of the Schiavo Family/Corbis; p. 599: © Comstock Images/PictureQuest RF; p. 600: Courtesy of the family of Mary Monteiro; p. 601: © Per-Anders Pettersson/Getty Images; p. 602: © Ned Frisk Photography/Corbis RF; 20.2: © Eastcott/Momatiuk/ The Image Works; p. 604: © Photodisc/Getty Images RF; p. 606: © Stockbroker/PhotoLibrary RF; p. 608: © Tao Ming/Xinhua Press/Corbis; p. 609 (top): © Thomas Hinton/Splash News/Newscom; p. 609(bottom): © Peter Power/Toronto Star/Getty Images; p. 611(top left): © Russell Underwood/Corbis; p. 611(top right): © Paul Almasy/Corbis; p. 611(middle): © Glenn Fawcett/Baltimore Sun; p. 611(bottom): © Robert Mulder/Godong/Corbis.

name index

Dorn, L. D., 29, 30, 342–344, 467
Dorner, J., 547
Dorszewska, J., 517
Doss, B. D., 446
Dotterer, A. M., 378
Doty, R. L., 130
Dougall, A. L., 466
Douglas, D. H., 535
Dow, B. J., 439
Dowdy, S., 351
Downs, J., 347
Dozier, M., 62, 250
Draghi-Lorenz, R., 169
Drake, B., 250
Drake, K. M., 351
Drake, R. E., 558
Dreby, J., 256
Drollette, E. S., 270
Dryfoos, J., 394
Dryfoos, J. G., 394
Drygas, W., 529
Du, D., 345
Duarte, A., 545, 551
Duberstein, P. R., 575
Dublin, S., 560
Dubois, J., 77, 106
Dubois, N., 112–113
Dubowitz, H., 249
Duchesne, S., 362
Duggan, K. A., 294
Dunbar, G. L., 561
Duncan, G. J., 10, 11, 256, 329
Duncanson, K., 7
Dunlosky, J., 544, 550
Dunn, C. B., 29
Dunn, D. W., 275
Dunn, E. C., 250
Dunn, J., 250, 251, 499
Dunn, M., 274
Dunnewold, A., 96
Dunsmore, J. C., 237, 238
Dupre, M. E., 446
Durham, R., 95
Du Rocher-Schudlich, T. D., 236
Durrant, J. E., 249
Durrant, R., 17, 49
Durston, S., 269
Dutta, R., 8
Dvornyk, V., 343
Dvorsky, M. R., 275
Dweck, C., 332, 336
Dworkin, S. L., 346
Dwyer, J. W., 583
Dykas, M. J., 379, 380
Dy-Liacco, G., 479
Dzewaltowski, D., 204

Eagan, K., 404
Eagly, A. H., 242, 317, 319
Easterbrooks, M. A., 18, 168–170, 174–175, 234, 236, 379
Eastwick, P. W., 438
Eaton, D. K., 346–348, 351, 352, 392
Ebemeier, K. P., 409
Ebmeier, K. P., 559

Eccles, J. S., 320, 341, 362, 363, 365
Echevarria, J. J., 298
Eckerman, C., 179
Edeas, M., 517
Edelman, M. W., 9–10
Edelstein, R. S., 582
Edgington, C., 384
Edmonds, G., 372
Ednick, M., 111
Edwardson, C. L., 270
Efron, D., 275
Egan, S. K., 241
Eggers, D., 401, 402
Eggum, N. D., 318
Egloff, B., 494
Ehnes, J., 578
Ehrlich, K. B., 380
Eibach, R. P., 414
Eichorn, D., 406
Eichorn, D. H., 494
Eidelman, A. I., 93
Eiferman, R. R., 260
Einarsen, S., 419
Einstein, G. O., 545
Eisenberg, M. E., 350
Eisenberg, N., 239, 314, 318
Eisner, B., 125
Ekas, N. V., 171
Ekin, A., 59
Elashi, F. B., 235, 306
Elavsky, S., 589
Elbourne, P., 153
Elder, G. H., 583
Eldreth, D. A., 518–519
El Haj, M., 545
Eliasieh, K., 520
Elkind, D., 208, 308, 358–359, 367
Elliott, E. M., 544
Elliott, G. R., 340
Elliott, W. J., 463, 464, 525–526
Ellis, B. J., 17, 49, 343
Ellis, L., 235
Ellis, M. A., 424
Ellis, M. L., 542
Elmes, D. G., 31–32
Elmore, B., 10, 407
Elsabbagh, M., 220
Else-Quest, N., 242, 316, 319
El-Sheikh, M., 201, 202, 253
El-Sohemy, A., 533
Emery, C. F., 463, 466, 525
Emery, R. E., 186, 354
Emes, R. D., 107
English, G. W., 10
English, T., 571, 572, 588
Ensor, R., 217, 220, 236
Eppinger, R., 547
Erickson, E., 29, 334
Erickson, E. N., 89
Erickson, K. I., 519, 531
Erickson, K. L., 548, 552
Erickson, S. J., 187
Ericson, N., 325
Ericsson, K. A., 281, 294
Eriksen, S. H., 476

Erikson, E. H., 20–21, 26, 27, 39, 177, 178, 180, 181, 193, 234, 258, 262, 308, 370, 372, 373, 375, 396, 438–439, 456, 486, 505, 564, 569, 570, 589
Erikson, J., 20
Eriksson, U. J., 83
Eriksson Sorman, D., 476
Erkut, S., 350
Escalante, Y., 269–270
Escobar-Chaves, S. L., 261
Espana-Romero, V., 203
Esther, R. R., 525
Estrada, S., 361
Etaugh, C., 501, 503
Evaldsson, A-C., 198
Evans, G. W., 10, 255, 256, 387
Evans, L., 582
Evans, S. W., 275
Evans, W. J., 522
Eveleth, D. D., 524
Everett, C. J., 532
Evers, A. W., 466
Evers, C., 50
Eviatar, Z., 106
Ewen, D., 227
Exline, J. J., 606
Eymard, A. S., 535
Ezell, G., 203
Ezkurdia, L., 52

Fabbri, R., 272
Fabian, S. G., 517
Fabiani, M., 545–546
Fabiano, G. A., 275
Fabre, B., 464
Fabricius, W. V., 253
Fagan, A. A., 390
Fagan, J. F., 151–152
Fagot, B. I., 243
Fagundes, C. P., 466
Fahlberg, B., 598
Fais, L., 155
Faja, S., 200, 216, 217, 237, 282, 308, 359
Fakhoury, J., 516
Falbo, T., 251
Falk, M. C., 550–551
Fall, A. M., 364, 365
Fang, L., 463
Fantz, R. L., 124, 127, 134
Farajinia, S., 520
Farb, A. F., 348
Farioli-Vecchioli, S., 520
Farley, F., 361
Farley-Hackel, P., 594
Farlow, M., 553
Farr, R. H., 254, 255, 448
Farrell, M. J., 525
Farrell, M. P., 488
Farrell, S. K., 555
Farrell, S. W., 530
Fasig, L., 177–178
Fatusi, A. O., 406
Fava, N. M., 347
Federmeier, K. D., 553
Feeney, S., 225, 259

Fees, B., 204
Fegert, J. M., 249
Feinberg, M., 186
Feinberg, M. E., 250
Feiring, C., 183, 434
Feldman, D. H., 214
Feldman, H. M., 274
Feldman, R., 93, 185, 187
Feldman, S., 216, 340, 346, 347, 378
Feldon, J. M., 606
Fenelon, A., 609
Feng, B., 362
Feng, L., 513
Feng, X., 559
Feng, Z., 513
Fenning, R. M., 238
Ferguson, C. J., 247
Ferguson-Rome, J. C., 562
Fergusson, D. M., 114, 249
Fernald, A., 159
Ferrari, M., 547
Ferraro, K. F., 527
Ferreira, J. A., 261
Ferris, S. H., 553
Fetterolf, J. C., 417
Feubner, C., 183
Fiatarone Singh, M. A., 269
Field, D., 502
Field, N., 86, 470
Field, R. D., 85, 243
Field, T., 94, 128, 143, 146
Field, T. M., 81, 90, 94, 96
Fielder, R.L., 412
Fiez, J. A., 106
Finch, C. E., 473, 517, 542
Fincham, F. D., 412, 450
Fine, M., 321
Finegood, E. D., 159
Finer, L. B., 348
Finger, B., 184
Fingerhut, A. W., 414, 415, 448
Fingerman, K., 498, 501–504, 582–584
Finkel, E. J., 438
Finkelstein, E. A., 407
Finkelstein, L. M., 555
Finlay, B. L., 49
Fiocco, A. J., 525
Fiori, K. L., 583
Firth, K.M.P., 490
Fischer, C. E., 553
Fischer, K. W., 420
Fischer-Baum, S., 274
Fischhoff, B., 359
Fisette, J. L., 203, 204, 269
Fishel, E., 374, 402
Fisher, B. S., 418
Fisher, C. B., 210, 339, 577
Fisher, G. G., 555
Fisher, P. A., 249
Fiske, A., 558
Fitzgerald, A., 352
Fitzgerald, N., 352
Fitzpatrick, K. K., 356
Fitzsimmons, C., 222

Fivush, R., 147, 148, 215, 216, 281
Fizke, E., 219
Fjell, A. M., 518
Flaherty, E. G., 249
Flamini, R., 529
Flavell, E. R., 218, 219
Flavell, J., 218, 279
Flavell, J. H., 218, 219, 284, 286
Flegal, K. E., 544, 553
Fleming, A. S., 184
Fletcher, B. R., 29–30, 473, 551
Fletcher, J. M., 52, 58
Flicek, P., 52
Flicker, L., 532
Flint, M. S., 53
Flint-Wagner, H. G., 528
Floel, A., 551, 552
Flom, R., 146
Flook, L., 446
Florsheim, P., 384, 450
Flouri, E., 308
Flynn, J. R., 290
Foddy, M., 582
Foehr, U. G., 261, 387–388
Fogel, A., 151
Foley, J. T., 204
Follari, L., 225, 228, 290
Fontana, L., 532
Fontenot, H. B., 63
Forbes, S. C., 530
Forcella, E., 57
Ford, D. Y., 294
Ford, L., 235
Forde, D. R., 30
Forget, H., 489
Forget-Dubois, N., 223
Forster, D. A., 82
Forstmeier, S., 570
Forte, R., 546
Fosco, G. M., 251, 390
Foster, E. M., 393
Fowler, C. D., 558
Fowler, C. G., 462
Fowler, M. G., 114, 214
Fox, B. J., 296
Fox, B. R., 513
Fox, J.A., 30
Fox, M. K., 112, 202
Fox, N. A., 105–106, 108, 109, 168
Fozard, J. L., 526
Fraiberg, S., 123
Fraley, R. C., 184, 434, 582
Franchak, J. M., 117–119, 123, 125, 131
Francis, A. L., 283
Francis, J., 374
Franco, D. L., 406
Franco, P., 111
Frank, G.K.W., 356
Frank, J. L., 390
Frank, M. C., 127
Frankl, V., 478–480, 482
Franz, C. E., 432
Fraser, G., 374

Gump, B., 477
Gunderson, E. A., 316
Gunes, C., 516
Gunn, P. W., 272
Gunnar, M. R., 29, 129, 168, 184, 185, 249
Gunning, T. G., 259
Guo, Q., 599
Guo, Z., 52
Gupta, S., 443
Gur, R. C., 316
Gurwitch, R. H., 310
Gustafsson, J-E., 290
Gutchess, A. H., 552
Gutmann, D. L., 587
Guttentag, C. L., 349
Guttmannova, K., 354

Haase, R. F., 261
Hackel, A., 594
Hadani, H., 217, 218
Haden, C. A., 216
Hadfield, J. C., 500, 501
Hagekull, B., 173
Hagen, J. W., 227
Hagestad, G. O., 500
Hagman, J. O., 356
Hagopian, W., 113
Hairi, N. N., 562
Haith, M. M., 142
Hakuta, K., 298
Hale, D. E., 271
Hale, N., 86
Haley, M., 298
Hall, 490
Hall, C. B., 549
Hall, D. T., 425
Hall, G. S., 340, 379
Hall, L. J., 276
Hall, S. E., 237
Hall, S. S., 56
Hall, W. J., 511
Hallahan, D. P., 277
Hall Haley, M., 37, 298
Halonen, J., 404
Halperin, J. M., 276
Halpern, C. T., 392
Halpern, D. F., 315–317
Halpern, G. T., 384
Halpern-Felsher, B. L., 347
Halpern-Meekin, S., 412
Halt, K., 75
Haltigan, J. D., 184
Haltiwanger, E. P., 515
Hamann, K., 147, 236
Hamilton, B. E., 348
Hamilton, J. L., 344
Hamilton, L. D., 489
Hamlin, J. K., 144
Hammond, R., 390, 391
Hammond, S. I., 217
Hamon, R. R., 586
Han, B., 513
Han, J. J., 281
Han, K. S., 530, 531, 589
Han, W-J., 252
Handler, A. S., 115

Handrinos, J., 243
Hanger, D. P., 559
Hanish, L. D., 324
Hannon, E. H., 126, 128, 130, 131, 141, 143, 144, 149
Hans, J., 448
Hansell, N. K., 392
Hansen, M., 578
Hansen, M. L., 272
Hansen, M. V., 541
Hansen, N. L., 473
Hansson, R., 599, 601, 602
Hanusa, B. H., 96
Haran, C., 95
Harari, Y., 516
Hardaway, C. R., 9, 256, 329, 341, 387
Hardcastle, A. C., 528
Harden, K. P., 64, 344
Hardy, M., 556
Hardy, S. A., 314
Harel, J., 171
Harkins, S. W., 525
Harkness, S., 110, 121, 184
Harley, A. E., 170
Harlow, H. F., 180
Harold, G. T., 187
Harper, K. M., 80
Harrell, R., 555
Harrington, S. E., 599
Harris, C. D., 578
Harris, G., 583
Harris, J., 160, 222, 259
Harris, J. R., 67
Harris, K. L., 274
Harris, K. M., 406
Harris, K. R., 297
Harris, L., 524
Harris, P. L., 201, 217, 220
Harrison, C., 516
Harrison, G. G., 115
Harrison, K., 597
Harrison, M., 270
Hart, B., 158–159, 290
Hart, C. H., 226
Hart, C. N., 202
Hart, D., 177, 314
Hart, S., 169
Harter, S., 234–236, 305, 307, 371
Hartley, A., 473
Hartshorne, H., 240
Hartup, W. W., 67, 258, 323, 326
Harward, S., 276
Harwood, L. J., 114
Hasher, L., 544–547
Hashim, H. A., 351
Haslam, A., 513
Haslam, C., 563
Haslam, S. A., 563
Hassija, C. M., 417
Hasson, F., 599
Hastings, P. D., 318
Hathaway, N., 607
Hatzfeld, J. J., 586
Hauck, F. R., 111

Haugrud, N., 553
Havighurst, R. J., 570
Havighurst, S. S., 170
Hawkes, C., 524
Hawkins, J. A., 362
Hawkins, P., 416
Hawkley, L. C., 584
Hawley, J. A., 462
Hay, P., 356
Hayatbakhsh, R., 205
Hayden, K. M., 548
Haydon, A., 384
Haydon, A. A., 346
Hayes, J. R., 274
Hayes, R., 130, 131
Hayflick, L., 516
Hayslip, B., 599, 601, 602
Hayward, R. D., 478, 563, 564
Hazan, C., 433–435
Hazen, A. L., 249–250
Hazen, C., 142
He, C., 129
He, K., 52
He, N., 520
He, W., 93
He, X., 463
Healey, M. K., 547
Heaney, J.L.J., 531
Heath, V., 407
Hebl, M. R., 426
Hecht, M. A., 318
Hefferman, M. E., 434
Hegaard, H. K., 92
Heiman, G. W., 31
Heimann, M., 146, 148, 180
Hein, D., 249
Heine, C., 524
Heir, T., 608
Hekman, E. E., 520
Helgeson, V. S., 439
Helman, C., 520
Helman, R., 557
Helmreich, R., 318
Helmuth, L., 546
Helson, R., 486, 492, 494, 495, 497, 498, 506
Helwig, C. C., 313–314
Hemmingsson, T., 425
Hemmy, L. S., 521, 553
Henchoz, Y., 409
Henderson, J., 90, 97
Henderson, V. W., 468
Hendrick, J., 225
Hendricks-Munoz, K. D., 93
Hendrie, G., 271
Hendriks, A.A.J., 575
Henggeler, S. W., 390
Henkens, K., 556
Hennessey, B. A., 285
Henninger, D. E., 547
Henninger, M. L., 225, 259
Henretta, J. C., 446
Henriksen, T. B., 80
Hensley, B., 513
Herberman Mash, H. B., 607
Herbers, J. E., 283
Herd, P., 584

Herdt, G., 346
Herek, G. M., 415
Herman-Giddens, M. E., 343
Hernandez, D. C., 9
Hernandez, D. J., 10
Hernandez-Reif, M., 94, 128, 143, 146
Herold, K., 223
Heron, M., 467
Herpertz-Dahlmann, B., 274
Herrera, A. M., 29, 168
Herrera, S. G., 37
Hershey, D. A., 556
Hertel-Fernandez, A., 577
Herting, M. M., 351
Hertzog, C., 544, 550, 551
Herzog, E., 243
Hespos, S. J., 142
Hetherington, E. M., 26, 252–254, 321, 322, 446–447, 451, 452, 454
Hewitt, J., 531
Hewlett, B. S., 188
Heyman, G. D., 235, 306
Hickey, M., 468
Hicks, J. A., 570
Higginbotham, B., 321
Highfield, R., 144
Highhouse, S., 424
Higo, M., 555
Hill, C., 191
Hill, C. R., 320
Hill, P. L., 493, 494, 496, 575
Hill, T. D., 586
Hillemeier, M. M., 189, 190, 227
Hilliard, L. J., 242, 315, 319, 324
Hillman, C., 531, 542, 548, 550
Hillman, C. H., 270
Himes, C. L., 460
Hinderliter, A. L., 408
Hindin, M. J., 406
Hindman, A. H., 227
Hines, M., 92, 241, 414
Hinkle, J. S., 270
Hinshaw, S. P., 275
Hinze, S. W., 587
Hirsch, B. J., 362
Hirsch, J. K., 527
Hirsh-Pasek, K., 153, 155, 156, 158, 160, 161, 222, 258–260
Hita-Yanez, E., 520–521
Hjern, A., 275
Ho, C., 112–113
Ho, G. W., 256
Ho, L. Y., 417
Ho, M., 269
Ho, M. J., 384
Ho, S. C., 464
Hoare, E., 351
Hochberg, C., 522
Hock, R. R., 346
Hockenberry, M., 199
Hodapp, R. M., 293
Hodge, A. M., 588, 589

Hodges, E.V.E., 324, 325
Hodis, H. N., 468
Hoefnagels, M., 48–49
Hoekstra, R. A., 220
Hoerl, C., 121
Hoeve, M., 379
Hofbauer, L. C., 462
Hofer, A., 316
Hofer, B. K., 330–331
Hofer, J., 486
Hofer, S. M., 547
Hoff, E., 161, 221, 256, 298
Hofferth, S. L., 188, 348–349
Hoffman, E., 227
Hoffmeyer, K., 516
Hogan, C., 111
Hogan, C. L., 531, 544, 548
Hogan, D., 378
Hogan, M. J., 546
Hogan, P., 571
Hogerbrugge, M. J., 502, 583
Holahan, C. J., 529
Holden, G. W., 187, 188
Holder, M. K., 343
Holland, C. R., 151–152
Holland, J. C., 202, 203, 607
Holland, J. M., 609
Hollich, G., 130
Hollister, M., 424
Holloway, R. G., 599
Holmes, L. B., 79
Holmes, R. M., 437
Holmes, T. H., 488
Holmin, J. S., 543
Holsen, I., 344
Holt-Hale, S., 202, 269
Holtz, P., 261
Hong, H. G., 249–250
Honig, L. S., 560
Honzik, M., 406
Hood, B. M., 201
Hoogendam, Y. Y., 542, 544
Hooker, K., 576, 577
Hooker, S. A., 479
Hooper, S. R., 56
Hoover, K. W., 407
Hooyman, N., 8, 10
Hooyman, N. R., 604
Hope, D.A.M., 414
Hopkins, B., 120, 121
Hoppmann, C. A., 576
Horn, J. L., 471, 482
Horn, M. C., 489, 490
Horne, R. S., 111
Horner, G., 249
Horowitz, E. K., 298
Horwood, L. J., 249
Hoshino, O., 519
Hoskins, I. A., 90
Hossain, N., 84
Hostinar, C., 68
Hostinar, C.E., 168
Hottensen, D., 607
Houde, O., 209
House, B., 579
Houston, D., 159

Howard, A., 54
Howard, A. L., 353
Howard, E., 580
Howard, K. S., 97
Howe, G. W., 426
Howell, D. C., 30
Howes, C., 258
Hoyer, W. J., 16, 461–462, 476, 522, 525, 529
Hoyert, D. L., 510, 511, 528
Hoyt, J., 286
Hoyt, M. A., 466
Hsu, J. L., 473
Hsu, W. L., 528, 531
Hu, F. B., 532
Hu, J., 514
Hu, J. C., 469
Hu, J. K., 55
Huang, H. W., 553
Huang, J-H, 409
Huang, K., 58
Huang, L., 308
Huang, P. M., 443
Huang, Y., 142, 143
Huart, C., 519–520
Huebner, A. M., 313
Huesmann, L. R., 261, 322
Huettel, S. A., 547
Hugel, H., 599
Hughes, C., 217, 219, 220, 236, 501, 522
Hughes, M., 446
Hughes, T., 448
Huh, S. Y., 112
Hull, S. H., 316
Hulton, L., 467
Hultsch, D. F., 549
Hulur, G., 549
Hummel, T., 519–520
Hummer, J. F., 410
Hunnius, S., 112
Hunt, R. R., 545
Hunt, S. R., 534
Hur, K., 205, 411
Hurley, K. M., 112, 202
Hurst, C., 255
Hurt, H., 81
Hurt, T. R., 354
Husain, M., 544
Hustedt, J. T., 227
Huston, A. C., 256, 320, 322, 341
Hutchinson, S. L., 573
Hutchinson, S. R., 406–407
Hutson, J. R., 75
Huttenlocher, J., 159
Huttenlocher, P. R., 107
Huxhold, O., 584
Huyck, M. H., 475
Huynh, V. W., 352
Hwang, A. C., 463
Hyatt, G., 365
Hybels, C. F., 558
Hyde, D. C., 143
Hyde, J. S., 8, 35, 50, 242, 255, 313, 315–317, 319, 346, 350, 413, 414
Hymel, S., 325
Hyson, M. C., 225, 226

Iacono, W. G., 375, 392
Iams, H. M., 557
Ibrahim, R., 106
Ickovics, J. R., 85, 86, 348
Igarashi, H., 502
Ikenoue, T., 91
Impett, E. A., 371
Imura, T., 126
Ingels, S. J., 364
Ingram, D. D., 478
Inhelder, B., 207
Insana, S. P., 95
Insel, P. M., 7
Iolascon, G., 528
Iovannone, R., 277
Ip, S., 113, 114
Iqbal, M., 75
Irish, C., 578
Irwin, C. E., 407
Irwing, P., 289
Isaac, M., 604
Isaacs, B., 225
Ishak, S., 119, 123, 131
Ishmael, H., 58
Isidori, A. M., 469, 526
Issel, L. M., 86
Ivanenko, A., 202
Iwasa, H., 575
Iwata, S., 93
Izard, C. E., 168
Izard, V., 143

Jacelon, C. S., 599
Jack, B. A., 604
Jackson, A., 604
Jackson, C. A., 10, 388
Jackson, J. J., 575
Jackson, J. S., 563, 586, 587
Jackson, S. L., 28
Jacob, J. I., 190
Jacob, R., 489
Jacobs, C. B., 572, 573
Jacobs, J. M., 549
Jacobs-Lawson, J. M., 556
Jacobson, K. C., 410
Jaeggi, S. M., 214–215
Jaffee, S., 313
Jaffee, S. R., 502
Jager, J., 379, 381
Jahanfar, S., 80
Jalles, J. T., 425
Jalongo, M. R., 223
Jambon, M., 314
James, W., 126
Janicki-Deverts, D., 466
Jansen, J., 113–114
Janssen, L., 203
Jardri, R., 129
Jaremka, L. M., 466
Jarosinska, D., 111, 205, 411
Jaswal, V. K., 201
Jelalian, E., 202
Jellinger, K. A., 518
Jenkins, J. M., 219
Jensen, W., 276
Jesse, D. E., 88
Jeste, D. V., 515, 547
Ji, B. T., 85

Ji, G., 251
Ji, H. F., 533
Ji, Y., 584
Jia, R., 248
Jiang, H. Y., 461, 559
Jiao, S., 251
Jimmieson, N. L., 578
Jin, K., 520
Jin, L., 78
Jin, Y., 182, 297
Jing, Q., 251
Jinyao, Y., 435
Jitendra, A., 273
Joh, A. S., 201
Johansson, M., 286
John, O. P., 494, 495, 497, 498
Johnson, A. A., 516
Johnson, C. L., 582
Johnson, E. J., 513
Johnson, G. B., 49
Johnson, J. S., 297
Johnson, K. J., 588
Johnson, L., 420
Johnson, M., 144
Johnson, M. H., 268, 297
Johnson, R. B., 28
Johnson, S. P., 126–128, 130, 131, 141, 143, 144, 149
Johnson, W., 294, 578
John-Steiner, V., 23, 210
Johnston, A. M., 235
Johnston, J., 275
Johnston, L., 577
Johnston, L. D., 353–354, 409, 410
Jokela, M., 556
Jokinen-Gordon, H., 579
Jolivette, K., 276
Jones, B. F., 421
Jones, B. L., 598
Jones, D., 395
Jones, J., 225, 226
Jones, K., 513
Jones, L., 88–90
Jones, M. C., 344
Jones, M. D., 375
Jones, N. A., 91, 170, 174
Jones, P. S., 583
Jones, R. M., 359
Jones, S., 149, 237
Jones, S. C., 381
Jones, S. M., 228
Jonides, J., 214–215
Jonson, H., 577
Jonson-Reid, M., 250
Joo, E., 556
Joosten, H., 548
Jopp, D., 589
Jordan, C. H., 306, 371
Jordan, K. F., 327
Jose, A., 443
Joseph, J., 48
Joshi, H., 308
Joyner, K., 383–384
Juang, L. P., 374, 375, 380
Juarez, C. A., 249
Judas, M., 78
Judd, F. K., 468

Julian, A. M., 489
Julian, M. M., 62
Jun, J., 570
Jung, C., 4, 459
Jung, W. P., 122
Jungert, T., 324
Juraska, J. M., 519
Jusczyk, P. W., 129
Just, M. A., 220, 276
Jutengren, G., 325

Kaczynski, T., 3, 5, 6, 10, 12, 17, 18
Kadivar, H., 351
Kaelber, D. C., 272
Kaffashi, F., 93
Kagan, J., 168, 169, 171, 173, 174, 183, 432, 534
Kagan, S., 534
Kagitani, H, 467–468
Kahn, J. A., 351
Kahrs, B. A., 122
Kail, M., 553
Kail, R. V., 215
Kalder, M., 90
Kalish, C. W., 222
Kalish, R. A., 602, 605, 611
Kalladka, D., 521
Kalmijn, M., 556
Kalousova, L., 425
Kaloustian, G., 184
Kamiya, M., 560
Kamp, B. J., 578
Kamphaus, R. W., 276
Kan, M. L., 186
Kan, P. F., 222
Kancherla, V., 78, 83
Kane, H. S., 466, 517, 522
Kang, C. B., 530, 531, 589
Kang, H. K., 88
Kang, J. Y., 298
Kannass, K. N., 146
Kanner, A. D., 490
Kantak, C., 60
Kantowitz, B. H., 31–32, 233
Kaplan, A. L., 347, 469
Kapornai, K., 393
Kappeler, E. M., 348
Kar, B. R., 115
Karahuta, E., 314
Karantzas, G. C., 582
Karasik, L. B., 121
Karasik, R. J., 586
Karatsoreos, I. N., 519
Karavia, E. A., 463, 464
Karlamangia, A. S., 466
Karmel, M. P., 177
Karmiloff-Smith, A., 109
Karney, B. R., 444
Karniol, R., 318
Karoly, L. A., 228
Karreman, A., 248
Karmel, M. P., 177
Kaski, D., 561
Kassahn, K. S., 52, 58
Kastenbaum, R., 602, 613
Kastenbaum, R. J., 595, 599, 603
Kasznak, A. W., 571

Kato, T., 441
Kattenstroth, J. C., 549
Katz, J., 412
Katz, L., 228
Katz, P. R., 534
Katzmarzyk, P. T., 532
Kauffman, J. M., 277–278
Kaufman, J. C., 284, 285, 421
Kaur, A., 56
Kautzky-Willer, A., 426
Kavanaugh, R. D., 217
Kavsek, M., 146, 151–152
Kawabata, Y., 317
Kawagoe, T., 544
Kawamoto, K., 8, 10
Kayama, H., 545–546
Kaynak, O., 354, 377–378
Kazakoff, E. R., 579
Kearney, P. M., 80
Kearsley, R. B., 171
Keating, D. P., 294, 360, 361, 420
Keen, R., 117, 122, 126, 131, 201
Keen, S. M., 248, 250
Kehle, T. J., 286
Keigher, S., 563
Keijsers, L., 378
Keiley-Moore, J., 467
Keith, J. D., 376
Kelber, S. T., 606
Kell, H. J., 294, 424
Kelleher, C. J., 90
Keller, A., 235
Keller, H., 177
Keller, M., 519–520
Kelley, A. S., 599
Kelley, G. A., 204
Kelley, J., 531
Kelley, K. S., 204
Kellman, P. J., 123, 127
Kellough, J., 557, 562
Kelly, A. J., 545
Kelly, D. J., 126
Kelly, E., 475
Kelly, J., 322, 451, 452
Kelly, J. P., 127
Kelly, M. E., 545–546
Kelly, Y., 80
Keltner, K. W., 333
Kemp, H., 524
Kemp, J., 524
Kempermann, G., 519
Kempner, S. G., 320, 333
Kendler, K. S., 65
Kendrick, C., 251
Kendrick, K., 325
Kennedy, J. L., 187
Kennedy, K. M., 518, 519
Kennedy-Bergen, R. M., 8
Kennell, H. H., 97
Kennell, J. H., 97
Kenney, C., 274
Kennis, E., 530
Kenny, L. C., 348
Kenny, S., 128
Kensinger, E. A., 552
Kerns, K. A., 258, 321

Lempers, J. D., 218
Lengua, L., 433
Lenhart, A., 388
Lennon, E. M., 150
Lenoir, C. P., 111
Lenroot, R. K., 200
Leon, J., 548
Leonard, C., 286
Leone, J. E., 343
Leong, D. J., 212, 283
Leong, F.T.L., 36
Lepage, J. F., 56
Lereya, S. T., 324
Lerner, H. G., 431
Lerner, J. V., 11, 339,
    341, 375, 377
Lerner, R. M., 345
Lerner-Geva, L., 468
Lesaux, N. K., 298
Leshikar, E. D., 545, 551, 552
Lessow-Hurley, J., 298
Lester, B. M., 81, 91
Leung, P.W.L., 393
Leuschen, J., 523
Levelt, W.J.M., 6
Levenson, R. W., 318
Leventhal, T., 329, 341, 387, 390
Lever-Duffy, J., 388
Levin, J. A., 30
LeVine, S., 492
Levine, T. P., 81
Levinson, D., 505, 506
Levinson, D. J., 476,
    486, 487, 495
Levy, F., 519–520
Levy, J. C., 23
Lewin, K., 19
Lewis, C., 188
Lewis, J., 47
Lewis, J. A., 47
Lewis, M., 169, 177, 183,
    236, 328, 434, 526
Lewis, M. D., 237, 576
Lewis, T. L., 131
Lhila, A., 92
Li, B. J., 82
Li, C., 112
Li, D., 255
Li, D. K., 111
Li, F. J., 533
Li, H., 60, 584
Li, J., 91
Li, S-C., 572
Li, W., 78, 191, 463
Li, Y., 325, 610
Liang, J., 205, 411
Liang, Y. J., 271
Liben, L. S., 241, 242, 244,
    313, 315, 316, 319
Libertus, K., 121, 122
Lichtenstein, P., 274
Lickenbrock, D. M., 171
Lickliter, R., 53, 187
Lie, E., 148
Liebergott, J., 155
Liebkind, K., 10
Liekweg, K., 261

Liets, L. C., 520
Lieven, E., 156
Lifter, K., 156
Lifton, R. J., 604
Light, L. C., 553
Lightner, C., 607
Li-Korotky, H. S., 524
Lillard, A., 259
Lillard, A. S., 217
Lillenes, M. S., 560
Lim, J. H., 60
Lim, K. O., 553
Lin, C. C., 82
Lin, F. R., 491, 523, 524
Lin, I-F., 581
Lin, J., 587
Lin, S. Y., 205, 411
Lin, X., 503
Lindau, S. T., 470, 526
Lindberg, S. M., 316
Lindblad, F., 275
Linde, K., 548
Lindenberger, U., 5, 147, 460,
    541, 542, 550, 572, 573
Lindholm-Leary, K., 298
Lindsay, R. K., 82
Lindsey, D.T., 127
Lindstrom, M., 447
Lindwall, M., 550
Lippa, R. A., 414
Lippman, L. A., 376
Lipschitz, J. M., 393
Lipton, J., 56, 143
Lira, F. S., 521
Lisha, N. E., 403
Liszkowski, U., 222
Little, J. P., 530
Little, K. C., 437
Littleton, H., 417
Liu, G., 52
Liu, R. X., 386
Liu, S., 126
Liu, Y. H., 90
Liu, Z., 464
Liu-Ambrose, T., 548, 552
Lively, A., 329
Lively, W., 305
Livingston, G., 562
Lleo, A., 56
Llewellyn, C. H., 271
Lliffe, S., 589
Lloyd, J. W., 296
Lloyd, S. A., 383
Loaiza, V. M., 474
LoBue, V., 128
Lochman, J. J., 122
Lock, J., 356
Lock, M., 468
Loeber, R., 390
Logan, A. G., 463
Logsdon, M. C., 96
Lohaus, A., 152
Lok, D. P., 572
Londono-Vallejo, J. A., 516
Long, S., 92
Longman, P., 578
Longo, M. R., 128

Loosli, S. V., 281
Lopez, B., 109
Lopez, E. I., 320
Lopez, L., 281
Lopez-Tello, G., 378
Loponen, M., 465
Loprinzi, P. D., 558
Lorenz, K., 25
Lovden, M., 542
Love, J. M., 228, 290
Love, V., 82
Lovinsky-Desir, S, 79
Low, J., 218
Low, S., 384
Lowdermilk, D. L., 83, 85, 89
Lowe, J. R., 179
Lowe, K., 378
Lowenstein, A., 227
Lowes, L., 607
Lowry, N. C., 519
Loya, F., 275
Lozoff, B., 112, 202
Lu, C. J., 55
Lu, P. H., 518, 544
Lubinski, D., 294
Lucas, R. E., 425, 494
Lucas-Thompson, R., 252
Lucchetti, A. L., 478, 563
Lucchetti, G., 478, 563
Lucovnik, M., 92
Luders, E., 316
Ludington-Hoe, S. M., 93
Ludwig, M., 488
Luijk, M. P., 184
Luiselli, J. K., 220
Lukowski, A. F., 147–149, 286
Lumpkin, A., 204, 269, 271
Lumpkin, G. T., 494
Luna, B., 345
Lund, D., 609
Lund, H. G., 353
Lundervold, A. J., 474
Lundh, L. G., 393
Lundin, A., 425
Lungu, O., 542
Luo, J., 406
Luo, L., 544, 545
Luo, Y., 142, 513, 585
Luong, G., 432
Luptak, M., 607
Luque-Contreras, D., 559
Luria, A., 243
Lusardi, A., 476
Lusby, C. M., 105
Lushington, K., 109, 201
Lustig, C., 544, 553
Luszcz, M., 545, 546
Luszczynska, A., 466, 488
Luyster, F. S., 407
Lykken, D., 48
Lynch, A., 10, 407
Lynch, E., 92
Lynch, J. L., 271
Lynch, M., 327
Lynchard, N. A., 572
Lyndaker, C., 467
Lynn, S. J., 417

Lyon, G. J., 52
Lyon, G. R., 274
Lyon, T. D., 286
Lyons, H., 412
Lyons, J. L., 500
Lyons, K. E., 283
Lyons, M., 277
Lyseng-Williamson, K. A., 92
Lyubomirsky, S., 244

Ma, L., 271
Ma, Y-Y., 294
Maalouf, F. T., 392
Macari, S., 149
Macartney, S., 581
Maccallum, F., 62, 607
Maccoby, E. E., 243, 245
MacDonald, S.W.S., 464
MacDougall, B. J., 597
MacFarlan, S. J., 188
MacFarlane, J. A., 130
MacGeorge, E. L., 319
Machado, B., 356
Machado, L., 546
Machado-Vidotti, H. G., 530
Maciejewski, P. K., 607
Mack, W. J., 468
Mackin, R. S., 548
Maclennan, A. H., 468
Macneil, L. G., 522
Madanat, F., 272
Madden, D. J., 520, 543,
    544, 547
Mader, S. S., 17, 49, 54
Madill, A., 29
Madrid, J. A., 517
Maercker, A., 608
Maffei, L., 109
Magee, C. A., 381
Magennis, R., 475
Maggs, J. L., 353
Magnuson, K., 10, 11
Mah, L., 599
Mahalik, J. R., 412
Maher, J. P., 409
Maher, M., 205
Mahn, H., 23, 210
Maholmes, V., 256, 290
Mahoney, J. R., 543
Maier, H., 459
Maillard, P., 463
Maines, D. R., 491
Malamitsi-Puchner, A., 349
Malik, R., 52
Malinen, S., 577
Mall, J. F., 515
Mallet, E., 111
Maloy, R. W., 261
Manard, M., 6
Manca, T., 478
Mandal, S., 55
Mandara, J., 321
Mandell, A. R., 544
Mandler, J. M., 147–149,
    163, 206
Manenti, R., 520, 552
Maner, J. K., 436

Mann, N., 524
Mann, T., 408
Manore, M., 112, 271, 409
Mansvelt, J., 584
Manthos, M., 412
Manton, K. I., 479
Mantyh, P. W., 524
Manuck, S. B., 67, 68
Maramara, L. A., 93
Marcdante, K., 105
Marceau, K., 343
Marcell, J. J., 462
Marcello, E., 519
Marchetti, D., 81
Marcia, J. E., 373, 374, 396
Marcotte, T. D., 353
Mares, M-L., 261
Margraf, J., 274
Margrett, J. A., 474
Marie, C., 129
Markant, J. C., 13, 107, 109,
    200, 268, 308, 345
Markham, C. M., 347
Markham, K. B., 92
Markides, K. S., 585
Markman, E., 156, 222
Markman, H. J., 445, 446
Markowitsch, H. J., 547
Marks, A. K., 255–256
Markus, H., 497, 576
Marmorstein, N. R., 392
Marques, L., 607
Marquie, J. C., 548
Marsh, H., 235, 306
Marshall, B. L., 526
Marshall, N. E., 83
Marshall, P. J., 148
Marshall, S. K., 378
Marshall, T. R., 170
Marsiske, M., 522
Martin, A., 215
Martin, A. J., 306
Martin, C., 198
Martin, C. L., 87, 91,
    92, 243, 315
Martin, J. A., 88, 245, 348
Martin, L. R., 16, 575
Martin, M., 460, 488
Martin, P., 488, 513
Martinelli, M., 525
Martins, W. P., 467
Maruyama, N. C., 610
Mascalo, M. F., 420
Mash, C., 131
Mash, E. J., 275
Mason, C., 531
Mason, K. A., 51
Mason, L., 274
Mason, M. J., 381
Masoodi, N., 560
Masselli, G., 59
Mastekaasa, A., 394
Masten, A. S., 10, 183, 283,
    309, 403
Master, A., 332
Mastergeorge, A. M., 227, 228
Masters, K. S., 479

Masters, R. K., 532
Masters C., 437
Mata, J., 531, 544, 548
Matamura, M., 64
Matas, L., 171
Mate, I., 517
Mateus, V., 146
Mather, M., 572
Matheson, E. M., 532
Mathews, B., 321
Matlow, J. N., 75
Matos, A. P., 261
Matsuba, M. K., 314
Matsuda, H., 82
Matthews, C. E., 530
Matthews, K., 477
Matthews, N. L., 220
Mattison, J. A., 533
Mattock, K., 129
Mattson, M. P., 521
Mattys, S. L., 553
Maurer, D., 131
Maurizio, S., 275
Maxson, S. C., 64
May, D., 242
May, M. S., 240
Mayas, J., 542, 550
Mayer, K. D., 81
Mayer, S. D., 526
Mays, K. L., 276
Mayton, M. R., 276
Mazzucato, V., 256
Mbugua Gitau, G., 84
McAdams, D. P., 496
McAuley, E., 570
McAuley, P. A., 532
McBride-Chang, C., 224
McBride Murry, V., 67
McBurney, W., 513
McCabe, D. P., 474
McCabe, F., 96
McCaffery, J. M., 67, 68
McCardle, P., 224
McCarthy, M. R., 329
McCartney, K., 10,
    11, 190, 192
McClain, C. S., 604
McClellan, M. D., 568
McClelland, A., 329, 387
McClelland, K., 54–55
McCormack, L. L., 271
McCormack, S. E., 269
McCormack, T., 121
McCormick, C. B.,
    285, 286, 297
McCourt, J., 594
McCourt, R., 594
McCourt, S. N., 395
McCoy, D. C., 237
McCoy, K. P., 186, 253
McCoy, M. L., 248, 250
McCrae, R. R., 488, 493,
    494, 505
McCullough, B. M., 585
McCullough, M. E., 478, 604
McCutcheon, V. V., 411
McDaniel, M. A., 545

McDermott, B., 309
McDermott, J. M., 61–63
McDonald, J., 388
McDonald, S., 61
McDonald, S. D., 61
McDonough, I. M., 543
McDonough, J. E., 578
McDonough, L., 149
McDougall, S., 579
McDuffie, A., 56
McElhaney, K. B., 378
McElvaney, R., 378
McElwain, N. L., 171
McEwen, B. S., 519
McGarry, J., 96
McGarvey, C., 111
McGee, H., 597
McGee, K., 277
McGee, T. R., 390
McGinley, M., 241
McGough, E. L., 531, 548,
    550, 552, 588
McGrath, S. K., 97
McGue, M., 375
McGuffin, P., 52
McHale, J., 248
McHale, S., 252
McHale, S. M., 250, 378, 499
McIlfatrick, S., 599
McInerney, M., 579
McIntosh, E., 489
McIsaac, C., 383, 384
McKay, A. S., 421
McKenna, K.Y.A., 438
McKenna, L., 465
McKenzie, B. E., 127, 128
McKinney, E. S., 83
McLaughlin, K., 600
McLaughlin, K. A., 105–106
McLellan, J. A., 377
McLeod, G. F., 249
McLeod, S., 272
McLoyd, V., 9, 11, 256,
    329, 341, 387
McMahon, C. G., 469
McMahon, D. M., 78
McMillan, C. T., 559
McMillan, J. H., 328
McNeal, D., 109
McNeil, D. A., 85, 86
McNicholas, F., 93
McNulty, J. K., 417, 435
McRae, K., 308
McWilliams, L. A., 435
Meacham, J., 235
Meade, C. S., 348
Meadows, S. O., 446
Measelle, J., 187
Mechakra-Tahiri, S. D., 609
Meeks, S., 602
Meeks, T. W., 547
Meerlo, P., 95
Mehari, A., 57
Meikle, J., 531
Meiksins, P., 460
Meins, E., 220
Meisel, V., 275

Melendez-Moral, J. C., 570
Melhuish, E., 191
Melia, K. M., 599
Mellor, J. M., 579
Meltzer, A., 147, 438
Meltzer-Brody, S., 95
Meltzoff, A. N., 141, 143–148,
    163, 315
Melzi, G., 187
Memari, A., 276
Menchola, M., 571
Mendes, W. B., 168, 170
Mendle, J., 64, 344
Menec, V. H., 585
Menendez, S., 186
Meng, X., 588, 599
Menn, L., 125, 155, 221
Mennecke, A., 411
Mennella, J. A., 130
Menon, R., 60, 75
Menyuk, P., 155
Mepham, S. O., 104
Merad, M., 519
Meras-Rios, M. A., 559
Mercy, J. A., 205
Meredith, N. V., 199
Merewood, A., 114
Merrell, K. W., 276
Merrill, D. M., 498, 503
Merrill, J. E., 410
Mersy, E., 60
Merz, E-M., 321
Mesman, J., 179
Mess, F., 203, 271
Messiah, S. E., 81
Mestre, T. A., 561
Mesulam, M. M., 559
Metcalfe, J., 286
Metha, A., 327
Metzger, A., 377–378
Metzger, A., 377–378
Meyer, A. M., 553
Meyer, M. H., 587
Meyer, S. C., 241
Meyer, S. L., 90
Meyer, U., 270
Mezzacappa, E., 308
Michael, R. T., 413, 414, 469
Michalska-Malecka, K., 523
Michaud, P. A., 86
Miche, M., 584
Mickelson, K. D., 186
Midouhas, E., 308
Miga, E. M., 379
Mike, A., 493
Mikulincer, M., 433, 435
Milan, S., 379
Milberg, A., 608
Milburn, N. G., 394
Milesi, G., 60
Miljkovic, M. D., 598
Miller, B. C., 347
Miller, C., 11, 68, 244,
    446, 448, 514
Miller, C. F., 315
Miller, J. G., 313
Miller, K., 598
Miller, L. M., 579

Miller, M., 275
Miller, M. D., 219, 607
Miller, P. H., 21, 23, 216,
    219, 358
Miller, R. A., 517
Miller, R. L., 79
Miller, S., 395
Miller-Perrin, C. L., 250
Mills, B., 361
Mills, C., 214
Mills, C. M., 235, 306
Mills, D., 214
Mills, K., 13, 106–108,
    344, 345
Mills-Koonce, W. R., 172
Milman, N. B., 327
Milne, E., 85
Milner, A., 426
Milte, C. M., 588
Mindell, J., 201
Mindell, J. A., 110
Miner, J. L., 189, 190
Miner, M. M., 469
Ming, X., 93
Miniussi, C., 520, 552
Minkler, M., 501
Minnes, S., 81
Minniti, F., 113
Minsart, A. F., 83
Miotto, E. C., 544
Mireles-Rios, R., 378
Mirvis, P. H., 425
Mischel, W., 24, 216
Mishara, B. L., 598
Mishra, G. D., 467
Miskovsky, M. J., 406
Mission, J. F., 83
Mistry, J., 8
Mistry, R. S., 9, 256, 319,
    329, 341, 387
Mitchell, A. B., 317
Mitchell, A. J., 93, 513
Mitchell, B. A., 497
Mitchell, J. R., 532
Mitchell, M. B., 550, 551
Mitchell, O. S., 476
Mitchell, V., 492
Mitchell, W., 190
Miyake, K., 182
Miyakoshi, K., 91
Mize, K. D., 169, 174
Moak, G. S., 562
Mobley, A. S., 519–520
Mock, S. E., 414
Moen, P., 423, 426, 460,
    475, 555–557
Mohamed-Ali, M. I., 179
Moilanen, J. M., 468
Moise, K. J., 60
Molina, B. S., 275
Molina, R. C., 349
Mollee, P., 58
Moller, J., 609
Molton, I. R., 525
Monahan, K., 345
Money, K. M., 107
Monsell, S. E., 559

Monserud, M. A., 500, 503
Montagna, P., 111
Montague, M., 273
Monteiro, M., 600
Montessori, M., 225
Montgomery-Downs, H. E., 95
Monti, J. M., 270
Montirosso, R., 91
Montoya Arizabaleta, A. V., 85
Moon, R. Y., 111
Moore, B. S., 216
Moore, D., 52, 384
Moore, D. S., 18, 30, 52–55,
    58, 67, 68, 187, 514
Moore, M. K., 143, 148
Moore, M. W., 106
Moore, S. R., 344
Moorefield, B. S., 321
Moos, B., 535
Moraes, W., 520
Moran, S., 289
Morasch, K. C., 105, 108, 168
Moravcik, E., 225, 259
Moreau, C., 441
Moreira, S. R., 531
Morgan, S., 80
Morin, C. M., 521
Morison, V., 125
Moro, M. R., 256
Moro-Garcia, M. A., 531
Morra, L., 548
Morra, S., 280
Morris, A. S., 239, 314, 318
Morris, B. H., 392, 514
Morris, B. J., 130
Morris, P., 25
Morris, P. A., 25, 26
Morris, R. J., 309
Morris, Y. P., 309
Morrison, G. S., 225,
    228, 279, 290
Morrison, R. S., 599
Morrison-Beedy, D., 347
Morrissey, T. W., 189
Morrow, C. E., 81
Morrow-Howell, N., 570
Mortensen, O., 186
Mortimer, J. T., 424
Moscovitch, M., 520
Moses, A.M.R., 541
Moses, L. J., 217, 282
Mosher, W. D., 443
Mosing, M. A., 575
Moskalev, A. A., 514
Moss, E., 434
Moss, M. S., 609
Moss, P., 189, 252
Moss, S. Z., 609
Motowidlo, S. J., 424
Motti-Stefanidi, F., 10
Moulson, M. C., 105–106, 179
Moutsiana, C., 182
Moyer, A., 443
Moyer, M. W., 533
Mparmpakas, D., 84
Mroczek, D., 495, 496
Mroczek, D. K., 496, 572

Perry, N., 137
Perry, N. B., 237, 238
Perry, S. E., 83
Perry, T. B., 326
Persky, H. R., 297
Pesce, Crova, L., 270
Peskin, H., 344
Pessia, E., 58
Peterman, K., 122
Peters, K. F., 55
Petersen, I. T., 68
Petersen, J. L., 413
Peterson, C. C., 220, 531
Peterson, G. W., 245–246
Peterson, S. R., 307
Petersson, B., 62
Petrick-Steward, E., 210
Petrill, S. A., 55
Pettigrew, T. L., 124
Pfefferbaum, B., 309
Pfeifer, M., 173
Pfeiffer, U. J., 126
Phadke, S. R., 56
Philbin, J. M., 348
Phillips, A. C., 531
Phillips, D. A., 227
Phillips, L. R., 578
Phillips, S. M., 570
Phinney, J. S., 255–256, 374, 375
Piaget, J., 21–22, 26, 27, 39, 131, 134, 136–145, 148, 149, 162, 163, 206–211, 213, 214, 224, 230, 236, 239, 258, 259, 263, 278–280, 301, 310, 313, 357, 358, 367, 401, 419, 428
Piaget, L., 136–138, 145
Piantadosi, S. T., 145
Piazza, J. R., 489, 490, 558, 580, 581, 583
Picasso, P., 208
Piccinin, A. M., 547
Pick, A. D., 121, 146
Pick, H., 131
Pickens, T. B., 520
Piehler, T. F., 317
Pieperhoff, P., 473
Pierce, R. S., 542
Piette, J., 597
Pike, A., 186
Pilkington, P. D., 585
Pillai Riddell, R., 129
Pinderhughes, E., 61–63
Pines, A., 468
Ping, H., 113
Pinninti, S. G., 83
Pinquart, M., 183, 570
Pinsker, J. E., 56
Piper, B. J., 81
Pirutinsky, S., 479
Pisoni, D. B., 129
Pitzer, L. M., 502
Pixley, J. E., 488
Pizza, V., 467
Place, S., 298
Place, S. S., 436
Platt, B., 392

Plischke, H., 579
Plomin, R., 67, 68, 174, 187, 291
Plucker, J., 284
Plumert, J. M., 121
Pohanka, M., 559
Poil, S. S., 560
Polat, U., 522
Polen-Petit, N., 346
Poll, J., 604
Pollack, P., 561
Pollack, W., 318–319
Polo-Kantola, P., 465
Pomerantz, E., 336
Pomerantz, E. M., 320, 333, 378
Pontifex, M. B., 276
Pooler, A. M., 559
Poon, L. W., 513, 516
Popenoe, D., 443, 444
Popkin, B. M., 271
Portman, J., 327
Posada, G., 184
Posner, J., 215, 275
Posner, M. I., 30, 145, 214–215
Postolache, P., 464
Poston, D. L., 251
Potapova, N. V., 175
Potochnick, S., 386
Potter, J. D., 533
Potthast, N., 249
Poulin, F., 381
Poulin-Dubois, D., 124
Powell, B., 184
Powell, D., 274
Powell, S. A., 7, 327
Power, T. G., 258, 260
Powers, C. J., 323, 326
Prabhakar, H., 423
Prado, E. L., 115
Prager, K. J., 438
Prakash, R. S., 549
Prameela, K. K., 113
Pratt, C., 218
Pratt, L., 160–161, 223, 224
Prendergast, C., 271
Pressler, E., 9
Pressley, M., 286, 328
Preston, S. H., 532
Preville, M., 489
Price, C. A., 556, 581
Price, C. D., 504
Price, D. D., 525
Price, J., 448
Price, P., 274
Prickett, K. C., 557
Pridham, K. A., 112
Prigerson, H. G., 607
Principe, G., 216
Prinstein, M. J., 325, 382
Prinzie, P., 250
Priyadarshi, B., 544
Propper, C. B., 172
Proulx, C. M., 446
Pryor, J. H., 375
Przbyksi, M., 437
Puccini, D., 222
Pudrovska, T., 488, 498, 501

Pufal, M. A., 271
Pugh, L., 89
Puhl, R. M., 324
Pullen, P.C., 277
Puma, M., 227
Pursell, G., 326
Purtell, K. M., 11
Putallaz, M., 317
Puzzanchera, C., 389, 390

Qian, Z., 532
Qin, J. B., 82
Qin, L., 333
Qu, H., 289
Quereshi, A. I., 598
Quigley, C., 542–543
Quinlan-Davidson, M., 351
Quinn, J. F., 476
Quinn, P. C., 148, 149
Quintino, O., 94
Quoidbach, J., 494, 496

Rabaglietta. E., 374
Raby, K. L., 18, 183–184, 434
Rachner, T. D., 462
Radey, C., 250
Radmacher, K. A., 372
Radulovich, S., 513, 514
Radvansky, G. A., 572
Rahe, R. H., 488
Rahnema, C. D., 469
Raikes, H., 160
Raikes, H. A., 182
Raiser, S. N., 522
Raj, T., 52
Raj, V. R., 105
Rajaraman, P., 82
Rakison, D. H., 142, 148, 149
Rakoczy, H., 217–218
Raley, R. K., 443
Ram, K. T., 113
Ram, N., 186
Ramani, G. B., 179
Ramasamy, R., 469
Ramchandani, P. G., 188
Ramey, C. T., 291
Ramey, S. L., 191, 291
Ramirez-Rodriguez, G., 519
Ramos, E., 58
Ramos, J. S., 377
Ramsey, D. A., 105
Ramus, F., 274
Rancourt, D., 381
Randall, G. K., 513
Randall, W. L., 569
Randel, B., 330–331
Randolph, S. M., 500
Ranhoff, A., 529
Ransmayr, G., 561
Rao, S. L., 115
Rapkin, B. D., 362
Rapp, B., 274
Rapp, P. R., 29–30, 473, 551
Rast, P., 547
Rasulo, D., 581, 584
Ratelle, C. F., 362
Rathunde, K., 7
Ratner, N. B., 159–160

Rau, B. L., 557
Raulin, M. L., 28
Rauner, A., 203, 271
Ravaglia, G., 558
Raven, P. H., 51, 53
Raver, C. C., 237, 245, 256
Ray, J. G., 443
Raz, N., 518, 545, 551
Raznahan, A., 200, 269, 344
Razza, R. A., 215
Razza, R. P., 283
Read, J. P., 410
Reale, M. A., 560
Realini, J. P., 350
Rebbechi, D., 518–519
Rebok, G. W., 6, 50, 550, 551, 588
Reddel, R. R., 516
Redeker, N. S., 202
Redford, L., 249
Redshaw, M., 97
Reeb-Sutherland, C., 168
Reed, S. D., 468
Reedy, E. J., 421
Reese, B. M., 347
Reeve, C. L., 289
Regalado, M., 246
Regan, P., 346
Regev, R. H., 92
Rehbein, M., 108, 109
Reibis, R. K., 526
Reich, S. M., 112, 113
Reichstadt, J., 556
Reid, L., 348–349
Reid, P. T., 35–36
Reiff, M. I., 274
Reijmerink, N. E., 55
Reijntjes, A., 325
Reilly, D., 316
Reindollar, R. H., 61
Reis, S. M., 294
Reisman, A. S., 608
Rejeski, W. J., 522
Rendall, M. S., 446
Rengasamy, M., 379
Reno, V. P., 578
Renz, M., 603–604
Renzetti, C. M., 8
Renzulli, J. S., 294
Repacholi, B. M., 218
Repetti, R., 446
Resick, P. A., 417
Resnick, B., 585
Resnick, B., 585
Reuter-Lorenz, P., 7, 549, 552
Reuter-Lorenz, P. A., 551
Reutzel, D. R., 296
Reyes, S., 521
Reyna, V., 361
Reyna, V. E., 282
Reyna, V. F., 282, 344, 358–361
Reynolds, D. K., 602, 611
Reynolds, E. H., 78, 84
Reynolds, G. D., 106
Reznick, J. S., 28, 30, 280
Rhoades, G. K., 441
Rhodes, A. E., 393
Rice, J., 555
Richards, J. E., 106, 146

Richardson, C. R., 409
Richardson, G. A., 81, 584
Richardson, M., 555
Richardson, M. S., 425, 426
Richardson, V. E., 608
Richards-Tutor, C., 298
Riche, D. M., 469
Richens, J. L., 560
Rickman, A., 385
Rideout, V., 387–388
Riediger, M., 530, 572, 573, 588, 589
Riesch, S. K., 202
Rietjens, J. A., 597
Riggins, T., 81, 148
Righi, G., 105–106, 126, 144
Riksen-Walraven, J. M., 113–114
Riley, K. P., 521
Riley, M., 203
Rimsza, M. E., 406
Rinehart, S., 93
Ripke, N. N., 320, 322
Rippon, I., 577
Risley, T. R., 158–159, 290
Ritzmann, R., 531
Riva Crugnola, C., 349
Rivas-Drake, D., 372, 375, 376, 387
Rivers, S. E., 359, 361
Rix, S., 554
Rizzo, M. S., 58
Rizzo, V. M., 562
Rizzuto, D., 532
Roane, B. M., 202
Robbers, S., 252
Roberie, D. R., 463, 464, 525–526
Roberto, K. A., 439, 583
Roberts, B. W., 372, 493–496, 575
Roberts, C., 612
Roberts, D. F., 261
Roberts, D. P., 387–388
Roberts, G., 364, 365
Robertson, L. T., 532
Robine, J. M., 511
Robins, R. W., 371, 372, 494, 575, 576
Robinson, S.R.R., 117, 119, 120, 131, 132, 179
Robinson-Zanartu, C., 327
Robitaille, A., 542
Robles, T., 466, 517, 522
Robson, S., 389, 390
Rochan, P. A., 15
Rochette, L. M., 204–205
Rochlen, A. B., 188
Rocke, C., 467
Rode, S. S., 97
Rodgers, C., 93
Rodgers, S., 489
Rodin, J., 535, 604
Rodkey, E. N., 129
Rodkin, P. C., 381
Rodriguez, E. T., 223
Rodrique, K. M., 518, 519
Rodriquez Villar, S., 607

subject index

Binge drinking, 354, 410, 529
Biological influences
  on emotional development, 168–169
  on gender development, 241–242
  on language development, 157–158
  on temperament, 174–175
Biological parents, adopted children and, 63
Birth order, 251
Birth process
  childbirth methods and, 88–91
  childbirth setting and attendants and, 87–88
  stages of, 87
Birth weight, low, 92–93
Bisexuality, 414
Blastocyst, 74
Blood type incompatibility, prenatal development and, 82
Body image, 343–344
Body mass index (BMI), 203
Bond density, 462
Bonding, parent-infant, 97
Bottle feeding, 112–113
Boys. See Males
Bradley Method of childbirth, 89
Brain/brain development
  in adolescents, 344–345
  attention deficit hyperactivity disorder and, 275
  autism spectrum disorders and, 276–277
  changes in regions of, 107–108
  in early childhood, 200
  early experiences and, 108–109
  gender differences in, 316
  in infants, 105–109
  language development and, 157–158
  in late adulthood, 518–521, 551–552
  lateralization of, 520
  mapping of, 106
  memory and, 147
  in middle and late childhood, 268–269
  neuroconstructivist view of, 109
  neurogenesis and, 78, 519–520
  in prenatal period, 77–78
  self-regulation and, 308
Brain death, 597
Brain-imaging techniques, 59–60, 552
Brainology workshop (Dweck), 332
Brain size, primate vs. human, 49
Brainstorming, 285

Brazelton Neonatal Behavioral Assessment Scale (NBAS), 91, 116, 150
Breast cancer, 113
Breast feeding, 112–113
Breech position, 90
Bringing Home Baby Project, 186
Broca's area, 157
Bronfenbrenner's ecological theory, 25–26
Bulimia nervosa, 356
Bullying, 324–325, 393

Caffeine, 80
Calorie restriction, 532–533
Cancer
  breast feeding and, 113
  in middle and late childhood, 272
Cardiovascular disease
  in late adulthood, 525–526
  in middle adulthood, 463–464
  in middle and late childhood, 271–272
Cardiovascular system, stress and, 466–467
Career counselors, 42, 405
Careers. See also Work
  in early adulthood, 423–424
  impact of work and, 424–425
  occupational outlook and, 424
Careers in life-span development
  audiologist, 43
  career counselor, 42, 405
  child-care director, 190
  child life specialist, 44, 272
  clinical psychologist, 42
  college/university professor, 41, 479, 504
  counseling psychologist, 42
  developmental psychologist, 36, 218
  director of children's services/Head Start, 227
  drug counselor, 43
  early childhood educator, 41
  educational psychologist, 36, 42
  elementary/secondary school teacher, 41
  ELL teacher, 299
  exceptional children (special education) teacher, 41
  family and consumer science educator, 42
  genetic counselor, 44, 58
  geriatric nurse, 43, 534
  geriatric physician, 43
  gerontologist, 42
  health psychologist, 391
  home health aide, 44
  home hospice nurse, 600
  infant assessment specialist, 151

marriage and family therapist, 44, 248
neonatal nurse, 43
nurse-midwife, 43
obstetrician/gynecologist, 43
occupational therapist, 43
parent educator, 451
pediatrician, 43, 116
pediatric nurse, 43
perinatal nurse, 89
physical therapist, 43
preschool/kindergarten teacher, 42
psychiatrist, 42, 331
rehabilitation counselor, 42
researcher, 41, 363
school counselor, 42
school psychologist, 42
social worker, 42–43
speech therapist, 43–44
therapeutic/recreation therapist, 43
Caregivers/caregiving
  attachment and, 183, 184, 244
  eating behavior and, 202
  emotional expressiveness and, 237
  for individuals with Alzheimer disease, 560–561
  maternal and paternal, 188–189
Care perspective, 312, 313
Case studies, 29
Cataracts, 523
Categorization, in infants, 149
Causality, 142
Cellular clock theory of aging, 516
Centenarians
  factors involved in increased life span of, 514–515
  opinions of, 513–514
  statistics related to, 511
  studies of, 511–513
Centration, 208
Cephalocaudal pattern, 104
Cerebral cortex, 269
Cesarean delivery, 90–91
Chastity, 445
Child abuse, 248. See also Child maltreatment
Childbearing, trends in, 451
Childbirth. See Birth process
Child care
  parental leave and, 189
  quality of, 190–192
  strategies for, 192
  variations in, 189–190
Child-care directors, 190
Child-centered kindergarten, 225
Child-directed speech, 159–160
Childhood amnesia, 148
Child life specialists, 44, 272

Child maltreatment
  contexts of, 249
  developmental consequences of, 249–250
  overview of, 248
  types of, 249
Child neglect, 249
Child psychiatrists, 331
Children. See also specific periods of childhood
  adopted, 61–64
  age of bearing, 451
  average, 323
  bullied, 324–325
  controversial, 323
  in divorced families, 252–254
  neglected, 249, 323
  popular, 323
  poverty among, 9–11
  rejected, 323–324
  remarriage and, 447–448
  social policy and, 8–11, 341
  temperament in, 433
Child welfare workers, 44
Chinese Longitudinal Healthy Longevity Survey, 511, 513
Cholesterol, 269, 463, 464
Chorionic villus sampling (CVS), 60
Chromosomal abnormalities, 55–56
Chromosomes
  explanation of, 51
  genes and, 53–54
  sex differences and, 241
Chronic disorders, 466. See also Health; Illness and disease
Chronosystem, 26
Cigarette smoking. See Tobacco use
Circumcision, 129–130
Climacteric, 467
Clinical psychologists, 42
Cliques, 382
Cocaine, as teratogen, 81
Cognitive control, in adolescents, 359–360
Cognitive development. See also Information processing
  in adolescents, 357–362
  attention and, 145–147
  components of, 5
  concept formation and categorization and, 148–149
  conditioning and, 145
  in early childhood, 206–220
  exercise and, 270, 549–550
  gender differences in, 244, 316–317
  imitation and, 148
  in infants, 137–161
  memory and, 147–148

in middle adulthood, 470–474
in middle and late childhood, 278–286
Piaget's theory of, 21–23 (See also Piaget's cognitive developmental theory)
play and, 258
religion and, 376–377
sleep and, 112
Vygotsky's theory of, 23, 210–213
Cognitive flexibility, 360
Cognitive function. See also Intelligence; Memory; Thinking
  in late adulthood, 541–553
  multidimensionality and multidirectionality of, 541–547
Cognitive mechanics, 541–542
Cognitive neuroscience, 551–552
Cognitive pragmatics, 542, 543
Cognitive processes, in infants, 137–139
Cognitive skills training, 550–551
Cognitive theories
  evaluation of, 23
  information-processing, 23
  of Piaget, 21–23 (See also Piaget's cognitive developmental theory)
  of Vygotsky, 23 (See also Vygotsky's sociocultural cognitive theory)
Cognitive training programs, 525
Cohabiting adults
  explanation of, 443–444
  older adults as, 581–582
Cohort, 32
Cohort effects
  explanation of, 32–33
  midlife development and, 491
Colleges/universities
  binge drinking in, 410
  rape in, 417, 418
  transition from high school to, 404
  work during attendance at, 425
College/university professors, 41, 479, 504, 587
Color vision, 127, 523
Commitment
  identity and, 373
  in marriage, 450
  understanding joint, 236
Communication
  about divorce, 254
  with dying persons, 605, 606
  social media and, 388
Complicated grief, 607
Concept formation, 148–149

Concepts, 148
Concrete operational
    stage (Piaget), 22,
    278–280, 357
Conditioning, operant, 145
Confidentiality, 35
Conscience, 240
Consensual validation, 437
Conservation, 208–209
Constructivist approach, 327
Consummate love, 440
Contemplative science, 284
Contemporary life-events
    approach, 488–490
Context of development, 6–7
Continuity-discontinuity issue,
    18, 23–24
Contraceptive use, among
    adolescents, 347–348
Control groups, 31–32
Controversial children, 323
Conventional reasoning
    (Kohlberg), 311
Convergent thinking, 284
Convoy model of social
    relations, 584
Cooperative (co-op)
    programs, 425
Coordination of circular
    reactions, 140, 141
Coparenting, 248
Coping
    with bereavement, 608
    emotional regulation and,
    171–172
    religion, spirituality
    and, 479
    with stress, 309–310
Core knowledge approach, 143
Corpus callosum, 344, 345
Correlational research, 30–31,
    306–307
Correlation coefficient,
    30, 31
Cortisol, 29, 489
Counseling psychologists, 42
Counselors
    career, 42
    drug, 43
    genetic, 44, 58
Crawling, 119
Creativity
    in early adulthood,
    420–421
    explanation of, 284
    strategies to develop,
    285, 422
Crisis, identity, 373
Critical thinking
    in adolescents, 361–362
    explanation of, 283
    in middle and late
    childhood, 283–284
Cross-cultural studies. See also
    Culture/cultural diversity;
    Ethnicity
    of academic achievement,
    330–332

of adolescent pregnancy, 348
of adolescents, 385–386
explanation of, 8
of marriage, 444–445
in parent-adolescent
    conflict, 380
of retirement, 556
Cross-sectional research
    approach, 32
Crowds, 382
Crying, 170, 172
Crystallized intelligence, 471
Cultural bias, in research,
    36–37
Cultural-familial intellectual
    disability, 292, 293
Cultural identity, 374–375
Culture/cultural diversity. See
    also Ethnicity
    adolescent development and,
    384–386
    adolescents and, 384–386
    of adopted children and
    adoptive parents, 61–62
    birth attendants and, 88
    child-care policies and,
    189, 190
    death and, 595–596
    development and, 7
    emotional development
    and, 169
    explanation of, 8
    families and, 255–256
    grandparenting and, 500
    grieving and, 608–610
    growth patterns and, 199
    infant sleep patterns
    and, 110
    intelligence and, 289
    intergenerational
    relationships and,
    503–504
    late adulthood and, 587–588
    life expectancy and, 510
    life span and, 50
    midlife and, 492
    motor development and, 121
    in mourning, 611–612
    parenting and, 246, 255
    physical punishment and,
    247–248
    puberty and, 343
    school dropout rate and, 364
    separation protest and, 171
    sexual initiation and, 347
    workplace and, 426
Culture-fair tests, 292
Cumulative personality model
    of personality
    development, 496
Curriculum, controversy
    over, 228
Cyberbullying, 325, 393
Cystic fibrosis, 57

Data-collection methods
    case studies as, 29
    observation as, 28

physiological measures as,
    29–30
    standardized tests as, 29
    surveys and interviews
    as, 29
Date rape, 417
Dating, 383–384
Death
    in adolescents, 353
    advance care planning and,
    597–598
    attitudes toward, 601–602
    care for dying individuals
    and, 599
    causes of, 600–601
    communicating with dying
    persons and, 605
    contexts for, 604
    culture and, 595–596
    in early adulthood, 406
    in early childhood, 204–205
    euthanasia and, 598–599
    forms of mourning and,
    611–612
    grieving and, 605–609
    historical changes and, 596
    in infants, 111, 113
    issues in determining, 587
    Kübler-Ross' stages of
    dying and, 603–604
    in late adulthood, 528
    of life partner, 609–610
    making sense of the world
    and, 609
    in middle adulthood, 464, 467
    perceived control and denial
    and, 604
Debriefing, 35
Deception, in research, 35
Decision making
    in adolescents, 360–361
    in older adults, 547
Deferred imitation, 148
Delivery. See Birth process
Dementia, 559
Denial and isolation stage of
    dying, 602, 603
Dependent variable, 31
Depression
    in adolescents, 391–392
    infant sleep patterns and
    maternal, 110
    in late adulthood, 558
    postpartum, 96–97
    prenatal development and
    maternal, 84–85
    suicide and, 392
Depression stage of dying, 603
Depth perception, 128, 523
Descriptive research, 30
Desires, in young children, 218
Development. See also Life-
    span development;
    specific age groups
    age and, 15–17
    biological, cognitive, and
    socioemotional processes
    in, 12–13

child maltreatment and,
    249–250
    contextual nature of, 6–7
    continuity-discontinuity
    issue and, 18
    explanation of, 4
    genetic foundations of,
    51–58
    growth, maintenance, and
    regulation of loss in, 7
    lifelong nature of, 5
    multidimensional nature
    of, 5
    multidirectional nature of, 6
    periods of, 13–15
    plasticity of, 6
    stability-change issue
    and, 18
Developmental cascade
    model, 183
Developmental cognitive
    neuroscience, 144, 345
Developmentally appropriate
    practice (DAP),
    225–226
Developmental psychologist,
    36, 218
Developmental
    psychology,
    evolutionary, 49–50
Developmental quotient
    (DQ), 150
Developmental research. See
    Research
Developmental social
    neuroscience,
    184–185, 345
Development theories
    behavioral and social
    cognitive, 23–24
    cognitive, 21–23
    comparison of, 27
    eclectic orientation to,
    26, 27
    ecological, 25–26
    ethological, 24–25
    psychoanalytic, 19–21
Diabetes
    breast feeding and, 113
    description of, 57
    gestational, 83
    maternal, 78, 83
    metabolic syndrome
    and, 464
    in older adults, 548
Diet
    calorie-restricted,
    532–533
    in early adulthood, 408
    longevity and, 514
    during pregnancy, 83–84
Dietary supplements, 533,
    550–551
Difficult child, 172, 173
Direct instruction
    approach, 327
Director of children's services/
    Head Start, 227

Disabilities
    attention deficit hyperactivity
    disorder, 274–276
    autism spectrum, 276–277
    emotional and behavioral, 276
    intellectual, 292–293
    learning, 272–274
    overview of, 273
Disasters, coping with,
    309–310
Disease. See Illness and
    disease; specific
    conditions
Disenfranchised grief, 607
Disequilibrium, 138
Dishabituation, 124–125, 146
Divergent thinking, 284
Divorce. See also Remarriage
    adjustment to, 252–254
    challenges related to,
    446–447
    children of, 502
    communicating with
    children about, 254
    dealing with, 451–452
    in middle adulthood,
    497–498
    older adults and, 581
    statistics related to, 446
Dizygotic twins, 54
DNA (deoxyribonucleic acid),
    51–54, 58, 65, 68
Domain theory of moral
    development, 312–314
Dominant genes, 54
Dominant-recessive genes
    principle, 54
Dopamine, 561
Dose-response effects, 309
Doulas, 88
Down syndrome, 55–56
Dropout rate, school, 364–365
Drug counselors, 43
Drugs
    for childbirth, 88–89
    prescription and
    nonprescription, 80
    psychoactive, 80–82
    teratogenic, 80–82
Dual-career couples, 426
Dual-process model
    adolescent decision making
    and, 361
    of coping with bereavement,
    608
Dynamic systems theory of
    motor development,
    116–117
Dyscalculia, 274
Dysgraphia, 274
Dyslexia, 274

Early adulthood
    attachment in, 433–435
    attraction to others in,
    436–438
    careers and work in,
    423–426

Early adulthood—*Cont.*
cognitive stages in, 419–420
cohabiting adults in, 443–444
creativity in, 420–421
divorced adults in, 446–447
divorce in, 451–452
eating and weight in, 407–408
exercise in, 409, 465
falling out of love in, 440–4412
gays and lesbians in, 448
health issues in, 406–407
love in, 438–440
married adults in, 444–445, 449–450
parents in, 450–451
physical development in, 405–406
rape in, 417–418
remarried adults in, 447–448
sexual activity in, 412–413
sexual harassment in, 418–419
sexually transmitted infections in, 415–417
sexual orientation and behavior in, 413–415
single adults in, 442
substance abuse in, 409–411
temperament in, 432–433
transition from adolescence to, 402–404
transition from high school to college in, 404
Early childhood
adopted children in, 63
attitude toward death in, 601
birth order and, 251
brain in, 200
child maltreatment and, 248–250
cognitive development in, 206–220
development of self in, 234–236
emotional development in, 236–238
exercise in, 204
family variations and, 251–256
gender in, 241–244
illness and death in, 204–205
information processing in, 214–220
language development in, 221–224
moral development in, 238–241
motor development in, 200–201
nutrition in, 202–203
parenting and, 244–248
peer relations in, 257–258

perceptual development in, 201
physical development in, 199–200
play in, 258–260
sibling relationships in, 250–251
sleep in, 201–202
television viewing and, 261
Early childhood education
child-centered kindergarten and, 225
controversies in, 228–229
developmentally appropriate and inappropriate, 225–226
disadvantaged children and, 226–228
Montessori approach to, 225
Reggio Emilia approach and, 198, 224
Early education educators, 41
Easy child, 172, 173
Eating behavior. *See also* Nutrition
in early adulthood, 407–408
in infants, 112
Eating disorders, 355–356
Eclectic theoretical orientation, 26, 27
Ecological theory
explanation of, 25–26
of perceptual development, 123, 131
Economic issues, 577
Ectoderm, 74
Education. *See also* Academic achievement; Colleges/universities; Schools
accountability in, 328
bilingual, 298
for children with disabilities, 277–278
constructivist approach to, 327
controversies in, 228–229
developmentally appropriate and inappropriate, 225–226
direct instruction approach to, 327
disadvantaged children and, 226–228
early childhood, 224–229
family-life, 349
for gifted children, 294
influence of, 7
for older adults, 547–548
parenting and, 320
premarital, 445–446
service learning, 365
single-sex, 316–317
Educational psychologists, 36, 42
Education for All Handicapped Children Act of 1975, 277
Effortful control, 173

Egocentrism
adolescent, 358–359
explanation of, 207
in preoperational stage, 207
self-talk and, 211
Eight frames of mind theory (Gardner), 288–289
Elaboration, 281
Elder abuse, 562
Eldercare, 578
Electroencephalogram (EEG), 30, 105
Elementary/secondary school teachers, 41
ELL teachers, 299
Embryonic period, 74–76
Emerging adulthood, 374, 402–404. *See also* Adolescents; Early adulthood
Emotional abuse, 249. *See also* Child maltreatment
Emotional and behavioral disorders, 276
Emotional development. *See also* Socioemotional development
biological and environmental influences on, 168–169
in early childhood, 236–238
in infants, 168–172
in middle and late childhood, 308–310
Emotional expression
caregivers and, 237
gender and, 318
in infants, 170–172
Emotion-coaching parents, 237–238
Emotion-dismissing parents, 237–238
Emotions
explanation of, 168
expression of, 236
in older adults, 571, 572
postpartum fluctuations in, 95–96
prenatal development and, 84–85
primary, 169
regulation of, 237–238
self-conscious, 169
understanding of, 236–237
in young children, 218
Emotion security theory, 253
Empiricists, 130
Employment. *See* Careers; Work
Empty nest syndrome, 498
Endoderm, 74, 75
English language learners (ELLs), 298, 299
Environmental experiences, shared and nonshared, 66–67
Environmental hazards, 82

Environmental influences
alcoholism and, 411
on emotional development, 168–169
on intelligence, 290–292
on language development, 158–161
obesity and, 271, 408
Epidural block, 88–89
Epigenetic view, 67–68, 187
Equilibration, 138–139
Erectile dysfunction (ED), 469
Erikson's psychosocial theory
adolescents and, 372–373
early childhood and, 234
identity and, 372–373
infant development and, 181
intimacy *vs.* isolation in, 438–439
late adulthood and, 569–570
middle adulthood and, 486
middle and late childhood and, 308
stages in, 20–21
Estradiol, 343
Estrogen, 343, 468
Ethical issues
bias and, 35–37
in research, 35
Ethnic bias, 36–37
Ethnic gloss, 36
Ethnic identity, 374–375
Ethnicity. *See also* Culture/cultural diversity; *specific groups*
academic achievement and, 330–332
adolescent pregnancy and, 348
adolescents and, 386–387
bias and, 36–37
education and, 329–330
explanation of, 8
immigration and, 386–0387
intelligence tests and, 291–292
late adulthood and, 586
parenting and, 255–256
poverty and, 387, 579
school dropout rate and, 364
socioeconomic status and, 387
Ethology, 24, 25
Euthanasia, 598–599
Evocative genotype-environment correlations, 65–66
Evolution, 49–50
Evolutionary psychology
evaluation of, 50
explanation of, 49–50
gender development and, 241–242
Evolutionary theory of aging, 516

Exceptional children teachers, 41
Executive attention
in adolescents, 359
explanation of, 214
in older adults, 543
Executive function
attention deficit hyperactivity disorder and, 275
explanation of, 545
in late adulthood, 545–546
in middle and late childhood, 282–283
theory of mind and, 220
in young children, 216–217
Exercise
in adolescents, 351–352
aerobic, 409, 464, 522, 546
attention deficit hyperactivity disorder and, 276
cognitive development and, 270, 549–550
in early adulthood, 409, 465
in early childhood, 204
health and, 269
in late adulthood, 530–532, 546, 548–549, 551, 560
in middle adulthood, 464, 465
in middle and late childhood, 269–270
during pregnancy, 85–86, 92
Exosystem, 26
Expanding, 160
Expectations, perceptual development and, 141–143
Experimental groups, 31–32
Experimental research, 31–32, 306
Experiments, 31
Expertise
memory and, 281
in middle adulthood, 474
Explicit memory
explanation of, 146, 147
in older adults, 543
Expressive vocabulary, 155
Extracurricular activities, 365
Extraversion/surgency, 173
Extremely preterm infants, 93
Eye-tracking equipment, 125–126

Face-to-face play, 179
False beliefs, 218, 219
Familiarity, attraction and, 436–438
Families. *See also* Divorce; Fathers; Marriage; Mothers; Parents
adolescents and, 385
adolescent substance abuse and, 355
attachment in, 321
changing nature of, 251

cross-cultural studies
of, 255
divorced, 252–254
dual-career couples in, 426
effects of child care on,
191–192
ethnicity and, 255–256
with gay and lesbian parents,
254–255
immigrant, 255–256,
386–387
managing and guiding infant
behavior in, 187–188
maternal and paternal
caregiving in, 188–189
moral development and, 313
reciprocal socialization and,
186–187
single-parent, 255
socioeconomic status
and, 256
stepfamilies, 321–322
as subsystems, 186
transition to parenthood
and, 186
transnational, 256
with two working
parents, 252
Family and consumer science
educators, 42
Family-life education, 349
Family Matters program, 355
Family policy, strategies to
improve, 11
Fast mapping, 222
Fast Track program, 395
Fathers. *See also* Caregivers/
caregiving; Parents
as caregivers, 188–189
gender development
and, 242
infant care involvement
of, 110
postpartum adjustments
for, 97
prenatal development
and, 85
Fear, in infants, 171
Feelings. *See* Emotions
Females. *See also* Gender
differences; Gender/
gender development;
Pregnancy; Prenatal
development
eating disorders in, 355–356
educational opportunities
for, 9
gender development and,
241–244
infertility in, 61
life expectancy and,
510–511
menopause in, 467–468
in middle adulthood,
491–492
postpartum period in,
95–97

poverty among, 578–579
puberty in, 342–344
self-esteem and, 371
socioemotional development
in, 317, 318
widowed, 609, 610
in workforce, 554
Fertilization, 53
Fetal alcohol spectrum
disorders (FASD), 80
Fetal MRI, 59–60
Fetal period, 76–77
Fetal sex determination, 60
Fetus. *See also* Prenatal
development
development of, 74–86
hearing in, 128–129
Fight-or-flight, 490, 491
Fine motor skills
in early childhood, 201
in infants, 121–122
First habits and primary
circular reactions,
139–140
Fish, in maternal diet, 84
Fixed mindset, 332
Fluid intelligence, 471
Flynn effect, 290
Folic acid, 83–84
Formal operational stage
(Piaget), 22–23,
357–358, 419, 420
Foster care, 62
Fragile-X syndrome, 56
Fraternal twins, 54
Free-radical theory of aging,
516–517
Freudian theory, 20
Friendship
in adolescents, 381, 382
cross-gender, 439–440
depression and, 392
in early childhood, 258
functions of, 325–326, 439
gender differences in, 439
intimacy and, 326
Frontal lobes, 106
Functional age, 515
Functional magnetic resonance
imaging (fMRI), 29–30
Funerals, 611
Fuzzy trace theory, 282

Games, 260. *See also* Play
Gametes, 53, 54
Gastrointestinal infections,
breast feeding and, 113
Gays. *See also* Same-sex
couples
adolescent dating among, 383
attitudes and behavior of, 415
lifestyle characteristics of, 448
as parents, 254–255
Gender bias
Kohlberg's moral
development theory and,
313, 315

in research, 35
stage theories of
development and, 491
Gender differences. *See also*
Females; Males
in adjustment to
divorce, 253
in adolescents,
378, 385
biological influences on,
241–242
in body image, 344
in brain development, 316
cognitive development and,
316–317
in divorce process and
outcomes, 447
in friendship, 439
in intergenerational
relationships, 503
in life expectancy,
510–511
in moral development, 313
in physical development,
315–316
in prevalence of depression,
391, 392
in relationships with adult
parents, 582–583
in school dropout rate, 364
in self-esteem, 371
in socioemotional
development, 317–318
in stress, 490–491
suicide and, 393
Gender/gender development.
See also Females; Males
in context, 319
in early childhood, 241–244
explanation of, 8
in middle and late
childhood, 315–318
social influences on,
242–243
Gender identity, 241
Gender roles
classification of, 318–319
explanation of, 241
in late adulthood, 587
Gender schema theory, 244
Gender stereotypes, 315
Gender typing, 241
Gene-gene interaction, 55
Gene-linked abnormalities,
56–58
Generational inequity, 578
Generation X, 33
Generativity *vs.* stagnation
stage (Erikson), 21, 486
Genes
chromosomes and, 53–54
collaborative, 52–53
depression and, 392
dominant, 54
environmental influences
and, 67–69 (*See also*
Nature-nurture issue)

explanation of, 51
identification of, 52
longivity, 54
recessive, 54
sex-linked, 54–55
sexual orientation
and, 414
susceptibility, 54
Genetic counselors, 44
Genetic expression, 53
Genetic imprinting, 55
Genetics
alcoholism and, 411
autism spectrum disorders
and, 277
behavior, 64–65
chromosomal abnormalities
and, 55–56
collaborative gene and,
51–53
depression and, 392
gene-linked abnormalities
and, 56–58
genes and chromosomes
and, 53–54
intelligence and, 289–290
longevity and, 512, 514
obesity and, 407
principles of, 54–55
Genetic variability, 53–54
Gene x environment (G x E)
interaction, 68
Genital herpes, 82–83
Genome-wide association
method, 52
Genotype, 54
Georgia Centenarian Study,
511, 513
Geriatric nurses, 43, 534
Geriatric physicians, 43
Germinal period, 74
Gerontologists, 42
Gestational diabetes, 83
Gestures, in infants, 155
Giftedness
characteristics of, 293–294
domain-specific, 294
education and, 294
explanation of, 292, 293
Ginkgo biloba, 550, 551
Girls. *See* Females; Gender
differences; Gender/
gender development
Glaucoma, 523
Goodness of fit, parenting and,
175–176
Grammar, in middle and late
childhood, 295–296
Grandparenting, 500–501.
See also Great-
grandparenting
Grasping reflex, 118
Great-grandparenting, 583
Grief/grieving
cultural differences in,
608–609
dimensions of, 606–608

dual-process model and, 608
explanation of, 605–606
Gross motor skills
in early childhood, 200–201
in infants, 118–121
Growth, 7, 104. *See also*
Physical development;
specific age groups
Growth hormone deficiency,
199–200
Growth mindset, 332
Gynecologists, 43

Habituation, 124–125, 146, 152
Head Start programs,
227–228, 237
Health. *See also* Illness and
disease; *specific
conditions*
adolescent, 350–353, 385
in early adulthood, 406–407
exercise and, 269
function of, 7
in late adulthood, 527–529,
548–549
in middle adulthood,
465–467
in middle and late
childhood, 270–272
overweight and obesity
and, 462
religion, spirituality
and, 478
Health care
for dying individuals, 599
in late adulthood,
533–535, 578
Health psychologists, 391
Hearing
by fetus, 128–129
in infants, 129
in late adulthood, 524
in middle adulthood,
263, 462
Height
in adolescents, 342
in early childhood,
199–200
in infants, 104–105
in middle adulthood,
461–462
in middle and late
childhood, 268
Hemophilia, 57
Heredity-environment
correlations, 65–66. *See
also* Nature-nurture
issue
Heteronomous morality
(Kohlberg), 239, 311
Heterosexuality, 413
High-amplitude sucking, 125
High school
explanation of, 364–365
transition to college
from, 404
Hispanics. *See* Latinos

HIV/AIDS
  breast feeding and, 114
  prenatal development and, 83
  protection strategies for, 416–417
  statistics related to, 416
Home births, 87–88
Home health aides, 44
Home hospice nurses, 600
Hormonal stress theory, 517
Hormone replacement therapy (HRT), 468
Hormones
  explanation of, 343
  flow of, 53
  gender development and, 241
  puberty and, 30, 343
  stress and, 29
Hospice, 599
Hospitals, 604
Human faces, perception of, 126–127
Human Genome Project, 52
Huntington's disease, 57
Hypertension, 464, 548
Hypnosis, during childbirth, 90
Hypotheses, 19, 28
Hypothetical-deductive reasoning, 358
Hysterectomy, 468

Identical twins, 54
Identity
  in adolescents, 372–375
  cultural and ethnic, 374–375
  developmental changes and, 373
  in emerging adulthood, 374
  Erikson's view of, 372–373
  explanation of, 372
  religion and, 376
Identity achievement, 373
Identity diffusion, 373
Identity foreclosure, 373
Identity moratorium, 373
Identity vs. identity confusion (Erikson), 372–373
I Have a Dream (IHAD) program, 365
Illness and disease. See also specific conditions
  breast feeding and, 114
  in early childhood, 204–205
  in late adulthood, 523–524
  poverty and, 205–206
Imaginary audience, 358
Imitation, 148
Immanent justice, 239
Immigration
  adolescents and, 386–387
  families and, 255–256
Immune system, in late adulthood, 522
Implicit memory, 146, 147
Income, 578–579. See also Poverty; Socioeconomic status (SES)

Independence, in infants, 178
Independent variable, 31
Individual differences, in intelligence, 286
Individualism, instrumental purpose, and exchange stage (Kohlberg), 311
Individualized education plans (IEPs), 277
Indulgent parenting, 245
Industry vs. inferiority stage (Erikson), 21, 308
Infant assessment specialists, 151
Infantile amnesia, 148
Infants. See also Newborns
  with adolescent mothers, 348, 349
  adopted, 63
  attachment in, 180–185, 434
  brain in, 105–109
  breast feeding benefits for, 112–113
  child care and, 189–192
  cognitive development in, 137–161 (See also Cognitive development)
  eating behavior in, 112
  emotional development in, 168–172
  empathy in, 238
  imitation by, 148
  language development in, 154–161
  malnutrition in, 114–115
  measures of cognitive development in, 150–151
  memory in, 147–148
  motor development in, 116–122
  nutrition in, 112–114
  perceptual-motor coupling in, 121, 131–132
  personality development in, 176–178
  physical development in, 104–105
  preterm and low birth weight, 92–93
  role of family in, 186–189
  sensory and perceptual development in, 122–132
  sleep in, 109–112
  social orientation/ understanding in, 179–180
  temperament in, 172–176
Infertility, 61
Infinite generativity, 152, 153
Information processing. See also Cognitive development
  in adolescents, 359–362
  attention and, 214–215
  in early childhood, 214–220
  in infants, 149
  in late adulthood, 542

in middle adulthood, 473–474
  in middle and late childhood, 280–286
  speed of, 473
Information-processing approach
  attention and, 214–215
  executive function and, 216–217
  memory and, 215–216
  theory of mind and, 217–220
Information-processing theory, 23
Informed consent, 35
Initiative vs. guilt stage (Erikson), 20–21, 234
Inner speech, 211
Insecure avoidant babies, 182
Insecure disorganized babies, 182
Insecure resistant babies, 182
Insight, in infants, 180
Insomnia, 202
Institutional abuse, 562
Integrity vs. despair stage (Erikson), 21, 569
Intellectual disability, 292–293
Intelligence
  crystallized, 471
  culture and, 289
  explanation of, 286
  extremes of, 292–294
  fluid, 471
  genetics and, 289–290
  individual differences in, 286
  in middle adulthood, 470–473
  predicting infant, 151–152
  theories of, 288–289
  types of, 288–289
Intelligence quotient (IQ), 151, 287
Intelligence tests
  Binet, 287
  ethnicity and, 291–292
  intellectual disability and, 292–293
  interpretation of, 289–293
  Stanford-Binet, 287
  use of, 292
  Wechsler scales, 287–288
Interactionist view, of language, 158, 160–161
Intergenerational relationships
  benefits of, 502–503
  culture and, 503–504
  gender differences in, 503
  in midlife, 501–502
  overview of, 501
Intermodal perception, 130
Internalization of schemes, 140
Internet
  cyberbullying and, 325
  dating services on, 437–438
Interviews, 29

Intimacy
  explanation of, 438–439
  in friendship, 326
Intimacy vs. isolation (Erikson), 21, 438–439
Intuitive thought substage (Piaget), 208
In vitro fertilization (IVF), 61, 62

Jealousy, 169
Joint attention, 146–147
Judaism, 612
Junior high school, transition to, 362–363
Justice, immanent, 239
Justice perspective, 312, 313
Juvenile delinquency, 389–390

Kamehameha Elementary Education Program (KEEP), 211
Kangaroo care, 92, 93
Kindergarten, child-centered, 225
Klinefelter syndrome, 56
Knowledge, memory and, 281
Kohlberg's moral development stages, 310–313
Kübler-Ross stages of dying, 603–604
Kwashiorkor, 114–115

Labeling, 160
Laboratories, 28, 29
Language
  explanation of, 152, 153
  rule systems of, 153–154
Language acquisition devices (LADs), 158
Language development
  biological influences on, 157–158
  in early childhood, 210–211
  environmental influences on, 158–161
  in infants, 154–161
  interactionist view of, 158, 160–161
  in late adulthood, 553
  literacy in young children and, 223–224
  in middle and late childhood, 295–298
  phonology and morphology and, 221–222
  pragmatics and, 223
  socioeconomic status and, 158–159
  syntax and semantics and, 222
  theory of mind and, 220
  Vygotsky's theory of, 210–211
Late adulthood
  attitude toward death in, 602
  biological theories of aging and, 516–516–517

brain in, 518–521, 551–552
  centenarians and, 511–515
  circulatory and respiratory systems in, 525–526
  cognitive functioning in, 541–553
  cognitive neuroscience and, 551–552
  cognitive skills training in, 550–551
  education in, 547–548
  ethnicity, gender, and culture and, 586–588
  exercise in, 530–532, 546, 548–549, 551, 560
  facing one's own death in, 602–604
  families and social relationships in, 580–585
  health in, 527–529, 548–549
  health treatment in, 533–535
  immune system in, 522
  language development in, 553
  life expectancy and, 510–511
  mental health in, 557–562
  nutrition in, 532
  personality in, 575
  physical appearance and movement in, 522
  policy issues affecting, 577–579
  possible selves and, 576
  relationships with adult children in, 582–583
  religion and spirituality in, 563–564
  retirement in, 555–557
  self-control in, 576–577
  self-esteem in, 563, 575–576
  sensory development in, 522–525
  sexuality in, 526
  sleep in, 520–521
  socioemotional development in, 569–574
  statistics related to, 11
  stereotypes of, 577
  "use it or lose it" concept in, 549
  victimization and maltreatment in, 561–562
  weight in, 532–533
  well-being in, 10–12
  work in, 548, 554–555
  young-old and oldest-old in, 515–516
Late-onset alcoholism, 529
Lateralization, of brain, 106
Latinos. See also Ethnicity
  adolescent pregnancy and, 348
  education and, 329
  in late adulthood, 586
  research issues and, 36–37
  sickle-cell anemia and, 57
  as single parents, 255
L-dopa, 561

Narcissism, 372
Narcolepsy, 202
National Longitudinal Study of Child Care (NICHD), 191, 192
Native Americans
school dropout rate and, 364
suicide among, 392
Natural childbirth, 89
Naturalistic observation, 28, 29
Natural selection, 48–50
Nature-nurture issue
behavior genetics and, 64–65
conclusions regarding, 68–69
epigenetic view and gene x environment interaction and, 67–68
explanation of, 17–18
giftedness and, 294
heredity-environment correlations and, 65–66
infant development and, 143–144
perceptual development and, 130–131
phenylketonuria and, 57
shared and nonshared environmental experiences and, 66–67
Negative affectivity, 173
Neglected children, 249, 323
Neglectful parenting, 245
Neonatal Intensive Care Unit Network Neurobehavioral Scale (NNNS), 91, 150
Neonatal nurses, 43
Neural connectivity, 78
Neural tube, 78
Neural tube defects, 78
Neuroconstructivist view, 109
Neurogenesis, 78, 519–520
Neuronal migration, 78
Neurons
explanation of, 78, 79
in infants, 106–107
in prenatal brain development, 78
Neurotransmitters, 107
Newborns. See also Infants
assessment of, 91
gross motor skills in, 118
kangaroo care for, 92, 93
massage therapy for, 93–95
pain in, 129–130
perceptions in, 124–126
physical growth in, 104–105
preterm and low birthweight, 92–93
New England Centenarian Study, 511–512

Next-generation sequencing, 521
Nicotine, 81, 411. See also Tobacco use
Nightmares, 202
No Child Left Behind Act of 2002 (NCLB), 317, 328
Noninvasive prenatal diagnosis (NIPD), 60
Nonnormative life events, 6–7
Non-Piagetians, 280
Nonprescription drugs, as teratogens, 80
Non-REM sleep, 110
Nonshared environmental experiences, 66–67
Normal distribution, 287
Normative age-graded influences, 6, 7
Normative history-graded influences, 6, 7
Nun Study, 521
Nurse-midwives, 43
Nurses
geriatric, 43, 534
home hospice, 600
neonatal, 43
pediatric, 43
perinatal, 89
Nursing homes, 534–535
Nutrition
in adolescents, 351
in early childhood, 202–203
in infants, 112–115
in late adulthood, 532
poverty and, 115, 203
during pregnancy, 83–84

Obesity. See also Overweight
breast feeding and, 113
in early adulthood, 203, 407–408
health risks of, 462
heredity and, 407
in late adulthood, 522, 532
in middle adulthood, 462
in middle and late childhood, 270
prenatal development and maternal, 78, 83
screen time and, 270
Object permanence
explanation of, 140–141
method to study, 142
Observation, 28, 29
Obstetricians, 43
Occipital lobes, 106
Occupational outlook, 424
Occupational therapists, 43
Older adults. See Late adulthood
Oldest-old, 558. See also Late adulthood
Omega-3 polyunsaturated fatty acids, 550–551
Operant conditioning, 24, 145
Operations, 206

Organic intellectual disability, 292, 293
Organization, cognitive development and, 138
Organogenesis, 75–76
Orienting response, 125–126
Osteoporosis, 528
Otitis media, breast feeding and, 113
Ovarian cancer, 113
Overweight. See also Obesity
breast feeding and, 113
depression and, 392
in early childhood, 202–203
in late adulthood, 532
in middle adulthood, 462
in middle and late childhood, 270–271
Oxidative stress, 559
Oxytocin, 89, 184–185, 491

Pain sensation
in infants, 129–130
in late adulthood, 524–525
Palliative care, 599
Palmer grasp, 121
Parental leave, 189
Parent educators, 451
Parenting. See also Caregivers/caregiving; Parents
academic achievement and, 320, 331–333
of adolescents, 377–380, 390
of adopted children, 63
authoritarian, 245, 246
authoritative, 245, 246
coparenting and, 248
cross-cultural variations in, 255
in early childhood, 244–248
effects of child care on, 191–192
emotional coaching and, 237–238
ethnicity and, 255–256
gender development and, 242–243
goodness of fit and, 175–176
indulgent, 245
of infants, 186–189
influence of, 7, 10
as influence on peer relations, 258
language development and, 160–161
moral development and, 240–241
myths and realities of, 450
neglectful, 245
overview of, 244–245
punishment and, 246–248
temperament and, 175–176
Parenting styles, 245–246

Parents. See also Caregivers/caregiving; Families; Fathers; Mothers; Parenting
adolescent conflict with, 379–380
adolescent substance abuse and, 354, 355
adoptive, 61–63
adult children living with, 498, 499
divorce of, 252–254
emotion-coaching and emotion-dismissing, 237–238
gay and lesbian, 254–255
as managers, 320–321
remarried, 320, 321
as role models, 270
socioeconomic status of, 256
working, 252
Parietal lobes, 106, 145
Parkinson's disease, 561
Passive euthanasia, 598
Passive genotype-environment correlations, 65
Pediatricians, 43, 116
Pediatric nurses, 43
Peer groups
adolescent, 381–382
bullying and, 325
function of, 257
Peer relations. See also Friendship
adolescent, 381–382, 385
adolescent substance abuse and, 354
delinquency and, 390
depression and, 392
developmental changes and, 257–258
early childhood, 257–258
emotion regulation and, 238
exercise and, 351–352
gender development and, 243
middle and late childhood, 322–324
parental influences on, 258
Peer status, 323–324
Perceived control, 604
Perception
explanation of, 123
intermodal, 130
visual, 126–128
in young children, 218
Perceptual categorization, 149
Perceptual development
ecological view of, 123
expectations and, 141–143
in infants, 122–132
measures of, 30
nature-nurture issue and, 130–131
Perceptual-motor coupling, 121, 131–132, 525
Perceptual narrowing, 127
Perceptual speed, 544

Perimenopause, 467
Perinatal nurses, 89
Personal fable, 359
Personality
big five factors of, 493–494
in late adulthood, 575
moral, 314–315
Personality development
cumulative personality model of, 496
independence and, 178
in infants, 176–178
in middle adulthood, 493–496
sense of self and, 177–178
trust and, 177
Perspective taking, 305–306
Phenotype, 54
Phenylketonuria (PKU), 56–57
Phonemes, 153, 154
Phonics approach, 296
Phonology, 153, 154, 221–222
Physical abuse, 249. See also Child maltreatment
Physical activity. See Exercise
Physical attractiveness, 438, 461
Physical development. See also Exercise; Growth; Health; Height; Weight
in adolescents, 342
in early adulthood, 405–406
in early childhood, 199–200
gender differences in, 315–316
in infants, 104–105
in middle adulthood, 461–465
in middle and late childhood, 268
Physical exercise. See Exercise
Physical punishment. See Punishment
Physical therapists, 43
Physician Orders for Life-Sustaining Treatment (POLST), 598
Physiological measures, for data collection, 29–30
Piaget's cognitive developmental theory
adolescents and, 357–358
early adulthood and, 419–420
early childhood and, 206–209, 239, 258
evaluation of, 141–144, 279–280, 358
infants and, 131, 137–141
middle and late childhood and, 239, 278–280
moral development and, 239, 310
overview of, 21
stages in, 22–23
Vygotsky's theory compared with, 209–210, 213

Pincer grip, 121, 122
Pitch, 129
Placenta, 75, 76
Planfulness, of attention, 214
Plasticity, 6, 109
Play
    functions of, 258–259
    gender behavior
        and, 243
    in infancy, 179
    trends in, 260
    types of, 259–260
Play therapy, 258
Polygenic inheritance, 55
Popular children, 323
Possible selves, 576
Postconventional reasoning
    (Kohlberg), 311–312
Postformal thought, 420, 421
Postpartum depression, 96–97
Postpartum period
    bonding in, 97
    emotional and psychological
        adjustments in, 95–97
    explanation of, 95
Posture, 118
Poverty. See also
    Socioeconomic status
    (SES)
    academic achievement and,
        328–329
    among children, 9–11
    early childhood education
        and, 226–228
    ethnicity and, 387
    health issues and, 527–528
    illness and, 205–206
    language development in
        infants and, 159
    in late adulthood, 578–579
    nutrition and, 115, 203
Practice play, 258, 259
Pragmatics, 153–154, 223
Preconventional reasoning
    (Kohlberg), 311
Prefrontal cortex, 269, 308,
    344–345, 519, 552
Pregaming, 410
Pregnancy. See also Prenatal
    development
    adolescent, 348–350
    diet and nutrition during,
        83–84
    exercise during, 85–86, 92
    prenatal programs and,
        85–86
    teratogens during, 78–85
Premarital education,
    445–446
Prenatal care
    diagnostic tests and, 59–60
    positive outcomes of, 85–86
Prenatal development
    brain and, 77–78
    in embryonic period, 74–76
    in fetal period, 76–77
    in germinal period, 74

normal, 86–87
prenatal care and, 85–86
prenatal testing and, 59–60
teratology and hazards to,
    78–85
Prenatal diagnostic tests,
    59–60
Preoperational stage (Piaget).
    See also Piaget's
    cognitive developmental
    theory
    centration and, 208–209
    explanation of, 22, 206
    intuitive thought substage
        of, 208
    symbolic function substage
        of, 206–208
Prepared childbirth, 89
Preschool education, universal,
    228–229
Preschool teachers, 42
Prescription drugs, as
    teratogens, 80
Pretense/symbolic play, 259
Preterm infants, 92–94
Primary circular reactions, 140
Primary emotions, 169
Problem solving, 474
Professional journals, 34
Progestin, 92
Project Head Start,
    227–228, 237
Prolonged grief disorder, 607
Prosocial behavior
    gender and, 318
    moral development and, 314
    television and, 261–262
Prospective memory, 545
Proximodistal pattern, 104
Psychiatrists, 42, 331
Psychoactive drugs, as
    teratogens, 80–82
Psychoanalytic theories
    Erikson and, 20–21 (See
        also Erikson's
        psychosocial theory)
    evaluation of, 21
    explanation of, 19, 238
    Freud and, 20
    of gender, 242
Psychological abuse. See Child
    maltreatment
Psychological adjustments,
    during postpartum
    period, 95–97
Psychology, evolutionary,
    49–50
Psychosocial moratorium, 372
Psychosocial stages, 20–21
Psychosocial theory. See
    Erikson's psychosocial
    theory
Puberty
    body image and, 343–344
    early and late, 344
    explanation of, 342
    hormonal changes in, 30, 343

physical growth and, 342
sexual maturation and, 342
timing and variations in, 343
Punishment
    effects of, 247–248
    views regarding, 246–247

Racism, 586
Rape, 417–418
Reading
    gender differences in, 316
    in middle and late
        childhood, 274, 296–297
Reading aloud, benefits of, 160
Reasoning
    conventional, 311
    hypothetical-deductive, 358
    moral, 239–240
    postconventional, 311–312
    preconventional, 311
    social conventional, 313–314
Recasting, 160
Receptive vocabulary, 155
Recessive genes, 54
Reciprocal socialization,
    186–187
Referral bias, 273
Reflexes, 117–118
Reggio Emilia approach,
    198, 224
Rehabilitation counselors, 42
Rejected children, 323–324
Relational aggression, gender
    and, 317
Religion
    in adolescents, 375–377
    coping and, 479
    explanation of, 477
    in late adulthood, 563–564
    marriage and, 445
    positive role of, 377
Religiousness, 477
Remarriage. See also Divorce;
    Marriage
    experiences related to,
        447–448
    older adults and, 581
    statistics related to, 447
    stepfamilies and, 320–321
    strategies for successful, 450
Reminiscence therapy, 570
REM sleep, 110
Reproductive technology, 61
Research
    bias in, 35–37
    correlational, 30–31,
        306–307
    data collection methods for,
        28–30
    descriptive, 30
    ethics and, 35
    experimental, 31–32, 306
    publication of, 34
    time span of, 32–33
Research designs, 30–32
Researchers, 41
Research scientists, 363

Resilience, 10, 403
Resistant hypertension, 464
Respiratory tract
    infections, 113
Retirement
    adjustment to, 556–557
    cross-cultural studies of, 556
    in middle adulthood,
        475–476
    in United States, 555–556
Ritalin, 275
Rites of passage, 386
RNA (ribonucleic acid), 54
Roles, gender. See Gender
    roles
Romantic love, 440
Romantic relationships,
    adolescent, 383–384
Rooming-in, 97
Rooting reflex, 118
Rubella, 82

Same-sex couples. See also
    Gays; Lesbians
    as parents, 254–255
    statistics related to, 448
Sandwich generation, 503–504
Sarcopenia, 462
Scaffolding, 187, 210, 212
Schemes, Piaget and, 137–138
School counselors, 42
School psychologists, 42
Schools. See also Early
    childhood education;
    Education
    accountability of, 328
    adolescent substance abuse
        and, 355
    antibullying programs
        in, 325
    dropout rate in, 364–365
    extracurricular activities
        in, 365
    high school, 363–364
    middle or junior high,
        362–363
    single-sex education in,
        316–317
    for young adolescents, 363
Scientific method, 19
Scientific thinking, 284
Screen time
    effects of, 261, 352
    exercise and, 409
    obesity and, 270
Seasons of a man's life
    (Levinson), 487
Seattle Longitudinal Study,
    471–473
Secondary circular
    reactions, 140
Second-language learning, in
    middle and late
    childhood, 297–298
Secure attachment style, 435
Securely attached babies, 181
Selective attention, 542–543

Selective optimization with
    compensation theory,
    572–574
Self
    in early childhood, 234–236
    in middle and late
        childhood, 305–308
    personality development and
        sense of, 177–178
Self-awareness, 177–178
Self-concept, 306–307
Self-conscious emotions, 169
Self-control, 576–577
Self-efficacy
    in adolescents, 360
    in middle and late
        childhood, 307–308
Self-esteem
    in adolescents, 371–372
    in late adulthood, 563,
        575–576
    in middle and late
        childhood, 306–307
    strategies to increase, 307
Self-image. See Self-esteem
Self-regulation
    in infants, 177
    in middle and late
        childhood, 308
Self-talk, 211
Self-understanding
    in early childhood, 234–235
    in middle and late
        childhood, 305
Self-worth. See Self-esteem
Semantic memory, in older
    adults, 544
Semantics, 153, 154, 222
Sensation, 123
Sensorimotor play, 258, 259
Sensorimotor stage (Piaget)
    evaluation of, 141–144
    explanation of, 22, 139
    object permanence in,
        140–141
    substages of, 139–140
Sensory development
    in infants, 122–132
    in late adulthood, 522–525
Separation protest, 171
Seriation, 278, 279
Service learning, 365
Sex hormones, 241
Sex-linked chromosomal
    abnormalities, 55–56
Sex-linked genes, 54–55
Sexual abuse, 249. See also
    Child maltreatment
Sexual activity
    in adolescents, 346–347
    in early adulthood, 412–413
    in middle adulthood, 469–470
Sexual harassment, 418–419
Sexual identity, 346
Sexuality
    in adolescents, 345–348
    in early adulthood, 412–416